MANAGING INFORMATION TECHNOLOGY

SIXTH EDITION

Carol V. Brown
*Howe School of Technology Management, Stevens
Institute of Technology*

Daniel W. DeHayes
Kelley School of Business, Indiana University

Jeffrey A. Hoffer
School of Business Administration, The University of Dayton

E. Wainright Martin
Kelley School of Business, Indiana University

William C. Perkins
Kelley School of Business, Indiana University

PEARSON

Prentice
Hall

Upper Saddle River, New Jersey 07458

Library of Congress Cataloging-in-Publication Data

Managing information technology / Carol V. Brown ... [et al].—6th ed.
    p. cm.
  Includes bibliographical references and index.
  ISBN 0-13-178954-6 (alk. paper)
  1. Management information systems. I. Brown, Carol V. (Carol Vanderbilt)

  T58.6.M3568 2005
  658.4′038011—dc22   2007044607

Editor-in-Chief: David Parker
Acquisitions Editor: Bob Horan
Assistant Editor: Kelly Loftus
Marketing Manager: Anne Fahlgren
Associate Managing Editor: Suzanne DeWorken
Project Manager, Production: Ann Pulido
Permissions Project Manager: Charles Morris
Senior Operations Supervisor: Arnold Vila
Operations Specialist: Michelle Klein
Cover Design: Bruce Kenselaar
Cover Image: Getty Images, Inc.
Director, Image Resource Center: Melinda Patelli
Manager, Rights and Permissions: Zina Arabia
Manager: Visual Research: Beth Brenzel
Manager, Cover Visual Research & Permissions: Karen Sanatar
Image Permission Coordinator: Kathy Gavilanes
Photo Researcher: Beth Brenzel
Composition: GGS Book Services
Full-Service Project Management: GGS Book Services
Printer/Binder: Edwards Brothers
Typeface: 10/12 Times New Roman

Credits and acknowledgments borrowed from other sources and reproduced, with permission, in this textbook appear on appropriate page within text.

Pearson Education LTD., London
Pearson Education Singapore, Pte. Ltd
Pearson Education, Canada, Inc.
Pearson Education–Japan

Pearson Education Australia PTY, Limited
Pearson Education North Asia Ltd, Hong Kong
Pearson Educación de Mexico, S.A. de C.V.
Pearson Education Malaysia, Pte. Ltd.
Pearson Education Upper Saddle River, New Jersey

10 9 8 7 6 5 4 3 2
ISBN-13: 978-0-13-178954-8
ISBN-10: 0-13-178954-6

BRIEF CONTENTS: CHAPTERS

CONTENTS: CHAPTERS AND CASES

CONTENTS: CASE STUDIES

PREFACE

Since the first edition of *Managing Information Technology* was published in 1991, an organization's dependence on information technologies for business survival and growth has continued to expand. Today's IS leaders have become more visible and strategically important, as both technological and business forces have continued to increase the IT management responsibilities and roles within their organizations.

Over the past decade alone, new enterprise-wide applications on client/server platforms have been expanded to provide secure, electronic linkages with suppliers and business customers and for workers to collaborate across organizational boundaries. At the same time, the Internet has become a trusted channel for communicating directly with end-consumers and enabling other new ways for businesses to compete. These types of business and IT innovations have also catapulted IT management concerns to the agendas of top management teams and sometimes boards of directors as well.

The overall objectives and targeted audience for this sixth edition remain the same: to provide a thorough guide to IT management practices and issues for advanced students and managers. We believe that our approach of providing both up-to-date chapter content and full-length case studies, written by the same authors, results in a unique set of materials for instructors to customize for their own instructional needs. Earlier editions of this textbook have been used for courses in MBA, MS in IS, and executive education programs, as well as in advanced undergraduate courses for students who seek careers as both business and IS managers, as well as IT specialists.

THE CHAPTER CONTENT

Following an introductory chapter that sets the stage for IT management roles and responsibilities, the text is divided into four main parts:

- **Information Technology** presents background knowledge about four major technology components: hardware, software, networks, and data. (Depending on the targeted audience, these chapters can be used for background reading only as a kind of "level-setting" for students from different backgrounds and experiences.)

- **Applying Information Technology** introduces in detail the capabilities of three categories of software applications: enterprise systems, managerial support systems, and e-business systems.

- **Acquiring Information Systems** prepares the reader for leading and participating in projects to implement and support the use of software applications—including methodologies for custom developed and purchased software.

- **The Information Management System** lays the groundwork for understanding the range of IS leadership roles and current best practices for managing IT assets.

THE TEACHING CASES

To demonstrate real-world IT management challenges—based on undisguised Fortune 500 companies and mid-sized companies as well as some camouflaged companies—the textbook authors have also developed a set of case studies for each part of the textbook. These 30 full-length case studies can only be found in this publication.

From these case studies, students can learn directly from both successful and problematic real-world situations about the challenges of implementing new technologies, the capabilities of new types of applications, managing systems projects of different sizes with different methods, leveraging new Internet opportunities, and addressing systems integration and leadership challenges.

The seven new cases not previously published that appear in this edition address such topics as:

- VoIP technologies and implementation
- open source project approaches
- data governance issues
- business intelligence
- developing a vendor-managed inventory capability
- managing a multi-year IT outsourcing contract.

NEW IN THE SIXTH EDITION: CHAPTERS

All prior chapters have been revised to reflect up-to-date technology trends and current IT management practices, and a totally new chapter on information security has been added.

Chapter 1 "Managing IT in an e-World" has been brought up-to-date, as well as shortened and simplified. Updated trends in hardware, software, and networks are used as motivators for learning more about information technologies and how they are managed in organizations. Examples of differing "modes" of dependency on IT found in different organizations and a sample organization chart are now provided in this first chapter to introduce students to the focus of this text: managing IT in organizations. Concerns about demands for IT workers in the U.S. being greater than the current supply are also presented as motivators for students considering entering the IT workforce.

Part 1: Information Technology

Chapter 2 "Computer Hardware" has been thoroughly updated to incorporate the latest information on microprocessor chips, REV and flash drives, optical disk storage, and multi-processor systems, as well as the technology developments and the major vendors in the microcomputer, midrange systems, mainframe, and supercomputer market segments. New topics covered include smartphones (also known as "killer" PDAs) and blade servers.

Chapter 3 "Computer Software" has also been thoroughly updated to include new developments in personal productivity software, open source applications and support software (with an emphasis on Linux), and Web programming. The concepts of service-oriented architecture and Web services are introduced, and the chapter takes a fresh look at the changing nature of software and the makeup of the software industry.

Chapter 4 "Telecommunications and Networking" has been changing even more rapidly than hardware and software, necessitating major revisions in this chapter. Among the new topics covered are city-wide Wi-Fi networks, WiMAX wireless networks, Voice over

Internet Protocol (VoIP) telephony, the Internet2 network, and Web developments such as blogs, wikis, and other social networking technologies. This chapter also includes an updated look at the ever-evolving telecommunications industry.

Chapter 5 "The Data Resource" provides additional coverage on why data management is important, including metadata as a tool for controlling data quality. Additional new material addresses master data management (subject area data across multiple systems and databases) and lays the groundwork for later chapter discussions on data integration.

Part 2: Applying Information Technology

Chapter 6 "Enterprise Systems" contains an important new section on service-oriented architecture and Web services, as well as expanded treatment of both portals and supply chain management systems. The chapter also incorporates significant updates in the enterprise resource planning, data warehousing, customer relationship management, and groupware sections.

Chapter 7 "Managerial Support Systems" includes new examples in every application area discussed in the chapter. The chapter has an increased emphasis on business intelligence applications, and it introduces the important idea of location intelligence (based on the Global Positioning System) as a growing subarea of geographic information systems.

Chapter 8 "E-Business Systems" has been substantially revised to include updated coverage on B2B and B2C applications that demonstrate how bricks-and-clicks firms have evolved to challenge dot-com pioneers, and how dot-com intermediaries have continued to leverage new technologies and an expanded base of Internet users. Updated statistics and case examples, including new discussions of Google, Netflix, Blockbuster, Staples, and Autobytel, are provided. New summaries have been written about what makes a successful e-tailer or dot-com intermediary.

Part 3: Acquiring Information Systems

Chapter 9 "Basic Information Systems Concepts" now better clarifies the distinction between systems analysis techniques and tools. A new E-R diagram helps students link data and process modeling, and a new section on design patterns (pre-packaged E-R and process diagrams) explains how these purchased artifacts can speed up and improve the development of system descriptions. The physical systems descriptions have been streamlined to match a wider student audience. The knowledge of basic systems concepts and tools is now also motivated by the need for organizations to adopt practices (such as ITIL) to comply with new financial reporting regulations (such as Sarbanes-Oxley and Basel II).

Chapter 10 "Methodologies for Custom Software Development" now emphasizes the need for risk assessment as a part of any software development process. More details on custom software development methods and a section on agile methodologies have been added. Comparisons with non-agile approaches are made and eXtreme programming is discussed as one of the principal methods used with agile methodologies. The Scrum technique is also motivated and explained. The coverage of managing offshore custom development work has been expanded.

Chapter 11 "Methodologies for Purchased Software Packages" includes leasing as an option for acquiring software packages (Software as a Service, or SaaS). The section on ASPs (leasing software on a hosted service) has been extensively updated. The chapter also expands the explanation of why organizations purchase (or lease) application software and elaborates on the factors to consider for package and vendor selection. The discussion of when to modify purchased software has been revised, including what this means for software contracts and managing vendors. Recent research on acquiring and managing ERP packages is incorporated, as well a new section on open-source software.

Chapter 12 "IT Project Management" has been revised to reflect recent research on managing IT project risks, including recognizing potential IT project failures. The concept of a Program Management Office (PMO) is introduced, and new guidelines are provided for engaging project sponsors and conducting a post-project review. The chapter now ends with a special section on managing virtual teams, including topics to include in training programs for increasing awareness of potential cultural differences.

Chapter 13 "Supporting Computer Users" has been shortened and simplified, as well as updated. Additional computer security issues are presented, and the section on supporting telecommuters has been expanded to address new support and security concerns. Issues to consider when introducing new social networking tools within organizations are discussed in a new section on managing intranets.

Part 4: The Information Management System

Chapter 14 "Planning Information Systems Resources" has been revised to incorporate IT architecture maturity stages, scenario planning (as a tool), and updated technology planning examples.

Chapter 15 "Leading the Information Systems Function" has been completely restructured to emphasize management of the three IT assets introduced in Chapter 1. Current management practices and recent field research have been incorporated in the discussions of IT governance, IT service delivery, managing an organization's portfolio of applications, IT staff retention, and managing offshore IT outsourcing arrangements. Relevant IT labor statistics have been incorporated, including research on IT skills that organizations consider to be critical to keep in-house.

Chapter 16 "Information Security" is a totally new chapter written for this edition. It emphasizes managerial approaches to managing information risks, including the development and distribution of security policies and business continuity planning. Recent laws that impact IT security practices are summarized, and electronic records management approaches and the role of the Chief Information Security Officer are introduced. E-crime statistics and the technical approaches to prevent and deter them have been updated.

Chapter 17 "Legal, Ethical, and Social Issues" has been substantially revised (and the discussions on e-crime and related issues were moved to Chapter 16). The opening section on ethics frameworks has been shortened and simplified. The remainder of the chapter focuses on individual and societal issues, with an emphasis on privacy issues, identity theft, and intellectual property rights.

NEW IN THE SIXTH EDITION: TEACHING CASES

In addition to the 17 prior published cases that are essentially unchanged, this edition includes 13 totally new or substantially revised cases, as described below.

Part 1: Information Technology

Case Study I-2: VoIP2.biz, Inc.: Deciding on the Next Steps for a VoIP Supplier NEW—This case study deals with product development issues faced by an IT industry company developing products and services for an emerging technology: Voice over Internet Protocol (VoIP).

Case Study I-3: The VoIP Adoption at Butler University NEW—The VoIP adoption decision process, and details about the implementation approach used to implement this new technology, are described in detail. Potential benefits for administrative departments and students are assessed, and the case ends as the impacts on the IS organization in this mid-sized university are beginning to be realized.

Case Study I-4: Data Governance at InsuraCorp   NEW—A corporate restructuring and new business pressures for data integration raise issues about data ownership, data quality, and other new data governance issues for a newly centralized IS organization in a large insurance firm.

Part 2: Applying Information Technology

Case Study II-1: Vendor-Managed Inventory at NIBCO   NEW—Following its initial Big-Bang implementation of multiple modules of an ERP system, NIBCO continuously improves its business processes and purchases additional vendor modules to pursue new strategic opportunities. A vendor-managed inventory initiative, in which NIBCO becomes a sole-source provider for selected business customers, is described in detail. The case study ends with NIBCO's management wondering how best to continue to leverage its new IT and business capabilities.

Case Study II-3: Real-Time Business Intelligence at Continental Airlines   NEW—Based on an award-winning case study, the Continental Airlines case study demonstrates how real-time data warehousing and business intelligence applications resulted in the organization's turnaround from a poor performer to an industry leader. The case is not heavy on technical details, but the essence of the technology is explained. The focus is on the process for delivery of data management services (data warehousing) for data sharing and decision making.

Case Study II-4: The Cliptomania™ Web Store: An E-tailing Start-up Survival Story REVISED—This case study has been expanded to cover Cliptomania's experience as the Web has evolved in ways that have challenged e-tailers to adapt or perish. A Web-based company's position on a search results page is paramount, and material on how Google ranks the results of a search is included as well as an example of what can happen to your sales if you do not understand the ranking algorithms.

Case Study II-5: Meridian Hospital Systems, Inc.: Deciding Which IT Company to Join REVISED—This case study builds on an earlier case about a real startup firm (Mezzia, Inc.). The focus now is entirely on a graduating student's career decision about whether to accept a position to work for a small startup company (now a fictional company) or for a well-established IT industry company (Hewlett-Packard).

Part 3: Acquiring Information Systems

Case Study III-5: The Kuali Financial System: An Open Source Project   NEW—Several universities have joined together to develop a comprehensive suite of financial systems tailored to the needs of higher education institutions and make it available to the educational community without charge under an open source license. The case study presents the organizational, management, and development approaches employed to overcome the challenges in getting agreement on system requirements by seven institutions and in successful development using personnel located from Hawaii to New York.

Case Study III-10: Purchasing a Student Management System at Jefferson County School System (Revised)   REVISED—The JCSS case study has been substantially revised to update the technology to the current infrastructure at the camouflaged organization. It is now purely a software purchase rather than a bundled hardware and software purchase. The issues in the case remain the same but some restructuring has been done to more clearly separate the purchase decision from its implementation.

Part 4: The Information Management System

Case Study IV-1: The Clarion School for Boys, Inc. – Milwaukee Division: Making an Information Systems Investment   REVISED—This case study has been revised to demonstrate decisions about technologies available today.

Case Study IV-4: IT Infrastructure Outsourcing at Schaeffer (A): The Outsourcing Decision   REVISED—The camouflaged context of the previously published IT outsourcing decision story at Schaeffer has been somewhat modified to incorporate insights learned from the development of a "B" case (see Case Study IV-5).

Case Study IV-5: IT Infrastructure Outsourcing at Schaeffer (B): Managing the Contract   NEW—Managing a 7-year IT infrastructure outsourcing contract at Schaeffer involves accommodating some anticipated business changes, as well as addressing some unexpected challenges in managing the vendor relationship. The case ends with management facing the decision of whether or not to renew the vendor contract in light of its experiences working with the vendor and its most recent business change.

Case Study IV-8: Mary Morrison's Ethical Issue (Revised)   REVISED—The issues in this version remain the same as before, but Mary's personal background has been modified to keep the focus on the ethical issues.

THE SUPPLEMENT PACKAGE: WWW.PRENHALL.COM/BROWN

A comprehensive and flexible technology support package is available to enhance the teaching and learning experience. All instructor and student supplements are available on the text's Web site. See: *www.prenhall.com/brown*. The Web site also includes a large number of "old favorite" case studies from earlier editions.

Instructor Resource Center

The following Instructor Resources are available on the secure faculty section of the Brown Web site:

- *Instructor's Manual* The Instructor's Manual includes syllabi for several courses (both undergraduate and master's level) that have used in this book. It also includes lecture notes on each chapter, answers to the review and discussion questions at the end of each chapter, teaching notes on the case studies, and a test bank for assistance in preparing examinations based on this book.

- *Test Item File and TestGen Software* The Test Item File is a comprehensive collection of multiple-choice, T/F, and fill-in-the-blank questions. The Test Item File is available in Microsoft Word and for use with the computerized Prentice Hall TestGen, as well as WebCT- and Blackboard-ready conversions. TestGen is a comprehensive suite of tools for testing and assessment. It allows instructors to easily create and distribute tests for their courses, either by printing and distributing through traditional methods or by online delivery via a local area network (LAN) server. TestGen features Screen Wizards to assist you as you move through the program, and the software is backed with full technical support.

■ *PowerPoint Slides* PowerPoint slides are available that illuminate and build on key concepts in the text. Professors can customize the presentation by adding their own slides or by editing the existing ones.

■ The *Image Library* is a collection of the text art organized by chapter. This collection includes all of the figures, tables, and screenshots (as permission allows) from the book. These images can be used to enhance class lectures and PowerPoint slides.

CourseSmart eTextbooks Online

CourseSmart is an exciting new *choice* for instructors and students. As an alternative to purchasing the print textbook, students can purchase an electronic version of the same content as the print text at a reduced cost. With a CourseSmart etextbook, students can search the text, make notes online, print out reading assignments that incorporate lecture notes, and bookmark important passages for later review. www.coursesmart.com.

ACKNOWLEDGMENTS

Our thanks go to our professional colleagues who have used one or more versions of the book and provided valuable feedback to us, as well as the reviewers who responded to the publisher's request. The list is too long to provide here, but we hope that they will accept our anonymous THANKS!

Special thanks also goes to current and prior Indiana University colleagues and former students who have authored content for specific chapters: Dwight Worker (information security chapter) and Susan A. Brown (data resource chapter). Other colleagues have also assisted us with important sections for the chapters: Dong-Gil Ko, Lisa Murphy, Jay Newquist, Madhu Rao, Andrew Urbaczewski, and Ramesh Venkataraman. The following individuals have also collaborated with us on case study research or co-authored teaching cases that appear in this book: Ron Anderson-Lehman, S. Balaji, Greg Clancy, Tony Easterlin, Dale Goodhue, Vijay Khatri, Scott A. Kincaid, Nicholas Lockwood, Stephen R. Nelson, John Sacco, Rebecca Scholer, Mohan Tatikonda, Iris Vessey, Hugh Watson, Taylor Wells, Bradley Wheeler, Michael Williams, and Barbara Wixom. Taylor Wells and Nicholas Lockwood also assisted with the development of the instructor resources for this edition.

We have also benefited from several sources of support for our research that have led to the development of teaching cases for this textbook, as well as for support for teaching case development specifically—including the IM Affiliates program at the Kelley School of Business at Indiana University, the EDS Corporation, British American Tobacco, SAP-America, Teradata Corporation, the Center for Information Systems Research at the Sloan School of Management, and the Society for Information Management (SIM).

Finally, each author extends their gratitude to the other four for their intellect, professionalism, and longtime interest in providing quality instructional materials for today's and tomorrow's business managers and IS leaders.

Carol V. Brown
Daniel W. DeHayes
Jeffrey A. Hoffer
E. Wainright Martin
William C. Perkins

October 2007

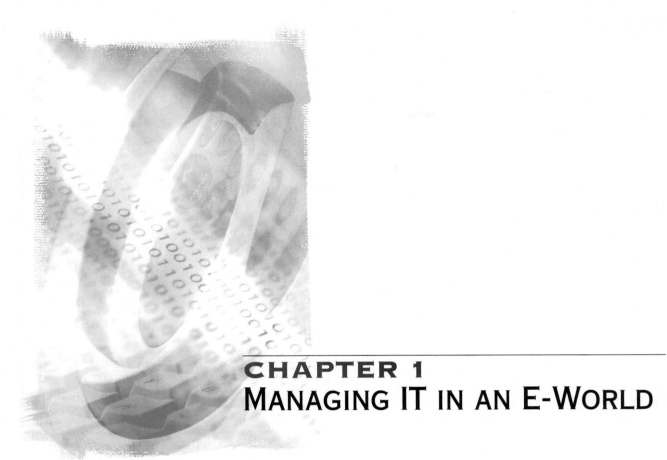

CHAPTER 1
MANAGING IT IN AN E-WORLD

THE USE OF INFORMATION TECHNOLOGY (IT) IN TODAY'S WORLD HAS become pervasive. Businesses have information systems that connect front-line employees with back-office accounting and production systems. Traditional companies compete with dot-com (Internet only) companies via Web-based stores that have become additional sales, marketing, and customer service channels. Some work teams never meet face-to-face but use group meeting tools, instant messaging, and video conferencing to collaborate. Office e-mail can be accessed anytime, anywhere. New workers may choose a BlackBerry or iPhone instead of a simple cell phone, and employees who travel can access high-speed wireless networks in airports and from a hotel room to keep them in contact with their businesses.

Many of today's consumers also live in an increasingly "flat world" in which IT linkages across emerging, developing, and developed economies help to "level" the economic playing field (Friedman, 2005). Schoolchildren learn to do research via Internet searches rather than using books in school libraries. Citizens across the globe can access world news online. People moving to a new geographic area within the United States don't have to change their cell phone numbers, and can use geographical positioning systems in their cars to help them find their way.

The day-to-day management of computer hardware, software, and networks to enable this pervasive IT world, or e-world, is the responsibility of IT professionals. However, all business managers, not just IT managers, are responsible for investing wisely in and effectively utilizing these information technologies. By the year 2000, more than half of capital expenditures by businesses in developed countries were for IT purchases.

The target audience for this IT management textbook therefore includes both current and future managers—both business and IT managers. Our primary objective is to increase your knowledge about managing IT within organizations. In the following chapters we will describe "best practices" for acquiring, implementing, and managing new and old IT system solutions, as well as proven approaches to developing IT capabilities that will generate the greatest value to a business.

The objective of this first textbook chapter is to set the stage for the remaining 16 chapters and 30 cases that follow. We first briefly describe some of the major IT trends that have led to (1) new ways for businesses to compete in today's world, and (2) new

> We define **information technology (IT)** as computer technology (hardware and software) for processing and storing information, as well as communications technology (networks) for transmitting information.

ways for employees to accomplish their work. Then we briefly introduce the IT leadership role in today's organizations—including three general IT assets that need to be managed and some typical managerial responsibilities in an IS department. The chapter ends with a brief summary of the topics that will be covered in the remaining four parts of this textbook.

RECENT INFORMATION TECHNOLOGY TRENDS

As a direct user of various computer and communication devices, you are probably already aware of some of the improvements in computer hardware, software, and communication networks that have been introduced by IT vendors over the past decade. This fast rate of innovation in the IT industry makes it difficult to accurately predict the IT products and services that will be "winners" tomorrow—and significant *mis*predictions about technologies have been common in the past (see the box "Mispredictions by IT Industry Leaders").

However, it seems safe to predict that computers and electronic communications devices will continue to touch almost every aspect of our lives. In Part I of this textbook, we will discuss in detail the key concepts underlying today's hardware, software, and communications technologies. For now, let us briefly consider some of the technology developments that have already led to ubiquitous computing in the first decade of this twenty-first century.

Computer Hardware: Faster, Cheaper, Mobile

Computer-on-a-chip (microcomputer) technology was available as early as the 1970s, and the introduction of the first IBM Personal Computer (PC) in 1981 was the beginning of desktop computing. Today, desktop and notebook-sized PCs produced by manufacturers around the world have become "commodity products" with processing power that is equivalent to an organization's entire computing center of the 1960s. The typical PC today has an easy-to-use operating system with graphical icons, point-and-click screen navigation, and preloaded software to play music and videos downloaded from the Internet—all at a cheaper price than what the same features would have cost 12 months earlier. Because of their

---

MISPREDICTIONS BY IT INDUSTRY LEADERS

This "telephone" has too many shortcomings to be seriously considered as a means of communication. The device is inherently of no value to us.
—*Western Union internal memo, 1876*

I think there is a world market for maybe five computers.
—*Thomas Watson, chairman of IBM, 1943*

But what [is a microchip] good for?
Engineer at the Advanced Computing Systems Division of IBM, 1968

There is no reason anyone would want a computer in their home.
—*Ken Olson, president, chairman, and founder of Digital Equipment Corp., 1977*

640K ought to be enough for anybody.
—*Attributed to Bill Gates, chairman of Microsoft, 1981*

Dell has a great business model, but that dog won't scale.
John Shoemaker, head of Sun's server division, 2000
[Sources: Kappelman, 2001; Jones, 2003]

---

portability and wireless capabilities, lightweight notebook computers have also replaced many of the larger desktop machines: They can be carried into meetings, taken on business trips, and used at home to connect to office e-mail.

Smaller, handheld devices have also become indispensable business tools to access e-mail and other applications inside and outside of the office, on the factory floor, or in hospital corridors. These devices have also continued to increase in functionality. For example, in mid-2007 Apple Computer began selling a new mobile phone with digital camera (iPhone) that simplifies calling from an address book and offers e-mail, text messaging, visual voice mail, video playing, and Web browsing via Wi-Fi connectivity and touch screen navigation and scrolling. As miniaturized computer devices and cellular phones have become ubiquitous in all types of locations. IT vendors have also developed new applications to help mobile users locate a specific business building or restaurant, to alert them of schedule changes, or to provide other business or customer support.

Computer Software: Custom and Prewritten, Standardized and Integrated

By the early 1990s, some version of Microsoft Corporation's Windows software had become the standard operating system for the vast majority of microcomputers being used as

---

We use the term **information systems (IS)** department to refer to the organizational unit or department that has the primary responsibility for managing IT.

desktop and portable computer "clients." By the mid-1990s, Microsoft's Office suite (word processing, spreadsheet, database, presentation, and e-mail software sold in a single bundle), and a few years later Microsoft's Web browser (Internet Explorer) had also become the *de facto* software in U.S. organizations and multinational companies. These software standards made it easier for individuals and organizations to work and communicate with other employees and business partners.

Over the past decade, many organizations have also invested in software packages with integrated modules that can share the same enterprise-wide database or pass data across dispersed work teams, business divisions, and national boundaries in "real time." These types of **enterprise systems** have now been widely adopted by manufacturing and service firms of all sizes, in the United States, and around the globe. Custom or purchased software applications that can access these databases are also used by suppliers to replenish materials for a manufacturing firm or retailer or by customers to check on order fulfillment.

Computer Networks: High Bandwidth, Global, and Wireless

The introduction of a Web browser in the mid-1990s that used an Internet communications standard (TCP/IP) led to a large wave of IT investments to link companies and individuals to the Internet. Subsequent investments by telecommunications firms and communities in fiber-optic (high-bandwidth) lines have made possible speedier Web page retrievals and downloads of large voice and video files. Today, many consumers pay their television cable company or telephone service provider for this type of high-bandwidth access to the Internet from their homes.

Today's companies have also invested in wireless technologies to provide mobile support to their employees. Satellite and cellular technologies also link remote workers to central support centers, travelers to travel services, and delivery personnel to transportation schedulers. Wireless technologies have also enabled some developing countries to bypass expensive investments in hard-wired telecommunications lines to new business buildings or rural communities.

NEW WAYS TO COMPETE

Since the 1960s, computers have been used to help companies compete by low cost, differentiation, or both (Porter, 2001).

- *Low Cost*—competing with other businesses by being a low-cost producer of a good or a service
- *Differentiation*—competing with other businesses by offering products or services that customers prefer due to a superiority in characteristics such as product innovativeness or image, product quality, or customer service

For example, computers can *lower the costs* of products or services by automating business transactions, shortening order cycle times, and providing operational data for decision making. In the 1980s a flood of IT innovations brought additional efficiency gains—such as shortening the time to develop new products with computer-aided design tools; optimizing a plant floor process with software that implements a human expert's decision rules; and speedily changing a production line with computerized planning systems based on sales information.

IT has also been used by companies to *differentiate* their products or services from those of competitors. By the 1980s, firms began to develop custom IT applications that provided sales personnel with information to help them better service a specific customer; just-in-time supplies for business customers; and new information-based products such as drug interaction information for health care providers.

More recently, companies have been looking for new ways to compete using the Internet. In the mid-1990s, most companies just used the Web to create a "presence" on the Internet: Managers registered memorable names for a URL for their company's public Web site and then posted information ("brochureware") for stockholders and other stakeholders. But by the late 1990s, traditional companies could see how Amazon.com and other dot-com innovators were using the Web, and they too began to use Web technologies as a new channel to their customers. However, since the features of a public Web site are also visible to competitors and can be quickly copied by them, in recent years it has become more difficult for companies to compete by product or service differentiation via the Web than it was in an offline world.

In addition, a company's customers may have direct access to Web sites that allow them to easily compare similar products and their prices. For example, airline companies no longer need travel agents to sell tickets, which saves them many dollars per ticket. However, consumers can now compare ticket prices and schedules online (via travel sites such as Expedia, Travelocity, or Orbitz) and even be electronically alerted to ticket price changes for a given route as they occur. This means the airlines face more severe pressures for low prices, and also find it difficult to differentiate their services from each other.

On the other hand, the Internet can increase a company's "reach" to new customers and new suppliers, which may even be on different continents. Web sites can be programmed to display screens using a different language, different currency, and even perhaps local pricing, depending on the user's browser location or selected preferences. Some businesses also buy, or sell, products using Web-based auctions with suppliers or customers that they will never meet face-to-face. Advertising via the Internet has also become increasingly common.

These new types of e-business systems have also greatly expanded the types of IT solutions that today's IT professionals need to develop and manage.

NEW WAYS TO WORK

Recent IT innovations in computer hardware, software, and networks have also enabled people to work more productively as employees in an office—as well as employees who are telecommuters at a work site far from a home office, are members of "virtual" teams, or are even "free agents" contracted by organizations for a short-term project.

For example, sales personnel and other traveling managers have become **telecommuters** with portable computers and other mobile equipment that give them access to company data anytime (24 hours a day, 7 days a week) and essentially anywhere (from an off-site office, home office, hotel room, airport, or on the road). Some cities have also experimented with laws that require businesses to support telecommuting by implementing work schedules that require less commuting—such as four days working in the office and one day working outside it—to help protect the environment.

Also common in many companies are **virtual teams**—that is, work teams with members who are separated too far geographically to work face-to-face. Team members may use software that facilitates document sharing and online video-conferencing from the desktop or in specially equipped videoconferencing rooms. Team members in different time zones now commonly participate in electronic meetings outside of regular office hours with individuals who are at different work sites or home offices on different continents.

Some new businesses might not even have a physical office building or headquarters. Instead, the company might operate as a "virtual organization" made up of individual professionals scattered across different domestic or global locations. Individuals with specialized skills may also choose to work independently as **free agents** who contract out their services without being a permanent employee of any organization. Organizations that hire free agents usually do so because they can obtain specialized skills that are temporarily needed for a specific project without having to make a long-term commitment to an employee for salary and expensive benefits (such as health care insurance).

These new ways of working have also greatly expanded the types of IT solutions that today's IT professionals need to develop and manage.

MANAGING IT IN ORGANIZATIONS

Supporting these new ways of competing and these new ways of working with computer hardware, software, and networks is the responsibility of the **information systems (IS) department** within a business. Although essentially all modern organizations are dependent on IT networks and applications for operational and decision-making support, not all organizations have the same level of dependency on IT. As shown in Figure 1.1, some organizations may still use IT primarily for back-office support (the Support quadrant), but rely heavily on person-to-person communications to operate their business; others may be heavily dependent on information systems up and running 24/7 for all their business operations, but don't actively invest in the latest new technologies to compete in new ways as a business (the Factory quadrant); and still others may be critically dependent on new IT applications for implementing new business strategies as well as running their business operations without interruption (the Strategic quadrant).

Organizations also don't always have the same level of IT dependency over time. For example, the business managers

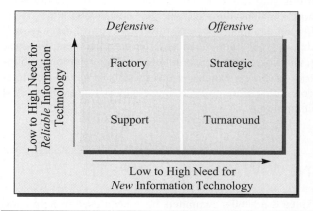

Figure 1.1   Four Modes of Dependency on IT (Based on Nolan and McFarlan, 2005)

Technology Asset
> Computer and communications infrastructure
> that enables information sharing over standard
> IT platforms

Relationship Asset
> Established partnering relationships for joint
> IT-business decision-making

Human Asset
> Pool of IT people talent for needed mix of
> technology and business skills

Figure 1.2   Three IT Assets (Adapted from Ross et al., 1996).

of an organization in the Support quadrant may see an opportunity to take advantage of a new technology, and move to the Turnaround quadrant, with the intent of moving into the Strategic quadrant. This type of change requires significant investments in IT assets—including not only new information technologies, but also new personnel with the necessary IT skill sets as well as new leadership talent, as described in the next sections.

Three IT Assets

Today's increased dependence on IT by businesses in many different industries requires IT leaders who know how to effectively manage three types of IT assets (see Figure 1.2): technology, relationship, and human assets (Ross, Beath, and Goodhue, 1996). Each of these IT assets is described in some detail next.

Technology Asset   Managing this asset requires effective planning, building, and operating of a computer and communications infrastructure—an information "utility"—so that managers and other employees have the right information available as needed, anytime, anywhere. Just like landline telephone users expect to receive a dial tone as they initiate a call, computer users expect computers to be up and running, and networks to be available and fast, so that they can access software applications and data quickly and easily. Organizations with high operational dependence on IT systems (organizations in the Factory and Strategic quadrants in Figure 1.1) are so dependent on IT that if an information system fails for a minute or more, or online response time exceeds a few seconds, employees can't get their work done. When customer transactions can't be processed, and suppliers can't receive orders for materials, business revenues suffer.

In a widely read but poorly titled article (called "IT Doesn't Matter") published in the *Harvard Business Review*

a few years ago, the author argued that the primary IT management role today is to manage the costs and vulnerabilities of the computing "utility"—the data centers and networks that provide access to business data and applications. However, while this is a critical IT management role, it is *not the only one*. Managing IT requires not only keeping computers and networks running, but also identifying what new technologies to invest in and how to specifically design and use these new IT solutions to improve the way a company does business. Effective management of the technology asset therefore requires not only successful IT managers and professionals, but also active participation by business managers—as captured by the next IT asset: the relationship asset.

Relationship Asset   This IT asset refers to how well an organization uses joint IT-business decision making for making investments in a firm's technology assets. IT is so integral to business today, that there needs to be a "blending" of IT and the business (see the box entitled "Blending IT and the Business"). Achieving business value from IT investments requires strong working partnerships between business managers and IT managers (Brown, 2004) to develop the business case for investing in new IT solutions and skill sets, for specifying the business requirements that will be used to design new IT applications, and for effectively implementing these new IT solutions so that the potential benefits become realized benefits.

BLENDING IT AND THE BUSINESS

Blending technology and the more traditional business disciplines has always been a challenge, one that I recognized in my early days at another company. I volunteered to do a job in what was then "data processing," generating projects and managing them, primarily to run the internal systems of the business. I was not embraced as part of the business but rather operated in my own little domain. I had a hard time getting their attention.

This experience began to teach me some important lessons. The business managers who refused to help got the worst outcomes: Their projects were delayed, inadequate, and more expensive than we had planned. I concluded that it wasn't intentional: They couldn't appreciate the potential of their involvement. Many of them didn't see technology as integral to their business; instead, they saw IT merely as a tool. Information technology is now so integral to business that a business leader must be smart about the key elements and trade-offs.

[Adapted from Pottruck and Pearce, 2000]

Human Asset Managing the human resources for any business function requires attention to recruiting, developing, and retaining the best talent available. Today there is a high demand not just for IT personnel with specialized technology skills, but also for personnel who have both technology skills *and* business knowledge. Business analyst and systems analyst roles require personnel who can understand the IT needs of workers in marketing, accounting, manufacturing, and other business functions. IT professionals who have a business education, as well as technical skills, are therefore especially in demand for these types of roles. These positions also are most effectively sourced "in-house" by people who are employees of the business—not by employees of an outsourcing firm or by temporary contract personnel.

Today within the United States there are concerns about the supply of new college and university graduates with IT-related majors being *lower than the demand* for entry-level, domestic IT workers. For example, Microsoft recently collaborated with chapters of the Society for Information Management (SIM) to help fund information sessions on college campuses to dispel common "myths" about the lack of domestic demand for IT workers (as summarized in Figure 1.3). Although companies in developed countries such as the United States have increasingly been utilizing IT workers in less developed countries to take advantage of lower labor costs, IT professionals are still critically needed to perform "in-house" IT responsibilities.

IT Leadership Roles

IT leaders in today's organizations come from a variety of backgrounds. Some managers are chosen to lead the IT

- IT is vital to business profitability
- Fast pace of technological change keeps IT careers interesting
- Offshoring threat overstated
- Globalization of IT is an opportunity
- U.S. IT worker demand will remain strong

Figure 1.3 Demand for IT Workers in the United States: Dispelling the Myths (Adapted from Future Potential of IT program held at Indiana University, October 2006, sponsored by Microsoft and SIM.)

organization because of their in-depth technical knowledge. Others may be chosen because of their abilities to work well with senior business leaders, not just their technical know-how.

Beginning in the 1980s, an officer-level position for IT leaders began to be created in many large organizations: the **chief information officer (CIO)**. Although not all heads of IT organizations are formally designated a CIO, all of today's IT leaders are expected to work closely with other senior managers to keep the company's IT resources aligned with the goals of the business. This IT leader may report directly to a CEO or president, or may report to another officer—such as a chief financial officer (CFO) or chief operating officer (COO).

A typical organization chart for an IS department in an organization with multiple business units is shown in Figure 1.4. Reporting to the CIO are other IS managers

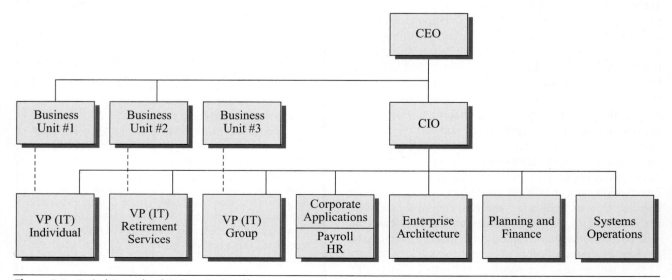

Figure 1.4 Typical Example of IS Organization Chart

responsible for system operations (data centers and networks), designing and building the company's IT architecture and strategic IT planning, as well as acquiring and maintaining software applications (here, applications for corporate functions such as payroll and HR and applications for the insurance company's three business units).

Some companies help ensure strong IT-business alignment by giving managers responsible for business unit applications a reporting relationship to the managers of the business units they support. For example, in the organization chart in Figure 1.4, the three IT vice presidents responsible for developing and maintaining software applications for the company's three different business units have a dotted-line reporting relationship to those business unit heads, in addition to their solid-line reporting relationship to the CIO.

As the dependency on reliable and secure IT networks and applications has increased, other new IS manager roles have also emerged. For example, some companies have created a chief information security officer position to plan for and monitor compliance with new federal reporting requirements and to ensure appropriate investments in technology policies and procedures to manage IT-related security risks.

Senior business managers also play IT leadership roles by serving on committees that approve and prioritize new IT investments, and by being the business sponsors of new software applications for their business areas. Less senior business managers often serve as subject matter (or business process) experts on IT project teams to develop custom software or to select, configure, and implement software packages. These business manager roles are critical ones because business leaders are the most knowledgeable about what changes in work processes will be needed to achieve the greatest business benefits from a new IT solution. Business managers can also best anticipate what obstacles might be encountered when implementing a new software application, and devise ways to avoid them.

THE TOPICS AND ORGANIZATION OF THIS TEXTBOOK

The primary objective of this textbook is to increase your knowledge about IT management so that as an IT manager, or business manager, you can effectively invest in and utilize new and old information technologies. The remaining chapters of this textbook have been grouped into four distinct parts. At the end of each part, we have included several full-length case studies that were written *by the*

authors specifically for this textbook. Although some of the company names are camouflaged, all of these cases are based on real-world practices and events.

Part I. Chapters 2, 3, and 4 on computer hardware, software, and networks provide the non-IS specialist with a good introductory understanding of fundamental technology concepts and major industry developments. For students that already have studied these technology topics, we incorporate recent industry reports and descriptions of technology developments and trends. Chapter 5 provides key concepts about managing data in organizations, another critical IT resource. Business managers are frequently the designated "owners" of different types of data (e.g., customer data, product data), and both IS and business managers share responsibilities for ensuring data accuracy and issuing the rights to data access for employees at all levels.

Part II. These three chapters provide in-depth descriptions of different types of software applications used in today's organizations. Chapter 6 focuses on enterprise systems, which include back-office enterprise systems for financial reporting and managing the company's human resources, internal supply-chain systems, as well as applications that link a company with its customers or suppliers. Chapter 7 describes different types of managerial support systems, which include software applications to support operational decision making by business managers or plant floor supervisors, as well as applications to support strategic decision making using sophisticated financial and marketing analytical tools. Chapter 8 focuses on e-business systems that leverage the Internet, including business-to-business (B2B) and business-to-consumer (B2C) applications, as well as Web sites that play intermediary roles, such as Google. Specific examples of both traditional and dot-com companies are used to generate some early "lessons" for how to use the Internet to survive in today's e-world.

Part III. The five chapters in Part III describe today's "best practices" for developing and implementing applications, managing IT projects, and supporting computer users in organizations. Chapter 9 introduces a broad range of systems concepts and development approaches that prepare the reader for the chapters that follow. Chapters 10 and 11 discuss in detail both traditional and newer methodologies for custom application development and purchased system packages, from the viewpoint of the implementing (client) organization. Chapter 12 discusses effective practices for managing IT projects, including managing specific risks and implementing business changes as part of a systems project. Finally, Chapter 13 focuses on strategies and tactics for supporting an organization's computer users—including remote workers.

Part IV. The first three chapters of Part IV focus on how to effectively develop and manage an organization's IT assets. Chapter 14 focuses on strategic IT planning of information resources from a portfolio perspective. Chapter 15 discusses today's IT leadership roles and responsibilities, including IT governance designs and outsourcing practices from a service management perspective. An entire chapter, Chapter 16, is devoted to discussing information security practices, including approaches to help ensure IT-related compliance with federal laws and other regulations. The final chapter in this textbook, Chapter 17, addresses IT-related issues that extend beyond an organizational setting: social, ethical, and legal issues from the perspective of individuals and societies. Included here are discussions about maintaining the privacy of an individual's personal information and reducing vulnerability to identity theft crimes—some "unintended" social impacts of today's Internet age—as well as examples of ethical dilemmas faced by managers and computer users in general.

As our sixth edition of this textbook is prepared for publication, we authors take pride in having witnessed firsthand the beginnings of an Internet age that holds great opportunities for those not just in developed countries, but also individuals and organizations in developing and emerging countries across the globe. Yet all of us—in our roles as managers, IS specialists, consumers, and world citizens—need to remain vigilant about not only our effective design and use of IT in organizations, but also our social responsibilities for the appropriate usage of today's and tomorrow's information technologies.

REVIEW QUESTIONS

1. Define what is encompassed in the term *information technology*.
2. What are some of the ways that IT has become "pervasive"?
3. What kinds of portable IT can help employees work more efficiently and effectively?
4. What kinds of IT can help support teams when team members work at different locations?
5. How have some businesses used the Internet to compete based on low cost or on product/service differentiation?

6. What kind of a business might be in the Factory quadrant of Figure 1.1?
7. What three IT assets have been identified as more important in today's Internet age, and why?
8. What does *CIO* stand for, and why has such a position been created?
9. For what reasons might an IS manager report not only to a CIO, but also to a business manager?
10. What types of IT leadership roles are performed by a business manager, not an IS department manager, and why?

DISCUSSION QUESTIONS

1. Provide an example of how a business function with which you are familiar (e.g., marketing, finance, operations/production, accounting, human resources) can be highly dependent on IT.
2. Describe some ways that today's information technologies make your life as a student different from students just a few years ago.
3. Some organizations purposefully select IT leaders that have strong business management backgrounds, not just technical experience. Under what circumstances do you think this might be an effective choice?
4. Describe a new business for which you think a "virtual organization"—which has no physical office or headquarters—could be an effective design, and some ways that the leaders of such an organization could use IT to help them effectively run their business.
5. Would you like to work as a free agent? Why or why not?
6. Using Internet resources, identify what is meant by the term *digital divide*. What actions do you think could be taken to lessen this divide—both within your own country and elsewhere in the world?
7. Identify some Web sites that could be useful supplementary resources for studying some of the IT management topics in this textbook.

REFERENCES

Brown, Carol V. 2004. "Seamless IT Alignment." in S. Chowdhury (ed.), *Next Generation Business Handbook*. New York: John Wiley & Sons, 1157–1168.

[*Business 2.0*] 2006. "10 Hot Jobs." *Business 2.0* (May): 96.

[*BusinessWeek*] 2007. "Cover Story: The Future of Work." *BusinessWeek* (August 20 & 27): 42–95.

Carr, Nicholas. 2003. "IT Doesn't Matter." *Harvard Business Review* (May): 41–49.

Clemons, Eric K. 1991. "Evaluation of strategic investments in information technology." *Communications of the ACM* 34 (January): 23–36.

Friedman, Thomas L. 2005. *The World Is Flat: A Brief History of the Twenty-First Century.* New York: Farrar, Strauss and Giroux.

Hilsenrath, Jon E. 2003. "Behind surging productivity: Immune sectors catch the bug." *Wall Street Journal* (November 7): A1, A8.

Jones, Kathryn. 2003. "The Dell Way," *Business 2.0* (February): 23.

Kappelman, Leon. 2001. "The future is ours." *Communications of the ACM* 44:3 (March): 46–47.

[Microsoft Corporation and Society for Information Management] 2006. Slide 17 from "Five Myths about Future Employment in IT," unpublished presentation for Future Potential in IT program at Indiana University-Bloomington (October).

Nolan, Richard and F. Warren McFarlan. 2005. "Information technology and the board of directors." *Harvard Business Review* (October). HBR Reprint R0510F.

Porter, Michael E. 2001. "Strategy and the Internet." *Harvard Business Review* (March): 63–78.

Pottruck, David S. and Terry Pearce. 2000. *Clicks and Mortar: Passion Driven Growth in an Internet Driven World.* San Francisco: Jossey-Bass.

Ross, Jeanne W., Cynthia Mathis Beath, and Dale L. Goodhue. 1996. "Develop long-term competitiveness through IT assets." *Sloan Management Review* 38:1 (Fall): 31–42.

MIDSOUTH CHAMBER OF COMMERCE (A): THE ROLE OF THE OPERATING MANAGER IN INFORMATION SYSTEMS

It was 7:30 P.M. on September 22, 1999, and Leon Lassiter, vice president of marketing with the Midsouth Chamber of Commerce (MSCC), was still in his office, reflecting on the week's frustrations. Lassiter had met with four territory managers, his marketing support supervisor, and a number of other members of his staff. All were upset about their lack of access to the new computer system and the problems they were having using the old PC systems. Lassiter had assured them that the problems were being addressed. He stressed that patience was needed during the ongoing conversion to the new system.

Now, during his private moment, Lassiter was beginning to recognize the problems and complexities he faced with the system conversion. The work of his marketing staff, who were unable to access the new computer system to handle their accounts, had ground to a halt. Even worse, something had happened to the data in most of the old PC systems, which meant that conference registrations and other functions had to be done manually. These inconveniences, however, were minor compared to Lassiter's uneasy feeling that there were problems with Midsouth's whole approach to the management of information technology. Lassiter knew that time was of the essence and that he might have to step in and manage the conversion, even though he had no information technology background. He wondered what he should do next.

Background

In the early 1900s, economic development in the Midsouth area was highly dependent on transportation systems. As a result of legislative decisions, many communities in the Midsouth area could not gain access to reasonable transportation services, thus retarding business and economic development. With no one to represent their concerns to Midsouth's

government, a group of powerful businesspeople formed the Midsouth Chamber of Commerce to lobby the state government on the issue of transportation.

The MSCC dealt with this single issue until the 1930s, when its charter was changed to include a broader range of issues affecting the business community, including state banking laws, transportation, industrial development, and business taxes. By the mid-1980s, the MSCC, under the new leadership of President Jack Wallingford, became an aggressive advocacy organization for the business community.

The shift in the MSCC's role brought substantial change to the organization. In 1978 the MSCC had a staff of 14, a membership of 4,000, and an annual budget of $720,000. Over the years, the MSCC had been able to develop a reserve account of just over $1 million.

By 1986, the staff had grown to 24, the $1 million cash reserve had been drawn down to $250,000, and membership had dropped to 2,300, largely because of local economic problems in the early 1980s. The reserve reduction, supported by the board of directors, had fueled considerable internal growth in terms of staff and capabilities. During this time MSCC also moved into larger offices and began to computerize some manual processes.

By the late 1980s, the MSCC was considered to be the most powerful business advocacy organization in the Midsouth area and one of the most innovative in its approaches and techniques in dealing with problems facing the business community. The greatest problem facing the MSCC at the time was the growing concern that its aggressive growth might have to be curtailed because it could no longer fund its annual operating budget.

Leon Lassiter

In mid-1988, Wallingford was faced with a serious dilemma. The MSCC was projecting a $330,000 deficit for the 1989 fiscal year. Wallingford realized he was going to have to reduce both the number of staff and the number of programs or find some way to grow revenue more aggressively in the organization. Wallingford called in his vice president of public affairs and operations, Ed Wilson, and asked him to find someone new to lead the sales and marketing function.

Leon Lassiter came to the MSCC in December 1988 with 8 years of experience in sales management and marketing with American Brands, where he had recently turned down a promotion to regional sales manager. The MSCC, he reasoned, offered more of an opportunity to have an impact than at American Brands. He reported to Wallingford. Lassiter quickly began making dramatic changes. He found that the marketing support functions were better coordinated and managed than the sales functions. Additionally, although the MSCC had purchased a personal computer for sales and marketing and had installed some custom software in 1986, the system was quite limited in capability. With these facts, Lassiter began to develop an entirely new sales and marketing system based on measurable goals, documented operating procedures, and regular training programs.

Early Computerization Activity

Ed Wilson, who joined the MSCC in 1981, performed a variety of duties at the MSCC. He coordinated the legislative lobbying team, managed Midsouth's operations, and, during the time that there was no vice president of marketing, managed that function as well.

Beginning in 1986, Wilson began introducing the MSCC to the world of microcomputers and database management. Most of the staff were skeptical of the automation effort and reluctant to accept this approach. However, with the help of a systems consultant, Wilson acquired equipment and hired a programmer to write custom software in each functional area. Three primary user groups were identified: the marketing division, the operations division, and the human resources division. One IBM PC and printer were ordered for each group.

Marketing Division   The marketing division's primary need was to track the activity occurring in membership. Primary uses of its computer system included:

- Developing a membership database
- Developing a prospective member database
- Making daily changes to both databases
- Generating a series of letters for personalized mail contact
- Generating prospect and member lists and labels by standard industrial classification (SIC) code, firm size (sales, employment), zip code, mailing designator, and other criteria
- Processing call-record activity by the territory managers
- Tracking member activities and concerns through a comment field
- Creating audit trails for reviewing changes
- General word processing

The marketing support area managed the database on the PC. They filled all requests for labels, lists, and changes from the sales and marketing staff. Requested changes to the member database sometimes backed up as much as 2 weeks. Lassiter felt this was unacceptable and required a 3-day turnaround on member-change activity.

Four territory managers, a marketing support supervisor, and two clerical people staffed the marketing division. The territory managers generated 75 to 80 call records per day that required database changes, letters, and invoice processing. Taking turns at the computer, both clerical people generally took a total of 12 hours to process these activities. In addition, the clerical staff processed commissions on membership sales, member cancellations, and general database maintenance. The clerical staff also prepared special-letter requests from the territory managers and performed all normal secretarial duties. Soon after the installation of the first PC system, the marketing staff began lobbying for additional capacity.

Operations Division   Ed Wilson managed the operations division. Fourteen managers and support staff worked in operations. This group needed a system capable of providing financial and accounting controls, because until 1986, all payment histories and financial and accounting transactions were recorded in a ledger book and tracked by hand.

During the late 1980s, Wilson and his accounting manager set out a series of needs for the information system to meet. These included:

- The general ledger system
- Fund balances
- Accrual accounting functions
- Payment history tracking
- Commission schedules
- Membership cancellation tracking
- Report generation

In addition, Wilson wanted the operations system to be able to track legislative bills from their introduction through their demise in committee or chamber, their passage, or their veto by the governor. This information would be keyed into the system, updated as changes occurred, printed, and sent to selected staff members on a daily basis. Soon after installing one PC system to handle both functions, financial and legislative, Wilson wished he had ordered two systems for the operations division.

Human Resources Division   The human resources division, with two managers and two support staff, was responsible for developing a conference and seminar tracking and reporting mechanism that would also have the capability of printing out badges for conference or seminar attendees. The division also maintained personnel records. Wilson's decision to buy a PC system for this group seemed to fit well with their needs.

From 1987 through 1992, use of the three systems grew steadily. In 1992, Wilson again hired an outside consultant to review the organization's information needs and select appropriate additional hardware and software. After a careful study, the consultant, Ted Vassici, recommended adding six more IBM PCs. In early 1993, the systems were ordered, each with HP laser printers, and allocated as follows: marketing (3), public finance (1), operations (1), and human resources (1). (See Exhibit 1 for the MSCC organization chart.)

In 1995, Vassici revised and updated the custom software used by each division. He also developed the MSCC's marketing software to sell to other membership-related organizations. Lassiter actively promoted the software, and the MSCC earned a small royalty on these sales.

Changing Times

By 1993, as a result of Lassiter's marketing and sales reorganization and Wilson's aggressive management of expenses, the MSCC was experiencing solid financial growth. While the two men were primarily responsible for the success, Wilson and Lassiter clashed on numerous occasions. Lassiter felt that much of the territory managers' work and marketing support activities could be automated to provide the MSCC with a significant reduction in labor and allied costs. Lassiter believed that a full-time systems analyst should be hired to meet the growing needs of the MSCC. Wilson, on the other hand, was worried about the cost of information systems. He felt that by maintaining the relationship with Vassici, he could control the rapidly growing demand for computer capabilities but not increase the number of employees. He knew that, as a nonprofit agency, there were limited funds for the expansion of computer capabilities. Adding a

EXHIBIT 1
MSCC Organizational Structure

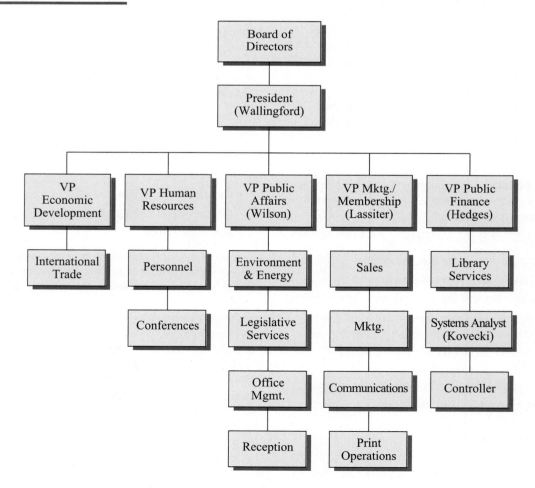

full-time systems analyst to the staff would make it significantly more difficult to contend with growing staff demands in other areas. Continuing the relationship with Vassici provided Wilson with the ability to specify exactly what Vassici worked on and what should be tabled until there was the time and budget for it.

Although Lassiter and Wilson continued to clash, Lassiter understood Wilson's desire to control costs in light of the limited resources of the MSCC. Lassiter knew that the slowly growing computer sophistication of the staff would explode once the tap was fully opened. However, Lassiter felt that the demand could be dealt with effectively once the MSCC determined the extent of the staff's needs.

In early 1996, Lassiter and Wilson joined forces on a concept by which the MSCC would offer a health insurance program to its members, now more than 4,500. Although the proposal was eventually rejected by the board of directors, Wilson and Lassiter, as a result of the study, determined that there were many revenue-producing opportunities the MSCC could pursue that would require a much higher level of information systems use. Wilson soon hired a systems analyst to increase the MSCC's capabilities.

Simon Kovecki, a young computer science graduate with no experience in a membership organization like the MSCC or with accounting software, joined the MSCC in June 1996 and spent his first 3 months on the job learning the organization and its computing systems. He worked exceptionally long hours as he struggled to understand software for which there was no documentation. Calls to Vassici for help were useless because his business had closed.

Through early 1997, Wilson continued to manage the computer systems and, with the help of Kovecki, upgraded the hardware in the PCs and printers with faster CPUs, memory upgrades, higher-capacity hard disks, and better monitors. With Kovecki's constant attention, the software continued to work relatively well. In 1997 Wilson, with Kovecki's assistance, developed an online legislative information system on a PC that was considered state of the art in the chamber of commerce industry. With this application and the growth in members and types of computer applications, the MSCC senior management began to worry about the separation of systems for membership and marketing, finance, conferences, and other applications which required constant data re-entry.

With annual dues approaching $2.8 million and approximately 4,750 member firms, the MSCC was among the largest statewide chambers of commerce in the country. By 1998, the staff had swelled to 42 and the financial reserve was nearly $2.6 million. Although Lassiter felt some satisfaction with the MSCC's growth and financial strength, he was bothered with the lack of forethought as to how the MSCC might develop a comprehensive plan to use information for competitive advantage. Wilson, too, recognized the value of information systems to an organization in the business of gathering, analyzing, and using information to affect legislative outcomes.

Catalyst for Change

By 1998, the MSCC had reached a point where change had to occur. Wallingford, at the urging of the board of directors, assigned Lassiter the additional areas of communications, graphic arts, and printing operations. Controller duties were assigned to Harry Taska, and Jeff Hedges, the new vice president of public finance, was assigned responsibility for computer operations. Wilson, nearing retirement, retained his public affairs activities and was asked to focus his efforts on developing an important public affairs project. (See Exhibit 1.)

Just after the staff changes took place, Kovecki confided to Lassiter that he was disappointed by the changes in staff responsibility. He felt he should have been elevated to manager of information systems and given additional staff. Hedges, who had little computer background, was also in charge of research on various issues of interest to the members of the MSCC as well as oversight of the controller's function. Kovecki was concerned that Hedges would not have the time to manage the growing computer operations properly.

Although the changes took place in early 1998, Lassiter had anticipated the changes in late 1997. His concern over the continued lack of attention to the information systems area led him to send out requests for information to a number of firms servicing the software needs of organizations like the MSCC. Primarily interested in sales and account tracking software, he focused on software systems from Cameo, MEI Colorado Association of Commerce and Industry, Connecticut Business and Industry Association, TelePro 2000, and Data Link. Lassiter sent the information he received from these vendors to other key managers but received little response. Wilson was involved in his new project, Taska was learning his new duties as controller, and Hedges had little time to examine the computer activities.

In August 1998, Lassiter attended a national association meeting where a session on management software led to his discovery of a small firm called UNITRAK. The company had developed a UNIX-based software system that was Y2K compliant. Lassiter was convinced that the software would meet the MSCC's needs. He based his assessment on the MSCC's current and anticipated future needs for computing capabilities that had been developed by Kovecki in 1997. (See Exhibit 2.)

Planning the New Data Processing System

Lassiter had identified areas in UNITRAK where he felt this more powerful information system would allow the MSCC to be more efficient. These improvements would enable staff members to:

- Input member information into a notes field (not then available)
- Generate telemarketing scripts that would allow "tree scripting" based on various sales objections (not then available)

EXHIBIT 2
MSCC Information Systems Needs

Information Systems Capabilities	Marketing	Operations	Public Affairs	Public Finance	Economic Development	Human Resources	Executive
Word Processing	X	X	X	X	X	X	X
Record Maintenance	X						
Legislative Services			X				
Online Publications			X		X		
List Processing	X						
Label Generation	X				X		
Database Management	X		X		X	X	
Financial Controls		X					
Conference Registration	X	X			X	X	
Seminar Registration	X	X	X			X	
Billings/Invoicing	X	X				X	
Publication Processing	X	X		X			
Data Search/Research				X			
Inventory Tracking	X	X					
Desktop Publishing	X					X	
Project Management	X	X	X		X	X	

- Utilize a statistical inquiry feature that would provide quantitative analysis of sales activity figures from all marketing activities (not attempted with the separate PC systems)

In addition, the new information system would allow territory managers to:

- Access their account information from their PCs rather than asking a staff member
- Develop letters and attachments from their PCs using information in the central database rather than manually linking information contained in several separate databases

In a memo to the management group, Lassiter commented, "The UNITRAK system not only meets our needs now, but it is also powerful enough to provide the MSCC with the room to grow over the next 5 years." The software also appeared to be user friendly, which Lassiter believed was the key to freeing up Kovecki's time. Lassiter explained the software to Hedges, who wanted the current accounting system left intact but agreed that now was the time to move forward in finding a more powerful software solution for the MSCC's problems. Hedges also agreed that other modules in the UNITRAK system could be activated at a later time.

In October 1998, Lassiter contacted Greg Ginder, president of the UNITRAK Software Corporation, and invited him to the MSCC for a demonstration of the system's capabilities. Wilson observed about 45 minutes of the three-hour demonstration and told Lassiter, "I'll support it if you want it. It will work for my project for public affairs." Hedges agreed that the new system would free up Kovecki's time and allow him to become more involved in planning and systems development. Kovecki's comments were different. He remarked, "Yeah, the software has its strengths and weaknesses and it probably would save some of my time. But, I don't like the idea of staff having uncontrolled access to so much data. It's not clear what they'll do with it."

The Proposal

Lassiter decided to move ahead quickly with a proposal to Wallingford and the board of directors. He developed simple flow charts that showed the hours it took to conduct certain activities, e.g., the staff time new member sales took with the current multiple-PC arrangement versus the time it would take with the new system. Lassiter knew that the executive committee of the board would require considerable justification to approve an "off-budget" capital expenditure that would significantly reduce reserves. He had also done some calculations to show that if the new system performed as he hoped, each territory manager would be able to generate $150,000 in increased sales through increased contacts. Although Lassiter knew this goal was aggressive and very difficult to justify, he wanted to be able to demonstrate a less-than-six-month payback if challenged by a member of the executive committee of the board.

Lassiter knew that UNITRAK would reduce the price of the software. The software was new, and UNITRAK had sold it to only one other statewide chamber of commerce organization, the Northern State Chamber of Commerce. Jeff Fritzly, vice president of marketing and development of the NSCC, told Lassiter:

> We looked at quite a few software packages as well as writing our own custom software, but our consultant chose the IBM AS/400 hardware and UNITRAK software. We purchased both the hardware and software from UNITRAK and got a good discount on the hardware. They have been very helpful and supportive of our needs.

A week before the executive committee meeting, Ginder and Lassiter agreed on a price for the software. Lassiter was pleased that the price was 30 percent less than Northern State had paid. With the help of Ginder and a member of the executive committee who headed the local branch office of IBM, Lassiter was also able to achieve an excellent discount on the AS/400. He felt this low cost was another justification for approval of the project. Lassiter also made it a point to meet with both Wilson and Hedges to keep them abreast of the negotiation and seek their advice. He felt that by increasing the level of communication with Hedges and Wilson, he would be able to gain their interest and support, which he felt was important to the success of the project.

When the executive committee of the board met in November 1998, Lassiter explained that the MSCC had reached the limit of its current system design, and that an investment in a central system connected to networked PCs was needed to allow the MSCC to meet current and future opportunities for growth. During his presentation, Lassiter said:

> While the MSCC has made significant and appropriate investments in the PC hardware necessary for the MSCC to increase its operational sophistication, we have reached the limit of these smaller machines. With the spectacular growth in revenue we've enjoyed over the last 5 years, our requirements and demands have increased dramatically. Without an immediate investment in increased capability, the MSCC's continued growth and services will be in jeopardy.

In response to challenges from the executive committee regarding what the new system would mean to the bottom line and the MSCC's reserves, Lassiter responded, "I believe we will see a 10–15 percent increase in sales and a 20 percent increase in staff productivity once the new system is operational." With these assurances and a price that would consume only 10–15 percent of reserves, the members of the executive committee complimented Lassiter on his work and approved the purchase of the software.

Implementation

Greg Ginder of UNITRAK was ecstatic over the decision and promised unlimited support at no charge to install the new system. But Kovecki continued to express concern about staff members using the new capabilities of the system. He said:

> I know that Lassiter expects this new software to be user friendly, but I'm uncomfortable with how strongly he feels about training the staff to use as many of the features as possible. He thinks that training the staff on whatever they want to learn will make the MSCC more effective, but I disagree. We would be opening Pandora's box and we would lose control over what was going on. The last thing we need is for people to be getting into things they don't need to be in.

By February 1999, Lassiter had heard nothing regarding the purchase of the new system. Kovecki told Lassiter that no one had approved the purchase order. Lassiter then questioned Hedges, who responded that he had heard nothing more and had been busy with research on issues of interest to the MSCC members. "Go ahead and purchase the software," Hedges told Lassiter. "It's your system anyway." Although Lassiter tried to explain that it was not his responsibility to implement the purchase or conversion, he felt the project would not move

forward without his purchasing the software. After signing the purchase order, Lassiter handed it to Kovecki and said, "You and Hedges are the project managers. I shouldn't be involved at this point. It's up to you guys to complete the project."

On March 30, Lassiter asked Kovecki how the project was proceeding. Kovecki stated that the hardware had been delivered but that he was busy with a project of Wilson's and didn't have time to work on the new software. Lassiter went to Wilson to inquire about the anticipated length of the project Kovecki was working on and Wilson indicated it should be finished by mid-April.

Although Lassiter felt uncomfortable about pushing Hedges and Kovecki, he was beginning to feel that he would have to use his influence to get things moving. Lassiter held a meeting with his staff, informing them that a new system had been approved that would improve operations in several areas. Several staff members expressed concern that they had not been consulted or informed of the idea before its approval. Specific questions were asked regarding word processing, new member recruiting, and general processing. Lassiter, anticipating that Kovecki had studied the documentation, asked Kovecki to answer the questions. Kovecki was unable to answer the questions and indicated he needed more time to study the documentation.

Lassiter set up an appointment with UNITRAK for training for Kovecki and himself. After a positive training visit, Lassiter asked Kovecki to spend half a day with him to set up a project flow chart and anticipate potential problems, but May and June passed with little forward progress on the conversion. Lassiter had told the executive committee that the project would be completed by the end of March 1999, yet little had been accomplished.

Upon Kovecki's return from a 2-week vacation at the end of June, Lassiter asked Wallingford to intervene and to strongly urge Hedges and Kovecki to complete the project. Lassiter stated:

> It really bothered me that I had to go over Hedges' head but we were coming up on the seventh month of what should have been an easy 3-month project. It's partly my fault because I didn't establish teamwork up front, nor did I make clear early in the process the responsibilities of those participating.

The Final Phase

With Hedges' agreement, Lassiter set up 2 days of staff training for the third week in August 1999. (See Exhibit 3.) Kovecki had assured Lassiter that the system would be up by the last day of training so that the staff could immediately use the new system. Lassiter broke the training into major segments and had Kovecki set up training sites in two separate conference rooms for staff. UNITRAK sent a two-person team that would act as project managers and trainers.

The training went well with the exception of the conference and seminar segment of the software. The users brought up

EXHIBIT 3
Staff Training

TO: All Staff Members
FROM: Leon Lassiter
DATE: August 12, 1999
RE: Computer Training Schedule

The following schedule has been designed to train all staff members on the new computing system:

August 18, 1999

9:30–11:30 Marketing Support
            Susan Devine
            Ann Triplett
            Dianne Hippelheuser
11:30–12:30 Lunch
12:30–2:30 Territory Managers
            Mitch Guiet
            Jim Wagner
            Gayle Roberts
            Dave Girton
2:30–3:00   Break
3:00–3:30   General Staff
            1._____
            2._____
            3._____
            4._____
            5._____
3:30–4:00   Economic Development Staff
            1._____
            2._____
            3._____
            4._____
            5._____
4:00–4:30   Public Finance Staff
            1._____
            2._____
            3._____
            4._____
            5._____

August 19, 1999

8:30–9:00   Human Resources Staff
            1._____
            2._____
            3._____
            4._____
            5._____

9:30–10:30 Conferences Staff
            Joyce Jones
            Kathy Neeb
            Carolyn Hosford
            Dianne Hippelheuser
            Gini Raymond
            Marge Price
            Amy Kerrick
10:30–11:00 Controller Staff
            1._____
            2._____
            3._____
            4._____
            5._____
11:00–11:30 General Staff
            1._____
            2._____
            3._____
            4._____
            5._____
11:30–12:30 Lunch
12:30–1:30 Legislative Services
            Darla Barnett
1:30–2:30   Doing Word Processing
            Joyce Jones
            Dianne Hippelheuser
            Gini Raymond
            Jean Wiles
            Carolyn Hosford
            Amy Kerrick
            Kathy Neeb
            Kathleen Johnson
2:30–3:00   Break
3:00–5:00   Open

significant complaints that the new software servicing this area was not as functional and user friendly as the existing custom-written PC software. Although Lassiter suspected that a large part of the problem was that the new software was just different, he asked UNITRAK to work with the users in adapting the UNITRAK software to better meet their needs. Ginder commented:

> Because our software is relatively new to the marketplace, we are open to adjusting and changing certain aspects of the software without rewriting major portions. We feel we could learn a great deal from the MSCC that would make our software more marketable.

On the final day of training, Lassiter told Kovecki to migrate the data in the current PC systems to the new system. Kovecki told Lassiter that he was having a few problems and would conduct the migration after work, and it would be ready first thing in the morning. The next morning Kovecki, in responding to Lassiter's query as to why the system was not up, said:

> When I attempted the migration last night, less than 15 percent of the data rolled over into the proper assignments. With no documentation on the old software to refer to, it will probably take me a week to work out the bugs. In the meantime, the new system won't work and some of the data in our current PCs seems to have been corrupted. I hope we can recover the latest backup, but some of the systems haven't been backed up for more than 3 months.

Although one of the marketing division's systems had been backed up recently, the rest of the MSCC's PCs were basically inoperable. Requests for lists and labels for mailings could not be fulfilled. Word processing, payment and invoice posting, changes, list management, and so on were all inoperable or partially inoperable. UNITRAK was finding it difficult to help because Kovecki had forgotten to order a new modem that would allow UNITRAK experts remote access to the system.

Lassiter was finding it very difficult to gain information from Kovecki on the progress and status of the system conversion. It seemed that Kovecki, frustrated with the problems he was having and irritated with the staff coming to him to ask for assistance, was going out of his way to avoid the staff. Lassiter said:

> I explained to Kovecki that I wasn't trying to grill him for information, but because the staff now considered me to be the project director, I needed information with which to make decisions affecting the work flow of the staff and determine what kind of help we could request from UNITRAK.

Although Lassiter knew that the staff felt he was responsible for the new system, he felt frustrated that there was little he could do in managing the conversion. Hedges remained disengaged from the project, and Kovecki did not report to Lassiter.

The Future

It was in this situation that Lassiter found himself as he sat in his office at 7:30 P.M. in late September of 1999. Kovecki had promised that the new system would be up on each of the last several Mondays. Each Monday brought disappointment and compounded frustration to the staff. Lassiter knew that the 2 days of training had been wasted because the staff had long forgotten how to use the new system. He also guessed that Kovecki had not made the old systems Y2K compliant, so time was running out. Something had to be done—but what?

PART I
INFORMATION TECHNOLOGY

After the important opening chapter, which sets the stage for the entire book, the four chapters in Part I focus on today's information technologies. A number of technical concepts will be introduced, and a large vocabulary of technical terms will be employed. However, Chapters 2 to 5 have been written with the objective of conveying to all readers what managers need to know about IT—and the data manipulated by that technology—in a straightforward way.

For those of you who have a background in information systems (IS), computer science, engineering, or one of the physical sciences, much of this technology material might already be familiar to you. For those of you without this background, our objective is to provide you with the terminology and concepts needed to understand the managerial issues in the remainder of this textbook, as well as to communicate with IS leaders and specialists today and in the future. These chapters will also enable you to be a knowledgeable reader of IT articles in the *Wall Street Journal*, *Business Week*, *Fortune*, and similar publications.

Our IT overview begins with a consideration of computer systems. Chapter 2 focuses on computer hardware, the physical pieces of a computer system, and introduces the basic stored-program concept. New technology developments and major IT industry vendors are highlighted, as well as current trends in the hardware arena. Chapter 3 discusses computer software, the set of programs that control the operations of the computer system. As a computer user, your interface with the computer system is through the software, whether you are working with microcomputer packages, enterprise systems, or a Web browser. As a manager, you will be involved in acquiring and developing new applications software for running your business. This chapter surveys the key types of software available today—including applications software, personal productivity packages, Web software, fourth generation languages, object-oriented languages, and database management systems. The concepts of service-oriented architectures and Web services are also introduced, and the makeup of today's software industry is discussed—including open source alternatives (such as Linux).

Telecommunications and networking are the topics of Chapter 4. Virtually all computers of all sizes communicate directly with other computers (at least part of the time) by means of a variety of networks, including the world-spanning Internet. In fact, "network-centric computing" is a characteristic of the computer industry today. Chapter 4 describes the main elements of telecommunications and networking, including transmission media and wireless communication, network topology, types of networks, and network protocols. Recent developments in wireless networks, Voice over Internet Protocol (VoIP) telephony, the Internet2 network, as well as Web developments such as blogs, wikis, and social networking applications, are also discussed. The chapter focuses on the business need for networking, as influenced by the ever-evolving telecommunications industry.

Chapter 5 describes issues related to managing the data resource in today's organizations. The chapter focuses on data modeling and data architecture issues, including key principles in managing data, the role of metadata, tools for managing data, and data management processes and policies within organizations. A well-managed data resource is essential to the effective organizational use of IT, and both IS and business managers play major roles in managing this critical organizational resource.

Five teaching cases related to managing information technology assets, written by the textbook authors, have been grouped at the end of Part I. The IMT Custom Machines Company case study investigates the choice between continued reliance on a large, mainframe-based computer system and newer IT platform alternatives: high-powered UNIX workstations or Linux-based machines. Two case studies focus on an important new Internet technology: VoIP telephony. The VoIP2.biz case study deals with product development issues faced by a VoIP business. The second case study, "VoIP Adoption at Butler University," describes in detail the selection and implementation issues faced by a midsized organization.

In the InsuraCorp case study, managers at a large (disguised) insurance company are wrestling with who in the organization should have ongoing responsibility for data quality and other data management issues that arise after a business restructuring. Finally, the Midsouth Chamber of Commerce (B) case study continues the saga—begun in Midsouth Chamber of Commerce (A) after Chapter 1 of this book—of the selection and management of hardware and software for this small organization.

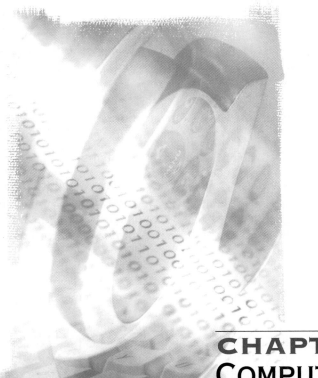

CHAPTER 2
COMPUTER HARDWARE

CHAPTER 1 HAS SET THE STAGE FOR THE DETAILED STUDY OF INFORMATION technology (IT) and your role in harnessing that technology. We can now take a closer look at the building blocks of information technology and the development and maintenance of IT systems.

Our definition of IT is a broad one, encompassing all forms of technology involved in capturing, manipulating, communicating, presenting, and using data (and data transformed into information). Thus, IT includes computers (both the hardware and the software), peripheral devices attached to computers, communications devices and networks—clearly incorporating the Internet—photocopiers, facsimile machines, cellular telephones and related wireless devices, computer-controlled factory machines, robots, video recorders and players, and even the microchips embedded in products such as cars, airplanes, elevators, and home appliances. All of these manifestations of IT are important, and you need to be aware of their existence and their present and potential uses in an organizational environment. However, two broad categories of IT are critical for the manager in a modern organization: computer technology and communications technology. Both of these technologies have had, and continue to have, a gigantic impact on the structure of the modern organization, the way it does its business, its scope, and the jobs and the careers of the managers in it.

Perhaps the first important point to be made in this chapter is that the division between computer and communications technology is arbitrary and somewhat misleading. Historically, computer and communications technologies were independent, but they have grown together over the past quarter century. Distributed systems (to be discussed in Chapter 6) exist in every industry, and these systems require the linking of computers by telecommunication lines. World Wide Web–based systems, delivered either via an intranet within the organization or via the Web itself, are becoming increasingly prevalent. Almost every manager at every level has a microcomputer on his or her desk. The computer is connected by telecommunication lines to a corporate computer and usually to the Internet. Today, the information systems organization often has responsibility for both computing and communications. The switches used in telephone networks are computers, as are the devices used to set up computer networks such as routers and gateways. It is still convenient for us to discuss computing technology as distinct from communications technology, but the distinctions are becoming even more blurred as time passes. In reality, computer/communications technology is being developed and marketed by the computer/communications industry.

This chapter concentrates on computer **hardware**, as distinct from computer **software**. Computer hardware refers to the physical pieces of a computer system—such as a central processing unit, a printer, and a disk drive—that can be touched. Software, by contrast, is the set of programs that controls the operations of the computer system. For the most part, our consideration of software will be deferred until Chapter 3, but the central idea behind today's computers—the stored-program concept—will be explored here to aid in our understanding of how a computer system works.

EVOLUTION OF COMPUTER SYSTEMS

At present, early in the twenty-first century, the computer/communications industry is easily the largest industry in the world in terms of dollar volume of sales. This is a remarkable statement, given that the first large-scale electronic computer was completed in 1946. The ENIAC (Electronic Numerical Integrator And Computer), which was built by Dr. John W. Mauchly and J. Presper Eckert, Jr., at the Moore School of Electrical Engineering at the University of Pennsylvania, was composed of more than 18,000 vacuum tubes, occupied 15,000 square feet of floor space, and weighed more than 30 tons (see Figure 2.1). Its performance was impressive for its day— the ENIAC could perform 5,000 additions or 500 multiplications per minute.

Mainframes and Minicomputers

The ENIAC was just the beginning. After several one-of-a-kind machines, the first production-line computers— the Sperry Rand Univac, followed shortly by the IBM 701—became available in the early 1950s. IBM quickly became the dominant vendor, but there were many other players. New machines were introduced every few years with new technology, more memory, faster execution speeds, and greater capabilities (see Table 2.1). As IBM and the other major vendors competed for industry leadership with more powerful, larger machines, a number of smaller, newer firms—such as Digital Equipment Corporation (DEC) and Hewlett-Packard—recognized a market niche for smaller machines aimed at smaller businesses and scientific applications. These minicomputers were just like the large machines (which came to be called mainframes) except that they were less powerful and less expensive. As the minicomputer market evolved, many of the mainframe vendors, such as IBM, moved into this area.

Figure 2.1   The ENIAC (Courtesy of Bettmann/CORBIS)

Table 2.1   Evolution of Computer Systems

Developments	Chronology	Key Technologies	Key Computer Systems/Vendors
First Generation of Computers	1946–1959	Vacuum tubes; magnetic drum memories	Sperry Rand Univac; IBM 650
Second Generation of Computers	1959–1964	Transistors; magnetic core memories	IBM 7000 series; IBM 1400 series
Third Generation of Computers	1964–late 1970s	Integrated circuits; semiconductor memories; introduction of an operating system	IBM System 360; IBM System 370
Fourth Generation of Computers	1980s–present	Large-scale integration (LSI) circuits, then very-large-scale integration (VLSI) circuits; communication between computers; use of multiple processors in a single machine	IBM mainframes
Minicomputers	1970s–present	Same as Third and Fourth Generations above, but with smaller machines aimed at smaller businesses and scientific applications	Digital Equipment Corporation; Hewlett-Packard; Data General; IBM
Microcomputers	late 1970s–present	Microprocessors; systems designed for a single user	Apple; IBM; IBM clones

The Development of Microcomputers

Another splintering within the industry took place in the late 1970s and 1980s with the introduction and success of the microcomputer, which is based on the computer on a chip (see Figure 2.2), or microprocessor. Apple and other companies pioneered the microcomputer business, finding a market niche below the minicomputers for home use, in very small businesses, and in the public school system. Then, in late 1981, IBM entered the market with the IBM Personal Computer, which quickly became the microcomputer

Figure 2.2   Intel® Core™2 Duo Processor (Courtesy of Intel Corporation)

standard for the workplace. In fact, the personal computer, or PC, became so much of a standard that most people use the terms *microcomputer*, *personal computer*, and *PC* interchangeably (and we will do so in this book, as well). Subsequent developments included greatly increased speed and capabilities of microcomputers, as well as the introduction of a variety of IBM "clones" in the marketplace by other vendors. The widespread acceptance of microcomputers in the business world placed significant computing power at the fingertips of virtually every manager. The connection of all these microcomputers (as well as the connection of the larger machines) through company intranets and the world-wide Internet changed the entire face of computing in the mid- and late 1990s. The Internet and intranets will be explored in Chapter 4 as well as in Chapter 8.

BASIC COMPONENTS OF COMPUTER SYSTEMS

For historical completeness, we should note that there are really two distinct types of computers—digital and analog. Digital computers operate directly on numbers, or digits, just as humans do. Analog computers manipulate some analogous physical quantity, such as voltage or shaft rotation speed, which represents (to some degree of accuracy) the numbers involved in the computation. Analog computers

MICROPROCESSOR CHIPS GET FASTER AND FASTER

In late 1971, Intel Corporation announced the first micro-processor in a trade-magazine ad that heralded "a new era in integrated electronics." But even Intel didn't anticipate the scope of the revolution it was unleashing on business and society. Today, the world's chip population (all types of semiconductor chips) has swollen to well over a trillion. In 2005, there were about 365 million microprocessor chips sold, with most of these embedded in products other than computers (such as automobiles, appliances, and game consoles). Ever since Intel's first microprocessor, the 4004, these chips have grown increasingly powerful in periodic leaps and bounds. The 4004 chip contained 2,300 transis-tors, sold for $200, and had a clock speed of 108 thou-sand cycles per second (kilohertz, or KHz).[1] Intel's first Pentium chip, introduced in 1993, contained 3.1 million transistors, sold for $878, and had a clock speed of 66 mil-lion cycles per second (megahertz, or MHz)—over 600 times faster than the 4004. In mid-2006, Intel introduced several versions of the Core 2 Duo microprocessor chip; one version, the E6700, contained 291 million transistors, sold for $530, and had a clock speed of 2,660 MHz—over 24,000 times faster than the 4004. And there doesn't appear to be any end in sight in terms of microprocessor chip speeds!

Of course, Silicon Valley-based Intel Corporation is not the only chip maker, but it is the largest and the most impor-tant. Intel supplies about 85 percent of the microprocessor chips used to power PCs, and about 50 percent of all micro-processor chips. Starting in 2006, Intel also supplies the chips for Apple's microcomputers. Advanced Micro Devices (AMD), which produces Intel-compatible chips, is the only other major player in the microcomputer market with about a 15 percent market share. Other manufacturers of proces-sor chips (largely for more powerful machines) include IBM and Sun Microsystems. As an interesting side note, IBM also provides the processor chips for all of the newest-generation game consoles (Sony, Microsoft, and Nintendo).

[Adapted from Hamm and Elgin, 2005; Intel Web site, 2006a and 2006b; and Edwards, 2006]

have been most useful in engineering and process-control environments, but digital machines have largely replaced them even in these situations. Thus, all of our preceding discussion relates to digital computers, as does that which follows.

---

[1]The internal clock speed in cycles per second is closely related to the number of instructions per second that the computer can carry out. Thus, millions of cycles per second (megahertz) would be the same as millions of instructions per second (MIPS) if one instruction were executed each cycle.

Underlying Structure

Today's computers vary greatly in size, speed, and details of their operation—from handheld microcomputers cost-ing around $100 to supercomputers with price tags of more than $30 million. Fortunately for our understanding, all these machines have essentially the same basic logical structure (as represented in Figure 2.3). All computers, whether they are microcomputers from Dell or mainframes from IBM, are made up of the same set of six building blocks: input, output, memory, arithmetic/logical unit, con-trol unit, and files. Our discussion of how computers work will focus on these six blocks and their interrelationships.

In addition to the blocks themselves, Figure 2.3 also includes two types of arrows. The broad arrows represent the flows of data through the computer system, and the thin arrows indicate that each of the other components is con-trolled by the control unit. A dashed line encircles the con-trol unit and the arithmetic/logical unit. These two blocks together are often referred to as the **central processing unit (CPU)** or as the **processor**.

Input/Output

To use a computer, we must have some means of entering data into the computer for it to use in its computations. There are a wide variety of input devices, and we will men-tion only the most commonly used types. The input device that you as a manager are most likely to use is a keyboard on a microcomputer. We will talk more about microcom-puters (PCs) later, but they include all of the building blocks shown in Figure 2.3.

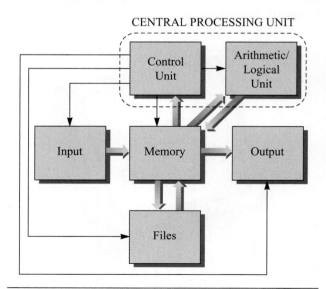

Figure 2.3   The Logical Structure of Digital Computers

A **terminal** is a simpler device than a PC; it is designed strictly for input/output and does not incorporate a processor (CPU), or at least not a general-purpose processor. Most terminals consist of a keyboard for data entry and a monitor to show the user what has been entered and to display the output from the computer. The terminal is connected to a computer via some type of telecommunication line. Although many terminals are being replaced by microcomputers today, terminals are still widely used by clerical personnel involved in online transaction processing (to be discussed in Chapter 6).

Special types of terminals are also in widespread use as computer input devices. Point-of-sale terminals are in use at most retail stores, and automatic teller machines (ATMs) are commonplace in the banking industry. These devices are simply terminals modified to serve a specific purpose. Like the standard terminals described previously, these special-purpose devices serve as both input and output devices, usually incorporating a small built-in printer to provide a hard-copy record of the transaction.

Terminals allow users to key data directly into the computer. By contrast, some input methods require that data be recorded on a special input medium before they can be entered into the computer. Until the 1980s, the most common form of computer input involved punched cards and a punched-card reader. Users keyed in data at a punched-card keypunch machine, which translated the keystrokes into holes in a punched card (employing a coding scheme known as Hollerith code). The punched cards were then carried to a punched-card reader directly attached to the computer; the reader read the cards one at a time, interpreting the holes in the cards and transmitting the data to the memory. For example, until the early 1980s, U.S. government checks and class enrollment cards at most universities were punched cards. Computers often had a card punch attached as an output device to produce checks, enrollment cards, and other punched-card output. However, punched cards were a nuisance to handle and store, and they have disappeared because of the communications developments of the past quarter century.

Some input methods read an original document (such as a typed report or a check or deposit slip) directly into the computer's memory. Check processing is handled this way in the United States through the **magnetic ink character recognition(MICR)** input method. Checks have the account number and bank number preprinted at the bottom using strange-looking numbers and a special magnetizable ink. After a check is cashed, the bank that cashed it records the amount of the check in magnetizable ink at the bottom of the check. A computer input device called a magnetic ink character reader magnetizes the ink, recognizes the numbers, and transmits the data to the memory of the bank's computer. **Optical character recognition (OCR)** is an input method that directly scans typed, printed, or hand-printed material. A device called an optical character reader scans and recognizes the characters and then transmits the data to the memory or records them on magnetic tape.

Imaging goes even further than OCR. With imaging, any type of paper document, including business forms, reports, charts, graphs, and photographs, can be read by a scanner and translated into digital form so that the document can be stored in the computer system. Then this process can be reversed so that the digitized image stored in the computer system can be displayed on a video display unit, printed on paper, or transmitted to another computer. However, the characters in the image cannot be easily processed as individual numbers or letters. Imaging is often accomplished through a specialized image-management system, which is a microcomputer-based system.

An increasingly important way of entering data into a computer is by scanning a **bar code label** on a package, a product, a routing sheet, a container, or a vehicle. Bar code systems capture data much faster and more accurately than systems in which data are keyed. Thus, the use of bar codes is very popular for high-volume supermarket checkout, department store sales, inventory tracking, time and attendance records, and health care records. Bar codes are also valuable for automated applications such as automotive assembly control and warehouse restocking. There is actually a wide variety of bar code languages, called *symbologies*. Perhaps the most widely known symbology is the Universal Product Code (UPC) used by the grocery industry.

Of course, if the data are already stored in computer-readable form, such as on a 3.5-inch floppy disk, a compact disk (CD), or a digital video disk (DVD), they can be input into the computer via a floppy disk drive, a CD drive, or a DVD drive, respectively. These devices can also serve as output devices if the data will be read back later into either the same or another computer.

Just as we must have a way of entering data into the computer, the computer must have a way of producing results in a usable form. We have already mentioned displaying results on a video display unit, printing a document on a small printer built into a special-purpose terminal, punching cards, or writing output on a floppy disk, a CD, or a DVD.

The dominant form of output, however, is the printed report. Computer printers come in a variety of sizes, speeds, and prices. At the lower end are serial printers, which are usually employed with microcomputers. They usually employ a nonimpact process (such as an ink-jet or laser-jet process), and they typically operate in a speed range of 5 to 25 pages per minute. Printers used with larger computers may be line printers or page printers. Line printers operate at high speeds (up to 2,000 lines per minute) and print one line at a time, usually employing an impact printing mechanism in which individual hammers force the paper and ribbon against the appropriate print characters (which are embossed on a rotating band or chain). Page printers, which produce up to 1,440 pages per minute, print one entire page at a time, often employing an electrophotographic printing process (like a copying machine) to print an image formed by a laser beam.

In part to counteract the flood of paper that is threatening to engulf many organizations, microfilm has become an important computer output medium. The output device is a **computer output microfilm (COM)** recorder that accepts the data from the memory and prepares the microfilm output at very high speeds, either as a roll of microfilm or as a sheet of film called a microfiche that contains many pages on each sheet. **Voice response units** are gaining increasing acceptance as providers of limited, tightly programmed computer output. Cable television shopping services and stock price quotation services often use voice output in conjunction with touch-tone telephone input.

To summarize, the particular input and output devices attached to a given computer will vary based on the uses of the computer. Every computer system will have at least

---

VOICE INPUT TO COMPUTERS

Voice input to computers is becoming a reality, although we cannot converse with today's machines as easily as Starfleet officers can talk with the computer system on the *USS Enterprise*. But we are certainly moving in that direction! Economical software packages are now available to run on microcomputers that permit users to "dictate" to the computer and have the computer produce a word-processed document. However, the accuracy of **speech recognition software** is still less than perfect, with the best packages achieving recognition accuracy in the 95 to 99 percent range. With these numbers, speech recognition software is close to becoming a productivity-enhancing tool—at least for users with limited typing skills, disabilities, repetitive stress injuries from overusing a computer keyboard, or no time to do anything except dictate (such as medical doctors). For most of us, speech recognition software might provide an interesting supplement to the keyboard and mouse, but it is not going to replace these traditional means of input in the short run.

Perhaps the best of the PC speech recognition software products is Dragon NaturallySpeaking 9 (from Nuance Communications; the Preferred edition costs about $200 and the Standard edition about $100), which received a World Class Award from *PC World* magazine as one of its 100 Best Products of the Year in 2006. Dragon NaturallySpeaking is tightly integrated with Microsoft Office (more on Microsoft Office in Chapter 3) and allows users to create new documents and e-mails, surf the Web, and navigate among programs, all by voice. When dictating, the software provides a useful list of alternatives when you tell it that it has made a mistake, and it allows you to correct your own verbal mistakes by selecting the error and then saying what you actually meant. Dragon NaturallySpeaking also contains automatic punctuation to save the user from dictating commas and periods, although some users have difficulty with this feature.

At least for the present, however, dictation to the computer is not the most important application of speech recognition—that honor falls to interactive voice response systems that provide up-to-date information and services through a call center, with the user providing voice input via a telephone. In this case, the software runs on a server (a larger computer) at the call center. The leading provider of these call-center speech recognition/voice response systems is Nuance Communications (see Dragon NaturallySpeaking), and industry giants IBM and Microsoft have also entered this market with IBM WebSphere Voice Server and Microsoft Speech Server, respectively. Such systems are now widely used for such activities as providing access to flight arrival and departure information, permitting phone-based Web browsing, tracking packages, and checking online brokerage accounts. Users prefer these speech recognition/voice response applications over the alternative of multiple touch-tone responses, but they are expensive to develop. For example, Amtrak has created a perky virtual attendant named Julie who provides schedule, fare, and train-status information from a speech recognition/voice response system. To develop this system, Amtrak spent $4 million over three years on speech-related hardware, software, and integration, but Amtrak executives think it was well worth the cost. Payback occurred in 18 months, according to Matt Hardison, chief of sales distribution and customer service at the railroad, because of reduced labor costs in call centers. Amtrak estimated that voice systems cost about $0.25 per call, compared to about $5.00 for a human responder. PC-based speech recognition software is getting close to being a mainstream application, and call-center speech recognition/voice response systems are already in the mainstream.

[Adapted from Keenan, 2002; Bannan, 2005; Claburn, 2006; Nuance Web site, 2006; Stafford, 2006; and Wildstrom, 2006]

one input device and at least one output device. On the computers you will be using as a manager, keyboards, video display units, printers, CD and DVD players, and disk drives will be the most common input/output devices.

Computer Memory

At the heart of the diagram of Figure 2.3 is the **memory**, also referred to as main memory or primary memory. All data flows are to and from memory. Data from input devices always go into memory; output devices always receive their data from memory; two-way data flows exist between files and memory and also between the arithmetic/logical unit and memory; and a special type of data flows from memory to the control unit to tell the control unit what to do next. (This latter flow is the focus of the section of this chapter entitled "The Stored-Program Concept.")

In some respects the computer memory is like human memory. Both computers and humans store data in memory in order to remember it or use it later. However, the way in which data are stored and recalled differs radically between computer memory and human memory. Computer memory is divided into cells, and a fixed amount of data can be stored in each cell. Further, each memory cell has an identifying number, called an *address*, that never changes. A very early microcomputer, for example, might have 65,536 memory cells, each capable of storing one character of data at a time. These cells have unchanging addresses varying from 0 for the first cell up to 65535 for the last cell.

A useful analogy is to compare computer memory to a wall of post office boxes (see Figure 2.4). Each box has its own sequential identifying number printed on the box's door, and these numbers correspond to the addresses associated with memory cells. In Figure 2.4 the address or identifying number of each memory register is shown in the upper-left corner of each box. The mail stored in each box changes as mail is distributed or picked up. In computer memory, each memory cell holds some amount of data until it is changed. For example, memory cell 0 holds the characters MAY, memory cell 1 holds the characters 2009, memory cell 2 holds the characters 700.00, and so on. The characters shown in Figure 2.4 represent the contents of memory at a particular point in time; a fraction of a second later the contents may be entirely different as the computer goes about its work. The contents of the memory cells will change as the computer works, while the addresses of the cells are fixed.

Computer memory is different from the post office boxes in several ways, of course. For one thing, computer memory operates on the principle of "destructive read-in, nondestructive read-out." This means that as a particular piece of data is placed into a particular memory cell, either by being read from an input device or as the result of a computation in the arithmetic/logical unit, the computer destroys (or erases) whatever data item was previously in the cell. By contrast, when a data item is retrieved from a cell, either to print out the item or to use it in a computation, the contents of the cell are unchanged.

Another major difference between post office boxes and memory cells is in their capacity. A post office box has a

0 MAY	1 2009	2 700.00	3 4	4 OSU	5 17	6 321.16	7 3
8 C	9 OMPU	10 TER	11 32	12 0	13 MARY	14 71.3	15 L
16 27	17 18	18 103.0	19 7	20 JOHN	21 41	22 100.00	23 0
24 0	25 0	26 0	27 37	28 B	29 0	30 62	31 1

Figure 2.4   Diagram of Computer Memory

variable capacity depending upon the size of the pieces of mail and how much effort postal employees spend in stuffing the mail in the box. A memory cell has a fixed capacity, with the capacity varying from one computer model to another. A memory cell that can store only one character of data is called a **byte**, and a memory cell that can store two or more characters of data is called a **word**. For comparability, it has become customary to describe the size of memory (and the size of direct access files) in terms of the equivalent number of bytes, even if the cells are really words.

Leaving our post office analogy, we can note that there are several important differences between the memory of one computer model and that of another. First, the capacity of each cell can differ. In a microcomputer, each cell might hold only 1 digit of a number, whereas a single cell in a mainframe might hold 14 digits. Second, the number of cells making up memory can vary from several million to many billion. Third, the time involved to transfer data from memory to another component can differ by an order of magnitude from one machine to another. The technologies employed in constructing the memories can also differ, although all memory today is based on incredibly small integrated (VLSI) circuits on silicon chips.

Bits and Coding Schemes   Each memory cell consists of a particular set of circuits (a small subset of the VLSI circuits on a memory chip), and each circuit can be set to either "on" or "off." Because each circuit has just two states (on and off), they have been equated to 1 and 0, the two possible values of a binary number. Thus, each circuit corresponds to a *bi*nary digi*t*, or a **bit**. In order to represent the decimal digits (and the alphabetic letters and special characters) for processing by the computer, several of these bits (or circuits) must be combined to represent a single character. In most computers, eight bits (or circuits) represent a single character, and a memory cell containing a single character, we know, is called a byte. Thus, eight bits equals one byte in most machines.

Consider a particular example. Assume that we have a computer where each memory cell is a byte. (A byte can contain one character.) Then memory cell number 327, for instance, will consist of eight circuits or bits. If these circuits are set to on-on-on-on-on-off-off-on (or, alternatively, 1111 1001), this combination may be defined by the coding scheme to represent the decimal digit 9. If these bits are set to 1111 0001, this may be defined as the decimal digit 1. If these bits are set to 1100 0010, this may be defined as the letter B. We can continue on like this, with each character we wish to represent having a corresponding pattern of eight bits.

Two common coding schemes are in use today. The examples given previously are taken from the Extended Binary Coded Decimal Interchange Code (commonly known as EBCDIC, pronounced eb'-si-dic). IBM originally developed EBCDIC in the 1950s, and IBM and other vendors still use it. The other common code in use is the American Standard Code for Information Interchange (ASCII), which is employed in data transmission and in microcomputers. Figure 2.5 lets you compare the ASCII and EBCDIC codes for the alphabet and decimal digits, but you do not need to know these codes—only that they exist!

Char-acter	EBCDIC Binary		Char-acter	ASCII-8 Binary	
A	1100	0001	A	1010	0001
B	1100	0010	B	1010	0010
C	1100	0011	C	1010	0011
D	1100	0100	D	1010	0100
E	1100	0101	E	1010	0101
F	1100	0110	F	1010	0110
G	1100	0111	G	1010	0111
H	1100	1000	H	1010	1000
I	1100	1001	I	1010	1001
J	1101	0001	J	1010	1010
K	1101	0010	K	1010	1011
L	1101	0011	L	1010	1100
M	1101	0100	M	1010	1101
N	1101	0101	N	1010	1110
O	1101	0110	O	1010	1111
P	1101	0111	P	1011	0000
Q	1101	1000	Q	1011	0001
R	1101	1001	R	1011	0010
S	1110	0010	S	1011	0011
T	1110	0011	T	1011	0100
U	1110	0100	U	1011	0101
V	1110	0101	V	1011	0110
W	1110	0110	W	1011	0111
X	1110	0111	X	1011	1000
Y	1110	1000	Y	1011	1001
Z	1110	1001	Z	1011	1010
0	1111	0000	0	0101	0000
1	1111	0001	1	0101	0001
2	1111	0010	2	0101	0010
3	1111	0011	3	0101	0011
4	1111	0100	4	0101	0100
5	1111	0101	5	0101	0101
6	1111	0110	6	0101	0110
7	1111	0111	7	0101	0111
8	1111	1000	8	0101	1000
9	1111	1001	9	0101	1001

Figure 2.5   EBCDIC and ASCII Computer Coding Schemes

The bottom line is that a coding scheme of some sort is used to represent data in memory and in the other components of the computer. In memory, circuits in a particular cell are turned on and off, following the coding scheme, to enable us to store the data until later. It turns out that circuits are also used to represent data in the control and arithmetic/logical units. In the input, output, and files, the coding scheme is often expressed through magnetized spots (on and off) on some media, such as a disk. In data transmission, the coding scheme is often expressed through a series of electrical pulses or light pulses. In summary, the coding scheme is vital to permit the storage, transmission, and manipulation of data.

Arithmetic/Logical Unit

The **arithmetic/logical unit**, like memory, usually consists of incredibly small integrated circuits on a silicon chip. In fact, the chip pictured in Figure 2.2 is the Intel Core 2 Duo processor chip used in many of today's top-of-the-line microcomputers. In many respects, the arithmetic/logical unit is very simple. It has been built to carry out addition, subtraction, multiplication, and division, as well as to perform certain logical operations such as comparing two numbers for equality or finding out which number is bigger.

The broad arrows in Figure 2.3 represent the way in which the arithmetic/logical unit works. As indicated by the broad arrow from memory to the arithmetic/logical unit, the numbers to be manipulated (added, subtracted, etc.) are brought from the appropriate memory cells to the arithmetic/logical unit. Next, the operation is performed, with the time required to carry out the operation varying, depending on the computer model. The speeds involved vary from several million operations per second up to billions of operations per second. Then, as indicated by the broad arrow from the arithmetic/logical unit to memory in Figure 2.3, the result of the operation is stored in the designated memory cell or cells.

Computer Files

As applications are being processed on a computer, the data required for the current computations must be stored in the computer memory. The capacity of memory is limited (although it can go over 500 billion bytes on some large machines), and there is not enough space to keep all of the data for all of the concurrently running programs (e.g., Microsoft Excel, Microsoft Word, Lotus Notes) in memory at the same time. In addition, memory is volatile; if the computer's power goes off, everything stored in memory is lost. To keep vast quantities of data accessible within the computer system in a nonvolatile medium and at more reasonable costs than main memory, file devices—sometimes called secondary memory or secondary storage devices—have been added to all but the tiniest computer systems. File devices include magnetic tape drives, hard (or fixed) disk drives, floppy (or removable) disk drives, flash drives, and CD or DVD (optical) drives. All but the optical drives record data by magnetizing spots on the surface of the media, using a binary coding scheme.

The broad arrows in each direction in Figure 2.3 illustrate that data can be moved from particular cells in memory to the file and that data can be retrieved from the file to particular memory cells. The disadvantage of files is that the process of storing data in the file from memory or retrieving data from the file to memory is quite slow relative to the computer's computation speed. Depending upon the type of file, the store/retrieve time may vary from a very small fraction of a second to several minutes. Nevertheless, we are willing to live with this disadvantage to be able to store enormous quantities of data at a reasonable cost per byte.

Sequential Access Files   There are two basic ways to organize computer files: sequential access and direct access. With **sequential access files**, all of the records that make up the files are stored in sequence according to the file's control key. For instance, a payroll file will contain one record for each employee. These individual employee records are stored in sequence according to the employee identification number. There are no addresses within the file; to find a particular record, the file device must start at the beginning of the sequential file and read each record until it finds the desired one. It is apparent that this method of finding a single record might take a long time, particularly if the sequential file is long and the desired record is near the end. Thus, we would rarely try to find a single record with a sequential access file. Instead, we would accumulate a batch of transactions and process the entire batch at the same time. (See the discussion of batch processing in Chapter 6.)

Sequential access files are usually stored on magnetic tape. A **magnetic tape unit** or magnetic tape drive is the file device that stores (writes) data on tape and that retrieves (reads) data from tape back into memory. Even with batch processing, retrieval from magnetic tape tends to be much slower than retrieval from direct access files. Thus, if speed is of the essence, sequential access files might not be suitable. On the other hand, magnetic tapes can store vast quantities of data economically. For example, a high-performance tape cartridge that can store up to 30 billion bytes of data can be purchased for under $40, or an extended length high-performance tape cartridge with a capacity of 60 billion bytes can be purchased for under $75.

Direct Access Files   A **direct access file**, stored on a **direct access storage device (DASD)**, is a file from which it is possible for the computer to obtain a record immediately, without regard to where the record is located in the file. A typical DASD for a computer consists of a continuously rotating stack of disks (or perhaps only one disk), where each disk resembles an old-style phonograph record (see Figure 2.6). A comb-shaped access mechanism moves in and out among the disks to record on and read from hundreds of concentric tracks on each disk surface. The hard drives found on almost all microcomputers are an example of direct access files. Typical internal hard drives for PCs store from 80 to 500 billion bytes (gigabytes) and cost from $50 to $250. The speed at which data can be read from or written on a hard drive is quite fast, with transfer rates up to 400 million bytes (megabytes) per second possible.

EMC Corporation, based in Hopkinton, Massachusetts, has become the market leader in storage systems for large computers by devising a way to link together a large number of inexpensive, small hard drives (such as those used in PCs) as a substitute for the giant disk drives that were previously used. EMC has developed a specialized computer and sophisticated software to control this **redundant array of independent disks (RAID)** approach so that data can be supplied to the mainframe or other large computer rapidly, reliably, and less expensively per byte than the giant disk drive approach (Judge, 1999). As an example, EMC's Symmetrix DMX-3 950 model can be configured with

from 32 to 360 hard drives, each with a storage capacity from 73 up to 500 gigabytes, giving a total storage capacity from 2.3 terabytes (trillion bytes) up to a maximum of over 173 terabytes (EMC Web site, 2006).

In contrast to these fixed-disk, large-capacity, fairly expensive file devices, direct access devices can also be portable or employ a removable disk, be relatively small, and be quite inexpensive. For instance, a removable 3.5-inch high-density disk for a microcomputer can store up to 1.44 million bytes (1.44 megabytes) of data and costs less than $0.50. The disk drive itself costs under $20.00. These 3.5-inch disks are protected by a permanent hard plastic case, but they are sometimes called floppy disks. "Floppy disk" is a misnomer for today's disks, but the name originated with their 5.25-inch predecessor disks for microcomputers, which were made of flexible plastic without sturdy cases and were in fact "floppy." The transfer rate to read to or write from a floppy disk varies, but a common transfer rate is 0.06 million bytes (megabytes) per second—a very slow rate compared to other DASDs.

A newer, higher-capacity DASD, with a removable disk, is Iomega Corporation's REV drive. A REV drive may be installed internally in a PC or attached externally; external REV drives are attached to a PC's standard universal serial bus (USB 2.0) port. A REV disk is slightly smaller than a conventional floppy disk, and about three times as thick; its capacity is either 35 or 70 gigabytes on a single removable disk, depending upon the REV drive. A 70-gigabyte REV drive costs about $600, and each disk for this drive is about $63; this REV drive reads or writes at speeds up to 25 megabytes per second. The smaller capacity 35-gigabyte REV drive has a similar transfer rate and costs about $400, and each disk for this drive is about $50 (Iomega Web site, 2006). This moderate cost and reasonably fast transfer rate have made the REV drive quite popular for backing up and transporting large data files.

Iomega Corporation also offers an attractive line of portable and desktop external hard drives, all of which can be attached to a PC's USB port. The portable drives vary from a lightweight (less-than-2-ounces), 4-gigabyte hard drive selling for $100 up to a 160-gigabyte drive for $230; all these drives have "drop shock technology" to make them truly portable. These portable drives permit the user to back up very large data files and move these large data files from one computer system to another. Iomega's desktop external hard drives, with capacities varying from 40 gigabytes to 750 gigabytes, can provide a backup capability as well as a significant addition to internal hard drive capacity. The 40-gigabyte drive costs $150, while the 750-gigabyte drive costs $460. When attached to a USB 2.0 port, all of these hard drives have a maximum sustained

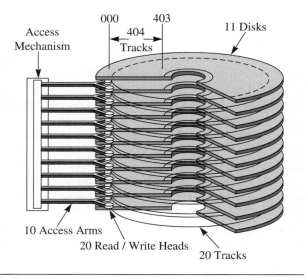

Figure 2.6   A Schematic Diagram of a Magnetic Disk Drive

data transfer rate of 60 megabytes per second (Iomega Web site, 2006).

The newest and smallest portable DASD for PCs utilizes flash memory—as used in digital cameras and portable music players—rather than a magnetizable disk. This **flash drive** goes by various names, including jump drive, mini USB drive, or keychain drive. **Keychain drive** is perhaps the most descriptive because the device is not much larger than the average car key—usually about 2 1/2 inches long (see Figure 2.7). As an example, SanDisk's Cruzer Micro USB Flash Drive is available in 512 megabyte and 1, 2, 4, and 8 gigabyte sizes, with prices of about $15, $25, $40, $70, and $140, respectively (SanDisk Web site, 2007). These flash drives, which are designed to plug into the standard USB port on a PC, have a maximum sustained data transfer rate of 60 megabytes per second. To use a flash drive, take off the top of the drive, exposing the USB connector. Plug the connector into the USB port on a PC, and the computer will recognize it automatically—then just use the flash drive as one does any other drive. The flash drive is an economical and extremely convenient way to save and transport significant amounts of data. The 3.5-inch floppy disk was on its way out even before the flash drive came on the scene, but the flash drive should certainly hasten the floppy disk into oblivion.

The key to the operation of direct access files is that the physical file is divided into cells, each of which has an address. The cells are similar to memory cells, except that they are much larger, usually large enough to store several records in one cell. Because of the existence of this address, it is possible for the computer to store a record in a particular file address and then to retrieve that record by

Figure 2.7 SanDisk Cruzer Micro 8 GB USB Flash Drive (Courtesy of SanDisk Corporation)

remembering the address. Thus, the computer can go directly to the file address of the desired record, rather than reading through sequentially stored records until it encounters the desired one.

How does the computer know the correct file address for a desired record? For instance, assume that an inventory control application running on the computer needs to update the record for item number 79032. That record, which is stored somewhere in DASD, must be brought into memory for processing. But where is it? At what file address? This problem of translating from the identification number of a desired record (79032) to the corresponding file address is the biggest challenge in using direct access files. Very sophisticated software, to be discussed in Chapter 3, is required to handle this translation.

Online processing (discussed in Chapter 6) requires direct access files, and so does Web browsing. Airline reservation agents, salespeople in a department store, managers in their offices, and Web surfers from their home or office machines will not wait (and in many cases cannot afford to wait) the several minutes that might be required to load and read the appropriate magnetic tape. On the other hand, batch processing can be done with either sequential access files or direct access files. Sequential access files are not going to go away, but all the trends are pushing organizations toward increased use of direct access files. First, online processing and Web browsing absolutely require direct access files. Second, advancements in magnetic technology and manufacturing processes keep pushing down the costs per byte of direct access files. Third, the newer optical disk technology (see the box "Optical Disk Storage") provides drastically lower costs per byte for applications where somewhat slower data retrieval speeds are acceptable. Fourth, and most important, today's competitive environment is forcing organizations to focus on speed in information processing, and that means an increasing emphasis on direct access files.

Control Unit

We have considered five of the six building blocks represented in Figure 2.3. If we stopped our discussion at this point, we wouldn't have much. Thus far we have no way of controlling these various components and no way of taking advantage of the tremendous speed and capacity we have described. The **control unit** is the key. It provides the control that enables the computer to take advantage of the speed and capacity of its other components. The thin arrows in Figure 2.3 point out that the control unit controls each of the other five components.

OPTICAL DISK STORAGE

A newer type of direct access file storage for computer systems, the **optical disk**, is becoming more and more important. The optical disk (together with the flash drive) spells the end of the floppy disk: Rewritable versions of the optical disk are now available that have thousands of times the capacity of a standard floppy disk, a transfer rate much faster than a floppy, and a price that is quite economical. An optical disk is made of plastic coated with a thin reflective alloy material. Data are recorded on the disk by using a laser beam to burn microscopic pits in the reflective surface (or in some cases alter the magnetic characteristics of the surface), employing a binary coding scheme.

Two primary types of optical disks are in common use with computers today: a **compact disk (CD)** and a **digital video disk**, or **digital versatile disk (DVD)**. Then each of these optical disk types has three primary variations: a read-only disk (**CD-ROM** or **DVD-ROM**, where ROM stands for Read Only Memory); a recordable disk (**CD-R** or **DVD-R**, where R stands for Recordable); and a rewritable disk (**CD-RW** or **DVD-RW**, where RW stands for ReWritable). A CD has much less capacity than a DVD: Standard capacity for a CD is 700 megabytes of data or 80 minutes of audio recording, while capacity for a DVD varies from 4.7 gigabytes (more than enough for a full-length movie) for a single-layer, single-sided DVD up to 17 gigabytes for a dual-layer, double-sided DVD. As the name suggests, dual-layer technology provides two individual recordable layers on a single side of a DVD disk. Some experts believe that DVDs will eventually replace CDs, but that won't happen overnight. A significant advantage of DVD drives is that they are backward compatible with CDs, so that a DVD drive can play all types of CDs as well as DVDs. The media are quite inexpensive, with standard blank CDs and DVDs costing $1 or less and dual-layer DVDs under $3.

The readable CD or DVD is familiar as a way of distributing music, computer software, and even movies. It can only be read, and cannot be erased; a master disk is originally created, and then duplicates can be mass produced for distribution. Thus, a readable optical disk is particularly useful for distributing large amounts of relatively stable data (such as music, computer software, a book, a movie, or multimedia material) to many locations.

A recordable optical disk was once called a **WORM** (Write Once-Read Many) disk. A recordable CD or DVD can be written on by the computer—but only once. Then it can be read many times. Recordable optical disks are quite appropriate for archiving documents, engineering drawings, and records of all types.

A rewritable CD or DVD is the most versatile form of optical disk because the data can be recorded and erased repeatedly. Writing on a rewritable optical disk is a three-step process: (1) Use laser heat to erase the recording surface; (2) use a combination of laser and magnetic technology to write on the recording surface; and (3) read, via a laser, what has been written to verify the accuracy of the recording process. This type of optical disk is a strong candidate to replace the venerable floppy disk, particularly now that software products let the user "drag" files to an optical disk (using a mouse) just like to any other drive.

One more complication arises with regard to recordable and rewritable DVDs—vendors have created multiple formats that are not always compatible. Thus, a rewritable DVD is only rewritable with the appropriate DVD writer drive. There are two different recordable formats, labeled DVD-R and DVD+R, and three different rewritable formats, labeled DVD-RW, DVD+RW, and DVD-RAM. Happily, many DVD drives will read and write all major CD and DVD formats. One such drive is Iomega's Super DVD 18x Dual-Format USB External DVD Burner, priced at about $130. This drive is rated 18x6x8x when using the DVD-RW format. The numbers mean that the speed of writing on this drive is 18x (which translates to 24.75 megabytes per second), the speed of rewriting is 6x (8.25 megabytes per second), and the speed of reading is 8x (11.0 megabytes per second). When using a CD with the CD-RW format, the drive is rated 48x24x32x, which translates to writing at 7.2 megabytes per second, rewriting at 3.6 megabytes per second, and reading at 4.8 megabytes per second. (Note that the baseline 1x differs from DVD to CD: With DVD, 1x equals 1.375 megabytes per second; with CD, 1x equals 0.15 megabytes per second.)

As an example of optical storage used with large computer systems, IBM offers the 3996 Optical Library, which is designed for archival storage applications that require secure, long-term data retention. The IBM 3996 Optical Library uses *either* rewritable or WORM 5.25-inch removable disk cartridges, with a cartridge holding up to 30 gigabytes of data. The 3996 Model 174 incorporates 174 cartridges, giving a total online capacity of 5.2 terabytes (5.2 trillion bytes) for the optical library system. IBM suggests the 3996 Optical Library as a low-cost complement to high-performance magnetic disk drives.

[Portions adapted from Webopedia, 2006; Iomega Web site, 2006; and IBM Web site, December 2006a]

How does the control unit know what to do? Someone must tell the control unit what to do by devising a precise list of operations to be performed. This list of operations, which is called a program, is stored in the memory of the computer just like data. One item at a time from this list is moved from memory to the control unit (note the broad arrow in Figure 2.3), interpreted by the control unit, and carried out. The control unit works through the entire list of operations at electronic speed, rather than waiting for the user to tell it what to do next. What we have just described is the **stored-program concept**, which is the most important idea in all of computing.

THE STORED-PROGRAM CONCEPT

Some person must prepare a precise listing of exactly what the computer is to do. This listing must be in a form that the control unit of the computer has been built to understand. The complete listing of what is to be done for an application is called a **program**, and each individual step or operation in the program is called an **instruction**. The control unit carries out the program, one step or instruction at a time, at electronic speed.

When a particular computer model is designed, the engineers build into it (more precisely, build into its circuitry) the capability to carry out a certain set of operations. For example, a computer may be able to read an item of data keyed from a keyboard, print a line of output, add two numbers, subtract one number from another, multiply two numbers, divide one number by another, compare two numbers for equality, and perform several other operations. The computer's control unit is built to associate each of these operations with a particular instruction type. Then the control unit is told which operations are to be done by means of a program consisting of these instructions. The form of the instructions is peculiar to a particular model of computer. Thus, each instruction in a program must be expressed in the precise form that the computer has been built to understand. This form of the program that the computer understands is called the **machine language** for the particular model of computer.

Not only will the form of the instructions vary from one computer model to another, so will the number of different types of instructions. For example, a small computer may have only one add instruction, while a large one may have a different add instruction for each of several classes of numbers (such as integer, floating point or decimal, and double precision). Thus, the instruction set on some machines may contain as few as 20 types of instructions, while other machines may have more than 200 instruction types.

In general, each machine language instruction consists of two parts: an operation code and one or more addresses. The operation code is a symbol (e.g., A for add) that tells the control unit what operation is to be performed. The addresses refer to the specific cells in memory whose contents will be involved in the operation. As an example, for a hypothetical computer the instruction

Operation Code	Addresses	
A	470	500

means the computer should add the number found in memory cell 470 to the number found in memory cell 500, storing the result back in memory cell 500. Therefore, if the value 32.10 is originally stored in cell 470 and the value 63.00 is originally stored in cell 500, the sum, 95.10, will be stored in cell 500 after the instruction is executed. Continuing our example, assume that the next instruction in the sequence is

M	500	200

This instruction means move (M) the contents of memory cell 500 to memory cell 200. Thus, 95.10 will be placed in cell 200, erasing whatever was there before. (Because of nondestructive read-out, 95.10 will still be stored in cell 500.) The third instruction in our sequence is which means

P	200	

print (P) the contents of memory cell 200 on the printer, and 95.10 will be printed.

Our very short example contains only three instructions and obviously represents only a small portion of a program, but these few instructions should provide the flavor of machine language programming. A complete program would consist of hundreds or thousands of instructions, all expressed in the machine language of the particular computer being used. The person preparing the program (called a programmer) has to know each operation code and has to remember what data he or she has stored in every memory cell. Obviously, machine language programming is very difficult and time-consuming. (As we will learn in Chapter 3, programs can be written in languages that are easier for us to use and then automatically translated into machine language, so almost no one programs in machine language today.)

Once the entire machine language program has been prepared, it must be entered into the computer, using one of the input methods already described, and stored in the computer's memory. This step of entering the program in memory is called loading the program. The control unit then is told (somehow) where to find the first instruction in the program. The control unit fetches this first instruction and places it in special storage cells called registers within the control unit. Using built-in circuitry, the control unit interprets the instruction (recognizes what is to be done) and causes it to be executed (carried out) by the appropriate components of the computer. For example, the control unit would interpret the add instruction shown previously, cause the contents of memory cells 470 and 500 to be sent to the arithmetic/logical unit, cause the arithmetic/logical unit to add these two numbers, and then cause the answer to be sent back to memory cell 500.

After the first instruction has been completed, the control unit fetches the second instruction from memory. The control unit then interprets this second instruction and executes it. The control unit then fetches and executes the third instruction. The control unit proceeds with this fetch-execute cycle until the program has been completed. Usually the instruction that is fetched is the next sequential one, but machine languages incorporate one or more branching instructions that, when executed, cause the control unit to jump to a nonsequential instruction for the next fetch. The important point is that the control unit is fetching and executing at electronic speed; it is doing exactly what the programmer told it to do, but at its own rate of speed.

One of the primary measures of the power of any computer model is the number of instructions that it can execute in a given period of time. Of course, some instructions take longer to execute than others, so any speed rating represents an average of some sort. These averages might not be representative of the speeds that the computer could sustain on the mix of jobs carried out by your organization or any other organization. Furthermore, some machines operate on four bytes at a time (older microcomputers), while others operate on eight bytes at a time (many larger machines). Thus, the speed rating for a microcomputer is not comparable to the speed rating for a larger machine.

In the 1980s the most commonly used speed rating was **MIPS,** or millions of instructions per second executed by the control unit. This measure has largely gone out of favor because of the "apples and oranges" nature of the comparisons of MIPS ratings across classes of computers. Another speed rating used is **MegaFLOPS (MFLOPS)**—millions of floating point operations per second. These ratings are derived by running a particular set of programs in a particular language on the machines being investigated. The ratings are therefore more meaningful than a simple MIPS rating, but they still reflect only a single problem area. As an example of MFLOPS ratings, see the box entitled "LINPACK performance ratings."

Published speed ratings can be useful as a very rough guide, but the only way to get a handle on how various machines would handle your organization's workload is

---

LINPACK PERFORMANCE RATINGS

One publicly available (and regularly updated) set of MFLOPS ratings is "Performance of various computers using standard linear equations software," authored by Jack J. Dongarra of the University of Tennessee and Oak Ridge National Laboratory. In these ratings, the problem area considered is the solution of dense systems of linear equations using the LINPACK software in a FORTRAN environment. For example, the MFLOPS ratings when solving a system of 100 linear equations on a single processor machine include 9.7 for an Apple Power Mac 6100/66; 62 for a Gateway G6-200 Pentium Pro; 558 for a Compaq Server D520e (667 MHz); 1,486 for an IBM eServer pSeries 655 (1.7 GHz); and 1,861 for an HP ProLiant DL140 G2 (3.8 MHz). For multiprocessor machines, the MFLOPS ratings when solving a system of 1,000 linear equations vary from 5,187 for a Sun UltraSPARC II (30 processors); 14,730 for an IBM eServer pSeries 655 (4 processors); 29,360 for a Cray T932 (32 processors); and 75,140 for a NEC SX-8/8 (8 processors). Of course, these LINPACK ratings are not very meaningful for applications where input/output operations are dominant, such as most business processing.

[Adapted from Dongarra, 2006]

---

benchmarking. Benchmarking is quite difficult to do, but the idea is to collect a representative set of real jobs that you regularly run on your computer, and then for comparison actually run this set of jobs on various machines. The vendors involved will usually cooperate because they want to sell you a machine, but there can be severe problems in getting existing jobs to run on the target machines and in comparing the results once you get them.

Computer publications often do their own benchmarking, as illustrated in Table 2.2 in which *PC World* identifies the top 10 computers in a class it calls "power desktop PCs." *PC World* has created a representative mix of 12 common applications it calls PC WorldBench 5, which it ran on all machines in this class; these applications include Adobe Photoshop, Microsoft Office XP, Mozilla, Roxio VideoWave, and WinZip. The test result score is a measure of how fast a PC can run this mix as compared with *PC World's* baseline machine, a high-end machine with a 2.2-GHz AMD Athlon 64 FX-51 processor, 1 gigabyte of memory, and a particular high-end graphics card. For example, the Dell XPS 410 in Table 2.2 is 1.38 times as fast as the baseline system.

PC World goes on to combine this PC WorldBench 5 test result score (valued at 30 percent of the overall

Table 2.2   Benchmarking: Top 10 Power Desktop PCs

System	Processor	Price	PC WorldBench 5 Test Results[a]	Overall Rating[a]
Dell XPS 410	2.4-GHz Intel Core 2 Duo E6600	$2,124	138 (good)	81 (very good)
Systemax Sabre	2.93-GHz Intel Core 2 Extreme X6800	$3,700	165 (superior)	81 (very good)
Polywell Poly 939N4-SLI2 FX60	2.6-GHz AMD Athlon 64 FX-60	$2,819	140 (good)	81 (very good)
CyberPower Gamer Infinity SLI Ultra	2.93-GHz Intel Core 2 Extreme X6800	$3,299	167 (superior)	80 (very good)
Micro Express MicroFlex 60B	2.6-GHz AMD Athlon 64 X2 FX-60	$1,999	139 (good)	80 (good)
Dell XPS 700	2.67-GHz Intel Core 2 Duo E6700	$3,999	153 (very good)	80 (good)
CyberPower Gamer Infinity 1950	2.67-GHz Intel Core 2 Extreme QX6700	$3,599	155 (very good)	78 (good)
Alienware Area-51 7500	2.67-GHz Intel Core 2 Extreme QX6700	$4,479	161 (very good)	78 (good)
ABS Ultimate X9	2.93-GHz Intel Core 2 Extreme X6800	$4,199	181 (superior)	77 (good)
ABS Ultimate M6 Sniper	2.6-GHz AMD Athlon 64 FX-60	$3,999	141 (good)	77 (good)

[a] The descriptive labels are those assigned by *PC World*.
Source: Ettenson (ed.), *PC World* Web site (2006).

rating) with other factors such as price (20 percent), features/specifications (30 percent), and design/usability (20 percent) to arrive at an overall rating for each machine, as shown in the far right column of Table 2.2. You will note that the Dell XPS 410 got to the top of *PC World*'s list with a combination of a good WorldBench test result and a relatively low price; the number two machine, the Systemax Sabre, reversed that combination, with a superior WorldBench test result and a much higher price.

Again, processing speeds vary across machines, but all computers use the stored-program concept. On all computers, a machine language program is loaded in memory and executed by the control unit. There is a great deal more to the story of how we get the machine language program, but suffice it to say at this point that we let the computer do most of the work in creating the machine language program. Neither you nor programmers working for your organization will write in machine language; any programs will be written in a language much easier and more natural for humans to understand. Chapter 3 is primarily concerned with the software, or programs, used to control computer systems.

EXTENSIONS TO THE BASIC MODEL

In the previous section, we considered the underlying logical structure of all digital computers, and we found that all computers are made up of the set of six building blocks shown in Figure 2.3. Now let us note that Figure 2.3 is an accurate but incomplete picture of today's computers (both microcomputers and larger machines), which often have multiple components for each of the six blocks rather than a single component. Machines might have multiple input devices, or multiple file devices, or multiple CPUs (processors). Let us introduce two of the most important extensions to the basic model: cache memory and multiple processors in a single computer system.

Cache Memory

Thus far we have considered two (or perhaps three) levels of storage devices: main or primary memory, which is very fast and quite expensive; and secondary memory, which we can subdivide into not-so-fast and not-so-expensive

DASDs and slow and inexpensive sequential access storage devices (magnetic tapes). Now add **cache memory**, which is very high-speed, high-cost storage used as an intermediary between the control unit and main memory. The term *cache* (pronounced cash) is French for a hidden storage place. The cache is intended to compensate for one of the speed mismatches built into computer systems—in this case, that between fetching data from main memory (and moving data to the arithmetic/logical unit or other internal registers) and executing an instruction.[2] The CPU can execute an instruction much faster than it can fetch data (which requires electronically moving the data from memory to the arithmetic/logical unit). Thus, in a conventional architecture, the critical CPU often waited for the completion of a data fetch.

With cache memory, an entire block of data is moved at one time into the cache, and then most data fetches take place from the higher-speed cache to the arithmetic/logical unit. The success of cache memory depends upon two characteristics of the data to be used by the CPU—locality of reference and data reuse. Locality of reference means that if a given piece of data is used, there is a high probability that a nearby piece of data will be used shortly thereafter. Data reuse means that a block of data will be kept in the cache until it has not been recently referenced; then it will be replaced by a block of data that has been requested. Figure 2.8 illustrates the use of cache memory in the CPU. As an example, the Intel Core 2 Duo

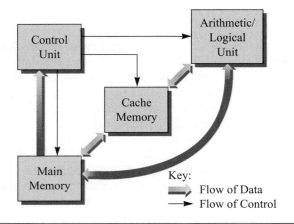

Figure 2.8   Partial Logical Structure of Computer Incorporating Cache Memory

---

[2]Cache memory is also used to compensate for other speed mismatches built into computer systems, such as that between a relatively slow DASD and the much faster communication channel that connects it to the main memory.

Processor (see Figure 2.2) incorporates 4 megabytes of cache memory in order to maximize the work done by the processor.

Multiple Processor Configurations

One of the most intriguing extensions to the basic model is the use of multiple processors as part of a single computer. The number of processors in a single computer system can vary from one (of course) or two (such as with the Intel Core 2 Duo Processor shown in Figure 2.2) up to over 100,000 in a large supercomputer. The terminology can be confusing for these **multiprocessor** systems, but let's make a few distinctions. A **dual-processor system** contains two physically separate processors (two integrated circuits, or chips) located in the same box (called a chassis), while a **dual-core system** has two complete processors manufactured as part of a single chip. There are now quad-core chips available, and there will eventually be 8-core and 16-core chips. In addition, a very large number of these chips (be they single-core, dual-core, or more) can be installed as part of a large computer system. The advantage of these multiprocessor configurations is greater computing power: Such multiprocessor machines can either work on several programs at the same time, or, in some cases, can process a single large program much more quickly.

The term **symmetric multiprocessor (SMP)** refers to multiprocessor machines in which all the processors are identical, with each processor operating independently of the others. The multiple CPUs equally share functional and timing access to and control over all other system components, including main memory and the various peripheral devices, with each CPU working in its own allotted portion of memory. On a large computer, one CPU might handle online transaction processing, while a second deals with engineering calculations, a third works on a batch payroll system, and a fourth operates as a Web server. On a PC, one CPU might be working on an Excel spreadsheet, while another is supporting Web browsing and virus scanning.

A **parallel processor (PP)** might have 16, 64, 256, or more processors, each of which would work on a separate piece of the same program. In order to use a parallel processing approach, the program must somehow be divided up among the processors and the activities of the various processors must be coordinated. Many supercomputers, to be discussed later in the chapter, employ a parallel processing architecture. The term **massively parallel processor (MPP)** is used to describe machines with some large number of parallel CPUs. There is no firm guideline to distinguish between a PP and an MPP; in general, however, 32 or more parallel CPUs would be considered an MPP if the different CPUs are capable of performing different instructions at the same time, or 1,000 or more parallel CPUs would be considered an MPP if the different CPUs must all carry out the same instruction at the same time. An example of a massively parallel machine is the Red Storm supercomputer, built by Cray Inc. and installed at the National Nuclear Security Administration's Sandia National Laboratories. Red Storm includes 26,544 processors operating in parallel, and has achieved a speed of 101.4 *trillion* calculations per second, making it the second fastest supercomputer in operation (Top 500, 2006). Red Storm performs a variety of tasks related to the U.S. nuclear stockpile, including the design of components and the virtual testing of components under hostile, abnormal, and normal conditions (Sandia National Laboratories, 2004). We are just beginning to learn how to take advantage of the incredible power of parallel processing machines. For the short term, parallel processors will be most useful in universities and research laboratories, and in a few specialized applications that demand extensive computations such as extremely high-volume transaction processing.

TYPES OF COMPUTER SYSTEMS

In our earlier discussion of the evolution of computer systems, we introduced some terminology—microcomputers, minicomputers, and mainframes—that has been applied to different types of computer systems. Now we want to expand our taxonomy of computer types to include the full range of computer systems available today. In our discussion, we will indicate the primary uses of each type of system as well as the major vendors. Our discussion must begin with a significant caveat: Although there is some agreement on the terms we will be using, there is no such agreement on the parameters defining each category or on the computer models that belong in each type.

Generally speaking, the boundaries between the categories are defined by a combination of cost, computing power, and purpose for which a machine is built—but the *purpose* is the dominant criterion. Listed in order of generally increasing cost and power, the categories we will use are microcomputers, midrange systems, mainframes, and supercomputers (see Table 2.3). You will note that the

Table 2.3 Types of Computer Systems

Category	Cost	MFLOPS	Primary Uses
Microcomputers	$200–$4,000	50–1,000	Personal computing
			Client in client/server[a] applications
			Web client
			Small business processing
Midrange systems	$4,000–$1,000,000	100–10,000	Departmental computing
			Specific applications (office automation, CAD[b], other graphics)
			Midsized business general processing
			Server in client/server applications
			Web server, file server, local area network server
Mainframes	$500,000–$20,000,000	400–10,000	Large business general processing
			Server in client/server applications
			Large Web server
			Widest range of applications
Supercomputers	$1,000,000–$100,000,000	10,000–1,000,000,000,000	Numerically intensive scientific calculations
			Very large Web server

[a] Client/server applications involve dividing the processing between a larger computer operating as a server and a smaller machine operating as a client; this idea is explored in depth in Chapter 6.

[b] CAD is an abbreviation for computer-aided design, to be discussed in Chapter 6.

ranges of cost and power in Table 2.3 are often overlapping, which reflects the differences in purpose for which the machines have been designed. Remember also that MFLOPS (millions of floating point operations per second) is only a very rough comparative measure of power.

Please note that the category boundaries in Table 2.3 are extremely fuzzy. The boundary between microcomputers and midrange systems has been arbitrarily set at $4,000, but the technology employed is quite similar on both sides of this boundary (at least in terms of PCs and the workstations subcategory of midrange systems). On the other hand, the type of work done on these classes of machines is quite different, as indicated in the table, so we have chosen to separate them. As we discuss midrange systems, we will find that this category grew from two distinct roots, but these subcategories now overlap so much in cost, power, and applications that we have chosen to combine them in a single category that stretches all the way from microcomputers to the much larger mainframes and supercomputers. Moreover, some midrange systems use similar technology to supercomputers—the primary difference might be the number of parallel processors. Low-end mainframes have significantly less power than high-end midrange systems, but have been designed for the widest possible range of applications. Some sources use the term *servers* instead of midrange systems, but we disagree with this label because a wide variety of machines including microcomputers, midrange systems, mainframes, and supercomputers can and do perform in a server capacity.

Microcomputers

Microcomputers, often called micros or **personal computers** or just PCs, cost from $200 to $4,000. They generally have less power than midrange systems, but the dividing line between these categories is faint. In general, microcomputers can be carried or moved by one person, and they usually have only a single keyboard and video display unit (which is why they are called personal computers). **Desktop PCs** are the most familiar, but PCs also come in **laptop** or **notebook** models in small briefcase-like packages weighing under 10 pounds and in newer, smaller **handheld** or **palmtop** models weighing in under a pound. An intriguing new variation of the notebook computer is the **tablet PC**, where the user writes on an electronic tablet (the video screen folded flat on top of the PC) with a digital pen (see Figure 2.9).

Let us be clear about the labels in this category. While PC is often used (in this book and elsewhere) as a synonym for microcomputer, in fact PC refers to the IBM Personal Computer or any one of the compatible machines built by other vendors such as Hewlett-Packard and Dell. For practical purposes, the PC label encompasses all microcomputers except those built by Apple. So in this section we will talk about PCs and we will talk about Apples.

By the second half of the 1980s, the most popular microcomputer for business use was the IBM Personal Computer, designed around microprocessor chips built by Intel and the PC-DOS operating system (a software package) created by Microsoft. In the first decade of the twenty-first century, IBM-compatible machines—PCs—still dominate the

Figure 2.9   Views of the HP Compaq tc4400 Tablet PC (Courtesy of Hewlett-Packard)

business marketplace, but *none* of the new PCs are being manufactured by IBM. In 2005, IBM sold its entire PC business to Lenovo, a Chinese firm, which immediately made Lenovo the world's third largest PC maker (McDougall, 2005). IBM was not happy with its profit margin on the PC business, and simply chose to exit the market. With the sale, Hewlett-Packard (HP) passed IBM as the world's largest IT firm, dropping IBM to second place. At present, HP and Dell are battling for market leadership in the PC business, although they achieved their premiere positions by different routes. Dell developed as a direct-sale vendor, originally by mail and telephone and now predominantly via the World Wide Web, while HP moved to the top by acquiring Compaq Computer in 2002. Other major players in the PC market include Gateway, Toshiba (Japan), Acer (Taiwan), and Fujitsu (Japan). [3]

Near the end of the first decade of the twenty-first century, about 85 percent of new PCs employ Intel microprocessor chips, either the newer Core 2 chips or older Pentium D or Pentium 4 chips, with the other 15 percent using AMD Athlon chips. Most of these machines use some version of the Microsoft Windows operating system (either Windows XP or Windows Vista).

The only microcomputer vendor that is not producing an IBM-compatible PC—and doesn't use the Windows operating system—is Apple. Initially, the Apple Macintosh found tough going in the business world against the entrenched PCs, but its easy-to-use graphical interface won it many converts in the late 1980s and early 1990s. Then, Macintosh sales hit a plateau, and Apple struggled until it introduced the iMac in 1998. The colorful iMac added a spark to the Apple product line and made Apple profitable again, and Apple continues to innovate with other computers such as the MacBook and MacBook Pro notebooks and the Mac Mini computer for the consumer market (a brushed aluminum square box, 6 1/2 inches on a side and 2 inches high). The Macs use Apple's own Mac OS X operating system (not Windows), and until 2006 used microprocessor chips manufactured by IBM and Freescale Semiconductor—but Apple has now shifted to an Intel chip. Apple's market share is still small—about 6 percent of the U.S. and worldwide microcomputer market. However, with its computers and other products such as the very successful iPod music player, the iTunes music distribution service, the innovative iPhone, and a variety of excellent software programs—including the iPhoto picture-managing program, iMovie video editing, and GarageBand music-creation software—Apple has

built a profitable and growing niche for itself (Wildstrom, 2005; Hesseldahl, 2006; and Moltzen, 2006). Between Apple and the various PC vendors, the microcomputer market is extremely competitive and should remain so for the foreseeable future.

Microcomputers have been put to a myriad of uses. In the home, they have been used for record-keeping, word processing, and games; in the public schools, for computerized exercises, educational games, and limited programming; in colleges, for word processing, spreadsheet exercises (more on this in Chapter 3), presentations, and programming. In the corporate environment they are used for word processing, spreadsheets, presentations, small database applications, and programming; as terminals into larger computers; and as clients in client/server applications. Stand-alone microcomputers in a large organizational setting are a thing of the past: For managers to do their jobs, they need microcomputers linked into the corporate computer network so that they can access data and applications wherever they exist. Microcomputers have also become important for small businesses, where they do operate as stand-alone machines or on small local area networks (LANs). The growing supply of software developed for a particular type of small business (for example, a general contractor, hardware store, or farmer), coupled with the relatively low price of microcomputers, has opened up the small business market. In the last half of the 1990s, microcomputers also became the point of entry for all types of users into the Internet and the World Wide Web—microcomputers are the universal Web client for all of us!

Midrange Systems

Midrange systems constitute the broadest category of computer systems, stretching all the way from microcomputers to the much larger mainframes and supercomputers. Somewhat arbitrarily we have defined this type of computer system as costing from $4,000 (the top of the microcomputers category) to $1,000,000 (near the bottom of the mainframes category), with power ranging from 100 to 10,000 MFLOPS.

Today's midrange systems have evolved from two earlier computer categories that have now largely disappeared—workstations and minicomputers. The term workstation, as used here, describes a powerful machine that is run by a microprocessor (just as a PC is run by a microprocessor), which may or may not be used by a single individual (whereas a PC is used by a single individual). **Workstations** are, in fact, grown up, more powerful microcomputers. Workstations at the lower end of the range tend to have only one "station"—a keyboard and a high-quality video

---

[3]From this point through the end of the chapter, all firms mentioned are based in the United States unless noted otherwise.

KILLER PDAS = SMARTPHONES

The smallest microcomputers—**palmtop** machines, also called **handheld computers** or **personal digital assistants (PDAs)**, which weigh under a pound and cost from $200 to $600—have been around for over a decade, and some commentators felt the PDA market was due to level off. However, by adding the ability to make phone calls to conventional handheld computer functions, BlackBerry and Palm (the two leading brands of PDAs) have reinvented themselves. These brands and other such hybrid devices from other vendors—often called smartphones or killer PDAs—permit the user to make phone calls, pick up and send e-mail, manage your calendar, keep your to-do list and address book up-to-date, and even entertain you with games, music, and video.

For example, the Palm Treo 750—available with AT&T (formerly Cingular) service—incorporates the Windows Mobile operating system from Microsoft and 128 megabytes of memory for running software applications, which makes it relatively easy to use Microsoft products such as Outlook, Excel, PowerPoint, and Word on the palmtop. The Treo has a tiny keyboard that will give your thumbs a good workout answering e-mail or using Microsoft Word. The Treo has a phone-like feel to it, and it has an integrated camera for snapping the occasional picture; it can also play music, audio books, and video clips (see Figure 2.10).

Another excellent smartphone is the BlackBerry Pearl from Research in Motion (RIM), a Canadian firm. Pearl is available through T-Mobile, and it uses the RIM OS (operating system); it also has 64 megabytes of memory, a digital camera, a multimedia player with a stereo headset jack, and an expandable memory slot.

Of course, all the PDAs sold today are not smartphones, but the proportion of smartphones sold is increasing every year—it passed 50 percent in 2006. BlackBerry is the market leader, followed by Palm; other major suppliers of smartphones are Danger, Inc., with its Sidekick model, which has achieved "near cult status" for young wireless-messaging users; HP; Mio Technology (Taiwan); Dell; Nokia (Finland); Samsung (Korea); and Motorola. Windows Mobile is the most

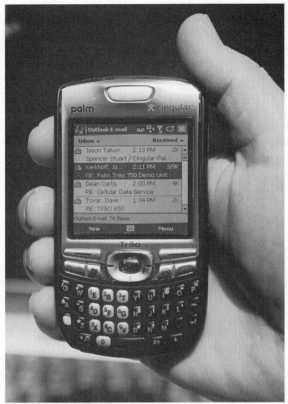

Figure 2.10   Palm Treo 750 (Courtesy of Palm, Inc.)

popular handheld operating system, with RIM OS and Palm OS also having significant market shares. Do you have your smartphone yet?

[Adapted from Gonsalves, 2006; Hesseldahl, 2006; and Malykhina, 2006]

monitor—at which to "work," although that is not usually true for the upper-end machines. Workstations are based on the microprocessor chip, but the chips tend to be more powerful than those used in microcomputers. Workstations were originally deployed for specific applications demanding a great deal of computing power, high-resolution graphics, or both, but they more recently have been used as Web servers, in network management, and as servers in client/server applications. (Chapter 6 will discuss client/server systems in more depth.) Furthermore, because of their very strong price-performance characteristics compared to other types of computers, workstations made inroads into the domains of traditional midrange systems (such as departmental computing and midsized business general processing) and mainframes (large business general processing). These inroads made by workstations into the midrange systems domain have been so significant that we have chosen to combine these categories for our discussion.

The development of the **reduced instruction set computing (RISC)** chip is largely responsible for the success of this class of machines, at least at its upper end. You will recall from our earlier discussion that some computers have a large instruction set (mainframes) while others have a considerably smaller instruction set (microcomputers). The designers of the RISC chips based their work on a reduced instruction set, not the complete instruction set used on mainframe chips. By working with a reduced instruction set, they were able to create a smaller, faster chip than had been possible previously. Variations of these RISC chips power most of the machines at the upper end of the midrange systems category today.

Let us turn to the second set of roots for the midrange systems category. Until the 1990s, these middle-of-the-road systems were called **minicomputers** (see the "Evolution of Computer Systems" section earlier in this chapter). Originally, these machines were just like the larger mainframe machines, except that they were less powerful and less expensive. For a while the larger minicomputers were even called **superminicomputers**, which is a strange name, using both *super* and *mini* as prefixes. These traditional midrange systems were very important, serving as departmental computers, handling specific tasks such as office automation, and acting as the server in a client/server architecture. Many mid-sized businesses used one or more of these systems to handle their corporate data processing. Some analysts suggested that these traditional midrange systems would disappear, squeezed between increasingly powerful microcomputers and workstations from the bottom and entrenched mainframe systems from above, but that did not happen. Instead, both workstations and minicomputers have "morphed" into the complex, intertwined category that we have chosen to call **midrange systems**. These systems are primarily employed as servers for client/server applications, Web serving, file and database serving, and network management. They vary from relatively small systems that serve one user or a single department up to enterprise-wide systems that have assumed many of the roles of mainframe computers.

It can be useful to divide midrange systems into several smaller categories. At the low-end come machines that are essentially high-powered PCs, typically built around Intel Pentium, Celeron, or Xeon processors or AMD Opteron processors and often using Windows Server as the server operating system. It is also possible to run the UNIX or Linux operating system on these Intel- or AMD-based servers, but this is not as common.[4] The major players in this market subsegment are Dell, Hewlett-Packard, IBM, Sun Microsystems, and Fujitsu (Japan). Other important vendors include Gateway, NCR, and NEC (Japan).

---

[4]Operating systems are considered in Chapter 3. UNIX and Linux are both "open" operating systems that are used on many midrange systems, supercomputers, and now mainframes. Both open and proprietary operating systems will be discussed in Chapter 3.

BLADES SERVERS: A NEW PARADIGM

In the ever-changing server world, the newest hot idea is the **blade server**. This is an idea that makes eminent sense—multiple server modules, called blade servers or just **blades**, are housed in a single chassis, saving space in the computer center, reducing the required cabling, and improving system management. The older options are to have each server module in a tower, much like an under-desk PC, or to mount them in an open rack, with all the connections leading from the rack. The blade server chassis provides the power supply for the blades, the management system, and the network switch; each blade has its own processor, memory, and hard drive. Diskless blades are also possible in larger blade servers, where the disk storage is external to the blades and shared among them.

As an illustration, IBM offers three variations of its blade server chassis—the BladeCenter, the BladeCenter T, and the BladeCenter H. The BladeCenter H chassis, which is less than 16 inches tall, offers up to 14 bays, each of which can hold a two-processor blade. The blade servers are 30 millimeters wide (about 1.2 inches) and are mounted vertically in the chassis—much like sliding a book into a bookshelf. The blade server slides into a bay and plugs into the chassis, sharing power, fans, floppy drives, switches, and ports with the other blade servers in the chassis. Interestingly, you can mix-and-match types of blade servers and the operating systems they use in a single chassis: BladeCenter permits the use of Intel Xeon blades, AMD Opteron blades, or IBM PowerPC blades in the same chassis. IBM is the market leader in blade servers, with significant competition from Hewlett-Packard, Dell, and Sun Microsystems.

[Adapted from IBM Web site, 2006e]

At the high-end are machines that are powered either by RISC processors developed by the vendor (such as Sun Microsystems or IBM) or top-of-the-line Intel or AMD microprocessors (such as the Intel Itanium). For the most part, these high-end machines run either the Linux operating system or some variation of the UNIX operating system. In this market subsegment, the leaders are IBM, Hewlett-Packard, and Sun Microsystems. Other vendors include Silicon Graphics, Inc. (also known as SGI), Fujitsu (Japan), and NCR. As an example, IBM's entry in this UNIX/Linux market subsegment is its System p5 server (formerly RS/6000), employing IBM-developed RISC chips. Among the many models of the System p5 are the System p5 550 Express with up to 8 processors and the System p5 595 with up to 64 processors. The p5 550 Express has a starting price of about $13,000, while the p5 595 can run into the hundreds of thousands of dollars. System p5 models are powered by IBM's POWER5+ 64-bit microprocessor,[5] described by IBM as a "server on a chip." The POWER5+ chip contains two processors, a high-bandwidth switch (for fast internal communications), a large memory cache, and an input/output interface. The processors can operate at speeds up to 2.3 GHz, and the p5 595 can have a total memory capacity of 2 terabytes (trillion bytes). The System p5 and its predecessor RS/6000 series have been a tremendous success for IBM, with well over 1 million systems shipped to commercial and technical customers throughout the world (IBM Web site, 2006b and 2006c).

A third subcategory is made up of machines that are most identifiable with the minicomputer roots of the midrange systems category. These machines have survived and prospered because they offer much better input/output capabilities than those from the workstations side of the mix and because an extensive array of easy-to-use commercial applications software has been developed for them. In addition, extensive specialized software has been developed by thousands of organizations to run on these middle-of-the-road systems, and these "legacy" systems cannot easily be converted to run on other types of hardware. On the other hand, these remaining midrange systems have incorporated RISC chips, have embraced UNIX and Linux, and are largely used as servers today. Thus, they are quite different from traditional minicomputers.

The primary example of such a midrange system is IBM's System i5 (formerly the AS/400) family of computers. In the 1980s, IBM's System/34, System/36, and System/38 became the most popular business computers (not including microcomputers) of all time. Most of these machines were replaced by IBM's AS/400 (which was first introduced in 1988 and has been a major success for IBM) and many additional AS/400s were sold. The name was changed in 2000 to the eServer iSeries and in 2006 to the System i5, and the beat goes on. In early 2006, IBM indicated that it had nearly 250,000 System i5 customers. Today's System i5 computers employ 64-bit RISC technology, with some models using the same POWER5+ chips discussed previously. System i5 models vary from relatively small machines, such as the single-processor System i5 520 Express with a sample configuration price tag under $12,000, to the System i5 595, which can incorporate as many as 64 processors and can cost hundreds of thousands

of dollars. All the System i5 machines use IBM's proprietary i5/OS (formerly OS/400) operating system, but even this operating system now incorporates support for the UNIX and Linux operating systems (Thibodeau, 2006 and IBM Web site, 2006d).

Mainframe Computers

Mainframes are the heart of the computing systems for many, perhaps most, major corporations and government agencies. Our earlier discussion on the evolution of computing dealt largely with the various generations of mainframe computers. The range of mainframe power and cost is wide, with MFLOPS varying from 400 to 10,000 and cost from $500,000 to $20,000,000. The strength of mainframes is the versatility of the applications they can handle: online and batch processing, standard business applications, engineering and scientific applications, network control, systems development, Web serving, and more. Mainframes also operate as very large servers in a client/server environment. Because of the continuing importance of mainframes in corporate computing, a wide variety of peripheral equipment has been developed for use with these machines, as has an even wider variety of applications and systems software. This development, by the way, has been carried out by computer vendors, other equipment manufacturers, and companies that specialize in producing software, known as software houses.

Historically, competition was fierce in the mainframe arena because of its central role in computing. The dominant vendor has been IBM since the late 1950s. The current generation of IBM mainframes is the System z9 family (formerly the zSeries, and before that the System/390). The newest machines in the System z9 family were introduced in 2005, and they vary from a single-processor model to a 54-processor model. All these machines are built around the IBM multichip module (MCM). For the high-end machines, the MCM contains a grouping of 16 chips (including 8 dual-core processor chips) employing leading-edge copper wiring and silicon-on-insulator technology and containing over 3.5 billion transistors.

The top-of-the-line, 54-processor System z9 Enterprise Class (see Figure 2.11) employs 4 such MCMs and can have up to 512 gigabytes (million bytes) of main memory. Even more impressive, the System z9 Enterprise Class can process 1 *billion* transactions per day, more than double the performance of its predecessor mainframe. In addition to more speed and capacity, the System z9 incorporates stronger security features such as the ability to encrypt backup tapes, making them less vulnerable to data theft if they are lost or stolen, and the centralized management of

---

[5]This means that the processor chip is capable of handling 64 bits of data at a time, whereas most microprocessor chips handle only 32 bits of data at a time.

Figure 2.11 IBM System z9 Enterprise Class (Courtesy of IBM Corporation)

encryption keys. Furthermore, multiple systems can be combined in a Parallel Sysplex, a multisystem environment that acts like a single system. Through a combination of hardware and software, especially the z/OS operating system, a System z9 Parallel Sysplex can incorporate up to 32 individual machines, each of which can have up to 54 processors (Marlin, 2005 and IBM Web site, 2005 and 2006f). IBM has maintained its preeminent position in the mainframe arena through solid technical products, excellent and extensive software, extremely reliable machines, and unmatched service.

Direct competition in the mainframe arena is less fierce than it used to be. Two vendors, Amdahl and Hitachi (Japan), dropped out of the mainframe market in 2000. Amdahl was purchased by Fujitsu (Japan), and Hitachi bowed out of the mainframe market to concentrate on other market segments. Amdahl and Hitachi are particularly interesting cases because they succeeded for many years by building machines that were virtually identical to IBM's, often with slightly newer technology, and then by selling them for a lower price. The only remaining major players in the mainframe market (in addition to IBM) are Fujitsu and Unisys. Unisys was formed years ago as the merger of Burroughs and Sperry (Sperry built the very first production-line computer), so Unisys has been in the mainframe business a long time. However, there is plenty of indirect competition in the mainframe arena, as vendors like Hewlett-Packard and Sun Microsystems try to get customers to migrate their mainframe systems to high-end servers.

All the mainframe vendors, including IBM, fell on hard times in the early 1990s. Because of stronger price/performance ratios from other classes of machines, the primary focus of new systems development in the first half of the 1990s was on client/server applications designed to run on these more cost-effective platforms. The last half of the 1990s saw a marked movement back to mainframes, although demand slackened before and after January 1, 2000, largely because companies were wrapped up in solving the year 2000 (Y2K) problem and then in attending to other IS problems they had let slip while working on Y2K. In recent years, IBM and other vendors have introduced new technology, added Linux options to proprietary operating systems, and slashed prices drastically. The addition of Linux capability has been particularly important in the twenty-first-century resurgence of the mainframe, with many companies finding out that it is more economical to run multiple Linux virtual servers on a single mainframe than to run (say) 40 Intel-based servers (Greenemeier, 2002). The role of the mainframe will continue to evolve as we move further into the twenty-first century, with more emphasis on its roles as keeper of the corporate data warehouse, server in sophisticated client/server applications, powerful Web server, and controller of worldwide corporate networks.

Supercomputers

Supercomputers are the true "number-crunchers," with MFLOPS ratings in excess of 10,000 and price tags from $1 million to $100 million (more for specialty machines). The high-end supercomputers are specifically designed to handle numerically intensive problems, most of which are generated by research scientists, such as chemists, physicists, and astronomers. Thus, most of the high-end supercomputers are located in government research laboratories or on major university campuses (even in the latter case, most of the machines are largely supported by grants from the National Science Foundation or other government agencies). Midrange supercomputers, however, have found a variety of uses in large business firms, most frequently for research and development efforts, Web serving on a massive scale, data mining, and consolidating a number of smaller servers.

Until the mid-1990s, the acknowledged leader in the high-end supercomputer arena was Cray Inc. However, IBM mounted a concerted effort in supercomputers in the 1990s, and IBM now clearly holds the top spot (see box entitled

WORLD'S FASTEST SUPERCOMPUTER

The competition is intense to build and operate the world's fastest supercomputer, and—for the present—that machine is the IBM Blue Gene/L system, developed in conjunction with the Department of Energy's National Nuclear Security Administration and installed at Lawrence Livermore National Laboratory. The Blue Gene/L system incorporates 65,536 dual-core IBM PowerPC processors and has achieved a sustained performance of 280.6 teraflops (*trillion* floating point operations per second). Blue Gene/L is used to conduct incredibly detailed materials science simulations to keep the U.S. nuclear weapons stockpile safe, secure, and reliable without underground nuclear testing.

Blue Gene/L took over the top spot from Japan's Earth Simulator in 2005. The Earth Simulator, which was built by NEC, is used to model global warming, hurricanes, earthquakes, and volcanic activity by researchers from around the world. Now the race is on to reach a new plateau of 1,000 teraflops, or 1 petaflop (*quadrillion* floating point operations per second). Perhaps a beefed-up Blue Gene system will be the first to hit the petaflop speed, or perhaps Japan's $1 billion Life Simulator project will be the first. Another contender is the Roadrunner project, being built by IBM at the Los Alamos National Laboratory in New Mexico, which is scheduled for completion in 2008. One interesting aspect of the Roadrunner project is that IBM will be employing 16,000 chips originally designed for Sony PlayStation 3 video consoles, in addition to other chips designed for computers.

After technology such as that used for Blue Gene/L is implemented for massive government laboratory machines, the vendor—IBM in this case—then tries to harness that power in smaller commercial versions of the system that can be sold to corporations to enable scientific and business breakthroughs in fields such as pharmaceuticals, manufacturing, and finance. In addition to selling a smaller Blue Gene system to a customer, IBM also offers a fractional ownership program—buy a piece of a Blue Gene system, which IBM will operate—or the customer can buy "Deep Computing Capacity on Demand" from IBM. With this option, a corporation buys an annual base membership and then purchases additional time on IBM high-performance computers, including an IBM Blue Gene system, as needed. Among other markets, IBM is targeting the automotive and aerospace industries, retail banking, the electronics industry, the petroleum industry, and health care with this "on demand" service.

[Adapted from Ricadela, 2005; Gaudin, 2006; Toner, 2006; and IBM Web site, 2006g]

"World's Fastest Supercomputer"). In the November 2006 online listing of the world's top 500 supercomputers, the top 100 machines were distributed as follows: IBM 44; Cray Inc. and Dell 9 each; Hewlett-Packard and Silicon Graphics, Inc., 7 each; Linux Networx 5; and 11 other vendors with 3 machines or less, plus 3 self-made machines (i.e., built by the using organization) (Top 500, 2006). These large computers use one or more of three high-performance computer architectures: parallel vector processing, massively parallel processing, and symmetric multiprocessing. As an example of a massively parallel machine, a sample configuration of the Cray XT4 supercomputer incorporates 548 dual-core AMD Opteron processors, giving a total of 1,096 massively parallel processors. This configuration has 4.4 terabytes of main memory and operates at speeds up to 5.6 teraflops (trillion floating point operations per second) (Cray Inc., 2006).

In addition to the vendors mentioned previously, some other important vendors of midrange supercomputers are Sun Microsystems and a trio of Japanese firms—NEC, Hitachi, and Fujitsu. An interesting development in the supercomputer arena occurred in 1996 when Silicon Graphics, Inc., acquired Cray Research, thus becoming (for a time) the world's leading high-performance computing company. Cray Research continued to operate as a separate unit, focusing on large-scale supercomputers. Then in 2000, Tera Computer Company purchased Cray Research from Silicon Graphics, Inc., with the combined company renamed Cray Inc. In the supercomputer arena as in other areas, sometimes it is hard to keep up with the players!

SUMMARY

There is a lot more to IT than the digital computer, but there is no doubt that the computer was the key technological development of the twentieth century. The computer has had an astounding impact on organizations and on our lives, and it has captured our imaginations like no other recent development.

To summarize, all computer systems are made up of some combination of six basic building blocks: input, output, memory, arithmetic/logical unit, files, and control unit. All of these components are controlled by a stored program that resides in memory and is brought into the control unit one instruction at a time, interpreted, and executed. The basic model has been extended in several directions over the years, such as by adding high-speed cache memory and employing multiple processors in a single computer system. Whatever the machine configuration, the computer system is still controlled by stored programs, or software. Chapter 3 explores computer software, concentrating on the programs that are most critical in running the computer system and the applications that you are most likely to encounter.

Let us end this chapter with the caveat that the numbers and specific details covered in the chapter will quickly become outdated, but the basic principles we presented should be valid for the foreseeable future.

REVIEW QUESTIONS

1. Distinguish between microcomputers, midrange systems, mainframes, and supercomputers. Give approximate speeds (millions of floating point operations per second, or MFLOPS) and costs.
2. List the six building blocks that make up digital computers, and describe the flows of data that occur among these blocks.
3. Distinguish between the *contents* of a memory cell and the *address* of a memory cell. Distinguish between a *byte* and a *word*. Distinguish between a *bit* and a *byte*.
4. What are the advantages and disadvantages of using direct access files versus using sequential access files? Why do organizations bother to use sequential access files today?
5. Explain in your own words the importance of the stored-program concept. Include the role of the control unit in your explanation.
6. Define the expressions in italics in the following sentence copied from this chapter: "In general, each *machine language* instruction consists of two parts: an *operation code* and one or more *addresses*."
7. Provide the full names for the following acronyms or abbreviations used in this chapter.

OCR	MIPS	UPC
CPU	MPP	CD-ROM
MFLOPS	DASD	PP
CD-RW	SMP	DVD

8. Four categories of computer systems were considered in this chapter: microcomputers, midrange systems, mainframes, and supercomputers. Provide the name of at least one prominent vendor in each of these categories (and you can only use IBM once!).

9. Describe what is meant by *benchmarking*. When and how would you carry out benchmarking?
10. What is cache memory? Where would it be used, and why?
11. Distinguish between a symmetric multiprocessor computer and a parallel processor computer. Which is the most important at this time for business information processing, and why?
12. What is a blade server, and why have blade servers become important in the last few years?

DISCUSSION QUESTIONS

1. From the discussion in this chapter and your own knowledge from other sources, what do you think is the most important advancement in computer hardware technology in the past five years? Why?
2. Carry out library or Internet research on the latest microprocessor chips available from Intel and AMD, collecting data similar to that contained in the box entitled "Microprocessor chips get faster and faster."
3. Some writers have suggested that mainframe computer systems could be squeezed out of existence in the next few years, with the incredible advances in the capabilities of midrange systems and the power of supercomputers combining to divide up the present mainframe market. What do you think? Why?
4. What are the advantages and limitations of palmtop or handheld computers? Do you have one? If so, for what do you use it? If not, what features would be particularly attractive to you?
5. What are the advantages and limitations of a tablet PC? Do you believe tablet PCs will be successful? Why or why not? Do you see yourself using a tablet PC in a few years?
6. As this chapter has indicated, IBM has been a dominant force in the computer industry since the late 1950s. Why do you think this is the case? More specifically, why were so many large corporations seemingly committed to "Big Blue" (as IBM is affectionately known), at least until the early 1990s?
7. Building on your answer to question 6, why did IBM suffer serious reverses in the early 1990s? Why did IBM bounce back in the latter half of the 1990s? Do you think that IBM will retain its dominant position as we move further into the twenty-first century? Why?
8. With one firm (IBM) dominating the mainframe hardware market in the United States since its inception, and with that same firm currently near the top in every

segment of the hardware industry (except microcomputers), has the computer hardware industry truly been competitive over the past five decades? Support your position.

9. List possible uses of a supercomputer in a business setting.

10. MIPS and MFLOPS were mentioned in this chapter as measures of the power of computer systems. If you were in charge of buying a new large computer system (and you might be some day), what measures of power would you want to find out? How would you go about determining these measures of power?

11. For most business information processing, what do you believe are the critical or limiting characteristics of today's computing systems—CPU speed, memory capacity, DASD capacity, internal communications speed, input-output speed, other factors, or some combination of these factors? Justify your answer.

12. For Web serving, what do you believe are the critical or limiting characteristics of today's computing systems? CPU speed, memory capacity, DASD capacity, internal communications speed, input-output speed, other factors, or some combination of these factors? Justify your answer.

REFERENCES

Bannan, Karen J. 2005. "Ernestine, meet Julie." *CFO* 21 (January): 26.

Beal, Vangie. 2005. "All about dual-core processors." Webopedia Web site, *www.webopedia.com/DidYouKnow/Hardware_ Software/2005/dual_core.asp* (May 6).

Claburn, Thomas. 2006. "PCs that listen perfectly . . . almost." *InformationWeek* 1100 (July 31/August 7): 29.

Cray Inc. 2006. "Cray XT4 and XT3 supercomputers." Cray Inc. Web site, *www.cray.com/products/xt4/index.html* (December).

Dongarra, Jack J. 2006. "Performance of various computers using standard linear equations software." Computer Science Department, University of Tennessee, and Computer Science and Mathematics Division, Oak Ridge National Laboratory, No. CS-89-85 (November 4).

Edwards, Cliff. 2006. "AMD: Chipping away at Intel's lead." *BusinessWeek* (June 12): 72–73.

EMC. 2006. "EMC Symmetrix DMX-3." EMC Web site, *www.emc.com/products/systems/symmetrix/DMX_series/ DMX3.jsp* (December).

Ettenson, Kalpana (ed.) 2006. "Top 10 Power Desktop PCs." *PC World* Web site, *www.pcworld.com/article/id,123846-page1/ article.html* (November 20).

Gaudin, Sharon. 2006. "IBM takes on petaflop barrier." *InformationWeek* 1105 (September 11): 24.

Gonsalves, Antone. 2006. "PDA shipments up, prices down." *InformationWeek* Web site, *www.informationweek.com/ showArticle.jhtml?articleID=194400740* (November 16).

Greenemeier, Larry. 2002. "Mainframes are still a mainstay." *InformationWeek* 911 (October 21): 74–78.

Hamm, Steve, and Ben Elgin. 2005. "IBM discovers the power of one." *BusinessWeek* (February 14): 80–81.

Hesseldahl, Arik. 2006. "Apple's Big Mac." *BusinessWeek* Web site, *www.businessweek.com/technology/content/oct2006/ tc20061018_006862.htm* (October 19).

Hesseldahl, Arik. 2006. "The swarm of killer PDAs." *BusinessWeek* (May 15): 100.

IBM. 2005. "New IBM mainframe designed as hub for collaborative business." IBM Web site, *www-03.ibm.com/press/ us/en/pressrelease/7803.wss* (July 26).

IBM. 2006a. "IBM 3996 Optical Library." IBM Web site, *www-03.ibm.com/servers/storage/optical/3996/* (December).

IBM. 2006b. "IBM unleashes world's most powerful server." IBM Web site, *www-03.ibm.com/systems/p/news/pressreleases/2006/jul/annc_0725.html* (July 25).

IBM. 2006c. "IBM System p5 550 Express" and "IBM System p5 595." IBM Web site, *www-03.ibm.com/systems/p/* (December).

IBM. 2006d. "Hardware—System i5." IBM Web site, *www-03 .ibm.com/systems/i/hardware/* (December).

IBM. 2006e. "BladeCenter." IBM Web site, *www-03.ibm.com/ systems/bladecenter/* (December).

IBM. 2006f. "System z hardware." IBM Web site, *www-03.ibm. com/systems/z/hardware/* (December).

IBM. 2006g. "IBM System Blue Gene Solution." IBM Web site, *www-03.ibm.com/servers/deepcomputing/bluegene.html* (December).

Intel. 2006a. "Intel unveils world's best processor." Intel Web site, *www.intel.com/pressroom/archive/releases/ 20060727comp.htm* (July 27).

Intel. 2006b. "Intel high-performance consumer desktop microprocessor timeline." Intel Web site, *www.intel.com/ pressroom/archive/kits/core2duo/pdf/microprocessor_ timeline.pdf* (December).

Iomega Corporation. 2006. "REV technology: safer, smarter, better backup," "External hard drive: features at a glance," "Super DVD 18x Dual-Format USB External DVD Burner." Iomega Web site, *www.iomega.com/na/landing.jsp* (December).

Judge, Paul C. 1999. "The inside story of how Mike Ruettgers turned EMC into a highflier." *BusinessWeek* (March 15): 72–80.

Keenan, Faith. 2002. "PCs and speech: A rocky marriage." *BusinessWeek* (September 9): 64, 66.

Malykhina, Elena. 2006. "Palm and BlackBerry compete for the all-you-need title." *InformationWeek* 1105 (September 11): 28.

Marlin, Steven. 2005. "IBM launches latest big iron." *InformationWeek* 1050 (August 1): 66.

McDougall, Paul. 2005. "IBM completes sale of PC business to Lenovo." *InformationWeek* Web site, *www.informationweek.com/showArticle.jhtml?articleID=162100445* (May 2).

Mitchell, Robert L. 2006. "Morphing the mainframe." *Computerworld* 40 (January 30): 29–31.

Moltzen, Edward F. 2006. "HP passes Dell as top PC maker worldwide." *InformationWeek* Web site, *www.informationweek.com/showArticle.jhtml?articleID=193400624* (October 19).

Nuance. 2006. "Nuance's Dragon NaturallySpeaking wins 2006 World Class Award from *PC World*." Nuance Web site, *www.nuance.com/news/pressreleases/20060531_pcworld.asp* (May 31).

Perenson, Melissa J. 2006. "New Intel Core 2 Duo systems reach top ranks." *PC World* (October): 72.

Ricadela, Aaron. 2005. "IBM supercomputer hits new top speed as competition looms." *InformationWeek* Web site, *www.informationweek.com/showArticle.jhtml?articleID=172901122* (October 27).

Sandia National Laboratories. 2004. "Red Storm to be assembled in New Mexico." Sandia National Laboratories Web site, *www.sandia.gov/news-center/news-releases/2004/comp-soft-math/redstormrising.html* (July 27).

SanDisk. 2007. "SanDisk Cruzer Micro USB Flash Drive." SanDisk Web site, *www.sandisk.com/Products/Catalog (1168)-SanDisk_Cruzer_Micro_USB_Flash_Drive.aspx* (October).

Stafford, Alan (ed.) 2006. "The 100 Best Products of the Year." *PC World* (July), 82–96, esp. 94.

Thibodeau, Patrick. 2006. "IBM's iSeries line gets upgraded hardware, OS." *Computerworld* Web site, *www.computerworld.com/hardwaretopics/hardware/server/story/0,10801,108246,00.html* (January 31).

Toner, Mike. 2006. "Nations in race to produce world's fastest, most powerful computer." *Atlanta Journal-Constitution.* (October 18): B1.

Top 500. 2006. "Top 500 list—November 2006." Top 500 Web site, *www.top500.org/list/2006/11/100* (November).

Webopedia. 2006. "DVD formats explained." Webopedia Web site, *www.webopedia.com/DidYouKnow/Hardware_Software/2003/DVDFormatsExplained.asp* (March 3).

Wildstrom, Stephen H. 2005. "And for Steve Jobs's next trick . . ." *BusinessWeek* (February 14): 20.

Wildstrom, Stephen H. 2006. "Hello again, speech recognition." *BusinessWeek* (May 22): 20.

CHAPTER 3
COMPUTER SOFTWARE

IN MANY RESPECTS THIS CHAPTER IS MERELY A CONTINUATION OF CHAPTER 2, which concentrated on computer hardware, or the physical pieces of a computer system. We learned that all the hardware is controlled by a stored program, which is a complete listing (in a form that the computer has been built to understand) of what the computer is to do. Such a stored program is an example of computer software, the topic of this chapter. Software is the set of programs (made up of instructions) that control the operations of the computer system. Computer hardware without software is of little value (and vice versa). Both are required for a computer system to be a useful tool for you and your organization. Thus, this chapter will explain more fully the symbiotic relationship between computer hardware and software.

As important as understanding computer hardware is, it is even more important for you as a manager to understand software. First, appropriate software is required before hardware can do anything at all. Second, most organizations spend several times as much money on software as they do on hardware. This ratio of software to hardware costs is rapidly increasing over time. In the first decade of the twenty-first century, a software company, Microsoft Corporation, is arguably the most successful and most influential company in the entire IT arena.

Third, and most personally relevant, you will be dealing directly with a number of important software products, such as spreadsheets, word processors, and Web browsers, whereas the only hardware you are likely to interact with is a PC. Whatever your job in an organization, you are also likely to be involved in software development or acquisition efforts as a member of a project team or as an end user. If your field is marketing, you might well be involved with the creation of a new sales reporting system; if your field is finance, you might develop a computer model to evaluate the impact of a possible merger; if you are an operations manager, you might participate in the development of a new inventory reporting system. (The role of the manager in software development and acquisition is discussed more fully in Chapters 10, 11, and 13.) For a variety of reasons, therefore, it is important that you understand the various types of computer software and the ways software is used within an organization.

EVOLUTION OF COMPUTER PROGRAMMING

First and Second Generation Languages

Computer software has, of course, been around as long as computer hardware. Initially, all software was written in machine language, as described in "The Stored-Program

Concept" section of Chapter 2. Each instruction in a machine language program must be expressed in the precise form that the particular computer has been built to understand. If, for instance, we want to subtract the number found in memory cell 720 from the number found in memory cell 600, storing the result in cell 600, then the machine language instruction (for a hypothetical computer) would be

Operation Code	Addresses	
S	720	600

A complete program to carry out a particular application (e.g., compute the payroll or prepare a management report) would consist of hundreds or thousands of similar instructions expressed in the machine language of the particular computer. The programmer would have to look up (or memorize) each operation code and remember what data have been stored in every memory cell. Machine language programming was (and is) an exacting, tedious, time-consuming process, but it was the only option available on the earliest computers.

Computer software developers soon created **assembly languages** that used the computer itself to perform many of the most tedious aspects of programming. For example, easily remembered mnemonic operation codes are substituted for the machine language operation codes (e.g., SUB for S or SUB for something as unintelligible as 67 on some machines). Symbolic addresses are substituted for a memory cell address (e.g., GPAY for 600). Thus, if our single instruction shown previously is part of a payroll program where we want to subtract deductions (DED) from gross pay (GPAY), we can write

SUB	DED	GPAY

Writing instructions such as this is much easier (and less error-prone) than writing machine language instructions, particularly when we consider that there are likely to be 50 different operation codes and hundreds of memory cell addresses to remember in even a moderate-sized program.

The entire assembly language program is written using instructions similar to the one shown previously. Then the computer, under the control of a special stored program called an **assembler**, converts these mnemonic operation codes and symbolic addresses to the machine language operation codes and memory cell addresses. The assembler program simply keeps a table of conversions for operation

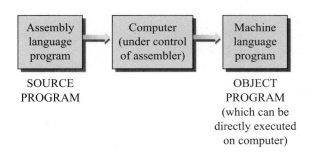

SOURCE   OBJECT
PROGRAM   PROGRAM
                                 (which can be
                                 directly executed
                                 on computer)

Figure 3.1   Assembler Translation Process

codes and addresses and makes the substitutions as necessary. Figure 3.1 illustrates this translation process from the assembly language program (the program containing mnemonic codes and symbolic addresses) to the machine language program. The assembly language program is also called the **source program**, and the resulting machine language program is the **object program**. Once the translation process has been completed, the outcome machine language program is loaded into memory and carried out by the control unit (as described in Chapter 2). The machine language for a particular computer is referred to as the first generation language (1 GL), and the assembly language that came along later is called the second generation language (2 GL).

Assembly language programming was popular for business applications for many years (until about 1970), and some computer professionals still use assembly language.[1] Popular assembly languages have included SOAP (Symbolic Optimization Assembly Program), Autocoder, and BAL (Basic Assembly Language). Assembly language programming is much easier than machine language programming, but it still requires the programmer to employ the same small steps that the computer has been built to understand; it still requires one assembly language instruction for each machine language instruction.[2] Thus, even after the advent of assembly languages, efforts continued

---

[1]The primary reason for the continued use of assembly language is computer efficiency. A well-written assembly language program will require less memory and take less time to execute than a well-written third or fourth generation language program.

[2]To be complete, assembly languages often provide for macroinstructions, where one macroinstruction may correspond to 5, 10, or more machine language instructions. A programmer writes a set of assembly language instructions that he or she expects to use repeatedly, and then gives this set a label (or a macroinstruction name). Then each time the macroinstruction is used in a program, the entire set of assembly language instructions is substituted for it.

to make it easier to tell the computer what the user wanted done. The results are today's third and fourth generation languages (3 GLs and 4 GLs).

Third and Fourth Generation Languages

The third and fourth generation languages represent a radical departure from the first two generations. Both machine language and assembly language programming require the programmer to think like the computer in terms of the individual instructions. With 3 GLs and 4 GLs, the programmer uses a language that is relatively easy for humans to learn and use but has no direct relationship to the machine language into which it must eventually be translated. Thus, the 3 GLs and 4 GLs are designed for humans, not computers! Typically, each 3 GL or 4 GL instruction will be translated into many machine language instructions (perhaps 10 machine language instructions per 3 GL instruction, or 100 machine language instructions per 4 GL instruction). Furthermore, although each type of computer has its unique 2 GL, the 3 GLs and 4 GLs are largely machine independent. Thus, a program written in a 3 GL or 4 GL can be run on many different types of computers, which is often a significant advantage.

Third generation languages are also called **procedural languages**, because they express a step-by-step procedure devised by the programmer to accomplish the desired task. The earliest procedural language was FORTRAN (an abbreviation for FORmula TRANslator), which was developed by IBM in the mid-1950s. Other popular procedural languages include COBOL (COmmon Business Oriented Language), PL/1, BASIC, PASCAL, ADA, and C. These third generation languages (particularly FORTRAN, BASIC, C, and COBOL) are still very important today, and a later section of this chapter will expand on these introductory remarks. Estimates vary, but it is likely that at least half of the programs in use today were written in 3 GLs.

A source program in any one of these languages must be translated into the machine language object program before the computer can carry it out. For 3 GLs (and for 4 GLs), the language translator is called a **compiler** if the entire program is translated into machine language before any of the program is executed, or an **interpreter** if each source program statement is executed as soon as that single statement is translated. Historically, the BASIC language was usually interpreted, while most other 3 GLs have been compiled. However, BASIC compilers now exist, and interpreted COBOL is sometimes used during program development.

Figure 3.2 depicts the process of compiling and running a compiled procedural language program, such as C, FORTRAN, or COBOL. This process is quite similar to that

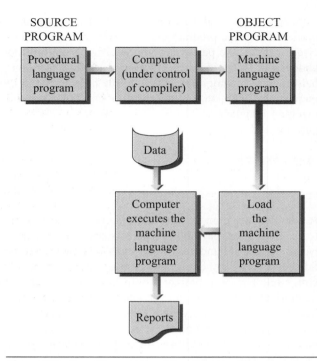

Figure 3.2   Compiling and Running a Procedural Language Program

used for assembly language programming (see Figure 3.1), with the labels changed as appropriate. The key is that the entire program is translated into an object program, and then the object program is loaded and executed. Dealing with the entire program in this manner has the advantage that an efficient machine language program (one that executes rapidly) can be produced because the interrelationships among the program statements can be considered during the compilation process; dealing with the entire program has the disadvantage that the programmer does not learn about errors until the entire program has been translated.

Figure 3.3 shows the process of interpreting and running an interpretive language program, such as BASIC.

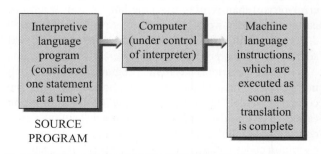

Figure 3.3   Interpreting and Running an Interpretive Language Program

With an interpreter, only one statement from the source program is considered at a time. This single statement is translated into machine language, and if no errors are encountered, it is immediately executed. The process is repeated, statement after statement. This interpretive process lends itself to a programming approach in which the programmer composes the program at a PC, keys in one statement at a time, and is almost immediately provided feedback if an error is made. If there are no errors, output is produced immediately after the last statement is entered. The machine language program resulting from the interpretive process is usually much less efficient than one resulting from compilation because only one source program statement is being considered at a time. On the other hand, program development might be sped up because of the immediate feedback to programmers when they make an error. With an interpreter, there is often no true object program, because the machine language instructions are discarded as soon as they are executed. Furthermore, if the program is executed repeatedly, each source statement is translated again each time it is executed, which is quite inefficient compared with the compilation process.

Fourth generation languages—also called **productivity languages** and **nonprocedural languages**—are even easier to use than the third generation languages. To employ a 3 GL, the programmer must devise a step-by-step procedure to accomplish the desired result and express this procedure in the form of 3 GL statements. With a 4 GL, the computer user merely gives a precise statement of what he or she wishes to accomplish, not an explanation of how to do it. Thus, the order in which statements are given in a 4 GL is usually inconsequential. Furthermore, each 4 GL statement is usually translated into significantly more machine language instructions than a single 3 GL statement, sometimes by a factor of 100. Thus, 4 GL programs are easier to write, shorter, and less error-prone than 3 GL programs, which in turn have the same advantages over their 2 GL predecessors. Some fourth generation languages use an interpreter to translate the source program into machine language, and some use a compiler. Please note that the 3 GLs and 4 GLs are essentially the same from one computer model to the next, but the translation programs (compilers and interpreters) must be specific to the particular computer model.

With these advantages, why aren't all programs written in 4 GLs today? First, some of the 4 GLs, like SAS and IFPS, are not general-purpose languages and cannot be used easily for many types of programs. On the other hand, FOCUS and CA-Ramis are indeed general-purpose 4 GLs. More important, many programs are not written in 4 GLs because of concern for efficient use of the computer resources of the organization. For the most part, 4 GL programs translate into longer machine language programs that take much longer to execute than the equivalent programs written in 3 GLs. The upshot of these arguments is many one-time programs or infrequently used programs (such as a decision support system or a specialized management report) are written in 4 GLs, while most production programs (those that will be run every day or every week) are written in 3 GLs. In the case of infrequently used programs, human efficiency in writing the program is more important than computer efficiency in running it; for production programs, the opposite is often the case.

In the late 1990s and early 2000s, new programming languages have gained popularity that are still predominantly 3GLs but also have some 4 GL characteristics. These languages are usually described as **object-oriented programming (OOP)** languages. OOP languages such as Smalltalk and C++ came first; these languages are built on the idea of embedding procedures (called methods) in **objects**, and then putting these objects together to create an application. Newer object-oriented programming languages, such as Java and Visual Basic .NET, provide a graphical programming environment and a paint metaphor for developing user interfaces. These newer entries in the programming arena as well as 3 GL and 4 GL languages will be described more fully later in the chapter. Overall, the programming environment in most large organizations is now more diverse than ever, with most organizations using some combination of conventional 3 GLs, 4 GLs, and object-oriented programming. The trend is toward more object-oriented programming, but significant 4 GL programming and even more 3 GL programming is still being carried out.

KEY TYPES OF SOFTWARE

In the previous section we considered the evolution of computer programming. These programming languages—from assembly language to COBOL to FOCUS to C++ to Java—have been used over the past several decades to create an incredible array of software products, including the language translators themselves. We now want to categorize the various types of computer software that have been created and gain an understanding of how they work together.

To begin our look at the key elements of computer software, let us step back from the details and view the big picture. It is useful to divide software into two major categories:

1. Applications software
2. Support software

Applications software includes all programs written to accomplish particular tasks for computer users. In addition to our payroll computation example, applications programs would include an inventory record-keeping program, a word-processing product, a spreadsheet product, a program to allocate advertising expenditures, and a program producing a summarized report for top management. Each of these programs produces output that users need to do their jobs.

By contrast, **support software** (also called **systems software**) does not directly produce output that users need. Instead, support software provides a computing environment in which it is relatively easy and efficient for humans to work; it enables applications programs written in a variety of languages to be carried out; and it ensures that the computer hardware and software resources are used efficiently. Support software is usually obtained from computer vendors and from specialized software development companies called software houses.

The relationship between applications software and support software might be more readily understood by considering the software iceberg depicted in Figure 3.4. The iceberg's above-water portion is analogous to applications software; both are highly visible. Applications software directly produces results that you as a manager require to perform your job. However, just as the iceberg's underwater portion keeps the top of the iceberg above water, the support software is absolutely essential for the applications software to produce the desired results. (Please note that the iceberg analogy is not an accurate representation of the numbers of applications and support programs; there are usually many more applications programs than support programs.) Your concern as a manager will be primarily with the applications software—the programs that are directly relevant to your job—but you need to understand the functions of the primary types of support software to appreciate how the complete hardware/software system works.

APPLICATIONS SOFTWARE

Applications software includes all programs written to accomplish particular tasks for computer users. Portfolio management programs, general ledger accounting programs, sales forecasting programs, material requirements planning (MRP) programs, electronic mail programs, and desktop publishing products are all examples of applications software. Each of you will be using applications software as part of your job, and many of you will be involved in developing or obtaining applications software to meet your organization's needs.

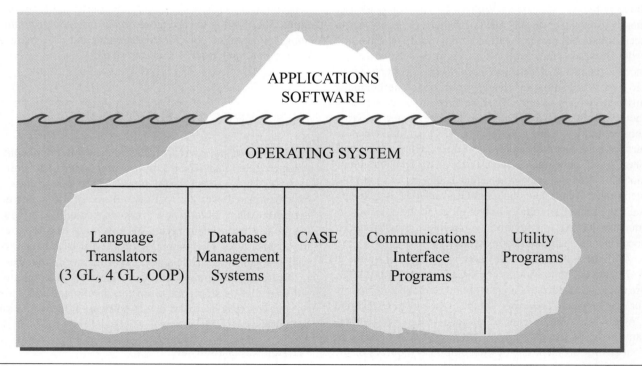

Figure 3.4 The Software Iceberg

Because applications software is so diverse, it is difficult to divide these programs into a few neat categories as we will do with support software later in the chapter. Instead, we will begin with a brief look at the sources of applications software, and then we will give two examples of accounting products to illustrate the types of commercial products that are available for purchase. Finally, we will look at personal productivity products for handling many common applications (e.g., word processing, spreadsheets).

Where do we obtain software? Support software is almost always purchased from a hardware vendor or a software house. Only the very largest information systems (IS) organizations would even consider writing utility programs or modifying operating systems or compilers. Applications software, however, is sometimes developed within the organization and sometimes purchased from an outside source. Standard applications products, such as word processing, database management systems, electronic mail, and spreadsheets, are almost always purchased. Applications that are unique to the organization—a one-of-a-kind production control system, a proprietary foreign exchange trading program, a decision support system for adoption or rejection of a new product—are almost always developed within the organization (or by a consulting firm or software company under contract to the organization). The vast middle ground of applications that are quite similar from one organization to the next, but which might have some features peculiar to the particular organization, might be either purchased or developed.

These middle-ground applications include accounts payable, accounts receivable, general ledger, inventory control, MRP, sales analysis, and personnel reporting. Here, the organization must decide whether its requirements are truly unique. Does the organization have the capability of developing this application in-house? What are the costs and benefits of developing in-house versus purchasing a commercial product? This make-or-buy decision for applications software is an important one for almost every organization, and this topic will be addressed further in Chapter 11. Let us note at this point that the rising costs of software development tend to be pushing the balance towards more purchased software and less in-house development.

Until the mid-1980s, virtually all software development done within an organization was done by the formally constituted IS organization. The exceptions were engineers, scientists, and a few computer jocks[3] in other user departments.

A revolution called end-user computing has occurred in the past two decades, and now end users such as you do much of the internal software development. There are at least three reasons for the end-user computing revolution. First, the IS organization was unable to keep up with the demand for new applications software, and significant backlogs of jobs developed. Second, a more knowledgeable, more computer-oriented group of users was created through the hiring of college graduates and the use of various internal and external training programs. Third, and perhaps most significant, powerful desktop computers became affordable, and software vendors developed relatively easy-to-use tools that made it possible for interested, but not expert, users to carry out significant software development. These tools include the fourth generation languages and the query languages associated with database management systems. This trend toward end-user computing will continue, in our view, with many of you becoming involved in software development early in your careers. Chapter 13 explores this phenomenon of user development.

Of course, not all internal software development is now done—or should be done—by users. For the most part, IS organizations have not shrunk because of end-user computing; they simply have not grown as rapidly as they might have otherwise. The IS organizations (or consulting companies or software vendors) continue to develop and maintain the large, complex applications. The IS organizations also tend to develop applications that apply to multiple areas within the organization and those applications for which efficiency is paramount, such as sales transaction processing. The IS organizations employ the same tools used by end users, but they also do a substantial portion of their work using COBOL and other 3 GLs, OOP, and, in some instances, CASE (computer-aided software engineering) tools. Chapters 10 to 13 explore the various ways in which applications systems are developed or procured.

Examples of Applications Products

Often applications software will be purchased from an outside source. To continue our look at applications software, we will consider one category of commercially available software—accounting products—as a representative of the many categories that exist. Many commercial accounting products are available, but we will focus on only two such products: one inexpensive product designed for small to midsized businesses and one somewhat more expensive product designed for larger businesses.

The product designed for smaller businesses is Peachtree by Sage Premium Accounting 2007, with a retail price of

---

[3]This is not meant as a term of derision. "Computer jock" is a common term used to indicate a person who spends great quantities of time and effort working with a computer.

$500 for a single-user version. This product has all the features that a small to midsized business would need, including general ledger, accounts receivable, accounts payable, inventory, payroll, time and billing, job costing, fixed asset accounting, and analysis and reporting tools. The Peachtree "Business Status Center" page, illustrated in Figure 3.5, provides a concise, integrated way for the business to review key financial information. The "Business Status Center" page displays up-to-date information on account balances, year-to-date income, customers who owe money, vendors to pay, aged receivables, aged payables, and top customers for the last 12 months. Other features built into Peachtree Premium Accounting include the ability to generate customer quotes, create and track sales orders and back orders, maintain an audit trail, track inventory items by detailed attributes, prepare progress billings, create departmentalized financial statements, and customize forms, reports, and screens. With the Comparative Budget Spreadsheet Creator, the user can create several different versions of budgets to better manage the business. *PC Magazine* gives Peachtree Premium Accounting an excellent rating—five out of five

possible dots—and named it an "Editors' Choice" in this category of software. "If you're looking to automate your business for the first time—especially if you need company consolidation and advanced inventory—make this product one of your top two choices," says *PC Magazine*'s Kathy Yakal (2006, p. 65).

The second product, or rather an extensive set of modules that can be purchased independently, is Sage Accpac 200 ERP. Sage Accpac 200 ERP (there is also Sage Accpac 500 ERP for midsized to large businesses and Sage Accpac 100 ERP for smaller businesses) is a Web-based, modular financial management system for midsized businesses that supports as many as 10 concurrent users. The Sage Accpac software resides on a Web server, with only a Web browser needed on PCs to access the application. The central module of Sage Accpac is the System Manager, which controls access to all Accpac accounting applications and data. The System Manager module manages security, ensures data integrity, handles bank reconciliation and tax processing, and permits creation of customized reports. Other available modules include General Ledger, Accounts Payable,

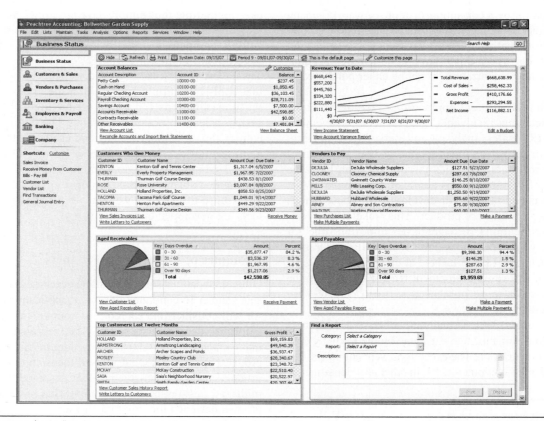

Figure 3.5 Peachtree "Business Status Center" Page from Peachtree by Sage Premium Accounting 2007 (Reproduced with permission of Best Software SB, Inc. The peach device, Peachtree Complete and Peachtree Today are registered trademarks of Best Software SB, Inc)

Accounts Receivable, Inventory Control, Order Entry, Purchase Orders, U.S. and Canadian Payroll, General Ledger Consolidations, Project and Job Costing, Multicurrency, and Intercompany Transactions. The idea, of course, is for each business to select and employ the modules needed to run its business. The System Manager module is priced at $1,250, and the other modules are priced at $1,000 each. In addition, there is a fee of $1,250 for LanPak (for use with the database) plus additional database license charges that vary with the number of users and the database management system used. Accpac options are also available, including a financial diagnostic and strategic analysis tool (CFO), an easy-to-use report generator (Query), an electronic funds transfer direct payroll option, a sales analysis tool, and a sales optimizer tool. These options cost from $500 to $1,000 each. Thus, the total cost of a Sage Accpac 200 ERP installation will be much higher than that for Peachtree by Sage Premium Accounting 2007, but Sage Accpac 200 ERP will be able to handle a much larger business.

DO YOUR ACCOUNTING ON THE WEB!

Accounting for small businesses can now be done on the World Wide Web! Several companies, including Sage Software (which includes the Peachtree line of accounting software), make accounting software accessible via the Web so that the bookkeeper, small business owner, or other designated employee can enter accounting data, check inventory levels or financial information, and create reports from anywhere at anytime. Sage Software calls its online accounting service ePeachtree, and the fees are quite reasonable. The ePeachtree basic accounting service—which includes general ledger, sales and receivables, purchasing and payables, inventory, job and project tracking, and sales tax tracking—is $150 per year for a single user (plus a single outside accountant at no additional fee), with an add-on fee of $102 per year for each additional user. ePeachtree also has available a payroll service add-on for an additional $96 per year. On its Web site, ePeachtree stresses its security measures, including the use of Secure Sockets Layer (SSL) encryption technology, regular data backups, 24x7 security guards, and video surveillance cameras (more on security measures in Chapter 16). From a small business standpoint, a big plus for using ePeachtree or a similar service is that the firm never again has to spend the money or take the time to upgrade its accounting software—the vendor automatically handles all upgrades. The only software the business needs is a Web browser!

[Adapted from Peachtree by Sage Web site, 2007]

Personal Productivity Software

From your personal standpoint as a manager, the category of applications software that we have chosen to call **personal productivity software** is probably the most important of all. These are the applications that you and your fellow managers will use on a regular basis: word processing, spreadsheets, presentation graphics, electronic mail, desktop publishing, microcomputer-based database management systems, Web browsers, statistical products, and other similar easy-to-use and extremely useful products. These products are microcomputer-based, and they have been developed with a friendly, comfortable graphical user interface (GUI).

Exciting things continue to happen in the personal productivity software area. The true beginning of this area came in 1979 with the introduction of VisiCalc, the first electronic spreadsheet. With VisiCalc, microcomputers became a valuable business tool, not just a toy or a hobby. The financial success of VisiCalc convinced many enterprising developers that there was money to be made in developing software products that individuals and companies would buy and use. Within a few years a deluge of products appeared—a mixture of good and bad—that has not stopped flowing. The results have been truly marvelous for the businessperson with a willingness to experiment and a desire to become more productive. Most of the microcomputer products are quite reasonably priced (often a few hundred dollars), because the successful products can expect to reap large rewards on their volume of sales. Furthermore, a number of excellent publications have developed (such as *PC Magazine* and *PC World*), which carefully review the new products to assist us in choosing the right ones. Hardly a month goes by without the announcement of an exciting new product that might become the new VisiCalc, WordPerfect, or Microsoft Excel.

Word Processing   Word processing might be the most ubiquitous of the personal productivity software products. In many organizations the first users of microcomputers were the secretaries using early word-processing products (often WordStar). As secretaries learned the advantages of word processing, particularly the ability to make corrections in a draft without retyping the entire document, managers began to think that it might be more convenient for them, too, to have a microcomputer on their desk so that they could draft letters and reports directly at the keyboard rather than writing them out longhand. There is an art to composing at the keyboard, but once a person has the hang of it, his or her productivity (in terms of written output) can easily be doubled or tripled, as compared to writing longhand. Thus, word processing has made major inroads into the corporate world at the managerial level.

The newest versions of the popular word-processing products make it easy to get addicted to them. For example, Microsoft Word underlines words that might be misspelled so that you can correct them as you type; lets the user change fonts, margins, and columns easily; rewrites sentences to make them grammatically correct with the click of a mouse; links any text directly to an Internet file; and converts Web files directly to Word format so they are ready to use. Another popular capability is mail merge—the ability to automatically print the same letter (with the address and salutation changed, of course) to everyone on a mailing list. Other popular word-processing products include Corel WordPerfect, Lotus Word Pro, and Sun's StarOffice Writer. In addition to these products that can be purchased, there are also some free options available, including OpenOffice's Writer (a free, downloadable version of StarOffice Writer) and Google's Docs & Spreadsheets product, which is Web-based. All these products try to achieve "what you see is what you get," or WYSIWYG, and all succeed to a great extent. The idea is that the text you see on the computer screen should be as close as possible to the resulting printed text. In choosing a word processor, most of us tend to prefer whichever word processor we worked with first. Increasingly, though, organizations have settled on a standard office suite (more on this later), and thus we use the word processor included in that standard suite, usually Microsoft Word.

Spreadsheets   Second only to word processing in popularity are electronic spreadsheet products, the most widely used of which is Microsoft Excel. Other popular spreadsheet products are Lotus 1-2-3 and Corel Quattro Pro. (Again, free products are also available, including OpenOffice's Calc and Google's Docs & Spreadsheets.) After the early success of VisiCalc, Lotus 1-2-3 became the spreadsheet standard in the early 1980s and held that leadership position for over a decade. With the growth of software office suites and the dominance of Microsoft in the operating system arena, 1-2-3 has fallen behind Excel as the spreadsheet of choice, but 1-2-3 is still an excellent product with a strong following.

The idea of the electronic spreadsheet is based on the accountant's spreadsheet, which is a large sheet of paper divided into many columns and rows on which the accountant can organize and present financial data. The spreadsheet approach can be used for any application that can fit into the rows and columns framework, including budget summaries for several time periods, profit and loss statements for various divisions of a company, sales forecasts for the next 12 months, an instructor's grade book, and computation of various statistics for a basketball team.

The intersection of a row and a column is called a cell. Each row in the spreadsheet is given a label (1, 2, 3, etc., from the top down), as is each column (A, B, C, etc., from left to right), and a cell is identified by combining the designations of the intersecting row and column. In a budget summary spreadsheet, for example, cell C4 might contain $32,150, the budgeted sales income for the second quarter. Similarly, cell C2 might contain the heading information "Second Quarter." To enter data into a cell, the cursor is positioned on that cell and the user merely keys in the appropriate data.

But the power of a spreadsheet program does not come from keying numeric data into particular cells, although that is certainly done. The power comes in part from the use of formulas to combine the contents of other cells, letting the program make the calculations rather than doing them by hand. For example, let us assume that cell C9 in our budget summary example is to contain the total income for the second quarter, which is the sum of cells C4, C5, C6, and C7. Rather than adding C4 through C7 by hand, the user enters a formula in cell C9 that tells the program to total the contents of those four cells. One way to express that formula in Microsoft Excel is = +C4+C5+C6+C7. The program then computes the sum and places it in cell C9. More importantly, if a change has to be made in one of the numerical entries, say in cell C5, the sum in cell C9 is automatically corrected to reflect the new number. This feature makes it very easy to modify assumptions and conduct "what if" analyses using a spreadsheet product.

Database Management Systems   After word processing and spreadsheets, the next most popular category of personal productivity software is microcomputer-based database management systems (DBMSs). The most widely used product is Microsoft Access; other popular products include FileMaker Pro, Corel Paradox, Alpha Five, and Lotus Approach. dBase was the desktop DBMS leader in the 1980s but has now disappeared. All these products are based on the relational data model, to be discussed later in this chapter. The basic ideas behind these products are the same as those for large machine DBMSs, but the desktop DBMSs are generally easier to use. With the aid of macros (the use of a macroinstruction name instead of the corresponding, oft-repeated string of commands) and other programming tools (such as Visual Basic for Applications in the case of Access), rather sophisticated applications can be built based on these DBMS products.

Presentation Graphics   Presentation graphics is yet another important category of personal productivity software. Most spreadsheet products incorporate significant graphics capabilities, but the specialized presentation graphics (sometimes called business graphics) products have even greater capabilities. Used for creating largely textual presentations, but with embedded clip art, photographs, graphs, and other media, the leaders in this field are Microsoft PowerPoint, Corel Presentations, and Lotus Freelance Graphics. For design of more complex business graphics, the leading products are Microsoft Visio, Adobe Illustrator, CorelDRAW, and Macromedia FreeHand.

Electronic Mail and Groupware   We will defer a full discussion of electronic mail (e-mail) and groupware until Chapter 6, but these clearly qualify as personal productivity software. Electronic mail has become the preferred way of communicating for managers in most businesses today. It is asynchronous (no telephone tag) and unobtrusive, easy to use and precise. Groupware incorporates electronic mail, but also much more. Groupware has the goal of helping a group become more productive and includes innovative ways of data sharing, such as Lotus Notes' threaded discussion groups.

Office Suites   There are still other important categories of personal productivity software to consider, but let's pause at this point to introduce the critical idea of **office suites**, which combine certain personal productivity software applications—usually all or most of those categories we have already considered—into integrated suites of applications for use in the office. With the strong popularity of the Microsoft Windows operating system, the major software players scrambled to introduce office suites, also known as **application suites**, that are compatible with Windows. Of course, Microsoft, as the developer of Windows, had the inside track in terms of producing a Windows office suite. In the first decade of the twenty-first century, the Microsoft Office suite is overwhelmingly the dominant entry in the marketplace. Three other commercial office suites are worth mentioning—Corel WordPerfect Office, Lotus SmartSuite, and Sun StarOffice—as well as one free suite—OpenOffice.

Microsoft Office (version 95, then 97, 2000, XP, 2003, and now 2007) was the first suite available and has captured a dominant market share, but the other suites have strong features and a distinct price advantage (sometimes even a zero price). The Microsoft Office 2007 suite includes Word (word processing), Excel (spreadsheet), PowerPoint (presentations), and Outlook (e-mail, contacts, and scheduling) in the standard edition. The small business edition adds Publisher (desktop publishing), Accounting Express (a small business accounting product), and a version of Outlook with Business Contact Manager, and the

professional edition adds Access (database management system) to the small business package. The suggested retail price is $399 for the standard edition, $449 for the small business edition, and $499 for the professional edition. The other players in the office suite arena have had difficulty keeping up with Microsoft. Microsoft was the first mover, controls the operating system, has good individual products (although not always the best individual products), and has done a better job of integrating the individual products than the other players.

Corel WordPerfect Office X3 includes four products in its standard edition: WordPerfect (word processing), Quattro Pro (spreadsheet), Presentations (presentations), and WordPerfect MAIL (e-mail). The professional edition adds Paradox (database management system). The retail price is about $270 for the standard edition and $350 for the professional edition, but the street price is under $40 for the standard edition and under $80 for the professional edition. Lotus SmartSuite Release 9.8 includes seven products: Word Pro (word processing), 1-2-3 (spreadsheet), Freelance Graphics (presentations), Approach (database management system), Organizer (time management), FastSite (Web publishing), and SmartCenter (information manager). The retail price is under $290, but the street price is often under $40.

The Sun StarOffice 8 office suite, which can be downloaded for $70, includes five key products: Writer (word processing), Calc (spreadsheet), Impress (presentations), Draw (graphics), and Base (database management system). For all three commercial suites, the price to upgrade from an earlier edition is considerably less than the retail price. Finally, OpenOffice is the free, downloadable version of StarOffice, and includes six products: Writer, Calc, Impress, Draw, Base, and Math (to create mathematical equations). All these suites provide excellent value for the investment. It seems clear that the future of certain personal productivity software products (word processing, spreadsheet, presentations, and database management system) lies in office suites because of the ability to move data among the various products as needed.

World Wide Web Browsers   A very important type of personal productivity software is the **Web browser** used by an individual to access information on the World Wide Web. The Web browser is the software that runs on the user's microcomputer, enabling the user to look around, or "browse," the Internet. Of course, the user's machine must be linked to the Internet via an Internet service provider (ISP) or a connection to a local area network (LAN) which is in turn connected to the Internet. The Web browser uses a hypertext-based approach to navigate the Internet.

Hypertext is a creative way of linking objects (such as text, pictures, sound clips, and video clips) to each other. For example, when you are reading a document describing the Grand Canyon, you might click on <u>The View from Yavapai Point</u> to display a full-screen photograph of that view, or click on <u>The Grand Canyon Suite</u> to hear a few bars from that musical composition.

The dominant Web browser in use near the end of the first decade of the twenty-first century is—no surprise—Microsoft's Internet Explorer. The Netscape browser had first mover advantage and was the most popular browser until the late 1990s, but has now essentially disappeared. There are, however, several other browsers in use, including the open-source Firefox browser from the Mozilla Foundation (more on open source in the "Sources of Operating Systems" section later in this chapter), Apple Computer's Safari browser, and the Opera browser (which is especially popular in Europe; Opera Software is based in Norway). Meaningful browser statistics are hard to come by, but one source reports that Firefox has about 30 percent of the browser market, compared to about 60 percent for Internet Explorer (W3Schools Web site, 2007). Because of the audience of this survey, these results likely understate Internet Explorer usage and overstate Firefox usage; more reasonable estimates are around 80 percent for Internet Explorer and 15 percent for Firefox. Many commentators prefer Firefox to Internet Explorer; for example, *PC Magazine*'s Davis Janowski summarizes his review of the new versions of both browsers by saying "Microsoft's offering is an overall good browser with a lot of features to recommend it, but Firefox 2.0, even though it represents smaller evolutionary steps beyond its predecessor, remains for now the best overall browser" (Janowski, 2006). From the standpoint of the user, the interesting thing about the browser battle is that all the products are free—the price is unbeatable!

Web browsers are based on the idea of **pull technology**. The browser must request a Web page before it is sent to the desktop. Another example of pull technology is the **RSS reader**[4] software (also called an **aggregator**) built into today's browsers and some e-mail programs. Such readers reduce the time and effort needed to regularly check Web sites for updates. Once a user has subscribed to an RSS feed from a particular site, the RSS reader checks for new content at user-determined intervals and retrieves syndicated Web content such as Weblogs, podcasts, and mainstream mass media reports.

Push technology is also important. In push technology, data are sent to the client (usually a PC) without the client requesting it. E-mail is the oldest and most widely used push technology—and certainly e-mail spam is the most obnoxious form of push technology. In the 1990s the most familiar Web example of push technology was PointCast (a free download product), which delivered customized news ticker-tape style to the user's desktop. However, this provider-to-end-user use of push technology has essentially gone out of existence (and so has PointCast) because of a flawed economic model. Other uses of push technology have been more successful. For example, it is commonplace for technology vendors (such as Microsoft) and corporations to distribute software patches and new versions of software via push technology, often on an overnight basis. Similarly, many organizations have pushed sales updates and product news to their sales representatives and field service technicians around the world. But what if the users are only occasionally online, with much of their work done offline?

BackWeb Technologies (based in Israel)—which describes itself as the "offline technology company"—has the answer with offline portal access and proactive delivery of information using its Polite technology. A **portal** is simply a standardized entry point to key information on the corporate network. When an employee is online, he or she goes through the portal to find the needed information. With the BackWeb system, a copy of the corporate portal is set up on the user's PC. When the PC is online, BackWeb's Polite technology takes advantage of otherwise unused bandwidth to update the portal's contents, such that network performance is never affected by the portal replication. Thus, the user can do most of his or her work offline using the offline portal. BackWeb's Offline Access Server product incorporates two-way replication, which lets users work in a portal offline and then automatically replicates changes and additions once they reconnect to the network. BackWeb has partnered with several software giants, including SAP and Oracle, to employ its Offline Access Server technology with their enterprise applications. Offline portals, serviced by push technology, can increase the productivity of today's mobile employees when they are on the road and disconnected from the network (Kontzer, 2003; and BackWeb Web site, 2007).

Other Personal Productivity Products Desktop publishing gives the user the ability to design and print an in-house newspaper or magazine, a sales brochure, an annual report, and many other things. The more advanced word-processing products, such as Microsoft Word and Corel WordPerfect, provide the capability to arrange the document in appropriate columns, import figures, tables, and photographs, and use appropriate type fonts and styles. The popular

---

[4]RSS refers to several standards, where the initials stand for Really Simple Syndication, Rich Site Summary, or RDF Site Summary.

specialized desktop publishing products, such as Adobe PageMaker, Adobe InDesign, Adobe FrameMaker, Quark XPress, Corel Ventura, and Microsoft Office Publisher, are even more powerful.

There are a number of other categories of personal productivity products. Two important security products are Norton Internet Security[5] (from Symantec), which is *PC Magazine*'s Editors' Choice for best security suite, and ZoneAlarm Internet Security Suite (from Zone Labs). We will consider computer security in more depth in Chapter 16. Personal information managers provide an easy-to-use electronic calendar plus storage of telephone numbers, addresses, and other personal information. For an individual not working as part of a group, AnyTime Organizer Deluxe (from Individual Software Inc.) and WinPIM Personal Edition (from YQSoft Inc.) are good choices; for those working in a group, groupware products such as Lotus Notes and Microsoft Outlook provide these capabilities. ACT! by Sage, GoldMine (from FrontRange Solutions), and NightHawk (from Now Software) are examples of contact management programs to let the user track past and potential customers.

A widely used and valuable product for creating, distributing, and commenting on electronic documents is Adobe Acrobat. Project scheduling software includes Microsoft Office Project, FastTrack Schedule (from AEC Software), and SureTrak Project Manager (from Primavera Systems). Among the popular products for image editing are Adobe Photoshop, Adobe Photoshop Elements[5] (a reduced-version product designed for hobbyists), Jasc Paint Shop Pro Studio, Serif PhotoPlus Studio Pack, and Corel Paint Shop Pro. For video editing, four strong software products are Pinnacle Studio (from Avid Technology), Adobe Premiere Elements, Roxio VideoWave, and Ulead VideoStudio Plus (from Corel). Valuable utility products include Roxio Easy Media Creator Suite[5] (to burn CDs and DVDs) and Mozy Remote Backup[5] (a PC backup solution), and valuable reference products include Microsoft Streets & Trips and Microsoft Encarta (a true multimedia encyclopedia).

The list of personal productivity software presented here could certainly be extended, but today's most important categories have been mentioned. New products and new categories will certainly be introduced in the next few years.

---

[5]*PC Magazine* named four products as "our top picks" for software in 2006: Adobe Photoshop Elements 5–best digital imaging software, Mozy Remote Backup 1.6–best personal backup solution, Norton Internet Security 2007–best security suite, and Roxio Easy Media Creator 9 Suite—best digital video software (2006).

SUPPORT SOFTWARE

Support software has been designed to support applications software from behind the scenes rather than to directly produce output of value to the user. There are several types of support software, such as the language translators we encountered earlier in this chapter. In our discussion of the evolution of computer programming, we noted that programs written in second, third, and fourth generation languages must be translated to machine language before they can be run on a computer. This translation is accomplished by support software called assemblers, compilers, and interpreters. We now want to take a systematic look at the various types of support software.

The Operating System

The most important type of support software is the operating system, which originated in the mid-1960s and is now an integral part of every computer system. The **operating system** is a very complex program that controls the operation of the computer hardware and coordinates all the other software, so as to get as much work done as possible with the available resources. Users interact with the operating system, not the hardware, and the operating system in turn controls all hardware and software resources of the computer system.

Before operating systems (and this was also before PCs), computer operators had to physically load programs and start them running by pushing buttons on the computer console. Only one program could be run at a time, and the computer was often idle while waiting for an action by the operator. Now the operator's job is much easier and the computer is used more efficiently, with the operating system controlling the starting and stopping of individual programs and permitting multiple programs to be run at the same time. The operating system on a PC also helps the user by providing an easy-to-use graphical user interface (GUI).

There are two overriding purposes for an operating system: to maximize the work done by the computer system (the throughput), and to ease the workload of computer users. In effect, the operation of the computer system has been automated through the use of this sophisticated program. Figure 3.6 illustrates some of the ways in which these purposes are advanced by the operating system. This somewhat complex diagram presents the roles of the operating system in a large computer system. To make these roles more understandable, we will concentrate on the individual elements of the diagram.

First, note that the human operator at the top of the diagram interfaces only with the operating system, the local

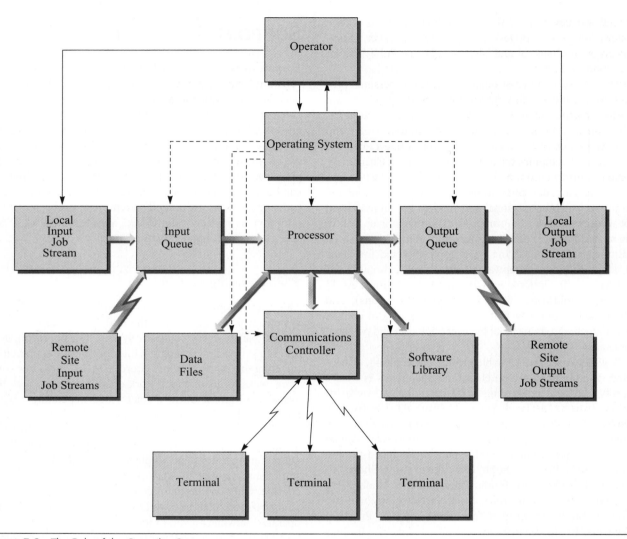

Figure 3.6 The Role of the Operating System

input job stream, and the local output job stream. The interface with the operating system is usually by entering simple commands at an operator console (a specialized terminal). The interface with the local input job stream usually involves loading tapes or changing removable disk packs, and the interface with the local output job stream means separating and distributing printed output.

The operating system, either directly or indirectly through other support software, controls everything else that takes place in Figure 3.6. It controls the inflow and outflow of communications with the various terminals and microcomputers (often through a specialized communications interface program). Using priority rules specified by the computer center manager, the operating system decides when to initiate a particular job from among those waiting

in the input queue; similarly, the operating system decides when to terminate a job (either because it has been completed, an error has occurred, or it has run too long). The operating system decides which job to print next, again based on priority rules. It stores and retrieves data files, keeping track of where everything is stored (a function sometimes shared with a database management system). The operating system also manages the software library, keeping track of both support and applications programs.

The advantage of letting the operating system perform all the previously mentioned tasks is that it can react at electronic speed to select the next job, handle multiple terminal sessions, select the appropriate software from the library, and retrieve the appropriate data file. Thus, the expensive and powerful central processing unit (CPU) can be kept as busy as possible, and the throughput from the system can be maximized. Further, the operating system can create a computing environment—in terms of what operators and other users see on their screens and what they need to key in to instruct the operating system what to do—in which it is relatively easy to work.

A microcomputer operating system, such as Windows XP or Windows Vista, performs many of the functions described previously, although the scale is smaller and the complexity is reduced. It is still true that the user employs the operating system to start a program, to retrieve data, to copy files, and so on. The purpose of a microcomputer operating system is exactly the same as the purpose of a large machine operating system: to maximize the work done by the computer system and to ease the workload of human users.

Job Control Language   As noted, it is necessary for computer users to communicate with the operating system, often by keying in instructions at a PC or terminal. These instructions must be expressed in the particular **job control language (JCL)** that is understood by the operating system being used. This job control language varies significantly from one operating system to the next, both in terms of the types of instructions and the detailed syntax. For example, with the PC-DOS or MS-DOS operating system (used on IBM and IBM-compatible PCs before Windows became popular), to change directories, one types CD\ followed by the name of the new directory; to list the current directory, one types DIR; to copy a file named MEMO from the A drive to the C drive one types COPY A:MEMO C:. These are examples of the job control language. The JCL is even simpler for a Macintosh or a PC operating under Windows XP or Vista. In this case, the user may click or double-click on an icon to start an application or retrieve a file. The JCL is much more complex for a larger machine, but the ideas are the same. To run a payroll program, for example, JCL is used to tell the operating system the name of the program to be run, the names of the data files that are needed, instructions for output of data, and the account number to be charged, among other things.

Multiprogramming, Multitasking, or Multithreading[6]
Operating systems often incorporate two important concepts—multiprogramming (or multitasking or multithreading) and virtual memory—in order to increase the efficiency of the computer's operations. These concepts are concerned with the management of the CPU time and the memory of the computer system.

On larger machines, **multiprogramming** is often employed to overlap input and output operations with processing time. This is very important because the time required for the computer to perform an input/output operation (such as reading from disk) is quite large compared to the time required to execute an arithmetic instruction. A typical computer might execute 100,000 arithmetic instructions in the time required to read a single record from a disk. Thus, it would be quite inefficient to let the CPU remain idle while input/output operations are being completed. Multiprogramming keeps the CPU busy by overlapping the input/output operations of one program with the processing time of another program.

For multiprogramming, several programs (say 5 to 10) must be located in memory at the same time. Then the operating system supervises the switching back and forth among these programs so that the CPU is almost always busy. When the currently executing program encounters an input/output instruction, an interrupt occurs and the operating system takes control. The operating system stores the status of the interrupted program in memory so that this information will be available when the interrupted program gets another shot at the CPU. The operating system then decides which of the waiting programs should be executed next, and it resets the computer with the new program's status. Then the operating system gives control to the new program, which executes until it encounters an input/output instruction. Thus, the operating system controls the switching back and forth among programs that is involved in multiprogramming.

The switching among programs in multiprogramming may be triggered by time as well as by an event (the occurrence of an input/output instruction). Time-driven multiprogramming (sometimes called **time-sharing**) is the usual mode of operation when large numbers of users are simultaneously using a computer (midrange or larger) from terminals or microcomputers serving as terminals. In this environment, each user is allocated a small slice of CPU time (e.g., a few milliseconds). When a particular user's turn arises, her program runs for those few milliseconds, carrying out thousands of instructions. Then a time interrupt occurs, and the operating system transfers control to the next user for his slice of time. Unless the number of concurrent users becomes excessively high, these bursts of available time occur so rapidly that it appears to the user that he or she is the only person who is using the computer.

On microcomputers, the term **multitasking** is used to describe essentially the same function as multiprogramming on larger machines. In both cases the operating system

---

[6]The material in the "Multiprogramming, Multitasking, or Multithreading" section and the "Virtual Memory" section is more technical than the rest of the chapter, and readers who only wish to obtain a basic understanding of operating systems may skip it. It is included to provide a more comprehensive picture to those who are interested.

controls the switching back and forth among programs stored in memory. There are two basic types of multitasking: *preemptive* and *cooperative*. In preemptive multitasking, the operating system allocates slices of CPU time to each program (the same as time-driven multiprogramming described previously). In cooperative multitasking, each program can control the CPU for as long as the program needs. In practice, multitasking means that a user can print a report at essentially the same time as he or she recalculates a spreadsheet, all the while monitoring for new electronic mail.

Finally, **multithreading** (*thread* is short for *thread of execution*) is almost the same as multitasking except that the multiple threads are different parts of the *same* program that are being executed near simultaneously, with the operating system controlling the switching back and forth among threads of the single program. All three terms—*multiprogramming*, *multitasking*, and *multithreading*—refer to the efforts of the operating system to maximize the work done by the CPU.

Virtual Memory[6]   Whereas multiprogramming or multitasking is primarily concerned with the management of CPU time, **virtual memory** is concerned with the management of main memory. Until the mid 1990s, virtual memory was used only on larger computer systems, but now it is used on microcomputers as well. Virtual memory makes it appear to the user that an unlimited amount of main memory is available, meaning that individual programs can be much larger than the actual number of memory cells. More importantly, virtual memory permits multiprogramming to operate more efficiently. How does this work?

The trick is the creative use of direct access storage devices (DASDs), with the operating system switching portions of programs (called pages) between main memory and DASDs. Unless all the programs are small, it is difficult to get enough programs stored in memory for multiprogramming to operate efficiently. For example, three large programs may occupy all of the memory, and it may be common for all three programs to be processing input/output instructions at the same time. This leaves the CPU idle, which is undesirable. The cost of adding enough real memory to store 10 programs at a time—to permit efficient multiprogramming—might be prohibitive. The virtual memory concept recognizes that only one segment of a large program is being executed at a time, while the bulk of the program is inactive. Therefore, with virtual memory, only a few pages of the program are kept in main memory, with the rest relegated to a DASD. Because only a small portion of each program is located in memory, portions of a sufficient number of programs can be stored in memory to permit efficient multiprogramming.

Of course, it is often necessary for the operating system to bring new portions of a program (new pages) into memory so they can be executed. This swapping of pages between a DASD and main memory is called, appropriately enough, paging. The size of pages varies, but each is often a few thousand bytes. When we combine the concepts of multiprogramming (switching among pages of programs already in memory) with virtual memory (requiring frequent page switches from DASDs to memory), then we begin to realize the incredible complexity of tasks carried out by the operating system.

Multiprocessing   Despite the similarity between the terms, multiprocessing is quite different from multiprogramming. **Multiprocessing** refers to the processing, or work, that takes place when two or more CPUs are installed as part of the same computer system. Each CPU works on its own job or set of jobs (often using multiprogramming), with all the CPUs under control of a single operating system that keeps track of what the various CPUs are doing. This is complexity piled on complexity! It is easy to see that today's computer systems would be much less efficient and of very limited use to us without the powerful operating systems that exist and are continually being upgraded.

Sources of Operating Systems   For the most part, operating systems are obtained from the manufacturer of the hardware, although some other company might have written the operating system. For example, when you buy a new microcomputer from Dell or Gateway, it likely comes equipped with Windows Vista, an operating system from Microsoft. Most of the popular operating systems are **proprietary systems** that were written expressly for a particular computer system. Examples are PC-DOS and MS-DOS, which are the same operating system written by Microsoft for IBM microcomputers and IBM compatibles, respectively; Windows XP and Windows Vista, which are newer systems written by Microsoft for PCs; z/OS and z/VM, which are two alternative mainframe operating systems offered by IBM; and i5/OS, which is the operating system for IBM's Series i (formerly AS/400) line of midrange systems.

In contrast to these proprietary systems, the UNIX operating system and the increasingly popular Linux operating system are **open systems**.[7] UNIX and Linux are not tied to

---

[7]UNIX and Linux are part of the larger open source software movement, which also includes the Firefox browser, the OpenOffice office suite, the Thunderbird e-mail client, and the Apache Web server software. Apache, by the way, has a 60 percent share of the Web server market, compared to a little over 30 percent for Microsoft (Netcraft Web site, 2007).

a particular computer system or hardware manufacturer. UNIX was originally developed by Bell Laboratories, with subsequent versions created by the University of California at Berkeley, AT&T, and a variety of hardware manufacturers. For example, Sun Microsystems and IBM have developed their own versions of UNIX—Solaris for Sun and AIX for IBM. UNIX is powerful and flexible, and it is portable in that it will run on virtually any computer.

Linux is a cut-down version of UNIX originally written by a young Finnish programmer, Linus Torvalds, in 1991. Torvalds made his new operating system compact and flexible, and he decided to share Linux freely. The only stipulation to the free use of Linux is that if a programmer makes modifications or extensions to Linux, he or she agrees to share them with the rest of the worldwide Linux community. Torvalds then has the final say on everything that goes into Linux. Although a knowledgeable computer programmer can download Linux for free and get it operating on his or her machine, most users (including corporations) need a bit more help and buy a Linux "distribution" from a vendor such as Red Hat, Corel, and Novell (with its SUSE distribution). This distribution includes the free Linux system plus additional software, documentation, and a way of installing the software. Linux received a significant boost when many of the major players in the information technology field, including IBM, Hewlett-Packard, Intel, and Dell, agreed to push the use of Linux. IBM, in fact, has made Linux the centerpiece of its information technology strategy, and now offers Linux on all of its varied computer platforms, from midrange machines to mainframes and supercomputers. Consequently, Linux has taken market share away from UNIX and is holding down the growth of Microsoft Windows on servers.

Many of the newer computers, such as high-powered workstations and supercomputers, run only UNIX or Linux. Many computer professionals would like to see UNIX or Linux become the standard operating system for all computer systems. That appears unlikely to happen, but the use of Linux in particular will continue to spread, at least for Web servers, network servers, and other larger machines. Some organizations have even adopted a strategy of carrying out all new applications software development in a UNIX or Linux environment, and gradually moving existing applications to UNIX or Linux. In particular, many client/server applications have been designed to run on a UNIX- or Linux-based server. Linux continues to move into the large computer arena, where it is likely to coexist with vendor operating systems like z/OS or i5/OS in major corporate and government data processing centers.

WHERE'S LINUX?

You might as well ask: Where's Waldo? Linux is almost everywhere. Because it was designed from the ground up to be the Swiss Army knife of operating systems, it can be easily adapted to many uses.

Vehicles: It's a brand-new thing. Sony uses Linux in one of its onboard auto-navigation systems in Japan. Volvo uses it in systems that track buses and trams for commuters in Sweden.

Servers: Linux is the number two server operating system, running everything from small networks at the neighborhood copy shop to mega-Web sites such as Google and eBay. Google taps an estimated 100,000 Linux computers for its search service.

Set-top Boxes: As cable-TV offerings get more sophisticated, operators are using computer-like set-tops. Sony boxes used by Cablevision in the New York metropolitan area run Linux. Ditto TiVo's personal video recorder.

Robots: The system is turning up in everything from outer space rovers to mechanical domestic servants. Wakamaru, developed by Japan's Mitsubishi Heavy Industries, is an experimental robot capable of being a caretaker and house sitter.

Cell Phones: As the manufacturers of cellular telephones shift to standard operating systems, Linux is a prime candidate. Already it's running some of the new mobile phones that are being put out by Motorola.

Desktops: Programmers at hundreds of companies use Linux on their PCs, and now large corporations are considering switching over. AT&T is thinking about swapping out Windows in favor of Linux for 70,000 employees.

Supercomputers: In the past five years, Linux has become the operating system of choice. It's used in a host of applications, from car-crash simulations to NASA's new Columbia space-exploration simulator. The Columbia is one of the world's fastest supercomputers, powered by 10,240 processors.

[*Business Week* (January 31, 2005): 65.]

A **server operating system**, also called a **network operating system (NOS)**, is software running on a server that manages network resources and controls the operation of a network. To state this in another way, a server OS is an operating system that has been enhanced by adding networking features. For example, a server OS allows computers on a network to share resources such as disk drives and printers; it also handles the server side of client/server applications (more on this in Chapter 6). Major players in the server OS market include several variations of UNIX, especially Sun's Solaris; several variations of Microsoft Windows Server, especially Windows Server 2003 and Windows Server 2008; and Linux. According to the Framingham, Massachusetts-based research firm IDC, Microsoft is dominant in this market, with a 58 percent market share. Linux comes in second, with 24 percent of the market, followed by the various flavors of UNIX. IDC also sees continued growth for Linux in the server OS arena—up to 33 percent in 2007—with Microsoft maintaining essentially the same market share (Hamm, 2005b).

At the microcomputer level, Microsoft Windows is even more dominant, with about 90 percent of the market. After subtracting a number of less-used operating systems with less than 0.5 percent each, the remainder is almost evenly split between Linux (for PCs) and Mac OS (for Apple's Macintosh machines) with about 3.5 percent each (W3Schools Web site, 2007). IDC projects the Linux share to grow to 6 percent by 2007 (Hamm, 2005b), but it is no real threat to Microsoft. Because most new PCs come preloaded with Windows Vista, it is the *de facto* standard for microcomputers as of this writing.

In summary, all of the widely used operating systems in use today will continue to evolve over the next several years, with each becoming more complex and more powerful. Paradoxically, microcomputer operating systems will at the same time become much easier to use. It appears likely that the movement towards Linux for larger machines will continue, and that Windows will continue to dominate the microcomputer market—although Linux might make some inroads here. The server operating system market is where a major Windows-Linux battle appears to be developing.

One of the important notions in the information technology area is that of an **IT platform**, which is defined as the set of hardware, software, communications, and standards an organization uses to build its information systems. Now we are in the position to point out that the operating system is usually the single most critical component of the platform. Thus, it is common to discuss a z/OS (mainframe) platform, a UNIX platform, a Windows Vista platform, or a Linux platform.

Third Generation Languages

As illustrated in Figure 3.4, the underwater portion of the software iceberg includes support software in addition to the critical operating system. It is useful to divide this support software into five major categories: language translators, database management systems, CASE tools, communications interface software, and utility programs. Let us consider languages and language translators first.

The third generation languages, which are more commonly called procedural or procedure-oriented languages, are the workhorses of the information processing field. As mentioned earlier, support software in the form of compilers and interpreters is used to translate 3 GL programs (as well as 4 GL and OOP programs) into machine language programs that can be run on a computer. The procedural languages do not enjoy the near-total dominance of 15 years ago, but they are still the languages of choice for many computer professionals, scientists, and engineers. During the 1990s and the early part of the 2000s, 4 GLs, DBMSs, application generators, and object-oriented languages have gained ground on the 3 GLs (in part because of the growth of end-user computing), but they will not replace the 3 GLs in the next few years. There are several reasons why the procedural languages will remain popular. First, most computer professionals are familiar with one or more procedural languages, and many of them are reluctant to change to something new. Second, the procedural languages tend to produce more efficient machine language programs (and thus shorter execution times) than the 4 GLs and other newer alternatives. Third, new versions of the procedural languages continue to be developed, each generally more powerful and easier to use than the previous version. For example, object-oriented versions of C, COBOL, and PASCAL are now available. Finally, there are literally millions of procedural language programs already in use in businesses and other organizations and, in most cases, it is more economical to maintain and update these "legacy" programs than to rewrite them in newer languages.

Using a procedural language requires logical thinking because the programmer must devise a detailed step-by-step procedure to accomplish the desired task. Of course, these steps in the procedure must be expressed in the particular statement types available in the given procedural language. Writing a procedural program is generally viewed as just one stage in the entire program development process. Table 3.1 provides one possible listing of the various stages in the program development process. Note that writing the program does not occur until stage four. Stage eight is debugging, which literally means to get the bugs or errors out of the program. The most difficult stages in this program development process tend to be one and two—the proper identification of the problem and the development of an algorithm, which is a step-by-step description (in English) of the actions necessary to perform the task. In stage three, the algorithm is converted into a structure chart, which is a pictorial representation of the algorithm, or pseudocode, which is an English-language-like version of the program. Throughout the entire process, logical thinking and a logical progression of steps are required to effectively use a procedural language.

Table 3.1   Stages in the Program Development Process

Stage 1	Problem identification
Stage 2	Algorithm development
Stage 3	Conversion of algorithm to computer-understandable logic, usually in the form of structure chart or pseudocode
Stage 4	Program preparation
Stage 5	Keying program into computer
Stage 6	Program compilation
Stage 7	Execution of program with test data
Stage 8	Debugging process using test data
Stage 9	Use of program with actual data

Perhaps the most significant change in the procedural languages from their beginnings is that they are more amenable to **structured programming**. A structured program is one that is divided into modules or blocks, where each block has only one entry point and only one exit point. When a program is written in this form, the program logic is easy to follow and understand, and thus the maintenance and correction of such a program should be easier than for a nonstructured program. The consequence of structured programming is that few if any transfer statements (often implemented as a GO TO statement) are required to transfer control to some other portion of the program. Therefore, structured programming is often referred to as GO TO-less programming, although the modular approach is really the central feature of a structured program. The newer versions of all the procedural languages encourage highly structured programs.

BASIC   BASIC is a good place to begin a brief look at the procedural languages because it is the simplest of them. BASIC, which is an acronym for **B**eginner's **A**ll-purpose **S**ymbolic **I**nstruction **C**ode, was developed in the early 1960s by John Kemeny and Thomas Kurtz at Dartmouth College. Their purpose was to create an easy-to-learn, interactive language for college students that would let the students concentrate on the thought processes involved in programming rather than the syntax.

The early versions of BASIC were interpreted rather than compiled, but BASIC compilers have popped up in the past two decades. Unfortunately, there are many versions of BASIC developed by various computer manufacturers and software houses, and they are often incompatible. Attempts at standardization came too late, which is one reason why businesses have been loath to adopt it. Also, BASIC has historically lacked the mathematical capabilities, data management capabilities, and control structures necessary to carry out business and scientific processing efficiently. Newer versions of BASIC have addressed these shortcomings, however, as well as added the capability of developing graphical user interfaces (more on this later).

To illustrate BASIC, consider the following sample problem: Write a BASIC program that will find the average of a set of numbers input by the user. Use a negative number to indicate the end of the data. A BASIC program to solve this problem is shown in Figure 3.7, together with the screen dialog that occurred when the program was run on a microcomputer using a simple data set. The details of programming are not important for our purposes, but you will note that most of the instructions are quite intuitive—even the uninitiated would correctly guess their meanings.

COBOL   COBOL, which is an acronym for **CO**mmon **B**usiness-**O**riented **L**anguage, is a language specifically devised for traditional business data processing tasks. It was developed by a computer industry committee (originally the short-range committee of the Conference on Data Systems Languages, or CODASYL; later the COBOL Committee of CODASYL) in order to provide an industry-wide common language, closely resembling ordinary English, in which business data processing procedures could be expressed.

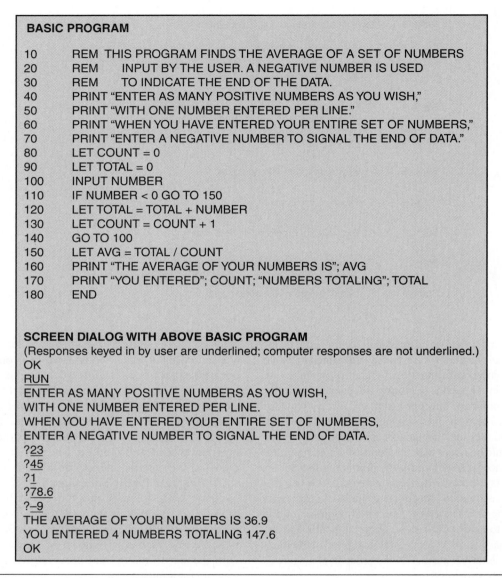

```
BASIC PROGRAM

10        REM  THIS PROGRAM FINDS THE AVERAGE OF A SET OF NUMBERS
20        REM      INPUT BY THE USER. A NEGATIVE NUMBER IS USED
30        REM      TO INDICATE THE END OF THE DATA.
40        PRINT "ENTER AS MANY POSITIVE NUMBERS AS YOU WISH,"
50        PRINT "WITH ONE NUMBER ENTERED PER LINE."
60        PRINT "WHEN YOU HAVE ENTERED YOUR ENTIRE SET OF NUMBERS,"
70        PRINT "ENTER A NEGATIVE NUMBER TO SIGNAL THE END OF DATA."
80        LET COUNT = 0
90        LET TOTAL = 0
100       INPUT NUMBER
110       IF NUMBER < 0 GO TO 150
120       LET TOTAL = TOTAL + NUMBER
130       LET COUNT = COUNT + 1
140       GO TO 100
150       LET AVG = TOTAL / COUNT
160       PRINT "THE AVERAGE OF YOUR NUMBERS IS"; AVG
170       PRINT "YOU ENTERED"; COUNT; "NUMBERS TOTALING"; TOTAL
180       END


SCREEN DIALOG WITH ABOVE BASIC PROGRAM
(Responses keyed in by user are underlined; computer responses are not underlined.)
OK
RUN
ENTER AS MANY POSITIVE NUMBERS AS YOU WISH,
WITH ONE NUMBER ENTERED PER LINE.
WHEN YOU HAVE ENTERED YOUR ENTIRE SET OF NUMBERS,
ENTER A NEGATIVE NUMBER TO SIGNAL THE END OF DATA.
?23
?45
?1
?78.6
?-9
THE AVERAGE OF YOUR NUMBERS IS 36.9
YOU ENTERED 4 NUMBERS TOTALING 147.6
OK
```

Figure 3.7   BASIC Program and Accompanying Screen Dialog

Since its inception in 1960, COBOL has gained widespread acceptance because it is standardized, has strong data management capabilities, and is relatively easy to learn and use. COBOL is by far the most popular language for programming mainframe computers for business applications.

COBOL programs are divided into four distinct divisions. The first two divisions are usually fairly short. The IDENTIFICATION DIVISION gives the program a name, and the ENVIRONMENT DIVISION describes the computer environment in which the program will be run. The ENVIRONMENT DIVISION is also the portion of the program that has to be changed to transport the program from one computer model to another. The DATA DIVISION, which is often quite lengthy, defines the file structures employed in the program. The PROCEDURE DIVISION corresponds most closely to a BASIC program; it consists of a series of operations specified in a logical order to accomplish the desired task. The combination of all these divisions, especially the DATA DIVISION, makes COBOL programs quite long compared with other procedural languages. COBOL has been correctly described as a verbose language.

Our sample COBOL program is designed to compute and print monthly sales commissions for the salespersons of a large corporation. Each salesperson earns a 1 percent commission on the first $50,000 in sales during a month and a 2 percent commission on all sales in excess of $50,000.

The data have already been keyed in and are stored as a data file on a magnetic disk. One record has been prepared for each salesperson, containing the person's name and sales for the month. The output is to be a line for each salesperson, showing the name, monthly sales, and sales commission. In addition, the program is to accumulate the total commis-

sions for all salespersons and to print this amount after all the salespersons' records have been processed.

Figure 3.8 provides a COBOL program to accomplish this processing. Again, the details are not important, but note the four divisions of the program and the sheer length of this relatively simple program.

```
1       8   12
            IDENTIFICATION DIVISION.
            PROGRAM-ID. COMMISSIONS-COMPUTE.
            ENVIRONMENT DIVISION.
            CONFIGURATION SECTION.
            SOURCE-COMPUTER. IBM-AS400.
            OBJECT-COMPUTER. IBM-AS400.
            INPUT-OUTPUT SECTION.
            FILE-CONTROL.
                SELECT SALES-FILE ASSIGN DA-4200-S-IPT.
                SELECT COMMISSIONS-FILE ASSIGN DA-4200-S-RPT.
            DATA DIVISION.
            FILE SECTION.
            FD SALES-FILE
                LABEL RECORD OMITTED
                RECORD CONTAINS 80 CHARACTERS
                DATA RECORD IS IN-RECORD.
            01  IN-RECORD              PICTURE X(80).
            FD  COMMISSIONS-FILE
                LABEL RECORD OMITTED
                RECORD CONTAINS 132 CHARACTERS
                DATA RECORD IS PRINT-RECORD.
            01  PRINT-RECORD           PICTURE X(132).
            WORKING-STORAGE SECTION.
            01  SALES-RECORD.
                05   NAME              PICTURE A(30).
                05   FILLER            PICTURE X(10).
                05   SALES             PICTURE 9(8)V99.
                05   FILLER            PICTURE X(30).
            01  COMMISSION-RECORD.
                05   FILLER            PICTURE X(10).
                05   NAME-OUT          PICTURE A(30).
                05   FILLER            PICTURE X(10).
                05   SALES-OUT         PICTURE $$$,$$$,$$$.99.
                05   FILLER            PICTURE X(10).
                05   COMMISSION        PICTURE $$$$,$$$.99.
                05   FILLER            PICTURE X(47).
            77  TEMP-COMMISSION        PICTURE 9(6)V99.
            77  TOTAL-COMMISSIONS      PICTURE 9(10)V99   VALUE 0.
            77  TOTAL-COMM-EDITED      PICTURE $$,$$$,$$$,$$$.99.
            01  MORE-DATA              PICTURE X          VALUE 'Y'.
                88   THERE-IS-MORE-DATA                   VALUE 'Y'.
                88   THERE-IS-NO-MORE-DATA                VALUE 'N'.
```

Figure 3.8 COBOL Program

```
1      8   12
           PROCEDURE DIVISION.
           MAIN-CONTROL.
               PERFORM INITIALIZATION.
               PERFORM READ-PROCESS-PRINT UNTIL THERE-IS-NO-MORE-DATA.
               PERFORM COMPLETE.
               STOP RUN.
           INITIALIZATION.
               OPEN INPUT SALES-FILE, OUTPUT COMMISSIONS-FILE.
               MOVE SPACES TO COMMISSION-RECORD.
           READ-PROCESS-PRINT.
               READ SALES-FILE INTO SALES-RECORD
                   AT END MOVE 'N' TO MORE-DATA.
               IF THERE-IS-MORE-DATA
                   MOVE NAME TO NAME-OUT
                   MOVE SALES TO SALES-OUT
                   IF SALES GREATER 50000
                       COMPUTE TEMP-COMMISSION = .01*50000+.02* (SALES-50000)
                   ELSE
                       COMPUTE TEMP-COMMISSION = .01*SALES
                   MOVE TEMP-COMMISSION TO COMMISSION
                   WRITE PRINT-RECORD FROM COMMISSION-RECORD
                       AFTER ADVANCING 1 LINES
                   ADD TEMP-COMMISSION TO TOTAL-COMMISSIONS.
           COMPLETE.
               MOVE TOTAL-COMMISSIONS TO TOTAL-COMM-EDITED.
               DISPLAY 'TOTAL-COMMISSIONS ARE' TOTAL-COMM-EDITED.
               CLOSE SALES-FILE, COMMISSIONS-FILE.
```

Figure 3.8   COBOL Program (*Continued*)

Other Procedural Languages   There are many other procedural languages in addition to BASIC and COBOL. The granddaddy of the procedural languages is FORTRAN. Originally introduced by IBM in the mid-1950s, it quickly became the standard for scientific and engineering programming. FORTRAN is still widely used today, in good part because of the significant investment made in the development of FORTRAN scientific software.

PL/1 (Programming Language One) was developed by IBM in the mid-1960s as a language to do both mathematical and business-oriented processing. IBM hoped that PL/1 would replace both FORTRAN and COBOL, but it obviously did not. Some companies switched from COBOL to PL/1 and have remained staunch PL/1 users, but their numbers are limited.

C, which was written by Dennis Ritchie and Brian Kernighan in the 1970s, is a very important language for scientific and engineering programming. C is a very powerful language, but hard to use because it is less English-like and closer to assembly language than the other procedural languages. C was originally developed for and implemented on the UNIX operating system, and its use grew as UNIX spread. In fact, the UNIX operating system was written in C. C programs have a high level of portability: A C program can usually be transported from one computer system to another—even from a mainframe to a microcomputer—with only minor changes. C has been adopted as the standard language by many college computer science departments, and it is widely used on microcomputers. On large research computers, it is not unusual for C and FORTRAN to be the only languages ever used.

In the 1980s, PASCAL was often the favorite language of college computer science departments, and it was widely used on microcomputers. PASCAL has greater mathematical capabilities than BASIC, and it handles data files better than FORTRAN. However, PASCAL never caught on outside of universities except as a microcomputer language, and its popularity has now waned in favor of C.

ADA is a language developed under the direction of the U.S. Department of Defense as a potential replacement for COBOL and FORTRAN. It was first introduced in 1980 and does have strong scientific capabilities. However, it was not widely adopted outside of the federal government. ADA has not disappeared, but its use has diminished even within the Department of Defense.

Special-purpose procedural languages have also been developed. For instance, SIMSCRIPT, GPSS, and SLAM are all special-purpose languages designed to help simulate the behavior of a system, such as a production line in a factory. Perl is a special-purpose language used primarily for writing Common Gateway Interface (CGI) scripts for World Wide Web applications. Our listing of procedural languages is incomplete, but it is sufficient for our purposes. The bottom line is that these workhorse languages are still important because they are the primary languages used by the majority of computer professionals.

Fourth Generation Languages

There is no generally accepted definition of a fourth generation language, but there are certain characteristics that most 4 GLs share. They generally employ English-like syntax, and they are predominantly nonprocedural in nature. With a 4 GL, the user merely gives a precise statement of what is to be accomplished, not how to do it (as would be done for a procedural language). For the most part, then, the order in which instructions are given in a 4 GL is unimportant. In addition, 4 GLs do not require the user to manage memory locations in the program like 3 GLs, resulting in less complex programs.

The 4 GLs employ very high-level instructions not present in 3 GLs, and thus 4 GL programs tend to require significantly fewer instructions than their 3 GL counterparts. This in turn means that 4 GL programs are shorter, easier to write, easier to modify, easier to read and understand, and less error-prone than 3 GL programs. Fourth generation languages are sometimes called very-high-level languages in contrast to the high-level third generation languages.

The roots of fourth generation languages date back to 1967, with the introduction of RAMIS (originally developed by Mathematica, Inc., and now sold by Computer Associates as CA-Ramis). Another early entry that is still in use today is FOCUS (from Information Builders). Initially, these products were primarily available on commercial time-sharing networks (like Telenet and Tymnet), but direct sales of the products to customers took off about 1980. By the mid-1980s, FOCUS was estimated to command about 20 percent of the market, with RAMIS following with 16 percent (Jenkins and Bordoloi, 1986).

In the late 1980s and early 1990s, the 4 GL market became even more splintered as new versions of the early 4 GLs were rolled out and a wide variety of new products entered the marketplace. The emphasis of the products appearing in the 1990s was on *portability*—the ability of the 4 GL to work with different hardware platforms, operating systems, and database management systems and over different types of networks (Lindholm, 1992). In the late 1990s and early 2000s, the 4 GLs changed again. First, most 4 GLs added a Web interface so that they could be used from a PC without requiring any special software on the PC. Second, and even more important, the focus of these products shifted to **business intelligence**, and the 4 GL label essentially disappeared. Today's business intelligence software tools are designed to answer queries relating to the business by analyzing data (often massive quantities of data), thereby providing "intelligence" to the business that will help it become more competitive. Of course, this focus on business intelligence is not that different from the focus of 4 GLs in the past; it really is an evolution, not a drastic change.

Some of the 4 GL products are full-function, general-purpose languages like CA-Ramis and FOCUS and have the complete functionality necessary to handle any application program. Thus, they are direct competitors with the 3 GLs. Other 4 GLs were created to handle a particular class of applications, such as statistics, decision support, or financial modeling. For example, SAS (from SAS Institute) began as a limited-purpose 4 GL focusing on decision support and modeling. SAS Business Intelligence has now expanded to an integrated suite of software for business intelligence in an enterprise, with extensive capabilities in data access, data management, data analysis, and data presentation. Among the more popular business intelligence products today are WebFOCUS (a Web-based, business-intelligence-oriented version of FOCUS), Cognos 8 Business Intelligence, MicroStrategy 8, BusinessObjects XI, Hyperion System 9 BI+, and Microsoft SQL Server Reporting Services and SQL Server Analysis Services. To gain a better perspective on the nature of a 4 GL, we will take a brief look at one of the most enduring 4 GLs, FOCUS.

FOCUS   FOCUS is an extremely versatile general-purpose 4 GL. Versions of FOCUS are available to operate under the control of all the mainframe and UNIX operating systems mentioned earlier in this chapter. Information Builders describes FOCUS as a "host-based reporting" system and as "the corporate standard for enterprise business information systems," while WebFOCUS is described as "the standard for enterprise business intelligence" (Information Builders Web site, 2007). FOCUS consists of a large number of integrated tools and facilities, including a FOCUS database management system, a data dictionary/directory, a query language and report generator, an interactive text editor and screen painter, and a statistical analysis product. Of particular importance, FOCUS has the ability to process data managed both by its own DBMS (FOCUS files) and by an external DBMS or external file system (non-FOCUS files). We will concentrate on perhaps the most widely used of the FOCUS capabilities, the query language and report generator.

Consider the following problem situation. A telephone company wishes to prepare a report for its internal management and its regulatory body showing the difference between customer bills under two different bill computation approaches. One of these bill computation methods is the traditional flat rate based on the size of the local calling area; the other is so-called measured service, in which the customer pays a very small flat rate for a minimum number of calls and then pays so much per call ($0.21 in the example) for calls above this minimum. Massive FOCUS data files already exist containing all the necessary raw data for an extended test period, with each record including customer number, area, type of service, number of calls during the time period, and the length of the time period (in months). The telephone company wants a report for present flat rate customers in area two only, showing the difference between the two billing approaches for each customer and the total difference over all flat rate customers in area two.

Figure 3.9 shows a FOCUS program (more commonly called a FOCEXEC) that can produce the desired report. As with our 3 GL examples, the individual instructions are not important, but let us consider the major pieces of the program. After some initial comments, the program begins with the TABLE command, which calls the query/report generator function of FOCUS. The data file is called TEST. Up to the first END, the instructions sum the variables TOT_CALLS and MONTHS for each customer in each area if the type of service is FL, and then divide one sum by the other to get an average number of calls per month (AVG_CALLS). The DEFINE FILE BDATA computes the rates by the two approaches as well as the difference between the two rates, storing these computed values in the temporary file BDATA. Finally, the TABLE FILE BDATA computes the average bill difference, AV_BILL_DIFF, and prints the report shown at the bottom of Figure 3.9.

Note that the FOCUS program is not particularly intuitive, but it is quite short for a reasonably complex problem. It is also largely nonprocedural in that the order of most statements does not make any difference. Of course, the conditional IFs and BYs must be appropriately placed.

Future Developments   The fourth generation languages are evolving even more rapidly than those in the third generation, particularly with the addition of easy-to-use business intelligence options and easy-to-interpret graphical output and colorful displays. However, the 4 GL label is disappearing in favor of the business intelligence (BI) tag. Furthermore, with the increasing capabilities of today's computers, the lack of efficiency of execution of 4 GL programs vis-à-vis 3 GL programs is of little concern. For these reasons and others mentioned earlier (increasing computer sophistication of managers, continuing backlogs in the information systems department), the use of 4 GLs (by whatever name) will continue to grow. The strongest element of growth will come from end-user computing, but IS departments will also shift toward 4 GLs, especially for infrequently used applications.

What comes after the 4 GLs? We already have markup languages, object-oriented programming languages, and languages for developing Web applications, and we will turn to these types of languages next. Another possibility is the development of **natural languages**, in which users write their programs in ordinary English (or something very close to it). Users will need little or no training to program using a natural language; they simply write (or perhaps verbalize) what they want done without regard for syntax or form (other than that incorporated in ordinary English). At present, there are no true natural languages, but some restricted natural language products have been developed that can be used with a variety of database management systems and 4 GLs. Commercial developments in the natural language area have, however, been slower than expected.

Markup Languages

Before turning to object-oriented programming languages, we should mention the markup languages, which are neither 3 GLs, 4 GLs, nor OOP languages. Currently the best known of the markup languages is **Hypertext Markup Language (HTML)**. HTML is used to create World Wide Web pages, and it consists of special codes inserted in the text to indicate headings, bold-faced text, italics, where images or photographs are to be placed, and links to other Web pages, among other things. Virtual reality modeling language (VRML) provides the specifications for displaying three-dimensional objects on the Web; it is the 3-D equivalent of HTML. HTML and the other markup languages are not really programming languages in the sense that we have been using this term; they are simply codes to describe the way the completed product (the Web page, the 3-D object, and so on) is to appear.

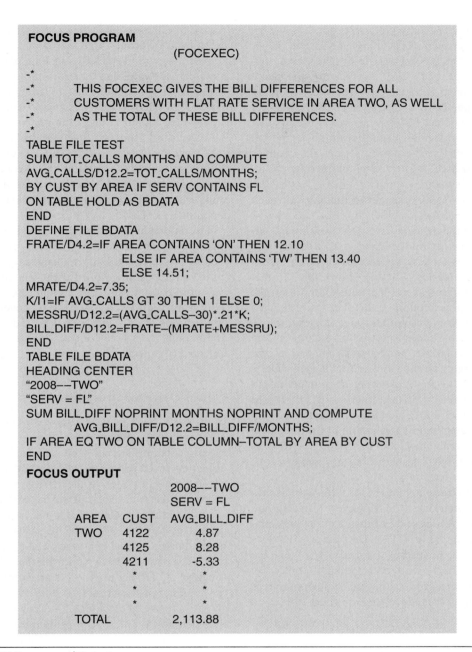

Figure 3.9   FOCUS Program and Output

eXtensible Markup Language (XML), is destined to become even more important than HTML. XML is used to facilitate data interchange among applications on the Web; it is really a metalanguage standard for specifying a document markup language based on plain-text tags. Let's see what this means. XML was developed by the W3C, the World Wide Web Consortium, whose goal is to develop open standards for the Web. Other W3C standards are **Hypertext Transfer Protocol (HTTP)** and HTML.

XML is a pared-down version of Standard Generalized Markup Language (SGML), which was itself developed by the International Standards Organization (ISO) in 1986. HTML is another subset of SGML with which we are more familiar. Both HTML and XML employ plain-text tags (i.e., made up of ordinary letters, numbers, and special characters) as a way to "mark up" a document. However, the similarities between HTML and XML end there. HTML tags tell a Web browser how to display various elements on a Web page, while XML tags identify the nature of the associated data. For example, one XML tag might identify a customer name as a customer name, another might identify a customer's address as an address, another might identify a number as a product number, and yet another might identify the quantity sold as the quantity sold. Entire sets of XML tags are being defined for particular industries and situations.

The key is that XML is a metalanguage: For each industry or unique situation, a set of XML tags can be created to identify the data elements employed in that situation. XML makes it relatively easy to identify and share data in order to achieve data integration across organizational boundaries. XML is "extensible" in that new tags can be defined as needed, and XML allows the separation of the presentation of the data from the data themselves. Through the use of text tags, for example, a company can identify specific pieces of data on a Web page (such as a customer order) and can extract the desired data for use in another application. It seems likely that the use of XML tags in Internet documents might eventually replace electronic data interchange (EDI) (see Chapter 8 for more on EDI). EDI depends upon carefully designed, rather cumbersome formatting of the data to be exchanged; XML replaces that formatting with customized tags. Thus, XML provides an easy and effective way to identify and share data.

An XML specification (like HTML) consists of tags (enclosed in angle brackets: < >). However, XML tags are intended to convey the meaning of data, not the presentation format. For example, an HTML tag such as <H1>This data to be displayed in Heading 1 format</H1> tells the browser to display data using the Heading 1 format. By contrast, the XML tags given below are an attempt to represent the meaning of the data related to games.

```
<Game type="College Football" date="10/14/2006">
Indiana vs. Iowa.
  <Score team="Indiana">31</Score>
  <Score team="Iowa">28</Score>
</Game>
```

The top-level tag <Game> specifies that what follows are details about a game. The attributes for Game (type and date) provide specific details about the information that follows. The end of details about the game is indicated by the </Game> tag. One of the key features of XML is its ability to have nested tags (i.e., tags within tags). The "Score" tags provide an example of how one can use this feature to add meaning to the information contained within the <Game> </Game> tags.

XML tags (unlike HTML tags) are not fixed. Programmers can use any tags that suit an application's needs. However, all applications that are going to process a given set of data need to understand and agree upon the tag names they intend to use. It is important to realize that data specified using XML do not provide any indication as to how to display the data. The data display for a set of XML documents is controlled by the use of eXtensible Style Language (XSL) specifications. These specifications indicate how to display XML data in different formats, such as HTML.

Let us emphasize that XML (used with XSL) is not merely a replacement for how HTML documents are created. It is also being used as a language to allow different applications residing on different machines (both inside and outside a company) to communicate with one another. This in turn allows a new way of developing business applications using Web services and service-oriented architecture (see box entitled "The Future is Service-Oriented Architecture").

Object-Oriented Programming

In the early years of the twenty-first century, the hottest programming languages (at least in terms of interest and experimentation) are not 4 GLs or natural languages, but **object-oriented programming (OOP)** languages. OOP is not new (it dates back to the 1970s), but it has received renewed attention because of the increased power of workstations and the excellent GUIs that have been developed for these workstations. OOP requires more computing power than traditional languages, and a graphical interface provides a natural way to work with the OOP objects. OOP is neither a 3 GL nor a 4 GL, but an entirely new paradigm for programming with roots in both the procedural 3 GLs and the nonprocedural 4 GLs. Creating the objects in OOP is somewhat akin to 3 GL programming in that the procedures (called methods) are embedded in the objects, while putting the objects together to create an application is much closer to the use of a 4 GL.

The fundamental ideas of OOP are to create and program various objects only once and then store them for reuse later in the current application or in other applications. These objects might be items used to create the user interface, like a text box or a check box, or they might represent an entity in the organization, such as Employee or Factory.

One of the first OOP languages was Smalltalk, a language developed by researchers at Xerox to create a way that children could learn how to program. Smalltalk never

THE FUTURE IS SERVICE-ORIENTED ARCHITECTURE

The next step in application development evolution is not something that is entirely new, but the way in which it is being approached is new. The bigger picture starts with what are called Web services. Web services are a way of sharing computer software in such a way that anyone, anywhere can use or reuse the logic or functionality provided by a computer program.

It has been a longstanding practice to reuse code to reduce software development time and costs. However, Web services allow an entirely different way of reusing code. Let's use an analogy of a familiar toy by comparing code reuse to LEGO blocks. By creating programs as if they were small building blocks (like LEGOs) and allowing these programs to be pieced together, companies have been able to save time and money by building systems faster. However, until the recent advent of Web services, these building blocks wouldn't necessarily fit with other blocks. This was analogous to having plastic building blocks from two different toy companies (e.g., LEGO and Mega Bloks).

With the era of Web services, we have entered a very different way of constructing systems. Web services are reusable programs like we have seen for years, and many times they are written in the same languages as before. The difference is that Web services allow us to make all the "blocks" fit together. Previously, developers had to concern themselves with what kind of computer hardware and what programming language would be used by a particular "block." With Web services these factors become transparent, and thus a nonissue when developing a system. The Web services "blocks" can work with any computer hardware and any programming language that can handle XML files.

Taking Web services a step further is an approach called service-oriented architecture (SOA). SOA works hand-in-hand with business process management. In this new way of developing applications, programmers will use standard programming languages such as Java, VB, or C# to create "services" that reflect small or atomic levels of a business process (think LEGO blocks). Then a business analyst (who is not necessarily a programmer) will piece these blocks together to create the whole system. When the business needs to make a change in the process, it will be the business analyst who will go into the tools and make the modifications to the process rather than having the programmer do this type of work. In support of the business analyst, the programmer will write additional services when a new specialized building block is needed. This move to SOA has been enabled by the recent emergence of tools such as Microsoft's BizTalk and SAP's NetWeaver. The SOA/Web services approach represents a radically different way of developing applications from what is done today.

---

really took off as a children's programming tool, but it was used marginally in the business world. Managers thought programming would become more efficient if programmers only had to create objects once, and then were able to reuse them in later programs. This would create a "toolbox" from which programmers could just grab the tool they needed, insert it into the program, fine-tune it to meet the specific needs of the program, and be done.

The most prominent OOP languages today are C++, an object-oriented version of the original C language; Java, a platform-independent language developed by Sun Microsystems; and Visual Basic .NET and C#, both developed by Microsoft. C++ is a superset of the C language, in that any C program can also be a C++ program, but C++ introduces the power of reusable objects, or classes. Java is a general-purpose programming language well-suited for use on the World Wide Web, and it has quickly gained widespread acceptance by most vendors and by programmers everywhere.

Java programs come in three flavors: stand-alone applications, applets, and servlets (see the section of this chapter entitled "Languages for Developing Web Applications"). Stand-alone applications are run on your desktop, whereas **applets** are programs that are downloaded from a Web server and run on your Web browser. **Servlets** are programs that reside in and are run on a Web server. Java programs are designed to run on a **Java virtual machine**, a self-contained operating environment (including a Java interpreter) that behaves as if it is a separate computer. Such an operating environment exists for most operating systems, including UNIX, Linux, Macintosh OS, and Windows, and this virtual machine concept implements the "write once, run anywhere" portability that is Java's goal. The Java virtual machine has no access to the host operating system (whatever it is), which has two advantages:

- *System independence*   A Java application will run exactly the same regardless of the hardware and software involved.
- *Security*   Because the Java virtual machine has no contact with the host operating system, there is almost no possibility of a Java application damaging other files or applications.

Other object-oriented languages that are gaining prominence are those that are part of the .NET framework from Microsoft. Introduced in 2002, the .NET framework allows programmers to write programs in a variety of OOP

J2EE VERSUS .NET

Java 2 Enterprise Edition (J2EE) and **.NET** are two competing frameworks proposed by an alliance of companies led by Sun Microsystems and Microsoft, respectively, as platforms for application development on the Web using the object-oriented programming paradigm.

J2EE, as the name suggests, is based on the Java language. In fact, J2EE is not the name of a product. Instead, it is a collection of 13 different Java-based technologies put together in a particular fashion. Thus, theoretically it is possible to buy each of these technologies from different vendors and mix-and-match them as needed. In practice, however, it is typical for a company to buy a product that implements the J2EE specification from a single vendor. Popular choices in this regard include WebSphere from IBM and WebLogic from BEA. One of the key advantages of J2EE is that because everything is Java-based, the products can be run on a variety of platforms (e.g., Windows, UNIX, and Linux).

By contrast, applications written for Microsoft's .NET framework are designed to run only on the Windows platform. However, unlike J2EE, where one is limited to using Java as the programming language, in .NET a programmer can choose among a variety of languages such as VB.NET, C#, J# (a variant of Java), and even C++. In fact, within a single application a programmer can, for example, choose to write portions of the program in VB.NET and others in C#.

There has been a lot of debate as to which framework is better. The answer depends on several tangible and intangible factors. In the end, we think that the decision regarding which technology to adopt will be based largely on the following factors:

- *Available programmer expertise*
- *Complexity of the Web application*   For large applications that have significant scalability and security requirements, the J2EE framework provides the flexibility needed to achieve the desired architectural and performance goals.
- *Degree of Web services support needed*   Both J2EE and .NET are quite comparable in terms of their support for Web services standards including XML. The difference lies in the fact that support for XML is an integral part of the .NET framework, whereas at this time XML support has to be "bolted on" in J2EE.

languages, including Visual Basic .NET (abbreviated as VB.NET) and C# (pronounced "C sharp") (see the box entitled "J2EE Versus .NET").

To work with an OOP language, one must think in terms of objects. The programmer must start by defining those entities that are referred to as classes. A class is the blueprint or specifications for creating an object. To work with the class, we must create an instance of the class, which is then referred to as the object. An object has attributes, or properties, that can be set by the programmer, or even by the user when the program is running, if the programmer desires. An object also has methods—predefined actions taken by the object. Objects can also respond to events, or actions taken upon the object. Objects, properties, methods, and events can all be a bit difficult to comprehend at first, so let's use an example that might be more familiar to you—the family dog.

We can think of a dog and identify various attributes, which programmers call properties, to differentiate one dog from another dog. Each dog has height, weight, color, coat thickness, eye color, snout shape, and many other features that might differ from other dogs (see Figure 3.10 left). Each of these properties thus has a value. Each dog, independent of its property values, also does several actions; programmers call these methods.

Eat, sleep, run, and fetch are examples of these methods. Dogs also respond to several actions done to them; these are called events. Hearing their name called, being petted, or even being kicked are examples of events to which the dog responds (see Figure 3.10 right). The code in Figure 3.11 shows an example of a class called Dog, written in Java.

We said that to work with a class, we must create an instance of the class called an object—this process is called instantiation. From our class definition of a dog (Figure 3.11), we know that it has various properties, methods, and events. For a family without a pet, however, all that family has is a class definition. When the family goes to the animal shelter to rescue a furry friend, they now have an instance of the class, or an actual dog.

The code in Figure 3.12 shows how a Dog can be instantiated from the class definition in Figure 3.11. We instantiate a new Dog and then call the display method in the newly created dog object.

Objects also have two important features that make them even more useful. One of them is **encapsulation**. Encapsulation allows the object's creator to hide some (or even all) of the object's inner workings from other programmers or users. This keeps the object's integrity very high, exposing only parts of the object that will not cause

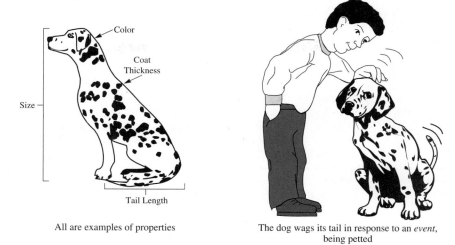

All are examples of properties

The dog wags its tail in response to an *event*, being petted

Figure 3.10 A Dog as an Object

```
public class Dog{
    double height;
    double weight;
    String color;

        public Dog (double someheight, double someweight, String somecolor)
    {
        height = sometype;
        weight = someweight;
        color = somecolor;
    }

        //methods
        public void sleep() {
        //code to make a dog sleep will go here
        }
        public void run() {
        //code to make a dog run will go here
        }

        public Object fetch() {
        //code to make a dog fetch will go here
        //this method will return the item fetched
        }
    public void display()
    {
    System.out.println("The Height of Animal is: " + height);
    System.out.println("The Weight of Animal is: " + weight);
    System.out.println("The Color of the Animal is: " + color);
    }
}
```

Figure 3.11 Java Class Called Dog

```
public class AnimalTest
{
        public static void main(String args[])
        {
                Animal myanimal;

                myanimal = new Dog("10.5", 30,"Black");
                myanimal.display();
        }
}
```

Figure 3.12   Java Instantiation of a New Dog

the object to crash. Let's apply this to our dog example. For a dog to survive, it needs vitamins, nutrients, proteins, and carbohydrates. These items must get into the dog's bloodstream and be carried to the muscles and organs that need them. However, we as dog owners do not try to inject the items directly into the bloodstream or the organs; we merely buy dog food at the store and set it out for our pet. The dog eats the food and digests it, and the nutrients are carried to their proper places. You could thus say that the digestive system of the dog has been encapsulated. We do not need to know how it works, nor in most cases do we even care. It has been created to work

the way it is, although if it were to start behaving incorrectly, we might take the dog to see a programmer—the veterinarian!

The second feature is called **inheritance**. Inheritance means that we can create subclasses and superclasses from classes, and they then automatically have properties, methods, and events of their related class. For example, if I have a class called animal, I know that dog should be a subclass of animal. A dog is a type of animal (not the other way around) and should take on the properties, methods, and events of the class animal.

Object-oriented programming continues to be one of the most sought-after skills in today's job market. Despite OOP's supposed natural way of thinking about the world, it is difficult to find good object-oriented programmers. Older programmers who learned programming in structured languages like C and COBOL often do not want to be retrained, and some younger programmers do not like OOP languages because they can be very difficult to learn. It can also take longer to develop an object-oriented program than a structured program, and objects must be reused several times before any overall cost and time savings are realized. However, with the advent of Web services and service-oriented architecture—which are essentially based on object-oriented concepts—the goal of reusing code and achieving cost and time savings might finally be realized.

WHY IS OBJECT TECHNOLOGY VALUABLE?

One reason that the term "object oriented," or "OO," is often confusing is that it is applied so widely. We hear about object-oriented user interfaces, object-oriented programming languages, object-oriented design methodologies, object-oriented databases, even object-oriented business modeling. A reasonable question might be: Is this term used because OO has become a synonym for "modern and good," or is there really some substantial common thread across all these object-oriented things?

I believe that there is such a common thread, and that it makes the object paradigm useful in all these diverse areas. Essentially it is a focus on the "thing" first and the action second. It has been described as a noun-verb way of looking at things, rather than verb-noun. At the user interface, first the object is selected, then the action to be performed on the object. At the programming language level, an object is asked to perform some

action, rather than a procedure called to "do its thing" on a set of parameters. At the design level, the "things" in the application are defined, then the behavior (actions) of these things is described.

Object technology provides significant potential value in three areas, all closely related: productivity, maintainability, and paradigm consistency. We must change application development from a people-intensive discipline to an asset-intensive discipline. That is, we must encourage and make feasible the widespread reuse of software components. It is exactly in this "reusable component" arena that object technology can contribute significantly. The aspects of object technology that help in reuse are encapsulation (which allows the developer to see a component as a "black box" with specified behavior) and inheritance (which encourages the reuse of code to implement identical behavior among different kinds of objects).

[Radin, 1996]

Languages for Developing Web Applications

The emergence of the Internet has led to the increasing need for developing Web-based applications. Although these applications range in complexity from very simple applications that allow user registration to applications that enable business-to-business transactions, they all have the following things in common:

- All Web applications are based on an n-tier architecture (where n >=2). The typical system consists of three tiers: a user interface (client), a Web or application server, and a database server.

- The user interacts with the system (on his or her machine) through Web-based forms. Data entered into the forms are sent to the server, where a server application program processes them. This program might write parts of this information to a database (residing on a different machine).

The most common user interface encountered by users is an HTML form. This form might either be static or dynamic (i.e., produced by a program). An example of a dynamic HTML form that can be used to order grocery items is shown at the top of Figure 3.13. The ASP.NET code needed to generate this page is shown below the HTML form. Please note that the user simply enters the heading, the labels, the items in the list, and the possible values of these items, and the code is automatically generated by Active Server Pages (ASP). The code is a mixture of general HTML tags and some tags that are specific to ASP.NET (e.g., asp:DropDownList). The *runat* portion of the form specifies that a program on the server that generated this page should be called when the user clicks on the button of type Submit (labeled Calculate Cost) on the form. The data from each of the user interface elements are passed on to the program on the server.

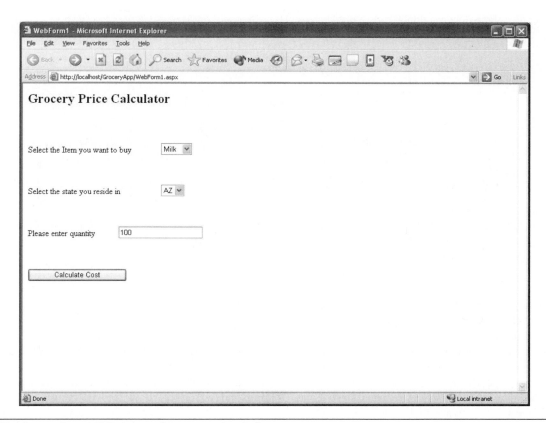

Figure 3.13 Grocery Store HTML Form and Accompanying Code

```
<%@ Page Language="vb" AutoEventWireup="false" Codebehind="WebForm1.aspx.vb"
Inherits="GroceryApp.WebForm1"%>
<!DOCTYPE HTML PUBLIC "-//W3C//DTD HTML 4.0 Transitional//EN">
<HTML>
        <HEAD>
                <title>WebForm1</title>
                <meta name="GENERATOR" content="Microsoft Visual Studio.NET 7.0">
                <meta name="CODE_LANGUAGE" content="Visual Basic 7.0">
                <meta name="vs_defaultClientScript" content="JavaScript">
                <meta name="vs_targetSchema" content="http://schemas.microsoft.com/intellisense/ie5">
        </HEAD>
        <body>
                <form id="Form1" method="post" runat="server">
                        <P>
                                <asp:Label id="Label1" runat="server" Width="340px" Height="40px" Font-
                                Bold="True" Font-Size="Large">Grocery Price Calculator</asp:Label></P>
                        <P> </P>
                        <P>
                                <asp:Label id="label3" runat="server" Width="242px">Select item you want
                                to buy:</asp:Label>
                                <asp:DropDownList id="item" runat="server">
                                        <asp:ListItem Value="Eggs">Eggs</asp:ListItem>
                                        <asp:ListItem Value="Milk">Milk</asp:ListItem>
                                        <asp:ListItem Value="OJ">OJ</asp:ListItem>
                                </asp:DropDownList></P>
                        <P> </P>
                        <P>
                                <asp:Label id="label2" runat="server" Width="242px">Select state that you reside
                                in:</asp:Label>
                                <asp:DropDownList id="state" runat="server">
                                        <asp:ListItem Value="IN">IN</asp:ListItem>
                                        <asp:ListItem Value="AZ">AZ</asp:ListItem>
                                        <asp:ListItem Value="IL">IL</asp:ListItem>
                                </asp:DropDownList></P>
                        <P> </P>
                        <P>
                                <asp:Label id="Label4" runat="server" Width="164px">Please enter
                                quantity:</asp:Label>
                                <asp:TextBox id="Qty" runat="server"></asp:TextBox></P>
                        <P> </P>
                        <P>
                                <asp:Button id="Submit" runat="server" Width="183px" Text="Calculate
                                Cost"></asp:Button></P>
                </form>
        </body>
</HTML>
```

Figure 3.13 Grocery Store HTML Form and Accompanying Code (*Continued*)

The program that processes the data is shown in Figure 3.14. This program retrieves the data from the form and stores the data items in session variables named item, state, and qty, respectively. After this, the program redirects control to the next page that needs to be displayed—that is, confirm.aspx. However, before this page is loaded, the load function shown in Figure 3.15 is called. Here, we retrieve the values stored in the session and assign them to various elements of our page to be displayed. The result is the new page shown in Figure 3.15.

The example shown in Figures 3.13 through 3.15 is written using ASP.NET. All Web application development technologies or server-side programming environments operate using a similar model in that they all provide mechanisms for generating dynamic Web pages, encoding complex business logic on the server-side as well as reading and writing to a variety of database management systems. Common examples of server-side programming environments are PHP, Java Servlets and Java Server Pages (JSP), Microsoft's Active Server Pages (ASP, ASP.NET),

```
Public Sub submit_Click(s As Object, e As EventArgs)

Session.add("item", item.SelectedItem.Text)
Session.add("state", state.SelectedItem.Text)
Session.add("qty", Qty.Text)
Response.sendRedirect("confirm.aspx")


End Sub
```

Figure 3.14 Program to Process Data from Grocery Store HTML Form

and Adobe's ColdFusion. Currently, Java Servlets/JSP (for all platforms, especially UNIX and Linux) and ASP/ASP.NET (primarily for Windows) are the preferred technologies for developing large e-business solutions. For small and medium-sized applications, developers prefer the flexibility and ease of development in languages such as PHP and ColdFusion.

Database Management Systems

A **database management system (DBMS)** is support software that is used to create, manage, and protect organizational data. A database management system works with the

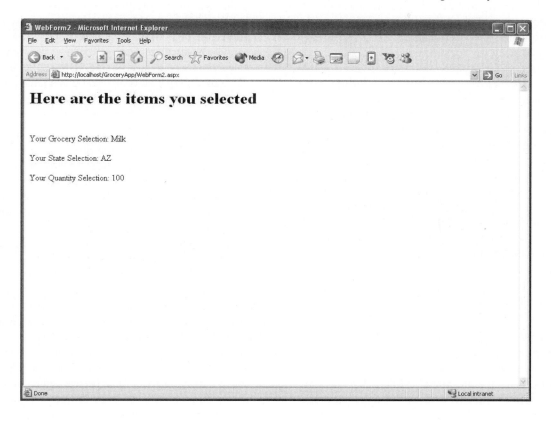

```
Private Sub Page_Load(ByVal sender As System.Object, ByVal e As System.EventArgs)
Handles MyBase.Load
    'Put user code to initialize the page here
    item.Text = Session.Item("item")
    state.Text = Session.Item("state")
    Quantity.Text = Session.Item("qty")
  End Sub

End Class
```

Figure 3.15 Grocery Store Confirmation Web Page and Code That Generates It

operating system to store and modify data and to make data accessible in a variety of meaningful and authorized ways.

A DBMS adds significant data management capabilities to those provided by the operating system. The goal is to allow a computer programmer to select data from disk files by referring to the content of records, not their physical location. This makes programming easier, more productive, and less error-prone. Also, this allows systems professionals responsible for database design to reorganize the physical organization of data without affecting the logic of programs, which significantly reduces maintenance requirements. These objectives are given the umbrella term *data independence*. For example, a DBMS would allow a programmer to specify retrieval of a customer record based only on knowledge of the customer's name or number. Furthermore, once the customer record is retrieved, a DBMS would allow direct reference to any of the customer's related order or shipment records (even if these records are relocated or changed). Thus, a DBMS allows access to data based on content (e.g., customer number) as well as by association (e.g., orders for a given customer).

A **database** is a shared collection of logically related data that is organized to meet the needs of an organization. A related term is a **data warehouse**, a very large database or collection of databases, to be considered in Chapter 6. A DBMS is the software that manages a database. A DBMS is a very complex and often costly software product, ranging in price from under $500 for a PC product to $200,000 or more for a DBMS on a large mainframe computer.

The **database architecture** refers to the way in which the data are structured and stored in the database. When selecting among database architectures, it is important to consider the types of data to be stored and how they will be processed and used. The five basic architectures are:

1. *Hierarchical*   Characterized by the IBM product Information Management System (IMS)—data are arranged in a top-down organization chart fashion.
2. *Network*   A good example is Integrated Database Management System (IDMS, now called Advantage CA-IDMS) from Computer Associates—data are arranged like the cities on a highway system, often with several paths from one piece of data to another.
3. *Relational*   Many such products exist, including Microsoft Access and Microsoft SQL Server, Corel Paradox, IBM DB2, Oracle, and Ingres—data are arranged into simple tables, and records are related by storing common data in each of the associated tables. The **relational DBMS** is the most common organizational approach to organizing data. In an interesting development, Ingres (from Ingres Corporation) is now an open source software product; it can be downloaded and used for free—the user pays only for service and consulting.
4. *Object-oriented*   Among the better known products are Versant Object Database, Progress ObjectStore, and Objectivity/DB—data can be graphics, video, and sound as well as simpler data types; attributes (data) and methods are encapsulated in object classes, and relationships between classes can be shown by nesting one class within another.
5. *Object-relational*   This hybrid approach to organizing data capitalizes on the capability of object-oriented databases to handle complex data types, and on the inherent simplicity of the relational data model. Although object-oriented data modeling tends to be well-suited for engineering and scientific applications, the object-relational approach is more appropriate for business applications. Object-relational database products include Oracle, IBM's DB2 and Cloudscape (which is also an open source product), and FFE Software's FirstSQL/J.

File Organization   The computer files are stored on the disk using the file organization provided by the operating system and special structures added by the DBMS. Although their exact details can be treated as a "black box" in most cases, it is useful to know some of the terminology and choices. Three general kinds of file organizations exist: sequential, direct, and indexed (see Figure 3.16).

A **sequential file organization** arranges the records so that they are physically adjacent and in order by some sort of key (usually the unique key that distinguishes each record from another). Thus, a sequential customer file would have the records arranged in order by customer name or identifier. Sequential files use very little space and are fast to use when the records are to be retrieved in order, but they are inefficient when searching for a particular record because they must be scanned front to back. Also, when records are added or deleted, the whole file must be rearranged to accommodate the modifications, which can be time-consuming.

A **direct file organization** also uses a key for each record, but records are placed and retrieved so that an individual record can be rapidly accessed. The records are located wherever they can most quickly be retrieved, and the space from deleted records can be reused without having to rearrange the file. The most typical method employed is a hashing function. In this case, the record key, such as the customer number, is mathematically manipulated (by some algorithm) to determine the location of the record with that key. It is possible that several keys can "collide" to the same location, but such synonyms are easily resolved. Direct files are extremely fast for accessing a single record, but because the keys that

Sequential File Organization

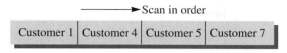

Direct File Organization

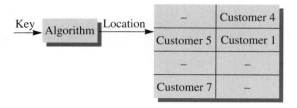

Indexed File Organization

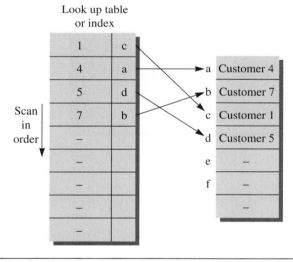

Figure 3.16 File Organizations

one entry at a time, and as each entry is encountered, its associated data record is retrieved. To access the records individually, the table is scanned until a match with the desired key is found and only the desired record is retrieved; if no match is found, an error is indicated. Because the table is quite small (just enough space for the key and location of every record, compared to possible hundreds or thousands of characters needed for the whole record—remember the analogy of the card catalog in a library), this scan can be very fast (certainly considerably faster than scanning the actual data). For a very large table, another table can be created to access the first table (which is, of course, nothing more than a specialized file itself). Popular names for such methods of indexes on top of indexes are indexed sequential access method (ISAM) and virtual storage access method (VSAM).

Finally, because in a database we want to be able to access records based upon content (e.g., by customer number) as well as by relationship (e.g., orders for a given customer), a DBMS along with the operating system must also provide a means for access via these relationships. Record keys and location pointers are these means. For example, we could store pointers in a customer record and its associated order records to link all these related records together (see Figure 3.17). Such a scheme is called *chaining* or a *list structure*. Alternately, we could store the customer number in each of its associated order records and use tables or hashing functions to locate the related record or records in other files. Relational DBMSs use this scheme.

Database Programming   Data processing activity with a database can be specified in either procedural programs written in a 3 GL or via special-purpose languages developed for database processing. In a relatively new development, languages such as XML and Java allow access to a database from a Web site. In the case of a 3 GL program, additional and more powerful instructions are added to the vocabulary of the programming language. For example, in a customer and order database, the storage of a new order record not only necessitates storing the order data themselves but also updating various linkages that tie together a customer record with its associated order records. In a regular 3 GL program, instructions to write new data to the customer record, its index, the order record, and its indexes would have to be provided individually. With the commands available through the special enhancements to the language provided by the DBMS, only one instruction is needed in the program and all the associated indexes and records are updated automatically, which makes the programming task more productive and less error-prone.

are being sought at any point in time are usually arbitrary, sequential processing of direct files requires a long and tedious scan and usually sorting of the records.

Indexed file organizations provide a compromise between the sequential and direct access capabilities. The record keys only are arranged in sequence in a separate table, along with the location of the rest of the data associated with that key (this location field in the table is called a pointer). This "lookup" table or index is similar to a card catalog in a library, in which the author name, book title, and topic are different types of keys and the book catalog number is a pointer to its location in the library. To access the records sequentially, the table is completely scanned

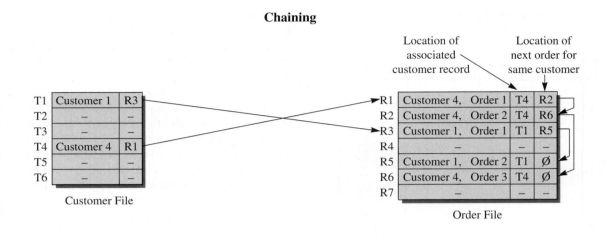

Figure 3.17 Schemes for Relationships Between Files

A DBMS also frequently provides a 4 GL, nonprocedural special-purpose language, called a **query language**, for posing queries to the database. For example, the following is a query in the SQL/DS command language:

SELECT ORDER#, CUSTOMER#, CUSTNAME,

ORDER-DATE FROM CUSTOMER, ORDER

WHERE ORDER-DATE > '04/12/08'

AND CUSTOMER.CUSTOMER# =

ORDER.CUSTOMER#

This is all that is required to request the display of the order number and date from each order record, plus the customer number and name from the associated customer record, for orders placed after April 12, 2008. The equivalent COBOL program might require 10 or more procedure division instructions. The popularity of such products as Access, Paradox, Ingres, and several SQL-based language products (a standard created by the **American National Standards Institute**, or **ANSI**) is due in great measure to the existence of such easy-to-use query languages.

Managing the Data Resource   Data are now recognized as a major organizational resource, to be managed like other assets such as land, labor, and capital. Chapter 5 will be entirely devoted to the data resource. For now, let us note that a DBMS is an important software tool for managing the data resource. From a managerial point of view, a DBMS helps manage data by providing the following functions:

■ *Data Storage, Retrieval, Update*   Providing a variety of commands that allow easy retrieval and presentation as well as modification of data

■ *Backup*   Automatically making copies of the database and the updates made to it to protect against accidental damage or deliberate sabotage

■ *Recovery*   The ability to restore the database after damage or after inaccurate data have gotten into the database

- *Integrity Control*   Ensuring that only valid data are entered into the database (so that, for example, data values only in a permissible range are entered)

- *Security Control*   Ensuring that only authorized use (reading and updating) is permitted on the database

- *Concurrency Control*   Protecting the database against anomalies that can occur when two or more programs attempt to update the same data at the same time

- *Transaction Control*   Being able to undo changes to a database when a program malfunctions, a user cancels a business transaction, or the DBMS rejects a business transaction that updates several database records

Along with the DBMS, many organizations also use a **data dictionary/directory (DD/D)**, which is a repository of data definitions that is shared among all the users. Such a central catalog is used by the DBMS and system users whenever the meaning, storage format, integrity rules, security clearances, and physical location of data need to be discovered. The DD/D is similar to an inventory accounting system for a parts warehouse—but in this case for a data warehouse, or a database. Many modern DBMSs have a built-in DD/D capability.

A DBMS and a DD/D are tools, and managers and database professionals in the information systems organization must use these and other tools wisely if data are to be readily accessible to all who have a need to know. Today, most organizations are highly computerized, and vast databases exist. The issue often is not whether the data are available, but rather which of several alternative versions of the data to use and how to gain access to these data. A DBMS with a variety of methods to store data and easy-to-use programming and query languages is essential for such access. Being able to use prewritten database processing routines and to write original database queries are necessary skills of today's general manager.

CASE Tools

It was originally predicted that CASE tools would have a major impact on computer professionals, and that has been true for some professionals in some firms. However, the growth of the use of CASE tools has been much slower than anticipated. **Computer-aided software engineering (CASE)** is actually a collection of software tools to help automate all phases of the software development life cycle. (The life cycle for software development is discussed in Chapters 9 and 10.) In those firms that have adopted CASE tools, CASE has radically changed the jobs of systems analysts and programmers. In particular, the job of the analyst or programmer involves more up-front work in clearly defining the problem and expressing it in the particular specifications required by the CASE tool. Then the tool assists in the back-end work of translating the specifications to the required output, such as a data flow diagram (see Chapter 9) or a COBOL program.

There has been a recent surge in the use of CASE tools for object-oriented development based on the **Unified Modeling Language (UML)**. UML is a general-purpose notational language for specifying and visualizing complex software, especially large, object-oriented projects. Examples of such UML-based CASE tools are IBM's Rational Rose, Borland's Together, and Sybase's PowerDesigner. We will defer a more complete treatment of CASE software until Chapter 10, where we will explore the variety of CASE tools and their role in the systems development process. For now, note that CASE is only beginning to make an impact. CASE has the potential of providing a productivity boost to an area of the company (the information systems organization) that needs such a boost.

Communications Interface Software

Communications interface software has become increasingly important with the explosion in the number of local area networks (LANs) and wide area networks (WANs) and with the growing importance of the Internet and the World Wide Web. We have already discussed perhaps the most important type of communications interface software, the Web browser, which is software that runs on the user's computer enabling the user to look around, or "browse," the Internet. We will defer discussion of most LAN, WAN, and Internet software until Chapter 4, but we will consider several other types of communications interface software now.

Communications products on large computers with many attached workstations have the awesome task of controlling the communications of these workstations, or terminals, with the central computer. This software collects the messages from the terminals, processes them as necessary, and returns the responses to the proper terminals. These products are often designed to work closely with a particular operating system. For example, IBM's CICS (Customer Information Control System) is a communications product designed to work with IBM's z/OS operating system (formerly the MVS operating system). Similarly, IBM's CMS (Conversational Monitor System) is designed to work with the z/VM operating system (formerly just VM). IBM has also created versions of CICS which work with AIX, IBM's UNIX operating system; Solaris, Sun's UNIX operating system; HP-UX, Hewlett-Packard's UNIX operating system; and Microsoft Windows Server. These UNIX/CICS and Windows/CICS combinations made it much easier for IBM's customers to move their applications to UNIX and Windows. Microcomputer communications products (in workstations attached to large computers) have the much simpler task of making the microcomputer act as if it were a particular type of terminal that can be handled by the large computer communications product.

In addition to the Web browser, two additional items of communication interface software became important in the last decade or so. **Telnet** is a communications interface product designed to permit a user to log into a remote computer from whatever computer he or she is currently using. The key is that the computer currently being used must be attached to the same network as the remote computer. In some cases, this "same network" might be a LAN on a corporate or educational campus, while in other cases this network might be the worldwide Internet. The user invokes the Telnet program and identifies the remote computer he or she wishes to log into. The connection is made, and then the user simply logs into the remote computer as if he or she were on-site. Another valuable communications interface product is **File Transfer Protocol (FTP)**. This product is designed to transfer files from one computer system to another. In effect, the user logs into the two computer systems at the same time, and then copies files from one system to the other. The files being transferred might be programs, textual data, images, and so on.

Utility Programs

This is obviously a catch-all category, but an important one nevertheless. On large computers, utility software includes programs that load applications programs into an area of memory, link together related programs and subprograms, merge two files of data together, sort a file of data into a desired sequence (e.g., alphabetical order on a particular data item), and copy files from one place to another (e.g., from a DASD to magnetic tape). Utility programs also give the user access to the software library. In most cases, the user communicates with these utility programs by means of commands in the job control language. On a microcomputer, utility programs are used to zip (compact) and unzip large files for easier transport, to reorganize the hard drive to gain disk space, to check for computer viruses, and for many other tasks.

THE CHANGING NATURE OF SOFTWARE

In the process of investigating the various categories of computer software, we have noted many of the important trends in the software arena. Building upon our earlier discussions, we can explicitly identify six key trends that have the most direct relevance to you as a manager:

1. Less concern with machine efficiency.
2. More purchased applications, and, conversely, more use of open source support software, such as Linux.
3. More programming using object-oriented languages.
4. More emphasis on applications that run on intranets and the Internet.
5. More user development.
6. More use of personal productivity software on microcomputers.

Less Concern with Machine Efficiency

The cost per instruction on computers will continue to drop dramatically, as it has for the past five decades. That is, machine cycles will continue to get cheaper. On the other hand, personnel costs, both for computer professionals and managers, will continue to climb. Thus, as time passes, we will be more concerned with human efficiency and less concerned with machine efficiency. This reduced concern for machine efficiency has both direct and indirect impacts on you as a manager. It means that software tools that improve human efficiency, such as object-oriented languages, query languages, and CASE tools, will become more popular for computer professionals and, where appropriate, for managers. Eventually it also will lead to the development of executive workstations with voice and natural language interfaces, which are terribly inefficient from the machine standpoint.

More Purchased Applications

The higher personnel costs for computer professionals mean higher costs for in-house development of new applications software. In addition, the present backlogs for internal development of new applications are not going to disappear in the short run. The demand for new applications is also not going to slacken, particularly with the infusion of an increasing number of computer-literate managers into organizations. Add to this mix a vigorous software industry marketing an incredible variety of software products, and it is easy to predict a continuing growth in purchased applications software. Furthermore, more of the purchased applications will be portable from one computing platform to another or will work with a variety of support software (especially database management systems). This gives companies more flexibility in their choice of computing platforms.

Another major reason for purchasing software is to correct internal business processes that are not working as well as they should. Most software products designed to handle standard business tasks such as payroll, accounts payable, general ledger, and material requirements planning incorporate excellent procedures in the product, and by implementing the product the organization is required to adopt these improved procedures. Thus, the organization is forcing the "reengineering" of its processes by implementing the software product. This is particularly true for so-called enterprise resource planning products, which we will discuss in Chapter 6. The advantage to you of the trend toward more purchased applications is that you will be able to get new applications you need implemented more quickly; the disadvantage is that the purchased software might not be able to do precisely what you want done in the way in which you want it done.

Although organizations are likely to purchase *more* of their applications in the future, it might be that they purchase *less* of their support software. The rising popularity of open source support software, such as the Linux operating system, means that more applications software is being developed to run on these open source platforms. As time goes on, organizations may be able to spend more of their information technology budget on applications and less on support software.

More Programming Using Object-Oriented Languages

In part because of the emphasis on GUIs, Visual Basic.NET, Java, and similar object-oriented programming languages will gain even more widespread acceptance. These languages lend themselves to developing GUI interfaces such as those used on the World Wide Web, and many believe that they are easier to learn and use than the traditional 3 GLs. The increased use of these languages is also consistent with the lessened concern over machine efficiency noted previously, because they tend to produce quite inefficient code. From the manager's perspective, the use of these languages will tend to give you the applications you need more quickly, and the GUI will make the screens more attractive and easier for you and your employees to use.

More Emphasis on Applications That Run on Intranets and the Internet

This is a very important and powerful trend, but we are somewhat premature in introducing it at this point in the book. We will explore the idea of intranets and the Internet in the next chapter. After that discussion, this trend will be more meaningful. For now, note that intranets are networks operating within an organization that use the same technology as the worldwide Internet, and that the Internet is a network of networks spanning the globe. More and more organizations are creating or buying applications that run on their internal intranet or the Internet because it is both easy and economical to make these applications available to everyone who needs them.

More User Development

This trend hits close to home because you and your fellow managers will carry out more software development efforts yourselves. For the most part, you will work with personal productivity software, 4 GLs, and query languages that are easy to learn and use. Why will this increase in user development occur? Because it is easier and quicker for you to develop the software than to go to the information systems organization and work with them on the development (often after an extensive wait). This will be the case for many situations where you need a one-time or infrequently used report, or a decision support system to help you with a particular decision. Managers will continue to rely on the information systems organization—or on purchased software—for major ongoing systems, such as production control, general ledger accounting, and human resource information systems. Because of its importance to you as managers, we have devoted much of Chapter 13 to user application development.

More Use of Personal Productivity Software

This final trend is the most important one for most of you. The use of personal productivity software, especially Web browsers, spreadsheet products, and database management systems, will grow for managers and other professionals. Products with a well-designed GUI will increasingly be the software of choice because a GUI makes the software easier to learn and use. Your workstation, linked to a LAN and the worldwide Internet (see Chapter 4), will become as indispensable as your telephone (and eventually might *become* your telephone). You will use it almost every hour of every working day for electronic mail, Web browsing, word processing, spreadsheets, database management, presentation graphics, and other applications. In fact, most of you will find the microcomputer so essential that you will carry a notebook version or an even smaller palmtop computer with you when you are out of your office.

THE SOFTWARE COMPONENT OF THE INFORMATION SYSTEMS INDUSTRY

Many software products have been mentioned in this chapter, as well as many software vendors, but we lack a frame of reference from which to view the software subindustry. There are two primary groups of players in the software arena: hardware manufacturers and software houses. Many of the major hardware vendors—companies such as IBM, Hewlett-Packard, Sun Microsystems, Hitachi, and Fujitsu—also have a major presence in the software arena. In the mainframe/midrange machine market, customers often buy much of their support software from their hardware vendors—and sometimes a significant proportion of their applications software as well. For example, IBM, the largest hardware vendor (excluding microcomputers), is the second largest software vendor in the world in terms of revenue, trailing only Microsoft.

The software houses form an interesting and competitive group, although they are dominated by a single firm. Microsoft, the largest and most influential software house, is based in Redmond, Washington, and until 2000 was headed by Bill Gates, reportedly the richest person in the world. Gates is still the Chairman of Microsoft, and he also served as Chief Software Architect until 2006. Other major software vendors include Oracle (based in Redwood Shores, California), which began by specializing in mainframe DBMSs but has now branched out into other areas, notably enterprise resource planning (ERP) systems (integrated software to run a business); SAP (Germany), which is the market leader in the ERP area with its R/3 product; Computer Associates (Islandia, New York), which produces a variety of mainframe and PC-based software products, with particular strength in mainframe database, job scheduling, security, and systems management software; and Symantec (Cupertino, California), which specializes in security tools and systems. Two smaller but important firms are Red Hat (Raleigh, North Carolina) and Novell (Waltham, Massachusetts), which are the leading vendors of Linux distributions. In addition to these big software houses, there is a multitude of medium-sized to small-sized software firms. Many of the smaller firms tend to rise and fall rapidly based on the success or failure of a single product, and often the most promising of these small firms are purchased by the major vendors.

Most of the large software vendors—including both Microsoft and IBM—have grown both by increased sales of products developed internally *and* by the purchase of other software firms, sometimes large firms. Oracle, for example, has grown its ERP business by the 2004 purchase of PeopleSoft for $10.3 billion, and it added strength in customer relationship management (CRM) software by the 2005 purchase of Siebel Systems for $5.85 billion. IBM purchased Rational Software in 2003 for $2.1 billion; Rational, which now operates as a division of IBM Software, produces software to assist in the development of major applications, especially when using an object-oriented approach. In 2006, IBM purchased FileNet Corp. (document management software) for $1.6 billion and Internet Security Systems, Inc., for $1.3 billion, as well as several smaller software companies. In total, IBM has purchased more than 30 software companies since 2003 (Hamm, 2006).Microsoft has also gotten into the act, purchasing PlaceWare, Inc., the number two player in Web conferencing, in 2003, and Groove Networks Inc., which uses peer-to-peer technology to let workers at different companies easily collaborate on projects through corporate firewalls, in 2005.

A third group of players in the software subindustry, not as important as the first two, is the consulting firms. The key players are changing so rapidly that it is difficult to keep up, as the major public accounting firms spin off or sell off their consulting practices, sometimes to hardware vendors (IBM purchased PricewaterhouseCoopers Consulting). For the most part, the software developed and sold by these firms has been an outgrowth of their consulting practices and, thus, tends to be applications software geared to particular industries in which they have consulted extensively. There are also many smaller firms in the information systems arena that are difficult to categorize as a software house or a consulting firm because they truly operate as both. Their consulting jobs often involve writing or modifying software for a particular firm and then moving to another firm within the same industry to do a similar job.

To complete the software story, we should mention that some excellent software can be obtained from noninformation systems companies that have developed software for their own use and then later decided to market the product. The software business is dominated, however, by the software houses and the hardware manufacturers. In Chapter 11, we will discuss the option of purchasing applications software.

SUMMARY

Both computer hardware and software are required for a computer system to perform useful work. The hardware actually does the work—adding two numbers, reading a record from disk, printing a line—but the software controls all of the hardware's actions. Thus, understanding software is critical to comprehending how computer systems work. From a financial perspective, most organizations spend several times as much money on software as they spend on hardware. Also, managers deal directly with a variety of software products but rarely deal with hardware other than their own workstation. For all these reasons, software is a vital topic for aspiring managers to understand.

Figuratively speaking, software comes in a variety of shapes and sizes. Applications software consists of all programs written to accomplish particular tasks for computer users; support software establishes a relatively easy-to-use computing environment, translates programs into machine language, and ensures that the hardware and software resources are used efficiently. The most important piece of support software is the operating system that controls the operation of the hardware and coordinates all of the other software. Other support software includes language translators, communications interface software, database management systems, and utility programs.

Applications software is often developed within the organization using third generation procedural languages like COBOL or C, fourth generation nonprocedural languages like FOCUS or SAS, or newer languages such as C++ or Java. Until the 1980s, nearly all the internal software development was carried out by computer professionals in the information systems organization. In the last two decades, however, more of the development has been done by end users (including managers), using 4 GLs and DBMS query languages. The trend that affects managers even more is the growing availability and use of personal productivity software such as spreadsheets and database management systems. We anticipate that these trends toward more user development of software and more use of personal productivity products will continue and will strengthen.

Almost all of an organization's support software and an increasing proportion of its applications software are purchased from outside the firm. The hardware manufacturers supply much of the support software and some of the applications programs for larger computers. Independent software houses (not associated with hardware manufacturers) are particularly important sources of large machine applications software and microcomputer software of all types. When purchasing software, the organization must consider the quality and fit of the software product and the services and stability provided by the vendor.

Hopefully, this chapter has provided you with sufficient knowledge of computer software to begin to appreciate the present and potential impact of computers on your organization and your job.

REVIEW QUESTIONS

1. Briefly describe the four generations of computer programming languages, concentrating on the major differences among the generations. How does object-oriented programming fit into these generations? How does HTML fit into these generations? How does XML fit into these generations?

2. List at least five categories of personal productivity software products. Then concentrate on one of these categories and describe a representative product in that category with which you are somewhat familiar. Provide both strong points and weak points of the particular product.

3. What are the purposes of an operating system? What are the primary tasks carried out by a mainframe operating system?

4. Differentiate between multiprogramming and multiprocessing.

5. Explain the concept of virtual memory. Why is it important?

6. List the six major categories of support software.

7. Explain the concept of structured programming. Why is it important?

8. What are the primary advantages of a fourth generation language over a third generation language? What are the primary disadvantages?

9. What are the primary characteristics of an object-oriented language? How does an object-oriented language differ from a third generation language or a fourth generation language?

10. Explain the difference between push and pull technology, and give an example of each.

11. Three general types of file organizations were described in the text: sequential, direct, and indexed file organizations. In general terms, describe how each type of file organization works. It may be helpful to draw a diagram to depict each type of file organization.

12. Three types of database architectures described in the text were hierarchical, network, and relational. Briefly describe how the data are arranged in each of these types of database architecture.

13. For what does the CASE acronym stand? In general, what is the purpose of CASE tools? What types of individuals are most likely to use CASE tools?

14. List at least three independent software houses (not associated with a computer vendor) that are major players in the software component of the information systems industry. List any software products that you

regularly use and indicate the firm that developed each product.

15. Some of the acronyms used in this chapter are listed below. Provide the full names for each of these acronyms.

JCL	HTML
4 GL	OOP
DBMS	DASD
COBOL	CASE
XML	BASIC

DISCUSSION QUESTIONS

1. From the discussion in this chapter and your own knowledge from other sources, what do you think is the most important advancement in computer software in the past five years? Why?

2. Which one category of personal productivity software is of most value to you now as a student? Why? Within this category, what is your favorite software product? Why?

3. Which one category of personal productivity software do you expect to be of most value to you in your career? Why? Is this different from the category you selected in the previous question? Why or why not?

4. Based on your own computing experience and your discussions with other computer users, which one category of personal productivity software needs the most developmental work to make it useful to managers? What type of development is needed?

5. List the pros and cons of the involvement of managers in the end-user computing revolution. What strengths and weaknesses do managers bring to the software development process? Is it appropriate for managers to be directly involved in applications software development?

6. In the mid-1980s, a movement developed within the information systems industry to "stamp out COBOL" and replace it with 4 GLs and other productivity tools. Manifestations of this movement included the slogan to "Kill the COBOL programmer" (not literally, of course) and T-shirts bearing the word *COBOL* within the international symbol for not permitted (a red circle with a red line diagonally across the word *COBOL*). Do you think the movement will ever be successful? Why?

7. You have probably had experience with at least one procedural (3 GL) language, either in high school or college. What are the strengths and weaknesses of the particular language that you know best? Based on what you have gleaned from the text, what primary advantages would a nonprocedural 4 GL offer over the 3 GL that you know best? What disadvantages? What primary advantages would a natural language offer over the 3 GL that you know best? What disadvantages?

8. Based on your reading in this chapter and other sources, what do you believe are the primary advantages of an object-oriented language over a third generation language or a fourth generation language? What are the primary disadvantages?

9. The box entitled "J2EE Versus .NET" introduced the differences between these two competing frameworks for developing Web applications. Explore J2EE and .NET in more detail by discussing the two frameworks with programmers you know and by conducting research using the Web. Are there other differences between the two frameworks? How would you modify the conclusions provided in the "J2EE Versus .NET" box?

10. Why is the concept of a Java virtual machine important? How does running a Java applet on a Java virtual machine differ from running a Microsoft VB.NET application on your Web browser?

11. As you have read in newspapers and magazines, one firm seems to dominate the worldwide software market—Microsoft. With this degree of dominance by one firm, has the software subindustry truly been competitive, particularly over the past decade? Support your position.

12. In the late 1990s, the United States government, joined by several state governments, brought suit again Microsoft, arguing that Microsoft unfairly exercised monopoly power in the software industry. What was the outcome of these lawsuits? The European Union has also brought suit against Microsoft for exercising monopoly power. What is the current status of the European Union lawsuit? (Use the Web to conduct your research.)

REFERENCES

2005. "Where's Linux?" *BusinessWeek* (January 31): 65.

2006. "Software: Our top picks." *PC Magazine* Web site, *www.pcmag.com/article2/0,1895,2060860,00.asp* (November 20).

Arar, Yardena, Michael S. Lasky, Matthew MacDonald, Harry McCracken, and Dennis O'Reilly. 2006. "Microsoft Office

2007: A worthy upgrade." *PC World* Web site, *www.pcworld. com/article/id,127919/article.html* (November 28).

BackWeb Technologies. 2007. "BackWeb mobilizes enterprise Web applications." BackWeb Technologies Web site, *www. backweb.com/* (January).

Eckel, Bruce. 2006. *Thinking in Java*, 4th ed. Upper Saddle River, NJ: Pearson Prentice Hall.

Greene, Jay. 2005. "Combat over collaboration." *BusinessWeek* (April 18): 64, 66.

Hamm, Steve. 2005a. "The gnat nipping at Microsoft." *BusinessWeek* (January 24): 78–79.

Hamm, Steve. 2005b. "Linux Inc." *BusinessWeek* (January 31): 60–66, 68.

Hamm, Steve. 2006. "A Big Blue feeding frenzy." *BusinessWeek* (September 4): 72.

Hoover, J. Nicholas. 2006. "The fight is on." *InformationWeek* 1110 (October 16): 25–27.

Information Builders. 2007. "Host-based reporting (FOCUS)" and "Enterprise business intelligence (WebFOCUS)." Information Builders Web site, *www.informationbuilders. com/products* (January).

Janowski, Davis D. 2006. "Battle of the browsers." *PC Magazine* Web site, *www.pcmag.com/article2/0,1895,2052335,00.asp* (November 6).

Jenkins, A. Milton, and Bijoy Bordoloi. 1986. "The evolution and status of fourth generation languages: A tutorial." Institute for Research on the Management of Information Systems (IRMIS) Working Paper #W611, Indiana University Graduate School of Business.

Kontzer, Tony. 2003. "Pervasive portal connections." *InformationWeek* 932 (March 24): 47.

Lindholm, Elizabeth. 1992. "The portable 4 GL?" *Datamation* 38 (April 1): 83–85.

Netcraft Web site. 2007. "January 2007 Web server survey." Netcraft Web site, *news.netcraft.com/archives/web_server_ survey.html* (January).

O'Reilly, Dennis. 2006. "WordPerfect Office: A better app mix, for less." *PC World* 24 (June): 75.

Peachtree. 2007. "Peachtree by Sage Premium Accounting 2007." Peachtree by Sage Web site, *www.peachtree.com/ peachtreeaccountingline/premium/* (January).

Peachtree. 2007. "ePeachtree." Peachtree by Sage Web site, *www.peachtree.com/epeachtree/* (January).

Port, Otis. 2002. "The next Web." *BusinessWeek* (March 4): 96–100, 102.

Radin, G. 1996. "Object technology in perspective." *IBM Systems Journal* 35, 2: 124–127.

Rubenking, Neil J. 2006. "Norton Internet Security 2007." *PC Magazine* Web site, *www.pcmag.com/article2/ 0,1895,2023974,00.asp* (October 4).

Sage Accpac. 2007. "Accounting and Operations." Sage Accpac Web site, *www.sageaccpac.com/products/accounting* (January).

Sage Accpac. 2007. "Sage Accpac Brochure." Sage Accpac Web site, *www.sageaccpac.com/products/pdflibrary/Sage_ Accpac_broch.pdf* (January).

Shadbolt, Nigel, Wendy Hall, and Tim Berners-Lee. 2006. "The semantic Web revisited." *IEEE Intelligent Systems* 21 (May/June): 96–101.

W3Schools. 2007. "Browser statistics." W3Schools Web site, *www.w3schools.com/browsers/browsers_stats.asp* (January).

Wildstrom, Stephen H. 2006. "Look out, Microsoft Office." *BusinessWeek* (July 10): 16.

Wildstrom, Stephen H. 2006. "Explorer's long-awaited update." *BusinessWeek* (November 13): 24.

Yakal, Kathy. 2006. "Peachtree Premium Accounting 2007." *PC Magazine* 25 (September 5): 65.

CHAPTER 4
TELECOMMUNICATIONS AND NETWORKING

THIS CHAPTER IS THE THIRD OF A QUARTET OF CHAPTERS DEVOTED TO the building blocks of information technology. So far we have considered hardware and software, but there are two more critical building blocks to go. The hardware and software must have *data* to be processed to produce useful results, and the data resource is the focus of Chapter 5. If every computer were a stand-alone unit with no connection to other computers, then hardware and software and data would be the end of the story as far as computers are concerned. In fact, until about 40 years ago, that *was* the end of the story. Today, however, virtually all computers of all sizes communicate directly with other computers by means of an incredible variety of networks. For computers in organizations, these networks include intraorganizational local area networks (LANs), backbone networks, and wide area networks (WANs) as well as the worldwide Internet. For home computers, the most important network is the Internet. In addition to computer (or data) communications, today's organizations also depend heavily on voice (telephone) and image (video and facsimile) communication. This chapter explores the increasingly important topic of telecommunications and networking.

This chapter's goal is to cover only the telecommunications and networking technology that you as a business manager need to know. You need to understand the roles and general capabilities of various types of transmission media and networks, but you do not need to know all the technical details. You certainly need to know the important terminology and concepts relating to telecommunications and networking. Most important, you need to understand the interrelationships between hardware, software, and telecommunications and networking so that you can use the full gamut of information technology to increase your productivity and your organization's effectiveness.

Change is everywhere in the information technology domain, but nowhere is this change more evident and more dramatic than in the realm of telecommunications and networking. A communications revolution is taking place that directly or indirectly affects the job of every manager, and the primary catalyst is the Internet and the World Wide Web (an application that runs on the Internet).

The breakup of American Telephone & Telegraph (AT&T) in 1984 created an environment in which a large number of firms competed to develop and market telecommunications equipment and services. Partially because of this increased competition, innovation in the telecommunications and networking arena has been at an all-time high. Digital networks, fiber-optic cabling, cellular telephones, the ability to send both voice and data over the same wires at the same time, and wireless networks have contributed to the revolution.

At the same time, most large U.S. businesses have restructured internally to reduce layers of middle management and create a leaner organization (as introduced in Chapter 1). They have also decentralized operations in order to respond more quickly to market opportunities and competitors' actions and have created cross-functional teams to improve business processes and carry out projects. The net result of these internal changes is that communication has become more important than ever for the remaining, often geographically dispersed, managers. They need rapid, reliable voice and data communication with other parts of the company and with suppliers and customers. Small businesses are also more dependent upon communication than ever before, and developments such as local area networks (LANs), cellular telephones, and increased functionality of the public wired telephone network have helped fill this need. Internal needs and external competition and innovation combined to create a latter-twentieth-century communications revolution that is continuing into the new millennium. The aim of this chapter is to help you become a knowledgeable participant in the communications revolution.

THE NEED FOR NETWORKING

Let us be more precise in justifying the need for networking among computers and computer-related devices such as printers. Why do managers or other professionals working at microcomputers need to be connected to a network? Why are small computers often connected to larger machines? Why are laser printers often attached to a LAN? Why is it critical for many businesses to be connected

to the Internet? In our judgment, there are five primary reasons for networking.

Sharing of Technology Resources

Networking permits the sharing of critical (and often expensive) technology resources among the various users (machines) on the network. For example, by putting all of the PCs in an office on a LAN, the users can share a variety of resources, such as a high-speed color printer that is a part of the network. The users can also share software that is electronically stored on a file server (another computer designated for that particular purpose). All these devices are connected by wiring and are able to communicate with one another under control of a LAN software package called a server (or network) operating system. When a particular user wants to print a color brochure or a color transparency, it is sent electronically from the user's machine to the network printer.

Sharing resources is also important for larger computers. It is quite common for mainframes or midrange computers to share magnetic disk devices and very high-speed printers. Further, WANs permit the sharing of very expensive resources such as supercomputers. The National Science Foundation has funded several national supercomputer centers across the United States, and researchers from other universities and research laboratories are able to share these giant machines by going through their local computer network into a national high-speed backbone network such as Abilene (more on this network later in the chapter).

Sharing of Data

Even more important than the sharing of technology resources is the sharing of data. Either a LAN or a WAN permits users on the network to get data (if they are authorized to do so) from other points, called nodes, on the network. It is very important, for example, for managers to be able to retrieve overall corporate sales forecasts from corporate databases to use in developing spreadsheets to project future activity in their departments. In order to satisfy customers, automobile dealers need to be able to locate particular vehicle models and colors with specific equipment installed. Managers at various points in a supply chain need to have accurate, up-to-date data on inventory levels and locations. Accountants at corporate headquarters need to be able to retrieve summary data on sales and expenses from each of the company's divisional computer centers. The chief executive officer, using an executive information system (see Chapter 7), needs to be able to access up-to-the-minute data on business trends from the corporate network. In some

NETWORKS WILL CHANGE EVERYTHING

In the early 1990s, Paul Saffo, a fellow at the Institute for the Future, developed a fascinating set of forecasts about the effect of information technologies on the way we would work, play, and conduct business in the years to come. So far, his projections have been right on. "The short answer is that networks will change everything," said Saffo. "In the next five years, networks will be supporting a shift to business teams from individuals as the basic unit of corporate productivity. In the 10-year time frame, we'll see changing organizational structures. In 20 to 30 years, we'll see a shift so fundamental, it will mean the end of the corporation as we know it." According to Saffo, organizations have started down the path to a pervasive interconnectivity of workstations that will result in an entirely new "virtual" corporate structure.

[Adapted from Wylie, 1993]

instances, data may be retrieved from a commercial, public database external to the firm, such as LexisNexis and Dow Jones Newswires.

Of course, the ultimate sharing of data is now occurring via the **World Wide Web** on the Internet. By conservative estimates, there are now at least *1 billion* users of the Web at sites around the world, and this number continues to grow rapidly. Each of these users has easy (and often free) access to an incredible array of information on any topic. The user begins by using a search engine such as Google or a favorite reference site, and then follows hypertext-based links to seek out the desired data. In short, the Web has created a new and exciting way of sharing data.

Distributed Data Processing and Client/Server Systems

With **distributed data processing**, the processing power is distributed to multiple computers at multiple sites, which are then tied together via telecommunications lines. **Client/ server systems** are a variant of **distributed systems** in which the processing power is distributed between a central server system, such as a midrange computer or mainframe, and a number of client computers, which are usually desktop microcomputers. Distributed and client/server systems tend to reduce computing costs because of their reliance on more cost-effective microcomputers and workstations.

There are many examples of distributed systems. One is the use of laptop computers by a company's sales force, where orders and sales data are transmitted over the Internet (using a virtual private network, to be discussed later in this chapter) to the corporate computer center. A second example is the use of a client/server application for general ledger accounting, with desktop microcomputers as the clients and a high-powered workstation as the server. In most cases, such a package is implemented over a LAN in a single building or a cluster of buildings (a campus). A third example, also a client/server system, involves the creation of a commercial real estate database on a server located at the real estate firm's main office. The client machines are microcomputers located in the firm's branch offices or customer offices, with the clients and server linked via the public telephone network. In any case, it is the existence of a telecommunications network that makes distributed data processing a feasible and attractive arrangement.

Enhanced Communications

Networks enhance the communications process within an organization (and between organizations) in many important ways. The telephone network has long been a primary means of communication within and between organizations. Electronic mail over the corporate computer network has become a mainstay of communication in most major organizations in the past two decades, and the development of the Internet has extended the reach of these electronic mail systems around the world. Electronic bulletin boards (including internal, regional, and national bulletin boards), blogs, and mass electronic mailing lists for people with common interests permit multiparty asynchronous communication on an incredible array of topics. Instant messaging permits synchronous text communication over the Internet. And video communication, especially videoconferencing, provides a richer medium to permit more effective communication.

Direct data communication links between a company and its suppliers or customers, or both, have been successfully used to give the company a strategic advantage. The SABRE airline reservation system is a classic example of a strategic information system that depends upon communication provided through a network. Recent developments to be discussed later in this chapter—such as DSL and IP telephony (voice over IP)—permit both voice and data communications to occur over the same telecommunications line at the same time. Starting with "plain old telephone service" (POTS) networks and continuing with today's LANs, WANs, and the Internet, networks have enhanced the communication process for individuals and organizations.

Marketing Outreach

In the last 15 years, the Internet has become an important marketing channel for a wide variety of businesses. Marketing is communication, of course, but it is a very specialized type of communication. Most midsized and larger business firms have a major presence on the World Wide Web, with extensive Web sites providing information on the firms' products and services and, in many cases, an online ordering capability. Many smaller firms are also using the Web for marketing outreach, perhaps by creating a Yahoo! store. Chapter 8 will consider the wide variety of marketing activities undertaken on the World Wide Web.

AN OVERVIEW OF TELECOMMUNICATIONS AND NETWORKING

Networking—the electronic linking of geographically dispersed devices—is critical for modern organizations. To participate effectively in the ongoing communications revolution, managers need to have a rudimentary understanding of the various telecommunications and networking options available to their organizations.

The prefix *tele-* simply means operating at a distance. Therefore **telecommunications** is communications at a distance. There are a number of other terms or abbreviations that are used almost interchangeably with telecommunications: *data communications*, *datacom*, *teleprocessing*, *telecom*, and *networking*. We prefer *telecommunications* because it is the broadest of these similar terms. It includes both voice (telephone) and data communications (including text and image). Teleprocessing means the computer processing is taking place at a distance from where the data originates, which obviously requires telecommunications. Networking is the electronic linking required to accomplish telecommunications.

One might think that only a wire (or some other conduit) or a wireless signal is needed for telecommunications, but it is much more complex than that! To begin a detailed consideration of telecommunications, first consider the primary functions performed by a telecommunications network, as listed in Table 4.1. The most obvious of these functions is the *transmission* of voice or data, or both, using the network and the underlying media. The *processing* involves making sure that an error-free message or data packet gets to the right destination. Subfunctions of processing include editorial, conversion, and routing. *Editorial* involves checking for errors and putting the communication into a standardized format, and *conversion* includes any necessary changes in the coding system or the transmission speed when moving from one device on the network to another. In networks where alternative paths are possible between the source and the destination

Table 4.1   Functions of a Telecommunications Network

Function	Brief Description
Transmission	Movement of voice and/or data using network and underlying media
Processing	Ensuring that error-free communication gets to right destination
Editorial	Checking for errors and putting communication into standardized format
Conversion	Changing coding system or speed when moving from one device to another
Routing	Choosing most efficient path when multiple paths are available
Network control	Keeping track of status of network elements and checking to see if communications are ready to be sent
Interface	Handling interactions between users and the network

of a communication (particularly WANs and the Internet), *routing*—choosing the most efficient path—is an important task. Closely related to the processing function is *network control*, which includes keeping track of the status of various elements of the system (e.g., which elements are busy or out of service) and, for some types of networks, checking each user periodically to see if the user has a communication to send. A not-so-obvious but critical function is the provision of an *interface* between the network and the user; hopefully this interface will make it easy and efficient for a manager or any other network user to send a communication. The next major section explores the variety of ways in which the functions listed in Table 4.1 can be delivered.

KEY ELEMENTS OF TELECOMMUNICATIONS AND NETWORKING

We believe that you as a business manager need to understand certain key elements about telecommunications and networking to participate effectively in the communications revolution—to know what the options are for the business systems you need. These key elements include certain underlying basic ideas, such as analog versus digital signals and switched versus private lines; the variety of transmission media available; the topology (or possible arrangements) of networks; the various types of networks, including LANs and WANs; and the network protocols employed on these networks. This section will be rather technical and will involve a number of difficult concepts, so it might require some effort on your part to keep sight of the big picture of telecommunications.

Analog and Digital Signals

Perhaps the most basic idea about telecommunications is that the electronic signals sent on a network may be either analog or digital, depending on the type of network. Historically, the telephone network has been an **analog network**, with voice messages sent over the network by having some physical quantity (e.g., voltage) continuously vary as a function of time. This analog signal worked fine for voice transmission because it required the significant variations provided by an analog signal (corresponding to variations in human speech characteristics) and was insensitive to minor degradations in the signal quality. On the other hand, computer data consist of a string of binary digits, or bits—a string of zeros and ones—to represent the desired characters. The form of this computer data does not mesh well with analog transmission.

First, only two distinct signals—representing zeros and one—need to be sent, and second, the data are extremely sensitive to degradations in signal quality. Noise in a telephone line could easily cause a zero to be interpreted as a one or vice versa, and the entire message might become garbled. Because of this problem with noise, data cannot be sent directly over the analog telephone network.

Two solutions are possible to the problem of transmitting computer data. The original solution, and one that is still widely used, is to convert the data from digital form to analog form before sending it over the analog telephone network. This conversion is accomplished by a device called a **modem**, an abbreviation for a *mo*dulator/*dem*odulator (see

Figure 4.1). Of course, the data must be reconverted from analog form back to digital form at the other end of the transmission line, which requires a second modem. The conversion (or modulation) carried out by the modem may be of different types. Figure 4.2 illustrates the use of amplitude modulation (two different voltage levels to represent 0 and 1), frequency modulation (two different frequencies of oscillations to represent 0 and 1), and phase modulation (the use of a phase shift to represent the change from a 0 to a 1 or vice versa). The use of modems and the analog telephone network is an acceptable way to transmit data for many applications, but it is severely limited in terms of transmission speeds and error rates.

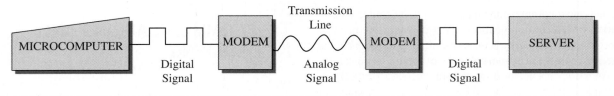

Figure 4.1   The Use of Modems in an Analog Network

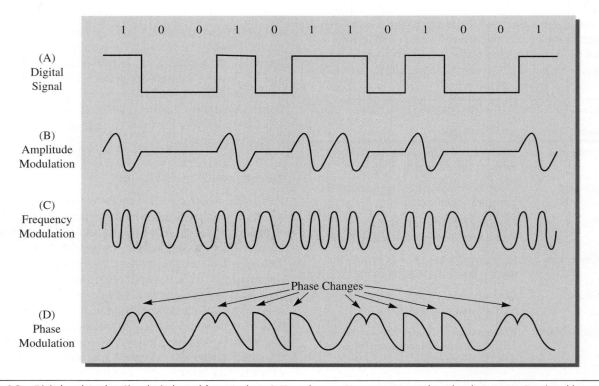

Figure 4.2   Digital and Analog Signals (Adapted from Andrew S. Tanenbaum, *Computer Networks*. 4th ed. © 2003. Reprinted by permission of Prentice Hall, Inc., Upper Saddle River, New Jersey.)

The second and longer-term solution to the problem of transmitting computer data is to develop **digital networks** specifically designed to directly transmit zeros and ones, as in Figure 4.2(A). Digital networks have the advantages of potentially lower error rates and higher transmission speeds, and modems are no longer necessary. Because of these advantages, the networks that have been specifically created for the purpose of linking computers and computer-related devices are digital. Furthermore, the telephone network is gradually being shifted from an analog to a digital network. Digital services such as ISDN and DSL (to be explored later in this chapter) are now available in many parts of the United States for users seeking higher-speed access to the Internet over the public telephone network.

This shift of the telephone network from analog to digital is due in part to the increasing volume of data being transmitted over the network, but there is also a significant advantage to transmitting voice signals over a digital network. Digital voice transmission can provide higher quality transmission—less noise on the line—just as digital recording provides higher fidelity CDs. Most of our telephone instruments are still analog devices, so the signal sent from the instrument to the nearest switching center (which may be operated either by the telephone company or your own organization) is still an analog signal. These telephone switches, however, are rapidly being converted from analog to digital switches. When the analog voice signal arrives at a digital switch, it is converted to a digital voice signal for transmission to a digital switch somewhere else, which may be across town or across the country. Thus, an increasing proportion of the voice transmission between switching centers is digitized. In the future, our telephone instruments will also be digital devices, so the entire telephone network will eventually become digital.

Speed of Transmission

Whether the signal is digital or analog, another basic question is the speed of transmission. Please note that by speed we *do not* mean how fast the signal travels in terms like miles per hour, but rather the volume of data that can be transmitted per unit of time. Terms such as *bandwidth*, *baud*, and *hertz* (*Hz*) are used to describe transmission speeds, whereas a measure such as bits transmitted per second (bits per second, or bps) would be more understandable. Happily, the three terms mentioned previously are essentially the same as bits per second in many circumstances. **Bandwidth** is the difference between the highest and the lowest frequencies (cycles per second) that can be transmitted on a single medium, and it is a measure of the medium's capacity. (Sometimes it is necessary to divide the bandwidth into multiple channels, all carried on a single medium, to utilize the entire capacity. Thus, the transmission speeds we discuss are really data rates for the one or more channels carried on the single medium.) **Hertz** is simply cycles per second, and **baud** is the number of signals sent per second. If each cycle sends one signal that transmits exactly one bit of data, which is often the case, then all these terms are identical. To minimize any possible confusion, we will talk about bits per second (bps) in this chapter. In information technology publications, *baud* was formerly used for relatively slow speeds such as 2,400 baud (2,400 bps) or 14,400 baud (14,400 bps), while *hertz* (with an appropriate prefix) was used for higher speeds such as 500 megahertz (500 million bps) or 2 gigahertz (2 billion bps). More recently, the term *baud* has fallen into disfavor, but *hertz* is still widely used in PC advertisements. For clarity, we will stick with *bps* in this chapter.

The notion of bandwidth, or capacity, is important for telecommunications. For example, approximately 50,000 bits (0s and 1s) are required to represent one page of data. To transmit 10 pages using a 56,000 bps (56 kbps) modem over an ordinary analog telephone line would take about 9 seconds. If one were transmitting a large data file (such as customer accounts), that bandwidth or capacity would be unacceptably slow. On the other hand, to transmit these same 10 pages over an 896 kbps DSL line would take only a little over half of a second. Graphics require approximately 1 million bits for one page. This would require about 18 seconds for transmission at 56 kbps over an analog telephone line, or a little over 1 second over an 896 kbps DSL line. Full-motion video transmission requires the enormous bandwidth of 12 million bps, and thus data compression techniques must be employed to be able to send video over the existing telephone network. The bandwidth determines what types of communication—voice, data, graphics, stop-frame video, full-motion video—can reasonably be transmitted over a particular medium.

Types of Transmission Lines

Another basic distinction is between private (or dedicated) communication lines and switched lines. The public telephone network, for example, is a switched-line system. When a communication of some sort (voice or data) is sent over the telephone network, the sender has no idea what route the communication will take. The telephone company's (or companies') computers make connections between switching centers to send the communication over the lines they deem appropriate, based on such factors as the length of the path, the amount of traffic on the various routes, and the capacity of the various routes. This switched-line system usually works fine for voice communications. Data communications, however, are more sensitive to the differences in line quality over different routes and to other local phenomena, such as electrical storms. Thus, a data communication sent from Minneapolis to Atlanta over the telephone network might be transmitted perfectly at 11 A.M., but another communication sent from Minneapolis to Atlanta 15 minutes later (a different connection) might be badly garbled because the communications were sent via different routes.

One way to reduce the error rate is through private lines. Most private lines are dedicated physical lines leased from a common-carrier company such as Verizon, Sprint, or AT&T. A company might choose to lease a line between Minneapolis and Atlanta to ensure the quality of its data transmissions. Private lines also exist within a building or a campus. These are lines owned by the organization for the purpose of transmitting its own voice and data communications. Within-building or within-campus lines for computer telecommunications, for example, are usually private lines.

The last basic idea we wish to introduce is the difference among simplex, half-duplex, and full-duplex transmission. With **simplex transmission**, data can travel only in one direction. This one-way communication is rarely useful, but it might be employed from a monitoring device at a remote site (monitoring power consumption, for example) back to a computer. With **half-duplex transmission**, data can travel in both directions but not simultaneously. **Full-duplex transmission** permits data to travel in both directions at once, and, therefore, provides greater capacity, but it costs more than half-duplex lines. Ordinary telephone service is full-duplex transmission, allowing both parties to talk at once, while a Citizen's Band (CB) radio provides half-duplex transmission, allowing only one party to transmit at a time.

Transmission Media

A telecommunications network is made up of some physical medium (or media) over which communications are sent. Five primary media are in use today: twisted pair of wires, coaxial cable, wireless, satellite (which is a special form of wireless), and fiber-optic cable.

Twisted Pair   When all uses are considered, the most common transmission medium is a **twisted pair** of wires. A twisted pair consists of two insulated copper wires, typically about 1 millimeter thick, twisted together in a long helix. The purpose for the twisting is to reduce electrical interference from similar twisted pairs nearby. Most telephones are connected to the local telephone company office or the local private branch exchange (PBX) via a

twisted pair. Similarly, many LANs have been implemented by using twisted pair wiring to connect the various microcomputers and related devices. For example, Category 5e cabling—which consists of four twisted pairs in a single cable jacket—is currently used for many new high-speed LANs.

The transmission speeds attainable with twisted pairs vary considerably, depending upon such factors as the thickness of the wire, the distance traveled, and the number of twisted pairs in the cable. On the analog voice telephone network, speeds from 14,400 to 56,000 bps are commonplace. When a digital service such as DSL is used on the telephone network, a speed of 256,000 bps is typical, with outbound DSL speeds ranging up to 896 kbps and inbound DSL speeds up to 7 million bps. Much higher speeds can be obtained when twisted pairs are used in LANs. Multiple twisted pairs in a single cable—such as Category 5e cabling—can support speeds up to 100 million bps when used in a Fiber Distributed Data Interface (FDDI) or Fast Ethernet LAN, or even up to 1 billion bps (1 gbps) with Gigabit Ethernet (more on these LAN types later). The speeds of twisted pair and other media are summarized in Table 4.2.

Coaxial Cable   **Coaxial cable (coax)** is another common transmission medium. A coaxial cable consists of a heavy copper wire at the center, surrounded by insulating material. Around the insulating material is a cylindrical conductor, which is often a woven braided mesh. Then the cylindrical conductor is covered by an outer protective plastic covering. Figure 4.3 illustrates the construction of a coaxial cable.

Table 4.2   Telecommunications Transmission Speeds

Transmission Medium	Typical Speeds
Twisted pair—voice telephone	14.4 kbps–56 kbps
Twisted pair—digital telephone	128 kbps–7 mbps
Twisted pair—LAN	10 mbps–1 gbps
Coaxial cable	10 mbps–1 gbps
Wireless LAN	6 mbps–100 mbps
Microwave	500 kbps–100 mbps
Satellite (per transponder)	500 kbps–100 mbps
Fiber-optic cable	100 mbps–640 gbps

KEY: bps = bits per second
kbps = thousand bits per second, or kilo bps
mbps = million bits per second, or mega bps
gbps = billion bits per second, or giga bps

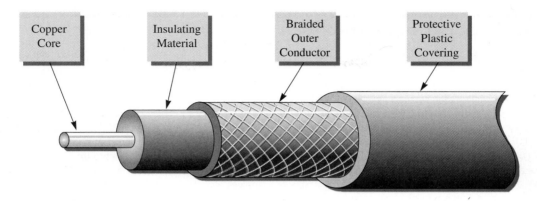

Figure 4.3   Construction of a Coaxial Cable

Because of its construction, coaxial cable provides a good combination of relatively high transmission speeds and low noise or interference. Two kinds of coaxial cable are in widespread use—**baseband coax**, which is used for digital transmission, and **broadband coax**, which was originally used for analog transmission but which is now used for digital transmission as well.

Baseband coax is simple to use and inexpensive to install, and the required interfaces to microcomputers or other devices are relatively inexpensive. Baseband offers a single digital transmission channel with data transmission rates ranging from 10 million bits per second (10 mbps) up to perhaps 1 billion bps (1 gbps), depending primarily on the distances involved (longer cables mean lower data rates). Baseband coax was widely used for LANs and for long-distance transmission within the telephone network, although much of this coax has now been replaced by fiber-optic cabling.

Broadband coax, which uses standard cable television cabling, was originally installed for analog transmission of television signals, but it increasingly employs digital transmission. A single broadband coax can be divided into multiple channels, so that a single cable can support simultaneous transmission of data, voice, and television. Broadband data transmission rates are similar to those for baseband coax, and high transmission speeds are possible over much longer distances than are feasible for baseband coax. Because of its multiple channels and additional capacity, broadband coax has been more enduring than baseband. Broadband coax is still widely used for cable television and LANs that span a significant area, often called metropolitan area networks.

Wireless   Strictly speaking, wireless is not a transmission medium. **Wireless** is broadcast technology in which radio signals are sent out into the air. Wireless communication is used in a variety of circumstances, including cordless telephones,

cellular telephones, wireless LANs, and microwave transmission of voice and data.

A **cordless telephone** is a portable device that may be used up to about 1,000 feet from its wired telephone base unit. This permits the user to carry the telephone to various rooms in a house, or take it outdoors on the patio. By contrast, a **cellular telephone** may be used anywhere as long as it is within range—about 8 to 10 miles—of a cellular switching station. At present, these cellular switching stations are available in all metropolitan areas of the United States and most rural areas. The switching stations are low-powered transmitter/receivers that are connected to a cellular telephone switching office by means of conventional telephone lines or microwave technology. The switching office, which is computer-controlled, coordinates the calls for its service area and links the cellular system into the local and long-distance telephone network.

Wireless LANs are growing in popularity. They have the obvious advantage of being reasonably easy to plan and install. A wireless system provides networking where cable installation would be extremely expensive or impractical, such as in an old building. A wireless LAN also permits users of mobile devices such as handheld or laptop computers to connect to the LAN (and thus the Internet) whenever they are within range of a wireless access point, such as in a coffee shop or an airport terminal. A wireless LAN is less secure than a wired LAN and more susceptible to interference, which might increase the error rate and force the wireless LAN to operate at a slower data rate. Most wireless LANs operate in the range of 6 to 54 mbps, with a few newer wireless LANs operating at speeds of 100 mbps or more.

Microwave has been in widespread use for long-distance wireless communication for several decades. Microwave is line-of-sight transmission—there must be an unobstructed straight line between the microwave

RFID SIGNALS GROWING STRONGER

Radio frequency identification (RFID) has been around since World War II, but it didn't gain public attention until 2003 when Wal-Mart announced that it would require its 100 top suppliers to begin using RFID for selected applications by January 2005. Since that announcement, the use of RFID has been growing every year, and now the RFID market is expected to grow at a compound annual growth rate of nearly 20 percent through 2012.

There are actually two flavors of RFID, passive and active. Both types of RFID are built around an RFID tag, which is a small piece of hardware—often the size of a postage stamp or smaller—that uses radio-transmitted codes to uniquely identify itself. A passive RFID tag combines a tiny chip with an antenna; it does not have an internal power source. Instead, a passive tag relies on the minute electrical current induced in the antenna by an incoming radio signal, providing enough power for the tag to send a brief response, typically just an ID number. An active RFID tag contains its own power supply and can transmit identifying information either continuously, on request, or on a predetermined schedule. Active tags are much

more expensive, usually over $1.00, while the prices of passive tags have dropped to the $0.10 to $0.17 level. At present, most of the RFID action involves passive RFID tags because of their lower cost. Passive RFID tags are beginning to appear on consumer electronics items, pharmaceuticals, and books. Active RFID tags are commonly found in cell phones, aircraft transponders, and other specialized applications such as the tracking of medical equipment.

How does RFID work? When a tag is placed on an item, it automatically radios its location to RFID readers on store shelves, checkout counters, loading bay doors, and possibly shopping carts. With RFID tags, inventory is taken automatically and continuously. RFID tags can cut costs by requiring fewer workers for scanning items; they also can provide more current and more accurate information to the entire supply chain. Thus, RFID provides significant advantages to businesses. As RFID prices continue to drop, the technology will become more viable for businesses of any size—not just the Wal-Marts of the world!

[Adapted from Khermouch and Green, 2003; Ohlhorst, 2005; Hoover, 2006; and Jones, 2006]

---

transmitter and the receiver. Because of the curvature of the earth, microwave towers have to be built, typically about 25 to 50 miles apart, to relay signals over long distances from the originating transmitter to the final receiver. These requirements for towers, transmitters, and receivers suggest that microwave transmission is expensive, and it is, but long-distance microwave is less expensive than burying fiber-optic cable in a very long trench, particularly if the right of way for that trench has to be obtained. Microwave is widely used for long-distance telephone communication and, to a lesser extent, for corporate voice and data networks; transmission speeds up to 100 mbps are possible.

Other line-of-sight transmission methods exist in addition to microwave. For short distances (such as from one building to another), laser or infrared transmitters and receivers, mounted on the rooftops, are often an economical and easy way to transmit data.

Satellite   A special variation of wireless transmission employs **satellite communication** to relay signals over very long distances. A communications satellite is simply a big microwave repeater in the sky; it contains one or more transponders that listen to a particular portion of the electromagnetic spectrum, amplify the incoming signals, and retransmit back to earth. A modern satellite may have around 40 transponders, each of which can handle an 80 mbps data transmission, 1,250 digital voice channels of 64 kbps each, or other combinations of data channels and

voice channels. Transmission via satellite is still line-of-sight transmission, so a communication would have to be relayed through several satellites to go halfway around the world (see Figure 4.4).

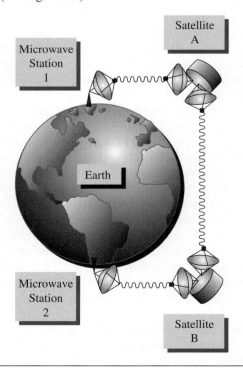

Figure 4.4   Satellite Communications

BLUETOOTH IS HERE!

Harald Bluetooth was a tenth-century Viking king in Denmark. Now a wireless technology named in his honor allows communication among a wide variety of devices, such as mobile telephones, desktop and notebook computers, palmtop computers, DVD players, and printers, eliminating cables and permitting communication where it used to be impossible. **Bluetooth** is short-range radio technology that has been built into a microchip, enabling data to be transmitted wirelessly at speeds of 1 mbps (Version 1.2) or up to 3 mbps (Version 2.0 + EDR). The Bluetooth Special Interest Group's founding members were two leading mobile phone manufacturers, Ericsson and Nokia; two leading notebook computer vendors, IBM (now Lenovo) and Toshiba; and Intel, the leading producer of microprocessor chips. They have been joined by many other companies, including Agere, Microsoft, and Motorola as promoter members. The Bluetooth Special Interest Group has developed Bluetooth technology standards that are available free of royalties to any company that wishes to use them. Products using Bluetooth technology have to pass interoperability testing prior to release. Thousands of Bluetooth products of all kinds are now available for purchase, and Bluetooth support is embedded in operating systems such as Microsoft Windows, Apple Computer's Mac OS, and Palm OS. Global shipments of Bluetooth-enabled devices—including hands-free cell phones, notebook computers, and palmtop computers—reached 318 million in 2005.

The possibilities are endless for the use of Bluetooth. By adding Bluetooth cards (containing the microchip) to a notebook computer and a palmtop, a business traveler is able to synchronize the data in a notebook computer and palmtop simply by placing both devices in the same room. Bluetooth can eliminate the need to use cables to connect the mouse, keyboard, and printer to a desktop computer. An array of Bluetooth-equipped appliances, such as a television set, a stove, a thermostat, and a home computer, can be controlled from a cellular phone—all from a remote location, if desired. The Bluetooth Special Interest Group has designed the microchips to include software controls and identity coding to ensure that only those units preset by their owners can communicate. As a specific example, UPS is using Bluetooth technology in the ring scanners used by package loaders. These ring scanners read bar-code data on packages and transfer it via Bluetooth to terminals they wear on their waists. Then, using wireless LAN access points deployed throughout all of UPS's buildings, the data are sent from the LAN via a landline to a global scanning system—which stores all of the information on packages—at one of two UPS data centers. Watch out for the Viking king—Bluetooth is here!

[Adapted from Wildstrom, 2005; Bluetooth Web site, 2007; and Malykhina, 2006]

One interesting, but annoying, aspect of satellite transmission is the substantial delay in receiving the signal because of the large distances involved in transmitting up to the satellite and then back down to earth. This is particularly true for the geostationary earth orbit (GEO) satellites, which are positioned 22,000 miles above the equator such that they appear stationary relative to the earth's surface. The minimum delay for GEO satellites is just under one-third of a second, which is an order of magnitude larger than on fiber-optic connections or earth-bound microwave covering the same ground distance.

In the 1990s a great deal of interest arose in low earth orbit (LEO) satellites, orbiting at a distance of only 400 to 1,000 miles above the earth—compared to 22,000 miles above the earth for GEO satellites. Because of their rapid motion, it takes a large number of LEO satellites for a complete system; on the other hand, because the satellites are close to the earth, the ground stations need less power for communication and the round-trip delay is greatly reduced. A decade ago it appeared as though nearly 1,700 LEO satellites would be launched by 2006—more than 10 times the 150 commercial satellites in orbit at that time (Schine, et al., 1997)—but that is not happening. Let's see why.

The first major LEO project was Iridium, which launched 66 satellites to offer mobile telephony, paging, and data communication services. Investors in the $5 billion Iridium project included Motorola, Lockheed Martin, and Sprint; Motorola managed the project. The satellites were all flying and the Iridium system went live in 1998, with two-page advertisements splashed in major magazines such as *Business Week*. The Iridium customer would have an individual telephone number that would go with him or her anywhere on earth, enabling the customer to make and receive calls from even the most remote places on the globe.

Unfortunately, the prices to use the Iridium service were too high, and it never caught on. Iridium filed for bankruptcy in 1999, and for a time it appeared likely that the satellites would be allowed to fall out of orbit. But Iridium got a second chance! A group of investors paid $25 million for the satellites and other assets of the original Iridium (quite a bargain!), and started satellite telephone service again in March 2001 (Ewalt, 2001). The old Iridium needed 1 million customers to break even; the new Iridium needed only tens of thousands. Many of these customers came from the U.S. military, which signed a deal for unlimited use for up to 20,000 soldiers. The British military is another customer, as are many news media representatives (Maney, 2003). The cost is still substantial for the reborn Iridium, but not nearly as high as before: The telephone, which weighs 13.2 ounces, costs about $1,300, and calls cost $1.39 per minute to a landline or cell telephone or $0.99 per minute to another Iridium phone. In addition, there is a $50 activation fee and a $34 basic monthly fee.

A competing LEO satellite system, Globalstar, has also had a troubled history. With its 40 LEO satellites, Globalstar does not provide complete coverage of the planet, but it does offer service in over 120 countries. The cost of Globalstar's Freedom 150 plan (in the United States and Canada) is $65 per month for 150 included minutes ($0.43 per minute), plus $0.99 per minute for additional minutes. The telephone for Globalstar costs about $750.

The plug was pulled on a third proposed LEO satellite system, named Teledesic, in October 2002. The original plan for Teledesic, which was sponsored by Craig McCaw (who built McCaw Cellular before selling it to AT&T), Bill Gates (Microsoft), and Boeing, was to create a 288-satellite network to provide low-cost, high-speed Internet access, corporate networking, and desktop videoconferencing. The number of satellites was later reduced to 30, each with a larger "footprint" on the earth, but even that plan was cancelled in 2002 before any Teledesic satellites were launched. All these LEO satellite systems seemed like good ideas at the time they were planned, but the expenses involved were massive. Furthermore, the LEO systems took so long from concept to deployment that competing, less expensive technologies—such as cell phones, DSL, and cable—had made massive inroads into the potential market before the satellites were launched.

Fiber Optics The last and newest transmission medium—**fiber-optic** cabling—is a true medium, not broadcast technology. Advances in optical technology have made it possible to transmit data by pulses of light through a thin fiber of glass or fused silica. A light pulse can signal a 1 bit, while the absence of a pulse signals a 0 bit. An optical transmission system requires three components: the light source, either a light-emitting diode (LED) or a laser diode; the fiber-optic cable itself; and a detector (a photodiode). The light source emits light pulses when an electrical current is applied, and the detector generates an electrical current when it is hit by light.

Fiber optics are much faster than other media and require much less space because the fiber-optic cable is very small in diameter. Fiber-optic cables are more secure because the cables do not emit radiation and, thus, are very difficult to tap. They are also highly reliable because they are not affected by

power-line surges, electromagnetic interference, or corrosive chemicals in the air. These benefits are leading telephone companies to use fiber optics in all their new long-distance telephone lines, lines connecting central office sites, and most of their new local lines from central office sites to terminuses located in subdivisions. (The advantages of speed and security are obvious; the size is important because many of the cable ducts already installed lack room for more coax, but can hold the thinner fiber-optic cabling.) The high cost of the required equipment and the difficulty of dealing with the tiny fibers make this an unattractive medium for most LANs, except when it is used as a backbone to connect multiple LANs and where very high speeds or high security needs exist.

Transmission speeds for fiber range up to 1 billion bits per second (1 giga bps or 1 gbps) for large diameter fiber (50 to 100 micron[1] core, which does not include any protective covering) to as high as 640 gbps for small diameter fiber (10 microns or less). The fact that the smaller diameter fiber has much larger capacity might be surprising, but light reflections are greatly reduced with a smaller fiber—the light ray bounces around less—permitting higher transmission speeds. The large diameter fiber is multimode, meaning that several light rays are traversing the fiber simultaneously, bouncing off the fiber walls, while the small diameter fiber is single mode, with a single light ray at a time propagated essentially in a straight line without bouncing. Single-mode fiber, unfortunately, requires higher cost laser light sources and detectors than multimode fiber. In a recent development, the light ray sent through a single-mode fiber can be split into 80 or more different colors, each carrying its own stream of data. In this process, called dense wave division multiplexing, prisms are used to send these multiple colors down a single fiber. Presently, much of the fiber being installed by telephone companies is 8-micron single-mode fiber with a transmission speed, using wave division multiplexing, of 160 gbps. The outside diameter (including protective covering) of this single-mode fiber is only 125 microns, which is about one-fiftieth the outside diameter of a typical coaxial cable. Thus, both the speed and size advantages of fiber optics are significant.

Topology of Networks

The starting point for understanding networks is to recognize that all telecommunications networks employ one or more of the transmission media discussed previously. But what do the networks look like in terms of their configuration or arrangement of devices and media? The technical

---

[1]A micron is one-millionth of a meter or one-thousandth of a millimeter.

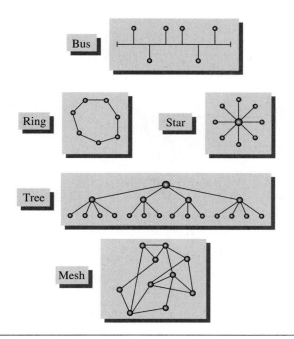

Figure 4.5   Network Topologies

term for this configuration is the topology of the network. There are five basic network topologies—bus, ring, star, hierarchical or tree, and mesh (see Figure 4.5)—plus an unlimited number of variations and combinations of these five basic forms.

Bus   The simplest topology is the linear or **bus topology**. With the bus, all network devices share a single length of cable (coax, fiber, or twisted pair). One of the network devices is usually a file server with a large data storage capacity. An obvious advantage of the bus is the wiring simplicity. A disadvantage is its single-point failure characteristic. If the bus fails, nodes on either side of the failure point cannot communicate with one another.

Ring   The **ring topology** is similar to the bus except that the two ends of the cable are connected. In this case, a single cable runs through every network device, including (usually) a file server. The wiring for the ring is slightly more complicated than for the bus, but the ring is not as susceptible to failure. In particular, a single failure in the ring still permits each network device to communicate with every other device.

Star   The **star topology** has a mainframe or midrange computer, a file server (usually a microcomputer), or a networking device at its center, with cables (or media of some type) radiating from the central device to all the other net-

work devices. This design is representative of many small-to-medium computer configurations, with all workstations and peripherals attached to the single midrange computer. Advantages of the star include ease of identifying cable failure because each device has its own cable; ease of installation for each device, which must only be connected to the central device; and low cost for small networks where all the devices are close together. The star's primary disadvantage is that if the central device fails, the whole network fails. A cost disadvantage might also be encountered if the network grows, for a separate cable must be run to each individual device, even if several devices are close together but far from the central device.

Tree   The fourth basic topology is the **tree**, or hierarchical. This topology is sometimes called a hierarchical star because with some rearrangement (spreading the branches out around the central device), it looks like an extension of the star. The configuration of most large and very large computer networks is a tree, with the mainframe at the top of the tree connected to **controllers** such as a multiplexer[2] and perhaps to other smaller computers. Then these controllers, or smaller computers, are, in turn, connected to other devices such as terminals, microcomputers, and printers. Thus, the tree gets "bushy" as one traverses it from top to bottom.

The tree has the same primary disadvantage as the star. If the central device fails, the entire network goes down. On the other hand, the tree arrangement possesses a great deal of flexibility. The cost disadvantage of the star might not appear when devices are added to the network, for the use of intermediate devices (multiplexers, small computers) removes the necessity of connecting every device directly to the center.

Mesh   In a **mesh topology**, most devices are connected to two, three, or more other devices in a seemingly irregular pattern that resembles a woven net, or a mesh. A complete mesh would have every device connected to every other device, but this is seldom done because of the cost. The public telephone network is an example of a mesh topology; another example is the system of networks that makes up the Internet.

The ramifications of a failure in the mesh depend upon the alternative paths or routes available in the vicinity of the failure. In a complex mesh, like the telephone network,

---

[2]A multiplexer is a device, usually located at a site remote from the mainframe or central device, whose function is to merge ("multiplex") the data streams from multiple low-speed input devices, such as terminals and microcomputers, so that the full capacity of the transmission line to the central device is utilized.

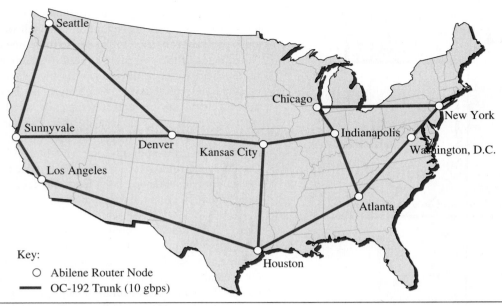

Figure 4.6 Abilene Network Map (Copyright © 2007 Internet2)

a failure is likely to have little impact, except on the devices directly involved.

More Complex Networks Now the fun begins because the previous five network topologies can be combined and modified in a bewildering assortment of networks. For example, it is quite common to attach multiple bus or ring LANs to the tree mainframe computer network. Multiple bus and ring LANs might be attached to a high-speed backbone cable, which is, in effect, a bus network with the LANs as nodes on the network.

National and international networks are much more complex than those we have considered thus far, because the designers have intentionally built in a significant amount of redundancy. In this way, if one transmission line goes out, there are alternative routes to almost every node or device on the network. As an example of a national network, the Abilene network—shown in Figure 4.6—is a leading-edge network for the U.S. research community created by the Internet2 consortium (more on Internet2 later), with its operations center in Indianapolis. Each link in the Abilene network has a capacity of 10 gbps; you can go online at *weathermap.grnoc.iu.edu/abilene_jpg.html* and see how busy the network currently is. Researchers from universities and research laboratories utilize regional networks to connect to Abilene at the nodes indicated on the map. The Abilene network is essentially a ring topology, but it has been enhanced with cross-ring links from Denver to Sunnyvale, Kansas City to Houston, and

Indianapolis to Atlanta. Abilene is a partnership of Internet2, Qwest Communications, Juniper Networks, Nortel Networks, and Indiana University.

Types of Networks

Thus far we have considered two key elements of telecommunications networks: the transmission media used to send the communications and the arrangement or topology of the networks. Now we turn to the categorization of networks into basic types, including computer telecommunications networks, LANs, backbone networks, WANs, the Internet, and Internet2.

Computer Telecommunications Networks It is almost easier to describe this initial type of network by what it is not. It is not a LAN, a backbone network, a WAN, or the Internet. What we are calling a **computer telecommunications network** is the network emanating from a single medium, large, or very large computer, or a group of closely linked computers. This type of network usually is arranged as a tree (see Figure 4.5) with coaxial cable and twisted pair as the media. Until the early 1980s, this was usually the only type of network (except for the telephone network) operated by an organization that did business in one building or a group of adjacent buildings (a campus). In many organizations even today, the predominant communication with the central computer is through the computer telecommunications network. This type of network is controlled by the

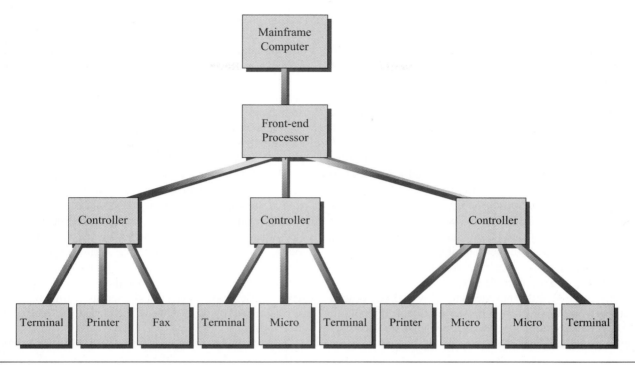

Figure 4.7   Computer Telecommunications Network

central computer, with all other devices (e.g., terminals, microcomputers, and printers) operating as subordinates or "slaves" on the network. IBM's mainframe architecture was originally based on this type of network, although LANs and other network types may now be linked to a mainframe or large computer.

This is not a bad arrangement, but it puts a tremendous communications control burden on the central computer. For this reason, it is quite common to add a front-end processor or communications controller to the network—between the central computer and the rest of the network—to offload the communications work from the central computer (see Figure 4.7). A front-end processor or communications controller is another computer with specially designed hardware and software to handle all aspects of telecommunications, including error control, editing, controlling, routing, and speed and signal conversion.

Local Area Networks   A **local area network (LAN)** is first and foremost a *local* network—it is completely owned by a single organization and generally operates within an area no more than 2 or 3 miles in diameter. LANs are data networks that generally have a high data rate of several million bps or more.

A LAN differs from a computer telecommunications network in that a LAN contains a number of intelligent devices (usually microcomputers) capable of data processing rather than being built around a central computer that controls all processing. In other words, a LAN is based on a peer-to-peer relationship, rather than a master-subordinate relationship.

There are five types of LANs in use today—three types of wired LANs and two types of wireless LANs—for which standards have been developed by the Institute for Electrical and Electronic Engineers (IEEE) and subsequently adopted by both national and international standards organizations. These five LAN standards are officially designated as IEEE 802.3 (contention bus design); IEEE 802.4 (token bus design); IEEE 802.5 (token ring design); IEEE 802.11, including 802.11a, 802.11b, 802.11g, and 802.11n (Wi-Fi wireless design); and 802.16, including 802.16d and 802.16e (WiMAX wireless design).

Wired Local Area Networks.   The **contention bus** design was originally developed by Xerox and subsequently adopted by Digital Equipment Corporation (now part of Hewlett-Packard) and Novell, among others. This design is usually referred to as **Ethernet**, named after the original Xerox version of the design. The contention bus is obviously a bus topology (see Figure 4.5), usually implemented using coaxial cable or twisted pair wiring. Communication on an Ethernet LAN is usually half-duplex—that is, communication in both directions is possible, but not simultaneously. The interesting feature of this design is its contention aspect—all devices must contend for the use of the cable.

With Ethernet, devices listen to the cable to pick off communications intended for the particular device and determine if the cable is busy. If the cable is idle, any device may transmit a message. Most of the time this works fine, but what happens if two devices start to transmit at the same time? A collision occurs and the messages become garbled. The devices must recognize that this collision has occurred, stop transmitting, wait a random period of time, and try again. This method of operation is called a **CSMA/CD Protocol**, an abbreviation for Carrier Sense Multiple Access with Collision Detection. In theory, collisions might continue to occur and thus there is no upper bound on the time a device might wait to send a message. In practice, a contention bus design is simple to implement and works very well as long as traffic on the network is light or moderate (and, thus, there are few collisions).

The original Ethernet design, now called **shared Ethernet**, employs a contention *bus* as its logical topology, but it is usually implemented as a physical *star* arrangement (see Figure 4.8). The usual way of creating a shared Ethernet LAN is to plug the cables from all the devices on the LAN into a **hub**, which is a junction box containing some number of ports (for example, 12) into which cables can be plugged. Embedded inside the hub is a linear bus connecting all the ports. Thus, shared Ethernet operates as a logical bus but a physical star.

Switched Ethernet is a newer variation of Ethernet providing better performance at a higher price. The design is similar to shared Ethernet, but a switch is substituted for the hub and the LAN operates as a logical star as well as a physical star. The switch is smarter than a hub—rather than passing all communications through to all devices on the LAN, which is what a hub does, the switch establishes separate point-to-point circuits to each device and then forwards communications only to the appropriate device. This switched approach dramatically improves LAN performance because each device has its own dedicated circuit, rather than sharing a single circuit with all devices on the network. Of course, a switch is more expensive than a simple hub.

The **token bus** design employs a bus topology with coaxial cable or twisted pair wiring, but it does not rely on contention. Instead, a single token (a special communication or message) is passed around the bus to all devices in a specified order, and a device can only transmit when it has the token. Therefore, a microcomputer must wait until it receives the token before transmitting a message; when the message is sent, the device sends the token on to the next device. After some deterministic period of time based on messages sent by other devices, the device will receive the token again.

The token bus design is central to **Manufacturing Automation Protocol (MAP)**, which was developed by General Motors and adopted by many manufacturers. MAP is a factory automation protocol (or set of standards) designed to connect robots and other machines on the assembly line by a LAN. In designing MAP, General Motors did not believe it could rely on a contention-based LAN with a probabilistic delay time before a message could be sent. An automobile assembly line moves at a fixed rate, and it cannot be held up because a robot has not

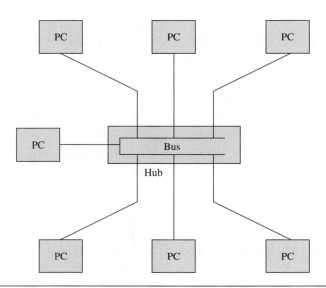

Figure 4.8   Shared Ethernet Topology: Logical Bus, Physical Star

received the appropriate message from the LAN. Therefore, General Motors and many other manufacturers have opted for the deterministic token bus LAN design.

The third LAN standard is the **token ring**, originally developed by IBM, which combines a ring topology (see Figure 4.5) with the use of a token as described for the token bus. A device attached to the ring must seize the token and remove it from the ring before transmitting a message; when the device has completed transmitting, it releases the token back into the ring. Thus, collisions can never occur, and the maximum delay time before any station can transmit is deterministic. The usual implementation of a token ring involves the use of a wire center into which cables from individual devices are plugged, creating a physical star but a logical ring.

All three types of wired LAN designs are in use today. Token bus dominates the manufacturing scene, and Ethernet leads token ring by a wide and growing margin in office applications. But the hottest type of LAN in the early twenty-first century is the wireless LAN, to which we will now turn.

Wireless Local Area Networks. Most **wireless LANs** in use today are of the **Wi-Fi** (short for wireless fidelity) variety, although WiMAX networks are beginning to appear (more on WiMAX later). Wi-Fi LANs are rapidly proliferating. Wi-Fi technology has obvious advantages for people on the move who need access to the Internet in airports, restaurants, and hotels and on university campuses. Wi-Fi is also gaining acceptance as a home or neighborhood network (see the box entitled "City-wide Wi-Fi Networks"), permitting an assortment of laptop and desktop computers to share a single broadband access point to the Internet. Wireless LANs are also moving into the corporate and commercial world, especially in older buildings and confined spaces where it would be difficult or impossible to establish a wired LAN or where mobility is paramount. Even in newer buildings, wireless LANs are often being employed as *overlay networks.* In such cases, Wi-Fi is installed in addition to wired LANs so that employees can easily move their laptops from office to office and can connect to the network in places such as lunchrooms, hallways, and patios (FitzGerald and Dennis, 2007, p. 249).

Today's Wi-Fi LANs use one of the standards incorporated in the IEEE 802.11 family of specifications. All these standards use the shared Ethernet design (logical bus, physical star; see Figure 4.9) and the **CSMA/CA Protocol**, which is an abbreviation for Carrier Sense Multiple Access with Collision Avoidance. CSMA/CA is quite similar to CSMA/CD used in traditional Ethernet, but it makes greater efforts to avoid collisions. In one approach to collision avoidance, any computer wishing to transmit a message first sends a "request to transmit" to the wireless access point. If no other computer is

---

CITY-WIDE WI-FI NETWORKS

An exciting trend in networking is the creation of city-wide public Wi-Fi networks. In Tempe, Arizona—the home of Arizona State University—the outdoor Wi-Fi network is called WAZTempe (Wireless Access Zones-Tempe) and is operated by Kite Networks. WAZTempe is a mesh network incorporating over 800 wireless access points (WAPs), most of which are mounted on street lamp poles. The network covers 95 percent of the city's 40 square miles, and it is currently being extended into the neighboring cities of Chandler and Gilbert. Access to the network is free in the downtown area and on the Arizona State University campus. Tempe residents may subscribe to a residential and outdoor roaming service for $29.95 a month, with speeds up to 1 mbps for downloads and 384 kbps for uploads. There are significant benefits to the city as well as to individuals; for example, police officers in Tempe can connect with their in-office network from their police cars while on patrol.

Other cities are also getting in on the act. Addison, Texas, a suburb of Dallas, has a city-wide Wi-Fi network operated by RedMoon, Inc., and Addison residents can buy wireless Internet access for $16.95 a month, much less than most other broadband alternatives. Other Wi-Fi networks are already operating or in various stages of development in Philadelphia, Minneapolis, Lexington, and 300 other cities.

[Adapted from Yang and Elgin, 2005; and WAZTempe Web site, 2007]

---

transmitting, the wireless access point responds by sending a "clear to transmit" signal to all computers on the wireless LAN, specifying the amount of time for which the network is reserved for the requesting computer.

In order to establish a wireless LAN, a wireless **network interface card (NIC)** must be installed in each computer. The wireless NIC is a short-range radio transceiver that can send and receive radio signals. At the heart of a wireless LAN is the **wireless access point (WAP)**, which is a radio transceiver that plays the same role as a hub in a wired Ethernet LAN. The WAP receives the signals of all computers within its range and repeats them to ensure that all other computers within the range can hear them; it also forwards all messages for recipients not on this wireless LAN via the wired network.

At the present time, there are three Wi-Fi LAN standards in use, with a fourth standard under development. The 802.11a Wi-Fi standard operates in the 5 GHz (gigahertz) band at data rates up to 54 mbps. The problem with 802.11a is that the range is only about 150 feet; in fact, the 54 mbps data rate can be sustained reliably only within about 50 feet of the WAP. The 802.11b standard operates in the 2.4 GHz band at data rates of 5.5 to 11 mbps. The range of 802.11b LANs is typically 300 to 500 feet, which is greater than that of 802.11a. The most popular Wi-Fi LAN standard is 802.11g,

WIRELESS MOOCHERS AND LOITERERS

Wireless Internet access—known by the term Wi-Fi, for wireless fidelity—is quickly gaining popularity among people seeking high-speed Internet connections when they are away from their home or office. The signal from a typical wireless access point (WAP) only extends for about 300 feet in any direction, so the user must find a "hot spot" to be able to access the Internet while on the road. Sometimes hot spots are available for free or for a small fee. For instance, some Schlotzsky's delicatessens, Omni Hotels, and Hampton Inns offer hot spots for free; some McDonald's restaurants, Starbucks coffee shops, and Borders bookstores offer hot spots for a fee. In early 2006 the number of public Wi-Fi hot spots topped 100,000 worldwide, with over 90 percent of these hot spots charging a fee for access.

The hot spots work; they do attract customers—and moochers and loiterers! The manager of a Hampton Inn in Michigan reports seeing local salespeople, who were not staying in the hotel, lurking in the lobby or sitting in cars as they checked their e-mail or surfed the Web using the hotel's wireless network. A homeowner in Oregon confirms that a digital moocher was parked at the end of his driveway using a hot spot that the homeowner had set up to share with his neighbors. One executive could not get a room at a Wyndham Hotel offering wireless access, so he checked into another hotel without Wi-Fi and ended up driving back to the Wyndham several times to check his e-mail in the lobby. Another executive sat outside a closed Starbucks after midnight, in frigid temperatures, to check his e-mail.

Loitering in wireless hot spots can also be a problem. In the Boston area, café owners who installed hot spots to draw customers say they are also drawing Internet users who tie up seats for hours, buy little or nothing, and make coffee shops feel like the office. To combat such loiterers, some owners are charging for wireless access, some are shutting off the wireless signal at peak hours, and others are confronting wireless users who don't buy food. Some hot spot owners have tried to set time limits for Internet use, telling them "Look, you've been here for three hours, and you've bought only a cup of coffee and it's time to move." Whether there is a fee to use the hot spot or not, owners become concerned when tables are occupied for hours and new customers cannot find seats. Wi-Fi is growing in popularity, and enthusiasts will go to great lengths to find hot spots and to occupy those hot spots for hours!

[Adapted from Wingfield, 2003; Hamblen, 2006; and Lobron, 2006]

which uses a different form of multiplexing in the 2.4 GHz band to achieve the same range as 802.11b (300 to 500 feet) with data rates up to the 54 mbps of 802.11a. The 802.11n standard is currently under development and is expected to be completed in 2009; it will use both the 2.4 GHz and 5 GHz frequency ranges simultaneously (by using multiple sets of antennas) in order to increase its data rates. The distance range for 802.11n is expected to be at least as great as 802.11g, with data rates expected to be from 100 to 300 mbps—considerably faster than the earlier standards! Happily, the 802.11n standard (like the 802.11g standard before it) will be backward compatible with the earlier Wi-Fi standards, so that it will have the potential to coexist with—and eventually replace—all of the earlier standards.

The newest type of wireless network is **WiMAX** (short for worldwide interoperability for microwave access), which is based on the IEEE 802.16 family of specifications. There are very few WiMAX users today, but the number is projected to grow to 15.4 million by 2010 because of the significant advantages offered by WiMAX (Edwards, 2006). In practical terms, WiMAX will operate very much like Wi-Fi, but at higher speeds, over greater distances, and for a greater number of

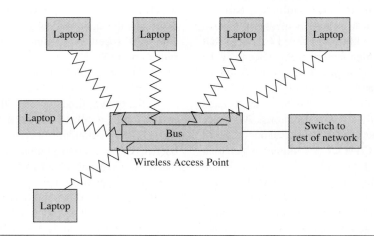

Figure 4.9   Wi-Fi Local Area Network Topology

users. Some prognosticators believe that WiMAX has the potential to do for broadband Internet access what cell phones have done to phone access. In the same way that many users have given up on wired phone service in favor of cell phones, WiMAX could replace cable and DSL services and provide Internet access just about anywhere you go.

There are actually two types of WiMAX. The IEEE 802.16d standard covers fixed-point wireless access, and it is used to connect a central access point to a set of fixed networks, such as from a branch office to a central office a few miles away. Under ideal conditions, 802.16d provides a data rate of 70 mbps for up to 30 miles, but actual data rates and distances are likely to be much less. An important use of 802.16d is to connect multiple Wi-Fi public access points (such as in a city-wide network) to a central switch so that users can connect to the Internet.

By providing access to mobile users, the 802.16e standard is designed to be direct competition for outdoor Wi-Fi networks. The network is expected to provide up to 15 mbps of capacity and to have an effective range of up to 6 miles with a line of sight to the access point or 2 miles without a line of sight. In 2006, Intel and Motorola invested nearly $900 million into a WiMAX company named Clearwire. Clearwire is headed by Craig McCaw, who in the 1980s built a cellular phone business that he sold to AT&T for $11.5 billion. Clearly, McCaw, Intel, and Motorola believe that WiMAX can compete with the cable and telephone companies in providing broadband access to the Internet.

Higher-Speed Wired Local Area Networks.   LAN technology continues to advance in the first decade of the twenty-first century. The top speed of a traditional Ethernet LAN is 10 mbps, but **Fast Ethernet**, operating at 100 mbps, is now the most common form of Ethernet in new LANs (and backbone networks, to be discussed in the next section). Fast Ethernet uses the same CSMA/CD architecture and the same wiring as traditional Ethernet. The most popular implementations of Fast Ethernet are *100 Base-T*, which runs at 100 mbps over Category 5 twisted-pair cabling (four pairs of wires in each cable), and *100 Base-F*, which runs at 100 mbps over multimode fiber-optic cable (usually two strands of fiber joined in one cable). Although the wiring for Fast Ethernet could handle full-duplex communication, in most cases only half-duplex is used.

Even newer and faster than Fast Ethernet is **Gigabit Ethernet**, with speeds of 1 billion bps and higher. Of the three varieties of Gigabit Ethernet in use today, the most widely used is 1-gbps Ethernet, commonly called **1 GbE**. 1 GbE running over twisted-pair cables is called *1000 Base-T*, and it operates over one Category 5e cable (four pairs of wires) by using an ingenious procedure to send streams of

bits in parallel. There are two versions of 1 GbE when running over fiber-optic cabling: *1000 Base-SX* uses multimode fiber and *1000 Base-LX* uses either multimode fiber or single-mode fiber depending on the distances involved (up to 1,800 feet with multimode fiber or over 16,000 feet with single-mode fiber). 1 GbE is often used in backbone networks, to be discussed in the next section. 10-gbps Ethernet, or **10 GbE**, is currently being deployed in circumstances where very high data rates are required, and 40-gbps Ethernet, or **40 GbE**, is just around the corner. These ultra-high speed networks have been designed to run over fiber-optic cables, but, amazingly, can also run over twisted-pair cables. Most of these Gigabit Ethernet networks are configured to use full-duplex communication, but only between two computers at a time. Ethernet speeds keep going up, suggesting that Ethernet will continue to be the preferred networking approach for high-speed LANs and backbone networks for the foreseeable future.

Just as Fast Ethernet is sort of a traditional Ethernet grown up, so is **Fiber Distributed Data Interface (FDDI)** related to a traditional token ring LAN. A traditional token ring LAN operates at a maximum speed of 16 mbps. By contrast, FDDI employs a token ring architecture to deliver 100 mbps. FDDI was originally developed to operate with fiber-optic cable (hence the name), but now operates on either copper media (usually Category 5 twisted-pair cable) or fiber-optic cabling. FDDI is actually a dual-ring technology, with each ring running in the opposite direction to improve fault recovery. With FDDI, the primary ring is active until a fault is detected, at which time the secondary ring is activated. Although still in use today, the future of FDDI seems limited because of advances in Ethernet technology.

Backbone Networks   **Backbone networks** are the in-between networks—the middle distance networks that interconnect LANs in a single organization with each other and with the organization's WAN and the Internet. For example, the corporate headquarters of a large firm might have multiple buildings spread out over several city blocks. Each floor of a large building might have its own LAN, or a LAN might cover an entire smaller building. All these LANs must be interconnected to gain the benefits of networking—enhanced communications, the sharing of resources and data, and distributed data processing. In addition, the LANs must also be connected to the company's WAN and, in most cases, to the Internet. A backbone network is the key to internetworking (see Figure 4.10).

The technology involved in backbone networks is essentially the same as that described for LANs, but at the high end. The medium employed is either fiber-optic cabling or twisted-

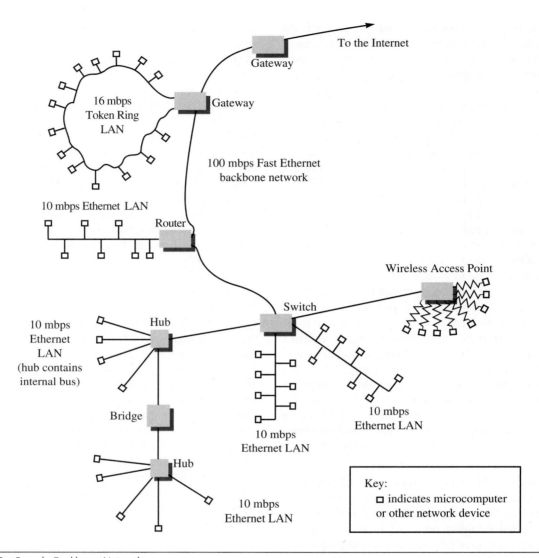

Figure 4.10   Sample Backbone Network

pair cabling, providing a high data transmission rate—often 100 mbps, 1 gbps, or more. The topology may be a ring (FDDI) or a bus (Fast Ethernet or Gigabit Ethernet) or some combination. The only new terminology we need to introduce relates to the hardware devices that connect network pieces together or connect other networks to the backbone network.

We have already introduced the hub, the switch, and the wireless access point. A **hub**, we know, is a simple device into which cables from computers are plugged; it can also be used to connect one section of a LAN to another. Hubs forward every message they receive to all devices or sections of the LAN attached to it, whether or not they need to go there. A **wireless access point** is the central device in a wireless LAN that connects the LAN to other networks. A

bridge connects two LANs, or LAN segments, when the LANs use the same protocols, or set of rules (more on this later); a bridge is smart enough to forward only messages that need to go to the other LAN. A **router**, or a **gateway** (a sophisticated router), connects two or more LANs and forwards only messages that need to be forwarded but can connect LANs that use different protocols. For example, a gateway is used to connect an organization's backbone network to the Internet. A **switch** connects more than two LANs, or LAN segments, that use the same protocols. Switches are very useful to connect several low-speed LANs (e.g., a dozen Ethernet LANs running at 10 mbps) into a single 100 mbps backbone network (running Fast Ethernet). In this case, the switch operates very much like a multiplexer. The top vendors of these hardware devices include Cisco, 3Com, and Alcatel-Lucent.

Wide Area Networks   Today's more complex, more widely dispersed organizations need **wide area networks (WANs)**, also called long-haul networks, to communicate both voice and data across their far-flung operations. A WAN differs from a LAN in that a WAN spans much greater distances (often entire countries or even the globe) and is usually owned by several organizations (including both common carriers and the user organization). In addition, a WAN employs point-to-point transmission (except for satellites), whereas a LAN uses a multiaccess channel (such as the bus and ring). We will note some exceptions, but for the most part WANs rely on the public telephone network.

DDD and WATS.   The easiest way to set up a WAN is to rely on ordinary public telephone service. **Direct Distance Dialing (DDD)** is available through a telephone company such as AT&T, Sprint, or Verizon and can be used for voice and data communications between any two spots served by the telephone network. Of course, the speed for data transmission is quite limited (up to 56 kbps), data error rates are relatively high, and the cost per hour is very expensive. **Wide Area Telephone Service (WATS)** is also available, in which the organization pays a monthly fee for (typically) unlimited long-distance telephone service using the ordinary voice circuits. WATS has the same advantages and disadvantages as DDD. However, the cost per hour of WATS is somewhat less than DDD, but the customer pays for it whether it is used or not, while DDD is only paid for when it is utilized. DDD is appropriate for intermittent, limited-volume data transmission at relatively slow speeds, while WATS is used for more nearly continuous, somewhat larger volumes of data to be transmitted at relatively slow speeds.

Leased Lines.   Another, sometimes attractive, alternative is to lease dedicated communications lines from AT&T or another carrier. If a manufacturing company has three plants geographically separated from corporate headquarters (where the mainframe computer or large servers are located), it might make sense to lease lines to connect each of the three plants to headquarters. These leased lines are generally coaxial cables, microwave, or fiber-optic cables of very high capacity, and they are less prone to data errors than ordinary voice lines. The leased lines are expensive, ranging from hundreds of dollars per month for distances of a few miles to tens of thousands of dollars per month for cross-country lines.

The most common leased lines operate at a data transmission rate of 1.544 mbps and are referred to as **T-1 lines**.

Table 4.3   SONET Circuits

SONET Level	Data Transmission Rate
OC-1	51.84 mbps
OC-3	155.52 mbps
OC-12	622.08 mbps
OC-18	933.12 mbps
OC-24	1.244 gbps
OC-36	1.866 gbps
OC-48	2.488 gbps
OC-96	4.977 gbps
OC-192	9.953 gbps
OC-768	39.812 gbps

KEY: mbps = million bits per second
       gbps = billion bits per second

In order to effectively use this high data transmission rate, organizations must employ multiplexers at each end of a T-1 line to combine (or separate) a number of data streams that are, individually, much less than 1.544 mbps.

Leased lines with capacities higher than T-1 are also available. Four T-1 lines are combined to create a T-2 trunk, with a capacity of 6.312 mbps, but T-2 trunks have largely been bypassed in favor of T-3 trunks (consisting of seven T-2s), with a data transmission capacity of nearly 45 mbps. T-3 links are available between major cities, although the costs are much higher than for T-1 lines. T-4 trunks also exist (made up of six T-3s), with a huge capacity of 274 mbps.

The newest and highest capacity leased lines (and also the most expensive) are fiber-optic transmission lines, or SONET lines. **Synchronous Optical Network (SONET)**, is an American National Standards Institute (ANSI) approved standard for connecting fiber-optic transmission systems. Data transmission rates for SONET lines are shown in Table 4.3. Note that the slowest SONET transmission rate (OC-1) of nearly 52 mbps is faster than the T-3 rate of 45 mbps. All the links in the Abilene network shown in Figure 4.6 are SONET lines operating at OC-192 (nearly 10 gbps). Abilene is truly a high performance, high bandwidth network.

Satellite.   Satellite microwave communication is being used by an increasing number of organizations that are setting up a WAN. The satellite or satellites involved are owned by companies such as Loral Space and Communications, Hughes Network Systems, and Intelsat, and the user organization leases a portion of the satellite's capacity. The user organization either provides its own ground stations or leases time on a carrier's ground stations, as well as communication lines to and from those ground stations. The use of Ku-band transmission with relatively inexpensive VSAT—very small aperture terminal (i.e., a small satellite dish)—ground stations is making satellite transmission very popular for organizations with many remote locations. Both Kmart and Wal-Mart, for example, use VSAT networks to link their thousands of stores with their corporate headquarters. V-Crest Systems, a member of the Volkswagen Group at the time—it has since been sold to Automatic Data Processing, Inc. (ADP)—created a VSAT network for all the Porsche, Audi, and Volkswagen dealerships throughout the United States. Through the VSAT network, V-Crest provided information services for order placement, warranty processing, parts and vehicle location, customer tracking, financing, insurance, accounting, inventory control, and service management.

ISDN. Another way of implementing a WAN is an **Integrated Services Digital Network (ISDN)**. ISDN is a set of international standards by which the public telephone network is offering additional telecommunications capabilities (including simultaneous transmission of voice and data over the same line) to telephone users worldwide. So-called narrowband ISDN is now available in many areas of the world. ISDN is digital communication, using the same twisted pairs already used in the present telephone network.

ISDN capabilities are made possible by hardware and software at the local telephone company office and on the organization's premises that divide a single telephone line (twisted pair) into two types of communication channels. The B, or bearer, channel transmits voice or data at rates of 64 kbps, faster than is possible using a modem. The D, or data, channel is used to send signal information to control the B channels and to carry packet-switched digital data.

So far, two narrowband ISDN services have been offered. The basic rate offers two B channels and one 16 kbps D channel (a total data rate of 144 kbps) over a single twisted pair. Each basic rate line is capable of supporting two voice devices and six data devices, any two of which can be operating simultaneously. The primary rate provides 23 B channels and one 64 kbps D channel (for a total data rate of 1.544 mbps) over two twisted pairs. Although not widely available, broadband ISDN—using fiber-optic cabling—offers data transmission rates of over 150 mbps. Therefore, ISDN provides a significant increase in capacity while still using the public telephone network.

Further, the D channel brings new capabilities to the network. For instance, the D channel can be used for telemetry, enabling remote control of machinery, heating, or air conditioning at the same time the B channels are being used for voice or data transmission. The D channel can also be used for single-button access to a variety of telephony features, such as call-waiting and display of the calling party's number.

A number of innovative uses of ISDN have been implemented. In a customer service application, an incoming call from a customer comes in over one of the B channels. The D channel is used to automatically signal the file server to send the customer's record to the service representative's workstation over the second B channel. In a marketing application, a salesperson sends alternative specifications or designs to a potential buyer's video screen over one B channel while simultaneously talking to the buyer over the second B channel. ISDN permits the user to be a more effective telecommuter (working from home), to share a computer screen display with another user at a distant location, to conduct desktop videoconferencing, to transfer large data files with relative ease, and to access the Internet at 128 kbps (combining the two B channels), over twice as fast as an ordinary modem.

The developments in ISDN are a part of the digitization of the public telephone network. However, ISDN has never caught on in a big way, and it now seems destined to be bypassed by other digital developments such as DSL (to be covered in a later section) and IP (Internet Protocol) telephony. At present, ISDN service is available on many telephone lines in the United States, but it is relatively expensive compared to other options such as DSL.

Packet-Switched Networks. **Packet-switched networks** are quite different from the switched-circuit (DDD and WATS, ISDN) and dedicated-circuit (leased lines, satellite) networks previously described. In switched- and dedicated-circuit networks, a circuit is established between the two computers that are communicating, and no other devices can use that circuit for the duration of the connection. In contrast, a packet-switched network permits multiple connections to exist simultaneously over the same physical circuit. **Packet switching** is a store-and-forward data transmission technique. Communications are sent over the common carrier network, divided into packets of some fixed length, perhaps 300 characters (see Figure 4.11). Control information is attached to the front and rear of this packet, and it is sent over a communications line in a single bundle. Packet switching is quite different from usual voice and data communications, where the entire end-to-end circuit is tied up for the duration of the session. With packet switching, the network is used more efficiently because packets from various users can be interspersed with one another. The computers controlling the network will route each individual packet along the appropriate path.

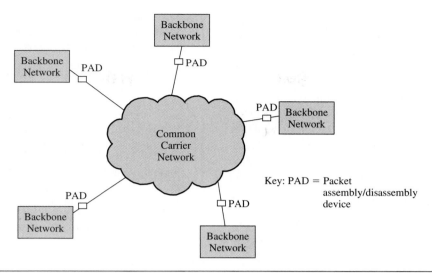

Figure 4.11   Packet-Switched Network Connecting Five Organizational Locations

A **packet assembly/disassembly device (PAD)** is used to connect the user organization's internal networks (at each of its locations) to the common carrier network. The organization must, of course, pay a fee to make use of the common carrier network. In some cases, the user organization provides the PADs and pays a fixed fee for a connection into the common carrier network plus a charge for the number of packets transmitted. In other cases, the user organization might contract with a firm that manages and operates the entire WAN for the user organization, including the PADs needed at each location. This contracting-out practice used to be called a **value added network (VAN)**, but that terminology has largely disappeared. Today such a packet-switched WAN is usually called a managed network. In the United States, managed network services are available from AT&T, Sprint, Verizon, BT Infonet, and other providers. Packet-switched networks are quite common, including some networks like Abilene that serve a limited audience and others like the Internet that are available to anyone or any organization that wishes to buy the networking service.

ATM.   One of the newer entries on the WAN as well as the backbone network scene is **Asynchronous Transfer Mode (ATM)**. ATM is based on the idea of packet switching as described earlier. For ATM, each packet is rather small—a total of 53 bytes, including 48 bytes of data and 5 bytes of control information attached to the front of the packet. ATM was originally created for use in WANs to carry both data and voice traffic, which helps explain the small packet size—the small packet is an appropriate size for voice traffic, but it is very small for

data traffic. ATM is a telecommunications standard for broadband ISDN.

ATM does not really describe a line transmission technology, such as contention bus or token ring; it is a switching technology with usual speeds from 155 mbps in each direction up to 622 mbps. ATM operates as a full-duplex circuit, so the total throughput varies from 310 mbps (155 mbps times 2) up to 1.24 gbps (622 mbps times 2). An ATM network uses switches arranged in a mesh topology (see Figure 4.5), usually running on fiber-optic cables or Category 5 twisted-pair cables. In brief, ATM is fast packet switching with short, fixed-length packets.

Because of the fast data transmission rates, ATM networks gained a foothold in the WAN arena and in backbone networks; they were also used in some LANs. However, ATM uses protocols that differ from the Internet's Transmission Control Protocol/Internet Protocol (TCP/IP), so it is necessary to convert ATM addresses into TCP/IP addresses (and back) to access the Internet from an ATM network. Thus, with the ascendancy of the Internet, ATM fell into disfavor. ATM has had some successes, and it is now widely used deep within the public telephone network (Tanenbaum, 2003, p. 62). It is not, however, a common choice for WANs or backbone networks.

Virtual Private Networks.   A **virtual private network (VPN)** provides the equivalent of a private packet-switched network (as discussed earlier) using the public Internet. A VPN provides a moderate data rate (up to 2 mbps) at a very reasonable cost, but the network's reliability is low. To establish a VPN, the user organization places a VPN device (a special router or switch) on each

Internet access circuit to provide access from the organization's networks to the VPN. Of course, the user organization must pay for the access circuits and the Internet service provider (ISP). The VPN devices enable the creation of VPN *tunnels* through the Internet. Through the use of encapsulation and encryption, these tunnels ensure that only authorized users can access the VPN. The primary advantages of VPNs are low cost and flexibility, while the disadvantages include low reliability, unpredictable transmission speeds, and security concerns. An organization can create a VPN itself, or it can contract with a vendor such as AT&T or Verizon to manage and operate the VPN.

Internet   Almost last, but certainly not least, of the network types we will consider is the ubiquitous Internet. The Internet could be considered a gigantic WAN, but it is really much more than that. The **Internet** is a network of networks that use the TCP/IP protocol (to be discussed later in the chapter), with gateways (connections) to even more networks that do not use the TCP/IP protocol. By January 2007, there were approximately 433 million hosts (number of IP addresses that have been assigned a name) on the Internet (Internet Systems Consortium, 2007). Internet World Stats estimated the number of Internet users in January 2007 as 1,093 million, with over 232 million users in North America (Internet World Stats, 2007). An incredible array of resources—both data and services—is available on the Internet, and these resources are drawing more users, which are drawing more resources, in a seemingly never-ending cycle.

The Internet has an interesting history, dating back to 1969 when the U.S. Department of Defense created ARPANET[3] to link a number of leading research universities. Ethernet LANs incorporating TCP/IP networking arrived in the early 1980s, and NSFNET was created in 1986 to link five supercomputer centers in the United States. NSFNET served as the backbone (the underlying foundation of the network, to which other elements are attached) of the emerging Internet as scores of other networks connected to it. Originally, commercial traffic was not permitted on the Internet, but this barrier was broken in the late 1980s and the floodgates opened in the early 1990s. In 1995 the National Science Foundation withdrew all financial support for the Internet, and began funding an alternate very high performance network named

---

[3]ARPANET is a creation of the Advanced Research Projects Agency of the U. S. Department of Defense. Much of the pioneering work on networking is the result of ARPANET, and TCP/IP was originally developed as part of the ARPANET project.

IM ABUSE IS RAMPANT IN THE WORKPLACE

Whatever it is that workers are doing with instant messaging, work is far down the list, a security company said in a study released Wednesday. Abusive language, gossip, sexual advances and complaints are among the chief uses of instant messaging in the workplace, the company [Blue Coat Systems] found during a survey of U.S. and U.K. workers with access to IM applications. Among the potential problems caused by IM abuse: lost productivity, potential exposure to litigation, compliance violations, risk of leaking confidential information, attachment of viruses, and transmission of links to illegal or malicious Web sites, among others.

"There are currently 40 million business users of IM, and there are genuine business benefits to the immediacy of IM," said Steve Mullaney, Blue Coat's marketing VP. "The technology is not going to go away. But left unchecked, instant messaging could ultimately cause more business problems than it solves."

The solution, from [Blue Coat's] point of view, is to make IM a full member of the enterprise IT club, subject to the same level of restriction, monitoring, and enforcement as e-mail, Internet use, and other better-established applications. Blue Coat also recommended development of company policies regarding appropriate use of instant messaging, basing those policies on a "log it, manage it, control it" triad.

[Ferrell, 2003]

vBNS—which was, in some respects, a forerunner of Internet2 (to be discussed next).

The Internet has no direct connection to the U.S. government or any other government. Authority rests with the Internet Society, a voluntary membership organization. The society is the organizational home for the groups responsible for Internet infrastructure standards, including the Internet Engineering Task Force and the Internet Architecture Board. Similarly, the Internet receives no government support now that NSF funding has ended. Users pay for their own piece of the Internet. For an individual, this usually means paying an Internet service provider (ISP) a monthly fee to be able to dial a local number and log into the Internet, or to access the Internet via a broadband service such as DSL or cable. The smaller ISPs, in turn, pay a fee to hook into the Internet backbone, which is a network of high bandwidth networks owned by major ISPs such as AT&T, Verizon, Sprint, Level 3 Communications, and Qwest.

The Internet provides the four basic functions summarized in Table 4.4: electronic mail, remote login, discussion groups, and the sharing of data resources. **Electronic mail** was really the first "killer app" of the Internet—the first application that grabbed the attention of potential users

Table 4.4   Internet Applications

Name of Application	Purpose of Application
Electronic mail, or e-mail	Easy-to-use, inexpensive, asynchronous means of communication with other Internet users
Instant messaging (IM)	Synchronous communication system that enables the user to establish a private "chat room" with another individual to carry out text-based communication in real time over the Internet
Remote login	Permits user to log into and perform work on a computer that is remote to the user's current location
Usenet newsgroups	Internet discussion groups, which are essentially huge electronic bulletin boards on which group members can read and post messages
Listserv	Mailing list such that members of a group can send a single e-mail message and have it delivered to everyone in the group
File Transfer Protocol (FTP)	Permits users to send and receive files, including programs, over the Internet
World Wide Web, or the Web	Hypertext-based tool that allows the user to traverse, or surf, the Internet by clicking on a link contained in one document to move to another document, and so on; these documents might include video clips, recordings, photographs, and other images
Search engine	An information retrieval program that permits the user to search for content that meets a specific criterion (typically containing a given word or phrase) and retrieves a list of items that match the criterion
Blog	A user-generated Web site where entries are made in journal style; blogs often provide commentary on a particular subject or serve as a personal online diary
Wiki	A Web site that permits users to add, remove, or modify the content of the site, often without the need for registration, thus making a wiki an effective tool for mass collaborative authoring
Social networking application	An application that permits users to post information about themselves and to view information posted by others

and turned them into Internet converts. Electronic mail provides an easy-to-use, inexpensive, asynchronous means of communication with other Internet users anywhere in the world. A newer variant of electronic mail, **instant messaging (IM)** is a synchronous communication system that enables the user to establish a private "chat room" with another individual to carry out text-based communication in real time over the Internet. Typically, the IM system signals the user when someone on his or her private list is online, and then the user can initiate a chat session with that individual. Major players in the IM market are AOL, Yahoo!, Microsoft, and IBM Lotus.

Remote login permits a user in, say, Phoenix, to log into another machine on which she has an account in, say, Vienna, using a software program such as Telnet or the more secure SSH. Then she can work on the Vienna machine exactly as if she were there. Discussion groups are just that—Internet users who have gathered together to discuss some topic. **Usenet newsgroups** are the most organized of the discussion groups; they are essentially a set of huge electronic bulletin boards on which group members can read and post messages. Google Groups now provides a Web interface into Usenet newsgroups. A **listserv** is a mailing list such that

members of the group can send a single e-mail message and have it delivered to everyone in the group. This usually works fine as long as users remember whether they are sending a message to an individual in the group or to the entire group. Do not use the reply function in response to a listserv message unless you intend your reply to go to the entire group!

The sharing of data resources is a gigantic use of the Internet. **File Transfer Protocol (FTP)** is a program that permits users to send and receive files, including other programs, over the Internet. For ordinary FTP use, the user needs to know the account name and password of the remote computer in order to log into it. Anonymous FTP sites have also been set up, however, which permit any Internet user to log in using "anonymous" as the account name. As a matter of courtesy (and to track accesses), most anonymous FTP sites ask that the user enter an e-mail address as the password. Once logged in, the user may transfer any files located at that anonymous FTP site.

FTP is still popular today, but by far the most important application for sharing data resources is the **World Wide Web (WWW)**, or just the **Web**. The Web is a hypertext-based way of traversing, or "surfing," the Internet. With hypertext, any document can contain links to other documents. By clicking on the link with the computer mouse, the referenced document will be retrieved—whether it is stored on your own computer, one down the hall, or one on the other side of the world. More than this, the Web provides a graphical user interface (GUI) so that images, photographs, sound bytes, and full motion video can be displayed on the user's screen as part of the document (provided your computer is appropriately equipped). All this material is delivered to the user's computer via the Internet. The World Wide Web is the second "killer app" of the Internet, and it has accelerated the already rapid telecommunications revolution.

To use the World Wide Web, the user's machine must have a Web browser program installed. This software package permits the machine to access a Web server, using a dial-up telephone connection (with a modem), a broadband connection via DSL or cable, or a connection through a local area network. As noted in Chapter 3, the most popular browser is Microsoft's Internet Explorer. When a user first logs into the Web, she is connected to a "home" server at her ISP or her own organization. She can then surf the Web by clicking on hypertext links, or if she knows the address of the site she wishes to visit—this address is called the **Universal Resource Locator (URL)**—she can enter the address directly into her browser. Alternatively, she can search for a particular topic using a **search engine** program such as Google, Yahoo!, MSN Search, or AOL Search. For Web site addresses, or URLs, she expects to visit frequently, she can save the address as a "bookmark" in her browser so that all she must do is click on the appropriate bookmark to return to the Web site.

In the early days of the Web (say, 1992 to 1995), a great deal of factual information was on the Web, but very little of commercial interest. Today, however, all major organizations, and many lesser ones, have a significant presence on the Web. The Web gives businesses a new way to provide information about their products and services, a new way to advertise, and a new way to communicate with customers and suppliers and potential customers and suppliers. With increasing frequency, the Web is being used to complete sales, particularly of products, such as software, that can be delivered via the Internet and of products such as books, CDs, and clothes that can be delivered via regular mail. (We will talk more about electronic commerce via the Web in Chapter 8.) Designing appealing Web pages has become an art—firms want to make sure that their pages convey the right image. Check out the home pages of some leading firms in any industry.

The Web has brought forth newer variations of discussion groups and communication tools, including blogs, wikis, and a variety of social networking applications. A **blog** (derived from We*b log*) is a user-generated Web site where entries are made in journal style, typically displayed in reverse chronological order. Blogs can deal with any subject—sometimes they serve as personal online diaries, and sometimes they provide commentary on a particular subject such as the environment, politics, or local news. Typically blogs include text, images, and links to other Web sites; sometimes blogs permit readers to leave comments in an interactive format. A **wiki** is a Web site that allows visitors to add, remove, or modify the content of the Web site, often without the need for registration. Thus, a wiki becomes an effective tool for mass collaborative authoring. A great example of a wiki is Wikipedia, the free online encyclopedia found at *www.wikipedia.org*. **Social networking applications**, which have really caught on in the twenty-first century, include the very popular MySpace, Facebook, and Classmates—these applications all permit users to post information about themselves and to view information posted by others. Taken as a group, these newer variations of discussion groups and communication tools are sometimes referred to as **Web 2.0**, a phrase that refers to a perceived second generation of Web-based services that emphasize online collaboration and sharing among users.

DSL, Cable Modem, and Satellite.   How does an individual user access the Internet? In the workplace, most users are connected to a LAN, which in turn is connected to the organizational backbone network, and then to the Internet. From home or a small office, there are several alternatives. Until a decade ago, connections were almost always made from a dial-in modem operating at speeds up to 56 kbps. Today, however, an increasing number of users are employing one of three newer, higher-speed alternatives: **Digital Subscriber Line (DSL)**, a **cable modem** connection, and a **satellite** connection. Taken together, these three alternatives are referred to as **broadband** connections.

DSL is a service offered by telephone companies using the copper wires already installed in homes and offices; it uses a sophisticated modulation scheme to move data over the wires without interfering with voice traffic—that is, both a voice conversation and an Internet hookup can be active at the same time over a single DSL line. DSL is sometimes called a "last mile" technology in that it is used only for connections from a telephone switching station to a home or office, not for connections between switching stations. Data transfer rates on DSL are very fast, varying from 256 kpbs to 7 mbps when downloading from the Internet to the home or office machine and from 256 kbps to 896 kbps when uploading from the home or office machine to the Internet. This differential in upload and download speed is not usually a problem because users typically do not send as much data *to* the Internet as they receive *from* the Internet. Furthermore, the DSL line is dedicated to the single user, so these speeds are guaranteed. As an example of the costs, installation of Qwest Choice DSL Deluxe with MSN Premium in Phoenix costs only $60 for the modem. This service provides speeds up to 1.5 mbps for downloading and up to 896 mbps for uploading. The monthly fee is $31.99, which does not include regular voice telephone service but does include MSN Premium ISP service.

A cable modem connection is very competitive to DSL in both price and speed. In this case, the service is obtained from the cable television company, and the data are transmitted over the coaxial cables already used by television. These cables have much greater bandwidth than twisted pair copper wires, but traditionally they transmitted data only in one direction—from the cable television company to the home. Reengineering of the cable television system was necessary to permit the two-way data flow required for Internet connections. Current download speeds with a cable modem range up to 12 mbps, with upload speeds considerably slower (up to 1 mbps). However, cable modem speeds might be degraded because users are sharing the bandwidth of the coaxial cable; as more users in a neighborhood log into the Internet, the slower the speed of the connections. As an example of the costs, installation of Cox Communications Preferred cable modem service in Phoenix costs only $60 for the cable modem. This service provides speeds up to 7 mbps for downloading and up to 512 kbps for uploading. The monthly fee is $44.95, which does not include cable television service. No additional ISP is needed; Cox Communications provides the connection to the Internet.

The third alternative, a satellite connection, tends to be the most expensive option, but for customers in rural areas it might be the only choice. The uplink typically operates from 128 to 200 kbps, with the downlink from 700 kbps up to 1.5 mbps. Satellite broadband connections can be one-way service or two-way service. For one-way service, the customer must contract with a wired ISP (dial-up, DSL, or cable modem) for the uplink, while the satellite supports the downlink. The downlink is just like the usual terrestrial link, except that the satellite transmits data to the computer via a satellite dish at the customer's home or office. The two-way satellite service transmits and receives signals directly via the satellite without needing a ground line to support the connection for the upstream portion of the broadband service. As an example of a two-way satellite service, HughesNet Home service (from Hughes Network Systems) provides download speeds up to 700 kbps and upload speeds up to 128 kbps and is available from any location in the United States with a clear view of the southern sky. With a 15-month service agreement, the installation fee is $400 (including a satellite dish, a modem, and installation) and the monthly charge is $59.99.

In the battle to provide high-speed Internet access in the United States, cable modem connections forged an early lead over DSL, but DSL came back strong to overtake cable. In March 2006, there were 84 million home broadband users in the United States, with half of them (50 percent) connected by DSL and 41 percent connected via cable modem (Horrigan, 2006). The strong growth of DSL is partly explained by the price differences—in December 2005, DSL users reported an average monthly bill of $32, while cable modem users reported an average monthly bill of $41. Nevertheless, the numbers of both cable modem and DSL users have been growing rapidly, and that growth should continue.

Even with this strong growth, the United States is far behind several other nations in the proportion of households with broadband service—in fact, the United States is not even in the top 10! In 2006, Denmark led the world with 29.3 broadband subscribers per 100 inhabitants, followed by the Netherlands, Iceland, Korea, and Switzerland in the top 5. By contrast, the United States had 19.2 subscribers per 100 inhabitants and found itself in 12th place (OECD, 2006). Furthermore, high-speed connections in the United States are often much slower than in other countries. A typical cable modem connection in the United States carries 5 mbps, while broadband connections in Asian countries such as Japan and Korea are as much as 20 times faster—and at a lower monthly cost. It is also true that about 20 percent of households in the United States have no way to obtain broadband Internet service (except for satellite), and another 5 to 10 percent only have a single choice—their local cable television provider (Lacy, 2005). If the United States is to catch up, it will require efforts on the part of the government to remove regulatory roadblocks and perhaps provide tax incentives for broadband investments, on the part of service providers to reduce prices and increase speeds, on the part of venture capitalists to promote broadband content startup companies, and on the part of content developers to promote legal file-sharing (Crockett, Ihlwan, and Yang, 2003).

Intranets.   An important spin-off from the success of the Internet has been the creation of **intranets** within many large organizations. An intranet is simply a network operating within an organization that employs the TCP/IP protocol. In most cases, an intranet consists of a backbone network with a number of connected LANs. Because the protocol is the same, the organization may use the same Web browser and Web server software as it would use on the Internet; however, the intranet is not

INTERNET TELEPHONY IS CATCHING ON!

The Internet is not just for data—**Internet telephony**, also called **Voice over Internet Protocol (VoIP)** is becoming a major factor in telephone communications, especially for corporations. VoIP allows the user to make voice calls using a broadband Internet connection instead of a regular (analog) telephone line. The advantage of VoIP is that it can significantly reduce telecommunications costs.

In order to use VoIP, a broadband Internet connection is required, either through a company network or a DSL or cable modem connection. The simplest and most common way to use VoIP is to plug your existing telephone into an analog telephone adapter—which is an analog-to-digital signal converter—that is, in turn, plugged into your DSL, cable modem, or LAN. VoIP providers such as Vonage and AT&T CallVantage bundle these adapters free with their service. Another option is to buy a specialized IP (digital) phone that plugs directly into a LAN connector; this is a popular option for businesses. The third option is to use your computer as a telephone; in this case your computer requires some software, a microphone, speakers, and a sound card, as well as an Internet connection. With this option, you can download the required software from the Internet, for free or a very small charge, and make local and long distance calls to other computers for free (except for your ISP fee). To interface with the public telephone network, however, you need to go through a VoIP provider. A variety of services (and, therefore, costs) are available, all of them quite reasonable compared to traditional telephone services. For example, both Vonage and AT&T CallVantage provide unlimited local and long distance service for $24.99 per month.

Because of the potential cost savings involved, businesses have been quicker than individuals to jump on the VoIP bandwagon. In the business marketplace, the leading VoIP vendors include Cisco, Avaya, Nortel, NEC, and 3Com. Gartner, a leading provider of research and analysis about IT, estimates that there were 14.7 million enterprise VoIP telephony lines installed in North America by the end of 2006, or about 21 percent of the total enterprise base. There are two primary approaches (and several variations thereof) to providing VoIP in businesses: With one approach, the business buys the IP phones, the Ethernet switches, and the servers that run the call-control software and operates the VoIP network itself; with the second approach, the business buys the IP phones but subscribes to a hosted VoIP service (from a vendor such as Covad or Vonage) for running the network. Many analysts contend that most companies will eventually move to VoIP. "IP telephony is absolutely inevitable, but the timing is up to each enterprise," says Jeff Snyder, Research Vice President at Gartner. "There's no reason to feel rushed to adopt that technology unless there is a legitimate business case," he says.

[Adapted from King, 2006 and FCC, 2007]

---

accessible from outside the organization. It might or might not be possible for people within the organization to access the Internet.

Some commentators have referred to the Internet as the "information superhighway." That is wrong, as Bill Gates, the chairman of Microsoft, has pointed out in his book, *The Road Ahead* (1995). The Internet is merely the predecessor of the information superhighway; we are not there yet. Before we have a true information superhighway, we need gigantic increases in bandwidth, more reliability and security, more accessibility by the entire population, and more applications. We are only beginning to scratch the surface of possibilities for the Internet and the information superhighway beyond.

Internet2   In reality, **Internet2** is not a network type, although it does run a leading-edge, very high-bandwidth network; it is a not-for-profit consortium of over 200 U.S. universities, working in cooperation with 70 leading technology companies, 45 government agencies and laboratories, and over 50 international partner organizations, to develop and deploy advanced network applications and technologies. Internet2 hopes to accelerate the creation of tomorrow's Internet, a true "information superhighway." The three primary goals of Internet2 are to

- create a leading-edge network capability for the national research community

- enable revolutionary Internet applications based on a much higher-performance Internet than we have today

- ensure the rapid transfer of new network services and applications to the broader Internet community

Until 2007, Internet2's "leading-edge network for the national research community" was named Abilene, with its operation center in Indianapolis (see Figure 4.6). In 2007, Internet2—in partnership with Level 3 Communications (who designed and built the network), Infinera (who provided the optical networking hardware and network operating system), and the Indiana University Global Network Operations Center (who manage the network)—rolled out a new, even higher-performance network, with the appropriate but nevertheless confusing name Internet2. Internet2 is an extremely high-performance digital optical network, with all the links in Figure 4.12 operating at 100 gbps—10 times the capacity of its predecessor Abilene network. Internet2 (the network) is a backbone network used by the Internet2 universities; it provides an effective interconnection among regional networks that have been formed by the Internet2

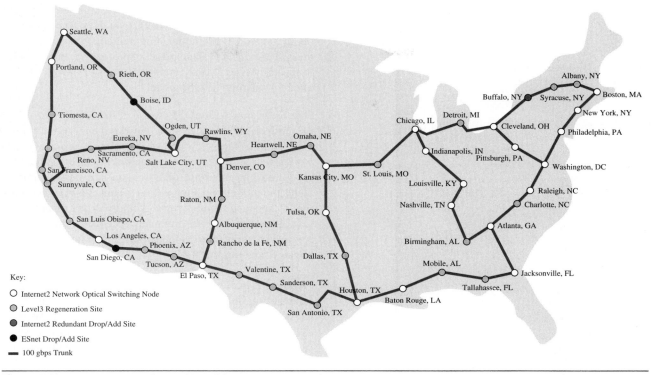

Figure 4.12   Internet2 Network Map (Copyright © 2007 Internet2)

universities. Connections from these regional networks and the commercial Internet can occur at any of the locations labeled on the map. The topology of Internet2 is similar to that of Abilene, with even more cross-ring links. The Boise and San Diego locations, each labeled as an "ESnet Drop/Add Site," are interconnection points with the Energy Sciences Network, which connects almost all U.S. Department of Energy (DOE) sites including DOE's super-computers. The Abilene and Internet2 networks and the other Internet2 projects are the precursors of tomorrow's Internet.

Network Protocols

There is only one more major piece to our network puzzle. How do the various elements of these networks actually communicate with one another? The answer is by means of a **network protocol**, an agreed-upon set of rules or conventions governing communication among elements of a network, or, to be more precise, among layers or levels of a network. In order for two network elements to communicate with one another, they must both use the same protocol. Therefore, the protocol truly enables elements of the network to communicate with one another.

Without actually using the protocol label, we have already encountered several protocols. LANs, for example, have four widely accepted protocols: contention bus, token bus, token ring, and wireless. Historically, the biggest problem with protocols is that there have been too many of them (or, to look at the problem in another way, not enough acceptance of a few of them). For example, IBM and each of the other major hardware vendors created their own sets of protocols. IBM's set of protocols is collectively termed Systems Network Architecture (SNA). IBM equipment and equipment from another vendor, say, Hewlett-Packard, cannot communicate with each other unless *both* employ the same protocols—IBM's, or H-P's, or perhaps another set of "open systems" protocols. The big challenge involved in integrating computers and other related equipment from many vendors into a network is *standardization* so that all use the same protocols.

In the past two and a half decades considerable progress has been made in standardization and acceptance of a set of protocols—although we are not ending up where most commentators would have predicted in the late 1980s. At that time, it appeared that the **Open Systems Interconnection (OSI) Reference Model**, developed by the International Organization for Standardization (ISO),

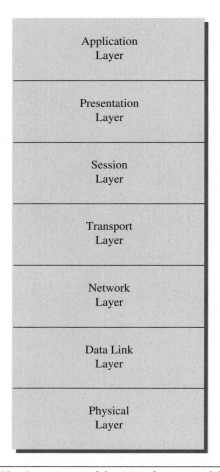

Figure 4.13   Seven Layers of the OSI Reference Model

would become the standard set of protocols. The OSI model defines seven layers (see Figure 4.13), each of which will have its own protocol (or protocols). The OSI model is only a skeleton, with standard protocols in existence for some layers (the four LAN protocols are part of the data link layer), but with only rough ideas in other layers. All major computer and telecommunications vendors—including IBM—announced their support for the OSI model, and it appeared that OSI was on its way.

For better or worse, the movement toward the OSI model was essentially stopped in the 1990s by the explosion of the role of the Internet and the creation of numerous intranets within major organizations. Both the Internet and intranets employ Transmission Control Protocol/Internet Protocol (TCP/IP) as their protocol. TCP/IP is not part of the OSI reference model, and it is a less comprehensive set of protocols than OSI, corresponding roughly to two of the seven OSI layers. Both the OSI model and TCP/IP are important, for different reasons, so we will explore both sets of protocols.

The OSI model provides an extremely useful framework for considering computer networks so it is a good place to begin. The TCP/IP model, augmented with some other ideas, is the *de facto* standard set of protocols for networking in the early twenty-first century, so we will turn to TCP/IP after considering the OSI model.

OSI Reference Model   Because of the importance of the OSI model, and because it will give us a conceptual framework to understand how communication takes place in networks, we will briefly discuss each of the layers in the OSI model and an example of how data can be transmitted using the model (see Figure 4.14). This is a very complex model because it must support many types of networks (e.g., LANs and WANs) and many types of communication (e.g., electronic mail, electronic data interchange, and management reports[4]).

Physical Layer.   The physical layer is concerned with transmitting bits (a string of zeros and ones) over a physical communication channel. Electrical engineers work at this level, with typical design issues involving such questions as how many volts should be used to represent a 1 and how many for a 0.

Data Link Layer.   For the data link layer to work, data must be submitted to it (by the network layer) in the form of data frames of a few hundred bytes. Then the data link adds special header and trailer data at the beginning and end of each frame, respectively, so that it can recognize the frame boundaries. The data link transmits the frames in sequence to the physical layer for actual transmittal and also processes acknowledgment frames sent back by the data link layer of the receiver and makes sure that there are no transmission errors.

Network Layer.   The network layer receives a packet of data from the transport layer and adds special header data to it to identify the route that the packet is to take to its destination. This augmented packet becomes the frame passed on to the data link layer. The primary concern of the network layer is the routing of the packets. The network layer often contains an accounting function as well in order to produce billing information.

Transport Layer.   Although not illustrated by Figure 4.14, the transport layer is the first end-to-end layer encountered. In the lower layers of the OSI model, the protocols are between a sending device and its immediate neighbor, then

---

[4]These applications and others will be described in Chapters 6 through 8.

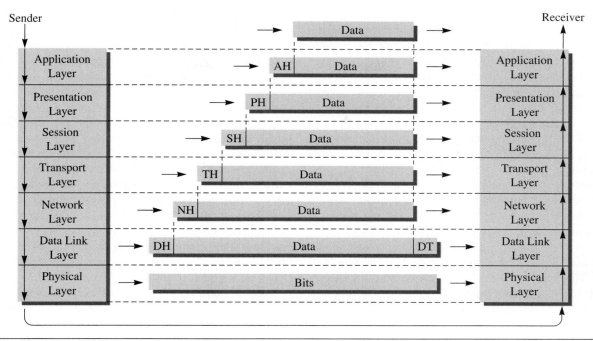

Figure 4.14   Data Transmission Based on the OSI Model

between the neighbor and its immediate neighbor, and so on until the receiving device is reached. Starting with the transport layer and continuing through the three upper layers, the conversation is directly between the layer for the sending device and the corresponding layer for the receiving device. Thus, the upper four layers are end-to-end protocols.

The transport layer receives the communication (of whatever length) from the session layer, splits it into smaller blocks if necessary, adds special header data defining the network connection(s) to be used, passes the packet(s) to the network layer, and checks to make sure that all the packets arrive correctly at the receiving end. If the network connection requires multiplexing for its efficient use, the transport layer also handles this (and in a manner transparent to the higher layers).

Session Layer.   Through the session layer, users on different machines may establish sessions between them. For most applications, the session layer is not used, but it would allow a user to log into a remote computer or to transfer a file between two computers. The session layer might provide several services to the users, including dialog control (if traffic can only move in one direction at a time) and synchronization (so that a portion of a communication received need not be retransmitted even if the network fails).

Presentation Layer.   The presentation layer, unlike the lower layers, is concerned with the information to be transmitted, rather than viewing it as a string of bits. The presentation layer accepts as input the communication as internally coded by the sending device and translates it into the standard representation used by the network. (The presentation layer on the receiving device reverses this process.) In addition, the data might be cryptographically encoded if it is especially sensitive. Like the layers below and above, the presentation layer adds a header to the data before sending it to the layer below.

Application Layer.   The uppermost layer deals with the wide variety of communications-oriented applications that are directly visible to the user, such as electronic data interchange, file transfer, electronic mail, and factory floor control. There will always be differences across different devices or systems, and a protocol is required for each application (usually implemented in software) to make each of these devices appear the same to the network. For a group of users to communicate using electronic mail, for example, the devices they employ must all use the same application layer/electronic mail protocol. The OSI electronic mail protocol, known as MOTIS, gained acceptance in some parts of the world but has largely been replaced by SMTP, which is at least unofficially part of the TCP/IP model.

Data Transmission Using the OSI Model.   Figure 4.14 provides an illustration of data transmission based on the OSI model. The sender has some data to be transmitted to the receiver. The sender, for example, might be a manager at a workstation who wishes to transmit a query to the corporate executive information system located on a large server in another state. The manager types in a query, which is temporarily stored in the workstation in electronic form. When the manager hits the Enter key, the query (data) is given to the application layer, which adds the application header (AH) and gives the resulting augmented data item to the presentation layer. The presentation layer converts the item into the appropriate network code, adds a presentation header (PH), and passes it on to the session layer. The session layer might not do anything, but if it does, it will end by attaching a session header (SH) and passing the augmented item to the transport layer. The transport layer does its work, adds a transport header (TH), and sends the resulting packet to the network layer. The network layer, in turn, does its work, adds a network header (NH), and sends the resulting frame to the data link layer. The data link layer accepts the frame, adds both a header (DH) and a trailer (DT), and sends the final bit stream to the physical layer for actual transmission to the receiver.

When the bit stream reaches the receiver, the various headers (and trailer) are stripped off one at a time as the communication moves up through the seven layers until only the original query arrives at the receiver, which, in our example, is a large server. Perhaps the easiest way to understand this entire process is that the original data go through a multilevel translation process (which is really much more than translation), with each layer acting as if it were directly communicating with the corresponding receiving layer. Most important, the entire process should take place in a device/system independent way that is totally transparent to the user.

TCP/IP   **Transmission Control Protocol/Internet Protocol (TCP/IP)** is not part of the OSI reference model, although it roughly corresponds to the network and transport layers. TCP/IP is used in many non-Internet networks, including Abilene, as well as in the UNIX and Linux operating systems and in Microsoft Windows. Most important, TCP/IP is the protocol used on the worldwide Internet and on numerous intranets operating within organizations. TCP/IP, not OSI, has become the *de facto* standard protocol for networking around the world. Nevertheless, TCP/IP is only a partial set of protocols, not a fully developed model. Thus, computer scientists and commentators have, in effect, developed an augmented TCP/IP model. First, we will

consider the TCP/IP protocols themselves, and then we will turn to the extended TCP/IP model.

The IP portion of the TCP/IP protocol corresponds roughly to the network layer of the seven-layer model, while the TCP portion corresponds approximately to the transport layer. TCP/IP accepts messages of any length, breaks them into pieces less than 64,000 bytes, sends the pieces to the designated receiver, and makes sure that the pieces are correctly delivered and placed in the right order (because they might arrive out of sequence). TCP/IP does not know the path the pieces will take and assumes that communication will be unreliable. Thus, substantial error-checking capabilities are built into TCP/IP itself to ensure reliability.

The original Internet developers envisioned the complete networking protocol as having four layers—the networking and transport layers as the middle layers, with a hardware layer below these two layers and an application layer above them (Dennis, 2003, p. 14). From a practical standpoint, this four-layer view of the world is not too different from the OSI model because the presentation and session layers are often not used. The four-layer model's hardware layer then corresponds to both the data link and physical layers of the OSI model. In this extended TCP/IP model, the application layer includes protocols such as SMTP (for e-mail), HTTP (for Web pages), and FTP (for file transfer). The transport layer is TCP, of course, and the network layer is IP. Then the hardware layer would include the various LAN standards, ATM, FTTP, ISDN, SONET, and DSL, among others. This extended TCP/IP model represents reality in terms of the standard set of networking protocols in the early twenty-first century.

SNA   The extended TCP/IP model, perhaps with some ideas borrowed from the OSI model, clearly represent the future in terms of network protocols. Nevertheless, IBM's **Systems Network Architecture (SNA)** remains an important standard. SNA, like OSI, is really a suite or grouping of protocols. IBM created SNA to allow its customers to construct their own private networks. In the original 1974 version of SNA, only a simple tree topology emanating from a single mainframe was permitted. By 1985, however, arbitrary topologies of mainframes, minicomputers, and LANs were supported, and by the early 1990s peer-to-peer networking was incorporated in SNA.

SNA is a very complicated suite of protocols because it was designed to support the incredible variety of IBM communication products, teleprocessing access methods, and data link protocols that existed before SNA. We do not need to explore the details of the SNA suite, but it might be useful to note that the newer OSI model was patterned after SNA in several ways: Both employ the concept of layering, use seven layers, and incorporate essentially the same functions. The contents of the two sets of layers, however, are quite different, especially in the middle three layers (called the network, transport, and session layers in OSI). Although IBM still supports SNA, it also supports both TCP/IP and elements of the OSI model under the umbrella of its late-1980s **Systems Application Architecture (SAA)**, which is really a philosophy rather than a set of protocols.

We now have all the pieces of the network puzzle. Network protocols provide the means by which various elements of telecommunications networks can communicate with one another. Thus, networks consist of physical media, arranged according to some topology, in a particular type of network, with communication throughout the network permitted through the use of particular protocols.

THE EXPLODING ROLE OF TELECOMMUNICATIONS AND NETWORKING

We have already stressed the critical role of telecommunications and networking several times, but to make the point even stronger, we will discuss how the role of telecommunications and networking is exploding in organizations today. In fact, many authorities suggest that the network (not the computer) is the most critical and most important information technology of the future. To illustrate this explosion, we will consider four areas of operation in which telecommunications networks are of critical and growing importance.

Online Operations

The dominant activities of many organizations have now been placed online to the computer via a network. For banks and other financial institutions, teller stations (as well as automated teller machines) are all online. Tellers directly update your account when you cash a check or make a deposit. The bank does not care what branch in what city you use because your account is always up-to-date. Not quite as obvious, insurance companies have most of their home office and branch office activities online. When an insurance claim is made or paid, when a premium is paid, or when a change is made to a policy, those activities are entered online to the insurance company network. These and other financial institutions (such as brokerage firms) simply could not operate as they do without telecommunications networks.

The computerized reservations systems of the major airlines are another example of an indispensable use of online systems. All travel agencies in the United States are now online, and computerized reservation systems constitute the core marketing strategy of the major airlines. The major airlines introduce new versions of their reservation systems every few years, with significant new features built into each revision. In the late 1990s the airlines and private vendors moved beyond the travel agencies by giving users the ability to make their own reservations online, effectively bypassing travel agencies entirely. Each of the major airlines has its own Web site where users can buy tickets and select seats on future flights. Even more capability is available on the Web sites of three major online travel companies: Travelocity (part of Sabre Holdings, a spin-off from American Airlines), Expedia (developed by Microsoft and spun off in 1996), and Orbitz (created by five airlines—American, Continental, Delta, Northwest, and United—and now part of Travelport). These sites provide information, process ticket sales for flights from all airlines, and offer other travel services such as hotel and rental car reservations. To access Travelocity, go to *www.travelocity.com;* for Expedia, go to *www.expedia.com;* and for Orbitz, go to *www.orbitz.com.*

Connectivity

Connectivity is a very popular buzzword among major U.S. and international corporations. Most large and mid-sized (and many smaller) organizations now provide a personal workstation for every managerial and professional employee, and these workstations are connected to a network structure (often an intranet) so that each employee has access to every person, and every system, with which he or she might conceivably need to interact.

Connectivity to persons and organizations outside the firm is also important. American Hospital Supply Corporation created a strategic advantage by providing connectivity with the hospitals it served. Chrysler Corporation has installed a system to tie its dealers to the corporation so that deviations from expected sales are spotted quickly. All the automobile manufacturers are stressing connectivity with their suppliers so that they can adjust orders efficiently. Thus, connectivity throughout the customer-manufacturer-supplier chain is a critical element.

Electronic Data Interchange and Electronic Commerce

Electronic data interchange (EDI) will be covered more completely in Chapter 8, but it is certainly part of the exploding role of networking. EDI is a set of standards and hardware and software technology that permits business documents (such as purchase orders, invoices, and price lists) to be transferred electronically between computers in separate organizations. For the most part, the transmission of EDI documents takes place over public networks, including the Internet. The automobile industry is perhaps the most advanced in the use of EDI, but many other firms and industries have also adopted this technology.

Electronic commerce (also called e-business) is a broad term that incorporates any use of telecommunications and networking to conduct commercial activities. EDI is part of electronic commerce, but the most explosive electronic commerce area involves commerce over the World Wide Web. Electronic commerce includes online catalogs, online ordering, online payment for goods and services, and sometimes online delivery of products. A number of virtual stores and shopping malls have been set up on the Web, and an incredible array of products is offered. One interesting and colorful electronic commerce venture is described in the box "Virtual Florist." Electronic commerce over the Web is burgeoning, and there is no end in sight. The authors of this book, for example, have purchased software and electronic books on the Web and immediately downloaded them; registered online for conferences; made hotel and airline reservations; and purchased books, CDs, and a variety of gifts on the Web for offline delivery. Shopping on the Web is becoming important for most consumers. As you will learn in Chapter 8, electronic commerce is even more important for businesses than for consumers.

Marketing

In addition to electronic commerce, telecommunications is being used for many exciting projects in the marketing area. Two examples are the use of laptop microcomputers by salespersons and the use of telecommunications for telemarketing and customer support. All business organizations sell products and services, although the distribution channels vary widely. The sales function is often performed either by sales representatives employed by the firm or by independent agents aligned with the firm (e.g., an insurance agent). In either case, telecommunications is being widely used to provide support for the sales personnel. In the last few years, instant messaging (IM) has become an important tool for customer support, especially for firms such as online retailer Lands' End and most of the major Wall Street stock and bond traders.

This sales support is not always as direct as the two examples previously mentioned. Such support often takes the form of online information describing product or service characteristics and availability. This up-to-the-minute

---

VIRTUAL FLORIST

The Virtual Florist is an Internet Web site operated by the Internet Florist, St. Paul, Minnesota, with a URL of *www. virtualflorist.com.* The home page includes the Virtual Florist logo—a bouquet of yellow tulips appearing to come out of a computer screen—in the upper left-hand corner, as well as a seasonal message just below the logo (e.g., "Send Love to Your Valentine" in late January or early February or "St. Patrick's Day: March 17" in late February or early March). Also at the top of the screen are two large buttons, one reading "SEND A Free Virtual Flower Card" and the other reading "PICK UP Your Virtual Flower Card." The rest of the home page includes a number of beautiful *real* bouquets that the Virtual Florist hopes you will buy.

You may send anyone a virtual flower card (as long as he or she has an e-mail address), and it really is free. The user picks out the appropriate virtual flower card from among a large number of screen displays of beautiful and interesting flower cards, some of which include animation. After the user personalizes the virtual flower card with a message and selects from among the available options for the card, which might include music, an animated banner, the background image, and the font style and color, an e-mail message is sent to the lucky person who is to receive the virtual flower card. Then the recipient "picks up" the virtual flower card from the Virtual Florist Web site and it is displayed on his or her screen. After several days, the virtual flower card and all records are destroyed. Of course, what the Virtual Florist wants the user to do is also to order a real bouquet. In addition to the real bouquets featured on the home page, links are available to shop by occasion, shop by product, or shop by price. The user may order online via the Web or call a toll-free telephone number. In most cases, same day delivery is available anywhere in the United States or Canada if the order is submitted by 2 P.M. in the time zone of the delivery.

[Adapted from Virtual Florist Web site, 2007]

---

information makes the sales representative or agent more competitive and increases the organization's profitability (as well as increasing the chances of retaining productive sales personnel). The importance of this instantaneous information is apparent for a St. Louis-based Merrill Lynch stockbroker talking to a client who is considering the purchase of a stock on the New York Stock Exchange, but it is almost as critical for a parts clerk at a Honda dealership in Oregon dealing with a disgruntled customer. The parts clerk can use his networked computer to check the availability of a needed part in Honda regional warehouses in the United States and can immediately place the order from the closest warehouse that has the part.

THE TELECOMMUNICATIONS INDUSTRY

There are three major segments of the telecommunications industry: (a) carriers, who own or lease the physical plant (cabling, satellites, cellular towers, and so forth) and sell the service of transmitting communications from one location to another; (b) equipment vendors, who manufacture and sell a wide range of telecommunications-related equipment, including LAN software and hardware, routers, hubs, wireless access points, digital switches, multiplexers, cellular telephones, and modems; and (c) service providers, who operate networks and deliver services through the network, or provide access to or services via the Internet. In the United States, the giant carriers are AT&T and Verizon, with the other major players including Sprint, Qwest, Alltel, and T-Mobile (Germany).[5] The major equipment vendors include Cisco Systems, Juniper Networks, Alcatel-Lucent (merged in 2006 and headquartered in France), Nortel Networks (Canada), Motorola, Nokia (Finland), and Ericsson (Sweden). The service providers include AOL, MSN, Google, Yahoo!, and a wide variety of ISPs.

As an important historical footnote, the entire complexion of the telecommunications industry changed in 1984 with the breakup of AT&T into the long-distance telephone and equipment-centered AT&T and the regional Bell operating companies (RBOCs). Although the various pieces that resulted from the divestiture were still large, there was no longer a single monolithic entity in control of most telecommunications in the United States. Just before the AT&T breakup, technological developments in long-haul communications (microwave, satellites, and fiber optics) made the development of long-distance networks to compete with those of AT&T economically feasible. Thus came the rise of MCI, Sprint, and other long-distance carriers.

The 1984 AT&T divestiture also had significant managerial implications for the telecommunications function in a user organization. Prior to 1984, the telecommunications manager had a relatively easy job, dealing with AT&T for almost all of his or her telecommunications needs and receiving high-quality, reliable service for a regulated price. After divestiture, the job got much tougher. Now the manager has to deal with a variety of carriers and equipment vendors, and also has to make sure that all the various pieces fit together. In the 1990s, the growth of

mobile telephony changed the landscape, with the rise of new wireless telephone companies, sometimes independent and sometimes associated with AT&T or one or more of the RBOCs. The recombining of the RBOCs into larger entities also began in the 1990s, culminating with SBC's merger with Ameritech in 1999 and the formation of Verizon from GTE and Bell Atlantic in 2000. In much of the world, the government-owned telephone carriers shifted to private ownership in the 1990s. In the United States, the Telecommunications Reform Act of 1996 resulted in increased competition for telephone service (both voice and data). To a great extent, everything was now up for grabs: Within limits specified by the act, the local telephone companies may enter the long-distance market and perhaps the cable television market; the cable television operators may enter the local and long-distance telephone markets; and the long-distance telephone companies may enter the local service market and perhaps the cable television market.

The twenty-first century is bringing even further changes to the telecommunications industry. In 2004, the number of cell phones in the United States passed the number of wired phones in homes. There are roughly 200 million cell phones in the United States, compared to 175 million wired home phones. The impact of Internet telephony is just beginning to be felt, but it will be big. The players in the telephone industry are changing as well. In 2005, Verizon acquired long-distance player MCI, and SBC pulled a major coup in acquiring AT&T (the long-distance leader) and subsequently changed its name to AT&T. Then in 2006, AT&T acquired BellSouth, one of the last two RBOCs that had not already been swallowed up by Verizon or AT&T. (The last remaining independent RBOC is Qwest.) AT&T's acquisition of BellSouth was doubly important because AT&T and BellSouth had jointly owned Cingular, the nation's number one wireless carrier. Thus, the new AT&T is the leading provider of wired home telephone service, the dominant supplier of telecommunications services to big U.S. businesses, the leading wireless carrier, and the leader in broadband subscribers. It seems that AT&T has been rebuilt! There is a difference, however: This time there is another giant, multifaceted telecommunications firm, Verizon, as well as three other strong competitors in the wireless arena—Sprint (which merged with Nextel), T-Mobile, and Alltel, growing competition from cable providers offering telephone and broadband services, and a number of other players (Ante and Crockett, 2005; Crockett, 2006; and Rosenbush, 2006). These are exciting—and nerve-racking—times for companies in the telecommunications industry and their customers.

---

[5]The companies listed in this section have their headquarters in the United States unless otherwise noted.

NETWORK-ENABLED UTILITY COMPUTING

Utility computing is a business model for computing in which resources (CPU power, storage space, bandwidth, etc.) are made available to the user on an as-needed basis, and the user pays for only the resources used. There are, of course, different approaches to utility computing. Some firms turn to outsourcers or service providers for these resources, while other firms are building a utility-computing infrastructure in-house so that they can provide on-demand computing resources from a pool of systems throughout the company. As an example of the external approach, Sun Microsystems has created the Sun Grid Compute Utility, where customers can access the Sun grid of servers via a Web portal. The service is quite affordable: only $1 per CPU-hour (Sun Microsystems Web site, 2007). For really big computing jobs, companies can buy time on an IBM Blue Gene supercomputer at IBM's Deep Computing Capacity on Demand Center in Rochester, Minnesota—starting at $10,000 per week (Dunn, 2005).

Development of in-house utility computing has been slower than expected, although some firms have rolled out streamlined operations through server consolidation and **virtualization** (running multiple applications with multiple operating systems on a single physical server). However, progress on in-house utility computing is occurring. In a November 2005 survey, 59 percent of the responding IT and business executives were planning for some type of utility environment in the near future, with proof-of-concept projects to be completed in 2007. For the most part, these are small, incremental projects that won't require a lot of human and financial resources—but they are a start! To be successful in a move to in-house utility computing, organizations must identify and deal with factors that might cause unintended consequences, and then must deploy services incrementally. For example, all departments must understand that utility-computing applications have to operate in a shared-resource environment, and thus departments have to be willing to cede control and management of all IT resources to the utility-operations group (Cassell and Guptill, 2006).

"Utility computing is the next biggest thing that will happen across the communications industry, the IT industry, and the consumer electronics industry," says David Tapper, an analyst with research firm IDC. "This may be the biggest disruptive technology in a century. This is real, and everybody better figure out how they are going to play in it because there will be winners and losers" (Dunn, 2004).

[Adapted from Dunn, 2004; Dunn, 2005; Cassell and Guptill, 2006; and Sun Microsystems Web site, 2007]

SUMMARY

The telecommunications and networking area has existed for considerably longer than computer hardware and software, but the developments in all three areas have merged in the past three decades to put more emphasis on telecommunications than ever before. The late 1990s and the first decade of the 2000s are the era of networking. Networks provide enhanced communication to organizations and individuals and permit the sharing of resources and data. They are also essential to implement distributed data processing and client/server systems. The exploding role of telecommunications and networking is evident in many organizational activities, including online operations and electronic commerce. There is an intense desire to improve organizational communications through universal connectivity. A communications revolution is underway, with networking—and particularly the Internet—at the heart of it.

The technology of telecommunications and networking is extremely complex, perhaps even more so than computer hardware and software. By concentrating on a number of key elements, we have developed a managerial-level understanding of networks. Communication signals may be either analog or digital. It is easier to transmit data digitally, and there is a concerted movement toward digital transmission today. Networks employ a variety of transmission media (such as twisted-pair and fiber-optic cable) and are configured in various topologies (such as rings and buses). Major network types include computer telecommunications networks, emanating from a mainframe or midrange computer; LANs for high-speed communication within a restricted area; backbone networks to connect LANs together and to connect to WANs and the Internet; WANs for communication over a long haul; and the Internet. The Internet, and especially the World Wide Web, has been front-page news over the past decade as the world has become wired. WANs and the Internet are highly dependent upon facilities owned and operated by the telephone companies and other carriers. To enable the devices attached to any type of network to communicate with one another, protocols (or rules of operation) have to be agreed upon. The success of the Internet has led to the acceptance of TCP/IP as today's *de facto* networking protocol.

We have now covered three of the four building blocks of information technology: hardware, software, and telecommunications and networking. In the next chapter, we focus on the data to be processed by the hardware and software and moved around on the networks. Whatever your personal managerial career involves, you are likely to be working both directly and indirectly with hardware, software, networking, and data. Knowledge of information technology is essential for understanding its present and potential impact on your organization and your job.

REVIEW QUESTIONS

1. What are the primary reasons for networking among computers and computer-related devices?
2. Explain the difference between analog and digital signals. Is the trend toward more use of (a) analog or (b) digital signals in the future?
3. What is a modem? When and why are modems necessary? What is a cable modem, and how does it differ from a traditional modem?
4. List the primary types of physical media in use in telecommunications networks today. Which of these media has the fastest transmission speed? The slowest transmission speed?
5. Describe the similarity between the bus and the ring topology; then describe the similarity between the star and the tree topology.
6. Identify the following acronyms or initials:

LAN	LEO	URL
WAN	FTP	ISDN
RFID	FDDI	SONET
DSL	VPN	VoIP

7. What is Bluetooth? Give examples of its use.
8. Explain the difference between Wi-Fi and WiMAX networks. Which of these network types is more important today? Is this likely to change?
9. Explain how packet switching works. Why is packet switching important?
10. What is the Internet? What is an intranet? How are they related?
11. What is the World Wide Web, and how does it relate to the Internet?
12. Three important protocols discussed in this chapter are OSI, TCP/IP, and SNA. In one or two sentences per protocol, tell what these names stand for and describe the basic purposes of these three protocols.

DISCUSSION QUESTIONS

1. Review Question 2 refers to the trend toward more digital (rather than analog) communication. In your judgment, what are the primary causes of this trend?

2. Discuss the advantages and disadvantages of the four primary types of local area networks—contention bus, token bus, token ring, and wireless.
3. What are the key differences between a LAN and a WAN? Are the differences between a LAN and a WAN becoming greater or less? Explain.
4. As noted in the chapter, the most common transmission medium is the twisted pair. Is this likely to continue to be true? Why or why not?
5. Explain the differences between accessing the Internet via a modem, ISDN, DSL, a cable modem, and satellite. Which of these access mechanisms are likely to become more important in the future?
6. List the seven layers of the OSI reference model, and give a description of the role of each layer in one or two sentences.
7. Why is the idea of a standard network protocol, such as the OSI reference model, important? What are the advantages and disadvantages of developing a single standard protocol?
8. Has the popularity of the Internet and the related adoption of TCP/IP by many organizations and networks helped or hindered the movement towards a single standard protocol such as OSI? Why?
9. Find out what types of computer networks are used at your organization (either the university at which you are taking this course or the company for which you work). Does your organization have an intranet? Does your organization have one or more LANs? What types of LANs does your organization use? Does your organization operate a WAN? Is your organization linked to the Internet? Speculate as to why your organization has developed this particular network structure.
10. Consider a large company with which you are somewhat familiar (because of your own work experience, a parent's work experience, a friend's work experience, or your study of the company). Use your imagination to suggest new ways in which the Internet could be used in this company.
11. Consider a particular small business with which you are familiar (as a customer, as a current or former employee, as a relative of the owner). Describe the current telecommunications employed by the business. In what ways might telecommunications and networking be used to improve the profitability of this business? Consider, as appropriate, such ideas as the use of facsimile communication, telemarketing, enhanced communication through a local area network, a Web home page, acceptance of orders over the Web, and cellular phones for employees.

12. What is Internet2, and how does Internet2 relate to the present Internet? What is the importance of Internet2 developments?
13. Discuss the advantages and disadvantages of wireless communication, such as Bluetooth and wireless LANs, compared to wired communication. Using your knowledge and your personal crystal ball, will wireless communication become more or less important in the future? Why?
14. Cellular telephone service has certainly become more important vis-à-vis wired telephone service over the past decade. Will this trend continue? How will the trend toward cellular service be affected by other developments in telephony such as massive increases in bandwidth through fiber-optic technology and the wider use of telephony over the Internet?
15. Explain, in your own words, the concept of utility computing. Do you believe that utility computing will have a major impact on the IT function in organizations? Why or why not? In your opinion, what are some factors that will hold back the growth of utility computing?

REFERENCES

Ante, Spencer E., and Roger O. Crockett. 2005. "Rewired and ready for combat." *BusinessWeek* (November 7): 110–113.

Bluetooth. 2007. "The official Bluetooth wireless info site." Bluetooth Web site, *www.bluetooth.com* (February).

Cassell, Jim, and Bruce Guptill. 2006. "What's holding up utility computing?" *Optimize* 52 (February): 58–62.

Crockett, Roger O. 2006. "Lord of the rings." *BusinessWeek* (March 20): 30–33.

Crockett, Roger O., Moon Ihlwan, and Catherine Yang. 2003. "How to get U.S. broadband up to speed." *BusinessWeek* (September 8): 92, 94, 96.

Dennis, Alan. 2003. *Networking in the Internet Age.* New York: John Wiley & Sons, Inc.

Dunn, Darrell. 2004. "Adopting a utility approach." *InformationWeek* 1002 (August 16/23): 62, 64, 66.

Dunn, Darrell. 2005. "Power up with utility computing." *InformationWeek* 1053 (August 29): 60, 62.

Edwards, Cliff. 2006. "A wake-up call from Craig McCaw." *BusinessWeek* (July 24): 34–35.

Ewalt, David M. 2001. "The rebirth of Iridium." *InformationWeek* Web site, *www.informationweek.com/story/showArticle.jhtml?articleID=6505188* (March 28).

FCC. 2007. "Voice over Internet Protocol." Federal Communications Commission Web site, *www.fcc.gov/voip/* (March).

Ferrell, Keith. 2003. "Report: IM abuse is rampant in workplace." *InformationWeek* Web site,*www.informationweek.com/story/showArticle.jhtml?articleID=14800189*(September 17).

FitzGerald, Jerry, and Alan Dennis. 2007. *Business Data Communications and Networking.* 9th ed. Hoboken, NJ: John Wiley & Sons, Inc.

Gates, Bill. 1995. *The Road Ahead.* New York: Viking Penguin.

Hamblen, Matthew. 2006. "Wi-Fi hot spots top 100,000." *Computerworld* Web site, *www.computerworld.com/mobiletopics/mobile/story/0,10801,107991,00.html* (January 23).

Hoover, J. Nicholas. 2006. "When RFID is everywhere." *InformationWeek* 1110 (October 16): 51–52.

Horrigan, John B. 2006. "Home broadband adoption 2006." Pew Internet & American Life Project Web site, *www.pewinternet.org/pdfs/PIP_Broadband_trends2006.pdf* (May 28).

Internet Systems Consortium. 2007. "ISC Internet domain survey, January 2007." Internet Systems Consortium Web site, *www.isc.org/index.pl?/ops/ds/* (March).

Internet World Stats. 2007. "Internet usage statistics—the big picture." Internet World Stats Web site, *www.internetworldstats.com/stats.htm* (February).

Jones, K. C. 2006. "2007 to see more RFID adoption, continuing need for training." *InformationWeek* Web site, *www.informationweek.com/story/showArticle.jhtml?articleID=196603236* (December 11).

Khermouch, Gerry, and Heather Green. 2003. "Bar codes better watch their backs." *BusinessWeek* (July 14): 42.

King, Rachael. 2006. "Internet telephony: Coming in clear." *BusinessWeek* online, *www.businessweek.com/technology/content/jul2006/tc20060710_291171.htm* (July 10).

Lacy, Sarah. 2005. "America: Still the high-speed laggard." *BusinessWeek* online, *www.businessweek.com/technology/content/apr2005/tc2005046_3472_tc206.htm* (April 6).

Lobron, Alison. 2006. "Wi-Fi wars: Loiterers can be a drag on businesses' bottom line." *Boston Globe, www.boston.com/news/local/massachusetts/articles/2006/07/09/wi_fi_wars* (July 9).

Malykhina, Elena. 2006. "Mobile handshake." *InformationWeek* 1081 (March 20): 56–57.

Maney, Kevin. 2003. "Remember those 'Iridium's going to fail' jokes? Prepare to eat your hat." *USA Today* (April 9): B3.

OECD. 2006. "OECD broadband statistics to June 2006." OECD Web site, *www.oecd.org/sti/ict/broadband* (October 13).

Ohlhorst, Frank J. 2005. "RFID signals growing stronger." *InformationWeek* Web site, *www.informationweek.com/ story/showArticle.jhtml?articleID=164903368* (June 24).

Rosenbush, Steve. 2006. "Wireless: Still too crowded?" *BusinessWeek* online, *www.businessweek.com/technology/content/may2006/tc20060501_332841.htm* (May 1).

Schine, Eric, Peter Elstrom, Amy Barrett, Gail Edmondson, and Michael Shari. 1997. "The satellite business blasts off." *BusinessWeek* (January 27): 62–70.

Sullivan, Laurie. 2005. "Where's RFID going next?" *InformationWeek* 1044 (June 20): 20–21, 24.

Sun Microsystems. 2007. "Utility computing." Sun Microsystems Web site, *www.sun.com/service/sungrid/index.jsp* (March).

Tanenbaum, Andrew S. 2003. *Computer Networks*. 4th ed. Upper Saddle River, NJ: Pearson Prentice Hall PTR.

Virtual Florist. 2007. Virtual Florist Web site, *www.virtualflorist.com* (March).

WAZTempe. 2007. "WAZTempe." WAZTempe Web site, *www.waztempe.com* (February).

Wildstrom, Stephen H. 2005. "The new Bluetooth: More on the beam." *BusinessWeek* (April 18): 24.

Wingfield, Nick. 2003. "WiFi moochers." *Wall Street Journal* (July 31): B1, B2.

Wylie, Margie. 1993. "Will networks kill the corporation?" *Network World* 10 (January 11): S9, S12.

Yang, Catherine, and Ben Elgin. 2005. "Wi-Fi with its own Zip Code." *BusinessWeek* (September 5): 39.

CHAPTER 5
THE DATA RESOURCE

THIS IS THE CONCLUDING CHAPTER OF PART I OF THIS BOOK, WHICH HAS been devoted to information technology. The previous three chapters have discussed computer systems, computer software, and telecommunications and networking—all central information technology topics. The fourth information technology component that is just as critical as those three is the data that are processed by the hardware and software and sent through the network both before and after processing. In fact, without the right data captured, stored, and disseminated, the other three components have no value. This chapter focuses on the all-important data resource.

The data resource consists of the facts and information an organization gathers while conducting business and in order to conduct business at all levels of the organization. The data resource's components include numeric, text, audio, video, and graphical data collected both within the organization and from sources external to it as well as the metadata, which describe the business and technical characteristics of the data resource. The variety and volume of data that are available to organizations has led to data being recognized as a major organizational resource, to be managed and developed like other assets, such as facilities, labor, and capital. In fact, many observers of trends in business believe that the organizations that will excel in the twenty-first century will be those that manage data and organizational knowledge as a strategic resource, understand the usefulness of data for business decisions, and structure data as efficiently as they do other assets.

Organizations are now able to collect more data than ever before through normal business activity, through the recording of data transactions from point-of-sale (POS) terminals and RFID readers, and via Web and electronic commerce sites. And the rate of growth in data is enormous. It is not uncommon for an organization to double the size of its data resource every 18 months. The amount of data added to databases in 2003 was twice that added in 1999 (*InformationWeek*, November 3, 2003). All this data can be an asset only if they are available and understood when needed and purged when no longer useful; and this cannot occur unless an organization actively organizes and manages its data. Financial resources are available to build a new plant or to buy raw materials only if a financial manager and other business managers have planned for enough funds to cover the associated cash requirements. A new product can be designed only if engineering and personnel managers have anticipated the needs for certain skills in the workforce. A business certainly would not ever think about not planning and managing facilities, labor, and capital. Similarly, data must be planned and managed.

The effort to manage organizational data is the responsibility of every business manager; some business managers, often called data stewards, are given defined roles to manage specified kinds of data like customer, product, or employee subject area data. In addition, a special management unit, usually called data or database administration, often provides overall organizational leadership in the data management function. Furthermore, some organizations have built knowledge management functions and appointed a chief knowledge officer. Every manager in an organization has some financial, personnel, equipment, and facilities/space responsibilities. Today, data must be added to this list of managed assets.

WHY MANAGE DATA?

One way to view the importance of managing the data resource is to consider the following questions:

- How much would it cost your company to not comply with Sarbanes-Oxley or other financial reporting laws because you failed to adequately control data integrity or document the source (lineage) of data in your financial statements?

- What would your company do if its critical business data, such as customer orders, product prices, account balances, or patient histories, were destroyed? Could the organization function? For how long?

- What costs would your company incur if sensitive customer, vendor, or employee data were stolen or you violated an HIPAA requirement on protecting health care data? What is the value of the trust you would lose? Can you identify fraud when customers return goods or make claims? Can you link all customer transactions together across different retail, online, and catalog sales channels to determine legitimate and unscrupulous patterns?

- How much time does your organization spend reconciling inconsistent data? Do account balances in your department always agree with those in central accounting? What happens when these figures do not agree? Are there problems with providing custom products because of different specifications by sales and engineering? Can you track a customer order all the way from receipt through production to shipping and billing in a consistent, logical way?

- How difficult is it to determine what data are stored about the part of the business you manage?

What data exist about customer sales in a particular market? In what databases do these data reside? What is the meaning of these data (e.g., do the data include lost sales, blanket orders, special orders, private label sales)? How can you gain access to these data, and who else has access to data you consider that you own?

- Do you know all the contacts a customer has with your organization? Do you know how profitable a customer is given their purchases, customer support, billing, and service and warranty activities, each with associated revenues and costs? And, based on profitability, can you make decisions on how to treat a customer whose flight is delayed, an account is temporarily overdrawn, or the customer registers a complaint?

All of these business questions have a foundation in managing data. Organizations win by making good decisions fast, and organizations cannot do so without a high-quality data resource. See the box entitled "Hurricane Windfall."

HURRICANE WINDFALL

What do customers of one of the largest retail chains, Wal-Mart, do as a hurricane is heading their way? Sure, they buy flashlights, but they also buy Pop-Tarts. This was the conclusion of Wal-Mart executives when they studied trillions of bytes of shopping history data from prior hurricane periods as they saw Hurricane Francis approaching the Florida Atlantic coast. Their ability to quickly react to changes that affect customer buying patterns turns into profits.

Wal-Mart gathers data on purchases at the POS terminals and using credit card numbers and other means enhances this data to match sales with customer demographics, inventory, supplier, and personnel data to insure that each store has enough of the right products on hand to meet customer demand—no more, no less. Even in times of emergencies.

Wal-Mart values its nearly 500 terabytes of data so much that it will not even share sales data with information brokers such as Information Resources, Inc., and ACNielsen, which buy data from retailers. Data and the ability to see patterns in the data are competitive weapons that allow Wal-Mart, for example, to dynamically reroute trucks from suppliers to better meet anticipated demand. Wal-Mart has been a leader in the use of their data resource to become a leader in their marketplace.

[Hays, 2004]

Although managing data as a resource has many general business dimensions, it is also important for the cost-effective development and operation of information systems. Poor systems development productivity is frequently due to a lack of data management, and some methods, such as prototyping, cannot work unless the source of data is clear and the data are available. Systems development time is greatly enhanced by the reuse of data and programs as new applications are designed and built. Unless data are cataloged, named in standard ways, protected but accessible to those with a need to know, and maintained with high quality, the data and the programs that capture and maintain them cannot be reused.

There are both technical and managerial issues regarding the data resource. The next section examines the technical aspects of managing the data resource that were not already covered in Chapter 3. It provides an overview of the most common tools used by database administrators (DBAs) and systems analysts for describing and managing data. As responsibilities for managing the data resource are distributed to the business units, these topics also become important to all managers.

TECHNICAL ASPECTS OF MANAGING THE DATA RESOURCE

The Data Model and Metadata

A key element in the effective management of data is an overall map for business data—a **data model**. A manufacturing company would never think about building a new product without developing a detailed design and using common components and parts from existing products where appropriate. The same is true for data. Data entities, such as customer, order, product, vendor, market, and employee, are analogous to the components of a detailed design for a product. Just as the detailed blueprint for a product shows the relationships among components, the data model shows the relationships among the data entities. A data model shows rules by which the organization operates, such as whether a customer order must be associated with a salesperson, an employee must have a social security number, or the maximum number of direct reports for a supervisor.

Data modeling involves both a methodology and a notation. The methodology includes the steps that are followed to identify and describe organizational data entities, and the notation is a way to show these findings, usually graphically. Managers must be integrally involved in these

Figure 5.1   Entity-Relationship Diagram

methodologies to insure that the data you need are planned for inclusion in organizational databases and that the data captured and stored have the required business meaning. Several possible methodologies are introduced in the following paragraphs, but the reader is referred to texts on database management for a detailed discussion of data modeling notations. Figure 5.1 shows a sample data model. Specifically, it is an **entity-relationship diagram (ERD)** that captures entities (i.e., customer, order, product) and their relationships (i.e., submits, includes).

The entity-relationship diagram is the most commonly accepted method for representing the data needs in an organization. It consists of **entities**, or the things about which data are collected, **attributes**, the actual elements of data that are to be collected, and **relationships**, the relevant associations between organizational entities. The model in Figure 5.1 could have the attributes of customer last name, customer first name, customer street, customer city, and so on to represent the data that would be captured about each customer. Because of its nontechnical nature, the ERD is a very useful tool for facilitating communication between end users who need the data and database designers and developers who will create and maintain the database.

However, an ERD is not sufficient for documenting data needs. An ERD is only part of **metadata**, or data about data, needed to unambiguously describe data for the enterprise. Metadata documents the meaning and all the business rules that govern data. For example, some metadata about an attribute of customer name would define this term, state it's properties such as maximum length and the type of data (alphanumeric characters) that a value of this attribute might have, whether every customer has to have a name to be stored in the database, whether the name can change in value over time, whether there can be multiple instances of the name, and who has rights to enter and change the name. These metadata rules come from the nature of the organization, so business managers are typically the source of the knowledge to develop these rules. You can purchase business rules and metadata repository software systems to help you manage the typically thousands of elements of metadata in an organization. Business rule software usually covers more rules than just those that address data (e.g., rules that govern when certain business processes must be used or which govern how processes are done).

Creating and maintaining high-quality metadata takes dedication, yet we cannot insure quality data without quality metadata. For example, unless everyone in the organization knows exactly what is meant by the attribute employee salary, different people might interpret values for this attribute differently. One of the authors of this text once worked in an organization that had 17 different definitions of the term customer, each relevant to different parts of the organization (e.g., billing, retail sales, and commercial sales). There were good business reasons to have 17 different interpretations, but it was confusing when people thought they were working off the same definition but were not. What this organization needed were 17 different, yet related, entities (e.g., retail customer, business customer, bill-to-customer). Eventually the organization made a commitment, using the concept of data steward, to actively manage the metadata for each subject area of the business. This allowed subtle differences in customer data to be recognized and accepted, and for data to be stored accurately. Until this was done, customers were inaccurately billed, product markets were not accurately understood, and many employees wasted much time trying to resolve misunderstandings.

Data Modeling

The role of data modeling as part of IS planning is essential. In practice, two rather different approaches are followed—one top-down, called enterprise modeling, and one bottom-up, called view integration. Many organizations choose to do both approaches because they are complementary methods that emphasize different aspects of data and, hence, check and balance each other.

The **enterprise modeling** approach involves describing the organization and its data requirements at a very high level, independent of particular reports, screens, or detailed descriptions of data processing requirements. First, the work of the organization is divided into its major functions (such as selling, billing, manufacturing, and servicing). Then each of these functions is then further divided into processes and each process into activities. An activity is usually described at a rather high level (e.g., "forecast sales for next quarter"). This three-level decomposition of the business is depicted in Figure 5.2.

Given a rough understanding of each activity, a list of data entities is then assigned to each. For example, quarterly forecasting activity might have the entities' product, customer order history, and work center associated with it. The lists of entities are then checked to make sure that consistent names are used and the meaning of each entity is clear. Finally, based on general business policies and rules of operation, relationships between the entities are identified and a **corporate data model** is drawn. Priorities are

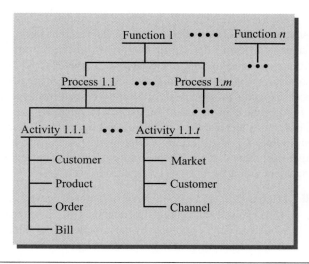

Figure 5.2 Enterprise Decomposition for Data Modeling

set for what parts of the corporate data model are in need of greatest improvement, and more detailed work assignments are defined to describe these more clearly and to revise databases accordingly.

Enterprise modeling has the advantage of not being biased by a lot of details, current databases and files, or how the business actually operates today. It is future-oriented and should identify a comprehensive set of generic data requirements. On the other hand, it can be incomplete or inaccurate because it might ignore some important details. This is where the view integration approach can help.

In **view integration**, each report, computer screen, form, document, and so on to be produced from organizational databases is identified (usually starting from what is done today). Each of these is called a user view. The data elements in each user view are identified and put into a basic structure called a normal form. **Normalization**, the process of creating simple data structures from more complex ones, consists of a set of rules that yields a data structure that is very stable and useful across many different requirements. In fact, normalization is used as a tool to rid data of troublesome anomalies associated with inserting, deleting, and updating data. When the data structure is normalized, the database can evolve with very few changes to the parts that have already been developed and populated.

After each user view has been normalized, they are all combined (or integrated) into one comprehensive description. Ideally, this integrated set of entities from normalization will match those from enterprise modeling. In practice, however, this is often not the case because of the different focuses (top-down and bottom-up) of the two approaches. Therefore, the enterprise and view-integrated data models are reconciled and a final data model is developed.

An alternative approach to enterprise modeling, which overcomes the difficulties of starting from a clean sheet of paper, is to begin not within the organization but rather from outside, using a generic data model developed for situations similar to your own. So called universal, logical, or prepackaged data models have been developed from years of experience in different industries or business areas. Consultants and database software vendors sell these starting points for your corporate data model. Such prepackaged corporate data models have several significant advantages, including:

- Data models can be developed using proven components evolved from cumulative experiences. These data models are kept up-to-date by the provider as new kinds of data are recognized in an industry (e.g., RFID).

- Projects take less time and cost because the essential components and structures are already defined and only need to be quickly customized to the particular situation.

- Because prepackaged data models are developed from best practices, your data model is easier to evolve as additional data requirements are identified for the given situation.

- Adaptation of a data model from your DBMS vendor usually means that your data model will easily work with other applications from this same vendor or their software partners.

- If multiple companies in the same industry use the same universal data model as the basis for their organizational databases, it may be easier to share data for interorganizational systems (e.g., reservation systems between rental car and airline firms).

Data modeling methods are neither simple nor inexpensive to conduct. They require considerable time, organizational commitment, and the assignment of very knowledgeable managers and data specialists. In order to deal with these concerns, certain guidelines have been developed:

- *Objective*   The modeling effort must be justified by some clear overriding need, such as coordination of operational data processing, flexibility to access data, or effectiveness of data systems. The less clear the goal, the higher the chance for failure.

- *Scope*   The coverage for a data model must be carefully considered. Generally, the broader the scope, the higher the chances for failure. Scope choices include corporate-wide, division, areas with particular high-impact needs, and a particularly important or willing business function (e.g., sales).

- *Outcome*   Choices here include a subject area database definition (e.g., all data about customers), identification of common data capture systems to be shared by several departments (replacing current separate databases), managerial and strategic databases (see Figure 5.3, which will be referred to several times in this chapter) and access services to support the information needs of these levels of management, and a more nebulous architecture for future databases. The more uncertain the outcome, the lower the chances for success.

- *Timing*   Few organizations can put all systems development on hold while a complete data model is developed. It is possible, for example, to do only a high-level data model (with just major data categories), and then fill in details as major systems projects are undertaken. This evolutionary approach might be more practical, but it must be done within the context of an initial overall, general enterprise data model.

Regardless of the approach, data modeling represents a radical change to the more traditional approach of making short-term fixes to systems. A business manager often simply wants access to needed data and is not interested in waiting for an entire data model to be built. Unless an overall data management approach is taken, however, the inconsistencies and excessive costs of poorly managed data will consume the integrity and viability of the data resource.

It should be clear that data modeling is not an issue of centralized versus decentralized control. In fact, the data administration approach (with database administrators and subject area data stewards) emphasizes placing decision-making power in the hands of those most knowledgeable about the data. Some managers (both business and IS), however, will resist data planning and modeling because they sense a loss of influence.

Database Programming

Data processing activity with a database can be specified in either procedural programs written in a 3 GL or via special-purpose languages developed for database processing. In the case of a 3 GL program, additional and more powerful instructions are added to the vocabulary of the programming language. For example, in a customer and order database the storage of a new order record not only necessitates storing the order data themselves but also updating various linkages that tie together a customer record with its associated order records. In a regular 3 GL program, instructions to write new data to the customer record, its index, the order record, and its indexes would

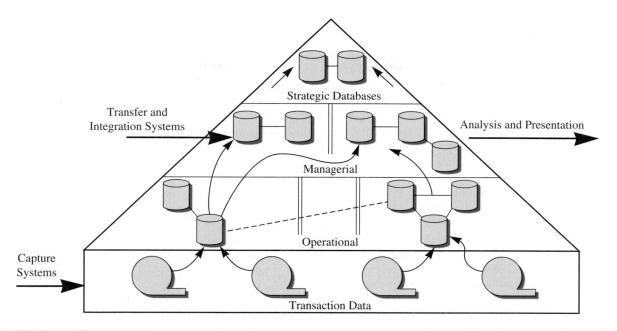

Figure 5.3   The Data Pyramid

have to be provided individually. With the commands available through the special enhancements to the language provided by the DBMS, only one instruction is needed in the program and all the associated indexes and records are updated automatically, which makes the programming task more productive and less error-prone.

More commonly today, two special purpose languages are used by themselves or in combination with 3 GLs for database access. One such 4 GL, nonprocedural special-purpose language, is called a **query language**, for posing queries to the database. The most common database 4 GL is **SQL** (Structured Query Language, often pronounced sequel), which is standardized by the International Standards Organization (ISO). Adopting such an international standard for writing database queries means that no or minimal changes will need to be made in a program you write if you change DBMSs. Using such a nonproprietary language, that is not particular to only one vendor, means that programming talent is more readily available, best practices are more common, and you are more likely protected from being locked in to one vendor.

Suppose you needed to see the order ID, customer ID, customer name, and order date for all customer orders since April 12, 2008. The following is an example SQL query to produce this result:

```
SELECT ORDER_ID, CUSTOMER_ID,
    CUSTNAME, ORDER_DATE
```

```
FROM CUSTOMER, ORDER
WHERE ORDER_DATE > '04/12/08' AND
CUSTOMER.CUSTOMER_ID =
    ORDER.CUSTOMERID;
```

The equivalent COBOL program might require 10 or more procedure division instructions. SQL can be used interactively, by entering one query at a time and getting a result for each query, or can be embedded in 3 GL programs. Languages such as COBOL, Java, C++, and PHP can include SQL with appropriate software to help these languages process the SQL. Software, called middleware, will allow SQL in programs on one computer to access data on another computer when software on both computers understand SQL, even if the SQL processors on the different computers come from different software vendors. Some software hides SQL from you. For example, statistical analysis software like SAS and business intelligence tools such as MicroStrategy actually generate very complex SQL code in order to retrieve the data needed, for example, to perform a sales forecast calculation.

When it is not possible to pass queries and data between computers using SQL, a data exchange language, **XML** (eXtensible Markup Language) often can be used. XML is used to describe the structure of data and to label data being exchanged between computer programs. XML has essentially become a standard for e-commerce data exchange because neither system (e.g., one in your company and one in one of your suppliers) needs to know anything about the database technology each is using. As long as the different organizations agree on a schema (similar to a data model) for data and what labels to use for different pieces of data, data can be exchanged.

XML is the basis for Web services, which is a scheme for sharing programs and data across the Internet. For example, suppose your organization, a manufacturing company, participates in an industry that has created a common schema for data the companies need to share (many industries, like automotive, travel, and health care, have done this). Further suppose that you allow your customers to place orders via the Web. Your organization writes programs, say in Java and Microsoft's ASP, to process orders via Web pages. When a customer places an order, your order entry program checks inventory to see if the order can be fulfilled without delay. When your warehouse is out of stock, you'd like to be able to check inventory in one of your suppliers. With XML you can send over the Internet a document with the product identifier being ordered to a Web Service on your supplier's computer systems; that Web Service will respond with the description of the item, its on-hand inventory level, and any costs associated with filling from the supplier's inventory. With this data, your e-commerce site programs can determine what to display to your customer. XML is used in this case to indicate what data are being exchanged by using labels or tags (similar to HTML) that both organizations understand. In neither case, however, does either organization have to understand the programs, computers, or database management systems the other is using.

MANAGERIAL ISSUES IN MANAGING DATA

Having considered key technical issues involved in managing data, let us now turn to managerial issues. How to plan for data, to control data integrity, to secure access to and use data, and to make data accessible are important to the business manager. As with any business resource, quality sources for data must be identified and the data acquired; enough space must be available for data storage; obsolete data must be identified, disposed of, or archived; and usage of data must be accounted for, and, if appropriate, usage fees should be charged to those utilizing the data. These are not just issues for the IS organization—the business manager should be equipped to deal with these issues as well.

Principles in Managing Data

Successful management of the data resource depends on understanding certain key guidelines:

The Need to Manage Data Is Permanent   Any organization has customers or clients, whether these are other organizations, individual consumers, or patients. Whether a company makes to stock or to order, there are vendors or suppliers, orders or reservations, products or services, and employees. Further, irrespective of how accounting, selling, billing, or any other management activity is performed, there still will be data about customers, vendors, orders, products, and employees. Data values might change, new customers might be added, products discontinued, and employees hired and retired, but a company will always have customers, products, employees, and other entities about which it needs to keep current data. Occurrences of data are volatile, but the existence of data is persistent and the need for excellent data management is constant. Business processes change, and so must information systems. If the company decides to change a sales forecasting method, programs will have to be rewritten, but customer, order, and general economic condition data are still needed. In fact, if data are well-managed, many of the databases will remain relatively unchanged when an organization decides to change the way it does business. At the same time, the programs that analyze, process, and report information might change drastically. Thus, data are fundamental to the business. Data remain over time and need to be managed over time.

Data Can Exist at Several Levels   Although the business retains vast amounts of data, there might be relatively few basic classes of data on which to base most information. One way to organize data is called the data pyramid (as depicted in Figure 5.3). Although new data can enter this pyramid at any level, most new data are captured at the base of the pyramid in operational databases. These databases contain the business transaction history of customer orders, purchases from suppliers, internal work orders, changes to the general ledger, personnel transfers, and other day-to-day business activities. Managerial control and strategic databases (often called data warehousing and used to support decision making and business intelligence) are typically subsets, summaries, or aggregations of operational databases, with key external data as supplements. For example, a database for sales forecasting (a managerial function) might contain past monthly summaries of sales by product family or geographical area derived from customer orders and product data. These data might be

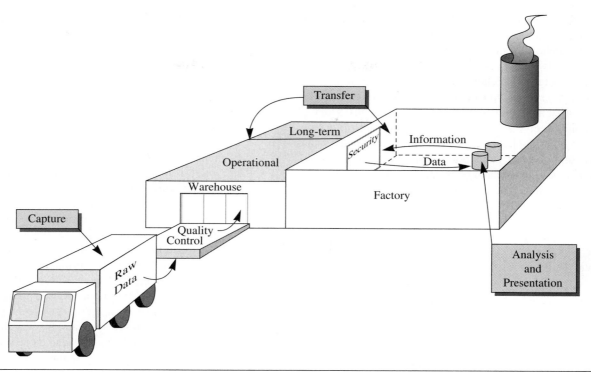

Figure 5.4   Categories of Information Processing with Application Independence

supplemented with external economic indicators and sales force judgments to produce sales estimates needed for production planning and scheduling.

When managerial databases are constructed from sources other than internal, shared operational databases, there can be significant inconsistencies. For example, the sales organization might track customer orders in a local database before passing these on to order entry. If they use these figures for forecasting final sales, they might not consider canceled orders, orders rejected due to insufficient credit, returned goods, or sales not met because of inadequate production capacity. These information items might not be considered because they enter the business at other points of contact with the customer. A well-run organization must consider all the transactions that define sales level to be able to build an accurate sales forecasting system.

Developing an understanding of the relationships between data in various databases is a critical element of managing the data resource. Ideally, aggregate data will be derived from operational data, not collected separately (and, hence, inconsistently), and different databases will receive data transferred from a common source. The systems that populate these databases, move data, and produce reports are described later in this chapter.

Application Software Should Be Separate from the Database   One goal of data management is **application independence**, the separation, or decoupling, of data from applications systems. This concept, embodied in Figure 5.3, is further illustrated in Figure 5.4.

In this figure the processing of data into **information** is viewed like the processing of the raw and component material resources into final products in a manufacturing company. Raw data are captured or received, inspected for quality, and stored in the raw material, or operational, warehouse. Data in storage are used in the production of any authorized information product (e.g., report). Data are retrieved from the warehouse when needed but, unlike raw materials, are not consumed when used. As operational data become obsolete (e.g., product price increase), they are replaced with new data. Somewhat different from our manufacturing analogy, in order to understand trends and patterns, snapshots of data are periodically transferred to a long-term data warehouse. The long-term data warehouse allows historical transactions to be understood within the context of the characteristics of customers, products, facilities, and the like at the time of the transactions, not just the current situation. Data are transferred from operational and historical sources to other parts of the organization or other organizations when authorized. As data are processed into information (e.g., sales forecast), this information is added to the warehouse, similar to the entry of products into finished goods storage. All operations and work centers use the raw material warehouse to produce information products (e.g., reports), but individual work centers (applications) may have their own work-in-process inventory of data and receive a few kinds of data that are not shared among other applications. Thus, data are cataloged, managed, and, at least conceptually, stored centrally, where they can be kept safe and uncontaminated for use throughout the business.

The central point of Figure 5.4 is that data and applications software must be managed as separate entities. When treated separately, data are not locked inside applications, where their meaning and structure are hidden from other applications that also require these data.

Application Software Can Be Classified by How They Treat Data   The concept of application independence suggests that different data processing applications can be classified into three groups, based upon their role in managing data: data capture, data transfer, and data analysis and presentation, as shown in Figure 5.3.

The process of transforming data into information useful for transaction management or higher-level decision making includes these steps:

1. *Data capture*   **Data capture applications** gather data and populate the database. They store and maintain data in the data pyramid of Figure 5.3. Ideally, each datum is captured once and fully tested for accuracy and completeness. Responsibility for ensuring the quality of data capture systems might be distributed across the organization. Localized data capture applications are developed for data with an isolated use or data for which coordination across units is not required. Still, because localized data might eventually be useful somewhere else in the organization (and they must then be consistent across sites), an inventory of data elements (in a metadata repository) must be maintained of all database contents.
2. *Data transfer*   **Data transfer and integration applications** move data from one database to another or otherwise bring together data from various databases to meet some processing need. These applications are often called bridges or interfaces because they connect related databases. Once raw data are captured, they might be extracted, transformed for new purposes, and loaded into various databases where they are stored for specific purposes. For

example, customer order data might be stored in multiple subject or target area databases supporting production scheduling, billing, and customer service. Also, this kind of application extracts and summarizes data, as well as distributes copies of original data. Ideally, this transfer would be event-triggered; that is, if new basic data are captured or changed in value, messages are sent as needed to all other databases that build on these data to alert these databases that changes have occurred.

3. *Data analysis and presentation*   **Data analysis and presentation applications** provide data and information to authorized persons. Data might be summarized, compared to history, reformulated into graphs, or inserted into documents being developed using a word processor. Data might be input to a decision support system or executive information system (to be discussed in Chapter 7). Data analysis and presentation applications can draw upon any and all data from databases the business manager receiving the presentation is authorized to see. Data and the way they are presented should be independent, and those who determine the format for presentation should not necessarily control the location and format for capture and storage of data.

Application Software Should Be Considered Disposable   A significant result of application independence is the creation of **disposable applications**. In many organizations, older systems cannot be eliminated or easily rewritten because applications and data are so intertwined. When the presentation capabilities of an application system become obsolete, but the application also maintains data that are essential to the business, an inefficient system might have to be kept alive only for its data access capabilities. With application independence, a company can replace the capture, transfer, and presentation software modules separately when necessary. Presentation systems are often the most volatile types of applications, and these types of systems provide management with business value. In addition, with modern programming languages and system generators, business managers can customize their own presentation and analysis software to meet personal needs.

Data Should Be Captured Once   Another implication of the separation of data from applications is that data should be captured at one source and, even when not shared from one common database, synchronized across different databases. It is simply too costly for an organization to capture the same data multiple times and reconcile differences across applications. For example, not long ago, a university discovered during a review of its application systems that 12 different systems captured a student's home address. The redundant data management cost was estimated at several hundred thousand dollars per year. Thus, an IT architecture based on application independence permits a more responsive, flexible, and beneficial approach for managing the data resource.

Figure 5.3 illustrates one way to view the data architecture (more on the information architecture, which includes the data architecture, in Part IV). The **data architecture** of an organization should contain an inventory of the uses of data across the business units. The architecture should also include a plan to distribute data to various databases to support the analysis and presentation needs of different user groups. The same data might be stored in multiple databases because that is the most efficient architecture to deliver data to users. To ensure that data are current, accurate, and synchronized across the organization, however, key business data should be captured once and transferred between databases as needed.

There Should Be Strict Data Standards   Because the same and similar data are used in various application software, data must be clearly identified and defined so that all users know exactly what data they are manipulating. Further, shared databases and data transfer systems require that database contents be unambiguously defined and described (metadata). The central responsibility in managing the data resource is to develop a clear and useful way to uniquely identify every instance of data and to give unambiguous business meaning to all data. For example, an organization must be able to distinguish data about one customer from data about another. Furthermore, the meaning of such data as product description and product specification must be clear and distinct.

Figure 5.5 lists the five types of **data standards** that must be established for a business: identifiers, naming, definition, integrity rules, and usage rights. Business managers, not IS managers, have the knowledge necessary to set these standards and therefore should actively participate in the standards-setting process. Often this participation happens through the role of **data steward**, who is a business manager responsible for the quality of data in a particular subject or process area.

1. *Identifier*   The identifier is a characteristic of a business object or event (a data entity) that uniquely distinguishes one instance of this entity from every other instance. For example, an employee number is a distinctive feature of each employee, and a unique bill-of-lading number clearly identifies each shipment. It is not uncommon to find applications in

Identifier:	Unique value for each business entity
Naming:	Unique name or label for each type of data
Definition:	Unambiguous description for each type of data
Integrity Rule:	Specification of legitimate values for a type of data
Usage Rights:	Security clearances for a type of data

Figure 5.5   Types of Data Standards

different units of a business using different identifiers for the same entity. As long as there is a one-for-one match of identifier values across the various systems, there is not a problem, but usually there is no such compatibility. The ideal identifier is one that is guaranteed to be unique and is stable for a long time. For example, a hospital might wish to use a social security number to identify a patient. Also, identifiers related to meaningful data tend not to be desirable because they are not stable. For example, a customer identification number based on geographical region and standard industrial classification (SIC) code will no longer be valid if a customer moves or changes primary businesses. Thus, it is wise to design a meaningless, sequentially assigned code as the identifier, and use such data as geographical location and SIC code as other descriptive data.

2. *Naming*   Distinct and meaningful names must be given to each kind of data retained in organizational databases. If two data elements have the same name, their meaning will be confusing to users. If the same data element is referred to by different names that are never associated, business managers will think that these are different pieces of data. Many organizations develop a naming scheme or template for constructing all data names, with common terms to be used for different elements of the scheme. For example, a data name of employee-monthly-pay indicates which entity, which time period, and which type of data. Each of the three components of this data name would be limited to a restricted vocabulary; for example, the time period would have values such as daily and weekly, and abbreviations for each could be assigned. Standard names make naming new data elements easier and give a user a quick start on knowing what data are on a report or in a certain database.

3. *Definition* Each data entity and element is given a description that clarifies its meaning. The definition should apply to all business circumstances and users. Terms such as *customer*, *employee*, and *product* might, surprisingly, not have universal meaning. For example, does customer refer to someone who has bought from you or any potential consumer of your products or services? Over the years different parts of the business might have developed their own interpretation of such terms, so definitions must be constructed through review by a broad range of organizational units.

4. *Integrity rules* The permissible range or set of values must be clear for each data element. These **integrity rules** add to the meaning of data conveyed by data definitions and names. For example, a data element of region is probably limited to some set of valid values based upon sales territories or some other artificial construct. In addition, a central and single standard for valid values can be used by those developing all data capture applications to detect mistakes. Also, because exceptions might be permitted, the integrity rules might specify who can authorize deviations or under what circumstances values outside of the valid set can be authorized.

5. *Usage rights* These standards prescribe who can do what and when to each type of data. Such security standards state the permissible uses for every type of data (e.g., whole databases, individual files in a database, particular records, or data elements in a file). For example, a business manager might be restricted to retrieving only the employee-monthly-pay data element, only during regular business hours, from an authorized terminal, and only about herself and those people she supervises.

These data standards should be retained in a standards database called a **metadata repository** or **data dictionary/directory (DD/D)**. This central repository of data about data helps users learn more about organizational databases. Database management systems should also use the DD/D to access and authorize use of data.

Master Data Must Conform Almost all information systems and databases refer to common subject areas of data (people, things, places), and often enhance that common data with local data relevant to only that application or database. All applications that use common data from these areas, such as customer, product, employee, invoice, and facility must refer to the same values or different parts of the organization cannot talk with one another without confusion. **Master data management (MDM)** refers to the

disciplines, technologies, and methods to ensure the currency, meaning, and quality of reference data within and across various subject areas (White and Imhoff, 2006). MDM ensures that everyone knows the current description of a product, the current salary of an employee, and the current billing address of a customer. MDM does not address sharing transactional data, such as customer purchases.

No one source system usually contains the "golden record" of all relevant facts about a data subject. For example, customer master data might be integrated from customer relationship management, billing, ERP, and purchased data sources. MDM determines the best source for each piece of data (e.g., customer address or name) and makes sure that all applications reference the same virtual "golden record."

There are three popular architectures for master data management: identity registry, integration hub, and persistent. In the registry approach, the master data remains in their source systems, and applications refer to the registry to determine where the agreed upon source of particular data (such as customer address) resides. The registry helps each system match its master record with corresponding master records in other source systems. Thus, an application may have to access several databases to retrieve all the data it needs, and a database may need to allow more applications to access it. In the integration hub approach, data changes are broadcast through a central service to all subscribing databases. Redundant data are kept, but there are mechanisms to ensure consistency yet each application does not have to collect and maintain all of the data it needs. In the persistent approach, one consolidated record is maintained and all applications draw on that one actual "golden record" for the common data. Thus, considerable work is necessary to push all data captured in each application to the persistent record so that it contains the most recent values and to go to the persistent record when any system needs common data.

MDM supports all uses of data, from operational to business intelligence. In good MDM, there is no delay for any application in knowing any fact about master data. For MDM to be successful, an organization must create a strong data governance process, often including data stewards. We will describe data governance later in this chapter. MDM requires a discipline around managing data.

But, does MDM pay off. The general benefit is that the whole enterprise works from a single version of the truth about key organizational data. This consistency and only planned redundancy reduces errors, misunderstandings, and wasted efforts to reconcile differences across business units and with stakeholders. Also, the impact of changes of key data values or even data models can be huge when master data are not carefully managed. MDM also greatly simplifies satisfying the data quality requirements of various regulations such as Sarbanes-Oxley, HIPAA, and Basel II (Russom, 2006). Here is an example of the logic to justify customer master data management and a strong program for data governance: Consistent data drives better data matching, better matching drives better customer identification and modeling, better identification and modeling drives better customer interactions and campaigns, better interactions and campaigns yields higher hit ratio, and higher hit ratios result in more revenues (Dyché, 2006). The root of this chain is MDM.

The Data Management Process

A manager of real estate, personnel, or finances is familiar with the basic but essential functions necessary to manage effectively those resources. Figure 5.6 lists the generic functions for managing any business resource. This section examines each of these functions within the context of data management. An important point to note is that, as with other resources, every business manager should be involved, in some way, in every one of these functions for data.

1. *Plan* Data resource planning develops a blueprint for data and the relationships among data across business units and functions. As with most plans, there will be a macro level data plan, typically called an enterprise data model, to identify data entities and relationships among the entities and more detailed plans to define schedules for the implementation of databases for different parts of this blueprint. The plan identifies which data are required, where they are used in the business, how they will be used (i.e., what they will be used to produce), and how much data are expected. This plan must then be communicated to all business functions that are involved in aspects of data resource management. For example, system capacity planning must be informed of this schedule, along with data and processing volumes, so that adequate computer and network technology can be in place to operate and access these databases.

2. *Source* Decisions must be made about the timeliest and highest-quality source for each data element required. For example, should customer sales data be collected at point-of-sale or entered later? Concerns over error rates, frequency of changes, chance of lost paper documents, technology costs, training requirements, and many other factors will influence this decision. For data to be acquired from sources external to the organization, the quality, cost, and timeliness of

- Plan
- Source
- Acquire and Maintain
- Define/Describe and Inventory
- Organize and Make Accessible
- Control Quality and Integrity
- Protect and Secure
- Account for Use
- Recover/Restore and Upgrade
- Determine Retention and Dispose
- Train and Consult for Effective Use

Figure 5.6 Asset Management Functions

these sources need to be considered. For example, different market research organizations might collect competitive sales data from retail outlets or telephone surveys. When selecting an external data source, the original source, the reliability of the data, the timing of when the data are needed and when they were collected, the precision and detail collected, and other factors should be checked. A master data management program often drives decisions about data sources.

3. *Acquire and Maintain* Once the best sources for data are identified and selected, data capture systems must be built to acquire and maintain these data. Changes in data need to be broadcast (via master data management techniques and technologies) to all databases that store these data. Users of the data need to know when the data are refreshed and perhaps automatically be informed of exceptional conditions (such as inventory being out of stock, stock price below a critical level, or receipt of an especially large customer order). Appropriate applications systems need to be built to track data acquisition and transfer. For example, suppose electronic files of customer list data are sent to telemarketing vendors for a promotional campaign and results are returned via the Internet. A system is needed to confirm that all files were sent and received, that all customers on the list were called, and that a status is received on each.

4. *Define/Describe and Inventory* A basic step in managing any resource is defining what is being managed. For a real estate manager, each property must be

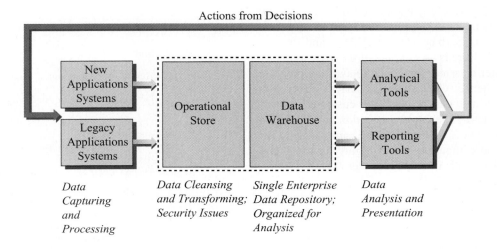

Figure 5.7   The Data Warehouse

described, standards and scales must be set to define the size and shape of each building or land parcel, and terminology must be defined to refer to different pieces of each building. Similarly, in managing data, each data entity, data element, and relationship must be defined, a format for storage and reporting established, and the organization of the data described so users know how to access the data. As mentioned earlier, a metadata inventory catalog must be maintained, usually using a DD/D, where all data definitions and descriptions are kept, volume statistics on data are maintained, and other data about data (such as access rights and integrity rules) are stored. All users can go to the metadata repository and data dictionary to find out what data exist and what the data mean.

5. *Organize and Make Accessible*   Databases need to be designed so that data can be retrieved and reported efficiently and in the format that business managers require. Data should be arranged and stored so that information can be produced easily. Although most of the work here is rather technical, this physical arrangement of data cannot be done unless potential uses of the data are well-defined, and this task is best done by business managers. The two aspects of data usage necessary for proper organization are what data are required and how the data are to be selected. For example, database designers need to know if customer data will be selected by markets, geographical regions, what products they have bought, through what sales staff they buy, or other criteria. Orders of magnitude improvements in processing speed can be achieved when the data organization is well-tuned to the

processing requirements. Of course, wise choices of database designs can similarly achieve significant reductions in the cost of maintaining and processing data.

One highly popular method for making data accessible to many people in an organization for decision making and business intelligence is the data warehouse (see Chapter 6 for more on data warehousing). Figure 5.7 depicts how a large division of a furniture manufacturer recently implemented a data warehouse. Prior to the creation of the data warehouse, the company operated several legacy applications systems, each containing data difficult to extract but needed by other units in the company. Likewise, because of the way data were organized, it was difficult to analyze the data residing in these application systems. A data warehouse was created whereby certain data from each existing system and data from new systems that were built were extracted on a regular basis and put in the operational store. In this facility the data were cleansed and organized for analytical applications (e.g., by product versus by order) and transferred to the data warehouse. Analysts thus have a historical set of data available from each plant and for all product lines. With the data warehouse in place, the furniture manufacturer is beginning to employ data mining techniques (to be discussed in Chapter 7) to aid in areas such as analysis and forecasting. Eventually, improvements in forecasting ability and reductions in lost analyst time from the creation of this data warehouse are estimated to generate a 31 percent return on investment. See the box "Birth of a Legend" concerning data warehousing.

BIRTH OF A LEGEND

If your job has anything to do with data warehouses, you have heard of the tale about the correlation between purchases of diapers and purchases of beer. The statistical oddity, duly reported in at least 200 articles, is variously attributed to Wal-Mart, Thrifty PayLess stores, or an unidentified grocery chain. Whichever, the retailer supposedly rearranged its shelves and sold more diapers and more beer.

Where did this tale start? It appears to have come from one Thomas Blischok, now chief executive of Decisioneering Group in Scottsdale, Arizona. As vice president of industry consulting for NCR, he was doing a study for American Stores's Osco Drugs in 1992 when he discovered dozens of correlations, including one connecting beer and diapers in transactions between 5 P.M. and 7 P.M.

Blischok recounted the tale in a speech, and it became the stuff of consultants' pitches, trade magazine articles, and ads. But did Osco rearrange its beer or diaper shelves as a result? Nope.

[Rao, 1998]

GOOD, CLEAN DATA

The costs of dirty data and poorly managed data are staggering. According to a survey by PricewaterhouseCoopers, poor data management costs global organizations more than $1.4 billion per year. A study conducted by the Data Warehouse Institute found that erroneous mailings cost U.S. business about $611 billion in 2002.

Data quality is a critical issue that is slowly coming to the forefront in businesses today. Two key reasons for poor data quality are the rush to install new systems and the failure to take an integrated view of the organization's data. In the rush to install a new system, many organizations fail to look critically at their existing data. Often, these new systems support a single function, and while the data might get cleaned up for that function, the source of the errors is often overlooked.

There are several critical steps in a data quality initiative:

1. Establish processes to prevent errors.
   a. Assign a person in each area to verify the data's quality.
   b. Structure databases so that fields are consistent across areas.
2. Clean up existing errors.
3. Verify that third-party data suppliers provide clean data.
4. Focus on the critical data.
5. Don't rely too heavily on cleanup tools; focus on prevention instead.

[Adapted from Turek, 2003, and Betts, 2001]

6. *Control Quality and Integrity*   As with employee certification, audits of financial records, and tests for hazardous materials or structural defects in buildings, quality and integrity controls must be placed on the data resource. The concept of application independence implies that such controls must be stored as part of the data definitions and enforced during data capture and maintenance. In addition, periodic checks of databases should be made as part of the audit of financial records. As with other quality assurance functions, the check of data quality should be assigned to an organization that is not directly responsible for storing and managing the data.

Data quality is an especially critical issue when data are considered a corporate asset (see the box entitled "Good, Clean Data"). The more data are used to support organizational operations, the cleaner the data should be. For example, when the data are combined with a customer relationship management (CRM) application, data quality problems can lead to mismanaged relationships and result in lost sales. Data are essential in enterprise resource planning (ERP) systems, CRM, and data warehousing. The quality of the data has a direct relationship to the quality of the processes performed by these systems.

Data quality initiatives, like master data management, can be difficult to justify. These programs look like overhead. So, where are the benefits? Most often the benefits come from greater confidence in

information. Greater confidence leads to more rapid decisions. Other benefits include less time spent reconciling data, increased customer satisfaction (because we deal with customers in consistent ways), and ultimately reduced costs and increased revenues.

7. *Protect and Secure*   The rights each manager has to each type of data must be defined. Privileges for use of data might include definition, retrieval, insertion, deletion, update, and retrieval of the datum by itself or in combination with other values. For example, a business manager might be permitted to see the salaries of everyone in his department but might not be able to match names with salaries. Privileges can be assigned to programs, databases, files, individual records or data elements, terminals, and workstations. Use of other equipment, data, and programs might be limited by time of day or days of the week. The decision on who has the right to do what with data is a delicate balance between the need to protect

the quality and integrity of data by protecting a valuable asset from damage or theft and the right of individuals to have easy access to the data they need in their jobs. Because security is so important and can be dysfunctional if managed improperly, security should be considered when databases and application systems are originally built and not developed as an afterthought.

8. *Account for Use*   Because there is considerable cost to capture, maintain, and report data, these costs must be identified and an accounting system developed to report them. Further, an organization might choose to distribute the costs to appropriate responsibility centers. Two conditions make accounting for the use of data especially difficult as compared to other information resources. First, frequently the organizational unit responsible for acquiring data is not the primary user of the data. Second, usage is shared because data are not consumed from usage. The operating system and database management systems can capture the actual costs of computer disk storage and computer processing time. The real issue is to develop a fair charging scheme that promotes good management of data but does not deter beneficial use. Because the value of data is so elusive, the linkage of readily identifiable costs to value is difficult. At a minimum, the costs for data storage and processing and who uses which data can be determined. Of course, how to charge to recover these costs is a separate and more difficult issue.

9. *Recover/Restore and Upgrade*   When an asset becomes old or damaged, it is often renovated and put back into operation. When an employee's skills become obsolete because of new technology or methods, the employee is trained for the new environment. The same process is true with organizational data. When a database is damaged because of some hardware or software malfunction, procedures must be in place to restore the database to a clean and uncontaminated condition. Usually, periodic backup copies of the database will be made and an electronic log will be kept of updates to the database so the restoration can happen quickly. The business manager must anticipate what needs to be done in the business when a database is not accessible because of a recovery or upgrading that temporarily takes the database out of action. In addition, the business manager must be able to determine what wrong actions or decisions might have been taken from the bad data and correct them before they cause excess costs or other problems for the business. For example, if an inventory file has been inaccurately changed and inventory

replenishment orders have been written, an inventory control manager should immediately analyze whether work, purchase, or expedited orders should be recalled.

10. *Determine Retention and Dispose*   Business managers must decide, on legal and other grounds, how much data history needs to be kept. Some data need to be kept in active databases, while other data may be archived to be used only when needed. Eventually, data should be summarized, eliminated, and/or moved to the data warehouse. Keeping data too long is not only costly in terms of storage space, but the use of out-of-date data can also bias forecasts and other analyses. With the trend toward data warehousing, a new mechanism exists to retain data to aid in organizational decision making. Wal-Mart, for example, has been storing data in its data warehouse since the late 1980s. Although this might not be appropriate for all organizations, Wal-Mart is in the enviable position of being able to examine and predict from over a decade's worth of buying trends. Every organization should have a policy on data retention that is consistent with the organization's strategy and use of data.

11. *Train and Consult for Effective Use*   Just because data exist, they will not necessarily be effectively used. What data are stored in databases, what they mean, what presentation systems report these data, and how they can be accessed in ad hoc ways all have to be explained to business managers who might want to use the data. This training might include review of the contents of the corporate data dictionary, with an emphasis on a particular user group (e.g., consumer marketing), or the training might be on how to use a statistical package (like SAS) to access a database for decision support.

Data Management Policies

The implementation of these concepts and processes for data management occurs differently in each organization. However, policies should be developed regarding data ownership and data administration. These policies are typically developed from a process called **data governance**. Data governance is an organizational process for establishing strategy, objectives, and policies for organizational data—that is, to oversee data stewardship, even overseeing local data stewards responsible for similar activities for specific data subject areas or business units. Data governance is a subset of IT governance, which will be reviewed in Chapter 15. The goal of data governance is to create and maintain an enterprise view of data through collaboration and a common agenda. Data governance includes high-level oversight of day-to-day data management activities.

Frequently data governance happens through a data governance council, whose members come from IT and a variety of key business areas, including data stewards. This council meets regularly—it is not ad hoc—to address high-level issues. The council sets standards by which day-to-day decisions about metadata, data ownership and access rights, data infrastructure and architecture, and other areas can be made. The council communicates to executive management about challenges and opportunities. The council gets its mandate from senior executives who see the value of managing the data asset. The council also communicates to data stewards, administrations, project managers, and other internal information system stakeholders about their decisions. The council may also audit that policies and processes it establishes are being followed, and may review periodic reports about data quality to determine if new policies need to be established, existing policies need to be better communicated, or policy violators (particular data stewards, application developers or project leaders, business managers, and others) need to be handled.

In today's world, a data governance council may have responsibility for insuring that regulations on quality of financial reporting are supported by sound data quality management practices. This means, in part, that policies must be transparent, procedures for enforcement are well-established and consistently followed, and that the policies are effective to ensure accurate and reliable information. Internal controls are a major focus of such regulations. The data governance councils oversee that proper data integrity controls are in place on databases and metadata repositories so that changes to data and metadata are properly processed and fraud and security breaches are deterred. Fundamentally, if proper controls are not placed on data, it is very difficult to show compliance with financial reporting rules.

Now, let us review two of the key policy areas for data governance: data ownership and data administration.

Data Ownership Business managers can become very possessive about data, for both business and personal reasons such as:

- the need to protect personal privacy
- the need to protect trade secrets
- the requirement to allow only those with a need to know to see sensitive business or product plans
- the desire to promote internal competition and to justify the use of scarce resources

- the desire to show commitment to one's job and ownership of the data needed to carry out one's job
- the desire to use information as power for political gain

This protectiveness is both good and bad. A commitment to quality data, cost control of data management, and use of data for strategic advantage are essential for obtaining the greatest benefits from managing the data resource. On the other hand, possessiveness about data can stifle data sharing, which can limit access to data (and, hence, reduce the ability to answer important business questions) and increase data processing costs for the whole enterprise. The culture about data must be managed as part of data resource management.

A **corporate information policy** is the foundation for managing the ownership of data. Figure 5.8 contains a data access policy statement developed in late 2000 for a large Midwestern manufacturer of truck parts. The president and the chief information officer (CIO) developed this policy after it was clear that many managers were not sharing data useful to others in the corporation. The new policy was communicated to all managers through a series of written announcements and staff meetings. This policy states that each manager has responsibility for managing data as a resource for the good of the whole enterprise, not just the gain of his area. Some policies will distinguish among classes of data—such as personal, departmental, and organizational—although the trend is to make all data organizational.

As organizations and the markets they serve become more global, issues of international regulations, standards, and cultures relating to data ownership can have major impacts on data management. One specific issue is relevant in the discussion of data ownership—regulation of the flow of data across international boundaries.

Transborder data flows are electronic movements of data that cross a country's national boundary for processing, storage, or retrieval of that data in a foreign country. Data are subject to the laws of the exporting country. Legislation to control transborder data flows varies widely from country to country. These laws are justified by the perceived need to

- prevent economic and cultural imperialism, including preventing the change of social values (a kind of antipropaganda mentality) and preventing the usurpation of local decisions by multinational headquarters outside the country

Data is a corporate resource. Much of our corporate data is stored electronically. Excellence in data management is key to achieving many of our business goals.

The following statements constitute our electronic data access policy:

- Corporate data will be shared internally. Data are not owned by a particular individual or organization, but by the whole organization.
- Data will be managed as a corporate resource. Data organization and structure will be planned at the appropriate levels and in an integrated fashion.
- Data quality will be actively managed. Explicit criteria for data accuracy, availability, accessibility, and ease of use will be written by the IS department.
- Data will be safeguarded. As a corporate asset, data will be protected from deliberate or unintentional alteration, destruction, or inappropriate disclosure.
- Data will be defined explicitly. Standards will be developed for data representation.
- Databases will be logically designed to satisfy broad business functions.

Figure 5.8 Example Data Access Policy

- protect domestic industry, including protecting the local computer hardware, software, and services industry
- protect individual privacy, including protecting individual citizens against storage of personal health, employment, and political affiliation data in databases held in foreign countries
- foster international trade, including measures to make the flow of data easy during desirable international trade and to promote the exporting of information technology and services

Mechanisms to control transborder data flows include tariffs, ministries of telecommunication and trade to formulate and implement policies, and formal application processes for conducting data processing activities in the country. Often no one administrative body has overall authority, and there is very little similarity of mechanisms from country to country. International standards bodies on data communications, programming languages, and electronics help to reduce many operational problems, but policy matters still have to be negotiated, often separately with each country.

Data Administration   To better manage data, many organizations have created a unit to lead the efforts in data management. Typically, this group is called **data**

administration, although other terms may be used. This group often reports as a staff unit to the IS director, although other structures are possible. In any case, the company should have a data governance policy that outlines the role of the data administration group and the role of business managers in data administration.

Typically, policies that assign the data administration group both operational and limited planning responsibilities work best. Data administration helps design databases to make them efficient for the processing requirements. Here, the group works with systems analysts, designers, and users to identify future databases and database technology requirements. Different data administration staff might address operational databases, data warehouses, databases used for e-commerce, and mobile applications. Members of the data administration group should include both technical (often called database administration) and managerial (often called data administration) staff, often with extensive experience and with considerable respect throughout the business and within IS management.

The data administration group should be a high-level function with responsibility for determining or coordinating data management from policy to implementation. A purely technical group, geared only to the optimization of database structures, might be insufficient to deal with the range of issues in data management.

Key functions of the data administration group should include the following:

- *Promote and control data sharing.*   The group should encourage all business units to define data and to increase the use of common sources of data for different application systems. The group should work to determine the appropriate ownership for each kind of data and the responsibilities data owners should have. An organization may have to make tradeoffs between data sharing and privacy (see the box titled "Data Privacy and Protection.")

- *Analyze the impact of changes to application systems when data definitions change.*   The application independence concept is usually not fully implemented, so evolution and change to databases might require programming modifications. A schedule of which systems need to be changed must be developed considering the needs of all database users.

- *Maintain metadata.*   When a metadata repository and data dictionary are started, data administration must clean up existing data definitions and write definitions where they do not exist. As new data are added or when unclear definitions or insufficient formats are identified, the dictionary needs to be changed.

- *Reduce redundant data and processing.*   The group should encourage dropping unnecessary copies of data and programs that maintain them, synchronizing purposefully redundant copies, and managing data distributed across the various computer systems within the organization (ranging from central system to desktop).

- *Reduce system maintenance costs and improve systems development productivity.*   Data administration should work to create database organizations that are easy to use, select database technology that reduces the amount of programming, and train database analysts and programmers in the most current methods. These efforts should improve the development and maintenance of application systems.

- *Improve quality and security of data.*   The group should take leadership in this area, helping business managers and the data governance council to define data quality standards, set security clearances, and work with data center operations to implement these guidelines.

- *Insure data integrity.*   Data administration must actively review databases to insure that the integrity of data has not been compromised. With the growing popularity of Internet-based hacking, the concern over data being corrupted has grown to make regular review a critical task.

Within the overall data administration function, the primary person responsible for the management of computer databases is the **database administrator (DBA)**. He or she might be placed in the technical unit that supports various system software and hardware. The DBA is concerned with the following:

- tuning database management systems
- selection and evaluation of and training on database technology
- physical database design
- design of methods to recover from damage to databases
- physical placement of databases on specific computers and storage devices
- the interface of databases with telecommunications and other technologies

---

DATA PRIVACY AND PROTECTION

Privacy guidelines are becoming a necessity in organizations today. With laws being enacted in the European Union and the United States, companies that collect data in a global environment via the Internet must attend to the privacy of that data. Many of these laws are a result of the fast-growing crime of identify theft, where confidential information is often obtained by hacking corporate databases. Additionally, large-scale data center breaches have prompted some laws.

Data privacy guidelines typically require that the data must be accurate, secure, and used for limited purposes. Legislation enacted in California in July 2003 takes this a step further. California Senate Bill 1386 requires organizations that experience a security breach to notify Californians if there is a chance that confidential information was accessed inappropriately. Although this law currently applies only in California, it is expected to spread to other states and potentially the United Kingdom. Any global organization that has Californian customers must comply with this law. Because data privacy laws have only recently come into effect, many organizations do not have policies regarding data privacy and are thus vulnerable to lawsuits.

In order for companies to properly manage data privacy, they need to know who is allowed to have access to the data. In the Internet environment, identifying authorized users can be a daunting task. Companies also need to have the ability to track access to the data by monitoring who is looking at the data and to deny access to those who should not be able to see it. Software is only beginning to be developed to address this critical concern.

But, data breaches occur. Personnel, health insurance claims, student academic and loan, and customer data records have been reported stolen from lost laptops and by hacking into computer systems. From January through August of 2006 over 160 serious data thefts were disclosed by U.S. companies and government agencies. In these cases, it may be necessary for the organization that had data stolen to purchase identity and credit tracking services for the affected parties, at potentially considerable cost.

[Adapted from Bloor, 2003; Vijavan, 2006]

SUMMARY

This chapter has presented the technical and managerial issues associated with designing, developing, and managing the data resource. Treating the data resource as an asset is essential in modern organizations. The value of the data must first be recognized, and steps to organize and structure the data must be taken in order to reap benefits from this vital asset.

The data model was introduced as a means of unambiguously describing organizational data. The data model is a tool that facilitates communication between the business manager and the database designer. Personal, departmental, and organizational data can all be described using this type of graphical model. Business managers should ensure that such a model exists for their organization. In addition, thorough metadata need to be kept to describe enterprise data and the rules that govern data.

An important distinction has been made among three types of data management systems: those that capture, transfer, or present data. This separation of data management functions leads to greater flexibility, longer life for some systems and the ability to easily dispose of others, and the benefits of greater sharing of data.

Finally, data governance processes are used to develop policies regarding the data resource. Issues regarding data quality, security, privacy, backup and recovery, and access are particularly important. These policies must balance the needs of business managers to use the data with the security and privacy requirements for the data. Careful attention to these policies is needed in order to protect the data resource while maximizing the potential benefits to be reaped from it.

The data resource in an organization is an essential asset that must be explicitly and professionally managed. This management requires a combination of efforts and cooperation by IS professionals and business managers. In the next three chapters, you will learn more about the role of data in the various types of information systems used in organizations.

This marks the end of the four-chapter technology component of this book. We have tried to cover only the technology that you, as a manager, need to know. Whatever your personal managerial career involves, you are likely to be working both directly and indirectly with hardware, software, telecommunications, and data. Knowledge of all four information technology components is essential for understanding the present and potential impact of IT on your organization and your job.

REVIEW QUESTIONS

1. Explain what the data resource is and why it is so important in today's organizations.
2. What is a data model? What does it contain? What are the objectives of data modeling?
3. What are metadata? Why is it important to manage metadata?

4. What are some examples of database programming languages? How do these languages interact with other programming languages?
5. Why do organizations often have several databases?
6. What are the different types of databases? How do they differ?
7. Define *application independence*.
8. Define *disposable applications*.
9. Describe the issues central to insuring the quality of the data resource.
10. What is master data management? What are the benefits of MDM?
11. Who is a data administrator and what does this person do?
12. What are the basic functions of managing the data resource?

DISCUSSION QUESTIONS

1. This chapter differentiates among data capture, data transfer, and data analysis and presentation systems. What are the major implications for the system developer of this division into three types of systems?
2. What are the different kinds of data standards and why are these an essential part of data management?
3. Do you think it is difficult to manage metadata? Why or why not?
4. What are the major differences between the two approaches to data planning and modeling outlined in this chapter—enterprise modeling and view integration? Why do these two methodologies usually yield different results? In what ways does the existence of prepackaged data models affect these approaches?
5. Discuss the problems or pitfalls of doing data planning and modeling. How can these be alleviated? Discuss the advantages and uses of data modeling.
6. Explain why, given the benefits of a coordinated, integrated data architecture, some organizations still maintain multiple databases. How does master data management assist in the management of multiple databases?
7. Identify the data that are captured about you—as a student, a professional, a customer, and so on. Discuss how this data can be an asset for the organizations that collect it.
8. Search the Web for examples of how organizations have treated their data as an asset and the benefits they have achieved through this approach.

REFERENCES

Berinato, Scott. 2002. "Take the pledge: The CIO's code of ethical data management." *CIO* 15 (July 1): 56–63.

Betts, Mitch. 2001. "Dirty data." *Computerworld* 35 (December 17): 42.

Bloor, Robin. 2003. "Data protection: IT chiefs' growing burden." *Computer Weekly* (August 19): 16.

Chang, Edward S. 1999. "Managing cyber security vulnerabilities in large networks." *Bell Labs Technical Journal* 27 (October–December): 252–256.

Crafts, Steven. 1997. "Data Warehousing: What Works?" Volume 4. New York: The Data Warehousing Institute.

Craig, Robert. 2000. "CRM and corporate data." *ENT* 6 (October 25): 24–25.

The Data Management Center. 2004. "Directory of data resource management and information resource management." The Data Management Center Web site, *www.infogoal.com/* (Last date accessed: April 2007).

Deck, Stewart. 2001. "Data storm ahead." *CIO* 14 (April 15): 96–100.

Dyché, Jill. 2006. "Rethinking Data Integration: The Rise of CDI." September 18. Presentation delivered at Teradata Partners conference, Orlando, FL.

Hayes, C. 2004. "What They Know About You." *New York Times* (November 14): section 3, page 1.

Hoffer, Jeffrey A., Mary B. Prescott, and Heikki Topi. 2009. *Modern Database Management*, 9th ed. Upper Saddle River, NJ: Pearson Prentice Hall.

Kay, Russell. 2003. "Data models." *Computerworld* 37 (April 14): 44.

Koch, Christopher. 2002–2003. "No more bogus data." *CIO* 16 (December 15–January 1): 40.

Lundberg, Abbie. 2002. "Do the right thing." *CIO* 15 (July 1): 18.

Myburgh, Sue. 2000. "The convergence of information technology and information management." *Information Management Journal* 34 (April): 4–16.

Purba, Sanjiv. 1998. "An approach for establishing enterprise data standards." *Information Systems Management* 15 (Fall): 14–20.

Rao, Srikumar S. 1998. "Diaper-beer syndrome" *Forbes* 160 (April 6): 128–130.

Russom, P. 2006. "Taking Data Quality to the Enterprise through Data Governance." Except of TDWI Report, *www.tdwi.org/Publications/WhatWorks/display.aspx?id=7980*

Singer, Peter. 2000. "Leveraging the power of your data warehouse." *Beyond Computing* 10 (May): 50–53.

Turek, Norbert. 2003. "Avoid bad-data potholes." *InformationWeek* 944 (June 16): 51–55.

Vijayan, J. 2006. "List of Data Breach Notices Lengthening." *Computerworld*. September 10 (reported on their Web site).

White, Colin and Claudia Imhoff. 2006. "Master Data Management: Creating a Single View of the Business." September, *www.beyeresearch.com/study/3360*.

White, Don. 2000. "Finding a life preserver for the data flood." *Brandweek* 15 (October 9): 26–29.

Whiting, Rick. 2003. "Intelligence or info overload?" *InformationWeek* 963 (November 10): 86–92.

Young, Debby. 2000. "An audit tale." *CIO* 13 (May 1): 150–115

IMT CUSTOM MACHINE COMPANY, INC.: SELECTION OF AN INFORMATION TECHNOLOGY PLATFORM

Carol Kallas watched an October rainstorm coming out of the west from her second-story executive office. Turning to a growing stack of paperwork, she also thought of the dark cloud hanging over her information systems (IS) area.

Something had to be done. Committee after committee had analyzed urgent systems problems and proposed incremental solutions. And Kallas' faith in her staff usually led her to approve the recommendations. But soon another "glitch" always seemed to develop, and another committee would have to be appointed. "Something fundamental was missing," she thought to herself. "We don't have a strategic direction for IS—we don't know where we want to be or how to get there. We have to get our arms around where we want to go with our information systems once and for all."

Kallas was a vice president and the division manager of a subsidiary within the International Machine and Tool–USA (IMT-USA) Company. The IMT Custom Machine Company built multi-million-dollar, large custom-made production machines. These machines were used in the manufacturing of various parts for large items such as automobiles. As division head, Kallas was responsible for two factories, which built about 150 machines per year, and a third factory that made smaller machined parts for the two factories. A service and spare parts group within the division supported the repair and maintenance business for any custom machine, including those built by IMT's competition. The Fort Wayne, Indiana, plant, where Kallas worked, was the largest custom machine factory in North America. (See Exhibit 1)

In early September, Kallas had decided to ask an experienced engineer to learn about the IS activities, investigate all the issues, and develop a recommendation, or at least offer some options for her to consider for getting IS on track for good. While she recognized she had undertaken an unconventional approach, she knew Charles Browning was the right

person for the task. Browning was a staff engineer with an extensive scientific computing background, finishing his MBA at a major Midwestern university. He reported to the development engineering manager at the Fort Wayne plant.

At a meeting on September 3, 2002, Kallas had given the charge to Browning:

> I need you to survey the total IS picture and give me three or four basic directional options which will satisfy our IS needs over the next several years. I want you to report your findings in six weeks. Plan on giving it to me straight. I will review the findings with you and then incorporate one of the alternatives into my business plan for 2003. There should be no limits on the type of recommendations you provide, Charlie.

By using Browning, Kallas hoped to cut through the layers of management that might have been filtering out the root causes of IMT's IS problems.

She heard the knock on her office door and assumed that Browning was ready with his report.

The Custom Machine Industry

Exhibit 2 summarizes the additions to production capacity for U.S. suppliers of custom production machines. Until the mid-1970s, there had been a clear upward trend of production capacity additions. But the growth in worldwide demand for the machines began to decline as industrial production in developed countries slowed.

As the market share of U.S.-based industrial production companies declined, demand decreases were soon felt in the U.S. custom machine industry. Excess production capacity suddenly became a reality. Underused plants became targets for closing, and plans for scores of new plants and additions were canceled. Annual capacity additions declined after 1975. By the mid-1990s, annual capacity additions had fallen below the level of the early 1960s. When the data were released for 2000, experts expected additions to capacity to be nearly zero.

The industry slowdown caused Williamson Machines and Engineering Corporation (WILMEC), which held about 30 percent of the U.S. market, to close its "medium horizontal"-type

EXHIBIT 1
Organization Chart: IMT Custom Machine Company, Inc.

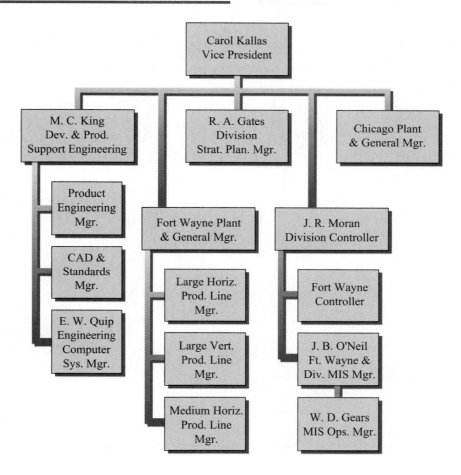

machine factory in Cleveland, Ohio, in 1983, moving its medium horizontal production capability to its one remaining custom machine factory in Fort Wayne, Indiana. The Fort Wayne facility was constructed in the early 1970s specifically to manufacture a similar, but technically different, type of custom machine called a "large vertical."

In 1988, General Engineering, Inc., which in previous years had been an equal market rival to WILMEC, abandoned its custom machine business by closing its Detroit, Michigan, plant. General Engineering (GE) sold its technology to WILMEC, and GE's production equipment was moved to WILMEC's Fort Wayne plant. The result of WILMEC's technology acquisition from GE was that a third, and very different, technology called "large horizontal" also started in Fort Wayne. At this time, WILMEC also expanded its custom machine reconditioning operation in Chicago to handle the assembly of one-third of its medium horizontal machines. By 1990, the Fort Wayne plant

produced all three custom machine types: large horizontal, large vertical, and medium horizontal.

Starting in late 1993, WILMEC refocused its strategy away from the machine fabrication industry into various service industries. WILMEC sold all of its custom machine engineering, manufacturing, and sales operations to International Machine and Tool (IMT) of Bonn, Germany, in mid-1995. IMT was itself the result of a 1987 merger between Europe's two largest machine manufacturers—International Machines (English translation) of Germany, and Tools of Commerce (English translation) of Italy. Numerous plant closings and consolidations had rippled through Europe as well as the United States in the late 1980s and early 1990s.

By 1995, the production capacity for custom production machines in the U.S. market had essentially stabilized at 95 percent of demand. As was true for most cyclical industries, a significant increase in demand would cause capacity problems and delivery delays. Indeed, some industry observers suggested

EXHIBIT 2

The U.S. Custom Machine Industry Production Capacity Additions from 1965 to 1995

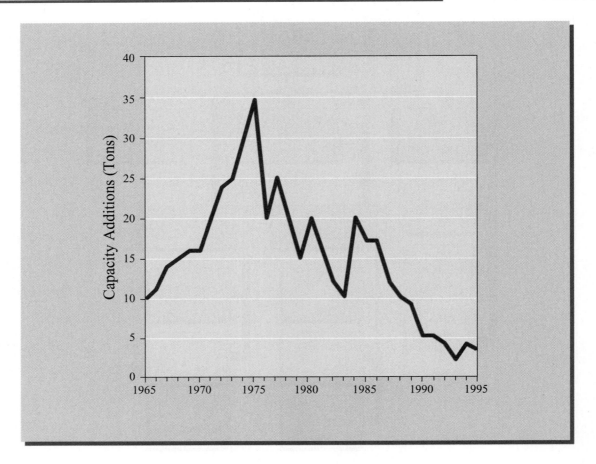

that the custom machine industry might return to a robust building program by 2005.

International Machine and Tool

International Machine and Tool used a matrix-style organization throughout its operations, modeled after the structure of other large, Europe-based global companies. Dr. Wilhelm Schlein, chairman of IMT, summarized the organization as "a federation of national companies with a global coordination center—a distributed organization which has many homes." Schlein's strategy for building a decentralized, multidomestic enterprise was critical to achieving IMT's goal of "think global, act local."

One side of IMT's matrix organization was country-based. Each country manager (president of the national holding company) was responsible for financial targets for all of IMT's products and services in that country. Country presidents coordinated synergistic relationships across IMT operations within the country

(e.g., the same distribution and service networks). They were also responsible for maintaining relationships with national government officials.

The second side of IMT's matrix was technology-based (product classes) and reported through a separate transnational technology management group, called a business group (BG). The mission of each BG was to support shared knowledge and operations among many international factories in the same industry. BG leaders served as business strategists who set global "rules of the game" and then let local managers (like Kallas) pilot the execution.

In 2002, IMT had eight international custom machine factories, two of which were located in the United States. The U.S. plants represented nearly one-half of IMT's global capacity. The combined capacity of the Chicago and Fort Wayne plants was far larger than any in the other countries.

Kallas reported to two managers in the matrix, the U.S. country manager and a Custom Machine BG manager, who often had conflicting goals. While she had to increase return on assets to support the U.S. country manager, she simultaneously was encouraged to maintain a leading technology position by the BG head. As was true for all custom machine factories, Kallas' division paid about one percent of sales to the BG for global research and development projects.

Carol L. Kallas

With more than 18 years of custom machine engineering experience, Kallas was widely known and highly respected throughout the custom machine industry. Earlier in her career, Kallas had worked her way through several engineering and manufacturing management positions at WILMEC. She had always been active in the industry by chairing and working on technical committees of various professional associations.

However, Kallas was not actively involved in the use of the information systems at IMT. Her personal use of a computer was limited to preparing short documents, maintaining a calendar, constructing and reviewing reports, sending e-mail at work, and browsing the Internet from home. She felt that her hectic schedule made it impossible to use the personal computer in her office for more than 50 minutes a day.

In 1999, Kallas was appointed a vice president of IMT Custom Machines Company, Inc. (CMCI), the IMT subsidiary in the United States. On the "country side" of the matrix, CMCI reported through the IMT-USA holding company in New York, which in turn reported to IMT's world headquarters in Bonn. On the BG side of the matrix, Kallas reported to the managing director of the Custom Machine BG. The headquarters for the business group was in Milan, Italy.

Shortly after taking the job, Kallas and other division managers worked with the IMT-USA president to develop universally applicable (to all IMT-USA companies) statements of the corporate mission, principles, and vision. After considerable discussion and many revisions, the IMT-USA president disseminated the final product on March 26, 1999. (See Exhibit 3.)

The Fort Wayne Plant

The work environment at the Fort Wayne plant over the prior 25 years was dynamic, to say the least. Over that period, the plant first transitioned from a busy single-product factory into a stagnant operation that nearly closed due to a lack of orders. A few short years later, it evolved into a facility that supported three technically different products (large horizontal, large vertical, and medium horizontal custom machines), each originating from a different company with different engineering design systems. In 2002, IMT's Fort Wayne facility was producing near its capacity and was staffed with about 1,200 employees.

Until the mid-1990s, all the engineering and marketing operations for the Fort Wayne and Chicago plants were located

EXHIBIT 3
IMT-USA Mission, Guiding Principles, and Vision Statements

The following was taken from a presentation given by the IMT-USA President on March 26, 1999.

Mission
- Serve U.S. customers to their individual needs and total satisfaction.
- Create an organizational environment that allows all IMT-USA's employees to add value.
- Promote an atmosphere of thirst and eagerness to perform that allows delegation of responsibility to the lowest possible organizational level and attracts good people.
- Generate a sense of urgency and results orientation in the development of capital and human resources to ensure proper return for both our employees and our shareholders.
- Expand the horizon of the organization to share in and contribute to our worldwide core competencies.

Guiding Principles
- Create a sense of urgency—concentrate on priority actions rather than procedural issues.
- Promote a unifying culture: "can do—do it."
- Remove barriers to performance.
- Shift organizational focus to servicing the customers and beating the competition.

Vision
- Demonstrate leadership in serving the U.S. marketplace in its transition to cleaner industry, where products are more efficiently produced, distributed, and applied.

in Cleveland, Ohio (200 miles from Fort Wayne and 350 miles from Chicago). In 1995, IMT closed the Cleveland site and transferred the engineering and marketing staffs to either Fort Wayne or Chicago.

As the Fort Wayne plant evolved to support multiple product lines, a number of informal procedures emerged to handle day-to-day situations. These undocumented processes worked well enough, despite the incompatibilities among the three machine technologies, which used three separate drafting systems as well as unique manufacturing processes. Very little capital had been invested in upgrading operations during the last several years of WILMEC's ownership. In fact, it was not until IMT had completed its purchase of WILMEC that a major capital upgrade was even considered. Low margins and strict capital budget limits always prevented significant upgrades. As a result, the informal processes continued under IMT ownership, as company executives focused on making the acquisition show a profit.

In early 1996, the plant was reorganized into three "machine-type" product lines, each operating as a separate product line and profit center. In June 1997, CMCI's quality assurance manager, Edward Fortesque, completed the mission statement for CMCI. (See Exhibit 4) Finally, the company's reorganization was coming together.

CMCI's Information Systems

Charles Browning began his investigation shortly after receiving his charge from Carol Kallas. By mid-September 2002, he had uncovered considerable data about the information systems at Fort Wayne and Chicago.

Support for Fort Wayne's information systems was split into two groups: an engineering systems (ES) group and a management information systems (MIS) group (again see Exhibit 1). The ES group consisted of eight of the 25 people who reported to Dr. Michael C. King, Fort Wayne's development engineering manager. Dr. King had been trained as an engineer and was known as an industry-wide expert on the design of automated fabrication technologies.

Twenty MIS support staff members reported to Bill Gears, who in turn reported to Joe O'Neil, the division MIS manager. Chicago had its own one-person MIS "group" who reported directly to O'Neil. O'Neil reported through the division controller's organization. O'Neil was a former IBM employee with extensive experience on large mainframes and on the IBM AS/400

EXHIBIT 4
Mission/Vision Statement
IMT Custom Machine Company, Inc.

The following was issued throughout the Fort Wayne plant on June 25, 1997 by Edward Fortesque, Manager of Quality Assurance.

Mission
- To be recognized as the outstanding custom machine manufacturer in the world.

Goals
- *Provide market leadership*
  - Customer satisfaction
    - Quality
    - Reliability
    - Delivery
    - Service
  - Serve the market with optional products and services
  - Be the technology leader

- *Achieve business (operational) excellence*
  - Zero failures
  - On-time performance
  - Low throughput time for orders through the factory
  - High productivity of labor
  - Return on capital employed >30% (pre-tax)
  - Revenue to total compensation growth of at least 5% per year

Vision
- To be perceived by each of our customers as superior to the best of our competitors in the overall quality of our products and services.

EXHIBIT 5
Fort Wayne MIS Direction and Objectives
IMT Custom Machine Company, Inc.

The following was issued to top division and plant management on July 30, 2002, by Joe O'Neil, division MIS manager.

Direction
- Pursue a more structured MIS strategy with a reasonable and manageable level of risk that will be consistent with our being a leader in the custom machine industry.
- Develop and execute a plan that will continually upgrade our hardware, software, applications, database, and network environments to accomplish the above.

Objectives
- Recognize our business is designing and producing custom machines, not chasing ever-changing computer technology and theories.
- Coordinate MIS strategy with our business objectives of:
  - Zero defects
  - Low throughput time
  - ROCE (return on capital employed) of 30%
- Control our own destiny.
- Minimize risk and hidden costs.
- Work from a total systems architecture plan to:
  - Develop an applications architecture
  - Select the hardware plan required to best accomplish our goals
- Maintain an integrated environment that supports the various functions of our division.

platform. He had been the MIS manager at another IMT site before coming to Fort Wayne in 1998.

On July 30, 2002, O'Neil circulated a memo to the top division and plant managers that summarized his objectives for Fort Wayne's MIS group. (See Exhibit 5) O'Neil later told Browning, "I do not have a formal mission for the MIS group, but essentially I am looking to provide an adequate, responsive, and economical network structure of data processing support for all sites within the division."

Browning found that a variety of computing hardware was used to support the division. (See Exhibit 6)

The division operated an IBM mainframe located at Fort Wayne that could be used by anyone in the division at no direct charge. All lease and operating costs for the mainframe were covered in the division's overhead. When they joined the company, new engineers and other professionals were supplied with a mainframe user account, a personal computer (PC) equipped with a board to enable it to communicate with the mainframe, and several PC software packages for local

work. The mainframe arrived in March 1999 on a 5-year lease. A mainframe upgrade in 2001 was driven by the need for improvements in computer-aided drafting (CAD) response time and an increasing number of users. From 1999 to 2001, 65 new users throughout the factory and front offices were connected to the mainframe.

CMCI also had an IBM AS/400 that it had inherited from General Engineering. Immediately after the acquisition, MIS personnel attempted to create a facility to move data between the two mainframes, but that proved to be difficult. Most exchanges were done by "pulling" data from one system to the other. Although a routine (called AMSERV) was available to "push" data to the other system, its use was not fully understood. Another reason AMSERV was not used was that the receiver's data file could be updated without the user's knowledge. As a result, data security issues slowed the practice of sharing data between the two systems. In sequential applications, where data were created in one system and used by another, identical data files were needed on each system.

EXHIBIT 6

Computing Systems and Applications: IMT Custom Machine Company, Inc.*

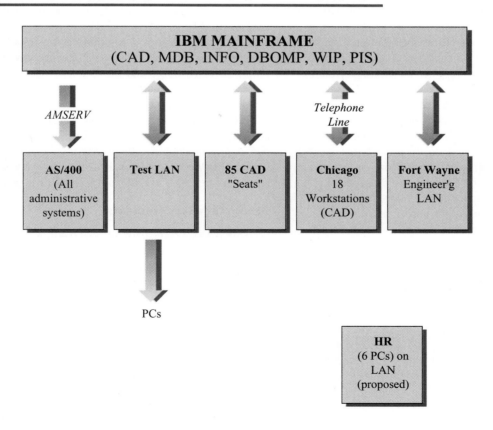

* Applications are in parentheses

From 2001 on, the heaviest use of the mainframe was by drafting and engineering staff. IMT Fort Wayne used IBM's CAD product on the mainframe. The CAD application, along with additional drafting and engineering programs, represented about 65 percent of mainframe use. Total usage in August 2002 was estimated at approximately 54 percent of the mainframe's CPU capacity.

The division also used personal computers extensively. The policy at Fort Wayne was that anyone who needed a PC could get one. Financial justification was not necessary, as PCs were considered a tool. Fort Wayne's standard PC configuration included the latest Intel processor running the latest version of Microsoft Windows as well as the Microsoft Office suite and several other popular packages—all connected to an ink jet printer. PCs were obtained under a three-year lease from a local supplier.

Many users felt that the lack of sufficient mainframe software support and lengthy systems development time on the part of the MIS group had been partially compensated by the use of PCs. For example, production scheduling in major work centers in the factory was done with a spreadsheet on PCs. However, the principal use for many PCs was as a "dumb" terminal to the mainframe for database inquiry or sending e-mail. In addition, secretaries and engineers routinely used PC word processing to write memos. Of the 300 users on Fort Wayne's mainframe, about 210 were accessing it through PCs. The remaining users were CAD users.

The division also had powerful personal workstations for technical work. As of 2002, Fort Wayne had six IBM workstations used by the development engineering group for special projects. They were connected through a local area network (LAN). Several Sun workstations were also linked into the LAN during the previous year. Personnel at the Chicago facility used 18 IBM CAD workstations for normal production work. At Fort Wayne, there were also 25 Sun and IBM workstations used for the production of drawings.

Drawings made in Chicago on workstations were stored on Fort Wayne's mainframe and uploaded and downloaded over a high-speed dedicated telephone line. Chicago's designers liked their CAD stations, but were having trouble with the connection between the mainframe and the Chicago LAN. Tom Goodman, the MIS support person in Chicago, told Browning, "I feel like we are the beta site for linking sites together."

Data Flow and Functional Responsibilities

Exhibit 7 illustrates the generalized data flow among the main functional areas of the Fort Wayne operation. Of the seven functions, only the human resources (HR) department was not connected to the main information flow. The remaining six organizational areas participated in a continuous sequential flow of information.

The flow of business information started with the interaction between marketing and the customer. Information originated from the customer when a technical description or specification (a "spec") was sent to IMT for a new machine. The length of the spec could be from ten to several hundred pages. A marketing engineer would then read the spec and enter his or her interpretation of it into a mainframe negotiation program. The negotiation program (MDB), inherited from WILMEC, required the input of about fifty computer screens of data, and was written in COBOL. For presentations, marketing used Excel and PowerPoint on their PCs.

If a marketing engineer had a question about a spec, he or she called a design engineer or another local expert. Most estimates had to be turned around in 10 working days. Because of the volume of requests and a staff of only two engineers covering all of the United States, negotiations were sometimes very hectic. Mike Truelove, a marketing engineer, told Browning, "We do the best we can, but we miss some things from time to time. Almost always after winning the order, we go back and negotiate with the customer over what we missed."

Another frequently used mainframe application was a query system (called INFO) automatically linked to data from the negotiation program. It was used to analyze data from ongoing negotiations as well as contracts after they were won or lost.

The administration and finance group was the home for most business support systems. The purchase order, accounts payable, and accounts receivable systems were applications used by purchasing, receiving, and other groups. All three systems had been custom developed on the AS/400 by the General Engineering MIS staff (some of whom now worked at CMCI). Although wages and salaries were maintained locally, an external data service company handled the payroll.

As of 2002, human resources used only stand-alone computers. HR had plans to install a LAN that operated customized corporate programs for handling HR functions, including benefits and pension/investment plans. There were no plans to connect the LAN with Fort Wayne's mainframe due to security concerns for the confidential personnel records residing on HR's computers.

Production Requirements

Each machine the company made was electrically and mechanically custom designed to a customer's exact specifications. Customization requirements, when mixed with the complexities of the economic and engineering limits, required sophisticated computer programs for modeling and design work. In 2002, Fort Wayne had three separate design systems, one for each of the three types of custom machines. Design engineers for each product line were experts on their own programs.

The first step in design engineering was to receive electronically the data previously entered into the negotiation program. The process entailed pulling the data records from the negotiation database. The design engineer reread the customer's spec and decided which additional data needed to be added to the input files for the design program. The program then generated

EXHIBIT 7
Data Flow Among Functional Areas*
IMT Custom Machine Company, Inc.

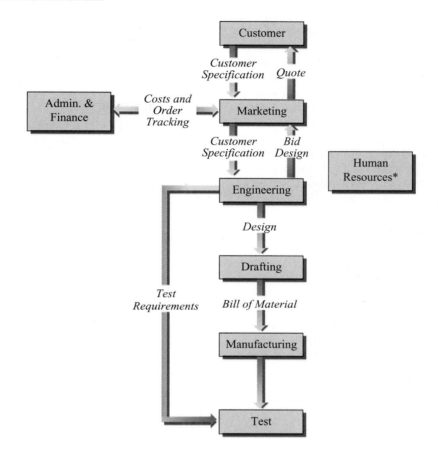

* Uses only applications supported by IMT-USA.

a design that the engineer reviewed in detail and often revised. After the design was accepted by the engineer, the electronic computer file and a paper folder with completed job forms were sent to a drafting supervisor for completion.

The ES group had created all of Fort Wayne's design systems. The number of routines used by each of the three systems was a relative measure of system size and complexity. Large vertical had about 500 routines, medium horizontal had about 400 routines, and large horizontal had about 2,400 routines.

All drafting at Fort Wayne and Chicago was performed on a CAD applications system. At Fort Wayne, the CAD application ran on the IBM mainframe, and in Chicago it ran on the local IBM workstations. There were 85 CAD "seats" at Fort Wayne and 18 at Chicago. (A "seat" is equivalent to one hardware CAD setup with

a high-resolution screen, keyboard, function-button box, and a pointing device that worked like a mouse.) During the prior 5 years, additional programs had been written to take output automatically from the design programs and create CAD drawings or references to drawings of standard parts. About 60 percent of the drawings for the average 4,000 parts per machine were created in this way. The remaining 40 percent of drawings had to be created by a draftsman from the design specifications. All jobs were reduced to drawings prior to being released to the factory.

A standard part drawing included the material specification on the drawing. Assembly work orders contained the bill of material (BOM). Having CAD and the design programs on the same platform made the development of the automatic drawing programs very convenient. Jennifer Velan, an engineer in the development group, told Browning, "There are things we have been able to do with this setup that would be impossible if the jobs were split between two separate systems."

When all the drawings for a machine were completed, the BOM was manually transferred from the drawings into the BOM database system, called DBOMP. DBOMP was originally written by IBM and extensively modified for Fort Wayne in the 1990s to handle bills of material for the vertical type machines. When production of the medium and large horizontal machines was transferred to Fort Wayne, DBOMP's limitations forced many "work-arounds." For example, when the General Engineering large horizontal technology was moved to Fort Wayne, it was discovered that DBOMP could not handle the longer General Engineering drawing numbers. Moreover, there was no one at Fort Wayne who knew the DBOMP code well enough to make a change in the software.

The work-in-process (WIP) inventory tracking system for the shop floor at Fort Wayne was very limited and worked only for items required for the main aisle assembly area. It could only handle made-to-order parts, not stock items. The system worked by having a main aisle supervisor request a "pull" from the storeroom to get parts delivered. The tracking systems for items within feeder aisles were done either manually or on a spreadsheet. Each item's information was maintained by its respective aisle. The WIP main aisle tracking system resided on the mainframe, and the data were loaded by hand from the DBOMP.

The parts inventory system (PIS) was very limited and similar to the tracking system except that it worked off all stocked inventory items for the main and all feeder aisles. It used a process identical to the WIP system.

The MIS group was backlogged in supporting the rapid changes occurring at the Fort Wayne plant. The lead time on most system upgrades was 3 weeks for emergencies and 6 to 9 months for non-emergencies. When a computerized system failed to provide needed functionality, paper systems were created to support information needs.

Because each custom machine was a significant investment—between $2 million and $8 million—all machines were fully tested at Fort Wayne or Chicago and the testing was personally witnessed by an employee or agent of the customer company. The test department, along with the witness, certified that every machine met the customer's test requirements set forth in the specification.

Scheduling information and other test details were forwarded to the test department by hand. Test information was written on a form that was interpreted or copied from the customer specification in marketing and engineering. The biggest complaint from the test department was that sometimes the marketing department did not properly interpret the customer's test requirement specifications. A failed or unnecessary test that resulted from misinterpreting a customer's specification could cost IMT well over $100,000.

The test department had several personal computers connected to a LAN. Although all PCs in the test department were also connected to the mainframe, this connectivity was used only occasionally. The test department was a part of the quality assurance organization at Fort Wayne, which was responsible for the data and production of the test reports sent to customers. Electronic test result data, however, remained only on the test department's LAN. The test department maintained its own LAN applications.

Personnel Issues

Browning uncovered some additional information about the information systems personnel at the company. The programmers in MIS had extensive backgrounds in COBOL and in RPG for the AS/400. None of them, however, knew the UNIX operating system or its related programming languages. Of the 14 programmers, four had over 25 years experience at Fort Wayne, two had about 12 years, and the remaining eight had 3 years or less.

Engineers who supported the engineering system in the development group had significant backgrounds in scientific computing and four had some experience with UNIX. Each engineer had more than 10 years of experience with the company. One of the recently added programmers in the engineering systems group knew UNIX very well.

Browning heard many comments during his investigation that suggested that the MIS and engineering systems staff at Fort Wayne always made the systems work—despite the constant change.

Browning concluded that as a result of employing informal systems, work-arounds, and an extraordinary amount of human effort, Fort Wayne was profitable in 2001—its first profitable year in several years. Slowly, things were stabilizing at Fort Wayne—the informal systems were being corrected and formalized. Restructuring into three product lines had helped to clarify the focus and purpose of operations systems and procedures. Overall, the primary reason many staff members saw progress was that each product line was allowed independent control and responsibility.

Computer systems support, however, remained an issue. The engineering systems group supported engineering and drafting, and the MIS group supported everything else. The HR organization was not considered a local issue because its applications were supported by the corporate MIS group in New York (IMT-USA). A small group within MIS maintained all PCs and miscellaneous computer hardware for all the functional groups across the plant.

Support for Engineering and Drafting Systems

Browning also discovered an ongoing debate over where the IT support for the engineering and drafting systems should be located. Browning summarized the three alternatives that arose from the debate on a legal pad at his desk:

1. *In the engineering support systems group:* Arguments for leaving support for engineering and drafting in the development engineering line of authority were strong. The design and drafting programs produced models for the three product line technologies. The three principal people supporting these design systems were engineers with strong computer backgrounds. Two of the three had master's degrees in engineering. Support for these programs required a balance of custom machine design knowledge, creativity, and programming. By working close to the user engineers in the product line, the support engineers could update the systems rapidly. The engineers feared that MIS programmers had little understanding of the underlying design technology. Some of the engineers speculated that the MIS people might make coding changes that "would cost millions to correct once a design was committed and the parts were made."

2. In the product lines: Arguments for product line support of engineering systems included the fact that product line engineers had extensive firsthand knowledge of how the system was used. As a result, feedback on problems would be more obvious to those who supported the system. Furthermore, it could be argued that ultimate control of the software should be in the hands of each of the profit centers. They should have the option to regulate the level of computer support based on their own strategy. However, if the engineering systems support responsibilities were located within the product lines, a programmer would need to be transferred from the engineering support systems group to each of the product lines.

3. In the MIS group: Arguments for MIS-based support of engineering and drafting systems included an alignment of all computer-related functions in one functional group—thus providing a common responsibility point for all computer support and integrated applications. Product line and development engineering would have to submit change requests that were more completely documented. Support through MIS would guarantee that coding changes would be better documented. If support were the responsibility of the product line engineers, MIS people argued that the end result might be "spaghetti code," which no one but the original programmer could understand.

The Move to a Common Machine Design System

Browning discovered that in early 2002, Kallas had received instructions that her subsidiary would have to use a redeveloped set of custom machine design programs from Germany. The BG management team believed it was appropriate to institute a common custom machine design system across all factories. The BG strategy was based on porting the German programs onto a UNIX workstation platform and then distributing and supporting it worldwide. When the announcement was made that the German programs would be used, however, none of the programs would work with UNIX. Nor did the German developers possess more than a few years of total experience in the UNIX environment.

A New Marketing and Negotiation System

Browning learned that marketing and engineering saw the existing negotiation program as inefficient and ineffective. Two years of studying how the IMT division should do business with its customers led the marketing group to propose a reengineered "front-end information" system. The proposed system would include capabilities to optically scan in all customer proposals, including text. Customer specs could then be analyzed and processed more quickly.

The proposed system had an initial price tag of over $2.5 million. The original idea for the system was conceived in the marketing department, which employed two staff engineers and an independent outside consultant as its own IS expert. Only recently had MIS been involved with planning the system. The project was being led by the division strategic planning manager, which isolated the project from division MIS and engineering input. Hardware purchases were to begin in November 2002, and the system was to be completed and operational by the end of 2003.

CMCI's Interface to Field Sales

Browning discovered that IMT's field sales group had itself been planning a new system for transferring order information to the factories. The new system, called SPEC, was planned to come on line in late 2003. By mid-2003, each factory was to have installed a LAN to accommodate the data downloaded from field sales personnel. As of September 2002, SPEC was plagued with delays because staff could not arrive at a consensus on the exact information that should be transmitted to each of the factories.

New Software Design Tools

After asking some questions in the controller's office, Browning found that payments from Fort Wayne and Chicago accounted for 25 percent of the funds used for the BG's R&D development budget. IMT's MIS group felt that about 30 percent of its investment was received back in the form of useful information technologies while the remaining 70 percent benefited production hardware improvements. The BG was definitely committed to additional investments in UNIX application tools.

Various software engineering and applications development tools had been mentioned, but the specific software and the number of seats that would be leased or purchased had not been finalized as of the end of September 2002.

Bill of Material (BOM) System Replacement

The production scheduling people told Browning that the DBOMP system was nearly 15 years old and could not handle the new German-developed design system that was to replace the three older systems. To support the new design system and its subsequent BOM structure, a new BOM system would be required. Fort Wayne systems staff had identified a system that would run on the IBM mainframe and could be acquired at no cost. The program, called PUFR, was free because it was in the process of being discarded by IMT-USA's corporate MIS group. The only requirement was that Fort Wayne MIS staff had to support PUFR.

By September 2002, over 4,000 staff hours had been consumed by Fort Wayne MIS personnel trying to make PUFR operational. Projections suggested that approximately 10 percent more work had to be done in order to get PUFR into a test mode. To get this far, Fort Wayne systems had already purchased additional modules that were not originally included in the free IMT corporate version of PUFR. The effort had also included converting some of the approximately 400 auxiliary programs that used the old DBOMP format. Occasional discussions of replacing PUFR "in a few years" were heard in the halls.

Browning's Meeting with Kallas

Browning summarized the findings of his six-week investigation at an October 2002 meeting with Kallas that went as follows:

"The best way to characterize the current information systems situation at Fort Wayne is as a lot of manual points where data are transferred between a patchwork of old, semiautomatic, outdated processes. The result is that since each place where information is transferred has a probability of introducing a new error, checking and rechecking is necessary to ensure integrity. And since the outdated processes require constant fixes and work-arounds, the newer processes never move ahead. What we really need is a clear vision to guide our decisions today, so we can be ready for tomorrow."

"I was afraid of that, Charlie. So do we have any options?" asked Kallas.

"We do." replied Browning. "But first we really need to develop a vision, architecture, and strategy statement for all information systems consistent with our business objectives. I see three options for the basic information technology architecture."

"Let me hear the first one," replied Kallas.

"OK," said Browning. "The first option is to move towards a centralized, likely IBM, computing environment. Under this option, we would commit to staying with the mainframe for all important applications, discourage the use of the Sun and IBM workstations, maybe allow the use of Linux on the mainframe, and eliminate the AS/400. This approach would maximize use of the lower cost, energy-efficient mainframe.

"Our commitment to the mainframe would have to be long term. To continue to maintain a large central mainframe and acquire new applications and full access for all users would require a systematic plan. The plan would include porting all the major AS/400 applications to the mainframe to assure central use, support, and control. Major mainframe packages would be reviewed for upgrades that could handle Fort Wayne's current capacity and requirements. Older packages used in Fort Wayne would be phased out over the next 5 years. PCs connected through LANs to the mainframe would do spreadsheet and word processing work, but almost all computational work would be done on the mainframe."

"OK," remarked Kallas. "I can see that as feasible even though a lot of people would be upset. Our engineers have become accustomed to using the Sun and IBM workstations whenever they want to. What is option two?"

"I call option two workstation computing," said Browning. "Here we would follow a strategy whereby the mainframe is phased out completely over time. At the same time, we would make significant investments in Sun and IBM workstations running UNIX, as well as PCs, big servers, and LANs. We could allow the use of Linux on the workstations. Such an architecture would allow migration to a full client/server environment.

"Our plans for a long-term shift to a distributed UNIX environment would include the migration of all applications to the new environment. A high-speed network would be installed to link all computers. Data and application servers would be distributed by functional areas and profit centers (e.g., marketing, development engineering, human resources, and testing). CAD seats would be slowly transferred from the mainframe to dedicated workstations. During the transition period, the mainframe would be connected to the network and available for access from all workstations.

"One database would serve the entire UNIX network system, but local databases could also exist as necessary. PCs would be linked via LANs, and gateways would be installed to bridge between networks.

"As CAD and other major applications were shifted off the mainframe, it would be downsized to a smaller, compatible midrange mainframe. The process could be expected to take approximately 10 years and two mainframe downgrades before all of Fort Wayne's applications would be migrated to UNIX workstations."

"All right," said Kallas, "but wouldn't this one be a lot more expensive and create a kind of 'disintegrated' computing environment? I have heard of other companies going this route only to have to reassert central control in a few years."

"It sure has that potential," said Browning. "And you are right ... it will likely be more expensive than the mainframe option, given what has happened to the cost of mainframes over the last several years.

"Before you decide, let me explain option three. This one is even more risky. We could go to a Linux environment. In this option, we would pursue a course of abandoning the mainframe, but converting the complete computing platform to a Linux environment. Though it is similar to UNIX as an operating system, Linux-based solutions offered by companies like Red Hat, IBM, and Nortel Information Network could cluster standard PCs or servers together to accomplish the same power as multiple UNIX workstations, a mainframe, or a supercomputer. While Linux started as a plaything for some younger computer junkies, it is now getting to be a mainstream offering by many of the major vendors. In the past few years, several large companies have adopted this environment for their architecture.

"Given the diversity of our needs across the company, the Linux solution could also provide more than adequate flexibility. Utilizing services provided by a recognized supplier like IBM, specialty Linux companies, or the in-house programming staff, Linux solutions could be used for anything from tracking quality control to managing machines and monitoring production. Furthermore, to accompany the resulting processing power, some providers of Linux solutions have guaranteed 99.7 percent or higher uptime to their Linux clients. I read that Linux has been useful for automobile simulations at DaimlerChrysler and Ford. In addition, the platform's durability has been proven at Amerada Hess and other oil companies through their exploration activities. Nevertheless, this is a major leap from IMT's current conservative environment."

"I guess," replied Kallas. "But at least we ought to consider it. Any more options?"

"Just one, to be complete," replied Browning. "We could consider just waiting and watching carefully. This option says do nothing fundamental at the present time. We wait and see what develops. We would decide on specific system changes only as circumstances force us to make decisions. Following the 'watch carefully' option would mean that each decision would be made in response to immediate demands. As part of this approach, we could bring in Linux and let some people experiment with it. If Linux is the wave of the future as some people claim, maybe the best idea is to not make a commitment now. It is not clear that Linux is ready for prime time now. But some experimenting could determine in a few years if it really is a long-term solution for the company."

A Decision and Direction for IMT IS

"OK," said Kallas. "Having the options is very helpful. I appreciate all the time you put into the project. Let me think about the options and make a decision."

After Browning left the office, Kallas began to reflect on the options he had presented. Change was going to be painful. Although Browning had captured the basic strategy alternatives, there were many considerations to take into account before a decision could be made on which option to follow. Years of neglect, restructuring, and a growing organization had finally caught up with CMCI's information systems. Kallas also recognized that changes in the division's IS architecture might require organizational changes as well. A decision had to be made soon. Or did it? Now the only question was, what to do?

VoIP2.biz, Inc.: Deciding on the Next Steps for a VoIP Supplier

Lawrence R. Milkowski, President and CEO of VoIP2.biz, Inc., an Indianapolis-based start-up supplier of Voice over Internet Protocol (VoIP) telephony to the small and midsize business market, knew he had a difficult job ahead of him. It was Friday, June 23, 2006, and he had to prepare his recommendations on the next steps for his fledgling company to the board of directors at its meeting on Tuesday, June 27, 2006. While Larry was a firm believer in the direction of the company, he knew that the board was anxious to resolve the future of the firm given the slower-than-hoped-for progress in getting the company's cash flow to break even.

The Company

In 2006, VoIP2.biz considered itself a systems integrator that worked with business customers to help them move their voice communications from legacy technology to VoIP technology. Through these activities, VoIP2.biz would become its clients' telephone company, thus earning a recurring revenue stream.

Management's plan was to continue to gain dominance in the Indianapolis market, expand the company's business activities throughout Indiana, and then open additional sales offices throughout the Midwest, gaining a first mover position in the marketplaces they served. Management believed that success in this strategy would make them an attractive acquisition target in the 2009 to 2010 timeframe.

Management thought that VoIP2.biz's business opportunity came from the recognition of five basic marketplace facts experienced by business customers with less than 400 voice telephone lines:

1. These businesses had often invested in separate voice networks, data networks, and Internet access technology whereby they had two distinct and separate monthly cost streams—a network for voice and one for data. Moreover, the voice network was often over configured and underutilized. In addition, specialized circuits for transporting voice calls often cost more, sometimes twice as much as the equivalent data circuit cost.

2. Most voice communication systems, called private branch exchanges (PBXs) or key telephone systems (KTSs), were special purpose machines with both proprietary hardware and software. As a result, they were expensive to buy, in the $1,000 to $2,000 per user range; expensive to maintain; and lacked the flexibility to easily adapt to specific user needs. They generally required specialized skills for moving, adding, or changing end-user stations—and therefore had a significant maintenance expense once installed.

3. Business customers understood that customer relationship management can be enhanced and additional sales can be made by the effective handling of their customer communication. For many businesses, the cost to purchase and implement the automated call distributors (ACDs) and the interactive voice response (IVR) applications required were just too expensive to be practical.

4. Business customers, particularly those with one to a hundred employees, or several hundred spread over several facilities, received very poor service from the traditional phone companies. They were often served by under-trained account managers with little technology experience or business knowledge, so it was difficult for the customer to get his or her questions answered or specific needs addressed.

5. Many customers lacked experienced networking people to help them make telephony decisions, and they often lacked a strong data processing staff with any experience in voice processing.

In order to meet these market needs, VoIP2.biz sold systems that:

1. Provided the economic benefits of collapsing the voice and data networks together into a consolidated network—one network instead of two,
2. Included the call origination and termination services in lieu of traditional phone company services, including low-cost long distance, E911, and all of the advanced features available through any traditional telephone carrier,
3. Utilized an open-source call processing platform that operated on commodity hardware in place of proprietary telephone systems, which was 10 percent to 20 percent of the cost of a competing technology, and
4. Were sold, engineered, installed, and supported by an experienced team of data and voice networking professionals.

Progress to Date

The concept behind VoIP2.biz came from some experimentation in early 2004 by personnel working for the Harley Services Corporation (HSC). HSC began business in 1995, providing outsourced engineering, installation, and marketing services to telecommunications carriers throughout the United States. By utilizing HSC's services, carriers were able to speed implementation of new customer services, such as DSL, and reduce costs by outsourcing central office engineering and equipment assembly. As a service provider to the carriers, HSC was in a unique position to understand and review new telecommunications technology prior to its general availability. In 2003, engineers at HSC started to investigate broadband applications, including video and voice over internet protocol (VoIP) applications.

During 2004, Milkowski and other personnel in HSC explored the market for VoIP and evaluated several then-current VoIP service providers. As a result of these investigations, the HSC project team designed a system to deliver a cost competitive IP PBX solution for implementing VoIP via an open source software platform. They selected an open source solution because it had the advantages of: (1) implementation on a commercially available commodity PC server, (2) high quality application code due to the ongoing review of a large user community, and (3) no licensing fees. Milkowski believed that the open source approach provided the best technological platform for smaller business customers due to its advanced call processing capability and significantly lower monthly telecommunications expense.

Beginning in October 2005, VoIP2.biz was spun out of HSC as a separate corporation, owned by several outside investors, Milkowski, and HSC. HSC retained 70 percent of the stock in VoIP2.biz. Milkowski then developed what was called internally the "Phase I Plan." In this plan, the infrastructure and staffing of

the business had to be completed and some presence in the market had to be accomplished. During late 2005 and the first half of 2006, employees at VoIP2.biz added to the functionality of the open-source IP PBX and entered into several reseller relationships with equipment manufacturers and carriers. These actions gave VoIP2.biz the ability to offer a complete end-to-end VoIP solution for business customers. Milkowski and his team of five engineers and sales professionals also sold the VoIP2.biz solution to several customers. VoIP2.biz signed agreements with four authorized distributors in Central Indiana to help sell the service to the business market. The team also developed a set of features for their product via internal work and relations with outside providers. Through its business activities to date, management was convinced that the open source solution offered by VoIP2.biz provided a small to midsize business customer a complete telephone system solution for 10 to 30 percent of the cost of a new proprietary solution from traditional vendors. For a detailed description of VoIP2.biz's services, see Exhibit 1.

By June 2006, VoIP2.biz was well on its way to completing the Phase I Plan. The company had sold several customers (the current count was 22), resolved several knotty technical issues, and completed hiring a small team of engineers (three) and sales/customer service people. However, the company was yet to break even financially from either a profit or cash flow standpoint. Revenue for October through December of 2005 totaled only $88,000 but resulted in a net loss of $86,000. Financial results for January through June 2006 were expected to be somewhat better with revenue expected to be nearly $150,000, but earnings before taxes were expected to be a negative $66,000. Several members of the board of directors thought that the company should be generating a profit or at least be at breakeven by June 30, 2006.

The Changing Telecommunications Landscape

By June 2006, many experts believed that the Internet would change business communication. However, while the impacts were dramatically changing data communications in a small or midsize business, voice communication often remained on the Plain Old Telephone Service (POTS). In the business market, voice communications was still important to business, and remained 10 to 20 times the size of Internet communication. Business still spent significant dollars every month on legacy telephony technology.

While the Internet had not yet had a major impact on business voice communication, several studies foresaw that business was at the beginning of the next phase in utilizing the Internet to further reduce costs. VoIP was seen as the next major breakthrough in voice communications.

In late 2005, several industry analysts predicted that much, if not most, of the voice traffic generated by businesses would

EXHIBIT 1
Detailed Description of VoIP2.biz's Services

VoIP2.biz Offerings

- The VoIP2.biz V2B System 1 IP PBX[SM], which provides the customer a VoIP solution for their enterprise
- The VoIP2.biz V2B Network Services[SM], which provides the customer connectivity to the telephone network for origination and termination of calls, and Internet access
- The VoIP2.biz Hosted Voice Services, which provides the customer a Centrex-like telephone system capability, including network services

VoIP2.biz V2B System 1 IP PBX[SM]

The V2B System 1 IP PBX is an Internet Protocol (IP)–based telephone system capable of originating, routing, delivering and managing voice communication for a customer enterprise. The IP PBX is implemented on an HP or IBM server running Linux and is installed by VoIP2.biz personnel on the customer's premises. VoIP2.biz integrates the system into the client's data network.

    The V2B System 1 IP PBX includes most of the commonly available communications features, including:

Automated Attendant	Conference Calling	"Meet Me" Capability
Call Forward	Do Not Disturb	Music on Hold
Call Park	External Line Access	Remote Users
Caller Log	Flexible Numbering Plan	Voicemail
Calling Name Display	Hunt Groups	Voicemail to E-Mail
Calling Number Display	Interactive Voice Response	

    Through VoIP2.biz's implementation process, the company defines the customer's specific call handling requirements and implements them in the V2B System 1 IP PBX. In most cases, these requirements include setting up specialized call handling, and applications such as voice mail, auto attendants, interactive voice response (IVR) and an automated call distributor (ACD). These applications are included in the V2B System 1 IP PBX.

    VoIP2.biz sells and installs, as an option, a graphical user interface (GUI) that runs on top of the Asterisk application and dramatically simplifies the administrative interface.

    As part of the system implementation, VoIP2.biz personnel interface the V2B System 1 IP PBX to the client's existing PBX or KTS so that the current analog phones can still be used; sells and installs new digital telephone sets; or does a combination of both.

    VoIP2.biz personnel often propose a migration plan to its customers. This plan calls for installing the V2B System 1 IP PBX first; then moving the voice network over to it, substituting IP trunking for POTS circuits; then moving the voice mail and call processing to the V2B System 1 IP PBX; and finally moving over all of the handsets and decommissioning the current system and voice network. This migration strategy reduces the perceived risk to the client and gets the network savings started as soon as possible.

VoIP2.biz V2B Network Services[SM]

While the V2B System 1 IP PBX can be installed and operate with an existing POTS telephone network, the operational savings of VoIP beyond the cost savings of the IP PBX itself, is best realized through consolidating the customer's voice and data network spending onto one network. Replacing voice telephone lines or trucks from the ILEC with data circuits from VoIP2.biz can generate a significant monthly savings for the customer. These new data circuits, combined with call origination and termination services, allow the V2B System 1 IP PBX to place and complete calls over the IP network. In summary, through VoIP2.biz's V2B Network Services, the company is providing:

- High-speed call trunking and Internet access
- Call origination and termination, including long distance and E911
- Local and toll-free number portability

The V2B Network Services Schedule includes:

- Internet Access—In order to assure quality of service, VoIP2.biz provides high-speed data circuits that also include Internet access. These circuits can augment or replace the customer's existing Internet access.

EXHIBIT 1 (*Continued*)

- Dial Tone—VoIP2.biz delivers dial tone to the desktop via the V2B System 1 IP PBX or remote user via VoIP2.biz provided facility.
- Phone Number Porting—At the customer's option, VoIP2.biz personnel can, in most cases, move the customer's existing direct inbound dial (DID) phone numbers into the VoIP2.biz service, and the customer will receive inbound phone calls on these numbers just as they have done in the past.
- Call Origination—Users of the VoIP2.biz service can originate or place phone calls, both local and long distance.
- Call Delivery—Calls will be delivered via the VoIP2.biz network to (1) other callers on the network, (2) local destinations, (3) long distance destinations, or (4) to other carrier facilities, as directed by the customer.
- Additional Services—including 911; E911; Directory Assistance or 411; and operator services.

VoIP2.biz V2B Hosted Voice Services

V2B Hosted Voice Services is a hosted Internet Protocol (IP)–based voice service that delivers the same feature functionality that is available in the V2B System 1 IP PBX bundled with the communications features of the V2B Network Services Schedule described above. This packaged offering allows the customer to utilize VoIP2.biz's capabilities and realize the savings of VoIP while paying a small start-up fee and a fixed monthly fee per user per month. This service bundles V2B System 1 IP PBX capabilities with the necessary network services into an easy to buy package. The V2B Hosted Voice Services Schedule includes:

- Internet Access—In order to assure quality of service, VoIP2.biz provides high-speed data circuits that also include Internet access. These circuits can augment or replace the customer's existing Internet access.
- Dial Tone—VoIP2.biz delivers dial tone to the desktop or remote user via VoIP2.biz provided facility.
- Phone Number Porting—At the customer's option, VoIP2.biz can, in most cases, move the customer's existing direct inbound dial (DID) phone numbers into the VoIP2.biz service, and will receive inbound phone calls on these numbers just as they have done in the past.
- Call Origination—Users of the VoIP2.biz service can originate or place phone calls, both local and long distance.
- Call Delivery—Calls will be delivered via the VoIP2.biz network to (1) other callers on the network, (2) local destinations, (3) long distance destinations, or (4) to other carrier facilities, as directed by the customer.
- Voice Mail—VoIP2.biz's Voice Services includes an integrated voice mail system, with voice mail to e-mail conversion.
- Additional Services—including 911; E911; Directory Assistance or 411; and operator services.

be delivered over Internet technologies. This change would happen for two key reasons:

- Businesses could consolidate voice and Internet connectivity into a single converged network that would carry voice, data, and video, reducing monthly communications expense *and* increasing Internet network capacity. By combining all communications over the Internet, the underutilized voice network capacity could be used to increase data network capacity. Because VoIP used less than half the network capacity of a traditional POTS phone call, customers would use less of their network capacity for voice.

- Delivering dial tone to the desktop and processing voice calls would become a commoditized application that would operate on standard PC hardware—eliminating the need for expensive, special use machines like traditional PBXs and KTSs, which require proprietary hardware and software.

Some experts argued that VoIP would also allow for integrating an organization's many locations, including remote workers,

into a single communications network. VoIP would also reduce communications cost and expand functionality by combining voice and data onto one network and by bringing advanced features not currently available to most small and midsize business customers.

In order for businesses to take advantage of these cost savings and functional enhancements, they would need to enhance or replace their existing telecommunications equipment, and replace their existing POTS telephone circuits with Internet connections. Utilizing open source voice applications and commodity Internet circuits, management at VoIP2.biz estimated that a business could achieve a four to six month payback on the required investment.

The Market for VoIP Services

As the telephone system in the United States was deregulated, technology vendors offered PBX systems for managing voice communication and optimizing the utilization of carrier services, reducing a company's monthly expense. Smaller versions of these systems, KTSs, were introduced next, making these savings available to smaller enterprises. Each manufacturer of PBXs and KTSs differentiated its products by integrating call processing features, like automated attendants and voice mail, into their systems. Eventually each manufacturer created a proprietary architecture of hardware, software, and telephone handsets for the market. Therefore, choosing Avaya as a business telephone system ruled out using components from Nortel, for example, to meet a future telecommunications need.

Over time, as the Internet expanded and became a business necessity, businesses deployed additional network services for Internet connectivity, and extended e-mail and Internet access to each desktop. Generally, these deployments were made totally independent of the existing voice communication infrastructure, including separate cabling systems and face plates.

The development of "open systems" standards, fundamentally meaning a defined interface for exchanging data between proprietary systems, created protocols like TCP/IP and made the Internet possible. In addition to speeding the development of application software and relational databases, these open systems standards made it possible for applications to be accessed from a standard browser, like Internet Explorer, dramatically reducing the cost to deploy and support Internet-based information services.

In time, engineers familiar with Internet technology began to reengineer traditional voice communication. Carriers began using Internet Protocol (IP) communication for voice traffic within their own networks, thus achieving significant savings. The broad acceptance of the need to adopt "open" standards drove traditional PBX manufacturers to accept Internet-based standard protocols for communicating within a network, making it possible for commodity priced components to be used with previously closed systems.

By 2006, many of the proprietary PBX and KTS manufacturers were reengineering their systems to include IP technology. However, they generally continued to deploy a proprietary system that limited the functionality available to their customer, and did not offer much cost savings. In order to take advantage of the cost savings available through IP networks, the customer had to go beyond the VoIP equipment sold to them, and reengineer their network. To see a savings, the POTS network needed to be replaced with an IP network. Then either the installed PBXs had to be replaced, or the customer would have to purchase expensive gateways that turned the new IP communication network back into POTS communication that the old PBXs could support. In short, achieving significant cost savings from network integration using the altered PBX or KTS systems was considered difficult by many smaller businesses.

Alternatively, organizations such as Digium, the authors of Asterisk, and Pingtel, developed application software that functioned just like a PBX, yet ran on commodity PC hardware under Linux. These systems, available for free and distributed as "open source" applications, provided virtually all of the features of a proprietary PBX, plus directly support IP trunking, and at a cost of as little as 10 percent of the cost of a traditional vendor's PBX.

In summary, as of June 2006, suppliers of voice communications systems for the small and midsize business market were selling:

a. Hosted VoIP solutions as replacements for long distance service, to both residential and commercial customers;

b. Proprietary telephone systems that utilized IP technologies for their internal workings; and

c. System integration solutions, such as VoIP2.biz's, which applied IP technology to address the entire business communications infrastructure and thereby deliver substantial enhancements in call processing *and* lower monthly costs.

The alternatives for the small and midsize business customer are summarized in the table on page 165. Hosted VoIP providers provided an additional phone number, sold long distance service, and linked to the existing Public Switched Telephone Network (PSTN) for delivering calls. . Either the supplier or provider could provide the telephone handsets. The provider didn't integrate with the rest of the business's telecommunications services and equipment, leaving that effort to the customer. System VoIP providers left even more functions to the customer. Management considered VoIP2.biz's solutions unique in offering the customer a single point of service and accountability for the entire telecommunications infrastructure.

The market for VoIP was typically measured in terms of how many POTS lines were available to be switched to VoIP service. In 2005, nearly 50 million POTS lines that could be switched to VoIP were installed in small enterprises in the United States. (The small enterprise market was defined as 100 telephone lines or less.) In Indiana, this market was estimated at 1 million POTS lines, and across the Midwest, it was estimated at 8.8 million POTS lines. Through 2005, it was estimated that less than 2 percent of these POTS lines had been converted to VoIP.

Management at VoIP2.biz summarized the small and midsize business market for their services as:

• These customers represented a large business opportunity;

• Currently, the customers were not appropriately served by the traditional telephone companies or carriers and were frustrated in their inability to work with these companies to get their business needs addressed;

• Most customers lacked the internal IT and telecommunications staff to manage their growth and required changes;

• A customer could dramatically decrease their monthly communications cost by moving to VoIP;

Implementation Type	VoIP Implementations			
	Residential	Commercial		
	Hosted	Hosted	System	VoIP2.biz
Phone Number	Vendor	Vendor	Customer	Either
Phone	Either	Either	Vendor	Either
Local Network	Customer	Customer	Customer	VoIP2.biz
PBX	—	—	Vendor	VoIP2.biz
Premise Switch / Router	Customer	Customer	Customer	VoIP2.biz
Wide Area Network/Internet	Customer	Customer	Customer	VoIP2.biz
Long Distance	Vendor	Vendor	Customer	VoIP2.biz
Public Switched Telephone Network (PSTN)	Vendor	Vendor	Customer	VoIP2.biz

- In order to take advantage of IP networking cost savings and enhanced features, a customer had to replace its existing PBX;
- Less than 10 percent of the PBXs on the market had some type of IP capability;
- The forecasted spending on IP PBXs was estimated to grow from $1 billion worldwide annually (2002) to $8 billion worldwide annually by 2008;
- Open source IP PBXs, such as Asterisk, could be implemented for 10 to 30 percent of the cost of a traditional vendor's IP PBX;
- To reach its objectives, the company would have to secure only 2 percent of the business market with 100 lines of less; and
- Expanding the target market to businesses with 400 lines or less would increase the market size an estimated 40 percent, and VoIP2.biz would need to only secure 1.4 percent of this expanded market.

VoIP2.biz's Differential Advantage

In a May 2006 presentation to a local venture capital company, Milkowski listed the following reasons why VoIP2.biz would be successful in the market:

"VoIP2.biz sells only to the business market. The big competitors (such as Vonage) are primarily targeting the residential market;

"VoIP2.biz focuses on the small and midsize business market where most of the competitors are not playing. We focus on the 20 to 100 line market primarily but will go up to 400 lines when an opportunity arises;

"We understand that delivering VoIP for business customers is not about saving money on long distance. Their long distance expense is typically only 5 to 10 percent of their telecommunications budget. VoIP for business customers is all about consolidating their networks and utilizing commodity-based technology to dramatically reduce their overall telecommunications costs.

"We believe we are the first company to offer an open-source VoIP IP PBX solution in the greater Indianapolis marketplace. We expect to be the best throughout the Midwest. The only competitors with a solution close to ours operate in New York, Atlanta, and California.

"VoIP2.biz's offerings are unique in that the company addresses the entire communications systems needs of its clients—from handsets through network connections.

"We believe our use of an open source platform instead of reselling a proprietary PBX manufacturer's product results in the customer realizing a savings in both the technology acquisition costs and in the ongoing operating costs of an IP PBX.

"Finally, our cost structure allows us to deliver a new PBX solution (the most popular alternative for these customers) cheaper than our competition as this chart indicates (see page 166). If you review the chart for several competitors, it is clear that VoIP2.biz offers a strong product in our target market. For both small systems (25 users) and for larger systems (200 users), our total cost of operation (TCO) per user at list price is substantially below all the known competitors . . . and the same is true for just the initial investment and for the ongoing cost with maintenance."

The Competition

In early 2006, management conducted an analysis of competing voice communication solutions offered to business customers. The results of this study were summarized in a report to the board of directors in April 2006:

- **National Hosted VoIP Solution Providers:** Starting with organizations like Vonage, these business entities use a national IP transport network to offer business customers low-cost long-distance service. Analogous to cellular phone service, these implementations are not integrated into the business's existing telecommunications environment. Through data gained by management,

Manufacturer	Model	Avg Cost per User (List)–5 Year TCO Analysis				
		25	50	75	100	200
3COM	NBX	$ 578	$ 533	$ 505	$ 470	$ 474
	with Maintenance	$ 1,127	$ 1,039	$ 985	$ 917	$ 924
Alcatel	Omni PCX Enterprise	$ 1,000	$ 900	$ 875	$ 850	$ 800
	with Maintenance	$ 1,950	$ 1,755	$ 1,706	$ 1,658	$ 1,560
Avaya	IP Office 403 & Definity Multivantage	$ 1,094	$ 909	$ 855	$ 800	$ 750
	with Maintenance	$ 2,133	$ 1,733	$ 1,667	$ 1,560	$ 1,463
Cisco	CallManager	$ 1,112	$ 918	$ 900	$ 899	$ 650
	with Maintenance	$ 2,168	$ 1,790	$ 1,755	$ 1,734	$ 1,268
Mitel	3300 ICP	$ 1,020	$ 720	$ 620	$ 560	$ 547
	with Maintenance	$ 1,989	$ 1,404	$ 1,209	$ 1,092	$ 1,067
Nortel	BCM	$ 1,170	$ 1,040	$ 885	$ 800	$ 750
	with Maintenance	$ 2,282	$ 2,028	$ 1,726	$ 1,560	$ 1,463
Target	VoIP2.biz	$ 280				$ 120
	with Maintenance	$ 500				$ 320

these providers are experiencing problems with the lack of data experience in their channel partners and are having difficulty in dealing with customer concerns. Representative companies in this group include *www. vonage.com*; *www.packet8.com*; *www.broadband.com*; and *www.broadvoice.com*. Generally, these systems are priced from $29.95 to $40.00 per line per month, plus installation fees. Some market participants provide Internet access and sell telephone handsets.

- **Incumbent Local Exchange Carriers (ILECs):** The ILECs, principally AT&T and Verizon in Indiana, have long dominated the traditional market for voice communication. They sell network services through a variety of channels, based on business size. ILECs sell IP-enabled PBXs from manufacturers such as Nortel, Avaya and Cisco. Generally, the ILECs sell equipment, referred to as customer premise equipment (CPE), in order to enable their network sales and maintain an account presence. The systems they sell are generally proprietary implementations of VoIP and generally cost $1,500 to $2,000 a station, with "right-to-use" fees for additional software applications. ILECs offer better pricing for Internet access T1s than for T1s used for voice communication.

- **Competitive Local Exchange Carriers (CLECs):** These firms offer competitive data connectivity for businesses to access the Internet or buy dedicated point-to-point data connectivity in fractional as well as full T1s. Some CLECs implement a hosted VoIP solution using a Cisco platform, though none in the Indianapolis marketplace. Others are reselling the services offered by the national providers described previously. Generally, the infrastructure required to implement a VoIP solution using Cisco is reported to be too expensive to be profitable for most CLECs, and we have

learned that the margin available for reselling the national hosted offerings was also not attractive. In addition, most CLECs are not comfortable with selling and servicing voice solutions—they are data providers. Both eGix (*www.egix. com*) and Ultimate Medium (*www.ultimatemedium.com*) have attempted to sell hosted VoIP solutions in the greater Indianapolis marketplace. Management understands that Ultimate Medium has withdrawn these services. Management believes Ultimate Medium represents an attractive partnering opportunity for VoIP2.biz rather than an effective direct competitor.

- **Cable Companies:** The companies are preparing to enter the VoIP marketplace, beginning with residential service. BrightHouse launched a residential offering at year-end 2005. They plan to offer a business service in the future, but as most businesses are not cabled and linked to the existing cable network, a significant capital expense would have to be incurred by the cable company or the customer in order for cable to be an effective alternative.

- **Internet Service Providers (ISPs):** ISPs see VoIP services as an attractive service extension, particularly for residential customers. Clearly, AOL, MSN, and other national ISPs should soon be rolling out residential VoIP services. ISPs that service business customers have long searched for an additional value-added service they could offer in addition to Internet access. With VoIP, an ISP could add a profitable service. To date, few local business-oriented ISPs have implemented a VoIP business strategy. Management expects wireless ISPs would also be interested in adding VoIP services.

- **Interconnects and PBX VARs:** VARs and interconnects have traditionally provided a competitive alternative to the ILECs for smaller firms, usually at a lower cost point. Many of these firms sell systems from existing PBX manufacturers, such as Nortel, Avaya, and Siemens. Rarely have they had the data expertise to sell and install a Cisco solution. In marketplace discussions, several firms have started selling lower-cost PBXs, including Mitel, NEC, Toshiba, and ShoreTel. These enterprises may prove to be good channel partners for VoIP2.biz. In the Indianapolis marketplace, these competitors included VanAusdell & Farrar (*www.vanausdell.com*) and MVD Communications (*www.mvdcommunications.com*).

- **Data Networking Solution Providers:**   These organizations have historically sold, installed, and serviced data networking infrastructure. They are in a strong position to add on VoIP equipment and services to their customer base. Organizations such as Fusion Alliance (*www.fusionalliance.com*) and Advanced Micro (*www.advancedmicro.com*) have expressed an aversion to management to working on voice communications solutions and an interest in partnering with experienced firms such as VoIP2.biz.

The Phase II Plan

Overview of the Plan   Beginning in July 2006, management planned to implement VoIP2.biz's "Phase II" plan. This plan was divided into two segments, the first from June 2006 through June 2007 with these objectives:

- Expansion of sales and marketing activities in Indianapolis to achieve two new system sales per week;
- Expansion of sales and marketing activities in Indiana beyond Indianapolis;
- Targeting specific opportunity areas such as large call center opportunities;
- Beginning sales and operations in five additional markets; and
- Developing a franchise strategy for smaller geographic markets.

Management would select suitable new geographic markets during the third quarter of 2006. The new markets would be entered in stages, beginning in the fourth quarter of 2006. These markets would be located in the Midwest and selected based upon having:

1. a population of at least 500,000 and the presence of approximately 200,000 business telephone lines;
2. no other competitor selling an open source IP PBX platform;
3. an effective reseller relationship with a CLEC operating in the marketplace;
4. the availability of suitable authorized distributors; and

5. the availability of local staffing with the appropriate experience, skills, and prospect network.

These market expansions would be supported by systems engineering, network engineering, network provisioning, and equipment configuring work from VoIP2.biz's Indianapolis headquarters. For geographic markets below a population of 500,000 people, VoIP2.biz would develop and market VoIP2.biz franchises. The company would begin sales of these franchises by the end of Phase II.

The marketing plan for these new markets would commence with:

1. identifying a general/sales manager for the market;
2. recruiting a sales support/project management resource;
3. partnering with the selected local CLEC and its sales force for low-cost T1 capacity;
4. recruiting appropriate authorized distributors to help reach the business market;
5. securing and installing the initial pilot customers;
6. launching advertising for VoIP2.biz;
7. securing editorial coverage in local business press;
8. purchasing local National Public Radio sponsorship during morning drive time;
9. conducting direct mail campaigns with follow-up cold-call prospecting; and
10. offering local seminars to business groups regarding the benefits of VoIP and VoIP2.biz's unique business model.

The second segment of the Phase II Plan would start in July 2007 and last until June 2010. During this time period, the company would enter an additional two markets per quarter for six quarters bringing VoIP2.biz's Midwest presence to 18 markets by late 2008 and achieving a revenue exceeding $60 million by the end of 2009. The plan called for selling the company to a larger provider sometime during 2010.

Sales and Marketing   The company planned a three-fold channel strategy: selling through indirect channels, direct marketing to potential business customers, and selling VoIP "telco-in-the-box" turnkey solutions to network providers. The company's franchise strategy would allow entry into smaller geographic markets by partnering with knowledgeable solution providers. These partnerships would use technology and business processes from VoIP2.biz and the sales and installation resources of the partner.

In addition to using authorized distributors to reach the market, the company planned to use direct sales efforts by selling to small and midsize business owners and financial officers as well as information technology leaders in these companies. Both direct mail and cold calling were being planned in this effort. Previous experience had shown a good response to these campaigns as businesses are generally aware of VoIP as a topic that could save their company money and that they should spend time to learn more about it. While company personnel had had excellent success in obtaining interviews with the client and gaining permission to write a proposal for converting their voice communications network to VoIP, Milkowski knew that the Phase II Plan had to solve the problem of a low close rate. While most clients did not say "no," the length of time to gain a "yes" was estimated to be six to nine months.

In addition to selling directly and through authorized distributors to businesses, Milkowski wanted to build a "telco-in-the-box" offering that provided smaller telecommunications carriers and ISPs with the capability of adding voice services to their existing data networking services. In June 2006, management was negotiating with its first carrier customer for these services and had discussions with several additional carriers.

In terms of growing the business, Milkowski planned that as VoIP2.biz entered new markets, the company would execute an advertising and promotion plan that introduced the benefits of VoIP, the advantages of an open source platform. They also planned to secure reference accounts in each local marketplace.

Upon entering each market, Milkowski planned to launch a substantial local advertising campaign. Management planned to begin promoting VoIP through local business groups, advertising through local business media, and obtaining drive time "sponsorships" on the local National Public Radio station. A sample of an advertisement run during June 2006 in the *Indianapolis Business Journal* is shown in Exhibit 2.

As shown earlier, VoIP2.biz offered solutions under both a hosted and a system sales pricing structure. Under the Phase II Plan, these hosted solutions would be priced at $25 to $30 per user per month, plus the monthly cost of Internet access. They planned these contracts to normally be three-year agreements. The company planned to charge for nonrecurring services, which included an installation fee of $1,000 plus the cost of any telephone handsets and any optional data networking equipment and services the customer needed.

System sales pricing would include nonrecurring charges for installation, hardware and software installed on the client site, telephone handsets and one-time network charges; and recurring charges for network, direct inbound dial phone numbers (DID's), long-distance telecom, and software support.

The Phase II Plan called for these systems to be priced at a 50 percent gross margin basis for the initial installation, with annual maintenance fees for the software. The customer also had monthly fees for the network connection and the call origination and termination service. The monthly networking price was quoted at very low margins, 20 to 30 percent, as T-1 pricing was broadly advertised in the market and was a generalized way to measure competition, but the monthly call origination and ter-

EXHIBIT 2
Sample Marketing Materials

Getting hosed?

Time to review what your business is spending for telephone service.

With VoIP2.BIZ, you get:

- Fully functional phone systems
- Voice mail delivered through e-mail
- Low cost call center and call recording technology
- Monthly communications cost savings at 40% to 60%

Get smart answers about VoIP
Call 317.888.XXXX or visit www.voip2.biz

mination service could be priced very profitably—at 80 to 90 percent margin. The following example (see page 169) shows target margins for different system sizes up to 128 stations.

Since late 2005, management had also been successful in securing presentation engagements at business forums to discuss VoIP. Information technology leaders were interested in open source solutions, and in extending their data networking to include voice processing capabilities. Many had heard of Asterisk, and a few had installed it as an R&D activity. Generally, they were open to learn more about it. The Phase II Plan called for several presentations in each market early in the market entry process.

Operations Milkowski felt that VoIP2.biz conducted business similar to a traditional professional services firm, implementing complex voice and data networking solutions. Therefore, he organized the sales support and operations functions accordingly in the Phase II Plan.

During the presales process, VoIP2.biz sales personnel planned to conduct a site survey and identify the prospect's current voice and data infrastructure components, including reviewing its telecommunications bills. In this process, VoIP2.biz personnel gained an understanding of future communications

System Configurations		Stations			
		16	32	64	128
	Processors	Single	Single	Single	Dual
	Margin				
Revenue					
Non-recurring Charges (NRC)					
System	40%	$ 2,907	$ 4,247	$ 5,704	$ 8,533
Implementation	50%	$ 2,200	$ 2,200	$ 3,400	$ 7,000
Network	20%	$ 300	$ 300	$ 600	$ 900
Sets	30%	$ 4,606	$ 9,211	$ 18,423	$ 36,846
Annual Recurring					
Software Fee		$ 1,800	$ 1,800	$ 3,600	$ 6,000
User Support Fees		$ 67	$ 134	$ 269	$ 538
Monthly Recurring – annualized					
Network	20%	$ 3,600	$ 3,600	$ 7,200	$ 10,800
DIDs	80%	$ 1,920	$ 3,840	$ 7,680	$ 15,360
LD	58%	$ 1,114	$ 2,227	$ 4,454	$ 8,909
Costs					
System		$ 1,980	$ 2,870	$ 3,830	$ 5,720
Implementation		$ 653	$ 1,057	$ 2,113	$ 3,627
Network		$ 2,880	$ 2,880	$ 5,760	$ 8,640
DIDs		$ 384	$ 768	$ 1,536	$ 3,072
Sets		$ 3,224	$ 6,448	$ 12,896	$ 25,792
LD		$ 472	$ 945	$ 1,889	$ 3,779
Margin					
NRC		$ 3,705	$ 5,622	$ 9,629	$ 18,147
Recurring		$ 4,123	$ 5,726	$ 11,453	$ 20,986
System Margin %		48%	45%	44%	46%
LD		$ 641	$ 1,283	$ 2,565	$ 5,130
LD Margin %		58%	58%	58%	58%
First 12 months revenue		$ 18,514	$ 27,560	$ 51,330	$ 94,885
First 12 months margin		$ 8,469	$ 12,631	$ 23,647	$ 44,263
Second 12 months margin		$ 4,764	$ 7,009	$ 14,018	$ 26,116

needs such as opening a new office, hiring significant additional employees, or a planned business relocation. With this information, VoIP2.biz engineers would prepare an initial statement of work, and then a prospect proposal would be presented. Experience had taught Milkowski that the prospect would want to see a demonstration and experience VoIP2.biz's service so the plan called for sales personnel to install a demonstration phone at the client site.

Once the business deal is closed, the plan called for VoIP2.biz engineers to follow a structured implementation process to complete station reviews, specify a dial plan and voice processing applications, build the appropriate IP PBX system software, order and install the necessary equipment, and complete customer training and cutover to the new system.

The plan called for billing activities to be triggered at both the installation of network facilities and at system installation time.

VoIP2.biz planned to provide post-installation support through its technical support center, which had been outsourced to HSC's technical support center team. VoIP2.biz managed its own network operations center (NOC).

Key Milestones Milkowski strongly believed in setting firm, measurable milestones during the Phase II Plan.

The operations team would be expected to:

- Deploy a second co-location site in order to have tandem network and call processing facilities and back up connectivity. This facility was planned for the third quarter of 2006, and would be implemented in downtown Indianapolis.

- Complete implementation of a graphical user interface for end user management via a Web-based tool by the fourth quarter of 2006.
- Implement the recently available extensions to Asterisk that provided for end user integration with Microsoft Outlook by the fourth quarter of 2006.
- Implement a billing system for automating the billing of clients for end user long-distance minutes by the fourth quarter of 2006.

The business development team would be expected to:

- Add additional sales resources for business expansion in Indianapolis during the third quarter of 2006. Close at least 8 new business contracts per month starting six months after entry into a market. Close at least 12 new business contracts per month starting a year after entry into a market.
- Select the appropriate markets and begin staffing for the expansion into additional geographic markets by August 2006.
- Initiate targeted sales activities to Midwest call centers and smaller carrier prospects by the fourth quarter of 2006.
- Complete the development of the franchise business approach for smaller geographic markets and

begin recruiting franchise partners during the fourth quarter of 2006.

The Investment Required   In order to carry out the Phase II Plan, management at VoIP2.biz planned to raise an additional investment of $3 million. Milkowski believed that his plan was an excellent investment because the company had successfully sold and implemented several customers in the greater Indianapolis marketplace, and the firm was poised to enter several additional Midwestern markets. The successful implementation of the Phase II Plan would require significant expenditures in marketing and working capital investment. The $3 million investment would be used primarily to fund this market expansion, and to fund general corporate and operating needs. A detailed breakdown of anticipated cash flows from the implementation of the plan is included in Exhibit 3.

Milkowski knew that this investment would have to come from outside sources. While HSC and some angel investors had provided the funding for VoIP2.biz to date, HSC management had determined that they would be investing only internally for the next two years. While some of the other investors could provide some investment capital, no current investor was willing to invest the entire $3 million.

Financial Projections   As part of the process of preparing the investment proposal, Milkowski had prepared a set of detailed assumptions about the future of the business. A summary of those assumptions is shown next:

EXHIBIT 3
Projected Statement of Cash Flow

Statement of Cash Flow (All figures in $000)

Forecasted		2006		2007		2008		2009		2010
Net (Loss) Income	$	(428)	$	(1,193)	$	1,151	$	9,738	$	22,866
Adjustments for non-cash item										
Depreciation	$	43	$	124	$	215	$	196	$	148
Working capital changes										
Accounts Receivable (Increase)	$	(384)	$	(1,633)	$	(3,611)	$	(3,902)	$	(3,147)
Inventory (Increase)	$	(36)	$	(290)	$	(535)	$	(343)	$	914
Accounts Payable Increase	$	304	$	1,644	$	3,743	$	4,129	$	3,292
Accrued Payroll Increase	$	26	$	108	$	144	$	81	$	(14)
Cash used for operations	$	(476)	$	(1,238)	$	1,106	$	9,899	$	24,058
Cash used for investments	$	(68)	$	(244)	$	(244)	$	(100)	$	(100)
Cash from financing activities	$	3,000			$	(250)				
Change in cash for period	$	2,456	$	(1,482)	$	612	$	9,799	$	23,958
Cash beginning of period	$	250	$	2,706	$	1,224	$	1,836	$	11,635
Cash ending of period	$	2,706	$	1,224	$	1,836	$	11,635	$	35,593

- The company would enter additional markets on the following schedule:

  - One market in October 2006
  - Two markets in 1Q 2007
  - Two markets in 2Q 2007
  - Two markets in 3Q 2007
  - Two markets in 4Q 2007
  - Two markets in 1Q 2008
  - Two markets in 2Q 2008
  - Two markets in 3Q 2008
  - Two markets in 4Q 2008

- The average customer fee per line would be $26.50 per month.
- Sales would be 65 percent systems and 35 percent hosted.
- Sales would come from:

  - In Indiana: 75 percent direct/25 percent authorized distributors
  - In additional markets: 25 percent direct/75 percent authorized distributors

- The cost to acquire a new customer would be around $120.

- 20 percent of the current customer base would leave after the first year of service.
- VoIP2.biz would outsource call center technical support at $0.55 per minute.
- Network engineering would be conducted at the Indianapolis headquarters; local market staff would conduct station reviews and installations.

Using these assumptions, Milkowski developed a projected statement of earnings (see Exhibit 4) and balance sheets (see Exhibit 5) through 2009.

The Options

As Milkowski thought about what he was going to present to the board, he began considering his options. The first option was to move forward with the Phase II Plan. He was very proud of the progress made in Phase I. For an investment of about $1 million to date, VoIP2.biz had the following accomplishments:

- Completed the installation of the network technology to support deploying VoIP solutions at customer sites,
- Tested and debugged the technology, making selections on the components to be included in its solution set,

EXHIBIT 4
Projected Statement of Earnings

The summary included below includes the forecasted income statement for the Indianapolis operation, which includes sales and delivery for the Indiana marketplace, plus centralized engineering, procurement and material management, and corporate management. The summary also includes the forecasted income statement used in building this business plan for each additional market that VoIP2.biz enters. While the experience and results for each market will likely be unique and may vary significantly from the forecast shown, the forecast was based on the experience the management team has had opening and operating in the greater Indianapolis marketplace.

The overall financial projections in this business plan were derived by applying a specific phased launch schedule and totaling financials for each period by matrix math against the "each additional market" forecast. The launch schedule for additional markets as used in this business plan was:

Phase I - First Segment:

- One market in July 2006
- Two markets in October 2006
- Two markets in January 2007

Phase II - Second Segment
- Two markets in 1Q FY2008
- Two markets in 2Q FY2008
- Two markets in 3Q FY2008
- Two markets in 4Q FY2008
- Two markets in 1Q FY2009
- Two markets in 2Q FY2009

Exhibit 4 (continued)

VoIP2.Biz
Business Model Income Statement Summary (All dollar figures in $000)

2006	Jan-06	Feb-06	Mar-06	Apr-06	May-06	Jun-06	Jul-06	Aug-06	Sep-06	Oct-06	Nov-06	Dec-06	Total
Total Cumulative Users							608	848	1152	1488	1824	2176	2176
Revenue							$ 69	$ 125	$ 129	$ 166	$ 163	$ 171	$ 1,023
COGS							$ 42	$ 82	$ 83	$ 105	$ 116	$ 120	$ 618
Gross Margin							$ 26	$ 43	$ 46	$ 61	$ 47	$ 52	$ 405
S, G&A Expense							$ 71	$ 76	$ 76	$ 103	$ 103	$ 103	$ 832
Earnings before Tax								$ (44)	$ (33)	$ (30)	$ (42)	$ (56)	$ (52)

2007	Jan-07	Feb-07	Mar-07	Apr-07	May-07	Jun-07	Jul-07	Aug-07	Sep-07	Oct-07	Nov-07	Dec-07	Total
Sales per Period	10	12	13	17	24	26	32	40	44	48	58	61	385
Total Cumulative Users	2512	2976	3488	4048	5040	5856	6896	8512	9936	11552	14000	16064	16064
Revenue	$ 199	$ 190	$ 265	$ 285	$ 308	$ 523	$ 447	$ 564	$ 868	$ 782	$ 924	$ 1,363	$ 6,718
COGS	$ 127	$ 130	$ 173	$ 194	$ 220	$ 357	$ 330	$ 413	$ 591	$ 581	$ 656	$ 905	$ 4,687
Gross Margin	$ 72	$ 61	$ 92	$ 91	$ 89	$ 166	$ 117	$ 151	$ 277	$ 200	$ 268	$ 448	$ 2,032
S, G&A Expense	$ 171	$ 170	$ 167	$ 230	$ 228	$ 220	$ 311	$ 301	$ 289	$ 386	$ 382	$ 370	$ 3,224
Earnings before Tax	$ (99)	$(110)	$ (75)	$(139)	$(140)	$ (54)	$(193)	$(150)	$ (12)	$(185)	$(114)	$ (78)	$(1,193)

Exhibit 4 (continued)

2008	Jan-08	Feb-08	Mar-08	Apr-08	May-08	Jun-08	Jul-08	Aug-08	Sep-08	Oct-08	Nov-08	Dec-08	Total
Sales per Period	67	79	81	91	704	105	116	130	130	142	156	156	1357
Total Cumulative Users	18320	21664	24432	27472	31792	35344	39184	44496	48848	53552	59856	65072	65072
Revenue	$ 1,184	$ 1,335	$ 1,896	$ 1,648	$ 1,848	$ 2,483	$ 2,211	$ 2,426	$ 3,136	$ 2,826	$ 3,099	$ 3,851	$27,942
COGS	$ 865	$ 947	$ 1,284	$ 1,202	$ 1,315	$ 1,709	$ 1,597	$ 1,718	$ 2,166	$ 2,028	$ 2,165	$ 2,656	$19,652
Gross Margin	$ 319	$ 388	$ 613	$ 446	$ 533	$ 773	$ 614	$ 708	$ 969	$ 798	$ 934	$ 1,195	$ 8,291
S, G&A Expense	$ 471	$ 467	$ 445	$ 564	$ 558	$ 534	$ 651	$ 644	$ 618	$ 744	$ 735	$ 709	$ 7,140
Earnings before Tax	$ (152)	$ (78)	$ 167	$ (118)	$ (25)	$ 239	$ (37)	$ 64	$ 351	$ 54	$ 199	$ 486	$ 1,151

2009	Jan-09	Feb-09	Mar-09	Apr-09	May-09	Jun-09	Jul-09	Aug-09	Sep-09	Oct-09	Nov-09	Dec-09	Total
Sales per Period	168	182	182	190	202	200	208	216	210	218	224	220	2420
Total Cumulative Users	70640	77936	84016	90352	98416	105168	112080	120656	127696	134896	143632	150960	150960
Revenue	$ 3,544	$ 3,838	$ 4,631	$ 4,326	$ 4,613	$ 5,378	$ 5,114	$ 5,326	$ 6,023	$ 5,713	$ 5,937	$ 6,540	$60,985
COGS	$ 2,501	$ 2,643	$ 3,172	$ 3,005	$ 3,117	$ 3,637	$ 3,453	$ 3,543	$ 4,031	$ 3,796	$ 3,874	$ 4,326	$41,099
Gross Margin	$ 1,043	$ 1,195	$ 1,460	$ 1,322	$ 1,496	$ 1,741	$ 1,661	$ 1,783	$ 1,992	$ 1,917	$ 2,063	$ 2,214	$19,886
S, G&A Expense	$ 796	$ 787	$ 761	$ 846	$ 840	$ 816	$ 879	$ 875	$ 855	$ 905	$ 901	$ 887	$10,148
Earnings before Tax	$ 247	$ 408	$ 699	$ 475	$ 656	$ 925	$ 782	$ 908	$ 1,137	$ 1,012	$ 1,161	$ 1,328	$ 9,738

EXHIBIT 5
Projected Balance Sheets

Balance Sheets (All figures in $000)

	7/1/2006	12/31/2006	12/31/2007	12/31/2008	12/31/2009	12/31/2010
Assets						
Cash	$ 250	$ 2,706	$ 1,224	$ 1,836	$ 11,635	$ 35,593
Accounts Receivable	$ 50	$ 434	$ 2,066	$ 5,678	$ 9,580	$ 12,727
Inventory	$ 10	$ 46	$ 336	$ 872	$ 1,215	$ 301
Total Current Assets	$ 310	$ 3,187	$ 3,626	$ 8,385	$ 22,429	$ 48,620
Fixed Assets	$ 60	$ 128	$ 372	$ 616	$ 716	$ 816
Accumulated Depreciation	$ -	$ (43)	$ (167)	$ (382)	$ (578)	$ (726)
Net Fixed Assets	$ 60	$ 85	$ 205	$ 234	$ 138	$ 90
Total Assets	$ 370	$ 3,272	$ 3,832	$ 8,619	$ 22,567	$ 48,710
Liabilities						
Accounts Payable	$ -	$ 304	$ 1,948	$ 5,691	$ 9,820	$ 13,112
Accrued Payroll	$ -	$ 26	$ 134	$ 277	$ 358	$ 344
Notes Payable	$ -	$ -	$ -	$ -	$ -	$ -
Total Current Liabilities	$ -	$ 329	$ 2,082	$ 5,968	$ 10,178	$ 13,456
Notes Payable	$ 250	$ 250	$ 250	$ -	$ -	$ -
Total Liabilities	$ 250	$ 579	$ 2,332	$ 5,968	$ 10,178	$ 13,456
Owners Equity						
Common Stock	$ 1,000	$ 4,000	$ 4,000	$ 4,000	$ 4,000	$ 4,001
Retained Earnings	$ (880)	$ (1,308)	$ (2,500)	$ (1,349)	$ 8,389	$ 31,253
Total Owners Equity	$ 120	$ 2,692	$ 1,500	$ 2,651	$ 12,389	$ 35,254
Total Liabilities and Equity	$ 370	$ 3,272	$ 3,832	$ 8,619	$ 22,567	$ 48,710

- Evaluated several graphical user interfaces (GUIs) and reporting packages for the Asterisk platform improving its general suitability for the small and midsize business markets,

- Secured distribution and reseller agreements for the necessary network and equipment service components,

- Developed processes for provisioning network, implementing systems, providing customer service, managing materials and billing,

- Developed and implemented processes for prospecting, seminar selling, and mass marketing,

- Secured sales channel relationships with four authorized distributors,

- Hired and trained required staffing in software systems engineering, network engineering and project management,

- Contracted with and installed an initial 22 customers, and

- Operated in late June 2006 at a rate of nearly 20,000 calls per week with a quality rating exceeding 98 %.

Milkowski knew that in order for the board of directors to accept the option of implementing Phase II, he would have to explain how he and his team were going to increase acceptance of the technology at a much faster pace without spending huge amounts of money. The board at their last meeting had indicated that they would invest only another $500,000 through the end of 2006 *if* an acceptable plan were to be developed.

Of course, continuing with the Phase II Plan was not the only option. Milkowski was aware that at least some members of the board were concerned about the future of VoIP as a viable commercial venture given the recent history of the best known VoIP firm—Vonage. Their stock's history since the IPO was anything but stellar. Several speculated that VoIP was just a few years ahead of its time. They recognized that Vonage was primarily a service for the residence market, and VoIP2.biz attacked the small and midsize business market. Still they were concerned. They did not believe that the firm could be sold for very much given the lack of a positive cash flow. These board members thought the firm should be shut down. Milkowski knew that closing down service would cause major disruptions for his 22 customers. He also did not like this alternative as it would put his people out of a job. While jobs were plentiful for skilled engineers, he knew that it would take longer to find positions for his more senior employees, each of whom had a sizeable mortgage and ongoing expenses. These people had joined the firm over the last year, each taking a substantial cut in salary.

Finally, Milkowski knew that the company could be sold to another firm. He had been contacted by two firms who had related businesses in the Indianapolis area. In order to recommend this course of action, Milkowski knew that he would have to develop and justify a proposed sale price. He knew the price should be based on the potential of future earnings. He also

was aware that earlier investors would like to at least recover their investment to date. Finally, he knew he should consider in setting the price for the firm that the 22 contracts already obtained represented pretty certain cash flow for the life of the contract. He was certain that most if not all of those contracts would transfer easily to the surviving company.

As he was trying to decide what option to recommend, his Vice President of Sales and Service, Jim O'Neil, came into the office. Jim said, "Larry, remember that large call center we have been trying to land? Well, it worked. . .they said they will sign the contract. . .and it is for 100 seats, expanding to 300 seats in three locations over the next year. We have a meeting on Monday to pick up the signed contract."

THE VOIP ADOPTION AT BUTLER UNIVERSITY

As CIO Kincaid looked back over the past 12 months, he took pride in the fact that Butler University had taken a major step forward with a network capability for the twenty-first century—the convergence of its data and voice networks. Yet the choices that had been made in the past year were not for the "faint of heart": his IT organization had taken on a lot more in-house responsibility for voice communications than in the past at a time in which network security risks were heightened concerns. This also meant 24/7 visibility for the telephony staff people who for the first time were working alongside their data network counterparts.

Kincaid wondered: *Did we make the right decisions? Have we taken on too much?*

IT at Butler University

Butler University is a private liberal arts college in Indianapolis, Indiana. Founded in 1855 by attorney Ovid Butler, the university was comprised of five colleges and 20 buildings on 290 acres, and a student enrollment of 4,400 students in 2005, the year it celebrated its 150th anniversary. More than half of the enrolled students lived on campus and depended on the university for network and telephone services.

Butler's Information Resources (IR) department (see Exhibit 1) consists of 40 staff members that service the technology needs of not only its students, but also approximately 900 faculty and staff members. The CIO, Scott Kincaid, reports to the president of the university; formerly a CIO at a major financial services firm, Kincaid was the first IT leader at Butler to be given the CIO designation. Reporting to Kincaid are four directors responsible for the university's IT services: Network and Systems, Administrative Computing, Web Applications

Development, and Instructional Technology. Part-time student workers are employed in all four of these areas, with an especially heavy dependence on students for help desk and instructional lab support services.

Campuswide, the IT organization was responsible for supporting over 125 servers, over 1,400 university-owned desktops, and approximately 7,000 network connections. Since 2001, the university's administrative systems have included PeopleSoft[1] ERP modules for Human Resources, Finance, Campus Solutions (student administration), and Enterprise Portal.

Prior to 2005, Butler had utilized SBC's[2] Centrex service to provide 3,000 phone stations, with most faculty and staff having basic single-line analog phones. The Centrex system was an outsourced solution: essentially, all call switching was handled by a local telephone provider (SBC), rather than by a university-owned system, and Butler paid for the services on a monthly basis. Over the past decade, the SBC Centrex system had been very reliable, but it lacked more modern functions, such as intelligent call queuing. Voice mail was provided by a Centigram 640 system that provided a single voice mailbox to each dorm room, which meant that students had to share both their phone number and voice-mail box with their roommates.

The outsourcing arrangement enabled the university to avoid the costs of ownership and the day-to-day management of the communications equipment that would be required if it had implemented its own private branch exchange (PBX). While very reliable, the Centrex system was based on features over a decade old, and was not easily customizable. It had therefore become an impediment to implementing customer call center service features, such as advanced call routings. As departments grew and personnel changed, moving phones

---

[1] PeopleSoft was acquired by Oracle in January 2005.
[2] SBC was formed through the mergers of Ameritech, Southwestern Bell, and Pacific Telesis. SBC purchased AT&T Corp in 2005 and took the name AT&T Inc. They then merged with BellSouth in 2006 and consolidated ownership of Cingular, all under the AT&T name.

EXHIBIT 1

IT Organization Chart at Butler University with Key Players in Deployment of New System Highlighted

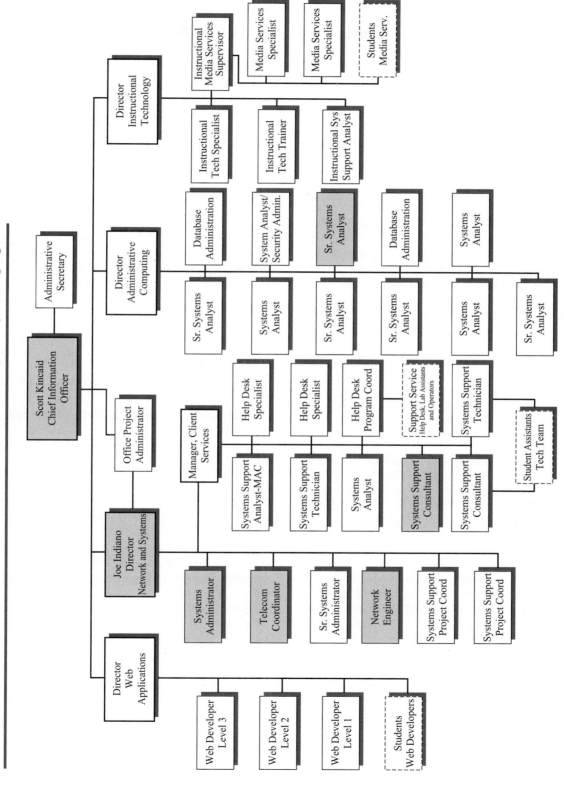

and phone lines was a labor-intensive process. SBC's billing system was antiquated, prone to error, and required constant reconciliation efforts by Butler's telecom coordinator.

Since Centrex was only partially meeting Butler's needs, Information Resources had begun researching the telephony landscape in early 2004. Many vendors and many trade magazines were predicting that an in-house PBX would be more cost-effective than the outsourced Centrex system for telephone services. Butler could acquire and control its own system and then customize it accordingly. Even more intriguing was a newer alternative that would bring voice communications onto the same network as data communications: a VoIP[3] network solution. Like the other alternatives, a VoIP solution appeared to be neither simple nor cheap.

A new in-house PBX would improve the treatment of callers with its Automatic Call Distribution capability, which put callers in a queue if all available staff were busy. Multiline telephone sets, an online caller directory capability, and better management reports would help to improve telecommunications services throughout the university and provide quicker access to personnel. For students, private voice mailboxes could be assigned with each student having their own phone number. Many organizations own and manage an in-house PBX system utilizing traditional voice circuits, but newer VoIP solutions was an interesting trend in the communications industry. The potential cost savings from placing voice traffic on the data network—VoIP—caught the eye of Butler's technology group. However, VoIP was a relatively new technology, and embarking on a marketplace solution that was this new would mean that there wasn't yet a "clear path to success."

> Only twelve to thirteen percent of the market had VoIP installed in 2004. Even though the telecommunications landscape was changing with an emerging trend of increasing IP lines, the current statistics were still daunting and left us wondering if this was a good path to take. Needless to say, we became intrigued.
>
> —Scott Kincaid, CIO

The limited adoption rates weren't the only risks Butler had to consider. By converging traditional data networks and voice networks into one, the reliability of the voice services on campus would likely be less than what the campus had experienced for telephone services in the past: The VoIP phone sets would depend on network operations that weren't used by traditional analog phones. The Butler data network was known to be prone to occasional outages due to equipment failure, insufficient capacity at times, or odd behavior from rogue student-owned computers. Several constituents were concerned about the potential voice quality of IP-based telephony.

Coincidentally, in January 2004, the Information Resources group at Butler had obtained formal approval to begin a three-year program to upgrade all of the network switches, routers, and hubs, a major endeavor. The network upgrade funding would come from two sources: two-thirds would be supplied by university gifts and the remaining third would come from the annual IR operations budget spread over three years. So Butler was on a path to improve the network, but it was not in place now.

The thought of a data network being capable of accommodating high-quality, business-class phone calls was a real source of apprehension. This meant that perhaps the biggest risk that a VoIP PBX solution posed was introducing a less proven technology to its users and gaining their buy-in to this emerging solution. Gaining buy-in would entail accepting the adoption of a new method of communication and new performance risks. Everyone was also worried about virus attacks that commonly affected data networks, but not traditional voice lines.

> People were concerned we'd drag down our voice systems to the quality of data network. Our goal, however, was to bring the data network up to the quality of our traditional voice network.
>
> —Joe Indiano, Director Network and Systems

Matching Butler's Needs with the Network Alternatives

In order to look at the alternatives, the Telephony Evaluation Team was formed in March 2004 (Exhibit 2). The team was led by Joe Indiano, IR's director of network and systems. The team included the telecom coordinator, a data network engineer, the university's Facilities Management telecom technician, and the CIO, Scott Kincaid.

Given that this evaluation was a new project to Butler, but had been done by many other organizations, Joe Indiano made the recommendation to engage an experienced consulting firm to coordinate a formal needs analysis, including end-user surveys. To find a qualified outside firm without spending months of analysis on that alone, Butler utilized the expertise of a professional trade group (ACUTA[4]) of which it was a member. Through the ACUTA listserv, they asked peers for recommendations regarding consultants who had helped other similar organizations with telephony system evaluations. This quickly identified two primary candidates, who Butler contacted and interviewed.

---

[3]Voice over Internet Protocol allows for transmission of voice traffic over an Internet protocol network that is either public (the Internet, for example) or private.

[4]ACUTA: Association for Communications Technology Professionals in Higher Education.

EXHIBIT 2
Project Participants at Cutover, July 2005

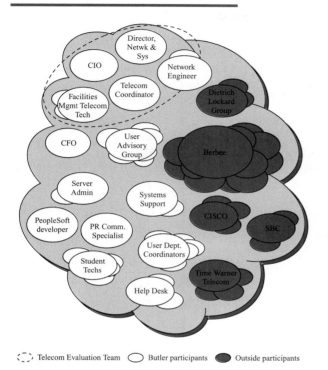

Telecom Evaluation Team ⬭ Butler participants ⬤ Outside participants

Butler decided to engage Dietrich Lockard Group, an independent telecommunications consulting firm based in St. Louis, Missouri, to help determine if the investment in a new phone system could improve communication and advance Butler's mission.

To engage the university community in the telephony needs analysis, a formal User Advisory Group was created to work alongside the consulting firm. This committee included end users of the phone system: administrative staff from Admission, Finance, Student Life, Facilities Management, the libraries, and faculty. In June 2004 the IR Telephony Evaluation Team, a Dietrich Lockard Group consultant, and most of the User Advisory Group went to Chicago to attend the SUPERCOMM telephony conference. SUPERCOMM hosted leading-edge technology forums and exhibits and allowed the Butler staff to get a jump-start on industry trends. The team was able to "window shop" to get a feel for what products were available and to help devise an appropriate solution for enhancing telecommunications on the Butler campus. The trip also allowed the User Advisory Group and technical staff to become more acquainted and begin to work as a team. The Butler participants began to feel more comfortable with the possibility of acquiring a PBX and implementing newer VoIP technology as they learned about ways to address some of the risks.

After returning to campus, Dietrich Lockard Group consultants conducted surveys, interviews, and focus groups with staff, faculty, and students. The team found that many administrative users were displeased with the outdated Centrex and Centigram capabilities, although they lauded the communication system's high reliability. For example, all the offices with heavy call volumes had only basic calling trees to help route calls and lacked management reporting; the analog phones could only handle one call at a time. Moves, additions, and changes to current phones required a technician to physically visit each phone. Like many other universities, Butler also lacked any means to communicate to the entire campus if time-sensitive emergency information needed to be disseminated.

The student surveys revealed that nearly 92 percent of students residing on campus had a cellular phone, but virtually the same number of students used their regular room phone as well. While almost two-thirds of the students preferred cell phones, one-third still preferred a regular telephone. Moreover, 73 percent of the students indicated that their campus-provided voice mail was important and they clearly wanted a private voice mailbox. These results were somewhat of a surprise to the Telephony Evaluation Team and the User Advisory Group, given the visible penetration of cell phones on campus. It meant that cell phones, with their limited minutes and sometimes spotty coverage, did not meet all of the needs of the typical residential student.

> Conventional wisdom in the cellular age would be that traditional land line phones are not important. However, facts don't always line up with intuition. We discovered that our peer institutions were continuing to provide regular phone service in dorm rooms, and therefore it was a no-brainer to continue to provide it as well. I would have bet money that the phones could have been pulled out, so it was a great surprise to me.
>
> —Scott Kincaid, CIO

From all of the needs analysis discussions, a long list of needs and potential opportunities had been identified. In June 2004, based on the analysis of the data collected, a list of key criteria for a new system was developed, with three priority groupings: must haves, very important, and nice-to-haves (see Exhibit 3). Joe Indiano and Dorothy Lockard (president of the Dietrich Lockard Group) then used these needs analysis results to help pinpoint the best opportunities within the context of Butler's strategic plan, and five strategic goals were established:

- Improve communications with the students and within the student community, including the allotment of private voice mailboxes

- Improve the handling of callers to high-volume call areas on campus

EXHIBIT 3
Key Criteria for New System (based on focus groups, surveys, and consultant interviews)

Critical Issues (from master list)	
Improved handling of calls to high volume offices	M
Performance reporting to manage calling to high volume offices	M
Improved handling of callers to operator position	M
Emergency alert campus-wide	M
Position for future services/technology & changing expectations	M
Improved training for end-users	M
Communication with students using their preferred medium (e.g., IM)	M
VM privacy for students in administratively efficient method	I
Indication of message waiting to student	I
Ensure donors reach Advancement anywhere, anytime	I
Ensure campus police can locate key administrators in an emergency	I
Standard features and functionality that improve efficiency and are common at many institutions (at minimal recurring cost)	I
Telephone instruments that reduce need for training and relabeling	I
Long delay in 911 cell call response, not routed to campus police	I
Administratively efficient means of assigning a single phone number for a student while at Butler	I
Enable faculty/staff to make and receive calls using Butler identity (i.e., Butler athletics recruiters, advancement, faculty at-home.)	I
Easy to use video conferencing	I
Conference calling for up to 6 parties at no extra cost	N
Efficient means to integrate VM with E-mail	N
Larger conference calls, ad hoc and meet-me	N
Cell phone coverage inadequate	N
Time saving system administration tools	N
M = Must Have, I = Very Important, N = Nice to Have	

- Leverage newer services such as multiline and self-labeling telephone devices and online directories as well as improve training
- Provide more immediate access to specific Butler personnel
- Remain competitive with peer institutions in the level of services offered, particularly those that impact students and their families

As part of the business case, cost estimates for various alternative telephony systems were determined. These cost estimates incorporated the investments in hardware, software, phone equipment, and on-going expenditures, based on projections of what each option would cost given industry research on pricing and the effort it would take to support each option ongoing.

Based on the cost-benefit estimates, the decision was made to consider four alternative scenarios:

1. Continuing with the current solution: Centrex service outsourced to SBC
2. Continuing with the outsourced Centrex service—but with a significant investment in upgrades and new "bolt-on" equipment
3. Acquiring an in-house PBX system, using either traditional equipment or VoIP
4. Continue with the current solution (Option 1)—but adding an independent 50-seat VoIP system for a few selected offices

With Butler's needs analysis completed, the results were presented to the university vice presidents in July 2004. Butler management then gave the team the go-ahead to solicit bids from vendors, but was nervous about the potential investment.

Request for Proposal to the Selected Vendors

Based on the strategic goals and the key criteria developed by the User Advisory Group, the Telephony Evaluation Team and the consultants crafted a detailed request for proposal (RFP). Dietrich Lockard Group identified vendors that appeared to be well-aligned with the needs of Butler. Dietrich Lockard Group contacted the six vendors and identified the best local implementation partners (manufacturer resellers) for each of the manufacturers. Four of the vendors, through the local resellers, submitted bids. SBC presented Butler with three bids: continue the outsourced Centrex service option, add equipment to the service, or move to an in-house PBX using Nortel equipment.

Then the User Advisory Group and the Telephony Evaluation Team began the journey of listening to vendor presentations, interviewing vendor representatives, evaluating all of the features, making visits to selected vendor customers, and striving to do an apples-to-apples comparison of the various proposals. The number of features and factors considered was extensive with 400 different data points provided in the RFP. To summarize the criteria, a three-level priority scheme (shown in Exhibit 3) would be used as a weighting scale to help ensure that the selected alternative would best address Butler's critical issues.

Butler's main criteria were total overall cost and meeting the needs defined in the RFP (as summarized in Exhibit 3), and most venders could meet Butler's requirements. However, during the comparative analysis, issues bubbled up as key differentiators. Local support from an experienced reseller was proving to be imperative if Butler was going to move all of its telephony in-house. Experience with new VoIP systems and integrating other enterprise systems (i.e., PeopleSoft, LDAP[5]) would be crucial as well. With Macintosh users representing 25 percent of the faculty population at Butler, the university also wanted a system that offered equivalent features, such as video conferencing capabilities, for both Mac and PC users. An effective and flexible integrated emergency notification system, which allowed for a simultaneous broadcast of text and audio to all campus phones, as well as other data network security concerns were other key differentiators reflecting their increased priorities in a post-9/11, Internet era.

In addition, what the manufacturers were planning to invest in R&D were also considered. Most telephony vendors currently sold both IP-based PBX systems and also traditional analog systems, with several promoting the ability to interconnect the two types of systems. But during last-minute visits to several of the manufacturers' headquarters, it became obvious to the Telephony Evaluation Team that the manufacturers were putting all of their R&D dollars into IP-based systems. While VoIP was certainly the more risky approach, the Telephony Evaluation Team came to the uncomfortable realization that if they invested in a new analog PBX, they might end up with a system that had a limited life. Suddenly, staying with the SBC Centrex service for a couple more years looked like a serious option.

Vendor Selection

Butler narrowed the field down to five main candidates from a list of nine potential options presented to them.

The final alternatives included the following:

- Continue with SBC's current Centrex service (outsourcing option)
- Continue with SBC's Centrex service, but add a Nortel 50-seat IP system
- Implement a new system to support VoIP PBX in-house
  - Cisco (represented by Berbee Information Networks)
  - Mitel (represented by MVD Communications)
  - Nortel (represented by SBC)

Side-by-side comparisons were made of what each vendor solution offered in regard to each critical issue, and what additional capital and/or ongoing support costs would be incurred to satisfy these requirements.

Following the review of this range of options, and the scorings of the options, the Telephony Evaluation Team, working in conjunction with the User Advisory Group, chose option 3: to acquire its own in-house system and to acquire a Cisco IPT system, with products and implementation services provided by a Midwest Cisco partner, Berbee Information Networks. Joe Indiano and Scott Kincaid presented this to the Butler senior management, and after careful consideration, obtained the go-ahead to proceed. Butler informed Berbee and Cisco they had won the bid on the day before the Christmas holidays began.

Contrary to what was seen in the popular press, the team's analysis did not show that an in-house IP-based system would be cheaper than the old Centrex solution. However, most of the needs identified by staff, faculty, and students would be addressed with only a minimal increase in costs. For example, each high-volume call area on campus would now have Automatic Call Distribution capabilities. Butler would be gaining a system to issue campuswide emergency alerts via the new IP-based phones. Additionally, each student who previously shared a line in a residence hall room would now have their

---

[5]Lightweight Directory Access Protocol provides an online, fully-indexed telephone directory service developed and freely distributed by the Regents of the University of Michigan. [Eudora]

own unique phone number and private voice mailbox, which also moved with them as they changed rooms from year to year. (Changes to room assignments would be entered into PeopleSoft and an automated interface would carry the change into the telephony system.) When students received voice mail, they would also receive an e-mail notifying them of the message.

The strategic objective was to support IR's mission of providing good services and communication between students and faculty. Cisco's system fulfilled the identified needs for voice communication, but Butler was concerned about more than just equipment specs and cost.

> During the sales cycle, vendors usually promise all types of grand improvements and outcomes. But the written contracts they provide promise only to deliver specific pieces of hardware and software, with very limited warranties, and customers often spend most of their time negotiating on price. In this project, we were able to successfully negotiate for the original RFP and the vendor's proposal to Butler to become part of the final contract. This kept everyone focused on delivering a fully integrated system, instead of just focusing on the hardware, and held the vendor accountable to the claims in their proposal."
>
> —Dorothy Lockard, President, Dietrich Lockard Group.

Furthermore, what Butler was ultimately implementing was an integrated set of software applications that operate on the IP network, not just a "black box" phone system. The understanding of the IP protocol and how it would fit into Butler was, in the end, second to how the multiple components of the system were to work together in a secure and quality fashion. Additionally, identifying who within Butler owned each piece, how the data would flow from point-to-point, and where data was being replicated were all important questions that needed to be answered for this application system. Creating seamless integration with other systems such as PeopleSoft, the housing system, and Butler's LDAP directory was one of the values of the newer software-based systems. Essentially, there were multiple interfaces to existing systems, more options, and a vast array of decisions to make about how all of these features were going to work in unison.

Thus, when choosing the primary vendor, the implementation support provided by a Cisco partner was extremely important.

> Since this was really an application system, we were more concerned with who was going to help us deploy the system. Of course, the manufacturer is important as we are using their equipment, but even more important is someone with large-scale application implementation experience.
>
> —Scott Kincaid, CIO

The new Cisco system configuration included the following investments:

- Cisco Call Manager with multiple forms of redundancy
- 1200 IPT stations for faculty and staff
- 1800 Analog ports via VG248 gateways for student phones
- Cisco Unity Voice mail with mailboxes for each student
- Cisco IPCC Express for six call centers
- Cisco Emergency Responder for campuswide E911 capability
- Berbee InformaCast alert system
- ISI Infortel call accounting

The IR team considered leasing the new telephony system, but after analysis chose to purchase and finance it in-house by redeploying the monthly fees they had been paying for the Centrex solution.

Butler's business model for its original data network replacement investment was a three-year funding plan. However, given the change from an outsourced telephony solution to an in-house solution that depended on the data network, there would have been a lot of risks if Butler continued on the three-year implementation plan for the data network. Instead, Butler decided to compress its three-year network replacement project into one year, using the bulk of their allotted funds at the beginning of the project to reduce the total implementation time.

After the new telephony system was chosen, Butler had to select a vendor to supply local voice circuits. Another RFP had to be initiated for the circuits, and the decision was made to change to a new voice carrier, Time Warner Telecom. The university negotiated the installation of two independent communication links to the campus, and Berbee helped split the new telephony servers between two campus locations—a capability not possible with traditional PBX systems. A total of 17 Windows servers ranging from Call Managers, to an E911 Emergency Responder, to a Call Accounting Database server, were implemented between the two onsite locations to provide backup and disaster recovery capabilities. The Berbee InformaCast software would make it possible for university-wide alerts to be made in audio and/or text, simultaneously or by zone, within seconds, to all IP phones.

The new focus became deploying a single network that would continue to provide reliable service for voice as well as provide more reliable services for traditional computer applications. Butler already had the necessary fiber backbone in place but needed to replace selected old wiring with new Ethernet cable. Improvements in the new converged network, such as installing an uninterruptible power supply (UPS[6]) in all network

---

[6]Uninterruptible Power Supply provides a backup power supply for a cable voice adapter and the telephone attached to it. [Cisco]

closets and replacing old wiring, would now benefit the new telephony system as well as aid in the support of the traditional data network services.

Contract work began during the holiday break, and the contracts were signed in mid-January 2005. Additionally, the department accelerated the pace on the network replacement project and began to implement new routers and switches across campus. To mitigate the reliability risks of the new system, the new network design included more segmentation, protections such as intrusion detection, and quality of service (QoS[7]) levels. With functions such as QoS levels—new for Butler—the network would be able to logically separate traffic on the converged network to protect voice transmissions from other traffic, including malicious activity. New monitoring tools would be incorporated in the VoIP system as well to observe where calls were originating and going, and to measure the quality of calls placed through the university. This would help the IR group pinpoint where problems were occurring and help them manage the network in order to provide a level of quality for voice communications similar to what was traditionally provided via old-style analog lines.

Implementing the VoIP System

The number of people formally involved in the project quickly began to increase. Berbee assigned a full-time project manager to the Butler project in January 2005. The director of network and systems, Joe Indiano, would serve as Butler project coordinator and play a key role by ensuring integration with other existing systems. The CIO would serve as project sponsor and had the role to eliminate roadblocks within the organization and to facilitate communication between key stakeholders in the university, such as the deans and other vice presidents. The CIO would also need to communicate the strategic vision of the project and address any concerns that staff, faculty, and student users had with regard to the new system.

The newly formed IP Implementation Team included other key IR personnel as well—telephony staff, network engineers, PeopleSoft developers, and help desk staff, as well as Butler's Facilities Management staff to help with the logistics of the installation. A majority of the IP Implementation Team members were from the implementation partner, Berbee Information Networks with Cisco staff helping as needed. Additionally, Berbee Information Networks's security practice was engaged to ensure that the new network design would allow data and voice traffic to coexist but with telephony servers that were protected from student desktops and outside security threats. While not anticipated at the beginning of the project, it was also decided to keep the Dietrich Lockard Group

consultant on the team to ensure that Berbee and Cisco implemented a system with all the items defined by the RFP and vendor contracts. Lastly, some 18 students were used to help with the testing and rollout.

Through this implementation, not only were data and voice network technologies converging, but also the former data and telecommunications personnel that had previously worked in separate units were merging:

> You have to keep in mind that convergence within the project not only refers to the convergence of technologies but also the integration of processes and people as well. When you have voice and data traffic merging, the respective personnel also merge. Data people approach projects differently than telephony people and use different terminology. So managing this merging of the staff and disciplines was essential. Along with the size of the implementation team, there were a lot of people to coordinate to pull this off.
>
> —Scott Kincaid, CIO

Butler's "Infinitely Personal" Communication Plan

A communications coordinator was added to the team to help establish the message that the university would send to all users to help ensure acceptance of the new system. Managing the fear factor of a major system overhaul was viewed as critical, because Butler's users had experienced data network failures before. One of the techniques used for this was to redefine "IP" to stand for "infinitely personal." This set the tone for the teams to focus on the ways the network changes were empowering people to communicate more freely, not on the fact the calls were being transported via IP data packets.

> We chose an IP system not because it was VoIP, but because, overall, it could provide the best set of services to meet our needs.
>
> —Joe Indiano, Director Network and Systems

Reassuring users that a personal approach was being taken helped communicate that this was a decision to help everyone, not just to improve the technology of the university. The IP—infinitely personal—communications plan sought to educate users by first raising awareness and then holding training forums (see Exhibit 4a). Communicating important system information to users in person via departmental staff and management reminders for attending training sessions were emphasized. Although much of the communication was done via e-mail, other media included all-campus voice mails and printed materials distributed throughout the campus.

Messages sent out to the university community included why a new system was being implemented, where and when

---

[7]Quality of service is the set of techniques to manage network resources. [Cisco]

EXHIBIT 4A
Communication Plan: Sample Page

New Phone System Project Communication Plan

What	Who/Target	Purpose	When	Type/Method(s)
New Phone and Voice Mail System Teaser	Bluemail and my. butler users	Raise awareness	May 31–June 27	On Bluemail, IR labs and my.butler homepages
New Phone and Voice Mail System Teaser	All Campus	Raise awareness that a new phone system is coming	May 26	Email
Sign up for training and when and where	Fac/Staff on campus now	Get people to go to training	May 27	Email
Training Dates and times on web	All Campus	Make training information available at all times in a central location	May 27	butler.edu/ir/ documentation/ telecom.html
New Phone and Voice Mail System & Training	Fac/Staff on campus now	Raise awareness and get people to training	June 1	All campus Voice mail
Ask for support	Scott to Cabinet	Ask VPs/Deans to encourage their staffs to attend training.	June 1	Email
Coordinator verification of phones in their areas	Coordinators	Ask coordinators to verify the phones in their areas.	June 3	Email
Early notification of cut dates.	Pilot team and coordinators	Give early notice of anticipated dates for phone system cut to groups.	June 6	Email
Emergency Broadcast System info	Greek house corps and presidents	Make Greek organizations aware of the opportunity to receive emergency information from Butler	June 7	Email
Messages to communicate in training	Students in training	Communicate important system information in person	June 13 in training class	Verbal and Print
Last reminder about training	All campus	Final reminder about going to training	June 15	All Campus Voice Mail
Phone delivery	Fac/Staff	Announce phone delivery and training reminder	June 15	Fac/Staff Alert

training would occur, how to transition from the old voice mail to the newer version, who to call with problems, the date and time of cutover, and how to return old phones after users began using their new equipment (see Exhibit 4b).

Pilot Program

Before a full-scale dissemination of the new VoIP phones, a pilot program was implemented to help test features and gain user feedback. In April 2005, approximately six weeks before the system was to "go live," 40 phones were issued to high-volume phone users, such as department coordinators and high-level secretarial staff. Over roughly three weeks, the users helped to test the various features of the new system and to fine-tune any other aspects that pilot users had noted. The overall goal of the pilot program was to gain buy-in from the user community. Ideally, pilot users would not only share their enthusiasm for the new system with their coworkers, but would also become a coordinator and trainer within their department.

IR needed input from the people who would be using the phones the most. They wanted someone from Admission involved because of our large call volume. Since I manage the team that handles incoming calls, it made sense for me to volunteer to be a phone coordinator.

—Susie Bremen, Senior Associate Director of Admission

The pilot program began with an information session, followed by a series of training sessions that took place in three labs

EXHIBIT 4B
Example of Communication Message to Staff

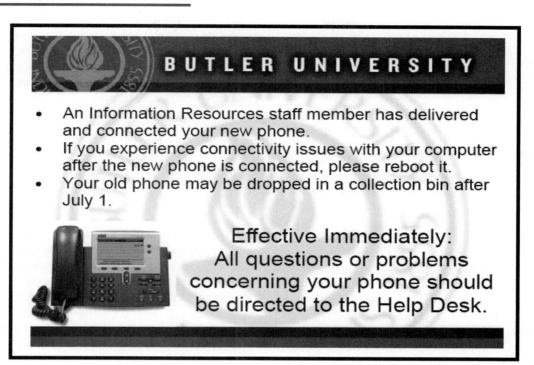

BUTLER UNIVERSITY

- An Information Resources staff member has delivered and connected your new phone.
- If you experience connectivity issues with your computer after the new phone is connected, please reboot it.
- Your old phone may be dropped in a collection bin after July 1.

Effective Immediately:
All questions or problems concerning your phone should be directed to the Help Desk.

and were run by a firm that Berbee had contracted with for the training. Members from the implementation team and consultants from Dietrich Lockard and Berbee were on hand to facilitate information sharing and initial training. Pilot users were provided with the opportunity to try various features of the new phone and interact with the new capabilities through role-playing.

> They made the training fun. They had gift bags and giveaways, and encouraged questions and discussion from the very beginning. They started out with a PowerPoint presentation to explain terminology, benefits, and how the new technology was going to improve our departments. The training sessions became very interactive. . . . The IR team sent out information regularly—leaflets with timelines, cards with contacts, and worksheets to complete after testing various features available with the new phones. We tested such features as "parking" calls, forwarding calls, and setting up conference calls, and we completed Phone Feedback Forms after experimenting with newly-learned features.
>
> —Susie Bremen, Senior Associate Director of Admission

The pilot program helped to create a type of "phone envy" among some users; some of those without IP phones had a chance to see how they were used and became intrigued with

the new features of the technology. By bringing the technology closer to the users, it also brought home the message of being "infinitely personal."

While many users were excited about the new phones and their functionality, others did not fully understand how the IP phone would actually work and were apprehensive about the change:

> It was a smooth transition for me [but] it was hard for a lot of people to comprehend; they didn't understand the concept of running the phone through a computer connection instead of a telephone jack.
>
> —Kristine Butz, Associate Director of Financial Aid

> I already had exposure to call routing and advanced phone systems. There is a learning curve. Some people were apprehensive because the phone was complicated, and they were also afraid that the system would crash and service would not be available.
>
> —Kathy Harter, Senior Assistant Director of Operations

Managers of high call-volume offices were aware that the capabilities of the new system would greatly improve their department's call center processes, as the functionality allowed for detailed reporting and could help department managers analyze and benchmark their call center employees. But these capabilities also contributed to additional concerns by users:

> Some of the functionality was actually scaring some users; they feared they would be monitored because we would have the capability to evaluate call volume and length. It gave some users the notion that "Big Brother" would be watching.

—Susie Bremen, Senior Associate Director of Admission

The Cutover to the New System

With the pilot behind them, the implementation team felt confident in their ability to move forward with the full roll-out planned for June 2005. Butler's move from traditional telephony to an IP-based system meant they didn't have to do a traditional cutover where the old phones are pulled and new ones installed at the exact same time. Instead, the new IP-based phones were distributed to all users during the weeks before the cutover, training sessions were arranged for all faculty and staff, and yet the old analog phones were still available. Even users at the new call centers were able to make and receive internal calls on their new IP phones while the old Centrex phones handled all external calls prior to the cutover.

However, a variety of technical problems threatened to derail the roll-out plan—and later became known as a "Week from Hell":

- The supposedly simple "plug and play" process of connecting the new IP-based phones failed due to a software bug; all multiline phones had to, unexpectedly, be manually registered one-by-one using their unique machine address code (MAC).
- The new telephony servers were rebooting haphazardly, and the vendor decided to replace and rebuild every single unit.
- After a two-month effort, 2,000 extra phone numbers, which Butler needed to provide private numbers and voice-mail boxes, were found to be missing—and SBC claimed it would take 45 days to resolve the issue.
- Both the Food Service and Bookstore offices, which are independent non-Butler companies but located on campus, were found to have no Ethernet wiring in their areas.

To further complicate matters, the SBC service representative whom Butler had come to rely upon for the past four years suddenly resigned, and the IR telecom coordinator's husband was robbed at gunpoint, bound and gagged with duct tape!

> Our week from hell was a huge setback . . . but I didn't want this project to be delayed, and neither did any of the team.

—Joe Indiano, Director Network and Systems

One of the options allowed for in the Berbee contract was for Butler to alter the implementation plan to allow for a split roll-out: phase one of the roll-out could be done in the summer to make sure things went according to plan, and then the phase two users would be implemented during the Thanksgiving holiday break. However, the team decided to push through and not let the unexpected setbacks create more damage than necessary, and the decision was made to delay the cutover date by just two weeks.

> We decided not to split the roll-out since everyone was motivated to do it all at once. We didn't want to kill that spirit. Also, we felt that creating more work during Thanksgiving time would place even more of a burden on our team members and the vendors.

—Scott Kincaid, CIO

On July 11 the system went live! SBC migrated all Butler's phone numbers to Time Warner Telecom, who then routed all calls to the new system, and Centrex was turned off. Calls got through to the right places and the new call center software managed the calls. Only a few lines and features were missed, so the planning, testing and roll-out was clearly valuable. However, none of the departmental burglar alarms worked! The alarm panels depended on analog phone lines to communicate with the campus police department and were now being connected via a Cisco analog-to-VoIP gateway device. However, the alarm panels, based on 1970's technology, would not work even with the analog-to-VoIP gateway; apparently Butler had not tested the devices before implementation. So Butler found some unused Centrex lines, and the alarms were reconnected using traditional analog circuits.

Otherwise, the newly converged, in-house voice-and-data system was fully functional. No one reported any problems with the voice quality.

> Having been a part of various large system changes in the past, I have seen my fair share of "blips" and overall catastrophes and I was pleasantly surprised that I have seen no such issues from this transition, at least not yet."

—Kathy Parsons, University Budget Director

Post-Implementation Reality

Altogether, the new system took approximately one year from the initial planning process to the final implementation (see Exhibit 5) and included a $1.5 million investment by Butler. The new system gave Butler a robust "soft-PBX" capability based on a series of integrated servers linked to PeopleSoft, LDAP, and the network. This also resulted in six full-featured call centers allowing students and outside callers to get better help regarding

EXHIBIT 5
Project Milestones: January 2004–August 2005

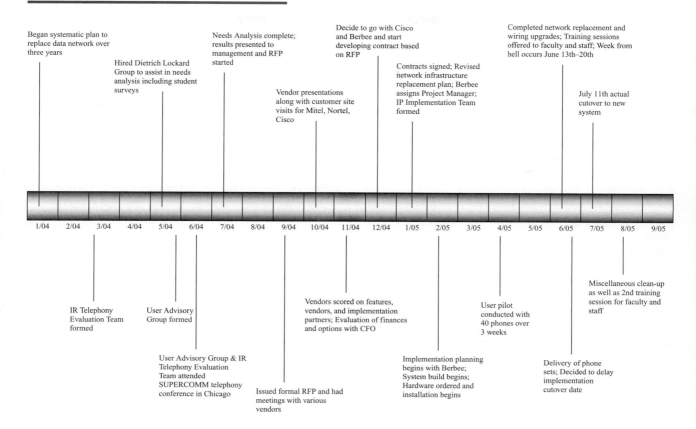

Began systematic plan to replace data network over three years

Hired Dietrich Lockard Group to assist in needs analysis including student surveys

Needs Analysis complete; results presented to management and RFP started

Vendor presentations along with customer site visits for Mitel, Nortel, Cisco

Decide to go with Cisco and Berbee and start developing contract based on RFP

Contracts signed; Revised network infrastructure replacement plan; Berbee assigns Project Manager; IP Implementation Team formed

Completed network replacement and wiring upgrades; Training sessions offered to faculty and staff; Week from hell occurs June 13th–20th

July 11th actual cutover to new system

IR Telephony Evaluation Team formed

User Advisory Group formed

User Advisory Group & IR Telephony Evaluation Team attended SUPERCOMM telephony conference in Chicago

Issued formal RFP and had meetings with various vendors

Vendors scored on features, vendors, and implementation partners; Evaluation of finances and options with CFO

Implementation planning begins with Berbee; System build begins; Hardware ordered and installation begins

User pilot conducted with 40 phones over 3 weeks

Delivery of phone sets; Decided to delay implementation cutover date

Miscellaneous clean-up as well as 2nd training session for faculty and staff

1/04 2/04 3/04 4/04 5/04 6/04 7/04 8/04 9/04 10/04 11/04 12/04 1/05 2/05 3/05 4/05 5/05 6/05 7/05 8/05 9/05

such items as student accounts, admissions, financial aid, and box office tickets. When departments moved to different offices, they could simply take their IP phone with them and the number was automatically redirected, without IR intervention. Additionally, faculty and staff were able to utilize a directory of campus phone numbers (available on the telephone's display area) that was updated daily by the PeopleSoft system.

However, the new IP system was not cheaper and, in fact, was actually somewhat more expensive as IR had to add a full-time staff member to manage the new system. The new system involved many more components than existed with the outsourced Centrex system. In addition, the IR group at Butler now has the responsibility of maintaining networks not just for data, but also voice.

Soon after the euphoria of a successful initial implementation ended, CIO Kincaid was wondering, "did we make the right choices?" In their quest to improve communications, should Butler have taken on the responsibility of managing an integrated voice and data network, given the current security threats to computer networks?

CASE STUDY I-4

DATA GOVERNANCE AT INSURACORP

InsuraCorp has several business units that provide financial products, services, and support for one or more of the company's three major lines of business: (1) individual insurance, such as term life, universal life, and whole life policies; (2) retirement services, such as retirement plans—401(k) and 403(b); and (3) group insurance, such as group life and disability insurance, long-term care insurance. InsuraCorp has grown through acquisitions, and until recently, the business units have continued to operate autonomously. In the past, there was also no attempt to market products to customers across business units.

Under the current CEO, however, there has been a new focus on achieving synergies across the business units by cross-marketing product offerings. The company's first CMO was hired in 2005, and under his direction, a new branding effort of the company was begun to help InsuraCorp achieve its new synergy goals. In addition to providing a consistent brand image, the branding initiative will result in a single point of contact for customers, including an integrated website that gives sales personnel and customers access to all product and service offerings. The CMO was well aware of the problems of the silos that had developed over time:

> In the past, if you had an individual insurance policy, had retirement services, and also had a group policy, you'd go to three different Web sites and you'd have three different passwords. . . . All of that is being consolidated. We are completely revamping the underpinnings of our Web sites so that it looks and feels the same across the board. We are also eliminating a lot of Web sites and reducing them down to where there is really one focal point where you come in as a customer, and you'll see all the information about you presented.

—VP of Enterprise Architecture

To help facilitate this initiative, the marketing VPs who used to report only to their respective business unit heads now also have a dotted-line relationship to the CMO. This dual-reporting relationship implies that the primary direction for the marketing group is set by the line head, but all marketing leads need to also work with the CMO to establish and achieve marketing plans at the enterprise level. The dotted-line relationship has also helped the marketing leads learn about what other business units are doing and how their own business unit plans fit with enterprise-level initiatives.

Achieving synergies across product offerings and developing a consistent brand image also requires the ability to view sales agents[1] and customers "holistically." The same agent could be selling products offered by different business units within InsuraCorp. Under its legacy systems, however, it is very difficult to capture the fact that a business or individual customer is interacting with the same agent. With respect to customers, it is also important to understand not only which InsuraCorp products they have, but also which products they *could have*. For individual customers, for example, the CMO realizes the importance of being able to recognize cross-sales opportunities for different InsuraCorp business units due to "life changing events," such as having children, buying homes, or sending children to college (empty nesters). Many customers simply buy one product and are not aware of the broad range of other products offered by InsuraCorp.

The InsuraCorp branding initiative, therefore, also requires investing in enterprise-level IT initiatives to capture, and facilitate access to, integrated enterprise-level data.

IT at InsuraCorp

Until recently, each business unit had an IT leader with their own IT staff. This decentralized IT organization structure led to processing inefficiencies and duplicate IT resources and was

---

[1]A sales agent can be a *career agent*—an agent who works for InsuraCorp—or an *independent agent* who is licensed to do business in a certain state and is designated to sell products for InsuraCorp.

also seen as a barrier to the company's data integration initiatives—such as the ability to cross-market products of the different business units under the new InsuraCorp brand.

In early 2006, a new centralized structure for the IT organization was announced in which essentially all IT resources were consolidated at corporate headquarters. Under the centralized structure, the former business unit IT leaders have a solid-line report to the CIO and a dotted-line report to the business unit they support (see Exhibit 1). The CIO's four other direct reports are the VPs of Corporate Applications, Enterprise Architecture, Planning and Finance (including a Project Management Office) and Systems Operations (Data Centers and Telecommunications). The new centralized IT organization has a total of about 300 IT personnel. About 25 other IT personnel are located at other sites. In addition, IT contractors are typically hired for on-site work when the company does not have the required skill set for a particular IT initiative, and InsuraCorp utilizes outsourcing for IT services such as 401(k) statement printing and spam protection.

The VP of Enterprise Architecture position was created in early 2006 and filled with an outside hire in response to the need to develop a new IT architecture to support enterprise-level infrastructure services. One of this VP's early initiatives was to establish 11 IT working groups to focus on particular aspects of IT architecture—such as desktop computing, networks, security, IT storage, and so on. Each group was charged with the task of setting standards and generating ideas for IT projects that would be needed to accomplish the new integration and standardization objectives of the company. The activities of the IT working groups are coordinated under an Enterprise Architecture Development Committee (EADC), which includes a few of the working group leads and the VP of Enterprise Architecture.

The move to a centralized IT organization also meant that new processes and committees needed to be established to review, approve, and prioritize IT projects. A new standing committee that includes a representative from InsuraCorp's corporate planning department was given the responsibility for initially approving requests for IT work. Approved IT project requests are then passed on to the company's Executive Committee (which includes the CEO, CMO, CIO, and all business unit heads) for final approval and prioritization.

Another initiative under the current CIO was the development of a set of IT principles to define the role of IT and communicate the standardized IT practices to be used throughout InsuraCorp (see Exhibit 2). The members of the IT Committee referred to as ITC (which includes the CIO's seven direct reports) developed a detailed rationale and a set of implications for each principle. The CIO understood the significance and necessity of the enterprise-wide IT principles:

> It's amazing to me once you develop those IT principles how pervasive they've become throughout the organization. . . You hear business people say "yeah, we buy versus build," and we do. . . It has been more powerful than I thought it would have been.
>
> —CIO

These IT principles are used to guide all business and IT managers and other staff involved in IT decision making. For

EXHIBIT 1
Centralized IT Organization

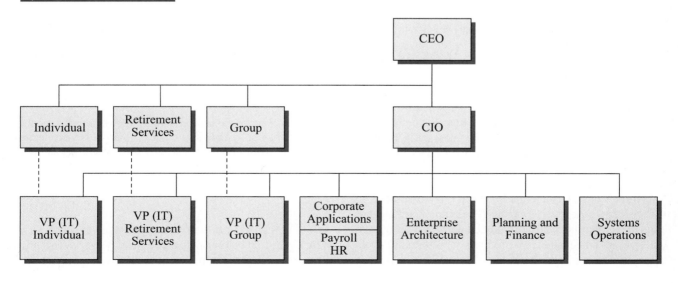

EXHIBIT 2
IT Principles at InsuraCorp

1. We will make our top priority supporting the uninterrupted processing of day-to-day business operations—Production is number 1.
2. We will see to leverage existing technology solutions before an alternative is purchased or developed.
3. We will purchase solutions or services rather than develop them unless business requirements can only be met, or competitive advantage gained, by developing them internally.
4. We will use common, shared technology solutions and processes consistently for similar functions throughout the enterprise.
5. We will select and develop technology solutions built on mainstream components and utilize commonly accepted industry standards.
6. We will select and develop technology solutions that have capacity for growth and allow easy integration with other systems.
7. We will engineer technology solutions from the outset to be secure, reliable and recoverable.
8. We will select and prioritize IT initiatives using an evaluation process that considers alignment, costs, value delivered, risks and capacity.
9. We will develop processes to provide technology services to be easy to access and use from the perspective of the customer.
10. We will select technology solutions to provide highest long term value.
11. We will favor integrated solution sets over separate stand-alone solutions.
12. We will change business processes rather than customize purchased solutions.
13. We will effectively manage the full life cycle (i.e., plan, acquire, use, dispose) of our valuable technology assets.
14. We will define and maintain a single, "master source" of data with a clearly defined owner.
15. We will develop and equip staff for success through mentoring, proactive training, and a variety of IT experiences.

example, Principles 1 and 9 define the primary IT role at InsuraCorp as providing "uninterrupted" support for company operations (principle 1), and establish the importance of providing technology tools that business users find easy to access and use (principle 9). The "working model" for investing in and using IT solutions includes a buy-versus-build preference (principle 3), based on criteria that include "alignment" (principle 8), and favoring integrated over stand-alone solutions (principle 11) supported by a "master source" of enterprise data (principle 14) that utilize standard industry solutions (principle 5). Principle 15 states the company's commitment to developing internal IT staff through mentoring and proactive training.

These principles clearly communicate InsuraCorp's move toward enterprise-level solutions that leverage mainstream IT products that can be purchased in the marketplace. They also signal that the company will modify its business processes to fit purchased software standards as necessary in order to achieve the corporation's data integration goals. The company's recent selection of Salesforce.com to provide a common IT platform for sales and customer service across InsuraCorp's dispersed internal workforce is an example of an initiative that is clearly in synch with the company's recently adopted IT principles: customized solutions at the business unit level are being forfeited for a common, easy-to-use, Web-based "self-service" approach.

Data Integration Initiatives and Challenges

Under the sponsorship of the CMO, an enterprise data repository (EDR) project was initiated in 2006. The objective of this project was to develop for the first time an enterprise-level data warehouse for customer and product data for all business units. Previously, all product and customer data existed in separate legacy systems at the business unit or function level. The goal of the EDR project is to have a single source of data for the entire enterprise. The EDR will provide an enterprise source for tracking and reporting on marketing campaigns. It will also be the source of a master list of products offered by InsuraCorp, which will allow sales agents to cross-sell products from business units across the enterprise to their customers. As one of the IT architects noted, EDR will help "connect the dots":

> They know what money is coming in. They know what money is coming out. . . They kind of know what they're paying the agents, but they can't correlate all of those dots together. They know they're doing these e-mail campaigns and these conferences, but again they can't tie that all together.

—Data Manager

The EDR project has been conducted totally in-house. Early work focused on building data models and data-flow diagrams. Nine months into the project, the EDR was ready to be populated with data, which involved more than 300 data elements across the enterprise. First, "trusted" electronic sources of data within InsuraCorp were identified, and the business analysts on the project team interviewed the subject matter experts and data stewards in the business areas to map the data fields of those trusted sources. The data fields were then mapped to the EDR itself, and it was connected to the source file for data transfer. Finally, the business analysts go back to review the data. Through this multistep process, the project team has identified and resolved inconsistencies within and across the source files. Once data is transferred to the EDR, the business analysts will be responsible for reviewing it for accuracy. Under the EDR project manager, alternative products for business intelligence reporting by either business or IT personnel (such as Microsoft Reporting Services Tools or ProClarity) were also being assessed.

However, bringing together data that was siloed in multiple administrative systems maintained by the separate business units in the past also surfaced several data management issues.

> Earlier they were more decentralized just within those divisions and so all they focused on was their little piece of the world and nothing else. . . Now they're kind of being pushed to kind of look beyond that.
>
> —Data Manager

These included data quality concerns and issues related to determining the "trustworthiness" of data from different legacy systems. For example, one of the data quality issues that surfaced was the absence of product description information. Products that do not have an associated description cannot be used, for example, by computer users in the marketing department. Incorrect categorizations of products have also been uncovered. Further, the same customer (or purportedly the same customer) may have different addresses in the legacy systems maintained by different business units, making it difficult to determine if two or more administration systems are indeed referring to the same customer. Although tools and services that can check for data accuracy as it is being entered are available, managers at InsuraCorp realize that data quality cannot be totally automated, nor does it come for free.

Predicting the credibility of data at InsuraCorp has been difficult for two reasons: (1) the large number of source systems (e.g., 11 different systems support sales and service), and (2) the resource-intensive manual processes that are involved in integrating such data. Additionally, the programs to manage and award compensation to sales agents are hard coded in the applications, thus complicating issues related to understanding the trustworthiness of data.

> There is certain data that is known to be incorrect in the fields, and there are some fields that are not populated. As we extract that data and move it into the data warehouse, we publish exception reports.
>
> —Project Manager

InsuraCorp's IT leaders knew that developing an EDR would also not resolve all of their data management challenges: Maintaining an enterprise-wide view of company data would require new data management approaches and decisions about data governance. For example, who in the organization should be responsible for data quality, and how would data quality be evaluated? Who in the organization should be the data owners? Who should be responsible for determining who should be given access to what data, and who should be enforcing the data access controls to ensure the right level of data security? Who should decide what data should be archived and how long should it be kept?

CASE STUDY I-5

MIDSOUTH CHAMBER OF COMMERCE (B): CLEANING UP AN INFORMATION SYSTEMS DEBACLE

As Sage Niele, the newly appointed vice president of operations and chief financial officer for the Midsouth Chamber of Commerce (MSCC), walked over to the microwave in her office, she recalled her excitement when she first started in this position. Only a few weeks earlier, Sage was the owner/operator of a successful information systems and financial consulting business that kept her in the office or on the road an average of 80 hours per week. With a family and dreams of a simpler life, Sage decided to start working for someone else, where she thought her schedule would be much less hectic. Today, it did not seem as though her life had changed that much. She was still working 80 hours a week, and her life was just as hectic as before. Sage thought that she could see hope on the horizon, however.

A few days after Sage began her position, Leon Lassiter, MSCC president, gave her the daunting task of managing the MSCC's information systems. In most organizations, this role would be challenging, but it was especially so at MSCC due to its history. Over the last several months, the MSCC had been receiving what it considered erroneous charges from its software vendor and consultant, Data Management Associates (DMA). DMA had been charging the MSCC for work related to errors in and/or the implementation of the relational database system and customized report-writing software the MSCC had purchased nearly 2 years earlier. Now it was clear that this was another incident in a long history of poor operational decisions for the MSCC's information systems. And it was Sage's job to correct the situation and build a direction for the future.

As Sage looked down at the calendar, she realized that she had just 2 more days until her 100-day action plan was due to Lassiter, on September 24, 2003. Among her list of things "to do" was to determine the deficiencies of the current information system, to ascertain the MSCC's future information system needs, and to investigate the alternatives that existed should

the MSCC need to scrap the DMA system. Beyond that, however, some items needed to be fixed immediately—including the deteriorating relationship with DMA and the implementation of the new software. While she knew that she did not have all the answers now, her 100-day plan had to lay out a process for getting the answers.

Given Sage's consulting experience, she decided the best way to start was to investigate the troubled history of the MSCC's information systems to help find the clues necessary to avoid disaster in the future. "How ironic," she thought. "The situation at the MSCC has the same potential to explode as the popcorn does when I hit the start button."

The Midsouth Chamber of Commerce

A more extensive description of the MSCC and its history and computing systems can be found in Case Study 1, Midsouth Chamber of Commerce (A).

The Midsouth Chamber of Commerce (MSCC) was created in the early part of the twentieth century, but its information systems history began in 1986 when personal computers and database management were first introduced into the organization by Ed Wilson, the vice president of public affairs. Many staff members were skeptical of the automation effort and reluctant to accept this approach. However, with the help of Jon Philips, a small business consultant, Wilson acquired the equipment and hired a programmer to write custom software for each functional area—the marketing division, the operations division, and the human resources division. One IBM PC and printer were ordered for each group.

From 1987 through 1992, the use of these three systems grew steadily. In 1992, Wilson selected another outside consultant, Ted Vassici, to review the organization's information systems needs and to select the hardware and software solutions the MSCC required. After a careful study, Vassici recommended six more IBM workstations. And in 1995, Vassici revised and updated the custom software used by each division and developed marketing software at the request of Leon Lassiter, the vice president of marketing.

In June 1996, Wilson hired a systems analyst, Simon Kovecki—a recent computer science graduate—to increase the MSCC's computing capabilities. Through early 1997, Wilson managed the computer systems and with the help of Kovecki, upgraded the hardware with more powerful CPUs, memory upgrades, higher capacity hard drives, and better monitors. Under Kovecki's watchful eye, the systems operated very reliably.

The Necessity for Change

By 1998, Lassiter was bothered by the lack of a comprehensive information systems plan that would provide the MSCC with a competitive advantage. Even though the system was stable, Lassiter felt the information systems area needed more attention, and eventually he sent out requests for information to a number of firms servicing the software needs of organizations like the MSCC. In August 1998, Lassiter attended a national association meeting where a session on management software led to Lassiter's discovery of a small firm called UNITRAK, which had developed a Y2K-compliant UNIX-based software system that Lassiter felt the MSCC should consider—based on his (and Kovecki's) 1997 assessment of the MSCC's current and anticipated divisional needs.

Planning the New Data Processing System

Lassiter had identified features provided by the UNITRAK software that he felt would allow the MSCC to be more efficient—including quicker access to account information, the ability to use a centralized database of information, and increased quantitative analysis of activities. In a memo to the management group, Lassiter commented, "The UNITRAK system not only meets our needs today, but this user-friendly package is also powerful enough to provide the MSCC with the room to grow over the next 5 years." Eventually, management agreed to move forward with this project.

In October 1998, Lassiter invited Greg Ginder, president of the UNITRAK Software Corporation, to give a short demonstration of the system's capabilities. Wilson observed about 45 minutes of the three-hour demonstration and told Lassiter, "I'll support it if you want it. It will work for my project in public affairs." Kovecki's comments were different. He remarked, "The software has its strengths and weaknesses and it probably would save some of my time. But, I don't like the idea of the staff having uncontrolled access to so much data. It's not clear what they'll do with it." Lassiter was able to convince the MSCC board of directors to approve the purchase of the UNITRAK system, including an IBM AS/400 computer system and the UNITRAK software.

Implementation of the System

Despite Lassiter's interest and urging, implementing the new system took much longer than was planned. Delays in issuing the purchase order and testing the software only added to the time to make the system operational. Training finally took place in August 1999. The training went well but data migration became a serious problem. On the final day of training, Lassiter told Kovecki to migrate the data in the current PC systems to the new system. Kovecki had considerable problems doing so as less than 15 percent of the data rolled over into the proper assignments. Because there was no documentation on the old software to refer to, it took him until the end of 1999 to get the system up and running. In the meantime, most of the MSCC PCs were essentially inoperable. Requests for lists and labels for mailings could not be fulfilled. And word processing, payment and invoice posting, data changes, and list management were very difficult during this time.

Lassiter was also finding it very difficult to gain information from Kovecki as to the progress and status of the system conversion. It seemed that Kovecki, frustrated with the problems he was having and irritated with the staff coming to him to ask for assistance, was going out of his way to avoid staff members.

UNITRAK came through, however, and by the end of the year the system was not only up and running but was also Y2K compliant—all at no additional cost (beyond the initial hardware and software cost) to the MSCC. Problems still remained, however, as it soon became clear that the system had severe limitations—most importantly the lack of a relational database management system. And by mid-2000, a more severe problem cropped up—UNITRAK was experiencing serious financial problems and its president decided to move its software towards a Windows-based (and away from its current UNIX-based) environment. Soon thereafter, UNITRAK's existing support staff was dismissed and the MSCC was left with no technical support. To alleviate this problem, Lassiter hired an outside consultant, Zen Consulting, to write programs, generate new reports, and assist in the maintenance/support of the software.

Moving Past the UNITRAK Implementation

In September 2000, Kovecki became concerned about his future with the MSCC. As a result, he resigned to take a position with a local law firm operating a similar hardware platform. In late October, Dick Gramen, a former staff computer trainer for a locally based insurance broker, was hired to replace Kovecki. Gramen came from an IBM RS/6000 computing environment where he established and maintained a mainframe and a local area network. Gramen, however, had no experience working with the AS/400 computer and did not think much of it.

Additionally, Gramen had no previous exposure to the UNI-TRAK software or trade associations generally. Soon after he arrived, Gramen realized that this new environment would be very difficult to learn as he struggled with even the most basic system management tasks. These struggles made him wonder why the MSCC's needs could not be satisfied on an RS/6000 and a personal computing network.

Determined to confirm his views, Gramen consulted one of his college roommates, John Harter, about the proper system for the MSCC to have in place. Harter was now an RS/6000 consultant. Harter said,

> Obviously, Dick, I'm going to tell you to buy the IBM RS/6000 system. The RS/6000 is the perfect system for your type of organization. It runs UNIX so UNITRAK should operate on it. IBM has changed the nameplate on the unit—to an eServer pSeries designation—but the system is still essentially the same. And it should be simpler for you to maintain. I have to be honest with you, though. It's going to be a tough sell to your board. There are cheaper systems out there that would also meet your needs. If you do get the RS/6000 system, however, our company could provide some support if you had difficulties.

Gramen was certain that with the help of Harter and by avoiding the learning curve on the old system, he would be able to handle the maintenance and support and succeed at the MSCC. Now, all he had to do was to convince the MSCC's managers to move to the RS/6000 system. So, one month into his tenure, Gramen began by telling Leon Lassiter, the vice president of marketing,

> The MSCC can no longer afford to stay with its current computer hardware platform. The AS/400 just cannot meet your needs today, let alone tomorrow. The current online legislative information services system is maxed out, and without new hardware I just can't support the emerging political action program. If we don't get this situation addressed soon . . .

Eventually, this combination of reasons led Lassiter to support Gramen's general hardware proposal. Lassiter was very pleased that finally the IS person was taking some initiative. He was convinced that the MSCC's information systems were the key to maintaining Midsouth's preeminence among business trade associations, and thus the key to its financial success. Lassiter was also fearful that the MSCC would not be able to be of real value to its members in the legislative tracking arena without a change. As a result, Lassiter told Gramen to quietly pursue acquisition cost estimates.

Gramen realized, however, that if he were to be successful in moving the MSCC to the new hardware, he would have to have support from the president of the association, Jack Wallingford. When Gramen approached Wallingford, however, he was not prepared for the response:

> Dick, I agree that we may need entirely new hardware, but we cannot repeat the problems that occurred with our previous information system purchase. We made some pretty serious errors when we purchased the UNITRAK system and those simply cannot occur again. And we don't have anyone from IBM on our board any longer. Plus, I don't see how you can make this decision yet. You have not had enough time to learn about our current hardware (the AS/400 system), software (UNITRAK), our data structure, or even what the MSCC is engaged in and how the organization operates.

To alleviate some of Wallingford's concerns, Gramen agreed to arrange several meetings throughout the first quarter of 2001 with members of senior management for the purpose of outlining the organization's IS needs and the general operations of the MSCC.

Moving to the IBM RS/6000

After listening to Gramen outline the gravity of the situation, Ed Wilson decided to help Gramen by going to Lassiter and Wallingford individually to persuade each to support the RS/6000 system. Lassiter's support was of the greatest importance, though, due to his influence within the executive committee and the fact that his division was the largest user of information systems. Nevertheless, when Wilson went to Lassiter, Lassiter was incensed:

> I told Gramen to *quietly* pursue acquisition cost estimates so that we would be prepared when we knew exactly what we needed. Apparently he did not honor my request. I am not willing to rush into this blindly and I will not support taking this to the executive committee until we know what we need. We can't just rush into a purchase.

Even though Lassiter's logic was sound, Wilson remained convinced that something needed to be done immediately—with or without Lassiter's support. Subsequently, even though they knew doing so would alienate Lassiter, Wilson and Gramen took their proposal to the executive committee. Wilson began,

> Ladies and gentlemen, this decision is one that must be made expeditiously. The high cost of paying a consultant to support and maintain the UNITRAK software on hardware that is undersized is becoming a drain on our increasingly scarce resources. And with needs in the legislative services arena on the horizon, we must act quickly before we can no longer serve our members well. Our proposal is the perfect solution to this crisis situation. From a technology standpoint, the IBM RS/6000 technology is state-of-the-art with impeccable stability and reliability. As important, however, is that we have received assurances from IBM that they will recommend a software vendor to meet our needs once a purchase is made. This proposal gives us the best of all worlds.

Uncharacteristically, Lassiter sat in the back of the room listening in complete silence. He felt confident that even without his input the executive committee—comprised of CEOs from twenty of the top companies in the state—would never accept this proposal. Because of the economic downturn in 2000 and,

EXHIBIT 1
Midsouth Chamber of Commerce, Revenues vs. Expenditures (1995–2003)

Year Ended October 31	Revenues	Expenditures	Difference
1995	1,853,402	1,565,522	287,880
1996	1,968,185	1,799,287	168,898
1997	2,115,646	1,903,688	211,958
1998	2,278,019	2,110,010	168,009
1999	2,561,345	2,381,965	179,380
2000	2,515,601	2,720,121	(204,520)
2001	2,698,045	3,189,617	(491,572)
2002	2,783,365	3,197,345	(413,980)
2003	3,468,698	3,642,836	(174,138)

in Lassiter's opinion, the limitations of the UNITRAK software system, the MSCC's revenue growth had slowed considerably while its expenditures continued to increase. (See Exhibit 1.) This had quickly sliced the MSCC's financial reserves in half to just over $1 million which would make an off-budget purchase difficult to justify.

Lassiter, however, had miscalculated the power of the crisis argument, as the executive committee instructed Wilson and Gramen to inquire into the acquisition cost of the RS/6000 with only one limitation—that they use "due diligence" in developing the entire information systems solution.

Realizing that the MSCC was starting down a dangerous path, Lassiter drafted a memo to Wallingford and Wilson in which he wrote,

> The MSCC must hire an outside consultant to conduct a thorough needs analysis and establish a long-range vision and IS goals before any decisions are made. Furthermore, we must recognize and learn from the mistakes we made with our first system. Hardware and software decisions cannot be made in isolation.

Neither Wallingford nor Wilson responded to his memo.

Enter Data Management Associates (DMA)

Immediately after the meeting of the executive committee, Gramen contacted IBM for its recommendation on an appropriate vendor. Without hesitation the IBM representative suggested a local value-added reseller (VAR) that not only sold and installed IBM hardware, but that also, for a fee, would search for software solutions that matched the MSCC's needs with the proposed RS/6000 hardware platform. With Gramen's shaky understanding of these matters, this seemed like the ideal solution. Because his friend, John Harter, worked for the local VAR, Gramen thought that this approach was the right way to go.

This arrangement, however, turned out to be far from ideal. Without ever visiting the MSCC—and based only on Gramen's view of the MSCC's operations and information systems needs—the VAR (for a $5,000 fee) contacted Data Management Associates (DMA) on behalf of the MSCC. DMA was a 54-employee operation located 61 miles from the MSCC offices and was headed by Dittier Rankin, a Stanford University alumnus and computer science Ph.D. DMA had recently undergone a shift in its focus and had begun developing custom software for small trade associations and local chambers of commerce throughout the country. Nonetheless, even with their lack of significant experience, the VAR was confident in DMA's abilities. After several phone conversations between Gramen and DMA, arrangements were made for DMA to demonstrate its capabilities at the DMA office in May of 2001.

While the meeting only lasted 45 minutes, Wilson and Gramen left it very impressed. With screen shots, report samples, and specification sheets in hand, Gramen was prepared to present this proposal to the executive committee. In the interim, however, a new situation had developed. John Hilborn, one of Lassiter's most trusted friends—and a member of the MSCC's executive committee—approached Lassiter inquiring about his silence at the prior meeting. Hilborn was not pleased with what he had heard. As a result, at the next executive committee meeting, Hilborn asked Lassiter—during Gramen's presentation—for his input on the proposal. With that cue, Lassiter only made one comment: "Guys, if the proposed solution turns out to be ideal for the MSCC it would be pure luck, as the software selection process has not been comprehensive." And then Lassiter sat down.

Those few words unnerved Gramen and made several members of the executive committee very uncomfortable. Immediately, a motion passed to table the proposal for a month while more information was gathered from and about DMA.

With his proposal—and potentially his job—on the line, Gramen arranged for DMA's president and two other members of DMA's management to visit the Chamber's offices and conduct an IS needs analysis. Those individuals visited for 2 days. They spent the morning of the first day providing a complete overview of DMA and demonstrating, on a laptop, the capabilities of the software system they offered. The remaining day and a half was spent interviewing the MSCC's staff on their job duties, on how they used the current system, and on any unmet needs they could identify.

Additionally, Lassiter provided DMA with a very complete look at his division's IS needs and his personal vision of the information system that the MSCC needed. Additionally, in an effort to explain the MSCC's capabilities and to impress upon DMA the diversity and complexity of its operations, Lassiter gave DMA lots of materials. These included examples of every report and every type of document that the existing system could produce as well as explanations of the purpose and meaning (to the MSCC) of the information in each of these reports. Furthermore, he gave DMA an operations manual, detailing each task of each employee in the marketing division, and a lengthy report on the information that was currently in the database that could not be retrieved and printed in a useable report format. In all, this was a two-foot-deep stack of reports and data. Lassiter was also unwilling to allow DMA to leave until he was given a detailed thesis on DMA's capabilities and its software systems.

After two weeks, and in time for the June 2001 executive committee meeting, Rankin reported that DMA had reviewed the information gathered on its fact-finding visit and had successfully analyzed the IS needs of the MSCC. In doing so, DMA determined that its Association Plus software was the ideal match for the MSCC's needs and the RS/6000 platform. Lassiter remained undeterred, however, as he urged the approval of travel funds to allow someone to visit at least one DMA customer to see the software in action. The executive committee, in deference to Lassiter—and to the fact that his division was by far the most extensive user of the current information system—agreed to delay the final decision and to approve funds to send him and Gramen to visit the Lake Erie Chamber of Commerce—one of DMA's most recent clients.

More Visits/Interviews

While DMA had willingly given out the Lake Erie Chamber of Commerce's (LECC) name, this proved to be a bad choice for DMA. One hour into their visit, Gramen and Lassiter met with LECC's president, George Franks. Mr. Franks explained,

> We were thoroughly impressed with DMA when we went through our due diligence process. They showed us reports and screen shots that gave all of us hope that this was our panacea. But guys, we have had serious and persistent data conversion problems from the moment of implementation. And, I still don't know whether we will ever see any value from this system.

With this information in hand, Lassiter (and a reluctant Gramen) reported these findings back to the executive committee. Even though Gramen continued to argue that time was of the essence, the executive committee needed additional assurances. As such, they sent Lassiter and Gramen to DMA headquarters with two goals: (1) to determine what DMA's capabilities were, and (2) to see an operational version of DMA's software.

Immediately upon arriving at DMA headquarters, Lassiter and Gramen were given a tour and were introduced to some of DMA's senior staff. Soon thereafter they were led into a conference hall where they were treated to a lengthy demonstration of what appeared to be a fully operational version of DMA's software. However, DMA had actually used the MSCC's data and reports to prepare sample reports and screenshots to create the appearance of a fully operational software system. As one former DMA employee would later tell Sage Niele,

> They used the sample reports and other information they received from Lassiter to create representative screens and reports. DMA so badly wanted to get into the trade association market with a big customer like the MSCC that they believed if they could just land this contract they could develop the software and stay one step ahead of the MSCC. The long and short of it is that they sold "vaporware."

During the demonstrations, Lassiter and Gramen repeatedly asked for and received assurances that DMA could, with "relatively minor and easily achievable modifications," develop the software and convert the UNITRAK database to produce the demonstrated reports and lists for the MSCC. To every question and contingency raised, DMA responded that the development would be no problem, and that, additionally, the MSCC would receive the source code if it purchased the software.

Satisfied with what they had seen, Lassiter and Gramen flew home. At the August 2001 executive committee meeting, they reported that this system (the RS/6000 and the DMA software) was acceptable for purchase. Hearing this, the executive committee instructed Gramen to request design specifications and specific cost estimates on this software system. Under the new configuration, a relational database management system called Progress, created by DMA, would be loaded on the RS/6000. (See Exhibit 2.) Existing data were to be converted by DMA into the new system. In addition, DMA was to use its Association Plus software to enable the MSCC's staff to produce the desired

EXHIBIT 2
Midsouth Chamber of Commerce, DMA's System Configuration

Association Plus	Results
DMA Developed Custom Software	User-Friendly Reporting Tool

Progress

Relational Database Management Software

IBM RS/6000 Computer

reports, lists, and other documents through a user-friendly report-writer software package known as Results. These detailed estimates were presented at the September 2001 executive committee meeting where they were approved. The total price was $277,000. Gramen immediately contacted DMA and asked the company to prepare a proposed contract.

The DMA Contract

In late September, DMA sent its standard contract to Gramen for the acquisition of the Progress relational database management system, the Association Plus custom software module, and several packaged software components. When the proposed contract arrived, Gramen, recognizing that he had neither the expertise nor the inclination to review the contract, sent the contract to Wallingford with a note saying, "It looks fine." Wallingford signed the contract and within the day it was headed back to DMA without any other staff member nor the corporate counsel or any outside specialist having reviewed the document.

Had someone with greater legal acumen reviewed the contract, however, they would have immediately recognized that it was extremely one-sided and contained none of the assurances that Lassiter and Gramen were given during their visit. In laymen's terms, it gave no specific or quantifiable performance standards for the services to be provided and gave DMA the right to increase the price of services and products provided at its discretion, while limiting DMA's financial and performance liabilities.

Troubles in Implementing the DMA Software

Nevertheless, for the first time in several years, excitement filled the air at the MSCC as it appeared as if a new computing era had begun. On November 11, 2001, the MSCC held a kickoff celebration and invited DMA management to help commemorate the event. Just as important, however, were the meetings associated with this celebration. In these meetings DMA was attempting to set the project's implementation schedule by determining (1) the complexity of the various customization components, (2) the length of time necessary to implement the customized software, and (3) the tasks that the MSCC needed to complete in order to facilitate the conversion. By the end of that day, the broad outline of an implementation schedule had been laid out with the first week of July 2002 set as the target completion date.

Two weeks after the initial meetings, Stacey Porter, a DMA consultant, arrived at the MSCC offices to install the first version of the telemarketing module and to provide training on the constituents, territory management, and committees modules. This training served as the staff's first look at the software. The territory managers, however, were not impressed with the layout or content of the software, as it often forced them to work through more than twenty screens to perform relatively simple tasks. As a result, Lassiter demanded a significant rewrite of the territory management module, and by March 2002, similar delays were a part of the PAC, accounting, meetings, and legislative modules as well.

With the scheduled conversion to the DMA software quickly approaching and delays becoming the norm, Gramen and Wallingford decided to continue running the old system until the staff was completely comfortable with the new system. Within 3 months, however, even though the DMA software was still not fully operational, the MSCC abandoned this directive as it had simply become too expensive to pay the consulting fees to keep UNITRAK operational.

As implementation pushed into late July, DMA began encountering substantial problems converting the membership database from UNITRAK into the DMA custom software package. As progress ground to a halt on the software installation, Lassiter summoned Gramen and Porter into his office. During this meeting, the working relationship between the MSCC and DMA began to deteriorate further as Gramen warned Porter, "I think we've been pretty patient with you so far, but that is about to change. I've heard of far less serious situations ending up in court before. And I know you understand that this all falls on you."

The Start of Additional Problems

Further complicating this relationship had been a series of billing issues. In the process of installing the system, DMA ran into a myriad of problems with solutions in one area often leading to problems in other areas. By the middle of July 2002, no less than five MSCC staff members were in regular contact with DMA identifying problems and requesting assistance. As a result, DMA had quickly used up the development hours specified in the contract, and had subsequently started billing the MSCC for the work beyond the free hours guaranteed.

As the problems worsened, Lassiter became increasingly involved in the daily implementation problems. Feeling as if he was the only one who could right the ship, Lassiter went to Wallingford and argued that he should be given the responsibility of overseeing the entire project. Wallingford gladly consented to Lassiter's request.

Immediately, Lassiter arranged a conference call between himself, Gramen, and Porter to address the many outstanding items past completion date. In the call Lassiter emphasized,

> We are in our eleventh month, and we still cannot use your software to close our books each month. This is completely unacceptable. You could at least provide the system documentation you promised so that we can reduce our own learning curve. It's no wonder that you cannot get the more complicated modules complete, though. All I've been making is simple requests and for some reason you can't meet them. And one more thing, we

were promised the source code when our negotiations began, and now I've been told by one of your team members that this will cost us $20,000. What type of dishonest organization are you running? This is completely unacceptable and my patience is thinning. If this situation doesn't improve. . . .

The exchanges between DMA and the MSCC continued to become increasingly strained, and disagreements on what items were and were not promised as part of the system installation became a key point of contention. Given the nature of the relationship, Lassiter ordered that all DMA billings were to be carefully reviewed by Gramen for inappropriate charges. Furthermore, Lassiter asked to review the DMA contract.

There first appeared to be a glimmer of hope, as the contract specified that roughly half the cost of the software system had been due as a down payment with the balance due upon Gramen signing acceptance certificates after the satisfactory installation of each individual module. After meeting with Gramen, however, Lassiter learned that although none of the acceptance certificates had been signed, the full system had nonetheless been paid for in full. Lassiter could not believe that they had given up one of the most important pieces of leverage that the MSCC had. Lassiter quickly decided it was time to go back to Wallingford for his input.

"Jack, we have two problems," Lassiter said. "First, it goes without saying that there are serious problems with the software and with DMA's capacity to support and deliver it. Just as important, however, is that Dick does not seem to have the requisite ability to maintain and support the hardware platform and is really of little value in terms of overseeing or solving problems with the software implementation. As a result, we are completely dependent on DMA for this project's success or failure. I think it's time we go in a different direction."

Wallingford replied, "I agree with you. I trust your judgments in these matters. But before we go any farther, there is something I want to tell you. I am planning on retiring at the end of the year. This week the executive committee will appoint a search committee and begin accepting resumes from interested parties. I really would like you to consider applying for this position."

Lassiter was speechless, but by this point he no longer had any desire to stay with the MSCC. In his mind, he had taken the marketing effort at the MSCC about as far as he could—especially given the information system's limitations. Lassiter had already received a lucrative offer to be the chief operating officer of a local investment management company and was ready to accept it. Lassiter was not alone, however, as Ed Wilson had just had a final interview with a new government policy think tank. But, while Lassiter did not throw his name into consideration, Wilson did because his final outside interview had not gone well. Nevertheless, the search committee was acutely aware that Wilson would just be a temporary fix as he was nearing retirement; Lassiter was their preference.

As a result, after reviewing the other available candidates again, two search committee members contacted Lassiter and urged him to apply. After two lengthy meetings—in which the two members intimated that they would not take no for an answer—Lassiter relented and agreed to have his name offered for the presidency. At the November 2002 meeting two weeks later, the board of directors ratified that selection.

A Lack of Progress

The search for a president had not slowed down the MSCC's problems, however. In late November 2002, Lassiter gave Porter an updated list of problems with the software—as compiled by MSCC staff—and asked her to estimate the time to address these tasks in hours. Three weeks later DMA sent back the time estimates and a series of work orders with cost estimates. DMA indicated in that correspondence that it would initiate the work when the orders were signed and returned by the MSCC. Lassiter refused to sign the work orders and informed DMA that he considered the work to be part of the initial installation and that DMA was in breach of contract.

On January 1, 2003, Lassiter officially took over as president, and shortly thereafter, Ed Wilson announced he would retire on June 30. Instead of replacing him, Lassiter decided to disperse his duties among existing staff members. Knowing that he had to shed some of his IS development responsibilities and realizing that he could no longer afford to leave Gramen as the sole person responsible for the MSCC's information systems, Lassiter began looking for a candidate with a strong management, information systems, and financial background to oversee the MSCC's information systems and to serve as chief financial officer. In the interim he had Gramen report directly to him while temporarily retaining the role of overseer of the ever-tenuous relationship with DMA.

Meanwhile, DMA seemed to be creating as many problems as it fixed. Confidence in the new software was dwindling, and paper systems began to proliferate as some modules were not installed and others were completely non-operational. Due to the slow response time, the staff often had to work evenings and weekends to complete simple tasks, which further diminished morale. In addition, the integrity and dependability of the membership database had become increasingly suspect as a result of the data conversion problems and the general unreliability of the system.

At the end of January, Rankin and Porter spent a full day in meetings with the MSCC staff and senior management. Each division outlined its problems and frustrations with the software system. By the final meeting that day, Lassiter was livid, "We have to bring the initial installation to an end! It is time for your company to deliver the system that we contracted for. I am tired of missed deadlines, unreturned phone calls, and partial solutions."

"I understand your frustration, Mr. Lassiter," Rankin said. "But I want to reiterate our desire to keep you as a customer. We will redouble our efforts to finish the installation, and I will personally send a letter to you outlining the dates for completion of the outstanding problems."

Two months later, Gramen and Porter held a conference call to once again discuss the discrepancies between the promised and actual delivery dates. Per Lassiter's instructions, they also requested and received a listing of DMA's client list. Lassiter instructed Gramen to conduct a phone survey of these businesses to determine their level of satisfaction with DMA. To Lassiter's dismay, this phone survey revealed that there was overwhelming dissatisfaction with DMA's products and services. The Lake Erie and Great Lakes Chambers were already in litigation with DMA due to contract non-performance and many of their other clients were calling for a multi-party lawsuit.

On May 7, Lassiter sent Rankin another letter outlining the items still unfinished and demanding a speedy resolution to these problems. In response, Rankin instructed Porter to phone Lassiter with a pointed message. "Mr. Lassiter," Porter said, "I just wanted to let you know that DMA has already incurred $250,000 of expenses it has not charged you in an attempt to meet your concerns. Nevertheless, DMA has decided to discontinue programming support for the MSCC until the Chamber pays its outstanding invoices."

"In that case," Lassiter responded, "I guess we'll see you in court." At which point the phone conversation ended abruptly.

Enter Sage Niele

On June 30, 2003, Ed Wilson retired—although he was retained as a part-time consultant and given the title of the political action committee's executive director—and Sage Niele arrived as vice president of operations and chief financial officer. Niele held an MBA from the Wharton School of Business and had previously performed systems manager responsibilities for a large pharmaceutical company in the Midsouth area. More recently, she had operated her own information systems and financial consulting business. With two small children at home she had decided to pursue something less rigorous and time-consuming than running her own business, but it soon became clear to her that this position might not fit that billing.

A few days into her new position, Lassiter met with Niele in his office:

Sage, it's good to have you on board. I need you to begin a planning and assessment process to determine the deficiencies of the current information system, along with the MSCC's needs, and the alternatives that exist in the event the MSCC needs to scrap the DMA system and start over. From this day forward, you are to be the exclusive contact person between the MSCC and DMA. I have begun the process of finding a suitable, top-notch replacement for Dick, which will help you in your cause. I'll give him 2 months to find a new job, but we have to let him go.

That next week, Lassiter, Niele, and Gramen met with an attorney specializing in computer software contracts who had also been a past chairman and current executive committee member of the MSCC. Lassiter outlined the situation for her, but her assessment was far worse than Lassiter had imagined.

"The way I see this contract," she began, "The MSCC has few, if any remedies. I wish you had contacted me earlier—before the contract was signed. The absence of performance standards leaves you with only one real remedy, the avoidance of payment. Because you have already made full payment, you have given a tacit acceptance of the software system. From speaking with Leon earlier, I understand that your goal is to either receive reimbursement and the source code from DMA—so you can hire a consultant to make the software usable—*or* to get your money back and buy another system. These outcomes are unlikely. In my opinion, you need to tone down your demeanor with DMA and try to get as much additional progress out of them as possible until you decide what to do. If DMA does get serious about cutting off their support, pay what you think you owe and we'll go after them for specific performance."

Taking that advice to heart, several additional pieces of correspondence were internally generated and sent to DMA with a more temperate tenor. Meanwhile, Niele continued to send DMA payments for only those items the MSCC deemed to be billable. Each time she crossed her fingers that DMA would not pull the plug.

With the help of the MSCC librarian, Niele identified a list of eight software packages that would run on an RS/6000 hardware platform, that were designed for use in a trade association environment, and that appeared to be worthy of further investigation. At the same time, she began interviewing MSCC staff members to prepare an inventory of the current system deficiencies as well as the needs for the future. An outgrowth of this effort was the creation of an *ad hoc* information systems committee that she used to help flatten her learning curve about the MSCC and its current information systems.

Furthermore, Niele also spoke with Lassiter and key board members to determine their vision for the operational future of the MSCC. And Niele arranged for six CEOs from the executive committee to have their IS managers or other key IS staff members serve on a steering committee to assist her in evaluating systems alternatives. Not only did that give her additional points of view, but she hoped this would make it easier to sell her final recommendation to the executive committee.

Unfortunately, Niele also knew that her assessment of the current situation and the alternatives she had identified to date would not be attractive to the executive committee. On a legal pad in her office, she wrote down the problems as she saw them: (1) The modules will likely never become operational, (2) DMA is unwilling to commit the resources necessary to finish the job, (3) the DMA relationship is still deteriorating quickly, (4) any costs already itemized are likely sunk due to poor contracting, (5) it will be expensive to start over from scratch, and (6) it is equally expensive to do nothing. Now the big question was, where to go from here?

As the microwave sounded to signal that her popcorn was ready, Sage wondered which problems she would be putting to an end through her recommendations and which problems she would create by making additional changes.

PART II
APPLYING INFORMATION TECHNOLOGY

THE PURPOSE OF THESE THREE CHAPTERS IS TO INCREASE AWARENESS AND UNDERSTANDING of specific IT applications being used in today's organizations. Rapid changes in business conditions and management methods, the types of applications available, and the IT platforms and networks that support them all provide new opportunities for organizations to use IT in new ways in order to survive and grow. Chapters 6 through 8 offer a comprehensive view of the capabilities of a wide range of IT applications that can be considered for adoption by business and IT managers. For those readers with considerable business experience, these chapters will help you categorize and assess the capabilities and features of systems that you might have already worked with.

The first two chapters in Part II focus on IT applications used *within* an organization's boundaries: enterprise systems (Chapter 6)—systems that support the entire organization or large portions of it—and managerial support systems (Chapter 7)—systems designed to provide support for one or more managers. At the beginning of Chapter 6 we first introduce several concepts critical to the understanding of IT applications in general: batch versus online processing, client/server systems, and service-oriented architecture. Then we discuss transaction processing concepts in general, followed by enterprise resource planning, data warehousing, customer relationship management, office automation, groupware, intranets, factory automation, and supply chain management applications. Among the managerial support systems discussed in Chapter 7 are decision support and group support systems in general, as well as geographic information systems, knowledge management systems, expert systems, neural networks, and virtual reality applications.

The focus of Chapter 8 is e-business systems—applications designed to interact with customers, suppliers, and other business partners. The chapter begins with a brief survey of Internet technologies that enable e-business applications and the roles that legal and regulatory environments play. A framework is provided for evaluating business opportunities and threats for individual firms within an industry context. Business-to-business (B2B) applications (including EDI and online marketplaces) are then described, followed by detailed business-to-consumer (B2C) examples of traditional (catalog, store) retailers that compete online with dot-com retailers, as well as online intermediaries (e.g., Google, eBay, Autobytel). The chapter ends with some considerations for what makes a good Web site from a customer perspective.

Part II concludes with a set of five original teaching cases. A supply chain management initiative that builds on an enterprise system capability is described in "Vendor-Managed Inventory at NIBCO." The MaxFli case study describes a multiphase project to provide information via handheld computers to sales teams located in different South American countries. The Continental Airlines case study illustrates how an organization invested in data warehousing and business intelligence applications to turn a poor performing organization into an industry leader.

The final two case studies involve start-up firms. The Cliptomania Web Store case study traces the changes made by a B2C start-up to continue to be a successful e-tailer. Finally, the Meridian Hospital Systems case study highlights the pros and cons of starting a career with a small software start-up in the health care industry versus an established IT industry player, from the perspective of a new college graduate.

CHAPTER 6
ENTERPRISE SYSTEMS

INFORMATION TECHNOLOGY (IT) IS A KEY ENABLER FOR ORGANIZATIONS OF all sizes, both public and private. Businesses and other organizations are not the same as they were a decade ago. They are more complex but have fewer layers of management; they tend to offer more customized products and services; they are increasingly international in scope; and they are heavily dependent on the accurate and timely flow of information. And this change in organizations is accelerating, not decelerating.

As a current or future manager, you must be aware of IT and its potential impact on your job, your career, and your organization. You cannot afford to leave consideration of IT solely to the information systems (IS) specialists. As a business manager, you must perform many critical roles if you and your organization are to be successful: conceptualize ways in which IT can be used to improve performance; serve as a consultant to the IS specialists who are developing or implementing applications for your organization; manage the organizational change that accompanies new IT applications; use the technology applications and help enhance them; and facilitate the successful implementation of new IT applications.

Where do we start getting you ready for your new roles? We start with an *awareness* of how IT is being used in a variety of organizations. The first five chapters of this book have already begun the process of building awareness of IT applications.

This chapter and the following two chapters will provide a systematic introduction to a wide variety of IT applications. We think you will be impressed with the breadth of areas in which IT is being employed to make organizations more efficient and effective. We hope these three chapters will stimulate your thinking about potential applications in your present or future organization. Most of the obvious applications are already in place. Nearly every organization uses a computer to handle its payroll, keep inventory records, and process accounts receivable and payable; almost every organization uses a telephone system and facsimile machines. But many applications remain to be discovered, most likely by managers like you.

APPLICATION AREAS

To consider a topic as broad as IT applications, some type of framework is needed. We have divided applications into those which are *interorganizational* systems and those which are *intraorganizational* systems. Electronic commerce or e-business applications, including electronic data interchange (EDI) systems, represent obvious examples of

CRITICAL IT APPLICATIONS AND TECHNOLOGIES

In a 2006 survey of Society for Information Management (SIM) members—primarily chief information officers (CIOs) or other senior IS executives—the executives placed "Web services" at the top of their to-do lists. According to Jerry Luftman, professor and associate dean of graduate IS programs for the Stevens Institute of Technology, in Hoboken, New Jersey, and SIM vice president of academic community affairs, the survey sample represented a cross-section of SIM members in a variety of different businesses and from companies large and small. Luftman said that the emphasis on Web services is tied to increased interest in virtualization and service-oriented architecture (SOA). "Business intelligence" ranked second among the applications and technologies of importance to IS executives, with "security" ranking third, "business process management" fourth, "customer portals" fifth, and "systems integration" sixth. "Security" had been at the top of the executives' list for the previous two years, but dropped in 2006 to third place. Luftman felt that this lessening of interest in security probably reflects the progress that IT professionals believe they have made in the past several years to make their IT systems less vulnerable to attack.

[Adapted from Gibson, 2006]

All six of these critical applications and technologies will be discussed in this chapter or in later chapters in the book. "Web services" will be considered as one of the critical concepts in the first major section of this chapter; virtualization was already introduced in the telecommunications chapter, and SOA will be considered along with Web services. "Business intelligence" will be covered in Chapter 7, and "security" will be the focus of Chapter 16, entitled "IT Security and Risk Management." IT can be used to improve "business process management" through enterprise systems such as enterprise resource planning (ERP), customer relationship management (CRM), and supply chain management (SCM)—all three of which will be discussed in this chapter. The important notion of "portals" will be introduced near the end of this chapter, with more added in Chapter 8. And "systems integration" is the goal of many applications and technologies, including Web services, SOA, and ERP systems. Thus, the topics covered in this chapter and the next two chapters directly relate to five of the top six critical applications and technologies, with the sixth topic dealt with in depth in Chapter 16.

Knowledge about e-business applications is so important today that we devote all of Chapter 8 to this topic.

To provide some structure to the broad range of intraorganizational systems, we have divided these applications into two major categories: enterprise systems, designed to support the entire enterprise (organization) or large portions of it, and managerial support systems, designed to provide support to a specific manager or a small group of managers. This chapter covers enterprise systems, such as transaction processing systems and groupware, as well as the critical concepts of client/server architecture and service-oriented architecture. Chapter 7 deals with systems specifically designed to support managers, such as decision support systems and expert systems.

Figure 6.1 lists these two major categories of applications, along with representative application areas that fall within each category. This figure provides the primary framework for our discussion of intraorganizational IT applications in this chapter and the following chapter. Please note that the application areas are neither unique nor exhaustive. For example, some specific applications fall in two or more application areas (such as enterprise resource planning systems also being transaction processing systems). Further, it is easy to argue that an application area such as groupware is both an enterprise system and a management support system. Somewhat arbitrarily, we

Enterprise Systems
   Transaction Processing Systems
   Enterprise Resource Planning Systems
   Data Warehousing
   Customer Relationship Management Systems
   Office Automation
   Groupware
   Intranets and Portals
   Factory Automation
   Supply Chain Management Systems

Managerial Support Systems
   Decision Support Systems
   Data Mining
   Group Support Systems
   Geographic Information Systems
   Executive Information Systems
   Business Intelligence Systems
   Knowledge Management Systems
   Expert Systems
   Neural Networks
   Virtual Reality

Figure 6.1   Types of Application Systems

interorganizational systems, or systems that span organizational boundaries. The importance of applications that link businesses with their end consumers (B2C) or link businesses with other business customers or business suppliers (B2B) has been fueled by the growth of the Internet.

have chosen to discuss group support systems, which is an important subset of groupware concerned with supporting the activities of a small group in a specific task or a specific meeting, as a management support system while discussing the broader category of groupware as an enterprise system. Despite these caveats, however, the application areas given in Figure 6.1 encompass the overwhelming majority of specific applications.

CRITICAL CONCEPTS

Before we turn to specific examples of the various application areas, we must consider a number of important concepts that are intertwined throughout all the applications. An understanding of these concepts is a prerequisite to an understanding of the applications.

Batch Processing Versus Online Processing

One of the fundamental distinctions for computer applications is **batch processing** versus **online processing**. In the early days of computers, all processing was batched. The organization accumulated a batch of transactions and then processed the entire batch at one time. For example, all inventory transactions (in and out) were recorded on paper during the day. After the close of business for the day, the transactions were keyed into a type of computer-readable medium, such as magnetic tape. The medium was then physically carried to the computer center, and the entire inventory was updated by processing that day's batch against the master inventory file on the computer. By the beginning of the next business day, the master inventory file was completely up-to-date and appropriate inventory reports were printed. Figure 6.2 represents this batch processing approach in a simplified form.

The major problem with batch processing is the time delay involved before the master file is updated. Only at the beginning of the business day, for example, will the master inventory file be up-to-date. At all other times the company does not really know how many units of each product it has in stock.

As the technology improved, online processing was developed to avoid the time delay in batch processing. With a fully implemented online system, each transaction is entered directly into the computer when it occurs. For example, in an online inventory system a shipping clerk or sales clerk enters the receipt or sale of a product into a workstation (perhaps a sophisticated cash register) connected by a telecommunications line to the server com-

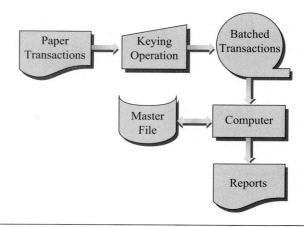

Figure 6.2   Batch Processing (simplified)

puter, which holds the inventory master file. As soon as the entry is completed, the computer updates the master file within a fraction of a second. Thus, the company always knows how many units of each product it has in stock. Figure 6.3 depicts such an **online system**.

A fully implemented online system is also called an **interactive system**, because the user is directly interacting with the computer. The computer will provide a response to the user very quickly, usually within a second. Not all online systems, however, are interactive. Some systems, often called **in-line systems**, provide for online data entry, but the actual processing of the transaction is deferred until a batch of transactions has been accumulated.

A fully online system has the distinct advantage of timeliness. Why then aren't all present-day systems online? There are two reasons—cost and the existence of so-called natural batch applications. In most cases batch systems are much less expensive to operate than their online counterparts. There are usually significant economies associated with batching, both in the data-entry function and the transaction processing. But if the data-entry function can be accomplished when the original data are captured

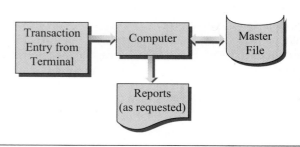

Figure 6.3   Online Processing

(such as with a sophisticated cash register), an online data entry/batch processing system might be less expensive than a straight batch system. The decision of batch versus online becomes a trade-off between cost and timeliness. In general, online costs per transaction have been decreasing and the importance of timeliness has been increasing. The result is that most applications today use online data entry and an increasing proportion also use online processing.

The exception to this movement to online processing has been the natural batch applications. An organization's payroll, for example, might be run once a week or once every two weeks. There is no particular advantage to the timeliness of online processing; the organization knows when the payroll must be run. Even in this instance, there might be advantages to online data entry to permit convenient changes in employees, exemptions, deductions, and wage rates. Thus, hybrid online data entry/batch processing systems will continue to exist.

Functional Information Systems

Instead of considering the two major categories and associated application areas of Figure 6.1, it is possible to create a framework based strictly on the organization's primary business functions—a **functional information systems** framework. For example, consider an organization in which the primary business functions are production, marketing, accounting, personnel, and engineering. Applications may then be categorized as part of the production information system, part of the marketing information system, or part of the accounting information system, and so on. This functional approach is simply an alternative way of classifying applications.

In this alternative view, the overall IS is composed of multiple subsystems, each providing information for various tasks within the function. In turn, each functional subsystem consists of a possibly interrelated series of subsubsystems. For example, the production information system is likely to include interrelated subsystems for sales forecasting, production planning, production scheduling, material requirements planning, capacity requirements planning, personnel requirements planning, materials purchasing, and inventory. The marketing information system may include subsystems for promotion and advertising, new product development, sales forecasting (hopefully tied into the production sales forecasting subsystem), product planning, product pricing, market research, and sales information. The accounting information system, which is generally the oldest and most fully developed functional system, is likely to include computerized versions of the entire journal and ledger system, plus a cost or responsibility accounting system and a financial reporting system for preparing reports for stockholders and other external groups.

One of the most important trends in the latter 1990s and the early 2000s is the movement toward integration of these functional information systems. Often these integration efforts have begun by focusing on a **business process**—the chain of activities required to achieve an outcome such as order fulfillment or materials acquisition—rather than on functions. Such a focus on process makes it easier to recognize where formerly distinct information systems are related and thus where they should be integrated (e.g., use common data and perform an activity only once). Sometimes the internal IS department has developed these integrated systems, but more often software packages called enterprise resource planning (ERP) systems have been purchased from outside vendors. We will return to these ERP systems later in the chapter.

Vertical Integration of Systems

Another important characteristic of some systems is that they operate across levels of the organization or, in some instances, across independent firms occupying different levels in an industry hierarchy, such as an automobile manufacturer and the associated independent dealers. (More on these interorganizational systems will be covered in Chapter 8.) A system that serves more than one vertical level in an organization or an industry is called a **vertically integrated information system**. For example, in a single firm, a vertically integrated sales information system might capture the initial sales data and produce invoices (acting as a transaction processing system), summarize these data on a weekly basis for use by middle managers in tracking slow- and fast-selling items as well as productive and unproductive salespeople (acting as a decision support system), and further analyze these data for long-term trends for use by top managers in determining strategic directions (acting as an executive information system).

In a somewhat similar way, a national fast-food chain might develop a sales information system with modules both for operating units (company stores and franchises) and for the national organization. Thus, data collected at the store level using the operating unit module are already in the appropriate form to be processed by the national organization module. These basic data are transmitted via telecommunication lines to the national organization on a periodic basis, perhaps each night. The extent of vertical integration is an important characteristic of applications.

Distributed Systems

Distributed systems, sometimes called **distributed data processing**, refers to a mode of delivery rather than a traditional class of applications like transaction processing or decision support systems. With distributed systems, the processing power is distributed to multiple sites, which are then tied together via telecommunications lines. Local area networks (LANs) and wide area networks (WANs) are both used to support distributed systems. Thus, distributed systems are systems in which computers of some size (microcomputers, midrange computers, mainframes, and so forth) are located at various physical sites at which the organization does business (headquarters, factories, stores, warehouses, office buildings) and in which the computers are linked by telecommunication lines of some sort in order to support some business process.

The economics of distributed systems are not perfectly clear, but have tended to favor distribution. For the most part, communication and support costs go up with distributed systems while computer costs go down. Placing smaller microcomputers and workstations at noncentral sites is generally less expensive than expanding the capacity of a large system at the central site. Distributed systems do have disadvantages, such as greater security risk because of easy accessibility, dependence on high-quality telecommunications lines, and greater required coordination across sites. In most instances, however, the disadvantages are outweighed by the economic advantages. The distributed mode of computing has become the norm for business firms around the world.

Client/Server Systems

In the 1990s a particular type of distributed system known as a **client/server system** moved to center stage, and this type of system continues to enjoy the spotlight in the twenty-first century. With this type of system, the processing power is distributed between a central server computer, such as a midrange computer or a powerful workstation, and a number of client computers, which are usually desktop microcomputers. The split in responsibilities between the server and the client varies considerably from application to application, but the client usually provides the graphical user interface (GUI), accepts the data entry, and displays the immediate output, while the server maintains the database against which the new data are processed. The actual processing of the transaction may occur on either the client or a server. For example, in a retail client/server application, the client might be the sophisticated cash register on the sales floor while the server is a workstation in the back office. When a credit sale is made, the data are entered at the register and transmitted to the server, the server retrieves the customer's record and updates it based on the sale, the server returns a credit authorization signal to the register, and the sales document is printed at the register. At the close of the billing cycle, the server prepares the bills for all of the customers, prints them, and produces summary reports for store management.

Now that we have a general idea about the nature of a client/server system, let us explore the three building blocks of such a system. First, the client building block, usually running on a PC, handles the user interface and has the ability to access distributed services through a network. Sometimes the client also does the processing. Second, the server building block, usually running on a bigger machine (a high-end PC, midrange computer, or even a mainframe), handles the storage of data associated with the application. This associated data might be databases, groupware files (to be discussed later), Web pages, or even objects for object-oriented programs. Sometimes the server (or even another server) does the processing. The third building block is **middleware**, a rather vague term that covers all the software needed to support interactions between clients and servers. The *Client/Server Survival Guide* refers to middleware as ". . . the slash (/) component of client/server. In this first approximation, middleware is the glue that lets a client obtain a service from a server" (Orfali, Harkey, and Edwards, 1999, p. 44).

Middleware can be divided into three categories of software: server operating systems, transport stack software, and service-specific software. The server operating system, also called a network operating system, has the task of creating a *single-system image* for all services on the network, so that the system is transparent to users and even application programmers. The user does not know what functions are performed where on the network—it looks like a single system. The primary server operating systems include several variations of Microsoft Windows Server, several variations of UNIX, and Linux. Transport stack software allows communications employing certain protocols, such as Transmission Control Protocol/Internet Protocol (TCP/IP) (see Chapter 4), to be sent across the network. The server operating system often encompasses some elements of the needed transport stack software, but other middleware products might also be required. The service-specific software is used to carry out a particular service, such as electronic mail or the World Wide Web's Hypertext Transfer Protocol (HTTP).

Consider the split in responsibilities between the client and the server. The question is where the actual processing of the application is done. Originally, all client/server systems had only **two tiers**—a client tier and a server tier. If most of the processing is done on the client, this is called a *fat client* or *thin server* model. If most of the processing is done on the server, then it is a *thin client* or *fat server* model. For example, Web servers and groupware servers are usually fat servers (i.e., the processing is largely done on the server for Web and groupware applications), while database servers are usually thin servers (i.e., the processing is largely done on the client). In the mid-1990s, **three-tier client/server systems** became popular. In the most common three-tier configuration, an application server that is separate from the database server is employed. The user interface is housed on the client, usually a PC (tier 1); the processing is performed on a midrange system operating as the application server (tier 2); and the data are stored on a large machine (often a mainframe or midrange computer) that operates as the database server (tier 3).

Let us consider some examples of client/server systems. An East Coast electric utility company used a three-tier approach to revamp its customer service system. The new system enables the utility's 450 service representatives to gain access to the multiple databases the company maintains on its 1.5 million customers. The service representatives use PCs as clients (tier 1) working through four servers that process the customer inquiries (tier 2) by accessing data from the company mainframe (tier 3). A Canadian supplemental health insurer began its migration to client/server technology by concentrating on getting its most mission-critical system—processing claims for prescription drugs sold at more than 3,500 pharmacies across Canada—into a three-tier environment. The clients were PCs, running Windows, located in the pharmacies (tier 1); the application servers were Sun workstations and Hewlett-Packard midrange systems (tier 2); and the database server was a Unisys mainframe computer (tier 3). Programmers initially used the C and C++ programming languages to develop the tier 1 and tier 3 components of the system. They used a specialized development tool, BEA Systems' Tuxedo, to develop the transaction processing component (tier 2). Later development work was done using Information Advantage's DecisionSuite (Ruber, 1997).

In the early twenty-first century, there is a renewed emphasis on the thin client model to service remote areas, small locations, and traveling employees, where it is difficult to update the client software regularly. As an example, Maritz Travel Company, a $1.8-billion travel management company, used a thin client approach based on Microsoft's Windows NT Terminal Server Edition and MetaFrame software, from Citrix Systems. With the Citrix approach, applications execute on a server and are merely displayed on the client, with the client acting as a "dumb" terminal. Maritz initially licensed 15,000 Citrix users and plans to extend the applications to nearly 50 of its remote offices. Richard Spradling, the Chief Information Officer of Maritz, identifies many advantages to the thin client approach. According to Spradling, it is much easier to update only the servers; users automatically access the most current version of an application; performance of the applications has improved; and, over time, Maritz will spend less money on hardware by purchasing thin client devices rather than standard PCs or other fat clients (Wilde, 1999).

Xerox Corporation is also adopting a thin client approach. Until recently, Xerox replaced employees' PCs every three years, meaning about 10,000 employees got new machines each year. Starting in 2005, Xerox adopted less expensive thin clients, moving many key applications—such as those supporting sales and service personnel—to servers. Centralizing software will reduce support costs, and will also provide better security because the applications are not scattered among tens of thousands of client devices. "We're trying to be more efficient and want to do more with less money," says Janice Malaszenko, Xerox's Vice President and Chief Technology Officer for Information Management Strategy, Architecture, and Standards (Chabrow, 2005).

Service-Oriented Architecture and Web Services

As we near the end of the first decade of the twenty-first century, client/server systems are still important, but service-oriented architecture and Web services are the hot buzzwords when considering the development and deployment of application systems. **Service-oriented architecture (SOA)** is an application architecture based on a collection of functions, or services, where these services can communicate (or be connected) with one another. A service is a function that is well-defined and self-contained, and that does not depend on the context or state of other services. Then there must be some means of connecting services to each other, when the services might be running on different machines, using different protocols, and using different operating systems and languages. The key advantage of SOA is that once services are created, they can be used over and over again in different applications—only the connections will vary. Furthermore, the services could be developed within an organization, or the software for the services could be purchased from a vendor, or the services could be obtained from a vendor on a fee-for-use basis.

Though built on similar principles, SOA is not the same as **Web services**, which is a particular collection of technologies built around the XML (eXtensible Markup

SERVICE-ORIENTED ARCHITECTURE HAS ITS RISKS

Companies want what service-oriented architectures promise: easier integration, more productive programmers, and faster ways to change business processes. But delivering on that vision has been fairly ad hoc for many companies.

Service-oriented architecture has its risks. One is losing sight of business goals, so SOA becomes just another tech conversion. Another is testing, which can take longer because apps interact more. There's security, since SOA can make it easier to link outside the company. And there's reliability. ADP's Bongiorno [see example in text] found the company has had to increase reliability standards on applications, since one app's failure could take down many processes. Just one of the many hard-knock lessons companies will learn as they embrace SOAs.

[Greenemeier and Babcock, 2006]

Language; see Chapter 3) standard of communicating.[1] In practice, Web services might be the means by which SOA services communicate with one another, but that would not have to be the case—other connecting technologies could be used. However, most commentators today use the terms *SOA* and *Web services* almost interchangeably.

SOA is slow in coming, although there are numerous vendors pushing their SOA-oriented products, including IBM, BEA Systems, and TIBCO Software. Based on a 2006 survey by IDC, only 23 percent of companies have an SOA project "in production," with another 18 percent having one "in pilot stage." In the same survey, 37 percent plan to invest in SOA in the next one to two years, while 22 percent either "don't know" if they will invest or have "no plans" to invest (Maguire, 2007).

Among firms that have invested in SOA are Automatic Data Processing (ADP), The Hartford, and Pep Boys. As ADP expanded from a payroll company to a full-services human resources (HR) company, it wanted better integration and more reuse of code. For example, all of its HR services require people to enter data for new employees, so ADP wanted to use the same code in each application—which resulted in an SOA approach. According to Bob Bongiorno, ADP's Senior Vice President and Chief Information Officer for Employer Services, SOA let ADP deliver an HR product for a new market segment in about one-third of the time it normally would have taken. The Hartford, a major financial services and insurance provider, began its SOA approach with an initiative to make it easier for insurance agents to use its Web-based system to get quotes—the agents could enter information one time and use it for several applications. Auto parts seller Pep Boys is using IBM's SOA strategy to help give its point-of-sale system a tune-up, including the rewriting of an inventory application linked to it. SOA's ability to let companies reuse application modules appealed to Pep Boys. After an application is reconfigured as a service—as Pep Boys' tax module was at the point of sale—it can be reused with other applications, such as customer service (Greenemeier and Babcock, 2006).

TRANSACTION PROCESSING SYSTEMS

Let us begin our survey of applications with the "grand-daddy" applications, the ones that started it all—**transaction processing systems**. These systems process the thousands of transactions that occur every day in most organizations, including sales; payments made and received; inventory shipped and received; hiring, firing, and paying employees; and paying dividends. In addition to producing the documents and updated records that result from the transaction processing (such as invoices, checks, and orders), these systems produce a variety of summarized reports that are useful to upper-level management.

Transaction processing systems are life-or-death systems for "paperwork" organizations, such as banks and insurance companies, and critical systems for the overwhelming majority of medium and large organizations. These systems were the first computerized systems, and they still use the majority of large-machine computing time in most organizations. For the most part, these transaction processing systems can be justified by traditional cost-benefit analysis. These systems are able to process transactions more rapidly and more economically (and certainly more accurately) than a manual (human) system. Transaction processing systems might be mainframe-based or midrange-based, or they might be two-tier or three-tier client/server systems, or they might involve the use of service-oriented architectures (SOAs). Most of the latest systems being implemented are client/server systems or employ SOAs, but there are many mainframe- or midrange-based transaction processing systems still in use.

---

[1]In the Web services approach, XML is used to tag the data. Other protocols used in Web services include Web Services Description Language (WSDL) to describe the services available, Universal Description, Discovery, and Integration (UDDI) to list the services available, and SOAP (originally Simple Object Access Protocol, but now just the initials) to transfer the data.

As a manager, you do not need to know the details of these systems. You only need to have an understanding of a transaction processing system's general nature, importance, and complexity. Therefore, we will limit our discussion to two representative transaction processing systems for single business functions—payroll and a sales order entry system.

Payroll System

At first glance, a payroll system seems fairly simple. Operators input the number of hours worked for each employee (usually employing online data entry), and the system batch processes these transactions to produce payroll checks. While this one-sentence description is correct, it represents only the tip of the iceberg, because it involves only about 10 percent of the system. The payroll processing subsystem also must keep year-to-date totals of gross income, social security income, individual deductions, various categories of taxes, and net income. It also must incorporate the ability to compute federal, state, and local taxes, as well as social security contributions, and it must handle both mandatory and voluntary deductions.

What other subsystems are necessary? Figure 6.4 lists the primary subsystems in most payroll systems and the tasks the subsystems must accomplish. Thus, the payroll system is both commonplace and complex. The payroll system is usually easy to justify on a cost-benefit basis because it would take an incredible number of payroll clerks to complete a modern payroll and maintain all the associated records.

Subsystems to accomplish:

Payroll processing, including updating year-to-date master file

Capture hours-worked data

Add/delete employees

Change deduction information for employees

Change wage rates and salaries

Creation of initial year-to-date master file

Calculate and print payroll totals for pay period, quarter, and year

Calculate and print tax reports for pay period, quarter, and year

Calculate and print deduction reports for pay period, quarter, and year

Calculate and print W-2 forms at end of year

Interface with human resources information system

Interface with budget information system

Figure 6.4   Components of a Payroll System

Order Entry System

We will illustrate a mainframe- or midrange-based order entry system, but an order entry system could certainly employ client/server technology. The basic idea behind an online order entry system is simple. As orders are received (whether in person, by mail, or by telephone), the sales representative enters the information into the system. The data entry might be via a microcomputer on the sales representative's desk or possibly through a point-of-sale transaction recording system (a sophisticated cash register that doubles as a terminal). The computer then updates the appropriate files and prints an invoice, either at the point-of-sale terminal, the sales representative's desk, or in the computer center.

Once again, this basic explanation tells only a small part of the story. Figure 6.5 provides a more complete description and shows how each transaction (sale) interacts with as many as six files on the computer system. In addition to the invoice, more than a dozen types of computer output might be generated. For example, the computer can check the credit status of the customer and reject the sale if the customer's credit limit will be exceeded. If the item ordered is in stock, a multipart shipping document is printed; if the item is not in stock, a message is sent (via the PC) to the customer to ask if he or she wants to back order the item. Periodically or on demand, the order entry system will print out sales reports organized by item or by customer, customer statements, inventory reports, back order status reports, and accounts receivable reports. The system will also generate reports when exception conditions occur, such as when an item is out of stock or when a customer attempts to exceed the established credit limit. In these cases management action might be necessary. The order entry system can automatically print out purchase orders when an item is out of stock; it can also print out past-due billing notices for customers. A primary advantage of such an online system is that inquiries can be answered in a few seconds.

An important order entry system variant is an interorganizational system in which the orders are placed directly by the customer or the customer's computer (more on e-business applications in Chapter 8). An early, pre-Internet example was the American Hospital Supply Corporation's ASAP system in which order entry terminals, linked to AHSC's computer, were placed on the customers' (hospitals') premises, and hospital personnel placed orders themselves by keying them in. This made placing orders much more convenient for the customers and at the same time greatly reduced the delays and costs associated with printing and mailing order forms. More recently, orders have been placed by the customer's computer to the seller's computer

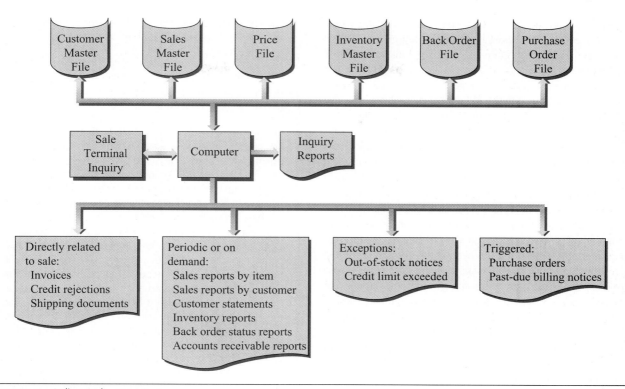

Figure 6.5 Online Order Entry System

using electronic data interchange (EDI)—which will be discussed in Chapter 8. By the late 1990s, the World Wide Web had taken the order entry process one step further by making it easy for both consumers and businesses to do their own order entry via a Web browser and an Internet connection. For example, many businesses use the Web to order networking equipment from Cisco Systems, and both businesses and consumers use the Web to order PCs from Dell Inc. In fact, several of the authors of this book have used the Web to order PCs from Dell.

ENTERPRISE RESOURCE PLANNING SYSTEMS

Enterprise resource planning (ERP) systems are also transaction processing systems, but they go well beyond traditional transaction processing system functionality— and thus deserve treatment as a separate application area. An ERP system is a set of integrated business applications, or modules, that carry out common business functions such as general ledger accounting, accounts payable, accounts receivable, material requirements planning, order

management, inventory control, and human resources management. Usually these modules are purchased from a software vendor. In some cases a company might buy only a subset of these modules from a particular vendor, mixing them with modules from other vendors and with the company's existing applications.

An ERP system differs from earlier approaches to developing or purchasing business applications in at least two ways. First, the ERP modules are integrated, primarily through a common set of definitions and a common database. As a transaction is processed in one area, such as the receipt of an order, the impact of this transaction is immediately reflected in all other related areas, such as accounting, production scheduling, and purchasing. Second, the ERP modules have been designed to reflect a particular way of doing business—a particular set of business processes. Unlike a functional IS approach, ERP systems are based on a value-chain view of the business in which functional departments coordinate their work. To implement an ERP system, then, a company is committing to changing its business processes. If a company is purchasing an ERP system, the company might need to change its processes to conform to those embedded in the software package. The company adapts to the ERP software package, not vice versa.

Why has ERP become such a hot topic in the late 1990s and early 2000s, with most large and medium-sized firms either installing ERP systems or seriously thinking about it? The benefits from ERP will be specific to a given firm, but some common benefits have emerged. In many cases the companies are not happy with the old way of doing business—by separate functional departments—and they do not have the *integration* of applications (and therefore the data) to support their decision-making and planning needs. The current applications often do not "talk" to each other, making it a time-consuming and difficult job to gather data, present a coherent picture of what is happening in the firm, and make informed decisions and plans. This situation is not new, but, until recently, packaged solutions were not available to companies. The cost to develop a set of integrated applications internally is prohibitive; even if the company had the IS resources to perform the task, it would take years. From previous reengineering efforts, many companies know that their internal business processes need to be changed, and they believe that the best and easiest way to fix them is by adopting the processes built into an ERP system that can be purchased. Thus, implementing an ERP system is a way to force business process reengineering.

In the late 1990s, the **Year 2000 (Y2K)** problem also added to the demand for ERP systems. At that time it became clear to many companies that their key application programs would cease to function correctly when dates past December 31, 1999, were used. When these programs were coded—often using COBOL—the programmers allowed only two digits to represent the year. They did not imagine that their programs, written in the 1970s and 1980s, would still be used when the millennium arrived. For companies with this problem, the effort and cost to change every reference from a two-digit year to a four-digit year in their programs would be substantial. Adopting an ERP system that correctly provided for dates beyond the year 2000 was a good, albeit expensive, solution to the problem. Rarely was the year 2000 problem the sole reason to implement an ERP system, but if the company was not happy with its existing, nonintegrated set of applications, then the year 2000 problem might well have tipped the balance.

It should be emphasized that implementation of an ERP system is extremely difficult because the company must change the way it does business. Further, ERP systems are very expensive. A typical large-scale ERP implementation costs tens of millions of dollars and takes a year or more. These implementation costs include not only the software licenses but also hardware and network investments and often consulting costs.

Further, choosing the right ERP software is a difficult task. The two giants in the ERP marketplace are SAP and

WHY PURCHASE AN ERP PACKAGE?

In a recent research study, three researchers—including one of the authors of this book—identified seven benefits gained by purchasing an ERP package. Three of these factors were overall business benefits, two were IT-related benefits, one benefit included both business and IT benefits, and the final factor was the avoidance of year 2000 maintenance costs. The three overall business benefits were data integration (improving access to data across business units, functions, processes, and the enterprise), new ways of doing business (implementing redesigned business processes, moving to a process orientation, and reducing costs of doing business), and global capabilities (supporting globalization with common processes and country-specific capabilities). The flexibility/agility benefit provided both business benefits (supporting competitive agility and business growth) and client/server architecture benefits. The two IT-related benefits were IT purchasing benefits (achieving time, cost, and reliability advantages from purchasing as opposed to building the system) and IT architecture cost reduction (reducing costs associated with systems operations and maintenance).

In considering the relative importance of these seven benefits, the authors distinguished between the purchase of an ERP by a company for its *value-chain* activities of materials management, production and operations, and sales and distribution, and the purchase of an ERP for *support* activities such as financial accounting and human resources. Data integration was the most highly sought-after benefit for both value-chain and support purchasers, and it was significantly more influential for value-chain purchasers than for support purchasers. Global capabilities were rated significantly higher by value-chain purchasers than support purchasers. Both IT purchasing benefits and year 2000 compliance were rated higher by support purchasers.

[Adapted from Brown, Vessey, and Powell, 2001]

Oracle. SAP (based in Germany) has been the leading ERP vendor since the beginning, and Oracle has grown in part by acquiring ERP vendor PeopleSoft in a hostile takeover in 2005 (PeopleSoft had, in turn, acquired ERP vendor J.D. Edwards in 2003). Other ERP vendors include The Sage Group (United Kingdom), Microsoft with its Dynamics applications, and Infor with its SSA ERP offering. For ERP purchases, there are strong arguments for picking a single vendor, such as the tight integration of applications that is possible and the standardization of common processes. On the other hand, choosing a single vendor could also reduce flexibility for the adopting company.

ENTERPRISE SYSTEMS SHOW RESULTS, BUT NOT ALWAYS RIGHT AWAY

The infamous reputation of enterprise systems (ERP, CRM) is lots of money for little value. Yet more than three-quarters of companies implementing enterprise systems say they've achieved at least half of the value they initially expected from the technology, according to a study by Accenture. The companies that extracted value had two things going for them: time and follow-through. Within a year of implementation, most companies failed to realize many hoped-for benefits, such as reduced headcount and more accurate business planning. But after two years, the majority saw payback of every type of benefit except increased revenue.

[Ware, November 1, 2003]

A "best of breed" or mix-and-match approach with multiple vendors might enable the company to meet more of its unique needs and reduce reliance on a single vendor; conversely, such an approach typically makes implementation more time-consuming and complicates system maintenance. With either approach, it is usually essential to employ the vendor or another consulting firm, or both, to assist in the implementation process. For large, multidivisional firms, implementing an ERP system is a very complex, challenging task that needs the best minds and careful attention of internal IS specialists, internal business managers, and external consultants. Most ERP implementations show positive results, but not always right away (see the box entitled "Enterprise Systems Show Results, But Not Always Right Away"). The potential payoff of an ERP system, in terms of better information for strategic and operational decision making and planning, and greater efficiency, profitability, and growth, makes the efforts and the costs worthwhile.

An Example ERP System: SAP ERP

The most popular of the ERP systems is SAP ERP, developed by SAP AG, headquartered in Walldorf, Germany. On the strength of SAP's R/3 system and its newer variants (the current version is SAP ERP 6.0), SAP is one of the top software firms in the world. According to an SAP brochure, 30,000 organizations worldwide run SAP software solutions. These organizations use SAP software at more than 100,000 locations in over 120 countries.

SAP R/2 was a mainframe-based ERP; R/3 is a client/ server system employing a common, integrated database with shared application modules. SAP developed R/3 using its own fourth generation language (4 GL), named ABAP, and customers may use this language, if they wish, to modify or enhance the standard R/3 modules. Today, however, if companies are interested in developing new SAP-related applications or extending SAP modules, the best option is to use SAP's NetWeaver platform, especially SAP NetWeaver Developer Studio, to carry out the development work. SAP NetWeaver Developer Studio offers a convenient user interface and rich functionality for developing Java 2 Enterprise Edition (J2EE; see Chapter 3) applications.

In 1999, SAP launched mySAP, which was both an umbrella concept for SAP's strategy of allowing its users to work through the World Wide Web *and* a brand name for the new Web-enabled versions of its R/3 software. In 2007, SAP dropped the mySAP label, calling the newest version of its ERP package simply SAP ERP 6.0. The all-encompassing SAP Business Suite includes a wide variety of enterprise software modules, including the robust ERP module (see Figures 6.6 and 6.7).

The family of SAP ERP software products fits the general description of an ERP system given previously. It is a tightly integrated system consisting of several modules. A company may choose to implement some or all of these modules. Most important, implementation of SAP ERP requires that the company change its business processes to conform to the processes built into the software.

Let us take a closer look at SAP ERP and the SAP Business Suite. SAP ERP consists of four primary sets of modules—SAP calls each set a "solution"—financials, human capital management, operations, and corporate services. In addition, modules are available for end-user service delivery and performance management (or analytics, to use SAP's term). End-user service delivery includes both employee self-service and manager self-service. The employee self-service area is an interesting one—it gives employees more active participation in the organization's human resources programs by permitting them to review and update their own address data, submit travel expenses or leave applications, view and print summary pay information, and check their own benefits selections and vacation balances. Manager self-service provides support for managers in the budgeting area (including budget planning, budget monitoring, and cost analysis) and in the staffing area (including recruitment, employee reviews, and compensation planning). As examples of the various analytics available, strategic enterprise management includes products for balanced scorecard, value-based management, risk management, and financial statement planning, while financial analytics includes products for financial and management reporting, payment behavior analytics, and working capital and cash flow management.

Financials
- Financial Supply Chain Management
- Financial Accounting
- Management Accounting
- Corporate Governance

Human Capital Management
- Talent Management
- Workforce Process Management
- Workforce Deployment

Operations
- Procurement
- Inventory and Warehouse Management
- Inbound and Outbound Logistics
- Transportation Management
- Production Planning
- Manufacturing Execution
- Product Development
- Life-Cycle Data Management
- Sales Order Management
- Aftermarket Sales and Service
- Professional-Service Delivery

Corporate Services
- Real Estate Management
- Enterprise Asset Management
- Project and Portfolio Management
- Travel Management
- Environment, Health and Safety Compliance Management
- Quality Management
- Global Trade Services

End-User Service Delivery
- Manager Self-Service
- Employee Self-Service
- Employee Interaction Support Center

Analytics
- Financial Analytics
- Workforce Analytics
- Operations Analytics
- Strategic Enterprise Management

Figure 6.6 Key Functional Areas of SAP ERP

Customer Relationship Management (CRM)
- Marketing
- Sales
- Service
- Partner Channel Management
- Interaction Center
- Web Channel

Enterprise Resource Planning (ERP)
See Figure 6.6

Product Lifecycle Management (PLM)
- Life-Cycle Data Management
- Program and Project Management
- Life-Cycle Collaboration
- Quality Management
- Enterprise Asset Management
- Environmental, Health, and Safety

Supply Chain Management (SCM)
- Supply Chain Planning and Collaboration
- Supply Chain Execution
- Supply Chain Visibility Design and Analytics

Supplier Relationship Management (SRM)
- Sourcing
- Procurement
- Supplier Enablement

Figure 6.7 SAP Business Suite Applications (in bold), with a Sample of Key Capabilities for Each Application

All the various modules run on the SAP NetWeaver platform, which is SAP's integration and application platform to ensure seamless interaction with virtually any other SAP or non-SAP software. Figure 6.6 lists the key functional areas of SAP ERP. Note that SAP ERP is a relatively comprehensive package, with strength in the operations area as has historically been the case for SAP.

In addition to the modules in SAP ERP, other available applications in the SAP Business Suite include customer relationship management (CRM), product lifecycle management (PLM), supply chain management (SCM), and supplier relationship management (SRM) (see Figure 6.7 for a sample of the key capabilities for each application). The names and sample capabilities of the applications should provide a reasonable understanding of what most of the applications do, but let us mention a few of the particularly interesting capabilities. Within the CRM application, the Web channel capability permits your business to carry out business-to-business (B2B) or business-to-consumer (B2C) sales on the Web; it also provides support for Web catalog management, content management, customer segmentation, and personalization, as well as a Web store locator. Within the PLM application, the enterprise asset management capability supports the selection, purchase, and installation of equipment, tracks the costs of individual assets and aggregates these costs as desired, and assists in determining the optimal time to replace equipment. Within the SRM application, the supplier enablement capability permits the electronic exchange of documents in any format with suppliers and provides the tools to create and manage a supplier portal (more on portals later in this chapter).

All of the previously mentioned SAP applications are generic software packages that would work in many businesses. In addition, the early years of the twenty-first century have seen the development of *industry solutions* by SAP and other ERP vendors that are tailored to the special needs of particular industries. SAP, for example, currently offers 26 specific industry solutions, including automotive, banking, chemicals, health care, insurance, pharmaceuticals, retail, and wholesale distribution. The trend is for more specialization of ERP packages, with variations for smaller businesses being introduced and more industry solutions under development.

Companies choose to implement the SAP modules or applications that make sense for them. MassMutual Financial Group has implemented several modules of mySAP, including employee self-service, payroll, and benefits administration from the human resources area; general ledger, budget, treasury, fixed assets, and travel and expenses from the financials area; and business-to-business procurement (buying) (SAP, 2000). More recently, Harry & David Operations Corporation, the premium gourmet food retailer, has selected the SAP for Retail solution, including the SAP Merchandise and Assortment Planning and SAP Forecasting and Replenishment applications, to drive business benefits in inventory management and retail and channel sales. These applications will support Harry & David's ability to offer more targeted merchandise selections in its retail stores. Harry & David will begin its implementation with food and beverage capabilities, followed by SAP ERP Financials. "We are poised for tremendous growth, both as a direct retailer and as a wholesaler to numerous retail outlets," said Joe Foley, Chief Information Officer of Harry & David Holding, Inc. "The seasonality of our business demands a platform that can rapidly scale and meet our ever-changing needs. Only SAP's fully integrated business model can provide us with a single operating platform that will take costs out of our infrastructure and give us a solid basis for growth" (SAP, 2007).

In other examples, Hyundai Motor Company has deployed mySAP modules, including the SAP automotive industry solution, to consolidate and automate its supply chain, financial, human resources, and procurement processes in its first North American assembly plant, recently constructed in Montgomery, Alabama (Bacheldor, February 3, 2003). As part of an outsourcing agreement with EDS, Dial Corporation has scrapped enterprise software packages from Oracle, Siebel Systems, and Manugistics and moved to a single suite from SAP. The SAP implementation included manufacturing, supply chain, finance, accounting,

performance management, and customer relationship management software and cost about $35 million, including licenses, implementation services, and maintenance. According to Dial Chief Information Officer Evon Jones, Dial went with SAP because "SAP and the processes with SAP's software are regarded as best in class and will drive operational efficiencies, particularly when you start to get greater visibility within your supply chain" (Bacheldor, July 25, 2003).

For more detailed descriptions of SAP implementations at several firms, see the section entitled "What is the Experience with ERP?" in Vollmann, Berry, Whybark, and Jacobs (2005, pp. 123–130). Also see the box entitled "Toyota Motorsport Accelerates Formula One Operations with SAP." Today, ERP software systems are still a hot commodity.

TOYOTA MOTORSPORT ACCELERATES FORMULA ONE OPERATIONS WITH SAP

SAP announced that Toyota Motorsport GmbH, Toyota's German-based motorsport subsidiary, is implementing software from SAP's automotive industry solution to streamline ERP processes across its Formula One racing operations. Toyota Motorsport is replacing its existing, nonintegrated systems with SAP for Automotive, including mySAP Product Lifecycle Management, mySAP Supply Chain Management, mySAP Human Resources, and mySAP Financials.

Having won seven world championship titles with its World Rally Championship program, Toyota decided to enter Formula One racing in 1999. The entire car, including the engine and chassis, is completely designed and constructed at Toyota Motorsport's headquarters in Cologne, Germany. In order to operate a Formula One racing program, 20,000 to 30,000 made-to-order parts are required, and these parts must be quickly available. Further, the parts must be analyzed on an ongoing basis. Toyota Motorsport felt that SAP software was the best choice to efficiently manage the enormous amount of data required for the racing program's success, as well as to control its supply chain, production, and financial processes cost effectively.

"Applying knowledge effectively translates into competitive edge," said Thomas Schiller, IT General Manager for Toyota Motorsport. "After comprehensive evaluation of several vendors, we found that SAP could best enable the solid data foundation that is critical to our business. SAP gives us a strategic advantage, ensuring high availability of reliable information across our operations to make faster and more informed decisions. With its integrated solutions and powerful scope of functionality, SAP enables us to effectively execute these decisions and accelerate our production and supply chain processes."

[Adapted from SAP, 2003]

DATA WAREHOUSING

In order to create a data warehouse, a firm pulls data from its operational systems—the transaction processing systems we have just discussed—and puts the data in a separate "data warehouse" so that users may access and analyze the data without endangering the operational systems. Thus, **data warehousing** is the establishment and maintenance of a large data storage facility containing data on all (or at least many) aspects of the enterprise. If the data warehouse is to be useful, the data must be accurate, current, and stored in a useable form; in addition, easy-to-use data access and analysis tools for managers and other users must be provided to encourage full use of the data.

Establishing a data warehouse is time-consuming and expensive. Three types of software tools are needed: warehouse construction software, warehouse operation software, and warehouse access and analysis software. Warehouse construction software is required to extract relevant data from the operational databases, make sure the data are clean (free from error), transform the data into a useable form, and load the data into the data warehouse (see Figure 6.8). Software tools to construct the warehouse include products such as Advantage Data Transformer (from Computer Associates), IBM WebSphere DataStage, Informatica PowerCenter, Oracle Warehouse Builder, and SAS/Warehouse Administrator. Operation software is required to store the data and manage the data warehouse. Data warehouse storage is typically accomplished by database management systems such as IBM DB2, Microsoft SQL Server, Oracle, Sybase ASE, and Teradata Warehouse; specialized warehouse management software is offered by Computer Associates, IBM, Oracle, SAS Institute, and others.

The widest variety of software tools is available in the warehouse access and analysis area. Information catalog tools, such as Computer Associates' AllFusion Repository, tell the user what is in the warehouse. Analysis and reporting tools enable a user to produce customized reports from the data warehouse, perhaps on a regular basis. Among these tools are Computer Associates' AllFusion ERwin Data Modeler, Information Builders' WebFOCUS, MicroStrategy 8, Oracle OLAP, and SAS Institute's Enterprise Miner. Visualizing the data might be important, using tools such as Computer Associates' CleverPath Forest & Trees and SAS Institute's SAS/INSIGHT. Some software packages, such as IBM's DB2 Data Warehouse Edition, include tools to accomplish warehouse construction, operation, and access and analysis. We will defer further consideration of these analysis tools until the next chapter, when we consider decision support systems, data mining, executive information systems, and especially business intelligence systems in more detail. In our judgment, creation and maintenance of the data warehouse is an enterprise system, while these end-user reporting and analysis tools are designed for management support—the topic of Chapter 7.

Data warehousing is being used successfully by organizations of all shapes and sizes. Let us consider some examples. The U.S. Postal Service has assembled a gigantic 32-terabyte data warehouse, and is using the system to analyze many areas of its business, including sales at individual post offices, the efficiency of mail-processing facilities, and the use of manpower and transportation resources. The data warehouse is based on hardware and software from Teradata. The warehouse collects retail data from 37,000 post offices, data from mail-processing facilities, package-tracking data, air-transportation data, and data from the Postal Service's ERP and CRM applications. At present, the data warehouse generates about 20,000 reports for 1,800 users every day, using software from Microstrategy; the number of reports is expected to grow to 60,000 reports for more than 5,000 users, according to Wayne Grimes, Customer-Care Operations Manager for the Postal Service. The data warehouse provides the Postal Service with a much clearer picture of its finances and operations. In the past, it took three to four months to close the books at the end of the fiscal year, but last year—using the data warehouse—it took less than five weeks (Whiting, 2005).

Wal-Mart operates a massive data warehouse containing—as of January 2006—583 terabytes of sales and inventory data. The data warehouse is built on a massively parallel 1,000-processor system from Teradata. "Our database grows because we capture data on every item, for every customer, for every store, every day," say Dan Phillips,

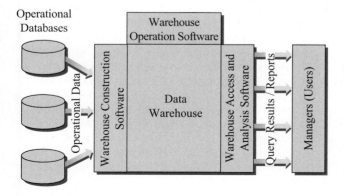

Figure 6.8 Key Elements of Data Warehousing

Wal-Mart's Vice President of Information Systems. Phillips goes on to indicate that Wal-Mart deletes data after two years and does not track individual customer purchases. Wal-Mart refreshes the information in its data warehouse every hour, and thus has turned its data warehouse into an operational system for managing daily store operations. Managers can check the database hourly and see what is happening at an individual store or stores throughout a region. As an example of the use of the data warehouse, Phillips relates an interesting story: On the morning after Thanksgiving a few years ago, the IT staff at Wal-Mart's headquarters checked the data warehouse and noticed that East Coast sales of a computer-monitor holiday special were far below expectations. When the marketing staff contacted several stores, they learned that the computers and monitors were not being displayed together, so customers could not see what they were getting for the posted price. Calls went out to Wal-Mart stores across the country to rearrange the displays, and by 9:30 A.M. CST the data warehouse showed that the pace of sales was picking up. Through its data warehouse, Wal-Mart is leveraging massive amounts of data for competitive advantage (Babcock, 2006).

Continental Airlines, Inc., won the 2003 Data Warehouse Institute Award for the best enterprise data warehouse. The original objective of the warehouse was to accurately forecast passenger bookings, but it is now used for a much wider variety of applications, including revenue management, customer relationship management, fraud detection, and management of crew payrolls. Continental's data warehouse, which is based on hardware and software from NCR's Teradata division, incorporates data from 41 sources, including flight schedules, seat inventory, revenue and ticketing data, profiles of OnePass frequent flyers, employee records, and crew payrolls. Thirteen hundred employees in 35 departments have access to the data, with most using Brio Software's query and reporting software. According to Continental, the data warehouse has been a big success, with millions of dollars in savings as well as revenue increases of several million dollars.

As user demands on the warehouse increased over time, Continental's data warehousing team reworked the data warehouse to operate on a near-real-time basis. The mainframe and COBOL tools that originally handled the transformation and loading of the data have been replaced by custom-built C++ software running on a network of Windows-based servers. Now users analyze flight operations and reservations data that is only seconds old. The data warehouse's near-real-time architecture and automated data transformation capabilities are two of the best practices that earned Continental the best enterprise data warehouse award (Whiting, 2003). Data warehousing has the potential to let companies understand and utilize the data that they are already collecting as they run their businesses.

HARRAH'S EARNS "TOTAL REWARDS" THROUGH DATA WAREHOUSING AND CUSTOMER RELATIONSHIP MANAGEMENT

Harrah's Entertainment, with 36 casinos in 13 states (plus 2 other casinos in Canada and Uruguay), has created an enterprise data warehouse to track and analyze customer spending in all its casinos through its Total Rewards system. All casino guest transactions are captured, including those at slot machines and gaming tables, through the use of a magnetic membership card. To encourage use of the card, members receive regular points and bonus points each time it is used. After a certain number of regular points have been earned, the cardholder qualifies for a Gold, Platinum, or Diamond membership, which offers privileges such as club memberships and expedited check-ins. The bonus points can be turned in for free food, drinks, and other perks at the casinos. The Total Rewards loyalty program has been a big success, with 6 million members who have used the card in the past year and 26 million members overall.

Total Rewards has been designed to appeal to both big-time spenders and small but steady gamblers, and it seems to be working. The program offers members powerful incentives to consolidate their gambling at Harrah's properties. Overall, Harrah's estimates that its customers spent about 43 percent of their annual gambling budgets at Harrah's properties in 2002, up from 36 percent when the program began in 1997.

Through the program, Harrah's can track who plays what games, where, when, and how often. From the information gathered, Harrah's can offer special deals aimed at generating repeat business, such as free hotel rooms to its big spenders and lesser rewards, such as free movie passes, to small but steady gamblers. The result is that Harrah's hotel occupancy rate exceeds 90 percent versus an industry average of 60 percent. David Norton, Senior Vice President of Relationship Marketing for Harrah's, attributes the high occupancy rate directly to the Total Rewards program.

Harrah's has implemented its data warehouse on an NCR massively parallel processor server, using Teradata database and warehousing software. The system employs SAS software for modeling and Cognos business intelligence software for queries and reports. This unique data warehouse/customer relationship management system is working: Harrah's executives believe that the Total Rewards program is the cornerstone of Harrah's growth strategy.

[Adapted from Young and Stepanek, 2003]

CUSTOMER RELATIONSHIP MANAGEMENT SYSTEMS

A type of application that often pulls much of its data from the organization's data warehouse is **customer relationship management (CRM)**. A CRM system attempts to provide an integrated approach to all aspects of interaction a company has with its customers, including marketing, sales, and support. The goal of a CRM system is to use technology to forge a strong relationship between a business and its customers. To look at CRM in another way, the business is seeking to better manage its own enterprise around customer behaviors.

A variety of software packages have been created to manage customer relationships, most based on capturing, updating, and utilizing extensive profiles of individual customers. These profiles are often stored in a data warehouse, and data mining (discussed in Chapter 7) is used to extract relevant information about the firm's customers. Furthermore, customer profiles are made available online to all those in the company who might interact with a customer. In addition, Web-based front-ends have been created so that a customer can interact with the company online to obtain information about products and services offered by the company, to place an order, to check on the status of an existing order, to seek answers from a knowledge base, or to request service. CRM software packages enable organizations to market to, sell to, and service customers across multiple channels, including the Web, call centers, field representatives, business partners, and retail and dealer networks.

There are many players in the CRM marketplace, so let's attempt to differentiate them in various ways. For the first cut, we will look at the leading firms that market to larger firms versus those that market to small and medium businesses. ISM, Inc., a strategic advisor to organizations planning and implementing CRM initiatives, names the top 15 CRM enterprise (larger firms) winners and the top 15 CRM small and medium business (SMB) winners each year—in other words, the top 15 vendors to larger firms and the top 15 vendors to small and medium businesses. Both rankings are based on ISM's surveys and testing, and both lists are presented alphabetically (ISM, 2007).

Most of the top 15 CRM enterprise vendors offer a traditional out-of-the-box CRM application, including call-center support, sales-force automation, and marketing support, as well as a traditional CRM with templates for specific vertical industries, such as health care, manufacturing, distribution, and financial services. Two of the firms in this category are major software vendors SAP (with SAP CRM) and Oracle (with PeopleSoft CRM and Siebel, which is now part of Oracle after its purchase in 2006). Smaller vendors in this category include Clear C2 (C2 CRM), Infor (Infor CRM), Onyx Software (Onyx), and Saratoga Systems (Saratoga CRM). A few vendors have chosen to focus on a particular industry—for example, Amdocs Ltd. (Amdocs CRM) focuses on telecommunications carriers and Internet service providers. Among the top 15 CRM enterprise vendors, one offers only a **hosted** or **on-demand solution** (also called **Software as a Service**, or **SaaS**)—Salesforce.com. With a hosted solution, the software runs on the vendor's hardware, and the customer pays a subscription fee on a per user, per month basis to use the application. Other top 15 enterprise vendors, notably SAP and Oracle, also offer a hosted CRM application, but Salesforce.com is clearly the leader in this market subsegment with over 50 percent of the on-demand market.

Turning to the top 15 CRM SMB vendors, we find a few repeats, including Salesforce.com. Microsoft enters this list with its Microsoft Dynamics CRM 3.0 product, which is also available as a hosted application. Other hosted applications on the SMB list include NetSuite's CRM+, Sage Software's CRM.com (Sage Software is based in the United Kingdom), RightNow CRM, and Siebel CRM OnDemand. A few of these top 15 SMB vendors offer a Lotus Notes–based product (more on Lotus Notes later in this chapter), including Ardexus Mode (Canada) and Relavis CRM. Other products in this top 15 SMB list include FrontRange Solutions' Goldmine, Sage Software's SalesLogix, and StayinFront CRM.

We have already described one example of a CRM project using a data warehouse in the box discussing Harrah's Entertainment. Other examples abound: Online brokerage Quick & Reilly, Inc., is using Siebel's sales-force automation tools to offer its customers investment options based on what it already knows about them. Quick & Reilly began investing $10 million in call-center and sales-force automation software in 1998. Within six months of initial implementation, the CRM system boosted the rate at which brokers convert sales prospects into customers by up to 20 percent. "That's a real return on investment," said Edward M. Garry, Quick & Reilly's Vice President for Customer Relationship Management (Kerstetter, Hamm, and Greene, 2002).

Pharmaceutical manufacturer Eli Lilly & Company has implemented sales-force automation, call-center, and other CRM applications from Siebel to support its efforts in branding its drugs (Lilly manufactures antidepressant Prozac as well as many other drugs). "Branding is more important to drug companies nowadays," said Roy Dunbar, Chief Information Officer at Lilly. "Patients used to call their doctors; now, a patient on one of our drugs can pick

CRM: DESPERATELY SEEKING SUCCESS

Not all CRM projects are successes, but that does not seem to be deterring corporate investment in CRM applications. An AMR Research study shows that only 16 percent of CRM initiatives have returned value to the company. The remaining projects include some that have failed but more that are unclear whether they have succeeded or failed because the companies have not defined successes or goals for their CRM projects. "Companies must define their CRM strategy up front, and that strategy will define what success looks like and which metrics are important," according to Kevin Scott, a senior research analyst with AMR Research.

Despite these mixed results, 35 percent of executives surveyed in a recent *CIO Magazine* Tech Poll indicated that their organizations will launch CRM projects in the next year. Similarly, a recent IDC forecast calls for a 6.7 percent annual growth rate for CRM expenditures, resulting in $12.1 billion in CRM software annual revenue in 2007.

Given this continued growth in CRM projects with only limited success thus far, what must companies do to give their CRM initiatives the best chance of succeeding? *CIO Magazine* suggests three best practices:

- Be prepared for organizational change—collaboration across the enterprise will be required.
- Keep it simple—make sure your application has an easy-to-use interface and that your vendor will work with you to provide user training.
- Align your vendor's definition of success with your own—make sure your vendor understands your company's definition of success.

[Adapted from Ware, August 1, 2003]

up the phone and call us." Based on its CRM systems, Lilly has initiated the Lilly Answer Center, which uses the Web and call-center technology to stay in close contact with customers (Greenemeier, 2003).

Another pharmaceutical research firm, Applied Biosystems Group, has opted for a hosted, Web-based approach for its CRM implementation, choosing several of Salesforce.com's software modules, including sales-force automation, marketing, and analytics. The global company had no central database or CRM in place until it recently went with Salesforce.com; instead, it relied on time-consuming spreadsheet tools as well as inconsistent local data entry by sales representatives around the globe, often in a foreign language. The Salesforce.com implementation permits the sales staff to store sales data in a central database that facilitates multiple languages. "[Multiple languages] make it easy for our partner network to enter and access data in their native languages, with only a few critical fields requiring English, while we benefit from the availability of local data which we leverage for local campaigning," said Anthony Watson, Applied Biosystems Senior IT Shared Commercial Systems Manager. The implementation began in 2005 and is already operating in the Asia-Pacific region and in the United States, with the entire global network scheduled to be operating by 2008. The initial two-year deal with Salesforce.com cost about $380,000 (Pauli, 2006).

In perhaps the largest implementation of CRM software ever, Hewlett-Packard is scrapping a number of different CRM applications across its business channels and installing the eBusiness Applications package from Siebel as a unified platform. The CRM project will consolidate Hewlett-Packard's direct and indirect sales channels,

including thousands of direct-sales representatives, marketing professionals, contact-center representatives, and partner resellers. Eventually, the project could involve over 50,000 users. "From a customer-experience perspective, it was absolutely imperative to move rapidly," said Mike Overly, Vice President of Customer Operations for HP Global Operations. Hewlett-Packard expects to gain a unified view of customers across all channels and drive operating efficiencies, saving the company tens of millions of dollars (Dunn, 2003). In recent years, many companies have publicly stated that they were becoming more customer-focused—and some companies are carrying through on such statements in a very significant way by installing a CRM system.

OFFICE AUTOMATION

Office automation refers to a set of office-related applications that might or might not be integrated into a single system. The most common applications are telephony, electronic mail (and its variants), word processing, voice mail, copying, desktop publishing, electronic calendaring, and document imaging, along with document preparation, storage, and sharing.

Office technology has taken major strides since World War II. Document preparation has evolved from manual typewriters, to electric typewriters with a moving carriage, to the IBM Selectric typewriters with the "golf ball" typing element, to memory typewriters, to expensive terminals connected to a minicomputer, to stand-alone microcomputers, and now to microcomputers linked via a LAN.

Copying has moved from mimeograph machines to fast photocopiers, and today's computer printers often double as photocopiers and facsimile machines. The telephone has moved from a simple wired instrument with no dial or keys to a dial telephone, and then from a simple touch-tone telephone to a versatile instrument (often wireless) with features such as call forwarding, call waiting, multiparty calling, and caller identification. Even today, however, these devices do not always talk to each other—but IT is changing that! With recent innovations—especially Internet telephony (see Chapter 4)—we are moving ever closer to an integrated voice/data/image network as shown in Figure 6.9. Please note that the connections shown in Figure 6.9 might turn out to be wireless rather than wired. In the discussion that follows, we will consider several components of this figure.

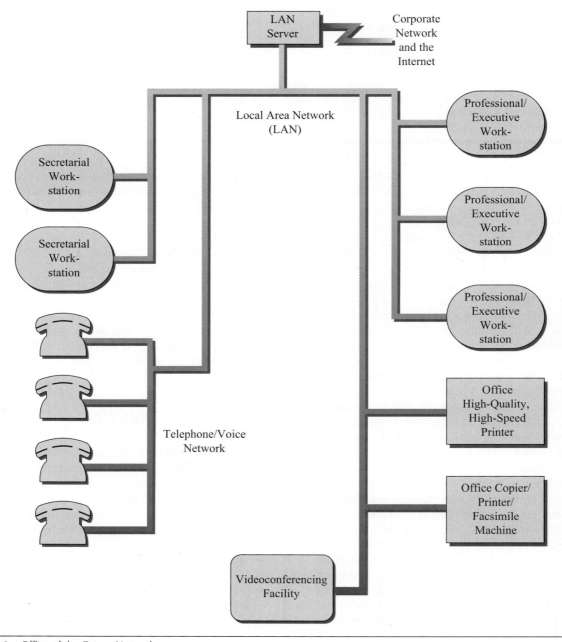

Figure 6.9   Office of the Future Network

Word Processing and Application Suites

A number of excellent word-processing packages have been developed for microcomputers, the most common workstations in today's offices. Microsoft Word is clearly the market leader, but other fine products exist—some of them free. As noted in Chapter 3, these software packages are typically sold as part of an application suite that includes spreadsheet, presentation, database, and possibly other applications. The advantage of a suite is that it is possible to copy and paste from one application to another in the same suite; for instance, a Microsoft Office user can copy a portion of an Excel spreadsheet to the clipboard and paste the portion directly into a Word document she is preparing. In a small office or high-print-volume situation, a high-quality printer can be connected directly to a PC. It is more common, however, for office PCs to be on a LAN so documents can be sent electronically from the preparing workstation to a high-quality, high-speed printer, as depicted in Figure 6.9.

Electronic Mail

Electronic mail (e-mail) systems permit rapid, asynchronous communication between workstations on a network, eliminating telephone tag. Most systems incorporate such features as sending a note to a distribution list, forwarding a note to someone else with an appended message, replying to a note without reentering the address, and filing notes in electronic file folders for later recall. All the authors of this book use electronic mail on a regular basis, and we feel we could not do without it.

Of course, there are potential drawbacks to e-mail communication. Because it is so easy to use, the volume of e-mail can become overwhelming, particularly standard messages sent to a distribution list. Spam—unsolicited e-mail that most of us regard as junk—is the bane of e-mail users. E-mail is also less personal because it is dependent on text signals alone (but some users spice it up a bit by using e-mail smileys such as :-) or :-( ). Some people use offensive words and phrases that they would never use in face-to-face conversation, called "flaming." Privacy issues arise because of the opportunity for electronic monitoring by supervisors. For most organizations and most users, however, these drawbacks are totally overshadowed by the advantages of rapid, asynchronous communication.

Variants of e-mail include electronic bulletin boards, listservs, computer conferencing, chat rooms, and, most recently, instant messaging (IM) and blogs. An electronic bulletin board is a repository (a disk on a computer) on which anyone with access to the bulletin board can post

messages and read other messages. Bulletin boards can be operated within an organization (employing the usual communication links), or over the Internet. A listserv is a computerized mailing list that accepts a message sent to the listserv address and forwards it to everyone on the particular mailing list.

Computer conferencing is similar to a bulletin board, but it is set up around a particular topic. For example, a professional society can set up a computer conference to consider changes in its annual meeting program. The announcement of the topic and the Web address at which the conference will be held are published in the society's newsletter, which can be distributed electronically via a listserv. Users participate in the conference by logging into the conference, entering an opinion, and reading other participants' opinions. Chat rooms are real-time versions of computer conferencing (synchronous communication) conducted on the Internet, with an incredibly wide array of topics. Group chat has emerged as an important real-time collaboration tool for businesses, providing communication support for far-flung project teams and reducing the need for in-person meetings, voice conferencing, and videoconferencing (Strom, 2006).

IM is a synchronous communication system that enables the user to establish a private chat room with another individual to carry out text-based communication in real time over the Internet. IM is a hit in business, with research firms estimating that 20 percent or more of employees use IM—and, of course, many workplace acronyms have popped up (see box entitled "Most Popular IM Workplace Acronyms"). A blog is a user-generated Web site where entries are made in journal style, typically displayed in reverse chronological order. Blogs can deal with any subject—sometimes they serve as personal online diaries, and sometimes they provide commentary on a particular subject such as the environment, politics, or local news.

The first popular e-mail systems were mainframe or minicomputer-based, which makes sense because e-mail predated client/server systems. They were also designed to run under proprietary operating systems (e.g., not UNIX). Examples are Digital Equipment's VaxMail and ALL-IN-ONE and IBM's OfficeVision and PROFS (Professional Office System). The more advanced mainframe-based systems, such as PROFS, packaged e-mail together with electronic calendaring and other related features. In this mainframe environment, the e-mail system runs on the mainframe, with the workstation being used as a terminal; there is no GUI interface. With PROFS, the main menu included a calendar with the current date highlighted, a clock, a message area where other users could directly communicate with this workstation, and a menu of other

MOST POPULAR IM WORKPLACE ACRONYMS

Omnipod, an enterprise IM software vendor (now part of MessageLabs Ltd.), conducted a survey of 2,000 of its end users to determine the most popular IM acronyms in the workplace. Note that acronyms that are used in everyday speech, such as FYI and ASAP, were not included in the survey. "It is interesting to see how IM slang evolves year after year," observed Gideon Stein, Chief Executive Officer of Omnipod. "People seem to be getting more comfortable in their general use of IM as a conversational medium with more and more slang entering their acronym use—LMAO and NCIH are prime examples."

Here are the 10 most commonly used acronyms while using IM in the workplace:

1.	NP	No Problem
2.	JK	Just Kidding
3.	LMAO	Laughing My Ass Off
4.	CB	Call Back
5.	TTYL	Talk To You Later
6.	WTG	Way To Go!
7.	NCIH	No Chance In Hell
8.	DHT$	Don't Have The Budget (or Dollars)
9.	WRUV4	Who Are You Voting For?
10.	RFL?	Ready For Lunch?

[Adapted from TechWeb News, 2004]

choices, such as process schedules (electronic calendaring), open the mail, search for documents, and prepare documents.

The second wave of e-mail systems was designed to run on UNIX servers (high-powered workstations running the UNIX operating system). Popular systems include Pine and Elm. This type of e-mail system runs on the server, with the PC being used as a terminal; again, there is no GUI interface. These systems do not have the functionality of mainframe systems like PROFS, but they are much more economical to operate on a per-user or per-message basis. It should come as no surprise that some colleges and universities still use these UNIX systems.

The development of POP-servers and POP-mail demonstrates how PC-based front-ends can be used to provide a friendlier interface for users. POP stands for post office protocol, and POP-mail is based on an analogy with post office boxes. To use POP-mail, a POP-client such as Eudora or Pegasus must be loaded on the PC. Various e-mail systems, including Pine, can be used as a POP-server. All incoming mail is kept on the POP-server until the user logs on and asks for mail to be downloaded to his or her own machine; this is analogous to traditional mail being kept in a post office box until the patron opens the box and empties it. The user processes the mail on his or her own machine, using the GUI provided by Eudora or Pegasus. The user can read mail, throw some of it away, store some in electronic file folders, and prepare responses to some of it. After processing the mail on the PC, the user reopens a connection to the POP-server on the host computer and uploads any outgoing messages.

The third wave of e-mail systems were LAN-based client/server software systems that incorporated well-designed GUI interfaces, complete with small inboxes, outboxes, wastebaskets, attractive fonts, color, and other GUI features. Example packages are cc:Mail by Lotus and Microsoft Mail. If an organization wants e-mail only, these packages are sufficient. LAN-based e-mail systems were very popular in the 1990s, but have largely been replaced in the 2000s by the more robust groupware systems such as Lotus Notes/Domino and Microsoft Outlook/Exchange. A variation of this third wave of client/server e-mail systems is Internet mail, which has become very popular for small business and home use. For Internet mail, the client software is the user's Web browser, and the server software is located on a high-powered Web server operated by an Internet service or software provider. The user must, of course, have access to the Internet via an Internet service provider (ISP) or an organizational link to the Internet. Examples of these Internet mail systems, which are usually free, are Microsoft Hotmail, Google Gmail, and Juno E-mail on the Web.

Most organizations, however, have moved beyond simple e-mail. They want the greater functionality of the older mainframe systems plus the GUI interface of the POP-mail and LAN-based systems. They want electronic calendaring and document sharing. The answer is groupware. We will discuss groupware as a separate category of applications later, after we have completed our discussion of the office of the future. Groupware is, in fact, a significant step toward the office of the future.

Future Developments

Today, the telephone/voice network in most companies is independent of the computer/data network. The situation is changing, however, as more and more businesses adopt Internet (VoIP) telephony. Gartner, an IT research and analysis firm, estimates that there were 14.7 million enterprise

VoIP telephony lines installed in North America by the end of 2006, or about 21 percent of the total enterprise base. Many of these VoIP lines use the old analog telephone wiring, but they could use the company's computer network (if it made economic sense to do so), and the two networks do both link to the Internet. The two networks are moving together! Newer workstations include a voice receiver and a voice speaker and can function as a telephone. Some users are already using their workstations to make telephone calls over the Internet, and their numbers are growing. As the technology matures, the workstation is likely to subsume the functions of today's telephones (and replace those telephones) for many workers.

Today, almost all offices have facsimile machines to receive electronically transmitted documents and produce a hard copy version. Faxes can also be sent and received via a PC. However, conventional copying machines are still stand-alone devices. In the future, the copying machine will be integrated into the office network and will absorb the function of the stand-alone facsimile device—and the function of the printer as well, although we suspect that in most offices there will continue to be a need for a high-speed, high-quality printer where the printing is not constantly interrupted for copying and faxes. Single or multiple copies of a document may be printed either at the copying machine, from a workstation in the same office, or from a remote site. The all-in-one or multifunction machines (printer, copier, scanner, and facsimile), such as the Hewlett-Packard CM8060 color multifunction business printer, are examples of these integrated devices.

Document storage is another evolving area of office automation. It is not unusual for today's organizations to store their business documents online, often using magnetic or optical disk technology (discussed in Chapter 2). More and more of these documents will be stored digitally in the future, particularly with the growing use of imaging technology. With imaging, any type of paper document—including reports, graphs, and photographs—can be read by a digital scanner and translated into digital form so that it can be stored in the computer system. Later this process can be reversed, so that the digitized image stored in the computer system can be printed on paper, displayed on a monitor, or transmitted to another workstation.

A facility possessed by a growing number of organizations—a videoconferencing facility—is shown at the bottom of Figure 6.9. Such facilities permit face-to-face, or, more properly, image-to-image meetings and conferences without the need for costly and time-consuming travel. By tying the videoconferencing facility into the integrated office network, computer-generated reports and graphics can also be shared during the conferences.

Desktop videoconferencing is becoming popular for one-on-one and small group conferences. The screen on a desktop PC is so small, however, that desktop videoconferencing is not satisfactory for large group conferences. Splitting an already small screen into multiple smaller images reduces the sense of being there, reducing the effectiveness of the conference. Thus, an increasing number of organizations now employ a separate videoconferencing facility (usually a conference room) where a large group of people can participate in a conference with a large group at another location.

As an example of both group and desktop videoconferencing, let us consider offerings from Polycom, Inc., headquartered in Pleasanton, California. With its 2001 acquisition of PictureTel Corporation, Polycom solidified its position as the worldwide market leader in voice- and videoconferencing. Polycom's VSX 8800 Presenter MP VTX conference room videoconferencing unit has a list price of $18,549, not including a floor stand or a monitor. This unit is designed to work in a custom boardroom, a large room, or an auditorium. The 8800 includes a voice-tracking camera, data-sharing capabilities, and a top-of-the-line conference phone. This system provides premium quality video with Polycom's Pro-Motion, and excellent audio with Polycom's StereoSurround. The data-sharing capabilities permit users to share content from laptops or PCs (e.g., a spreadsheet or a PowerPoint presentation) that have an IP network connection (they do not have to be connected to the VSX system). In the VSX Executive Collection, the customer can add a floor stand and dual 50-inch plasma monitors for a total of $58,000. Less expensive conference room units are also available. The VSX 7400s Presenter is designed for medium to large rooms with up to 40 people, and the price is $9,000 (again, no stand or monitor).

At the desktop level, Polycom offers Polycom PVX software, which is designed to work with your PC and your own high-quality USB camera attached to the PC. The price of a single-user license is only $149, with a 100-user license available for $10,900. Polycom PVX includes the data-sharing capability described previously, and it is designed to operate at 30 frames per second over a broadband or LAN connection.

In summary, the ideal office network shown in Figure 6.9 does not exist—but we are getting closer every year. Offices have secretarial and professional/executive workstations in ever-increasing numbers, and these devices are almost always linked via a LAN. Today most telephony is not accomplished on the same network, but Internet telephony is changing that. The use of videoconferencing is increasing, but still not commonplace. Office automation is moving forward, slowly but steadily, and the key to further development appears to be the use of collaboration tools, or groupware.

GROUPWARE

Earlier in this chapter, we argued that ERP systems deserved treatment as a separate application area because of their currency and importance, despite the fact that ERP systems are, indeed, transaction processing systems. Now we wish to make the same argument for including groupware as an application area vis-à-vis office automation. Clearly, groupware is part of office automation, but it is a very critical part that deserves special attention.

Groupware is an industry term that refers to soft*ware* designed to support *groups* by facilitating collaboration, communication, and coordination. Nowadays, the term **collaboration** or the phrase **collaborative environment** is often used as a synonym for groupware. In choosing a groupware product, the decision maker must decide what functions are required, and seek a product (or a combination of products) that provides these features. Some groupware features are electronic mail, electronic bulletin boards, computer conferencing, electronic calendaring, group scheduling, sharing documents, electronic whiteboards, shared workspace, meeting support systems, workflow routing, electronic forms, Internet telephony, desktop videoconferencing, learning management systems, and IM. One groupware feature needed to support real-time collaboration is presence awareness, or the ability to detect others' online availability (which is the key technology underlying IM). None of the leading groupware packages provide all the functions that a company might want, but in many cases add-on packages can be purchased to fill the gaps.

One might guess that the heart of a successful general-purpose groupware product is electronic mail, and that is certainly right—both industry leader Microsoft Exchange[2] and top contender Lotus Notes[3] (from IBM) have excellent e-mail capabilities. Until 2004, Lotus Notes held the top position based largely on its outstanding ability to share documents of all types. However, for a variety of reasons—Exchange is somewhat less expensive to operate, Exchange has a user interface that some find easier to use, and Microsoft's marketing prowess—Exchange has now passed Notes in terms of its installed base (Lyons, 2005). In terms of market share, no other contenders come close to the top two. However, there are other players in the market with exciting groupware products, including Oracle with its Collaboration Suite, Novell GroupWise, Thruport Technologies with its HotOffice product, Web Crossing, and EMC's Documentum eRoom.

The top two players are even introducing new products. For example, Microsoft has added Microsoft Office Groove to the enterprise version of Microsoft Office. With Groove, which incorporates presence awareness, it is easy to create a Groove workspace that others can use at your invitation, to share files, to host online discussions and meetings, and to share business forms. Microsoft also offers Microsoft SharePoint Server, an integrated suite of server capabilities including extensive collaboration services such as shared workspaces, shared calendars, presence awareness and IM, document management, workflow routing, wikis, and blogs. Then Microsoft Office Communications Server delivers streamlined communications including presence awareness and IM, VoIP telephony, videoconferencing, and mobile access.

IBM has introduced a brand new product, IBM Workplace Collaboration Services, that includes e-mail, calendaring and scheduling, presence awareness and IM, learning, team spaces, Web conferencing, and document and Web content management. IBM Lotus Sametime provides unified communications including presence awareness and IM, Web conferencing, VoIP telephony, videoconferencing, and mobile access. IBM-watchers assume that eventually Lotus Notes and IBM Workplace Collaboration Services will morph into a single product. An interesting specialized groupware area deals with electronic meeting support systems, and we will talk more about this area in the next chapter.

Groupware, like ERP systems, is a growth area in the software industry as well as an evolving area (see the box entitled "Real-Time Collaboration"). To gain a greater understanding of this area, let us take a closer look at a leading groupware product, Lotus Notes.

An Example Groupware System: Lotus Notes

Lotus Development Corporation's first important product was 1-2-3, and it became the dominant spreadsheet package in the 1980s and early 1990s. The second important

---

[2]Actually, Microsoft Exchange is the name of the server program, while Microsoft Outlook is the name of the client program that runs on a PC. However, it is common for users to refer to the Microsoft Outlook/Microsoft Exchange combination as a Microsoft Exchange groupware system.

[3]In this case, Lotus Notes is the name of the client program that runs on a PC. Lotus Domino is the name of the server program. However, it is common for users to refer to the Lotus Notes/Lotus Domino combination as a Lotus Notes groupware system.

REAL-TIME COLLABORATION

Many business-technology managers see a lot of value in using the Internet to keep people in constant and instantaneous communication with one another, yet they're not certain when that vision will become reality. It's happening, but only in bits and pieces, as with telecommuters who communicate with co-workers using IM and employees who attend project-team meetings via Web conferencing. This concept, known as real-time collaboration, focuses on the person-to-person aspect of a company's broader collaboration strategy. On occasion, technologies such as IM and Web conferencing are being used to collaborate in real time with customers, partners, and suppliers.

But are the technologies and concept advanced enough to build a strategic organizational plan around real-time collaboration? That's a question business-technology managers are asking, and there are numerous challenges to achieving that goal in the near future. Many of the technologies available don't follow standards and don't link to each other easily, and the performance of multimedia delivery over the Internet hasn't reached a high degree of consistency. Then there are the cultural issues involved in getting people to embrace a completely different way of working. "Real-time collaboration apps aren't ready for prime time," says Forrester Research analyst Erica Rugullies.

On a positive note, analysts think it will be only a few years before big visions for real-time collaboration are realized. Big-name vendors such as IBM Lotus Software, Microsoft, Oracle, Siemens, and Sun Microsystems are promising—and in some cases already offering—collaboration tools that embrace standards-based technologies such as XML, Web services, Java 2 Enterprise Edition, and voice over IP. The resulting flexibility will let collaborative components be sewn together to create an always-on architecture. The plan from the IT community is to let collaborative features be embedded in various enterprise applications, launched from numerous communication tools, and consumed by just about any device. "There's a larger vision here than a group of disconnected services," says Rob Koplowitz, Senior Director of Product Marketing for Oracle. "Customers are beginning to see this as an infrastructure play."

[Kontzer, 2003]

---

product was Notes, a groupware system originally featuring strong document-sharing features and a reasonable e-mail package that has grown into a more full-featured product. Notes—and Lotus's expertise in developing PC and client/server software—were important to IBM, which paid $3.5 billion to purchase Lotus in 1995. IBM was already a software powerhouse, as we have noted earlier in this book, but its strength was in large machine software. IBM felt it needed to bolster its PC software prowess to compete with Microsoft in that market, and it also wanted the Notes groupware product. IBM has allowed Lotus to operate as a separate business unit, and the buyout seems to have benefited both IBM and Lotus.

Users can configure the welcome page of Lotus Notes to their liking; Figure 6.10 shows the slightly customized welcome page used by one of the authors of this book. At the top left of the screen is the menu bar containing the menus of commands used to perform tasks within Notes. Just below the menu bar is a row of icons that permit the user to perform tasks quickly by clicking the mouse on an icon. Below the row of icons is an address box. To go to a Web address you have not visited before, enter the Uniform Resource Locator (URL) in the address box; to go to a page you have previously visited, click the down arrow at the right end of the address field and select the appropriate URL from the drop-down list. To the right of the address field is the navigation bar that allows the user to navigate in Notes just as you would in a Web browser

(Notes is, in fact, a Web browser). Down the left side of the screen are the bookmark buttons, which represent a powerful way to navigate to Web pages as well as to Notes databases, views, and documents. In the big area of the screen, the upper left quadrant shows the most recent entries in the user's Notes inbox, the upper right quadrant shows the calendar entries for the current week, and the lower half contains "hot spot" links to the user's mail, calendar, contacts (address book), "to do" list, and personal journal.

When the user opens the mail—either by clicking the mail bookmark button on the left side of any page (the top icon, which looks like a piece of mail) or the mail hot spot in the bottom area of the welcome page—the inbox view of the mailbox is displayed, as shown in Figure 6.11. In addition to the bars and icons appearing on the welcome page, a view action bar appears above the listing of e-mail messages in the larger window to the right. The actions listed relate to the current view. For the inbox view, the entries include new memo, reply, reply to all, forward, delete, follow up, folder (i.e., move to folder), and copy into new—all common actions used in processing e-mail. Most of the screen is divided into a navigation pane on the left and an active view pane on the right. In the inbox view, the active view pane lists the user's mail messages, tells who sent the message, the date and time it was sent, the size of the message, and the subject assigned by the sender. To open a message a user double-clicks on it. A star immediately to the left of the sender's name indicates an unread message.

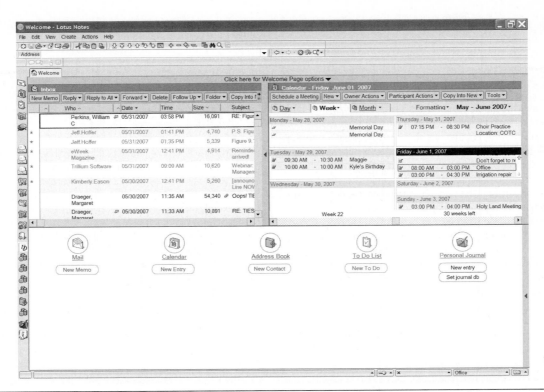

Figure 6.10 Lotus Notes® Welcome Page (IBM Lotus Notes Screen Captures © 2004 IBM Corporation. Used with permission of IBM Corporation. IBM, Lotus, Notes and Domino are trademarks of IBM Corporation, in the United States, other countries, or both.)

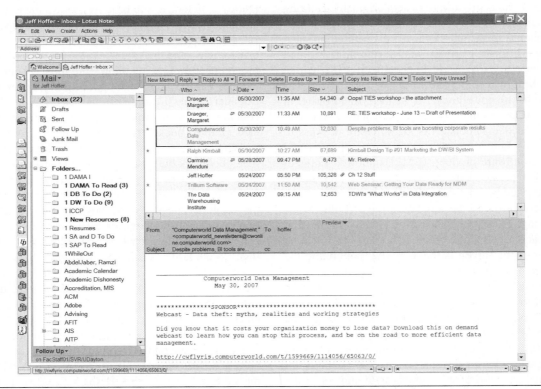

Figure 6.11 Lotus Notes® Inbox (IBM Lotus Notes Screen Captures © 2004 IBM Corporation. Used with permission of IBM Corporation. IBM, Lotus, Notes and Domino are trademarks of IBM Corporation, in the United States, and other countries, or both.)

The navigation pane on the left lists a number of views and folders that can be used to manage the mail. For instance, the folder "drafts" contains messages you are working on but have not yet sent, and the set of file folders with names such as Academic Calendar, Academic Dishonesty, Accreditation MIS, ACM, and Advising constitute the electronic filing system for this user. Notes also has a valuable electronic calendaring feature that you access by clicking on the calendar bookmark button on the left side of the page (the second icon, which looks like a page of a desk calendar) or by clicking on the calendar hot spot on the welcome page. Several different calendar views are available, including a one-day view, a one-week view, and a one-month view.

The user's mail files, as described previously, constitute a Notes database. The calendar files are another database, and the contacts are yet a third database. In fact, the various databases are the heart of Notes. Each database contains a collection of documents (of some sort) relating to the same topic. An experienced Notes user most likely will

have created databases for the variety of activities in which he or she is engaged, such as a significant committee assignment, an ongoing research project, a graduate information systems course, and a faculty discussion group. These are databases that the user most likely does not want to share with other users. However, there are other databases—created by users throughout the company—that are intended for sharing. As mentioned previously, the real strength of Notes is its document-sharing abilities. This is done through various *shared* databases. Some of the databases might be set up so that the user can only read documents, not modify them or add new ones; in other databases, such as discussion groups, all participants are encouraged to enter into the discussion.

To open a particular database, first click on the database bookmark button on the left side of the page (this button appears to be two cylinders, or hard drives, in front of a file folder). This opens the database bookmark page, showing all the databases that the user has bookmarked. The user opens a database by double-clicking on the relevant database

AT HERTZ, LOTUS NOTES/DOMINO IS NUMBER 1

Hertz rents cars from approximately 7,000 locations in more than 150 countries. Given this global span, Hertz employees must communicate and collaborate on an ongoing basis with people all over the world. Forms must be completed and routed to people in other offices or countries. Changes in policies and regulations must be quickly distributed to a widely dispersed workforce. To streamline these and other global tasks, Hertz depends on IBM Lotus Notes and Domino and on related Lotus technologies such as IBM Lotus Instant Messaging, Web Conferencing, Team Workplace, and Domino.Doc.

"For us, Lotus Domino is key to efficiency," says Claude Burgess, Senior Vice President of Technology and e-Business at Hertz. "It takes so many of the mundane procedures we have as a global organization and lets us automate them to cut costs, eliminate travel, speed processes, and add security. The processes won't go away, and so making them more efficient is extremely important."

One Domino application that touches the lives of most of Hertz's 15,000 Lotus Notes users is its home-grown eForms system. With eForms, Hertz employees can electronically complete and process any of about 500 types of forms that used to exist only on paper. "With eForms I can submit the forms in seconds," says Burgess. "Our Domino-based workflow application routes it to the appropriate people automatically, and any questions or annotations stay with the form, creating a history for the next person who gets it and eliminating questions that slow things down." Burgess indicates that eForms has reduced the amount of paper Hertz prints by 70 percent and has greatly speeded up forms processing. "Form contents are more secure,

and we don't lose data. Everything is routed and processed correctly not just by luck, but because the software makes it happen."

Other Lotus communication and collaboration applications at Hertz include:

- The use of IBM Lotus Team Workplace to create Web-based workrooms where project teams formed to digitize processes within the company can manage the associated documents and track progress.
- The use of Domino.Doc to publish the company's employee policy and procedure manual, as well as other internal documents. Domino.Doc is a Domino-based solution that enables collaborative document management throughout the entire document life cycle.
- The use of Lotus Web Conferencing to hold regular meetings between multidisciplinary teams in dispersed locations. "For instance," Burgess indicates, "we can all be looking at a graphical display of information while making changes to it on the shared screen as the team interaction dictates."
- The use of Lotus Domino Everyplace to send critical information to profit center managers' phones, personal digital assistants (PDAs), or other mobile devices. "These people are always on the move, and aren't often in their office or at their desks to receive messages," says Burgess. "But the faster we can get them crucial information, such as a last-minute change in fleet availability, the better they're able to do their jobs."

[Adapted from IBM, 2003]

listing. What if the user has not bookmarked the desired database? The database bookmark page also contains "Find a Database" and "Browse for a Database" selections. The opening screen of any database looks similar to Figure 6.11, with appropriate tool buttons, a navigation pane to the left, and a list of topics or documents in the view pane to the right. The user double-clicks on a document to display it.

How does all this work? Lotus Notes is a client/server system, with the large files (databases) stored on the server, which Lotus calls a "Domino server powered by Notes." The user can opt to store databases on the PC hard drive, but master copies of the large corporate or departmental databases of documents are stored on the server. Corporate files are replicated from one Notes server to another on a regular basis, so that everyone in the organization has access to the same version of a document. The Lotus Notes client, operating on a PC, is used to access the server with appropriate password protection. This access might either be directly across a LAN or via an Internet connection. Any Web browser on the Internet can also access Notes. Of course, the Notes client is itself a Web browser. A major advantage of using Notes as the browser is that Notes gives you the ability to store copies of Web pages as documents in a Notes database.

Finally, another strength of Lotus Notes is its ability to serve as a development platform, allowing companies to create their own Notes applications customized for their needs. In fact, a growing number of these specialized applications are available commercially through third-party vendors, including project management, human resources, help desk, document management, health care, sales and marketing, and imaging applications.

INTRANETS AND PORTALS

The notion of an intranet was introduced in Chapter 4: An **intranet** is a network operating within an organization that employs the TCP/IP protocol, the same protocol used on the Internet. In most cases, an intranet consists of a backbone network with a number of connected LANs. Because the protocol is the same, the organization may use the same Web browser, Web search engine, and Web server software that it would use on the Internet. The intranet, however, is not accessible from outside the organization. The organization decides whether or not people within the organization have access to the Internet.

An intranet presents some incredible advantages to the organization. If an organization already has an internal

network of interconnected LANs plus Web browsers on most workstations and an operating Web server, as most organizations do, then implementing an intranet is a relatively easy task involving some programming on the Web server. With minimal effort the full functionality of a localized World Wide Web, including e-mail and document sharing, is available within the organization. The Web browser is a "universal client" that works with heterogeneous platforms. Furthermore, virtually no training is needed to implement an intranet because users already know how to use a browser. Deploying a new intranet application is simple—just send an e-mail message containing the URL (address) of the new application to users.

Even if the organization does not have a Web server and Web browsers, the costs are not overwhelming. Web browsers are free, and a minimal Web server complete with software can be obtained for well under $10,000. Intranets are easy enough to set up that in some organizations the first intranet was set up by end users (such as engineers), not by the IS organization, to enable sharing of particular documents.

Intranets serve a variety of important uses within organizations. None is more important than those of the CareWeb intranet at the Boston-based CareGroup HealthCare System. The CareGroup includes six hospitals, 2,500 health care professionals, and 800,000 patients in the northeastern United States. The CareWeb intranet, introduced in 1998, consolidates medical records from geographically dispersed patients, clinics, and laboratories into a single clinical database and makes these records accessible to health care professionals via a Web browser.

One of the early applications on the CareWeb intranet was the Secure Patient/Physician Communication application, a clinical database. "With our clinical systems on the Web, if I am an E. R. doctor and a 53-year-old patient rolls in with chest pain, I am able to compare that day's events with what happened [to him] a year ago," says Dr. John Halamka, Chief Information Officer of CareGroup. Furthermore, CareGroup officials firmly believe that CareWeb has enabled them to increase the quality of patient care while reducing expenses by about $ 1 million per year.

With patients' medical histories available on the intranet, health care professionals can easily determine information such as past surgeries, medications used, and allergies. Patients can also access their own medical records over the intranet—as long as they have a browser and the requisite password—to check prescriptions and request referrals to specialists. Another intranet application gives insurance providers access to CareWeb so that insurance transactions can be conducted over the Web. Insurance providers can transmit information on benefits and eligibility of patients to CareGroup, and CareGroup has made referral and authorization applications available on the intranet. Insurance claims can also be submitted over CareWeb. Nearly 300 different applications are currently available on CareWeb. They run the gamut from those discussed previously to a signature authorization program to financial analysis to medical analysis, such as an application used for calculating kidney functions (Henry, 2000).

In 2006, IBM's intranet—known inside the company as "w3 On Demand Workplace"—was selected as one of "The Year's 10 Best Intranets" by Nielsen Norman Group, a research firm that advises companies on human-centered product and service design. IBM was the only IT company selected in the top 10, and one of only four U.S. companies (the others were Capital One, Merrill Lynch, and Staples). Nielsen Norman said that IBM achieved consistency and personalization in its intranet, which facilitates collaboration between 329,000 employees in 75 countries.

Among the features of IBM's intranet recognized by Nielson Norman are:

- the personalization of news based on self-created profiles

- the creation of role-specific portlets for employees in finance, sales, and management (A **portlet** is a specialized content area, or window, within an intranet opening page, or within a portal.)

- a robust employee directory, which permits its employees to search for other employees in many ways, including particular areas of expertise

- a facility for blogging—employees can create their own blogs through BlogCentral or they can subscribe to each other's blogs via RSS (**RSS** is the *de facto* standard for the syndication, or distribution, of Web content—in this case, employees' blogs, but also news feeds, event listings, project updates, or corporate information.)

- accessibility—the intranet is designed to be accessible for people with disabilities, memory issues, and low vision (Jones, 2006)

When originally introduced, intranets were seen as competing with full-service groupware products such as Lotus Notes and Microsoft Exchange. Both fostered communication within the organization. Intranets did not provide the full range of groupware services, but they were much less expensive. Over time, intranets and groupware have grown closer together. Groupware has fully embraced the Internet, and groupware clients such as Lotus Notes are now Web browsers. Today some intranets employ the groupware client as the Web browser. At the same time,

intranets became so complex and cumbersome to use that it was necessary to provide some structure, some organization so that users could find what they needed on the intranet. The answer was a **portal**—software that provided a structure and thus easier access to internal information via a Web browser. (If the organization desires, those external to the organization can also use the portals—see the Haworth, Inc., example later in this section and the Volkswagen box.) This added software meant that intranets became more expensive. Portal software is available from a number of software firms, both large and small, including groupware vendors IBM (with IBM WebSphere Portal) and Oracle (with Oracle Portal). Among other portal products are BEA WebLogic Portal, Sun Java System Portal Server, Tibco PortalBuilder, and Vignette Portal.

Ball Memorial Hospital in Muncie, Indiana, has successfully used a portal for its physicians, and it is currently extending the portal to be useful for all its employees. Ball Memorial has used portal development tools from Bowstreet, Inc. (purchased by IBM in late 2005), along with IBM's WebSphere Portal, to build more than 20 applications for its physicians. Christina Fogle, e-Systems Manager at Ball Memorial, estimates that the tools helped shave 40 percent off the development time for complex applications and as much as 70 percent for simpler applications. The hospital is currently using the same tools for new employee self-service applications, including benefits management and travel (Whiting, January 2, 2006).

Furniture maker Haworth, Inc., which reported $1.26 billion in sales for 2003, upgraded its dealer portal, which it calls dNet, in 2004—and the upgraded portal has proved valuable for both Haworth's dealers and Haworth's own employees. Before the upgrade, the number of visitors to the portal averaged about 12 a month. After the improvement, the portal garnered about 4 million hits in 7 months, according to Mike Stock, dNet's manager. To rework the portal, Haworth employed systems integrator Ascendant Technology, which helped the company upgrade dNet using IBM's WebSphere Portal and Lotus Workplace for Web Content Management.

The company's dealers use dNet to obtain real-time financial information, inventory status, and marketing materials. Before the upgrade, Haworth's sales representatives would spend more than 30 minutes per customer call to search various databases for product availability, pricing, and order-status information. Much of this work dealers can now do for themselves. The portal has also increased productivity for other Haworth employees. "Internally, all of our employees now have a centralized place to access order-entry, marketing materials, and product-development information," Stock says. "They no longer have to walk down the hall or call across the room

---

PORTALS POWER VW

Two major portals—one internal and one external—are helping Volkswagen AG manage the production of five million cars a year at 40 factories in 16 countries. "This is a core element of our borderless enterprise," said Meike-Uta Hansen, Director of e-Supply Chain Integration and Services. Implementing an internal portal for procurement and an external business-to-business portal for suppliers wasn't easy. There were skeptical questions and some resistance from employees and suppliers. But the initiative had strong support from VW's board of managers, which believed the company could improve its processes "by delivering the right information to the right person at the right time," Hansen said.

VW procurement employees were spending 70 percent of their time looking for information on parts, and the company wanted a process to deliver the data they needed faster. The automaker created the Integrated Purchasing Agent's Desk portal, known as iPAD. "In the past, purchasers looked for data; now the information comes in to the purchaser," Hansen said. The portal is being used by purchasing agents in most parts of the company, including research and development, quality assurance, logistics, production, and finance. "It provides 360-degree views of suppliers, parts, and projects," Hansen said.

VW also collaborates more closely with suppliers through its business-to-business portal that features 30 applications, links to 16,000 supplier sites, and has 55,000 users. "It's now a deep-seated part of all of our business processes," Hansen said. Suppliers get personalized views of the information they need to track VW projects and procurement needs, and they receive event-driven alerts to keep them up-to-date on changes.

[Travis, 2005]

---

to get information like part numbers" (Hulme, 2005). For organizations such as CareGroup HealthCare System, IBM, Ball Memorial Hospital, Haworth, and many others, intranets and portals have brought improved performance and improved communication.

FACTORY AUTOMATION

The roots of **factory automation** lie in (1) numerically controlled machines, which use a computer program, or a tape with holes punched in it, to control the movement of tools on sophisticated machines, and in (2) **material requirements planning (MRP)** systems, which rely on extensive data input to produce a production schedule for the factory and a schedule of needed raw materials. The newer **computer-integrated manufacturing (CIM)** combines these basic ideas not only to let the computer set up the schedules (as with MRP) but also to carry them out through control of the various machines involved (as with numerically controlled machines).

Computer-integrated manufacturing is one of the primary ways by which manufacturers are facing the challenges of global competition. Through the various components of CIM, manufacturers are increasing productivity and quality while simultaneously reducing the lead time from the idea stage to the marketplace for most products. A list of strong proponents of CIM reads like a who's who of manufacturing—General Motors, John Deere, Ford, Weyerhaeuser, FMC, and Kodak, among others.

CIM systems fall into three major categories: engineering systems, manufacturing administration, and factory operations. Table 6.1 lists the acronyms used in this section on factory automation. The engineering systems are aimed at increasing the productivity of engineers and include such systems as computer-aided design and group technology. Manufacturing administration includes systems that develop production schedules and monitor production against these schedules; these systems are usually termed manufacturing resources planning systems. Factory operations include those systems that actually control the operation of machines on the factory floor. Computer-aided manufacturing and shop floor control are examples of such systems.

Table 6.1 Abbreviations Used in Factory Automation

Acronym	Full Name
CIM	computer-integrated manufacturing
CAD	computer-aided design
CAE	computer-aided engineering
GT	group technology
CAPP	computer-aided process planning
MRP	material requirements planning
MRP II	manufacturing resources planning
SCM	supply chain management
CAM	computer-aided manufacturing
AGV	automated guided vehicle
MAP	Manufacturing Automation Protocol
SFC	shop floor control

Engineering Systems

Computer-aided design (CAD) is perhaps the most familiar of the engineering systems. CAD involves the use of computer graphics—both two-dimensional and three-dimensional—to create and modify engineering designs. **Computer-aided engineering (CAE)** is a system designed to analyze the functional characteristics of a design and simulate the product performance under various conditions in order to reduce the need to build prototypes. CAD and CAE permit engineers to conduct a more thorough engineering analysis and to investigate a wider range of design alternatives. Advanced CAD/CAE systems store the information they generate in a database that is shared with the other components of CIM, such as CAM.

Group technology (GT) systems logically group parts according to physical characteristics, machine routings through the factory, and similar machine operations. On the basis of these logical groupings, GT is able to identify existing parts that engineers can use or modify rather than design new parts, simplifying the design and manufacturing processes. **Computer-aided process planning (CAPP)** systems plan the sequence of processes that produce or assemble a part. During the design process, the engineer retrieves the closest standard plan from a database (using the GT classification of the new part) and modifies that plan rather than starting from scratch. The resulting plans are more accurate and more consistent, thereby reducing process planning and manufacturing costs.

Manufacturing Administration

Manufacturing resources planning (MRP II) systems usually have three major components: the master production schedule, material requirements planning, and shop floor control. The master production schedule component sets the overall production goals based on forecasts of demand. The MRP component then develops a detailed production schedule to accomplish the master schedule, using parts explosion, production capacity, inventory, and lead-time data. The shop floor control component releases orders to the shop floor based on the detailed production schedule and the actual production accomplished thus far. Using recent buzzwords, MRP II systems attempt to implement just-in-time (JIT) production. Note that MRP II does not directly control machines on the shop floor; it is an information system that tries to minimize inventory and employ the machines effectively and efficiently.

In our discussion of enterprise resource planning (ERP) systems earlier in this chapter, we noted that MRP is often one of the key modules of an ERP system. Thus, such an ERP system ties together the manufacturing production schedule with the other important aspects of running an enterprise, including sales and distribution, human resources, and financial reporting. The latest type of manufacturing administration system—supply chain management (SCM)—goes beyond ERP and outside the boundaries of the firm itself. In our view, SCM systems are so important that we have chosen to treat them as a separate application area in a section that immediately follows the factory automation section.

Factory Operations

Factory operations systems go a significant step further than MRP II—they control the machines. By definition, **computer-aided manufacturing (CAM)** is the use of computers to control manufacturing processes. CAM is built around a series of computer programs that control automated equipment on the shop floor. In addition to computer-controlled machines such as automated drill presses and milling machines, CAM systems employ automated guided vehicles (AGVs) to move raw materials, in-process materials, and finished products from one workstation to another. AGVs are loaded using robot-like arms and then follow a computer-generated electronic signal (often a track under the floor that has been activated) to their next destination. Workers are used only to provide maintenance on the equipment and to handle problems. Because job setups (preparing a machine to work on a new part) are automated and accomplished in minimum time, CAM permits extremely high machine utilization. With the low setup time, very small batches (even as small as one) can be produced efficiently, shortening production lead times and reducing inventory levels.

As this brief description has implied, a CAM system is very sophisticated and requires a great deal of input data from other systems. Product design data would come from CAD, process design data from CAPP, and the master production schedule and material requirements from MRP II. The CAM system must also be able to communicate electronically with the machines on the shop floor.

The manufacturing communications network is likely to employ the **Manufacturing Automation Protocol (MAP)**, pioneered by General Motors and now accepted by nearly all major manufacturers and vendors. MAP is a communications protocol (a set of rules) to ensure an open manufacturing system. With conformance to MAP by all vendors, seamless communication between all equipment on the factory floor—regardless of the vendor—is possible. MAP is a user-driven effort, and the details of the concept are evolving. Nevertheless, MAP is a reality in factory automation upon which future systems will be based.

Within factory operations applications, **shop floor control (SFC)** systems are less ambitious than CAM but are still important. These systems provide online, real-time control and monitoring of machines on the shop floor. For example, the SFC might recognize that a tool on a particular milling machine is getting dull (by measuring the metal that the machine is cutting per second) and signal this fact to the human operator on duty. The operator can then take corrective measures, such as instructing the SFC to change the tool or changing it himself or herself, depending on the system.

Robotics

Outside the broad area of CIM, robotics is one other aspect of factory automation that deserves mention. Robotics is, in fact, one branch of the artificial intelligence tree. (Artificial intelligence, especially expert systems and neural networks, is discussed in the next chapter.) With robotics, scientists and engineers are building machines to accomplish coordinated physical tasks in the manner of humans. For over two decades, robots have been important in manufacturing to accomplish simple but important tasks, such as painting and welding. Robots perform repetitive tasks tirelessly, produce more consistent high-quality output than humans, and are not subject to such dangers as paint inhalation or retinal damage. Newer robots incorporate a certain amount of visual perception and thus are able to perform assembly tasks of increasing complexity. Industrial robots are expensive, but they are becoming economically viable for a wider range of tasks as their capabilities are extended. Robots and CIM are producing a vastly different "factory of the future" based on IT.

SUPPLY CHAIN MANAGEMENT SYSTEMS

Supply chain management (SCM) systems are designed to deal with the procurement of the components a company needs to make a product or service and the movement and distribution of components and finished products throughout the supply chain. These supply chain management systems are often interorganizational in nature, involving two or more levels of the supply chain—such as a manufacturer and its suppliers or a retailer and its suppliers. There are five basic components of SCM: plan, source, make, deliver, and return. Planning means developing a strategy, with appropriate metrics, for managing all the resources that are needed to meet customer demand for your product or service. Sourcing is choosing the suppliers for the resources needed to produce your product or service, as well as developing pricing, delivery, payment, and inventory management processes for these resources. Making is the manufacturing step, including scheduling the activities required. Delivering is the logistics associated with getting your product or service to customers, and returning is creating a procedure for handling defective and excess products and supporting customers who have problems (Worthen, 2007).

Each of these five basic components actually consists of dozens of specific tasks, and SCM software has grown up around these specific tasks, such as demand planning, inventory management, and transportation planning. SCM software packages are available to handle a few of these specific tasks, or many of them, but no vendor has a complete package that is right for every company. Each company must carefully assess its needs, and select the package—or perhaps the combination of products from several vendors—that best meets its needs. Among large companies, the SCM market tends to be dominated by the ERP vendors, especially SAP and Oracle; Microsoft has a significant presence in the small and medium business SCM market. Other important SCM vendors are i2 Technologies, Manhattan Associates, and JDA Software Group. It is interesting to note that JDA Software Group, which traditionally has had strength in SCM for retailers, acquired Manugistics, with strength in SCM for manufacturers, in 2006.

As an example of SCM in the retail industry, let's consider J.C. Penney, an $18.4 billion company. In 2002, J.C. Penney implemented an inventory management system from i2 Technologies and a forecasting and replenishment system from Teradata. Based on the success of these systems and other changes in the supply chain and product development processes, J.C. Penney has reduced the time it takes to get a product from the design stage to the sales floor from as long as two years to just 45 days, according to Jeffrey Allison, J.C. Penney Executive Vice President and Director of Planning and Allocation.

In 2003, J.C. Penney created its factory-store system, which enables the store to replenish such basics as towels, sheets, and jeans on an as-needed, just-in-time basis. Because J.C. Penney can now get these items directly from its suppliers, who can produce them in a matter of days, the company no longer has to store them in warehouses, said Peter McGrath, J.C. Penney's Executive Vice President of Product Development and Sourcing. "The direct-to-store program allows J.C. Penney to ship weekly from global suppliers within five to seven days of receipt of an order. This saves J.C. Penney approximately $30 million in average

SCM HELPS DELIVER THANKSGIVING TURKEYS

Perdue Farms produces more than 48 million pounds of chicken products and almost 4 million pounds of turkey products each week. For Thanksgiving, Perdue will ship roughly 1 million whole turkeys—and all these turkeys will arrive at the supermarkets within 24 hours of processing. This logistics task is much easier for Perdue after the company invested $20 million in Manugistics supply chain management software, including forecasting and supply chain planning tools. With the aid of the SCM system, Perdue has gotten much better at delivering the right number of turkeys to the right customers at the right time, according to Chief Information Officer Don Taylor. "As we get to November, we have live information at our fingertips," he says.

Perdue also uses technology to make sure its products arrive fresh. Each of its delivery trucks is equipped with a global positioning system, so dispatchers always know where the trucks are and can send out replacement trucks if necessary. Some supermarkets have vendor-management inventory control systems, which allow Perdue to track sales of its products in real time. "We're always looking at new technologies as they come along to see what makes sense for us," Taylor says. And SCM certainly makes sense for Thanksgiving turkeys.

[Adapted from Luttrell, 2003]

---

monthly inventory investment. Beyond reducing our warehouse inventory and improving our in-stock percents, we believe that cycle time and turnover should improve as well," indicated McGrath. Virtually all the suppliers that manufacture J.C. Penney's private label merchandise are linked to this system. SCM is working for J.C. Penney (Levinson, 2005).

SUMMARY

Today virtually all large and midsized businesses and an increasing number of small businesses depend on enterprise IT systems. These systems support almost every function of the business, from procuring raw materials to planning the production schedule to distributing the product, from recording and summarizing sales figures to keeping track of inventory, from paying employees and suppliers to handling receivables, from maintaining the organization's financial records to enabling employees to communicate more effectively. Modern organizations simply require enterprise IT systems to do business.

Transaction processing systems are central to the operations of almost every business. These workhorse systems, which were the very first IT applications installed in most businesses, process the thousands of transactions that occur every day, including sales, payments, inventory, and payroll. In recent years, many larger businesses have turned to enterprise resource planning (ERP) systems as a way to achieve an integrated set of transaction processing applications. ERP systems typically consist of a number of modules to handle the sales and distribution, manufacturing, financial reporting, and human resources areas, and the organization can buy a subset of these modules to satisfy its needs.

Transaction processing systems handle the volume of transactions generated as a firm does business, and they also produce summary reports on these transactions. They do not, however, provide this transactional data in a form that enables managers to use the data in decision-making activities—data warehousing does this. With data warehousing, organizational data are made accessible from a storage area that is distinct from that used for operational transaction processing. When combined with easy-to-use analysis tools—which are discussed in the next chapter—the data warehouse becomes a critical information resource for managers to enable strategic and operational decision making.

Office automation systems affect every knowledge worker in a firm. Word processing, electronic calendaring, electronic mail, and many other applications are most commonly delivered via an employee's PC attached to the organization's network. Groupware is a popular way of providing office automation functionality in an integrated package. Microsoft Exchange and Lotus Notes, the most popular groupware packages today, provide e-mail, calendaring, document sharing, and other features. Intranets—networks within an organization that employ Internet standards—offer employees easy access to an organization's internal information via a Web browser, with portals providing a valuable structure for accessing these intranets. Factory automation applies IT to the task of increasing efficiency and effectiveness in the manufacturing process. A particularly important factory automation application is supply chain management, which enables more efficient management of the supply chain as a process from supplier to manufacturer to wholesaler to retailer to consumer (or at least some portion of that supply chain).

As important as these various enterprise systems are, they are certainly not the whole story in terms of IT applications. Chapter 7 focuses on managerial support systems designed to provide support to a manager or a group of managers, and Chapter 8 explores the topic of e-business applications.

REVIEW QUESTIONS

1. Consider the enterprise systems application areas listed in Figure 6.1. Which application area developed first? Which one is most common today? What is a "hot" application area today?
2. Describe the fundamental differences between batch processing and online processing. What is in-line processing?
3. What is a vertically integrated information system? Give an example.
4. What is a client/server system? What is a client? What is a server? Why would an organization choose to implement a client/server system?
5. Define *middleware*. What are the three categories of middleware?
6. What is service-oriented architecture, and how does it relate to Web services?
7. List the primary categories of modules that are likely to be offered by a major ERP vendor.
8. What are the primary reasons for implementing an ERP system?
9. What aspects of the automated office are you most likely to encounter in the workplace today? In the future, what additional features are likely to be added to the automated office?
10. What is groupware? What are the features likely to be included in a groupware product?
11. What is an intranet? Why would an intranet be implemented?
12. Some of the most important acronyms used in the factory automation area are listed below. Provide the full names for each of these acronyms, and give a one-sentence explanation of each term.

CIM	SCM
CAD	GT
MRP	MRP II

DISCUSSION QUESTIONS

1. Differentiate between a two-tier client/server system and a three-tier client/server system. Differentiate between a fat client and a thin client. Why would a firm choose one of these approaches over the others when implementing a client/server system?
2. In review question 5, you listed the three categories of middleware. In one sentence each, define the three categories. Explain the role of each category and how they interact.
3. In this chapter, payroll and order entry were used as examples of transaction processing systems. Another example with which all of us are somewhat familiar is the check-processing system employed by your bank. Consider how the check-processing system is similar to (and different from) the two examples in this chapter. Is the check-processing system likely to be batch, online, or some hybrid of the two? What subsystems would be required to operate the check-processing system?
4. Why do many firms find it difficult to implement an ERP system? List all the reasons you can think of, and indicate which reasons you think are most important and why.
5. Every large organization has large files or databases containing data used in operating the business. How does a data warehouse differ from these operational files or databases? Why are these differences important?
6. Consider an office environment with which you are somewhat familiar. Over the past decade, what changes in the way the office operates (including communication, document preparation, scheduling meetings, etc.) have been brought about by office automation? Why do you think these changes have occurred? Have they been technology- or people-driven, or both?
7. Based on your reading and knowledge from other sources, in what ways has the phenomenon of the Internet influenced office automation?
8. Many large organizations have adopted groupware, but others are still using UNIX server-based or LAN-based e-mail systems. What explains this difference? Why have some organizations quickly moved to groupware, whereas others are moving more slowly?
9. Find out if the university where you are enrolled, or the company where you work, or the company where a close relative or friend works, has developed a portal for employees (or students) to access information and applications on the organization's intranet. If possible, log into the portal and find out what services are available.
10. The terminology employed in factory automation is often confusing, in part because the names are so similar and in part because the subareas do indeed overlap. Carefully distinguish among CIM, CAD, CAE, CAM, and CAPP, indicating any overlaps.
11. All of us come into contact with distributed systems almost every day, even if it is only while shopping at

Wal-Mart or Sears. Describe a distributed system with which you have come in contact. In your view, what are the advantages and disadvantages of this system? Is the system you described a client/server system?

12. What factors are pushing organizations to adopt service-oriented architectures, and what factors are holding them back? Considering these factors, do you believe that SOA will be adopted, but slowly; that SOA will be adopted rapidly; or that SOA will disappear as another good idea that simply costs too much?

REFERENCES

Babcock, Charles. 2006. "Data, data, everywhere." *InformationWeek* 1071 (January 9): 49–52.

Bacheldor, Beth. 2003. "Hyundai steers business to SAP." *InformationWeek* 925 (February 3): 30.

Bacheldor, Beth. 2003. "Dial scraps its enterprise software, switches to SAP." *InformationWeek* Web site, *www.informationweek.com/story/showArticle.jhtml?articleID=12803187* (July 25).

Barry, Douglas K. 2003. *Web Services and Service-Oriented Architectures: The Savvy Manager's Guide.* San Francisco, CA: Morgan Kaufman Publishers.

Bendoly, Elliot, and F. Robert Jacobs, eds. 2005. *Strategic ERP Extensions and Use.* Stanford, CA: Stanford University Press.

Brown, Carol V., Iris Vessey, and Anne Powell. 2001. "Predicting ERP benefits: Towards a contingency model." Indiana University Working Paper.

Chabrow, Eric. 2005. "PC priority: Security drives move to thin clients and Macs." *InformationWeek* Web site, *www.informationweek.com/story/showArticle.jhtml?articleID=56800124* (January 3).

Chase, Richard B., F. Robert Jacobs, and Nicholas J. Aquilano. 2006. "Managerial briefing: Enterprise resource planning systems," *Operations Management for Competitive Advantage,* 11th ed. New York: McGraw-Hill/Irwin, 498–509.

Dunn, Darrell. 2003. "Siebel: The megadeal isn't dead yet." *InformationWeek* 950 (August 4/11): 24.

Gibson, Stan. 2006. "Study: Web services lead growing IT investment." eWeek.com Web site, *www.eweek.com/article2/0,1895,2017627,00.asp* (September 19).

Greenemeier, Larry. 2003. "Biotechnology & pharmaceuticals: Drug companies get customer-focused." *InformationWeek* 956 (September 22): 87.

Greenemeier, Larry, and Charles Babcock. 2006. "SOA has the buzz—and its fair share of risks." *InformationWeek* 1084 (April 10): 42.

Henry, Amanda Mitchell. 2000. "High-tech healthcare." Earthweb.com Web site, *itmanagement.earthweb.com/erp/article.php/621761* (June 1).

Hulme, George V. 2005. "Furniture maker Haworth reupholsters its portal." *InformationWeek* Web site, *www.informationweek.com/story/showArticle.jhtml?articleID=159901514* (March 17).

IBM. 2003. "IBM Lotus Domino is #1 at Hertz." IBM Web site, *www-3.ibm.com/software/success/cssdb.nsf/csp/ehon-5mxw5p* (November).

ISM. 2007. "ISM annual top 15 CRM awards announced." *ISM March 2007 eNewsletter,* ISM Web site, *www.ismguide.com/pdfs/2007-03-Newsletter.pdf* (March 26).

Jones, K. C. 2006. "Top 10 intranets: creative, mobile, multinational." *InformationWeek* Web site, *www.informationweek.com/story/showArticle.jhtml?articleID=177104515* (January 27).

Kerstetter, Jim, Steve Hamm, and Jay Greene. 2002. "The tech outlook: Software's hot spot." *BusinessWeek: The BusinessWeek 50 Special Issue* (Spring): 178–179.

Kontzer, Tony. 2003. "Real-time teamwork." *InformationWeek* 964 (November 17): 57–69.

Kontzer, Tony. 2006. "Better late than never? SAP spices up on-demand CRM." *InformationWeek* 1075 (February 6): 26, 28.

Levinson, Meridith. 2005. "CRM and SCM will help some retailers survive the holidays." *CIO* Web site, *www.cio.com/article/print/14759* (December 1).

Luttrell, Sharron Kahn. 2003. "Talking turkey with Perdue's CIO." *CIO* 17 (November 1): 44.

Lyons, Daniel. 2005. "IBM in denial over Lotus Notes." *Forbes* Web site, *www.forbes.com/2005/04/06/cz_dl_0406notes_print.html* (April 6).

Maguire, James. 2007. "SOA: Hype vs. reality." Earthweb Web site, *itmanagement.earthweb.com/erp/article.php/3671061* (April 12).

Orfali, Robert, Dan Harkey, and Jeri Edwards. 1999. *Client/Server Survival Guide,* 3rd ed. New York: John Wiley & Sons, Inc.

Pauli, Darren. 2006. "Biosystems applies CRM to global network." *Computerworld* Australia Web site, *www.computerworld.com.au/index.php?id=1701749749* (August 28).

Polycom, Inc. 2007. "Conference Room: Polycom VSX8000," "Conference Room: Polycom VSX7000s," and "Desktop: Polycom PVX." Polycom Web site, *www.polycom.com* (April).

Ruber, Peter. 1997. "Client/server's triple play." *Beyond Computing* 6 (March): 32–34.

SAP. 2000. "Premier financial services company, MassMutual Financial Group, to streamline its operations using mySAP.com." SAP press release, SAP Web site, *www.sap.com* (September 25).

SAP. 2003. "Toyota Motorsport accelerates Formula One operations with SAP." SAP press release, SAP Web site, *www.sap.com* (October 8).

SAP. 2007. "Harry & David selects SAP to support retail and wholesale growth strategy." SAP press release, SAP Web site, *www.sap.com* (March 22).

Singer, Peter. 2000. "Leveraging the power of your data warehouse." *Beyond Computing* 9 (May): 50–53.

Strom, David. 2006. "Group chat is all the buzz." *InformationWeek* 1119 (December 18/25): 51–54.

Sullivan, Laurie. 2005. "ERPzilla." *InformationWeek* 1047 (July 11): 30–40.

TechWeb News. 2004. "NP. JK. But CB, OK?" *InformationWeek* Web site, *www.informationweek.com/story/showArticle.jhtml?articleID=56700159* (December 29).

Travis, Paul. 2005. "Portals power VW." *InformationWeek* 1035 (April 18): 12.

Vollmann, Thomas E., William L. Berry, D. Clay Whybark, and F. Robert Jacobs. 2005. "Chapter 4, Enterprise resource planning (ERP)—integrated systems," *Manufacturing Planning and Control for Supply Chain Management*, 5th ed. New York: McGraw-Hill/Irwin, 108–132.

Ware, Lorraine Cosgrove. 2003. "CRM: Desperately seeking success." *CIO* 16 (August 1): 20.

Ware, Lorraine Cosgrove. 2003. "Enterprise systems show results." *CIO* 17 (November 1): 38.

Wettemann, Rebecca. 2005. "Trendspotting: Getting the most from CRM." *InformationWeek* Web site, *www.informationweek.com/story/showArticle.jhtml?articleID=164302018* (June 13).

Whiting, Rick. 2003. "The data-warehouse advantage." *InformationWeek* 949 (July 28): 63–66.

Whiting, Rick. 2005. "Data transformation." *InformationWeek* 1035 (April 18): 75.

Whiting, Rick. 2006. "Portal popularity drives IBM's Bowstreet deal." *InformationWeek* 1,070 (January 2): 23.

Whiting, Rick. 2006. "ERP gets a complete makeover: You look marvelous." *InformationWeek* 1099 (July 24): 33–39.

Wilde, Candee. 1999. "Citrix sees fortunes rise with thin-client model." *InformationWeek* 763 (November 29): 92–96.

Worthen, Ben. 2007. "ABCs of supply chain management." *CIO* Web site, *www.cio.com/article/print/28261* (January 18).

Young, Margaret L., and Marcia Stepanek. 2003. "Make every customer more profitable: Harrah's Entertainment Inc." *CIO Insight* Web site, *www.cioinsight.com/article2/0,1397,1419567,00.asp* (December 1).

CHAPTER 7
MANAGERIAL SUPPORT SYSTEMS

 MANAGERIAL SUPPORT SYSTEMS ARE THE TOPIC OF THIS SECOND OF three chapters devoted to our survey of information technology (IT) application areas. Managerial support systems are designed to provide support to a specific manager or a small group of managers, and they include applications to support managerial decision making such as group support systems, executive information systems, and expert systems. In contrast, the previous chapter dealt with enterprise systems designed to support the entire organization or large portions of it, such as transaction processing systems, data warehousing, groupware, and intranets. Together these two chapters provide a relatively comprehensive picture of the applications of IT within a single organization (*intraorganizational* systems). To complete the survey of IT applications, Chapter 8 will focus on *e-business applications* that span organizational boundaries, including B2C and B2B applications using the Internet. Taken as a set, these three chapters encompass the great majority of IT applications in use today.

The enterprise systems discussed in the previous chapter are critical for running a business or any other type of organization, and you will be dealing with many such enterprise systems, especially transaction processing systems and groupware. Nevertheless, these enterprise systems have been designed to support the organization as a whole, not you in particular or even a group of managers. Managerial support systems, in contrast, are intended to directly support you and other managers as you make strategic and tactical decisions for your organizations. For example, interactive decision support systems (DSSs) are designed to help managers and other professionals analyze internal and external data. By capturing the expertise of human experts, expert systems advise nonexperts in a particular decision area. Group support systems are designed to make group work, especially meetings, more productive. Executive information systems (EISs) provide easy-to-navigate summary data for the managers of an organization. This chapter will explore these and other managerial support systems that are increasingly important in running modern organizations.

DECISION SUPPORT SYSTEMS

A **decision support system (DSS)** is a computer-based system, almost always interactive, designed to assist a manager (or another decision maker) in making decisions. A DSS incorporates both data and models to help a decision maker solve a problem, especially a problem that is not well structured. The data are often extracted from a transaction processing system or a data warehouse, but that is not always the case. The model might be simple, such as a profit-and-loss model to calculate profit given certain assumptions, or complex, such as an optimization model to suggest loadings for each machine in a job shop. DSSs and many of the systems discussed in the following sections are not always justified by a traditional cost-benefit approach; for these systems, many of the benefits are intangible, such as faster decision making and better understanding of the data.

Figure 7.1 shows that a DSS requires three primary components: model management to apply the appropriate model, data management to select and handle the appropriate data, and dialog management to facilitate the user interface to the DSS. The user interacts with the DSS through the dialog management component, identifying the particular model and data set to be used, and then the DSS presents the results to the user through this same dialog management component. The model management and data management components largely act behind the scenes, and they vary from relatively simple for a typical spreadsheet model to quite complex for a mathematical programming-based scheduling model.

An extremely popular type of DSS is a pro forma financial statement generator. Using a spreadsheet package such as Microsoft Excel, a manager builds a model to project the various elements of the organization or division financial

statement into the future. The data employed are historical financial figures for the organization. The initial (base) model incorporates various assumptions about future trends in income and expense categories. After viewing the results of the base model, the manager performs a series of "what-if" analyses by modifying one or more assumptions to determine their impact on the bottom line. For example, the manager might explore the impact on profitability if the sales of a new product grew by 10 percent per year, rather than the 5 percent incorporated in the base model. Or the manager might investigate the impact of a higher-than-expected increase in the price of raw materials, such as 7 percent per year instead of 4 percent per year. This type of financial statement generator is a simple but powerful DSS for guiding financial decision making.

An example of a DSS driven by transactions data is a police-beat allocation system used by a California city. This system enables a police officer to display a map outline and call up data by geographic zone, which shows police calls for service, types of service, and service times. The system's interactive graphics capability lets the officer manipulate the maps, zones, and data to consider a variety of police-beat alternatives quickly and easily and takes maximum advantage of the officer's judgment.

Other DSS examples include an interactive system for capacity planning and production scheduling in a large paper company. This system employs detailed historical data and forecasting and scheduling models to simulate overall performance of the company under differing planning assumptions. A major oil company developed a DSS to support capital investment decision making. This system incorporates various financial routines and models for generating future plans; these plans can be displayed in either tabular or graphic form to aid in decision making. A major airline uses a DSS to help aircraft controllers deal with aircraft shortage problems that might arise at an airport because of delayed or canceled incoming flights or mechanical problems for aircraft on the ground. The DSS, which uses a network optimization modeling technique, helps controllers use spare aircraft more effectively as well as evaluate possible delay-and-swap options. Over an 18-month period, this DSS saved the airline more than $500,000 in delay costs.

All the DSS examples cited are more properly called **specific DSSs**. These are the actual applications that assist in the decision-making process. In contrast, a **DSS generator** is a software package that provides a set of capabilities to build a specific DSS quickly and easily (Sprague and Carlson, 1982). In the previous pro forma financial statement example, Microsoft Excel can be viewed as a DSS generator, whereas a specific Excel model to project financial statements for a particular division of a company is a specific DSS.

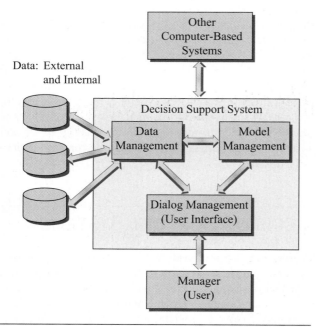

Figure 7.1 Decision Support Systems Components

A POTPOURRI OF DSS EXAMPLES

Virtually every issue of *Interfaces* contains a discussion of one or more new DSSs. To illustrate, we briefly describe three quite different DSSs presented in 2006 and 2007 issues of *Interfaces*.

"Supply chain collaboration through shared capacity models" (Shirodkar and Kempf, 2006) describes a multipart, integrated DSS developed to assist Intel Corporation and its six substrate suppliers in their utilization of existing capacity and in their planning for additional capacity. Intel, the world's largest chip maker, fabricates its own silicon wafers and then cuts these wafers into individual devices called die. These die are then assembled with packages known as substrates—which provide physical protection, electrical connectivity, and heat dissipation—to produce the final chips. Intel purchases the substrates from suppliers, and over time has had difficulty coordinating with these suppliers in terms of their short-term and long-term capacities. To deal with these capacity issues, Intel—in collaboration with its suppliers—has developed shared capacity models for itself and its suppliers and has created multiple decision tools to deal with different planning horizons. The first decision tool is the tactical substrate planning tool (T-SPT) that produces build plans for all substrates and substrate suppliers, based on a linear programming approach. The resulting plan spans eight weeks, with the first week numbers used to order substrates and the following seven weeks analyzed to detect future variations. The second decision tool, the midrange substrate planning tool (M-SPT), uses a similar linear programming approach to forecast over a nine-month horizon to give suppliers an early warning of capacity rearrangements that might be needed. The strategic substrate planning tool (S-SPT) employs a mixed-integer programming approach to provide quarterly forecasts of capacity requirements for a five-year horizon. These tools have proved to be highly successful: "The direct benefits include hundreds of millions of dollars in savings for the suppliers, tens of millions of dollars in savings for Intel, and a tenfold improvement in productivity for the suppliers' personnel and the Intel personnel involved" (p. 428).

A DSS developed for Omya Hustadmarmor, a Norwegian company that produces calcium carbonate slurry for use in the European papermaking industry, assists the company in a very complex maritime inventory and routing problem (Dauzère-Pérès, Nordli, Olstad, Haugen, Koester, Myrstad, Teistklub, and Reistad, 2007). Omya Hustadmarmor produces over 3 million metric tons of slurry a year at its facility on the west coast of Norway, and then ships the slurry in chemical tank ships of various sizes to tank farms throughout northern Europe. Transportation costs are lower for large ships than for small ships, but their use increases planning complexity and creates problems in production and inventory management. The DSS considers available ship sizes, production capacity, inventory levels at the plant and the tank farms, shipping times, transportation costs, demand for various types of slurries, and other factors in order to determine the shipment quantities and the schedules of the vessels. After experimenting with a mixed-integer programming approach, the development team settled on a complex heuristic-based algorithm for the final DSS. The DSS has helped planners make better, faster decisions and has saved production and transportation costs of $14 million a year; it has also enabled the company to react more quickly in the case of unexpected events, such as vessel delays or machine breakdowns.

A quite different type of DSS has been developed to assist Schlumberger, the leading oilfield services company, in bidding for and carrying out land seismic surveys (Mullarkey, Butler, Gavirneni, and Morrice, 2007). One of the services offered by Schlumberger is seismic surveying, the process of mapping subterranean rock formations with reflected sound waves, which is an important early step in the identification and recovery of oil and gas reserves. Carrying out a seismic survey is a complicated logistical operation lasting up to six months, covering hundreds of square miles, and involving many people. Schlumberger must bid for seismic survey projects, and thus it must be able to quickly and accurately estimate the cost of a survey. Mullarkey et al. developed a simulation tool to evaluate the impact of crew sizes, the amount of equipment employed, the survey area, the survey design, the geographic region, and weather conditions on survey costs and durations. The simulator involves stochastic elements to incorporate such factors as equipment failures and the varying speeds of the vehicles and crews used in the survey. Because the results are stochastic, the simulator is run multiple times for each scenario, that is, for each set of input factors. Then the scenarios are varied to arrive at the best cost figures for acceptable survey durations; Schlumberger can then use the costs in preparing its bid for the project. On four surveys, the use of the DSS resulted in savings of about $2 million, so the simulator should save Schlumberger $1.5 to $3 million each year. Although the simulator was constructed for bid estimation, it has also been used for production planning on existing jobs, and future plans include embedding the simulator in an "end-to-end decision-support framework for each land seismic job, making the simulator available for both bidding and executing surveys" (pp. 121–122).

DATA MINING

In Chapter 6 we introduced data warehousing—the idea of a company pulling data from its operational systems and putting the data in a separate data warehouse so that users may access and analyze the data without interfering with the operational systems. In that discussion we touched on the variety of software tools available for analysis of data in the warehouse, but deferred a more complete discussion until this chapter. Our argument was that the creation and maintenance of the data warehouse is an enterprise system, in that the data warehouse supports the entire organization by making the data available to everyone, whereas the analysis of the data is performed by and/or for a single manager or a small group of managers and is, therefore, a managerial support system. Without explicitly mentioning it, we have already begun the more detailed discussion of these tools for analyzing data in the warehouse, for the DSSs described in the previous section often pull the data they need directly from the organizations' data warehouses.

Data mining employs a variety of technologies (such as decision trees and neural networks) to search for, or "mine," "nuggets" of information from the vast quantities of data stored in an organization's data warehouse. Data mining, which is sometimes considered a subset of decision support systems, is especially useful when the organization has large volumes of transaction data in its warehouse. The concept of data mining is not new, although the term became popular only in the late 1990s. For over two decades, many large organizations have used internal or external analysts, often called management scientists, to try to identify trends, or patterns, in massive amounts of data by using statistical, mathematical, and artificial intelligence techniques. With the development of large-scale data warehouses and the availability of inexpensive processing power, a renewed interest in what came to be called data mining arose in recent years.

Along with this renewed interest came a variety of high-powered and relatively easy-to-use commercial data mining software products. Among these products are Oracle Data Mining, SAS Enterprise Miner, XLMiner for Windows (an add-in for Microsoft Excel from Resampling Stats), and KnowledgeSEEKER, KnowledgeSTUDIO, and Strategy BUILDER from Angoss Software Corp. IBM has embedded data mining capabilities in its comprehensive DB2 Data Warehouse Edition. One of the more interesting data mining products is SAS Text Miner,[1] which has the ability to handle textual information, pulling data out of letters, memos, medical records, and documents of all kinds and finding themes and patterns in these documents. These products vary widely in cost, ranging from under $1,000 for some desktop products to over $100,000 for some enterprise products that run on large servers. Consultants are often required to fully utilize the capabilities of the more comprehensive products.

What are the decision techniques or approaches used in data mining? One key technique, decision trees, is embedded

in many of the packages. A decision tree is a tree-shaped structure that is derived from the data to represent sets of decisions that result in various outcomes—the tree's various end points. When a new set of decisions is presented, such as information on a particular shopper, the decision tree then predicts the outcome. Neural networks, a branch of artificial intelligence to be discussed later in this chapter, are incorporated in most of the high-end products. Other popular techniques include linear and logistic regression; association rules for finding patterns of co-occurring events; clustering for market segmentation; rule induction, the extraction of if-then rules based on statistical significance; nearest neighbor, the classification of a record based on those most similar to it in the database; and genetic algorithms, optimization techniques based on the concepts of genetic combination, mutation, and natural selection.

For completeness, let us introduce a term related to data mining, but with a difference—**online analytical processing (OLAP)**. OLAP has been described as human-driven analysis, whereas data mining might be viewed as technique-driven. OLAP is essentially querying against a database, employing OLAP software that makes it easy to pose complex queries along multiple dimensions, such as time, organizational unit, and geography. The chief component of OLAP is the OLAP server, which sits between a client machine and a database server. The OLAP server understands how data are organized in the database and has special functions for analyzing the data. In contrast, data mining incorporates such techniques as decision trees, neural networks, and genetic algorithms. An OLAP program extracts data from the database and structures it by individual dimensions, such as region or dealer. Data mining software searches the database for patterns and relationships, employing techniques such as neural networks.

Of course, what you can do with data mining is more important to you as a manager than the decision techniques employed. Typical applications of data mining are outlined in Table 7.1. Whatever the nature of your business, the chances are good that several of these applications could mean increased profits. Most of these applications focus on unearthing valuable information about your customers.

Many examples of successful data mining operations have been reported in IT magazines. Farmers Insurance Group, a Los Angeles-based provider of automobile and homeowners insurance, uses data mining to develop competitive rates on its insurance products. For example, Farmers used IBM's DecisionEdge software to mine data on owners of sports cars. Typically, these drivers are categorized as high-risk and thus pay high insurance premiums. However, Farmers discovered that a sizeable group of

---

[1]SAS Text Miner was named *Datamation's* Data Mining and Business Intelligence Product of the Year for the most recent year for which the award was given, 2003.

Table 7.1 Uses of Data Mining

Application	Description
Cross-selling	Identify products and services that will most appeal to existing customer segments and develop cross-sell and up-sell offers tailored to each segment
Customer churn	Predict which customers are likely to leave your company and go to a competitor and target those customers at highest risk
Customer retention	Identify customer characteristics associated with highest lifetime value and develop strategies to retain these customers over the long term
Direct marketing	Identify which prospects should be included in a mailing list to obtain the highest response rate
Fraud detection	Identify which transactions are most likely to be fraudulent based on purchase patterns and trends
Interactive marketing	Predict what each individual accessing a Web site is most likely interested in seeing
Market basket analysis	Understand what products or services are commonly purchased together (e.g., beer and diapers) and develop appropriate marketing strategies
Market segmentation	Segment existing customers and prospects into appropriate groups for promotional and evaluation purposes and determine how to approach each segment for maximum results
Payment or default analysis	Identify specific patterns to predict when and why customers default on payments
Trend analysis	Investigate the difference between an average purchase this month versus last month and prior months

sports-car owners are married, 30 to 50 years old, own two cars, and do *not* have a high risk of accidents. Farmers adjusted the premiums for this group downward and believes that the company gained a competitive advantage in this market segment (Davis, 1999).

Vermont Country Store (VCS), a Weston, Vermont-based catalog retailer of traditional clothing, personal items, and housewares, uses SAS's Enterprise Mining data mining software to segment its customers to create appropriate direct marketing mailing lists. "We concentrate on profitability, which we have learned can be increased by identifying the top echelon of customers and mailing them the larger catalog," according to Erin McCarthy, Manager of Statistical Services and Research at VCS. VCS also uses data mining to determine the mailing lists to be used for special campaigns. For example, VCS uses Enterprise Miner to research Christmas buying patterns and create a special Christmas campaign list, selecting just customers who order during the holidays. These customers can be even further segmented by their level of purchases and the types of products they buy, with focused catalogs sent to each separate group. "Our ultimate goal," says McCarthy, "is to be able to limit, or stabilize, the number of contacts we have with customers and still grow our market. For instance, if we're going to mail a catalog to a certain group

DATA MINING WORKS AT AMERICAN HONDA

Engineers at American Honda Motor Co. hope you never have to take your car to the shop—except for routine maintenance. "People expect their cars to be perfect," says Tracy Cermack, Project Manager in the Service Engineering Information Department at American Honda. Cermack's group continually analyzes warranty claims, Techline [technician call center] data, customer feedback, parts sales, and vehicle sales to gauge quality and safety—looking at essentially anything that possibly could go wrong with a vehicle.

"We've implemented a system using SAS data mining and SAS text mining that gives us insight into what the data can tell us," Cermack explains. "American Honda has an excellent infrastructure for identifying problems and investigating issues that aren't clear on the surface. There's always something we could miss if we had to do it all manually, so we rely on SAS to identify and help us make sense of key information."

Using SAS, American Honda has developed an early-warning system that helps the automaker find and forestall potential problems and go back to previous data for more in-depth analysis. During the project's development phase, analysts identified emerging issues with three different vehicle models—issues that had not shown up earlier. With this help from SAS, American Honda was able to resolve the problems swiftly before they had widespread effects.

SAS Text Miner helps analysts zero in on a single performance issue that might be identified based on text. They can then compare hundreds of potential scenarios and drill into additional areas of information to quickly find key concepts or threads that provide a picture of what's really happening. By analyzing the text and related structured data, American Honda can pinpoint the real issue and identify key part numbers or other sources for further investigation.

[SAS Web site, 2007]

of people five times a year, we want to know the best five offers to make them. Data mining is helping us do that" (Dickey, 1999, and SAS Web site, 2007).

Florida Hospital, an 11-campus, Orlando-based health care organization, has implemented IBM's Intelligent Miner in an effort to identify relationships in its patient data. Florida Hospital's initial data mining project was to predict which patients suffering from congestive heart failure were most likely, after being treated and released, to be readmitted or, even worse, to die. Data mining identified unsuspected clusters of data involving patient care that the hospital used as a starting point for making changes in its clinical procedures. In another study, the hospital used Intelligent Miner to investigate patterns associated with the care being given by individual physicians and the total charges they generate. That study is helping the hospital's chief medical officers establish standard care guidelines and clinical best practices. Early in 2000, Florida Hospital created a new standard care plan for patients with pneumonia and acute pneumonia. "We're using Intelligent Miner to validate whether patients on the standard care plan at one campus do better than those who are not on the plan at other campuses," reports Alexander Veletsos, Information Systems Director at the hospital (Gwynne, 2000). Data mining offers exciting possibilities for learning about customers, particularly for companies that have well established data warehouses.

GROUP SUPPORT SYSTEMS

In our discussion of groupware in Chapter 6, we noted that the term *collaboration* or the phrase *collaborative environment* is often used as a synonym for groupware. Collaboration, of course, can be aided by many tools, including e-mail, IM, VoIP telephony, videoconferencing, shared workspaces, and shared document storage. But none of the major groupware systems includes a collaboration tool designed to provide comprehensive support for meetings, whether these meetings are in-person or virtual meetings. Such a collaboration tool—one that is specifically aimed at supporting meetings—is a specialized type of groupware called a **group support system (GSS)**.

GSSs are an important variant of DSSs in which the system is designed to support a group rather than an individual. GSSs, sometimes called group DSSs or electronic meeting systems, strive to take advantage of the power of a group to make better decisions than individuals acting alone. Managers spend a significant portion of their time in group activity (meetings, committees, conferences); in

fact, some researchers have estimated that middle managers spend 35 percent of their work week in meetings and that top managers spend 50 to 80 percent of their time in meetings. GSSs represent an attempt to make these group sessions more productive.

GroupSystems, developed at the University of Arizona (and now marketed by GroupSystems, formerly Ventana Corporation), is an excellent example of GSS software (Austin, Drakos, and Mann, 2006; GroupSystems Web site, 2007). GroupSystems customers include major corporations such as Agilent Technologies, IBM, Procter & Gamble, Southern California Edison, and Verizon, and government organizations such as the Environmental Protection Agency (EPA), the National Aeronautics and Space Administration (NASA), the U.S. Army, the U.S. Air Force, and the North Atlantic Treaty Organization (NATO). In a typical in-person implementation (see Figure 7.2), a computer-supported meeting room is set up containing a PC for each participant, all linked by a local area network (LAN). A large public screen facilitates common viewing of information when this is desired. GroupSystems, which is installed on each machine in the network, provides computerized support for idea generation, organizing ideas, prioritizing (such as voting), and policy development (such as stakeholder identification).

Each participant in a group session (for example, a brainstorming session) has the opportunity to provide input anonymously and simultaneously via the PC keyboard. This can encourage creative thinking because no one can be ridiculed for a "stupid idea." Each idea or

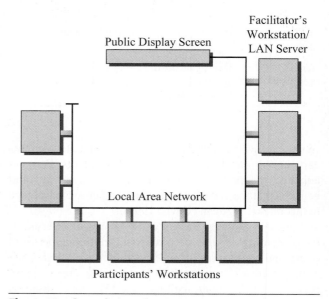

Figure 7.2   Group Support System Layout

comment is evaluated on its merits rather than by who offered it. Similarly, in a voting session the participants will not be swayed by how someone else votes. Thus, a GSS such as GroupSystems should generate more high-quality ideas as well as decisions that truly represent the group.

Recent work in the GSS area has moved beyond support of the traditional group session. The new focus is to support the work team in all its endeavors, whether the team is operating in a "same time, same place" traditional meeting or in a "different time, different place" mode—that is, as a **virtual team**. The client/server version of GroupSystems, called GroupSystems I MeetingRoom, provides rich support for a "same time, same place" traditional meeting, while GroupSystems II allows group members to use GroupSystems over the World Wide Web and/or an intranet via a standard Web browser, permitting group members to participate in the group session no matter where they are or when they are able to contribute. The newest version of GroupSystems is ThinkTank, which works seamlessly with the IBM Lotus Sametime platform to provide real-time collaboration and meeting support. Group sessions benefit from ThinkTank's presence awareness (knowing who is online), agenda management, anonymous contributions, multiple voting tools, and automatic documentation of the group's proceedings.

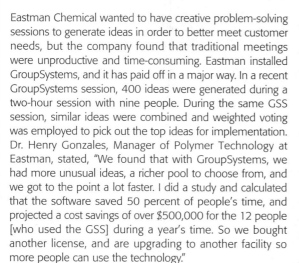

GSS WORKS FOR EASTMAN CHEMICAL, NOKIA TELECOMMUNICATIONS

Eastman Chemical wanted to have creative problem-solving sessions to generate ideas in order to better meet customer needs, but the company found that traditional meetings were unproductive and time-consuming. Eastman installed GroupSystems, and it has paid off in a major way. In a recent GroupSystems session, 400 ideas were generated during a two-hour session with nine people. During the same GSS session, similar ideas were combined and weighted voting was employed to pick out the top ideas for implementation. Dr. Henry Gonzales, Manager of Polymer Technology at Eastman, stated, "We found that with GroupSystems, we had more unusual ideas, a richer pool to choose from, and we got to the point a lot faster. I did a study and calculated that the software saved 50 percent of people's time, and projected a cost savings of over $500,000 for the 12 people [who used the GSS] during a year's time. So we bought another license, and are upgrading to another facility so more people can use the technology."

Finland-based Nokia, the world's second largest cellular telephone manufacturer, had developed an environmental policy with the objective of sustainable development in accordance with the International Chamber of Commerce charter. To implement this policy, the switching platforms research and development department decided that it was necessary to integrate environmental issues into the design process. To make this happen, idea-generating workshops using GroupSystems were held for the product design experts. As an example, the initial GroupSystems workshop generated 90 pages of ideas, voting results, and survey results, providing valuable feedback on both environmental and other aspects of product design.

The environmental ideas produced by the GSS sessions were carefully examined and rewritten as check lists, which in turn became the heart of Nokia's new "Design for Environment" system. The result was the integration of "Design for Environment" into the product design at key "influencing points" in the product life cycle process, such as writing requirements and specifications.

[Adapted from GroupSystems Web site, 2007]

GEOGRAPHIC INFORMATION SYSTEMS

Geographic information system (GIS), spatial decision support system (SDSS), location intelligence, geodemographics, computer mapping, and automated routing are names for a family of applications based on manipulation of relationships in space. Geographic technologies such as a GIS capture, store, manipulate, display, and analyze data spatially referenced to the Earth. As Figure 7.3 shows, a GIS—a generic term for any system that specializes in geographic data—features a rich user display and an interactive environment that is highly engaging to human decision makers.

Fields as diverse as natural resource management, public administration, NASA, the military, and urban planning have been using GISs for more than four decades. Scientists, planners, oil and gas explorers, foresters, soldiers, and mapmakers have matured this technology, developing sophisticated capabilities for creating, displaying, and manipulating geographic information. In the 1990s geographic technologies came to the attention of business users as the power of desktop computing merged with widespread access to geographic data. In the new century geographic technologies are moving into key business functions enabled by technologies such as radio frequency identification (RFID) tags, embedded Global Positioning System (GPS) capabilities, and spatial analysis features in mainstream database management systems (DBMSs). More important, many firms are learning that most business data have inherent

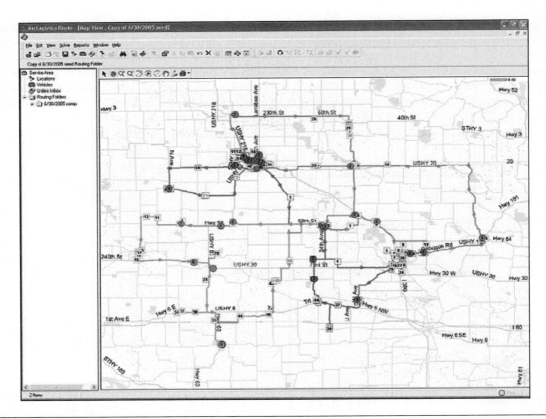

Figure 7.3 Apex Office Supply's GIS Displays Delivery Truck Routes and Stops (Data in this figure courtesy of Monkeytown Inc., formerly Apex Office Supply. The ArcLogistics Route graphical user interface is the intellectual property of ESRI and is used by permission. Copyright © 2007 ESRI.)

spatial meaning and they are taking steps to exploit this characteristic.

Business Adopts Geographic Technologies

Geographic technologies in business were a well-kept secret for many years; the earliest business adopters of GISs seldom talked about it because of its competitive value. Firms such as Arby's and McDonald's—whose ability to succeed depends on being in a better location than competitors—used GISs for site location to become among the first to recognize the business benefits of geographic technologies. Other applications include market analysis and planning, logistics and routing, real estate, environmental engineering, and the geographic pattern analysis that mortgage bankers use to show that they do not "redline" areas—that is, unfairly deny loans by location. Today, many sources provide high-quality geographically encoded data; few companies need to digitize their own maps or photographs.

Many functional areas in business are using spatial technologies to recognize and manage their geographic dependencies. Federated Department Stores, Inc. (Macy's and Bloomingdale's) provides an example: Beginning in the late 1990s, Federated used a GIS for simple map production and analysis. Dozens of proprietary, industry, and public data sources including internal sales information were underutilized because of the difficulty of linking them. The capabilities languished until a team of five analysts identified an integrated GIS as a key organizational tool. The resulting system came together just in time to support a major business initiative to find sites for a new type of small store in existing markets. Federated's GIS allowed comparison between potential and actual performance in hundreds of existing markets; mapping the data clearly showed untapped potential and supported market development (ESRI, 2003).

It is hard to find an industry or government agency that does not have spatial analysis needs. Health care, transportation, telecommunications, homeland security, law

SMALL IS BEAUTIFUL, SPATIALLY SPEAKING

Today, you don't have to be giant or global to use a GIS. Apex Office Supply, a small office supply company serving Waterloo and Cedar Rapids, Iowa, runs five delivery routes (each covering a 50-mile radius) and makes an average of 200 deliveries per day. Can geographic technologies keep Apex ahead of local and national competitors?

Apex chose ESRI's ArcLogistics Route software (see Figure 7.3). The software defines routes overnight for tomorrow's orders; in the morning, Apex's drivers load their trucks by delivery sequence. Provided with invoices, delivery directions, and timing, drivers are less likely to speed and total drive time has been reduced by about 7 percent.

"ArcLogistics Route has redefined how our business processes work," says Kurt Karr, the owner of Apex Office Supply. "We are more efficient than ever." Fuel use has decreased by 4 percent, labor hours are down nearly 20 percent, and the company retains its adaptability, high service level, and customer-centric focus.

[Adapted from ESRI, 2006]

enforcement, natural resources, utilities, real estate, banking, and media all need to locate people or assets, or both, in space and to predict their behavior. For example, the National Center for Health Statistics at the Centers for Disease Control and Prevention uses a GIS to improve policy making by mapping health concerns ranging from diseases to homicides (NCHS, 2004).

What's Behind Geographic Technologies

Two approaches to representing spatial data are widely used: the raster approach and the vector approach. Both types of data are commonly managed in a data model that stores related data in layers known as coverages or themes.

Raster-based GISs rely on dividing space into small, equal-sized cells arranged in a grid. In a GIS these cells (rasters) can take on a range of values and are aware of their location relative to other cells. Like pixels on a computer screen, the size of the cells relative to the features in the landscape determines the resolution of the data. Satellite imagery and other remote sensing applications exploit the ability of the raster approach to identify patterns across large areas. Although this approach offers continuous data, objects of interest must be inferred or extracted from the rasters, making the precision of the original data collection crucial.

Raster approaches have dominated applications in natural resources. Analysis of raster data using statistical techniques and mathematical models allows meteorologists to distinguish rain from snow, foresters to identify diseased areas within a forest, and farmers to more precisely apply herbicide to their fields. The Nature Conservancy compares handheld "ground truth" data collected with GPS devices to raster-based remote sensing data to aid in early detection and monitoring of invasive plants in the Hells Canyon region of Idaho and Oregon (Karl, 2007).

Vector-based GISs are widely used in public administration and utilities and, arguably, are the most common approach used in business. Vector systems associate features in the landscape with either a point, a line, or a polygon. Points are often used to represent small features such as ATMs, customer addresses, power poles, or items in motion, like trucks. Lines are for linear features such as roads and rivers and can be connected together to form routes and networks. Polygons represent areas and surfaces, including lakes, land parcels, and regions—such as sales territories, counties, and zip codes. The relationships between the vector elements are called their topology; topology determines whether features overlap or intersect. Vector systems can distinguish, for example, an island in a lake, two roads crossing, and customers within a 2-mile radius of a retail site. However, vector data are not continuous; the resulting overlaps and gaps between features affect presentation and analysis, and thus can require a specialist's attention.

The most common data model for both vector and raster data is the **coverage model** in which different layers or themes represent similar types of geographic features in the same area and are stacked on top of one another (see Figure 7.4). Like working with transparent map overlays, the layers allow different geographic data to be seen together, and they facilitate geographic manipulation and analysis.

Most GIS technologies today effectively combine both types of data, often using raster data sets for realism and vector data for roads, administrative boundaries, and locations. By employing both types of data, geographic analysis can answer questions such as the following:

- What is adjacent to this feature?
- Which site is the nearest one, or how many are within a certain distance?
- What is contained within this area, or how many are contained within this area?
- Which features does this element cross, or how many paths are available?
- What could be seen from this location?

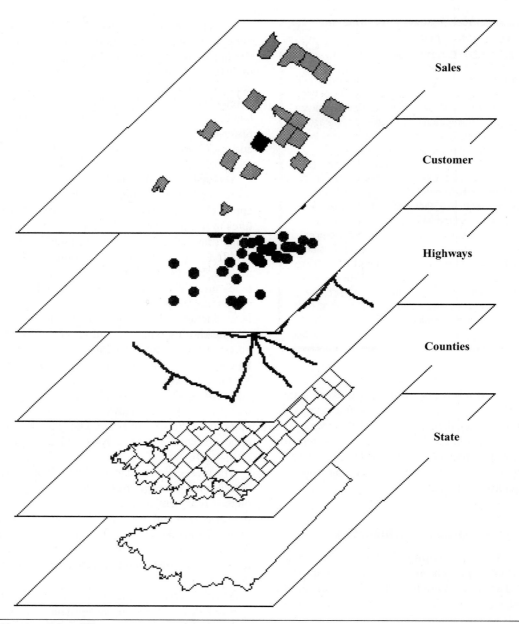

Figure 7.4 Map Layers in a GIS

If you have looked for your house on Google Earth, you have used the zoom feature as well as panning and centering your display based on a map overlay—these are basic capabilities of any GIS. Other basic capabilities include finding the distance between two points, searching for and labeling specific features, and turning symbols and layers on and off on demand. These functions underlie spatial manipulation such as intersection and union, the assignment of geographic references to addresses through geocoding, and standard query language support for interacting with descriptive (attribute) data. Once limited to high-end workstations, advanced GIS applications—now on the desktop or palmtop—automate sophisticated decision support tasks such as finding the shortest/fastest/safest route from A to B or grouping sales or service territories to minimize internal travel distance, equalize potential, or omit the fewest prospects.

Issues for Information Systems Organizations

Business applications of GISs are often initially introduced into a company to support a single function such as market research or field service. Experience shows us that GISs soon spread within and across groups. Thanks to the maturity of GIS tools, organizations can acquire off-the-shelf geographic technologies with scripting languages, application program interfaces with popular desktop software packages, and Internet-based interactive mapping packages (such as Microsoft's MapPoint Web Service). As the cost of GIS technologies has dropped and technical sophistication has risen, even computationally demanding functions such as route optimization and territory assignment are widely available (do your competitors already have these functions?).

Managing geographic technology options, now that they are available on familiar platforms, may be less challenging to a typical IS organization than managing spatial data. Obvious geographic data (which you will want to buy, not build) include base maps, zip code maps, street networks, and advertising media market maps. Other data with spatial elements are spread around in internal company databases, including customer locations, locations of company warehouses and distribution centers, and the location of fixed and movable assets. Recently, a new wrinkle in spatial data management has arisen: Handheld GPS devices now allow users to collect their own data and download it to a PC.

Because the value for a business in "going spatial" comes from bringing internal and external data together, IS personnel can expect to get an education in cost and quality issues for geographic data. For example, although geographic files for zip codes are often included at no additional cost in packaged desktop GIS software, the U.S. Postal Service updates zip codes on an ongoing basis, resulting in decay in the accuracy of existing data. For geodata coverage outside the United States, one can expect fewer choices in terms of available data, and the data that

---

INTELLIGENT LOCATIONS OR LOCATION INTELLIGENCE?

People are always someplace in space, whether at home, working, shopping, playing, or traveling. These days, they are likely to have a portable, wireless, location-aware, audio-visual device with them: their cell phone. And, if they are in Italy within a certain radius of a Dunkin' Donuts store, they might receive a discount coupon on their cell phone. And, a certain Dunkin' Donuts franchisee might see, oh, a 15 percent boost in sales (Reid, 2007). Or, they might be your 16-year-old, newly licensed, teenager driver speeding (?) home (AccuTracking, 2007). Or, they might be the crew on a multimillion-dollar racing sailboat in head-to-head competition for the coveted America's Cup. Or, they might be stranded mountain climbers, or a wandering dog, or a misplaced pallet in a warehouse. (These last two examples are not people with cell phones, but they still might have location-aware devices such as RFID chips.)

The application of spatial technologies to identifying where someone or something is in real time is called **location intelligence**. The technology most responsible for the shift in geographic technologies from being about maps to about location is the Global Positioning System (GPS).

GPS, created and operated by the U.S. Air Force, is a worldwide satellite-based system in which small receivers can determine longitude, latitude, and altitude. Fully operational in the 1990s, the 24 original satellites offered the U.S. military unprecedented accuracy in navigation and targeting anywhere in the world. An encrypted signal gave military personnel accuracy within 3 feet; the free public signal offered accuracy within 30 to 50 feet. The potential for GPS in nonmilitary applications, both public service (such as navigation and search and rescue) and commercial (such

as finding a discounted donut), quickly built up a multibillion-dollar market.

The importance of location for military, government, commercial, and personal pursuits is behind two new satellite initiatives: GPS III and Galileo. Not surprisingly, GPS III is a new and improved GPS funded by the U.S. government. More satellites in a different orbital pattern, carefully designed frequencies, and the addition of a "beam" antenna will enhance both military and commercial applications when GPS III is fully deployed sometime around 2013. Less dramatic is a pattern of regular upgrade and replacement of the existing satellite fleet (called GPS II), designed to maintain operational readiness and accuracy and improve the ability to locally disrupt the signal to hostile forces (while not impeding civilian use).

Galileo is the name for a satellite navigation system under development by the European Union and European Space Agency. Conceived as a primarily civilian alternative to the U.S.-military-controlled GPS, Galileo will provide higher accuracy and better signal coverage at latitudes closer to the poles. The core consortium members of Germany, France, Italy, and the United Kingdom have now been joined by China, Israel, Ukraine, India, Morocco, Saudi Arabia, and South Korea. Galileo will offer a free, lower-precision open service; a fee-based commercial service with higher accuracy; and an encrypted public service/safety-of-life signal for government use. As of spring 2007, one of the 30 planned satellites has been launched, with full deployment expected sometime in the 2014–2015 time frame.

[Adapted from AccuTracking, 2007; Reid, 2007; and Wikipedia, 2007a, 2007b, and 2007c]

are available are likely to be less accurate, more difficult to obtain, and more expensive.

Many people have been exposed to mapping technologies through household-name Internet sites such as Yahoo! Maps or Google Earth. The "GIS engines" behind these sites come from a less well-known pool of vendors including Environmental Systems Research Institute (ESRI), MapInfo, AutoCAD, Tactician, and Intergraph Corp. Ongoing developments in geographic technologies include:

- three-dimensional and dynamic modeling to simulate movement through time and space, such as reconstructing the path of Hurricane Katrina

- geography in your hand—the continued proliferation of spatial technologies such as GPS into handheld devices for consumer use in location-based services (see the box entitled "Intelligent Locations or Location Intelligence?")

- linking spatial capability with wireless capability for deployment and redeployment of the right assets—both human and nonhuman—to the right place, in real time, particularly for public safety or customer service

- forecasting models that include geography as a variable to predict, for example, the responses of consumers to a loyalty card program based on their proximity to other adopters and to billboard advertisements

- use of spatial technologies in a variety of new settings, such as taming out-of-control data warehouses and point-of-sale (POS) data, visualizing network security attacks, and identifying the country of origin of an Internet service provider (ISP) to be able to return a Web page customized for that country

EXECUTIVE INFORMATION SYSTEMS/BUSINESS INTELLIGENCE SYSTEMS

The key concept behind an **executive information system (EIS)** is that such a system delivers online current information about business conditions in an aggregate form easily accessible to senior executives and other managers. An EIS is designed to be used directly by these managers without the assistance of intermediaries. An EIS uses state-of-the-art graphics, communications, and data storage methods to provide the executive easy online access to current information about the status of the organization.

Dating only to the late 1980s in most cases, EISs represent the first real attempt to deliver relevant summary information to management in online form. Originally, EISs were developed for just the two or three top executive levels in the firm, but that caused many problems of data disparity between the layers of management. The most important internal data—dealing with suppliers, production, and customers—are generated under the control of lower-level managers, and they need to know what is being reported higher up in the organization. As a result, today the user base in most companies has been broadened to encompass all levels of management in the firm—and sometimes even managers in customer and supplier organizations. Largely because of this broadening of the user base, today the EIS label has often been replaced with the broader term **performance management (PM)** software.

EISs employ transaction data that have been filtered and summarized into a form useful for the executives in the organization. In addition, many successful EISs incorporate qualitative data such as competitive information, assessments, and insights. This emphasis on competitive information has become so important in the last few years that many organizations now call their EISs **business intelligence systems** or **competitive intelligence systems** (see the box entitled "Global Competitive Intelligence at Dow AgroSciences"). In summary, an EIS is a hands-on tool that focuses, filters, and organizes an executive's information so he or she can make more effective use of it.

Let us take Infor PM (formerly Extensity MPC) as an example of a software platform for developing a performance management/business intelligence system. Infor PM has its roots in an earlier product named Commander EIS, but it has now moved beyond a relatively simple EIS that summarizes data for top managers to a full-blown management planning and control system. Infor PM incorporates three core components, each in turn consisting of a number of modules. These modules may be deployed individually or as part of the full suite. The Business Process Applications component includes modules for strategic management, planning, budgeting, forecasting, financial consolidation, and financial reporting. The Business Specific Analytics component uses prebuilt analytic applications to present, in real time, decision-making information for specific industry and business functions. The third component, Infor Expense Management, includes modules for travel plans, expense reports, payment requests, and timesheets. The client for Infor PM is simply a Web browser.

Infor PM permits customization of a large number of easy-to-use and easy-to-interpret displays to present key information to managers; the software package allows

GLOBAL COMPETITIVE INTELLIGENCE AT DOW AGROSCIENCES

"Have you heard the latest about Monsanto? Can you believe the recent program Bayer launched? Rumors, news, and updates on competitors are everywhere. Yet how do we make sense of it all and stay focused on the information that really matters? Thanks to the newly launched Global Competitive Intelligence (GCI) Web site, all Dow AgroSciences employees can now efficiently learn competitive information while sharing what they hear in the marketplace." These lines begin an internal newsletter article that announced GCI to Dow AgroSciences employees in 1999.

In 1997, Dow AgroSciences management set an objective of establishing competitive intelligence as part of its company's culture. Eighteen months prior to this decision, two independent "skunk works" projects had yielded positive business results. The skunk works approaches were simple. One involved establishing HTML pages posted to a Web site on the company's intranet, where competitive information was posted and accessible by password. The other approach involved assigning an individual within each business unit as a competitive intelligence "focal point." Competitive information was fed to these focal points, who then distributed the information to all other focal points by e-mail, who in turn distributed information to sales and marketing personnel where appropriate.

Based on the business benefits realized from these early approaches, competitive intelligence was established as a global center of expertise within Dow AgroSciences. The result was the Global Competitive Intelligence (GCI) system. GCI is an intranet-based system that utilizes an Oracle database and is supported by a network of human resources (focal points) covering global operations. The intranet interface is simple to use yet is driven by a powerful database. The system is accessible to any Dow AgroSciences employee throughout the globe via the company's intranet. Currently, four levels of access have been built into the database. Level 1, which includes public information about the industry and competitors, is accessible to all employees who have access to the intranet. Competitive intelligence focal points and selected managers have access to additional information at Level 2, including public articles provided by a news service as well as reported competitive activities (rumors). Level 2 also includes detailed competitive profiles, updated annually. Level 3 is reserved for top management use, and Level 4 is for database administration.

The GCI system provides competitive observations and published news to permit employees to gain a clearer understanding of a competitor's strategy. Key competitive companies are profiled annually with the results of the analyses posted to dynamic pages within GCI. Information used in profiling companies includes corporate and divisional strategy assumptions, a history of business agreements, plant locations and research and development sites, product sales, financial assumptions, key personnel, and a SWOT analysis (see Chapter 14 for a discussion of SWOT analysis). Dow AgroSciences has integrated information from the GCI system into its business planning cycle and utilizes the analyses for licensing and acquisition activities. Through the use of the GCI system, the company has a designated network of people responsible for collecting, analyzing, and sharing competitive information with the entire organization on a global basis.

[Adapted from Fowler, 2000]

---

business users to view information in whatever way makes sense to them, including charts, dashboards, scorecards, gauges, spreadsheets, and even early warning alerts when results deviate from expected performance. In addition, it provides an intelligent "drill down" capability to identify relevant detailed information, multiple business perspectives (such as region or product), multiple scenarios for planning ("what if" analyses), and charting of cause/effect linkages among plan elements. Examples of Infor PM displays are shown in Figure 7.5.

Other EIS/PM products include Executive Dashboard from Qualitech Solutions, PilotWorks from Pilot Software, SAS/EIS, and SymphonyRPM from Symphony Metreo. Business intelligence platforms, which overlap considerably with EIS/PM products but sometimes have a broader focus (including, for instance, data mining) and sometimes a narrower focus (excluding performance management reporting features), include Business Objects XI, Cognos 8 Business Intelligence, Hyperion System 9 BI+ (Hyperion was acquired by Oracle in 2007), MicroStrategy 8 Intelligence Server, and SAS Enterprise Intelligence Platform.

Perhaps the earliest EIS described in print is the management information and decision support (MIDS) system at the Lockheed-Georgia Company (Houdeshel and Watson, 1987). The sponsor for MIDS was the Lockheed-Georgia President, and a special staff reporting to the Vice President of Finance developed the system. An evolutionary approach was used in developing MIDS, with only a limited number of displays developed initially for a limited number of executives. For example, a display might show prospective customers for a particular type of aircraft or might graphically depict both forecast and actual sales over the past year.

Over time, more displays were developed and more executives were added to the system. The initial version of MIDS in 1979 had only 31 displays developed for fewer than a dozen senior executives. By 1985, 710 displays had been developed, 30 senior executives and 40 operating managers were using the system, and the mean number of

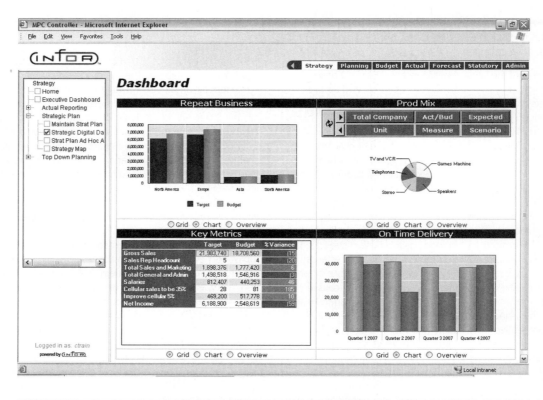

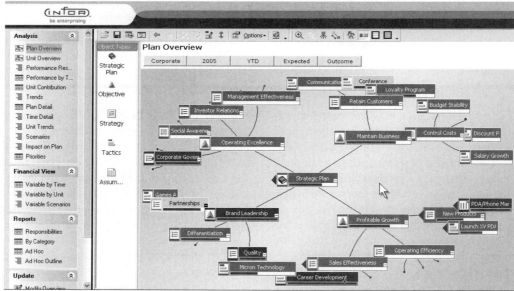

Figure 7.5 Example Infor PM Displays (Courtesy of Infor. Copyright © 2007 Infor Global Solutions.)

displays viewed per user per day was up to 5.5. Many factors had to come together for MIDS to be successful, but perhaps the most important was that the system delivered the information (based on quantitative and qualitative data) that senior executives needed for them and their company to be successful.

More recently, EISs have been created and used successfully in many other large companies such as Phillips

Petroleum, Dun & Bradstreet Software, Coca-Cola Company, Fisher-Price, Conoco, Inc., and CIGNA Corporation. The following paragraphs focus on three other companies that have recently installed EISs or PM systems.

Based in Calgary, Alberta, Petro-Canada is a leader in the Canadian petroleum industry. Petro-Canada's oil and gas division used Comshare Decision (now incorporated in Infor PM) to create an integrated information system with easier, more consistent, and timely access to information for business decision-making processes—an EIS. Petro-Canada calls the new system "The Dashboard Project," which means having the key performance measures and analytical data available for view on a dashboard so that managers can look forward through the "windshield of opportunity." By using Comshare Decision's integrated solution for analysis and performance measurement, all levels of decision makers have access to the same numbers and views and have confidence that the data are current, correct, and verifiable. The new system provides a single user interface for all required information in an intuitive, flexible manner, including executive views, graphs, charts, drill-down capabilities, alarms, and alerts. Furthermore, the data visualization capabilities permit decision makers to have the data presented in the way that makes most sense for them (*DM Review*, 2000).

Santa Clara Valley Health & Hospital System has implemented Extensity MPC (now Infor PM) to provide more depth and breadth in the budgeting and reporting processes. "We liked Extensity's scalability, analytic capabilities, and the fact that the system was Web-based," said Curtis Odle, MPC System Administrator. The system is used for detailed headcount planning as well as for reporting of budgets and expenses. The financial reporting data are consolidated by MPC and made available online. "Our managers are able to be much more productive and make better decisions now," according to Odle. "They see changes instantly and daily. They can see the bottom line on new proposals before submitting the budget, and can adjust on the fly based on the results. We feel we have a much better handle on interpreting information now." Odle added that "The best part is that [the data are] interactive and customizable. Users can define personal views, surfacing the information they need to do their jobs. We have general ledger drill-through, meaning details are instantly available. Now we have the tool we need to manage our resources in the most effective way possible" (Extensity Web site, 2007).

Universal Studios Hollywood (USH) has used Extensity MPC to achieve deep integration between finance and operations. Using data from an existing data warehousing system that tracks ticketing information and a new ERP system that provides financial performance data (see

BUSINESS INTELLIGENCE MOVES TO MARKETING

BI [business intelligence] has begun moving beyond the desks of financial analysts and other specialists to sales, marketing, and customer service professionals. About 50 marketing people at StubHub, the online marketplace for events tickets that eBay bought in January for $310 million, create their own Business Objects reports to make decisions about where to target promotions and online advertising. They can analyze customer buying patterns and demographic data to determine when purchases for a particular event are likely to peak so they know the right time to advertise, for example.

StubHub marketers don't have unfettered access to the BI. Using a drag-and-drop function, they create reports based on analysis already churned out by trained specialists. "My team does the real intricate analysis work," says Rob Singer, StubHub's Director of BI. "What we didn't want is people generating reports from scratch that could be wrong or misleading."

[Weier, 2007]

Chapter 6 for more on data warehousing and ERP systems), USH has built a real-time key-performance-indicator (KPI) reporting system. The system is also used to build daily and monthly budgets and to conduct scenario modeling for USH's 200 venues across seven businesses. USH has built KPI dashboards that link directly to monthly and quarterly analyses, show dynamic month-to-date and year-to-date calculations, and provide standard reporting templates. The budgeting process has also been streamlined through the use of MPC. "We've cut down our budgeting cycle time on a budgeting go-forward basis by about 50 percent," said Don Aptor, Director of Finance at NBC Universal, the parent company of USH. "But more importantly, Extensity's performance-based tools are enabling finance to create value, and that's really what it's all about" (Extensity Web site, 2007).

KNOWLEDGE MANAGEMENT SYSTEMS

Knowledge management systems (KMSs) are systems that enable individuals and organizations to enhance learning, improve performance, and, hopefully, produce long-term sustainable competitive advantage. Simply stated, a

KMS is a system for managing organizational knowledge. A KMS may be designed to support "communities of practice" focusing on different key knowledge areas; in this case, the KMS enables connections from people to people (e.g., expert directories), people to knowledge (e.g., knowledge repositories), and people to tools (e.g., community calendars, discussion forums). On the other hand, a KMS may consist of elaborate structuring of knowledge content (e.g., taxonomies), carefully packaged and disseminated to people. Hence, KMSs provide organizations the ability to leverage and extract value from their intellectual or knowledge assets.

KMSs use various hardware and software applications to facilitate and support **knowledge management (KM)** activities. What then is KM? KM is a set of management practices that is practical and action-oriented. In other words, KM involves the strategies and processes of identifying, creating, capturing, organizing, transferring, and leveraging knowledge to help individuals and firms compete (O'Dell and Grayson, 1998). KM is concerned with behavior changes to reflect new knowledge and insights. KM is not about relying on technology to improve processes; rather, KM relies on recognizing the knowledge held by individuals and the firm. Therefore, a KMS is the technology or vehicle that facilitates the sharing and transferring of knowledge for the purpose of disseminating and reusing valuable knowledge that, once applied, enhances learning and improves performance.

Why has KM received so much attention recently, and why are so many projects labeled KM projects? There are two explanations. First, one trigger leading to the development of KM projects is related to firm valuation. For example, Microsoft's net value was estimated by examining its market value based on stock prices minus net assets. The enormous difference was attributed to the knowledge held by individuals and the organization (e.g., routines, best practices). In a similar time frame, "knowledge assets" began to appear on a few firms' balance sheets in their annual reports. Hence, there is a growing awareness and consensus that "knowledge," or intellectual capital, will enable firms to differentiate themselves from others and to compete effectively in the marketplace, and this has led to a proliferation of KMSs for managing knowledge assets.

Second, tangible benefits accrue from implementing KM and KMS initiatives. Although the benefits are specific to a given firm, there are both *operational improvements* and *market improvements*. Operational improvements focus on internal activities and include cost savings (e.g., faster and better dissemination of knowledge), efficient processes (e.g., best practices), change management processes (e.g., behavior changes), and knowledge reuse (e.g., high quality

standards). In contrast, market improvements focus on external activities such as performance (e.g., increased sales), cost savings (e.g., lower costs of products and services), and customer satisfaction.

The goal of a KMS is to tap into the knowledge of the individual and the organization and disseminate it throughout the firm to derive operational and market improvements. Furthermore, a KMS is different from other systems because it considers the content contained within the system—that is, the system is only as good as what is in it! Based on a study of more than two dozen successful KMSs recently implemented in various firms, there are three KMS characteristics that need to be considered in describing a KMS: First, the extent to which there is formal management and control of the KMS; second, the focus of the KM processes, such as knowledge creation, capture, organization and packaging, access, search and dissemination, and application; and third, the extent to which reusability of knowledge is considered (e.g., the 80-20 rule, or 20 percent of the knowledge content that potentially could be contained in a KMS is likely to be of most value to 80 percent of the users) (Dennis and Vessey, 2005).

A KMS might have very little formal management and control, as in the case of "communities of practice" (COPs). Designed for individuals with similar interests, a COP KMS provides a vehicle to allow members of such a community to exchange ideas, tips, and other knowledge that might be valuable to the members of the community. There is no formal management or control of such a KMS; rather, the members are responsible for validating and structuring their knowledge for use within the KMS. Each member of the COP is responsible for the knowledge content, with a great likelihood that such knowledge will be applicable to only a few members. In other words, there is very little, if any, organizing and packaging of knowledge, making the search and applicability even more difficult. Hopefully, there will be occasions where a single item of knowledge content will be important to many members of the COP, although these occasions might be few in number.

In contrast, a KMS might have extensive formal management and control. There might be a KM team to oversee the process of validating the knowledge prior to dissemination. Such a team provides structure, organization, and packaging for how knowledge is to be presented to the users. These dedicated resources ensure that knowledge content entered into the KMS has been thoroughly examined and that it will meet the 80-20 rule.

This discussion does not imply that a KMS must be characterized as binary—that is, having either little or extensive formal management and control, knowledge processing, or knowledge reusability. Rather, there is a spectrum of KMSs that are designed to meet the specific needs of a given firm. In the case of a COP KMS, it is not clear whether the focus is either operational or market improvements. On the other hand, the KM team approach attempts to accomplish both operational and market improvements. Although KMSs are still growing with much room for advancement, many firms observe their KMS evolving from one form to another as they learn from their experience and as their strategic needs and resources change. Such evolution suggests that firms are enjoying the benefits accrued from tapping into their employees' and organizational knowledge. Moreover, they find a strategic need to continue their efforts to unveil the hidden treasures within and outside their organizational boundaries.

Two Recent KMS Initiatives Within a Pharmaceutical Firm

Corporate KMS A KM team was formed to develop an organization-wide KMS serving multiple communities of practice. The operation of a community of practice involves a combination of software and processes. Each community has a designated coordinator whose job is to ensure that the community thrives (some communities have two or three coordinators). The coordinators are volunteers and receive no extra compensation; however, they do tend to become highly visible members of their communities. The coordinator performs many specific functions such as welcoming new members, developing and maintaining standards of conduct and standards for knowledge within the community, maintaining the community calendar, monitoring the discussion forums, ensuring that the knowledge in the community is appropriate, and serving as the primary point of contact and external ambassador for the community.

The portal software used to support the communities of practice provides approximately 150 tools of which only a handful are regularly used. The three most commonly used tools are the discussion forum, tips, and calendar. As the name suggests, the discussion forum is a tool that enables question-and-answer discussions among members of the community. Any member of the community can pose a question or a request in the discussion forum; likewise, all members can respond to the items posted in the discussion. Each discussion item in the forum is typically started as its own thread and there are often two or three active discussion threads, depending on the community's size. The community's coordinator typically reviews the items in the discussion forum and archives older discussions. Sometimes the coordinator will decide that a particular item is useful and relevant over the long term and should be moved to the tips area. In that case the coordinator or the contributors to the discussion will prepare a more formal version to be stored in the tips area.

The tips tool enables any member of the community to write a short entry that documents some best practice advice that the contributor believes might be of interest to the community as a whole. The full text of all tips is searchable, so the members of the community can find tips of interest.

The coordinator maintains the community calendar. Members of the community typically e-mail the coordinator with suggested calendar items, which the coordinator posts. Typical calendar items include face-to-face meetings held by part or all of the community, seminars and workshops offered by members of the community, and more formal presentations likely to be of interest to the community.

Field Sales KMS A different KM team was formed to lead the development of the field sales KMS. Unlike the corporate KMS, this KMS team's mission was to design and build *both* the content and the structure of the KMS. Therefore, a knowledge taxonomy was developed so that knowledge about each of the drugs sold by the firm was organized separately. Sales representatives would have access to knowledge only about the drugs they sold.

Sales operations and brand management would develop initial drafts of the knowledge content, which they would provide to the KM team. The KM team would format the documents and put them in the proper locations in the KMS according to the taxonomy. The system was designed to be the primary knowledge repository used by the field sales representatives and the sales managers. In addition, all knowledge communication with the field sales representatives was expected to be conducted through the field sales KMS. Instead of mailing paper marketing materials and advisories, for example, managers would now create them in Word and PowerPoint and post them into the field sales KMS.

The KM team also realized that it was important to enable the field sales representatives themselves to contribute sales tips and practical advice for use by other sales representatives. However, because of strict government regulatory control over communication with the physicians, all such tips needed first to be approved by the firm's legal department. A formal four-step process was therefore developed for validating all content sent in from the field sales representatives. Tips were first vetted by the KM team itself to make sure the content was coherent and complete. Next, the tip was submitted to the legal group to ensure that the content was consistent with all rules, regulations, and good promotional practice guidelines. Then the tip was sent to the brand management team to ensure that it was consistent with the marketing strategy for the drug. Last, the tip was sent to the sales operations group for peer review by a panel of five sales representatives to ensure that the contribution had real value. Finally, once the tip had been approved, it was entered into the field sales KMS. Although this sounds like a lengthy process, most tips were processed within two weeks of receipt. Field sales representatives were rewarded by receiving sales points for each tip that was ultimately accepted (these points were part of the usual commission structure received by all sales representatives; the points received for each tip were equivalent to approximately $60).

Although there were several iterations of user interfaces to best align with changing taxonomies, the knowledge structure for the current system was designed in what the team called a "T-structure," which had two distinct parts. Across the top of the "T" (and presented horizontally near the top of the Lotus Notes screen) was the general sales knowledge designed to be pertinent to all sales divisions. This contained knowledge on topics such as rules and guidelines for sales promotions, templates for sales processes, forms for sales functions, and directories with phone numbers of key experts within the U.S. business unit. Down the middle of the "T" (and presented vertically near the left edge of the Lotus Notes screen) was the division-specific knowledge, which typically pertained to drugs sold by that division. This contained information such as fundamental sales information on the drugs sold by the sales representatives, competitive analyses, results in recent drug trials, and letters from expert physicians. Tips and best practices submitted by the field sales representatives would either fit across the top or down the side of the screen depending on whether they focused on general sales knowledge or on product-specific knowledge.

KMS Success

What does it take for a KMS to be a success? One stream of research suggests that both the supply (i.e., knowledge contribution) and the demand (i.e., knowledge reuse) sides of KM must be considered simultaneously. In other words, organizational support factors on the supply side—involving leadership commitment, manager and peer support for KM initiatives, and knowledge quality control—and on the demand side—involving incentives and reward systems, relevance of knowledge, ease of using the KMS, and satisfaction with the use of the KMS—are as important as the KMS itself, and that these factors must be managed carefully and concurrently (Kulkarni, Ravindran, and Freeze, 2006–2007). Another stream of research suggests the importance of social capital in determining whether benefits can be realized. KMS

success occurs when individuals are motivated to participate in the KM initiative, when individuals have the cognitive capability to understand and apply the knowledge, and when individuals have strong relationships with one another (Wasko and Faraj, 2005). Collectively, these "people" factors facilitate the success of a KMS.

ARTIFICIAL INTELLIGENCE

The idea of **artificial intelligence (AI)**, the study of how to make computers do things that are currently done better by people, is about 50 years old, but only in the last 25 years have computers become powerful enough to make AI applications commercially attractive. AI research has evolved into six separate but related areas; these are natural languages, robotics, perceptive systems (vision and hearing), genetic programming (also called evolutionary design), expert systems, and neural networks.

The work in **natural languages**, primarily in computer science departments in universities and in vendor laboratories, is aimed at producing systems that translate ordinary human instructions into a language that computers can understand and execute. Robotics was considered in the previous chapter. **Perceptive systems** research involves creating machines possessing a visual and/or aural perceptual ability that affects their physical behavior. In other words, this research is aimed at creating robots that can "see" or "hear" and react to what they see or hear. With **genetic programming** or **evolutionary design**, the problem is divided into multiple segments, and solutions to these segments are linked together in different ways to breed new "child" solutions. After many generations of breeding, genetic programming might produce results superior to anything devised by a human. Genetic programming has been most useful in the design of innovative products such as an energy-efficient halogen light bulb that is much brighter than a standard halogen light bulb and a satellite support arm with a novel shape that prevents vibrations from being transmitted along the truss.

The final two branches of AI are the ones most relevant for managerial support. The **expert systems** branch is concerned with building systems that incorporate the decision-making logic of a human expert. A newer branch of AI is **neural networks**, which is named after the study of how the human nervous system works, but which in fact uses statistical analysis to recognize patterns from vast amounts of information by a process of adaptive learning. Both of these branches of AI are described in more detail in the following sections.

EXPERT SYSTEMS

How does one capture the logic of an expert in a computer system? To design an expert system, a specialist known as a knowledge engineer (a specially trained systems analyst) works very closely with one or more experts in the area under study. Knowledge engineers try to learn everything they can about the way in which the expert makes decisions. If one is trying to build an expert system for estate planning, for example, the knowledge engineer works with experienced estate planners to see how they do their job. What the knowledge engineer has learned is then loaded into the computer system, in a specialized format, in a module called the knowledge base (see Figure 7.6). This knowledge base contains both the inference rules that are followed in decision making and the parameters, or facts, relevant to the decision.

The other major pieces of an expert system are the inference engine and the user interface. The inference engine is a logical framework that automatically executes a line of reasoning when supplied with the inference rules and parameters involved in the decision; thus, the same inference engine can be used for many different expert systems, each with a different knowledge base. The user interface is the module used by the end user—for example, an inexperienced estate planner. Ideally, the interface is very user-friendly. The other modules include an explanation subsystem to explain the reasoning that the system followed in arriving at a decision, a knowledge acquisition subsystem to assist the knowledge engineer in recording inference rules and parameters in the knowledge base, and a workspace for the computer to use as the decision is being made.

Obtaining an Expert System

Is it necessary to build all these pieces each time your organization wants to develop and use an expert system? Absolutely not. There are three general approaches to obtaining an expert system, and only one of them requires construction of all these pieces. First, an organization can buy a fully developed system that has been created for a specific application. For example, in the late 1980s, Syntelligence, Inc., developed an expert system called Lending Advisor to assist in making commercial lending decisions for banks and other financial institutions. Lending Advisor incorporated the many factors involved in approving or rejecting a commercial loan, and it was installed in several banks. In general, however, the circumstances leading to the desire for an expert system are unique to the organization, and in most cases this "off-the-shelf" expert system option is not viable.

Second, an organization can develop an expert system itself using an **artificial intelligence shell** (also called an **expert systems shell**). The shell, which can be purchased from a software company, provides the basic framework illustrated in Figure 7.6 and a limited but user-friendly special language with which to develop the expert system. With the basic expert system functions already in place in the shell, the system builder can concentrate on the details of the business decision being modeled and the development of the knowledge base. Third, an organization can have internal or external knowledge engineers custom-build the expert system. In this case the system is usually programmed in a special-purpose language such as Prolog or Lisp. This final approach is clearly the most expensive, and it can be justified only if the potential payoff from the expert system is quite high and no other way is possible.

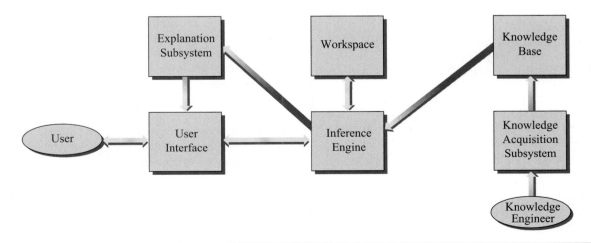

Figure 7.6 Architecture of an Expert System

Examples of Expert Systems

Perhaps the classic example of an expert system is MYCIN, which was developed at Stanford University in the mid-1970s to diagnose and prescribe treatment for meningitis and blood diseases. General Electric Co. created an expert system called CATS-1 to diagnose mechanical problems in diesel locomotives, and AT&T developed ACE to locate faults in telephone cables. Schlumberger, Ltd., an international oil company, developed an expert system named Dipmeter to give advice when a drill bit gets stuck while drilling a well. These examples and others are concerned with diagnosing problem situations and prescribing appropriate actions, because experts are not always present when a problem occurs.

Diagnosis of a different sort is accomplished by an expert system at the American Stock Exchange that has been built to help detect insider trading on the exchange. This expert system, named Market Surveillance, is designed to support analysts in making recommendations on whether to open an investigation of suspected insider trading. The relevant database of stock price activity is entered into the expert system, and the analyst responds to a series of questions from the system. The output consists of two scores—the first is the probability that an investigation should be opened and the second is the probability that an investigation should not be opened (Exsys Inc., 2007).

EXPERT SYSTEMS GO MOBILE

Traditionally expert systems have been run on a PC or a server (often via a Web interface), but that is changing. Software vendor Exsys Inc. now makes its Corvid expert systems software available to run on Hewlett-Packard's iPaq Pocket PCs as well as about 40 other handheld models. This expert systems mobility could be especially useful to sales representatives, field technicians, and repair workers—and anyone else who works outside of an office environment.

As an example, Exsys CEO Dustin Huntington indicates that the National Park Service (NPS) is considering the use of the handheld version of Corvid to evaluate areas in the parks that have experienced environmental damage. By using a mobile expert system, NPS could hire people with a limited environmental background to go to a site and evaluate the situation as if they were environmental experts. The expert system, in the form of a questionnaire, would guide the employees through the evaluation process, prompting them to seek specific new information based on the response to the last question they entered. "By having that knowledge there," Huntington says, "they're able to put the logic of the decision maker out there in the field."

[Adapted from Chabrow, 2006]

Earlier we mentioned that expert systems were used to assist in making commercial lending decisions as early as the 1980s. Today, over one-third of the top 100 commercial banks in the United States and Canada use FAST (Financial Analysis Support Techniques) software for credit analysis. The FAST expert system gives a credit analyst access to the expertise of more experienced analysts, speeding up the training process and increasing productivity. FAST also provides a complete range of traditional analytical reports on both a historical and a pro forma basis (Exsys Inc., 2007).

Expert systems often serve in an advisory role to decision makers of all kinds. For example, the IDP (individual development plan) Goal Advisor is an expert system that assists a supervisor and an employee in setting short-range and long-range employee career goals and the developmental objectives to reach these goals. Nestlé Foods has developed an expert system to provide information to employees on their pension fund status. Using the expert system, an employee can conduct a private "interview" with a pension fund expert and ask what-if questions about benefits. The expert system enables the employee to make more knowledgeable personal financial planning decisions without requiring extensive personnel department consultation. EXNUT is an expert system developed by the National Peanut Research Laboratory and the U.S. Department of Agriculture to help peanut farmers manage irrigated peanut production. Based on extensive data collected from individual peanut fields throughout the growing season, EXNUT makes recommendations for irrigation, fungicide treatment, and pest management. The results are quite positive: The fields managed by EXNUT have consistently produced higher yields and high-quality peanuts using less water and less fungicide than those managed without the expert system (Exsys Inc., 2007).

Scheduling is another important area for expert systems. Expert systems currently in use include a truck routing and scheduling system that determines the sequence of stops on a route to provide the best service and a factory design system that organizes machines and operators to provide an efficient flow of materials through the factory and use the resources efficiently. As another example, General Motors created the Expert Scheduling System (ESS) to generate viable manufacturing schedules. ESS incorporates heuristics that had been developed by an experienced factory scheduler into the system, and it also links directly into GM's computer-integrated manufacturing (CIM) environment so that real-time plant information is used to generate the plant floor schedules.

Some expert systems specialize in sifting through massive sets of rules or other data. For example, expert system

EXPERT SYSTEMS PAYING OFF FOR SOME FIRMS

Twenty years ago, some commentators felt that expert systems would revolutionize business operations. That hasn't happened, and you don't read or hear much about expert systems today. Nevertheless, expert systems are important tools in many organizations. Can expert systems help your enterprise run more effectively and efficiently?

In the early days of expert systems, "there was too much technobabble that wasn't backed up by actual business cases," according to Mike Will, Director of Research and Development for Picodoc Corp. Picodoc's product, PicoXpert, is used to create relatively small expert systems that have no more than 500 rules and run on the Palm handheld platform.

Automated network-based expert systems are more complex than the small-scale PicoXpert systems. These systems are often built into other products, such as the network protocol analysis and monitoring software developed by Network Instruments. According to Network Instruments President Douglas Smith, the software identifies a specific event such as a delay in data transmission and then the expert system component kicks in. Smith explained that the system examines all the streams of data. "It can determine, say, whether the delay is network-based or just that somebody left to go to the bathroom. It saves IT shops a lot of time."

Among the most complex expert systems are mainframe-based systems developed by organizations such as airlines and shipping companies in order to efficiently deploy equipment and crews. To make a profit, these organizations must allocate their aircraft, crews, and other equipment efficiently, and it would be exorbitantly expensive for them to hire enough people to perform such ongoing analyses. Instead, expert systems are widely used for these deployment decisions.

The bottom line, according to Will, is that expert systems can make many companies operate more efficiently, but they need to be ready to invest a lot of time and money developing and tweaking the systems.

[Adapted from Haskin, 2003]

online advisors have been created for more than a dozen complex areas of Occupational Safety and Health Administration (OSHA) regulations. One of these online advisors is the Asbestos Advisor, which is available for free download by building owners, managers, and contractors maintaining properties potentially contaminated with asbestos. Based on the user's input, the system provides guidance on how asbestos standards might apply to buildings. In the first year it was placed on the Internet, nearly 80,000

businesses used the Asbestos Advisor. Another example is the Case Worker Advisor, which has been developed to support the Navajo Nation's Tribal Temporary Assistance for Needy Families (TANF) welfare program. This expert system captures the expertise of case workers in making decisions about benefits to Navajo clients. The Case Worker Advisor incorporates the cultural aspects and philosophy of the Navajo case workers, streamlines the previous assessment methods, and assists less experienced case workers. "In programming the knowledge automation system we accounted for our unique cultural heritage, while following complex federal, state, and tribal guidelines," according to Alex Yassa, the Navajo Nation's TANF Project Director (Exsys Inc., 2007).

NEURAL NETWORKS

Whereas expert systems try to capture the expertise of humans in a computer program, neural networks attempt to tease out meaningful patterns from vast amounts of data. Neural networks can recognize patterns too obscure for humans to detect, and they adapt as new information is received.

The key characteristic of neural networks is that they *learn*. The neural network program is originally given a set of data consisting of many variables associated with a large number of cases, or events, in which the outcomes are known. The program analyzes the data, works out all the correlations, and then selects a set of variables that are strongly correlated with particular known outcomes as the initial pattern. This initial pattern is used to try to predict the outcomes of the various cases, and these predicted results are compared to the known results. Based on this comparison, the program changes the pattern by adjusting the weights given to the variables or by changing the variables. The neural network program then repeats this process over and over, continuously adjusting the pattern in an attempt to improve its predictive ability. When no further improvement is possible from this iterative approach, the program is ready to make predictions for future cases.

This is not the end of the story. As more cases become available, these data are also fed into the neural network and the pattern is once again adjusted. The neural network learns more about cause-and-effect patterns from this additional data, and its predictive ability usually improves accordingly.

Commercial neural network programs (actually, these are shells) are available for a reasonable price, but the difficult part of building a neural network application is data collection and data maintenance. Still, a growing number

Table 7.2   Uses of Neural Networks

Categorization	Prediction/Forecasting
Credit rating and risk assessment	Share price forecast
Insurance risk evaluation	Commodity price forecast
Fraud detection	Economic indicator predictions
Insider trading detection	Process control
Direct mail profiling	Weather prediction
Machinery defect diagnosis	Future drug performance
Character recognition	Production requirements
Medical diagnosis	
Bacteria identification	

of applications are being deployed. Neural networks are typically used either to predict or categorize, but to do so in an inductive manner rather than deductively. Table 7.2 lists examples of current uses of neural networks.

Let us consider some neural network examples. Bank of America uses a neural network to evaluate commercial loan applications. American Express uses a neural system to read handwriting on credit card slips. The state of Wyoming uses a neural system to read hand-printed numbers on tax forms. Oil giants such as Arco are using neural networks to help pinpoint oil and gas deposits below the Earth's surface. Mellon Bank installed a neural network credit card fraud detection system. When a credit card is swiped through the card reader in a store, the transaction is sent to Mellon's neural system. By analyzing the type of transaction, the amount spent, the time of day, and other data, the neural network makes a fraud prediction in a few seconds and either approves or denies the transaction or feeds the predictive score to a human analyst who makes the final decision. Spiegel Brands, Inc., which depends on catalogs to generate sales for its mail-order business, uses a neural network as a way of pruning its mailing list to eliminate those who are unlikely to order from Spiegel again.

Neural networks are also being used in investment and trading applications. In some cases major companies are using neural networks to manage their pension fund portfolios. Another application detects common characteristics among stocks to determine whether a stock is on the verge of a breakout. Neural networks have been used to predict the next day's closing prices of stocks and to group mutual funds based on performance measures. In a business setting, neural networks have predicted the probability of bankruptcy to help banks make lending decisions and have

also predicted the total contingency cost on a construction project. In one especially interesting application, a neural network was designed to predict the expected revenue range of a movie prior to its theatrical release—and the neural network resulted in a much better prediction than other statistical methods currently employed (NeuroDimension, 2007).

Another use of neural networks is in targeted marketing, where marketing campaigns are targeted to potential customers who have the same attributes that resulted in sales for previous campaigns. Neural networks are also being used to improve security. A security system has been developed that uses neural technology to recognize a person's face to grant that person access to a secured area. A computer network intrusion protection system, based on a neural network, conducts a real-time assessment of each visitor to a network, and if it notes behavior that indicates an attempted security breach, automatically terminates the intruder's access (Orzech, 2002).

At Anderson Memorial Hospital in South Carolina, neural networks embedded in a hospital information and patient prediction system have improved the quality of care, reduced the death rate, and saved millions of dollars in resources. Using California Scientific's BrainMaker software, a separate neural network has been trained (developed) for each of 473 primary diagnoses to enable the hospital to classify and predict the severity of illness and the use of hospital resources so that quality and cost issues can be addressed fairly. A neural network has also been used to predict the mode of discharge—from routine discharge through death—for each diagnosis. Based on the resulting predictions, expenses at the hospital have been reduced by fewer unnecessary tests and procedures, lowered lengths of stays, and other procedural changes. For a given diagnosis, about 400 to 1,000 cases were used for training the neural network, with length of stay in the hospital as the primary variable to be predicted based on 26 input variables such as the number of body systems involved (e.g., cardiac and respiratory), number of complications, smoker or not, diabetic or not, age, sex, race, marital status, and number of previous admissions (California Scientific Software, 2007).

In the late 1980s and 1990s, expert system and neural network applications received a great deal of hype in the popular press. The AI applications were supposedly going to solve many of the decision problems faced by managers. Today, industry has adopted a more realistic view of AI applications: AI is not a panacea, but there are a significant number of potentially valuable applications for AI techniques. Each potential application must be carefully evaluated. The result of these careful evaluations has been a steady growth, but not an explosion, in the development and use of expert

LOAN STAR

Household Financial Corporation is a $10 billion consumer finance business with headquarters in Prospect Heights, Illinois, and 1,400 branch offices in 46 states. In the late 1990s, Household developed an object-oriented software system named Vision to integrate all phases of the consumer lending process; Vision also connects to an intelligent underwriting system that returns lending decisions in minutes rather than hours or days. Built into the Vision system are neural network components that help Household make smarter decisions about its customers.

For instance, say a credit card holder calls, irate about a late fee. He's not a profitable customer for the company; he carries a single card with little or no balance and has spurned Household offers for credit insurance products and equity loans. Why should the Household service rep cancel the late fee? Vision knows why. The system "takes into consideration the potential lifetime value of the customer," says Ken Harvey, now Household's Chief Information Officer.

Turns out this customer took out a school loan six years ago and a small auto finance deal for a used car three years ago from another company. His modest income has gone up significantly two years running. Considering these variables, Vision can recognize this late fee as a first offense by a recent college graduate who handles his finances well and may be in the market for significant new loans in the next year. Vision authorizes the service rep to waive the fee. Then the system can prompt the rep with suggestive selling for this now-happy customer—does he know that Household can pay off that old car loan and offer attractive terms on a loan for a newer vehicle?

Taken in sum, the system ties the company more closely to existing and prospective customers. Loan approvals are faster, sales proposals more targeted, and customer service more responsive. Cutting out the waiting game and creating more desirable products helps Household forge a customer intimacy that ultimately translates to profits, which in today's stock-market-driven environment is the ultimate in enterprise value.

[Slater, 2000]

systems and neural networks to help businesses cope with problem situations and make better and more consistent decisions.

VIRTUAL REALITY

Virtual reality is a fascinating application area with rapidly growing importance. **Virtual reality (VR)** refers to the use of computer-based systems to create an environment that seems real to one or more senses (usually including sight) of the human user or users. The ultimate example of VR is the holodeck aboard the *U.S.S. Enterprise* on *Star Trek: The Next Generation*, where Data can be Sherlock Holmes in a realistic setting with realistic characters and where Jean-Luc Picard can play the role of a hard-boiled private eye in the early twentieth century.

VR exists today, but with nowhere near the reality of the *Enterprise*'s holodeck. You might have played a video game where you don a head-mounted computer display and a glove to get directly into the action. The use of VR in a nonentertainment setting falls primarily into three categories—training, design, and marketing. Training examples will be presented first, followed by examples of the use of VR in design and in marketing.

The U.S. Army uses VR to train tank crews. Through multiple large video screens and sound, the soldiers are seemingly placed inside a tank rolling across the Iraqi desert, and they have to react as if they were in a real tank battle. In the field of medicine, medical students are learning through collaboration and trial-and-error on virtual cadavers, which is much less expensive than using actual bodies. As an example, researchers have created 3-D animations of hematomas—bleeding between the skull and brain—of virtual patients who have suffered head damage in an automobile accident. Using a virtual-reality head-mounted display and virtual-reality gloves, students work together to diagnose and treat the patient (Hulme, 2002).

Amoco (now part of British Petroleum) has developed a PC-based VR system, called "truck driVR," for use in training its drivers. Amoco believed that the VR system was a cost-effective way of testing how well its 12,000 drivers performed under a variety of hazardous driving conditions. This immersive VR system, which cost approximately $50,000 to develop, employs a helmet that holds the visual and auditory displays and completely immerses the user in the virtual world. To make truck driVR realistic, multiple views are provided to the user, including views of both left and right rearview mirrors that are displayed only when the user moves his or her head to the left or right. Several manufacturers use VR in training for specialized jobs. As an example, you can view a short video at *www.osc.edu/research/video_library/ford.shtml* showing Ford's use of VR in training a forge hammer operator (Ohio Supercomputer Center, 2007).

Duracell also employs VR for training. Duracell was installing new equipment to manufacture a new line of rechargeable batteries, and the company needed to train its factory personnel on the new equipment in a safe and cost-effective manner. The Duracell system, which is nonimmersive (no helmet or special glasses), runs on a PC and incorporates a parts familiarization module, an operations module, and a troubleshooting module. With this system the user is able to completely explore the new piece of equipment within the desktop virtual world. "With the use of that special mouse [a Magellan space mouse], the user can walk around it [the equipment], they can get underneath it, they can get on top of it," says Neil Silverstein, a training manager at Duracell. "They can fly into the smallest crevices of the machine, something that you can never do in the real world because you might lose a finger." Duracell is quite pleased with the results. The training is standardized and completely safe, and there is no need for on-the-job training.

On the design side, several automobile manufacturers use VR to assist in the design of new automobiles. As an example, General Motors created the Envisioning Center, a three-screened, theater-like room where designers can view 3-D images of car designs. The image can be rotated to be viewed from any angle, and it is displayed at such an exact scale that the designers can walk up to the screen and use rulers to measure the width and height of any detail. A designer can manipulate the image until it almost seems that he or she can reach into the interior and manipulate the steering wheel. "Designers can study how much headroom a driver has, how ergonomic the dashboard controls are, and make absolutely sure that every aspect of the vehicle is perfect," says Robert DeBrabant, who runs the Envisioning Center. The center also has a collaboration capability that permits members of the design team to participate in VR sessions from remote sites—even on other continents—and these remote team members can manipulate the 3-D models as easily as their on-site counterparts (Konicki, 2002).

Arizona State University has created the Decision Theater for the New Arizona, an immersive 3-D visualization environment that has many similarities to GM's Envisioning Center. The Decision Theater, however, boasts seven screens and is primarily focused on "connecting the science of the university with the needs of the Arizona community," and thus it often serves as an aid to policy making (Arizona State University, 2007). For example, a detailed 3-D model of downtown Tempe, including Arizona State University, has been built to assist the city in making zoning decisions (particularly for height limitations) and to illustrate to all involved (e.g., developers, city officials, and the general public) the impact that a proposed multistory office building, condominium project, or university building would have on the nature of an area and on sightlines. One of the authors of

this book viewed a demonstration of this model in the Decision Theater—using 3-D glasses, of course—and was amazed at the impact of changing the angle at which the model was viewed and the ease of moving around within the model.

An air conditioning/furnace manufacturer is using VR to permit engineers to walk through an existing or proposed product. By walking through a furnace, for example, the engineer gets a perspective of the design from a completely different vantage point. The engineer starts thinking of all the ways in which the design could be improved that were not obvious before. VR also allows the mock-up of products long before physical prototypes are created. This enables designers to get the real look and feel of the product and even get feedback from focus groups. Imagine sitting in the cab of a large farm combine before it is ever built and getting an understanding of the line of sight that the operator will have. Is the steering wheel blocking important gauges? Where should the mirrors be placed?

VR is increasingly being used for marketing on the Web. Interactive 3-D images of a company's products and services are beginning to appear on company Web sites; these images provide a more comprehensive view of the product as well as differentiate the Web site from those of competitors. A very popular use of VR-like technology is the use of "virtual tours" for the real estate industry, the travel and hospitality industry, and educational institutions. On these virtual tours, the user logs on the appropriate Web site and can experience a 360-degree view from a particular camera location. If you are house hunting, you can get a 360-degree view of the great room and the kitchen in a home for sale; if planning a vacation, you can get a 360-degree view of the grounds and the lobby of a resort hotel; if selecting a college, you can get a 360-degree look at key buildings on campus. Figure 7.7 shows a virtual-tour view of the living room of a home for sale in California. By using the buttons at the bottom of the picture, the user can turn a full 360 degrees in either direction, stop the movement, or zoom in and out. At *www.campustours.com* you can find campus tours for most college campuses in the United States; some of these tours incorporate 360-degree photographs. Check out your college and see if it has a 360-degree tour!

The development of VR is in its infancy, and it will be a long time before anything remotely approaching the *Enterprise*'s holodeck is possible. Nevertheless, many vendors are developing VR hardware and software, and numerous valuable VR applications are beginning to appear.

Figure 7.7   CirclePix 360° Virtual Tour of Living Room (Courtesy of CirclePix.com, LLC. Copyright © 2007 CirclePix.com, LLC)

SECOND LIFE OPENS FOR BUSINESS

Second Life is an online 3-D virtual world entirely built and owned by its residents. Launched in 2003, Second Life now boasts over 6 million registered residents. Users create alter egos, called avators, to represent themselves. These avators, which can look like ordinary people or very weird nonhuman beings, can walk, run, sit, fly, buy property, build houses, start businesses, and buy and sell virtual products and services. All this sounds like escapist fun—and it is—but why then are real-world businesses establishing a presence in Second Life?

Companies such as Toyota, Dell, Sears, IBM, Cisco, Adidas, and Circuit City have all created buildings in Second Life that can be visited by residents. These companies all believe, to some extent, that some of the biggest design, marketing, and sales challenges in the real world are about to be solved by the virtual world. For example, the Second Life Sears store lets customers do things they can't do in real life, such as create a 3-D model of a kitchen and plan the equipment and cabinets to go in the kitchen. If your business has trouble understanding what your customers really want in a car, let them design their own car personally. Let them design their own jeans, or their home theater installation. Through your Second Life store, let shoppers browse your products and decide what products work for them—and then let them click on a link that sends them to your real-world Web site where they can actually buy the product.

Thus far, however, little of this positive "business" is really taking place. The virtual stores tend to be nearly empty, and the design simulations are too kludgy to attract users. "What the useful applications will be for business is the million-dollar question," according to Bob Moore, a member of the research staff at the Computing Science Laboratory at Xerox's Palo Alto Research Center. "A lot of it is just plain hype. We see corporations that are excited about it . . . but the jury is still out about the real business value."

[Adapted from Claburn, 2007, and LaPlante, 2007]

SUMMARY

We have now completed our two-chapter survey of *intraorganizational* IT application areas. Chapter 6 focused on application areas that support the entire organization or large portions of it, including transaction processing systems, data warehousing, and office automation. At the conclusion of Chapter 6, we argued that modern organizations cannot do business without these enterprise IT systems. In this chapter we have concentrated on managerial support systems such as decision support systems, business intelligence systems, and neural networks. These managerial support systems are just as critical to the individual managers in a business as the enterprise systems are to the firm as a whole. Modern managers simply cannot manage effectively and efficiently without managerial support IT systems.

Several types of managerial support systems are designed to support *individual* managers in their decision-making endeavors *without* the aid of artificial intelligence. Decision support systems (DSSs), data mining, geographic information systems (GISs), executive information systems (EISs), and business intelligence systems all fall into this broad grouping.[2] A DSS is an interactive system, employing a model of some sort, that assists a manager in making decisions in a situation that is not well structured. The prototypical example of a DSS is carrying out what-if analyses on a financial model. Data mining is concerned with digging out nuggets of information from a data warehouse, again using a model; thus data mining can be considered as a subset of the broader DSS construct. A GIS is based on spatial relationships; many, but not all, GISs incorporate a model and are used as a DSS. In contrast, an EIS does not usually involve a model. An EIS provides easy online access to current aggregate information about key business conditions. A business intelligence system is a newer variant of an EIS incorporating special tools to capture and display competitive information. In general, a DSS, data mining, or a GIS provides specific information of value to a manager working on a particular problem, while an EIS provides aggregated information of value to a wide range of managers within the firm.

Group support systems (GSSs) and knowledge management systems (KMSs) provide support to a *group* of managers, although in quite different ways. A GSS provides support to a group of managers engaged in some sort of group activity, most commonly a meeting, whereas a KMS is a system for managing organizational knowledge and sharing it with the appropriate group. A GSS, which is a specialized type of groupware, consists of software running on a LAN that permits all meeting participants to simultaneously and anonymously make contributions to the group discussion by keying in their ideas and having them displayed on a large public screen, if desired. The software facilitates various group tasks, such as idea generation, organizing ideas, prioritizing, and policy development. With a KMS, knowledge might be shared within a community of practice (a group of managers with similar interests) via knowledge repositories, discussion forums, and community calendars, or within a broader grouping of employees via a carefully structured package of knowledge content.

Artificial intelligence (AI) is used to support the *individual* manager in our third grouping of managerial support systems. By capturing the decision-making logic of a human expert, an expert system provides nonexperts with expert advice. A neural network teases out obscure patterns from vast amounts of data by a process of adaptive learning. In both cases the user is led to better decisions via AI. Closely related to AI is virtual reality (VR), where computer-based systems create an environment that seems real to one or more human senses. VR has proved particularly useful for training and design activities, and it is increasingly being used for marketing on the Web.

We hope that these two chapters have convinced you of the value of these intraorganizational systems. But how does an organization, or an individual manager, acquire one of these potentially valuable systems? The complete answer to this question will have to wait until Part III of this book, entitled "Acquiring Information Systems," but we already have some clues.

The enterprise systems, for example, are primarily large-scale systems that would be purchased from an outside vendor or custom developed by the internal IS organization or an external consulting firm. In particular, enterprise resource planning, office automation, groupware, and factory automation are almost always purchased from an outside vendor. These are all massive systems that require similar functionality across a wide variety of firms. Of course, the internal IS department or a consultant may customize them to the organization. Data warehousing and intranets are often implemented with purchased software, but there might also be internal or consultant development. Historically, the internal IS organization developed most transaction processing systems, but even these systems are likely to be purchased today,

---

[2]This generalization is not entirely correct. Data mining, in particular, may incorporate neural networks–a branch of artificial intelligence–as a technique employed to mine data. Nevertheless, the authors believe that the groupings of managerial support systems given here provide a useful way of summarizing the chapter.

as shown by the growth of ERP systems, unless the firm's requirements are unique.

By contrast, the business manager or a consultant (internal or external to the firm) is likely to develop many managerial support systems expressly for the manager. In most cases the business manager or consultant would start with an underlying software tool (such as a DSS generator, expert systems shell, neural network program, data mining tool, or business intelligence package) and develop a specific implementation of the tool that satisfies the need. The manager is unlikely, however, to develop a GSS, EIS, or KMS; these multiuser systems are more akin to enterprise systems in terms of their acquisition.

All these methods of IT system acquisition—purchase of a fully-developed system, development by the internal IS organization or an external consultant, and end-user development—will be explored in detail in Part III.

REVIEW QUESTIONS

1. Describe the three primary components that make up any decision support system (DSS) and how they interact.
2. Explain the difference between a specific DSS and a DSS generator. Give an example of each.
3. Describe two examples of specific DSSs that are being used to assist in decision making. You may use examples from the textbook or other examples you have read about or heard about.
4. Explain both data warehousing and data mining. How are they related?
5. List at least two techniques (decision technologies) that are used in data mining.
6. List at least three uses of data mining.
7. What is the purpose of a group support system (GSS)? What are the potential advantages and disadvantages of using a GSS?
8. Compare the raster-based and vector-based approaches to geographic information systems (GISs). What are the primary uses of each approach?
9. What are the distinguishing characteristics of an executive information system (EIS)? Why have these systems become a part of business intelligence in many companies?
10. What is knowledge management, and what is a knowledge management system? How does the concept of a community of practice relate to knowledge management?

11. Briefly describe the several areas of artificial intelligence (AI) research. Indicate why we in business are most interested in the expert systems and neural networks areas.
12. What are the three general approaches to obtaining an expert system? What are the pluses and minuses of each approach?
13. Describe two examples of expert systems that are being used to assist in decision making. You may use examples from the textbook or other examples you have read about or heard about.
14. Describe two examples of neural networks that are being used to assist in decision making. You may use examples from the textbook or other examples you have read about or heard about.
15. Describe two examples of the use of virtual reality in an organizational setting. You may use examples from the textbook or other examples you have read about or heard about.

DISCUSSION QUESTIONS

1. Review question 4 asked about the relationship between data warehousing and data mining. In addition to data mining, which of the other application areas discussed in this chapter may be used in conjunction with data warehousing? Explain.
2. Two of the important topics in this chapter are decision support systems (DSSs) and expert systems. Based on your reading of this chapter, you have undoubtedly noticed that these two application areas have a great deal in common. What are the primary distinctions between DSSs and expert systems?
3. Compare group support systems, as described in this chapter, with groupware, as described in Chapter 6. How do these two application areas relate to one another? Which one is more important today? Do you think this will be true in the future?
4. Several examples of geographic information systems were mentioned in the chapter. Consider an industry or a company with which you have some familiarity and identify at least one possible application of GISs in the industry or company. Explain why you think this is a good prospect for a GIS application.
5. Explain the concept of "drilling-down" as used in executive information systems (EISs). Is drilling-down used in other IT applications? How do these applications relate to EISs?

6. Explain the original role that was to be played by an EIS and then describe how this role has been modified over time. Why has this role change occurred?

7. According to the trade press, the success record of knowledge management systems has been spotty. Why do you think this is? What steps must organizations take to give their knowledge management efforts the best chances of succeeding?

8. Several examples of expert systems were mentioned in the chapter. Consider an industry or a company with which you have some familiarity and identify at least one possible application of expert systems in the industry or company. Explain why you think this is a good prospect for an expert system application.

9. Several examples of neural networks were mentioned in the chapter. Consider an industry or a company with which you have some familiarity and identify at least one possible application of neural networks in the industry or company. Explain why you think this is a good prospect for a neural network application.

10. Which of the application areas considered in this chapter is most useful to a small to midsized business? Defend your answer.

REFERENCES

1995. "How organizations are becoming more efficient using expert systems." *I/S Analyzer Case Studies* 34 (March): 1–16.

1997. "How businesses are cutting costs through virtual reality." *I/S Analyzer Case Studies* 36 (March): 1–16.

2000. "Comshare Decision delivers intuitive analysis solution to Petro-Canada." *DM Review, www.dmreview.com/article_sub.cfm?articleId=1962* (March).

AccuTracking, Inc. 2007. "Low cost GPS tracking service for everyone." AccuTracking Web site, *www.accutracking.com* (May).

Allaway, Arthur W., Lisa D. Murphy, and David K. Berkowitz. 2004. "The geographical edge: Spatial analysis of retail loyalty program adoption," in James Pick (ed.), *Geographic Information Systems in Business*. Hershey, PA: Idea Group Publishing.

Arizona State University. 2007. "Decision Theater, Arizona State University," "PRISM (Partnership for Research in Spatial Modeling) Research." Arizona State University Web site, *dt.asu.edu* (May), *prism.asu.edu/research/index.php* (May).

Austin, Tom, Nikos Drakos, and Jeffrey Mann. 2006. "Web conferencing amplifies dysfunctional meeting practices." Gartner Research, ID number G00138101 (March 13).

Blough, Kay. 2002. "Virtual reality to aid stroke therapy." *InformationWeek* 876 (February 18): 20.

California Scientific Software. 2007. "BrainMaker improves hospital treatment and reduces expenses." California Scientific Software Web site, *www.calsci.com/hospital.html* (May).

Chabrow, Eric. 2006. "Expert systems: A pocket full of knowledge." *InformationWeek* 1112 (October 30): 21.

Claburn, Thomas. 2007. "IBM and Sears build Second Life store." *InformationWeek* Web site, *www.informationweek.com/story/showArticle.jhtml?articleID=196801663* (January 8).

Dauzère-Pérès, Stéphane, Atle Nordli, Asmund Olstad, Kjetil Haugen, Ulrich Koester, Per Olav Myrstad, Geir Teistklub, and Alf Reistad. 2007. "Omya Hustadmarmor optimizes its supply chain for delivering calcium carbonate slurry to European paper manufacturers." *Interfaces* 37 (January–February): 39–51.

Davis, Beth. 1999. "Data mining transformed." *InformationWeek* 751 (September 6): 86, 88.

Dennis, Alan R., and Iris Vessey. 2005. "Three knowledge management strategies: Knowledge hierarchies, knowledge markets, and knowledge communities." *MIS Quarterly Executive* 4 (December): 399–412.

Dickey, Sam. 1999. "OLAP and data mining put profits first." *Beyond Computing* 8 (October): 18–22.

ESRI. 2003. "Federated Department Stores, Inc. uses GIS for advanced market research." *ArcNews Online*, Environmental Systems Research Institute Web site, *www.esri.com/news/arcnews/summer03articles/federated-department.html* (Summer).

ESRI. 2006. "Apex Office Supply: GIS transforms company's way of doing business." Environmental Systems Research Institute Web site, *www.esri.com/library/fliers/pdfs/cs-apex.pdf* (September).

Exsys Inc. 2007. "Case study: Credit analysis advisor and report system," "Case study: Detecting insider trading," "Case study: Individual development plan advisor," "Case study: Maximum yield/minimum resources farm advisors," "Case study: OSHA hazard compliance advisor helps thousands," "Case study: Pension fund advisor," "Case study: Web-based knowledge automation system helps the Navajo Nation." Exsys Inc. Web site, *www.exsys.com* (May).

Fowler, Bob. 2000. "Dow AgroSciences Global Competitive Intelligence." Personal correspondence (September). At the time, Mr. Fowler was global competitive intelligence/data compensation leader, Dow AgroSciences.

GroupSystems. 2007. "History: Group collaboration and Web meetings software," "GroupSystems structures group collaboration on IBM's Lotus Sametime 7.5 platform," "Eastman Chemical—creativity and team center," "Nokia

Telecommunications, Finland." GroupSystems Web site, *www.groupsystems.com* (May).

Gwynne, Peter. 2000. "OLAP and data mining: Making the right decisions." *Beyond Computing* 9 (September): 42–45.

Haskin, David. 2003. "Years after hype, 'expert systems' paying off for some." Earthweb.com Web site, *itmanagement. earthweb.com/netsys/article.php/1570851* (January 16).

Houdeshel, George, and Hugh J. Watson. 1987. "The management information and decision support (MIDS) system at Lockheed-Georgia." *MIS Quarterly* 11 (March): 127–140.

Hulme, George V. 2002. "Cadavers go virtual." *InformationWeek* 889 (May 20): 20.

Infor Global Solutions. 2007. "Infor PM (Performance Management)." Infor Web site, *www.infor.com/solutions/ pm/* (May).

Infor Global Solutions. 2007. "Santa Clara Valley Health & Hospital System." Infor Extensity Web site, *www.extensity. com/object/SantaClara_case_PM.html* (May).

Infor Global Solutions. 2007. "Universal Studios Hollywood." Infor Extensity Web site, *www.extensity.com/object/ universal_studios_PM.html* (May).

Karl, Jason. 2007. "The Nature Conservancy uses mobile GIS technology in fight against invasive species," *GIS Best Practices: Mobile GIS.* Environmental Systems Research Institute Web site, *www.esri.com/library/bestpractices/ mobile-gis.pdf* (May): 23–27.

Konicki, Steve. 2002. "How to design cars and scare children." *InformationWeek* 891 (June 3): 42.

Kulkarni, Uday R., Sury Ravindran, and Ronald Freeze. 2006–2007. "A knowledge management success model: Theoretical development and empirical validation." *Journal of Management Information Systems* 23 (Winter): 309–347.

LaPlante, Alice. 2007. "Second Life opens for business." *InformationWeek* 1127 (February 26): 45–49.

Mullarkey, Peter, Grant Butler, Srinagesh Gavirneni, and Douglas Morrice. 2007. "Schlumberger uses simulation in bidding and executing land seismic surveys." *Interfaces* 37 (March–April): 120–132.

National Center for Health Statistics (NCHS). 2004. "GIS and the public health." Centers for Disease Control and Prevention Web site, U.S. Department of Health and Human Services, *www.cdc.gov/nchs/gis.htm* (January).

NeuroDimension, Inc. 2007. "Neural network applications in investment and trading," "Neural network applications in business." NeuroDimension Web site, *www.nd.com* (May).

O'Dell, Carla, and C. Jackson Grayson, Jr. 1998. *If Only We Knew What We Know: The Transfer of Internal Knowledge and Best Practice.* New York: The Free Press.

Ohio Supercomputer Center. 2007. "Ford's use of virtual reality in training." Ohio Supercomputer Center Web site, *www. osc.edu/research/video_library/ford.shtml* (May).

Orzech, Dan. 2002. "Using neural networks to beat hackers." CIO Update Web site, *www.cioupdate.com/news/article. php/1561971* (December 27).

Port, Otis. 2000. "Thinking machines: Special report on smart manufacturing." *BusinessWeek* (August 7): 78–86.

Reid, Hal. 2007. Personal correspondence (May). Hal Reid is currently chief technical editor for Directions Media (*www.directionsmag.com*) and former manager of development systems at Dunkin' Donuts; Reid has been pivotal in expanding the use of GIS down to the parcel level for determining trade areas, generating demographic reports, and assessing retail sites and markets.

SAS. 2007. "Fast action drives customer satisfaction: American Honda saves millions using SAS," "Reliable CRM always in stock at the Vermont Country Store." SAS Web site, *www.sas.com* (May).

Shirodkar, Shamin, and Karl Kempf. 2006. "Supply chain collaboration through shared capacity models." *Interfaces* 36 (September–October): 420–432.

Slater, Derek. 2000. "Household Financial Corporation: Loan star." *CIO* (February 1): 100–106.

Sprague, Ralph H., Jr., and Eric D. Carlson. 1982. *Building Effective Decision Support Systems.* Englewood Cliffs, NJ: Pearson Prentice-Hall, Inc.

Wasko, Molly McLure, and Samer Faraj. 2005. "Why should I share? Examining social capital and knowledge contribution in electronic networks of practice." *MIS Quarterly* 29 (March): 35–57.

Weier, Mary Hayes. 2007. "Analyze this: How many employees really need BI?" *InformationWeek* 1137 (May 7): 27.

Wikipedia. 2007a. "Galileo positioning system." Wikipedia Web site, *en.wikipedia.org/wiki/Galileo_positioning_ system* (May).

Wikipedia. 2007b. "Global Positioning System." Wikipedia Web site, *en.wikipedia.org/wiki/Global_Positioning_ System* (May).

Wikipedia. 2007c. "GPS modernization." Wikipedia Web site, *en.wikipedia.org/wiki/GPS_modernization* (May).

CHAPTER 8
E-BUSINESS SYSTEMS

THIS CHAPTER FOCUSES ON APPLICATIONS THAT ARE DESIGNED TO extend an organization's electronic reach beyond its own organizational boundaries to customers, suppliers, and other business partners: **e-business** systems.

Although e-business systems to conduct business transactions beyond organizational boundaries did not originate with the Web, the development of the first commercial Web browser (Netscape Navigator) in the mid-1990s led to an explosive demand for the development of commercial Web sites: hypertext applications stored on Web servers connected to the Internet. This commercial potential of the Internet was first revealed by **dot-com** (also known as "pure-play") survivors such as Amazon.com, eBay, and Yahoo! as well as many other dot-com pioneers that did not survive.

Today, however, having an online channel for communicating and conducting business via the Internet has also become an *additional* channel for traditional companies. These traditional companies that integrate their *offline and online*

business channels as part of a multichannel strategy are referred to today as **bricks-and-clicks** (or **click-and-mortar**) firms.

Continued growth in e-business systems by companies around the globe have been forecast due to the proven benefits of conducting business via the Internet: a relatively cheap entry cost, a transmission speed measured in microseconds, a multimedia communications capability via the Web, and a growing number of business partners and customers that can be "reached" via the Internet. A more theoretical explanation for why the Internet is likely to become in future years an even more attractive vehicle for e-business is provided by **Metcalfe's Law**:

The value of a network to each of its members is a nonlinear increasing function of the number of users, expressed as $(n^2 - n)/2$.

Stated differently, there are increasing returns to be gained as more and more organizations create Web sites and more individuals gain access to the Internet.

In the next section, we provide a brief history of the Internet, including some of the major IT innovations that led to the rapid commercial growth of the Internet, as well as some aspects of the legal and regulatory environments in the United States that impacted its early growth. Since in-depth technology discussions

---

E-business systems enable the electronic transmission of business transactions or other related information between a buyer and seller.

can be found in the chapters in Part I, in this chapter we focus on the strategic opportunities (and threats) that e-business systems offer. Specific B2B, B2C, and dot-com intermediary examples are then discussed. The chapter ends with some ideas of what makes a good Web site from a customer perspective.

It should be noted, however, that the examples in this chapter are primarily from a U.S.-centric viewpoint. This is because the e-business systems have thus far been heavily shaped by U.S.-based firms. However, this is gradually changing, as more and more Internet users are non-U.S. and companies in other countries begin to take the lead in Internet innovations.

BRIEF HISTORY OF THE INTERNET

The commercial history of the Internet is actually quite short. The Internet has its roots in **ARPANET**, a network that initially included only U.S. government organizations and a select group of research and development firms in the private sector and then grew to include educational institutions and other nonprofit organizations outside of the United States. Two events in the first half of the 1990s paved the way for today's Internet. First, in 1991 the National Science Foundation (the nonprofit organization in the United States then responsible for managing the Internet backbone) lifted the ban on commercial usage of the Internet. Second, in 1994 Netscape Navigator (the first

commercial **Web browser**) was released as a free product, based on the Mosaic browser developed at the University of Illinois. This rapid diffusion of an easy-to-use Web navigation tool, followed shortly thereafter by Microsoft's Internet Explorer browser, quickly ushered in the opportunity for businesses connected to the Internet anywhere in the world to have an online reach to customers and suppliers. Today, the Internet is a network of computer networks that use the TCP/IP protocol with gateways to even more networks that do not use the TCP/IP protocol. The Web (World Wide Web) is a subset of the Internet, with multimedia capabilities. Web documents are composed in standard markup languages (HTML) and stored on servers around the globe with standard addresses (URLs) that are accessible via a hypermedia protocol (HTTP). No single organization owns the Internet; each organization or end user pays for its software and hardware (for clients and servers) and network access. Initially, these Web technologies were created for a scientific community to exchange documents. Today these Internet technologies have become "standards" for use by local communities, governments, nonporfit organizations, entrepreneurs, and both the poorest countries and the largest companies in the world.

As shown in Figure 8.1, the IT applications, services, and communications technologies that enable e-business are dependent on two types pillars: a technology pillar and a legal and regulatory pillar. The standards for the Web have evolved under the guidance of consortia such as the

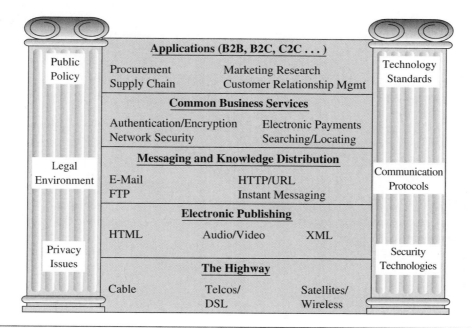

Figure 8.1   E-Business Framework (Adapted from Applegate, Holsapple, et al., 1996; Kalakota and Whinston, 1996)

cross-industry World Wide Web Consortium (**W3C**), other industry consortia, as well as various watchdog groups. Beginning in 1993, the rights for registering Web site addresses (domain names) were held solely by a U.S. federal contracter, Network Solutions Inc., but for the past decade the assignment of domain names and IP addresses has been overseen by the Internet Corporation for Assigned Names and Numbers (ICANN), a nonprofit organization headquartered in California, which has recently been taking on broader coordination and policy roles. The left-hand support pillar in Figure 8.1 includes actions by governments and legal systems. We discuss both of these pillars in more detail next.

E-business Technologies

In this section, we summarize some of the major IT developments that especially impacted B2C and B2B applications during the "first decade" after the introduction of the Web browser, as shown in Figure 8.2. (More detailed discussions on the technologies are provided in Part 1.) Initially, businesses only had the tools to create a "Web presence": Text documents with hyperlinks were loaded on a Web server to communicate with various stakeholders, including not just customers and the public, but also other financial backers. Web technologies to support interactivity with the user were then developed, followed by flashier designs to capture the "eyeballs" of Web site visitors.

The implementation of secure ways to transmit sensitive transactions and a standard for credit card processing were catalysts for the development of Web sites with online sales capabilities. A consortium that included banks, two major credit card players (MasterCard and Visa), and other major industry players (GTE, IBM, Microsoft, and Netscape) developed this new standard to support B2C transactions via the Web, and the first version of Secure Electronic Transaction (SET) was released in June 1997. Similarly, the implementation of a digital signature capability was a

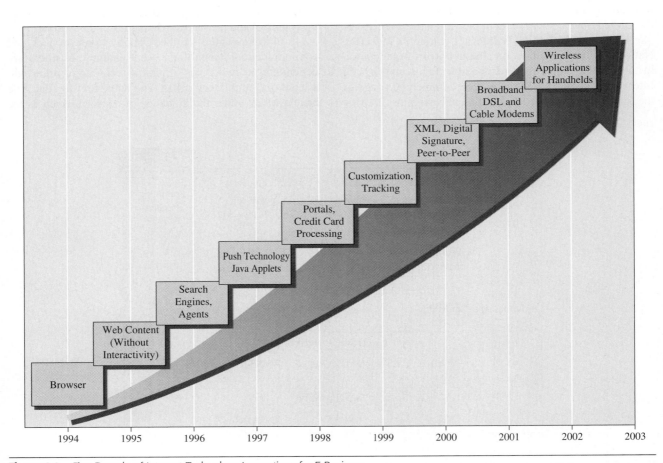

Figure 8.2   First Decade of Internet Technology Innovations for E-Business

DIGITAL SIGNATURES

Digital signatures use cryptography to convert data into a secret code for transmission over a public network. These technologies are often considered the most secure and reliable form of electronic signature because they use public-key infrastructure technologies to ensure that the electronic message has not been altered during transmission.

Say you wanted to draft and complete a contract with a customer using a digital signature. To do so, you'd first have to acquire a digital certificate—the electronic equivalent of an ID card. Several companies, including VeriSign and Entrust Technologies, are licensed to issue such certificates. Once you sign up, the provider transmits the certificate to your computer. You also receive two digital keys—one private and one public.

To sign a document, you enter a password or PIN and affix your electronic signature—the private key—to the document. The person or company receiving your document would then use the public key to unlock your certificate and verify that the signature is valid. Once confirmed, they could sign the document using their own digital tools and return it to you. Throughout the process, the software documents the date and time of each signing, while built-in security measures ensure that the documents haven't been altered anywhere along the process.

[J. Brown, 2000]

Internet   A worldwide network of networks, accessible to the public, that employs the TCP/IP protocol.

Intranet   A *private* network operating within an organization that employs the TCP/IP protocol, to provide information, applications, and other tools (such as collaboration tools), for use by the organization's employees.

Extranet   A *private* network that is a portion of a company's Intranet, which is made accessible (normally over the Internet) to business partners outside of the company (such as customers or suppliers).

---

catalyst for enabling secure business transactions via B2B applications by the year 2000 (see the box entitled "Digital Signatures").

By the late 1990s, the term "Web portal" emerged to refer to sites that were designed to be an initial point of access, or gateway, to other Web sites. Popular Internet portals today include Yahoo!, AOL and MSN, which include search engines, news stories, stock prices, and other sources of information and personal entertainment. Many businesses also began to establish internal portals for their business employees, with links to the company's intranet sites, which might include self-service applications to facilitate the collection of employee data for payroll and other HR systems. Some businesses have also established portals for business partners, which are accessed remotely using a URL separate from the company's public Web site, to provide selective access to company information (called extranets). Of course along with the introduction of public Web sites and extranet sites, firms also needed to provide online channels for around-the-clock customer service and ensure reliable and secure Web site hosting. Many firms today use external service providers to host their Web sites and manage the security risks associated with Internet sites.

By this time, Web masters had gained experience designing and operating Web sites for public use. Within traditional companies as well as new dot-com companies, developers began to focus on technologies to not only improve the online sales experience for individual end consumers, but also auction bidding or other B2B experiences for business customers and suppliers. The collection of click-stream metrics and personal data from Web site users, as well as the users' benign (and often unaware) acceptance of Web "cookies" stored on their personal computers, enabled the presentation of customized Web site content (or screens) for the individual or organizational user. Web browsers also continually improved in functionality and ease-of-use, and by the new millenium they were a standard interface to access not just text and graphics, but also interactive multimedia (audio, video, animation), with essentially no special end-user training.

By the early 2000s, broadband access (via cable modems or DSL telephone lines) became increasingly available in, or near, U.S. cities or towns with a sizable population. The widespread diffusion of mobile devices for wireless cellular communications has fueled the development of mobile e-business applications (**m-commerce**), including applications that provide customized content to the user based on the actual geographic location of the handheld device. Countries outside of the United States (e.g., Finland and Japan) were leaders in providing this type of Internet access to their citizens, but high-end handhelds with phone, camera, and Internet access capabilities are becoming widespread among business professionals and other early adopters in the United States, Europe, and Asia.

For B2B e-business, an important open technology standard endorsed by the W3C is **XML** (eXtensible Markup Language), a language for facilitating the transmission of common business data elements due to its precise "tagging" capabilities. Although prior to the commercialization of the Internet, many companies had developed offline systems for e-business with their trading partners, based on agreed-upon standards for business document transmission,

XML has enabled a flexible, lower-cost form of **electronic data interchange (EDI)** applications.

Prior to the commercialization of the Internet, over half of the *Fortune* 1000 had already implemented their own proprietary EDI applications using a private telecommunications network of leased lines or a value-added network (VAN) provided by a third party (see box entitled "How EDI Works"). For large discount retailers like Wal-Mart and large manufacturers, these systems enabled just-in-time (JIT) product replenishment and provisioning of materials for manufacturing processes that provided major B2B benefits, such as:

- reduced cycle times for doing business
- cost savings for automated transaction handling and the elimination of paper documents
- improved interfirm coordination and reduced interfirm coordination costs

Reduced cost savings and improved cycle times have also been enabled by new online e-marketplaces (or exchanges) for B2B transactions with buyers, suppliers, third-party service providers, or a consortia of buyers or suppliers. However, for large firms with extensive EDI implementations using older technologies and well-developed procurement channels, major investments in B2B transactions via the Internet may not have occurred until after the year 2000 when the security and reliability of Internet channels were well proven.

An early dot-com entrant for B2B exchanges was FreeMarkets, which provided behind-the-scenes experts to prepare for and then host online "reverse auctions" for client companies. In these auctions, preapproved suppliers could see their competitors' price bids online (in real-time), and then respond by lowering their own bid for a client's contract—and this bid would also become visible to other bidders (see Figure 8.3). Many client firms first

---

HOW EDI WORKS

EDI is usually implemented by computer-to-computer communication between organizations. A customer sends a supplier a purchase order or release to a blanket order via a standard electronic document. There is no manual shuffling of paperwork and little if any reentering of data. The supplier's computer system checks that the message is in an acceptable format and sends an electronic acknowledgment to the customer. The electronic order then feeds the supplier's production planning and shipping systems to schedule the shipment.

When the order is ready to ship, the supplier sends the customer an electronic notice of the pending shipment. The customer's computer checks that the shipment information corresponds to the order and returns a message authorizing the shipment. The supplier then sends a message that includes the truck number, carrier, approximate arrival time, and bill of lading The customer's computer alerts the receiving dock of the expected arrival; receiving personnel visually verify the shipment upon arrival for quality, and the shipment is accepted.

A contract signed by EDI business partners determines when an electronic order is legally binding, which could be when it is delivered, after the message is read, or after it has been checked. A contract also determines whether all messages must be acknowledged. Usually, the customer must guarantee that if it issues a correctly formatted and acknowledged order, then it is obliged to accept and pay for the requested goods.

The technical success of EDI depends on standards. Standards for EDI are necessary because computer file formats, forms, data and transaction definitions, and the overall methods of processing data can vary considerably across companies and especially across countries. Standards provide a way to decouple the different EDI participants as much as possible, yet still facilitate data exchange.

An electronic business document is called a transaction set. Header and trailer records contain batch control information, such as the unique identifiers of the sender and receiver, a date, the number of line segments, and so on. Each transaction set also has a unique identification number and a time stamp. An EDI translation program converts an incoming EDI format so that it can be read by an application program, and vice versa.

The specific standard for a transaction set is established between the business partners of an EDI relationship. EDI standards are of three types: proprietary formats designed for one or more organizations and their trading partners, industry-specific formats that are designed to match specific industry needs (e.g., automotive), and generic formats for use by any trading partners. In some industries a major industry player or a consortium of companies have established a standard, whereas in other industries a formal body with large representation may have established a standard.

The American National Standards Institute (ANSI) has coordinated standard-setting activities in the United States. ANSI X.12 formats exist for standard documents in many U.S. industries—including chemicals, automotive, retail merchants, textiles, and electrical equipment. Some of these U.S. standards were developed by an industry group. For example, the Automotive Industry Action Group (AIAG) was created by Ford, General Motors, and Chrysler along with 300 large suppliers. For some industries, the usage of uniform standards for product identification (product codes) is also key to EDI cost savings.

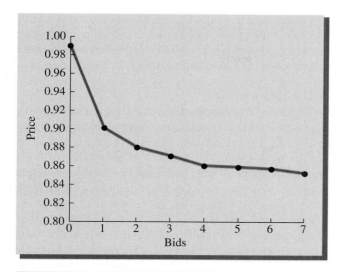

Figure 8.3 Price Changes During Internet Auction

> **Firewalls** are devices that sit between the Internet and an organization's internal network (or an individual's computer) in order to block intrusions from unauthorized users and hackers from remote sites. A firewall can be a router, a personal computer, a host, or a collection of hosts.
>
> **Encryption** systems are based on two decoding keys and mathematical principles for factoring a product into its two prime numbers. One decoding key is used to encipher (code) a message; a second decoding key is used to decipher it. The enciphering key makes it easy to encode a message, but deciphering requires a key only available to the intended recipient of the message. If the enciphering key is the product of two very large prime numbers, the key is expected to have a relatively long life before being vulnerable to a hacker.

learned how to conduct their own online auctions using such a service, and then linked their own procurement systems with off-the-shelf software from a B2B software vendor such as Ariba (which subsequently purchased FreeMarkets), and hosted their own reverse auctions without vendor support (Mabert and Skeels, 2002).

The lack of sufficient online security was one of the biggest initial constraints to the diffusion of Internet-based e-business systems for businesses as well as for end consumers. Two major security issues are:

1. how to control access to a computer that is physically networked to the Internet, and
2. how to ensure that the security of a given communication, such as a business transaction, is not violated.

The primary way to control access to corporate or individual computers is via a **firewall**. A company's public Web site typically sits outside the firewall, and many firms use outside vendors to host their external Web site for security reasons—as well as for peak load balancing. **Encryption** is the primary way to ensure the security of a business transaction or other communication.

Companies have also had to make major IT investments to protect their firms from intentional attacks and viruses that originate with Internet communications. Today's software vendors regularly make available security patches when vulnerabilities for a specific application program are identified. However, denial-of-service and intentional virus attacks are ongoing security concerns, and the legal systems of national governments have been slow to pass strong legislation or play aggressive oversight roles to help businesses and individuals avoid the high costs of recovering

from intentional security breaches. (See also the discussions on information security and privacy issues in Chapters 16 and 17.)

Legal and Regulatory Environment

Given the U.S. origins of the Internet, the legal and regulatory environment in the United States has played a major role in initially shaping the Internet's capabilities for e-business. One of these has been the government taxing (or rather, lack of taxes) on most Internet purchases.

Within the United States, taxes on sales of products and services are collected at the state level, not the national level. Given the lack of physical geography associated with online Web sites, a uniform sales tax policy at the federal level could have been initiated. However, under President Bill Clinton, the executive branch of the U.S. government supported a "hands-off" policy for taxing Web-based sales beginning in the mid-1990s. This fit the U.S. government's vision for a national information infrastructure (superhighway), funded by the private sector, that would link homes, businesses, and government. In October 2001, this "hands-off" federal policy was scheduled to be reconsidered by the U.S. legislature, but the 9/11 terrorist attacks took attention away from Internet tax revenues and focused it on national security concerns; therefore, the policy has continued.

An Amendment to extend the moratorium on taxes related to Internet purchases was passed by the U.S. Congress in October 2007. One argument against such taxation in the past has been a complexity argument, due to the different taxation laws that exist at the state level. However, several U.S. states have invested in a project to develop and implement a sales use tax system that can be used by Internet providers to identify and collect sales tax revenues at relevant rates. Besides state governments, local "brick-and-mortar" merchants have an interest in the current legal and online collection roadblocks being dismantled. Since online shopping is also more accessible to more affluent consumers, it has also been argued that the present laws result in benefits to those on the higher end of the socioeconomic scale rather than poorer consumers.

A second issue, concerns for the privacy of individual consumer data, has gained significant attention within the United States as Web-based e-business applications have grown and the new technologies to capture consumer data and behaviors, including the usage of cookies, continue to be introduced. For example, when a top Internet advertising firm, DoubleClick, revealed its plans for user profiling (by combining anonymous data about Web surfers with personal information stored in other consumer databases), advocacy groups sent out an alert, the Federal Trade Commission (FTC) began to investigate, and DoubleClick had to revamp its new project introduction (for more details, see Chapter 17).

To date, privacy-rights advocacy groups and nonprofit organizations in the United States have played a major role in ensuring that companies protect the privacy of their consumers by not sharing the personal data they have collected. Virtually all U.S.-based retailers today provide a copy of their company's privacy policy on their Web sites—explicitly stating what the firm will or will not do with any individual data collected from usage of their Web site. Nonprofit organizations such as TRUSTe also administer programs that validate a firm's "trustworthy" behavior toward Web site visitors. Dot-com companies particularly dependent on maintaining consumer trust, such as eBay and Facebook, then display a visible logo signalling their validated trustworthiness for protecting their customers' individual privacy (see box entitled "TRUSTe Program Continues to Ensure Consumer Privacy").

However, although the U.S. brand of capitalism and the U.S. laws protecting freedom of expression were the initial shapers of the Internet, today's Internet is truly a global marketplace. International agreements are therefore needed, but face considerable barriers due to major differences in national policies related to the rights of individuals and the protection of intellectual property.

TRUSTe PROGRAM CONTINUES TO ENSURE CONSUMER PRIVACY

TRUSTe is an independent, nonprofit organization founded in 1997 by the Electronic Frontier Foundation (EFF) and the CommerceNet Consortium. Its TRUSTe seal is intended to be a signal to Internet users that a given Web site is trustworthy. The seal is awarded only to sites that adhere to established privacy principles and agree to comply with ongoing TRUSTe oversight and consumer resolution procedures, which include the adoption and implementation of a **privacy policy** that discloses the company's information collection and use practices, and also gives users the opportunity to exercise some control over the use of their information.

By year-end 2006, about 2,500 Web sites were participating in the company's TRUSTe seal program, including about half of the 50 most visited Web sites, such as Web portals AOL and Yahoo!, computer industry leaders Apple and Microsoft, dot-com pioneer eBay, and newer dot-com social-networking and matchmaking sites such as Facebook and Match.com.

To celebrate its tenth anniversary in 2007, the company launched a new version of its seal to emphasize its "trustmark" for privacy assurance and its ongoing dedication to helping companies build a reputaton for being fair and honest. As stated by the chief privacy officer at financial software and services vendor Intuit, one of the participants in the company's program: "When we display the TRUSTe seal, our customers have a clear-cut symbol ensuring them that their data will not be shared with third parties or compomised in any way."

[www.Truste.org, last accessed December 17, 2007. Used with permission of TRUSTe.]

STRATEGIC E-BUSINESS OPPORTUNITIES (AND THREATS)

A well established, pre-Internet framework for assessing a firm's strategic opportunities and threats is Michael E. Porter's **competitive forces model** (Porter, 1985; Porter and Millar, 1985). This model can also be used to assess the commercial opportunities and threats to an industry or a business due to the influence of the Internet. Figure 8.4 summarizes Porter's general predictions of the influences from the perspective of a traditional company, which were published shortly after the first wave of Internet activity by U.S. firms (Porter, 2001).

The five competitive forces in the model are: supplier power, customer power, the threat of new entrants (same products/services), the threat of substitute products/services, and the responses of competitors within the same industry to any of these same forces. The potential opportunities are shown with a plus (+) sign, potential threats with a minus (−)

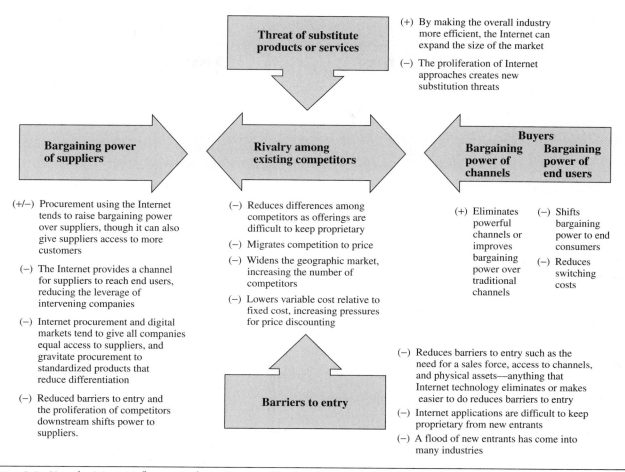

Figure 8.4   How the Internet Influences Industry Structure (Reprinted by permission of *Harvard Business Review*. "How the Internet Influences Industry Structure," by Michael Porter. *Harvard Business Review* March 2001. Copyright © 2004 by the Harvard Business School Publishing Corporation. All rights reserved)

sign. As shown in Figure 8.4, Porter identifies three major opportunities for traditional companies in general:

1. the procurement of supplies via the Internet can increase the traditional company's power over its suppliers,
2. the size of a potential market is expanded due to the Internet, and
3. powerful distribution channels between the traditional company and its customers can be eliminated.

The first and third opportunities here refer to the potential to "bypass" a company that was a traditional "intermediary" between a producer (or service provider) and the customer for that product (or service). For example, an airline company used to need a travel agency to sell and print airline tickets; today, airline companies can "bypass" this channel by selling tickets directly to customers via the

Web, and save the transaction fees paid to travel agents or their own customer service representatives.

However, as can be seen in Figure 8.4, Porter also identifies a large number of threats to the traditional company due to the Internet. Among these threats are the following: (1) there is greater competition based on price because the Internet makes it more difficult to keep product or service offerings proprietary, (2) the widening of the geographic markets results in an increase in the number of competitors, (3) the Internet reduces or eliminates some traditional barriers, such as the need for an in-person sales force, and (4) customers have more bargaining power because they can see prices for the same or similar products by just looking at Web sites, and can easily "switch" to a competitor. The first and fourth threats suggest that, using online channels, it is much more difficult to compete based on

	Prior to 2000–2001	Beginning 2000–2001
Source of innovation	Technology-driven	Business-driven
	Venture Capital	Less venture capital
Financial markets	Valuation based on potential for revenue growth	Valuation based on potential for earnings and profits
Taxation on sales	"Hands-off" policy	Some state sale tax
Business models	Dot-com (pure online)	Bricks-and-clicks
	First mover advantage	Strategic follower
	New types of intermediaries	New types of intermediaries

Figure 8.5 Before and After the Dot-Com Meltdown

differentiation of the company's products or services—such as visible quality, customer service, or some other unique value perceived by the customer.

Although Porter's five forces model establishes a starting point for thinking about competitive moves for companies within an industry, there is a potential danger in using a competitive model that was initially based on ways of doing business in earlier decades when we did not have a global computer network to link commercial businesses with their business partners and to provide global reach online. For example, users of this model need to take into account the potential impacts of new dot-com intermediaries between a firm and its customers, as well as between a firm and its suppliers—including Web sites that can serve as online "aggregators" that make it easy to compare prices (such as *www.hotels.com*) or competitor bids.

About the time that Porter's predictions were published in the *Harvard Business Review*, an economic recession in the United States severely "dampened" the rate of IT-related Internet innovations. After the huge IT expenditures for Y2K and euro compliance, an e-business "reality check" set in and the venture capitalists that had fueled the growth of the Internet in the United States began to reward profits, not revenue growth. Referred to as the "dot-com meltdown," first-mover advantages were also questioned, as it became apparent following the 1999 end-of-year holidays that many online retailers lacked B2C fulfillment capabilities and many online B2B exchanges lacked a robust enough business model to survive. See Figure 8.5.

As summarized by Marc Andreessen, the cofounder of the first commercial browser (Netscape) who saw his company lose its "first mover" advantage to Microsoft's Internet Explorer browser, being first does not guarantee survival:

Most first movers end up lying facedown in the sand, with other people coming along and learning

*from their mistakes. . . . **Being the first mover with the right approach** is very important. Being the first mover with the wrong approach means you're dead.*

—MARK ANDREESSEN
(as quoted in Anders, 2001)

Recent analyses of the business plans from Internet start-ups seeking private equity funding during the "bubble years" (1995–2000) suggest that this reflection is right on-target (see box entitled "Is There a First Mover Advantage?").

IS THERE A FIRST MOVER ADVANTAGE?

The common wisdom is that the "bubble years" of the Web (typically viewed as beginning with the Netscape IPO in August 1995 to the NASDAQ peak at 5100 in March 2000) was due to too many companies rushing into the market in defiance of all known business fundamentals.

An analysis of the business plans for Internet start-ups during this period document that the defining business strategy was to "get big fast." The assumption was that a business should grow as quickly as possible because the first successful entrant in a category could keep out challengers. This "first mover advantage" is certainly a characteristic of dot-com survivors like Amazon.com or eBay. Those who lived through these years can also still recall the colossal dot-com start-up flops of the earlier period—including Webvan (for groceries), Pets.com, and eToys.com. Yet new evidence suggests that the overall survival rates for start-ups during that period was on par with, if not slightly higher, than those in other major industries during their formative years.

Recent acquisitions of start-ups such as MySpace, Skype, and YouTube suggest that a variation on "get big fast" is also alive and well today.

[Adapted from Gomes, 2006]

Another key lesson learned from the early 1990s about IT for competitive advantage has also proved again to be true: IT innovations that are sustainable over some appreciable time period are those that leverage a unique competitive capability or strength of the company—because the impact of the application is more difficult to replicate when it is strongly linked with other unique organizational capabilities (Clemons, 1991).

Nevertheless, Internet technologies did not disappear: they just slowed down, and both technology and business innovations for e-business systems continue today across the globe. Within the United States, many of the software and Web site innovations have been part of what's been referred to as a wave of **Web 2.0** capabilities, including social-networking software for information sharing across individual Web users and virtual communities. This consumer-centric phenomenon was highlighted in the year-end *Time* magazine "Person of the Year" award for 2006, in which the winner was "You" (signalled by a mirror on the magazine cover). In addition to independent Web sites for information sharing (such as MySpace and YouTube), businesses have begun to implement information-sharing sites that will also yield benefits such as an additional marketing channel or advertising revenues from other businesses (for example, see the MyRide.com introduction by Autobytel discussed later in this chapter).

In the next two sections, we provide selected examples of how traditional companies that have evolved to include Internet e-business capabilities (bricks-and-clicks firms), as well as new dot-com companies, have evolved to take advantage of Internet-based applications. We begin first with B2B applications, which are not visible to consumers in the same way that public Web sites for B2C applications are.

B2B APPLICATIONS

As discussed in the prior section, the earliest B2B applications were proprietary EDI systems using private networks, and by the early 1990s there was a large installed base of these systems. Because these proprietary systems were also highly reliable and efficient, it took almost a decade for many of these businesses to migrate to Internet technologies to replace these early proprietary systems or use the Internet as a secure communications channel. Many of the custom EDI systems of the past were also not economically feasible for most smaller businesses, so the Internet has also created entirely new B2B opportunities for smaller firms. By 2003, the dollar volume of B2B e-business had grown to about $1.3 trillion (from about

---

E-SOURCING AT NESTLÉ

As part of one of the largest food and beverage companies in the world, the Nestlé North American procurement team recognized that a comprehensive IT sourcing solution could yield much higher savings than doing sourcing offline for many of its purchasing categories. The team first focused on strategic purchasing of raw materials and packaging. Using an online auction capability required significant changes in the sourcing process, and the support that it received from top management helped the team promote the new approach. After several events, it learned to use the auction system more wisely and shared the success stories about the cost savings that have been achieved. As it made sense to do, the team then made plans for using e-sourcing for MRO products and additional services such as IT consulting and car leasing as well.

[Adapted from Ariba Spotlight: Nestlé, 2005]

$250 billion three years earlier), in comparison to an approximately $1 billion from B2C transactions by 2003.

Some of the benefits achievable with B2B applications via the Internet are the same as those previously achieved by large companies with EDI applications. For example, B2B applications via the Internet can reduce the cycle times for doing business with customers and suppliers and decrease the cost of these business transactions. In addition, however, B2B applications via the Internet faciltiate electronic linkages with new suppliers and new business customers, including the creation of new marketplace exchanges for buyers and sellers that have no geographic boundaries.

For example, B2B exchanges for the procurement of commodity MRO (materials, repair, and operations) supplies can generate significant cost savings. Even companies that use B2B e-sourcing software for purchasing items that are commodity products, which typically have very low margins, have reported initial cost savings of 5 percent or more (see the box entitled "E-Sourcing at Nestlé"). However, to capture these benefits using auction software under the control of a purchasing department requires investing in new software as well as standardized procedures.

Another alternative is to use B2B exchange software run by independent companies. In the late 1990s, many dot-com exchanges emerged to attempt to capture these new Internet markets. However, as shown in Figure 8.6, if the number of buyers is small, the buyers will have a lot of "buyer power" and will not likely want to pay an independent intermediary for an online service that they could provide themselves. Similarly, if the number of sellers is small, the sellers will theoretically rely on their own

• If Buyers and Sellers are
  Fragmented, **Independent
  Intermediaries** are
  likely to be successful.

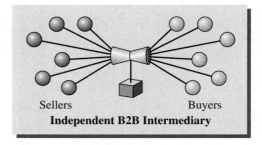

• If Sellers are Concentrated,
  Sellers are likely to dominate.

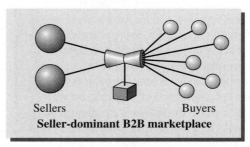

• If Buyers are Concentrated,
  Buyers are likely to dominate.

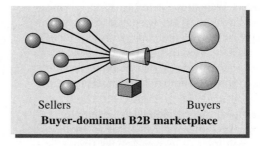

Figure 8.6   Dominant Providers for B2B Marketplaces

competitive power as a supplier or band together rather than pay an intermediary for an online service that they could provide themselves. As a result, many of these B2B intermediary ventures have since gone out of business.

An example of a consortium of competitors that included an exchange, but also didn't survive, was Covisint (pronounced coh-viz-int). This intermediary was established by the Big Three automobile manufacturers in the United States, and therefore had enormous joint "buyer power." However, it faced major roadblocks to operational and information sharing among the automakers in the consortium due to government antitrust laws, and has abandoned the broad initiative.

Another potential benefit from B2B systems via the Internet is improved information sharing with suppliers and customers. Many B2B applications use extranet portals: Web-based access to a password-protected site that provides access to a portion of a business partner's intranet. Improved relationships with business partners are a potential outcome because of the extensive information sharing about supply-chain transactions that is possible with this type of technology. Extranets for access to a customer's supply-chain information would typically be used only with a few selected business partners with which a strong interfirm relationship is considered to be highly beneficial.

Many other B2B applications are designed to specifically leverage prior enterprise system investments, especially ERP systems. For example, the e-sourcing initiative describe above at Nestlé USA leveraged a major supply chain initiative that was part of a global ERP system rollout (under the parent firm, headquartered in Switzerland) in which coordinated information to achieve major cost savings was a key driver (Vollman, 2005).

Similarly, customers and suppliers with access to centralized product and inventory information captured with a centralized database (as part of an ERP system) have been able to leverage this type of integrated data access to develop effective B2B applications for a vendor-managed inventory (VMI) partnership. VMI partnerships are dependent on timely electronic information sharing about sales, and the low cost of communications between businesses via the Internet have made this type of B2B application feasible for even midsized and smaller companies (for a detailed example, see Case Study II-1, "Vendor-Managed Inventory at NIBCO").

As more firms roll out standardized ERP platforms to more locations, and develop extranet portals for information sharing with key business partners, the benefits of B2B applications are expected to be realized by even more organizations of all sizes.

B2C APPLICATIONS

The growth of B2C e-business worldwide is dependent on the number of potential consumers that have Internet access, and the numbers of world Internet users has grown steadily. By 2004, within the United States, the demographics of Web users had become more mainstream. That is, the largest age group of Americans (ages 30 to 49) accounted for almost half of the total users, and the number of men and women across all age groups was approximately equal (Greenspan, 2004). By 2006, more than two-thirds of the U.S. population were reported to be Internet users (see Figure 8.7). However, North American Internet users represented only 20 percent of the world's Internet users by 2007, versus close to 30 percent in Europe and 36 percent in Asia. As can be seen in Figure 8.7,

since the population of North America is only about 5 percent of the world population, the ability to access potential Internet customers in Africa, Asia, and other world regions is just in its infancy.

The 1999 end-of-year holiday season within the United States is usually cited as a major milestone for B2C applications, as online sales approached 1 percent of the U.S. holiday sales for the first time. But besides online purchasing (24 percent of online users), consumers were already beginning to use Web sites for price comparisons (an additional 32 percent), and the remaining 45 percent were using the Web to search for gift ideas (Schwartz, 2001). By 2002, Internet users in the United States were buying products (62 percent), making travel reservations or buying travel tickets (50 percent), and banking online (32 percent). However, by 2006, the percentage of online retailing had grown to be just above 5 percent of all U.S. retailing.

Another widely recognized potential constraint for Internet users is the capacity of the "pipeline" that users have access to for different types of media and files. By midyear 2006, 143 million Americans used the Internet at home, and 72 percent of these users had a high-speed (broadband) connection. However, the U.S. experience has been that as more users have access to broadband Internet usage, companies modify their Web site content to make

WORLD INTERNET USAGE AND POPULATION STATISTICS

World Regions	Population (2006 Est.)	Population % of World	Internet Usage, Latest Data	% Population (Penetration)	Usage% of World	Usage Growth 2000–2006
Africa	915,210,928	14.1%	32,765,700	3.6%	3.0%	625.8%
Asia	3,667,774,066	56.4%	394,872,213	10.8%	36.4%	245.5%
Europe	807,289,020	12.4%	308,712,903	38.2%	28.4%	193.7%
Middle East	190,084,161	2.9%	19,028,400	10.0%	1.8%	479.3%
North America	331,473,276	5.1%	229,138,706	69.1%	21.1%	112.0%
Latin America/Caribbean	553,908,632	8.5%	83,368,209	15.1%	7.7%	361.4%
Oceania/Australia	33,956,977	0.5%	18,364,772	54.1%	1.7%	141.0%
WORLD TOTAL	6,499,697,060	100.0%	1,086,250,903	16.7%	100.0%	200.9%

Source: http://www.internetworldstats.com/stats.htm

NOTES: (1) Internet Usage and World Population Statistics were updated for Sept. 18, 2006. (2) [On web site] CLICK on each world region for detailed regional information. (3) Demographic (Population) numbers are based on data contained in the world-gazetteer website. (4) Internet usage information comes from data published by Nielsen//NetRatings, by the International Telecommunications Union, by local NICs, and other other reliable sources. (5) For definitions, disclaimer, and navigation help, see the Site Surfing Guide. (6) Information from this site may be cited, giving due credit and establishing an active link back to www.internetworldstats.com. © Copyright 2006, Miniwatts Marketing Group. All rights reserved worldwide.

Figure 8.7   Internet Usage and World Population Statistics. Copyright 2006. Miniwatts Marketing Group. All Rights Reserved.

File Type	Average Size	Ave. Download Time via Cable	Ave. Download Time via DSL
Single page text email	2.0 KB	0.0 sec.	0.0 sec.
20-page Word document	130 KB	0.3 sec.	0.5 sec.
Medium resolution photo	500 KB	1.1 sec.	1.9 sec.
MP3 file (5-minute song)	5 MB	11.0 sec.	19.5 sec.
60-second video clip	10 MB	22.0 sec.	38.9 sec.
2-hour movie, DivX format	700 MB	25 min.	45 min.
Full-length DVD	4.7 GB	2 hour 52 min.	5 hour 5 min.

Figure 8.8   Relative Download Times with Broadband for Common File Types (Adapted from Efrati, 2006)

use of the new capacity. Comparative download times for different types of file content are summarized in Figure 8.8.

The actual benefits for B2C e-business varies based on the market in which the seller competes, whether a company has traditionally sold directly to end consumers (either by catalog or retail store), and characteristics of the product or service. For example, products such as music and services such as aggregated information can be distributed directly to the customer in digital form using an online channel. However, the potential benefits are relatively clear, as summarized in Figure 8.9.

Next we describe how six companies have evolved their usage of the Internet for B2C applications. First, we describe two successful dot-com retailers (Amazon.com, Netflix); then, two traditional catalog retailers that were early innovators with using online Web technologies in combination with their supply chain systems (Dell, Lands' End); and finally, two traditional store retailers that are now competing with traditional and dot-com companies as "bricks-and-clicks" firms (Staples, Blockbuster). From these examples, we can learn about what makes an effective B2C application for direct-to-customer retailing.

Seller Benefits

24/7 access to customer for sales and support

Lower costs from online channel

Multimedia opportunities for marketing

New ways to research potential markets

New ways to distribute (if product/service can be digitized)

Global reach to buyers

Figure 8.9   Potential B2C Benefits to Sellers

Two Dot-Com Retailers

Amazon.com (www.amazon.com)   Amazon.com was a dot-com pioneer that began as an online bookseller in 1995. Under its founder Jeff Bezos, Amazon.com was able to leverage the publicity it received due to its successful "first mover" online retailing to quickly "brand" itself as a trusted dot-com company that provides a customer-friendly online shopping experience.

Named after the Earth's biggest river, Amazon.com was launched as a pure-play online retailer in 1994 with the slogan "Earth's Biggest Bookstore." Originally only a threat to traditional superstore booksellers (Borders, Barnes & Noble), by mid-1999 Amazon expanded into other third-party consumer products—from electronics to outdoor furniture—and reported having 17 million customers by the year 2000. Although traditional "big-box" retailers such as Wal-Mart, Target, and Sears became its new competitors, by August 2003 Amazon.com was the online "department store" with the most visitors, and by yearend 2003 the company finally reported its first profitable fiscal year.

Amazon.com has long been recognized for its superior online shopping experience for individual consumers, including its patented "one-click" method of online shopping and a tailoring capability that provides purchase recommendations based on a customer's own purchases as well as those by other online customers. In 2001, Amazon.com received the highest customer satisfaction score for any service company (online or offline) by the American customers that participated in the survey. (See the box entitled "Online Shopping at Amazon.com" in which personal computing critic for the *Wall Street Journal*, Walter Mossberg, described his online shopping experience as early as the year 2000.)

ONLINE SHOPPING AT AMAZON.COM

Amazon.com has won the loyalty of millions by building an online store that is friendly, easy to use, and inspires a sense of confidence and community among its customers. People trust Amazon.com, partly because it knows their tastes and does what it promises. Most purchases arrive on time and exactly as ordered. The company sends e-mails to tell when the order was processed and, later, when it was shipped. An order can be cancelled before it ships without going through the usual wrangling. If something goes wrong, Amazon usually forgives the shipping charge or upgrades the type of shipping.

The shopping experience is just terrific. The site is easy to navigate, even though it features 15 different departments. Searching is easy and excellent. The site intelligently personalizes the pages you see to highlight merchandise of a type you've bought before and to suggest similar items.

[Adapted from Mossberg, 2000]

Amazon.com was also one of the first Web sites to capture product reviews from its customers, which helped customers feel like they belonged to an online community. More recently, it launched a click-to-call customer service in which online shoppers can pose questions to a customer service representative: Users enter their phone numbers in a help screen, indicating how soon they would like to be contacted, and the customer's data—including usually what section of the site a customer is viewing—is made available to an Amazon.com employee.

Amazon.com has also leveraged its superior Web technology capabilities by selling its services as a Web site host for traditional retailers. For example, beginning in 2001 Target had a store tab on Amazon.com's site that linked Web users to selected Target products. In 2002, Target set up a contract with Amazon.com in which it could use Amazon.com's advanced search, personalization, product recommendation technology, 1-click shopping, etc. under Target's own URL. However, not all such Web hosting alliances have ended well. For example, in 2006 a state court ruled that Amazon.com had violated a 10-year agreement (begun in the year 2000) with Toys "R" Us that gave the toy retailer the exclusive right to sell toys and baby products on Amazon.com's Web site (Mangalindan, 2006).

Amazon.com's initial success as a dot-com book retailer has also been attributed to its early access to a major distribution infrastructure first built by another company. For example, when other dot-com retailers failed to deliver holiday purchases on time in late 1999, Amazon.com was able to fulfill 99 percent of its orders in time for the Christmas

holiday. When the company expanded its online store offerings in the following years, it also had to heavily invest in additional distribution facilities to handle products for which it kept its own inventory (including electronics).

Although as a *Fortune* 500 company, Amazon.com still generates relatively modest profits, its brand name is associated with superior customer service via its public Web site and innovative strategic alliances. For example, in 2005, the company introduced Amazon Prime, a flat-fee membership program for free two-day shipping benefits. In August 2007, it announced a new Books-on-Demand service via a company (CreateSpace.com) it had established several years earlier for on-demand CDs and DVDs of works by musicians and filmmakers.

Netflix (www.netflix.com)   Netflix is a newer dot-com, but one that has also achieved high brand recognition. The company was established in 1998 shortly after the DVD format had become the new standard for video rentals and sales. Under its founder and current CEO, Reed Hastings, the company began its flat-rate online movie rental business in 1999 with about 1,000 movie titles. In 2006, Netflix reported having 6.3 million subscribers (a 50 percent increase over the prior year), annual revenues close to $1 billion with profits close to $100 million, and an inventory of over 75,000 movies (and TV program) titles—including an extensive collection of documentaries and hard-to-find independent films.

The company's Web site (see Figure 8.10) features a bold red color scheme that promotes the dot-com's simple brand logo. Movie information is provided with images and text, and the site has an easy-to-use but sophisticated search and sorting capability. Subscribers create an ordered list (queue) of DVDs to be rented that are filled in the order listed, as available. Currently, U.S.-based customers can choose from several monthly subscription plans that vary in the number of movies that the customer can "check out" at the same time—such as 1 DVD at a time and up to 2 movies a month for a monthly fee of $5 all the way up to 8 movies at a time and an unrestricted total number of DVDs for a monthly fee of about $50. A smoothing (or "throttling") business rule reportedly gives priority selection and shipping to member plans with the fewest discs per month. By 2007, about 1.5 million DVDs were being mailed out daily to customers' mailboxes from over 40 distribution centers in 29 different states, using the U.S. Postal Service. Customers return the videos to Netflix by mail using the same preaddressed, prepaid envelope at a time of their own choosing. According to some assessments, one of the IT "secrets" behind its supply chain capabilities is the use of a bar code on the

Figure 8.10 Netflix Home Page. Reproduced by permission of Netflix, Inc. Copyright (insert copyright symbol 2007 Netflix, Inc. All Rights Reserved.)

envelope, as well as a bar code on the DVD in the envelope that is visible from a window opening (Zachary, 2006).

Similar to Amazon.com's customer reviews, members can create a "Friends List," with whom they share their movie queues, and provide movie ratings that can be viewed by other members. Sixty percent of customers reportedly select their rentals based on movie recommendations provided by the Web site, which uses an algorithm (similar to Amazon.com) that takes into account past rental titles by the subscriber and recommendations by other members who have similar tastes. Members can also sign up for e-mail notifications (press release information, video library updates, media reviews) and RSS feeds for account and video release information.

The company has filed several patents on its business model and recently settled a patent litigation suit against its bricks-and-clicks rival Blockbuster (see the Blockbuster description later in this chapter). In January 2007, the company also began launching a digital movie distribution service ("WatchNow") using a proprietary video streaming technology to existing subscribers' personal computers (with Microsoft XP or Vista operating systems and the Internet Explorer browser). Initially, this new service was offered for free (with one free hour per subscription dollar limit), and in these first six months subscribers reportedly had more than 5 million viewings. The company reported plans to invest about $40 million in this new Internet delivery service, with about 5,000 titles available to all of its subscribers, by yearend 2007. Netflix's goal is to eventually be able to deliver movies to any Internet-connected screen—including cell phones.

Two Traditional Catalog Retailers

Dell (www.dell.com) Within the PC industry, Dell Corporation (formerly Dell Computer Corporation) was one of the first to establish a customer-driven PC configuration capability. Its early mover advantage was due to its already existing business model: Unlike competitors that manufactured PCs for a distribution channel, Dell had a make-to-order assembly model that received orders from its own direct-to-customer retail channels—using call centers, fax, and phone orders—but no retail stores. Launched in July 1996, Dell's Web site leveraged the software applications and experiences of its own customer service representations to create an effective "self-service" Web application that let online customers create their own custom PC orders. Customers can experiment with different computer configurations using a "choiceboard" capability that shows them price differences for components and calculates the total price *before* finalizing their order. Customers submit their PC order via the Web site, and the order data is translated into a design, the components are ordered, and then the right resources are electronically scheduled to fulfill the order "Direct from Dell."

For retail sales to business customers (which is a larger customer segment than end-consumer sales), Dell's sales staff works with an organization's procurement managers to select a small number of PC configurations at a prenegotiated price to fit the company's infrastructure standards and employee needs. Only these options are displayed when the company's employees access the secure Web page (Premier Pages) customized for their firm. The configurations typically also include preloaded application software packages, sometimes with company-specific images.

By yearend 2002, Dell was number one in market share for desktop PCs and was also the number one Internet retailer. However, by mid-2006 Dell had lost its market share position to Hewlett-Packard (which had merged with Compaq Computer a few years earlier). The company's highly efficient supply-chain model and direct sales retail approach were still intact, but by then its competitors were also able to compete online as well as through their traditional distribution channels. In January 2007, its founder, Michael Dell, returned as CEO, and a few months later Dell announced that it had signed a pact to sell low-end, preconfigured desktop PCs in Wal-Mart stores in North America. Initially, only two models would be offered as part of an expanded electronics section in Wal-Mart stores, but the company suggested that this would be its "first step" into a global retail store market.

This announcement clearly signalled a recognition that the build-to-order, catalog model that its founder had leveraged during the first decade of online sales was at a disadvantage in today's multichannel, bricks-and-clicks world. Until then, Dell had been the major "holdout" in the U.S.-based PC industry, since Hewlett-Packard, Apple, Toshiba, and others already sold their products in retail stores, including superstores with bricks-and-clicks models like Best Buy and Circuit City.

Lands' End (www.landsend.com)   Founded in 1963 as a retailer of first sailing equipment, then clothes and home furnishings, Lands' End traditionally marketed its products via catalog. Like Dell, it took sales orders via mail, telephone, and fax. In the late 1990s, it began selling its products online via its Web site. Similar to Dell, its traditional distribution infrastructure for catalog sales was easily modified to also fulfill online orders, and the company quickly realized additional profits from its new multichannel capability.

In October 2001, Lands' End also was an early mover in offering online sales of custom-crafted clothing. The customer answers a few questions about fit preferences and body type, and can "try on" items and outfits using a 3-D model via its Web site. The customizaton product innovation was made possible by an alliance with Archetype Solutions, Inc. (ASI), a small start-up, founded by a prior Levi Strauss North America manager. Levi's had been an early experimenter with online orders of customized clothing but, unlike Lands' End, traditionally sold its products via distributors rather than direct to customers. ASI's algorithms translate a customer's measurements into a pattern for cutting fabric for a specific product, which is then electronically submitted to manufacturers of the custom clothing orders. Other Lands' End initial IT investments included software to track custom orders as they were passed between Lands' End, ASI, offshore manufacturing sites, and shippers.

Lands' End began with custom orders for a small number of products. By 2003, its Web site sales of custom chinos and jeans accounted for 40 percent of its sales for those product lines. The company kept in place its usual generous return policy for its custom orders and customers that experienced poor fit were encouraged to "try again" by providing additional information. The company then used this customer feedback to improve its software algorithms with ASI. However, by 2007 several competitors (including Levi's) were offering their own customization options and similar promises of money-back, customer-satisfaction guarantees.

Although Lands' End was acquired by U.S.-based retailer Sears in 2002 (just a few years prior to the merger of Sears and Kmart), its public Web site has not featured this relationship in any way, except for a listing of Lands' End "stores" within Sears stores across selected U.S. locations. Previously, Lands' End clothing had been found in different sections of the large Sears stores, which gave the brand an additional sales channel but diluted its image as a specialty apparel brand. The new Lands' End stores-within-a-store also were to offer lounge areas and Internet kiosks to help promote online sales. The companies' systems have also been integrated so that customers can return Lands' End clothing purchased online to a Sears store.

Two Traditional Store Retailers

Staples (www.staples.com)   Staples began as a superstore retailer of office products in 1986. Initially, the company focused on the small business and home office market, but by the late 1990s it had implemented separate Web sites to support the procurement of supplies and equipment by *Fortune* 1000 companies, midsize companies, and small businesses, as well as a catalog division, and 1,100 stores in six counties.

The company's public Web site has little aesthetic appeal but is designed to efficently facilitate first-time and repeat orders, with tabs, textual and graphical product descriptions, and search capabilities similar to other superstore sites. A store locator feature is prominently placed on its Web site, and in recent years it has also promoted its "Easy button" brand marketing. In its retail stores, kiosks enable customers to order products not available in a given store from an online inventory.

Beginning with its 1998 launch of its online division, Staples's strategy was to align its online and offline divisions to take advantage of its existing infrastructure for order fulfillment for retail store and catalog sales. Its early multichannel integration was also no doubt fostered by other external events: Its plan for an initial public offering (IPO) of the tracking stock for its online unit was abandoned due to the dot-com meltdown in the year 2000.

By yearend 2006, Staples was the world's largest office products company with $18 billion in revenues generated from its public Web site, extranet sites, catalogs, and stores, including almost $5 billion in e-business sales.

Blockbuster (www.blockbuster.com)   Until recently, Blockbuster had avoided becoming a "bricks-and-clicks" competitor with online sales to rival its major dot-com competitor Netflix. However, after several years of income losses, Blockbuster began its online rental site in 2004. By 2006, it remained the world's largest video rental company with 8,000 stores, including over 2,500 stores in 25 countries, renting movies and videogames on DVDs. In November 2006, it launched its Total Access program, in which it leveraged its multichannel capability to include in-store returns (and exchanges) for online rentals. After the first six months, which included a major advertising campaign during the most widely watched national football game in the United States (the Super Bowl), it had over 2 million new subscribers.

The Blockbuster Web site has similar capabilties to the Netflix site (see previous description), including a "Friends and Family" feature, and utilizes a customer profiling application that allows customers to set preferences that can be used to better target movie recommendations from the site. Like Netflix, its online rentals are also distributed via the U.S. Postal Service. In addition to its highly automated, centralized distribution facility in Texas, it operates about three dozen distribution centers throughout the United States.

However, in addition to being a laggard in developing a true multichannel capability, Blockbuster was also a laggard in developing a capability to digitally distribute movies online. In August 2007, following the replacement

of its CEO, the company announed its strategic move to address this major competitive shortcoming: the acquisition of Movielink, a movie download service that was a joint venture of five major movie studios. The stated vision is to offer online video delivery via the Web using its large library of movie titles and strategic alliances with movie studios to new customers, as well as customers who do not have access to its retail stores. To help address its continued operating losses, the company is also closing its less profitable stores.

Summary: B2C Retailing

The Initial Dot-Com Advantage   In the mid-1990s, as corporate America was beginning to learn about this piece of software called a Web browser, *the dot-com companies clearly had the online advantage*: They could focus on developing interactive customer experiences that helped them brand their Web sites, which "were" their companies in the eyes of their customers. Dot-com retailers also had the luxury of avoiding the costs and constraints associated with retailing via stores, such as owning or leasing physical stores and personnel costs.

The dot-com IT leaders also had a clear advantage as they focused on hiring workers with Web technology skills and interests, who had a kind of "green field" opportunity to develop systems. They could focus on developing superior online experiences without having to consider linkages with legacy applications or migrating historical data.

However, having the eyeballs of Internet users and online orders was not enough for a successful online retailer. Customer communications are primarily (if not completely) automated via the Internet and product delivery is typically via services such as UPS or FedEx, but the new dot-com businesses also faced significant challenges to develop efficient back-end processes and information systems to complete the order delivery process. In fact, the importance of a reliable order fulfillment capability, with delivery tracking capabilities for customers, became widely recognized after the publicized failures of dot-com companies to deliver holiday purchases in 1999. These consumer failtures, in turn, contributed to the "wake-up call" among venture capitalists that led to the rapid closedown of many U.S.-based dot-coms in the months that followed.

Dot-com pioneer Amazon.com was an innovator in using the new Web technologies to tailor content to match a customer's online ordering preferences, but it also recognized the importance of a reliable back-office order fulfillment capability. It initially was able to jump-start its fulfillment capability (for books and CDs) with a business alliance, but Amazon.com also continued to invest heavily in technology and process improvements for its warehouses as it expanded its third-party products to compete with discount department stores such as Wal-Mart and Sears. Although Amazon.com has struggled to achieve high profitability, the company's superior online Web site and back-office IT capabilities have enabled it to be an IT provider for other companies, while still surviving as a third-party retailer.

Dot-com Netflix had a later start-up and therefore less venture capital to support its growth. However, this company has also benefitted from being in an industry niche (movie rentals) where the largest traditional video rental competitor (Blockbuster) was slow to develop a multichannel capability. Given that video can be delivered online in digitizable form, the current challenge faced by both the dot-com and traditional companies in this industry niche will be to evolve easy-to-use digital online video capabilities. Blockbuster appears to at last be in a good position to do this, given a recent acquisition that leverages its multi-year alliances with major movie studios.

Today's Multichannel Advantage   By the middle of the first decade in the new millenium, *the online advantage had clearly shifted to traditional firms who had developed a multichannel capability*. In a direct sales model, the seller and buyer communicate directly. When a direct retailer who traditionally has sold products via a store or catalog implements an online sales capability, it creates an additional channel for the customer to gather information, purchase a product, or get customer service (via information on the site or other contact methods). The customer can still go to a store, or call a customer service rep, but there is also the option of using the retailing Web site when it's more convenient. From a customer perspective, however, an effective multichannel capability means that online purchases can also be returned or exchanged in a retail store, and perhaps purchased online and picked up from a nearby store by the customer a short time later. And to facilitate this type of multichannel capability requires significant IT investments.

Traditional catalog companies (such as Dell and Lands' End) were among the first to become "bricks-and-clicks" firms by leveraging not only their brand names, but also their distribution systems for offline catalog customers that were designed to deliver small product quantities to widely dispersed customers. Dell Computer had the additional advantage of selling build-to-order computer products to early Internet shoppers that were among the most computer literate, as well as typically eager to play with different configuration options as part of the online ordering process. As catalog retailers of their own products, Dell

and Lands' End were also both early Web innovators by offering online tools to enable a "mass customization" sales strategy: The customer designs their own products, which these companies then make-to-order.

However, within just a few years, both of these traditional catalog companies' innovations had been copied by other computer hardware and apparel companies, and their traditional customers now have lots of other Web-based retailers to choose from. These two companies have also recently linked themselves with large retail store chains. Although this relationship gives them the opportunity to learn about marketing and sales from a large retailer, both companies also face the challenge of not diluting their preestablished images as retailers of higher end products at low cost, with superior customer service.

Today, the multichannel advantage seems to be in the hands of companies that can offer *both in-person and online customer service and sales* via retail stores as well as the Web. This type of multichannel capability (like developed by Staples and Blockbuster) enables customers to use the Internet to find and order the product they want, and then choose whether to receive it via a delivery service or from a store. If a store is nearby, they might pick up their purchase (or rental) at the store that same day, or return an item ordered online in a store where they can be immediately serviced in-person. If a store is not nearby, or does not have the item wanted, their Web sites give the customer the opportunity for online shopping with a company not available in their geographic region or not able to immediately satisfy their purchase needs.

However, to provide this type of seamless multichannel capability, companies need to integrate their place (off-line) and space (online) business operations as well as their information systems. Sometimes barriers to this type of integration are preestablished incentive systems that reward for performance based on only a traditional channel (in-store). The business and IT personnel that support both off-line and online business operations also need to be linked in some way, in order to develop applications and processes that support a single face to the customer, no matter what sales channel is used.

Prior to the year 2000, a firm's new online systems for order fulfillment were typically developed separately from their legacy systems. Today, however, companies such as Staples and Blockbuster have recognized the need for a fully integrated approach and have made the necessary organizational and IT investments to have a truly multichannel e-business capability as part of their online strategy.

It should also be noted that all six of the B2C examples described here are companies that use the Web for retailing their own products or third-party products. However, when manufacturing or service firms that traditionally have sold their products or services through distributors first set up a new direct-to-customer Web site capability, they need to carefully take into account the potential responses of the companies that are their traditional intermediaries.

In the next section, we focus on how three companies created dot-com businesses that couldn't have existed prior to the Internet.

DOT-COM INTERMEDIARIES

In the mid-1990s, there was a widespread belief that the Internet would primarily have a *disintermediation* effect. As shown in Figure 8.4, the intermediaries between the companies that created the products and services and their end consumers would no longer be economically viable, because the producers could adopt a direct-to-consumer sales strategy. Disintermediation has certainly occurred in some industries—notably the disintermediation of travel agencies by airline companies that have developed their own Web sites for ticketing and other customer services. However, the Internet has also of course led to another phenomenon: the formation of dot-com companies that serve as online intermediaries between producer companies and their customers.

To be successful, an intermediary company needs to be able to attract a large enough user base that will generate revenues that pay for the unique service that it provides to buyers, or sellers, or both. The service provided could be an online marketplace that brings together buyers or sellers (such as an auction) for which a buyer and/or seller pays a fee; a single site with products and services from multiple sellers (such as a travel site) for which a buyer and/or seller pays a fee; or a Web navigation (or "finder") tool valued by individuals (such as a Web search tool) that also facilitates targeted advertising by businesses.

The three dot-com companies described in this section are each examples of companies that provide at least one of these types of services to generate revenues:

- eBay, (*www.ebay.com*), a pioneer in C2C electronic auctions that was one of the first dot-com companies to achieve profitability based on small fees paid for auction sales and other services, that today also generates major fees from being a B2C and B2B intermediary.
- Autobytel (*www.autobytel.com*), also a dot-com pioneer as an intermediary between automotive dealers and potential buyers, but which today is still struggling to be profitable.

- Google (*www.google.com*), a more recent dot-com with a superior Web search algorithm that currently supports more than half of the Internet searches submitted daily around the world, and has recently achieved record profitability as a dot-com due to targeted advertising revenues.

Additional ideas about what makes a successful intermediary can be learned from examining these three companies' business models in more detail.

eBay (www.ebay.com) EBay has been successful as an intermediary that brings together individual buyers and sellers from over the world who might not otherwise find each other (see Figure 8.11). Launched in 1995, the company had captured about 80 percent of the online auction market by the year 2000, with more than $5 billion in merchandise sales from 250 million auctions and global participants. By yearend 2006, it had over 6 million listings that generated $14 billion in trades during the fourth quarter alone.

The online auction model is based on revenues captured as a percentage of the auction sale, as a transaction fee for the sale, and/or as a listing fee. Initially, the eBay business model was a consumer-to-consumer (C2C) application; that is, the typical user assumed that they were part of a "community" of individual buyers and sellers. However, many eBay sellers today are small businesses: liquidators, wholesalers, small retail shops, or at-home entrepreneurs. EBay today is therefore also an intermediary for businesses of many sizes that sell to other businesses or individuals. To foster relationships with small businesses in particular, the company provides extensive online advice as well as periodically runs workshops in various geographic regions.

EBay has continued to add online services, often by buying other small companies that first developed them. For example, it created a fixed price trading capability for direct sales of previously owned goods when it purchased the dot-com startup Half.com. For auction sales there is also a "Buy It Now" capability in which the buyer agrees to pay a price specified by the seller before the auction period is scheduled to be over. In 2003, it also purchased PayPal, which provided eBay with their own third-party payment capability: An account can be established by users with debit cards, bank accounts, or stored balances, which enables usage by those who might not otherwise be able to book tickets online. Since PayPal also still provides payment services to other Web sites, it has become an additional revenue source for eBay. Fees are also collected from sellers for "extras" such as additional digital photos with a listing, the highlighting of a listing, and setting a

Figure 8.11 EBay Web Site

"reserved price" (such as a minimum price or a Buy-It-Now capability). In 2005, it purchased Skype, a peer-to-peer Internet telephony network, which also generates outside revenues.

As an intermediary that hosts millions of auction sales simultaneously, in real time, eBay's IT operations are of critical importance. In addition to capacity planning for its servers, the company has also had to quickly recover from denial-of-service attacks and other security breaches in recent years. Its primary value to sellers and buyers is low search costs, so the design and execution of its site search capabilities must also be of the highest quality. The actual transfer of the purchased good takes place between the buyer and seller, but eBay maintains data about the transaction and tracks sales for sellers, and purchases for buyers. However, the company is also not responsible for the quality or legal ownership of the items sold, as it clearly states on its Web site.

Like other online intermediaries dealing directly with the public, eBay faces considerable sales transaction risks, such as buyers with inadequate funds, sellers that misrepresent their goods, or sellers that do not deliver their goods. Since maintaining the trust of buyers and sellers is a key to its survival, one of eBay's early tactics for self-policing was to encourage buyers to rate their sellers, and vice versa. The company also offers insurance coverage for items of certain types and value, and facilitates a process to resolve disputes between buyers and sellers.

EBay also continually monitors its sites for the sale of inappropriate items, or even illegal items. For example, eBay has had to delete listings for items related to tragic events in the United States—including the 9/11 terrorist attacks and the explosion of the NASA space shuttle *Columbia* (see box entitled "EBay Items Yanked").

EBAY ITEMS YANKED

EBay deleted several items billed as debris from the space shuttle *Columbia* from the online auction site Saturday, warning that anyone attempting to sell fragments from the doomed shuttle could be prosecuted. It's unclear what kind of debris was listed, but eBay spokesman Kevin Pursglove said that many of the items were pranks. The listings were immediately yanked from the site, and executives may report the sellers to federal authorities. The San Jose-based company has become a barometer of pop culture and current events. But eBay must also deal with morbid postings and attempts to capitalize on human tragedy, and it frequently pulls items.

[Adapted from The Associated Press, 2003]

Autobytel (www.autobytel.com) Autobytel was the first online automotive intermediary. Launched the same year as eBay (1995), it also had a successful beginning (IPO) as a public company in 1999, and purchased a struggling competitor (Autoweb) in 2001. However, Autobytel has also struggled to achieve sustainable profitability, despite being the automotive Web site with the most traffic and close partnerships with other businesses to provide additional services to an auto buyer (including access to videos from auto manufacturers, and links to financial, warranty, and insurance services).

Autobytel's primary business model has been to provide sales "leads" to local automobile dealerships based on requests for information by Web site users. Potential customers provide characteristics that they are seeking (such as car make and model or category, model year, price, or payment range), and customer information is provided to dealers in the customer's geographical area that have cars with those characteristics.

Since most car manufacturers today have their own sophisticated Web sites featuring their own cars, a dot-com intermediary for customer leads to dealers—who pay for this service—is a potentially viable business model in the United States primarily because of a characteristic of the current legal environment for new car sales: State laws prohibit manufacturers from selling directly to consumers. In other words, the potential "supplier" threat of car manufacturers reaching directly to customers, and disintermediating car dealerships, is still quite low due to laws at the state level. This situation is expected to continue for some time due to the large state tax revenues generated from automotive sales for new cars in particular. However, Web sites for national conglomerates of automotive dealerships (such as AutoNation) that offer quick quotes, inventory searches, and dealer searches are major competitors.

In addition, the initial conventional wisdom that online purchasing of an automobile without a dealer would be unlikely because consumers would want to test-drive such an expensive purchase, has not proven to be entirely true. In particular, online intermediaries that link end consumers with used car owners (including eBay) have become a major threat to used car dealers, state tax coffers, and independent intermediaries such as Autobytel.

To remain successful as a "lead generator," Autobytel has also invested in helping car dealerships convert "serious" sales leads to actual sales. The company advertises itself as an "Internet marketing specialist" for the dealerships based on the capabilities of software applications that dealers can pay the compay to host for them, such as:

1. a software program that generates a phone call to a dealer within seconds after a Web user has submitted an online request for a price quote, and also allows dealers to request an automated phone call to that potential car buyer (who presumably can be reached while still using their computer).
2. lead management tools that coordinate and track follow-up contacts by e-mail and phone with prospective customers, which may include a series of customized e-mail messages from the local dealership that are automatically sent in a prescheduled sequence from the "most qualified" representative in the dealership, based on prespecified criteria.

In 2007, the majority of its revenues were still from fees for sales leads paid by both new and used car dealers, but with growing revenues from advertising and a smaller, stable percentage of revenues from fees for these types of customer relationship management (CRM) services.

By mid-2007, Auboytel had also launched a beta version of a new Web site designed to leverage recent consumer interest in social networking (Web 2.0) tools: MyRide.com. In addition to providing "vertical-search" tools to provide more focused results (than broad-based navigation searches on Google), the site is being marketed as a community "meeting place" for car owners and enthusiasts, with online tools for them to share stories (blogs), photos, and personal videos.

Google (www.google.com) Google was founded in 1998 by two Stanford University doctoral students in their 20s who put their studies on hold to develop a Web search capability with more relevant results than the dominant service player at the time (Yahoo!)—using a PageRank algorithm, in which pages that were linked to other pages were given higher weightings. (The company's name is a play on the word *googol*: the number 1 followed by one hundred zeroes.) Within two years, it was the ninth U.S. Web site in terms of unique monthly visitors (24.5 million) without the company having spent any money on marketing (see Figure 8.12 and the sidebar entitled "Google Timeline for Major Products and Services").

Although initially the company's revenues were only based on sales of its search engine, the company changed its business model in 2003 to capture advertising revenues. At first, ad revenues to search engine dot-coms were paid by companies who placed bids to pay more money than other companies to be listed based on the same keywords. By March 2003, Google had launched a targeted advertising service in which ads were posted based on "contextual" search results, and by 2007 the company was reportedly

price was determined by a Dutch aution rather than investment bankers.

Like other dot-com successes, the company has continued to grow by both internal innovations as well as acquisitions. For example, its purchase of Keyhole enabled it to launch Google Maps and other GIS applications (Google Earth), whose success are due to the tight integration of these applications with the company's search capabilities (see the box entitled "Google Mapping").

Since its IPO, the company has continued to broaden its offerings, and therefore its attractiveness to advertisers. Its acquistion of YouTube and alliance with the parent of MySpace (News Corp.) has greatly increased its attractiveness to users, and advertisers, as a Web portal. This relatively new company also played new roles in the 2007–2008 U.S. presidential race: YouTube postings were the sources for some televised candidate "debates," and Google searches on a candidate name revealed some interesting sponsored links (see the box entitled "Google Ads and Political Elections").

capturing about one-third of total Internet advertising dollars (see the box entitled "How to Help Online Customers Find You").

The company has been known in the past as a dot-com with distinctive corporate values, with a slogan of "Don't be evil" and other democratic ideals associated with computer science and engineering professionals in general and early Silicon Valley innovators. Its approach to its initial public offering (IPO) in mid-2004 reinforced its founders' insistence that it was a company of the people, as its initial IPO

GOOGLE TIMELINE FOR MAJOR PRODUCTS AND SERVICES

1995: Google cofounders, Sergey Brin from Moscow and Larry Page from Michigan, meet at a spring gathering of new Stanford University Ph.D. computer science candidates.

1997: Brin and Page create BackRub, the precursor to the Google search engine.

1998: Google becomes incorporated; founders raise $1 million in funding from family, friends and "angel" investors.

1999: Google raises $25 million in funding from venture capitalist firms (Sequoia Capital, Kleiner Perkins Caufield & Byers).

2000: Google becomes the largest search engine on the Web. Yahoo! picks Google as its default search results provider.

2001: Eric Schmidt, CEO of Novell and a former chief technology officer at Sun Microsystems, joins Google—first as chairman, then CEO.

2002: Google begins selling its enterprise search appliance (hardware and software product) to organizations to help users find information on their corporate intranets. Google launches a beta version of Google News, rolls out its key word advertising program worldwide, and launches a beta version of its shopping service Froogle (product search service).

2003: Google acquires Pyra Labs, creator of Blogger.com tools, and Applied Semantics. Google launches AdSense, an advertising program that delivers ads based on the content of Web sites (contextual ads).

2004: Yahoo! rolls out its own new Web search technology (phases out Google). Google announces its free e-mail service, Gmail, supported by advertising. Google acquires Keyhole (satellite image mapping). Google launches Google Book Search (formerly Google Print)—both a library digitizing project and a partner program for publishing PDF files of books—and Orkut (social networking). Amazon.com launches a beta version of Web search service using Google search technology.

April 29, 2004: Google files with the U.S. Securities and Exchange Commission to sell as much as $2.7 billion in stock in an initial public offering. The company said it would seek to list on either the NASDAQ or the New York Stock Exchange.

2005: Google launches Google Maps (for North American users) and Google Earth (using Keyhole), Talk (instant message and VoIP service), and Mobile Google Local.

2006: Google purchases YouTube, Inc., and signs pacts with eBay and News Corp's MySpace for use of search technology and carrying ads brokered by Google. Google purchases dMarc (for national radio advertising).

April 13, 2007: Google announces intent to purchase Internet advertising services company DoubleClick.

Figure 8.12   Google Home Page

However, its 2007 announcement of its intent to purchase DoubleClick began to generate concerns from potential business partners, due to the company's number one market position in online advertising revenues (an estimated $10 billion annually). The company already had access to aggregate data on millions of individuals' Web searches, and their responses to specific ads, which led to the speculation that the company could in the future create something like a NASDAQ for Internet ads. The company's large cash holdings and other acquisition targets also pointed to a strategy that would include a multichannel advertising capability—that is, ads delivered by television, radio, and print media, as well as online.

Summary: Successful Online Intermediary Models

Like some of the direct-to-customer retail examples we discussed earlier, online intermediaries have achieved their current success by continuously innovating with superior IT capabilities. EBay's business model requires superior IT operations capabilities, and except for some early server reliability problems, it has continuously maintained an outstanding record for systems availability and reliability. Google's success is primarily due to its superior search capabilities, still accessible today via a deceptively simple screen interface. Autobytel's new Web site (MyRide.com) is also based on providing an easy-to-use, superior search capability—for a specific (vertical) market—but its survival as a business is still highly dependent on local dealers paying for Internet leads provided by an independent intermediary.

In addition, all three of these intermediaries have continued to evolve their business models to provide enough value to buyers and sellers, so that they can capture relatively small fees from a large enough number of buyers or sellers. EBay has expanded into certification services in order to provide auction services for products that yield higher service fees (such as used cars), and has also considerably changed its original buyer/seller mix to include many small businesses selling their products online, as well as large brand companies that sell their inventory remainders. Google's continued success will depend on how well it continues to manage its growth by acquisition and create new types of markets.

The sustainability of Autobytel's B2C intermediary model will depend on its continuing ability to attract potential car buyers as well as to help local dealers (who pay them fees) to be more successful in their own sales business. Many consumers may not be aware that it is Autobytel's own software that is resulting in an immediate phone call from a local dealer as they are still using their computer to search for the right car purchase, or that the customized e-mail message from a given dealer is based on a customer relationship management tool hosted by Autobytel for any dealer that will pay for this service.

Finally, all three intermediaries have succeeded in branding themselves online. EBay and Autobytel appear to have benefitted from a "first mover" presence: both companies first launched their Web sites in 1995. However, Google's recent meteoric rise is a clear reminder that a strong brand is not enough to guarantee survival as an intermediary. Individual Web users were quick to "switch" loyalties away from another dot-com pioneer (Yahoo!) when they perceived a better "free" service by a much younger company, whose name also became a verb (Google).

SPECIAL ISSUE: WHAT MAKES A GOOD WEB SITE?

For e-business applications that use a Web site, the company's Web site "is" the company. This means that the design and operation of the Web site is of critical importance for dot-com as well as bricks-and-clicks firms.

A useful framework for thinking about Web site designs from a human-computer interface perspective is the 7Cs framework in Figure 8.13 developed by Rayport and Jaworski (2004). These 7Cs take into account both the functional and the aesthetic characteristics of a good Web site. Using Rayport and Jaworski's framework, Web sites known for their superior customer experience can be analyzed and then compared to the Web sites of other companies that are pursuing similar e-business models.

Note that the Rayport and Jaworski framework has a separate "C" for Community. Although companies in some industries (such as banks) may not highly value such a characteristic, "fostering community" has been associated with a more mature (level 5) site by other early researchers as well (Seybold, 1995). Investments in Web site features and tools to achieve a sense of community among their users have significantly grown in recent years, as business firms have observed the meteoric rise in popularity of social networking Web sites such as MySpace and YouTube.

Another widely disseminated framework is Microsoft's Usability Guidelines (MUG), which has the following categories (Venkatesh, 2003): content, ease-of-use,

Context	Site's layout and design—functionally vs. aesthetically dominant or both (integrated)
Content	Text, pictures, sound, and video that Web site contains, including offering dominant "store types"
Commerce	Site's capabilities to enable commercial transactions—functional tools and pricing
Community	Ways that the site utilizes user-to-user communication to enable feelings of membership and shared common interests
Connection	Extent to which the site is linked to other sites—links out and in
Customization	Site's ability to tailor itself to different users or to allow users to personalize the site
Communication	Ways that the site enables site-to-user, user-to-site, or two-way communications

Figure 8.13   7Cs Framework for Web Site Design

made-for-the-medium (including customer tailoring), promotion, and emotion (affective reactions to the site). Again, the recent investments in community features are directed at yielding high user ratings for the emotion category.

Other key attributes of a good Web site are related to the characteristics of the operational environment—both the client side and the Web server side—as well as the networks being accessed. Common technical problems that need to be anticipated include download delays, search problems, as well as security weaknesses (Straub, 2003). User tolerance for download times will likely be a function of the users' goals, where they are working (at home versus the office), whether they are connected to a high-speed communications line or not, and whether the download involves multimedia, and the user's expectations for the download time (see Figure 8.8). Delays in download times can be at the server side, the client side, and/or be a function of the network infrastructure between the client and server.

Given the increase in wireless networks and handheld devices that can access the Internet, today's developers must also consider what makes a good Web site display not only on desktop computer screens but also on much smaller devices. In addition to the differences in hardware (e.g., screen size, keyboard, etc.), developers also need to take into account differences in typical device usage. For example, the typical mobile user may use the device for shorter time periods, and in very different contexts (while traveling, shopping, walking down a street, etc.).

Lee and Benbasat (2003) have identified some of the design elements that address the consumer's limited attention as well as the deficient displays of today's typical handheld devices for each of the 7Cs shown previously. For Commerce, for example, a secure payment method that demands minimal cognitive attention is needed, as well as a condensed checkout process suitable for a small display (see Figure 8.14).

As noted at the beginning of this chapter, however, the examples provided here are primarily U.S.-centric. As more and more Internet users are non-U.S., and companies in other countries begin to take the lead in Internet innovations, we will also better understand what it takes to have a successful Web site for users in different countries. Some of the adjustments made by a Chinese dot-com e-tailer, for example, are shared in the box entitled "Building a Dot-Com Superstore in China."

M-Commerce Web Site Design Issues			
7Cs Framework		**Mobile Setting** to support consumer's limited attention	**Mobile Device Constraints** to complement the insufficient display of mobile devices
Context	*Focal Point*	Linking structure that connects pages seamlessly but efficiently	Section breakdown that organizes information in separate pages
	Interface Implementation	• Menu structured in a shallow rather than a deep hierarchy • Layered sequential process rather than field selection process	Summary and key words that give a whole picture of information separated over pages
Content	*Focal Point*	The adaptive supply of product information and promotional messages to a user's setting	Multimedia mix to utilize both visual and audio channels
	Interface Implementation	Proximate selection method that makes nearby located objects easier to choose (gas stations, bank accounts)	• Conversion of visual information to audio format • Use of non-speech sound
Community	*Focal Point*	Interactive communication by connecting the people with similar needs	To accelerate interactive information exchange despite inferior input/output devices
	Interface Implementation	Connection to shopping companions who share interests in common	SMS, and graphics describing products, transferred through a user's phone book
Customization	*Focal Point*	Tailoring enhanced by information on users' mobile setting	Filtering unnecessary information, so that a small screen contains only information that is highly useful
	Interface Implementation	Proximate selection method that emphasizes the objects of interest, by combining a user's mobile setting (location, time, and resource) with his or her personal interests	Personalized service based on known user profile (content and layout configuration without a need of log-in registration)
Communication	*Focal Point*	Broadcast messages relevant to a consumer's environment	Alternative methods for interactive communication that overcome text typing with awkward input devices
	Interface Implementation	Targeted advertising suitable at the point-of-purchase	Customer feedback in multiple-answer or multimedia formats
Connection	*Focal Point*	Pathways that present Web sites relevant to users' changing environment	To reduce the probability of feeling lost given pathways provided
	Interface Implementation	Adaptive map that shows the information about nearby stores	Icon that gives a link to the starting page with one click of the 'cancel' button
Commerce	*Focal Point*	Secure payment method demanding minimal cognitive attention	Condensed checkout process
	Interface Implementation	Insertion of authentication into mobile phones	One-click checkout process made available by storing a consumer's address, payment method, and preferred delivery options

Figure 8.14   Designing an Interface for Mobile Devices © [Source: Lee and Benbasat, 2003 Association for Computing Machinary, Inc. Reprinted by Permission.]

BUILDING A DOT-COM SUPERSTORE IN CHINA

In 1999, China had only about 4 million Internet users; by 2006, the number of users had mushroomed to 123 million—a national user population second only to the United States. Founded in 1999, Dangdang.com was a dot-com pioneer in China as an online bookseller, and by 2006 it was reported to be the country's largest online retailer with revenues of US$55 million.

Like Amazon.com, the business model for Dangdang.com has expanded beyond books to cell phones, appliances, and other products. Survival has also required making adjustments to the model pioneered by the U.S. pioneers like Amazon.com. For example, the vast majority of buyers of books pay with cash on delivery or with money orders—as credit cards are still relatively uncommon in China. The company therefore distributes about 2.2 million products a month from its three large warehouses (in Beijing, Shanghai, and Guangzhou) using about 50 different delivery companies that operate in about 170 Chinese cities.

In 2004, the company's founders rebuffed a takeover offer by Amazon.com, betting that China's business and regulatory environments will continue to make it difficult for foreign firms to be successful. For example, dot-com companies from outside China find it difficult to establish local business partners and distribution channels: EBay still trails rival site Taobao.com, Google trails Baidu.com, and Yahoo! handed over the control of its China operations to Alibaba.com, the company that owns Taobao. China also continues to set limits on foreign ownership and forces companies that provide online content to comply with Chinese censorship rules. However, Amazon.com bought Dangdang.com's Chinese competitor Joyo in late 2004, and by some accounts, the two competitors are neck-to-neck. Yet because the major Internet companies are not publicly listed, market-share data is hard to estimate.

[Adapted from Dean, 2006]

SUMMARY

Today we now have more than a decade of e-business applications that use the Internet, including companies that still survive as dot-com pioneers from the mid-1990s. As new technologies have become available, businesses have continued to innovate with new business models to increase their competitiveness with both traditional and dot-com rivals. The legal and regulatory environments of the United States have also shaped the current e-business landscape. However, current Intenet user populations are now growing faster on continents other than North America, and these other countries will undoubtedly have a much larger influence in the coming decades.

By evaluating how companies over the past decade have responded to the new business opportunities and threats created by the Internet, several trends can be identified. First, companies are expanding their investments in EDI capabilities to take advantage of the Internet's reach to companies of all sizes in locations across the globe. Although new types of online B2B exchanges that are owned by independent companies, or consortia, have proven to be difficult to sustain, companies are migrating to Internet-based EDI and online auctions for direct and indirect materials, with or without the support of specialized service providers. Other types of B2B applications, such as vendor-management inventory systems that leverage a company's investment in ERP or MRP investments, are also yielding major benefits in cost efficiencies and improved cycle time response.

Although dot-com companies had an initial advantage over traditional companies in developing effective B2C capabilities, both traditional catalog companies and store retailers that have developed integrated online and offline multichannel capabilities as bricks-and-clicks companies appear to hold the competitive advantage today. The dot-com pioneers, both retailing companies and online intermediaries, that have survived have had to continue to aggressively invest in not only new Web site capabilities for superior online customer experiences, but also new business models, to achieve profitability. Newer social networking tools and Web sites are currently generating a marketplace advantage for both dot-com and traditional companies that can foster a sense of community and attract targeted advertising revenues.

Today we have a good understanding of what makes a good e-business application for desktop and laptop users. In the coming decade, however, the focus will be on applications to better leverage the capabilities of wireless, multiuse computer and communication devices of handheld size that are being rapidly adopted by both business employees and end consumers around the globe.

REVIEW QUESTIONS

1. Define the terms *dot-com*, *bricks-and-clicks*, *extranet*, *B2C*, and *B2B*.
2. What e-business capabilities are supported by digital signatures and XML?

3. Describe some characteristics of the U.S. regulatory and legal environment that have influenced the growth of online sales?

4. What are some of the potential benefits of traditional EDI versus B2B applications using the Internet?

5. Choose one of the five competitive forces in Porter's model, and describe a new opportunity and a new threat due to the impact of the Internet on a specific industry of your choosing.

6. What privacy concerns of consumers should also be concerns of businesses pursuing an online capability?

7. Describe some of the reasons that dot-com companies had an initial advantage over traditional companies in developing an online sales capability.

8. What is meant by the term *multichannel capability*?

9. Describe some of the reasons that a typical traditional catalog firm may have had an advantage over a typical company that sold third-party products via retail store chains during the first decade of online sales.

10. What were some of the innovations using Web technologies that were introduced by Amazon.com, Dell.com, and Landsend.com?

11. Describe one of the ways that eBay evolved from its original C2C business model.

12. What is the major source of revenues today for a Web portal or a company like Google?

13. Why might a firm choose to use an external service provider to host their public Web sites?

14. What is one of the ways that the dot-com meltdown in the United States during the early 2000s has influenced the recent growth of e-business?

15. What is m-commerce and why is this the next e-business frontier?

DISCUSSION QUESTIONS

1. Provide evidence to support the following statement: The growth of e-business is due to both business and technological innovations.

2. Provide an argument to either support or refute the following statement: In trading partner applications, the customer holds the greatest power.

3. Briefly describe some ways that companies have used the Internet as a new customer service support channel.

4. Describe a customer experience that you have had on a retailing Web site, and how it has impacted your Internet usage.

5. Describe how the existence of (or lack of) state laws in the United States have been barriers or catalysts to online sales.

6. Choose three firms that compete within the same industry, and examine their public Web sites. Based on these sites, compare and contrast the potential B2C e-business benefits that these companies appear to be achieving.

7. Use the 7Cs framework of Rayport and Jaworski (described in the final section of the chapter) to evaluate the public Web sites of two competitors. Based on your analyses, what improvements could these companies make to their Web sites?

8. Find a company Web site that emphasizes community building, and examine the usage of social networking technologies supported by the site. What do you see as some of the pros and cons for supporting this type of software?

9. Identify some statistics on Internet users around the globe, and comment on some trends.

10. Describe some of the ways the Internet has or has not impacted the way you: (1) buy groceries, (2) make travel plans, (3) read news, (4) follow your favorite sports team, (5) decide which movie to see next, (6) decide what political candidate to vote for, and (6) do research for a business course.

REFERENCES

[Amazon.com] *www.amazon.com.*

Anders, George. 2001. "Marc Andreessen, Act II." *Fast Company* (February): 110–121.

Applegate, Lynda M., Clyde W. Holsapple, Ravi Kalakota, Franz J. Radermacher, and Andrew B. Whinston. 1996. "Electronic commerce: Building blocks of new business opportunity." *Journal of Organization Computing and Electronic Commerce* 6 (1): 1–10.

[Ariba, Inc.] 2005. "Ariba Spotlight: Nestlé," Ariba Web site, *www.ariba.com.*

[Autobytel] *www.autobytel.com.*

[Blockbuster] *www.blockbuster.com.*

Brown, J. 2000. "Signing on the digital line." *CIO* (October 15): 273.

Byrnes, Nanette, Peter Burrows, and Louise Lee. 2006. "Dark Days at Dell." *BusinessWeek* (September 4): 24–29.

Clemons, Eric K. 1991. "Evaluation of strategic investments in information technology." *Communications of the ACM* 34 (January): 23–36.

[Cyberatlas]. 2002. "B2B e-commerce headed for trillions." *http://cyberatlas.internet.com/markets/b2b/print/0,,10091_986661.00.html* (March 6).

Dean, Jason. 2006. "China's Web Retailers Beat U.S. Rivals at Their Own Game." *Wall Street Journal* (August 22): B1.

DeJesus, Edmund X. 2001. "EDI? XML? Or both?" *Computerworld* (January 8): 54–56.

Delaney, Kevin J. 2007. "How search-engine rules cause sites to go missing." *Wall Street Journal* (March 13): B1, B4.

[Dell] *www.dell.com*.

[eBay.com] *www.ebay.com*.

Efrati, Amir. 2006. "Neutral net: A battle for control of the Web." *Wall Street Journal* (June 24–25): A9.

Elgin, Ben. 2006. "MAPS: It feels like you're flying." *BusinessWeek* (January 16): 89.

Eisenmann, Thomas R., and Kerry Herman. 2006. "Google Inc." Boston, MA: Harvard Business School, Case No. 9-806-105 (rev. November 9, 2006).

Frei, Fances X. 2001. "eBay: The Customer Marketplace (A)." Boston, MA: Harvard Business School, Case No. 9-602-071 (rev. May 2, 2002).

Gates, Bill. 1995. *The Road Ahead*. New York: Viking Penguin.

Gomes, Lee. 2006. "The Dot-Com bubble is reconsidered—and maybe relived." *Wall Street Journal* (November 8): B1.

[Google.com] *www.google.com*.

Greenspan, Robyn. 2004. "Internet not for everyone." *http://Cyberatlas.internet.com/big_picture/demographics/article/0.1323.5901_2192251.00.html*.

Hudson, Kris. 2006. "New Lands' End Format Suits Sears." *Wall Street Journal* (October 17): B2.

Jones, Kathryn. 2003. "The Dell Way," *Business 2.0* (February): 61–66.

Kiley, David. 2007. "How to read the Google tea leaves." *BusinessWeek* (April 2): 10.

King, Julia. 2000. "B2B's surprise: The survivors," *Computerworld* (December 11): 1, 16.

[Lands' End] *www.landsend.com*.

Lee, Young Eun, and Izak Benbasat. 2003. "Interface design for mobile commerce," *Communications of the ACM*, 46:12 (December): 49–52.

Lewis, Christina S.N., and Jessica E. Vascellaro. 2006. "Finding the perfect pair of jeans—on the Internet." *Wall Street Journal* (January 19): D4.

Louie, Dickson L., and Jeffrey F. Rayport. 2001. "Amazon.com (D)." Boston, MA: Harvard Business School, Case No. 9-901-022.

Mabert, Vince A., and Jack A. Skeels. 2002. "Internet reverse auctions: Valuable tool in experienced hands." *Business Horizons* (July–August): 70–76.

Mangalindan, Mylene. 2006. "Court rules against Amazon in Toys dispute." *Wall Street Journal* (March 3): B1, B3.

Magretta, Joan. 1998. "The power of virtual integration: an interview with Dell Computer's Michael Dell, *Harvard Business Review* (March–April): 73f.

[Miniwatts Marketing Group] 2007. Internet World Stats: Usage and Population Statistics. *www.internetworldstats.com/stats.htm*.

Mossberg, Walter S. 2000. "The Amazon Way is still the best model for Web shopping." *Wall Street Journal* (September 21): B1.

[Netflix, Inc.] *www.netflix.com*.

[Nielsen, Jakob] 2001. "Jakob Nielsen Interview." *www.webreference.com/new/nielsen.html* (January 2).

[Nielsen/Net Ratings] November 2003. Table 1

[Pew Internet & American Life Project Surveys] 2002. Growth in selected online activities by U.S. consumers: 2000–2002.

Piccoli, Gabriel, Bill Bass, and Blake Ives. 2003. "Custom-made apparel at Lands' End." *MIS Quarterly Executive* 2:2 (September).

Porter, Michael E. 1985. *Competitive Advantage: Creating and Sustaining Superior Performance*. New York: Free Press.

Porter, Michael E. 2001. "Strategy and the Internet." *Harvard Business Review* (March): 53–68.

Pottruck, David S., and Terry Pearce. 1999. *Clicks and Mortar*. San Francisco: Jossey-Bass.

Rayport, Jeffrey F., and Bernard J. Jaworski. 2004. *Introduction to e-Commerce*. New York: McGraw-Hill/Irwin.

Rivkin, Jan W., and Michael E. Porter. 1999. "Matching Dell." Boston, MA: Harvard Business School: Case study #9-799-158.

Seybold, Patricia, and Ronni Marshal. 1995. *Customers.com*. NY: Random House/Crown.

Spector, Mike. 2007. "Easier ways to car shop online." *Wall Street Journal* (March 13): D1, D4.

Spors, Kelly K. 2007. "In search of traffic." *Wall Street Journal* (April 30): R1, R4.

[Staples Inc.] *www.staples.com*.

Straub, Detmar. 2004. *Foundations of Net-Enhanced Organizations*. Hoboken, NJ: Wiley.

Vollmann, T.E. 2005. "ERP as a resource for inter-organizational value creation." in Elliot Bendoly and F. Robert Jacobs (eds.), *Strategic ERP Extension and Use*. Stanford, California: Stanford Business Books, 140–152.

Weill, Peter, and Michael R. Vitale. 2001. *Place to Space: Migrating to eBusiness Models*. Boston, MA: Harvard Business School Press.

Wingfield, Nick. 2007. "Netflix vs. Naysayers." *Wall Street Journal* (March 27): B1–B2.

Zachary, G. Pascal. 2006. "Evolution of an envelope." *Business 2.0* (April): 70.

VENDOR-MANAGED INVENTORY AT NIBCO

Headquartered in Elkhart, Indiana, NIBCO is a worldwide provider of flow control products (valves, fittings, hangers, supports, seismic bracing, and struts) with over $400 million in revenues and a 100-year history. As a privately held firm, by 2003 NIBCO had about 3000 employees (referred to internally as *associates*) and manufactured more than 20,000 different stock-keeping units (SKUs) in manufacturing facilities primarily in the United States, but also in Mexico and Central Europe.

NIBCO's flow control products (made from plastics and metals manufacturing processes) are used in several industries, including the residential and commercial construction, industrial, and irrigation markets. Two-thirds of its sales are in commodity markets, and its major customers include large wholesalers such as F. W. Webb; large ("big box") retailers such as Home Depot, Lowe's, and Menard's; hardware cooperatives such as Ace Hardware and True Value; and a substantial number of smaller customers. The remaining one-third of its sales are from make-to-order products. These make-to-order products are marketed and sold by a direct sales force that works with engineering firms, architectural firms, and contractors that require specialized flow control products for custom projects.

NIBCO's mission is to be the worldwide choice in flow control products, competing on both low price and differentiation. Because of the low growth opportunities within its commodity markets, there is fierce competition for retaining existing customers and increasing market share. NIBCO therefore strives to be the manufacturer of choice not only as a result of its reliability as a supplier and low costs, but also as a result of its value-added services. Competing on service has therefore become an even more important way for the company to distinguish itself in commodity markets: Competing on superior product quality alone is not enough.

Copyright © 2007 by Carol V. Brown, Mohan V. Tatikonda, and Iris Vessey. This teaching case is based on a larger case study sponsored by SAP America for which the authors conducted interviews with managers at NIBCO. A full case report entitled "NIBCO: mySAP™ Supply Chain Management" is available from the authors.

Initial SAP R/3 Implementation Project

> Every time someone would stand up and [present their long-range plan], they'd say we could do this wonderful thing, *"but…"* and the "but" would be that we needed good systems. This led to a fundamental change in the way we viewed IT.
>
> —*Rex Martin, Chairman, President, and CEO, NIBCO*

In 1995, the firm developed a long-range strategic plan that called for radically improved information flows in an attempt to ensure company survival and growth. A business operations manager was released full time by early 1996 to develop task force recommendations for an enterprise resource planning (ERP) package and implementation partner selection. NIBCO's executive leaders endorsed the internal recommendation that SAP R/3 be purchased and implemented by December 1997. Its selected implementation partner was IBM. By the end of 1996, NIBCO had become one of the first midsized manufacturers in North America to begin planning a "big bang" SAP implementation for R/3 modules to replace most of its legacy systems—at its headquarters, 10 domestic manufacturing plants, and four newly consolidated distribution centers.

The internal project team was led by a trio of senior managers with accountabilities for business process, technology, and change management. Other company directors participated as business process experts (business review leaders), and power users from the various business functions were dedicated full time to the project team or played part-time roles as extended team members from October 1996 through the end of 1997. On December 30, 1997, NIBCO went live with version 3.0f of SAP R/3 sales and distribution, production planning, materials management (including warehouse management), and financial and controller modules. All company employees normally included in the bonus program were rewarded with a one-time project bonus for a successfully functioning system that was implemented as planned, on-time and within the approved $17 million budget.

In the four years following its initial SAP R/3 implementation (see Exhibit 1), NIBCO implemented new functionality (human resources modules and e-business) and also implemented

EXHIBIT 1
Timeline of NIBCO's Major Projects Following Initial SAP R/3 Implementation

1998	1999	2000	2001
01/98 NIBCO implements SAP R/3 in all locations with wide variety of core functionality	**03/99** Upgrades SAP R/3 to 4.0b	**01/00** Implements NIBCO E-Commerce **04/00** Implements Human Resources	**03/01** Upgrades SAP R/3 to 4.6c **12/01** Purchases mySAP SCM and other SAP business licenses

two SAP R/3 upgrades (to 4.0b and then to 4.6c). At the end of 2001, it also purchased mySAP SCM modules and other licenses. Instead of being a cost of doing business that would continuously be restricted, IT became a strategic investment in the business.

NIBCO's initial implementation of SAP R/3 resulted in a totally different focus for the company, improving the way it does business, facilitated by the integrated processes and information facilitated by its SAP systems. IT spending on an annual basis was almost doubled: New integrated systems were needed to enable a new cross-functional process orientation and greater returns on business and IT assets.

The two SAP upgrades (in 1999 and 2001) were treated as separate information systems (IS) projects with no new business functionality.

> We made a strategic alignment decision to stay relatively current on both hardware and software. We try to upgrade SAP every 18 to 24 months. We have done it efficiently, although it is going to become more complex [because of integrating non-North American operations and a recent domestic acquisition].
>
> —Gary Wilson, Vice President and Chief Information Officer, NIBCO

All other projects have had significant business management involvement.

Business Process Improvement Projects

Since the initial SAP R/3 implementation, the company has engaged in a series of continuous improvement projects that have involved business innovation initiatives. The following quotes from Ken Eme, VP of Supply Chain at NIBCO in the second half of 2002 articulated the company's vision:

We took the SAP implementation as an opportunity to redefine our supply chain business processes. The implementation was the trigger to make it happen. It also helped us define and communicate our supply chain philosophy.

Having a standardized system across our network of plants helps us do many more things remotely than before. Further, it reduces our personnel training expenses and helps us leverage expertise across our plants. Personnel can move from one factory to another and be ramped up very quickly—this makes our associates even more agile and flexible.

The standardization brought about by the SAP system provides us with complete, real-time visibility into inventory levels, production order status, and sales orders, helping us gain a better understanding of our total position and opportunities.

As part of its initial SAP R/3 implementation, NIBCO consolidated its distribution centers from 17 to 4 to better manage inventory and improve order fill rates. The improvements NIBCO made to its work processes involved all aspects of both its internal and external (both supply-side and customer-side) supply chains. Gordon McCrory, Director of Metals Manufacturing at NIBCO, highlighted the achievements that had been gained and the future benefits envisaged from changes in work processes:

> Some of the side benefits from SAP may potentially be of the greatest benefit: For example, the things that SAP can do for us from a high performance work organization standpoint . . . . If you believe that people closest to the work have the best ideas and can make improvements, then you need to be able to get the information to them.

When NIBCO had received a customer order in the past, it had been filled by a divisional distribution center closest to the customer. Traditionally, NIBCO had collected demand forecasts from customers and constructed an aggregate forecast of future demand. These forecast figures, in turn, drove medium-term and short-term production planning decisions in which the bulk of the manufacturing activity focused on make-to-stock production. This product was then pushed from NIBCO manufacturing plants to NIBCO distribution centers (DCs) regardless of emerging short-term demand patterns—information on immediate actual sales demand was not considered or even commonly available through NIBCO's stovepipe legacy systems.

The SAP implementation enabled the company to replace its long-established *forecast-push* approach to supplying product to customers, with a *demand-pull* approach. The new approach involved a complete change in the corporation's mind-set:

> That was a huge cultural shift for NIBCO: going from a push to a pull system. It took a while to get that ingrained.
>
> —Clyde Hayes, Director of Supply Management, NIBCO

Now, product would be "pulled" through the supply chain, with the customer triggering the pull process. A customer purchases product from NIBCO, which is supplied or "pulled" from the appropriate DC. Should the supply of the given product fall below a preestablished level (the reorder point), the DC places a replenishment order with the appropriate NIBCO plant. Here the DC "pulls" product from the plant. The plant then replenishes the stock of that product, either through provision from its own finished goods inventory or through rapid production and shipment of that finished good, often in *kanban quantities* (which are predetermined, fixed order quantity levels, often based on storage and shipment container sizes). In turn, the plant "pulls" raw materials and components from its own inventory and from suppliers for subsequent materials conversion at the plant. The pull philosophy embraced by NIBCO is consistent with tenets of *just-in-time manufacturing* and *lean supply chains*.

The new system is notable in two ways: first, the reliance on actual customer orders as the driver for day-to-day replenishment and production activity (versus demand forecasts as the driver) and, second, the direction of triggers for the movement of product (from the marketplace rather than from the manufacturer). The demand forecasts employed previously to guide supply of product to customers were necessarily speculative, typically inflated, and often inaccurate. In contrast, actual customer orders represent true immediate customer demand. NIBCO embarked on this radical change to its supply chain processes with two overriding goals: to significantly increase customer service through greater product availability (in turn further differentiating NIBCO's product/service bundle to customers in the marketplace) and to drastically cut inventory and other operating costs.

To make the demand-pull process possible, NIBCO implemented a system of *inventory zones*. Inventory zones are numerical values or ranges specifying desired inventory levels. The end product (an SKU) is typically stored at a specific DC, but in special cases, it may be stored at a manufacturing plant or even at a customer site (such as for vendor-managed inventory customers, as described in the next section). Statistical analyses are used to determine the maximum level of end product to maintain, the reorder point quantity, and the safety-stock level. This approach was implemented initially by evaluating the prior year's historical demand pattern for a given SKU and aiming for a 99 percent product availability service level. Currently, a rolling 12-month sales demand history, along with seasonality information and customer-specific inputs, is assessed periodically to reevaluate the zone levels. Zone levels may change as often as twice a year for a given end product.

This initiative has had a massive influence on all aspects of NIBCO's supply chain, cutting across customer service, the distribution system, manufacturing operations, and procurement. It also enabled the firm to embark on a new external supply-chain initiative: vendor-managed inventory.

The VMI Initiative

In order not only to retain customers but also to increase its market share, NIBCO needed to develop innovative ways to provide additional value-added services, particularly for key customers of its commodity products. NIBCO's objective was to become the easiest, most valued supplier with which to do business, and the company looked for ways to use mySAP SCM to develop electronic partnerships with its customers, which would increase customer loyalty and decrease its customers' switching costs.

One of its most successful innovations has been a vendor-managed inventory (VMI) program for its large wholesalers. VMI requires a large amount of transaction data on a daily or weekly basis across thousands of SKUs per customer. It therefore requires a robust enterprise system.

NIBCO's first VMI customer was a leading wholesaler whose president had challenged all current and potential copper suppliers to provide an efficient customer response capability. The company with the successful proposal would become their sole-source provider of copper products.

NIBCO captured the contract and developed first a manual process and then a fully automated replenishment process driven by mySAP SCM. Under VMI, the customer no longer places an order; instead, the customer provides a daily inventory level report electronically. NIBCO uses that report to monitor the customer's inventory levels on a daily basis, and inventory is replenished weekly. NIBCO guarantees that its customer will never run out of NIBCO products and that the customer's orders can therefore always be filled. Backup plans are developed to deal with extraordinary events.

By mid-2002, NIBCO had developed competency in VMI, providing these value-added services to eight strategic wholesale customers who entered into sole-sourcing agreements with NIBCO for specific, high-moving products. One of the primary benefits to NIBCO has been the smoothing of demand. One of the biggest difficulties in NIBCO's supply chain is that the demand from some of its large customers tends to fluctuate, which can create a *bullwhip-effect* type of response to a false demand, despite the fact that the yearly demand of its largest customers is fairly stable. Price changes, orders from a new large customer, or other events can create extreme fluctuations when the marketplace really does not need the product for 30 to 60 days.

> VMI has taken a tremendous amount of the bullwhip effect out of the supply chain response: our demand pull coming through the plants is now more related to what the final customer buys than it is to what our wholesaler buys.
>
> —John Hall, Director of Supply Chain Systems, NIBCO

NIBCO has developed a business model to identify potential VMI customers based on sales levels and the attractiveness of a sole-sourcing arrangement to both parties. A targeted customer also typically has a centralized inventory system servicing multiple branches.

> We have a very diverse customer base out there . . . and their ability to make investments in information technology is radically different. A $10 million or $20 million business in a single location has a radically different ability [to make investments] than a $5 billion or $10 billion firm, or a Home Depot at $60 billion.
>
> —Jim Drexinger, Vice President of Sales and Marketing, NIBCO

Many of NIBCO's domestic wholesale and retail customers have already made an investment in EDI. For those that need to start from scratch, the investment includes not only technology (hardware, software, and sometimes ongoing value-added network operational costs) but also ongoing technical support personnel. The alternative is outsourcing to an EDI trading partner. Four EDI transactions are currently involved: product data activity (transaction number 852), product order acknowledgment (855), advanced ship notice (856), and invoice (810).

> We replenish millions of dollars worth of inventory. But the first human intervention is literally when our distribution center gets the picking list out of SAP to fulfill an order to be shipped to our VMI customer.
>
> —Jim Drexinger, Vice President of Sales and Marketing, NIBCO

NIBCO and a few of its VMI partners work with a center of technology excellence in the American Supply Association (ASA), with whom the EDI standards for wholesale distributors were developed (ASA Express). For example, NIBCO has participated in the development of standards for electronic product catalogs.

> We are really dealing with an industry that is working hard to embrace technology.
>
> —Jim Drexinger, Vice President of Sales and Marketing, NIBCO

Since 1999, NIBCO's VMI team has honed its processes and systems so that a new VMI partnership can be established within a period as short as two to three weeks, once customer buy-in is achieved. A marketing team provides the initial presentation for the customer, informing them of the types of improvements that other VMI customers have already achieved; then, if there is buy-in, a statistical analysis is performed to model their purchase landscape and determine the potential benefits for the customer. The customer's past 24-month purchase activity is typically analyzed in conjunction with customer inventory data, growth forecasts, and seasonality effects. It is not uncommon for 300 to 600 SKUs to be involved. This approach is followed by a proposal for mutually agreed upon aspects of the contract, including reorder point levels for automatic replenishment. Implementing VMI in the short time frame is facilitated by the fact that mySAP SCM allows for multiple cross-references for Universal Product Code

(UPC) bar codes to accommodate a specific customer's product name and labeling needs.

> Before SAP, that was difficult. Now we can have a call in the morning . . . and by the end of the day we have a new trading partner. It can be that easy.
>
> —Diane Krill, Director of Customer and Marketing Services, NIBCO

After a new VMI implementation, the NIBCO core team typically stays on the project for three to four weeks to monitor issues on a weekly basis. Then, on a quarterly basis, NIBCO communicates to customers the benefits that have been delivered. The idea is to create a unique service that is available from NIBCO alone. Having a well-honed SAP architecture to build on, as well as the experience resulting from several years of internal SAP experience, gives NIBCO an initial competitive advantage in its industry.

> Without the SAP platform as the backbone, we would never have been able to get to that level of e-commerce commitment within the time frame that was being mandated [by the customer].
>
> —Jerry Whiteford, Vice President of Finance and Treasurer, NIBCO

The benefits of the VMI program have been compelling. The critical business metrics used by NIBCO's customers are the success measures that are tracked for the VMI program; the program, for example, is sold primarily on the basis of gross margin return on inventory (GMROI). Other metrics that are tracked are the increase in the customer's inventory turns, the decrease in the customer's inventory items and dollars, and the decrease in pallet or physical storage requirements. The proposed improvement levels for all VMI customers to date have been realized or exceeded.

> In some cases, we cut their inventory levels quite significantly because there was a lot of hedging on their part before this [VMI] process.
>
> —Chris Mason, Manager of Supply Chain Systems, NIBCO

Benefits Realized: 1997 to 2002

NIBCO became an IT leader within the flow control industry as a result of its early (1996 to 1997) investment in an ERP package (SAP R/3) to replace its legacy systems. By 2002, NIBCO had also positioned itself as a leader in business process innovation within its industry. The company had developed closer relationships to key customers as a result of its initiation of value-added services based on electronic integration capabilities, and it was the first company in its industry to leverage its IT infrastructure to offer VMI.

NIBCO also leveraged the project management knowledge that it had gained for two integration projects. These two projects involved replacing legacy systems of one of its international business units and a new acquisition, with little outside consulting help. In the company's Polish operations, SAP solutions were implemented in May 2002. This project was viewed as an internal pilot for integrating a new acquisition, and the project team created templates for future use. Five months after a domestic acquisition (TOLCO) in California was finalized in June 2002, a dedicated project team of business and IT associates implemented SAP in the acquired company as well. Although new make-to-order processes were also added, about 60 percent of NIBCO's business processes were used without configuration changes.

> We have been able to effectively take 60% of our business operating processes defined in SAP and implement them unchanged. . . . It standardizes them with our business functionality almost immediately.
>
> —John Hall, Director of Supply Chain Systems, NIBCO

By leveraging the capabilities of its SAP investments, NIBCO has measurably:

- Improved customer service by focusing on order accuracy and product availability
- Developed multichannel customer service capabilities and electronic partnerships for customers and suppliers
- Increased the effectiveness and reduced the costs of doing business through continuous business process improvements in both its internal and external supply chains

Looking Ahead

What other initiatives should NIBCO embark on to leverage its IT lead?

One of the CIO's first assignments when he joined NIBCO as an IS director almost a decade ago was to implement a data warehouse capability to improve business decision making. This initiative was abandoned when the decision was made to invest in an ERP package. Now there was an opportunity to implement a data warehouse capability with its SAP platform. Could NIBCO's business managers gain greater insights into its product manufacturing and distribution costs with an information warehouse? Could it improve its customer relationships? Could it selectively increase prices and achieve other increased revenues with investments in new CRM and business intelligence tools? Or should it focus instead on a more aggressive growth-by-acquisition strategy to both increase revenues and achieve cost savings, such as achieved with TOLCO?

When its customers or suppliers increase their own IT investments, NIBCO should also be in an even better position to leverage its enterprise system platform with expanded electronic linkages to them:

> We see cost reductions and some nice growth opportunities [by leveraging] our SAP engine.
>
> —Rex Martin, Chairman, President, and CEO, NIBCO

THE CHALLENGES OF LOCAL SYSTEM DESIGN FOR MULTINATIONALS: THE MAXFLI SALES FORCE AUTOMATION SYSTEM AT BAT

Will all direct-distribution markets eventually use MaxFli or a system like it? Yes. I believe yes, they will. And why? Because there is an absolute need to connect selling in and selling out together.

—Peter Brickley, Chief Information Officer, BAT Globe House

I have a very high view of MaxFli. [It] creates a selling process. It allows us to have a real competitive advantage in the field. It's really that . . . MaxFli allows you to direct your promotion, all your marketing strategies to the right outlet at the right time. That is why it gives us competitive advantage.

—Oscar Gonzalez, formerly at BAT Colombia, transferred to Globe House in 2001

Until today, there are some concerns [with MaxFli]. Why is that? The problem is the cost of MaxFli, and it is not paying off. That is the big concern. Why not use a more simple system to help us to sell? Selling is our business. So we [should think about] stopping the use of MaxFli.

—Juan Morales, a marketing executive in BAT Central America

MaxFli was a business change initiative: a sales force automation (SFA) system created to structure and automate the sales process within multiple locations around the globe. However, after three implementations, the success of MaxFli was in question.

Background: British American Tobacco

Founded in 1902, British American Tobacco (BAT) has grown through organic growth and acquisitions to be one of the top three global players in the tobacco industry. By 2002 it ranked number 271 in the *Fortune* Global 500 list of companies. Prior

Copyright © 2003 by Bradley C. Wheeler and Michael L. Wiliams. This case was prepared by Bradley C. Wheeler and Michael L. Williams at Indiana University's Kelley School of Business. The names and titles of some informants have been camouflaged as requested. The authors would like to thank the IU CIBER office for funding the research and the many BAT employees around the world who participated in the research.

to 1996, BAT Industries PLC had four tobacco businesses among a number of unrelated business interests. In 1996, this business strategy was revised to merge the four independent tobacco businesses into one. Nontobacco businesses (financial services, retailing, and others) were divested, and BAT became a stand-alone business focused only on tobacco. The company then merged in 1999 with the global cigarette company Rothmans International. In the fall of 2001 BAT's local and international brands were sold through five regional divisions: America Pacific, Asia Pacific, Europe, Latin America, and AMESCA (Africa, the Middle East, South and Central Asia). A sixth division, STC (Smoking Tobacco and Cigars), is global and operates in more than 120 countries.

The profit centers are 120 "end markets," each typically a country. End-market directors (general managers) report to regional directors, who are members of BAT's top executive board—the Tobacco Management Board (TMB). The company's strategy leverages global economies of scale while offering autonomy to end markets.

In general, end markets either distribute the product to retail outlets via their own trucks and sales force (direct distribution) or use other distribution-for-fee service companies. The direct distribution model is data- and resource-intensive and is used by many end markets worldwide. MaxFli was designed to facilitate the trade-marketing and distribution activities within direct distribution markets.

Birth of MaxFli in Latin America

The Origins of MaxFli

Several business and technical issues converged for the creation of MaxFli. The rapid maturation of trade marketing and distribution (TM&D) within BAT markets had outpaced the ability of existing technology. As sales, marketing, and cash-collection methods evolved, new systems were needed to support them. Additionally, BAT began to consider the implications of Y2K issues for their IT systems. By the mid-1990s many Latin

American markets recognized the need to replace their existing SFA system as a result of Y2K concerns and the rapid acceleration of trade-marketing and distribution practices. Because these were all direct-distribution markets with similar business processes, a codevelopment strategy emerged.

As end markets discussed strategies for a Y2K-compliant TM&D system, a new opportunity arose. BAT global headquarters (Globe House) reasoned that global economies of scale could produce a better system, at a lower per-user cost. In particular, executives at Globe House and several end markets saw the opportunity to develop a flexible, re-usable IT system to support trade marketing and distribution within direct distribution markets.

Choosing the Right Approach for Developing MaxFli

Based on experience with a recent Globe House–led IT initiative to develop a TM&D system for traditional distribution markets, there was a widely held belief that the primary design of the system should occur in the end markets, not in Globe House. Because TM&D includes many of the value-added processes that support the retailer, it was thought difficult for Globe House to understand or appreciate the nuances and complexities of regional differences. Hans Neidermann, global director of trade marketing for BAT, observed, "There are so many differences in terms of local processes relating to invoices, trading terms, taxation, etc., that we did not want to get involved in this in the first place."

In light of the complexities involved in local trade-marketing processes, Globe House decided on a distributed approach for the design and development of MaxFli. Globe House would coordinate much of the development effort in London with the help of Andersen Consulting (now Accenture), but the design would occur in the end markets of Latin America.

In February 1998, representatives from 15 markets including Colombia, Honduras, Venezuela, Brazil, Mexico, UK, USA, Belgium, and France began a 2-month feasibility study to develop the business case for MaxFli. Two specific goals for the feasibility study were to determine the "best practices" of direct distribution markets to be embedded in the software, and to determine if the direct distribution solution could fit within the existing technological platform at BAT. The business case from this feasibility study was presented to the TMB, which granted final approval to begin development in May 1998. The MaxFli steering committee planned for three separate implementation rollouts before the end of 2000: Chile, Colombia, and Central America. (See Exhibit 1.)

Chiletabacos, BAT's operating company in Chile, was selected to take the lead in designing and implementing MaxFli, for several reasons. Chiletabacos was one of the leaders among the BAT markets in Latin America. They were already a well-established company with a strong market presence in Chile. With 98.5 percent market share, Chiletabacos had demonstrated a consistent ability to develop successful business strategies and generate revenue. Additionally, Chiletabacos General Manager Roberto Friere was highly respected throughout the BAT community.

Designing and Building MaxFli

MaxFli was viewed as an important element in the continued maturation of the TM&D function in BAT direct distribution markets. Designing a system to incorporate the best practices from 15 end markets was a complex task. Much attention was given to the design objectives and issues to ensure the usefulness of the system.

Design Objectives

Hans Neidermann captured the essence of the design objectives for MaxFli by saying, "we needed a better integration of the selling process and the trade-marketing process." The goal for the system focused on four key strategic elements:

- Focusing on the in-store experience of the consumer
- Partnering with the retailer as the primary interface with the consumer
- Maximizing marketing costs by understanding in-store promotional successes
- Forecasting retail sales to maximize supply chain efficiency

To accomplish these goals, MaxFli had to provide accurate business information that would allow BAT to cross-reference retail sales and consumer information, which was the only way for BAT to continue succeeding in markets where advertising was increasingly restrictive. Finally, MaxFli needed to be integrated with accounting and inventory management to avoid the duplication of effort and accounting difficulties experienced with previous systems.

Design Issues

Because the system was to be used in markets of different sizes and market conditions, the design of MaxFli required agreement on several early decisions. According to Roberto Palacios, the MaxFli project manager in Chile, the IT strategic priorities that guided the development of MaxFli were:

- A common, reusable, and scalable technology platform
- Shared data between sales, accounting and marketing
- Appropriate use of packaged software

BAT faced a variety of options to attain these priorities. Should BAT use an existing product or develop their own?

EXHIBIT 1
A History of Handheld Sales Force Automation Systems in Latin America

Date	Event
1983	Chile's first handheld is developed
1986	Major upgrade to handheld in Chile
1993	BAT Colombia is started
1995	Six independent end markets of Central America form a single cluster market, BAT Central America
March – May 1998	2-month feasibility study of MaxFli case
May 1998	BAT Tobacco Management Board approves MaxFli concept
May 1998	BAT has commitment from Siebel Systems to build a handheld solution
May 1999	Siebel backs out of building handheld solution
Summer 1999	BAT replaces Andersen Consulting with Ernst & Young
Sept. 1999	Ciberion is started as a joint venture with E&Y and BAT
Nov. 1999	MaxFli 1.0 goes live in Chile
May 2000	MaxFli 1.0 goes live in Colombia
Nov. 2000	MaxFli 1.1 goes live in Central America

Should they develop a product independently or in partnership with a supplier? What platform provided maximum scalability, reusability, and stability? What were the implications of MaxFli for the Enterprise Resource Planning (ERP) applications being installed throughout BAT? What handheld device allowed for international support and maintenance? What implications did the variance in technical expertise throughout Latin America present?

After carefully reviewing the options, BAT negotiated with Siebel Systems to build a handheld solution for direct distribution markets within BAT. However, one month before development was to begin, Siebel withdrew to focus on other corporate priorities of its own.

Design Choices

In May 1998, BAT began developing MaxFli with the help of Andersen Consulting. The primary design work and project leadership were in Santiago de Chile and consisted of a team of BAT staff from Brazil, Chile, Colombia, Honduras, Mexico, and Venezuela. The development effort took place in London, performed by Andersen Consulting and managed by BAT personnel. The system was to be finished and first implemented in Chile in May 1999.

MaxFli was designed to deliver a globally transferable, leading-edge direct distribution system for BAT. In its final form MaxFli consisted of several interdependent systems to track sales, inventory, credit accounts, competitor information, merchandising, and outlet classification. (See Exhibit 2.)

The front end of MaxFli was a Visual Basic® application running on a handheld Hewlett-Packard Jornada 680™ using Windows® CE 2.1. This handheld was used by the sales representatives each day to place orders, issue credit, print invoices, track inventory, and monitor merchandising and competitor activity. At the end of each day, the sales reps synchronized their handhelds with the back-office system. Synchronization could occur through the office network, a dial-up connection from a land-based telephone, or from a mobile phone. The back-office system was a Siebel Systems customer relationship management

EXHIBIT 2
Main Technological Concepts in MaxFli

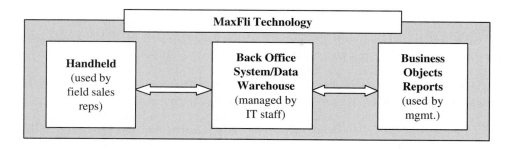

system (CRM) and an Oracle 8i data warehouse running on HP servers. The reporting engine was BusinessObjects 2.0 integrated into a Lotus Notes workspace. MaxFli reported sales and competitor information, outlet classification, and promotional material effectiveness. It was designed to be used by management at all levels from junior sales manager to senior executive.

Implementing MaxFli in Chile

Chile is a long, narrow country of 15 million people surrounded by the Andes Mountains to the east and the Pacific Ocean to the west and south. It covers about 50 percent of the western edge of South America and has been receptive to BAT products over the years. Chiletabacos held command over a large percentage of the cigarette market in Chile.

The IT function at Chiletabacos was a mature function with a strong presence in the business. Despite a history of difficult IT implementations, General Manager Roberto Friere expressed great confidence in the team of IT professionals in his organization. One senior executive argued that "[implementing MaxFli] was an important move for us, because our track record with large IT system implementations was poor."

MaxFli was the largest IT project in the history of Chiletabacos. Chiletabacos shouldered $8.9 million of the development costs, which cumulatively totaled nearly $15 million. Before taking on the project Friere asserted two conditions to Globe House: it had to be first and foremost a Chilean solution (as opposed to a global solution that required Chilean adoption); and he had to have final control over project development.

Palacios was selected as the project manager on the basis of his track record of managing large projects throughout his 20 years in finance at Chiletabacos. It did not take long for Palacios to develop a clear vision about the implementation of MaxFli. From the beginning he saw MaxFli as a business change project, not just an IT project:

> The IT tool is just one of the key components of the business change program. The tool by its own will not change anything. So people, processes, and IT systems need to be aligned.

MaxFli is a business change program that requires huge organizational effort with four major work-streams: management, communication, process/people, and technology.

Management

Friere and Palacios shared a belief that decisively addressing project challenges as they arose would be critical for success in the MaxFli implementation. Palacios demonstrated this by creating a well-defined plan for pre-implementation, implementation readiness, and post-implementation acceptance. Still, at one point in the development process, Friere believed that he needed to exercise his project control explicitly. When a series of events led him to question who was in charge of the project, he froze the development effort for two weeks until he was convinced that his two primary objectives, creating a Chilean solution and maintaining control, would be met. This helped the development team remain focused on the task at hand and ensured that they did the "right things, the right way, using the right tools."

Palacios also emphasized managing expectations:

> An implementation of this size represents a serious challenge; thus the organization needs to be aware that there will be problems. Delays and problems…should be communicated and explained to the whole organization. The business and technical learning curve is unavoidable. So level of service expectations need to be managed.

Palacios demonstrated a pattern of underselling the benefits of MaxFli while over-delivering on their realization in order to manage expectations.

Communication

Palacios crafted his communications about MaxFli very carefully. MaxFli was under very close scrutiny from management because of its cost. Consequently, Palacios spent much of his energies "managing upward—making sure management understood what we were doing and why we were doing it."

Palacios created "powermaps" to help monitor communication. These graphic representations displayed each important person on the MaxFli team, how they were all related, and what communications were essential. These maps helped Palacios keep management informed about the current struggles and successes of the project. This style worked well, according to GM Friere: "Everyone was well informed throughout the [different] stages of the process. It was not a 'black box' where we put in the money and hoped we got the right system."

This was important because MaxFli was intended to be a solution for many direct distribution markets in Latin America. By "managing upwards" Palacios secured the approval and protection of the most powerful force in the MaxFli implementation, the strategic steering committee.

There were several challenges to effective communication during the MaxFli development effort. First was the geographical distance between the design team based in London and the development team based in Santiago. Frequent teleconferences, video conferences, and pan-Atlantic trips helped to moderate the effect of time and distance on communication between designers and developers. A second constraint could not be moderated by travel or telephone. Most of the design team were native Spanish speakers while the development team in the UK were primarily English speakers. This issue was moderated somewhat by the fluent bilingual language skills of Friere, Palacios, and others on the team.

Processes and People

Palacios insisted that MaxFli was not primarily a technology innovation, but a business-process change project supported by technology. Therefore, successful implementation depended on much more than having a strong IT function to support it. He argued, "[T]o capture its full potential [MaxFli] requires an in-depth revision of current TM&D processes, organizational change and a strong commitment."

This view is illustrated by Exhibit 3, which Palacios used in describing MaxFli. It displays the role of the MaxFli system and the role of the implementing end market in determining system success with MaxFli. The unshaded areas represent end-market responsibilities for success while the shaded areas represent MaxFli's contribution toward system success. Accordingly, almost 75 percent of the final outcome depends on the efforts of the local end market, apart from MaxFli. MaxFli was not expected to single-handedly increase market share, streamline processes, and manage trade marketing in the end markets. It was a technological tool that enabled these desiderata but did not command them.

Palacios planned the implementation as a 13-month, 3-phase plan, consisting of awareness, presystem business preparation, and in-market implementation. Over 50 percent of the total effort was expended in end-market business process improvements and preparations before the system went live. The first 2 months were spent in developing awareness, studying the business case, and choosing a management team. The next 5 months were spent reviewing and optimizing current organizational processes to be ready to implement the system. Finally, the system implementation itself required 6 months and led to well-aligned processes, people, and systems.

Palacios gave considerable attention to training and support. Training in the new business processes as well as the MaxFli tool itself were offered in parallel with the process improvements for all employees who would use MaxFli. Palacios

EXHIBIT 3
Clarifying MaxFli and End-Market Responsibilities for Implementation Success

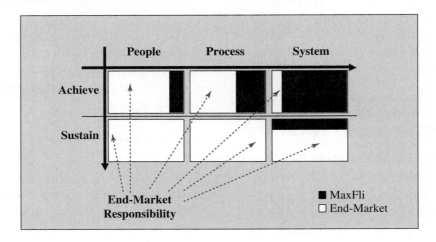

believed that ongoing support was just as critical as initial training. He argued that,

> [a]lthough thorough system testing and adequate training are essential before implementation, with any highly complex system, support plays a key role. The set-up of a local support team should be anticipated and ideally it should be in place before final implementation.

The support team had to be prepared to answer both technical questions (e.g., "How do I print an invoice?") and business questions (e.g., "Can I make a credit decision for this customer, or do I have to check with someone else?").

By focusing on training and support, Palacios wanted to pre-empt some of the personnel issues that often plague large IT implementations. As stated by GM Friere: "[T]here are personnel issues involved in any project this size. Treat [your people] well, but expect a lot."

Technology

Previous systems at Chiletabacos were designed to control and support basic sales rep activities, but did not provide valuable sales and marketing information. One of the primary objectives of MaxFli was to increase the information available to management, so that they could quickly identify market trends and competitor activity and make effective trade-marketing and distribution decisions. Before, MaxFli marketing managers had to rely mostly on instinct to select which marketing promotions to run in each outlet. MaxFli allowed managers to cross-index sales with promotional activities in individual outlets to better understand the effectiveness of marketing promotions in each category of outlet. This required a combination of technologies. (See Exhibit 4.)

When MaxFli was first proposed in 1997 there were no integrated, off-the-shelf systems that tied a handheld SFA system to a CRM system. The challenge faced by the MaxFli steering committee and project managers was to integrate off-the-shelf and custom components while maintaining low costs, maximum flexibility, and reliability.

Go Live in Chile

MaxFli went live in Chile in November 1999 on schedule and 2 percent over budget. Despite being over budget, the MaxFli implementation in Chile was viewed as a success: it provided valuable information to management about market trends and enabled efficient trade-marketing decisions. Chiletabacos GM Friere elaborated:

> The best thing about MaxFli is that I, or any of my managers, can sit at my desk and see exactly what happened yesterday throughout the country, region, city, or even a single outlet. That is incredibly powerful for making decisions about brands, promotions, and marketing.

By the spring of 2001 the success of MaxFli in Chile was secure: Managers at every level in the organization were using it. However, its biggest test would be its introduction to other end markets in Latin America and around the world.

MaxFli in Colombia

The next site for MaxFli was BAT Colombia. BAT Colombia planned to implement MaxFli in May 2000, 6 months after Chiletabacos completed implementation. BAT Colombia was a relatively young firm, founded by Chiletabacos in 1993.

EXHIBIT 4
Combining Custom and Off-the-Shelf Packages

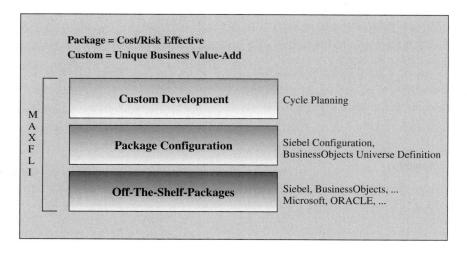

Beginning as a marketing operation, it had expanded to be a complete direct distribution market. Many of its business processes were imported from Chiletabacos, along with several members of the executive team. Consequently, according to Jorge Soto, the general manager of BAT Colombia, they run a very "Chilean business." The relationship between BAT Colombia and Chiletabacos continued to be both close and supportive.

Market Forces in Colombia

Although the business processes and leadership style in Colombia were similar to Chiletabacos, the competitive environment was quite dissimilar. There were four tobacco firms competing for the market in Colombia with each having approximately 25 percent of the market. Two of BAT Colombia's competitors were Colombian companies focused on value brands, while Phillip Morris, Inc., and BAT battled over premium brands.

Chiletabacos was primarily concerned with MaxFli as a competitive information tool; BAT Colombia was more concerned with consumer information, cutting costs, and creating efficiencies with MaxFli. The new system enabled BAT Colombia to more quickly identify and understand the consumer's tastes and preferences. This information helped them produce and target premium brands to those willing and able to buy them.

Project Team in Colombia

BAT Colombia had aggressively adopted new technologies to increase efficiencies for several years, but MaxFli was their largest IT project to date. The MaxFli project team in Colombia was led by one of their senior TM&D Managers, Patricio Imbert. The IT personnel assigned to the MaxFli project included some of the best and brightest IT talent in BAT Colombia, including System Administrator Juan Carlos Hidalgo, who had already spent 1 year in Chile working on MaxFli.

In July 1999, at the beginning of the MaxFli project in Colombia, Chiletabacos hosted a "MaxFli University," and several members of the project team spent one week in Chile becoming familiar with MaxFli. Upon returning home, the IT project staff began to dive into the MaxFli program. They carefully examined each component and module to discover its purpose, inputs, and outputs. This was essential because there was little existing documentation to describe the detailed specifications of MaxFli. In addition to the "MaxFli University," Chile sent two IT personnel on monthly 2-day visits to Colombia throughout the implementation process.

Implementation in Colombia

BAT Colombia implemented MaxFli on time and 11 percent under budget. Overall, the MaxFli implementation in Colombia was considered a success. Like Chiletabacos, BAT Colombia undertook an extensive training program.

BAT Colombia GM Jorge Soto attributes the success primarily to the quality of personnel in BAT Colombia and the training: "Here in Colombia, we have a lot of young, motivated people. We have been through many changes in the past few years and they are ready to handle more changes."

Mauricio Leon, the infrastructure manager for MaxFli in Colombia, agreed: "This is a very good experience we have here...because of the training."

Even though MaxFli was widely considered a success in Colombia, there were two major obstacles. First was the perception that MaxFli was inadequate as a trade-marketing system. This problem was exacerbated by BAT Colombia's decision to implement a multiphase rollout of the system. In May 2000 the full system went live, but only the basic sales force automation functionalities of MaxFli were used. The more advanced modules that allowed for gathering competitor activity, structuring the sales visit, and maintaining merchandising material were not activated until January 2001. BAT Colombia CIO Jaime Navas argued that this approach was beneficial because it reduced the initial complexity and smoothed the transition to MaxFli from legacy systems. While this strategy met their immediate need for a new sales system, it did not immediately tap into the true value of MaxFli as a competitive information tool.

Although the system was implemented on time and under budget, the limited initial usefulness of MaxFli may have affected some users' views of its value. One manager from trade-marketing suggested: "We need a new system for trade marketing. MaxFli does distribution very well but with it we cannot manage individual promotions or other trade marketing activities."

These concerns led to the development of a locally designed trade-marketing system named AMiT. This system was developed for use by sales managers to coach, monitor, and support individual sales reps. This system runs on palm-sized HP Jornadas and aggregates MaxFli data and automates a sales review process for the sales manager. Sales managers use this system to improve cycle planning and sales activities as well as to mentor sales reps. As of Fall 2001, AMiT was only being used in Colombia.

The second major obstacle for MaxFli in Colombia was the reliability and performance of the handheld device (Jornada 690). Based on Chiletabacos's experience, CIO Jaime Navas expected reliability problems with it. Consequently, he chose a different strategy for acquiring the devices. Instead of purchasing the devices from a local vendor and negotiating a service agreement for support, he leveraged the strength of BAT Colombia's relationship with HP to negotiate a leasing arrangement directly with HP Colombia.

While BAT Colombia experienced the same high failure rate with the Jornadas as Chiletabacos, they had lower support costs. CIO Navas claimed that this arrangement saved BAT Colombia $150,000 over 3 years compared to working with a local vendor. Eventually HP decided to provide newer Jornadas to BAT Colombia free of charge in order to reduce their support costs. Despite this beneficial leasing arrangement, the handhelds were a major obstacle for MaxFli in Colombia. Mauricio Leon described the problem:

> I think that the most important challenge was the handheld. Because the server we [could] manage. There were many new things in the server. Oracle was new for the company. All the processes that MaxFli runs were new…we understood what the process does, and there was no problem with that. There was some problem but they fix it. So for us, Oracle was new but it was not a problem. We had experience in databases so the operating system of the MaxFli was not a problem, we knew it. We had to change the communication links; we had to double [our bandwidth].…That was not a problem. We put in remote access services (RAS) in order to support some salespeople who work in very far away small cities. So they just dial in. That was not a problem. But the handheld has been a continuous challenge. And we spent a lot of money in the handhelds. At the beginning, we had many problems with the handhelds. A lot of problems. So I think that is the challenge, to find a powerful device and stable device is the main challenge.

MaxFli in Central America

The next test for MaxFli was BAT Central America (BATCA). BATCA is as different from Chiletabacos as BAT Colombia is similar. BATCA is unique in organizational structure, market conditions, IT capabilities, and business processes.

BATCA operates as a "cluster market," meaning that the six countries of Central America (Costa Rica, Honduras, Nicaragua, Guatemala, El Salvador, and Panama) form a single operating unit. The markets operated independently prior to 1995. In 1995 BATCA management was centralized in San Jose, Costa Rica, and production was centralized in Honduras. Each country maintained independent marketing and sales operations. By combining resources into a cluster, BATCA was able to centralize production and create efficiencies of scale in their operations. The larger size of the cluster allowed BATCA to implement larger, more expensive IT systems like MaxFli, although none of the independent countries of Central America would have been able to.

Market Forces in Central America

Coordinating six sets of business processes in one organization created many complications for BATCA. The six countries of Central America share a common language and religion but little else. Each country differs in terms of competitive environment, taxes, regulation, currency, market share, and business strategy. (See Exhibit 5.)

An important market feature in BATCA was that the sale of nontobacco products (e.g., matches) was an important source of revenue. However, in order to limit the complexity of the new system, the global steering committee decided not to support nontobacco products in MaxFli. Since MaxFli would be the

EXHIBIT 5
Breakdown of BAT Central America by Country

Volume (rank)	Country	Market Share	World Bank Income Classification *
1	Nicaragua	95 %	Low income, severely indebted
2	Honduras	90 %	Low-middle income, moderately indebted
3	Panama	75 %	Upper-middle income, moderately indebted
4	Costa Rica	50 %	Upper-middle income, less indebted
5	Guatemala	30 %	Low-middle income, less indebted
6	El Salvador	75 %	Low-middle income, less indebted

*Based on the World Bank's Country Classification Table (n.d.) accessed from Web site 9/18/01: *www.worldbank.org/data/databytopic/CLASS.XLS.*

only system in use by BATCA sales reps, the implementation of MaxFli implied an immediate decrease in revenue from lost match sales.

IT Infrastructure and History in Central America

Prior to 1995 each country in BATCA had developed independent information systems to monitor and track sales. Two markets, Guatemala and Costa Rica, had specific concerns about migrating to MaxFli because both of these countries had developed custom IT applications that mapped well to the contours of their existing business processes. The "best practices" embedded in MaxFli required the sacrifice of those customized applications. The business case for MaxFli in Central America identified eight important risk factors associated with the MaxFli project. (See Exhibit 6.)

Items 4 and 7 represented highly probable risks that would have a high impact. From the beginning, the implementation team was concerned about MaxFli's ability to achieve and sustain improvements in the way of doing business. These concerns would continue to be present throughout the implementation process.

Item 3 addressed possible "technical constraints" based on two specific concerns. First, BATCA's IT infrastructure relied on complicated relationships with telecommunications providers in six countries. It was a challenge to create an intercountry backbone capable of running MaxFli, because each country had an independent domestic telecommunications provider (See Exhibit 7.)

Based on previous experiences with its primary telecommunications vendor, BATCA estimated that a significant portion of the ongoing costs for MaxFli would be devoted to improving the communications infrastructure.

EXHIBIT 6
Risk Management Table for MaxFli Implementation in Central America

#	Summary Description of Risk	Keyword	Probability	Impact
1.	Implementation delays due to staffing problems	Resources	M	H
2.	Implementation delays due to readiness not achieved by end markets	Readiness	M	H
3.	Implementation delays due to technical constraints	Technical	H	M
4.	Organization does not achieve expected level of improvement in the way of doing business	Achieve	H	H
5.	Dedicated central team's performance not optimal	Team	L	M
6.	System/network configuration does not fully support vision of doing business	System	L	M
7.	The organization does not sustain achieved level of performance in the way of doing business	Sustained	H	H
8.	External factors delay system implementation	External	L	L

EXHIBIT 7
The Intercountry Communications Backbone for MaxFli in Central America

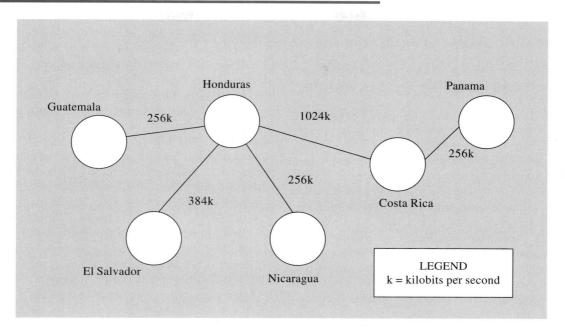

The communication infrastructure was an ongoing frustration during the initial phase of implementation. Juan Carlos Gracia, the project IT leader, noted:

> One of the challenges from an IT perspective that we faced was in terms of dealing with six different telephone companies when setting our wide-area network for centralizing the operations of MaxFli. That is something that you really have to take into consideration. Even though we are a cluster, we speak the same language, we have many things in common, even the same religion. But legally, there are many differences between countries....So [each] has to be treated differently. Telecoms are privatized in most countries [but are] publicly managed in Costa Rica and Honduras. [And] that's where we have most of our operations concentrated.

A second technical constraint was the challenge of finding a vendor able to support the Jornada handheld across the six cluster countries. The MaxFli project team faced a choice: find a vendor who could provide a service-level agreement to provide and maintain the handhelds locally in all six countries, or find a vendor in one country who could coordinate shipping the handhelds throughout Central America and perform all the maintenance from one country. They chose the first option and signed a service-level agreement with a vendor to provide all of the Jornada handhelds plus an additional 10 percent standing inventory to use as backups to all six countries and provide a 14-day repair/replace service locally in each country.

The Project Team in Central America

Similar to the Colombian team, the MaxFli implementation team in Central America was led by an experienced trade marketing manager. Walter Kruger had worked his way up through the BAT trade-marketing function in Central America. Unlike BAT Colombia, BATCA did not share many business practices with Chiletabacos, nor did it have strong relational ties with them.

One of the difficulties for the BATCA project team was a lack of training in MaxFli. Gracia remembers that the "flying doctors," a term he used to refer to the MaxFli support team, dogmatically insisted that no one on the implementation team needed MaxFli training. Instead, they suggested that reviewing the MaxFli documentation and system outputs were enough to prepare the implementation team. The "MaxFli University"–style training used by BAT Colombia, where several key project personnel spent time in Chile studying MaxFli, was not offered to BATCA. This was especially problematic to Gracia, who had built his IT career outside of BAT and joined BATCA at the beginning of the MaxFli project to provide expert assistance during this large system implementation. With no history within BAT, he felt at a disadvantage in learning the details of the MaxFli system. Gracia laments:

> Marco [a colleague IT manager] told me, "oh, you must go to Chile for two months where you'll be trained in MaxFli. How it has been done, how the implementation works, what are the

interfaces and fields, how do you do the change management, etc." Chile, however, decided to curtail the training to the markets embarked in this initiative. They said, "it is now your responsibility to get training"…[I]t was a nightmare. We had to rely on one particular resource that had been an integral part of the implementation in Chile, Luis Boesch. He became very important. Definitely, he was an ombudsman. Initially we were so reliant on him that he could not leave even to provide consulting to Colombia, which was the other market implementing MaxFli.

Through a long and difficult process of examining screens, reports, and documentation, the MaxFli project team began to form ideas about the inputs, outputs, and processes involved in MaxFli. However, apart from interactions with Luis Boesch and participation in several electronic discussion groups about MaxFli implementation, there was no way to verify their conclusions.

The BATCA project team struggled to find qualified IT personnel to support MaxFli in each country. While stronger economies like Panama and Costa Rica had adequate IT personnel, it was more difficult finding qualified IT personnel in struggling economies like Nicaragua and El Salvador. Consequently, the MaxFli project team hired and coordinated all development staff in Costa Rica. To confirm the capabilities of applicants, Gracia had applicants complete a small programming scenario along with their written application for employment. Those applicants who successfully completed the programming module were further considered for hiring. This process allowed Gracia to identify qualified personnel whom he believed added value to the development process. Ultimately Gracia was very satisfied with the quality of his team.

A final challenge faced by the project team in BATCA was turnover on the BATCA executive steering committee. Six months into the MaxFli project, the GM of BATCA transferred to Europe, and a new GM, Raymond Acorda, was selected from Souza Cruz, BAT's Brazil operation. Then shortly after the project rollout, a new marketing executive, Juan Morales, joined the steering committee. While both Acorda and Morales supported MaxFli, the mid-project leadership change created additional difficulties for the implementation team.

Implementation in Central America

The MaxFli implementation in Central America struggled. It was completed on time but over budget. Much of the budget overage was caused by the necessary transition from MaxFli 1.0 to MaxFli 1.1. This transition was required because MaxFli 1.0 was designed to handle a single currency and a single management structure. It could not support the complexity of multiple countries and multiple currencies required by BATCA's cluster structure. The software development challenges associated with a major system upgrade were made more difficult by another transition occurring with BAT globally.

In May 1999 Globe House decided to phase out all projects with Andersen Consulting. To continue the development and support of MaxFli, BAT began a joint venture with Cap Gemini/Ernst & Young, called Ciberion. In September 1999 formal responsibilities for the ongoing support, training, and development of MaxFli were given to Ciberion.

Ciberion was created to develop, market, and sell the MaxFli system to BAT end markets and external companies in the consumer goods industry. The transition was difficult for Chiletabacos and BAT Colombia, but especially difficult in Central America. To Gracia, Ciberion seemed too focused on future sales to pay attention to the present needs of BAT MaxFli users. Although Ciberion had committed to a 2-week turnaround for MaxFli problems, even "urgent" support requests took an average of 60 days to resolve. Gracia recalled waiting for weeks to hear from Ciberion even when his staff had already developed a solution to the problem.

Project IT Leader Gracia felt that several requirements that BATCA considered important were neglected by Ciberion. At least three are worth mentioning. First, the disagreement about the importance of MaxFli training for the implementation team caused continual frustration. Despite continual requests for training from Kruger and Gracia, Ciberion insisted that it was not required. This had long-standing implications for the success of the MaxFli implementation in Central America. As clearly stated by Rodrigo Palacios of Chile, "MaxFli is a business change program supported by an IT program." Without proper training, the BATCA implementation team was at a severe disadvantage in implementing the system.

Second, by the time BATCA implemented MaxFli it was clear that there were problems with the Jornada handhelds used by MaxFli. Both Chiletabacos and BAT Colombia had experienced problems with the limited durability and unreliability of the Jornadas. The BATCA project team felt that these difficulties would only be worse in Central America. Central America has a tropical climate with regular, often daily, periods of heavy rain. The project team felt that the climate might be too stressful for the handheld. Additionally, many of the sales routes in Central America are in remote, rugged, and isolated locations. Gracia was convinced early on that the handhelds were not adequate:

> We assessed the handheld ruggedness and therefore knew that it was not robust enough and was going to bring lots of trouble to our sales force. However, since there was a mandate that the system had to be implemented during Year 2000 and the decision from Ciberion was "Look, we are not going to test the code on any other machine besides this handheld unless you want to defer the implementation until later," we had no choice. If that was the decision, we had to go with it.

I explicitly communicated that decision to the project stake-holders. This was, in the long term, going to create a problem. But, there was this mandate that we had to implement regardless of the robustness of the hardware. And guess what, we have an average of 10 handhelds each week that need to be replaced!

Upgrading to newer, more rugged handheld devices was more complicated than it might have appeared to Gracia. Microsoft released Windows CE 3.0 during the final stages of MaxFli development. Because the new version was a major upgrade from Windows CE 2.1, it made fundamental changes in how MaxFli could interact with the hardware. The new CE 3.0-enabled handheld devices would not run MaxFli in its current version. Ciberion directed their efforts toward making the shift from CE 2.1 to CE 3.0. The Jornada 690 in use by Chiletabacos, BAT Colombia, and BATCA could not run CE 3.0 and was thus obsolete. Neil Coupland, a senior vice president for marketing and sales in Ciberion, argued that, "because of the fact that hardware reliability was an issue, we had to support new hardware, [and] the old hardware was now obsolete. You couldn't buy it. Therefore, the code was obsolete too. The focus was put on actually producing a working version on the new hardware."

Complicating the difficulties with the Jornadas, the service-level agreement with the supplier who provided and supported the Jornadas in all six countries was unsatisfactory. The average repair/replace order required 6 weeks instead of the contractually agreed 2 weeks. The delay required an additional 20 percent reserve supply of handhelds. Eventually, Gracia switched to a vendor in Costa Rica, who agreed to support all six countries centrally and manage the shipping to the sales reps in each country.

A third technical issue important to BATCA but largely unaddressed by Ciberion was the "suggested order" functionality. The suggested order routine is intended to provide the salesperson with a suggested order of brands and quantities at each outlet. This functionality was one of the major selling points of MaxFli in the minds of the trade marketing department. By giving the salesperson an accurate, up-to-date order history for each outlet, BAT hoped to increase sales and market share. However, due to technical problems with the Siebel and Oracle systems, this functionality was not implemented in initial MaxFli versions. This frustrated the project teams in Chile and Colombia as well as in BATCA. Kruger repeatedly pressed Ciberion about the importance of the suggested order routine. As of June 2001, the suggested order functionality was still not implemented in MaxFli 1.1.

BATCA installed multiple servers to manage MaxFli across six countries. Because of the communication infrastructure issues discussed previously, the management team chose to put the servers in Honduras and the IT support team in Costa Rica. The rollout occurred in three phases. Because Nicaragua was the strongest market in Central America, they were selected to go first. Costa Rica, Panama, and Honduras went live in the second phase of implementation, and finally El Salvador and Guatemala in the third phase. Like BAT Colombia, the BATCA MaxFli project team also chose a phased implementation strategy for the rollout. Instead of implementing the full MaxFli functionality, the project team chose to focus first on the basics of ordering, invoicing, and receiving payments. The value-added features of MaxFli, like brand coverage, competitive information gathering, and cycle planning, would be integrated one at a time every other month.

As in Colombia, this implementation decision created perceptual problems for MaxFli. The system had been billed as a panacea for Central America. Unfortunately, the enthusiastic expectations for MaxFli surpassed its initial capabilities. Because the initial system only handled the basics, it was essentially a replacement for the relatively low-tech handheld system previously in use. Without the value-added features of MaxFli, Central American users felt they had the worst of both worlds. They had given up the highly customized sales force automation system they were used to, without gaining the information benefits promoted for MaxFli. The morale and enthusiasm for MaxFli waned quickly. This sentiment was expressed by Morales, who said:

I think we oversold this as a tool....Our business is very, very simple. And now we're utilizing this big, big, very complicated tool. It is silly because we treat big complicated outlets like Shell, Exxon, and others the same as the little mom and pop shops. It is easy to sell this kind of system to Shell and Exxon. But when it comes to the mom and pop shops, this is not important. What they're looking for is that our salesperson will be there every week, be there on time, provide the right product, and so on. They don't care about all of this information gathering.

While initial user satisfaction was lower than in Chile and Colombia, there was reason to be hopeful. One of the technical challenges faced by the MaxFli team had become one of the technological strengths of BATCA. The MaxFli project team successfully negotiated with several telecom providers to implement the necessary communications backbone for MaxFli. As a result, BATCA now has one of the best communications infrastructures in Central America. Gracia argued:

What I can tell you right now is that we have the best communications infrastructure in Central America in terms of a company. We have received people from telecoms who say, "Look, the network capacity you have, no one else in Central America has." That sounds great, though we need to make a more effective use with additional services into it. But that is one of the challenges of implementing in different countries for one market.

As of the summer of 2001, the Central America implementation of MaxFli had been the most difficult implementation to date. However, it may also have been the most important. Neil Coupland of Ciberion summarized:

> [Central America] was critical frankly. Central America proved an awful lot of things. That MaxFli could work for example. Not just in another market outside of Chile. But that it could [work]. Really [work]. In six markets simultaneously. Frankly, I don't know that anyone had thought through how difficult that would be. But it worked, and is working still.

On the other hand, Morales summarized his concerns this way:

> Our business is very, very simple....In my opinion, until today we have a very, very simple business and a very complicated tool. I don't think it ought to be. We need to balance our tool with our business.

For the Globe House, the questions to be answered were: Is the MaxFli approach the best way to build custom-developed IT systems that can be shared by multiple end markets? Is this the systems development approach to replicate for future multinational systems that embody a business change initiative? Or are the needs of end markets unique enough to demand a more locally-tailored solution?

CASE STUDY II-3

REAL-TIME BUSINESS INTELLIGENCE AT CONTINENTAL AIRLINES

Continental Airlines was founded in 1934 with a single-engine Lockheed aircraft on dusty runways in the American Southwest. Over the years, Continental has grown and successfully weathered the storms associated with the highly volatile, competitive airline industry. With headquarters in Houston, Texas, Continental is currently the United States' fifth largest airline and the seventh largest in the world. It carries approximately 50 million passengers a year to five continents (North and South America, Europe, Asia, and Australia), with over 2,300 daily departures, to more than 227 destinations. Continental, along with Continental Express and Continental Connection, now serves more destinations than any other airline in the world.

In 1994, Continental was in trouble. There were 10 major U.S. airlines, and Continental ranked tenth in on-time performance, mishandled baggage, customer complaints, and denied boardings because of overbooking. Not surprisingly, with this kind of service, Continental was in financial trouble. It had filed for Chapter 11 bankruptcy protection twice in the previous 10 years and was heading for a third, and likely final, bankruptcy. It had also gone through 10 CEOs in 10 years. People joked that Continental was a "Perfect 10."

Continental's position in the industry changed dramatically over the period 1994–2004. In 1994, Gordon Bethune became Continental's CEO, and by 1998 he took the company from its "worst to first" position in the airline industry. A key to this turnaround was the Go Forward Plan, which continues to be Continental's blueprint for success and is increasingly supported by real-time BI and data warehousing. Currently, the use of real-time technologies has been critical for Continental in moving from "first to favorite" among its customers, especially among its best customers. Continental's president and COO,

---

This case is adapted from Anderson-Lehman, Ron, Hugh J. Watson, Barbara H. Wixom, and Jeffrey A. Hoffer. 2004. "Continental Airlines Flies High with Real-Time Business Intelligence." *MIS Quarterly Executive* 3 (December): 163–176. Revised case study copyright © 2007 by Jeffrey A. Hoffer.

Larry Kellner, describes the impact of real-time BI in the following way: "Real-time BI is critical to the accomplishment of our business strategy and has created significant business benefits." In fact, Continental has realized more than $500 million in cost savings and revenue generation between 1998 and 2004 from its business intelligence initiatives, producing an ROI of more than 1,000 percent.

The Role of Data Warehousing and Business Intelligence

Real-time business intelligence (BI) is taking Continental Airlines to new heights. Powered by a real-time data warehouse and strong management leadership around data, the company has dramatically changed all aspects of its business.

Information Wasn't Available

The movement from "worst to first" was only partially supported by information technology. Historically, Continental had outsourced its operational systems (e.g., reservations, payroll, billing) to EDS, and employees had very limited access to data from these systems. Data was locked away in systems that could support operations, but not decision making. Each department had its own approach to data management and reporting. There was no support for ad hoc queries. Employees had to make decisions based on intuition rather than on information.

The airline lacked the corporate data infrastructure for employees to quickly access the information they needed to gain key insights about the business. Data was not considered an asset, and was not governed for the good of the enterprise. However, senior management's vision was to merge data into a single source, with access by employees in all departments.

Enter Data Warehousing

Senior management decided to invest in an enterprise data warehouse that all employees could use for quick access to key information about the business and its customers. The CIO

EXHIBIT 1
Some of the Initial Data Warehouse Applications

Demand-driven Dispatch

Prior to the warehouse, flight schedules and plane assignments were seldom changed, regardless of changes in markets and passenger levels. Continental flew flights without fully understanding each flight's profitability. After the data warehouse, Continental created Demand-driven Dispatch, an application that identifies opportunities for maximizing aircraft usage. The application identifies opportunities to make short-term adjustments that do not disrupt operations. For example, it may be possible to swap one routing of an aircraft without disrupting the crews or the maintenance operations. The swap may assign a larger plane to a flight with unusually high demand. This application is very useful when large events, such as the Super Bowl or Mardi Gras occur. Continental uses this application to "cherry pick" schedule changes that increase revenue. Demand-driven Dispatch has lead to an estimated $5 million dollars a year in incremental revenue.

Good Will Letters

An eight-month good will test showed that even small gestures are very important to building loyalty. The warehouse first determined Continental's high-value customers by marrying profitability data and algorithms with customer records. The marketing department pulled this data from the warehouse and divided a sample of these high-value Continental customers into three groups. When individuals were delayed more than 90 minutes, one group received a form letter apologizing, a second group received the letter and a trial membership to the President's Club (or some other form of compensation), and a third group received no letter. Customers who received regular written communication spent 8 percent more in the next 12 months. Another unexpected benefit was that nearly 30 percent of those receiving the President's Club trial membership joined the club. This translated into $6 million. The concept was expanded across the company to include the top 10 percent of Continental's customers.

at the time, Janet Wejman, recognized that the warehouse was a strategic project and brought the development and the subsequent maintenance and support in-house. She believed that the warehouse was core to Continental's business strategy and should not be outsourced. Work on the warehouse began, and after six months of development, the warehouse was rolled out in June 1998.

The initial focus of the warehouse was to provide accurate, integrated data for revenue management. Before the warehouse, only leg-based (a direct flight from one airport to another) data was available. Continental could not track a customer's itinerary from origin to destination when it involved more than one stop because itinerary data were held in multiple databases. This limited Continental's ability to understand a market and customer behavior, and optimize its entire network. The warehouse integrated multiple data sources—flight schedule data, customer data, inventory data, and more—to support pricing and revenue management decision making based on origin-to-destination information.

The data warehouse provided a variety of early, big "wins" for the business. The initial applications for pricing and revenue management were followed by the integration of customer information, finance, flight information, and security. They created significant financial lift in all areas of the Go Forward Plan. Exhibit 1 provides two examples of how integrated enterprise data was initially used at Continental.

Taking Things a Step Farther, with "First to Favorite"

Once Continental achieved its goals of ranking first in the airline industry in many performance metrics and of returning the company to profitability, Gordon Bethune and his management team raised the bar with a new vision. Instead of merely performing best, they wanted Continental to be their customers' favorite airline. The First to Favorite strategy builds on Continental's operational success and focuses on treating customers extremely well, especially the high-value customers.

The Go Forward Plan identified the actionable ways in which the company could move from first to favorite. Increasingly, information technology was critical for supporting the plan's initiatives. At first, having access to historical, integrated information was sufficient to support the Go Forward Plan and to generate considerable value for the company. However, as Continental moved ahead with the First to Favorite strategy, it became increasingly important for the warehouse to provide real-time, actionable information to support tactical decision making and business processes.

Real-Time BI Applications

Continental moves real-time data (ranging from to-the-minute to hourly) about customers, reservations, check-ins, operations, and flights from its main operational systems to the enterprise data warehouse. The following applications, ranging from revenue management to flight operations to fraud detection, illustrate the variety of key applications that rely on real-time data.

Revenue Management and Revenue Accounting

The purpose of revenue management is to maximize revenue given a set of resources. An airline seat is a perishable good, and an unfilled seat has no value once a plane takes off. The revenue accounting area seeks to quickly and accurately record the revenues that Continental generates.

Fare Design Continental understands how important it is to offer competitive prices for flights to desired places at convenient times. Continental uses real-time data to optimize airfares (using mathematical programming models). Once a change is made in price, revenue management immediately begins tracking the impact of that price on bookings. And, knowing immediately how a fare is selling allows the group to adjust how many seats should be sold at a given price. Last minute, customized discounts can be offered to the most profitable customers, to bring in new revenue, as well as increase customer satisfaction. Continental has earned an estimated $10 million annually through fare design activities. Prior to the availability of real-time data, Continental's pricing was a less effective balance of filling seats and optimizing fares.

Ticket Facsimile Prior to the warehouse, paper tickets were scanned and archived on microfiche. To access a ticket for research purposes, required finding the ticket number, accessing microfiche, locating the particular ticket, and printing it. In 2001, the warehouse team built a report in Hyperion Intelligence (the software was called Brio at the time) to "look like" a facsimile of the ticket, and other airlines and agencies agreed to use this as the standard ticket copy for inter-airline transactions. The report is used to interactively search for one or more tickets in a variety of ways and query the real-time booking, customer, and flight information in the warehouse. The ability to find and print tickets from the warehouse reduced headcount by eight and saves hundreds of thousands of dollars for Continental.

Airline Reservations

The ability of customers to make reservations and airlines to accurately process those reservations is critical. While a data warehouse is not typically thought of as supporting airline reservations, Continental's warehouse sometimes serves as an emergency backup system because it includes real-time reservation data.

Recovering Lost Reservations In 2002, an error in Continental's reservation system resulted in a loss of 60,000 reservations. Within a matter of hours, the warehouse team developed an application whereby agents could obtain a customer's itinerary and confirm whether the passenger was booked on flights based on warehouse data.

Another similar situation happened recently when the reservation system had problems communicating with other airlines. In certain circumstances, the system was not sending reservation information to other airlines, and, consequently, other airlines weren't reserving seats for Continental's passengers. As a result, Continental customers would arrive for a flight and not have a seat. The data warehouse team was able to run a query to get the information on passengers who were affected and who had not yet flown. This information was fed back into the reservation system so that seats could be assigned, thus avoiding a serious customer relations problem.

Customer Relationship Management

The purpose of customer relationship management (CRM) is to increase revenues, profits, and customer service by knowing customers exceptionally well and giving them great service. Continental's marketing department uses the warehouse for customer segmentation and target marketing, loyalty/retention management, customer acquisition, channel optimization, and campaign management. In additional to these traditional CRM applications, marketing has created other innovative CRM applications that leverage the warehouse's real-time capabilities.

Customer Value Analysis A customer value model using frequency, recency, and monetary value gives Continental an understanding of its most profitable customers. Every month, the customer value analysis is performed using data in the warehouse, and the value is fed back to Continental's customer database. Although the value is not adjusted real-time (because some source systems needed for the value analysis can provide the data only once per month), the value is provided to Continental's customer–facing systems so that employees know who the best customers are.

This understanding helps Continental react effectively in tough situations. For example, post-9/11, Continental used the results of its customer value model to understand who and where their best customers were stranded around the world. Continental applied this information to its flight rescheduling priorities. And, while the schedules were being revised, the company worked with its lodging and rental car partners to make arrangements for its stranded customers. The highest value customer was in Zurich, and he used Continental's offices to conduct business until he was able to get home.

Marketing Insight Marketing Insight was developed to provide sales personnel, marketing managers, and flight personnel (e.g., ticket agents, flight attendants) with customer profiles. They can see how much someone has traveled with Continental and what the person's value is to the airline. Flight attendants receive the information by reading their "final report," which lists the passengers on their flights, expanded to include value information. Gate agents are able to pull customer information up on their screens and drill into flight history to see which high-value customers have had flight disruptions. A commonly told story is about a flight attendant who heard about a high-value customer's recent flight disruption and apologized on behalf of Continental. The passenger was floored that she would know about the incident and then care enough to apologize. President and COO, Larry Kellner, loves the Marketing Insight application because if someone calls him on the phone, he can input their frequent flier number to identify the customer. He knows immediately if he is speaking with a customer who flies every week or once a year and responds accordingly.

A Personal Touch   At Continental, like at most companies, a relatively small percentage of customers are responsible for a disproportionate amount of the company's profits. Using data from the warehouse, each quarter Continental's top 3,000 customers are sent handwritten notes from senior management. A note may say, "I see that you live in Houston. Hope that you have tried the Presidents Club, it has wireless Internet access," or "You checked in on Continental.com. I hope that you liked the service." Sometimes these customers are sent a personalized report card (based on up-to-the minute warehouse data) that shows the on-time performance of the flights that they were on. The response to this personal touch has been outstanding. Many fliers select carriers on the basis of price, but many of the most profitable customers do it on the basis of the relationships that are created and the attention and service that go along with the relationships.

Elite Access   Elite Access is one of the perks that Continental extends to its high-volume, high-profit customers. Qualifying travelers receive priority check-in, priority security screening, priority boarding, priority baggage handling, seat upgrades when available, and additional mileage credit when they happen to be assigned to a middle seat. Prior to the warehouse, marketing assumed that nearly all of the people who qualified for Elite Access were One Pass (Continental's frequent-flyer program) members. This proved to be incorrect. Through an analysis of warehouse data, Continental discovered that 60 percent of the high-value customers were not One Pass members, and as a result, were not receiving Elite Access service. These customers were going to the airport, standing in (long) lines, not benefiting from high-priority service, and not receiving any seat upgrades. In other words, they were receiving baseline service. With the real-time warehouse in place, these customers are identified as soon as they check in. They receive Elite Access treatment because Continental's systems can identify them at all of the customer touch points. They do not have to be One Pass members to be recognized.

Flight Operations

Operations is concerned with all aspects of getting people to their destinations safely, on-time, efficiently, and with their luggage. This is where customers have either a good or bad flying experience, and Continental works hard to provide excellent service. Good operations also can reduce costs by ensuring that ground personnel are in the right place at the right time. Special real-time applications have been developed to support this capability.

Flight Management Dashboard   The Flight Management Dashboard is an innovative set of interactive graphical displays developed by the data warehouse group. These displays are intended to help the operations staff quickly identify issues in the Continental flight network and then manage flights in ways to improve customer satisfaction and airline profitability.

Some of the dashboard's displays help Operations to better serve Continental's high-value customers. For example, one of the displays is a graphical depiction of a concourse, which is used to assess where Continental's high-value customers are or will be in a particular airport hub (see Exhibit 2). The display shows gates where these customers have potential gate connection problems so that gate agents, baggage supervisors, and other operations managers can assess where ground transportation assistance and other services are needed so these customers and their luggage avoid missing flights. In Exhibit 2 it can be seen that Flight 678 is arriving 21 minutes late to Gate C37 and two high-value customers need assistance in making their connections at Gates C24 and C29.

On-time arrival is an important operational measurement at Continental. Therefore, another critical set of dashboard displays helps Operations keep the arrivals and departures of flights on time. One display shows the traffic volume between the three Continental hub stations and the rest of their network (see Exhibit 3). The line thickness between nodes is used to indicate relative flight volumes and the number of late flights so that the operations staff can anticipate where services need to be expedited. The ratio of the number of late flights to the total number of flights between the hubs is also shown. The operations staff can click on the lines and drill down to see individual flight information. Another line graph summarizes flight lateness. Users can drill down to more detailed pie charts that show degrees of lateness, and then, within each pie, to the individual flights in that category. Another chart concentrates on flights between the United States and Europe and the Caribbean, and can show similar critical flight statistics. In all of these elements of the dashboard, high-level views can be

EXHIBIT 2
Concourse Display of High-Value Customer Activity

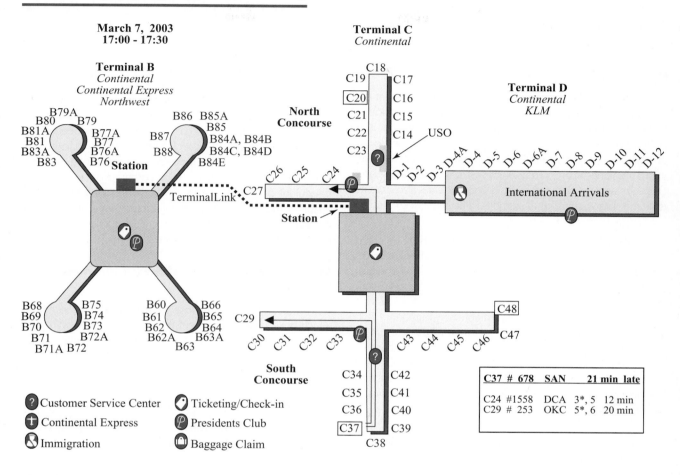

C37	# 678	SAN	21 min late
C24	#1558	DCA	3*, 5 12 min
C29	# 253	OKC	5*, 6 20 min

EXHIBIT 3
Display of Flight Lateness from/to Hubs

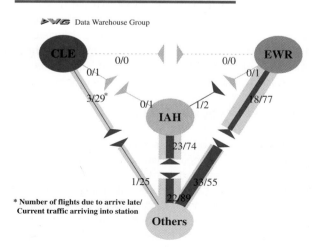

* Number of flights due to arrive late/
Current traffic arriving into station

broken down to show the details on customers or flights that compose different statistics or categories.

Real-Time Flight Statistics Continental management believes, "You can't manage what you can't measure." Therefore, management has an operations meeting every morning to review airline performance in terms of on-time arrival, on-time departures, baggage handling, and other key performance indicators. Prior to the real-time warehouse, information was refreshed at the end of each day; therefore, managers had to use historical information to try to improve the day's operations.

Operational data are now available in real-time (updated each minute), and users can submit queries and understand how the airline operation is performing at any moment. Upper management can see in real-time the revenue projections for any flight, where the most valuable customers are while in flight, which ones are affected by delays and cancellations, and bookings as they are made. This helps management make decisions in the event flights need to be delayed or cancelled for weather and other disruptions. They can also run "what-if" scenarios to determine the impact of cancellations, delays, or changes to specific flights.

Fraud Detection and Airline Security

Continental uses its warehouse to identify reservations that are not in fare and contract compliance and to profile suspicious booking and ticketing transactions. Fraud also includes the blocking of seat inventory, the selling of tickets at prices lower than allowed (an estimated $60 to $70 million annual risk), fictitious booking records, fraudulent lost baggage claims, and One Pass account redemption abuse. Continental also uses its real-time data warehouse to support airline security efforts.

Fraud Profiles   Some interesting applications have emerged as different kinds of fraud have been identified. More than 100 "profiles" of fraud are run regularly against the data. As potential fraud is detected, it is handed off to a case worker who conducts a formal investigation. For example, one profile looks for reservations agents who make an extraordinary number of first-class bookings. Last year, Continental was able to convict an agent who was manufacturing fake tickets and then exchanging them to purchase new first-class tickets that she would then sell to friends. Continental received over $200,000 in restitution from that one case. In total, Continental was able to identify and prevent more than $15 million in fraud last year alone.

Too Much Travel to Be True   A daily report lists Continental's most profitable customers. A man appeared out of nowhere one day as number one on the list. An alert user did not recognize the name and investigated. She discovered that he had made all of his deposits for frequent flyer points on the same day. She then looked at all of the deposited flights and discovered that he had not flown on any of them. He had counterfeited boarding passes and tickets and bundled them up and sent them in to the One Pass service center. The "revenue" from the dummy tickets shot him to the top of the customer profitability report. A timely report, an alert employee, and the ability to drill into One Pass flight data caught this attempted fraud.

Is It Safe to Fly   Immediately after 9/11, planes were ordered to land at the nearest airport. Continental had 95 planes that did not reach their planned destination. Sometimes there were three or four planes at a little airport in a town with no hotels, and passengers had to move in with the local people. At Continental's headquarters, FBI agents moved into a conference room with a list of people they wanted to check.

Queries were run against flight manifest data to see if potential terrorists were on flights, and it was only after a flight was deemed safe that it was allowed to fly. Continental Airlines was recognized by the FBI for its assistance in the investigations in connection with 9/11.

Fraud Investigations   In the wake of 9/11, Continental realized that they had the technology and data in place to monitor passenger reservation and flight manifests in real-time. A "prowler application" was built so that corporate security can search for names or patterns of activities that have been identified as being fraudulent. When matches are found, an e-mail and page message is sent immediately to a contact at corporate security. This capability helps corporate security identify fraudulent activity as it occurs. Not only does this feature enable corporate security to prevent fraud that is occurring, but it enhances their ability to gather critical intelligence through more timely interviews with suspects, victims and witnesses.

Supporting First to Favorite with Information Technology

Real-time BI requires the use of appropriate technologies, which build upon and extend those that are used with traditional BI and data warehousing. At Continental, real-time technologies and the associated processes are critical for supporting the First to Favorite strategy.

The Data Warehouse

Real-time BI is built on a real-time data warehousing foundation. At the core of Continental's real-time efforts is an 8-terabyte enterprise data warehouse running on a 3 GHz, 10-node Teradata 5380 machine. The warehouse supports 1,292 users who access 42 subject areas, 35 data marts, and 29 applications. Exhibit 4 shows the growth of the warehouse over time.

The basic architecture of the warehouse is shown in Exhibit 5. Data from 25 internal operational systems (e.g., the reservations system) and two external data sources (e.g., standard airport codes) are loaded into the warehouse. Some of these sources are loaded in real-time and others in batch, based on the capabilities of the source and business need. Some results of analysis (e.g., customer value analysis) are fed from the warehouse back into the operational systems.

Data Access   The users access warehouse data in various ways (see Exhibit 6). Some use standard query interfaces and analysis tools, such as Teradata's QueryMan, Microsoft Excel, and Microsoft Access. Others access data using custom-built applications. Still others use either the desktop or Web versions of Hyperion Intelligence to access data. An estimated 500 reports have been created in Hyperion Intelligence, and many

EXHIBIT 4
Warehouse Growth over Time

	1998	2001	2004
Users	45	968	1,292
Tables	754	5,851	16,226
Subject Areas	11	33	42
Data Marts	2	23	35
Applications	0	12	29
DW Personnel	9	15	15

of these reports are pushed to users at scheduled intervals (e.g., at the first of the month, after the general ledger is closed). Other products include SAS's Clementine for data mining and Teradata's Campaign Manager for campaign management.

Real-Time Data Sources   The warehouse's real-time data sources range from the mainframe reservation system, to satellite feeds transmitted from airplanes, to a central customer database. For example, files of reservation data are sent from a mainframe application on an hourly basis. Within the reservation system, the records are not structured in a useful way for analysis. The records are leg-based instead of trip-based (i.e., a trip recognizes a passenger's true origin and destination), and they are stored in a hierarchical format that cannot be easily queried. Therefore, a passenger name record (PNR) server application reads each file into memory and changes the

EXHIBIT 5
The Data Warehouse Architecture

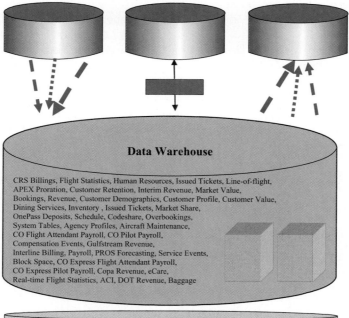

External and Internal Operational Data Sources

Continuous and Batch Updates from the Data Sources

Warehouse Data Back to the Internal Operational Data Sources

Data Warehouse

CRS Billings, Flight Statistics, Human Resources, Issued Tickets, Line-of-flight, APEX Proration, Customer Retention, Interim Revenue, Market Value, Bookings, Revenue, Customer Demographics, Customer Profile, Customer Value, Dining Services, Inventory , Issued Tickets, Market Share, OnePass Deposits, Schedule, Codeshare, Overbookings, System Tables, Agency Profiles, Aircraft Maintenance, CO Flight Attendant Payroll, CO Pilot Payroll, Compensation Events, Gulfstream Revenue, Interline Billing, Payroll, PROS Forecasting, Service Events, Block Space, CO Express Flight Attendant Payroll, CO Express Pilot Payroll, Copa Revenue, eCare, Real-time Flight Statistics, ACI, DOT Revenue, Baggage

Enterprise and Restricted Views

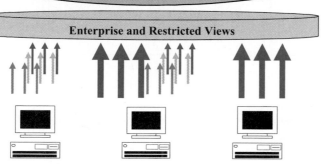

Short, Tactical Queries

Complex Queries (predefined and ad-hoc)

Business Users and Applications

EXHIBIT 6
Data Warehouse Access

Application or Tool	Types of Users	Number of Users
Hyperion Intelligence — Quickview (web)	Enterprise	300
Hyperion Intelligence — Explorer (Desktop)	Enterprise	114
Access	Enterprise	200
Custom Applications	Enterprise	700
Teradata Campaign Manager	Marketing	20
Clementine Data Mining	Revenue Management	10
Teradata QueryMan	Enterprise	150
Excel	Enterprise	many

format of the records from a leg-based perspective to one that includes origin and destination information. The PNR server application then sends the updated records to the warehouse. Passenger data are referenced by many applications, so it is important to control this critical master data.

Other data feeds are streams of real-time data. The flight data (called FSIR, or flight system information record) is sent real-time from the airplanes via satellite to an operations control center system, which supports the command center for Continental where the actual flights are coordinated. FSIR data may include time estimates for arrival, the exact time of lift-off, aircraft speed, etc. This data is captured by a special computer and sent within seconds to the warehouse.

Other data sources are pushed real-time by the sources themselves. For example, Continental's reservations system, One Pass frequent-flier program, Continental.com, and customer service applications all directly update a central customer database. Then, every change that is made to a customer record is sent to the warehouse.

The Data Warehouse Team

Continental has 15 people on its data warehouse team. They are responsible for managing the warehouse, developing and maintaining the infrastructure, data modeling, developing and maintaining ETL processes, and working with the business units. The organization chart for the data warehouse staff is shown in Exhibit 7.

Data Warehouse Governance

The Data Warehouse Steering Committee provides direction and guidance for the data warehouse. It is a large, senior-level committee with 30 members, most at the director level and above. The members come from the business areas supported

EXHIBIT 7
The Data Warehouse Organization Chart

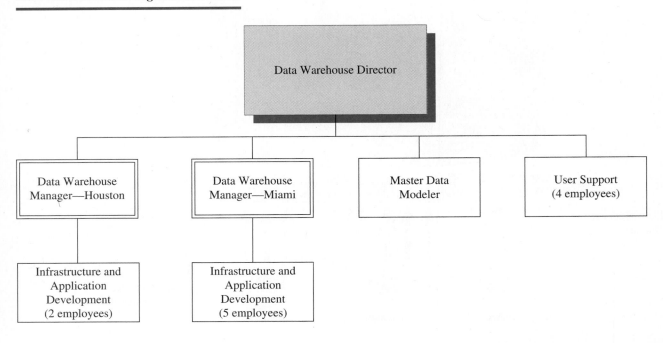

by the warehouse and are the spokespersons for their areas. The warehouse staff meets with the committee to inform and educate the members about warehouse-related issues. In turn, the members identify opportunities for the warehouse staff to become involved with the business areas. They also help the warehouse team justify and write requests for additional funding. Another responsibility is to help set priorities for future directions for the warehouse.

Securing Funding   The business areas drive the funding for the warehouse. There has always been one area that has helped either justify the initial development of the warehouse or encourage its later expansion. Revenue Management supported the original development. The second and third expansions were justified by Marketing to support the First to Favorite strategy. Corporate Security championed the fourth, and most recent, expansion. This approach helps ensure that the warehouse supports the needs of the business.

The funding does not come directly from the business areas (i.e., their budgets). Rather, the funding process treats proposals as a separate capital expense. However, the business areas must supply the anticipated benefits for the proposals. Therefore, any proposal must have a business partner who identifies and stands behind the benefits.

The Benefits of Business Intelligence

Continental invested approximately $30 million into real-time data warehousing from 1998 to 2004. Of this amount, $20 million was for hardware and software expenses, and $10 million for personnel costs. Although this investment is significant, the quantifiable benefits from real-time warehousing are magnitudes larger. Specifically, over this same period, Continental realized over $500 million in increased revenues and cost savings, resulting in an ROI of over 1,000 percent.

The benefits from real-time BI at Continental range from better pricing of tickets to increased travel to fraud detection. Exhibit 8 identifies some of the benefits that have been realized. Because there are 1,300 users with warehouse access, it is impossible to keep track of all the ways in which the warehouse has impacted Continental's bottom line. The data warehouse team knows that many other benefits exist that have not been identified. However, when big "wins" are achieved, the benefits are recorded and communicated throughout the company. This helps to preserve the excitement around warehouse use, and it encourages business users to support warehouse expansion efforts.

Lessons Learned

The experiences at Continental confirm the common keys to success for any enterprise-wide IT initiative—the need for senior management sponsorship and support, close alignment

EXHIBIT 8
Sample Benefits from Real-Time BI and Data Warehousing

Marketing
- Continental performs customer segmentation, target marketing, loyalty/retention management, customer acquisition, channel optimization, and campaign management using the data warehouse. Targeted promotions have produced cost savings and incremental revenue of $15 million to $18 million per year.
- A targeted CRM program resulted in $150 million in additional revenues in one year, while the rest of the airline industry declined 5 percent.
- Over the past year, a goal was to increase the amount of travel by Continental's most valuable customers travel. There has been an average increase in travel of $800 for each of the top 35,000 customers.

Corporate Security
- Continental was able to identify and prevent over $30 million in fraud over the last three years. This includes more than $7 million in cash collected.

IT
- The warehouse technology has significantly improved data center management, leading to cost savings of $20 million in capital and $15 million in recurring data center costs.

Revenue Management
- Tracking and forecasting demand has resulted in $5 million in incremental revenue.
- Fare design and analysis improves the ability to gauge the impact of fare sales, and these activities have been estimated to earn $10 million annually.
- Full reservation analysis has realized $20 million in savings through alliances, overbooking systems, and demand-based scheduling.

between business and IT strategies, a careful selection of technologies, and so on. In terms of data management, Continental learned two very important lessons:

1. **Recognize that some data cannot and should not be real-time.** Although the initial movement to real-time was relatively easy for Continental, the decision to move additional data to real-time is made with care for several reasons. First, real-time data feeds are more difficult to manage. The real-time processes, such as the flow of transaction data into queues, must be constantly monitored, and problems with these processes can occur throughout the day (rather than just when a batch update is run). And, when problems with data occur, they must be addressed immediately. This puts pressures on staffing requirements. Second, there is a need for additional hardware. Additional capacity is needed to store the data, and each real-time feed requires two servers, one to run the load and a second to back it up. Third, obtaining a real-time data feed from some source systems can be prohibitively expensive (or even impossible) to implement. Because of these time, cost, and difficulty-related factors, data should only be as fresh as its cost and intended use justify. Some daily, weekly, or monthly updates may be adequate for the business.

2. **Have the right people in the right positions.** Developing and operating a real-time warehouse requires a team with excellent technical and business skills. At Continental, data warehouse staff members in the more technical positions (e.g., design of ETL processes) have degrees in computer science. Some of them previously built and maintained reservation systems before they joined the warehouse team. Consequently, they have experience with transaction-oriented, real-time systems, which serves them well for real-time BI and data warehousing. The warehouse team members who work closely with the business units have previous work experience in the business areas they now support.

   In some companies, the warehousing staff has strong technical skills but limited business knowledge, and the business side has limited technical skills but good business knowledge. At the intersection of the warehousing and business organizations, there is a dramatic change in the technical/business skills and knowledge mix. Continental ensures that the warehouse is used to support the business.

   The right people are also on the data governance council. The council has authority from senior management and includes a balanced membership from IT, business, and data stewardship roles.

Conclusion

The leadership of Gordon Bethune, the Go Forward Plan, and Continental's employees moved the airline from "worst to first." They helped Continental do what an airline should do—get people to their destinations, safely, on-time, and with their luggage.

Continental's initial improvements were made in spite of the company's limited information systems, but management recognized that better information was critical if the company was to improve, grow, become more profitable, and provide even better customer service. The company developed better performance reporting systems, shared this information with everyone in the company, and rewarded outstanding performance when the airline as a whole improved.

Even after Continental had moved from "worst to first," management wanted more. It wanted Continental to move from "first to favorite." With the First to Favorite business strategy, Continental would strive to become the preferred airline of Continental's most profitable customers. Meeting this objective, however, required much better information than was currently available. Continental had to learn who its most valuable customers were and what kinds of programs and offers were most appealing to them, and then the airline had to use information to provide exemplary service.

To meet these requirements, Continental developed and rolled out its data warehouse in 1998. At the time, management recognized that real-time BI was needed in order to fully support the First to Favorite strategy. Consequently, Continental moved systems to real-time as much as was possible given the source systems and the current technology and made plans for real-time data warehousing. In 2001, ahead of other airlines and most other companies, Continental implemented real-time BI and data warehousing. The use of real-time BI has fundamentally changed how the company operates and its ability to compete in the marketplace.

As noted, data warehousing is commonly described as "a journey rather than a destination." This is certainly true at Continental. For example, although the Continental data warehouse currently contains 90 percent of the operational systems' subject areas, the warehouse team is currently working to enhance existing subject areas and to convert more subject areas to real-time.

Continental's journey is likely to be relatively easy because of the approaches they have taken with real-time BI and data warehousing. The business strategy and real-time BI are in sync. The business units feel that they own the warehouse; the warehouse team maintains the warehouse, and the business areas develop their own applications, with assistance from the warehouse staff. With its approach, Continental is able to use real-time business intelligence to move from First to Favorite.

THE CLIPTOMANIA™ WEB STORE: AN E-TAILING START-UP SURVIVAL STORY

Cliptomania, LLC, a limited liability corporation, sells clip-on earrings on the Internet at *www.cliptomania.com*. Cliptomania is owned and operated by the Santo family—father Jim, mother Candy, and daughter Christy. Its business is conducted from the lower level of the Santo home in Indiana, but it sells non-pierced earrings throughout the United States, Canada, Ireland, Australia, and New Zealand.

Most people who wear earrings have pierced ears, so stores offer a limited assortment of non-pierced earrings. Those who want clip-ons have a very difficult time finding appealing choices. Cliptomania sells nothing but non-pierced earrings, and it offers its customers a choice of hundreds of different styles of clip-ons. Although the percentage of people who want clip-ons is small, the total number of potential customers available to Cliptomania on the Web is huge. The Santos have found an underserved market niche. According to Candy:

A lot of our buyers are first-time buyers on the Internet, and some of them are older women. But you would be surprised how many teens and young twenties buy because for one reason or another they have had trouble with pierced ears. There are young mothers whose babies ripped the earrings out of their ears and their ears cannot be pierced again. And there are people like me who have problems with scarring forming keloids and don't want any unnecessary scars. There are people for whom piercing their ears is against their religious beliefs.

Some women are so thrilled to find us they will tell me that they have this problem or that problem and ask which of the earrings will work best for them. Because there are several different types of clip mechanisms, I can often help them out.

Our customers are pretty evenly distributed by age from pre-teens to the elderly. We had not anticipated it, but we estimate that we get some 5% of our sales from the cross-dresser and transgender population.

The Santos want Cliptomania to become the Kleenex[1] of clip-on earrings (i.e., the first name someone thinks of when looking for non-pierced earrings). They concentrate on providing a quality product at a competitive price with outstanding customer service. They have worked diligently to provide quality, honesty, and friendliness through the Cliptomania Web site. For example, Cliptomania has a very liberal return or exchange policy that allows customers to return or exchange any item within 30 days for any reason without question. Less than 1 percent of their customers return any items.

First established as a Yahoo! store in November of 1999, Cliptomania has had spectacular growth in sales during a very difficult period for retailing. Although it sells only clip-on earrings, by June, 2003 Cliptomania was the fifth largest jewelry store on Yahoo! in terms of gross sales.

Yahoo! store customers are encouraged to rate their satisfaction (or lack thereof) with their experience with the store. If they choose to rate the store, in two weeks (by which time they should have received their purchases) they are sent an e-mail pointing to an online rating form to complete. The ratings are on the following scale: Excellent, Good, OK, Bad, Awful. Although the default rating (already checked) is Good, an amazing 81 percent of Cliptomania's ratings have been Excellent! Ninety-eight percent of Cliptomania's ratings have been either Excellent or Good, so Cliptomania quickly earned a five-star Yahoo! rating for service.

In addition to a numerical rating, the rating form provides space for customers to submit specific comments that are available to the store through a database. Cliptomania has received a great deal of effusive praise such as the following:

I am very pleased and satisfied with the service I received from Cliptomania. The customer service representative was polite, helpful, and patient with me being a new customer ordering

---

[1]Kleenex is the brand name that is often used as a generic term for paper tissues.

with a credit card. The service was superb! I am also very pleased with the earrings. They are light, comfortable, and no pinching of my ears. And the cost you cannot beat. I am so thrilled with this. I plan on ordering more earrings from them, and have told several of my friends about this Web site. It is hard to find good quality clips, and I found just what I was looking for, and more. Working with the customer service representative was just like talking to a friend. I appreciated that.

History

In the mid 1990s Jim and Candy Santo were living in New Jersey near New York City. Candy was the development director for a large nonprofit organization that provided a broad continuum of care for the homeless, and before that she had been executive director of a crisis line. Jim had a long-time career in insurance sales that he still continues. According to Jim:

> In 1998 I went out to buy earrings for an anniversary present for Candy, and I could not find a good selection of nice clip-on earrings anywhere. I looked everywhere I could think of in the New York metropolitan area. I could find plenty of earrings for pierced ears, but it was clear that all the stores had decided that they could not sell enough clip-ons to justify carrying an adequate stock in their stores.
>
> I knew that there must be millions of people in the world who wanted clip-ons and could not find what they wanted, so this appeared to be a great opportunity to sell them on the Internet. This intrigued me, but I knew little about the Internet or jewelry so I started staying up at night and working weekends doing research on jewelry and how to sell via the Internet.
>
> After 13 months of research I concluded that the Internet was the ideal medium for this type of business. Earrings had a high markup, you could get started with little capital, and the Internet was the way to access the widely distributed market for clip-on earrings.

The Santos decided to try to sell clip-ons on the Web and Candy came up with the name Cliptomania for their new Web store. They decided that if the URL cliptomania.com was available and the name Cliptomania had not been registered as a corporate name they would go forward with the endeavor. They employed a patent and trademark attorney who checked and found that the corporate name appeared to be available. And they were able to purchase the URL cliptomania.com from Network Solutions, so they decided to go ahead.

On Thanksgiving day, 1999, traditionally the beginning of the Christmas holiday sales season in the United States, they went live with the Cliptomania store on the Web, operating out of one small room of their home in New Jersey. Their total capital investment was $10,000, which came from their savings. Although Jim had hopes that Cliptomania would grow, they expected it to be a sideline activity that they would take care of in their spare time while continuing their regular jobs.

Setting Up the Web Store

Neither Jim nor Candy had any expertise in the creation of a Web site, so Jim had devoted a lot of time and effort to determining how they would go about setting up the Cliptomania Web site. Jim found that one way would be to contract with an Internet service provider (ISP) for the computer resources required, purchase several software packages to perform the various functions that would be needed to run the store, and design the site and write the HTML code to set up the pages. The problem was that they did not have the personal experience or any IT development background to design the site and write the code or to integrate the various software packages. To hire someone to do all of that would be expensive and they might have little control over the process or the result.

The other alternative was to pay a vendor for hosting a store. For a price the vendor provides the computer resources and integrated software as well as templates for setting up the Web pages that provide the basic Web store structure but allow you to customize them to suit your business. The Santos chose this option and contracted with Yahoo! to establish their Cliptomania Yahoo! store.

Yahoo! provided templates for setting up the home page and the pages that displayed images of and described the items offered, as well as for navigation across the site. Yahoo! made it easy to add and delete items offered for sale and to make changes in the images and descriptions of these items. It used a shopping cart approach that holds selected items there until the customer wishes to place an order. Then it provides an online order form with the selected items detailed, and accepts a credit card number and other billing information from the customer. Yahoo! then sends the completed order to Cliptomania, and presents the customer with a page confirming that the order has been placed with Cliptomania. By checking a box, the customer can request that the order also be confirmed by e-mail.

Another company, Paymentech, is integrated with Yahoo! to validate the credit card by making sure that the customer address on the order is the same as the billing address of the credit card. After Cliptomania accepted the order, Paymentech collected the money from the credit card company and deposited it in Cliptomania's bank account once a week.

Jim was very concerned with transaction security via the Internet. When he was doing his research, he had read that 40 percent of the transactions on the Internet were fraudulent. He also read that Yahoo! had the best security among the vendors providing support for Internet stores. In addition to encryption to restrict access by outsiders to credit card numbers and other financial data, the Yahoo!/Paymentech combination detected and eliminated most fraudulent purchases, and that was crucial to Jim. The outstanding security and the ease of setting up and operating the store were the main reasons the Santos decided to go with Yahoo! as their vendor.

The Yahoo! store also had a "back office" that collected and made available data about Cliptomania's Web site transactions. The Santos got a historical report for each month showing the number of customers that visited the store, the number of page views, the average number of page views per customer, the number of orders, the income, the number of items sold, the average number of items per order, and the dollar value of the average order. This report also included daily and yearly totals. They could also print out graphs showing the volatility and seasonality of their orders. On many orders they could find what search engine sent the customer to Cliptomania and what search terms were used, and this information could be summarized by search engine. All of this information was of great value to the Santos in managing the store and evaluating the effect of their marketing efforts.

When Cliptomania was started in 1999 there was only a $100 monthly charge for the Yahoo! store. However, over the years Yahoo! has changed its pricing structure and as of 2003 it charged $49.95 per month for hosting, $0.10 per item carried per month, a .5 percent fee on all sales, and a 3.5 percent revenue share on sales that originate through a Yahoo! Store search.[2] Paymentech charged $0.20 for each credit card transaction it processed, in addition to the percentage of the amount of the sale charged by the credit card company (typically 2.5 to 3.5 percent).

Designing the Cliptomania Web Site

Jim and Candy did most of the set up work on the original Web pages themselves, with some help from a freelance consultant they employed to help them with problems that were beyond their technical capability. Since then Candy has learned the basics of the HTML language. The consultant is still available to the Santos via telephone and the Internet for tougher questions, although they have had to turn to him less and less often.

Before starting the store the Santos examined a number of Web stores and they had a pretty good idea of what they liked and what they didn't like in these Web sites. Candy explains what they wanted to do:

I designed the logo in the banner at the top of our page. I wanted the "t" to be dangling down from the "p" like an earring hanging down. We chose the burgundy and gold colors for our page because we wanted to give the impression of a quality jewelry store and not look like the typical Web store with bright colors crying for your attention. We put our names—Jim, Candy, and Christy—on the front page and we use personal pronouns throughout the site because people need to know that we are real people. Some people call before they will place an order on the Internet because they feel the need to talk to a real

person and have a sense that we are legitimate. A lot of our buyers have been first-time buyers on the Web. We are asking them to make a leap in faith and we want them to feel comfortable about making that leap.

From the start we put the various categories of products that customers can click on down the left side of the page. The names of these categories are very important because they must guide the customers to the products that they like. I have set things up so that no more than six items appear on one page. I do this because I think that most people don't like to scroll down a page—they will only look at the top items. Also, our pages load fast, which is important when people are coming in through regular phone lines. Customers often mention how nice it is that our pages load so fast.

Getting Items to Sell

Initially one of their biggest problems was finding sources from which they could get earrings to offer in the Cliptomania store. They searched yellow pages on the Internet for jewelry wholesalers and manufacturers and called lots of them. Half of them did not exist any more and the rest were not very helpful. They finally found a man in Virginia who bought overruns and closeouts, so in the beginning most of their stock was not the most attractive. Jim remembers:

We were very naive in the beginning. We got any stock we could get because we were almost desperate. We didn't know anything about jewelry, about what styles were popular, or about fashion. And we are in the fashion industry, so there was a big learning curve there. But somehow we survived.

I knew there was a jewelry district in Manhattan, so I took a day off from my insurance business and went to the city to the fine jewelry area, the diamond district. I tromped around for five or six hours before I concluded that I was in the wrong area. Finally someone had mercy on me and told me where to find the fashion jewelry area. That was a major breakthrough.

We finally found the wholesalers that would provide the kind of product we were looking for. These wholesalers had the product, but they were relatively expensive because they were several layers down from the manufacturers, and each layer tacked on its expenses and profit. After searching everywhere for manufacturers, we finally found this woman manufacturer/wholesaler out on Long Island who got all excited about what we were doing. We started getting stock from her and developed a relationship with her. She told us that we should go to the manufacturers' International Fashion Jewelry, Accessories and Gifts (IFJAG) national show in Rhode Island, which is very difficult to get admitted to. She got us an invitation that allowed us to get into that invaluable show that we now go to each February and September.

Before we went to the show, manufacturers' reps wouldn't talk to us because at that point we weren't buying in large enough quantities to interest them. But when we went to the show and got to talk directly to the manufacturers some of

[2]For current charges see *http://smallbusiness.yahoo.com*.

them connected with our passion to offer quality products for women who don't want to pierce their ears. Some of the manufacturers would say: "I think you've got a good idea, and you remind me of my wife and I when we were your age. We're going to gamble on you. I'm going to take orders from you that I would kill any rep of mine if he came in with them." They started providing stock to us that we couldn't have gotten otherwise.

That was the beginning of some mutually beneficial relationships. Since then we have grown to the point that we are ordering in such volumes that we are higher up on their customer lists. Some manufacturers will now make special manufacturing runs for us. At the 2003 February show one of the manufacturers said that it was time that we had our own exclusive earrings, and that manufacturer designed some for us and we have had our own special designs ever since.

Early Growth

The year 2000 showed steady growth in Cliptomania's sales. The Santos had only three orders in January, but by the end of the year they were up to more than one order a day. In 2001 Cliptomania's sales continued to grow rapidly to where sales had more than quadrupled over its sales for the year 2000. Candy recalls:

Jim and I both had full-time jobs and Christy was a student. We took no pay out of the business for the first two years—we just plowed everything back in. We started with pure sweat equity.

It started very, very slowly. When we got to one order a week we were celebrating. But it just grew and grew. Around October of 2001 I left my full-time development director job because I was really burning-the-candle-at-both-ends at that point. I took a part-time job where I could just go to work and leave it behind when I came home.

The Move to Indiana

In December 2001, the Santos sold more than they had in the entire year 2000. They were running out of space for operating out of their small house in New Jersey. Candy was originally from Indianapolis, Indiana, and she began to think about getting away from the high costs of New Jersey to the Midwest where the costs of space were much lower. She explains:

I could see after the holiday season of 2001 that we would not be able to handle the next holiday season out of the space in which we were working. If you needed packing material you either went up into the attic or out into the garage. We didn't have separate offices—we were all trying to work out of one room. After we searched for a suitable space in our area and found that everything available was far too expensive, it dawned on me that the people on the Internet don't care whether you are doing it out of high-cost New Jersey or lower-cost Indiana.

Jim provides another perspective on the move:

Another reason we moved to Indiana was to change our lifestyle. Candy and I recognized that if I continued to work 80 hours a week I was going to kill myself. Our expensive lifestyle wasn't giving us any quality of life.

Also, I think that the events of 9/11/2001 had something to do with it. We lost several friends and some neighbors in the World Trade Center disaster. Moreover, after 9/11 thousands of people who felt vulnerable living in Manhattan wanted to move out of the city. They bid up real estate by 50 percent in our neighborhood across the river in New Jersey, so we could sell our house easily and at a very good price.

In March 2002, we took a trip out to Indiana, and after that trip we decided to move. We sold our house in New Jersey and bought our present one in Indiana. We got twice the house for half the money, the equity in our New Jersey house paid for our new home, and we now have no mortgage. That was a big plus in enabling us to devote the time necessary to bring Cliptomania to the point where it could fully support the three of us and enable us to hire adequate help to make sales 24/7 without having to cover every day on our own.

When they moved to Indiana, Candy quit her part-time job. She has been full time with Cliptomania since then. Also, Jim cut back his insurance agent job to half time and has since hired his own help to continue to build his insurance clientele in Indiana.

Later Developments

In 2004 Candy began to question the use of Paymentech to verify and process credit cards. She explains:

Paymentech proved to be very expensive and difficult to work with. In credit card processing there are three costs to us: The monthly fee we pay for the service, a per transaction fee, and the percentage that the credit card company gets. In addition to a hefty monthly fee, Paymentech was charging us 20 cents for each transaction, and in addition was charging us 30 cents for any credits or voids.

I went to our local bank and they set me up with a group called Nova that was much lower cost to us. Nova only charges us 10 cents per transaction and they charge nothing on the credits. Also, the monthly fee is less and I'm almost a full percentage point less on the percentage that the credit card company keeps. That adds up quickly.

Furthermore, I am dealing with either my local bank or Nova, and they are much easier to deal with than was Paymentech. They provide much better support at substantial savings.

After its start in 1999 as a part-time mom-and-pop operation, Cliptomania has grown steadily to where in 2007 it has yearly sales of close to $500,000 and a staff of three full-time and several part-time employees.

Cliptomania's Operations

Candy is Cliptomania's CEO and Christy is customer relations manager. In addition to sharing responsibility for receiving and processing orders with Christy, Candy maintains the Web site, chooses the styles of earrings to stock, orders the stock, sets the prices, and manages the inventory.

Customers access the items for sale by clicking on one or more of the categories arranged vertically along the left side of the main page. Therefore Candy's choice of and wording of these categories is carefully selected. Candy also produces the images of the items that are shown and writes the descriptions that appear alongside the pictures. According to Jim:

Candy describes each earring very honestly so that the customer knows exactly what she is getting. But she has the gift of wording it in such a way that the person reading about it thinks that she will look like a million bucks when she wears our $10 earrings.

The quality of the pictures is critical. The customer cannot pick up an earring and look at it like you would in a brick-and-mortar store, so if she does not feel she is seeing the real thing and is not attracted to the earring, she is not going to buy it. Candy also does all of our imaging and her pictures look great!

Earrings are fashion items, so the market is continually changing. Candy changes Cliptomania's Web page almost every day as new items are added, old ones are removed, items are featured during special times of the year, items are put on sale, categories are reorganized, and so on.

Buying Earrings to Stock

About half of their sales are for fairly standard items that sell year in and year out. But the other half are fashion items that are very dynamic. Candy and Christy try to keep abreast of fashion trends to choose what to stock. There is a long lead time in ordering and receiving fashion items—in fact many decisions must be made at the national manufacturers' show in February. Therefore, they depend heavily on the manufacturers' whose judgment they trust to help them decide what will be hot for the next year.

With Cliptomania's rapid growth and the dynamism and long lead times of the fashion business, keeping adequate stocks of the good sellers while not getting stuck with items that don't sell is a continuing challenge for Candy. She describes the problem:

We do about 60% of our business in the last third of the year—September through December. September is the latest that I can order fashion items and expect to get delivery before Christmas, so I have to make decisions as quickly as I can figure out what items are going to be hot for Christmas. In mid-December the manufacturers worldwide close down, and don't open back up until mid-January. They have the IFJAG show in February, so they won't really start making the stock to fill the IFJAG orders until March and I will be lucky to get the new stock in May. When I order in September I figure it is going to have to hold me until May, but I don't want to overbuy on something that will have passed its peak by the time February rolls around so I will be sitting on it forever.

Many of the newer fashion items are designed and manufactured in the United States. Many of the standard items that do not change are made overseas where costs are much lower. Even the standard items can be difficult to maintain in inventory because the lead times on them are long and delivery schedules can be uncertain. Candy sometimes runs out of some of her standard earrings that are best sellers because of shipping problems in getting deliveries from China.

Candy gets lots of helpful information that is gathered by the Web site, which helps her with stocking decisions. She can see how many people visited, how many put items in the basket but have not bought yet, what they put in the baskets, and which search engine they came from and what search terms they used. She can get online graphs showing sales trends by item as well as for total sales. She can request summaries for various time periods and sort by gross receipts or number of items sold.

Candy also uses an Excel spreadsheet she developed that has a line for each item Cliptomania sells. It shows the Cliptomania product code, the name of the item, the cost per unit, the total number she has received, the dollars she has invested in the item, how many they have sold, the number damaged or lost in the mail, gross receipts for the item, total net margin, the vendor of the item, the vendor's product code, the current inventory, and the value of the current inventory. But even with all this information there is still a lot of judgment involved in deciding what to stock and how much to order.

Processing Orders

Cliptomania operates out of the lower level of the Santos' home in Bloomington, Indiana. There is a large workroom that contains the inventory in wide shallow drawers in cabinets and small plastic containers in cubbies along one wall. There also is room for assembling and packing orders, two desks with computers, and workspace for receiving orders. In addition there are two offices and a storeroom for packing materials and reserve stock.

There are four PCs connected by a network, along with a fax machine and a printer. They have two high-speed lines coming into a router on the network, one from a telephone company and the other from a cable company, so that they can continue operations if one vendor's lines go down for some reason. Once a month Candy backs up key records onto a zip drive and puts it into their safe deposit box at the bank.

In addition to the security features provided by the Web site provider, they have firewalls to deter break-ins to their own computers. They have many different layers of security to make it more difficult to break into their store either physically or electronically, including central security alarm systems for their house.

When an order comes in on the computer, Candy or Christy checks Nova's assessment of whether the billing address the customer has given matches the address for that card in a central database. If these addresses are not the same, it is a red flag that the order may be fraudulent. She also looks all orders over for other indications that they may be suspicious. If it appears that there might be problems she can call Nova to obtain the telephone number of the issuing bank and call it to determine whether or not the card is legitimate. If she cannot verify that the card is legitimate she can cancel the order, which does occur, but rarely.[3] If everything seems all right, she checks the inventory to make sure the items are available and, if so, prints out the picking ticket and the mailing label for shipment. The order is then assembled. Each pair of earrings is wrapped in plastic padding; the more expensive ones are placed in an attractive box. Once the earrings are protected, they are placed in a small corrugated cardboard shipping box. For some kinds of clip-ons a set of printed instructions for putting on the earrings is inserted. Then the box is sealed and the mailing label is affixed. Once a day the completed orders are taken to the local U.S. Post Office[4] and mailed. Most orders go out the same day that they are received. The shipping options and charges for shipping and handling are detailed on Cliptomania.com.

After the orders are put into the mail, Christy sends each customer an e-mail thanking her for the order, telling her it has been shipped, spelling out the return policy and, where appropriate, encouraging her to read the instructions in the box describing how to put on the earrings. Candy explains:

> We found early on that customers were having trouble with some of the earclips because they didn't know how they worked—they were twisting them and breaking them. So I made a graphic and wrote directions showing how to put them on properly and we include these instructions in the box with the earrings.

Some customers are not comfortable ordering over the Web, so Cliptomania also accepts orders by mail, fax, or phone. Such orders are relatively rare (less than 2 percent) which is fortunate because it is more work to process them as the information has to be manually entered into the computer and the credit card processing must be done manually. Mail orders sometimes include items that were in stock when the buyer decided to make the purchase, but are sold out by the time the order is received by Cliptomania. Initially the Santos accepted personal checks in payment of mail orders, but they have had enough problems with this that they now only accept credit cards and U.S. Postal Money Orders as payment.

One of Cliptomania's PCs is a laptop. The office printer has two trays, one with plain paper and the other with mailing labels. Things are set up so that if the Santos go on a trip they can log onto the network via the laptop, process orders from the Web as though they were in the Cliptomania office, and print out the orders and mailing labels. Workers can come in and pack and mail the orders, and Cliptomania's operations can continue uninterrupted.

Foreign Sales

About 10 percent of Cliptomania's sales are to customers outside of the United States. Selling overseas has some challenging aspects. There is the language problem—their overseas sales are restricted to English-speaking countries—Canada, Ireland, Australia, New Zealand, and English-literate persons in Japan. Initially Cliptomania sold earrings in the United Kingdom, but because of long delays in clearing British customs they no longer accept orders from there.

The cost to a foreign customer is considerably higher than in the United States because of higher shipping cost and import duties that may be charged. A major problem is verifying the validity of credit cards. On the other hand, currency exchange is not a problem as the credit cards take care of that—Cliptomania bills in dollars, and the customer's credit card is charged in his or her local currency at a reasonably good exchange rate.

Although Canadian import duties on jewelry make Cliptomania's earrings cost as much as 60 percent more for Canadians than they cost for Americans, the majority of their foreign sales are to Canadians. Overseas customers may pay even more than Canadians because shipping costs are higher.

In July 2003, Cliptomania attempted to expand its presence in Japan. They had been told that Japan could be a big market for clip-ons. They tried to set up a Japanese language Web site, but were not successful. Eventually they wrote off the Japanese experiment as a failure, but they still accept orders from there as long as they are in English.

In 2003 a man from Mexico e-mailed Cliptomania and was adamant about needing three pairs of thin hoop earrings. Although they do not usually sell in Mexico, Candy worked with him and reports:

> Mail theft is rampant in Mexico, and has been for at least 10 years. As the U.S. Postal Service does not serve his area, the customer said he would pay for UPS or FedEx shipping. The shipping costs exceeded the costs of the earrings as neither company would ship by ground due to theft problems. The

---

[3]Their credit card verification process has been very effective. There have been very few instances in their history where they were charged back on a credit card transaction.

[4]The boxes are too small to make it feasible to use a package service such as UPS.

customer was afraid a money order would not reach us, so he sent his credit card number by three different e-mails and the expiration date by a fourth. And then the whole order had to be manually done. The time it took to research this and all the e-mails sent back and forth added up to a loss to us if we add the value of my time. He was thrilled with his earrings, but I am convinced we have made the right choice not to sell in Mexico!

Marketing on the Web

Marketing on the Web is primarily a matter of getting potential customers to visit your Web store. Jim spends one-quarter of his time as Cliptomania's vice president for marketing and three-quarters of his time with his insurance business. Jim's son, Greg, recently joined the family business and assists Jim in Cliptomania's marketing efforts.

The primary way that potential customers find the Cliptomania store is by searching on a term such as *clip earrings* on a search engine such as Google, Yahoo! Search, or MSN Search. When Cliptomania got started in late 1999, search engines on the Internet were still listing sites by relevance based on the site's fit with the search terms. In very quick order, Cliptomania was listed number one on all the search engines when someone searched for clip-on earrings. But soon the environment changed radically. Jim explains:

> When the dot-coms went "dot bomb" in 2000, the whole environment got even more dynamic—it went ballistic. Since I was devoting lots of time to keeping up with what was going on, I quickly caught on to the fact that the industry somehow had to generate revenue and profits instead of just expanding its customer base. This is when Yahoo! went from a modest fixed monthly charge to adding fees based on volume.
>
> About this time the GoTo search engine started charging for listing position. There was not a fixed price for the top positions. You stated how much you would pay per click for each of your search terms, and if you bid high enough you could be number one or number two on a GoTo search. But if you did not pay you might be down on the second or third page where 95% of the people would not find you. I jumped on this and immediately agreed to pay GoTo (which changed its name to Overture and became Yahoo! Search in 2005). We had an instant increase in our business! Within a week it was very obvious that our sales were up significantly, and they stayed up.
>
> At the start we paid one cent whenever GoTo sent a person to our site. However, only 1.2% of these clicks resulted in a sale, so the cost was about 83 cents per sale. That cost was quite acceptable, but since that time our cost per click has increased to where the cost per sale can eat up most (or sometimes all) of the profit on that sale. However, we are willing to pay a high price because we view this as an acquisition cost— hopefully a good proportion of these buyers will be repeat customers who will come directly to Cliptomania without going through a search engine (which is one reason why we encourage people who visit our store to bookmark us).

People search the Web by entering combinations of key-words and the search engine produces lists of Web pages that are related to these search terms. Today there are two ways that your Web store may appear on search engine results— sponsored links and relevancy ranked listings. The sponsored links appear at the top and along the right-hand side of the results page. Search results ranked by relevancy appear below the top-level sponsored links and may go on for page after page. A Web site may appear both as a sponsored link and on the relevancy ranked listings.

Search Engine Advertising

Sponsored links are the major way Cliptomania advertises on the Web. Your sponsored link is an advertisement and you get to write the short description that is displayed as the sponsored link. You want this description to attract potential customers so that they will click on it to visit your store, but you want it to realistically describe your offerings because you do not want persons who have little probability of buying to click and cost you money.

To establish a sponsored link, you bid a specified amount that you are willing to pay per click on a search for a specific search term. Thus, you must specify the search terms that you are interested in and you may bid a different amount for each of your specified terms. You may not pay the amount you bid for each click as you actually are charged $0.01 more than the next lower bid on that term. You can specify your search-targeted keywords as broad matches, phrase matches, exact matches, or negative matches.[5]

The amount that you bid determines your position among the sponsored links for that term—the highest bid gets the top position, the next bid gets the second position, and so on. Jim tries to be among the top three positions on his major search terms.

The Cliptomania site includes over a hundred search terms, but most customers access them through a small number of terms such as *clip earrings* or *clip-on earrings*. Jim only pays for the terms that are used by most customers because it doesn't make sense to pay for a search term where a person will click on your site and find that she has no interest in buying your product.

The placement of your sponsored links can change instantaneously as your competitors can change their bids at any time. If you want to stay at the top of the sponsored listings, you have to pay close attention to what is going on so that you can respond to competitors' moves. However, there are limits to what you can afford to pay per click without losing money on each resulting sale. The search engines provide tools that allow you to analyze the results you get from your sponsored links so that you can make informed decisions about how much to bid on each of your search terms.

---

[5]Explanations for these terms can be found on the Google Web site.

Jim and Candy's son, Greg, has been examining their strategy in pay-per-click advertising and sharpening its focus. Greg explains:

On searching the term "clip-on earrings" we have what is called a general match, which means that if we don't have a specific term set up that matches the search term then the search engine will default to a general search on clip-on earrings. So if somebody does a search on "little girl clip-on earrings" and we don't have that term a Cliptomania advertisement will come up, but we don't pay the 10-cent minimum. Instead we pay what we bid on the term "clip-on earrings," which is much higher. So I am researching and creating ads for specific terms to bid on. These terms tend to have a higher conversion rate for us because they are very specific terms and they cost less per click because there is less competition for them.

Jim is experimenting with site targeted advertising through search engines where the search engine company places an ad for you on Web pages that are found via related searches. These ads would not appear on one of Cliptomania's competitor's pages, but might appear on the page of someone who sells scarves or beauty products or on categories that you specify. Jim explains:

We choose the Web sites and submit them to Google. They review them and don't approve all of them, and the target sites must also agree to accept the ads. You have to be highly relevant. For example, earrings seem to appeal to people who are doing new hair styles, so they have approved all of those ads we have submitted. We have targeted certain niches where we know the customers may be interested in our product.

Here you do not pay by the click, but rather by how many persons view your ad—you pay a certain amount per thousand impressions. The search engine company pays the person on whose page your ad appears a certain amount and charges you a certain amount per thousand impressions, but neither you nor the other person knows exactly what these amounts will be! After the fact you know what you paid or received and you can analyze whether or not the results were worthwhile, but beforehand everything is pretty hazy.[6]

Jim is closely monitoring this form of advertising and has removed his ads from some sites where the impressions were high and the conversions were low. The jury is still out on whether this form of advertising is effective for Cliptomania.

Jim will not accept ads for related products on Cliptomania's Web pages. He says:

We don't like the idea of cluttering up our store with links that send people away and they may not come back. Furthermore,

we have worked hard to provide superior service and achieve an outstanding excellence rating. We have control over how you are treated when you deal with us, but if we refer you out to another site we lose that control. If someone gets bad service from a store we sent them to, they might associate that experience with us, and our good reputation is too important to risk.

The Relevancy Listings

Although the sponsored links are important, according to Greg about three-fourths of the clicks Web sites receive come from the relevancy listings, so it is very important to appear among the top few relevancy listings. If you are not on the first page, most of the searchers will not find you. Therefore it is very important to understand how the search engines work and how they determine their relevancy rankings. For competitive reasons Google and the other Web search companies are reluctant to explain exactly how their search engines determine their rankings, but each of them has a different algorithm for determining its relevancy rankings. As of this writing Google is the dominant search engine, and it seems to have the most complex approach to its relevancy rankings. The following excerpts from the Google Web site explain in general how its search engine works:

The process by which we find content to include in our search index is known as "crawling." Google is a fully automated search engine that uses computer programs known as "spiders" to "crawl" the web and find sites for inclusion in our search index.

The spiders analyze the Web pages for relevant terms and phrases that characterize the content of the site and includes these terms in the giant index that it uses when you perform a Google search. Google's Web page explains:

Google goes far beyond the number of times a term appears on a page and examines all aspects of the page's content (and the content of the pages linking to it) to determine if it's a good match for your query.

The following presents what Google reveals on its Web site about its relevancy rankings.

Search results are generated automatically using algorithms that weigh numerous factors about the quality of a given Web page and its relevance to a user's search query. Google doesn't accept payment either to include sites in our search results or to improve or alter the ranking of sites in our search results.

Google uses PageRank to examine the entire link structure of the Web and determine which pages are most important. It then conducts hypertext-matching analysis to determine which pages are relevant to the specific search being conducted. By combining overall importance and query-specific relevance, Google is able to put the most relevant and reliable results first.

PageRank Technology: PageRank performs an objective measurement of the importance of Web pages by solving an equation of more than 500 million variables and 2 billion terms.

---

[6]At this writing some start-ups are beginning to compete for this type of advertising, and they are much more open about the costs. It is likely that the big search engine providers will have to become more open in this area.

Instead of counting direct links, PageRank interprets a link from Page A to Page B as a vote for Page B by Page A. PageRank then assesses a page's importance by the number of votes it receives. PageRank also considers the importance of each page that casts a vote, as votes from some pages are considered to have greater value, thus giving the linked page greater value. Important pages receive a higher PageRank and appear at the top of the search results. Google's technology uses the collective intelligence of the Web to determine a page's importance.

Hypertext-Matching Analysis: Google's search engine also analyzes page content. However, instead of simply scanning for page-based text (which can be manipulated by site publishers through meta-tags), Google's technology analyzes the full content of a page and factors in fonts, subdivisions and the precise location of each word. Google also analyzes the content of neighboring Web pages to ensure the results returned are the most relevant to a user's query.

In summary, Google combines at least two major factors to determine the ranking of Web sites in response to a search: (1) How well the content of the site matches the search terms; and (2) The quality of the Web site defined primarily by the number and quality of the Web sites that link to it.

In regard to the page content component of the ranking, it is important that the crawlers find indications of the content that people may be searching for on the page. For example, Cliptomania has a number of what they call "bead earrings," but many potential customers search for these as "beaded earrings" and may not find Cliptomania's store under that search term. Also, Web crawlers cannot deal with images, so if your content is in images it will not show up on searches unless the images are also described in text. For example, if you are a dude ranch that features horseback riding and emphasize that in pictures but not in text, the Web crawlers will not rank you high on "horseback riding" searches.

Other Marketing Approaches

Like many Web businesses, Cliptomania also owns quite a number of URLs with names that are similar to Cliptomania or have to do with clip-on earrings. For example, if someone in desperation keys in the URL www. cliponearrings. com into the address field on their browser, the browser will pull up the Cliptomania Web site. Cliptomania gets some business via these URLs, and it is relatively inexpensive as it only costs a few dollars a year to maintain a URL.

The Santos have established another Web site, www. earringinformation. com, that contains a lot of interesting information about non-pierced earrings including information on how to adjust them, what styles are best with different shaped faces, and other interesting information and ideas. This site also extols the virtues of Cliptomania and encourages visitors to click to visit Cliptomania, so this site is a marketing tool for the Santos.

Although Jim will not accept advertising on Cliptomania.com, he does allow ads on Earringinformation.com and receives some revenue from this source.

Another marketing approach involves the use of e-mail. Cliptomania has a file containing the e-mail addresses of all its customers. It also has a box on its home page where a visitor can provide an e-mail address. About eight times a year Candy sends everyone in this file a promotional e-mail. Candy cites examples:

> For the Twelve Days of Christmas (December 26 through January 12) everything in the store is a fixed percent off. I give our customers a jump on that by sending out an e-mail that lets them get the discount a few days before other visitors so that they can get the most desired stock before it sells out.
>
> These e-mails can be very effective. I sent out an e-mail around April 25 that said "Here comes Mother's Day, graduation, wedding season and proms. If you or someone you know doesn't have pierced ears we have what you need for these occasions." That produced a tremendous spike in our sales over a two-week period.

Incidentally, repeat customers provide a healthy percentage of Cliptomania's business. Through their eclectic product offerings and outstanding service, the Santos have built a very loyal customer base, so a sale to a first-time customer is just the beginning of a very productive relationship for Cliptomania. They also get a lot of new business by word of mouth from satisfied customers.

Jim is always seeking ways to increase sales so he continues to search for and experiment with new marketing approaches so that Cliptomania doesn't fall behind. However, the Internet is such a dynamic environment that not all Jim's initiatives work out well. He has spent several thousand dollars each year on experiments that were failures, but he realizes that in such a dynamic environment you must take some calculated risks.

Changing Web Service Providers

In 2006 the Santos began to have problems with the service that Yahoo! was providing. Customers were reporting that they were having trouble placing orders, and Cliptomania was being charged more than once for some transactions. They called in their consultant to help them deal with these problems but were not able to resolve them all.

To make a long story short, it turned out that the consultant's company, NetProfits Internet Consulting, had also become a Web service provider and was serving a number of former Yahoo! customers. In the fall of 2006 Cliptomania switched to this new Web service vendor with the URL Cliptomania.net. The new vendor charged substantially less than Yahoo! and provided services that in many ways were better than those Yahoo! offered, so Cliptomania is no longer a Yahoo! store.

An Unforeseen Consequence of the Change

When the Santos changed Web service providers from Yahoo! to NetProfits Internet Consulting, they operated the two stores in parallel for a while, giving the new store the URL Cliptomania.net and keeping the old one as Cliptomania.com. When they switched over to the new store, its URL remained Cliptomania.net rather than Cliptomania.com. Although this small change did not affect Cliptomania's position on its sponsored links, it had serious consequences for Cliptomania's relevancy rankings. Before this change Cliptomania.com was among the top five in the relevance rankings on most searches for non-pierced earrings. However, by late December the Santos discovered that neither Cliptomania.com nor Cliptomania.net was in the top 100 of the relevancy rankings on the major search engines—they had fallen off the radar! The Santos had been so busy handling the Christmas rush that they had not monitored the relevancy rankings so they do not know exactly when the rankings collapsed.

The Santos had retained both the Cliptomania.com and the Cliptomania.net URLs, but the information on all the earrings for sale was on Cliptomania.net. If someone went to Cliptomania.com, he or she was automatically transferred to Cliptomania.net, so the store was indirectly available via Cliptomania.com.

This change seems to have confused the search engines, some more than others. Cliptomania.net gradually rose in the relevancy rankings on Yahoo! Search and MSN Search to where by February they appeared on the first or second pages. However, neither Cliptomania.net nor Cliptomania.com appeared in the top 100 of the Google relevancy rankings. Greg tweaked the content of their pages every way he could think of to improve their relevancy on Google, the most popular search engine, to no avail. On March 1 the Santos opted to redirect the store content back to its original URL, Cliptomania.com. In about a week, Cliptomania.com was near the top of the Google relevancy rankings and also near the top of the other search engines. Things were back to normal, but the Santos have no idea how many sales Cliptomania lost due to this episode. They do know, however, that their advertising costs grew significantly during the time when people who were looking for Cliptomania could not find it on the Google relevancy listings and instead had to click on its pay-per-click sponsored link.

Challenges

Although the Santos have had to overcome many difficulties and problems, Cliptomania has been an outstanding success. During a period where most Internet retailers have struggled, Cliptomania has grown rapidly. Started as a part-time sideline for Jim and Candy, Cliptomania is a thriving business employing four members of the Santo family and a number of part-timers.

Up through 2005 Cliptomania's yearly dollar sales grew at least 20 percent a year. However, in 2006 Cliptomania's sales leveled off for the first time. Jim explains:

> I am sure that some of our lack of revenue growth was due to the problem with our search engine relevancy rankings, but there were also other factors involved. When the price of gasoline hit $3.00 a gallon last summer we got the number of orders that we expected, but they were much smaller. That has not bounced back totally yet. Our average size of order is still down about 20%. It is obvious that people were buying earrings with their disposable income. Although our number of orders in 2006 was up about 20% over 2005, the total dollar sales for 2006 was about the same as 2005.

In 1999, when Jim and Candy started Cliptomania, they had little competition as a specialized Web store. Today, however, competition is fierce. If you do a search on "clip-on earrings" you will get over a million responses. Jim explains his competitive situation:

> We still do not have serious competition from stores that exclusively sell clip-on earrings. A couple of people have tried this approach, but they tend to not last long. Our main competitors today are big portals like eBay, BizRate, Shop.com, etc. They are emerging as huge malls on the Internet and they are trying to capture everything they can. They do not stock products themselves but present the goods of others. They direct traffic to stores that give them the highest rate of return. These competitors can outbid us for position on the sponsored links and are driving up the cost of our basic advertising because we must stay near the top of the sponsored links.

> The Web is so dynamic and so competitive that we have to keep running hard to keep up. I look at other successful Web stores and try to learn from them. And I devote a lot of time and energy to identifying and keeping up with new developments and trends relating to the Internet. For example, we just bought some more URLs. An obvious trend in this country is to go mobile. Everyone has a cell phone, and we think the Internet is going on the cell phone. The URL for mobile ends with .mobi, so we have purchased our most critical URL terms with the .mobi ending. It is still speculative at this time, but I think that sometime in the future everyone will be wearing a portable computer or have it strapped to them or built into their cell phone or some other means. If they want to find clip earrings we want Cliptomania to be found, so I have purchased those URLs just to protect our turf.

> We are lucky that we started when we did. Today there is no way that we could be successful starting Cliptomania on a shoestring, but we have reached the point where we can continue to prosper despite competition, downturns in the marketplace, and a few missteps like we had when we changed service providers.

MERIDIAN HOSPITAL SYSTEMS, INC.: DECIDING WHICH IT COMPANY TO JOIN[1]

It was late October of 2005, and Willis "Willie" Stahe was running late. As president of Midwest University's Computing and Information Systems student club, he had helped organize a student-alumni networking event and was relieved to find the room packed for lunch and the afternoon seminar. He threw his backpack into a corner and headed for the podium. After a short introduction and thank you to everyone for coming, he stopped at the buffet table and filled a plate.

As he reached for a crescent roll, he crossed arms with a tall, older man, surprisingly dressed casually. Willie thought his long-sleeved shirt looked like it was flannel. "Sorry. I guess I'm still rushing," Willie said.

"Quite all right. After you," flannel shirt said quietly.

"I feel like I've just been hit by a truck," Willie continued. "I just attended a presentation by this speaker in our Management of Information Systems class. He co-founded a local start-up software firm."

"Sounds interesting," flannel shirt said. Willie raced on, "See, I graduate this semester and I have an offer from Hewlett-Packard to start as a software developer in January. I told them I would get back to them at the end of this week. I just told them that because I was playing it cool. But now, I'd really like to interview with this start-up company. They're here today and Friday only."

"Seems to me like you should go through the interview first. That may help make the decision for you," flannel shirt said.

"The start-up sounds so cool. But Hewlett-Packard—how could I turn that offer down?" Willie thought out loud.

"A lot of software start-ups crash and burn. But in the last few years, some of the large IT companies have had their problems as well. Before you turn HP down, perhaps you should really study this other company," flannel shirt said.

"The speaker did give us some handouts. Plus, I guess I could do some additional library and Internet research myself," Willie said. "Thanks for talking me through this. When did you graduate from Midwest?"

"Alum? Is that why there are so many people here? Is this an alumni event?" flannel shirt asked.

"Yes. Why? You're not an alum?" Willie asked.

"No. I'm here interviewing. We haven't done a lot of campus interviewing, so I don't know the layout here. One of the interviewers said there was a break room down the hall," flannel shirt said.

"Oh. That's down the hall the other way," Willie said.

"Whoops," flannel shirt said. "I was surprised at the crowd, but I thought Midwest was going all out to retain recruiters!" Willie and flannel shirt laughed. Then flannel shirt said, "It's time I get back. Good luck with your decision."

"Thanks," Willie said and shook flannel shirt's hand. As Willie started to ask his name, the caterer interrupted to ask what Willie wanted to do with the extra food. "Just leave it out. Someone will eat it," Willie said. "No. Wait. Put it in the Placement Office break room. For the recruiters."

As Willie picked up his backpack, he thought about what flannel shirt had said. He would sign up to interview with the start-up Friday. But before that, he would need to do a lot of research. He was going to stop by the gym after the seminar, but decided he had better stop by the library instead.

The Job Opportunity at Meridian Hospital Systems, Inc.

In his class, Willie had been impressed by guest speaker Jim Stone, co-founder and Executive Vice President of Meridian Hospital Systems (MHS), not so much by his colorful charts and demonstration of the company's software as by what he said. He had not expected the cofounder of a Midwest company to be so insightful about the current developments in the software industry from both a technology and competitive

---

[1]Copyright © 2007 by Daniel W. DeHayes. This case was developed by Professor Emeritus Daniel W. DeHayes at Indiana University. The case was written to provide a basis for class discussion rather than to illustrate either effective or ineffective management practices. Some figures, names, and dates have been disguised.

standpoint. He had always assumed that anybody who was somebody in software was on the West Coast.

And the job sounded interesting. Willie would be assigned to a team that was developing MHS's next product offering. As a software developer, Willie would have access to all the tools he had heard about and used in his classes. He would join a small group of eight developers, most of who graduated only one or two years ago. The group would be headed by a 30-year-old with a Ph.D. in computer science.

He found himself excited by the prospects of this company, about how he could have an important role so early in his career. He was excited about Hewlett-Packard, too, but not about what he would be doing so much as that he would be working for Hewlett-Packard. He had already made sure all his friends knew he had been given an offer. And his mom had made sure everyone in the family, the church, her bridge group, the whole neighborhood knew it, too. Even Aunt Nellie in Dallas wrote to congratulate him on the offer. The HP opportunity was even better than when he interned at a large public accounting firm in their IT group last summer.

However, Willie also felt that the offer from HP had its uncertainties. Willie knew from his research that the company had had some troubles in the last few years, starting with the questions about the success of the acquisition of Compaq, the troubles and eventual dismissal of the CEO earlier in 2005, and current rumblings in the trade press about problems on the HP Board of Directors. These matters made Willie a little uncertain of this employment option. But he knew that job offers at HP were tough to come by, especially during these difficult times for the company and he was happy to have received one. At the same time, Willie began to wonder how long he might be employed by the company—particularly if all the current turmoil resulted in layoffs. He knew that he would be low on the seniority list. If the company ran into more problems, he might be among the first to go. And, as had happened to some of his friends at other firms, the offer might even be revoked after he had accepted.

In his class notes, he read that MHS was founded in 2003 by three software veterans who had worked together for a company that was eventually acquired by IBM. All three had at one time in their careers worked for large corporations. Willie also learned that the founders named Meridian Hospital Systems to reflect their Indianapolis roots (Meridian is the main north/south street in Indianapolis) as well as their target market (hospitals). The focus of the company was to make the process of assembling and processing product orders from diverse units in the hospital easier.

From the MHS Web site, Willie found some additional information about the founders of MHS (see Exhibit 1). Willie knew MHS had not been in business too long, but to its credit it had received several rounds of venture investment so someone felt

EXHIBIT 1
Meridian Hospital Systems's Management

Management

Joseph A. Dobbins, Co-Founder, President, and CEO.
Dobbins has over 20 years of experience in technology and software. He serves as director of the Midwest Information Technology Association, which focuses on the development of technology companies in the Midwest. He has held executive-level responsibility for all aspects of a technology company, including sales, marketing, product development, and operations. Previously, he was vice president and COO for an IBM company focused on enterprise software for customer relationship management. Dobbins has delivered dramatic revenue growth, routinely overachieving all financial and operational targets. Dobbins has also been senior vice president for a software vendor for the consolidated service desk market (help desk, asset management, change management, decision support). Once this company was acquired, he became senior vice president for worldwide operations, establishing a global direct and indirect sales organization. Dobbins directly managed creation of North American, European, and Asia-Pacific operations. Dobbins began his career at Xerox and Honeywell in sales/sales management. He holds a B.S. degree from the University of Detroit.

James S. Stone, Co-Founder and Executive Vice President, Product Group.   Stone was previously vice president and CTO for IBM's Corepoint, where he had responsibility for all product and business strategy aspects and where he managed a 550-person global product effort across five geographic sites and four product families. Earlier Stone managed a shift in product direction toward integrated technologies and applications. Prior to Corepoint, Stone was general manager and vice president for a software vendor for the consolidated service desk market (help desk, asset management, change management, decision support) where he was responsible for product development. He led the effort to launch a new business unit into the fast-growing customer relationship management (CRM) enterprise software market. Stone started his technology career at BorgWarner Automotive Research Center, developing advanced vision-guided robotics. He then spent several years at Eli Lilly, a leading pharmaceutical firm, developing enterprise-level applications and very large databases for Lilly Research Laboratories. Stone holds an M.B.A. degree from Indiana University and a B.S. degree in computer science from Ball State University.

Matthew B. Mahoney, Co-Founder and Executive Vice President, Marketing.   Mahoney has spent 19 years in marketing management and entrepreneurial business development, ranging from start-ups to Hewlett-Packard. Previously, he was vice president of worldwide marketing for Corepoint where he was responsible for a $26 million marketing budget and

45 people across five global regions. He successfully planned and executed a comprehensive marketing launch of the company in a remarkable 12 weeks, attaining significant awareness levels within the Global 1000. Mahoney spent the first nine years of his career at Hewlett-Packard where he marketed UNIX, manufacturing automation systems, and software to major accounts, and consulted with the company's value-added reseller channel partners. One client, a leading industrial engineering simulation and production scheduling software firm, recruited him to manage their newly formed alliance with IBM. There, he headed marketing and developed the company's first channel marketing program. For the past 15 years, Mahoney has participated as investor and director in local entrepreneurial ventures. He holds a B.S. degree in electrical engineering technology from Purdue University.

Source: Company Records.

---

the company was a long-term survivor. Although the risk associated with working for a company that was not well established was great, so was the reward if the company grew as expected. Regardless of the current corporate controversy, even Hewlett-Packard started with just two founders and a garage.

MHS's Strategy

Once he had a reasonable idea of the job he would be interviewing for, Willie reviewed what he knew about MHS's market and product strategy from Stone's presentation and some materials he distributed in class.

When creating their business plan in early 2003, MHS's founders decided to focus first on applying the company's software development skills to a single industry. They were aware from business publications of the difficulty many organizations had in obtaining the best price and terms for products and services, especially if they had diverse operations. They had also read an article about some retailers that had difficulty determining exactly how much product to order in a fast-moving competitive environment with a set of stores spread around a large geographic area.

Accordingly, the founders of MHS decided to focus on a specific market segment that met the following requirements:

- was of significant size with a high volume and velocity of dollars and transactions
- had a readily identifiable block of buying organizations and influencers
- had a need for consolidation of orders from diverse organizations
- did not currently have ways to consolidate orders from departments

- wanted to maintain the role of demand determination in decentralized organizations, yet have centralized accountability and control
- had a unique procurement processing and documentation requirement
- was not especially sensitive to privacy issues or excessive regulatory burdens pertaining to its procured goods and services
- was not overcrowded with first or early movers with software designed to solve the problems

After an analysis of several industries, MHS's founders chose hospitals as their initial targeted industry. They found that hospitals met all the criteria. They next conducted 12 interviews with hospital administrators to verify that the reported problems in procurement did indeed exist. They also found that it was typical for hospitals to spend between 20 to 40 percent of their annual revenue on goods and services. The diverse nature of hospitals made it very difficult to effectively control the procurement process to insure the most favorable pricing and terms. The hospital market was well-known for not being very efficient in taking advantage of quantity discounts in its purchasing procedures. Stories about hospitals placing an order today for some product and tomorrow ordering the same product were quoted during MHS's market research. During these interviews, hospital administrators expressed considerable interest in software that would help solve their problems in procurement.

Hospitals were traditionally highly decentralized in their operations due in part to the wide variety of special knowledge needed in order to procure the correct products. In turn, departments guarded their decision-making authority closely. It was also true that these departments often developed close relationships with certain suppliers that negated the effects of competition when it came to buying. It was only after the continuing increase in cost pressures that more centralized processes could be instituted. In addition, the hospital industry traditionally was slow compared to many other industries to adopt new information technology. Hospitals spent a smaller percentage of their overall operations budget on information technology as compared with many other industries.

Based on the founders' market research, MHS's first strategy was to create online purchasing processes for hospitals, using reverse auctions and other techniques to help lower costs. MHS developers spent eight months in late 2003 and early 2004 developing such Web-based systems for hospitals. However, the slow acceptance rate of their product during 2004 made MHS's founders go back to the market for additional interviews. After these interviews, MHS's management changed strategy in September 2004 and decided to focus on helping hospitals understand and aggregate their demand better.

In their second round of interviews with buyers, MHS's founders discovered that buying *per se* was not the immediate problem. In order to achieve real savings, hospital buyers must first be able to forecast and aggregate demand from a number of diverse departments and laboratories. If this information could be aggregated somehow, then a comprehensive and longer-term view of demand could be created.

This rapid change in strategy made Willie worry about the stability of MHS. The change also reminded Willie of some material covered in an entrepreneurship class he took with Professor Morphen at Midwest University. The professor pointed out that the short-term cash difficulties small businesses faced (e.g., from lack of demand for their products) sometimes caused managers to make dramatic changes in direction of the firm with little or no notice to employees. Morphen underlined the dangerous implications of this behavior on the ability of the small company to move forward toward its vision consistently. However, Morphen also tried to make sure the students understood the need for small businesses to change and innovate quickly when circumstances required it.

MHS's second software product was delivered to hospitals in very late 2004 and helped the procurement department understand current demand across several departments. This Web-based software tool allowed diverse departments to enter demand for a variety of products and services for the next month. In turn, the centralized purchasing department could use these aggregated figures to obtain the best prices and terms from suppliers. Several upgrades to this product were released over the next several months. Demand for the product started to grow rapidly in mid-2005.

The company had plans to introduce additional improvements in the current software product and to roll out new software tools to facilitate the longer-term forecasting of demand based on historical data and using department input. Details of the software were not yet released by MHS.

Willie's First Interview with MHS

Willie signed up to interview with MHS on campus Friday. He was pleased that Jim Stone was there to do the interviewing. Willie found Stone's description of MHS's software developer job, positioning Willie "closer to the road" and accountable for making a major contribution to an application and a customer, exciting.

After asking Willie about his grades (a 3.42 on a 4.0 scale), his internship experience, and the extra computer science courses he had taken, Stone extended him an invitation for a second interview on Tuesday morning. Willie called Hewlett-Packard to ask if he could postpone his decision to the end of next week. His sponsor replied that they needed to know no later than Wednesday so they could extend the offer to another candidate should Willie decide not to accept. Willie would have

little time to make the most important decision of his career. But he had no choice.

The Second Interview with MHS

It took Willie longer than normal to get dressed for Tuesday's interview. He was not sure whether he wanted to wear a full suit or slacks, a button-down and tie. A full suit seemed to be the safest bet. He would make a horrible impression if he did not wear one and was expected to. But, the button down and tie seemed to say "confident."

He opted for gray dress pants, a black long-sleeved turtleneck and a black jacket—kind of a Steve Jobs look. He felt comfortable and well prepared.

When he entered MHS's office, he was surprised. Unlike the huge marble reception area at Hewlett-Packard, there was only a desk, unstaffed, in MHS's entry. Two chairs and a small table with business magazines were off to the side. He was not sure whether he should just start roaming the halls or if he should sit down and hope someone showed up. He sat down.

"Has someone helped you?" Willie looked up and was surprised to see flannel shirt, the interviewer he had run into at the alumni event! "Hi. I'm Joe Dobbins," flannel shirt said as he extended his hand. "I guess we didn't introduce ourselves properly last time we met."

"Willie Stahe," Willie said as he shook hands.

"Have you solved your dilemma over whether or not to go with Hewlett-Packard?" Joe asked.

"Not yet. I'm here for a second interview," Willie said.

"Oh. So we're the cool start-up you want to work for," Joe said.

"I think so," Willie answered. "It's such a huge change from where I thought I'd be and what I thought I'd be doing."

"It's a big decision, a big challenge," Joe said as he sat in the chair next to Willie. "We're less than three years old and have money in the bank to last only through January of next year, assuming the worst case. I'm out raising more equity capital now. Our product is selling but revenue has to grow substantially if we are to cover our costs. It's a challenge. Tell me, what kinds of challenges have you faced?"

"Getting to college was a big one. My Dad's business was close to filing for bankruptcy my senior year in high school. Not only did I not get to go to prom and stuff like that, but I wasn't sure I would be able to get to college," Willie said.

"That's a big hit for an 18-year-old. How'd you handle it?" Joe asked.

"I wasn't eligible for most of the government programs because need is based on the previous April's tax return, which for us wasn't great, but it was enough to make us ineligible. So I looked at holding off a year and working and saving or trying to get a bank loan and working while going to school. With my Dad's situation, it was unlikely I'd get the bank loan," Willie said.

"So you held back a year?" Joe asked.

"No. Actually, I went into the bank anyway. My Dad and I worked on why we thought his business still had potential and then we laid all the cards out on the table and convinced the bank I'd be a good credit risk," Willie said.

"Seems like that was a creative and effective solution," Joe noted.

"In addition, we met with a financial aid counselor and ended up getting a low interest loan for most of the money," Willie paused, deep in thought. "I think what's more important is that my confidence in my Dad and his business, and working with him to look at the positives when everything seemed doomed really helped him reenergize and get the business back on track. Of course, that helped me as well," Willie said.

"Kind of like not running from the smoke," Joe said.

"Huh?" said Willie.

"It's a saying we have here. Don't run from the smoke. If you see something's wrong, run to it, not away from it," Joe said.

"I guess it was a lot like that," Willie said.

"I see you've met Joe," Stone said as he walked toward them. "You'll be meeting with him later on."

"I don't think that'll be necessary, Jim," Joe said. "He's answered my questions. Willie," he extended his hand, "it was a pleasure talking with you. I hope we have the opportunity to work together sometime."

Willie wished he had been paying more attention to what he had been saying. "Wow. I didn't even know I was being interviewed," he said.

"That's what everyone says after talking with Joe," Stone said. "He pretty much can tell within the first five minutes whether someone will fit with MHS. Looks like you left a favorable impression. About your next interview—normally the founders don't all interview a candidate. But since you've gotten an offer from Hewlett-Packard, I thought you might like to talk with Matt Mahoney."

"He's the one that started out at Hewlett-Packard, isn't he?" Willie said.

"Right. I thought he might be able to answer a lot of your questions," Stone said. "Hey, Matt, this is the Midwest student I was telling you about, Willie Stahe."

"Good to meet you," Matt said as he extended his hand. "Have a seat."

As he sat down, Willie was struck by how neat Matt's office was and how neatly he was dressed. Matt had a soft voice and disarming smile, and Willie immediately felt comfortable.

"Jim tells me you're interested in working with us, but that you've also gotten an offer from Hewlett-Packard," Rich said.

"I'm really torn. It's like a dream come true to be offered the chance to work for Hewlett-Packard. Move out to the West Coast. I haven't even told my family that I'm interviewing with you. I don't think they would understand," Willie said.

"What don't you think they would understand?" Matt asked.

"That I'd be turning down big bucks for incredibly smaller bucks that may or may not turn into big bucks," Willie said.

"Considering you wouldn't be living on the West Coast, I think you'll find our salary is pretty competitive. And predicting future big bucks is largely dependent on each of us who work here and how much you believe in our vision and business model," Matt said. "Disregarding salary, which job would you take?"

"Hmm—that is a tough question. I think that I would take this job," Willie said.

"Why?" Matt asked.

"Because what I'd be doing would matter, would have a significant impact. I could be part of something new that will be the leader in industry, first health care and then others after that. I'd be on the ground floor of the next Microsoft, or the next Hewlett-Packard," Willie said. "You worked at Hewlett-Packard. Why did you leave?"

"In a large corporation, if you want experience with other perspectives, you pretty much have to displace someone else. And the higher up you go, the more difficult it is to get different experiences," Matt said. He added, "With a start-up like MHS, everyone will share in the company's good fortune and can take on additional responsibility as we grow. There's always an opportunity to expand your set of experiences."

"How come you chose to start MHS after you left IBM rather than take a position with another established company?" Willie asked.

"All the other opportunities I looked at were all start-ups. I'm interested in making an impact, in creating something. To me, that's where the challenge, and the excitement, lies," Matt said. "Plus, our business is still evolving. It's exciting working in a dynamic environment. Although Hewlett-Packard changes, it's incremental change. They know their products and their markets well. Have you looked at working for other start-ups?"

"No. This is the only one. I fully intended to work for Hewlett-Packard. It's a goal I've had for about two years, and I was pretty focused on attaining it," Willie said.

"Then I guess you have a big decision to make," Matt said.

"I do," Willie said sadly. "Thanks for meeting with me."

"Good luck," Matt said as he shook hands with Willie.

"What did you think?" Stone asked Matt.

"The main question for Willie isn't whether he wants to work with us. I think it's whether he wants to say no to Hewlett-Packard," Matt said.

Willie met with a few other software developers and the chief architect. He really liked the software design tools and the design of MHS's second product. But it was all over in two hours. During the exit interview, Stone offered him a software developer job to start in January at an annual salary that was $6,000 less than the one from Hewlett-Packard, but with comparable benefits. He then showed him the space on the floor where his new cubicle would be constructed.

Decision Time

As Willie left the building, he was torn. He secretly had hoped he would not like someone—anyone—at MHS. But he found that not only did he like everyone he met, he felt stimulated by their enthusiasm and energy.

He could work for Hewlett-Packard for a few years and then leave to work for a start-up, or maybe start his own company. But, if that was really what he wanted to do in a few years, then why not do it now while there was an opportunity? But how could he say no to Hewlett-Packard? That was a prestigious opportunity that would open many doors. Just working for them would establish his credibility.

But there was definitely reason to be concerned about this employment option. The difficulties at HP caused him to worry a little about what might happen if he was to join that firm.

Regardless, if Willie chose Hewlett-Packard for employment, he was very unsure of how long he would stay. He had heard from friends at Midwest University who used to work for large software companies that outsourcing the development function to other countries was always possible.

However, he still questioned whether he should accept the offer at MHS. As he had found in his search for information on the health care software industry over the weekend, many of the smaller companies were showing signs of rapid future change because of a more demanding competitive environment. How would MHS's management team keep the direction of the company focused, but still give employees the sense of ownership they wanted? If the company began to have more serious financial troubles, would Willie be asked to leave quickly?

Again, he headed for the library instead of the gym. He needed to review his notes from the two-day interview at HP and the visit to MHS. He also needed to make a list of pros and cons for working for Hewlett-Packard versus working for MHS. Then he would talk to some friends. Once he had the options clearer, he knew they would help him make the final decision. He had to give Hewlett-Packard his answer tomorrow.

PART III

ACQUIRING INFORMATION SYSTEMS

OBTAINING AND SUCCESSFULLY IMPLEMENTING A NEW INFORMATION SYSTEM IS FAR from trivial. Whether a system is custom-built for a business organization, or purchased (or leased) from a software vendor, both business and IS managers need to be accountable for achieving the business benefits and managing the potential business risks from these application investments. These chapters therefore describe key capabilities for every IS organization, large or small. For readers preparing to be IS professionals or have taken courses on systems analysis and design techniques, you will have already had some experience using a subset of these system methodologies. For readers with experience managing non-IT projects in organizational settings, you will likely be familiar with some of the project management practices discussed here, but others will be specifically related to IT projects.

Chapter 9 presents some fundamental systems principles, including how systems thinking underlies business process design and can be used for recognizing the technical *and* organizational aspects of introducing new systems in an organization. A life-cycle view of systems development is introduced, as well as a variety of structured techniques, both procedural-oriented and object-oriented. The chapter also highlights the importance of disciplined approaches to ensure operational reliability and data integrity, as well as compliance with financial reporting requirements (such as Sarbanes-Oxley and Basel II).

Chapter 10 focuses on methodologies used by IS professionals for developing custom software applications. Four approaches are described and compared in some detail: the traditional systems development life cycle (SDLC), an evolutionary prototyping approach, a rapid application development (RAD) approach (for delivering system modules in short timeboxes), and newer so-called "agile" methodologies. In addition to describing methodology steps, we discuss project team roles, some project characteristics associated with successful system delivery, and advantages and disadvantages of the custom development approach. The chapter concludes with some guidelines for managing software projects that involve an IT outsourcer.

Chapter 11 details a methodology for purchasing (or leasing) large software packages. Over the past decade, organizations of all sizes have begun to "buy" rather than build custom applications whenever it is feasible and cost-beneficial to do so. We begin the chapter by discussing the importance of the make-or-buy decision and then describe in detail the process steps for identifying, selecting, and implementing packaged software. Next we discuss project team roles, some project characteristics associated with successful system implementation, advantages and disadvantages of a purchasing approach, and under what circumstances to modify purchased software. The chapter ends with a discussion of three special packaged system situations: the benefits and critical success factors associated with enterprise system packages, the special opportunities presented by open source software projects, and the advantages and downsides for implementing a packaged solution hosted by an application service provider (ASP).

Chapter 12 discusses practices for effectively managing IT projects. After introducing the concept of an IT application portfolio, the project initiation, planning, execution and control, and closing phases of an IT project are described. Techniques are then presented for addressing two IT project management challenges that also require effective business manager participation: managing the business risks of an IT project and managing business change. The chapter concludes with a discussion of practices to address two special issues: managing complex IT software projects and managing virtual teams.

Chapter 13 focuses on the critical IS role of supporting computer users. It begins with a discussion of support for user-developed applications (such as complex spreadsheet programs or database applications)—including the potential advantages of user-developed applications, some characteristics to help if a user-developed application is the best alternative, and pitfalls to try to avoid. Then strategies and tactics for providing desktop support to all computer users—including common support services and computing policies—are discussed in detail. The chapter concludes with some special issues for supporting telecommuters (and other remote workers) and managing internal networks using Web technologies (intranets) for employees.

Ten original teaching cases, written by the textbook authors, accompany Part III. The Consumer and Industrial Products case study describes the roles of both business managers and IT professionals using an SDLC approach for the development of a complex system. The Zeus case study describes the development of a large interorganizational system designed to serve a network of independent distributors— and the politics involved.

The Baxter case study is concerned with a make-or-buy decision for a critical software application, and the Benton case study describes the viewpoints of various organizational stakeholders as the organization considers whether or not to acquire an enterprise resource planning (ERP) system. The Kuali Financial System case study demonstrates potential development and managerial challenges when multiple independent organizations develop a suite of applications with the intention of providing them under an open source license.

Two cases are concerned with major changes to an organization's business processes. The Naval Surface Warfare Center case study explores the role of the IS organization in supporting a business process reengineering effort to improve the competitiveness of an organization. The NIBCO's "Big Bang" case study describes a 15-month project to implement multiple modules of an ERP suite at a midsized manufacturing firm, with the help of consultants as implementation partners. The project entails major changes to the way the organization purchases materials, manages its factories, uses its distribution centers, conducts transactions with its customers, and manages its accounting functions. The BAT Taiwan case study describes the challenges faced when implementing a standard ERP package in a small country office in which expertise from other BAT units in Asia is utilized in lieu of external consultants.

The final two case studies describe problematic implementation projects in disguised organizations. In the Modern Materials case study, managers are faced with the dilemma of what to do with a runaway (troubled) IT project. And finally, the Jefferson County School System case study provides an example of the potential pitfalls involved in purchasing and installing a packaged system in an organization that previously relied on custom-developed applications.

CHAPTER 9
BASIC INFORMATION SYSTEMS CONCEPTS

"It's the SYSTEM's fault!"
"The SYSTEM is down."
"My SYSTEM can't be beat!"
"Don't buck the SYSTEM."

Pʜʀᴀꜱᴇꜱ ꜱᴜᴄʜ ᴀꜱ ᴛʜᴇꜱᴇ ʀᴇᴍɪɴᴅ ᴜꜱ ᴛʜᴀᴛ ᴛʜᴇ ᴛᴇʀᴍ *SYSTEM* ᴄᴀɴ ʙᴇ used to refer to an information system with hardware, software, and telecommunications components (discussed in Part I) or that the term *system* can be used to refer to something much broader than an information system. For example, a systems perspective helps us to understand the complex relationships between different business units and different types of events within an organization so that when we change one aspect of a business we can anticipate the impact on the entire business. The ability to manage organizations as systems with interrelated processes is crucial for success in today's fast-changing business environments.

Today's business managers are being asked to play major roles in systems project teams with internal information systems (IS) specialists and/or outside vendors and consultants, and one of their key roles will be to help provide a high-level systems perspective on the business. Business and information technology (IT) managers must work together to determine the best scope for a systems project to meet the business's needs, as well as the business's requirements for financial returns on its IT investments. With IS personnel, business managers will also help develop and review graphical diagrams of the ways in which the organization currently works, as well as new ways. This chapter will therefore familiarize you with some of the specific methods and techniques that software developers use to describe both current (As-Is) and future (To-Be) systems in the abstract.

Today there is also a heightened sensitivity to system security and reliability. At the end of this chapter we describe a variety of controls that are associated with best practices for system development and implementation in particular. In Chapter 12 we will more fully discuss how a project manager needs to manage the business risks associated with a systems project.

THE SYSTEMS VIEW

Peter Senge and other management gurus have argued that more holistic systems thinking is needed to enable organizations to more quickly adapt to today's complex, fast-changing environments. According to Senge (1990), systems thinking is

- a discipline for seeing wholes
- a framework for seeing interrelationships rather than things
- an antidote to the sense of helplessness one feels when confronted with complexity

This section provides some templates for analyzing, describing, and redesigning systems. The systems concepts we discuss are general ones, although we will use many information systems examples.

What Is a System?

A **system** is a set of interrelated components that must work together to achieve some common purpose. An example of what happens when system components do not work together appears in Figure 9.1. This house has all the components (rooms, doors, windows, plumbing, electrical wiring) necessary for a functioning home, but the components just do not fit together. For example, the outside steps do not lead to a door. The lesson here is that even when a given component is well-designed, simple, and efficient to operate, the system will malfunction if the components do not work together.

Further, a change in one component could affect other components. For example, if the marketing group (one component part of a business) sells more of some product than expected, the production group (another component) would have to special-order materials or pay overtime to produce more than the planned amount. If the interrelationships between these functions (components) are not well managed, an unanticipated result might be a rise in the costs of goods sold, leading to the company actually losing money from increased sales.

An **information system (IS)** can be defined in a very broad way as the collection of IT, procedures, and people responsible for the capture, movement, management, and

Figure 9.1   An Example of Poor Design

distribution of data and information. As with other systems, it is crucial that the components of an IS work well together. That is, the components must be consistent, minimally redundant, complete, and well connected with one another.

Seven Key System Elements

Systems share the seven general system elements briefly defined as follows:

1. **Boundary**   The delineation of which elements (such as components and storage) are within the system being analyzed and which are outside; it is assumed that elements within the boundary are more easily changed and controlled than those outside.
2. **Environment**   Everything outside the system; the environment provides assumptions, constraints, and inputs to the system.
3. **Inputs**   The resources (data, materials, supplies, energy) from the environment that are consumed and manipulated within the system.
4. **Outputs**   The resources or products (information, reports, documents, screen displays, materials) provided to the environment by the activities within the system.
5. **Components**   The activities or processes within the system that transform inputs into intermediate forms or that generate system outputs; components may also be considered systems themselves, in which case they are called subsystems, or modules.

6. **Interfaces**   The place where two components or the system and its environment meet or interact; systems often need special subcomponents at interfaces to filter, translate, store, and correct whatever flows through the interface.
7. **Storage**   Holding areas used for the temporary and permanent storage of information, energy, materials, and so on; storage provides a buffer between system components to allow them to work at different rates or at different times and to allow different components to share the same data resources. Storage is especially important in IS because data are not consumed with usage; the organization of storage is crucial to handle the potentially large volume of data maintained there.

Figure 9.2 graphically illustrates how these seven elements interrelate in a system.

These elements can also be used to describe specific computer applications. For example, in Figure 9.3 a payroll application and a sales-tracking application are described in terms of five system elements, excluding boundary and environment.

Another important system characteristic is the difference between **formal** versus **informal systems** within organizational contexts. The formal system is the way an organization was designed to work. When there are flaws in the formal system, or when the formal system has not been adapted to changes in business situations, an informal system develops.

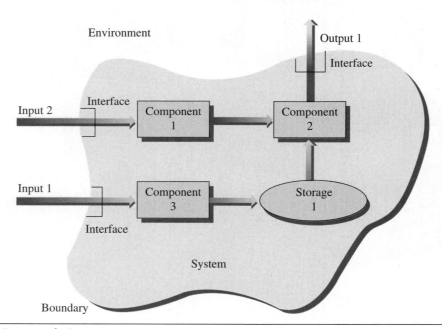

Figure 9.2   General Structure of a System

System	Payroll	Sales Tracking
Inputs	Time cards Vouchers	Customer orders Customer returns of goods
Outputs	Paychecks W-2 forms	Monthly sales by product Monthly sales by territory
Components	Calculate total pay Subtract deduc- tions	Accumulate sales by product and compare to forecast
Interfaces	Match time cards to employees Sort paychecks by department	Translate cus- tomer zip code into territory code
Storage	Employee benefits Pay rates	Product list Sales history Sales forecasts

Figure 9.3   System Component Examples

Recognizing that an organization's formal system is not necessarily equivalent to the real system is crucial when analyzing a business situation or process. For example, if workers continue to reference a bill-of-materials list that contains handwritten changes rather than a computer-printed list for a new shop order, an informal system has replaced the formal information system. In this case, the real system is actually the informal system or some combination of the formal and informal systems.

Three system characteristics that are especially important for analyzing and designing information systems are: determining the system boundary, breaking down a system into modules (decomposition), and designing interfaces between old and new systems.

System Boundary   The system **boundary** delineates what is inside and what is outside a system. A boundary segregates the environment from the system or delineates subsystems from each other. A boundary in the systems world is often arbitrary. That is, we can often choose to include or exclude any component in the system. The choice of where to draw the boundary depends on factors such as these:

1. **What can be controlled**   Recognizing you can't control everything . . . Elements outside the control of the project team are part of the environment, and the environment often places a constraint on the system scope. For example, if a preexisting billing system is

treated as part of the environment of a new product management system, the product management system would be limited to devising products that can be priced and billed in ways already supported.
2. **What scope is manageable within a given time period**   Make progress and move on to the next job . . . Complex systems often take so long to design and develop that the envisioned systems solution could no longer be the best choice by the time the project is complete.
3. **The impact of a boundary change**   While you were gone over the weekend, we decided to . . . As the business changes or new information about the organization is uncovered, a different system boundary can appear to be beneficial. This decision requires careful analysis of the impact of such a change.

Component Decomposition   A system, like an assembled product, is a set of interrelated components. A component of a system that is itself viewed as a system (or a set of interrelated components) is called a **subsystem (module)**. The components of a subsystem can be further broken down into more subsystems. The process of breaking down a system into successive levels of subsystems, each of which shows more detail, is called hierarchical (or functional) decomposition. An example is provided in Figure 9.4. Figure 9.4(A) shows a high-level view of the system with two subsystems. Figure 9.4(B) shows details about one of these subsystems, Produce Sales Summaries. One important relationship between the two views of the Product Sales Summaries subsystem is that there are two inputs to each view and the consolidated output in (A) matches with the detailed outputs in (B).

Five important goals of **hierarchical decomposition** of a system are the following:

1. **To cope with the complexity of a system**   Decomposition of a complex system allows us to break the system down into understandable pieces.
2. **To analyze or change only part of the system**   Decomposition results in specific components at just the right level of detail for the job.
3. **To design and build each subsystem at different times**   Decomposition allows us to respond to new business needs as resources permit while keeping unaffected components intact.
4. **To direct the attention of a target audience**   Decomposition allows us to focus on a subset of components of importance to a subset of the total user population.
5. **To allow system components to operate more independently**   Decomposition allows problem

(A) Sales Summary System

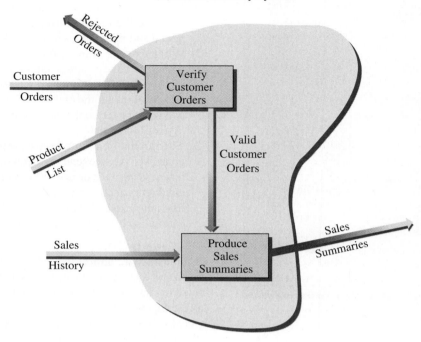

(B) Produce Sales Summary Subsystem

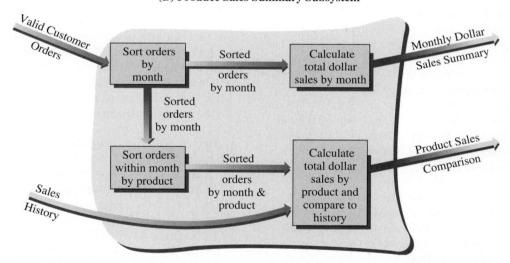

Figure 9.4 Sales Summary Reporting System and Subsystem

components to be isolated and components to be changed, moved, or replaced with minimal impact on other components.

Interfaces An **interface** is the point of contact between a system and its environment or between two subsystems. In

an information system, the functions of an interface are generally as follows:

Filtering Disposing of useless data (or noise)
Coding/decoding Translating data from one format into another (for example, switching between two-part

numbering schemes, one used by marketing and another used by engineering)

Error detection and correction Checking for compliance to standards and for consistency; by isolating this task in interfaces, other components can concentrate on their more essential responsibilities

Buffer Allowing two subsystems to work together without being tightly synchronized, as by having the interface collect data until the next component is ready to accept the data

Security Rejecting unauthorized requests for data and providing other protection mechanisms

Summarizing Condensing a large volume of input into aggregate statistics or even mathematical parameters to reduce the amount of work needed by subsequent subsystems

Interfaces also can be built between preexisting independent systems. For example, a company might contract with an outside organization (possibly a bank) to process payroll checks or with a market research firm to capture competitor sales data. In each case an interface is built that allows the external system to communicate with the company's internal systems. Different formats for data, different identifications for customers or employees, and various other differences in definitions and coding need to be translated to support this type of interface. Sometimes these interfaces are called bridges because they connect two "island" systems.

Bridge programs are relatively common. Bridges are expedient ways to accomplish the goal of expanding the capabilities of any one system. Rather than take the time to redesign two systems into one (e.g., to reduce redundant steps, to share common data, and to discontinue duplicate processing and calculations), the two systems are simply interfaced. In fact, many methods for integrating two or more information systems are really different ways to build interfaces. You may hear or read the term *federated systems*; a federation is simply multiple systems coupled by interfaces.

Another important objective of an interface is **system decoupling**. Two highly coupled system components require frequent and rapid communication, thus creating a dependence and bottleneck in the system. If one of the components fails, the other cannot function; if one is modified, the other might also have to be modified. Appropriately designed interfaces result in the decoupling of system components. The principal methods of system decoupling are these:

Slack and flexible resources Providing alternative paths to follow when one component breaks down or slows down, such as having an interface reroute data transmissions to public carriers if the company's private data communications network becomes busy

Buffers Storing data in a temporary location as a buffer or waiting line that can be depleted as the data are handled by the next component, as in collecting customer orders over the complete day and allowing an order-filling batch program to allocate scarce inventory to highest-need jobs

Sharing resources Creating shared data stores with only one program (part of the interface component) maintaining the data, thus avoiding the need to synchronize multiple step updating or to operate with inconsistent multiple copies of data

Standards Enforcing standards that reduce the need for two components to communicate, as in adopting a business policy that requires all interunit transfer of information about customers to be done using the company standard customer identification code

Decoupling allows one subsystem to remain relatively stable while other subsystems change. By clustering components into subsystems and by applying various decoupling techniques, the amount of design and maintenance effort can be significantly reduced. Because business is constantly changing, decoupling can significantly reduce an organization's systems maintenance burdens.

Organizations as Systems

Several useful frameworks exist to conceptualize how information systems fit into organizational systems. The framework in Figure 9.5, based on the Leavitt diamond, graphically depicts four fundamental components in an organization that must work in concert for the whole organization to be effective: people, information technology, business processes, and organization structure.

Figure 9.5 also suggests that if a change in IT is made in an organization—such as the introduction of a new software application—this change is likely to affect the other three components. For example, *people* will have to be retrained,

Figure 9.5 Fundamental Components of an Organization

methods of work (*business processes*) will have to be redesigned, and old reporting relationships (*organization structure*) will have to be modified. The important principle here is that:

> *Each time we change characteristics of one or more of these four components, we must consider compensating changes in the others.*

This raises an interesting question: With which of the four components do we start? There is no universal answer to this question, and organizational politics can play a key role in this decision. For example, organization theorists have argued that changes in technology can lead to organizational changes (technological imperative); that organizational factors can drive changes in technology (organizational imperative); and that changes are difficult to predict because of variations in purpose, processes, and organizational settings (Markus and Robey, 1988). In the 1990s many large U.S. companies chose to make large-scale changes in the way they conducted business by replacing custom information systems with a large software package (such as an enterprise resource planning [ERP] system) in which a vendor embedded the "best practices" for a business function or even an industry.

Systems Analysis and Design

A major process used in developing a new information system is called **systems analysis and design (SA&D)**. SA&D processes are based on a systems approach to problem solving. Here we describe several fundamental principles associated with good SA&D techniques that stem from the key system characteristics described previously.

The first two principles are these:

- *Choose an appropriate scope* Selecting the boundary for the information system greatly influences the complexity and potential success of an IS project.

- *Logical before physical* You must know what an information system is to do before you can specify how a system is to operate.

System Scope Often the fatal flaw in conceiving and designing a system centers on choosing an inappropriate system scope. Apparently the designer of the house in Figure 9.1 outlined each component separately, keeping the boundaries narrow and manageable, and did not see all the necessary interrelationships among the components. Turning to a business situation, when a salesperson sells a cheaper version of a product to underbid a competitor, that salesperson has focused only on this one sale. However, the costs of handling customer complaints about inadequacy

of the product, repeated trips to install upgrades, and other possible problems make this scope inadequate.

The system boundary indicates the system scope. As discussed earlier under the topic of system boundary, defining the boundary is crucial to designing any system or solving any problem. Too narrow a scope could cause you to miss a really good solution to a problem. Too wide a scope could be too complex to handle. Choosing an appropriate scope is difficult but crucial in problem-solving in general and in IS projects in particular.

Logical Before Physical Any description of a system is abstract because the description is not the system itself, but different system descriptions can emphasize different aspects of the system. Two important general kinds of system descriptions are logical and physical descriptions. Logical descriptions concentrate on *what* the system does, and physical descriptions concentrate on *how* the system operates. Another way to say this is "function before form."

Returning to our example of a house as a system, as an architect knows, function precedes form with the design of a new house. Before the house is designed, we must determine how many people will live in it, how each room will be used, the lifestyle of the family, and so on. These requirements comprise a functional, or logical, specification for the house. It would be premature to choose the type of materials, color of plumbing fixtures, and other physical characteristics before we determine the purpose of these aspects.

We are often anxious to hurry into designing the physical form before we determine the needed functionality. The penalty for violating the function before form principle is increased costs—the cost and efforts to fix a functional specification error grow exponentially as you progress to the physical. We must get the logical or functional specifications right to understand how to choose among alternate physical implementations.

As an example of the difference between a logical and a physical information system, consider a class registration system. A **logical system** description would show such steps as submitting a request for classes, checking class requests against degree requirements and prerequisites, and generating class registration lists. A **physical system** description would show whether the submission of a request for classes is via a computer terminal or a touch-tone telephone, whether the prerequisite checking is done manually or by electronic comparison of transcript with course descriptions, and so on.

Some people find logical system descriptions to be too abstract to confirm what functionality is really needed and if business requirements will be met. To overcome this disconnect, a physical system can be used to communicate the logical system. Some systems development methods (which we describe in Chapter 10 under the general category of prototyping) intermix logical and physical design. In these methods, building a physical, working prototype of an information system is done for the purpose of developing, communicating, and testing ideas about the functionality (logical system). The prototype is very likely NOT the physical design that will be used for the information system. The final prototype is interpreted as a concrete logical system to inform the actual physical design process. For very small information systems, the final prototype may have evolved into a workable physical design.

Problem-Solving Steps   The three following principles, or problem-solving steps, have also been associated with good SA&D processes. In fact, they are recommended as good principles for problem-solvers in general.

- A problem (or system) is actually a set of problems; thus, an appropriate strategy is to keep breaking a problem down into smaller and smaller problems, which are more manageable than the whole problem.

- A single solution to a problem is not usually obvious to all interested parties, so alternative solutions representing different perspectives should be generated and compared before a final solution is selected.

- The problem and your understanding of it could change while you are analyzing it, so you should take a staged approach that incorporates reassessments; this allows an incremental commitment to a particular solution, with a "go" or "no-go" decision after each stage.

Later in this chapter we will introduce a generic life cycle process for developing new systems, as well as some specific techniques used by SA&D professionals. First, however, let us develop a shared understanding of the "what" that is driving many IS development and implementation projects today: systems to support cross-functional business processes.

BUSINESS PROCESSES

In the 1990s many organizations began to transform their businesses in an effort to sense and respond more quickly to global threats and demands for cost-cutting. Many of these transformation efforts were directed at moving away from a functional "silo" approach to a more process-oriented approach. Organizing work and work structures around business processes—rather than business functions or business products—requires a new mind-set in which basic assumptions are challenged and change is embraced. A **business process** is the chain of activities required to achieve an outcome such as order fulfillment or materials acquisition. Information systems are used to facilitate radical restructuring from silos to true core business processes.

Identifying Business Processes

According to Peter Keen (1997), the identification of a firm's core processes is a key analytical task. For example, a typical manufacturing firm may have six core processes: sensing the market, developing product, sourcing of materials, manufacturing product, selling product, and fulfilling customer order. A firm's core processes should not be viewed just as its workflows. Rather, these business processes should be viewed as the firm's assets and liabilities. By evaluating the worth of a given process to a firm's competitiveness, managers should be able to identify a small number of processes that need their attention the most.

Figure 9.6 shows one way in which managers can evaluate the importance of a given business process. Folklore processes are those processes that are carried out only because they have been in the past; they are often difficult to identify because they are so embedded in an organization's tasks. When they are identified, they should be abandoned because they create no economic value. Keen also warns that the importance (salience) of a given process is not necessarily the same in different companies in the same industry or even in the same company under different circumstances.

Business Process Redesign

In a seminal article published in the *Harvard Business Review*, reengineering expert Michael Hammer urged companies to start with a "clean slate" and use IT to radically change the way they did business: "Don't automate; obliterate!" By the early 1990s, consulting firms had developed expertise in what came to be referred to as **business process reengineering (BPR)**: radical business redesign initiatives that attempt to achieve dramatic improvements in business processes by questioning the assumptions, or business rules, that underlie the organization's structures and procedures, some of which could have been in place for decades. New, disruptive, technologies can be the catalyst for such radical redesigns (e.g., telecommunications, in general, and group meeting tools such as WebEx, in particular have changed the way

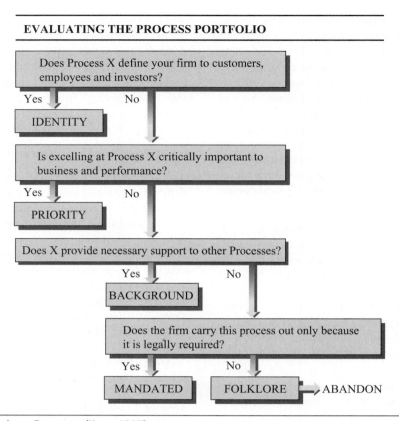

EVALUATING THE PROCESS PORTFOLIO

Figure 9.6   Evaluating Business Processes (Keen, 1997)

meetings among geographically dispersed employees are conducted).

Simple questions like "why," "what if," "who says so," and "what do our customers think," can lead to break-through insights that result in totally new business processes. The goal is to achieve an order of magnitude improvement, rather than incremental gains.

Two BPR success stories described by Hammer (1990) have now become classic examples.

Accounts Payable at Ford Motor Company   During an initial redesign of its accounts payable process, Ford concluded that it could reduce head count by 20 percent in this department. The initial solution was to develop a new accounts payable system to help clerks resolve document mismatches. This solution was based on the assumption that problems with coordinating purchase orders, shipment documents, and invoices are inevitable. The proposed new system would help prevent the document mismatches.

Ford's managers were reasonably proud of their plans until the designers discovered that Mazda Motor Corp. accomplished the same function with just five people. The

difference was that Ford based its initial system solution on the old business assumptions. In particular, Ford had not questioned its assumption that it could not pay a vendor without an invoice. When Ford questioned its assumptions, a truly reengineered solution was identified, as follows: capture the receipt of goods at the loading dock using computer scanners and use the negotiated price to pay the vendor based on a validated receipt of goods—instead of an invoice. When Ford took a "clean slate" approach, the company achieved a 75 percent improvement gain—not the original projected 20 percent.

Mutual Benefit Life Insurance   Mutual Benefit Life's old insurance application processing was a 30-step process that involved 19 people in 5 departments. Rather than automating the old workflows across multiple people in multiple departments, the process was radically redesigned. Under the reengineered process, an individual case manager is empowered to handle the entire loan application process. This was accomplished by supporting the case manager with an advanced PC-based workstation, expert system software, and access to a range of automated systems.

Old Ways to Work	Information Technology	New Ways to Work
Field personnel (such as sales and customer support staff) need to physically be located in an office to transmit and receive customer and product data	Portable computers with communications software and secure networks that allow remote access to company data	Field personnel access data and respond to messages wherever they are working
Client data is collected in different databases to support different points of contact with the client	Centralized databases that capture transactions from different parts of the business and are accessible via a network	Client data can be accessed simultaneously by employees working in different business units
Only experts can do a complex task (see Mutual Benefit Life Insurance example)	Expert systems that have knowledge rules used by company experts when they do this task	Generalists can do a complex task previously only done by an expert

Figure 9.7 How IT Enables New Ways to Work

Time to issue a policy dropped from three weeks to about three hours.

In both of these examples IT played a key role as an enabler of radical business process redesign. Hammer and Champy (1993) encourage managers to go through exercises that help them think about how IT can be used to break old assumptions and rules. Three examples of rule-breaking IT are provided in Figure 9.7.

Hammer (1990) advocated the use of key principles for redesigning business processes. A consolidated list of six principles is presented next.

1. **Organize business processes around outcomes, not tasks** This principle implies that one person should perform all the steps in a given process, as in the case of Mutual Benefit Life, where one manager handles the whole application approval process. IT is used to bring together all the information and decision-making resources needed by this one person. Often this principle also means organizing processes around customer needs, not the product.

2. **Assign those who use the output to perform the process** The intent of this principle is to make those most interested in a result accountable for the production of that result. For example, Hammer reports the case of an electronics equipment manufacturer that reengineered its field service function to have customers perform simple repairs themselves. This principle reduces nonproductive overhead jobs, including liaison positions. Principles 1 and 2 yield a compression of linear steps into one step, greatly reducing delays, miscommunication, and wasted coordination efforts. Information technologies, like expert systems

and databases, allow every manager to perform functions traditionally done by specialty managers.

3. **Integrate information processing into the work that produces the information** This principle states that information should be processed at its source. For example, at Ford this means that the receiving department, which produces information on goods received, should also enter this data, rather than sending it to accounts payable for processing. This puts data capture closest to the place where data entry errors can be detected and corrected, thus minimizing extra reconciliation steps. This principle also implies that data should be captured once at the primary source, thus avoiding transmittal and transcription errors. All who need these data work from a common and consistent source. For example, the true power of electronic data interchange (EDI) comes when all information processing related to an EDI transaction works from a common, integrated database. This principle also implies that process design should begin early in the information systems development process, when enabling technologies can influence breaking long-standing business rules before they are perpetuated by new information processing.

4. **Create a virtual enterprise by treating geographically distributed resources as though they were centralized** This principle implies that the distinction between centralization and decentralization is artificial with IT. Technologies such as teleconferencing, group support systems, e-mail, and others can create an information processing environment in which time and space are compressed. Hammer reports on the experience of Hewlett-Packard, which treats the purchasing

departments of 50 manufacturing units as if they were one giant department by using a shared database on vendor and purchase orders. The result is 50 percent to 150 percent improvement in key performance variables for the purchasing function.

5. **Link parallel activities instead of integrating their results**   This principle says that related activities should be constantly coordinated rather than waiting until a final step to ensure consistency. For example, Hammer suggests that different kinds of credit functions in a financial institution could share common databases, use communication networks, and employ teleconferencing to coordinate their operations. This would ensure, for example, that a customer is not extended a full line of credit from each unit.

6. **Have the people who do the work make all the decisions, and let controls built into the system monitor the process**   The result of this principle is the drastic reduction of layers of management, the empowerment of employees, and the shortcutting of bureaucracy. This principle emphasizes the importance of building controls into a system from the start, rather than as an afterthought (see the section entitled "Information Systems Controls to Minimize Business Risks" at the end of this chapter).

However, not all BPR projects of the early 1990s were successes. In fact, Keen (1997) points out that Mutual Benefit Life, whose radical reengineering example was described previously, was taken over by regulators due to insolvency about the time Hammer lauded it as a success story. By the mid-1990s many firms began to acknowledge that a combination approach of both radical change and incremental change (such as continuous improvements as part of quality management initiatives) was more successful (El Sawy, 2001).

By the mid-1990s client/server versions of enterprise system packages had also become widely available, making it possible for large companies to implement systems that would support complex processes across multiple functions for the first time: Earlier attempts to become more process-oriented had been aborted because systems to support their reengineered processes were too difficult to custom develop. For example, as described in Chapter 6, enterprise resource planning (ERP) packages offered by vendors such as SAP and Oracle provide integrated software modules that use the same centralized database for manufacturing, purchasing, and accounting transactions. Similarly, packages to support customer relationship management (CRM) by vendors such as Siebel from Oracle provide modules that can integrate customer data from multiple communication "channels," which are typically managed by different business units (marketing, sales, and customer support).

PROCESSES AND TECHNIQUES TO DEVELOP INFORMATION SYSTEMS

We turn now to processes and techniques for developing information systems. Our intent here is to introduce the key concepts that underlie the toolkits of system professionals. We also emphasize topics of use to both IS specialists and business managers who are asked to participate in, or lead, systems projects.

The Information Systems Development Life Cycle

Figure 9.8 presents the three phases of a generic **systems development life cycle (SDLC)** model: Definition, Construction, and Implementation.

In the *Definition* phase, end users and systems analysts conduct a multistep analysis of the current business operations and the information system or systems in the area of concern. Current operations and systems are described via both process-oriented and data-oriented notations. Process-oriented analysis concentrates on the flow, use, and transformation of data. Data-oriented analysis focuses on the kinds of data needed in a system and the business relationships between these data. Problems with current operations and opportunities for achieving business value through new IT capabilities are identified. A business case is made for the feasibility of new systems, and one solution is chosen. This solution is detailed in a requirements statement agreed to by all parties. If a software vendor has already developed a "packaged" system that meets these requirements, this phase also includes steps to identify and select the best packaged solution. The Definition phase of the life cycle is very much a cooperative effort between business and systems professionals. Doing this phase right can have significant impact on the competitive use of IT.

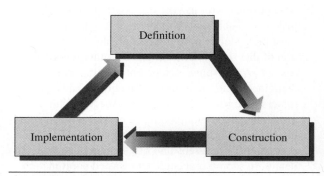

Figure 9.8   Generic Systems Development Life Cycle

The *Construction* phase entails the designing, building, and testing of a system that satisfies the requirements developed in the Definition phase. The system first is logically described, and then its physical design is specified. Programs and computer files are designed, and computer technology is chosen. Inputs such as business forms and computer screens are designed, as well as outputs such as reports. After the physical design is accepted as feasible (technically, economically, and operationally), the computer software is programmed, documented, and tested. Users play a major role in acceptance testing to verify that the system requirements have been met.

In the *Implementation* phase, business managers and IS professionals work together to install the new system, which often involves converting data and procedures from an old system. The installation of a new system can occur in a variety of ways, such as in parallel with operation of the old system or in a total and clean cutover. The implementation phase also includes the operation and continued maintenance of the system. Maintenance is typically the longest stage of the systems life cycle and incurs the greatest costs. It includes system changes resulting from flaws in the original design, from changing business needs or regulations, and from incorporating new technologies. Each maintenance activity is a mini–life cycle following the same three phases. By monitoring an information system for both performance and satisfying business needs, it will eventually be discovered that the information system has major flaws or inadequacies. Then work is begun on a new information system by cycling back to the Definition phase.

In the following chapters we will discuss in more detail some specific methodologies for developing and implementing custom software solutions (Chapter 10) and for purchasing and implementing packaged software solutions (Chapter 11). All these methodologies are based on the generic three-phase life cycle for systems development described previously. Although many IS organizations customize these approaches—including expansion or contraction of the specific number of phases or steps, or using different names—there is agreement among IS specialists on the generic activities that are required for developing a quality system that meets the organization's needs.

Structured Techniques for Life Cycle Development

Just as architects use blueprints as abstract representations of a house, IS professionals have developed techniques for representing system requirements and designs. In this section we describe some of these techniques.

Today, IS development projects range in size from a single-user application for a desktop machine to one that will be used by thousands of people in a large organization. The scope of today's large development projects has brought system builders up against both cognitive and practical limitations: The scale and complexity of these projects exceed the capacity of one developer or even a single team of manageable size. Effective large system development requires more systematic approaches that allow partitioning of the problem so that many developers can work on the project simultaneously. Increasing the scale also increases the number of parties involved. Systems projects today can require coordination across multiple project managers and even involve IS professionals in a customer or supplier organization (such as some B2B applications discussed in Chapter 8). System builders must be able to communicate with other IS professionals about what system modules do and how they do what they do. IS project managers must be able to coordinate and monitor progress and understand the commitments they are asking business managers and IS project team members to make.

A body of tools has emerged to document system needs and requirements, functional features and dependencies, and design decisions. Called **structured techniques**, these techniques exist for all phases of the systems development process, and many variations have emerged. Additionally, the techniques could be embodied within a larger approach called a **system development methodology**. A methodology is a framework consisting of guidelines, processes, tools, and techniques for managing the application of knowledge and skills to address all or part of a business issue. In addition to the types of structured techniques discussed in the sections that follow, these methodologies prescribe who should participate and their roles, the development stages and decision points, and specific formats for system documentation.

This section will provide a conceptual introduction to the most common structured techniques in a general life cycle development framework. Two major approaches to systems building have emerged: procedural-oriented and object-oriented. Procedural-oriented systems have historically been the most common, as they appropriately represent a large class of business activities. They include data-oriented as well as sequential, process-oriented activities such as tabulating time cards and printing paychecks, inventory handling, and accounts payable. Object-oriented (O-O) techniques are a newer approach to systems development which often are used with prototyping-like methodologies. Considered by some to be revolutionary and by others to be evolutionary, O-O techniques are better suited to the development of graphical user interfaces

(GUIs) and multimedia applications, but they require an entirely new way of thinking for veteran IS professionals.

Procedural-Oriented Techniques

In the past the vast majority of IS development projects have involved automating an existing paper-oriented business process or updating and expanding an existing automated or partially automated business process. This reality is reflected in the fundamental procedural approach to systems development: describe what you have, define what you want, and describe how you will make it so. This process is akin to the general problem-solving approach of analysis (detect problems), design (develop solutions and select the best), and take action (operationalize the chosen solution).

As shown in Figure 9.9, this approach involves documenting the existing system (the As-Is model), creating a model of the desired future system (the Logical To-Be model), and then interpreting the logical future model as a physical system design (the Physical To-Be model). The motivation for following such a process derives in part from human nature. Most people find it easier to imagine the future by conceiving of how it is different from today. A systematic effort to document the existing system can also yield important insights about its deficiencies and worker ideas about improvements.

This sequential approach is also effective when a new business process is being implemented at the same time that a new system is being implemented; it helps ensure that the new process will work in concert with the new IS, not against it. As described previously, business process redesign became increasingly common during the 1990s.

Describing the three models in Figure 9.9 requires a significant amount of effort prior to building the software. Business managers are often surprised at the demands placed on them to support this definition phase. The objective of this process is to have a thorough description of what the construction phase for the system will entail, so that the project risks can be assessed and planned for with some level of confidence or the decision can be made to abandon the project. In fact, actual software coding during the construction phase typically represents less than one-quarter of the entire systems development effort (Page-Jones, 1988). The As-Is model provides a baseline for the system: Why build a new one if it will not do more than the old one, do it faster, or avoid existing problems? The As-Is model typically includes both logical and physical models.

Although developing the As-Is model can be user-intensive, the majority of the effort is typically involved with developing the second model: abstracting the As-Is model into the Logical To-Be. Logical To-Be modeling involves a critical appraisal of existing work processes in order to

■ identify major subprocesses, entities, and their interactions

■ separate processing from the flow of data

■ capture relationships between data elements

■ determine those entities and processes within the project scope, and those that are not

Creation of the Physical To-Be model is a task dominated by IS specialists, as it requires technology expertise to map the logical requirements to available technology. Although information systems are implemented with specific hardware and software, participants in systems development efforts are cautioned to resist the urge to make decisions related to design and implementation until as late as possible in the project. Premature fixation on a particular technology has often led to unsatisfactory outcomes because it can cause important aspects of the system to go undiscovered or put undue emphasis on *how* to do something before there is certainty about *what* needs to be done. In reality, although no IS project is truly a "clean slate," delaying judgment until the Physical To-Be stage is the recommended strategy.

After a new system has been implemented and is operational, a diagram like that in Figure 9.10 would be used to show a physical model of the key system components and their relationships. It uses the following symbols:

Boxes	for	Major modules
Cylinders	for	Databases
Arrows	for	Flow of data

Note, however, that this diagram makes no references to details such as what type of computer hosts the software or what language it is written in. Instead, the Physical To-Be model is a high-level model. It communicates how the new system will work and helps identify any dependencies that might lead to downstream impacts, such as data integrity problems or inadequate process definitions.

Distinct techniques are used at each stage of procedural-oriented development. The output from one stage serves as the input for the next. As firms gain experience with systems development, they often develop a preference for certain techniques or adopt variations in the notation. The following section introduces some of the most common

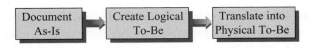

Figure 9.9 Three-Step Modeling Approach

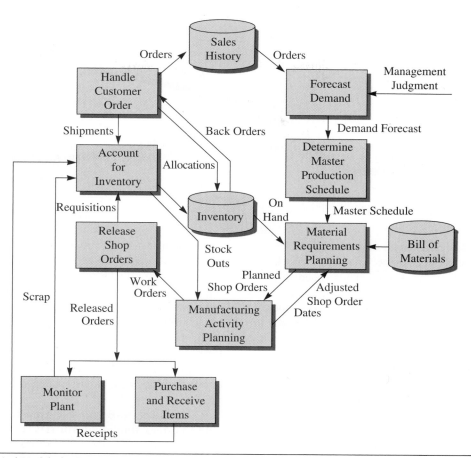

Figure 9.10   Physical Model of a System

techniques, concepts, and terminology using widely recognized notation. The techniques will be presented with the model (As-Is, Logical To-Be, Physical To-Be) with which they are most closely associated, using a common business example throughout: accounts payable. An accounts payable example is useful because accounts payable activities interact with other business activities (such as purchasing and receiving), are familiar to most managers and business students, and are common across industries.

Techniques for the As-Is Model

Whether a system is entirely manual or highly automated, the functions and flows of the existing business activity must be captured. Knowledge of a business process is rarely entirely in the possession of a single person, and there could be disagreements on the actual or preferred processes. Procedures, policies, manuals, forms, reports, and other documentation are used along with individual and group interviews to identify existing processes, external participants such as vendors and other functional departments, other databases or applications, and the inputs and outputs of the activities concerned.

A **context diagram** positions the system as a whole with regard to the other entities and activities with which it interacts. This provides a common frame of reference for project participants and helps define the project scope. Figure 9.11 illustrates a context diagram for an accounts payable system. We can see from this diagram that the accounts payable function both receives input from vendors and sends output to them. Other accounting functions receive summary information about payables activities, whereas purchasing provides the input needed to process payables. Vendors, accounting, and purchasing are all considered to be outside the project scope for this development effort.

Another common technique for documenting the As-Is system is a work process flow diagram, as shown in Figure 9.12. This flow chart identifies the existing information sources (purchase order file, receipts file), information

Figure 9.11 Context Diagram for Accounts Payable System

sources that are updated (changes to invoices/payables), the order in which steps occur (approvals before checks are printed), and some of the dependencies (need to know whether vendor is new or not). The way in which exceptions are handled should also be captured (e.g., what happens to invoices not approved). No two workflow diagrams are identical, because they capture the unique patterns and procedures—formal and informal—of an organization.

The work process flow diagram and other As-Is techniques serve to point out where the existing system does and does not perform as desired. Common problems include repeated handling of the same document, excessive wait times, processes with no outputs, bottlenecks, and extra review steps. This shows how systems development efforts are closely associated with business process redesign efforts. To emphasize process flows across organizational units—where errors can be introduced and delays can occur—one variation of the diagram in Figure 9.12, called a swimming lane diagram, shows which steps are processed in which area of the organization. Moving of data across organizational boundaries (swimming lanes) cause analysts to consider more efficient designs. Recall that the principles of BPR suggest that one person (or one organization) should perform all the steps in one process.

Techniques for the Logical To-Be Model

In this step, systems developers build a high-level model of a nonexistent system: the system that the users and managers would like to replace the one they have now. The Logical To-Be model is an abstraction that identifies the processes and data required for the desired system *without* reference to who does an activity, where it is accomplished, or the type of computer or software used. The model describes the "what," rather than the "how." Stated differently, it separates the information that moves through the business process from the mechanisms that move it (e.g.,

forms, reports, routing slips). This is important because IT enables information to be in more than one place at the same time; paper does not possess this attribute. By leaving physical barriers behind, the analyst can better determine how to exploit IT. This abstraction step can be difficult for first-time business participants because it appears to ignore issues crucial to their daily work (e.g., specific forms, reports, routing slips). Understanding that the Logical To-Be model encompasses information flows, rather than physical flows (paper, money, products), is the key.

The Logical To-Be model is most closely associated with the **data flow diagram (DFD)** (see Hoffer et al., 2008, for a thorough discussion of DFDs). The DFD notation itself is technology independent; the symbols have no association with the type of equipment or the humans that might perform the process activities or store the data. DFD creation typically involves groups of people and is accomplished through multiple iterations.

Four types of symbols are used in DFDs:

External Entity   A square indicates some element in the environment of the system that sends or receives data. External entities are not allowed to directly access data in the system but must get data from processing components of the system. No data flows between external entities are shown. External entities have noun labels.

Data Flow   Arrows indicate data in motion—that is, data moving between external entities and system processes, between system processes, or between processes and data stores. Timing and volume of data are not shown. Data flows have noun labels. Because data flow labels often sound similar, and there could be hundreds of distinct data flows in a project, numbers might also be assigned.

Process   Circles represent processing components of the system. Each process has to have both input and output

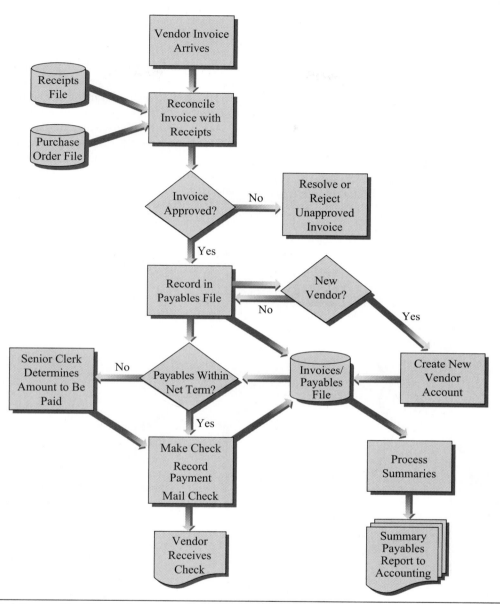

Figure 9.12   Work Process Flow Diagram for Accounts Payable

(whereas an external entity may have either input, output, or both). Processes have verb-phrase labels as well as a numerical identifier.

Data Store   Rectangles depict data at rest—that is, data temporarily or permanently held for repeated reference by one or more processes. Use of a data store implies there is a delay in the flow of data between two or more processes or a need for long-term storage. Each data store contained within the system must have both input and output (i.e., be populated and be used) within the

system. Data stores that are outside the system may provide only input or only output. Data stores have noun labels and a unique identifier.

The process of creating data flow diagrams is as follows:

■ Identify the entities that supply or use system information.

■ Distinguish processes from the data that they use or produce.

- Explicate business rules that affect the transformation of data to information.
- Identify logical relationships.
- Pinpoint duplicate storage and movements of data.

In Figure 9.13(A) a "top-level" DFD for the accounts payable system is shown. Consistent with the context diagram of Figure 9.11, the dashed line delineates the system boundary. The system includes four processes (circles). Data stores internal to this system (D2, D3, and D4) serve as buffers between the process components (e.g., to compensate for different processing rates of the components or to permit batch processing of transactions), as well as semipermanent storage for auditing purposes. Because this is a top-level DFD, or macro view, processing details are not depicted. For example, this top-level diagram does not show what happens to exceptions—such as what the process does to deal with invoices that do not match purchase orders or shipment receipt records.

A key to the effectiveness of DFD modeling is the enforcement of strict hierarchical relationships. Each process (circle) on the top-level DFD has a lower-level DFD that documents the subprocesses, data stores, and data flows needed to accomplish the process task. This

(A) Top-Level DFD

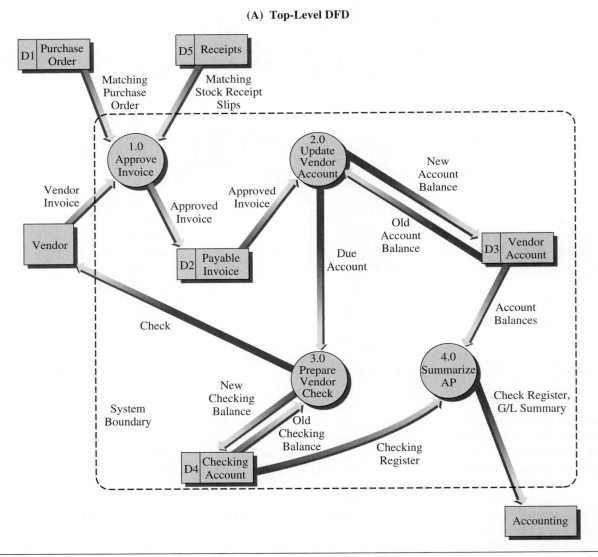

Figure 9.13 Two Levels of Data Flow Diagram for Accounts Payable System

"explosion" continues for each subprocess until no further subprocesses are needed to describe the function. A process at the lowest level in the model must be definable by a few descriptive sentences. Figure 9.13(B) is the next-lower-level explosion DFD for Process 1.0 (Approve Invoice) in Figure 9.13(A). The process decomposition relationship is shown by the process numbering scheme (1.1, 1.2, etc.).

The lower-level DFDs can result in the identification of additional data stores and data flows as well as subprocesses, but the exploded DFDs must balance with their higher-level counterparts. All data flows identified in a lower-level DFD must be accounted for in the description, source, and destination of data flows at the higher level. During the Logical To-Be defining process, external entities and data flows sometimes will need to be added to higher-level DFDs to assure completeness. It is not uncommon for business systems to have four or five levels of DFDs before exhausting all subprocesses.

When complete, DFDs tell a story about the business process that does not depend upon specific forms or technology. The rigor imposed by the explosion, aggregation, balancing, and documentation of DFDs results in more than simple circle-and-arrow diagrams. For example, from reviewing the accounts payable DFDs, we see:

1. Purchase orders and shipment receipt records are produced by systems outside the accounts payable system (because they are shown as inputs from the environment—that is, outside the system boundary).
2. The payable invoice data store temporarily stores and groups invoices after invoice approval and before subsequent vendor account updating and check writing (data flows into and out of D2).

These statements describe two aspects of the accounts payable organizational data flows as we want them to be without implying computerization or any other form of new system implementation.

In addition to diagrams such as in Figure 9.13(A) and(B), each external entity, process, data flow, and data store is documented as to its content. The documentation also shows how the components are related; for example, the description

(B) Second-Level DFD for Process 1.0 in Top-Level

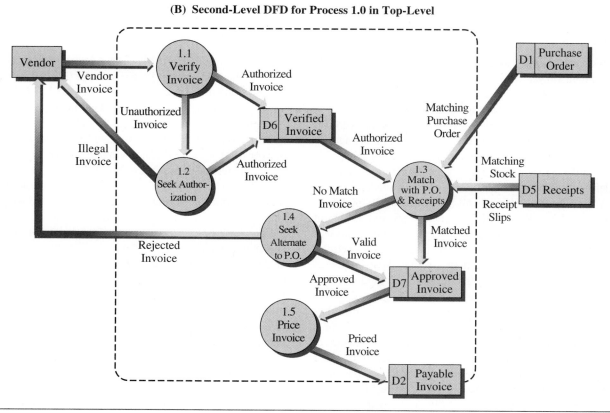

Figure 9.13   (continued)

Accounts Payable Project Data Dictionary Entry for PO Number

Label	PO Number
Alternate Names	Purchase Order Number. PO Number. PO#
Definition	Unique identifier for an individual purchase order: alpha character designates the division. The five digit number is assigned in sequential order at the time of creation.
Example	C07321
Field Name	PO_Num
Input Format	A##### (single alpha followed by five integers, no spaces or symbols allowed)
Output Format	Same as input format
Edit Rules	No values below 1000 allowed in numeric portion: currently using A–E as division code indicators.
Additional Notes	At conversion to the former system in 1991, numbers below 1000 were discontinued. Each division writes about 700–1,000 purchase orders per year. PO Numbers cannot be re-used.
Storage Type	Alphanumeric, no decimals
Default Value	None
Required	Each purchase order must have one PO Number.

Prepared by: JDAustin	Date: 8/27/07	Version No.: 1

Figure 9.14 Data Dictionary Sample Entry

for the Vendor entity would include both inbound and outbound data flows. Similarly, the data store documentation includes the individual data elements that are input into the store and matches them to output descriptions.

The accuracy and completeness of a DFD model is crucial for the process of converting the Logical To-Be model into the Physical To-Be design. However, prior to commencing this physical design step, additional logical modeling is required to define the system's data elements and relationships.

A **data model** (defined and illustrated in Chapter 5) is created by logically defining the necessary and sufficient relationships among system data. A data model, as was discussed in Chapter 5, consists of data entities (people, places, things, concepts) and their associated data elements (characteristics), relationships between the data entities, and instances of the entities and relationships.

The most common approach to maintaining the metadata in a DFD is to create a **data dictionary/directory (DD/D)**, a concept introduced in Chapter 5. The goal of the DD/D is to maintain the metadata as completely as possible; these entries should err on the side of too much information, rather than too little. This is also the place to capture whether elements are calculated, how many decimal places are required, and how an element may be referred to in external systems

that reference it. Figure 9.14 shows a typical data dictionary entry for the data element Purchase Order (PO) Number.

In addition to the detail at the data element level, the relationships between entities must be determined. A technique for capturing this information was introduced in Chapter 5: the **entity-relationship diagram**, also known as the E-R diagram or ERD. Figure 9.15 shows that the data entity "Vendor Invoice" is related to the data entity "Purchase Order" by the relation type "Includes." Furthermore, the notation next to the data entities show that a many-to-one relationship has been defined. This means that one invoice can refer to only one purchase order but that a purchase order number may have many invoices associated with it. The attributes of each data entity are shown inside the rectangles (only a sample of attributes are included); that attribute which is unique to each instance of the entity is underlined (e.g., PO_No for Purchase Order) and any attribute whose value must be present for each instance of the entity is in bold (e.g., any purchase order must have a date).

The E-R diagram in Figure 9.15 thus reflects an existing business rule:

Vendor invoices cannot include items from more than one purchase order.

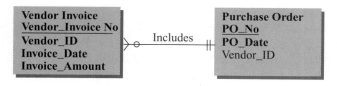

Figure 9.15   Entity-Relationship Diagram for Invoice and PO

The motivation for such a business rule could lie in difficulties related to manual paper processing. However, IT can be used to break this rule by eliminating the problems of manually reconciling invoices to multiple purchase orders. If this decision rule is changed, the E-R diagram would be changed to reflect a new many-to-many relationship desired in the Logical To-Be system.

In summary, creating a Logical To-Be model requires the abstraction of existing business processes from the As-Is model into representations that separate data flows from processes and entities, accurately identify business rules, and capture the relationships among data. Though a demanding effort, the creation of a complete To-Be model for complex systems is our best assurance that the new system will improve upon the existing one.

The next step is to develop a physical model based on the Logical To-Be model—including all the decisions necessary to determine how the logical requirements can be met. In preparation for the following Physical To-Be model discussion, Figure 9.16 identifies relational database terminology (as used in a physical model) that corresponds to the various logical data modeling terms. For each pair of terms, a corresponding example from the accounts payable system is also provided.

To-Be Patterns   Recall that in Chapter 5 we introduced the notion of universal, or prepackaged, data models. Such database patterns provide reusable starting points for new To-Be logical data modeling. Few new information systems are so unique that we need to start with a clean sheet of paper. It is likely that some similar system has been developed before, so we can learn from past experience by starting from a pattern that is considered best practice for the type of system we are developing. For a systems development team unfamiliar with the type of system they are developing, patterns can greatly assist in communication of potential requirements. We can then customize the pattern with local terminology and unique requirements. Patterns can also be used to evaluate the capabilities of purchased software.

For many years, IT organizations have maintained libraries of documentation and computer code so that these artifacts can be reused and adapted for new needs. Today, such analysis and design libraries can be purchased from consulting firms and software companies so best and proven practices can be shared across organizations. Patterns might exist of a data model for a manufacturing company or data flow diagrams for credit card application processing. Purchased patterns for the physical To-Be system descriptions are also available.

These patterns are abstractions that address all aspects of a domain; that is, they are comprehensive and cover the most general of circumstances. Several patterns may need to be combined to cover the design of a new information system. These patterns then need to be adapted to use terminology for data and processes in the specific organization. Special business rules may need to be added to accommodate industry regulations or organizational customs. Kodaganallur and Shim (2006) provide a taxonomy of To-Be patterns.

Techniques for Documenting the Physical To-Be System

The end deliverables from the Logical To-Be modeling process are called the **system requirements**. Requirements are embodied in the kinds of diagrams illustrated in the prior section along with metadata contained in the DD/D. Other textual documents, which may or may not be contained in the DD/D, contain business rules and other

Logical Data Modeling Terms	Physical Data Terms	Example
Data Store	Database or File	Accounts Payable Database
Entity	File or Table	Purchase Order (D1)
Entity Instance	Record or Row	All information on purchase order number C07321
Data Element	Field or Column	PO Number

Figure 9.16   Key Terms for Logical Data Modeling

narrative explanations of agreed upon expectations. Any proposed system design must address the need for each requirement, provide a substitute, or justify its exclusion. Of course, the objective is to meet as many of the requirements as possible without jeopardizing project scheduling and budget constraints. For this reason, often requirements are categorized into mandatory (has to be handled exactly as specified), required (may be handled in an alternative way), and desired (can be delayed to a later maintenance phase or could be rejected as infeasible). Any physical design that does not satisfy mandatory and required features should not be proposed.

Making the Logical To-Be model "physical" requires additional analysis and a host of decisions. Techniques for physical design include those that represent how processes and data stores will be partitioned, how program control will be handled, and how the database will be organized.

One of these techniques is called a **program structure chart**. Figure 9.17 shows the program structure chart for a subsystem called "Handle Customer Order." Boxes represent subprocess modules, and arrows represent the flow of control during program execution. The diagram is read from top to bottom starting from the left and moving to the

right. Flags (arrows with circles) come in two forms: data couples (open circle) and control flags (filled circle). Both flags direct the program modules to take action. Data couples cause action to be taken based on the data passed to the module, whereas control flags cause program execution based on the result of another module's processing. The module at the top controls all these processes and is the only means by which other program modules can interact with any of the subprocesses. Managers may be asked to review such a diagram to ensure that business rules are being precisely followed and that adequate controls are included. Similar to DFDs, a complex system will have many program structure charts organized in a hierarchy of greater to lesser detail.

Data design issues must also be resolved for a specific database and application architecture. The number, content, and relationship of data tables and their data elements must be defined. For example, a closer look at the accounts payable system reveals that purchase orders, receipts, and invoices may contain several similar data elements. An Item Master table is created into which data about all invoiced items must be entered. Figure 9.18 shows the Item Master table and its relationship to other tables in the

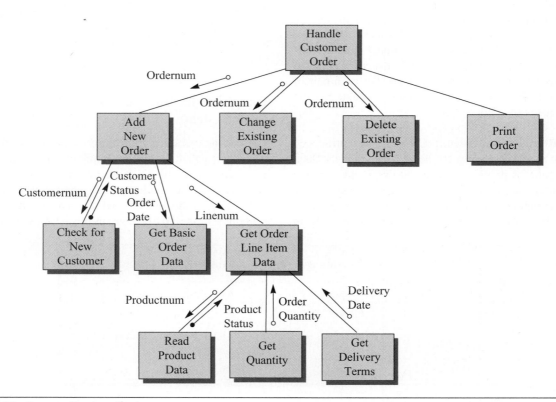

Figure 9.17 Program Structure Chart

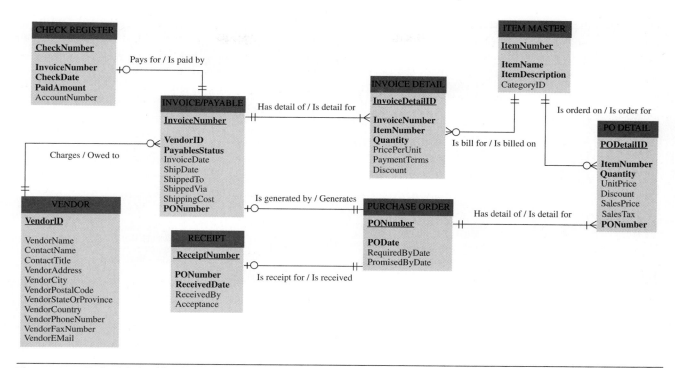

Figure 9.18   Entity-Relationship Diagram for Accounts Payable Database

accounts payable database. In each table there is a data attribute which uniquely identifies each instance of that data; for example, ItemNumber is the identifier for the Item Master table (so it is in boldface and underlined). Attributes that must have a value for each row in a table are in boldface; for example, each Item Master must have an ItemName and an ItemDescription. Notation on the relationship lines between tables indicate how many rows of one table may relate to rows in another table. For example, there may be many Invoice Detail rows for each row in the Item Master table, and an Invoice Detail row must have an associated Item Master row (this makes sense; why have an Invoice Detail entry that isn't for some item). Invoice Detail also includes the ItemNumber attribute, which is the way an Invoice Detail row implements the relationship to its associated Item Master row. The names on the relationship lines help people to read the diagram; for example, a Check Register entry Pays for an Invoice, and each Invoice Is paid by some Check Register entry. All of this notation shows important business rules that the database and information system must enforce.

Our final example for the Physical To-Be model is layouts for system interfaces with end users. The most common interfaces are online screen layouts and report layouts. In the Logical To-Be modeling, the need for an interface was identified, as well as its frequency of use and information content. In the Physical To-Be modeling, the specific interface design is addressed.

Figures 9.19 and 9.20 show draft layouts for an input screen and a report for the accounts payable system. Layouts such as these are often developed in close consultation between systems designers and the end users who will be directly working with a computer display. Today's system building tools allow for easy prototyping of such interfaces by end users before the system itself is actually built. Systems today are also frequently built with some flexibility, so that the user can directly control design options for reports and data entry forms in order to adapt to changing needs of the business or the user of the report.

You have now considered some of the techniques used to capture system needs, document business rules, and uncover hidden dependencies and relationships as part of the process of developing a new computer system using procedural-oriented techniques.

Object-Oriented Techniques

An object orientation (O-O) to systems development became common in the 1990s as the demand grew for client/server applications, graphical interfaces, and multimedia data.

Vendor Invoice Form

*Indicates Required Field
For existing Invoice, enter InvoiceNumber
For existing Vendor, enter VendorID

InvoiceNumber		*	NEW
PONumber		*	
PayablesStatus		*	
InvoiceDate		mm/dd/yyyy	
Shipped To			
Shipped Via			
Shipping Cost			

VendorID	NEW
Vendor Name	
Contact Name	
Contact Title	
Vendor Phone	
Vendor Fax	

Address	
City	
St/Province	
Postal Code	
Country	
E-Mail	

Click NEW button to add a new Detail, Click in Detail and REMOVE button to delete Detail

InvoiceDetailID *	ItemNumber *	Quantity *	PricePerUnit	PaymentTerms	Discount

NEW
REMOVE

SUBMIT FORM
CLEAR FORM

Figure 9.19   Vendor Invoice Maintenance Form

Check Register

Account Number 2936

	CheckNumber	CheckDate	InvoiceNumber	VendorID	PONumber	InvoiceDate	InvoiceAmount	PaidAmount
	482441	8/3/08	C1523	178	A00702	7/20/98	1,925.50	1,925.50
	482442	8/3/08	1398752	52	C00321	7/24/98	408.92	408.92
	482443	8/3/08	E17982	104	E00052	7/23/98	1,500.00	1,200.00
	482444	8/3/08	175632	89	C00323	7/24/98	10,328.72	10,328.72
TOTAL							14,163.14	13,863.14
	482445	8/4/08	R1689	13	B00824	7/27/98	505.17	505.17
	482446	8/4/08	M568930	97	B00825	7/28/98	12,327.18	11,094.46
	482447	8/4/08	897532	152	A00704	7/28/98	765.15	765.15
	482448	8/4/08	C1527	178	D00376	7/30/98	1,534.83	1,534.83
TOTAL							15,132.33	13,899.61
MONTHLY TOTAL							29,295.47	27,762.75

Figure 9.20   Check Register Report Layout with Sample Data

Objects can be used with any type of data, including voice, pictures, music, and video. An object approach is also well suited for applications in which processes and data are "intimately related" or real-time systems (Vessey and Glass, 1994). As described in Chapter 3, common O-O programming languages include C++, Java, and Visual Basic.

One of the primary advantages of an O-O approach is the ability to reuse objects programmed by others (see Figure 9.21). According to industry observers, successful O-O approaches can produce big payoffs by enabling businesses to quickly mock up prototype applications with user-friendly GUI interfaces. Application maintenance is also simplified.

	Procedural Approach	Object-Oriented Approach
Defining the Task	A team of business managers prepares a detailed design document specifying, as precisely as possible, how the program should do the task.	The O-O programmer searches a library of objects (prewritten chunks of software) looking for those that could be used for the business task.
The Process	Programmers divide up the design and write thousands of lines of code from scratch. If all goes well, the pieces work together as planned and the system fulfills the design requirements.	Within days, a few objects have been put together to create a bare-bones prototype. The business user gets to "test-drive" the prototype and provide feedback; by repeatedly refining and retesting the prototype, the business gets a system that fulfills the task.
Elapsed Time	Months.	Weeks.

Figure 9.21   The Promise of Object-Oriented Approaches (Adapted from Verity and Schwartz, 1991)

Software objects are also a key concept behind the sharing of software for an emerging type of network-centric computing: Web services. A Web service enables computer-to-computer sharing of software modules via the Internet on an as-needed basis: A computer program (which could be another Web service) "calls" a Web service to perform a task and send back the result. This type of "dynamic binding" occurs at the time of execution and therefore greatly increases application flexibility as well as reduces the costs of software development: The computer program's owner who uses the service could pay the owner of the Web service on a subscription basis or per use. Existing examples of Web services include currency conversions (e.g., U.S. dollars to euros), credit risk analysis, and location of a product within a distribution channel. (For a discussion of the software standards, communication protocols, and development environments that enable Web services, such as .NET by Microsoft Corp., see Chapter 3.)

encapsulation. Encapsulation also means that systems developed using O-O techniques can have loosely coupled modules, which means they can be reused in other O-O applications much more easily. This is why O-O approaches should theoretically result in faster project completion times: New systems can be created from preexisting objects. In fact, vendors can sell libraries of objects for reuse in different organizations.

A second major O-O principle is **inheritance**. That is, classes of objects can inherit characteristics from other object classes. Every object is associated with a *class* of objects that share some of the same attributes and operations. Object classes are also typically arranged in a hierarchy, so that subclasses inherit attributes and operations from a superclass. For example, if a bird is a superclass, the bird object's attributes and operations could be inherited by a specific type of bird, such as a cardinal.

Core Object-Oriented Concepts

An **object** is a person, place, or thing. However, a key difference between an entity in data modeling and an object is that data attributes as well as the methods (sometimes called operations or behaviors) that can be executed with that data are part of the object structure. The attributes of an object and its methods are *hidden* inside the object. This means that one object does not need to know the details about the attributes and methods of another object. Instead, objects communicate with each other through *messages* that specify what should be done, not how it should be done (see Figure 9.22).

Storing data and related operations together within an object is a key principle of O-O approaches, referred to as

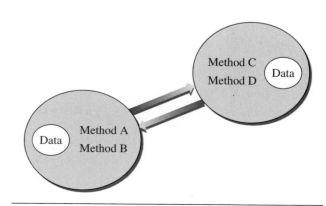

Figure 9.22   Message Passing

Unified Modeling Language (UML)
for O-O Modeling

Techniques and notations for O-O analysis and design modeling have now been standardized under a Unified Modeling Language (UML).

Logical modeling begins with a use-case diagram that captures all the actors and all the actions that they initiate. (The actors are similar to external entities in a data flow diagram.) For example, the actors for a software application to support the renting of videos would include customers who are registered members, noncustomers (browsers) who could choose to become members, a billing clerk, a shipping clerk, and an inventory system. As shown in Figure 9.23, nine different functions initiated by these actors are modeled as Use Cases.

Each Use Case is also described in a text format using a standard template. Common elements in a template are Use Case Name, Actor, Goal, Description, Precondition, and Postcondition, as well as Basic, Alternate, and Exceptional Flow events, which describe the actor's actions and the system's response. The events to be documented for one of the use cases (Become Member) in Figure 9.23 are shown in Figure 9.24.

UML also has many other types of diagrams. Three examples for a student registration system are shown in Figure 9.25:

- An extended relationship use-case diagram to logically model event flows beyond initial requirements

- A sequence diagram to capture the messages that pass between object classes

- A class diagram with each object's attributes and methods as well as a model of the relationships between object classes

Summary of Processes and Techniques
to Develop Information Systems

Yes, information systems development is very detailed, and it is easy to become overwhelmed by the many diagrams and documents. Why so detailed? The reason is quality. Quality information systems support every circumstance with repeatable, correct actions. Everyone touched by the system has to agree on the business rules to govern each process, and on the usability and adequacy of all data inputs and information outputs. The builders of the system are usually not the same persons who will use the system and conduct the organizational tasks being supported by the information system, so the builders have to be told explicitly what to build. (Alternatively, as we will see in Chapter 11, these specifications are necessary to evaluate possible purchased solutions, as well.) New regulations such as Sarbanes-Oxley require that systems and system changes be thoroughly documented so there is transparency and controls in place that will allow executives to sign financial statements and stay out of jail! The design documentation also makes subsequent design work more efficient, just as

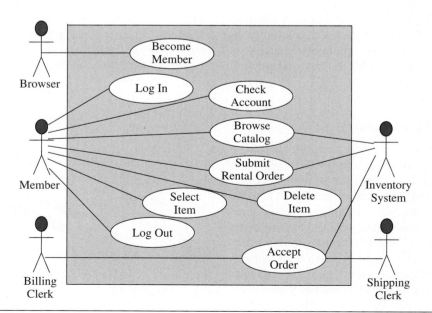

Figure 9.23 Use Case Diagram (Reprinted from Chand, 2003)

Use Case Name:	Become Member	
Actors:	Browser	
Goal:	Enroll the browser as a new member	
Description:	The Browser will be asked to complete a membership form. After the Browser submits the application form, the system will validate it and then add the Browser to the membership file and generate a password that is e-mailed to the Browser.	
Pre-condition:	The systems is up and the Browser is logged in as a guest	
Post-condition:	The Member password e-mailed to the Browser/ Member is logged	
Basic Flow		
	Actor action:	System response:
	1. This use case begins when the Browser clicks the membership button	
		2. Display the membership form
	3. Browser completes and submits the application	
		4. Check for errors
		5. Check the membership database for prior membership
		6. Create a password
		7. Add new or updated member record to the membership database
		8. Send an e-mail to the actor with the password
		The use case ends
Alternate Flow	Prior membership handling	
		5.1. Update membership record
		5.2. Inform the browser
		Continue from step 6 of Basic Flow
Exception Flow	Errors in membership application	
		4.1. Identify errors
		4.2. Return errors to Browser
	4.3. Browser corrects errors	
		Continue from step 4 of Basic Flow

Figure 9.24 Become Member Use Case (Reprinted from Chand, 2003)

having blueprints of a home make it easier to build an addition by knowing the capacity of the furnace to support the added space, where the plumbing and wiring might be in a wall to be exposed, and what building codes have to be followed. Fortunately, managers will be asked to review specifics of the diagrams and documentation, not all of the gory details. But, the diagrams are shared by the many business and technical people working on a systems development project, so they have many uses and must have much detail.

(A) Use-Case Diagram for Student Registration System

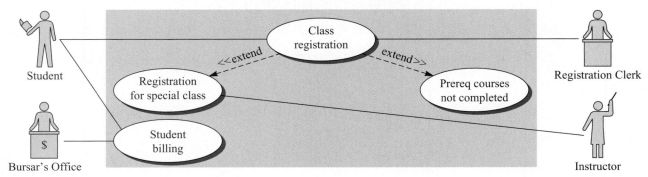

(B) Sequence Diagram for Class Registration Scenario with Prerequisites

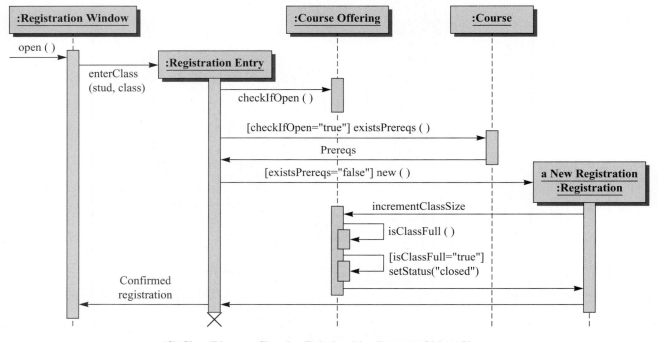

(C) Class Diagram Showing Relationships Between Object Classes

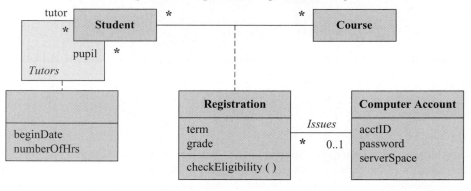

Figure 9.25 UML Diagrams for Student Registration System

INFORMATION SYSTEMS CONTROLS TO MINIMIZE BUSINESS RISKS

Suppose you and your partner with whom you have a joint savings account separately go to the bank one day to withdraw the same $500 in savings. Or suppose an inventory clerk enters a wrong part number to record the issue of an item from the storeroom, which results in an out-of-stock status, which automatically generates a purchase order to a supplier, who then begins production, and so on. These situations illustrate just some of the ways in which potential human errors when interacting with information systems can create business risks. However, they are only a small part of the potential risks associated with the use of IT.

Other common system security risks include: (1) risks from criminal acts, (2) risks due to staffing changes and project management deficiencies, and (3) risks from natural disasters. All these risks have the potential for not only dissatisfied customers, but also considerable business expenses for error correction. There is also the risk of potential losses due to lawsuits and negative publicity, which even the world's largest software vendors don't want to receive (see the box entitled "Regaining Customer Trust at Microsoft").

REGAINING CUSTOMER TRUST AT MICROSOFT

Computer users worldwide raced to protect themselves from a malicious electronic "worm" designed to allow hackers to gain access to infected PCs. Whatever the origin of the worm, one thing is clear: The outbreak increases pressure on Microsoft to make its Windows software more reliable and secure. In 2002, Bill Gates launched an initiative, called "Trustworthy Computing," to change the way the company designs and builds software. Among other actions, Microsoft added 10 weeks of training for 8,500 of its software engineers. The company also reportedly spent more than $200 million in 2002 to improve the security of its Windows program for corporate servers.

But experts give Microsoft mixed grades for its follow-through, saying the company hasn't changed its methods enough to avoid the kinds of flaws that make attacks by viruses and worms possible in the first place. Ultimately, that could hurt Microsoft where it matters most—in the corporate wallet.

[Adapted from Guth and Bank, 2003]

Because of the importance of this subject, elsewhere in this textbook we will also provide discussions of potential IT-related business risks and how to manage them. For example, in Chapter 12 we provide some guidelines for managing the risks of IT projects, and in Chapter 17 we discuss information security issues to help ensure compliance with Sarbanes Oxley (SOX) and other recent laws.

What is your data quality ROI? No, we don't mean return on investment. Rather, we mean risk of incarceration. According to Yugay and Klimchenko (2004), "The key to achieving SOX (Sarbanes-Oxley) compliance lies within IT, which is ultimately the single resource capable of responding to the charge to create effective reporting mechanisms, provide necessary data integration and management systems, ensure data quality and deliver the required information on time." Poor data quality can put executives in jail. Specifically, various sections of the SOX act yields requirements for organizations to measure and improve metadata quality; ensure data security; measure and improve data accessibility and ease of use; measure and improve data availability, timeliness, and relevance; measure and improve accuracy, completeness, and understandability of general ledger data; and identify and eliminate duplicates and data inconsistencies.

Here we discuss some of the management controls to address risks that are specifically associated with the three phases of the software life cycle. Although the security and reliability issues will differ somewhat due to the nature of the software application, this list of control mechanisms provide a starting point for understanding the role of the IS professional (including project managers, analysts, and programmers) in helping to ensure that business risks have been accounted for. However, the identification of potential control risks is to a large extent a business manager's responsibility.

First we describe different types of control mechanisms that need to be considered. Then we describe specific examples of control mechanisms for error detection, prevention, and correction that need to be addressed during the three life cycle phases (Definition, Construction, and Implementation). Although these "proven" mechanisms are recommended responses, both business and IS managers also need to recognize that when new information technologies are introduced they likely will also introduce new control risks.

Types of Control Mechanisms

Control mechanisms include management policies, operating procedures, and the auditing function. Some aspects of control can be built into an information system itself,

Life Cycle Phase	Control Mechanism
Definition and Construction	• Methodology Standards • Validation Rules and Calculations • System Testing
Implementation	• Security • Backup and Recovery • Auditing Roles

Figure 9.26   Pre- and Post-Installation Controls

whereas others are the result of day-to-day business practices and management decisions. Information system controls, for example, are needed to maintain data integrity, allow only authorized access, ensure proper system operation, and protect against malfunctions, power outages, and disasters. Throughout the systems development process, the needs for specific controls are identified and control mechanisms are developed to address these needs. Some mechanisms are implemented during the system design, coding, or implementation. Others become part of the routine operation of the system, such as backups and authorization security, and still others involve the use of manual business practices and management policies, such as formal system audits. Figure 9.26 shows some of the control approaches usually employed in the indicated phases of the systems life cycle.

Security controls related to the technology infrastructure—such as backup power supplies, network access control, and firewall protection—are typically the purview of the IS organization. In addition, IS developers will include some standard controls in all applications. However, specifying checks and balances to ensure accurate data entry and handling is a business manager's responsibility. Managers must carefully identify what are valid data, what errors might be made while handling data, what nontechnical security risks are present, and what potential business losses could result from inaccurate or lost data.

Some new technologies, such as advanced software tools for system testing, have improved an organization's control processes, whereas other new technologies (such as Web applications) have introduced new control risks. The increase in distributed computing applications over the past two decades in general has significantly increased a company's reliance on network transmission of data and software—which requires additional technical and managerial controls (Hart and Rosenberg, 1995). Next we discuss only some of the most common control mechanisms that apply to a wide range of application development situations.

Controls in the Definition and Construction Phases

In the initial two phases of the systems life cycle, the accurate and reliable performance of the system can be assured by the use of standards, embedded controls, and thorough testing.

Methodology Standards   The reliable performance of a system depends upon how well it was designed and constructed. No amount of automated checks can override errors in the software itself.

One way to avoid errors is to develop standard, repeatable, and possibly reusable methods and techniques for system developers. The use of standard programming languages and equipment means that systems developers will be more familiar with the tools and will be less likely to make mistakes. A common method is to create a library of frequently used functions (such as calculation of net present value or a sales forecasting model) that different information systems can utilize. Such functions can then be developed and tested with great care and reused as needed, saving development time and reducing the likelihood of design and programming flaws. Most organizations also have standards for designing user interfaces, such as screen and report layout rules and guidelines.

The importance of standards also extends to the documentation of the system during construction and the following period of maintenance and upgrades. If future programmers do not have access to systems documentation that is complete and accurate, they could be unaware of prior changes. Documentation for the system's users also needs to be complete and accurate so that system inputs are not incorrectly captured and system outputs are not incorrectly used.

Standards are also important for supporting information systems and users. A rather extensive set of international guidelines have been developed called Information Technology Infrastructure Library (ITIL). ITIL documents best practices for management of incidents, problems, system changes, technology configuration, software releases, service/help desk operations, service levels, service and support availability, capacity, continuity (recovery), and financials, Many organizations are benchmarking their implementation management practices against these guidelines, which originated in 1989 in Great Britain's Office of Government Commerce. The goal of using these standards include to reduce IT costs, increase IT resource utilization, better align IT with business requirements, reuse proven methods and tools, and generally refocus IT operations around customer satisfaction. The IT Service Management Forum (ITSMF) professional society fosters the ITIL methods through education, and certification of its members and other IT professionals, and promotion of the value of ITIL.

Validation Rules and Calculations   Each time a data element is updated, the new value can be checked against a legitimate set or range of values permitted for that data. This check can be performed in each application program where these data can be changed (e.g., in a payables adjustment program that modifies previously entered vendor invoices) and in the database where they are stored. Edit rules, ideally stored with the database, are also used to ensure that data are not missing, that data are of a valid size and type, and that data match with other stored values (e.g., a price of a new product is within some tolerance of the price of similar existing products).

Providing a screen display with associated data can be a very useful edit check. For example, when a vendor number is entered, the program can display the associated name and address. The person inputting or modifying data can then visually verify the vendor information. Edit rules can also ensure that only numbers are entered for numeric data, that only feasible codes are entered, or that some calculation based on a modified data value is valid. When feasible, data being entered should be selected from drop-down lists of possible values, thus minimizing the chance of keystroke mistakes. These edit checks are integrity rules that control the data's validity.

Well-designed user interfaces also will prevent data entry mistakes. Clear labels to identify each field to be entered, edit masks that show standard formats for data, examples of valid data formats, buttons to quickly clear fields when a user recognizes data entry errors, and similar user interface guidelines help to control data entry. When possible errors are identified, immediate and direct error messages should indicate exactly what data is in error and why so the user can correct any mistakes. Overriding data entry rules should be allowed only when necessary and should be logged so they can be traced after the fact during auditing of databases.

Various calculations can be performed to validate processing. Batch totals that calculate the sum of certain data in a batch of transactions can be computed both manually before processing and by the computer during processing; discrepancies suggest the occurrence of data entry errors such as transposition of digits. Though they are not foolproof, such approaches, along with automated edits, go a long way toward assuring valid input.

A **check digit** can be appended to critical identifying numbers such as general ledger account numbers or vendor numbers; the value of this check digit is based on the other digits in the number. This digit can be used to quickly verify that at least a valid, if not correct, code has been entered, and it can catch most common errors.

Business managers and their staffs are responsible for defining the legitimate values for data and where control calculations would be important as a part of the information captured in the data dictionary. Furthermore, business managers must set policy to specify if checks can be overridden and who can authorize overrides. Validation rules should permit business growth and expansion, yet reduce the likelihood of erroneous data.

System Testing   Certainly the most common and effective of all IS controls is complete system testing. Each program must be tested individually and in combination with the other programs in the application. Managers develop test data that have known results. Programs are run with typical and atypical data, correct and erroneous data, and the actual results are compared to what should be produced. Testing occurs not only when systems are initially developed, but also when systems are modified. (See Chapter 10 for a description of additional roles played by users when testing a system.)

Controls in the Implementation Phase

Not all the elements necessary to assure proper systems operation can be built into an application. Avoiding and detecting inappropriate access or use, providing data backups and system recovery capabilities, and formally auditing the system are all ongoing control mechanisms. As mentioned earlier, many application-level controls work in concert with managerial controls. User-managers are responsible for being familiar with any firm-wide control mechanisms and identifying when additional ones are needed for a specific application.

Security The unauthorized use of data can result in a material loss, such as the embezzlement of funds, or in losses that are harder to measure, such as the disclosure of sensitive data. In any case, the security of data and computers is necessary so that employees, customers, shareholders, and others can be confident that their interactions with the organization are confidential and the business's assets are safe.

Security measures are concerned with both logical and physical access. Logical access controls are concerned with whether users can run an application, whether they can read a file or change it, and whether they can change the access that others have. Managers work with systems personnel to identify and maintain appropriate authorization levels based on work roles and business needs. Two mechanisms for controlling logical access are authentication and authorization (Hart and Rosenberg, 1995):

Authentication involves establishing that the person requesting access is who he or she appears to be. This is typically accomplished by the use of a unique user identifier and a private password.

Authorization involves determining whether or not authenticated users have access to the requested resources and what they can do with those resources. This is typically accomplished by a computer check for permission rights to access a given resource.

Encryption techniques are used to encode data that is transmitted across organizational boundaries. Data may be stored in an encrypted form and then decrypted by the application. Unless a user knows the decryption algorithm, an encrypted file will be unreadable.

The physical security of specific computers and data processing centers must also be established. Badge readers; voice, fingerprint, and retina recognition; or combination locks are common. Formal company statements about computer ethics raise awareness of the sensitivity of data privacy and the need to protect organizational data. When combined with knowledge of the use of transaction or activity logs that record the user ID, network location, time stamp, and function or data accessed, many security violations could be discouraged.

Because no security system is foolproof, detection methods to identify security breaches are necessary. Administrative practices to help deter computer security abuses have been compiled by Hoffer and Straub (1989). Detection methods include:

- Hiding special instructions in sensitive programs that log identifying data about users
- Analysis of the amount of computer time used by individuals
- Analysis of system activity logs for unusual patterns of use

With the rise of end-user computing and use of the Internet, additional risks due to inappropriate behaviors while using these tools have emerged, as well as issues stemming from work-related use of home PCs. Some specific end-user computing risks and controls are discussed in Chapter 13. Today, organizations are developing similar controls to manage intranets and access to external Web sites from intranets.

Backup and Recovery The ultimate protection against many system failures is to have a backup copy. Periodically a file can be copied and saved in a separate location such as a bank vault. Then, when a file becomes contaminated or destroyed, the most recent version can be restored. Of course, any changes since the last copy was made will not appear. Thus, organizations often also keep transaction logs (a chronological history of changes to each file) so these changes can be automatically applied to a backup copy to bring the file up to current status.

A common flaw in backup plans is storing the file backup in the same location as the master file. If stored in the same location, a backup is no more likely to survive a fire, flood, or earthquake than its source file. A secure, off-site location for the backup must be provided, along with a foolproof tracking system.

Some organizations (such as airlines, banks, and telephone networks) can operate only if their online computer systems are working. One approach is to provide redundant systems and operations that "mirror" the production system and data located at a distant facility. This improves the chances of an effective recovery from a widespread power or network outage or a natural disaster. If data recovery processing via another location is immediately available, these locations are known as "hot sites."

Managers and IS professionals together need to determine how frequently backup copies are needed, the business cost of recovering files from backup copies, and how much should be spent on specialized backup resources. As with any security procedure, the ongoing backup and recovery costs need to be in line with the potential organizational benefits and risks.

Auditing Roles Critical business processes are subject to periodic formal audits to assure that the processes operate within parameters. Such audits may be part of the annual accounting audit for a publicly traded company or part of activities to show compliance with financial reporting regulations like Sarbanes-Oxley and Basel II, or with health care regulations such as HIPAA. As more and more organizations have become dependent on information systems in order to operate their business, the importance of IS auditing has increased. IS auditing is still frequently referred to as **EDP auditing**—a name chosen when the term *electronic data processing* was used to refer to computer operations. EDP auditors use a variety of methods to ensure the correct processing of data, including compliance tests, statistical sampling, and embedded auditing methods.

Compliance tests check that systems builders use high-quality systems development procedures that lead to properly functioning systems. Statistical sampling of a portion of databases can identify abnormalities that indicate systematic problems or security breaches. Embedded auditing methods include reporting triggers programmed into a system that are activated by certain processing events. The flagged records are then analyzed to determine if errors or security breaches are occurring in the system.

The most commonly used EDP auditing technique in the past has been an **audit trail**. Audit trails trace transactions from the time of input through all the processes and reports in which the transaction data are used. Audit trail records typically include program names, user name or user ID, input location and date/time stamps, as well as the transaction itself. An audit trail can help identify where errors are introduced or where security breaches might have occurred.

Managers need to participate in the identification of elements that should be captured in the audit trail to detect errors and assure compliance with all relevant laws and regulations. Furthermore, the frequency and extent of formal information system auditing is a management decision that should take into account the system's breadth and role, its relationship to other business processes, and the potential risks to the firm.

notation systems for modeling processes and data separately. Object-oriented (O-O) techniques, including a new modeling language (UML), have become more prevalent as newer software applications have required graphical user interfaces, multimedia data, and support for "real-time" transactions. O-O approaches will also be important in the development of Web services. Common IS control mechanisms to minimize business risks due to internal and external threats are described; many of these controls need to be identified with the help of business managers and then addressed during the development and maintenance of an information system.

REVIEW QUESTIONS

1. Define the term *system*. Give an example of a business system and use a context diagram to show its boundary, environment, inputs, and outputs.
2. Define the term *subsystem*. Give an example of a business subsystem and identify some subsystems with which it relates.
3. Define the term *business process reengineering* and describe its importance for IS work.
4. Describe how logical and physical representations of a To-Be system will differ.
5. Describe the relationships between a context diagram, as in Figure 9.11, and the top-level and second-level diagrams of a data flow diagram, as in Figure 9.13(A) and(B).
6. What is a data dictionary and why is it important?
7. Why are software objects more "reusable" than other types of computer code?
8. What are analysis and design patterns and why are they useful for information systems development?
9. Compare a context diagram (using DFD modeling) and a use case diagram (using UML); what is the same and what is different?
10. Briefly describe some common information system controls that need to be implemented by business managers, not IS professionals.
11. What is an audit trail and why is it a useful mechanism for controlling business risks due to an information system?
12. In what way does thorough documentation for an information system help in compliance with regulations such as Sarbanes-Oxley?
13. What is the Information Technology Infrastructure Library (ITIL) and what benefits does it provide for implementation of information systems?

SUMMARY

Systems thinking is a hallmark of good management in general. Systems thinking is also core to many basic concepts on which modern information systems are defined, constructed, and implemented. Three systems characteristics especially important for IS work are: determining the system boundary, component decomposition, and designing system interfaces.

This chapter also introduced a generic life cycle model for software systems as well as some of the processes and techniques for systems analysis and design used by IS professionals for developing software. Procedurally oriented techniques for structured system development include

DISCUSSION QUESTIONS

1. Explain and give an example that supports the following statement: Each time we change characteristics of one or more of the components of the organization (organization structure, people, business processes, information technology), we must consider compensating changes in the other components.

2. Explain the function of hierarchical decomposition in systems analysis and design and discuss the reasons for viewing and analyzing systems in this way.

3. Why do informal systems arise? Why should systems analysts be aware of them?

4. Some observers have characterized business process reengineering (BPR) as evolutionary, others as revolutionary. Develop an argument to support one of these sides.

5. Explain why many companies were unable to implement new cross-functional processes that were identified by BPR project teams in the early 1990s, before ERP packages became widely available.

6. Describe why analysts begin with the As-Is system, rather than starting with the design of a To-Be system.

7. Develop a context diagram and a top-level DFD to model the data flows involved in registering for classes at your college or university. Then model the student registration system in a use case diagram and write a textual description for one of the use cases.

8. Identify the construction controls for the class registration system of the previous question. Justify why these controls would be adequate for data quality, security, and recoverability.

9. Web services have been called a second wave of net-centric computing that will have broad implications for software development approaches in the future. Develop an argument to support or refute this viewpoint.

10. Explain why some organizations have adopted more rigid control mechanisms in recent years and whether or not you think they are justified, given the added costs to implement them.

REFERENCES

Chand, Donald R. 2003. "Use case modeling." Carol V. Brown and Heikki Topi (eds.), *IS Management Handbook*, 8th ed. New York: Auerbach.

Dennis, Alan, and Barbara Haley Wixom. 2000. *Systems Analysis and Design*. New York: John Wiley & Sons, Inc.

El Sawy, Omar A. 2001. *Redesigning Enterprise Processes for E-Business*. Boston: Irwin/McGraw Hill.

Fitzgerald, Jerry, and Alan Dennis. 1999. *Business Data Communications and Networking*, 6th ed. New York: John Wiley & Sons, Inc.

Guth, Robert A., and David Bank. 2003. "Online 'worm' puts new stress on Microsoft." *Wall Street Journal* (August 15): B1, B5.

Hammer, Michael. 1990. "Reengineering work: Don't automate, obliterate." *Harvard Business Review* 68 (July–August): 104–112.

Hammer, Michael. 1996. *Beyond Reengineering*. New York: HarperCollins.

Hammer, Michael, and James Champy. 1993. *Reengineering the Corporation*. New York: HarperCollins.

Hart, Johnson M., and Barry Rosenberg. 1995. *Client/Server Computing for Technical Professionals: Concepts and Solutions*. Reading, MA: Addison-Wesley Publishing Company.

Hoffer, Jeffrey A., Joey F. George, and Joseph S. Valacich. 2008. *Modern Systems Analysis and Design*, 5th ed. Upper Saddle River, NJ: Pearson Prentice Hall.

Hoffer, Jeffrey A., and Detmar W. Straub, Jr. 1989. "The 9 to 5 underground: Are you policing computer crimes?" *Sloan Management Review* 30 (Summer): 35–43.

Keen, Peter G. W. 1997. *The Process Edge*. Boston: Harvard University Press.

Kodaganallur, Viswanathan, and Sung Shim. 2006. "Analysis Patterns: A Taxonomy and Its Implications." *Information Systems Management* 23, 3 (Summer): 52–61.

Markus, M. Lynne, and Daniel Robey. 1988. "Information technology and organizational change: Causal structure in theory and research." *Management Science* 34 (May): 583–598.

Hoffer, Jeffrey A., and Mary B. Prescott. 2007. *Modern Database Management*, 8th ed. Upper Saddle River, NJ: Pearson Prentice Hall.

McNurlin, Barbara C., and Ralph H. Sprague, Jr. 2004. *Information Systems Management in Practice*, 6th ed. Upper Saddle River, NJ: Pearson Prentice Hall.

Page-Jones, Meilir. 1988. *The Practical Guide to Structured Systems Design*, 2nd ed. Englewood Cliffs, NJ: Yourdon Press.

Senge, Peter M. 1990. *The Fifth Discipline*. New York: Doubleday.

Yugay, Irina, and Victor Klimchenko. 2004. "SOX mandates focus on data quality & integration." *DM Review* 14, 2 (February): 38–42.

Valacich, Joseph S., Joey F. George, and Jeffrey A. Hoffer. 2006. *Essentials of Systems Analysis & Design,* 3rd ed. Upper Saddle River, NJ: Pearson Prentice Hall.

Verity, John W., and Evan I. Schwartz. 1991. "Software made simple." *Business Week* (September 30): 92–100.

Vessey, Iris, and Robert L. Glass. 1994. "Applications-based methodologies." *Information Systems Management* (Fall): 53–57.

CHAPTER 10
METHODOLOGIES FOR CUSTOM
SOFTWARE DEVELOPMENT

UNTIL THE LATE 1980S, SOFTWARE APPLICATIONS THAT WERE CUSTOM-developed systems for a specific firm were very common. If an organization had its own information systems (IS) professionals, the organization's own IS staff most likely developed these custom applications in-house. If an organization did not have the resources (or IS expertise) to develop custom applications, an outside vendor would be employed either to provide IS contract personnel on a temporary basis or to completely develop the custom software for the organization. As we will discuss in Chapter 11, today's firms are likely to purchase software packages whenever they can. However, custom software development skills are still in high demand in a variety of organizations, as well as in software vendor and consulting firms.

In this chapter we first describe two common approaches to developing customized applications: a traditional systems development life cycle (SDLC) approach and an evolutionary prototyping approach. Although our methodology descriptions assume that the IT project is being managed in-house, most of what we describe holds true for application development approaches used today within commercial software houses. A key difference, of course, is that when custom applications are being built for a specific organization—rather than for sale to many organizations—business managers and end users who will use the application on a day-to-day basis will play key roles in the development process.

Next we describe two newer development approaches: rapid application development (RAD) and an "agile" development approach, including some characteristics of an "extreme programming" approach. The chapter closes with a brief description of some of the special issues related to developing custom software using external contract (outsourced) staff.

SYSTEMS DEVELOPMENT LIFE CYCLE METHODOLOGY

In Chapter 9 we introduced three generic phases of a systems **life-cycle process:** Definition, Construction, and Implementation. We turn now to a detailed discussion of these three phases in the development of a new software application using a highly structured approach. This traditional life cycle process for developing customized applications is referred to as the **systems development life cycle (SDLC).**

The SDLC approach also provides a baseline for understanding what is involved in developing an application system, whether by IS professionals employed by your organization, by IS professionals employed by a software development firm or consultancy, or by some combination of internal and external IS specialists. The processes for purchasing a software package (described in Chapter 11) or developing an application as an end user (described in Chapter 13) will also be better understood after becoming familiar with the traditional SDLC approach.

The SDLC Steps

The generic SDLC methodology includes three phases and eight steps. This template is shown in Figure 10.1. The specific steps in this figure can vary across organizations. For example, an organization could have developed its own version of an SDLC methodology that includes a total of five steps or even ten steps. Nevertheless, an organization's internally developed SDLC methodology should also essentially correspond to the steps for each of the three phases in Figure 10.1.

The overall thrusts of the three phases of the SDLC are quite straightforward. The Definition phase is critical: It justifies the systems development work and defines precisely what the system must do in sufficient detail for IS specialists to build the right system. In the Construction phase, the IS specialists produce a working system according to the specifications set forth in the earlier phase. These include many of the structured techniques—data flow diagrams, E-R models, structure charts—and IS control concerns discussed in Chapter 9.

A key characteristic of the SDLC approach is extensive formal reviews by project team members and business management at the end of each major step. Without formal approvals, the project team cannot begin the next step of

the methodology. The completion of each phase therefore represents a milestone in the development of the system.

In the Implementation phase, the new system is installed, becomes operational within the organization, and is maintained (modified) as needed so that it continues to reflect the changing needs of the organization. These last two steps—Operations and Maintenance—are included in the life cycle as a way to formally recognize that large custom applications are major capital investments for an organization that will have ongoing operational and maintenance costs.

In large organizations in the 1980s it was not uncommon to find many custom software applications that were more than a decade old. These systems had often been modified multiple times—the Maintenance step—in response to the organization's changing requirements. As we will learn later in this chapter, it often took a major external crisis, such as potential system failures due to the program's handling of the year 2000, for the organization to invest in a replacement system after having made significant dollar investments in these systems over many years.

In Figure 10.2 a typical breakdown of IS costs is presented for these three phases for a medium-sized project with a total development cost of $1 million. This breakdown does not include costs that a business unit might bear for training or replacing a business manager who is working on the project team. As can be seen from this hypothetical example, the Requirements Definition step is the costliest. As will be emphasized in the following sections, this is a hallmark of the SDLC approach: Extensive, upfront time is spent determining the business requirements for the new custom software application in order to

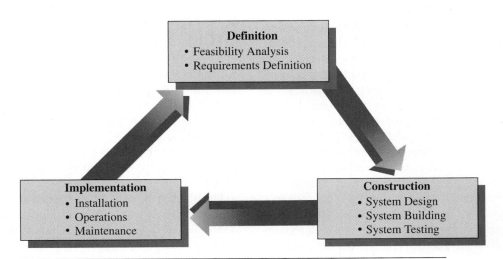

Figure 10.1 Phases and Steps of Systems Development Life Cycle

Development Activities	Percentage of Total Cost	Dollar Cost
Definition Phase		
Feasibility analysis	5	$ 50,000
Requirements definition	25	250,000
Construction Phase		
System design	15	150,000
Coding and initial testing	15	150,000
System testing	13	130,000
Documentation and procedures	12	120,000
Implementation Phase		
Installation planning, data cleanup, and conversion	15	150,000
Total	100%	$1,000,000

Figure 10.2   Cost Breakdown for $1 Million SDLC Project

avoid expensive changes later in the process due to inadequate definition of the requirements.

Most SDLC methodologies result in a lot of documentation. In the early steps, before any computer code is even written, the specific deliverables from each step are written materials. An SDLC step is not complete until a formal review of this documentation takes place.

The traditional SDLC approach has often been referred to as the "waterfall" model (Boehm, 1981): The outputs from one step are inputs to the next step. However, in practice, an organization could have to take more of a "spiral" approach, returning to earlier steps to change a requirement or a design as needed. Later in this chapter (see the section entitled "Newer Approaches") we will discuss an approach that builds on both the waterfall and spiral concepts: rapid application development (RAD).

Initiating New Systems Projects

Organizations use a number of approaches to decide which new applications to invest in. In many organizations the process begins with the submission of a formal proposal by a business department. Some large organizations require that these proposals first be reviewed and prioritized by a committee at the department or division level. When substantial investments and resources are involved, the department might be required to wait for an annual approval and prioritization process to occur. Very large, high-budget projects could also require approval by the corporation's top management executive committee and board of directors.

Some organizations require that a business sponsor, rather than an IS manager, present his or her proposals to these approval bodies. Smaller, low-budget projects might be approved on a much more frequent basis with fewer hurdles.

At a minimum, a proposal that describes the need for the software application with a preliminary statement of potential benefits, costs, scope, and risks will be prepared by business management or an IS manager assigned to a particular business unit (an account manager). The extent to which IS professionals need to be involved in this preliminary phase varies greatly across organizations.

Once the proposal has been approved and IS resources are formally assigned to the project, the formal SDLC process begins. For some projects, the initial approval might only be an endorsement to proceed with a feasibility analysis, after which additional approvals will be required. The documents for the feasibility analysis then become the basis for a decision on whether or not to invest in the custom application (that is, a business case for investment). In many situations, because of the phased nature of the SDLC, the commitment to move forward applies only to the next phase or step, at which time the business case will be readdressed. This approach of reviewing a program after each phase or step, with options to continue, continue with changes, or terminate the project, is called **incremental commitment**.

Descriptions of each of the eight steps outlined in Figure 10.1 follow.

Definition Phase

Feasibility Analysis   For this first step of the SDLC process, a project manager and one or more systems analysts are typically assigned to work with business managers to prepare a thorough analysis of the feasibility of the proposed system. Three different types of feasibility will be assessed: *economic, operational*, and *technical*.

The IS analysts work closely with the sponsoring manager who proposed the system and/or other business managers to define in some detail what the new system will do, what outputs it will produce, what inputs it will accept, how the input data might be obtained, and what databases might be required. An important activity is to define the scope or boundaries of the system—precisely who would it serve, what it would do, as well as what it would not do— and what data processing would and would not be included. The IS analyst is primarily responsible for assessing the system's technical feasibility, based on a knowledge of current and emerging technological solutions, the IT expertise of in-house personnel, and the anticipated infrastructure needed to both develop and support the proposed system. The business manager is primarily responsible for assessing the proposed system's economic and operational feasibility. In some organizations, business analysts who are knowledgeable about IT, but are not IT professionals, play a lead role in this process. Operational feasibility entails assessing the degree to which a proposed system addresses the business issues or opportunities that gave rise to the idea for a new or changed information system. The motivation may be discretionary (e.g., "I think we can improve sales with an X system") or imposed (e.g., a new EPA or FTC regulation or new language in a labor contract).

Both business managers and IS analysts work together to prepare a cost/benefit analysis of the proposed system to determine the economic feasibility. Typical benefits include costs to be avoided, such as cost savings from personnel, space, and inventory reductions (which might be due to reducing errors); new revenues to be created (which might come from increased speed of decision making, improving planning and control, or opening new sales opportunities); and other ways the system could contribute business value overall. However, for many applications today, some or all of the major benefits might be intangible benefits; they are hard to measure in dollars. Examples of intangible benefits include better customer service, more accurate or more comprehensive information for decision making, quicker processing, or better employee morale. (For a further discussion of system justification, see the section later in this chapter entitled "Managing an SDLC Project.")

The IS analyst takes primary responsibility for establishing the development costs for the project. This requires the development of a project plan that includes an estimated schedule in workweeks or months for each step in the development process and an overall budget estimate through the installation of the project. Estimating these project costs and schedules is especially difficult when new technologies and large system modules are involved. (Note that these costs usually do not include user department costs, which might be substantial during both the Definition and Implementation phases.)

Any project, not just systems development, has risks, and these risks need to be considered. Not every project needs to be low risk. Often an organization will undertake a portfolio of systems development projects that range from low to high risk and low to high net value. Risks can arise from barriers to achieving the benefits (e.g., overcoming resistance from some key players—often called political feasibility—or differences of opinion about system requirements), uncertainties of economic estimates, inexperience of development staff with the application area

or technologies to be used, and the sheer size of the project (large projects tend to be more risky than small projects). Projects with high risks and low rewards may not be approved.

The deliverable of the Feasibility Analysis step is a document of typically 10 to 20 pages that includes a short executive overview and summary of recommendations, a description of what the system would do and how it would operate, an analysis of the costs, benefits, risks of the proposed project and system, and a plan for the development of the system. Sometimes referred to as a systems proposal document or a business case, this document is typically first discussed and agreed to by both the executive sponsor and the IS project manager and then reviewed by a management committee that has authority for system approvals and prioritization.

Before additional steps are undertaken, both IS and business managers need to carefully consider whether to commit the resources required to develop the proposed system. The project costs up to this point have typically been modest in relation to the total project costs, so the project can be abandoned at this stage without the organization having spent much money or expended much effort. As described earlier, the approval of a large system request might not actually occur until after the completion of a formal feasibility analysis and may be reassessed after each step in the SDLC. For large projects, the executive sponsor of the application is typically responsible for the presentation of a business case for the system before the approving body.

Requirements Definition If the document produced from the feasibility analysis receives the necessary organizational approvals, the Requirements Definition step is begun. Both the development of the "right system" and developing the "system right" are highly dependent on how well the organization conducts this step in the SDLC process. This requires heavy participation from user management. If this step is not done well, the wrong system might be designed or even built, leading to both disruptive and costly changes later in the process.

Although in the past new systems often automated what had been done manually, most of today's systems are developed to do new things, to do old things in entirely new ways, or both. Although the executive sponsor plays a key role in envisioning how IT can be used to enable change in what the sponsor's people do and how they do it, the sponsor is often not the manager who helps to define the new system's requirements and will not be a primary user of the system. Rather, the sponsoring manager must make sure that those who will use the system and those managers responsible for the use of the new system are involved in defining its detailed requirements.

Also referred to as systems analysis or logical design, the requirements definition focuses on processes, data flows, and data interrelationships rather than a specific physical implementation. The systems analyst(s) is responsible for making sure these requirements are elicited in sufficient detail to pass on to those who will build the system. It might appear easy to define what a system is to do at the level of detail with which system users often describe systems. However, it is quite difficult to define what the new system is to do in the detail necessary to write the computer code for it. Many business applications are incredibly complex, supporting different functions for many people or processes that cross multiple business units or geographic locations. Although each detail might be known by someone, no one person knows what a new system should do in the detail necessary to describe it. This step can therefore be very time-consuming and requires analysts who are skilled in asking the right questions of the right people and in conceptual system design techniques. In addition, there might be significant disagreements among the business managers about the nature of the application requirements. It is then the responsibility of the IS project manager and analysts to help the relevant user community reach a consensus. Sometimes outside consultants are used to facilitate this process.

A variety of methods are used to elicit requirements, and several are often used on the same project. Interviews of key personnel (from the sponsor to a representative set of users) are often done. These may be individual interviews or group interviews, sometimes called Joint Application Design (JAD) sessions (described later in this chapter). Review of documents related to the application area (e.g., business plans, communications complaining about the current system, job descriptions, even descriptions of commercial applications or academic research about similar systems) is also common. Sometimes it makes sense for the systems analyst to observe people doing the job that will be supported by the new or changed system, so that bottlenecks, errors, and confusions can be seen firsthand. It is best to triangulate on requirements by using a variety of these methods.

Furthermore, some new applications are intended to provide decision support for tasks that are ill-structured. In these situations, managers often find it difficult to define precisely what information they need and how they will use the application to support their decision making. Information needs might also be highly variable and dynamic over time. As noted in Chapter 9, many of today's large systems development projects might also arise in conjunction with reengineering an organization's business processes. Redesign of the organization, its work processes and the development of a new computer system could go on in parallel. The ideal is to first redesign the process, but even then work processes are seldom defined at the level of detail required for a new business application.

Because defining the requirements for a system is such a difficult and a crucial task, analysts rely on a number of techniques and approaches to document and communicate the requirements. Examples of some of the techniques were described in detail in Chapter 9. Later in this chapter we also describe an evolutionary prototyping approach that can be used to help define systems requirements—for the user interface in particular.

The deliverable for the Requirements Definition step is a comprehensive *system requirements document* that contains detailed descriptions of the system inputs and outputs and the processes used to convert the input data into these outputs. It typically includes several hundred pages with formal diagrams and output layouts, such as shown in Chapter 9. This document also includes a revised cost /benefit analysis of the defined system and a revised plan for the remainder of the development project.

The system requirements document is the major deliverable of the Definition phase of the SDLC. Although IS analysts are typically responsible for drafting and revising the requirements specifications document, business managers are responsible for making sure that the written requirements are correct and complete. Thus, all relevant participants need to carefully read and critique this document for inaccuracies and omissions. Case studies have shown that when key user representatives do not give enough attention to this step, systems deficiencies are likely to be the result.

The deliverable from this step is typically subject to approval by business managers for whom the system is being built as well as by appropriate IS managers. Once formal approvals have been received, the system requirements are considered to be fixed. Any changes typically must go through a formal approval process, requiring similar sign-offs and new systems project estimates. All key participants therefore usually spend considerable time reviewing these documents for accuracy and completeness.

Construction Phase

System Design In this step, IS specialists design the physical system, based on the conceptual requirements document from the Definition phase. In system design, one decides what hardware and systems software to use to operate the system, designs the structure and content of the system's database(s), and defines the processing modules (programs) that will comprise the system and their interrelationships. A good design is critical because the technical quality of the system cannot be added later; it must be designed into the system from the beginning.

As shown in Figure 10.3, a quality system includes adequate controls to ensure that its data are accurate and that it provides accurate outputs. It provides an audit trail that allows one to trace transactions from their source and confirm that they were correctly handled. A quality system is highly reliable; when something goes wrong, the capability to recover and resume operation without lost data or excessive effort is planned for. It is also robust—insensitive to minor variations in its inputs and environment. It provides for interfaces with related systems so that common data can be passed back and forth. It is highly efficient, providing fast response, efficient input and output, efficient storage of data, and efficient use of computer resources. A quality system is also flexible and well documented for both users and IS specialists. It includes options for inputs and outputs compatible with its hardware and software environment and can be easily changed or maintained. Finally, it is user-friendly: It is easy to learn and easy to use, and it never makes the user feel stupid or abandoned.

To ensure that the new system design is accurate and complete, IS specialists often "walk through" the design first with their colleagues and then with knowledgeable business managers and end users, using graphical models such as those described in Chapter 9. This type of technique can help the users understand what new work procedures might need to be developed in order to implement the new system.

The major deliverable of the System Design step is a detailed design document that will be given to programmers and other technical staff. Models created by various development tools, such as diagrams of the system's physical structure, are also an important part of the deliverable. The documentation of the system will also include detailed descriptions of all databases and detailed specifications for each program in the system. Also included is a plan for the remaining steps in the Construction phase. Again, both

users and IS managers typically approve this document before the system is actually built.

System Building   Two activities are involved in building the system—producing the computer programs and developing or enhancing the databases and files to be used by the system. IS specialists perform these activities. The major involvements of users are to answer questions of omission and to help interpret requirements and design documents. The procurement of any new hardware and support software (including the database management system selection and new telecommunications network infrastructure) is also part of this step, which entails consultation with IS planners and operations personnel.

System Testing   Testing is a major effort that might require as much time as writing the code for the system. This step involves testing by IS specialists, followed by user testing. First, each module of code must be tested. Then the modules are assembled into subsystems and tested. Finally, the subsystems are combined and the entire system is integration tested. Problems might be detected at any level of testing, but correction of the problems becomes more difficult as more components are integrated, so experienced project managers build plenty of time into the project schedule to allow for problems during integration testing. The IS specialists are responsible for producing a high-quality system that also performs efficiently. Tests are done to assure requirements are met, performance is adequate even under high-load and stress situations, and security is as expected.

The system's users are also responsible for a critical type of testing—*user acceptance testing*. Its objective is to make sure that the system performs reliably and does what it is supposed to do in a user environment. This means that users must devise test data and procedures that completely test the system and that they must then carry out this extensive testing process. Plans for this part of the application testing should begin after the Definition phase. Case studies have shown that end-user participation in the testing phase can contribute to end-user commitment to the new system, as well as provide the basis for initial end-user training.

Both user and IS management must sign off on the system, accepting it for production use, before it can be installed. **Documentation** of the system is also a major mechanism of communication among the various members of the project team during the development process: Information systems are simply too complex to understand when they are described verbally.

Once the users sign off on this part of the testing, any further changes typically need to be budgeted outside of

Accurate	Reliable
Auditable	Robust
Changeable	Secure
Efficient	User friendly
Flexible	Well documented

Figure 10.3   Characteristics of High Quality Systems

the formal development project—that is, they become maintenance requests.

Implementation Phase

The initial success of the Implementation phase is highly dependent on business manager roles. Systems projects frequently involve major changes to the jobs of the people who will use the system, and these changes must be anticipated and planned for well before the actual Implementation phase begins. Ideas for user training as well as other "best practices" for change management will be discussed in a subsequent project management chapter (Chapter 12).

Installation Both IS specialists and users play critical roles in the Installation step, which includes building the files and databases and converting relevant data from one or more old systems to the new system. Depending on the extent to which the data already exist within the organization, some of the data conversion burden might also fall on users. In particular, data in older systems could be inaccurate and incomplete, requiring considerable user effort to "clean it up." The cleanup process, including the entering of revised data, can be a major effort for user departments. Sometimes the cleanup effort can be accomplished in advance. In other situations, however, the data cleanup is done as part of the new system implementation. This means users that have a lot of data verifications to do and conversion edits to resolve, sometimes without the benefit of additional staff, as they also learn the new system.

Another crucial installation activity is training the system's end users, as well as training other users affected by the new system. If this involves motivating people to make major changes to their behavior patterns, planning for this motivation process needs to start well before the Implementation phase. User participation in the earlier phases can also help the users prepare for this crucial step. Similarly, user training needs to be planned and carefully scheduled so that people are prepared to use the system when it is installed but not trained so far in advance that they forget what they learned. If user resistance to proposed changes is anticipated, this potential situation needs to be addressed during training or earlier.

Installing the hardware and software is the IS organization's responsibility. This can be a challenge when the new system involves technology that is new to the IS organization, especially if the technology is on the "bleeding edge." The major problems in system installation, however, usually lie in adapting the organization to the new system— changing how people do their work.

Converting to the new system might be a difficult process for the users because the new system must be inte-

grated into the organization's activities. The users must not only learn how to use the new system but also change the way they do their work. Even if the software is technically perfect, the system will likely be a failure if people do not want it to work or do not know how to use it. The **conversion** process therefore might require attitudinal changes. It is often a mistake to assume that people will change their behavior in the desired or expected way.

Several strategies for transitioning users from an old system to a new one are commonly used (see Figure 10.4). This is a critical choice for the effective implementation of the system, and this choice needs to be made well in advance of the Implementation phase by a decision-making process that includes both IS and business managers. Good management understanding of the options and trade-offs for the implementation strategies discussed next can reap both short-term and long-term implementation benefits.

In the *parallel* strategy, the organization continues to operate the old system in parallel with the new system until the new one is working sufficiently well to discontinue the old. This is a conservative conversion strategy because it allows the organization to continue using the old system if there are problems with the new one. However, it can also be a difficult strategy to manage because workers typically must operate both the old system and the new while also comparing the results of the two systems to make sure that the new system is working properly. When discrepancies are found, the source of the problem must be identified and corrections initiated. Parallel conversion can therefore be very stressful. A parallel strategy also might not even be feasible due to changes in hardware and software associated with the new system.

The *pilot* strategy is an attractive option when it is possible to introduce the new system in only one part of the

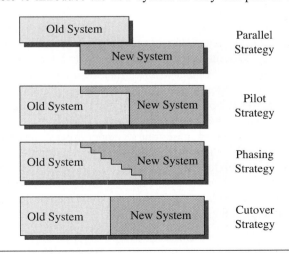

Figure 10.4 Implementation Strategies

organization. The objective is to solve as many implementation problems as possible before implementing the system in the rest of the organization. For example, in a company with many branch offices, it might be feasible to convert to the new system in only one branch office and gain experience solving data conversion and procedural problems before installing the system companywide. If major problems are encountered, companywide implementation can be delayed until they are solved. Pilot approaches are especially useful when there are potentially high technological or organizational risks associated with the systems project.

For a large, complex system, a *phased* conversion strategy might be the best approach. For example, with a large order processing and inventory control system, the firm might first convert order entry and simply enter customer orders and print them out on the company forms. Then it might convert the warehouse inventory control system to the computer. Finally, it might link the order entry system to the inventory system, produce shipping documents, and update the inventory records automatically. The downside to this approach is that it results in a lengthy implementation period. Extra development work to interface new and old system components is also typically required. On the other hand, a phasing strategy enables the firm to begin to achieve some benefits from the new system more rapidly than under other strategies. A phased strategy may relate to not only the implementation of a system but also prior steps in the SDLC, thus breaking a large project down into a series of smaller, coupled projects. Later in the chapter we will describe a formal process that takes this incremental approach called agile methods.

In the *cutover* (or cold turkey) strategy, the organization totally abandons the old system when it implements the new one. In some industries this can be done over holiday weekends in order to allow for a third day for returning to the old system in the event of a major failure. The cutover strategy has greater inherent risks, but it is attractive when it is very difficult to operate both the old and new systems simultaneously. Some also argue that the total "pain is the same" for a system implementation, whether implemented as a cutover or not, and that this strategy moves the organization to the new operating environment faster.

Combinations of these four strategies are also possible. For example, when implementing system modules via a phased conversion strategy, one still has the option of a parallel or cutover approach for converting each phase of the system. Similarly, a pilot strategy could include a parallel strategy at the pilot site.

Operations The second step of the Implementation phase is to operate the new application in "production mode." In the Operations step, the IS responsibility for the application is turned over to computer operations and technical support personnel. The project team is typically disbanded, although one or more members may be assigned to a support team.

New applications are typically not moved into production status unless adequate documentation has been provided to the computer operations staff. Implementing a large, complex system without documentation is highly risky. Documentation comes in at least two flavors: system documentation for IS specialists who operate and maintain the computer system and user documentation for those who use the system.

Successful operation of an application system requires people and computers to work together. If the hardware or software fails or people falter, system operation might be unsatisfactory. In a large, complex system, thousands of things can go wrong, and most companies operate many such systems simultaneously. It takes excellent management of computer operations to make sure that everything works well consistently and to contain and repair the damage when things do go wrong.

Maintenance The process of making changes to a system after it has been put into production mode (i.e., after the Operations stage of its life cycle) is referred to as **Maintenance**. The most obvious reason for maintenance is to correct errors in the software that were not discovered and corrected prior to its initial implementation. Usually a number of bugs in a system do elude the testing process, and for a large, complex system it might take many months, or even years, to discover them.

Maintenance could also be required to adapt the system to changes in the environment—the organization, other systems, new hardware and systems software, and government regulations. Another major cause for maintenance is the desire to enhance the system. After some experience with a new system, managers typically have a number of ideas on how to improve it, ranging from minor changes to entirely new modules. The small changes are usually treated as maintenance, but large-scale additions might need approval as a new development request.

Because both business and technology environments change rapidly, periodic changes to large systems are typical. In the past the total costs over a typical system's life cycle have been estimated to be about 80 percent on maintenance and only 20 percent on the original development of the application. As a result, many IS organizations have to allocate a significant number of their IS specialists to maintaining systems, rather than developing new ones. In the early 1990s maintenance resources were consuming as much as 75 percent of the total systems development resources in many large organizations (see Figure 10.5). The IS organization is responsible for making the required changes in the system throughout its life, as well as for eliminating any bugs that are identified prior to launching the new system in a production mode.

To make a change in a system, the maintenance programmer must first determine what program(s) must be changed and then what specific parts of each program need to be changed. The programmer must also understand the logic of the part of the code that is being changed. In other words, one must understand the system in some detail in order to change it.

Because systems can be very complex, system documentation is critical in providing the necessary level of understanding. This brings up another difficulty—the documentation must be changed when the system is changed or the documentation will provide misleading information about the system rather than assistance in understanding it. Most programmers are primarily interested in programming and are not rewarded for updating the documentation, so in many IS organizations the documentation of old systems becomes outdated and includes inaccuracies.

Furthermore, when changes are made in complex systems, a **ripple effect** might be encountered such that the change has an unanticipated impact on some other part of the system. For example, a change in a program can affect another program that uses the output from the first program. A change to a line of code can affect the results of another line of code in an entirely different part of that program. Another change must be made to correct those problems and that change might cause unanticipated problems elsewhere.

Another major problem with maintenance is that most IS professionals prefer to work on new systems using

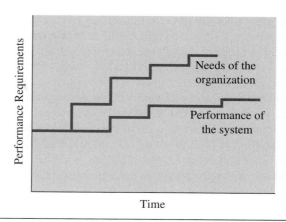

Figure 10.6   The Widening Gap Between the Organization's Needs and the System's Performance

new technologies rather than maintain old systems. Maintenance is therefore often perceived as low-status work, although it is critical to the business. Maintenance is often the first assignment of a newly hired programmer, and most organizations do not have mechanisms to ensure that really good maintenance people are rewarded well.

From the business manager's perspective, the major maintenance challenges are getting it done when it is needed and dealing with new system problems introduced as part of the maintenance process. A high proportion of operational problems are caused by errors introduced when making maintenance changes. Changes to production systems need to be carefully managed. Maintenance changes are typically made to a copy of the production system and then fully tested before they are implemented. An effective **release management** process for changing from an older to a newer version of the system is critical to avoid introducing large numbers of new problems when maintaining operational systems.

If adequate numbers of IS specialists are not available for systems maintenance projects, the manager often must suffer long delays before needed changes are made. Figure 10.6 graphically displays the widening gap that can occur between the organization's needs and the system's performance over time. Also, as a system gets older and is repeatedly patched, the probability of performance problems becomes even greater and reengineering or replacement solutions might be required.

The SDLC Project Team

Most application systems are developed by a temporary project team. When the system project is completed, the team is disbanded. Most project teams include representa-

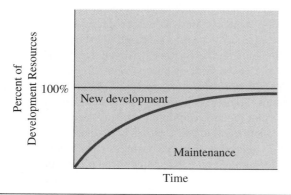

Figure 10.5   Percent of Development Resources Devoted to Maintenance

tives from both the IS organization and relevant business departments. If several organizational units or several levels of people within a unit will use the system, the project team might include representatives from only some of these different units, including higher-level managers and experienced end users who will work with the new application on a day-to-day basis. The selection of the project team is therefore critical to the success of a given systems project.

The project team also can vary in membership during the system's life cycle: A few members might be assigned full-time to the project for its entirety, while others might join the project team only temporarily as their specific knowledge or skills are required. In addition to an IS manager in a project leadership role, other IS personnel will be assigned as needed for the specific application, including systems analysts, application programmers, data administration specialists, telecommunications specialists, and others. It is also not unusual for IS specialists from outside the organization to also be used on systems projects. The IS specialists hired from a contract firm might bring specific IS knowledge to the project or might be needed due to the lack of internal resources available to assign to the project. These personnel could be so well integrated into the project that they are almost indistinguishable from the firm's internal IS personnel.

Historically, the **project manager** for a custom application was always an IS manager. Today, however, a business manager with information technology (IT) management knowledge might be asked to be the project manager, or a project might have two project managers: a business manager responsible for all user activities, especially for the implementation phase, and an IS manager responsible for the activities of all IS personnel. Some guidelines on whether the manager of a specific project should come from the IS organization, a business unit, or both, are provided in the box "Who Should Lead the IT Project?" The practitioner press suggests that assigning both IT and business managers to lead IT projects is a way to tighten the overall alignment between the IT organization and the business. According to a recent report, Cisco Systems, Inc., is giving IT and business leaders joint responsibility for every IT project (Hoffman, 2003).

Whether or not this role is shared, the project manager(s) is held responsible for the success of the project—for delivering a quality system, on time, and within budget. Managing a systems project typically involves coordinating the efforts of many persons from different organizational units, some of whom work for the project only on a part-time or temporary basis. The project manager must plan the project, determine the SDLC tasks that must be carried out and the skills required for each task, and estimate how long

WHO SHOULD LEAD THE IT PROJECT

If the project involves new and advanced technology,
   Then it should be managed by someone from the IS department.
If the project's impact would force critical changes in the business,
   Then it should be managed by someone from the business unit.
If the project is extremely large and complex,
   Then it should be managed by a specialist in project management.
If a project shares all of the above characteristics,
   Then senior management should consider multiple project leaders.

[Radding, 1992, based on Applegate]

each will take. The skills of the IS resources assigned to the project can be just as important as the number of resources assigned.

The system documentation produced at each step of the SDLC methodology provides a major tool for communication across team members and for assessing the quality of the development effort throughout the life of the system. Most organizations require that systems for which an SDLC process is appropriate include business management beyond those on the project team to provide formal sign-offs at each milestone of the project.

The **systems analyst** role is also a critical one. These IS professionals are trained to work with business managers and end users to determine the feasibility of the new system and to develop detailed system requirements for the custom application. During the Construction phase, they work with other IS specialists in designing the system and help to monitor the adherence to the system requirements. A good systems analyst has problem-solving skills, a knowledge of IT capabilities, and a strong understanding of the business activities involved in the application. The role of the systems analyst needs to be played well in order for *multiple* user perspectives to be taken into account. Sometimes the systems analyst also provides the important function of providing checks and balances for IS specialists eager to work with new, but unproven, technologies by ensuring that the business risks associated with new technologies are accounted for in project decisions.

Other key roles, including key business roles (sponsors, champions), are discussed in the chapter on IT project management (see Chapter 12).

Managing an SDLC Project

All systems projects are typically measured by three primary success criteria: (1) on-time delivery of an IS that (2) is of high quality and meets business requirements and (3) is within project budget. Additional project management techniques for achieving these goals will be considered in Chapter 12.

Particularly critical for the success of custom development projects using an SDLC methodology are three characteristics: manageable project size, accurate requirements definition, and executive sponsorship.

Manageable Project Size   Experience has convincingly shown that very large custom IT projects are very difficult to deliver within budget, which is one reason these types of projects are considered riskier when developing the business case. On the other hand, projects that take fewer technical people a year or less to complete are more likely to meet the success criteria for the project. This suggests that large systems should be broken down into relatively independent modules and built as a sequence of small, manageable projects, rather than as a single monster project.

Accurate Requirements Definition   The SDLC waterfall process is based on the premise that requirements for a new system can be defined in detail at the beginning of the process. The downside is that if the requirements are not well defined, there could be large cost overruns and the system could be unsatisfactory. Early studies have shown that about half of the total number of requirements errors (or omissions) is typically detected in the Requirements Definition step. Further, as shown in Figure 10.7, an error detected in the Implementation phase costs about 150 times as much to fix as an error detected in the Definition phase. Every effort must therefore be put into obtaining as accurate a requirements definition document as possible. This requires systems analysts skilled in eliciting requirements as well as in process and data representation techniques. It also requires *access to business users* knowledgeable about both current business operations and the envisioned system.

Executive Sponsorship   Although all large systems projects require business sponsorship, the intensity and length of time involved with the typical SDLC project means that executive-level sponsorship is critical to success. Key business managers need to understand the potential benefits of the proposed system and be dedicated to contributing resources to the systems project team, as well as the sustained usage of the new custom application. Because some business managers and end users will also be assigned to the project team, business sponsors need to be willing to dedicate these resources to the project team, sometimes on a full-time basis for the life of the project.

Although not every project team has end users as formal team members, end users frequently participate by

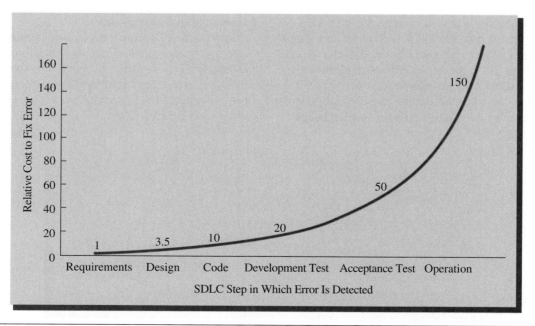

Figure 10.7   Costs of Error Correction by SDLC Step (Adapted from Boehm, 1976)

providing information about current work processes or procedures and evaluating screen designs from an end-user perspective. This, too, takes time away from normal business activities. User involvement in a systems project has in fact been associated with user acceptance and usage of the new system (Hartwick and Barki, 1994). However, business managers must be willing to dedicate these business resources throughout the project as needed, not just at the time of implementation.

Beath and Orlikowski (1994) have pointed out that systems development methodologies can differ in their assumptions about IS and user roles over the life of the project. For example, two methodologies that have been practiced more commonly outside of the United States (the ETHICS method and the Soft Systems Methodology) are specifically designed to facilitate more user involvement.

System implementation also requires managing organizational changes. Unless there is strong business sponsorship, there will not be a strong initiative to make changes to the business as part of the systems project effort. (See Chapter 12 for some guidelines for managing business change.)

SDLC Advantages and Disadvantages

The SDLC process is a highly structured approach to the development of large, complex applications for one or more business units. A summary of the advantages and disadvantages of the SDLC approach is provided in Figure 10.8 and is discussed in the following paragraphs.

In the hands of competent IS specialists and knowledgeable business managers, the SDLC process sets up formal steps with clear IS and user roles, formal checkpoints, and techniques for analysis, design, testing, and implementation. These tools and the rigorous discipline associated with an SDLC methodology help the systems project manager produce a well-engineered system on time and within budget.

The major disadvantages are inherent in the methodology. First, the project's success depends on the accurate and complete specification of detailed requirements at the beginning of the development process (Definition phase). There are several serious problems with this dependency. For example, many customized applications today are unique solutions. Because the project begins with an incomplete understanding of what this unique information system will do, it might be necessary to try several approaches before discovering the optimal one. New technologies might also be involved, and until the capabilities of these technologies are better understood, it might be hard to develop a firm set of requirements or to estimate the time to perform some project steps. With pressure to meet what were ill-conceived deadlines, shortcuts can be taken that affect project and system quality. Another problem with upfront detailed requirements specification is that today's business environment is changing so rapidly that there can be significant differences in business needs between the time the requirements are specified and the time the system is installed. Although the SDLC allows for backtracking to previous steps if necessary, this feedback loop is often ignored in practice. Rather, the output of one step is frozen; requested changes are recorded and handled only during maintenance.

Note that the SDLC process also requires a total system cost/benefit analysis based on the initial Definition phase. The justification process can be difficult to accomplish using traditional approaches such as return on investment (ROI) calculations when new technologies are involved or requirements are incomplete.

Second, the SDLC process is time-consuming. In the 1980s the typical systems project took several years, and the pace of business change accepted this. Today, with personnel turnover, threats from new competitors, and conditions changing at Internet speed, such long delivery times are not acceptable Third, because the SDLC process is both

Advantages
- Highly structured, systematic process
- Thorough requirements definition
- Clear milestones with business management sign-offs

Disadvantages
- Does not account well for evolving requirements during project
- Time-consuming (and costly) process
- Top-down commitment required

Figure 10.8 Advantages and Disadvantages of Traditional SDLC Approach

lengthy and costly, strong executive sponsorship is required. Without strong business sponsorship, business managers and users will be reluctant to dedicate their time to a systems project instead of working on other activities for which they are typically measured.

Next we look at an alternative approach to systems development that addresses some of these disadvantages.

PROTOTYPING METHODOLOGY

The SDLC methodology is based on the premise that business requirements for the system will be static over the life of the project. Thus, the system requirements must be completely and finally specified before the Construction phase is begun. Once the requirements have been agreed upon, changing them leads to significant project costs and potential schedule delays.

In the second half of the 1980s, the growing availability of fourth generation nonprocedural languages and relational database management systems began to offer an alternative approach. These tools make it possible to initially build a system (or part of a system) more quickly and then revise it after users have tried it out and provided their feedback to the developers. Thus, rather than first initially defining the system on paper and then building it, the initial system can be revised based upon the user's experience and understanding gained from the earlier versions.

This approach is very powerful because, although most people find it very difficult to specify in great detail exactly what they need from a new system, it is quite easy for them to point out what they do not like about computer screens that they can try out and use.

This general approach is most commonly known as **prototyping**. It is a type of **evolutionary development** process. The prototyping concept can also be applied to a process in which a real system is developed for the user to try out as well as for situations in which only a "toy" (nonoperational) prototype is developed. For example, prototype input and output screens are often developed for users to work with as part of the requirements definition or detailed design steps. Other examples of prototyping include a "first-of-a-series" prototype in which a completely operational prototype is used as a pilot and a "selected features" prototype in which only some essential features are included in the prototype and more features are added in later modules (Kendall and Kendall, 1999).

In the next section we first discuss prototyping as a *complete alternative* to the traditional SDLC methodology: its steps, project management considerations, and its overall advantages and disadvantages in comparison to an

SDLC methodology. This approach is particularly attractive when the requirements are hard to define, when a critical system is needed quickly, or when the system will be used infrequently (or even only once)—so that operating efficiency is not a major consideration. Note that these are all system characteristics that apply to some types of managerial support systems.

Prototyping as an alternative to an SDLC methodology is impractical for large, complex system efforts. However, when prototyping is used *within* an SDLC process to help determine requirements of a new custom application, it can increase the likelihood that the system project is a success. Prototyping provides a practical way for organizations to experiment with systems where the requirements are not totally clear and where the probability of success is unclear but the rewards for success appear to be very high.

The Prototyping Steps

Figure 10.9 presents the steps for an evolutionary methodology for developing a new, working system. The process begins with the identification of the *basic* requirements of the initial version of the system (step 1). The analyst/builder(s) and user(s) meet and agree on the inputs, the data processing, and the system outputs. These are not complete detailed requirements; rather, this is a starting point for the system. If several builders and users are involved, a joint application design (JAD) session may be used to determine requirements (see the description of JAD in the section entitled "Newer Approaches" later in this chapter).

In step 2 the system builders produce an initial prototype system according to the basic requirements agreed on in step 1. The system builders select the software tools, locate the necessary data and make these data accessible to the system, and construct the system using higher-level languages. This step should take from a few days to a few weeks, depending on the system's size and complexity. Note, this step works best when high-quality data already exist in some current databases and access to the existing data can be quickly acquired.

When the initial prototype is completed, it is given to the user with instructions similar to the following: "Here is the initial prototype. I know that it is not what you really need, but it's a beginning point. Try it and write down everything about it that you do not like or that needs to be added to the system. When you get a good list, we will make the changes you suggest."

Step 3 is the user's responsibility. He or she works with the system, notes the things that need to be improved, and then meets with the analyst/builder to discuss the changes.

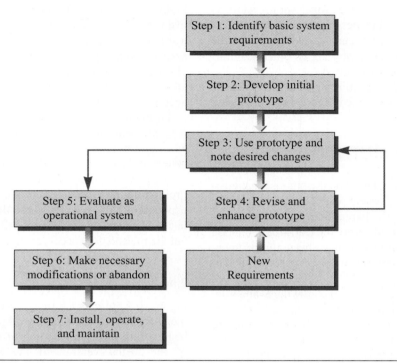

Figure 10.9   The Prototyping Life Cycle

In step 4 the builder modifies the system to incorporate the desired changes and any additional requirements that have surfaced from further analysis work. In order to keep everyone actively involved, speed is important. Sometimes the builder can sit down with the user and make the changes immediately; for larger systems, the changes might take several weeks. Steps 3 and 4 are repeated until the user is satisfied with the current version of the system. These are *iterative steps* within the prototyping process. When the user is satisfied that the prototype has been sufficiently developed, step 5 begins.

Step 5 involves evaluating the final prototype as an operational system. It should be noted, however, that not all prototypes become operational systems. Instead, it might be decided that the prototype system should simply be thrown away. Or, it could be decided that no additional costs should be devoted to the application because a system could not be developed that solved the original problem. That is, the prototyping process helped the organization decide that the system benefits do not outweigh the additional development or operational costs, or both, or that the expense of developing an operationally efficient system is too high. At this point it could also be decided that the system will be implemented but that the system needs to be built using different tools in order to achieve performance efficiencies.

If the prototype is to become an operational system, in step 6 the builder completes the Construction phase by making any changes necessary to improve operational efficiency and to interface the new application with the operational systems that provide it with data. This is also the step in which all necessary controls, backup and recovery procedures, and the necessary documentation need to be completed. If the prototype is only slightly modified, this step differs from the end of the Construction phase of an SDLC methodology in that most (or all) of the system has already been tested. Step 7 is similar to the Implementation phase of the SDLC: The new system is installed and moved into operational status. This is likely to be a much easier Implementation phase than under the traditional SDLC process because at least some of the intended users are already familiar with the system. Step 7 also includes maintenance. Because of the advanced tools that likely were used to build it, changes might be easier to make.

The Prototyping Project Team

Managing an evolutionary development process is clearly a joint IS and user management responsibility. Whether the project manager role is played by IS alone, business personnel alone, or both IS and business personnel, both groups need to jointly determine when to continue to request revisions to a prototype and when to end the iterative tryout-and-revise steps. The business manager needs to determine whether a satisfactory solution has been developed, and the IS manager needs to determine whether all relevant technology capabilities have been explored.

Because only basic requirements are being defined, the systems analyst and prototype builder (which might be one and the same) need to have some different skill sets than required for the SDLC process. Techniques to elicit abstract requirements and an emphasis on detailed documentation under the SDLC process are replaced by a heavy reliance on skills to build systems quickly using advanced tools. The initial prototypes are assessed more in terms of their look-and-feel from a user perspective and less in terms of technical quality from a systems performance perspective. Interactions between IS specialists and users center around creative development solutions and personal reactions to user-system interfaces and outputs.

A prototyping methodology also requires a dedicated business user role. Because there is continual user involvement with the various versions of the system, the designated business user needs to be able to be freed from other responsibilities to work with the application and to suggest changes over the life of the project. Sometimes more than one person plays this critical end-user role, which will require a structure and process for reaching agreement when suggested changes from different users are in conflict. The business user also needs to be patient and to understand that each iteration results in a system that may be "not quite right."

Managing a Prototyping Project

Managing new development projects with a methodology based on an iterative or evolutionary process requires a different mind-set than managing projects using an SDLC methodology based on a highly structured development approach. IS project managers and system builders need to approach the project differently: The objective is to respond quickly to user requests with a "good enough" prototype multiple times rather than to produce a tightly engineered actual system at the outset of the project. This might require some cultural changes within the IS organization. IS professionals who have built their careers on skills and attitudes required by an SDLC approach might need to acquire new skills for prototyping approaches.

IS managers also find managing prototyping projects more problematic because it is difficult to plan how long it will take, how many iterations will be required, or exactly when the system builders will be working on the system. Project managers need to have sufficient IS resources

available for system building in order to quickly respond to user requests for system changes within an agreed-upon timetable. Users who will be trying out each prototype version must be committed to the process and must be willing and able to devote the time and effort required to test each prototype version in a timely fashion. IS managers might rightfully feel that they have less control over the project's scope. One of the potential hazards of prototyping is that the iterative steps will go on and on and that the project costs will keep accumulating. Good working relationships between IS personnel and users responsible for the project are required to move to the prototype evaluation step (step 5) at the optimal time. Joint IS-user accountability would appear to be a key to success for these types of projects.

Depending on the software tools used to build the prototype, the operational efficiency of a prototype that is evaluated in step 5 might be significantly inferior to systems developed using the traditional SDLC methodology. Technical standards established by the organization also might not be rigorously followed, and the documentation might be inadequate. A substantial investment in computer-aided software engineering (CASE) tools (see the final section of this chapter entitled "Newer Approaches"), database management tools, and IS specialist training might be required before an IS organization can successfully implement the end prototype as the final system.

Prototyping Advantages and Disadvantages

The advantages of the evolutionary development methodology address the disadvantages inherent in the SDLC methodology. First, only *basic* system requirements are needed at the front end of the project. This means that systems can be built using an evolutionary approach that would be impossible to develop via an SDLC methodology. Furthermore, prototyping can be used to build systems that radically change how work is done, such as when work processes are being redesigned or a totally new type of managerial support tool has been envisioned but never seen. It is virtually impossible to define requirements for these kinds of systems at the beginning of a systems development process. Prototyping also allows firms to explore the use of newer technologies, because the expectations under an evolutionary methodology are that the builders will get it right over multiple iterations, rather than the first time.

Second, an initial working system is available for user testing much more quickly. In some cases business managers might actually use a working prototype to respond in some way to a current problem or at least to quickly learn that a given systems approach will not be the best solution. Although the complete process might take several months, users might have a working prototype in a few weeks or months that allows them to respond to a problem that exists now and is growing in importance; often a business manager cannot wait many months, let alone years, for a particular system to be built.

Third, because of the more interactive nature of the process, with hands-on use of working system models, strong top-down commitment based on a well-substantiated justification process might be less necessary at the outset of the project. Instead, the costs and benefits of the system can be derived after experience with an initial prototype.

Fourth, initial user acceptance of an application developed with an evolutionary process is likely to be higher than with an SDLC process. This is partly because the evolutionary process results in more active involvement and more joint control of the process on the part of the user.

The disadvantages of an evolutionary methodology are related to the evolutionary build process. The end prototype typically lacks some of the security and control features found in a system developed with an SDLC process. It also might not undergo the same type of rigorous testing. Documentation of the final version can be less complete because of the iterative nature of the process. Because the focus is on getting the requirements right as well as the look and feel of the user interface, other critical infrastructure features of the system may not be quite right. However, many of these flaws can be corrected in step 6 when the final prototype is converted to a system that can go into production. In some cases, it will be necessary for this final prototype to go through the same audits and controls testing of systems developed by the SDLC before it can be approved to go into production. Of special concern will be any dependencies the new system has with existing systems, usually for the exchange of data.

In the past the operational inefficiencies of fourth generation tools also contributed to the inadequacies of end prototypes. However, with recent advancements in hardware and software tools for developers and end users, these issues have become much less important than implementing a system that meets user needs. As described earlier, these potential deficiencies are assessed in step 5 and corrected in step 6 of the evolutionary methodology in Figure 10.9.

Another potential disadvantage is related to managing user expectations. Frequently, a prototype system appears to be so good that users are reluctant to wait for a well-functioning, well-documented operational system.

Prototyping Within an SDLC Process

As fourth generation tools have become commonplace, the incorporation of a few steps of an evolutionary process into an SDLC methodology has also become common. In the following paragraphs we describe two ways that prototyping is commonly incorporated into an SDLC process.

First, prototyping is used in the Definition phase to help users define the system requirements, particularly for the user interface (computer screens and navigation). As shown in Figure 10.10, the SDLC process still begins with a feasibility analysis. However, for the requirements definition step, IS specialists use screen-painting tools to produce initial versions of screens and reports that users can experiment with. This might be an example of a nonoperational prototype, in which the screen designs are not connected to a live database. After the requirements have been determined with the help of the prototype, the remainder of the steps in the SDLC process remain the same. However, the system builders can also make use of the screens during the design and build steps, and they may actually use computer code generated by the prototyping tools in the final system.

The second way prototyping is used is more complex, and includes a pilot implementation of a working prototype. This type of prototype is typically a first-of-a-series type of pilot system. Unlike the pilot rollout strategy discussed for the Implementation stage of the SDLC process, in which a complete system is first implemented in only a portion of the organization, here the intent is to use a scaled-down prototype in only a minimal number of locations within the organization in order to assess its feasibility in an operational setting. As shown in Figure 10.11, the Definition phase of the SDLC process is replaced by three steps in a Prototyping/Piloting phase. After basic requirements are determined (step 1), a working prototype is developed (step 2). The initial prototype is sufficiently developed to demonstrate a technical solution using hardware and software components that typically had not been used before in the organization. In step 3 the prototype is

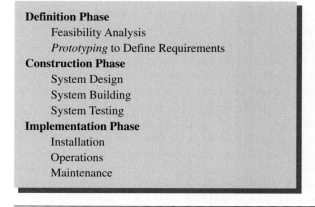

Definition Phase
    Feasibility Analysis
    Prototyping to Define Requirements
Construction Phase
    System Design
    System Building
    System Testing
Implementation Phase
    Installation
    Operations
    Maintenance

Figure 10.10 SDLC with Prototyping to Define Requirements

Prototyping/Piloting Phase
   Determine Basic Requirements
   Prototype the System
   Pilot the Prototype
SDLC Construction Phase
   System Design Modifications
   System Building
   System Testing
SDLC Implementation Phase
   Installation
   Operations
   Maintenance

Figure 10.11 Prototyping/Piloting Phase Replaces SDLC Definition Phase

extended to become a working prototype that can be piloted with a subset of the targeted users.

This prototyping/piloting approach within an SDLC is especially useful for large, risky projects that involve technological risks or organizational risks, or both. For example, one major objective might be to demonstrate the basic capabilities or provide a proof-of-concept test of a technical solution. A second major objective might be to get executive sponsors to buy in to the proposed system. By working with a prototype with live data, business managers can evaluate the potential benefits (and risks) of the new application in an operational setting. The expectation is that this is only a prototype, developed at minimal cost, which will be modified before the actual system is built.

For example, changes in functionality based on using the prototype in a pilot setting, as well as changes in the technology, are anticipated before the final system will be implemented at all locations. The prototype is used to help "sell" the system to key users as well as those who have budgeting authority. If the pilot is successful, what was learned from using the working prototype can now be incorporated into the design that will be used for the building of the actual system. The learning from the pilot step also helps users prepare for the organizational changes needed to implement the full system. The remaining steps match the typical SDLC process.

NEWER APPROACHES

The demands for speedier development of new application systems have steadily increased over the past decade. In this section we briefly discuss two approaches that have

been proven to result in faster development of high-quality customized applications of a certain size: a RAD methodology and "agile" software development approaches.

Rapid Application Development (RAD)

Rapid application development (RAD) is a hybrid methodology that combines aspects of the SDLC methodology and prototyping. Similar to the SDLC methodology, several RAD variants exist within organizations and consultancies. The goal is to produce a system in less than a year. Some organizations adopting RAD approaches require that all projects fit within a short timebox—such as six months (Clark et al., 1997). RAD is usually applied, much like prototyping, in isolation from other systems, so interdependencies between systems are not considered.

The RAD life cycle developed by guru James Martin includes four steps, with iterations between and parallel conduct among steps 2 and 3, similar to a prototyping methodology (see Figure 10.12). The Requirements Planning step incorporates elements of the traditional IT project proposal initiation and steps from the SDLC Definition phases. For the User Design step, **Joint application design (JAD)** sessions and software automation (CASE) tools are used to accomplish the work more quickly.

A JAD session could last several hours or could be held over several consecutive days. It is often held at a location removed from the participants' usual workplace so that the task can be concentrated on without interruption. A remote location also helps set up a forum for user representatives to work through areas of disagreement; achieving shared

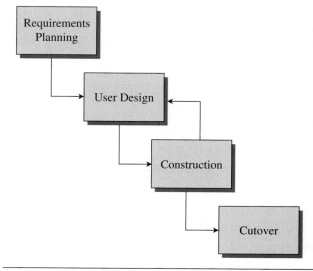

Figure 10.12 Four-Step RAD Life Cycle

understanding is especially important when cross-functional systems are being developed. The JAD session is led by a facilitator who is not only skilled in systems analysis and design techniques but is also skilled in managing group interactions; a person outside the organization is sometimes used in this facilitator role in order to have a neutral third party who can help resolve conflicts and keep the group focused on the JAD session outcomes.

As shown in Figure 10.13, **computer-aided software engineering (CASE)** tools include *front-end* analysis tools such as diagramming tools, analysis tools, and computer display and report generator tools to support requirements definition and system designs; *back-end* tools for generating code (in one or more computer languages) from diagrams and other design documents; and *central repositories* for the processing logic, data structures, other specifications, and project management documents for a software system. Full-cycle CASE systems, also called **Integrated-CASE (I-CASE)** tools, combine front-end and back-end functions to produce a working system.

Returning to Figure 10.12, in the Construction phase computer code is generated using the CASE tool. The business team members help validate screens and other design features, and an iterative approach is then used to make design changes and generate new code for validation. A cutover approach is used to convert the organization to the new system. By using this implementation approach, system testing must be undertaken at virtually the same time that user training and other organizational preparations are being accomplished.

The structured checkpoints and system reviews that are hallmarks of an SDLC approach are also used in a RAD approach. However, unlike the traditional SDLC approach, when users sign off on the CASE-based design document, the expectation is that they will also be involved in the Construction step, during which additional design changes can be made as necessary. Besides intensive usability testing with end-user involvement, rigorous quality assurance procedures are also built into the RAD methodology.

RAD is a methodology that works well in a business environment characterized by rapid change. The smaller design teams and shorter development times associated with RAD also can lead to considerably lower total development costs. For example, the U.S. Navy has reported system development savings of up to 50 percent and annual maintenance savings of 20 percent (Valacich et al., 2006). On the other hand, increased speed can sometimes also have its downside. For example, noncritical functionality or quality standards might be sacrificed, such as consistent user interfaces across screens and data element naming standards.

Figure 10.14 summarizes some of the advantages and disadvantages of RAD. Like prototyping, a RAD methodology is highly dependent on involvement by key users. If these key users are not freed up to work on the RAD project, the custom application might still be produced quickly, but is less likely to be an optimal software solution for the business.

Agile Methodologies

No one systems development methodology works in every circumstance better than all other methodologies. This is why structured, rapid, and other methodologies all have

- *Diagramming tools:* support graphic representations for process, data, and control structure diagrams
- *Computer display and report generators:* used to prototype user interface for input (screen displays, forms) and reports as part of requirements definition
- *Analysis tools:* automatic checkers for missing, inconsistent, or incorrect specifications in diagrams, forms, and reports
- *Central repository:* integrated storage of system specs, diagrams, reports, and project management documents
- *Documentation generators:* produce technical and user documentation in standard formats
- *Code generators:* automatic generation of program and database definition code from diagrams, forms, reports, and other design documents

Figure 10.13 Types of CASE Tools (Adapted from Valacich, George, and Hoffer, 2006)

Advantages
- Dramatic savings in development time
- Focuses on essential system requirements
- Ability to rapidly change system design at user request

Disadvantages
- Quality may be sacrificed for speed
- Time-consuming commitments for key user personnel
- Possible shortcuts on internal standards and module reusability

Figure 10.14   RAD Advantages and Disadvantages

been developed. Systems development is difficult for a variety of reasons, including:

- Requirements are about dealing with business problems not software features, yet how we apply different methods often tries to separate these two aspects too much

- The business (and developers, too) may not know what is possible with IT, so they may limit their requirements to what they think is possible or to current business rules rather than what could be done with "out of the box" thinking

- Business conditions are constantly changing, so freezing requirements always means being out of step once the system is implemented (by the way, there is a similar truth with textbooks!)

- There is often not a consensus about what is required (due to different situations or cultures in different user groups), so agreements may not be able to be reached until well into a project.

- Personnel turnover during a project, from both the user community and the development team, means new ideas, new skills, and relearning.

Different methodologies attempt to deal with these issues in different ways.

In recent years a more "agile" software development discipline has emerged as an alternative methodology for smaller projects (e.g., project teams not larger than 20) in order to address some of these issues. The objective is to deliver software with very low defect rates, based on a set of four key values:

- Simplicity
- Communication
- Feedback
- Courage

A project is not a full application, but rather one module or working piece of a full application.

A "whole team" approach is taken in which business representatives (customers) and technical team members (programmers) work in a co-located workspace (sometimes called a bullpen) on a daily basis. Daily, face-to-face conversations among these core team members, rather than documentation and interviews with subject matter experts, dominate requirements determination. Team members use processes utilizing adaptation rather than planning. Working versions of software, not artifacts, are measures of progress, and these working components or increments (pieces of the whole) are produced very frequently. Proponents suggest that the more engineering approach of traditional systems development methods fails because it is not designed to handle the changing requirements (due to business changes or better understanding of needs) in most software development activities. Late changes to requirements are welcomed by agile methods. Learning occurs through repletion and readdressing requirements in increments.

Agile methods are similar to other iterative methods, such as prototyping and RAD, but differ in that cycles for delivery of new code products are much shorter (in fact, timeboxed to be weeks not months) and the very close collaboration of team members. Figure 10.15 characterizes an agile approach, with frequent software releases and rapid

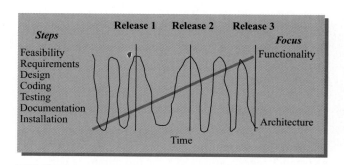

Figure 10.15   Agile Systems Development Process

cycling over the systems development phases of definition, construction, and implementation and their various steps. Some see this chart as the route of a yo-yo over time. Each release is a refactoring and enhancement of the accumulation of prior releases; prior work is not scrapped. The software gets better with each release. Early releases focus more on architecture issues (the glue that will hold the pieces together) whereas later releases drill deep into specific functionalities. The application is composed of the set of all releases, and can be under continuous change. There is a need for an initial step to establish an overall architecture for the application system so that each piece can be developed and all pieces will fit together (remember Figure 9.1).

Agile methods are a radical change in systems development and can be resisted by systems development staff (Wailgum, 2007). Some see agile methods too dominated by users who do not understand IT or too dependent on the scarce resource of expert developers to be used for many systems development projects. Individuals on the team may be called "purple people," because they are generalists, neither business or IT specialists (an odd reference to combining "red" and "blue" to get purple). Others feel that the lack of deep up-front design compromises a sound architecture needed for robust and easy to maintain organizational systems. Because testing occurs throughout the development cycle, rather than at fixed points controlled by quality assurance staff, some believe testing is too ad hoc and myopic. Some believe the lack or limited conduct of planning and documentation is a hazard. For these and other reasons, agile methods are still emerging as accepted approaches to systems development. Successful projects using agile methods are making organizations pay more attention to the potential of agile methodologies.

Fowler (2003) recommends that agile methodologies are best suited for situations with dynamic requirements, dedicated and motivated team members, customers willing to be members of the core team, and the core team can be kept relatively small (20 or fewer members).

Agile is a general term that encompasses various specific methods and techniques. Several of the more widely used agile methods and techniques are Crystal Clear, Adaptive Software Development, Scrum, Feature Driven Development, and eXtreme Programming. The remainder of this section presents overviews of several of these methods and techniques as a way to illustrate what might happen on a project using the agile approach and to illustrate some of the important principles that transcend all agile methods.

eXtreme Programming   In one agile approach, called **eXtreme Programming (XP)**, the programmers write production code in pairs. By using simple designs (definition and construction are fused together) and frequent testing, the team produces small, fully integrated releases that pass all the customers' acceptance tests in a very short time period (e.g., every two weeks). The cycle of analyze, design, code, and test are integrally linked and iterated until a working solution is developed. Programming teams test their own code (which is a radical change from traditional testing methodologies). Both members of the programming pair do coding and testing in parallel, so duties are not divided by one person coding and the other testing. It is claimed that such a process produces higher-quality code faster (for those situations outlined previously). The programming pairs then might disband to form new pairs and thus quickly share their specialized knowledge and completed code. Another hallmark of the XP approach is the obsession with feedback and testing. As team-tested programs are released to a collective repository, any pair of programmers can improve any of the collective code at any time, following the common coding standards adopted by all teams.

XP focuses on the immediate problem, not anticipating future requirements. This and other factors keep the design simple, a major goal of this technique. Three traits characterize simple design:

- The system must communicate everything you want to communicate (i.e., be complete and self-documenting)
- The system must contain no duplicate code (so reusing code modules is essential, hence simplicity and standards are key for reusability)
- The system should have the fewest number of components as possible

Scrum   Yes, for you rugby fans, the origins of the **Scrum** agile method are in this team sport, in which well-orchestrated movement between team members is important. A Scrum Master (SM) organizes the Scrum team work, serves as the team's liaison with other teams and with clients, and monitors team performance. Scrum emphasizes independent project teams, coordination and communication between and within teams, iterative and continuous monitoring of work, and highly efficient work methods. A major vehicle that Scrum uses for this purpose is meetings (Cho et al., 2006):

- *Daily Scrum meeting*   A very short (5 to 15 minutes) "stand up" session for each team in which developers on that team report on accomplishments since the last meeting, what is to be done before the next meeting, and issues that might impede progress.

- *Scrum of Scrum meeting* The team SMs gather for short ("stand up") daily meetings and monthly for longer meetings to review coordination between teams and interteam issues.

- *Sprint planning meeting* Each team meets monthly (for up to a day in length) to allocate work units in the project backlog to team members. Each work unit is prioritized, and based on these priorities, interdependences, and estimated work times, tasks are scheduled and assigned so they can be completed over the next month.

- *Sprint review meeting* This team meeting reviews (in a meeting that might last up to a day) accomplishments of the monthly work plan, identifies areas for improvement, and highlights what has gone well. In some instance this meeting becomes a "products fair" to which members from other teams, clients, and IT support staff (e.g., from quality assurance and data administration) are invited to see intermediate results.

Additional meetings or presentations are required to share project results with clients.

These frequent and varied meetings facilitate communication and sharing of ideas, and provide peer pressure to show real progress. Quality assurance (QA) is built into each team by including a QA staff member on each team. The role of SM is key and must be carefully staffed. Work products are considered the output of the team. Hence, the team nature of Scrum tends to foster team ownership and sharing of ideas and solutions to problems among team members.

MANAGING SOFTWARE PROJECTS USING OUTSOURCED STAFF

Although hiring on-site contractors to help with custom software projects has been a widespread practice for decades, today there is a renewed focus on keeping down the costs of software development by outsourcing portions of the project to off-site workers, especially offshore workers in a different labor market. Other advantages of using external resources to assist or substitute for internal staff for custom development work are to make use of technical expertise not available in-house (some contractors specialize in certain technologies or application areas), to hire capacity above a baseline for the amount of development work the organization can justify at any given time, to free up internal staff to work on more strategic or proprietary projects that must be kept in-house, and to be able to complete the project more

quickly (due to when internal staff is available or expertise). Some organizations have actually outsourced their whole systems development group; this usually occurs when the organization feels its mission does not include managing information systems development. Some small organizations may feel they cannot afford to retain quality IT development staff.

Off-site outsourcing can involve contracting with companies within the same country or region ("onshore") or not ("offshore"). Offshore outsourcing is often driven by price because labor costs have traditionally been 40 to 60 percent less by offshoring work to systems development groups in India, Eastern Europe, or Asia. As will be discussed in more detail in Chapter 15, some significant risks of offshore outsourcing are loss of some control (or at least control is more difficult due to time zone differences), language and cultural barriers, and threats of piracy of intellectual property. According to Poria (2003), the offshore alternative is likely a very favorable option when the following conditions exist:

- The system requirements can be well-defined and will remain relatively stable over the project.

- Time is of the essence and 24/7 availability of resources to work on the project is advantageous.

- The cost of the project (or program) is an important consideration.

Research by Holmström et al. (2006) suggests that the agile methods of Scrum and eXtreme Programming are useful in overcoming some of the risks of offshore software development projects. These methods, with their explicit communication and coordination mechanisms, can reduce the negative effects of distance between team members. Guidelines for effectively managing the day-to-day interactions with an offsite outsourcer have also been developed. For example, some of the key guidelines published by a Sourcing Interests Group (and summarized in McNurlin and Sprague, 2003) and by Rottman and Lacity (2004) are as follows:

Manage expectations, not staff The outsourcer's staff is not under the direct control of the client company nor are their rewards tied to those of the client, so a facilitative mode of working is best in which the focus is on the outcomes.

Take explicit actions to integrate the offsite workers Managing projects across workgroups requires more formality, such as explicit, agreed-upon outcomes and measures. In-house staff might even benefit from moving to the outsourcer's firm in order to work side-by-side with them and learn how they work together internally.

Communicate frequently Managers responsible for the relationship with the outsourcers need to keep the lines of communication open.

Abandoning informal ways may result in increased rigor Because of their business model, a service provider might have more disciplined processes than the client organization, which can lead to higher quality solutions.

Create a centralized project management office A PMO is a center of excellence for managing projects; a specialized unit of the PMO can concentrate on managing offshore projects, which can become very inefficient due to risks mentioned earlier.

Begin with pilot projects Small pilot projects will test working relationships, build trust, and develop experience for the more important projects later.

Hire offshore legal expertise Specialized legal consultants can assist in writing contracts to manage tax implications, protect intellectual property, address differences in legal systems and regulations, handle visa issues for workers who have to travel between your organization and the contractor, define precise deliverables and terms (often called service level agreements), and assist in resolving disputes.

Use secure and redundant communication links Such communication links help to insure sensitive documentation that must be shared between your organization and the contractors arrive and are protected from theft.

SUMMARY

The choice among the traditional systems development life cycle (SDLC), prototyping, RAD, and the newer "agile" methodologies for developing a customized application is essentially an IS management decision. Within firms that have their own capable IS staffs, the methodology choice might be based on factors such as the degree to which system requirements can be easily determined, and the application's functionality, size, and complexity. Custom application development using the multistep SDLC methodology, with well-defined sign-offs, is now the traditional way to develop new computer systems and to maintain them; it is still the preferred approach when the system is large, complex, and serves multiple organizational units. A prototyping methodology is a more effective approach for small, simple projects. A prototyping approach is also used within an SDLC methodology to help users and IS professionals begin with a set of basic requirements and then develop a fuller set of functional requirements. A combination prototyping/piloting approach within an SDLC methodology is

especially useful when the systems project is characterized by significant technological risks or organizational risks, or both, that can be tested out early in the project using a prototype.

Whether the traditional SDLC, prototyping, or some combination of the two is used, it is the responsibility of both business managers and IS specialists to ensure that the system that is installed meets the needs of the business at the time of installation. IS specialists typically hold primary responsibility for most system analysis and all system building steps. However, the systems project may be managed by an IS manager, a business manager, or both.

Rapid application development (RAD) methodologies have become more important as businesses seek to deliver high-quality applications within shorter time frames. A RAD methodology combines the iterative development benefits of prototyping with the quality controls of the SDLC; this approach also typically relies on JAD sessions and software automation (CASE) tools to generate code. In recent years there has also been a movement to develop more "agile" development methods based on the principles of simplicity and feedback, with relatively small project teams. One of the characteristics of an agile method called eXtreme Programming is an obsession with testing code early and often, in order to have zero defects. Another method called Scrum utilizes many work teams and frequent meetings to coordinate and share work experiences.

The chapter ends with a discussion of some guidelines for managing the interactions between project team members when there are off-site (including offshore) contract workers on a project.

REVIEW QUESTIONS

1. Briefly describe the typical steps in the typical systems development life cycle (SDLC) as presented in this chapter.
2. Describe the key activities performed by IS professionals in each step of the SDLC.
3. Select three characteristics of a high-quality application system, as shown in Figure 10.3, and provide a rationale for why each is important.
4. Describe the importance of documentation under an SDLC methodology.
5. Describe a distinct advantage of each of the four strategies for implementing a new system, as shown in Figure 10.4.
6. Briefly describe the elements of a business case for a new information systems project under the SDLC methodology.

7. Why is an accurate and complete requirements definition especially critical when using the SDLC "waterfall" approach?

8. Briefly describe the steps of a pure prototyping methodology as an alternative to an SDLC approach.

9. Which disadvantages of an SDLC methodology are addressed by a prototyping approach?

10. Describe two ways that a prototyping approach can be used within the Definition phase of a traditional SDLC methodology.

11. Why are JAD techniques a key characteristic of RAD methodologies?

12. Describe how a RAD methodology builds on the strengths of both an SDLC methodology and prototyping.

13. Why does the use of contractors increase the complexity of an IT project?

14. Describe the underlying principles of agile systems development methodologies.

DISCUSSION QUESTIONS

1. Discuss why you think the SDLC methodology for developing application systems was widely adopted in U.S.-based organizations by the early 1990s.

2. IS department managers often believe that they are responsible for making sure the requirements of the system are properly defined, but in this chapter the business manager's responsibility for defining requirements is emphasized. How can you reconcile these two points of view?

3. There have been many failures in the development of application systems using the traditional SDLC. Discuss some characteristics of the methodology that could contribute to the high failure rate under certain situations.

4. Compare the role of the systems analyst in the development of an application system using the SDLC and using a prototyping approach.

5. Some IS specialists contend that end prototypes are usually poor technical solutions. Comment on why this perception might (or might not) be valid.

6. Discuss why an application might be built using prototyping as part of the SDLC methodology, rather than by a pure prototyping methodology alone.

7. Discuss the role of the project manager in the in-house development of a customized application and in what situations both IS and business managers might serve as co-leaders of a project.

8. It has been said that "a system without good documentation is worthless." Provide support for this statement. Then comment on how today's advanced tools might alleviate the documentation burden.

9. Discuss how some modern tools (such as CASE), techniques (such as JAD), and new methodologies (such as eXtreme Programming) help IS organizations overcome the disadvantages of the traditional SDLC methodology.

10. Discuss the role of testing in each of the SDLC, RAD, and eXtreme Programming methodologies.

11. Discuss and contrast the role of application clients in the SDLC, RAD, and agile methodologies.

12. Discuss some factors that would encourage an organization to outsource some or all of its information systems development work.

13. Discuss the unique issues that arise with offshore outsourcing of information systems development.

REFERENCES

Beath, Cynthia M., and Wanda J. Orlikowski. 1994. "The contradictory structure of systems development methodologies: Deconstructing the IS-user relationship in information engineering." *Information Systems Research* 5 (December): 350–377.

Boehm, Barry. 1976. "Software engineering." *IEEE Transactions on Computers* C-25 (December): 1226–1241.

Boehm, Barry. 1981. *Software Engineering Economics*. Upper Saddle River, NJ: Pearson Prentice Hall.

Bollinger, Terry B., and Clement McGowan. 1991. "A critical look at software capability evaluations." *IEEE Software* (July 1): 25–46.

Cho, Juyun, YongSeog Kim, and David Olsen. 2006. "A case study on the applicability and effectiveness of Scrum software development in mission-critical and large-scale projects." In Proceedings of 12th Americas Conference on Information System (AMCIS-06), Acapulco, Mexico, 2006.

Clark, Charles E., Nancy C. Cavanaugh, Carol V. Brown, and V. Sambamurthy. 1997. "Building change-readiness capabilities in the IS organization: Insights from the Bell Atlantic experience." *MIS Quarterly* 21 (December): 425–455.

Colter, Mel A. 1984. "A comparative examination of systems analysis techniques." *MIS Quarterly* 8 (March): 51–66.

Davis, Gordon B. 1982. "Strategies for information requirements determination." *IBM Systems Journal* 21: 4–30.

DeMarco, Tom. 1982. *Controlling Software Projects*. New York: Yourdon Press, Inc.

Gane, Chris, and Trish Sarson. 1979. *Structured Systems Analysis: Tools and Techniques*. Upper Saddle River, NJ: Pearson Prentice Hall.

Hartwick, Jon, and Henri Barki. 1994. "Measuring user participation, user involvement, and user attitude." *MIS Quarterly* 18 (March): 59–79.

Hoffman, Thomas. 2003. "Corporate execs try new ways to align IT with business units." *Computerworld* (October 27): 13.

Holmström, Helena, Brian Fitzgerald, Pär J. Ågerfalk, and Eoin O. Conchúir. 2006. "Agile practices reduce distance in global software development." *Information Systems Management* 23, 3 (Summer): 7–18.

Kannan, Nari. 2007. "Agile Outsourcing: Requirements Gathering and Agile Methodologies." SourcingMag.com, www.sourcingmag.com/content/c061002a.asp

Keen, Peter G. W. 1991. "Managing the economics of information capital." *Shaping the Future: Business Design Through Information Technology*. Boston: Harvard Business School Press.

Kendall, Kenneth E., and Julie E. Kendall. 1999. *Systems Analysis and Design*. 4th ed. Upper Saddle River, NJ: Pearson Prentice Hall.

Lindstrom, Lowell, and Ron Jeffries. 2003. "Extreme Programming and Agile Software Development Methodologies." in Carol V. Brown and Heikki Topi (eds.), *IS Management Handbook*, 8th ed. New York: Auerbach.

McNurlin, Barbara C., and Ralph H. Sprague, Jr. 2004. *Information Systems Management in Practice*, 6th ed. Upper Saddle River, NJ: Pearson Prentice Hall.

Mueller, John Paul. 2007. "ABC: An Introduction to Agile Programming." *CIO*, www.cio.com/article/100501 (March 28).

Parker, Marilyn M., and Robert J. Benson. 1987. "Information economics: An introduction." *Datamation* 33 (December 1): 86–96.

Poria, Bharat C. 2004. "Strategic Outsourcing." *CIO Wisdom*. Upper Saddle River, NJ: Pearson Prentice Hall.

Radding, Alan. 1992. "When non-IS managers take control." *Datamation* 38 (July 1): 55–58.

Robey, Daniel. 1987. "Implementation and the organizational impacts of information systems." *Interfaces* 17 (May–June): 72–84.

Rottman, Joseph W. and Mary C. Lacity. 2004. "Twenty Practices for Offshore Outsourcing." *MIS Quarterly Executive* (September): 117–130.

Valacich, Joseph S., Joey F. George, and Jeffrey A. Hoffer. 2006. *Essentials of Systems Analysis and Design*, 3rd ed. Upper Saddle River, NJ: Pearson Prentice Hall.

Wailgum, Thomas. 2007. "From here to agility." *CIO: Business Technology Leadership* (June 1): 43–50.

CHAPTER 11
METHODOLOGIES
FOR PURCHASED
SOFTWARE PACKAGES

IN MOST LARGE COMPANIES TODAY, APPLICATION SOFTWARE IS BOTH custom developed by in-house information systems (IS) staff and procured from an outside source. In fact, the trend for more than a decade has been for midsized and larger organizations to purchase (or lease, often from a service provider) application packages rather than custom develop their own solutions with in-house IS personnel, whenever it is feasible and cost-beneficial to do so. Capital expenditures for implementing purchased or leased software packages are therefore a large part of the total IS budget. Of course, many small businesses have no, or very few, IS professionals, so they essentially procure all their software from outside sources. In some cases, the software is not even run on in-house hardware but rather accessed from an external service using telecommunications, often the Internet. An often cited example of this kind of application service provider (ASP)—or "software as a service" (SaaS)—is Salesforce.com.

Firms in the software industry have grown across the globe over the past decades, so that today companies can choose from thousands of products that can be purchased or leased as "off-the-shelf" packaged software to be deployed in-house or accessed as an external service. The software industry firms that survive attract new and seasoned IS professionals to be their employees so that they can quickly develop information technology (IT) solutions to respond to new marketplace needs.

Firms that purchase or lease a software package also typically need to purchase services from the software vendor to help install and maintain the software for their business. Besides working with the software vendor or software service provider, the purchasing firm's own system and business analysts work on project teams with business managers to purchase and install new systems. Some team members also typically are part of an ongoing support team for the business users after a new purchased or leased system has been deployed.

Packaged software applications are often built today with standard Windows or Web browser interfaces for the end user. These types of interfaces are also available for large client/server systems (such as the enterprise resource planning [ERP] and customer relationship management [CRM] packages introduced in Chapter 6). Some of these enterprise-level systems have industry-specific versions of their packages to facilitate their implementation. Other software vendors develop packages for a specific industry only, such as sales and inventory management systems for retailers, commercial loan systems for banks, claim-processing systems for insurance companies or health care providers. Yet additional software vendors provide software tools, such as for statistical analysis and forecasting, report writing, business analytics, and graphical design. Wherever there is a sizable market for a standard package, a software company is likely to be developing applications to sell to that market.

For firms that have their own IS department resources, a make-or-buy analysis is undertaken in order to decide whether to procure a product or service from an outside source or to produce the software or perform the service using internal IS resources. In this chapter, therefore, we begin by better understanding the overall business and IT benefits that an organization needs to consider when it has a choice between purchasing a software application and developing a customized application. Next we will describe in detail the process steps for selecting, preparing for, and implementing a software application package, as well as some of the project team roles and keys to success.

THE MAKE-OR-BUY DECISION

The choice between building a custom application and purchasing (or leasing) a software package—a **make-or-buy decision**—should be made jointly by the business managers who need the software and the IS professionals who have the knowledge to assess the technical benefits and risks. For organizations with their own skilled IS personnel, the two most obvious advantages of packaged software are (1) cost savings and (2) faster speed of implementation. A software package usually costs less than a custom solution because the software vendor will be selling the package to many organizations. That is, the companies that acquire the software will be sharing the development and upgrade costs of the package. A software package also typically can be implemented sooner than a custom application because it already exists; in today's fast-changing business environments, this can be a very important advantage. This can be important when IT and business staff lack sufficient experience with the application, thus making a development project especially risky. A package may be preferred to support core, generic business functions on which your organization does not compete with other organizations that could also acquire the same technology. Of course, the real advantage comes from intelligently using the package in ways competitors cannot.

However, there also are some downsides. One major downside of buying an application solution is that packaged software seldom exactly fits a company's needs. For the organization that is acquiring a package to replace an older, custom-developed system, this type of change can have several important ramifications for the business. Most commonly, it means that business users might be asked to "give up" features of the older custom software that the package does not support. The package may be

able to be customized to add distinctive features, but customization can make upgrading the package much more difficult as new releases occur, and may be limited by what the software license allows for the package to be supportable by the vendor. Another choice is for the organization to change its processes to match those supported by the software. This could be desirable, albeit painful, if organizational processes are inefficient or not current best practices. This downside alone means that organizations should have a very good process in place that will help them make the best trade-off decisions about software features and capabilities for the organization. As described next, this requires a methodology that will take into account knowledge of the package's capabilities as well as informed business and technical judgments about how well the package will meet the organization's needs.

Other issues that play a role in making the make-or-buy decision are the financial viability of the major or desired vendors, whether the software fits with the chosen system software of the organization, whether the vendor has a vision for enhancement of the package that is compatible with the future (not just current) needs of your organization, the reliability of the vendor in delivering new releases on time, and the total cost of ownership (that is, considering not just the purchase cost but also longer term costs to maintain and upgrade the software—an especially critical factor to consider with open-source packages, which we discuss later in the chapter).

At the end of this chapter we also briefly discuss the procurement option that includes contracting with a vendor to "host" (run) one or more applications (such as Salesforce.com) for a business firm under a leasing contract (see the section of this chapter entitled "New Purchasing Option: Application Service Providers"). The process for deciding on an application service provider is similar to the process for deciding on a purchased software package, with some special considerations because of the remote connection to data and software.

PURCHASING METHODOLOGY

Let's turn now to the detailed steps of a life-cycle process for selecting, modifying, and implementing software application packages. After describing the individual steps in detail, we then briefly discuss the project team roles, how to effectively manage a purchased system project, and the major advantages and disadvantages of purchasing a packaged system.

Although at first glance it appears relatively easy to purchase packaged software, many instances of systems implementation problems have arisen because an organization simply did not understand what was involved in acquiring and installing the software package that was purchased. Our description of the purchasing steps assumes that an initial approval has been received for a new system that is of sufficient size to merit a full purchasing process. As we will discuss, the package selection should be a joint decision between business managers who can assess the organizational benefits and risks and IS professionals who can help assess the benefits and risks from a technical as well as ongoing support perspective.

Note that our focus here is on what has been referred to as a "dedicated" package that offers a solution to a particular business problem, rather than a personal productivity suite (such as Microsoft Office). Our discussion also assumes that an organization has its own IS specialists. Organizations that have no IS specialists will need to rely on the vendor or outside consultants, or both, to provide the necessary IS expertise.

The Purchasing Steps

The template for the purchasing process steps is shown in Figure 11.1. The steps for purchasing application packages fit into the three life-cycle phases introduced in Chapter 9: Definition, Construction, and Implementation. In the systems development life cycle (SDLC) methodology described in Chapter 10, detailed systems specifications (what the system is to do) are documented in the Definition phase; the system is built in the Construction phase; and the system is installed, operated, and maintained in the Implementation phase.

Because customized application development using an SDLC process historically came first, the process for purchasing packages is referred to here as a *modified SDLC approach*. In the Definition phase, an organization not only defines its system needs but also then uses these requirements to identify potential vendors and solutions and then collect enough information to be able to evaluate them. In comparison to the SDLC process for custom software, the Definition phase is expanded to include five additional steps, beginning with creating a short list of potential packages.

Because an off-the-shelf packaged solution has already been designed, built, and tested by a vendor, the Construction phase is radically reduced. An exception here is when the package has not yet been fully released and the purchasing organization contracts with the vendor to serve as an **Alpha site** or a **Beta site** for the software vendor. Being involved as an Alpha site often means that the company can play a significant role in determining the final functionality and user interface design for the new package; in turn, this is a major commitment to providing both business and IS resources to work with the vendor. Being

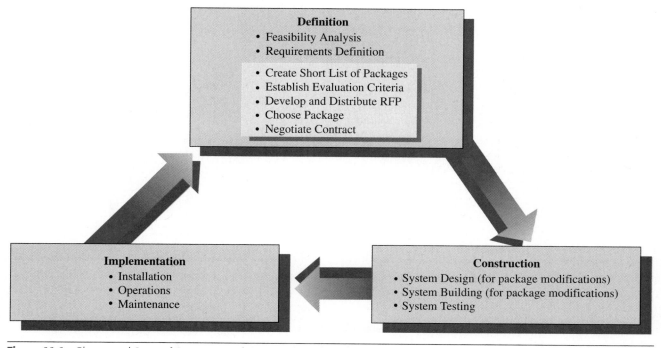

Figure 11.1 Phases and Steps of Systems Development Life Cycle when Purchasing a Package

involved as a Beta site typically means significant involvement in a user acceptance test role for the software vendor (such as described in Chapter 10): A vendor does Beta testing with organizations that are not Alpha sites in order to closely monitor the system for potential errors in a different setting.

The Implementation phase includes the same steps as in the SDLC. For a purchased system, however, the software vendor might be highly involved in the Installation. Further, the maintenance of the package is usually a task performed by the vendor. The negotiation of this part of the purchase contract is therefore a critical step.

Initiating the Purchasing Process   Similar to the decision for customized application investments, organizations use a number of approaches to decide whether to invest in a purchased system. Some organizations do not require a detailed formal request to begin an investigation of a possible system purchase because there is an assumption that fewer IS resources are needed. At a minimum, the business manager prepares a document that briefly describes the proposed application needs and outlines the potential benefits that the application will provide to the organization.

A high-level cost estimate for a proposed purchase will need to be developed with both business manager and IS analyst input. Estimating the system costs involves much more than identifying the purchase costs of candidate packages. For example, Figure 11.2 provides a hypothetical comparison of the costs for a $1 million custom-developed system using in-house resources (a midsized system) with the costs for selecting and purchasing an off-the-shelf package with the same overall functionality. The total cost for the purchased solution ($650,000) is about two-thirds of the total cost of building the system in-house. Note, however, that the software purchase price ($100,000 for purchasing the licenses to the software package) is less than one-sixth of the total costs—a characteristic that is often not fully realized by business managers who don't have extensive experience with purchasing packaged software. Further, in the Construction phase costs for this example, there is an assumption that no major modifications to the package are required and that linkages with other systems are not a part of this project.

As when building the system using the SDLC, a systems project team should be established and given the responsibility for acquiring the software. The team should include representatives from the business units that will implement the system, IS analysts, and other IS specialists who will operate and support the packaged system and other systems that will interface with the package. Some of the specific team roles will be described later in this chapter.

Definition Phase   The Definition phase begins with the same two steps as in the SDLC process. However, five additional steps are specific to the purchasing process.

Feasibility Analysis   Similar to the SDLC, the objective of this step is to determine whether the proposed system is

Stages	Cost of Building System	Cost of Buying System
Definition Phase		
Feasibility Analysis	$ 50,000	$ 50,000
Requirements Definition	250,000	200,000
Construction Phase		
System Design	150,000	—
Coding and Testing	150,000	—
System Testing	130,000	100,000
Documentation and Procedures	120,000	25,000
Implementation Phase		
Installation Planning, Data Cleanup, and Conversion	150,000	175,000
Software Purchase Price	—	100,000
Total	$1,000,000	$ 650,000

Figure 11.2   Comparison of Costs for Building Versus Purchasing a System

economically, technically, and operationally feasible. When purchasing a system, the feasibility of purchasing rather than building a system solution is also being considered. This step would therefore include a preliminary investigation of the availability of packaged systems that might be suitable candidates, including a high-level investigation of the software features and capabilities provided by the vendors. In this step a more detailed cost-benefit analysis is undertaken for project budgeting and monitoring purposes.

Requirements Definition   The requirements definition is a critical step in the SDLC approach. The SDLC deliverable is a detailed specification of what the system must do in terms of the inputs it must accept, the data it must store, the processes it must perform, the outputs it must produce, and the performance requirements that must be satisfied. It must be accurate, complete, and detailed because it is used to design and program the system and because it determines the quality of the resulting system.

When purchasing the system, this step is equally critical. In order to select the best software package, one must first have at least a high-level conceptual understanding of the system requirements. Here, however, the focus is on defining the functional requirements of the system to the degree needed for developing a request for proposal (RFP) from a short list of vendors. The requirements need to be more fully developed than the basic requirements used to build a prototype but less detailed than the requirements elicited under an SDLC process when they are used to design the actual system. Research has shown that uncertainty about an organization's needs is a significant barrier to packaged software adoption.

Create Short List of Suitable Packages   In this step the organization's requirements are used to eliminate all but a few of the most promising candidate packages that were identified in the feasibility analysis step. For example, packages should be eliminated if they do not have particular required features or will not work with existing hardware, operating system and database management software, or networks. Further research on the vendor's capabilities can be undertaken to eliminate vendors due to problems experienced with other users of the package, a vendor's inadequate track record or firm size, or other concerns about long-term viability. Independent consultants with expertise on specific types of applications or specializing in a given industry can also be key resources here and might be able to help the project team eliminate inappropriate candidates.

Establish Criteria for Selection   In this step both business and IS team members need to work together to determine relevant criteria about the candidate packages and vendors in order to choose the best one. Some criteria can be categorized as mandatory requirements, whereas others could be categorized as desirable features.

Some areas in which detailed criteria should be developed are shown in Figure 11.3. For example, the vendor's business characteristics could include items such as how long the vendor has been in the software business, the number of employees, financial reports over the past five years, its principal products, its yearly software sales revenue, and the location of its sales and support offices. The packaged system's functional capabilities should include the degree to which the package allows for multiple options and the ease with which it can be tailored to fit company needs using parameters or other approaches that do not require system coding.

The technical requirements to be evaluated include the hardware and system software (system platform) required to run the system and the database requirements for the package. This information allows one to evaluate how well the package will conform to current organizational standards for hardware, software, and networks. The types, amount, and quality of the documentation provided should also be evaluated, as well as the quality and amount of vendor support available, including training, consulting, and system maintenance.

In addition to detailing the evaluation criteria, consideration should be given to the measures that will be used in the evaluation process. It is not uncommon to evaluate packages using a scale with numbers (such as 1 through 10) or qualitative labels (such as outstanding, good, average, fair, or poor). If a scale with numbers is used, each criterion can be assigned an importance weight, and a weighted score can be computed for each evaluation category for each package. Although quantitative scores might

The Package
  Functional capabilities of the packaged system
  Technical requirements the software must satisfy
  Amount and quality of documentation provided

The Vendor
  Business characteristics of the vendor firm
  Vendor support of the package—initial
    and ongoing

Figure 11.3   Key Criteria for Software Package Selection

not be the sole means for selection, they help to quantify differences among the candidate packages.

Develop and Distribute the RFP A **request for proposal (RFP)** (sometimes called a request for quote, or RFQ) is a formal document sent to potential vendors inviting them to submit a proposal describing their software package and how it would meet the company's needs. In organizations with prior experience purchasing software, a template for the RFP could already have been developed. A sample table of contents is shown in Figure 11.4. However, the specific requirements sought in Section III in this example will greatly depend on the type of package and the specific business needs.

The project team uses the criteria for selection to develop the RFP. The RFP gives the vendors information about the system's objectives and requirements, the environment in which the system will be used, the general criteria that will be used to evaluate the proposals, and the conditions for submitting proposals. Specific questions might need to be developed to capture the system's performance characteristics, whether source code is provided, and whether the purchasing organization is allowed to modify the package without voiding the vendor warranty. In addition to pricing information for the package itself,

any additional costs for training and consulting need to be ascertained. The RFP can also be used to capture historical information about the package, such as the date of the first release, the date of its last revision, and a list of companies in which the package has been implemented—including contact information to obtain references from these companies.

This step ends when the RFP is sent to the short list of qualified vendors.

Evaluate Vendor Responses to RFP and Choose Package In this step the vendor responses to the RFP are evaluated and additional actions are taken to evaluate the candidate packages and their vendors. The overall objective of the evaluation process is to determine the extent of any discrepancies between the company's needs as specified by the requirements and the weighting system and the capabilities of the proposed application packages. Aggregate evaluations (scores) need to be calculated for each set of criteria and for the overall package. The team then uses these figures to discuss the major strengths and weaknesses of the candidate packages. This can be a large data collection and analysis task and might involve independent evaluations by all project team members. Both IS and business team members might need to confer not only

	Page		Page
I. Introduction		III. Requirements	
A. Structure and Scope of the RFP	3	A. Vendor Information	12
B. Objective of RFP	3	B. Vendor Support/Training	13
C. Company Background and Philosophy	3	C. Documentation	15
D. Hardware/Software Environment	4	D. Package Hardware and System Software Environment	17
E. Current Business Environment	5	E. Application and Database Architecture	21
		F. Tuning and Measurement	26
		G. Functional Requirements	28
II. Guidelines for Vendor Response		IV. Costs	
A. Guidelines	6	A. Summary	33
B. Vendor Response	8	B. Nonrecurring	35
C. General Evaluation Process	10	C. Recurring	37
		D. Price Guarantee	39
		E. Maintenance Agreement	40
		F. New Releases	41
		V. Signature Page	42

Figure 11.4 Sample RFP Table of Contents

with other project team members, but also with other members of their departments.

In addition to evaluating the vendors' responses from the formal RFP process, two other types of data collection are commonly pursued, at least for the leading candidate packages. First, demonstrations of the leading packages can usually be arranged. Sometimes it is feasible for the vendor to set up a demo on-site at your organization; at other times, another location is required—either at a vendor location or at another company that has installed the package. Detailed requirements for software demos should be provided to the vendors to ensure equitable conditions for demonstrating system performance, because response times and other characteristics of system performance can vary greatly depending on the hardware and system software being used to run the package. An example of demo specifications for a financial modeling package, and a form for evaluating the demo specified, are provided in Figures 11.5A and 11.5B. In addition, it may be possible for the vendor to install the software on an organization's computer for some short period to allow for a test drive of the application. This way you can explore firsthand some features for which there was not time in the demo to show and which can be used by your staff to investigate potential idiosyncrasies that the vendor staff quickly passed over during the demo.

Second, references from users of the software package in other companies are usually obtained. Each vendor might be asked to provide a reference list, to your specifications, as part of the RFP. You might ask for references from similar-sized organizations, some geographically close, who have a mix of experience (e.g., some recent and some long-term purchasers), or from similar businesses. You might even want to talk with a reference that chose not to purchase the package. One especially effective technique is to require the vendor to provide the names of users as well as IS specialists for each customer organization on their reference list. Task force members can then divide up the names with, for example, IS specialists contacting their counterparts in companies that have already implemented the package. Site visits to one or more of these companies might also be possible. Evaluations of the vendor's support, consulting, and training services can also be obtained from these sources. You need to understand the situation with the reference organization to understand how to evaluate their experiences. For example, a reference where the package was thrust on users by the IT unit will likely provide different comments than a reference from an organization in which the package was selected by a careful process, as outlined in this section.

Based on all the previously mentioned information sources, the project team needs to assess how well the

---

Presentation Directions

The format must follow the outline provided.

The mainframe to which the PC is connected for this presentation must be an IBM running under MVS. If your MVS is not exactly like ours (as outlined in the RFP) you must provide a written explanation of how the differences (i.e., response time, color, etc.) affect the demonstration.

The presentation is limited to 2 hours, including 30 minutes for questions at the end. You will be given 30 minutes to set up.

With the data and formulas provided, create a relational database so that the following Profit and Loss (P&L) statements can be modeled and reported.

Fiscal 2000 Plan:

Item P&L: by month with total year at the right.
Control Unit P&L: by item with total at the right.
Business Unit P&L: by Control Unit with total at the right.

Fiscal 2001 Projection:

Business Unit P&L: by Control Unit with total at the right.

Combined Fiscal 2000 & Fiscal 2001:

Control Unit Change Analysis: by item for total Fiscal 2000 vs. proj. Fiscal 2001.
Business Unit Change Analysis: by Control Unit for total Fiscal 2000 vs. proj. Fiscal 2001.

Provide a listing of the populated database relations and/or tables.

Provide an example listing of the programs/models and report format files for each type of P&L and Change Analysis above.

Figure 11.5 Forms for Managing Vendor Demonstrations. (A) Example of Requirements for Vendor Demonstration

---

company's needs match with the capabilities of the available packages (see Figure 11.6). This is a critical step that requires both business and technical expertise. The results of this process step will also have broad ramifications for the project's success.

Once the discrepancies between the package's capabilities and the company's needs are identified, the team needs

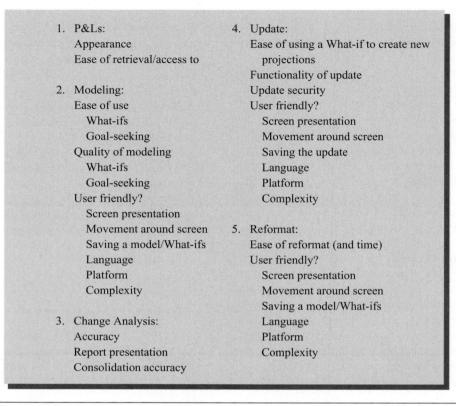

1. P&Ls:
   Appearance
   Ease of retrieval/access to

2. Modeling:
   Ease of use
      What-ifs
      Goal-seeking
   Quality of modeling
      What-ifs
      Goal-seeking
   User friendly?
      Screen presentation
      Movement around screen
      Saving a model/What-ifs
      Language
      Platform
      Complexity

3. Change Analysis:
   Accuracy
   Report presentation
   Consolidation accuracy

4. Update:
   Ease of using a What-if to create new
      projections
   Functionality of update
   Update security
   User friendly?
      Screen presentation
      Movement around screen
      Saving the update
      Language
      Platform
      Complexity

5. Reformat:
   Ease of reformat (and time)
   User friendly?
      Screen presentation
      Movement around screen
      Saving a model/What-ifs
      Language
      Platform
      Complexity

Figure 11.5   (continued) (B) Example of Evaluation Worksheet for Vendor Demonstration

to choose the best way to deal with these discrepancies for the top candidate packages. Assuming that the company decides that it still wants to invest in one of these packages, there are three major alternatives to choose from. As shown at the bottom of Figure 11.6, the company can change its own procedures to fit the package, investigate the feasibility and costs of modifying the package, or implement the package "as is" and work around the differences.

An important factor when choosing among these alternatives is fully understanding the additional development effort and costs that would be required to modify the package in order to tailor it to the company's needs and integrate it into the company's environment. These alternatives therefore need to be made in collaboration with internal IS specialists and the vendors of the top candidate packages in order to be sure that the extent of the discrepancies havebeen fully identified and that the feasibility and advisability of modifying a given package have been fully considered.

If system modifications are a viable alternative, the plans for which organization will be responsible for programming the changes and the total costs of these changes

will need to be taken into consideration. Further, the impacts of modifying the package need to be evaluated for not just the initial system project, but also for subsequent

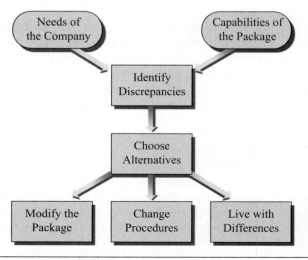

Figure 11.6   Matching Company Needs with Capabilities of the Package

maintenance and package upgrade projects. For example, many companies that purchase today's large complex enterprise system packages, such as an ERP system, are advised to avoid reprogramming portions of the package in order to avoid the costs of continually modifying new releases of the package in the future (see the section below entitled "Special Case: Enterprise System Packages").

Instead, many purchasing companies have decided to take the middle alternative in Figure 11.6: Change Procedures. That is, they decide that it is better for the company to change its own procedures to match the way the software package operates than to modify the package. A company might in fact even find that the procedural assumptions incorporated into the package are better ways of doing things than those specified by the company during the Requirements Definition step of the process. This could occur if the software vendor has worked with one or more leading organizations in the same industry in order to develop the software package. For example, the vendors of today's large ERP packages might have worked with industry consortia to develop modules around industry-specific processes, and then the vendors can market their packages as having "best practices" for the industry embedded in their software package.

The decision to purchase a system is therefore not only a commitment to purchase the best of the available systems, but also a commitment to whatever organizational changes (sometimes compromises) need to be made in order to implement the system. Packaged software is a vendor's solution to a problem that is perceived to exist in a significant number of firms. In many cases, the solution implements best practices—at least best for many organizations. Thus, it is likely that discrepancies between the organization's needs and the package's capabilities will exist. Before finalizing the purchase decision, the project team should ensure that the relevant business managers support the decision to buy the selected package and agree that they will do whatever is necessary to implement it successfully. Similarly, the project team should ensure that the IS specialists agree that the system can operate in the current environment and that they can satisfactorily support it in-house as required.

Negotiate Contract.   The deliverables from this stage are a legal contract with the vendor of the selected software package and a detailed plan for the remainder of the lifecycle steps. The contract with the software vendor specifies not only the software price, number of licenses, and payment schedule, but also functional specifications, acceptance-testing procedures, a timetable of the delivery process, protection of trade secrets, repair and maintenance

responsibilities, liabilities due to failures, required documentation, and options to terminate the agreement (Gurbaxani and Whang, 1991). Another important element of the contract is the rights of the customer to future upgrades of the package—including the cost, and whether upgrades can be skipped yet a prior release will still be supported by the vendor.

Contract negotiations should be an integral part of the purchase process. When working with vendors to determine how to reduce the discrepancies between the company's needs and the packages' capabilities, one is actually prenegotiating a contract with the selected vendor.

Many organizations have software purchasing specialists who work with system project managers in the contract writing and negotiation steps. Because the contract will be the only recourse if the system or the vendor does not perform as specified, the use of an attorney also reduces the likelihood of future legal wrangling or a loss of rightful claims. Once the project is underway, the project manager needs to be familiar enough with the contractual agreement in order to know whether an unanticipated need for vendor services will require a formal change to the vendor contract.

The contract type also has implications for the risk level of the purchasing company. For example, under a fixed-price contract, the buyer knows in advance the total price that will be incurred for a specified product and vendor services. Under a cost-reimbursement type of contract, in which the buyer agrees to pay the vendor's direct and indirect costs, the purchasing company assumes a much greater risk.

Construction Phase   In the SDLC process, the Construction phase includes three steps: system design, system building, and system testing. With purchasing, the extent to which the first two steps are needed depends on whether or not the purchased package is modified, as well as the complexity of the package itself.

Significant savings in time and money might be realized if no major modifications are made to the package's code. Looking back at the cost comparisons in Figure 11.2, the Construction phase costs are the major source of the total cost savings from purchasing a package versus building a custom application: Even when adding in the software purchase price itself (shown under Implementation Phase), the costs for the Construction phase of a purchase package are less than half as great as the Construction costs for the customized solution. However, as stated earlier, the example in Figure 11.2 assumes that no major modifications to the package are required and that linkages with other systems are not a part of this project. The

$350,000 difference in total costs between the cost of building and the cost of purchasing this particular system could therefore quickly vanish if the assumption of no system modifications does not hold true.

If no modifications to the system are to be made, the firm can move to the system testing step after the purchase contract is signed. Many off-the-shelf packages for single functions, such as accounting applications, are often not modified because the business practices they support are quite standardized and the vendor did not develop the package with modifications in mind (Rockart and Hofman, 1992). Packaged systems have typically been Beta-tested in companies in the targeted industry before they are sold on the open market. Despite the fact that the package might have been thoroughly tested and already used in other organizations, user acceptance testing still needs to be conducted to ensure that the system works properly with the company's data and on preexisting or newly installed hardware. This could require significant time and effort because the purchasing organization is not familiar with the system's detailed design. The vendor provides user documentation for those who will use the system and technical systems documentation for those who install the system and operate it. However, new procedures for the system's business users might need to be developed to fit the purchasing organization.

If the package is modified, there might be several options to consider for how to accomplish the changes: a contract with the vendor, a contract with a third party, or modifying the software with in-house resources. Many vendors routinely contract to make the desired modifications. If a vendor will furnish only the machine-language code for the application—not the source code in which the program was written—the only alternative might be to contract with the vendor to make the modifications.

If the vendor or another outside supplier makes the modifications, the purchaser also needs to test them. User acceptance testing is especially important and typically requires significant time and effort by the business users. Revised user and system documentation also needs to be reviewed. If the purchaser modifies the package, the system design and building activities in the SDLC methodology will likely be followed, similar to the way these steps would be for traditional custom development. Because IS staff must devote substantial effort to understanding the details of the software package's design and structure in order to modify it, it is not uncommon for the initial estimates of the time and costs for these steps to be insufficient.

The scope of the project might also include modifications to existing company systems in order to interface them with the new package. Creating these interface programs can be difficult and costly, and integration testing is typically time-consuming. According to Keen (1991), the total costs of system modifications can be hard to predict and the total life-cycle costs for a purchased system can be up to seven times greater than the original estimate.

The previous discussion focused on actual modifications to the functionality or architecture of the purchased package (e.g., changing the way inventory is valued in an accounting package or changing the software to work with a specific database management system). In contrast, some modifications and enhancements are not as significant. Most purchased packages have routines that allow certain customization (e.g., including your company name and logo on reports and invoices, or tailoring the layout of standard reports). Also, the package may include tools to allow the purchasing organization to build additional reports, display screens, or data extracts (the latter to assist in interfacing the purchased system with other "downstream" systems). These changes do not affect the underlying architecture or code of the purchased software and tend to be much easier to maintain as new versions of the purchased system are released.

Implementation Phase   The Implementation phase of the SDLC involves installation, operations, and maintenance. As seen in Figure 11.1, these are all major activities in the purchasing life cycle.

Installation   The installation stage in the SDLC involves installation planning, training, data cleanup, and conversion. The installation of a packaged system also includes all these activities. A key factor in a successful installation of a packaged system is the quality of vendor support during this step (Lucas et al., 1988). The package's size and complexity can also greatly affect the installation plan. For example, large ERP system packages can entail multiple years of work by in-house IS specialists as well as outside consultants to prepare for the initial installation of these integrated systems. This is because not only do these systems include many optional choices with which to configure the system to fit the organization, but also because ERP systems typically require significant changes in day-to-day business processes. As a result, the costs for installation planning, data cleanup and conversion efforts to install such packages exceed those for a custom application effort (see Figure 11.2). In large organizations, especially those with different types of business units in different geographic locations, it is also often necessary to implement the package in phases, which can also increase project costs.

Special attention also needs to be given to the training needs for a purchased system as part of the implementation activities. Depending on the extent to which the new system will require significant changes in how employees currently do their jobs, the project might require a large investment in preparing the users for the new system, including in-house or vendor-led training programs. Business managers and representative users must be actively involved in these activities and committed to devoting the time necessary to anticipate and resolve problems that arise.

To help organizations that will be making significant changes in the way people do their jobs, many consulting firms have developed an expertise in what is referred to as "change management." Some of the change management activities are specifically designed to help overcome resistance by business users to the new system being implemented. For projects implementing complex enterprise systems, for example, the systems budget for change management activities can be greater than the budgeted cost for the initial software purchase. (See the section entitled "Managing Business Change" in Chapter 12.)

Operations   Ongoing operations tasks for a new application are similar whether the company purchases the system or builds it using the SDLC. However, a key to success in the initial days of operation for a new packaged system is good lines of communication with the vendor in order to quickly resolve any problems. Long-term success depends on the degree to which the organization has successfully integrated the system into the company's ongoing operations.

Maintenance   As described previously, it is common for a vendor to do package maintenance, and this needs to be specified in the software purchase contract. A well-designed contract can lead to considerable cost avoidance to a firm over the life of the system. The potential downside, however, is that the purchasing company becomes totally dependent upon the vendor for future system changes. (This is especially true for so-called proprietary software—but, as we discuss in a subsequent section, open-source software is built on a different purchasing-maintenance business model). Because the vendor must balance the desires and needs of all the organizations that use the system, a purchasing company might not get all the changes it wants and it might even have to accept some changes it does not want. The worst case scenarios here are as follows: (1) the purchased system has a significantly shorter useful life than originally intended, so the system costs may exceed the expected benefits for the company

that purchased the software, or (2) the vendor goes out of business before the company achieves its expected return on the packaged software investment.

If the original package was modified, the installation of a vendor's new version of the package might not be the optimal solution for the purchasing organization. With the vendor's help, the company needs to compare the functionality of the new version of the package with its current modified version and then decide on the best way to deal with these discrepancies. The choices are similar to those shown in Figure 11.6, except the "do nothing" choice means that the organization might be left operating a version of the package that the vendor might or might not continue to support. If the organization modified the original package in-house or built extensive interfaces to the package's earlier version, the implementation of a new version of the package can also result in considerable maintenance costs for the organization.

In the case of large ERP system packages, the purchasing organization needs to anticipate that new releases of the software might be relatively frequent, and the vendor might continue to support prior package releases only for a certain time period. When implementing a system upgrade that includes significant new functionality, the company will need to decide whether to first implement the new version of the system and then initiate projects to make better use of the business capabilities supported by the new release or whether to implement the new business capabilities as part of the system upgrade project.

Project Team for Purchasing Packages

Successfully implementing a packaged application typically requires a major commitment on the part of business managers and users because of the extensive changes in business processes and procedures that are needed to effectively implement the purchased software. As a result, it is not uncommon for business managers to be asked to take a **project manager** role for a packaged application system project. However, because IS expertise is still required in order to manage the technical aspects of implementing a package, IS managers also need to play project leadership roles. As mentioned previously, small organizations that have no IS specialists will need to rely on the software vendor or outside consultants, or both, to provide the necessary IS expertise.

The software vendor initially provides information on the package capabilities in response to an RFP. Vendors of leading packages might then be asked to provide a demonstration and to consult with the purchaser about potential system modifications or new interfaces to older systems.

The vendor company might also be contracted to perform modifications to the package prior to implementation in order to reduce mismatches between the packaged system's capabilities and the organization's needs after a careful assessment of the benefits and risks of doing so. The vendor could also play a major role in the system installation, as well as provide ongoing maintenance support for the purchasing organization. In the case of large enterprise system packages, it is also common for companies to contract with a consulting firm (that might have been certified by the software vendor) as a **third-party implementation partner** on the project.

Because of the initial and ongoing dependence on the software vendor, purchasing specialists (contract specialists) within the purchasing company can also be critical to the success of a packaged system implementation, whether or not they are formal members of the project team. For example, if an RFP is sent to vendors, a purchasing specialist will help prepare or at least review the RFP document before it is distributed to vendors. Firms with prior software purchasing experience might have developed boilerplate sections to be adapted to the type of purchase. Purchasing specialists are also skilled in negotiating contracts that provide for contingency actions that can reduce financial and other business risks for the purchasing company. For example, many of today's contracts include specific agreements about levels of service during an installation period (see the section entitled "Service Level Agreements" in Chapter 15).

As described earlier under the negotiate-contract step, attorneys (who may also be purchasing specialists) should oversee the writing and approval of the external contract with software vendors. All associated licensing agreements should also be reviewed in order to minimize the associated costs and risks for the business.

Managing a Purchased System Project

Purchased system projects are successful when the organization has selected a product, and a vendor, that is able to satisfy the firm's current and future system needs. This requires an effective project team with members who have the business and technical skills and knowledge needed, including the skills and knowledge needed for the project team roles described previously. Unlike the traditional SDLC process in which a long Construction phase buffers the Definition phase from the Implementation phase, the purchase of a software package might entail large capital expenditures by the company within just a few months (unless other terms are negotiated with the vendor). The right business managers, end users, and IS specialists need

to be a part of the project team to ensure that the best package is purchased from the best vendor and that both technical and business risks have been adequately considered.

A typical problem with managing the life cycle of a purchased system project is ensuring that adequate attention is given to the steps in the initial Definition phase. A common mistake is that business managers learn about a particular packaged solution from another company or a salesperson at an industry conference and they begin negotiating with the vendor without adequate attention to the functional requirements definition step. Project teams that do not do a good job identifying their requirements will not be able to do a good job assessing the discrepancies between the company's needs and the capabilities of candidate packages. This increases the short-term and long-term investment risks, because a contract with an external vendor is not as easily changed as a project agreement between users and internal IS developers. It is therefore critical that the Definition phase be performed well.

For the project team members from the business side who also have implementation responsibilities, it is also imperative that they be *representative* business managers and users. Steps should be taken to ensure that they are committed to the project goals at the outset, including the time schedule and budget.

The success of the Implementation phase also depends on how well the Definition phase was performed, because this is where the team members assessed the organizational changes needed to successfully implement the purchased system. As discussed earlier, users of the packaged system might be asked to make significant changes in how they do their jobs in order to conform to a package's features. This requires a well-planned installation step under the leadership of committed business managers who are very knowledgeable about the needed changes.

In addition, purchased system projects introduce several new types of risks. First, the success of the project is highly dependent on the performance of a third party. The quality of the implemented system will depend not only on the vendor's software engineering capabilities, but also on how well the implementing organization understands the package's capabilities and on the vendor's training and installation capabilities. As discussed earlier, a key aspect of the vendor selection process is the accurate assessment of the vendor's capabilities, not just an evaluation of the current software package.

The project's initial success, as well as the long-term effectiveness of the system being installed, is also highly dependent on the contract negotiation process. In most situations system implementation does not simply involve "turning the key." Vendor expertise might be required to install the package, build interfaces to existing systems, and perhaps modify the package itself to better match the purchasing organization's needs. Service expectations between the purchaser and vendor need to be a part of the contract developed at the end of the Definition phase. The contract will be the only recourse for the purchaser if the system modifications, vendor training, or the implementation of the package do not go well.

Purchasing Small Systems   The discussion in this chapter has focused on the purchasing process for large, complex systems. If a smaller, simpler system is being considered, the time and effort put into the process can, of course, be scaled back. However, a small system can still be a major investment for a small business. Unfortunately, many small businesses have limited experience with and knowledge of evaluating and installing such systems. The services of a hardware vendor, a local software supplier, as well as external consultants might therefore be needed.

Purchasing Advantages and Disadvantages

Figure 11.7 summarizes the advantages and disadvantages of purchasing packaged systems, as well as some potential long-term advantages and disadvantages for buying packaged software solutions.

Advantages   The primary project advantage is that, compared to customized application development, less time is needed to implement the system. Nevertheless, for mid-sized systems, the entire process will still require several months, and for large-scale enterprise software implementations (with packages such as ERP systems) the process

---

Purchasing Advantages
- Reduced time to implement
- Lower overall acquisition costs
- Reduced need for internal IS resources
- High application quality (debugged and best practices)
- Infusion of external expertise (IS, business)

Purchasing Disadvantages
- Risks due to lack of package knowledge
- Risks due to extent of organizational changes required
- Initial and ongoing dependance on vendor

Figure 11.7   Advantages and Disadvantages of Purchasing Packaged Software

can take several years to implement enough modules of the software to achieve a net benefit.

A second major advantage is that packaged software implementations can be very attractive from an economic standpoint. For example, a small business can obtain a complete accounting system for less than $25,000, which is very low compared to the cost of developing a comparable customized application. Assuming that the vendor has more than 10,000 installations of this small package ($250 million in revenues), the vendor will have an incentive to spend millions of dollars on improving the package in order to issue new releases. Everyone comes out a winner because each purchaser has cost avoidance from purchasing a package, and the vendor makes a large enough profit to stay in business and provide upgrades and other support services on an ongoing basis. As shown in Figure 11.2, the initial purchase price of a software package might be a relatively small fraction of the total cost of acquiring and installing a software package.

A third temporary advantage is that in-house IS resources could be freed up to develop mission-critical applications that could provide the firm a competitive advantage if software packages can be implemented for relatively common processes that provide no specific strategic advantage.

Two potential long-term advantages are application quality and the infusion of external expertise. The quality of a software package might be substantially better than that of a custom system, because a vendor can afford to spend much more time and effort developing the system than an individual company. Also, the package may include best practices or choices of best practices for different situations. The documentation can be much better than the typical in-house documentation, and new releases of the package might incorporate improvements recommended by companies that are using the system. Furthermore, each release is usually thoroughly tested, including a Beta test in a client organization.

Finally, a packaged solution is a quick way to infuse new expertise—both IT expertise and business expertise—into the organization. Given the fast pace of technological change, most organizations today find it difficult to train and retain IS personnel with expertise in new, emerging technologies. Software vendors often have the funds and motivation to develop systems using newer technologies. Packaged solutions for a particular industry, or large ERP systems, also frequently have best-in-class processes and procedures embedded in the software. By purchasing the software, companies can also adopt better business processes.

Disadvantages   Two major project risks are also associated with implementing purchased packages. One risk is the lack of package knowledge. The package implementation can require significant training for IS as well as business personnel, which increases the implementation costs. Because of an organization's relative unfamiliarity with the software package, the organization might also not be as quick to leverage the capabilities of the package as it would be to leverage the capabilities of a system that members of the organization had designed and custom developed. Some organizations also make the mistake of initially modifying the package, or adding other functionality, only to learn later that the package could have provided the same functionality if it had been implemented differently.

Another related project risk is that since implementing a packaged system often requires significant business process changes, there are greater project risks. Knowledgeable business managers and skilled IS specialists need to be significantly involved in the Definition phase to understand what organizational changes need to be made. Furthermore, there often is more user resistance due to the extent of changes required in order to implement the packaged solution.

The long-term disadvantage is that the organization becomes dependent on an external IT provider not only for the initial installation and perhaps some package modifications, but also for the ongoing maintenance of the package. Although in many cases this can result in a strategic alliance of value to both the vendor and purchaser, the purchaser might not fully anticipate the coordination costs associated with managing the vendor relationship. In addition, of course, there is the risk that the vendor will go out of business or be unresponsive to the needs of the purchasing firm. There can also be pricing hazards if the vendor makes it difficult for third parties to compete for support services.

SPECIAL CASE: ENTERPRISE SYSTEM PACKAGES

By the end of the 1990s, the majority of U.S.-based *Fortune* 500 companies and more than one-fourth of European-based midsized organizations had invested in a first wave of enterprise system packages: enterprise resource planning (ERP) systems. Most companies purchased these systems in order to achieve business benefits (e.g., cost reduction, more efficient business processes, and faster compliance with legal requirements), but ERP investments are also IT platform investments (see the discussion of major vendors and ERP benefits in Chapter 6).

One of the primary business benefits associated with ERP systems is to enable access to integrated data, sometimes real-time data, for better management decision making. This is accomplished by getting most business applications on a common platform, the ERP system. Because most ERP systems are built to support cross-functional business processes, there will be fewer system interfaces to maintain. Further, ERP modules that can be "configured" to be used by different types of firms in different industries enable those firms that have already conducted projects to reengineer their business processes to now implement them; building custom systems to support new cross-functional processes would require a much larger system investment over a much longer time. However, an ERP system is not a total information system for an organization; rather, an ERP system itself will meet only roughly 70 percent of the needs of the organization (Markus, 2000). Thus, it is important in selecting an ERP system to consider how the ERP system will interface with existing operational systems with which it must share data. Such interfaces may not be trivial because the software platforms of legacy applications can be quite different than the platform for the more modern ERP system.

Adopting an ERP system is a major undertaking for any organization, and there are potential risks and costs (see Fuß et al., 2007). ERP systems are very expensive to purchase, plus there likely will be significant consulting fees to assist in configuration and installation. Like any package, but more so because of the comprehensive nature of ERP, the package confines an organization to the capabilities of the particular package. The ERP package may establish standards for the platform for all systems that will interface with it. Also, an organization becomes very dependent on one vendor for a sizeable portion of its core business applications. The task of deploying the ERP package, which includes turning off legacy applications in the organization, is complex and can be perilous to continuing operations. These are all important risks and costs, hence, the decision to acquire an ERP package and how to manage its deployment are critical.

For the IS departments within firms that purchase an ERP package, this could also be the first time that their project team personnel would be asked to configure a package in the best way possible, rather than to custom develop an application based on the requirements of their business users. IS and other project team personnel, as well as business users, must be sent to training classes, typically conducted by the software vendor, so that they can learn the packaged software as well as learn new vendor-specific languages for writing interfaces and queries. Because, out of the box, an ERP system is a generic, semifinished product, IS and other personnel must learn how to configure the software for the options that are best for your organization. New "business analyst" skill sets may also be required to effectively manage the process steps for a packaged software project, rather than a customized life cycle methodology.

Another key characteristic of the early ERP projects has been the heavy reliance on third-party consultants who are not employees of the software vendor, such as consultants in the Big Four or smaller consulting firms. These "implementation partners" are usually invaluable for helping an organization quickly learn how the software package operates, as well as how the complex business process options embedded in each module would work. Because of the large scope and complexity of some of these ERP package implementations, one of the key management challenges has been to what extent to rely on the external consultants to lead an ERP project and how to make sure the purchasing company captured the needed knowledge to continue to operate and "fine-tune" the configurations after the consultants left. More recently, firms that host ERP installations for several clients (see the subsequent section on ASPs) can be relied on to keep the ERP application running and maintained to the latest releases of the software, as well as to provide some of the up-front and ongoing consulting services. Nevertheless, even with the help of third-party consultants, many initial ERP implementation projects have not been successful.

According to Brown and Vessey (2003), five factors need to be managed well for an ERP project to be successful. These factors are described in some detail next.

- *Top management is engaged in the project, not just involved.*   Because enterprise systems demand fundamental changes in the way a company performs its business processes, its business executives need to be visibly active in the funding and oversight of the project. Lower-level managers will not have the clout needed to ensure that not only will the ERP modules be configured to align with the best business process solutions for the company, but also that all relevant business managers buy in to the organizational changes that will be necessary to take advantage of the software package's capabilities. Turnover among project sponsors (given the length of most ERP projects) may mean that new top management is less engaged in the project, so the job of the project leader to keep top management engaged requires constant effort. Also, it is common that benefits from the ERP implementation will take time to occur, well after significant initial costs. Initial reactions from some

stakeholders (e.g., employees, customers, and suppliers) may be negative due to start-up difficulties and the initial net cash outflow (Markus, et al. 2003). Again, top management engagement is needed to stay committed to the ultimate expected goals through each project phase.

- *Project leaders are veterans, and team members are decision makers.*   Because ERP system implementations are extremely complex, the leaders of the project need to be highly skilled and have a proven track record with leading a project that has had a major impact on a business. The team members who are representing different business units and different business functions (e.g., finance, marketing, manufacturing) need to also be empowered to make decisions on behalf of the unit or function they represent. If the team members do not have decision-making rights, the project leaders will likely not be able to meet the agreed-upon project deadlines. It is also important to try to keep the project team members intact for as long as possible because of the need for the right people on the team and because of the ramp-up time needed to become an effective team member.

- *Third parties fill gaps in expertise and transfer their knowledge.*   As described previously, ERP systems are typically implemented with the help of third-party implementation partners (consultants), as well as the software vendor. The skill sets of the consultants needed will depend on the skill sets and experiences of the purchasing company's own business and IT managers. If there are no internal project leaders with the necessary project management skills, consultants should also be used to help manage the project. However, before the consultants leave, the internal staff needs to acquire the knowledge needed to continue to operate the new system. Many organizations develop agreements with consultants that explicitly refer to the transfer of knowledge to internal staff as a part of the consultant contract.

- *Change management goes hand-in-hand with project planning.*   Many of the early adopters of ERP systems underestimated the need for project resources to help prepare the business for implementing the new system. ERP systems typically require training not only in how to use the new system, but also in how to perform business processes in new ways to take advantage of the package's capabilities. Because of the tight integration of the ERP modules, workers also typically need to learn much more about what happens before and after their own interactions with the system. Companies with the fewest problems at the time of implementation began to plan for these types of changes as part of the overall project planning activities. The fundamental changes are to business processes. It has been found that it is better to change business processes to adapt to the best practices embedded in ERP systems than to try to modify the purchased software; not modifying business processes to fit the ERP software is a main reason for ERP project failure. Remember, the reason an ERP solution is being adopted is to reengineer business processes to best practices and better integration across business units. Not all ERP systems are created equal. Each has its roots in some industry (e.g., manufacturing, banking), sector (public or private), or country (e.g., U.S. or European), Thus, it is important to select an ERP package that is based on the set of best practices and business processes you want to adopt (see Kien and Soh for more on this topic).

■ *A satisficing mind-set prevails.* Because of the integrated nature of the modules of an ERP package, companies typically implement the package in as "vanilla" a form as possible. This typically means that business personnel will be asked to "give up" some functionality that they had in a system that the ERP is replacing. In other words, the company needs to be in a "satisficing" mind-set, as opposed to expecting an "optimal" solution for every aspect of the system. For companies with many business units across the globe, business managers will also typically be asked to accept some less-than-optimal ways of doing things in their unit in order to have a standard configuration across the enterprise. A typical rule-of-thumb here is to try and keep a standard solution for about 80 percent of the package configuration, recognizing that some local customization will even be required due to specific country or regional regulations. Related is the need to carefully select measures of ERP project success in different phases of the project. In general, big picture measures of success need to be used (e.g., "achieving commonality of systems and business practices in a decentralized organization") in order for the organization to sustain support for the project.

Brown and Vessey also point out that later adopters of a new kind of enterprise system always have the advantage of learning from the mistakes of early adopters. For example, companies that purchased an ERP package in the second half of the 1990s could talk with other companies in their industry who had already implemented an ERP and then they could benchmark their own implementation plans in order to avoid making costly mistakes. These authors also suggest that much of what is learned from ERP projects will help the early adopters of the next wave of enterprise systems (e.g., customer relationship management and supply chain management systems).

Other researchers (e.g., Ross, 1998) have emphasized the importance of recognizing that large, complex enterprise system initiatives really don't end with the initial "Go Live" date. Rather, managers should anticipate that there will be a period of time following the initial implementation in which the system and new processes become more stabilized (a "shakedown" period). After the new ways of doing business have become more routinized and the technical operations of the new system are running smoothly, the company can begin to make smaller changes (continuous improvement) to help it achieve the promised business benefits from implementing this new type of software package. For example, many companies report having achieved cost efficiencies in materials procurement within the first calendar year after an ERP implementation, but other value-chain improvements might not be realized for several more years.

OPEN SOURCE SOFTWARE

Although the open source movement began with system software like the Linux operating system, the Firefox Web browser, and the MySQL database management system, open source is now viable for application software. **Open source software** goes beyond freeware, which can be downloaded from various bulletin boards. With open source you obtain the source code and the right to modify it. Depending on the license for acquiring the software, if you change it you may be obligated to share your changes with the community of organizations that are using the software.

Although an open source application is free to acquire, the provider of the software as well as third parties often provide fee-based products and services to extend the product with advanced features, maintenance and training, and documentation and books about use of the software. Thus, for some, the real advantage of open source software is not the lower cost but rather the independence from a single software provider that may not have the same priorities as you do for enhancements and that may lock adopters into their services and add-on components by not allowing third parties to be involved.

What makes open source an attractive type of purchased software? Certainly the up-front acquisition cost is important, but the total cost of ownership (for maintenance, upgrades, support, training, thorough documentation, etc.) may make proprietary packages not much more expensive. However, an open source application also has other advantages, including (see Hoffer et al. 2009):

- A large pool of volunteer testers and developers facilitate the construction of reliable, low-cost software in a relatively short amount of time; in other words, the future viability of the application software does not depend on one vendor.

- The ability to modify source code to add new features you want, not those on the priority list developed by the marketing department of the software vendor; your new code can be easily inspected by others; even the ability to review the original source code (rather than having to treat it as a "black box") means that you can inspect it thoroughly before deployment.

- You do not become dependent on one vendor or proprietary code, which may not allow you to enhance the software as your needs change.

- The acquisition cost is the same for one copy or thousands, so it can be much less expensive to make the software available to a large number of users throughout your (perhaps global) organization than would acquiring multiple-user licenses for proprietary applications.

- You may use the software for any purpose (e.g., for your own use, to distribute with software you write, for profit-making activities).

- Because the source code is open, it may be easier to interface different open source packages with each other, and you would not have to be dependent on the software vendor to provide this service.

However, there are some risks with open source application software, including:

- The absence of complete documentation without paying for it from some service provider.

- Only commodity type applications (that is, applications that are generic and common to many organizations—e.g., a catalog-type e-commerce Web site) are viable; otherwise, there is no motivation among a large enough community of users for

you to expect that the software will advance with the general needs of users like yourself.

- Unless there is some cooperative group of users, different adopters may not know what others are doing, so there can be duplication of efforts; at least with proprietary software, vendors usually announce what future enhancements are coming and when; however, it is possible through cooperation to join forces on the development of features desired by several open source adopters.

- There are different types of open source licensing agreements, so you must be careful to choose software with a license that suits your needs (e.g., whether you must share code changes or whether you can sell new applications you might build from the open source code you acquire).

NEW PURCHASING OPTION: APPLICATION SERVICE PROVIDERS (ASPs)

A new trend (or a renewal of an old practice) related to implementing packaged solutions began to emerge in the IT industry during the first decade of the new millennium: **application service providers (ASPs)**. Note that we do not distinguish here between an ASP and a newer term—*software as a service (SaaS)*—or the alternative term, *on-demand software*. Under this kind of purchasing option, the purchaser elects to use a "hosted" application rather than to purchase the software application and host it on its own equipment. The ASP is therefore an ongoing service provider, and the ASP option is a different kind of make–versus-buy decision. Instead of having a software licensing agreement with a firm that developed the software, a company pays a third party (ASP) for delivering the software functionality over the Internet to company employees and sometimes the company's business partners. The ASP host owns the licenses for the software. Almost any software can be delivered via an ASP, from basic office automation (e.g., Microsoft Office) to specialized application software (e.g., Salesforce.com) and large ERP systems (e.g., the Oracle ERP suite). The most common ASP services are for Web site hosting, e-mail, financial/accounting applications, and e-commerce. The ASP client pays for as much or as little of the software service as they need (based on number of users and which modules of the package the client uses), rather than having to buy a minimal number of licenses from the original vendor.

The ASP provider may be a specialist in the particular hosted software or in some vertical industry suite of software (e.g., software for firms in the health care industry). Many ASP hosts are oriented to supporting small to medium-sized businesses in a particular geographical area (when they can meet directly with clients). Some ASPs provide auxiliary services, such as arranging for the local networking and ISP service to provide Internet access, and purchasing and maintaining thin-client workstations for their customers (when thin clients are sufficient because all software and data storage are maintained at the ASP host site).

The two major *advantages* associated with purchasing a package, which were discussed at the beginning of this chapter, are also advantages for choosing an ASP: (1) cost savings and (2) faster speed of implementation. A subscription-based service with an ASP typically involves monthly fees (pay as you go) rather than large up-front IT investments in both the software package and additional infrastructure investments to host the package. You can stop the service at any time without large "sunk costs" associated with purchasing. For companies with widely dispersed employees requiring remote access, an ASP solution can also reduce network access and other service delivery costs. Because the package is also typically already up and running on the ASP's host computer, the implementation project should also be less time-consuming. Also, the hosting service provides all software maintenance and operational support, freeing up your IT staff to work on other applications. Often, your organization can afford to use a package with more functionality (arguably the best or industry standard software) than you might be able to afford by directly purchasing the software.

However, there are also some potential downsides, including dependence on an external vendor not just for the software package, but also for ongoing operations. Good processes for making the best purchasing decision and contracting for the needed service levels are even more critical when an organization enters into an ASP agreement. A purchasing process that carefully assesses the capability of an ASP to provide reliable performance and the likelihood of the ASP surviving in the marketplace are especially important for ASP contracts, because this market is still in its infancy. Some of these risks appear to be diminished when the ASP host is also a large software vendor—such as SAP or PeopleSoft for ERP modules or Siebel Systems for CRM modules. The ASP host may not be in the business of integrating their hosted software with

client-hosted software; thus, the ASP model works best for stand-alone applications. Also, the host will not customize the software for the client (beyond any customization features built into the software such as including your organization's logo in computer-generated documents). Security (ensuring your data will be protected from access by others, especially those in competitor organizations using the same hosting service) can be a concern, but most ASPs provide high-end security services. Finally, the hosting service may require you to convert to new versions of the packaged software, which may not be when you want to convert.

Metrics for vendor performance and penalties for noncompliance should be a key part of the contract. A **service level agreement** should be part of the contract, in which specific performance expectations are set for various operational metrics—such as system uptime, recovery time, wait time on calls to the help desk, notifications about software upgrades, and other factors important to the customer. As described in the box entitled "A Dream Versus a Nightmare," if you do not do a good job with the ASP selection process up-front, you risk paying the price later.

A DREAM VERSUS A NIGHTMARE

It was an IT manager's worst nightmare. The OshKosh B'Gosh Company online store was open, but the orders went nowhere: The communications link between the clothing retailer and the company that hosted its Web application had gone down. Resolving the nightmare was further complicated because the ASP with which OshKosh had contracted had subcontracted with another firm to host their application. And OshKosh's telecommunications carrier needed to get into the hosting site to repair the equipment. According to CIO Jon Dell-Antonia at OshKosh, "It was like the Three Stooges and the Keystone Cops combined. If I went through the whole litany, you'd be rolling on the floor laughing. But we were not laughing at the time."

One common mistake companies make when choosing an ASP vendor is that they involve their application specialists in the meetings with the prospective ASPs, but not their computer operations specialists. According to an analyst with the Gartner Group, customers should concentrate not just on the A in ASP—the application that will be provided—but also the S—the service. You need to carefully document your needs first, before you start talking to an ASP.

[Adapted from Anthes, 2000]

SUMMARY

Purchasing packaged software is an alternative to custom software development that has been increasingly pursued by organizations of all sizes since the early 1990s. The fact that packaged solutions can be implemented more quickly than a custom-developed solution with the same, or similar, functionality is a major advantage in today's fast-changing business environment. A major disadvantage can be increased dependence on a vendor that could go out of business.

The process for purchasing an application is based on the same life-cycle phases as a custom approach: Definition, Construction, and Implementation. Even if an application is to be purchased, an organization first must define its basic system needs before attempting to select the best off-the-shelf application solution. The Definition phase also includes the development of an RFP to be sent to software vendors and an evaluation of the vendor responses. If successful, the Definition phase ends with a vendor contract, which should be negotiated with the help of contract specialists.

The time spent on Construction phase activities varies greatly depending on whether or not the source code of the package is modified, which may be done by the vendor, another outside supplier, or the purchasing company. In the case of large packaged systems for which there are expected to be frequent future releases (such as ERP modules), modifications are typically kept to a bare minimum. In contrast, the Implementation phase for a software package can be more challenging than for a custom application because of the purchasing company's lack of familiarity with the details of how the package operates as well as the need for large-scale changes in the way the company will operate once the new package has been implemented. The software vendor might be heavily involved in the installation step and is also typically relied on for ongoing maintenance. Large enterprise system vendors (such as SAP) typically release new versions on a frequent basis and support older versions of the package only for a set period of time.

Expertise in the implementation of packaged systems has become an important IT capability. In some firms new manager positions have been created in order to manage relationships with IT vendors. Organizations are increasingly considering open source packages in addition to proprietary application packages. Open source packages can be obtained with low up-front investment; support can be obtained for a fee from various service providers. A new procurement option is to pay an application service provider to host a software application for remote access by company employees via the Internet.

REVIEW QUESTIONS

1. What are the major trade-offs in a make-or-buy decision?
2. Summarize the five additional steps for purchasing a system that are not part of the Definition phase of a traditional SDLC process.
3. What is an RFP, and what critical tasks does it facilitate in the purchasing process?
4. Why is making a lot of modifications to a packaged system sometimes a risky approach, and what are the alternatives?
5. Briefly summarize how the phases of the traditional SDLC are similar to or different from the phases of the modified life-cycle approach in support of the cost comparisons in Figure 11.2.
6. Describe the role of the vendor for each of the three phases of the purchasing life cycle.
7. Describe why the methodology for purchasing a small system could differ from purchasing a large system.
8. Describe what a purchasing company might want to learn from a vendor demonstration of a packaged system.
9. What do you think are the most important advantages and disadvantages of purchasing a package?
10. What are some of the major differences between a process to implement an ERP package and the process to implement a less complex package?
11. What are the critical success factors for running an ERP project?
12. What are the relative advantages and disadvantages of open source software versus proprietary application packages?
13. What is an ASP and why is this an attractive purchasing alternative?

DISCUSSION QUESTIONS

1. Critique the following statements: It would cost us $800,000 to build this system, but we can purchase an equivalent package for $125,000. Therefore, we can save the organization $675,000 by purchasing the software package.
2. Discuss the options an organization needs to choose from when the best packaged-system solution is not a perfect fit with the needs of the organization.

3. You run a small business. You have no IS specialists on your staff and plan to purchase all your software. What might be your three most important concerns?

4. You are a manager in a company that has a lot of in-house IS expertise. What might be your key decision rules for when to purchase a system versus when to develop it in-house?

5. Discuss why an assessment of the financial stability of the vendor can be a critical consideration when evaluating responses to an RFP.

6. Choose one of the five factors associated with successful ERP implementations (presented in the section entitled "Special Case: Enterprise System Packages") and comment on how different this really is (or is not) from other packaged system implementations.

7. Many midsized firms are investing in ERP system packages, such as SAP and Oracle/PeopleSoft. Comment on what you think might be particularly important parts of the decision-making process when the purchasing organization has only a small IS department

8. Revise Figure 11.3 to make it a list of criteria for assessing an application service provider (ASP).

9. Research two competing packages for some application, one proprietary and one open source. Develop a list of criteria for selecting between these packages and then compare these packages on the criteria. What advantages does the open source package have? What disadvantages?

10. Modify Figure 11.7 to focus just on ERP packages.

11. Modify Figure 11.7 to focus on open source packages.

REFERENCES

Anthes, Gary H. 2000. "Asking the right questions up front can mean the difference between a dream relationship and a nightmarish one." *Computerworld* 34 (October 10): 21.

Applegate, Lynda M., Robert D. Austin, and F. Warren McFarlan. 2003. *Corporate Information Strategy and Management,* 6th ed. Boston: McGraw Hill.

Bailey, Jeff. 1999. "Trash haulers are taking fancy software to the dump." *Wall Street Journal* (June 9): 1.

Brown, Carol V., and Iris Vessey. 2003. "Managing the next wave of enterprise systems: Leveraging the lessons from ERP projects." *MIS Quarterly Executive* 2, 1 (March).

Everdingen, Yvonne van, Jos van Hillegersberg, and Eric Waarts. 2000. "ERP adoption by European midsize companies." *Communications of the ACM* 43 (April): 27–31

Fuß, Carolin, Ralf Gmeiner, Dirk Schiereck, and Susanne Strahringer. 2007. "ERP Usage in Banking: An Exploratory Survey of the World's Largest Banks." *Information Systems Management* (24): 155–171.

Gurbaxani, Vijay, and Seungjin Whang. 1991. "The impact of information systems on organizations and markets." *Communications of the ACM* 34 (January): 59–73.

Hoffer, Jeffrey A., Mary B. Prescott, and Heikki Topi. 2009. *Modern Database Management,* 9th ed. Upper Saddle River, NJ: Pearson Education.

Hoffman, Thomas, and Sarwar Kashmeri. 2000. "Realistic ASPirations." *Computerworld* 34 (August 7): 46.

Keen, Peter G. W. 1991. "Managing the economics of information capital." *Shaping the Future: Business Design Through Information Technology*. Boston: Harvard Business School Press.

Kien, Sia Siew, and Christina Soh. 2003. "An Exploratory Analysis of the Sources and Nature of Misfits in ERP Implementations." in Graeme Shanks, Peter B. Seddon, and Leslie P. Willcocks (eds.), *Second-Wave Enterprise Resource Planning Systems: Implementing for Effectiveness*. Cambridge, UK: Cambridge University Press.

Lucas, Henry C., Jr., Eric J. Walton, and Michael J. Ginzberg. 1988. "Implementing packaged software." *MIS Quarterly* 12 (December): 525–549.

Markus, M. Lynne. 2000. "Conceptual Challenges in Contemporary IS Research." *Communications of the Association for Information Systems* 3(4): 141–170.

Markus, M. Lynne, and Robert I. Benjamin. 1997. "The magic bullet theory in IT-enabled transformations." *Sloan Management Review* 38 (Winter): 55–68.

Markus, M. Lynne, Sheryl Axline, David Petrie, and Cornelis Tanis. 2003. "Learning from Experiences with ERP: Problems Encountered and Success Achieved." in Graeme Shanks, Peter B. Seddon, and Leslie P. Willcocks (eds.), *Second-Wave Enterprise Resource Planning Systems: Implementing for Effectiveness*. Cambridge, UK: Cambridge University Press.

Martin, E.W. 1988. "Halsted, Inc." Indiana University teaching case.

Rockart, John F., and J. Debra Hofman. 1992. "Systems delivery: Evolving new strategies." *Sloan Management Review* 33 (Summer): 21–31.

Ross, Jeanne. 1998. "The ERP revolution: Surviving versus thriving." MIT Sloan School CISR Research Paper.

Schwalbe, Kathy. 2004. *Information Technology Project Management,* 3rd ed. Canada: Thomson Learning.

CHAPTER 12
IT PROJECT MANAGEMENT

THE OVERALL GOALS OF SYSTEMS PROJECTS ARE TO IMPLEMENT A QUALITY system that meets the needs of the targeted business and its users, on schedule and within budget. Achieving these project goals requires not only an appropriate systems methodology (such as the SDLC, prototyping, "agile" approaches, and purchasing life cycle discussed in the previous chapters), but also "best practices" for managing projects.

The Project Management Institute (PMI), an international society of project workers, has developed detailed guides for managing projects (PMBOK Guide) and certified thousands of project management professionals for more than two decades (www. pmi. org). The management competencies certified by the PMI include nine areas (see Figure 12.1). Four of these have traditionally been associated with project management: managing the project scope, time to completion, project costs, and human resources. The five other competency areas have been developed more recently: managing project communications, procurement (including contract management), quality management, risk management, and project integration. Managers of IT projects therefore need to be skilled in these nine project management competencies, as well as "best practices" for managing systems projects in particular.

In today's fast-changing business environment, IT project work also needs to stay in synch with changes in the business.

Although an IT project has been approved, and resources have been committed to it, unanticipated events may also need to be addressed. These range from new corporate initiatives that affect a company's products or customer base, as well as external events such as unexpected changes in national or international laws, political events, natural disasters, or even health epidemics. Reevaluating IT projects in light of such events is the responsibility of both business and IT managers, and many organizations have implemented a committee of senior business leaders to approve, prioritize, and oversee such projects from an **IT portfolio management** perspective.

Even more common today is a "project office," or **program management office (PMO)**, to ensure that projects in different stages of completion are coordinated. The PMO is staffed with managers experienced in managing project budgets, scheduling resources, and using tools that keep track of projects across work teams and business stakeholders. Their objective is to help ensure projects are run well and are successful. The PMO might be a temporary unit set up for a large, enterprise-wide systems project (such as a multiyear ERP or CRM systems project described in Chapter 6), a permanent unit within an IS organization, or a permanent unit within a corporate office that serves many functional areas.

Project scope	Project time	Project cost
Human resources	Quality management	Risk management
Project communications	Procurement	Project integration

Figure 12.1 Nine Project Management Competencies

A **project** is a temporary endeavor undertaken to create a unique product or service. It typically is a one-time initiative that can be divided into multiple tasks, which require coordination and control, with a definite beginning and ending.

Project management is the application of knowledge, skills, tools, and techniques to a broad range of activities. In order to meet the requirements of a particular project (PMBOK Guide, 3rd ed.)

A **program** is a group of projects managed in a coordinated way to obtain benefits not available from managing them individually (PMI, 1996).

A **Program Management Office (PMO)** or "project office" is an organizational unit responsible for ensuring that standard approaches to project management are utilized across projects and "best practices" are shared across project teams.

In this chapter we first briefly discuss the growing issue of how to manage an organization's portfolio of IT projects; we will return to this topic in Part 4 of this textbook. Then we introduce the key project management roles and describe in detail some approaches to managing the four stages of an IT project once it has been prioritized and initially funded: (1) project initiation, (2) project planning, (3) project execution and control, and (4) project closing. In the project execution and control section we focus on two capabilities that are especially important for successfully managing IT projects: managing project risks and managing business change.

The chapter ends with some guidelines for two special IT project management issues: (1) managing large, complex IT projects (such as enterprise system package implementations) and (2) managing a project with "virtual teams" (in which team members are geographically dispersed).

IT PORTFOLIO MANAGEMENT

As organizations have become highly dependent on integrated data for their strategic and operational decision making, there has been an increasing emphasis on a portfolio approach to IT investments. **IT portfolio management** is typically the responsibility of a committee of senior business leaders and IT leaders who approve and prioritize IT project requests for an entire organization, and then monitor progress on approved IT projects until they are completed. An organization's IT portfolio usually includes investments in new IT applications as well as IT infrastructure investments (networks, servers, storage equipment, data warehouses) to support these applications.

New IT project requests are typically submitted using an organization-specific template that captures the expected business benefits and both the initial resource costs for the project and the ongoing resource costs for maintaining the new system (see the example in Figure 12.2). Most organizations also want to review an initial return on investment (ROI) analysis, or other formal financial assessment to help the committee of business and IT leaders assess what are the right set of IT projects to work on (given the organization's current competitive environment) and what priority should they be given for resource allocation. For large, complex projects, however, only a rough order of magnitude (ROM) cost estimate may be possible at the time of the initial request.

As part of the system prioritization process, an evaluative categorization scheme for all projects of a certain size is typically applied. One such scheme, based on Denis et al. (2004), would categorize projects into four buckets:

- *Absolute Must*   A mandate due to security, legal, regulatory, or end-of-life-cycle IT issues

- *Highly Desired/Business-Critical*   Includes short-term projects with good financial returns and portions of very large projects already in progress

- *Wanted*   Valuable, but with longer time periods for returns on investment (more than a 12-month period)

- *Nice to Have*   Projects with good returns, but with lower potential business value

In most organizations projects in the top two categories would most likely be funded for the budget year in which they were submitted. The "Wanted" projects might involve the most contentious prioritization decisions. The business leaders who will be paying for the projects (business sponsors) typically present the business cases for the project. Many practitioners emphasize that a senior committee

PROJECT DESCRIPTION	**MAJOR MILESTONES**
Implement Learning Delivery system to build and deliver virtual classes, conference calls, Web meetings, and other e-learning events. Implementation target is 18 months from project initiation.	· Project Scope and Approval · Publish RFP · Vendor Screening/Evaluation/Selection · Architecture Review · Implementation · Training · Go-Live
BUSINESS BENEFIT	**LEVEL OF EFFORT/COST**
Creates dependable, cost-effective, scalable solutions that offer all learners rich distance learning experience to expand their knowledge in the way that works best for them. Cite savings and revenue generation expected.	· 100 hrs ERP Interface · 300 hrs Build Learning · 100 hrs customization · Estimated Licensing, Time & Materials (500 hrs × hrly rate = $$$$) · Total Cost of Ownership (annual or per user) · FTE support required
DEPENDENCIES/RED FLAGS	
Project budget, Resource & skill sets, Technology	

Figure 12.2   Project Prioritization Template (Vavra and Lane, 2004)

approach to IT project approvals and prioritization results not only in a list of current prioritized IT projects for funding, but also in a better understanding among the organization's business and IT executives about the reasons for why a given IT project was funded, or not funded.

Besides assessing new requests, the same committee typically will also be charged with monitoring the status of all current IT projects underway in order to ensure that the company's IT investments are staying aligned with the company's business goals. Some organizations are now doing this on a quarterly basis—referred to as a "dynamic" portfolio management process.

PROJECT MANAGEMENT ROLES

Every IT project will have at least one assigned IT project manager and a project sponsor (the business owner of the project). We describe these two roles next, as well as a third

role that is critical for some projects: the business manager role of project champion.

Project Manager

A systems project is typically led by an IT project manager with technical and managerial skills. This manager is responsible for managing relationships with the project sponsor and other stakeholders, as well as leading and managing all technical activities for the project. Some projects involve managing not only in-house IT professionals assigned to the project, but also employees of IT vendors associated with the project.

In some situations, a business manager could also be selected as a project manager or co-manager. The choice of the project manager depends not only on the degree to which the application project could affect a specific business unit or division, but also on the degree to which the project requires technical expertise, both internal and external.

Leadership Skills: Sets example, energetic, vision (big picture), delegates, positive attitude

Organizational Skills: Planning, goal-setting, analyzing

Communication Skills: Listening, persuading

Team-Building Skills: Empathy, motivation, esprit de corps

Coping Skills: Flexibility, creativity, patience, persistence

Figure 12.3 Nontechnical Skills for Effective Project Management

The project manager's responsibilities in general are to plan and execute the project, including controlling for project risks and ensuring that necessary business changes have been implemented. This requires several different types of skills, including team management skills (see Figure 12.3). A major characteristic of any project is "uniqueness," so all projects are learning experiences for the project manager (Meredith and Mantel, 1989). This is especially true for a systems project, because the typical IT project involves new technologies. In other words, no amount of planning can take into account the variety of unexpected events that occur during the course of the project. Effective project managers also are good leaders. Sometimes this entails being politically savvy—aware of what not to do as well as what to do in a given organizational context. Riskier projects, such as when new, unproven technologies are involved, also require coping skills and a high tolerance for ambiguity (Frame, 1994).

Project Sponsor and Champion Roles

Most IT projects have multiple business stakeholders: managers and users with vested interests in the outcome of the project. Two business stakeholder roles, if played well, have been associated with successfully managed systems projects: the project sponsor and the project champion.

The **project sponsor** role is typically played by the business manager who financially "owns" the project (i.e., the person who "writes the check" for the project). The sponsor participates in the development of the initial project proposal, including an assessment of the feasibility of the project. The sponsor also argues for the approval of the systems project before the committee members responsible for new system project approvals. For systems projects that will be implemented in multiple business functions or

business units, the sponsor is likely to be an officer of the company (CEO, president, CFO) or the designated owner of a major business process (such as a supply chain process). For systems projects that are major hardware and telecommunications infrastructure investments only, the CIO is likely to be the designated project sponsor.

Once the systems project has been initiated, the project sponsor provides the funds for the project and helps play an oversight role during the life of the project. For example, the sponsor typically takes responsibility for ensuring that the most appropriate ("best") business managers and other users are assigned to the project team, and that these project team members are empowered to make decisions for the business units they represent. The sponsor also is relied on to provide business personnel who are not formal team members as needed at certain points in the project— such as providing information about current work processes or procedures in the Definition phase, evaluating screen designs from a user perspective early in a Construction phase, performing system tests at the end of a Construction phase, or training other users during an Implementation phase. Because the business unit often cannot easily spare the most capable business managers and users for part- or full-time IT project work, the business sponsor makes the necessary financial and work arrangements to "free up" these project team members from their normal tasks and responsibilities, so that they can put forth the level of effort that is needed for the project to succeed.

It is critical for the project manager to have a strong relationship with the project sponsor from the very beginning of the project. Suggestions for how a project manager can keep a typically busy executive engaged in an IT project are provided in the box entitled "Tasks to Engage and Maintain Project Sponsors." Once the system project has been completed, the sponsor should also be held accountable for ensuring that the projected system benefits are achieved after the system is installed.

The **project champion** role is another business stakeholder role associated with successful IT projects. In essentially all situations, the champion role needs to be played by a business manager for the following reason: A business manager with high credibility among the business users most affected by the new system solution will be best able to prepare workers for any process changes required. This involves continual communications throughout the project about its goals and the milestones achieved. Personal traits of an effective project champion include an enthusiasm that never wanes and the capability to "rally the troops" as problems arise that require exceptional efforts.

TASKS TO ENGAGE AND MAINTAIN PROJECT SPONSORS

- Schedule regular meetings with the sponsor to ensure the project is on track, according to current business priorities
- Create a list of expectations with the sponsor to clarify the project manager role and the sponsor's role
- Agree on how handoffs between the project manager and sponsor will occur
- Discuss the sponsor's preferences for when and how project issues will be brought up with the sponsor
- Learn how the sponsor will communicate the status of the project to peers and the company's top management
- Determine what metrics the sponsor will use to judge the completion of the project
- Agree on how the sponsor will participate in the post-project review

[Adapted from Russell, 2007]

In contrast to the project sponsor role, the champion role is not always a formally designated one, although the champion's contribution to the project's success can be critically important. For some IT projects, the project sponsor and the project champion may be the same person. For example, for enterprise-wide system projects a CEO, CFO, COO, or CMO might play both roles. However, for other projects in which the sponsor's daily responsibilities are far removed from the business activities to be affected by the new system, the champion role is better played by a lower level business manager whose direct reports will be highly impacted by the project.

PROJECT INITIATION

The first phase of a project life cycle is the project initiation phase. A key deliverable for this phase is a project charter that states in some detail the project's specific objectives, its intended scope, any underlying assumptions, and the estimated benefits based on the feasibility analysis step of the IT project. A broad statement of scope for a large ERP package implementation project would include the specific ERP package modules to be purchased (e.g., finance/accounting, materials management) as well as the number of divisions and geographic locations within the enterprise to be included in the proposed project.

The scoping of a project involves setting boundaries for the project's size and the range of business functions or processes that will be involved. A high-level diagram is used to capture the major actors (entities) that provide inputs or receive outputs from the proposed system. (For examples, see the context diagram and the use case diagram descriptions in Chapter 9).

As described in Chapter 10, three types of feasibility analyses are typically conducted for systems projects as part of the Definition phase of a systems life cycle: economic feasibility, operational feasibility, and technical feasibility. Some of the technology feasibility questions to consider are the expected maturity level of the technologies to be used and the ease with which the needed technical expertise can be acquired (bought) or transferred to sufficient numbers of internal IS specialists. A common pitfall here is that the potential for major "technical shortfalls" is not adequately taken into account. To do so may require IS managers with strong relationships with the vendors of the IT products to be utilized.

The economic feasibility investigation usually involves a formal cost-benefit analysis based on the overall objectives and scope of the project as well as an estimate of the project budget. For projects with benefits that are easily measured, an ROI will be easy to calculate. However, for projects that involve a business innovation, such as building a new organizational capability, it is much more difficult to quantify the potential benefits. For these types of strategic application projects, a technique such as rank-ordering the alternatives can be used to overcome total reliance on ROI measures that could be very difficult to calculate (see Figure 12.4).

Several other types of feasibility concerns can also be studied in order to better understand the best way to manage a systems project and its interdependencies, including schedule feasibility, legal and contractual feasibility, and political feasibility. Schedule feasibility takes into account the potential impact of externally imposed deadlines, such as the effective date of a new federal regulation or a seasonal date of importance for competing in a given industry. Legal and contractual feasibility concerns might need to be investigated to understand the issues related to partnering with one or more IT vendors for delivering the product solution. Political feasibility involves an assessment of support for the proposed system on behalf of key organizational stakeholder groups, which may not have been captured as part of an operational feasibility study. For example, a systems innovation with major potential impacts for the way an organization conducts its business could require special capabilities that organizational members do not yet possess, or the innovation could be perceived as a major

Rank Alternatives	Even if it is not possible to compute explicit numerical values, it may be possible to estimate with enough accuracy to rank the alternatives.
Sensitivity Analysis	Use sensitivity analysis to deal with uncertainties. If a precise value is not known for a parameter, repeat the analysis with alternative values.

Figure 12.4 Alternatives to ROI for Justifying Investments

competitive threat to one organizational group but not another.

As described earlier, a committee of business and IT leaders is typically charged with new system project approvals and prioritization. This committee also typically approves the project charter from the project initiation phase before additional resources are committed. If approved, the charter document also serves as a tool for the project manager, the project sponsor, and the IS and business oversight committees to monitor adherence to the agreed-upon project objectives and scope over the life of the project.

PROJECT PLANNING

The three major components of project planning are project scheduling, budgeting, and staffing. These components are obviously interrelated, and poor planning for one component can severely affect another. Good estimation techniques are especially important for systems projects that involve immature or emerging technologies. In general, conservative (rather than optimistic) estimations are recommended, as well as control mechanisms that focus on the areas of greatest project uncertainty and organizational vulnerability. Although we emphasize next some proven techniques for good project planning and control, it should also be kept in mind that experienced project managers will tailor their approaches to match the special circumstances of a given project or organizational situation (see the box entitled "256 Project Characteristics To Be Managed").

"Scope creep" is often touted as a potential pitfall to watch out for during project planning. However, sometimes changes in the project scope are positive changes that result from a better understanding of business needs or technology capabilities during the planning phase. According to

256 PROJECT CHARACTERISTICS TO BE MANAGED

Projects can have an overwhelming number of different characteristics. They can be high-risk or low-risk, long-term or short-term, state-of-the-art or routine, complex or simple, single-function or cross-functional, large or small, technology-driven or market-driven, contracted out or performed in-house, and so on. These eight characteristics alone can lead to 256 different combinations that might entail a different approach to project planning, execution, or control.

[Adapted from Roman, 1986]

Russell (2007), "scope creep" only becomes a problem when the project manager and business stakeholders don't agree that the scope has been changed and the impacts of these changes aren't formally and realistically accounted for in the project schedule, budget, and staffing.

Scheduling

Developing a project schedule typically involves a **work breakdown analysis**: identifying the phases and sequence of tasks that need to be accomplished to meet the project goals—as well as the goals for other organizational and external party obligations—and then estimating the time of completion for each task. For systems projects, the project phases as well as the detailed activities for each step and their sequence can typically be derived from the systems methodology being used for the project.

Work breakdown is a basic management technique that systematically subdivides blocks of work down to the level of detail at which the project will be controlled.

Time estimates are typically based on the relevant past experiences of the organization or the project manager, or both. Other sources for time estimates include benchmarking studies for similar projects in other organizations, activity estimates embedded in software estimation packages, and project databases of system consultants.

The detailed work activity list, the task interdependencies, and the time estimates for each task are then used to develop a master schedule for the project that identifies the **project milestone** dates and deliverables. The level of detail provided in a master schedule depends upon project characteristics such as size, functional complexity, and task interdependencies, as well as organizational practices.

Some project milestone dates will also be highly influenced by time demands particular to the organization. System implementation activities are frequently scheduled to coincide with calendar periods when transactions affected by the new system solution are much lower in number or can even be temporarily left unprocessed during the conversion to the new system. For example, it is very common for major system tests and new system cutovers in U.S.-based organizations to be scheduled for three-day holiday weekends. In other situations, a project implementation date near the end of a fiscal period will be targeted in order to minimize historical data conversions.

The project scheduling process is somewhat different when an organization has adopted a timeboxing philosophy. The term **timeboxing** refers to an organizational practice in which a system module is to be delivered to the user within a set time limit, such as six months. (This technique is a characteristic of the rapid application development [RAD] methodology discussed in Chapter 10.) Because the intent of timeboxing is to deliver new IT solutions as rapidly as possible, a work plan might be designed in which a given module is initially implemented during the timebox without full functionality, and then the functionality is increased in subsequent releases.

A common pitfall in developing a master schedule is a failure to understand the interdependencies among project tasks and subtasks. Including a customer verification step as part of the master scheduling process can help identify misunderstandings at an early stage of the project planning cycle. Another common pitfall is estimating task completion times based on a level of expertise associated with an experienced worker, rather than the average worker typically available in the organization.

Effective scheduling is critical to the project's success and is a key input to the project budgeting component. However, the master schedule is also meant to be a living document. A good planning process therefore also provides for change-control procedures to request schedule changes. Aside from a process to request the necessary management approvals, changes to the master schedule should be documented with the date of the change, the nature and reason for the change, and the estimated effects of the change on other project components (budget, resource allocations) and related project tasks.

Budgeting

The project budget documents the anticipated costs for the total project. These costs are typically aggregated into meaningful categories at the level at which the project costs will be controlled.

There are two traditional approaches to estimating project costs: bottom-up and top-down. The project work plan from the scheduling process is typically used for a bottom-up process: Cost elements are estimated for the lowest level of work plan tasks and then aggregated to provide a total cost estimate for the project. According to Frame (1994), a top-down approach "eschews" the cost details and provides instead estimates for major budget categories based on historical experience. A top-down approach (also called parametric cost estimating) could be used in the project initiation stage because not enough is known about the project to do a work breakdown analysis. However, once a master schedule has been developed, a bottom-up process is recommended, especially if the project is large and complex. These two approaches can also be used as checks for each other.

No matter which approach is used, the budgeting process needs to build in cost estimates to cover project uncertainties associated with changing human resources, immovable project deadlines (that could require overtime labor), as well as changes in technology and contract costs outside the organization's control.

Like the master schedule, the project budget is a living document of anticipated total costs. A good planning process therefore also provides change-control procedures to request approvals for deviations from an estimated budget. Changes to the budget should be documented with the date of change, the nature and amount of the requested budget deviation, the reason for the change, and the estimated effects of the change on other project components (scope, schedule, resource allocations).

According to Frame (1994), inexperienced estimators typically fall into three estimation traps: They (1) are too optimistic about what is needed to do the job, (2) tend to leave components out, and (3) do not use a consistent methodology, so they have difficulty recreating their rationales. Good training in how to estimate project steps and organizational checklists of items to include in estimates can help the amateur estimator quickly improve.

HIGHBALLING VERSUS LOWBALLING PROJECT COSTS

Budget padding is a common approach. Often there is no useful precedent to serve as a guide for a budget projection; past authorizations can be misleading or only partially applicable. Further, sometimes project budgets receive across-the-board cuts, favoring those who have submitted a padded budget in the first place. Budget padding is therefore sometimes the best defensive measure to ensure that adequate resources will be provided to get a job done.

Lowballing project costs can be conscious or unconscious. Sometimes lower estimates are provided in order to gain initial project approval. Other times the technical glitches that can arise are underestimated. Sometimes ignorance of an environmental event invalidates what was thought to be a well-informed estimate.

[Adapted from Frame, 1994; and Roman, 1986]

Even for the experienced project manager, cost estimations can be complicated by many types of unknowns, including the lack of precedents, unpredictable technical problems, and shifting business requirements. Projects that use standard and mature IT components are generally the easiest to estimate. Both budget padding and lowballing are apparently widely used, but both of these techniques can also cause dysfunctional consequences (see the box entitled "Highballing Versus Lowballing Project Costs").

Staffing

Project staffing involves identifying the IT skill mix for specialists assigned to the project, selecting personnel who collectively have the skills needed and assigning them to the project, preparing team members for the specific project work, and providing incentives for them to achieve the project goals.

In project work the human resources are a critical production factor. As part of the project planning, the project manager should be able to estimate the skill type, proficiency level, quantity, and time frame for personnel to execute each project phase and critical task. Some human resources need to be dedicated to the project full-time, whereas others (such as a database administrator) will likely be shared with other project teams. Still others (such as users who help test a system) might not be formal team members, but will be relied on for their expertise at critical points in the project.

Wherever possible, individual employees with the best qualifications for the project work should be selected.

However, in an organizational setting this is not always possible, due to the size and talent of the specialist pool internal to the organization. Because of the diverse set of specialist skills that might be needed across projects, it is not uncommon for at least a portion of the team members to undergo specialized training in anticipation of a project. Some IS organizations use a skill centers approach in which IS specialists belong to a **center of excellence** managed by a coach who is responsible for developing talent and selecting personnel for project assignments based not only on the project's needs for specific skill sets, but also on individual development needs (see the box entitled "Centers of Excellence at Bell Atlantic"). In addition, personnel from a PMO may be involved to help plan communications with key stakeholders and other business employees, as well as to ensure that the must current documents are available to all employees who need access to them.

For systems projects it is also not uncommon to hire outside contractors for project work for either quality or workload reasons. This is especially desirable if a distinct IT specialty is required for a single project but it does not make economic sense to develop and maintain these specialized resources in-house. It also might be impractical to use internal resources if a project requires a significant number of additional personnel for just a short period of time. The downside in these situations is that the company can become highly dependent on a talent base that is temporary. In the late 1990s, many companies began to focus on decreasing dependence on outside contractors by developing their own IT specialist talent. One way to do this is to build in a requirement for "knowledge transfer" to internal

CENTERS OF EXCELLENCE AT BELL ATLANTIC

Prior to its merger with another telecommunications company, Bell Atlantic began to implement 12 skill centers, also called Centers of Excellence. Each skill center was a semipermanent team of technical specialists or people trained in a specific IT skill, such as client/server, database management, or quality assurance. Each skill center was a "virtual homeroom" managed by a coach who was responsible for assigning IT personnel to specific application projects in order to achieve the project goals as well as the employee's career goals. The objective was to build an IT talent base of skilled IT professionals. Processes were developed to anticipate the skill sets needed for new development projects and to move people from older (e.g., COBOL) skill sets to newer ones.

[Adapted from Clark et al., 1997]

employees from the outside consultants or contractors as part of the external vendor contract.

Another key aspect of systems project team staffing is the selection of business personnel for the project team. Business personnel with enough authority and credibility to work with both business leaders and other business workers who will be using the new software need to be selected with the help of the project sponsor. The careful selection of business employees can obviously be a critical step in the staffing process. IS specialists are dependent on business users for their functional expertise (referred to as subject matter expertise, or SME). Formal documented procedures are not always the way that work tasks actually get done, and the project team must also be able to elicit these differences from business users as part of the Definition phase. Further, making major changes in the ways that business personnel get their work done can be a major project objective. Changes in business processes are most common when an organization is implementing a new software package without modifications (referred to as "vanilla" implementations), and the right business personnel need to be part of the project team to accomplish this objective. In addition, business personnel who are not formal team members may have a role as "extended" team members to help with defining the systems requirements, testing, and training over the life of the project.

Even after a well-managed selection process, there is sometimes a need for special team-building exercises to build team spirit and to help team members who have not worked together before to get to know each other quickly. The degree to which team-building is needed will depend on the characteristics of the project, the prior experiences of the team members, and the degree to which the systems methodology or other project practices will be new to the team members. Team-building and fostering ongoing motivation for meeting the project objectives are easiest when team members are in the same physical location (co-located), there is a stable roster of team members, and the project manager is able to manipulate the appropriate motivating factors. (See the section "Special Issue: Managing Virtual Teams" at the end of this chapter.)

Because project incentives can influence individual performance and productivity, projects that require especially intense efforts, personal sacrifices (such as postponed vacations), and possibly geographic relocation might also have attractive project-based incentives to help ensure that the project goals are achieved. The dot-com IT start-up culture within the United States in the late 1990s epitomized this highly intensive lifestyle for which stock options were the primary reward. Similar motivators are sometimes needed for IT projects with highly aggressive schedules in order to meet project deadlines. (Unlike a dot-com start-up, however, the duration of the project is usually known and the rewards can be more certain.) For example, key project team members on multi-year enterprise implementation projects could be asked to make commitments to the project in return for special project completion bonuses or even stock options. (See the box entitled "Project Completion Incentives when the Stakes Are High.") When designing incentives, it should also be kept in mind that an individual's response to a particular incentive can vary over time due to changing personal needs (such as family pressures for work-life balance).

PROJECT COMPLETION INCENTIVES WHEN THE STAKES ARE HIGH

When NIBCO's project planning phase ended, the company's leaders had a better understanding of the level of change that would be required for a successful "Big Bang" ERP project and the potential impacts of this project on the company's bottom line. To help motivate the right behaviors throughout the company, management established an incentive plan that would reward all NIBCO employees for a successful on-time, within budget project completion, as well as a special bonus for all project team members. The specific metrics were clearly communicated, and the board of directors was charged with the responsibility of determining whether the metrics were met. For example, for every $1 over the project budget, the incentive pool would be reduced by a half dollar. (For more details, see Case Study III-7, "NIBCO's 'Big Bang.'")

One of the public goals for the merger of Sallie Mae and the USA Group was a 40 percent reduction in costs, including a 25 percent headcount reduction that would partially come from a consolidation of the two companies' data centers, as well as the elimination of one of the two loan processing systems that had been custom-developed at each company. This meant that the new company was at risk for losing IT talent before these IT integration projects had been completed. To mitigate this serious risk, Sallie Mae quickly offered a retention package to the IT workers most likely to leave. The incentives offered were perceived by these workers as being "generous" ones, and the CIO was able to keep the IT talent that he needed to successfully complete a complex data center move within an aggressive timetable. (For more details, see Case Study IV-3, "Fast Track IT Integration for the Sallie Mae Merger.")

Planning Documents

Two documents are typically created from the project planning phase: a **statement of work (SOW)** for the customer and a project plan to be used by the project manager to guide, monitor, and control the execution of the project plan.

The SOW document is a high-level document that describes what the project will deliver and when. It is in effect a contract between the project manager and the executive sponsor. It therefore can be used as a high-level guide for business managers to plan for their own unit implementation as well as to monitor the project's progress toward the project goals of on-time completion within budget.

All program managers or committees that oversee the project typically review the project plan. For example, a program manager and other IT project managers may initially review the project plan, and then a project oversight committee of business managers and IS leaders may be asked to endorse it.

Two types of project management charts are also typically developed during the planning phase and used during project execution: (1) PERT (or CPM) charts and (2) Gantt charts. These are two complementary techniques for project scheduling and resource planning, as described next.

A PERT chart (a Program Evaluation and Review Technique developed for a missile/submarine project in 1958) graphically models the sequence of project tasks and their interrelationships using a flowchart diagram. (Note: Some organizations use an alternative method called CPM [Critical Path Method] developed by DuPont about the same time.) As shown in Figure 12.5, each major task is represented as a symbol (such as a circle or rectangle) and lines (arrows) are used to show predecessor and successor tasks. A PERT chart depicts what is referred to as a critical path—a sequence of activities that will take the longest to complete. Any delays in completing the activities on the critical path will result in slippage on the project schedule. A PERT chart therefore helps managers estimate the effects of task slippage and shows the tasks not on the critical path for which there will be some slack resources. Researchers have found that projects in which PERT (or CPM) techniques are used are less likely to have cost and schedule overruns (Meredith and Mantel, 1989).

A Gantt chart graphically depicts the estimated times (and later, the actual times) for each project task against a horizontal time scale. Tasks are presented in a logical order along with a bar graph depicting the estimated time duration for each task on an appropriate linear calendar (minutes, hours, days, or weeks) for the number of months and years planned for the life cycle of the project (see Figure 12.6). The precedence relationships in the PERT/CPM chart are reflected in the start and end dates of the activities, and overlapping tasks can be easily seen. Although time periods for tasks can also be shown on PERT or CPM charts, Gantt charts are particularly useful for displaying a project schedule and for tracking the progress of a set of tasks against the project plan (as discussed in the "Project Execution and Control" section next).

An important project management skill is to determine at what level of detail to plan the project tasks. Too much detail can be stifling and result in too much time being spent on tracking rather than on more critical project tasks. Too little detail can result in inadequate project management controls and both missed deadlines and cost overruns.

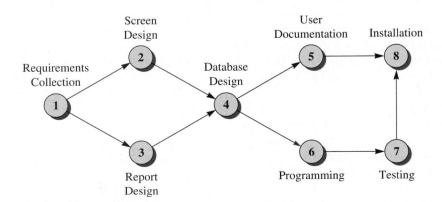

Figure 12.5 PERT Chart Example (Reprinted from Valacich, Joseph S.; George, Joey F.; and Hoffer, Jeffrey A., *Essentials of Systems Analysis & Design,* 1st Edition. Copyright © 2001. Reprinted by permission of Pearson Education, Inc., Upper Saddle River, NJ)

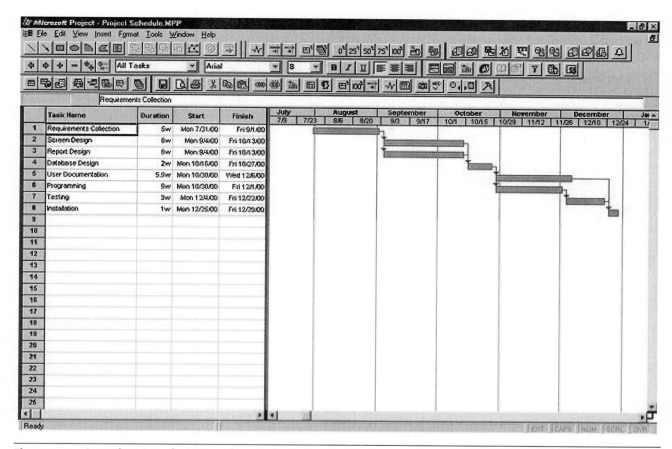

Figure 12.6 Gantt Chart Example (Reprinted from Valacich, Joseph S.; George, Joey F.; and Hoffer, Jeffrey A., *Essentials of Systems Analysis & Design,* 1st Edition. Copyright © 2001. Reprinted by permission of Pearson Education, Inc., Upper Saddle River, NJ)

PROJECT EXECUTION AND CONTROL

The *project plan* documents described in the preceding section are best recognized as living documents that need to be refined and reassessed throughout the life of the project. In large, complex projects, the planning activities still continue after a project team has been selected and some initial tasks have been undertaken, and the revised plan goes through the same endorsement procedures a few months into the project, as described previously.

Although projects vary by size, scope, time duration, and uniqueness, most projects share the three following life-cycle characteristics (PMI, 1996):

1. Risk and uncertainty are highest at the start of the project.
2. The ability of the project stakeholders to influence the outcome is highest at the start of the project.

3. Cost and staffing levels are lower at the start of the project and higher toward the end.

Software project management tools such as Microsoft Project are commonly used to help the project manager and other team leaders initiate and monitor the project tasks. In some cases an organization develops its own project management tools, or a consulting firm might provide such a system. Our focus here is not on the software tools used, but on three general project management practices: communication, coordination, and measuring progress.

Communication about the project to all affected stakeholders and potential users is key to successful implementation for systems projects in particular. For large projects with major business impacts, a project "kickoff" event is frequently scheduled at which the project's sponsor or champion explicitly communicates the project objectives and perhaps also presents some general ground rules for project team members to make decisions on behalf of their constituents.

It is the project manager's responsibility to have an external communications plan appropriate for the project. This includes formally communicating the project status on a regular basis (typically weekly or monthly) to any oversight groups, all key stakeholders, and the user community that will be affected by the project. Using the planning charts mentioned earlier, variances from the forecasted project budget and project milestones can be reported in a way that highlights deviations from the project plan and their causes (see Figure 12.7). When outside consultants are used, the tracking of consultant costs and utilization is also a key project manager responsibility.

Some organizations have also adopted a red-yellow-green (or red-amber-green, RAG) traffic light approach to signal what is "on track," potential problem areas, and project problems to business oversight groups:

■ Green indicates a project is on track

■ Yellow flags potential problems

■ Red means a project is behind

This type of high-level approach helps ensure that business managers focus on corrective actions to avoid a bottleneck, or consider major revisions to the project plan, to better manage project risks.

Good communications among the project team members are also critical for task coordination and integration. The mechanisms here include both formal activities (such as weekly meetings of team leaders) and informal (such as e-mail communications and in-the-hall progress reporting). Recently researchers (Kappelman et al., 2006) have provided evidence that potential project failures can be avoided if project managers and team members pay attention to "early warning signs" of people-related and process-related issues and then take appropriate actions to mitigate these risks. The 12 dominant "early warning signs" their study identified are shown in Figure 12.8.

Managing Project Risks

All projects carry some risks, and one of the goals of project management is to reduce the risk of failing to achieve the project's objectives. Standard risk management practices include: identification and classification of project risks, planning how to avoid them, and establishing plans to otherwise detect, mitigate, and recover from problems if they occur (see the summary in Figure 12.9). The extent of risk exposure for approved projects can vary widely across projects as well as across organizations. The culture of an organization can lead some managers to take a more defensive approach overall, while managers in a different organization might purposely pursue high-risk projects because of the potential for higher competitive rewards.

Risk identification should be undertaken at the project's outset, based on experience with similar projects. A common risk management approach is to develop a list of risk factors and then to weight them according to their potential impact. Identified risks are typically classified on several dimensions, including the nature and cause, the likelihood of occurrence, and the potential consequences. Risks can be due to a variety of causes, including characteristics of the project itself (project size, availability of business experts, newness of the technologies to be utilized), as well as characteristics of the external environment (competitive risk for not completing a project, extraordinary economic events).

The risk assessment for a given project is then used for decisions about project staffing or technical platform alternatives that lower the total risks, beginning with the planning stage. A potentially serious risk should be addressed by

- **Schedule Status**
    1. Scheduled and actual or forecasted completion dates
    2. Explanations of deviation(s)

- **Budget Status**
    1. Total project funding
    2. Expenditures to date of report
    3. Current estimated cost to complete
    4. Anticipated profit or loss
    5. Explanation of deviation, if any, from planned expenditure projection

Figure 12.7   Status Reporting (Roman, 1986)

People-Related Signs	Process-Related Signs
Lack of top management support	Lack of documented requirements and/or success criteria
Weak project manager	No change control process
No stakeholder involvement and/or participation	Ineffective schedule planning and/or management
Weak commitment of project team	Communication breakdown among stakeholders
Team members lack requisite knowledge and/or skills	Resources assigned to a higher priority project
Subject matter experts are overscheduled	No business case for the project

Figure 12.8   Early Warning Signs of IT Project Failure (Adapted from Kappelman et al., 2006)

Risk Identification and Analysis	Elicit, identify, and classify major project and process risks and determine the values of impact, likelihood, and time frame.
Risk Planning	Translate risk information into decisions and actions (both present and future) and implement those actions.
Risk Avoidance	Where possible, modify to minimize likelihood/impact of particular risk type.
Risk Monitoring	Track risk indicators and mitigation actions. Anticipate increasing likelihood of particular risks. Detect impending (or actual) occurrences where possible.
Risk Mitigation	If a problem occurs, take steps to limit its scope and impact to prevent a cascade of related problems.
Risk Management, Recovery, and Control	If a problem occurs, take steps to get the project back on track. Correct for deviations from the planned risk actions.

Figure 12.9   Risk Management Phases (Based on Mohtashami et al., 2006)

detailed plans and dedicated tasks. Some examples of common strategies for resource decisions are shown in Figure 12.10. For example, an exchange strategy could result in subcontracting with vendors, and a reduction strategy could result in allocating the "best and brightest" to a project team to minimize the potential for failure. Sometimes the project budget includes monetary resources allocated to a contingency fund that can be used at the discretion of project team members to resolve anticipated thorny problems that cannot be specifically defined at the outset of the project.

Exchange Strategy: An unknown risk or known critical risk is exchanged for a more acceptable level of risk. For example, the risk can be shifted to a third party by subcontracting with another organization under a fixed-cost contract for a specific project deliverable.

Reduction Strategy: By allocating to the project the best human resources available, a specific project risk can be reduced.

Avoidance Strategy: An alternative technical approach to a problem may be chosen in order to avoid risk exposure.

Figure 12.10 Common Strategies for Managing Risks (Based on Roman, 1986)

The highest level of project risk typically occurs at the project's outset. Once the project is underway and the team members learn more about a business unit's needs, a new technology, or a vendor's software package, the project risks will typically decrease. After more resources have been invested, the organization's stake in the project also increases and thus its risk exposure also increases: More will be lost if things go wrong (see Figure 12.11). However, in the earliest stages of the project fewer resources have been invested and it is easier to terminate the project.

Good risk management depends on accurate and timely information on project characteristics that managers view as likely indicators of risk (Hamilton, 2000). Deviations from expectations need to be clearly highlighted, and this information needs to reach the right people at the right time in order for further investigation and corrective actions to be taken. One of the major pitfalls in monitoring the risks of

projects that are already underway is to ignore negative feedback: Project managers need to be careful not to "turn a deaf ear" to bad news or to downplay symptoms of what could be major problems (Keil and Robe, 1999). An outside consultant may be needed to evaluate a troubled project and to help devise alternative courses of action.

Managing Business Change

When new systems are implemented, they typically involve major changes in business processes, which in turn require changes in the way employees do their work and information flows into and out of their work activities. **Change management**, or the ability to successfully introduce change to individuals and organizational units, is therefore key to successfully implementing a new system.

When a new information system will affect organizational power structures, strategies and tactics to deal with these political aspects of the project need to be explicitly developed. According to Markus (1983), the sources for resistance to the implementation of a new information system can often be anticipated by comparing the distribution of power implied by the new system and the distribution of power existing in the organization prior to the new system. Faced with potential shifts in organizational responsibilities, key stakeholders could consciously, or unconsciously, employ counterimplementation tactics that result in preventing or delaying the completion of a new system or in modifying its initial requirements. Examples of explicit or implicit resistance tactics include:

■ withholding the people resources needed for a task (including designating a representative who is not qualified to make the decisions needed)

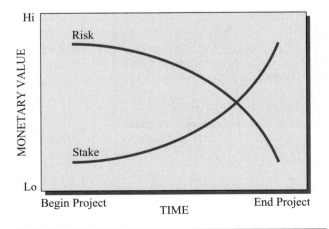

Figure 12.11 Risk Exposure: Risk Versus Stake (Adapted from Frame, 1994)

- raising new objections about the project requirements, resulting in schedule delays

- expanding the size and complexity of the project (rescoping)

Recognizing from the beginning of a project the potential political implications and then devising solutions to avoid them is usually more effective than overtly trying to overcome resistance tactics. Devising system solutions that will be viewed as desirable by all stakeholders is of course an ideal outcome. One key way to achieve this type of win-win situation is to involve potential objectors in the implementation process so that they participate in negotiating the requirements as well as the implementation schedule for a new system.

As business managers have come to recognize the importance of change-management practices in general, researchers have proposed multistage models for managing changes in organizations. Most of these change models have their roots in the simple three-stage **Lewin/Schein change model** shown in Figure 12.12.

In the first stage, Unfreezing, those individuals affected by the new system must realize the need for change. To help motivate change, a work environment in which it is "safe to change" needs to be created. That is, those individuals who need to change have to be convinced that giving up the old ways of doing things will not personally disadvantage them.

The Moving stage requires knowledge transfer and training. Until the knowledge and skills required for the new roles are acquired, change cannot take place. New ways to work need to be assimilated, and adequate time needs to be allocated for the people to learn these new skills and behaviors.

In the last stage, Refreezing, the new behavior becomes the accepted way of doing things. New incentive systems could be needed to reinforce the new behaviors, and the change might not be routinized until new informal norms have also been adopted within relevant workgroups across an enterprise.

Based on a study of successful and failed efforts to transform an organization, Kotter (1995) has proposed the eight-step model for leaders of major organizational change efforts in Figure 12.13.

The first four steps bring an organization to the Moving stage (described previously) by establishing a sense of urgency for the change and both creating and communicating a vision to help direct the change effort. The eighth step is similar to the Refreezing stage. According to Kotter, for a change to be institutionalized, it must be rooted in the organization's norms and values.

Today's common wisdom is that modern organizations and their people need to be able to accept change easily. This suggests that the institutionalization step, or Refreezing stage, might be pursued somewhat differently than when it was originally conceived. That is, a more typical organizational goal today is to have a workforce that has been reskilled but is also "change-ready," rather than becoming refrozen (Clark et al., 1997). Change-ready personnel also view change as a desirable, ongoing state for competing in today's business world.

Kotter and other change-management researchers have recently emphasized that major organizational change efforts cannot be entirely planned in advance. Instead, change efforts should be expected to be somewhat "messy" and "full of surprises" (Kotter, 1995). A successful change-management effort therefore requires both planned (preplanned) activities as well as "improvisational" responses to unforeseen circumstances (Orlikowski and Hofman, 1997). Similar to risk management, then, a major systems project trap is to ignore negative feedback. Paying careful attention to those in the organization who are closest to the people who will be affected by the systems project will help avoid implementation failure.

Three major categories of change-management activities have been associated with successful IT projects: communicating, training, and providing incentives. Communication activities are part of good project management, and communicating the need for change (the vision)

- Unfreezing
  - Establish a felt need
  - Create a safe atmosphere
- Moving
  - Provide necessary information
  - Assimilate knowledge and develop skills
- Refreezing

Figure 12.12 Three Stages of Lewin/Schein Change Model

---

1. Establish a sense of urgency
2. Form a powerful guiding coalition
3. Create a vision
4. Communicate the vision
5. Empower others to act on the vision
6. Plan for and create short-term wins
7. Consolidate improvements and produce still more change
8. Institutionalize new approaches

Figure 12.13 Change Model (Kotter, 1995)

is one of the first activities that needs to be addressed. The second category, training, is part of the installation step in a systems life cycle implementation phase. According to the practitioner press, however, the amount of user training required for an initial implementation success is typically underestimated. The third category, incentive system changes (such as performance rewards), helps motivate the attitudes and behaviors needed for the Lewin/Schein moving stage and helps institutionalize the behaviors for a Refreezing stage. Special project incentives may be used for high-risk projects and be under the control of the project manager(s). However, long-term incentive schemes to influence behavioral changes are clearly beyond the scope of a single project.

In many situations, the budget for an IT project does not include change management activities. Not allocating sufficient resources for managing business change when the implementation of an IT project includes major changes in business processes can be a major barrier to implementation success (Brown and Vessey, 2003). In organizations with a PMO (or project office), specific activities to ensure "change-readiness" are more likely to be a part of the project plan. These include formal assessments of the project's impacts on different types of job positions. Based on the level of these impacts, resources are then allocated for training workers. This type of approach was taken by Motorola (in their Semiconductor Products Sector) in preparation for a major ERP release that affected 5,700 employees worldwide. Under the leadership of their change-readiness unit, individual workers were assigned to instructor-led, train-the-trainer-led, or computer-based training depending on the anticipated impacts of the new system on the individual's job role (Roberts et al., 2003).

How close to the scheduled completion date was the project actually finished?
    What was learned about scheduling that will help us with future projects?

How close to budget were the final project costs?
    What was learned about budgeting that will help us with future projects?

At completion, did the project meet client specifications without additional work?
    If additional work was required, what was it?

What was learned that will help us with future projects about:
- communications during the project?
- writing specifications?
- staffing?
- managing conflict through negotiation?
- monitoring performance?
- taking corrective action?

What technological advances were made on this project?

What tools and techniques were developed that will be useful on future projects?

What was learned from our dealings with service organizations and outside vendors?

If we had the opportunity to redo the project, what would be done differently?

Figure 12.14   Questions for an IT Project Review [Adapted from Russell, 2007]

PROJECT CLOSING

A project close-out process begins when the IT project deliverables have been completed and a formal user acceptance or a user sign-off has occurred. Project managers should be required to document whether or not the project met its budget, schedule, scope, and other project success criteria.

A project closing should also include a formal post-project review step in which a set of "lessons learned" from managing the project are shared. This step might occur a few months later than the user acceptance sign-off.

Some common questions for team members to respond to in general are (based on Schwalbe, 2004):

- What went right on this project?
- What went wrong on this project?
- What would you do differently on the next project, based on your experience with this project?

The team member responses can be aggregated and summarized in a lessons-learned section of the report. Once collected, these lessons then need to be made accessible to other project team leaders, perhaps as part of a knowledge management initiative within the IT organization.

In today's complex business environments, one of the best survival strategies is to share expertise about what went right, what went wrong, and what project leaders would do differently (Wheatley and Kellner-Rogers, 1996; Schwalbe, 2004). Yet if there is no formal post-project review step, project team leaders typically do not take the time to document what actions helped the project succeed. A list of sample questions to be used in an IT project review process is provided in Figure 12.14.

SPECIAL ISSUE: MANAGING COMPLEX IT PROJECTS

Experienced IT project managers or IT program managers are increasingly likely to be asked to lead large, complex systems projects across an enterprise, such as ERP package implementations. Consulting firms are also frequently contracted to help with these complex projects because of their experiences in implementing the same package in other organizations.

According to Accenture consultant Hugh Ryan (2000), complexity must be accepted as a key characteristic of systems development and implementation projects in today's world. To deliver quality solutions in this type of environment, business managers must realize that complexity is unavoidable and that they must manage the associated project risks. A multiyear field review of how large, complex projects were implemented led to the identification of three high-level factors that are critical to success:

1. The business vision was an integral part of the project.
2. A testing approach was used at the program level (not just at the individual application level).
3. The projects used a phased-release approach (rather than a single-release rollout strategy).

Another source of project complexity comes from the use of outside contractors on a project. As shown in Figure 12.15, project complexity increases when contract workers are off-site rather than on-site during the project and when project team members are located in a different country, commonly referred to as "offshore." The management of off-site and offshore workers and projects is becoming an important IT capability as more programming work in particular is being outsourced to countries with significantly lower labor costs. Next we discuss the issue of managing virtual teams. In Chapter 15 we will address the challenges of managing IT outsourcing in general.

SPECIAL ISSUE: MANAGING VIRTUAL TEAMS

Project teams with members working at different locations within the same company have become increasingly common as distributed tools have facilitated working across organizational boundaries. These so-called "virtual teams" in which team members cannot work side-by-side are often formed to take advantage of unique skill sets or business knowledge not available at a single geographic location. More recently, IT project resources are also being selected in order to take advantage of lower labor costs. As a result, a single team in one location working under the same management team has become much less common. For example, a multinational company may assign some of their own IT workers based in offshore IT centers (in India, Brazil, or Macedonia) to an IT project led by a project manager in the United States or the United Kingdom—a practice referred to today as "best shore" offshoring.

In addition, as IT outsourcing has become more common over the past decade, companies in developed countries have also increasingly been *outsourcing* IT work to firms headquartered in the same country (domestic outsourcing) or in a different country (offshore outsourcing). In particular, IT projects to develop or maintain software applications may be contracted out to an offshore vendor in countries like India where software engineering skills and

Type of Resource	Project Characteristics
On-site Contract Worker	Delivery team in the U.S. Hourly charges Managed by the client company
On-site Project Teams	Delivery team in the U.S. Hourly charges; may also be milestone fees Managed by the client company
Mixed On-site–Offshore Projects	Project management and internal customer services in the U.S. Delivery team offshore Fees normally project-based Requires client investment in development infrastructure Requires client efforts in building trust
Pure Offshore Projects	Project management by offshore vendor Fees normally project-based Requires client investment in development infrastructure Requires client and vendor efforts in building trust Requires increased efforts to transfer intellectual capital

Figure 12.15   Complexity Increases with Off-site and Offshore Resources [Adapted from Poria, 2004]

English language skills are plentiful, but at a lower unit cost. However, project coordination can be hampered by time zone differences: morning in the United States is mid-afternoon in Europe and nighttime in Asia.

These less centralized ways to source a project team therefore require new approaches to project management to ensure successful project completion. Some of these new approaches are common across virtual teams for different types of tasks, such as the six guidelines in Figure 12.16 from a very readable book by Jaclyn Kostner.

Virtual teamwork also introduces new IT project risks due to three related factors: differences in communication norms, unfamiliarity with a different culture, and a lack of trusting relationships across team members (Mohtashami et al., 2006). According to these researchers, communication risks are intensified when there is a greater likelihood of imprecision in communicating project requirements or other deliverables with high information content, and interpersonal relationships are less developed due to communications that are not face-to-face and often asynchronous.

Cultural differences include cross-national social differences as well as differences due to an organizational style, even if team members are from the same country. Training programs to increase awareness of potential cultural differences and their impacts on "virtual" project work can help reduce this source of project risk. An example of the topics that might be included in such a training workshop can be found in Figure 12.17.

Trusting relationships are also key to effective collaboration across team members. As personal trust increases, team members and other project stakeholders exchange information in more detail and more freely. They are also

Six Leadership Secrets For Managing Remote Workers

1. Aim to build trust through every interaction.

2. Create symbols and structures that unify the dispersed work group.

3. Establish ongoing opportunities for the team to learn more about each other, both professionally and personally.

4. Develop a daily alignment tool to focus the effort of the team.

5. Be scrupulously fair in treating all team members.

6. Be crystal clear about project objectives.

Figure 12.16 Six Leadership Secrets for Managing Remote Workers [Adapted from Kostner, 1996]

Behavior Dos and Don'ts
    Dos: Be proactive, be positive, respect, celebrate success, be compassionate
    Don'ts: Blame, embarrass, say one thing and do another, be defensive

Communications
    Seek first to understand…then to be understood
    Feedback: give honestly, accept with grace, be constructive, provide frequently
    Priority order: face-to-face, phone, e-mail—as appropriate

Organization
    Understand your role and process
    Share priorities and goals
    Work within the organization defined
    Continuous improvement

Relationships
    Be supportive: cooperation, affirmation, give credit to others
    Teamwork: be inspirational, take ownership, strive for excellence
    Value diversity: understand, leverage, blend, value styles
    Trust: be trustworthy, understand others, give benefit of doubt

Figure 12.17 Workshop Topics for Enhancing Global Teamwork [Adapted from Ranganathan et al., 2007]

more likely to endorse mutual goals and use common processes. All of these behaviors increase a team member's confidence that unanticipated problems will be surfaced and misunderstandings will be avoided.

SUMMARY

Many organizations are adopting an IT portfolio approach to IT investments to help identify the "right" projects to work on. A PMO (project office) structure can help ensure that the company utilizes best practices for managing approved projects. Today's IT project managers therefore need not only technical skills but also more general project management competencies identified by the Project Management Institute. Two business stakeholder roles—the project sponsor and project champion—have also been associated with successful project implementations.

The planning phase for an IT project includes project scheduling, budgeting, and staffing. PERT charts, Gantt charts, and project management software are typically used to help execute and control project team activities. Managing IT project risks involves identifying and classifying potential risks, assessing the potential consequences, developing responses for risk minimization, and ongoing risk monitoring. Successfully managing business change as part of an IT project requires change management activities throughout the project, as well as timely responses to unanticipated situations. Capturing the lessons learned from each project, as part of a project closing phase, can help project managers learn from the successes and mistakes of other projects in the same organization.

The successful management of complex software projects is an important IT capability that often requires outside consulting help. Today's IT project teams are also likely to have some "virtual" team members working at different company centers, perhaps in different countries, or working for an IT outsourcing vendor. In many of today's organizations, IT project managers that have repeatedly delivered quality IT solutions, on-time and within-budget, using project teams of IT and business workers in different locations and time zones, are therefore especially highly valued.

REVIEW QUESTIONS

1. Describe the difference between project management and program management.
2. What is a PMO and why should organizations implement one?
3. What managers are involved in managing an IT portfolio, and why?
4. What information is typically included in an initial IT project request? In a project charter?
5. What types of skills have been identified as important for successful IT project managers?
6. What are the business manager roles of project sponsor and project champion, and why are they important?
7. What is a work breakdown analysis and why is this concept important?
8. Why is timeboxing becoming a common IT project management technique?
9. Contrast the strengths of bottom-up and top-down approaches to project budgeting.
10. What are some key issues related to IT project staffing that need to be well managed?
11. Describe the key uses of PERT, CPM, and Gantt charts.
12. Describe one technique used to manage IT project risks.

13. Describe one technique associated with effectively implementing business change (change management).
14. Compare and contrast the Lewin/Schein model with the Kotter framework. What is the same and what is different?
15. Why is management of large complex system projects an important IT capability?
16. What is a virtual team, and why do IT managers need new approaches for managing such a team?

DISCUSSION QUESTIONS

1. If a person has been certified by the PMI but has never been on an IT project team, would you even consider hiring that person to manage an IT project? Justify your answer.
2. Several approaches for time and budget estimations are provided in this chapter. Why are these types of project estimates difficult to "get right," and what techniques can be used to improve them?
3. Select an IT project that you are familiar with and comment on whether there was a formal project sponsor and champion, which business managers played these roles, and whether or not you think their roles positively affected the project outcomes.
4. Use the Web to identify at least two software products used to support project managers in general. Briefly contrast their features and costs.
5. Select any project that you have participated in. Describe how well the project budget and schedule were controlled, and evaluate why you think this outcome occurred.
6. A project monitoring technique called a traffic approach (red, yellow, and green lights) is mentioned in the chapter. Comment on what you see as the pros and cons of this approach.
7. A large number of U.S.-based mergers over the past two decades have failed to achieve the forecasted business benefits of the merger. Develop an argument for why poor IT project management could contribute to this type of failure.
8. Not all organizations conduct a formal post-project review. Provide an argument for why you think organizations should include such a step as part of their project closing.
9. Describe which one of the training topics in Figure 12.17 would be most helpful to you, and why.

REFERENCES

Applegate, Lynda M., Robert D. Austin, and F. Warren McFarlan, and James L. McKenney. 2002. *Corporate Information Strategy and Management*, 6th ed. Chicago: Irwin.

Bashein, Barbara J., M. Lynne Markus, and Jane B. Finley. 1997. *Safety Nets: Secrets of Effective Information Technology Controls.* Morristown, NJ: Financial Executives Research Foundation.

Clark, Charles E., Nancy C. Cavanaugh, Carol V. Brown, and V. Sambamurthy. 1997. "Building change-readiness capabilities in the IS organization: Insights from the Bell Atlantic experience." *MIS Quarterly* 21 (December): 425–456.

Clemons, Eric K. 1991. "Evaluation of strategic investments in information technology." *Communications of the ACM* 34 (January): 22–36.

Denis, Bob, Maureen Vavra, and John Dick. 2004. "Budgeting." in *CIO Wisdom.* Upper Saddle River, NJ: Pearson Prentice Hall, Chapter 13.

Duffy, Dainty. 1999. "Making lemonade." *CIO* (December 1): 71–77.

Duncan, William R., and Duncan Nevison. 1994. "Software methodology vs. project management." *SIM Executive* 4:14 (Spring).

Frame, J. Davidson. 1994. *The New Project Management*. San Francisco: Jossey-Bass.

Grover, Varun, Seung Ryul Jeong, and James T. C. Teng. 2000. "Reengineering project challenges," in Carol V. Brown and Heikki Topi (eds.), *IS Management Handbook*, 7th ed. New York: Auerbach, Chapter 46.

Hamilton, Stewart. 2000. "Information and the Management of Risk." in Donald A. Marchand (ed.), *Competing with Information*. England: John Wiley & Sons, Ltd., 195–207.

Highsmith, Jim. 2000. "There are projects—and there are Internet projects." *Computerworld* (March 27): 64.

Hoffman, Thomas. 2003. "Corporate execs try new ways to align IT with business units." *Computerworld* (October 27), 13.

Kappelman, Leon A., Robert McKeeman, and Lixuan Zhang. 2006. "Early warning signs of IT project failure: The dominant dozen." *Information Systems Management*, 23:4 (Fall): 31–36.

Kay, Ira T., and Mike Shelton. 2000. "The people problem in mergers." *The McKinsey Quarterly*, No. 4.

Keil, Mark, and Daniel Robey. 1999. "Turning around troubled software projects: An exploratory study of the deescalation of commitment to failing courses of action." *Journal of Management Information Systems* 15 (Spring): 63–87.

Kostner, Jacyln. 1996. *Virtual Leadership—Secrets from the Round Table for the Multi-Site Manager.* New York: Warner Books, Inc.

Kotter, John P. 1995. "Leading change: Why transformation efforts fail." *Harvard Business Review* (March–April): 59–67.

Lewin, Kurt. 1947. "Frontiers in group dynamics." *Human Relations* 1:5–41.

Lindstrom, Lowell, and Ron Jeffries. 2003. "Extreme Programming and Agile Software Development Methodologies," in Carol V. Brown and Heikki Topi (eds.), *IS Management Handbook*, 8th ed. New York: Auerbach, Chapter 41.

Markus, M. Lynne. 1983. "Power, politics, and MIS implementation." *Communications of the ACM* 26 (June): 430–444.

McNurlin, Barbara C., and Ralph H. Sprague, Jr. 2004. *Information Systems Management in Practice*. 6th ed. Upper Saddle River, NJ: Pearson Prentice Hall.

Meredith, Jack R., and Samuel J. Mantel, Jr. 1989. *Project Management: A Managerial Approach*. 2nd ed. New York: John Wiley & Sons.

Mohtashami, Mojgan, Thomas Marlowe, Vassilka Kirova, and Fadi P. Deek. 2006. "Risk management for collaborative software development." *Information Systems Management*, 23, 4 (Fall): 20–30.

Montealegre, Ramiro, and Mark Keil. 2000. "De-escalating information technology projects: Lessons from the Denver International Airport." *MIS Quarterly* 24 (September): 417–447.

Orlikowski, Wanda J., and J. Debra Hofman. 1997. "An improvisational model for change management: The case of groupware technologies." *Sloan Management Review*, 38 (Winter): 11–22.

PMI Standards Committee. 2003. *A Guide to the Project Management Body of Knowledge* (PMBOK Guide), 3rd ed. Newton Square, PA: Project Management Institute.

Poria, Bharat C. 2004. "Strategic Outsourcing." in *CIO Wisdom*. Upper Saddle River, NJ: Pearson Prentice Hall, Chapter 9.

Ranganathan, C., Poornima Krishnan, and Ron Glickman. 2007. "Crafting and Executing an Offshore IT Sourcing Strategy: Globshop's Experience." *Journal of Information Technology,* 22:4 (December): 440–450.

Roberts, Betsy, Sirkka Jarvenpaa, and Cherie Baxley. 2003. "Evolving at the speed of change: Mastering change readiness." *MIS Quarterly Executive*, 2(2): 58–73.

Roman, Daniel D. 1986. *Managing Projects: A Systems Approach*. New York: Elsevier.

Russell, Lou. 2000. "Managing the end for new beginnings: Post-project review for year 2000." *Cutter IT Journal* 13 (July): 28–39.

Russell, Lou. 2007. *10 Steps to Successful Project Management.* Alexandria, VA: ASTD Press.

Ryan, Hugh W. 2003. "Managing development in the era of complex systems," in Carol V. Brown and Heikki Topi (eds.), *IS Management Handbook.* 8th ed. New York: Auerbach, Chapter 44.

Schwalbe, Kathy. 2004. *Information Technology Project Management.* 3rd ed. Canada: Thomson Learning.

Valacich, Joseph S., Joey F. George, and Jeffrey A. Hoffer. 2005. *Essentials of Systems Analysis and Design.* 3rd ed. Upper Saddle River, NJ: Pearson Prentice Hall.

Vavra, Maureen, and Dean Lane. 2004. "Strategic Planning," in *CIO Wisdom.* Upper Saddle River, NJ: Pearson Prentice Hall, Chapter 11.

Wheatley, Margaret, and Myron Kellner-Rogers. 1996. *A Simpler Way.* San Francisco: Berrett-Koehler.

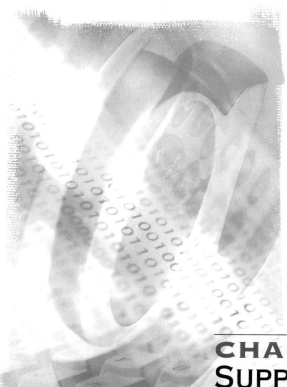

CHAPTER 13
SUPPORTING COMPUTER USERS

THIS CHAPTER FOCUSES ON THE STRATEGIES AND TACTICS USED BY IS managers to support computer users who are not IT professionals. Computer users today typically are working from microcomputer platforms with graphical user interfaces, but both the user's computer skills and the nature of the applications can vary widely. One of the responsibilities on an IS department is to provide desktop assistance to employees using personal productivity tools (using spreadsheets such as Excel and database software such as Access) as well as to support employees working at remote sites. As described in Chapter 1, this could include employees who are telecommuters working from home, at a customer site, or while traveling.

In addition, many non-IT specialists may also be developing software applications using programming languages for enterprise systems (such as SAP's ABAP programming language), statistical analysis tools (such as SAS), other business intelligence tools (such as Hyperion), Web-authoring tools, and so forth. Both business and IS managers need to take responsibility for secure access to these tools and company databases. However, IS managers have the primarily responsibility for ensuring a secure and reliable computing and communications infrastructure for computer users throughout the organization.

We begin the chapter discussing how to support these types of *systems development* activities by users. As early as the 1970s, workers in accounting, finance, marketing, and other business departments have been using computer software to develop programs to capture and analyze data and to generate reports. We provide some guidelines for thinking about differences between user-developed and IS-developed applications and how to balance the potential benefits with the potential risks to the organization.

Then we turn to strategies, support services, and control issues for managing user computing environments in general. Although the potential productivity gains from what's referred to as **user computing** (or **end-user computing**) are well recognized, these benefits do not come without organizational costs for supporting computer users. For example, the initial purchase of a personal computer is generally only 20 percent of the total cost of supporting an employee using a networked computer over its typical three-year life cycle. This is because the **total cost of ownership (TCO)** for desktop and portable computers includes not only the initial purchase costs for the equipment, but also ongoing costs such as application software licenses, network access, communications services, user training and support services, as well as virus and spam protection, e-mail storage costs, and so on. The chapter ends with two special cases related to providing support for computer users: (1) supporting computer users who are working remotely (telecommuters) and (2) managing corporate intranets (including the introduction of collaborative tools such as blogs and wikis).

SUPPORTING USER APPLICATION DEVELOPMENT (UAD)

When microcomputers first became available in the late 1970s, many IS department managers did not expect them to be used in a corporate setting. This is because the first microcomputers were distributed by mail order to hobbyists as electronic toys. Compared to the mainframe computers and minicomputers installed in most businesses, they had very limited processing and storage capabilities. But especially after IBM Corp. introduced its first microcomputer (called the "personal computer" or PC) in late 1981, microcomputers did begin to appear on the desktops of users. Many of these PCs were purchased by business managers using office equipment budgets without the knowledge or support of the IS department. Until there was a "call for help" from a computer user or business manager, the IS department may not have even known what hardware and software was in use in the business.

By the early 1990s, when local area networks that enabled the sharing of microcomputer resources (including printers) began to be installed in organizations, IS managers began to implement less reactive approaches to supporting microcomputer users. The use of desktop computers also became more widespread due to the rise in computer literacy among entry-level employees who had learned PC (or Mac) applications as part of their college programs. Computer-literate business managers recognized that small spreadsheets and database applications, as well as reports with graphics, could usually be more quickly developed by their own workers. This meant that the business manager didn't have to fill out a formal project request for an application to be developed by IS staff, which would typically take much longer or possibly not be approved for IS resources at all.

Today, the overall challenge in managing user application development is to find the best ways to maximize the potential benefits of application development by users without creating unacceptable levels of risks to the organization for using applications developed by minimally trained users.

Advantages and Disadvantages of User-Developed Applications

Understanding the potential advantages and disadvantages of user-developed applications is critical for making good choices about whether a new application should be user-developed or IS-developed. More than 25 years ago, the prolific IT guru James Martin shocked many IT professionals by advocating that organizations invest in software products for users to develop their own applications:

The continuing drop in cost of computers has now passed the point at which computers have become cheaper than people.

—James Martin, *Application Development Without Programmers,1982*

The main advantages to UAD are due to users (1) not having to explain their information requirements to an analyst who is not familiar with the business context and (2) not having to wait for IS resources to be assigned to work on their project. Rather, the business manager can determine when his or her own workers should spend time on using computer tools to develop a new application. This can often result in a more timely response to a specific information need. Business managers also gain total control over the development costs: There are no cost chargebacks from an internal IS department or contractual obligations with an outside vendor if the manager's own employees can develop the application. User application development (UAD) can also be a clear advantage when internal IS resources are relatively scarce: In this situation, it may be best for an organization to use its IS resources to work on projects that require more sophisticated, specialized IT skill sets.

However, organizations also need to recognize the potential downsides to applications developed by non-IS specialists (see Figure 13.1). First, a major downside can be the potential loss of quality controls. By virtue of their training, IS professionals are knowledgeable about how to design controls into a new information system: controls for data access and inputs, controls for calculations and other outputs, and application controls for backup and reliability. As in any profession, products developed by those with less training and experience will, on the average, be of lower quality. Depending on the type and size of the application, there is also an organizational cost associated with having an untrained, or partially trained, employee spend considerable amounts of time on what could be much more efficiently achieved by an IT professional. Undetected bugs in processing logic, the lack of audit trails, inadequate backup and security procedures, and undocumented systems are much more common in user-developed systems than in those developed by a trained IS professional (Schultheis and Sumner, 1991). Errors in spreadsheet programs are particularly common and business decisions based on faulty data can imperil the survival of the business (see the box entitled "Errors in Spreadsheets").

Lack of application controls (security, data quality)
Loss of opportunities for IT integration
Increased operational risks due to developer turnover

Figure 13.1 Potential Disadvantages of User-Developed
Applications

In addition to concerns about the quality of the application design, user-developed applications that are utilized on an ongoing basis can pose operational risks. Corporate systems run on servers in a data center are monitored and maintained by computer specialists. However, the responsibilities for the ongoing operation and maintenance of a user-developed application typically belong to the business unit that created and owns the application—and might in fact be managed by a single employee who originally developed it. If the original developer of a database application or a spreadsheet application (especially one with complex logic) moves on to a different work unit, or even a different organization, the user-developed system may have to be abandoned due to the lack of resident knowledge within the business unit (Klepper and Sumner, 1990). This risk exposure is especially great when the application is being used as a managerial support tool for decisions with high impact or as a regular transaction processing and reporting system at the work-group or department level.

Finally, when systems are developed outside of an IS organization, there is also a greater likelihood that opportunities for data integration are missed and employee time is being spent "reinventing" an application with functionality that is similar to an application already in use by another work group. Duplicated efforts within the same department, let alone across business units within an organization, are common when projects to develop applications are not part of an organization-wide IS application portfolio. When business units throughout an organization independently develop applications using software and data definitions of their own choosing, the result is dozens, or even hundreds, of what has been referred to as isolated silos or "islands" of automation. The risks include not only unsharable data, but also conflicting reports of key business indicators, especially if different data sources, business rules, or time periods are utilized by the different applications.

These types of organizational risks associated with user application development increase considerably when user-developed applications are allowed to proliferate without adequate coordination and oversight. The first management

ERRORS IN SPREADSHEETS

End users produce countless spreadsheet models each year, often to guide mission-critical decisions. Some consultants have claimed that something like a third of all operational spreadsheet models contain errors. One Price Waterhouse consultant reported auditing four large spreadsheet models for a client and finding 128 errors.

Different types of errors contained in spreadsheets that have been identified include:

- *Mechanical errors*   Typing errors, pointing errors, and other simple slips. Mechanical errors can be frequent, but they have a high chance of being caught by the person making the error.
- *Logic errors*   Incorrect formulas due to choosing the wrong algorithm or creating the wrong formulas to implement the algorithm. Pure logic errors result from a lapse in logic, whereas domain logic errors occur because the developer lacks the required business area knowledge. Some logic errors are also easier to identify than others: easy-to-proof errors have been called Eureka errors, and difficult-to-proof errors have been called Cassandra errors.
- *Omission errors*   Things left out of the model that should be there. They often result from a misinterpretation of the situation. Human factors research has shown that omission errors have low detection rates.
- *Qualitative errors*   Flaws that do not produce immediate quantitative errors, but can lead to quantitative errors during later "what-if" analyses or when updates are made to a spreadsheet model, or errors that cause users to misinterpret the model's results or make maintenance difficult, leading to increased development costs and the potential for new errors.

To reduce error rates requires aggressive techniques—similar to the discipline followed by developers of more complex applications.

[Adapted from Panko, 1996, and Panko and Halverson, 1996]

responsibility is to identify when an application should be user-developed or IS-developed—by assessing the benefits and risks.

Assessing the Risks from UAD

Let us turn now to the issue of under what conditions a specific application should be developed by business users rather than IT professionals. As summarized in Figure 13.2, three types of factors should be considered: characteristics of the application to be developed, the tools available for UAD, and the human resources (IS or user) needed for both a high-quality application and reliable, ongoing operations and maintenance over the life of the application.

> **Application Characteristics**
> Scope (personal, departmental, organizational)
> Criticality/Impact (risk exposure)
> Size and usage (one-time, periodic, ongoing)
> Business problem complexity (commonality of task, problem structure)
>
> **Tool Characteristics**
> Tool sophistication/complexity
> Interconnectedness
>
> **Developer Characteristics**
> User developer skills, experience, and availability
> IS specialist skills, experience, and availability

Figure 13.2 Application, Tool, and Developer Risk Factors

Application Characteristics Several characteristics of the application need to be taken into account. First, the organizational risks associated with UAD differ depending on the intended scope (or organizational usage) of the application to be developed. Some firms make decisions based on just two categories of risk: applications developed for personal use only and those intended to be used by more than one person. Other organizations assess risks based on three levels of *application scope* that typically have significantly different risk levels (Pyburn, 1986–1987), as shown next. Personal applications typically have the least risk, whereas organizational applications have the greatest risk.

- *Personal* applications developed and used (operated) by the primary user for personal decision making, often replacing work formerly done manually

- *Departmental* applications developed by a single user but operated and used (and perhaps enhanced) by multiple users in a department; departmental applications often evolve from applications originally developed for personal use

- *Organizational* applications used by multiple users across a number of departments

In addition to application scope, the potential impact of managerial decisions based on the application, as well as the actual size of the application and its intended frequency of usage, also need to be considered. Small, one-time applications are typically good candidates for user-developed applications, although the application also needs to be assessed in terms of risk exposure for the organization due to its usage.

Finally, the complexity of the business problem supported by the application needs to be assessed in two different ways: the degree to which the task is common and the degree to which the problem being addressed is well-defined. If the application is addressing an ill-structured analytical problem, a combination of business and IS specialist expertise may be required to develop the best software application to address it. On the other hand, applications to support business tasks that are already well understood (common), such as a system to track the status of multiple departmental projects or to track communications with various suppliers, are usually better candidates for user-developed solutions.

Tool Characteristics Two important tool characteristics to consider are the complexity of the software tools to be used to develop the system and the degree to which the application is to be interconnected with other applications (or databases). User tools vary greatly in complexity and technology sophistication. For example, spreadsheet functions are relatively simple to design and spreadsheet applications are relatively simple to implement, whereas data mining tools based on neural network technologies are much more complex and require more sophisticated tool training.

Applications can also vary greatly on the extent to which they rely on other applications for data inputs. Some applications do not use data from any other computer-generated source (unless it is manually input), and do not provide inputs to other applications. At the other end of the spectrum, an application may receive automatic data feeds from other applications over an internal or external network. If an application requires sophisticated tools and access to data distributed via a network, then an IS-developed solution may be the only appropriate approach. However, it is not uncommon for users to first develop a stand-alone application to address a business problem, and then later for this application to be used as a prototype for a more integrated application developed by IS specialists.

Developer Characteristics The application developer characteristics to be considered of course include the relevant skills and experience of the potential programmers. A second consideration here is the availability of the user developer resources in relation to the time period allotted for the development of the new application. As discussed earlier, the lack of dependence on scarce IS department resources is a frequent catalyst for UAD if the user developers have, or can be trained to have, the tool skills and application development expertise required. One management challenge here is that the business manager who wants the application might not have the knowledge to adequately assess the user developer's skills and expertise prior to the project getting underway. Consultation with IS experts inside or outside the organization may therefore be needed to adequately assess this potential risk factor.

Guidelines for User Developers

When systems are developed by IS professionals, they use a methodology appropriate for the specific application. For user-developed systems, the user developer (or the accountable business manager) typically chooses the development methods to be used. Panko (1988) suggests that the most appropriate methodology for a user-developed application depends on three of the application characteristics: scope (personal or departmental use), size (small to large), and the nature of the business problem being supported by the application (simple to complex).

As shown in Figure 13.3, not all user-developed applications require a strict adherence to a formal systems development life cycle (SDLC) methodology, which was described in earlier chapters. For example, small applications for simple problems that will be used by the person developing the application (personal scope) could be developed with a simplified ("collapsed") life cycle approach. However, when the application for personal use is of larger size and requires more complex logic, a more disciplined approach needs to be taken to ensure a quality application.

If the application is for other users (a work group or department), then one or more of the other intended users should be involved in the application's development, even if a formal project team for the application is not established. If a large, complex application is being developed for multiple users, it should be developed using an SDLC methodology (as described in Chapter 10) with formalized user and developer roles. In fact, the Definition phase should include a reassessment of whether the project should be user-developed or IS-developed, using factors such as those summarized earlier (see Figure 13.2).

Prototyping and other iterative methods are especially well suited for user-developed applications: the screen designs can be tried out with multiple users, and today's UAD tools have graphical interfaces that support prototyping well. However, as described in Chapter 10, a basic set of requirements for the application should first be defined to guide the development of the prototype; selected users then try out the prototype and suggest changes; and the prototype is then modified by the developer until there is agreement that the application meets the business users' needs. Managing user expectations during this process can also be important (see the box entitled "Lessons Learned by User Developers").

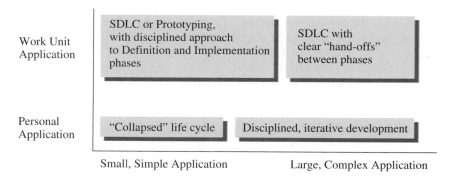

Figure 13.3 Guidelines for Choosing the Development Approach (Adapted from Panko, 1989)

LESSONS LEARNED BY USER DEVELOPERS

In developing a contact management system for our work group, I learned that it was important to stay in touch with the end users of the product throughout the development cycle. Not only does this assure that their needs are being met and the program will be useful to their productivity, but it also entices excitement, which is vital to the acceptance of the final product. Even with the use of a prototyping methodology with rapid development tools, the several months required to develop a quality product can be enough of a lapse in the anticipation of the end users such that acceptance of the product is less than enthusiastic. Another valuable lesson learned was that when the program gets close to being completed is always when the intricate, hard-to-find bugs seem to be found.

I employed a prototyping methodology to develop a project tracking database for my work group using Lotus Notes. I spent most of the first couple of days working with the Lotus Notes tool to become proficient as a user before diving into the developer world. My goal was to have a usable prototype as quickly as possible so I could take it to three key users: my manager and two colleagues. I chose one colleague who was very computer literate and one that seems to merely know where the "ON" switch is on his workstation. I had a usable prototype in three days. One key lesson I learned in developing this system overshadows all others: managing user expectations is paramount to user satisfaction early in a project. My "key users" believed that since I had a prototype with the user screens developed very rapidly, that the workable system with "everything they wanted" would follow equally as fast; although the bugs they found were corrected quickly, the changes to the system that they wanted required several iterations over several weeks. Another lesson I learned is the value of the prototyping methodology: It enabled our group to develop a powerful system with little time and little money invested.

[Evening MBA students, Indiana University]

Figure 13.4 lists a number of important questions that can serve as a guide for user developers during the Definition and Construction phases. It is common for user developers to underestimate what it takes to define a system's requirements, especially if other users will also be using the application. A key learning point for most first-time user developers is not to move to the Construction phase, or the building of the prototype, too soon. In contrast, the typical IT professional is trained in various systems analysis techniques as well as interviewing techniques to elicit requirements. The larger and more complex the system, the more critical the need for developers to devote more time to the up-front requirements analysis and

other steps in the Definition phase. In the Construction phase, the design steps should take into account security features, such as input and output controls (including application backup and recovery controls).

Two common UAD pitfalls are not doing enough testing of the application and not providing sufficient documentation. Significant time and a rigorous test process are needed to ensure that an application works the way it is intended to. The lack of adequate testing for decision support applications can lead to serious consequences for a business. Errors in spreadsheet applications, for example, are known to have resulted in business losses ranging from hundreds of thousands to millions of dollars (Galletta et al., 1996), and inadequate debugging practices can be a major cause (Panko, 1996; Panko and Halverson, 1996). For example, studies have found that many spreadsheet developers apparently do not attempt to reduce their spreadsheet errors systematically, and do not have other workers check their programs. Since research on the work practices of IS professionals has found that spotting errors by inspection is difficult for the original programmer, user developers should regularly involve others in debugging their applications rather than relying wholly on self-testing.

The documentation that is necessary for a user-developed application depends upon the application's characteristics. If the application is to be used by someone other than the user-developer, including a possible successor in a specific organizational role, formal documentation should be provided and kept up to date; documentation that is not embedded in the application itself is needed in the event of a system crash. The documentation for a multiuser system, or a stand-alone application used by different people in different work groups, typically requires relatively detailed user documentation, such as that produced for users by IS documentation specialists. If user-developed systems are regularly audited, it is obviously a good idea to consult with these auditors while defining and constructing the system to ensure that the organization's auditing concerns are adequately addressed from the start. Depending on the organizational context, a formal internal audit or other oversight mechanism may be needed before the application is utilized to ensure that it does not expose the organization to unacceptable levels of risk.

Even users formally educated in IS development methodologies typically face a significant learning curve as a user developer. This learning involves both tool learning and process learning. IT professionals have also learned that a simple system that works reliably is much more useful than an elaborate failure. It often is a good idea to start with a limited version of a user-developed system and then to expand it after some having experience with the initial version. Indeed, user-developed systems

Definition Phase
What outputs should the system produce?
What processes are necessary to produce the needed outputs?
What should the system be able to do?
What input data are needed?
> How can data best be obtained?
> How can data accuracy, completeness, and timeliness be assured?

Construction Phase
What data must be stored in the system?
> How should data be organized?
> How can data be maintained?
How can this system be decomposed into modules?
> How do these modules relate to each other?
> In what sequence should the modules be executed?
How can the system be recovered if anything happens?
Is an audit trail necessary?
What level of documentation is necessary?
What system tests need to be run?

Figure 13.4   Questions to Guide User Developers

sometimes also lead to more complex systems projects that require custom development work by IS professionals.

PROVIDING DESKTOP SUPPORT

Although only a subset of users may be involved in developing applications, virtually all users rely on IS specialists to provide desktop support. Figure 13.5 presents a framework that can be used to help design an organization's approach to supporting end-user computing activities in general. The Individual-Level box at the bottom right includes factors that were discussed previously, including the characteristics of the user developer, the business tasks for which computers are used, and the end-user tools. Highly skilled computer users can be found in most organizations today, but it is important to remember that not every user, or user department, may have the same level of computer skills or the same complexity of computer tasks.

The box at the far left, labeled Organizational Context, explicitly acknowledges that the location of the IS specialists providing the support (which could include personnel that work for an outsourcer) and the different needs of different business units need to be taken into account when designing strategies and tactics for providing desktop support. For example, if an IS group is physically located alongside the users to be supported, there is a greater likelihood that these "local" IS professionals will have a high degree of business-specific knowledge that will help them to anticipate the need for support services at the time of a new system implementation or for playing a *consultant* role for users developing their own applications. Similarly, if a business manager is highly computer-literate, there is a greater likelihood that this user department will be more self-reliant.

The Organization-Level box has three factors that are the responsibility of both IS *and* business managers:

- *Strategy*   The strategic objectives and overall approach to supporting end-user computing
- *Technology*   The range and accessibility of tools for computer users
- *Tactics for Support Services, Control Policies and Procedures*   The organization's specific support services as well as its control policies and procedures for end-user computing

The two-headed arrow between the Organization-Level and Individual-Level boxes in Figure 13.5 reflects the importance of designing a support approach that takes into account unique aspects of the organization as well as the needs of different individuals: a rigid, one-size-fits-all approach to supporting users is not likely to be as effective.

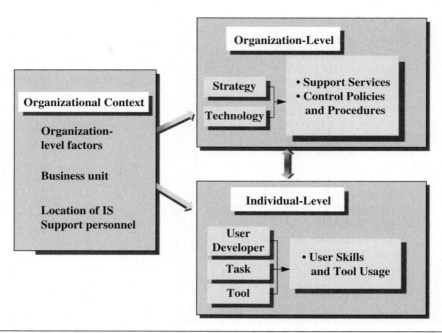

Figure 13.5 Framework for Designing User Support (Adapted from Brancheau and Brown, 1993)

Since the technologies for user computing are discussed in Part I of this textbook, the remainder of this chapter focuses on the other two factors: Strategies and Tactics.

Strategies for User Computing

Most organizations today have developed an explicit strategy and have a designated support staff for providing desktop support. However, the laissez-faire ("hands-off") approach shown in Figure 13.6 was commonly found in the 1980s when microcomputers (PCs) were first being brought into corporations. Today, a laissez-faire approach can also be used when new technologies are involved. For example, workers may be purchasing personal digital assistants (PDAs) based on their own product preferences, or implementing instant messaging software, without formal authorization or support of an IS department, and it may be some period of time before an organization establishes a PDA standard and implements policies and procedures appropriate for this type of technology.

For more established user technologies, the three other management approaches in Figure 13.6 are commonly used. For example, organizations that invest heavily in resources to support user computing, but implement minimal formal controls and procedures (to be described later), have an *Acceleration* strategy. Their objective is to enable users to acquire and learn appropriate computer tools and perhaps also develop their own innovative computer applications,

with few constraints. In contrast, firms with a *Containment* strategy opt to bring in new user technologies more slowly, after specific controls are put in place, to minimize organizational risks. Business units can only purchase "standard" computer tools unless they have received permission for an exception, and stricter guidelines for tool usage and security are heavily enforced.

The *Controlled Growth* strategy (high expansion, but also high control) is the most mature approach, and is common in many organizations today. However, even organizations in this mature stage need to select a different strategy

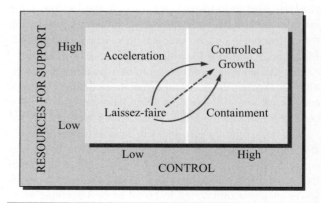

Figure 13.6 Strategies for User Computing (Adapted from Munro et al., 1987–1988; Brancheau and Amoroso, 1990)

when implementing newer user technologies. For example, many organizations initially took an Acceleration approach helping users develop Web pages for organizational intranets in the late 1990s, and then introduced more restrictive approaches as they would for a Controlled Growth stage. Other organizations, however, chose a Containment strategy: from the start, they established a committee to develop rules for Web page content and a standard "look-and-feel" format for all Web pages (see the section on "Managing Intranets" at the end of this chapter).

Those organizations that started with a Laissez-faire or Acceleration approach with new technologies, however, have sometimes encountered heavy user resistance when they implemented a product standard and appropriate control policies. As depicted by the dotted line in Figure 13.6, these experiences have lead many organizations to take a more middle-ground, or balanced, strategy for bringing in a new technology. A balanced strategy typically involves starting with a pilot implementation of a new technology (such as a specific instant messaging tool) that involves just a subset of users to help the organization learn what support services and control policies are needed. Then they roll out the technology across the entire organization with a set of support services and control policies in place that eventually evolve to a Controlled Growth strategy.

A critical success factor for effective desktop support is the staffing of the support unit. In the early 1990s, a typical staffing ratio was 1 support member for each 100 PCs, but ratios as low as 35 staff members supporting 10,000 users have been reported (McNurlin and Sprague, 1998). As with other personnel responsible for customer services in general, support staff for computer users need to have not only knowledge about the technologies being used, but also the ability to relate well to business users. Providing quick turnaround time in response to user requests for help is a key performance metric. Different support "levels" are typically established in consultation with business unit managers, and different types of computer problems will have different maximum time periods in which they should be solved (see Figure 13.7).

Today's more proactive approaches to desktop support typically involves both IS and business managers working together to best leverage investments in technologies for business users and support personnel. For example, it is not uncommon for "power users" in business units that have experience in developing sophisticated applications for decision support to be hired away by an IS department to provide consulting and troubleshooting support for other business users.

No matter what strategy is adopted, all organizations need to design an appropriate set of support services and

---

Service Level Agreements (SLAs) by Severity Level of Desktop Problem

80% of Severity 1 problems will be resolved in 4 hours; 95% in 24 hours

80% of Severity 2 problems will be resolved in 8 hours; 95% in 24 hours

80% of Severity 3 problems will be resolved in 3 business days; 95% in 5 days

80% of Severity 4 problems will be resolved in 5 business days; 95% in 15 days

Figure 13.7   Service Level Agreements for Desktop Support

---

control policies to help realize their strategy for user support. Next, we discuss first some typical services and then control policies and procedures for desktop computer users.

Support Services

A list of services for desktop support is provided in Figure 13.8. One critical service is help desk support, which the user typically accesses via a telephone number. Some organizations have used help desk positions as an initial training ground for entry-level IS department positions; in a very short time, the new employee gained a firsthand appreciation of the difficulties faced by the organization's business users. However, just as many companies today are outsourcing some of their customer service support to organizations that can easily support customers in different time zones at a lower cost, many help desks for internal computer users are also being outsourced. Help desk personnel (both in-house and those working directly for an external vendor) typically are guided by computer tools that provide them with "scripts" to follow to help them document and/or diagnose a problem in response to telephone inquiries. Today's network administrators also have an array of sophisticated tools to help them troubleshoot problems at remote sites.

Supporting users also involves preparing employees for new application systems and upgrades of existing software that can impact the way a user gets their work done. For example, when new versions of an operating systems (such as Microsoft's Vista) or a major revision of a personal productivity package (such as Microsoft's Office) is involved, user training may be required, as well as perhaps upgrading a user's computer equipment (for example, adding more memory or disk storage space to support the new software). By the late 1990s many organizations adopted a three-year replacement strategy for personal computer hardware to more easily handle such upgrades. However, some organizations have found that a five-year replacement strategy can be sufficient for some computer users (Delaney, 2003).

- *Troubleshooting* A hotline or help desk 24/7 or as needed

- *Consulting* One-on-one consulting with IS specialists on application development, query tools, and so on

- *Training and Education* Technology (tool) training in classroom setting as well as self-paced e-learning modules; education in system development methodologies, security procedures, and so on

- *Tool research and evaluation* Identifying and evaluating new end-user tools and recommending products for trial by users

- *Tool purchasing, installation and maintenance* Hardware, software, networks

- *Information sharing* Formalizing communications between support personnel and end users, as well as across end-user groups; typical sharing mechanisms include newsletters, Web pages on an intranet, and periodic meetings for users to evaluate new tools and share development and technology "tips"

Figure 13.8 Common Support Services

The list in Figure 13.8 also includes not just tool training but also user education: Training refers to learning to use a specific tool or software application. IS education refers to more general computer literacy—such as learning "best practices" and alternative methodologies for user-developed applications or better managing their e-mail (see the box entitled "Training for E-Mail Hoarders").

Many organizations have attempted to reduce classroom training costs by providing self-paced training alternatives. Large firms in particular have found it cost-effective to invest in "learning portals" (see the box entitled "Reinventing Training at Cisco Systems"). Sharing solutions to common problems via intranet postings, such as answers to frequently asked questions (FAQs), can also reduce support costs.

The outsourcing of user training has also become more popular as firms have begun to standardize on office

TRAINING FOR E-MAIL HOARDERS

E-mail users tend to be Hoarders or Deleters. Hoarders keep thousands of e-mails in their inbox and use it as a searchable archive. Deleters keep only a few messages in their e-mail inbox; after reading a message they immediately answer it, file it, or delete it. To avoid the high storage costs of e-mails left on corporate servers, some companies are adopting stricter policies for what e-mails to store and for how long. The policies vary since some companies and industries are subject to special legal requirements about what e-mail documents must be retained. Other companies are emphasizing user training programs that provide suggestions for using alternative storage options that minimize organizational storage costs and for altering work habits that lead users to hoard e-mails.

[Adapted from Zaslow, 2006; Tam, 2007]

REINVENTING TRAINING AT CISCO SYSTEMS

Tom Kelly, vice president of worldwide training at Cisco Systems, joined the company with a clear mandate: to make Cisco a model of Web-based excellence in the one part of its business in which it was a laggard—Cisco's training division. According to Kelly: "There are very few high-tech companies that truly respect how much learning has to happen to allow them and their people to stay current." The learning model that Kelly is building at Cisco distinguishes between "structured learning" and "emergency learning," and tries to customize each form to the needs of the individual. Users will be able to create a customized Web page where they can chart a long-term, structured learning plan; get all relevant short-term updates; and automatically receive critical information based on their job title, area of operation, field of interest, and learning preferences—including time-critical content for emergency-learning situations. Ultimately, Kelly says, e-learning will be most effective when it no longer feels like learning—when it's simply a natural part of how people work.

[Adapted from Muoio, 2000]

productivity tools and other purchased software whenever possible. However, it should be noted that by turning over classroom training to an outside firm, a desktop support organization may lose a valuable opportunity for education on company-specific IS issues as well as an opportunity to establish a support-service relationship with business users. In other words, cost efficiencies alone should not be the only criterion for choosing whether to provide a support service in-house or via a third-party supplier.

In addition, the vendors of software for large numbers of users have also improved their online self-help features for their products and are paying more attention to the "user experience" with their products in general. For example, tools have more sophisticated help functions that include searching by key words as well as context-specific help functions. Some vendors offer wizards that help users with tasks such as creating graphs in spreadsheet programs, new tables for common entities in database management programs, and formatting text, spreadsheets, data entry forms, and reports. Some vendors have also experimented with cartoon pop-up screens that offer help to the user, or software tips, based on keystroke patterns by the user.

Control Policies and Procedures

A list of typical policies and procedures for business users is provided in Figure 13.9. In the past, one of the most contentious issues has been policies and procedures related to what hardware and software can be purchased and how.

The development and enforcement of user computing "standards" is typically an IS department responsibility, but some organizations have set up a committee that includes business unit representatives to establish these types of policies and an exception process for requests of nonstandard hardware or software. The degree to which organizational policies are guidelines versus mandates, and the manner in which they are enforced, varies widely across organizations and sometimes even across different departments within the same organization (Speier and Brown, 1997). However, the willingness of business unit managers and individual users to comply with computing standards has increased in recent years as the business advantages associated with using common tools has increased and employee awareness of the need to avoid potential business losses due to external threats such as virus attacks has become widespread.

Keeping users up to date on the latest policies and procedures has been a challenging management issue; organizations have typically done a better job communicating all of them to new workers via orientation programs than to informing currently employees of changes in policies and procedures. However, user computing policies and forms for technology and password approvals are typically accessible to all employees via a company's intranet, and changes in policies and procedural deadlines can also be broadcast to all relevant employees via e-mail.

Organizational compliance with copyrights and licensing agreements is also a responsibility of senior IS managers. Many organizations invested in mechanisms to monitor

Required (or recommended) product standards (hardware and software)
Requirements (recommendations) for workstation ergonomics
Approval process for product purchases
Requirements for product inventorying
Upgrade procedures

Application quality review process
Guidelines to identify high-impact applications and sensitive data
Policies for corporate data access
Guidelines for program and data backup procedures
Policies for document retention
Requirements for audit trails
Documentation standards

Policies to control unauthorized access and file sharing
Policies to control unauthorized software copying
Policies for acceptable use of computing resources
Virus protection procedures
Spam filtering procedures

Figure 13.9   Common Policies and Procedures

software licenses and to inventory user-developed applications and other software on desktop machines as part of their Year 2000 compliance initiatives, but not all of these organizations have continued to monitor for compliance. Although enforcing control policies for software copyrights is certainly easier to accomplish in networked environments in general, software vendors are reportedly still losing significant revenues due to software copyright violations. To put pressure on companies to proactively monitor for copyright and software licensing violations, software vendors in the United States have created entities such as the Business Software Alliance (BSA) through which civil suits for copyright infringement can be filed (see also the box entitled "Software Companies Identify U.S. Pirates").

SOFTWARE COMPANIES IDENTIFY U.S. PIRATES

One of the most lucrative squealing operations in America is run out of the K Street lobbying district in Washington, D.C. The Business Software Alliance (BSA) does all the things that most D.C. lobby groups do, but it also has "power of attorney" to enforce the copyright claims of its members against companies using pirated software. The members of the BSA include large software companies like Microsoft. If the BSA finds out that your company is using more software than you have paid for, they can demand not only that you buy the programs, but also that you pay a penalty—a negotiated settlement fee that will serve as a reminder of the error of your ways. The alternative is to face a civil suit for copyright infringement, something few companies would want to risk.

In fall 2005 BSA launched its Rewards program in which individuals are given incentives to confidentially submit detailed information about software piracy infringements in a U.S. business to the BSA. In July 2007 BSA was scheduled to launch a "Blow the Whistle" national advertising campaign that encourages employees to report software piracy. In addition to national radio and online advertisements, BSA planned to target states such as California, Texas, Illinois, New York, New Jersey, Pennsylvania, and Florida.

A May 2007 study conducted by IDC for the BSA found that 21 percent of software in the United States is unlicensed, and in 2006 alone the commercial software industry was estimated to have losses of over $7.3 billion due to the usage of unlicensed software on office computers in this country alone. During that year several manufacturing companies settled with the BSA for a total of $1.43 million for claims that they had unlicensed copies of Adobe, Autodesk, Microsoft, SolidWorks, and Symantec software on their company computers. In 2006 over 20 percent of BSA settlements were in the manufacturing industry, bringing the industry total to $3.79 million since 2005.

[Based on Gomes, 2003; and www.bsa.org (accessed July 2007)]

Some of the greatest increases in costs for desktop computing are related to security issues: preventing viruses, worms, and other hacker software to enter a company's network. Providing regular updates to standard tools and filters to reduce the amount of unsolicited bulk e-mail messages (referred to as **spam**) is a service usually only offered for an organization's "standard" software. Nevertheless, greatest control challenges today are preventing, and recovering from external threats. Although laws against hackers have existed, and been enforced, in recent years, organizations have faced increasingly frequent and more costly digital attacks from viruses and worms—especially those directed at Microsoft products that have been widely adopted. Although security procedures can be implemented centrally and users can be given procedures to follow to avoid these security risks, the company's network is only as secure as its weakest link. For 2003 alone, estimates of economic damage worldwide due to viruses, worms, and other hacker attacks was estimated to be more than $120 billion, which was more than twice as large as the estimated damage for the preceding year (Langley, 2003).

Control policies and procedures need to be continually modified in response to new technologies, new ways of working, new laws, and new external threats. Because of the increased important of information security issues in general, we devote a whole chapter to this topic in Chapter 16. We conclude here by addressing two special user support issues: (1) supporting users (telecommuters) who are working remotely and (2) managing corporate intranets.

SPECIAL CASE: SUPPORTING TELECOMMUTERS

Providing support for workers outside of the physical walls of a business has become increasingly important as computer and communications devices have become more portable. The United States is still the leader in telecommuting, with more than a quarter of all corporate workers telecommuting at least one day a month. Gartner has estimated that more than 80 million workers worldwide worked from home at least one day per month in 2005, up from 38 million in 2000, and in the fist quarter of 2006 a larger than normal increase in telecommuters was reported (InfoWorld, 2006). Given the accelerated diffusion of mobile devices and wireless networks, as well as broadband connections from the home that support fast data transfers of large data streams and multimedia applications, the number of telecommuters is likely to continue to increase.

> **Telecommuters** spend at least a part of their regular business hours using IT to perform their jobs outside of a company's physical facilities, using a mobile office, an office in their personal home, or at a temporary office at a shared work center away from the company's main office.

However, not all "white collar" work (knowledge work) is suited to a telecommuting arrangement and not all telecommuters have the same needs for remote work support. One way to think about these differences is to categorize job positions in terms of to what extent an employee is "tethered" to a physical building in which they work:

- *Office-bound*   Office-bound employees are "tethered" to an office in a building, where they typically use IT that might or might not be portable.

- *Travel-driven*   Travel-driven employees take their office with them to whatever location they are working in, which can change during the workday or workweek. For example, many sales force personnel have travel-driven jobs; they were likely to be among the first employees within their organizations to become telecommuters.

- *Independent*   Independent workers do not have a permanent office work space owned or leased by an employer. Instead, the worker uses IT in a home office or a mobile office, or both.

More recently, however, many organizations have implemented telecommuting options for individual employees who weren't necessarily independent or travel-driven workers, but who desired more flexibility in their work arrangements to achieve a more positive work-life balance. For example, an employee might normally go to an office building to work but occasionally would be able to work at home. Other telecommuters might simply be "day extenders"—employees working full days at a permanent office but then working at home during evenings and weekends. Some companies' programs are designed to facilitate working at home for different types of projects that might require uninterrupted work time. Companies having trouble recruiting full-time employees with specific skills have also developed work-at-home programs for new hires.

For those knowledge workers in positions that are not highly office-bound, the benefits from implementing telecommuting programs can be compelling. According to self-reports by telecommuters, many personal benefits are associated with telecommuting, including those that contribute positively due to a worker's productivity:

- *Increased workday flexibility*   Remote workers gain flexibility in their work schedules that can reduce work stress and could allow them to avoid rush-hour traffic.

- *Improved work-life balance*   Employees who work at home typically are able to spend more time with family members by working very early in the morning or very late in the evening.

- *Easier accommodation of communications across time zones*   Employees who need to communicate with others in different time zones sometimes find it easier to integrate meeting times that extend their workdays if they can communicate from their homes.

In addition, some companies have also realized significant savings from implementing telecommuting programs of various types. For example, over a period of more than five years, 12,500 employees at IBM gave up dedicated office space in company buildings, and the company achieved multimillion annual dollar savings (Agpar, 1998). In some geographic regions within the United States with major air pollution problems (for example, Los Angeles), governments have experimented with requiring companies of a certain size (or setting up tax incentives for them) to establish telecommuting programs so that only a certain percentage of their employees are physically commuting to work within a given workweek.

Given these organizational and individual benefits, why have the number of telecommuters not increased more rapidly? One reason is that telecommuting programs require portable equipment (which is still more expensive than the equivalent desktop equipment) and remote access with sufficient bandwidth. Another reason is that, although the costs of mobile devices and networks continue to decline, telecommuters might also require immediate help desk support outside of normal work hours, due to more flexible work schedules and the time zone in which they are working; in many large organizations, 24/7 user support, at some level, has become the norm.

Other reasons for the relatively slow diffusion of telecommuting arrangements over the past decade are not technology obstacles, but managerial and behavioral obstacles. For example, it has been learned that organizations need to redesign their performance appraisal systems to focus on performance outcomes so that the telecommuter is not penalized for different (and less visible) approaches to achieving work objectives. Some companies only allow "proven stars," not newcomers, to telecommute, and some managers still believe that telecommuting weakens loyalty to the company (Dunham, 2000).

Another obstacle is that some employees who are telecommuters feel a sense of isolation: Remote workers don't have the opportunity for informal social interactions that working in an office building fosters. Some organizations have therefore instituted regular meetings at times that telecommuters can attend in order to increase social interactions with supervisors and among coworkers and make electronic communications more meaningful. Some telecommuters have also voiced concerns about missing advancement opportunities due to the belief that being "out-of-sight" would mean that they are less well known and therefore less likely to be considered for a given career opportunity. Training programs for not only telecommuters, but also supervisors of telecommuters, can be developed to help avoid some of these nontechnical obstacles.

Telecommuting programs also need to take into account security and legal issues. Employees need to be aware of organizational policies for maintaining the confidentiality of company data and the use of company equipment for personal reasons. Many financial services companies have reported placing restrictions on who can take confidential records out of the office or use their own PDAs on company computers. Other companies (like Boeing) require laptops to be physically locked to a stationary object at all times (see also the box entitled "Equipping Teleworkers").

EQUIPPING TELEWORKERS

Teleworkers need to have access to all the same data communication services that are available to employees with a permanent office, although not always at the same speeds. Virtual private networks (VPN) and other remote access technologies provide seamless, location-independent access to corporate data resources. The importance of sufficient bandwidth to support mobile workers cannot be overemphasized. Today, wireless cards (with antennas that link computers to wireless networks) can be cost-effective solutions in more densely populated areas. E-mail, instant messaging, and other Internet access can also be provided via mobile phones and PDA devices.

Tech-savvy travelers have also learned how to fit their electronic gear into overhead bins of airplanes and avoid computer theft. Yet battery power is still a constraint, and road warriors with layovers at airports frequently find themselves without access to a power socket to keep them working.

SPECIAL CASE: MANAGING INTRANETS

As described in Chapter 6, Intranets are networks operating within organizations that employ the TCP/IP protocol, the same protocol used on the Internet. When Web authoring tools designed for business users (such as Microsoft FrontPage) became readily available in the late 1990s, IS managers had to select an approach for developing intranet content. For example, Boeing initially took a "let-the-flowers-bloom" approach (similar to an Acceleration strategy shown in Figure 13.6). IS managers deliberately sought to keep intranet restrictions to a minimum to facilitate exploration with Web tools by computer users in different units across the organization. A standard Web authoring tool was distributed without cost to user departments, and it led to a very quick growth of Web pages developed by users on the corporate intranet (Jordan, 1997). Other organizations chose a Containment strategy to develop their intranets. The IS department or a corporate committee first established the rules for Web page content and set specific parameters for look-and-feel formats, and then continued to serve as an oversight committee. Organizations like Boeing that began with an Acceleration strategy eventually implemented more rules and standards, and organizations that began with a Containment strategy also moved to a Controlled Growth strategy over time.

Companies also implement intranets for different reasons. Some companies view the intranet as a major cost savings tool and cite metrics for cost savings due to not having to duplicate and distribute revised procedure documents as changes occur or policy manuals and other documents for employees. Cost savings may also be attributed to self-service applications delivered via an intranet, such as for updates to personnel records or benefit calculations that previously required in-person contacts with HR staff. However, these types of cost savings can only be realized if users can find the documents and information that they need.

In recent surveys, only 47 percent of business users said they could easily find what they were looking for on their intranet, and 59 percent of middle managers in large organizations reported that almost every day they missed information that could have been valuable to them because they couldn't find it. Just as with other new information systems, user feedback is critical to ensure that documents are easy to find due to the way sites are designed, documents are linked, and common terminology is used to facilitate searching. Another common challenge is the monitoring and management of content for currency. Royal Dutch Shell recently reported saving more than $1 million by consolidating separate country and regional sites into a single Asia-Pacific intranet—which reduced the amount of content from more than 1,000 sites and 212,000 pages to 20 sites and 30,000 pages (Blackman, 2007).

Some companies are also experimenting with collaboration tools used on the Internet—such as blogs and wikis—to increase the usage of their intranets as sites for employees to informally interact with each other and share information informally. However, bringing blogs and wikis into a corporate intranet requires a supportive corporate culture. Successful blogs on the Internet have two common characteristics (Singh, 2007): (1) the blogger needs to have something important to say, and (2) the blogger needs to be able to share opinions that are "uncensored." If the corporation's culture does not encourage the sharing of personal viewpoints ("free expression"), then few employees will likely share their views and blogs will gain few readers.

Similarly, wikis—a kind of Web page that can be added to and edited by many different users—can be a useful platform for informal information sharing among employees, including providing tips for new employees in a division. However, if a workplace culture doesn't value unfettered collaboration by employees and a less structured kind of publication, then wikis might only be useful in a more restricted setting—such as to support collaboration among members of a specific project team.

Other firms have also reported "taking a cue from YouTube" (White, 2007) and using online video, delivered over their intranets, for communicating messages from top managers to employees located at different sites or for delivering training to a dispersed sales team.

SUMMARY

Providing support for desktop and remote computer users is the responsibility of IS managers. Effective desktop support for an organization's employees requires strategies and tactics that take into account unique organizational context characteristics and the range of needs of computer users with different skill levels. IS and business managers need to collaborate on policies and procedures to ensure that computer users have a work environment that enables them to be productive without placing the business at risk. Today's network technologies make it easier to provide some support services and to enforce some control policies and procedures. In particular, the increasing use of networks has made it easier to place the tasks of hardware and software inventorying and upgrading, as well as the enforcement of some security controls and procedures, in the hands of network administrators rather than individual

users. The IT industry has also become more responsive to some support needs by embedding context-specific support and control mechanisms in the software itself.

The development of computer applications by business employees who are not IS specialists has become commonplace. Although there can be clear benefits to having business users develop applications, both business and IS managers should carefully consider the characteristics of the application to be developed, the technologies to be used, and the skills and experience of the available user developers to ensure that the benefits are not outweighed by the risks to the organization for an application developed and maintained by a non-IS specialist. User developers should also use a development methodology that is appropriate for the specific application, and consultation with IT professionals and auditing personnel should be encouraged, as appropriate.

Effective support strategies for new user technologies (such as PDAs or blogs) may initially be different from the strategies and tactics implemented for more mature user computing environments. Supporting a remote workforce (telecommuters) in different time zones may also require not only mobile technologies, but also 24/7 help desk support. Both employees and supervisors may also need special training programs to increase the likelihood of successful telecommuting programs. Participation by managers and users is also important for ensuring that an intranet's content and tools are aligned with the company's goals and culture.

REVIEW QUESTIONS

1. What are some of the reasons that business users want to develop computer applications (user application development) rather than rely on only IS-developed applications?
2. What are some of the major business risks associated with user application development?
3. Describe one application, tool, and developer characteristic that should be assessed when evaluating whether or not a given application should be user-developed, including what you see as the potential business risk associated with each characteristic.
4. Choose three of the Definition questions in Figure 13.4 that the user developer should address and explain why they could be important.
5. What are some of the key causes of spreadsheet errors in user-developed applications?
6. Compare the Acceleration and Containment strategies for supporting user computing and provide a rationale for why a firm might choose one or the other.

7. What support services are most important for you as a computer user today, and why?

8. Describe how a company policy could minimize a specific business risk associated with user computing.

9. What types of companies are members of the Business Software Alliance, and what role is played by the BSA in enforcing software copyright laws?

10. What are some of the reasons that the number of workers who are telecommuting has been increasing?

11. Why do companies implement intranets, and what are some of the challenges in managing an intranet?

DISCUSSION QUESTIONS

1. From the perspective of an organization's managers, discuss what you see as some of the primary tradeoffs between the benefits and risks of user application development.

2. Describe a situation in which one of the advantages of user application development might be more important to a business manager than an IS manager. Then describe a situation in which one of the disadvantages might be more important to a business manager than an IS manager.

3. Summarize the lessons learned from the user developers' remarks in the box entitled "Lessons Learned by User Developers."

4. Describe the extent to which you think the support services for computer users listed in Figure 13.8 are being offered to business users in an organization that you are familiar with.

5. Develop a few guidelines for spreadsheet developers to follow to help prevent spreadsheet errors.

6. Describe a circumstance under which you think it will be difficult to enforce a corporate "standard" for purchasing a newer user technology—such as a BlackBerry (or other type of handheld device or PDA).

7. The number of telecommuters in the United States did not grow as fast during the 1990s as some had predicted it would. Provide a rationale for why you think telecommuting has increased more rapidly in more recent years.

8. If you were employed as a salesperson, but were asked to work from your home (as a telecommuter) on days that you were not out in the field, what would you like, and dislike, about this arrangement—and what could the company do to address some of your "dislikes"?

9. Use the Internet to find examples of blogs and wikis. Provide some ways that companies could make good

use of these tools (a) as part of their corporate intranets and (b) as part of their public Web sites.

REFERENCES

Agpar, Mahlon IV. 1998. "The alternative workplace: changing where and how people work." *Harvard Business Review* 76:3 (May/June): 121–136.

Blackman, Andrew. 2007. "Dated and confused." *Wall Street Journal* (May 14): R5.

Boynton, Andrew C., Robert W. Zmud, and Gerald C. Jacobs. 1994. "The influence of IT management practice on IT use in large organizations." *MIS Quarterly* 17 (March): 299–318.

Brancheau, James C., and Donald L. Amoroso. 1990. "An empirical test of the expansion-control model for managing end-user computing." *Proceedings of the 11th International Conference on Information Systems*: 291–303.

Brancheau, James C., and Carol V. Brown. 1993. "The management of end-user computing: Status and directions." *Computing Surveys* 25 (December): 437–482.

[BSA] 2007. "Manufacturing Companies Pay Substantial Amounts for Unlicensed Software Use: Damages Total $1.43 Million." June 11. BSA Web site, *www.bsa.org* (July 20, 2007).

[BSA] 2007. "BSA Raises the Stakes in Fight Against Software Piracy." July 2. BSA Web site, *www.bsa.org* (July 20, 2007).

Carlton, Jim. 2006. "Secrets of the tech-savvy traveller." *Wall Street Journal* (April 3): R1, R4.

Delaney, Kevin J. 2003. "Old computers don't fade away anymore." *Wall Street Journal* (May 1): B3.

Dunham, Kemba J. 2000. "Telecommuters' lament." *Wall Street Journal* (October 31): B1, B18.

Galletta, Dennis F., K. S. Hartzel, S. Johnson, J. Joseph, and S. Rustagi. 1996. "An experimental study of spreadsheet presentation and error detection." *Proceedings of the 29th Hawaii International Conference on System Sciences*: 336–345.

Gerrity, T. P., and John F. Rockart. 1986. "End-user computing: Are you a leader or a laggard?" *Sloan Management Review* 27 (Summer): 25–34.

Glick, James. 2003. "Tangled up in spam." *New York Times Magazine* (February 9): 42–47.

Gomes, Lee. 2003. "Software companies flex real muscle in search for pirates." *Wall Street Journal* (October 20): B1

Green, Jeff. 2006. "Implementing a telecommuting program." Faulkner Information Services.

Hall, M. J. J. 1996. "A risk and control oriented study of the practices of spreadsheet application developers."

Proceedings of the 29th Hawaii International Conference on System Sciences: 364–373.

Hammond, L.W. 1982. "Management considerations for an information center." *IBM Systems Journal* 21 (2): 131–161.

Hansel, Saul. 2003. "How to unclog the information artery." *New York Times* (May 25): BU1, 10.

Harmon, Amy. 2003. "Re: What people love to hate." *New York Times* (May 11): WK7.

Huff, Sid L., Malcolm C. Munro, and Barbara H. Martin. 1988. "Growth stages of end-user computing." *Communications of the ACM* 31 (May): 542–550.

Jordan, Graeber. 1997. "The Boeing Web," Keynote Address at SIM Interchange, San Francisco.

Kaiser, Kate M. 1993. "End-user computing," *Encyclopedia of Computer Science and Technology.*

Karten, Naomi. 1990. "The two stages of end-user computing," *Mind Your Business: Strategies for Managing End-User Computing.* Wellesley, Massachusetts: QED Information Sciences, Inc. pp. 3–24.

Klepper, Robert, and Mary Sumner. 1990. "Continuity and change in user developed systems." in K. M. Kaiser and J. J. Oppelland (eds.), *Desktop Information Technology.* Amsterdam: North-Holland, 209–222.

Langley, Alison. 2003. "Computer viruses are frustrating insurers, too." *New York Times* (October 12).

Martin, James. 1982. *Application Development Without Programmers.* Upper Saddle River, NJ: Pearson Prentice Hall.

Mathews, Anna Wilde. 2003. "As workers grab web freebies with 'peer-to-peer' software, employers move to prevent it." *Wall Street Journal* (June 26): B1, B7.

McLean, Ephraim R., L. A. Kappelman, and J. P. Thompson. 1993. "Converging end-user and corporate computing." *Communications of the ACM* 36 (December): 79–92.

McNurlin, Barbara C., and Ralph H. Sprague. 1998. Information Systems Management in Practice, 4th ed. Upper Saddle River, NJ: Pearson Prentice Hall.

McQueen, M.P. 2006. "Laptop lockdown." *Wall Street Journal* (June 28): D1.

Munro, Malcolm C., Sid L. Huff, and G. C. Moore. 1987–1988. "Expansion and control of end user computing." *Journal of Management Information Systems* 4 (Winter): 5–27.

Muoio, Anna. 2000. "Cisco's quick study." *Fast Company* (October): 286–295.

Panko, Ralph R. 1988. *End User Computing: Management, Applications, and Technology.* New York: Wiley.

Panko, Ralph R. 1996. "Minitrack on risks in end-user computing." *Proceedings of the 29th Hawaii International Conference on System Sciences.*

Panko, Ralph R., and R. P. Halverson, Jr. 1996. "Spreadsheets on trial: A survey of research on spreadsheet risks." *Proceedings of the 29th Hawaii International Conference on System Sciences*: 326–335.

Pender, Lee. 2000. "How personal is the personal computer?" *CIO* (October 15): 185–192.

Pyburn, Philip J. 1986–1987. "Managing personal computer use: The role of corporate management information systems." *Journal of Management Information Systems* 3 (3): 49–70.

Rivard, Suzanne, and Sid L. Huff. 1988. "Factors of success for end-user computing." *Communications of the ACM* 31 (5): 552–561.

Rockart, John F., and L. S. Flannery. 1983. "The management of end-user computing." *Communications of the ACM* 26 (10): 776–784.

Schultheis, Robert A., and Mary Sumner. 1991. "The relationship of application risks to application controls: A study of microcomputer-based database applications." *Computer Personnel* 13 (3): 50–59.

Shellenbarger, Sue. 2007. "Reasons to hold out hope for balancing work and home." *Wall Street Journal* (January 11): D1.

Singh, Shiv. 2005. "Intranet Trends to Watch for in 2006." *CIO,* December 19.

[Spam calculator]. 2003. Trend Micro Web site. *www.trendmicro .com/en/products/gateway/spam/evaluate/spam-calculator .htm* (August 13).

Speier, Cheri S., and Carol V. Brown. 1997. "Differences in end-user computing support and control across user departments." *Information & Management* 32 (February 15): 85–99.

Tam, Pui-Wing. 2007. "Cutting files down to size." *Wall Street Journal* (May 8): B4.

Topi, Heikki. 2003. "Supporting telework: Obstacles and solutions," in Carol V. Brown and Heikki Topi (eds.), *IS Management Handbook*, 8th ed., New York: Auerbach Publications, 807–817.

White, Bobby. 2007. "Firms take a cue from YouTube." *Wall Street Journal* (January 2): B3.

Williford, Steven M. 2003. "Reviewing user-developed applications," in Carol V. Brown and Heikki Topi (eds.), *IS Management Handbook*, 8th ed., New York: Auerbach Publications, 781–798.

Zaslow, Jeffrey. 2006. "Hoarders vs. deleters, revisited." *Wall Street Journal* (September 7): D1.

MANAGING A SYSTEMS DEVELOPMENT PROJECT AT CONSUMER AND INDUSTRIAL PRODUCTS, INC.

Late Friday afternoon, T. N. (Ted) Anderson, director of disbursements for Consumer and Industrial Products, Inc. (CIPI), sat staring out the wide window of his 12th-floor corner office, but his mind was elsewhere. Anderson was thinking about the tragic accident that had nearly killed Linda Watkins, project director for the Payables Audit Systems (PAS) development project. Thursday night, when she was on her way home from a movie, a drunken driver had hit her car head on. She would survive, but it would be months before she would be back to work.

The PAS system was a critical component of a group of interrelated systems intended to support fundamental changes in how billing and accounts payable at CIPI were handled. Without Watkins, it was in deep trouble. Deeply committed to the success of these new approaches, Anderson did not know exactly what he could do, but he knew he had to take drastic action. He picked up his phone and told his secretary, "Please get me an appointment with IS Director Charles Bunke for the first thing Monday morning." Anderson would have the weekend to decide what to do.

The Origin of the PAS Project

Consumer and Industrial Products, Inc., is a Fortune 100 manufacturer of a large variety of well-known products for both individuals and industry. Headquartered in the United States, CIPI is an international company with facilities in Europe, Asia, and North and South America.

The PAS project was one of several interrelated projects that resulted from a fundamental reevaluation of CIPI's accounts

payable process as part of CIPI's companywide emphasis on total quality management (TQM). Anderson recalls:

In late 1991 we began to look at what we were doing, how we were doing it, the costs involved, and the value we were adding to the company. We realized that, even with our computer systems, we were very labor-intensive, and that there ought to be things we could do to increase our productivity and our value added. So we decided to completely rethink what we were currently doing and how we were doing it.

Since we were a part of the procurement process, we needed to understand that total process and where accounts payable fit into it. We found that procurement was a three-part process—purchasing the goods, receiving them, and finally paying for them. And we concluded that our role was pretty extensive for someone who was just supposed to be paying the bills. We were spending a lot of effort trying to match purchase orders with receiving reports and invoices to make sure that everyone else had done their job properly. We typically had about 15,000 suspended items that we were holding up payment on because of some question that arose in our examination of these three pieces of information. Many of these items spent 30 to 60 days in suspension before we got them corrected, and the vast majority of the problems were not the vendor's fault but rather the result of mistakes within CIPI. For some of our small vendors for whom we were a dominant customer, this could result in severe cash flow problems, and even bankruptcy. With today's emphasis upon strategic partnerships with our vendors, this was intolerable.

We finally recognized that the fundamental responsibility for procurement rests with purchasing, and once they have ordered the goods, the next thing that is needed is some proof that the goods were received, and we are outside that process also. We concluded that our role was to pay the resulting bills, and that we should not be holding the other departments' hands to make sure that their processes did not break down. And we certainly should not be placing unfair burdens upon our vendors.

So we decided to make some fundamental changes in what we did and how we did it. We told the people in our organization what we wanted to do and why we wanted to do it and gave them the charge to make the necessary changes. After about 9 months we discovered that we were getting nowhere—it was just not moving. Obviously we could not just top-down it and get the results we wanted. With the help of a consultant we went back to the drawing board and studied how to drive this thing from the ground up rather than from the top down. We discovered that our people were very provincial—they saw everything in terms of accounts payable and had little perspective on the overall procurement process. We had to change this mind-set, so we spent almost a year putting our people through training courses designed to expand their perspective.

Our mind-set in accounts payable changed so that we began to get a lot of ideas and a lot of change coming from the floor. There began to be a lot of challenging of what was going on and many suggestions for how we could reach our strategic vision. In cooperation with the other departments involved, the accounts payable people decided to make some fundamental changes in their role and operations. Instead of thoroughly investigating each discrepancy, no matter how insignificant, before paying the bill, we decided to go ahead and pay all invoices that are within a reasonable tolerance. We will adopt a quality-control approach and keep a history of all transactions for each vendor so that we can evaluate the vendor's performance over time and eliminate vendors that cause significant problems. Not only will this result in a significant reduction in work that is not adding much value, but it will also provide much better service to our vendors.

We also decided to install a PC-based document imaging system and move toward a paperless environment. We are developing a Document Control System (DCS) through which most documents that come into our mail room will be identified, indexed, and entered through document readers into the imaging system. Then the documents themselves will be filed and their images will be placed into the appropriate processing queues for the work that they require. The Document Control System will allow someone to add notes to the document, route it from one computer system to another, and keep track of what has been done to the document. This will radically change the way we do business in the department. Things that used to take 18 steps, going from one clerk to another, will take only 1 or 2 steps because all the required information will be available through the computer. Not only will this improve our service, but it will drastically reduce our processing costs. It will also require that all of our processing systems be integrated with the Document Control System.

In addition to developing the new Document Control System, this new accounts payable approach required CIPI to replace or extensively modify five major systems: the Freight Audit System (FAST); the Computerized Invoice Matching System (CIMS), which audited invoices; the Corporate Approval System (CAS), which checked that vouchers were approved by authorized persons; the vendor database mentioned above; and the system that dealt with transactions that were not on computer-generated purchase orders. The PAS project was originally intended to modify the CIMS system.

Systems Development at CIPI

Systems development at CIPI is both centralized and decentralized. There is a large corporate IS group that has responsibility for corporate databases and systems. Also, there are about 30 divisional systems groups. A division may develop systems on its own, but if a corporate database is affected, then corporate IS must be involved in the development. Corporate IS also sells services to the divisions. For example, corporate IS will contract to manage a project and/or to provide all or some of the technical staff for a project, and the time of these people will be billed to the division at standard hourly rates.

Similarly, computer operations are both centralized and decentralized. There is a corporate data center operated by corporate IS, but there are also computers and LANs that are operated by the divisions and even by departments. Corporate IS sets standards for this hardware and the LANs, and will contract to provide technical support for the LANs.

Because the accounts payable systems affected corporate financial databases, Anderson had to involve corporate IS in the development of most of these systems. The Document Control System (DCS), however, did not directly affect corporate databases, so Anderson decided to use his own systems group to develop this imaging system.

Corporate IS had just begun using a structured development methodology called Stradis. This methodology divides the development into eight phases: initial study, detailed study, draft requirements study, outline physical design, total requirements statement, system design, coding and testing, and installation. This methodology provides detailed documentation of what should be done in each phase. At the end of each phase detailed planning of the next phase is done, and cost and time estimates for the remainder of the project are revised. Each phase produces a document that must be approved by both user and IS management before proceeding with the next phase. Stradis also includes a post-implementation review performed several months after the system has been installed.

Roles in the PAS Project

The Stradis methodology defined a number of roles to be filled in a development project: Anderson was the executive sponsor, Peter Shaw was the project manager, and Linda Watkins was the project director. (Exhibit 1 shows the Disbursements Department organization chart and Exhibit 2 shows how Corporate IS Systems Development is organized.)

Executive Sponsor

Ted Anderson, director of disbursements, is responsible for all CIPI disbursements, including both payroll and accounts payable. Starting with CIPI in 1966 in the general accounting

EXHIBIT 1
Partial Organization Chart of Disbursements Department

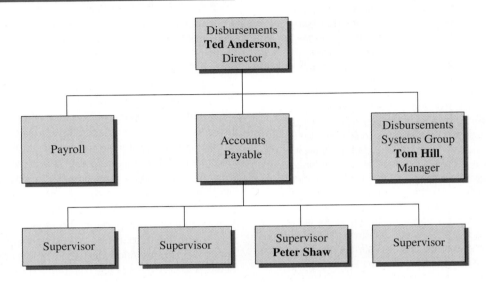

area, Anderson had a long history of working as the user-manager on systems development projects, including projects in payroll, human resources, and accounting. He spent a year doing acquisitions work for CIPI and in 1978 served a stint in Europe as area treasurer. He made steady progress up the CIPI management ladder.

In the Stradis methodology the executive sponsor has budgetary responsibility and must approve all of the expenditures of the project. He or she must sign off at the end of each phase and authorize the team to proceed with the next phase.

According to Watkins, Anderson was a very active executive sponsor:

> Ted was determined that this project would produce a quality system and get done on time and that his people would commit themselves to the project. He not only talked about these priorities, but he also led by example by attending working sessions where lower-level people were being interviewed and participating in data modeling sessions. By visibly spending a lot of his personal time on the project, he showed his people that it was important for them to spend their time.

"The area manager has to take an active role in the development of systems," Anderson asserts:

> particularly when you are trying to reengineer the processes. If you do not have leadership from the manager to set the vision of where you are going, your people tend to automate what they have been doing rather than concentrating on what really adds value and eliminating everything else, so I took a fairly active role in this project. I wanted to make sure that we were staying on track with our vision and on schedule with the project.

User Project Manager

Peter Shaw was the user project manager. He had worked for CIPI for 18 years, starting as a part-time employee working nights while going to college. Over his career he had worked in payroll, accounting, and human resources, spending part of the time in systems work and part in supervisory positions. For the past 3 years, he had been a supervisor in accounts payable.

The user project manager is responsible for making sure that the system meets the user department's business needs and that the system is completed on time. He or she manages the user department effort on the project, making sure that the proper people are identified and made available as needed. He or she is also responsible for representing the user view whenever issues arise and for making sure that any political problems are recognized and dealt with.

The user project manager and the project director work closely together to manage the project and are jointly responsible for its success. Shaw also served in the role of business analyst on this project.

Project Director

Linda Watkins, senior analyst in the corporate IS department, was the project director. Watkins, who had recently joined CIPI, had an MBA in MIS and 7 years of experience as an analyst and project manager with a Fortune 500 company and a financial software consultant. She had experience using Stradis to manage projects, which was one of the reasons she had been hired by CIPI. Because they were being charged for her time,

EXHIBIT 2
Partial Organization Chart of Corporate IS

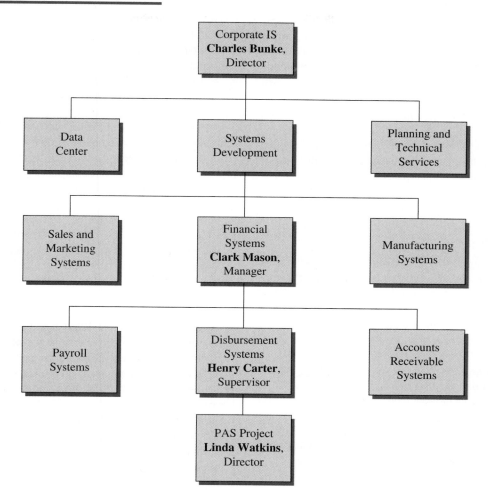

Watkins viewed the disbursement department managers as clients for whom she was working as a consultant.

The project director was responsible for managing the IS people on the project. "My job resembled that of the general contractor on a construction project who has to deal with all the subcontractors and manage the budget and schedule," Watkins explains.[1] She developed the project plans, determined what each phase would cost, managed the budget, involved the necessary technical people at the right time, and worked through Shaw to make sure that the proper client people were available when needed to be interviewed or make decisions.

"I felt like I was ultimately responsible for the success of the project," Watkins reports, "because if things fell apart I would be the one that would take the blame, both from IS management and client management. Therefore my major concern was to look ahead and foresee problems and make sure that they were solved before they impacted the success of the project."

"That is what I look for in a project manager," Ted Anderson asserts. "Most of the day-to-day work just happens if you have good people, but the crucial thing is to anticipate potential problems so that you are preventing them rather than just reacting."

Watkins also tried to make her clients aware of what was possible with computer technology so that they would not simply automate what they had been doing. "I tried to help them think about why they were doing things instead of just how they were doing them," Watkins says. "Because I was not an

---

[1]The interviews for this case were conducted while Watkins was recovering from her accident, a few months after the events described.

expert in accounts payable, I could ask the dumb question that might lead to a new perspective."

Another important part of Watkins' job was communication. "I tried to make sure that the client managers knew what was going on at all times and that they knew all the options when there were decisions to be made. I trusted them to make the right decisions if they had the information they needed." Anderson found that to be a refreshing change from his past experience. "Previously IS has not told its customers any more than it had to. But Linda was very open and we felt that we could trust her."

That trust was very important to Watkins, for her ultimate responsibility was to ensure that everyone worked together effectively on the project. She devoted a lot of effort to selecting technical people who had good communications skills and could interact positively with her clients.

IS Management

Henry Carter, IS supervisor of disbursements systems, was Watkins' supervisor. He was responsible for integrating all projects in the disbursements area and for allocating IS people to these projects. His role included advising and coaching the project directors, reviewing their project plans, and making sure that they got the technical assistance they needed from the IS organization.

Carter had been responsible for maintenance of the Disbursement Department's systems for many years. When the new development projects were initiated, Carter became responsible for them also, but he had little experience with systems development and was of little help to Watkins.

Carter reported to Clark Mason, IS manager of financial systems, who was aware of some of Carter's limitations but who valued him for his knowledge of the existing systems. To compensate for Carter's weaknesses, Mason had tried to get the best available project managers, and he told them to come directly to him when they had strategic questions or problems with client relationships.

Steering Group

The steering group was chaired by Anderson and included three accounts payable supervisors whose areas were affected by the project, Shaw, and the manager of the disbursements systems group, Tom Hill. Watkins and Carter were ex officio members of this group. The role of the steering group was to approve budgets, determine the business direction of the project, and make any necessary decisions.

The steering group met on alternate Wednesdays at 3:30 p.m. The agenda and a project status report, such as the one prepared for the steering group meeting on October 6, 1993 (see Exhibit 3), were distributed at least 24 hours before each meeting.

Under the "Recap Hours/Dollars" section, the "Original" column refers to the original plan, and the "Forecast" column gives the current estimated hours and cost. The "Variance" column is the original plan minus the current estimate, whereas the "Actual-to-Date" column shows the hours and cost incurred up to October 5. A major function of the steering group was to deal with problems and issues. Problems require immediate attention, and issues are potential problems that will move up to the problem category if they are not dealt with.

At the start of each steering group meeting, Anderson would ask whether or not everyone had made themselves available when they were needed, and if not he would talk to them afterward. According to Watkins, "Ted was very vocal with his opinions, but he was not autocratic. When there were differences of opinion within the steering group, he would subtly hint at the direction he wanted to go, but it was still up to the interested parties to work out their own resolution of the problem. On the other hand, if he thought the project was getting off the track, he would put his foot down hard!"

Shaw was knowledgeable about the political climate, and he and Watkins would meet to plan the steering group meetings. They would discuss the issues that might come up and decide who would present them and how. If there were significant decisions to be made, Watkins and Shaw would discuss them with Anderson ahead of time to see where he stood and work out an alternative that he could support. Watkins did not try to force a recommendation on the committee; rather, she presented the problems in business terms along with a number of possible alternatives. Because the agenda was well organized and all the information was in the hands of participants ahead of time, the steering group meetings were quite effective, usually ending before the scheduled hour was up.

Several of the steering group members were the sponsors of other projects, and after the PAS steering group meetings were finished they would stay around and discuss these projects and their departmental problems with Watkins. She was pleased that she was viewed as a Disbursements Department colleague and not as an outsider.

Project Planning

The Stradis methodology requires that the project director estimate two costs at the end of each phase of the project: the cost of completing the rest of the project and the cost of the next phase. At the beginning, estimating the cost of the project was mostly a matter of judgment and experience. Watkins looked at it from several perspectives. First, she considered projects in her past experience that were of similar size and complexity and used their costs to estimate what the PAS system would cost. Then she broke the PAS project down into its phases, did her best to estimate each phase, and totaled up

EXHIBIT 3
PAS Project Status Reportas of October 5, 1993

Recap Hours/Dollars	Original	Forecast	Variance	Actual-to-Date
Initial Study:				
Hours	577	448	129	434
Dollars	$20,000	17,000	3,000	16,667
Detailed Study:				
Hours	1,350	1,337	13	1,165
Dollars	$45,000	47,927	−2,927	42,050
Total:				
Hours	1,927	1,785	142	1,599
Dollars	$65,000	64,927	73	58,717

Milestone Dates	Original	Revised	Completed
Complete Context DFD—Current	8/3		8/4
Complete Level 0 DFD—Current	8/6		8/13
Complete Level 1 DFD—Current	8/22	9/12	9/14
Complete Level 0 DFD—Proposed	9/17	9/21	9/21
Map System Enhancements to DFD	9/17	9/21	9/24
Complete Data Model (key-based)	10/2	10/11	
Complete Detailed Study Report	10/8	10/15	

Accomplishments This Week:
Project Team:
    Completed the documentation library for the current system.
Lucy Robbins:
    Completed the PAS system's Business & System Objectives.
    Documented the PAS system's constraints.
    Started compiling the Detailed Study Report (DSR).
    Completed the documentation library for the current system.
Arnold Johnson:
    Completed the documentation library for the current system.
Linda Watkins:
    Reviewed the estimates and work plan for the three enhancements.
    Drafted the authorization for the enhancements.
    Initiated the Draft Requirements Statement (DRS) work plan.
Peter Shaw:
    Identified the new system's Business & System Objectives.
Carol Hemminger and Paul Brown:
    Completed the documentation of the workshop findings.
    Refined the ERM diagram.

Plans for Next Week:
    Finish and distribute the draft DSR.
    Finish the data modeling workshop documentation.
    Complete the DRS work plan.
    Distribute the finalized Initial Study Report (ISR).

Problems That May Affect the Project Status:
1. The DSR will not be finalized until the documentation from the data modeling workshops is completed.
2. Two walkthroughs are still outstanding, the key-based data model workshop and current system task force. Both will be completed when client schedules allow.

Issues:
1. Due to delays in scheduling interviews with AP, Robbins' time has not been utilized as well as possible. If this continues it may cause delays.

these costs. When she compared these two estimates, they came out to be pretty close. Finally, she went over the project and her reasoning with several experienced project managers whose judgment she respected. This initial estimate was not too meaningful, however, because the scope of the project changed radically during the early stages.

Estimating the cost of the next phase requires that the project director plan that phase in detail, and then that plan is used to set the budget and to control the project. According to Watkins:

> The Stradis methodology provides an outline of all the steps that you go through to produce the deliverables of a stage. I would go through each step and break it down into activities and then break down each activity into tasks that I could assign to people. I would estimate the time that would be required for each task, consider the riskiness of that task, and multiply my estimate by a suitable factor to take the uncertainty into account. I would also ask the people who were assigned the task what kind of effort they felt it would require and would consult with experienced people in the IS area. Finally, by multiplying my final time estimate by the hourly rate for the person assigned to the task I would get a cost estimate for each task and add them all up to get a total cost for the phase. Again I would go over this with experienced project managers, and with Peter and Ted, before making final adjustments.
>
> Then I could start scheduling the tasks. I always included the tasks assigned to user department people, although I did not need them for controlling my budget and many other project managers did not bother with them. I wanted Peter and Ted and their people to see where they fit into the project and how their activities impacted the project schedule.

To help with the scheduling, Watkins used a tool called Project Manager's Workbench that included a PERT module and a Gantt Chart module. With the possibility of time constraints and different staffing levels, she often had to develop several different schedules, for discussion with Shaw and Anderson and for presentation to the steering group.

Staffing the Project

In addition to Watkins, Arnold Johnson was assigned to the project at the beginning. Johnson had worked for Carter as a maintenance programmer for many years. Carter valued him highly as a maintenance programmer and therefore only assigned about 20 percent of Johnson's time to the PAS project. According to Watkins:

> Arnold did not see any urgency in anything he did, and being primarily assigned to maintenance, he never had any commitment to our deadlines, and he would not even warn me when he was going to miss a deadline. When you are on a project plan that has tasks that have to be done by specific times, every person

must be fully committed to the project, so the project plan was always in flux if we depended on him to get anything done.

Johnson had a detailed knowledge of the existing CIMS system, and Watkins had planned for him to document the logical flow of the 14,000 lines of spaghetti code in the main program of the CIMS system. Watkins reported:

> He knew where things were done in the existing program, but he never knew why they were being done. He would never write anything down, so the only way to get information from him was verbally. We eventually decided that the only way to use him on the project was as a consultant and that we would have an analyst interview him to document the existing system.

A few weeks after the start of the project, Watkins obtained Lucy Robbins from a contractor firm to be her lead analyst. Robbins had managed a maintenance area at a medium-sized company and had also led a good-sized development project. She could program, but her main strength was in supervising programmers and communicating with the technical specialists in IS. Watkins was able to delegate much of the day-to-day supervision to Robbins so that she could concentrate on the strategic aspects of the project.

The Stradis methodology required the use of a CASE tool, and Robbins became the CASE tool "gatekeeper" who made sure that the critical project information stored therein was not corrupted. She said,

> We used the CASE tool to keep our logical data dictionary, data flow diagrams, and entity/relationship data models. The CASE tool keeps your data repository, and then uses that repository to populate your data flows, data stores, and entity/relationship models. It also assists in balancing the diagrams to make sure that everything that goes into a diagram is necessary, and everything that is necessary goes in.

Because IS had far more projects under way than it had good people to staff them, Watkins was never able to convince Henry Carter or Clark Mason to assign a qualified CIPI person to the project full time, so she had to staff the project with temporary employees from outside contractors:

> After I determined what resources I could get from CIPI, I would look at the tasks the project team had to perform and then try to find the best persons I could that fit our needs. I took as much care hiring a contractor as I would in hiring a permanent CIPI person. I tried to get people who were overqualified and keep them challenged by delegating as much responsibility to them as they could take. My people had to have excellent technical skills, but I was also concerned that their personalities fit in well with the team and with our clients.

Watkins hired two contractor analysts who had skills that the team lacked. One was a very good analyst who had experience with CIPI's standard programming language and database management system and had been a liaison with the database people on several projects. The second contractor analyst had a lot of experience in testing.

The project got excellent part-time help from database specialists in the CIPI IS department. Watkins recalls:

> We used IS database people to facilitate data modeling workshops and to do the modeling. We also used a data analyst to find a logical attribute in the current databases or set it up in the data dictionary if it was new. There were also database administrators who worked with the data modelers to translate the logical data model into physical databases that were optimized to make sure we could get the response time we needed.

Watkins also used consultants from the IS developmental methodologies group:

> Because my supervisor was not experienced in development, I used people from the methodologies group to look at my project plans and see if they were reasonable. We also used people from this group as facilitators for meetings and to moderate walkthroughs, where not being a member of the team can be a real advantage. Also, when we needed to have a major technical review, the methodologies group would advise me on who should be in attendance.

Carrying Out the Project

The project began in mid-June 1993 as the CIMS Replacement Project. The Computerized Invoice Matching System (CIMS) was an old, patched-up system that matched invoices to computer-issued purchase orders and receiving reports, paid those invoices where everything agreed, and suspended payment on invoices where there was disagreement.

The Initial Study

Because of strategic changes in how the department intended to operate in the future, a number of significant changes to the system were necessary. The project team concluded that it was impractical to modify the CIMS system to include several of these important enhancements. Therefore, Shaw and Watkins recommended that a new system be developed instead of attempting to enhance the existing CIMS system. They also suggested that the scope of this system be increased to include manual purchase orders and some transactions that did not involve purchase orders, which effectively collapsed two of the planned development projects into one. At its meeting on August 8, 1993, the steering group accepted this recommendation and authorized the team to base the Initial Study Report on the development of a new system that they named the Payables Audit System (PAS).

The Initial Study Report was a high-level presentation of the business objectives of the new system and how this system would further those business objectives. A seventeen-page document released on September 21, 1993, it discussed two major problems with the old system and described five major improvements that the new system would provide. The estimated yearly savings were $85,000 in personnel costs and $50,000 in system maintenance, for a total of $135,000. On October 9, 1993, the Initial Study Report was approved by Anderson, and the team was authorized to proceed with the Detailed Study.

The Detailed Study Report

The Detailed Study Report begins with an investigation of the current system, and with production of level 1 and level 2 data flow diagrams and an entity/relationship diagram of the existing system. Then, given the business objectives of the new system, the project team considers how the current system can be improved and prepares data flow diagrams and entity/relationship diagrams for the proposed system. Much work on the Detailed Study Report had been done before it was formally authorized, and this report was issued on October 26, 1993. This report was a 30-page document, with another 55 pages of attachments.

The major activities in this stage were initial data modeling workshops whose results were stored in the CASE tool logical data dictionary. Most of the attachments to the Detailed Study Report were printouts of data from this logical data dictionary providing information on the data flow diagrams and the entity/relationship models that were included in the report.

The body of this report was mainly an elaboration of the Initial Study Report. It included the following business objectives of the new system:

- Reduce the cost of voucher processing over the next 3 years to less than the current cost.
- Reduce the staff required for processing vouchers by 50 percent over the next 5 years.
- Significantly reduce the time required to pay vouchers.
- Provide systematic information for the purpose of measuring quality of vendor and accounts payable performance.
- Support systematic integration with transportation/logistics, purchasing, and accounts payable to better facilitate changes due to shifts in business procedures.

Among the constraints on the PAS system cited in the Detailed Study Report were that it must be operational no later than September 30, 1994; that it would be limited to the IBM mainframe hardware platform; and that it must interface with six systems (Purchase Order Control, Supplier Master, Front-End Document Control, Electronic Data Interchange, Corporate

Approval, and Payment). Four of these systems were under development at that time, and it was recognized that alternative data sources might need to be temporarily incorporated into PAS.

The estimated savings from the new system remained at $135,000 per year, and the cost of developing the system was estimated to be between $250,000 and $350,000. It was estimated that the next phase of the project would require 1,250 hours over 2.5 months and cost $40,000. The Detailed Study Report was approved on October 31, 1993, and the team was authorized to proceed with the Draft Requirements Study.

The Draft Requirements Study

As the Draft Requirements Study began, Watkins was concerned about three risks that might affect the PAS project.

> First, so many interrelated systems were changing at the same time that our requirements were a moving target. In particular, the imaging Document Control System that was our major interface had not been physically implemented and the technology was completely new to CIPI. Second, the schedule called for three other new systems to be installed at the same time as PAS, and conversion and testing would take so much user time that there simply are not enough hours in the day for the accounts payable people to get that done.
>
> Finally, I was the only full-time person from the CIPI IS department. Although the contractors were excellent people, they would go away after the project was over and there would be little carryover within CIPI.

Watkins discussed her concerns with Carter and Mason and with Anderson and the steering group. They all told her that, at least for the present, the project must proceed as scheduled.

The Draft Requirements Study produces detailed information on the inputs, outputs, processes, and data of the new system. In addition to producing level 3 data flow diagrams, the project team describes each process and produces data definitions for the data flows and data stores in these data flow diagrams, and describes the data content (though not the format) of all input and output screens and reports of the new system. The project team was involved in much interviewing and conducted a number of detailed data-modeling workshops to produce this detail.

The major problem encountered was the inability to schedule activities with Disbursements Department people when they were needed. For example, in early December, Anderson came to Watkins and told her that his people would be fully occupied with year-end closing activities for the last 2 weeks of December and the first 2 weeks of January and that they would not be available for work on the PAS project. He was very unhappy with this situation and apologized for delaying the project. Watkins told him that she understood that the

business came first and that she would reschedule activities and do what she could to reduce the impact on the schedule. This potential problem had been brought up at the steering group meeting in early November, but the group had decided to go ahead with the planned schedule.

The PAS Draft Requirements Statement (DRS) was completed on March 21, 1994, 4 weeks behind schedule, but only $5,000 over budget. The DRS filled two thick loose-leaf binders with detailed documentation of the processes and the data content of the inputs, outputs, data flows, and data stores in the new system. Preparation of the Outline Physical Design was projected to require 600 hours over 6 weeks at a cost of $25,000. The DRS was approved on April 3, 1994, and the Outline Physical Design phase was begun.

The Outline Physical Design

In the Outline Physical Design phase the IS technical people become involved for the first time. They look at the logical system and consider alternatives as to how it can be implemented with hardware and new manual procedures. The approach in this phase is to map the processes in the logical data flow diagrams and the data models to manual processes and hardware and to make sure that this proposed hardware can be supplied and supported by the organization. Programming languages and utilities are also considered, so at the end of this phase the project team knows what kind of programming specifications and technical capabilities will be required.

The PAS system was originally planned to run on the IBM mainframe, but given the use of a LAN for the Document Control System, the technical people decided to move as much of the PAS system to the LAN as possible. This was a radical change that increased the estimated development cost substantially.

Watkins' new estimate of the total cost of the PAS system was $560,000. This was a substantial increase from the previous estimate of $250,000 to $350,000, and it caused some concern in CIPI management. Peter Shaw asserted:

> The company treasurer doesn't care a bit about the PAS project. All he cares about is how many dollars are going to be spent and in which year. When the cost went up so that we were substantially over budget for this year, that got his attention. If the increase were for next year it would not be a major problem because he would have time to plan for it—to get it into his budget. But this year his budget is set, so Linda and I have to figure out how we can stay within our budget and still get a usable system this year as version 1 and upgrade it to what we really need next year.

On June 27, just as the Outline Physical Design report was being completed, Watkins' car accident occurred, taking her away from work for several months.

Anderson's Concerns

Watkins' accident focused Anderson's attention on some long-standing concerns. He was worried because among the directors of the five projects he was sponsoring, Watkins was the best. All of his other projects were behind schedule and in trouble, and now he did not know what would happen to the PAS project.

Anderson was fully committed to his strategic direction for the disbursements area, and he felt that his reputation would be at risk if the systems necessary to support his planned changes could not be completed successfully. He was convinced that he had to take decisive action to get things back on track. He needed a plan of attack to present to IS Director Charles Bunke at tomorrow's meeting.

DEVELOPMENT OF AN INTERORGANIZATIONAL SYSTEM AT ZEUS, INC.

Zeus, Inc., headquartered in the United States, is a leading global designer and manufacturer of heavy equipment. Zeus employs approximately 17,000 persons in its manufacturing, assembly, and research and engineering facilities. With some 300 U.S. and 125 overseas locations where Zeus-trained service personnel and Zeus parts are available to repair and maintain its products, Zeus has an outstanding reputation for customer service. In 1999 Zeus reported net earnings of $35 million on sales of over $2.1 billion.

Zeus has a strong emphasis on quality which focuses on providing a comparative advantage to customers. This emphasis, supported by extensive training programs, has resulted in improved product quality with significantly reduced warranty expense to Zeus, better work processes emphasizing cross-functional teams, and smoother product introductions. Zeus' management believes this emphasis on quality is a key to improving Zeus' financial performance.

Electronic controls—the use of a computer to control the equipment—are a major development in Zeus' efforts to gain market share in its highly competitive industry. Zeus first started shipping electronically controlled equipment in the late 1980s. Today most of Zeus' products are electronically controlled, which means that each product includes at least one computer. These computers not only control the engine, they also manage how the horsepower is used by the machine and its operator and provide the owner with information to help run his or her business more efficiently.

Zeus' North American Distributors

There are 24 Zeus distributors covering the United States and Canada, each of which handles Zeus' products in a specified geographic area. These distributors are independent businesses, although most of their owners have some past relationship to Zeus (such as a major customer or former employee). Each distributor has a contract with Zeus specifying

the rights and responsibilities of each party and the conditions under which the contract may be canceled by either party. The typical distributor has been associated with Zeus for many years—there has been very little turnover.

The typical distributor has a headquarters location and several branches in its territory. The Memphis distributor, for example, has branches located in Memphis, Little Rock, and Cairo, Illinois, and has about $50 million a year in revenue.

Zeus has a special sales force that deals with the large, national customers, but the Memphis distributor territory includes about 30 large equipment dealers to which the distributor sells equipment and repair parts. This is a very competitive and cyclical business. Product quality has greatly improved over the recent past, causing the replacement and repair business to stagnate. The only way to increase equipment sales has been to take market share from competitors. In addition to designing and producing superior products, an important competitive factor is providing outstanding service to customers.

Another response to this stagnation in the equipment business has been to diversify into selling services. Zeus' management expects that within 5 years information and information-related products will be a very significant proportion of the distributors' business. This represents a major change for distributors, for these products seem strange and intangible in comparison to the traditional business of selling and fixing equipment.

The ZOCS Project

In Zeus' very competitive situation, one way to obtain a competitive advantage is through outstanding customer service. Consequently, Zeus is committed to customer service that ensures that the customer will be delighted with every aspect of his relationship with Zeus. The performance of the distribution channel is critical to providing outstanding customer service and Zeus' management wants a world-class distribution network.

Due to the highly competitive nature of its business, Zeus has instituted and is in the process of implementing the **ZOCS** (**Zeus Outstanding Customer Service**) system, a computer system to support operations for both Zeus and its distributors.

The purpose of the ZOCS system is to secure a comparative advantage for Zeus and its distributors by providing uniform outstanding service to their customers. To this end ZOCS will implement **uniform processes** throughout the Zeus distribution system. ZOCS also includes the installation of a computer/communications network to connect all of the distributorships and their branches to Zeus headquarters and thereby to each other.

According to Jonathan Buthman, marketing vice president:

When our customers come into their home distributorship they are well taken care of. But if they break down far away—in Salt Lake City or San Diego or Vermont—they might not get the same good treatment because the local distributor may not know who is responsible for taking care of warranty work or the exact configuration of the equipment. We want to have a common standard of performance nationwide just like McDonald's or Budweiser beer. We want our customers to get the same good service in the same way no matter where they may be. That is why we need the best uniform business processes supported by instantly available information throughout our distribution system.

Nathan Byars, controller of the Memphis distributorship, explains:

Today if a product we sold here breaks down in Salt Lake City they have to get on the phone and call us and we have to go through our records to look up the product to find warranty information, the history and configuration, etc. With the new system the person in Salt Lake City will put the product's serial number into his computer and it will bring up its history record. That will be such a great benefit to both us and our customers. The phone calls will go away.

We also have a lot of information that goes between us and Zeus and other distributors. We are now going to have a visible inventory nationwide. The first time one of our people keys in the number of a part that we need but don't have and sees one in Texas that can be shipped to us immediately, he is going to say "Wow! This is great!"

Also, as mentioned previously, Zeus products are rapidly incorporating computer technology, and management foresees the day soon when providing information will be a major contributor to the bottom line. Computers must have software to operate properly, and that software may have bugs or need to be upgraded to improve the equipment's performance or to provide better information to customer management. Today, when a software change is made, Zeus must send the change to each distributor location on a disk, and managing the disks and making sure that the current version is always used is an almost impossible task. The solution to this problem will be to maintain the latest version of all software on a central database at Zeus headquarters and download it directly to the equipment when and where it is needed. This, of course, requires a communications network that will be a part of the ZOCS system.

Computer systems are critical to a good distribution system, both at Zeus headquarters and the distributors, and the systems at these two levels must be coordinated so that they work together effectively. Unfortunately, the distributors have had a wide variety of local systems to manage their operations. Half of the distributors used systems provided by Milroy Systems, Inc. (MSI), a software house that specializes in software for heavy equipment sales and service organizations. Five distributors had systems provided by another software house, Titanic Systems. Each of the remaining seven distributors used a system that was different from all the rest. Consequently, the Zeus IS group was in an impossible position whenever any aspect of Zeus' distribution computer system must be changed. According to Harvey Snider, Zeus' IS distribution systems leader:

Whenever we need to make a change, my first task is to figure out who is doing what today, which takes a lot of time and money. Then I have to develop a solution to deal with each unique case, which takes a lot more time and money. Moreover, by the time I am finished with all this, what I did is no longer what we need because it took me too long to get it done. We must have uniform systems at all our distributors.

The ZOCS project was begun in July 1994 and was scheduled to complete the rollout of the system to all distributorships by the end of 1998. System design and development was to take 15 months, with the Alpha test scheduled for the fourth quarter, 1995. The Beta test was scheduled for the second quarter, 1996, and two pilot installations were to be completed during the third quarter, 1996. Rollout to all distributorships was scheduled to begin in the fourth quarter, 1996, with all distributors up and running by the end of the third quarter, 1998.

This project was expected to cost about $60 million, about half invested by the distributors and half invested by Zeus. The total cost was to be spread over 7 years. The annual benefits after system installation were projected to total around $27 million per year, with about $18 million going to the distributors and $9 million going to Zeus. The direct benefits to Zeus did not meet Zeus' normal investment criteria, but Zeus management felt strongly that this project was necessary for Zeus to continue to be successful in the U.S. market.

The project team included some 40 people from Zeus, along with some 60 other people from contractors and the distributorships who worked on the project.

The Computer/Communications Network

The architecture of the proposed computer/communications network (see Exhibit 1) has three layers: branch, distributor headquarters, and Zeus headquarters. These three layers are connected via a TCP/IP wide area network (WAN).

EXHIBIT 1
ZOCS Architecture Overview

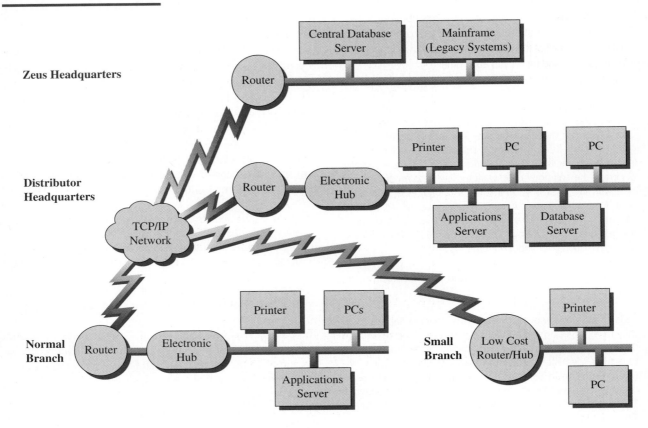

Consider first the distributor headquarters, where there is a LAN connected to the WAN through a router. The LAN connects an applications server, a database server, and various PCs and printers to each other and through the WAN to branches and Zeus headquarters, and thence to the other distributors and Zeus' subsidiaries. The applications server stores the applications software and makes it available to the PCs on the LAN, but does no processing itself. The database server maintains the databases for the distributorship and provides data to the PCs upon request. The PCs, located throughout the distributorship, run the applications software to support the business processes of the distributor.

The normal branch has a LAN similar to the one at the distributorship, except that it has no database server so its data are provided by the database server at the distributor headquarters. Again, the branch's PCs run the applications software that is furnished upon demand by the branch's applications server. A small branch with only a few people is treated like a PC on the distributor's LAN and obtains both its software and data from the distributor headquarters via the WAN.

Zeus headquarters also has a LAN that connects a national database server (which Zeus calls its central database server) to the mainframe at the Zeus Data Center that supports Zeus' legacy systems. The central database server (CDS) will provide common cross-distributor information such as the parts master database, national parts inventory database, standard repair times, and product service history summary database.

The Business Processes

A major objective of the ZOCS project was to produce and institute good, uniform business processes throughout the system so that a customer gets the same treatment no matter where he may be in the country. The ZOCS project plan has identified some 28 common processes that support all 24 distributorships' operations. The order fulfillment process, for example, includes activities from when the order is placed until the bill is paid. The preparation of a proposal to sell equipment to a particular customer is another common process. When a breakdown occurs anywhere in the United

States, there is a process that determines Zeus' liability under the warranty and reimburses the distributorship that performs the required work. Many of these distributorship processes interact with corresponding processes at Zeus headquarters, so the ZOCS project must include these processes at both levels.

The Applications Software

Computer applications have been identified that support these 28 business processes. These applications are categorized in the following four areas: financial, marketing, service, and parts.

The distributorship financial applications include accounts payable, general ledger, and accounts receivable.

The main application in the marketing area is customer management, which includes maintaining contact lists, call reports, a history of proposals, and other information that assists the sales force in dealing with the customer.

The service applications include work orders, warranty, and shop management. The work orders application keeps track of progress on the work order, parts used, labor hours used, and so forth. The warranty application maintains information that enables the distributor to determine what work is required under the warranty and to assure that it is done and that the appropriate money transfers are made. The shop management application manages all the active work orders in the shop, provides standard times and costs to the work order application, and gathers data on actual times and costs that can be used to measure performance of the shop and to improve the standards when necessary. There is also a preventive maintenance application that helps manage preventive maintenance contracts. Another application is project management, where the distributor will take responsibility for a complex project that integrates Zeus equipment with other equipment for special applications.

Parts applications include order entry, inventory control, and physical inventory. Zeus also must track used or damaged components that can be reconditioned. The customer must be given credit for the component he or she provides, the component must be sent to the vendor who will recondition it, and the vendor must be billed for that component.

Reaction to the ZOCS Project

The ZOCS project received a varied reaction among the distributors, which are all independently owned businesses.

Hiram Patterson, owner of the Salt Lake City distributorship, opposed the ZOCS project:

> That project will cost me roughly a million dollars, which will eat up most of my profits for several years. Surely there is some way to allow us to share information without all that expense. Furthermore, I am not happy with Zeus trying to tell me in detail

how to operate my business. This is a family business, and we've been operating this distributorship and providing excellent service to our customers for over 50 years. I seriously doubt that the people at Zeus headquarters know as much about running our business as we do!

Jack Claiborne, owner of the Memphis distributorship that uses the MSI system, saw the need for the ZOCS system and was a strong supporter of its development. He said:

> Of course I am not thrilled at having to invest over a million dollars in a new system, especially since I have a pretty good system already that I have paid a pretty penny for. However, our business will live or die on the basis of customer satisfaction, and the ZOCS system figures to give us a substantial improvement in the ability to serve our customers the way we would want to be served. It's just something that we have to do to prosper in this business.

A number of alternative approaches to developing the system were considered. The distributors who already were using the MSI system thought that the first step should be to standardize on that system throughout all the dealerships and then upgrade that system where needed. Other approaches considered were (1) having the Zeus IS group develop the new system, (2) outsourcing the development of the system to EDS or Andersen Consulting or some other organization, and (3) employing a systems integrator to put the systems together, primarily from purchased components.

After a good deal of discussion the following approach was adopted: The Zeus IS group would manage the project, but hire MSI to upgrade the existing system that was in use at 12 of the distributorships. One reason for not adopting the existing MSI system was that it was based on a minicomputer with dumb character-based terminals, and a LAN-based system with a graphic user interface (GUI) was thought to be a better approach. Although the applications would be upgraded and the systems would be integrated into the new network environment, the present MSI users would not see many exciting improvements in the basic systems.

Implementation of the ZOCS System

While MSI was developing the software, Zeus put on a big push to get the computer/communications infrastructure in place by offering to pay part of the hardware cost for distributorships that would install the equipment early. Quite a few distributorships installed this equipment before the first Beta test of the software was completed. When it was learned that some of the hardware was inadequate for the system and had to be replaced, Zeus ate the cost. The problem of deciding on the technology can be frustrating. Jacob Hickson, Zeus project manager for the ZOCS project, reflected on the problems that rapid technological change poses for a project like ZOCS that takes several years from inception to completion:

> One of the most frustrating aspects of this project is the turmoil that faces everyone in the choice of technology. Pick any component—the applications servers, the database servers, the network, the workstations—and within a 12-month period the price/performance capability changes dramatically. You are faced with rolling something out quickly, but at the same time keeping up, which is an almost impossible task! You have to draw a line somewhere, and that is the part that no one is very good at doing.

The Alpha Test

The Alpha test was started in the second quarter of 1996, 6 months late. They did not have a suitable environment for testing at that time, so they set the system up as best they could on a server and workstation at Zeus headquarters and brought in a number of distributors and walked them through the processes and applications, trying to validate functionality and capability. This testing turned out to have been inadequate, to say the least.

The First Beta Test

They started the first Beta test at the distributorship at Green Bay in July 1996, only 3 months behind schedule. It was a disaster, and the system was pulled out after only 10 weeks of attempting to operate it. According to Hickson:

> We made about every mistake that you could make. The software was full of bugs. A hardware/software component of the initial architecture was inadequate—we literally couldn't keep the server up and running for more than a 24-hour period. The users were not ready—they didn't manage the training and we didn't follow up on it the way we should have. The implementation process wasn't capable, and we didn't have the right leadership. Nothing was really up to snuff.

One of the underlying causes of this disaster was that they tried to maintain an original schedule that was totally unrealistic. They had several teams involved in different aspects of the project—information systems, the MSI development team, a business process team, a training team, and distributor people—and each team was under intense pressure to meet its deadline. The result was that there was no overall teamwork, little communication, and no understanding of where they stood on the overall process. They did not have a cohesive team that could look at the overall process, evaluate where they were at the time, and decide what they needed to do before attempting to install the system. Consequently, they launched blindly into something for which they were woefully unprepared.

The disaster at Green Bay was a tremendous blow to the Zeus team's morale, and resulted in a lot of voluntary turnover. Many of the most capable members of the team, whose skills were in great demand, transferred to other projects within Zeus or were hired away by outside firms. Also, the morale of the distributors plummeted. According to Byars:

> This was almost the end of the project. With the distributors being independently owned, there was a lot of skepticism and a lot of people saying: "You're requiring me to spend a lot of money that I'm not going to get anything for." And when you go through a disaster like that it is easy for them to resist the project. The only thing that saved the project was the unwavering support of the project sponsor, Zeus marketing VP Jonathan Buthman, who just insisted that everyone fall in line and continue the project to a successful conclusion, no matter what the problems. He made it clear that if you dropped out of the project you would not continue to be a Zeus distributor.

The Second Beta Test

The team learned a lot from the experience of the first Beta test. They spent several months working to eliminate the problems with the software and training that had surfaced in Green Bay, and then started the second Beta test at Oklahoma City in April 1997. It went much better. According to Hickson:

> The major difference in our approach was that in Green Bay we tried to implement everything at once, but at Oklahoma City we had three major phases, and some minor ones in between. We started with the finance applications on April 1, 1997, started the service applications on July 1, and started the parts applications on August 1. By the end of September the whole thing was operational, and we fixed the problems and the distributorship signed off on it on May 1, 1998.

One of the problems that they struggled with in implementing the ZOCS system was the cultural differences between the distributors and the Zeus project team. Hickson explains:

> The distributor organizations are used to operating on a crisis basis. A customer comes in with a broken-down piece of equipment and you deal with the problem and get him on his way, and then you deal with the next customer's problem. They are used to that kind of interaction. Then we come in and say: "Here is the schedule, and here is what you need to do to get the job done. Now do these things and we'll come back and see you next week." That doesn't work because that is not the way they operate. We came in and changed the rules on them, and didn't even tell them what the new rules are. So we have had to learn how to identify and develop leaders and train them to manage the implementation of all of this change that is inherent in converting to the ZOCS system.

The Memphis Pilot

The Memphis pilot began in March 1998, when the distributor started selecting process leaders. They already had the hardware up and running because they had been scheduled for conversion much earlier. On June 15 they brought up accounts payable and general ledger. Simultaneously they began training their trainers who would train the operations and service people before starting to bring up the operations components on August 15. They completed the conversion to the new system by the end of September. Incidentally, the ZOCS project was originally scheduled to have all distributors up and running by that time, so the project was seriously behind schedule, with only 2 of the 24 distributors up and running by then.

On April 15, 1999, Byars evaluated the Memphis experience as follows:

> We had a lot of problems, but have gotten to the point where our heads are above water. We haven't solved everything, but problems are not coming at us so fast and furious now. This has been a typical family squabble—there has been a lot of finger-pointing and frustration.
>
> We were the first group that the Zeus implementation team has taken through the new training process. A lot of their folks were learning at the time, and a lot of the documentation was weak. They have learned a lot from our experience and they have upgraded their training again. We are going to send some of our people to the first upgraded training session next week.
>
> Although there are a couple of things that they really have to do some work on, most of the software flaws are just a lot of irritants. The major problems are in things that Oklahoma City did not have as part of their business, or they didn't have on a big scale. For example, Oklahoma City did not have a preventive maintenance program, but we do have that business, and we had a rude awakening because that module had serious design flaws. We are still trying to work through these problems.
>
> Converting data from our old system to the new one was my most frustrating problem. The new database is really good in that it contains a lot of new data fields that will help us with marketing, keeping track of customers and equipment, etc. When we did the conversion those fields were entered as blanks. Then the first time someone used that record the system stopped him on a dime and said, "fill it in." That really frustrated the operations people who were trying to use the system to do their work for the first time. As a result of this, I had to spend a couple of months personally recreating a lot of entries. Where I usually get our books closed the third week in January, I got it done the first of April.
>
> We are concerned that we still need to make a lot of corrections, but Zeus is back on a rapid deployment plan. They argue that it is better to get a system out there that everyone is using, even if it is imperfect, and we can see the logic in that. But we still think it would be better to take a couple of extra months to get things fixed so that it will be a little easier when they go to other places. We should have devoted more time and effort to reducing the pain, but they didn't see it that way.

At this time there were four distributorships up and running, although not yet running smoothly. Zeus was pressing forward with plans to have seven more distributorships up and running by the end of 1999.

Status as of May 1, 2000

As of May 1, 2000, 17 distributorships were running or in the process of installing the new system. According to Hickson:

> We have made progress in the installation process, but they are still rough. On the basis of what we learned from the first four installations, we have developed a good plan—we know what has to happen when, and we are able to provide the right tools to support the key events that have to happen and the key work that a distributor has to do.
>
> Between the Oklahoma City and Memphis installations we took about 4 months to get the bugs out of the system that had been revealed by the Oklahoma City experience. But Memphis still had a lot of problems because of the components that had not been implemented in Oklahoma City, so we had to start back at square one with them. The reality is that some of these changes are just being put into place right now.
>
> We have had a real struggle in determining how much effort to devote to getting the system to have the kind of capability that we all want it to have. We see the need to get everyone up quickly and say "O.K., you can invoice customers and you can track inventory, so let's go." And they say, "Yeah, but how do I manage this particular activity?" Well, they did it manually before, or they didn't do it. There are lots of different dynamics that come into play there.
>
> Despite all we have learned, as we go from distributor to distributor we still have uniquenesses in terms of where they are coming from. We know where they are going to—that is crystal clear to us. What we don't know, and what we really don't put a lot of energy into, is where are they starting from. We give them the tools, and we give them a gentle nudge and tell them how to get there, but we can't attempt perfection. Our goal is 24 up and running on the system, not one running perfectly, and that has been a source of conflict.

Each of the Zeus distributorships in North America, all 24 of them, are now network capable. They have deployed 145 file servers and 145 network connections, all to the same specifications. Lotus Notes email has also been deployed to all those locations and is being used throughout the distribution system. The central database server (CDS) is up and operational, but they have had serious problems with its data because of problems with other Zeus information systems that supply the data. According to Hickson:

> One of the key pieces of information that distributors need is data about parts. Whenever a new part is released or a price changes, that information must be available to the distributors, and in the new system parts information is available to everyone through the central database server (CDS). Zeus management decided to centralize our warehousing, and in the process of doing that they installed new purchased software to manage our inventories. That has been a horrible mess, a complete disaster, and the result was that we had to turn off the CDS parts system for several months until they could get the data cleaned

up. The distributors on our new system were dependent on that information, and all of a sudden it is not there. Now what do I do?

We had a similar problem with the Zeus system that manages information on standard repair times (SRTs), the information the distributors use to do repairs. During the time when they were having those problems Zeus released four new machines, so these should have been lots of parts and SRT information going out to the distributors, but we had to shut off the system until they could get the SRT data cleaned up. The people in the field are trying to repair equipment and submit warranty claims on Zeus, and they don't have the SRT data they need for these activities. What a mess! These problems were not the ZOCS team's fault, but they damaged the credibility of the new system. And they point out how vulnerable a tightly integrated system can be.

The problems with the CDS data were extremely frustrating for the distributorships. Byars explains:

We have worked like galley slaves to get this system installed and working, and many of the most important functions are dependent upon the data available through the CDS But much of this data has not been usable for 9 months! Now, we can understand having problems with a system—we've had our share of them. But 9 months go by and the system still doesn't work! They forced us onto the system and we can't use it! What are they doing up there?

We still don't have uniform processes, which was a major objective of the new system. But putting in a system doesn't change processes, especially when the system doesn't work. The CDS not working has provided lots of excuses for not changing our processes.

Despite all the problems, there were indications that the new systems were having a very beneficial impact on those distributorships that had installed them. According to Hickson:

We have done an analysis of the sales and profit history of the first four distributorships that were implemented. We found that although there was a sharp drop during installations, sales increased by 22 percent during the first year after installation was completed, while sales only increased by 12 percent for all distributors during that period. The effect was even more pronounced for profit before income taxes—a 60 percent increase for the first four installations versus a 15 percent increase for all distributors. These are very impressive figures on year-to-year changes.

Nathan Byars was not impressed by this analysis:

We do not agree that our good performance was due to the new system. We were so tied up trying to get the new system working during the first year after installation that our good performance was in spite of the new system, not because of it. We still expect that the new system will improve our performance, but we haven't gotten to that point yet. I suspect that the first four installations performed better than average because the Zeus team chose the best-run distributorships to implement first.

In 2000 the ZOCS team was starting one new installation each month, with the process taking from 4 to 6 months depending upon the distributorship. The team anticipated that all distributors would be up and running by the end of the second quarter of 2001, almost 3 years behind the original schedule. According to Hickson:

We are implementing one distributor a month now, with a 4-month cycle from start to finish, so we have 4 to 6 of them going all the time, all in different phases. We have three two-person implementation teams that manage the contact with the distributor during the installation. Each team has one to two active projects at a time, depending on scheduling and how many delays they encounter. The teams have a predefined number of visits that they make that are scheduled around events such as kickoffs, training sessions, starting a phase, etc. The implementation teams are on site about 3 weeks during the four months, broken up into 2- to 4-day trips. There are additional training people that are used—the implementation team doesn't do much training.

Our biggest problem is the organizational adjustment that is required by the distributorships—getting their heads around the fact that this takes a different mind-set than they are used to. The notion of making changes is what is different for a lot of them. They have to understand and accept that people are going to have to go through some training and make some adjustments, and at the end do something different. This whole mind-set change has been the biggest challenge so far.

The Future

With the end of this long project in sight at last, the question for the Zeus ZOCS team is "Where do we go from here?" Hickson explains:

Zeus has distributorships in some 27 countries outside North America, and we originally thought that we would move this new system into our international distributorships after we got the system implemented in North America. However, we tried it in Taipei and had a disaster. One would think that the distributorship function would be about the same no matter where it is located, but the issues are broader than that. It is clear that, in addition to cultural differences, there are differences in financial systems, inventory management capability, repair shop operations, and a host of other areas. We definitely have learned that an overseas distributorship is not just another distributorship—it's a different animal.

We also intended to go back and do some serious reengineering of our processes. The question is "What does that mean?" We have a wealth of opportunities in many areas to tighten up the flows and improve the business. But which of them are we going to do? Where is the most value, both for Zeus and for the distributors? Although we have some ideas, we don't have a plan—we haven't had time to think about that yet. And with the distributors exhausted and in a certain degree of turmoil, there is a great deal of uncertainty about the future. What do we prepare for? Are we going to do something major, or are we just going to keep the system running for the time being?

The long, difficult ZOCS project has had a decidedly negative impact on the relationships between Zeus and its distributors. Nathan Byars expresses his view of the future of the system:

> We are very frustrated because there are a lot of big gaps in the system that is being installed that we have known about for years, but nothing has been done about them because all the available resources have been used getting the system running in all the distributorships. There are a lot of changes that we need, and the distributors are getting organized to see that they get done.
>
> We have set up a Z/D steering committee, half of whose members represent the distributorships and half represent Zeus. It is co-chaired by a distributor and a Zeus manager. This steering committee will study the things that need to be done and define projects and do a cost/benefit analysis of them. Then they will prioritize them and present them to the distributorship council made up of all the distributorship owners and several top Zeus managers.
>
> For the recommended projects the Distributorship Council will determine: (1) Are we going to do it? (2) How much will it cost? and (3) Who is going to pay for it? The intention, of course, is that everyone will pay their fair share. I hope that we can work through it and make good progress.

Both Byars and Hickson agree that, up to this point, the focus of the project has been on the needs of Zeus and the distributors, and the customers' needs have not had a high priority. They are hopeful that these needs will be emphasized in the future, but the distributorship council will have to determine who is going to pay for those things that primarily benefit the customer.

A MAKE-OR-BUY DECISION AT BAXTER MANUFACTURING COMPANY

It is late Friday afternoon, and Kyle Baxter, president of Baxter Manufacturing Company, Inc., and his sister, Sue Barkley, vice president for customer relations, are discussing whether or not to purchase the Effective Management Systems manufacturing software package proposed by manufacturing Vice President Lucas Moore.

"I'm really fearful of buying such a large, complex software package given our past experience," Baxter exclaims. "What do you think?"

"I really don't know," Barkley replies. "We do need manufacturing software, and there are some obvious advantages to purchasing this software. We have had bad experiences in past attempts to buy such software, but we have learned from some of our mistakes, so we might be successful this time. But I have been impressed by the success that MIS has had in building new systems for us, so I am in a quandry right now."

"We're going to have to decide before long," Baxter notes, "but we need to talk with some of our people first."

Baxter Manufacturing Company Background

Baxter Manufacturing Company (BMC), located in a small Midwestern town, is a leading manufacturer of deep-drawn stampings, particularly for electric motor housings. (Exhibit 1 shows a few of BMC's products.) The company was founded in 1978 by its chairman, Walter R. Baxter, as a supplier of tools and dies, but it soon expanded into the stamping business. BMC is a closely held corporation, with the family of the founder holding most of the stock.

BMC's engineers have implemented some of the most complex stamping concepts in the industry, as the company has established its niche as a quality supplier of deep-drawn stampings to the automotive (85 percent of sales) and appliance (15 percent of sales) industries. BMC's major customers include Ford, General Motors, Honda of America, General Electric, Whirlpool, Amana, and Maytag. BMC puts great emphasis on quality and has achieved Q-1 status from Ford, a QSP Award from GM and quality awards from Honda, and is recognized as a world-class supplier within its niche.

Producing a deep-drawn part is a complex process requiring repeated stampings, each with a different male/female die pair. This process is performed on a heavy press, using a very complex die that consists of perhaps 10 individual dies assembled together in a line. A coil of steel of the proper width and thickness is fed into one end of the press. After each stamping cycle a precision transport mechanism moves the material forward exactly the right distance so that a part that has completed one stage is positioned correctly at the next stage to be struck by the next die on the next cycle of the press. Thus each cycle of the press performs a different forming operation on each of 10 parts, and a finished part comes off the machine at the end of each cycle. (Exhibit 2 shows the different stages of a motor housing stamping.)

EXHIBIT 1
Some of BMC's Stamped Parts

EXHIBIT 2
The Stages of a Motor Housing Stamping

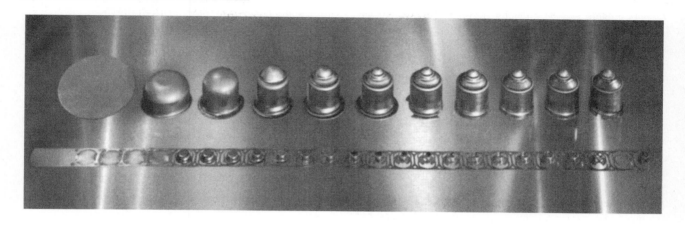

BMC's strength lies in its ability to produce efficiently large volumes of high-quality complex stampings. It may take 6 to 8 hours to install the dies and set up the huge stamping presses for a production run, so BMC cannot efficiently produce short runs and therefore does not serve the replacement market well.

BMC uses state-of-the-art equipment to develop and manufacture the necessary tooling for the needs of its customers. With the use of wire electrical discharge machines (EDM), computer numerical control (CNC) vertical machining centers, and CNC horizontal lathes, it is able to produce quality tooling efficiently. For the life of a part, BMC's computerized equipment can reproduce identical die components for replacement of worn or damaged dies.

BMC's 140,000-square-foot manufacturing facility is one of the best in the country, with 39 presses that range from 50-ton to 600-ton capacity. Every press is equipped with accessory items such as feeds, reels, and electronic detection systems. In addition to the presses, BMC has recently added the capacity to weld, drill, tap, and assemble stampings into more complex· parts to suit the needs and desires of its customers.

BMC employs about 420 people and is nonunion. Management believes that these employees are BMC's greatest asset. According to Chairman Walter Baxter:

> We have a great group of people! We are fortunate to be located in a farming area where the people have a strong work ethic and a "do whatever it takes" attitude. We started out as a family company and we have a lot of families—husbands and wives, their children, aunts and uncles—working here. My son, Kyle, is now President, and my daughter Sue is Vice President for Customer Relations. We cherish our family atmosphere.

Over its 19-year history, BMC has grown at about 20 percent a year. The last 5 years of sales have been as follows:

1992	$32,000,000	1995	$61,976,000
1993	$37,292,000	1996	$74,130,000
1994	$49,900,000		

This rapid growth has caused problems at times. For example, in 1990 its sales were so close to BMC's production capacity that, even when running its production 24 hours a day 7 days a week, it became almost impossible to meet promised delivery schedules. According to Sue Barkley:

> In 1991 we had to turn down business from existing customers who wanted to give us new parts to make. For almost a year we did not accept any new business. That was the most difficult thing we ever did because we were fearful that customers who had to go to our competitors might never come back. We told our customers that we hated to refuse their business, but we had to because if we took more business we couldn't handle it—we would be late and couldn't provide the level of service that we are committed to providing. Most of our customers understood. They were not happy about it, but they respected us for being up front about it. We did lose some good orders because we weren't accepting business when they came out, but I don't think that there are any customers who haven't come back to us with more business.

By 1992 BMC had made the large investment necessary to significantly increase capacity and was back on its historical growth track.

In the late 1980s BMC's automotive customers started to go to a just-in-time (JIT) philosophy in which they carried minimal inventories of raw materials and parts. Rather than sending an order for a month's parts at a time as they had in the past, the customers began telling BMC one day what to ship on the next. BMC was provided with a blanket order for planning, but the customers reserved the right to change the amounts at the last minute.

Including the time to procure the raw materials, run them through the presses to make the parts, clean and pack them, and ship them out, BMC's production process requires at least 2 weeks if things go well. Thus the automotive companies are forcing their suppliers to maintain their inventories for them, which places great pressure on BMC to reduce its cycle times. Because of its 2-week production cycle and long setup times, BMC is often forced to maintain a finished goods inventory that is substantially above its target of a 3-day supply.

About 5 years ago its automotive customers began to pressure BMC to convert to electronic data interchange (EDI), where all paper document flows between customer and supplier are replaced by electronic flows directly between the customer's computer and BMC's computer. Thus BMC receives all purchase orders and shipping schedules electronically and sends out electronic shipping notices and bills. EDI has the potential to be quicker and more efficient for both parties, but BMC's factory computer systems were incomplete and fragmented, so for several years BMC accepted the data electronically, printed it out, and then rekeyed the data into those relevant systems that existed. The IS department is now building interfaces to enter the EDI data directly into some of BMC's systems. One reason for this delay was that their automobile customers use one EDI standard while their appliance customers use another, and each customer has its own variation on the standard it uses. BMC has had to build a separate subsystem to handle each of its customers.

Information Systems at BMC

BMC's managers have been very receptive to the introduction of new technology. They were early adopters of CAD/CAM, and are at the forefront of stamping technology. However, they have had little experience with the use of computers in business applications and have limited understanding of what the technology can do for them.

BMC got its first PCs in 1987 and a few managers started experimenting with Lotus spreadsheets. One of the first applications they set up was a spreadsheet for generating customer quotes by calculating what price to charge for a part based on estimates of raw material cost, tooling costs, the costs of stamping, and the expected quantity to be produced. Another early use of the PC was a scheduling spreadsheet developed by the company president, Kyle Baxter, when serving as vice president for manufacturing. This spreadsheet, which is still used today, contains data for each part, including the machine used, the number produced per hour, and the setup time. The quantity required and the delivery date are entered and the spreadsheet determines when each part should be started into production and generates a schedule of what should be run when on each machine group. If the schedule is not feasible (e.g., some parts must be started last week), the scheduler can

make manual adjustments in due date, quantity required, overtime, and other factors to produce a feasible schedule.

Realizing that they needed someone to lead and educate them in the use of computers, in 1989 BMC management set up an MIS department and hired an MIS manager, Nancy Shaw. BMC installed a Data General MV minicomputer, and the first application was interoffice e-mail. This was a great way to start because it demonstrated how helpful the computer could be in sharing information. According to Sue Barkley:

> E-mail was very well received because we were growing so rapidly and the need to communicate within the plant was so important. It wasn't until we got on e-mail that we realized how much time we had been spending running around the plant trying to find somebody and leaving little notes on their desk. We really became dependent on our e-mail system.

During the next 2 years Shaw led the purchase and successful installation of a package of financial applications, including payroll, accounts payable and receivable, and general ledger. Also, in 1989 BMC was beginning to encounter problems in production because of its growing capacity problems and its customers' switch to JIT. When customers changed their requirements the production schedule had to be changed, which forced changes in the schedules of other parts, and production people seemed to be spending all their time rescheduling things. Because demand was so near to capacity it was difficult to get all the orders done on time and there was a lot of expediting going on, which again led to the need to reschedule. Although there was no computer support for manufacturing other than the spreadsheet used for scheduling, BMC's management decided that if scheduling could be speeded up the problems would be alleviated. Consequently, the decision was made to purchase a software package for scheduling.

Sue Barkley, who was involved in the process, remembers:

> Our MIS manager, Nancy Shaw, did some research and selected four packages from which we tried to choose the best one. That was my first exposure to software, and it was a terrible experience. Each vendor claimed that his software would do anything you wanted to do, and there were so many questions we should have asked but didn't.
>
> Vendors all offered integrated packages that included production scheduling, but you also got sales, inventory, purchasing, shipping, etc. We made our selection and paid about $120,000 for the system, including both hardware and software, which was a large expenditure for us at the time.
>
> Then we started to load the data and implement the scheduling package. The training the vendor provided was poor, the manual was full of errors, and support from the vendor was minimal. We worked and worked, and finally became so frustrated by our inability to get the system to do what we wanted it to that we just gave up. On top of everything else the vendor went bankrupt. It was a total disaster—$120,000 down the tube!

As mentioned previously, by 1991 the problems in meeting shipping schedules had gotten so bad that BMC began to have to turn down new business. Management again decided that they had to do something about machine scheduling, so again they decided to purchase a scheduling package. Sue Barkley remembers:

> This time things went better. Nancy Shaw and I got more people involved in the decision on what package to buy. This vendor provided some in-depth training to our MIS people, and vendor people came down here for 2 weeks to help us load the data and get the production scheduling module working. Again, we found that the manual was full of errors and that the vendor people did not fully understand the logic that the system was using. But we got the system up and working and taught the production scheduling people how to use it.
>
> The problem was that whenever we had to expedite something—give it top priority because it had to be shipped quickly—the schedule had to be regenerated, and that took 2 hours. Then we had to take the schedule for each machine and examine it to see what the impact on its schedule was and change what it was going to do. Because we were always expediting something, we were constantly churning.
>
> After about a month the production scheduler came to me and said, "I'm not getting anything done. It takes me 2 hours to regenerate a schedule. I look at it and I then have to change five or six machines because of what the system did. Then it takes me 2 more hours to generate a new schedule and I have to change another five machines, and I have to go through the cycle again. It's just a continuous process of change, change, change!"
>
> We tried for another month to make the system work for us, but we were in such bad shape with our capacity that we just couldn't take the time to try to cope with the system anymore. So we abandoned it and went back to our Lotus spreadsheet. The $150,000 that we had spent for that system was down the drain!

The Present MIS Department

In 1994 Shaw left and BMC hired Don Collins to replace her as MIS manager. Collins had 20 years of experience as a lead systems analyst with a large manufacturer and broad experience with manufacturing systems. In 1996, Collins has a programming staff of four. The 1996 capital budget for hardware, software, and other information technology items was about $200,000. The MIS expense budget for payroll, supplies, and education was about $350,000.

The MIS department is using a development tool called Cyber Query Cyber Screen (CQCS) from Cyber Science, but Collins is giving some thought to what BMC's development environment of the future should be. The Data General MV computer is becoming obsolete and is reaching capacity, so BMC will have to obtain additional capacity soon.

In order to plan a production schedule you need to know what you have in inventory, so the MIS group has created systems to track raw-material, in-process, and finished-goods inventories. MIS has also developed a minicomputer system that accepts EDI orders from customers and allows the customer service group to create a shipping schedule on the computer. Collins believes that within 2 more years the MIS group can build and install a set of manufacturing systems that will satisfy BMC's basic needs and provide quite satisfactory EDI service to customers.

This success in building new systems opened BMC managers' eyes to the possibilities for using the computer, and they have generated so many requests for new systems that an MIS steering committee has been established to approve projects and set systems development priorities. The members of the MIS steering committee are President Kyle Baxter, Controller Lou Wilcox, Sue Barkley, and Don Collins.

The New Proposal

In late 1996 Lucas Moore, vice president of manufacturing, suggested that BMC purchase and install an integrated package of manufacturing software sold by Effective Management Systems, Inc. (EMS). Moore had worked as an engineer with the company for 7 years and then took a leave for 2 years to get an MBA. The vice president of manufacturing retired soon after Moore returned, and Moore was promoted to that management position.

Moore supports the proposal that BMC install the EMS Time Critical Manufacturing package consisting of eight modules: shop floor control, EDI integration, inventory management, factory data collection, standard routings, labor collection, engineered product configurator, and general ledger. The purchase price of this software package is $220,000, including documentation, training by EMS, and consulting help during installation of the software. The cost of a software maintenance contract is $55,000 a year, and EMS will make limited changes requested by BMC at a cost of $60 per hour.

The EMS software will run on several minicomputers, including BMC's Data General MV. However, additional computer capacity will be needed whether BMC purchases the EMS package or builds its own manufacturing systems.

Moore's Views

Moore is relatively new to the manufacturing area, having taken over that area about a year ago, and was not involved in the past attempts to purchase scheduling software. Moore explained to Baxter that BMC should purchase the EMS package for the following reasons:

> We are still fudging our EDI and still scheduling with a Lotus spreadsheet. The entire industry has passed us by in our use of the computer in manufacturing and we are in danger of losing

our reputation as a world-class parts manufacturer. Both my MBA studies and our experience with the new inventory systems that Don has installed have convinced me that computer systems can significantly enhance our efficiency and improve our service to our customers, but we can't wait another 2 years to complete home-grown manufacturing systems that will still need to be upgraded before they are really first class.

I have had extensive discussions with EMS manufacturing specialists, read their literature, and seen the proposed systems demonstrated, and am convinced that the proposed system will do everything that we will ever want to do. EMS has assured me that there will be no problem integrating these manufacturing modules with our existing financial systems, and that we can be up and running with the entire system in 6 months.

"Given that our MIS group is doing a good job developing new systems," Baxter asked, "why should we purchase the EMS package rather than build manufacturing systems in-house?" Moore's reply was:

> The time and cost differences between purchasing and building are too significant to ignore: 6 months to install this advanced system versus 2 years to build our own basic system, and a firm $220,000 to purchase this system versus over $400,000 to build our own. These costs do not include new hardware, but we will need to increase our capacity whether we purchase or build our new systems.
>
> Furthermore, we will get a high-quality state-of-the-art system instead of a simple "first try" system. EMS has sold this system to hundreds of manufacturers, and thus has been able to spend much more time and money developing it than we could possibly afford. EMS has a large staff of more creative and sophisticated programmers than we can get, and EMS has gone through several cycles of improvement of this system based upon the experience of hundreds of users of the earlier versions of the system.
>
> It is true that the EMS system will not always do things the way we currently do them. But is the way we do them better than the way that is based on the experience of hundreds of manufacturers? We are always making changes in how we do things, so it will not be difficult for us to make some changes to conform to this new software, and I expect that these changes will improve our operations.

"We have not been successful in two tries to use purchased software packages in the manufacturing area," Baxter noted. "What makes you think that we would be successful this time?" Moore replied:

> There are a number of important differences this time. First, in the past there was little ownership of the new system by the factory people, but this time I am the champion of the new system and my people will make it work. Second, in the past the conversion strategy was flawed—BMC tried to install scheduling without having inventory data under control, but this time we will go at it a module at a time in the sequence that EMS has been very successful with in many previous installations. Third,

during the previous attempts we were pushing capacity and no scheduling system was going to work when we were having to expedite everything, but today capacity is not a major problem and things are reasonably calm in our factory so we can devote our energy to making the new system successful.

Collins' Views

Baxter also talked with Collins, who argued that BMC should continue its process of building the manufacturing systems that it needed. He estimated that the needed systems could be completed in about 2 years at a cost of around $420,000—$220,000 for outside help (including training his people in new development tools) and $200,000 in internal costs.

When Baxter asked Collins why BMC should not purchase the EMS software, Collins replied:

> First, the EMS software is far more complicated than we need. For most general manufacturers each part may require six operations on six different types of machines, and each part has a routing that is different than other parts. Then several parts may be assembled into a subassembly, so you have two- or three-level bills of material. We typically take a coil of steel, stamp out the part, clean it, box it, and ship it out, so both our routings and our bills of material are very simple, as is our production process. The EMS system is designed for much more complex manufacturing.
>
> Second, we have had little or no experience with computerized production systems. Does it make sense for us to try to jump to a very complex and sophisticated system like the EMS proposal? Lucas has a very superficial understanding of this software package, and he doesn't know any of the details of how it will work. Therefore, he has no idea of the difficulties that his people will run into in adapting to this complex package. It will require them to do many tasks that they have never done, or even considered doing. And they don't need this complexity. Wouldn't it be better to build our own systems that correspond to where we are on the learning curve and plan to upgrade them as we progress in our understanding of our systems needs?
>
> Third, it is likely that the system does not fit the way we are running the business. Do we change the system or do we change how we run our business? We probably can't change a purchased system, so we would have to change the way we run the business. Do we really want to do this?
>
> Fourth, we are constantly changing our manufacturing facilities and processes, and they may be unique to our business. If you purchase a package you are at the mercy of the vendor to make changes in it. He may or may not make the changes that you want, and in fact he may make some changes that you do not want. If you do not expect the system to change and it is a common system, you probably should purchase it. For example, one general ledger system is just like any other, and they haven't changed in 20 years, so you should purchase this application. But we are continually changing things out in the shop, and if we build our own systems we can change them when we need to.

Finally, we have demonstrated that we can build and successfully install our own systems, but our record with purchasing and installing manufacturing systems is dismal. The EMS proposal may fulfill our needs, but then again it may not. We failed twice in the past because the system we purchased did not fit our needs. Why take that chance again?

"You seem very concerned that the EMS system might not suit our needs or that our needs might change," Baxter replied. "Could we modify this system if it does not suit our needs?" Collins said:

Because we will not have a source-code version of the software, it will not be feasible for our programmers to modify the functionality of this system. However, we can write interface software to change the form of the system's input and output.

When Baxter noted the cost and time differences between purchasing and building the system as estimated by Moore, Collins replied:

The figures Lucas quotes are very misleading. The purchase price is but a part of the total cost of buying, installing, and maintaining the software. To be sure you are choosing software that truly meets your needs, you must put a substantial effort into defining your needs and evaluating each candidate package against those needs. One of the major weaknesses of the present proposal is that this process of defining needs and evaluating possible packages has been completely ignored. In my opinion we must go through this process before buying any packaged software, and this will affect both the proposed cost and how long it will take to install the system.

Another cost of purchasing a system is the cost of modifying your existing systems so that they can feed data to or receive data from the purchased package. If the systems that must be interfaced with the purchased systems are also purchased systems that you cannot modify, you may have to create additional systems to translate from one packaged system to the other packaged system. In addition there will be costs of training the users, data conversion, and the changeover to the new system. A good rule of thumb for the total cost of installing a purchased package would be twice the purchase price of the software, which in this case would be $440,000. I doubt that we could do it for any less, and that compares with about $420,000 to build our own systems, which includes all the costs involved, such as training, conversion, and defining the needs of our manufacturing people.

It will take at least a year to properly evaluate and install a purchased system. This is less than the 2 years we will need to complete our own system, but we will be installing and using components of the new system as we complete them, so the time advantage is not that great.

When asked what it would take to do a more complete evaluation of the proposal to purchase the EMS system, Collins replied:

We would need to spend about 6 months studying our manufacturing area to determine what we are doing now and what the new systems should do. Then we would take some time to explore the many packages that are available, and winnow them down to the three or four most suitable. Then we would invite the chosen vendors to submit proposals so we could study and evaluate each of these proposals in detail and pick the best one. Meantime, we would prepare a proposal for building the new system that would describe the proposed system in detail and include a plan for its development including schedules of both time and dollars. Finally, we would compare the best proposal with the plan for building the system ourselves and decide which to do. That would take at least a year and cost between $50,000 and $90,000.

Decision Time

After his discussions with Moore and Collins, Baxter sat down with his sister, Sue Barkley, to discuss what to do about Moore's proposal. "Sue," Baxter began, "you were able to get the second manufacturing software system we bought up and running, but conditions in the shop were so chaotic that we abandoned trying to use it. Why don't we go back and try it again?" Sue replied:

We recently considered trying again to use this system, but the special computer we bought to run it died and the software vendor has gone out of business, so we were out of luck.

"Lucas claims that BMC is losing its reputation as a world-class parts manufacturer because its systems are inadequate, and therefore BMC must purchase a system without delay," Baxter said. "Do you believe that it is critical that we get these new systems immediately?" Sue thought a while before replying:

I don't think that our customers care about our systems as long as we provide high-quality products at a good price and deliver them when they are needed, which we are doing. From their perspective, we are already interacting with them via EDI, so that is a problem for us rather than for them. It would be great to have the proposed systems as soon as possible, but we have been getting along without them for a long time.

"Well, Sue," Baxter said, "I still don't know what we should do. What do you think?"

CASE STUDY III-4

ERP PURCHASE DECISION AT BENTON MANUFACTURING COMPANY, INC.

Benton Manufacturing Company, Inc., is a U.S. manufacturer of a varied line of consumer durables. Although its stock is publicly traded, a single family holds a controlling interest in the company. In 1998 Benton had net sales of almost $1 billion and an operating profit of about $180 million.

Benton's 5,200 employees operate seven factories and 57 distribution centers located throughout North America. In the past few years Benton has acquired several companies, and two of Benton's factories have been added as the result of acquisitions that broadened Benton's product line. Benton's products are sold through thousands of independent dealers who may sell both Benton's and competitors' products.

Benton is the leader in its industry with its products claiming some 40 percent of the market. However, industry demand is growing very slowly while the structure of the industry is undergoing rapid change as formerly independent dealerships are being acquired by large chains. This consolidation is changing the power relationships between Benton and its dealers and causing Benton's traditional profit margins to erode.[1] Benton has responded to this pressure by pursuing a Continuous-Improvement strategy that so far has increased productivity more than 25 percent, reduced in-process inventory 30 percent, freed up thousands of square feet of factory space, and reduced new product development cycle times.

Benton has a history of continuous growth in sales and profits. In order to continue this growth in today's increasingly competitive environment, Benton management has focused on growth through the following strategies: (1) customer-driven new product development, (2) the acquisition of new businesses that complement existing ones, (3) international expansion, and (4) emphasis on the Continuous-Improvement approach.

Enterprise Resource Planning Systems

As one response to growing competitive pressure, Benton management is considering acquiring an Enterprise Resource Planning (ERP) system. An ERP system is a comprehensive set of software modules that integrate a company's financial, human resources, operations and logistics, and sales and marketing information systems, storing the data for all these systems in a central database so that data are entered only once and the results of each transaction flow through the system without human intervention. An ERP system can replace many separate poorly integrated computer applications systems that a company has purchased or developed over the years. During the 1990s the use of purchased ERP packages exploded among Fortune 500 companies, making the leading vendor, Germany's SAP, the fastest-growing software company in the world.

Thomas H. Davenport[2] explains why ERP systems—sometimes called Enterprise Systems (ES)—are so popular:

> An ES streamlines a company's data flows and provides management with direct access to a wealth of real-time operating information. For many companies, these benefits have translated into dramatic gains in productivity and speed.
>
> Autodesk, a leading maker of computer-aided design software, used to take an average of 2 weeks to deliver an order to a customer. Now, having installed an ES, it ships 98 percent of its orders within 24 hours. IBM's Storage Systems division reduced the time required to reprice all of its products from 5 days to 5 minutes, the time to ship a replacement part from 22 days to 3 days, and the time to complete a credit check from 20 minutes to 3 seconds. Fujitsu Microelectronics reduced the cycle time for filling orders from 18 days to a day and a half and cut the time required to close its financial books from 8 days to 4 days.

[1]This is a disguised case. Because of confidentiality issues further details about Benton's products or its industry cannot be disclosed.

[2]Thomas H. Davenport, "Putting the enterprise into the enterprise system," *Harvard Business Review*, July–August, 1998, pp. 123–4.

Along with the successes, however, there have been a number of resounding failures in attempts to utilize ERP systems. Davenport[3] reports on problems with enterprise systems:

The growing number of horror stories about failed or out-of-control projects should certainly give managers pause. FoxMeyer Drug argues that its system helped drive it into bankruptcy. Mobile Europe spent hundreds of millions of dollars on its system only to abandon it when its merger partner objected. Dell Computer found that its system would not fit its new, decentralized management model. Applied Materials gave up on its system when it found itself overwhelmed by the organizational changes involved. Dow Chemical spent 7 years and close to half a billion dollars implementing a mainframe-based enterprise system; now it has decided to start over again on a client/server version.

Some of the blame for such debacles lies with the enormous technical challenges of rolling out enterprise systems–these systems are profoundly complex pieces of software, and installing them requires large investments of money, time, and expertise. But the technical challenges, however great, are not the main reason enterprise systems fail. The biggest problems are business problems. Companies fail to reconcile the technological imperatives of the enterprise system with the business needs of the enterprise itself.

An enterprise system, by its very nature, imposes its own logic on a company's strategy, organization, and culture. It pushes a company toward full integration even when a certain degree of business-unit segregation may be in its best interests. And it pushes a company toward generic processes even when customized processes may be a source of competitive advantage. If a company rushes to install an enterprise system without first having a clear understanding of the business implications, the dream of integration can quickly turn into a nightmare.

The ERP Study

Aware of the growing use of ERP systems and concerned that Benton might be missing an important development, Benton President and CEO Walter S. McHenry has formed a two-person team, composed of Adam T. Meyer and Jerry L. Cook, to investigate whether or not Benton should purchase such a system. Meyer is a senior systems analyst who has been a star with the Benton IS department for 15 years and has led many successful projects. Starting in engineering 12 years ago, Cook has worked in several areas throughout the company, including production, finance, and market research. Although not an IT professional, Cook is quite comfortable with computer technology and has led the introduction of CAD and LANs into engineering. McHenry told Cook and Meyer:

ERP seems to be the direction that our industry is going, and we probably need one too. However, I don't know the specifics of what an ERP system involves or what it might bring to the company, so I want you to do a quick study and determine whether ERP is for us, and if so how we should approach it.

The study team found that there are four major ERP software vendors they might consider: SAP, J.D. Edwards, Oracle, and PeopleSoft. Each of these vendors is financially stable, supports global companies, has a full line of highly integrated modules, and is a leader in R & D. There are a number of "Tier 2" vendors, but Cook and Meyer believe that none of them is suitable for a long-term partnership.

After a great deal of study, attending a number of conferences, and talking with several people from companies that are using ERP systems, the study team is convinced that Benton should replace its legacy "back office" systems with an ERP system. Meyer explains:

We believe that information technology is crucial to survival in today's competitive environment. Our present systems are growing old and hard to maintain, and will have to be replaced in the next few years. ERP systems have much more functionality and much better integration than our internal IT staff can possibly provide, so we have to use them just to keep up with our competitors who are starting to install them.

Furthermore, Benton management has established strategic business plans that cannot be realized without an ERP system. These plans include the following emphases that cannot be fully supported by our present information systems:

- International expansion
- Mergers and acquisitions
- Use of IT as a strategic weapon
- Integration with suppliers and customers
- Reduction of operational costs
- Product line expansion
- Process standardization across different units of the company

Adopting an ERP system will be a monumental undertaking for Benton. According to Cook:

An ERP system is not just a huge infusion of software and technology. We have learned that this is not just an IT project. Rather, it will require wholehearted commitment from all departments. They have to be willing to change their work processes to conform to those dictated by the ERP–the software is almost an afterthought. Benton has never faced change of this magnitude!

Reactions to the ERP Proposal

Cook and Meyer know that there is strong support for an ERP system from IT management, and they are confident that, although President McHenry does not seem to want to get personally involved, he is supportive of an ERP system. To make sure that McHenry understands the issues involved in adopting an ERP, Cook and Meyer have urged him to visit with a friend of his who is the CEO of a company that installed an ERP 2 years ago and is reported to be very pleased with the results.

---

[3]*Ibid.*, pp. 122–3.

There is also a great deal of support for an ERP system from operating-level management. But the reaction of VP-level management (see the partial organization chart in Exhibit 1) is mixed. According to Cook:

> Contrary to what Benton management believed in past years, we're going to have to change. Although the structure of our industry is changing, our dealers are changing, and the economy is changing, the need for us to change is not universally recognized in the company management. We have some managers whose view is more defensive and who are less willing to embrace change.

Benton's present human resources information systems are old and inadequate. Susan R. Hamilton, human resources vice president, is an enthusiastic supporter of an ERP system. Hamilton says:

> I have talked with human resources managers who have ERP systems from several different vendors, and they are all enthusiastic about their systems. I know that an ERP system will enable us to increase productivity, serve the needs of our employees much better, and significantly improve the management of our human resources at Benton. Although I realize that converting to such a system will be a long and difficult process, I can't wait to get started.

Tracy C. Scott, vice president for distribution, has 7 years' experience with Benton and is one of the few top managers that have management experience outside the company. Scott advocates an ERP system:

> Our present computer systems work well at the distribution centers, but they only provide local information—I can't get a quick picture of the entire distribution system. Better information would enable us to significantly reduce our finished goods inventory and at the same time provide better service to our customers. The integration of sales, production, and inventory information that an ERP system provides would enable me to do a much better job of managing my department.

Pat L. Miller, vice president for manufacturing, joined Benton as an engineer 20 years ago and worked in many positions in the manufacturing area prior to becoming a vice president four years ago. Miller is concerned about the possible impact of an ERP system on the manufacturing area:

> For the past several years we have been concentrating on lean manufacturing through the Continuous-Improvement approach, and have increased productivity over 25 percent and reduced inventory by 30 percent in our factories. The Continuous-Improvement approach avoids going for the "home run." Rather, it concentrates on producing many relatively small improvements, each of which can be quickly and easily implemented. It seems to me that an ERP project costing over $30 million is the antithesis of our Continuous-Improvement approach that has been so successful. First, it is one huge step, not a progression of small improvements. Also, in the ERP approach you must use the process dictated by the designer of the ERP system, and that is inflexible. How can you do Continuous Improvement?
>
> I have another concern. We have a unique culture here at Benton that, in my opinion, is responsible for the success we

EXHIBIT 1
Partial Benton Organization Chart

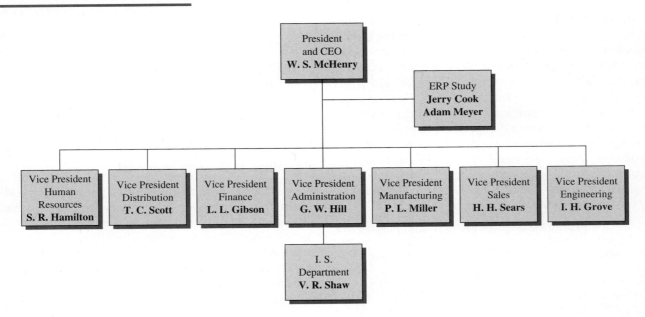

have enjoyed. I have read that installing an ERP system may well force you to change your culture to be more compatible with the ERP system. That sends shivers down my back!

Lee L. Gibson has been vice president for finance for 10 years. Until about 3 years ago the information systems department reported to Gibson. Gibson, who is responsible for financial analysis of Benton's investments, asserts:

> The IS department has developed excellent financial systems for me that are quite adequate for our needs, so I see no major need for an ERP system as far as the finance department is concerned.
>
> Also, I am very concerned about the high cost of an ERP implementation and about whether the bottom-line return from such a system would justify this huge expense. We have always subjected our IT investments to a rigorous cost/benefit analysis, and I don't see any reason why we should treat an ERP system any differently. In my view, the larger the investment the more important it is that it be carefully justified, and an ERP system would cost many times as much as the largest IT system we have ever developed.

Cost/Benefit Analysis

Meyer shudders at the thought of trying to use cost/benefit analysis to justify an ERP system:

> The costs of an ERP system are readily apparent up front, but many of the benefits are results of more complete and timely information that enable you to better manage the enterprise. These intangible benefits do occur, but they are not easy to identify and quantify beforehand.
>
> At conferences we talked with a number of people that are delighted with the results of their ERP systems, and we

always asked how they cost justified the system. We got a lot of strange looks and blank stares. The identifiable cost reductions will seldom justify the cost of an ERP system, but people are installing them because they realize that they have to in order to compete in the future. And many companies are beginning to get bottomline results that they ascribe to their ERP investments.

Gibson's concern prompted Cook and Meyer to develop the analysis presented in Exhibits 2 and 3 This analysis is based on a study they obtained that reported the experience of over 60 firms that have successfully installed ERP systems and used them for at least 3 years. Using the figures from this study, the team estimates that it will cost Benton some $34 million to install an ERP system and $750,000 a year for a maintenance contract. The benefits are estimated to be about $11.593 million a year after installation is complete. Over a 7-year period this produces an Internal Rate of Return of 20 percent and a Net Present Value (at a 20 percent discount rate) of just over $156,000, which just barely meets Benton's criteria for such investments.

Cook explains how the yearly benefits were developed, as shown in Exhibit 2:

> In each area of benefits (inventory, centralized operations, etc.), the table shows the industry low and high as a percent of the Base Amount column, which contains the current cost to Benton of the category in each line, except for the last line where it contains Benton's total revenue. The three Estimated Benefits columns are calculated as follows: The Low $ column is the Base Cost times the Low percent; the High $ is the Base Cost times the High percent; and, the Medium $ is the average of the High $ and Low $ columns.

EXHIBIT 2
Industry-Based Annual Benefits of Benton's ERP

	Industry Low	Industry High	Base Amount	Estimated Benefits			Benton Projected
				Low $	Medium $	High $	
Inventory	10%	40%	$7,800	$780	$1,950	$3,150	$780
Centralized Operations	15%	50%	$3,000	$450	$975	$1,500	$450
Procurement	10%	20%	$1,750	$175	$263	$350	$263
Logistics	5%	10%	$68,000	$3,400	$5,100	$6,800	$5,100
Incremental Revenue	1%	5%	$1,000,000	$5,000	$15,000	$25,000	$5,000
					Total Projected Yearly Benefits		$11,593

Note: Dollar figures are in thousands.

For each row we considered Benton's situation and chose a Low $ or Medium $ figure depending on our judgement, trying to be conservative. In the Inventory row we chose the Low $ column because we had already reduced inventory by 30 percent. In the Centralized Operations row we chose the Low $ figure because we think we are already pretty lean. And in the Incremental Revenue row we chose the Low $ figure because we are already growing revenues by 6 to 7 percent, and doubt that we will be able to do much better than that given the industry conditions. Incidentally, in that line we took only 50 percent of the increased revenue as the benefit because labor and materials cost is half the revenue. We think that the $11,593,000 estimate of total yearly benefits is conservative.

Meyer explains Exhibit 3:

We based our estimate of total cost of converting to an ERP on the concept of "cost per seat." The industry "cost per seat" ranges from $15,000 to $35,000, which includes hardware, networks, software, consulting, conversion, customization, and the cost of our people who work on the project. Because we expect to have to do a good amount of reengineering and will need a lot of help from outside consultants, we took $25,000 per seat and multiplied by the number of PCs we expect to

have on the system (1360) to get the $34 million cost estimate. We also included $750,000 a year for a maintenance contract. We used judgement to spread both the costs and the benefits over the 7 years.

Recommendation

Although they understand that there are legitimate concerns about the cost of an ERP and that there will be many difficulties to be overcome to install an ERP, Cook and Meyer are convinced that Benton should acquire an ERP system as quickly as possible. They are aware that this proposal has generated controversy, but the team believes that most of Benton's top management is supportive of installing an ERP system. To force a decision on this matter the team has proposed to President McHenry that Benton begin the process of acquiring an ERP by employing a nationally known consulting firm to help select an ERP system vendor and assist in the process of implementation of the system. Because the recommended consulting firm has worked with each of the four major ERP vendors, it should be prepared to help select and install the ERP system that best suits Benton's needs.

EXHIBIT 3
Cost/Benefit Analysis for Benton ERP

	Year 2001	Year 2002	Year 2003	Year 2004	Year 2005	Year 2006	Year 2007
Costs	20,000,000	10,000,000	4,000,000	750,000	750,000	750,000	750,000
Benefits		6,000,000	9,800,000	11,593,000	11,593,000	11,593,000	11,593,000
Net Benefits	−20,000,000	−4,000,000	5,800,000	10,843,000	10,843,000	10,843,000	10,843,000

IRR = 20%
NPV @ 20% = $156,046.83

CASE STUDY III-5

THE KUALI FINANCIAL SYSTEM: AN OPEN SOURCE PROJECT

The Kuali Financial System is an open source enterprise financial information system for colleges and universities that is being developed by seven higher education institutions for free and unrestricted use by anyone, including the entire higher education community.

The Kuali Financial System (KFS) is being developed by staff from Cornell University, Indiana University, Michigan State University, San Joaquin Delta College, The rSmart Group, The University of Arizona, and the University of Hawaii, with guidance from The National Association of College and University Business Officers (NACUBO). In March 2005, the initiative received a grant of $2,500,000 from the Andrew W. Mellon Foundation. The University of California Office of the President, along with University of California campuses at Davis, Irvine, and Santa Barbara, joined the project in 2006. The KFS is based on the proven design of the Indiana University Financial Information System. Built on open standards and featuring a robust enterprise workflow engine that enables effective institutional business processes, the KFS is designed to meet the needs of any Carnegie Class institution, regardless of size or complexity.

The KFS consists of the following modules: Chart of Accounts, Financial Transactions and General Ledger, Workflow, Capital Assets, Budget, Labor Distribution, Accounts Receivable, Purchasing and Accounts Payable, and Research Administration/ Contracts and Grants. A higher education institution can choose whether to install all or just some of these modules, so the system can be tailored to suit the needs of institutions of varying size and complexity ranging from small colleges to large multicampus research universities.

The Indiana University Financial Information System has a number of characteristics that made it desirable as the basis for

a system to serve the higher education community. The system was designed and built for higher education institutions whose needs are quite different from the needs of most business organizations. It is used at all seven IU campuses, both large and small, so it can be tailored to the needs of small undergraduate-oriented campuses as well as large research-oriented campuses. It is a paperless system that can be accessed from desktops throughout the university system.

The chart of accounts is table driven and is therefore very flexible and can be tailored to the needs of any institution. The system makes it possible for an institution to produce all its GASB-required financial statements including segment reporting. On demand one can produce, for example, snapshots of the financial status of auxiliary organizations or provide a dean with a report on the total travel expense across all funds within a college.

The workflow engine is a general-purpose electronic routing infrastructure. Client applications use the workflow engine to automate and regulate the routing and approval processes for the transactions/documents they create. It starts with an eDoc that users compose in a client application such as one of the other modules of the KFS or some other Web application, which requires routing and approval of documents. The workflow engine routes the eDoc electronically to the attention of designated individuals, based on university or departmental business rules and policies. For example, the Business School may route a transaction directly to an administrative officer while the College of Arts may route the same type of transaction first to the department chair and then to the dean's office. This routing is table-driven so that it can be easily tailored to the characteristics of the transaction and organizational unit without modifying the software code; you just change the table values. Therefore the workflow engine can be used by any institution, and when there is a reorganization the workflow may be easily changed to suit the new organization structure.

The Kuali Financial System is being developed and distributed using the "community source" model, a type of open source approach. System development is managed by the Kuali Financial System board and is staffed by employees of the partner institutions. Except for the fact that the developers operate in a virtual organization and are geographically distributed across the country from Ithaca, New York, to Hawaii, the development process is managed just like any other large systems development project. However, the software is being distributed under the open source Educational Community License that provides:

> Permission to use, copy, modify, merge, publish, distribute, and sublicense this Original Work and its documentation, with or without modification, for any purpose, and without fee or royalty to the copyright holder(s) is hereby granted,....

Thus, anyone can take the Kuali software and do whatever they want to do with it. Anyone, including for-profit companies, can take the code and documentation, modify it as they wish, and use it or sell it without restriction. A large trove of information on the KFS is available on the Web at *www.kuali.org* including both user and technical documentation. Also, anyone can download the software from this site.

History of the Project

The Kuali Financial System project was initiated by Indiana University. IU had an excellent Financial Information System (FIS) that had been developed in the early 1990s. By 2002, however, it had become clear that the client/server technology on which the IU FIS was based was rapidly becoming obsolete and was not likely to be supported for much longer. Furthermore, the other administrative systems at IU were migrating to Java Web technology. It was becoming difficult to keep good technical people in this area because the client/server technology had become a dead end in the career paths of IU development staff. So, although the users were quite happy with the existing FIS, it was decided that the FIS would have to be replaced.

There were two traditional possibilities—build a replacement system for the FIS using newer technology or install a financial system from a software vendor. Both of these alternatives were quite expensive. IU was using the Student and Human Resources systems that were part of the PeopleSoft ERP suite. There was initial support from the IT department for installing the PeopleSoft Financials, but the estimates of the cost of this conversion ranged from $20 to $22 million. Furthermore, it was clear that in terms of functionality the PeopleSoft system would be a step backward, so that was not an attractive option. The option of building a replacement for the system in-house was estimated to cost $8 million, which would be a very painful expenditure for Indiana University. There would be additional costs of converting to the new system, but these would be far less than for converting to the PeopleSoft system.

Experience with the Sakai Project

IU had previously experienced growing pains with its homemade OnCourse course management system, and established partnerships with other institutions with similar problems to develop a course management system that could be used by all. In late 2003 then IU Assistant Vice President Bradley C. (Brad) Wheeler joined with representatives of the University of Michigan, Stanford University, and MIT to found the Sakai Project to develop an open source course management system for higher education by assigning staff at the participating institutions to develop course management systems software under the direction of a multi-university project board. With a $2.4 million grant from the Andrew W. Mellon foundation and a $300,000 grant from the William and Flora Hewlett Foundation, the Sakai project was launched and soon began to upgrade and integrate classroom management software components from the founding institutions. Within a short time Harvard, Columbia University, Cornell, Northwestern, the University of Cambridge, and a host of other outstanding universities were supporting this effort, and by 2006 the Sakai software was being used by dozens of higher education institutions on five continents.

In 2003, Wheeler and John F. (Barry) Walsh, Senior Director of e-Business Services at IU, decided to try to adapt the approach that had been pioneered by Sakai to the replacement of the IU FIS and began discussions with the National Association of College and University Business Officers (NACUBO), the rSmart Group, and the Andrew W. Mellon foundation regarding an open source financial system that could be used for all higher educational institutions. The Mellon Foundation provided a small grant to NACUBO to assess the feasibility of an open source financial system. NACUBO sponsored a survey of higher education finance officers that concluded that there was "affirmative ambivalence" about building open source financial systems for universities. The proponents took that as a ringing endorsement and ploughed ahead.

One problem with selling this idea to university financial officers was that they had little understanding of the term *open source*, and even less understanding of what was being proposed. Wheeler recalls:

> In May of 2004 I went to a meeting in Chicago of financial officers and IT officers that was jointly convened by the two professional societies. We were in the early days of talking about doing an open source financial system. When we said open source to these people the image in their minds was of strange people in foreign countries who dress funny making changes to their mission-critical systems by dark of night. It was very clear that there was a chasm in understanding what open source actually meant, so we explained to them that we were really talking about our developers in our institutions creating the software with rigorous processes and structured releases. We were

talking about an investment model as much as we were talking about a software creation model. So to avoid confusion we quit using the term "open source" and started using the term "community source" instead.

Formation of the Kuali Partnership

In early 2004 IU started to try to find some partners to develop a community source financial system based on the IU FIS. Hawaii joined up immediately, and NACUBO and the rSmart Group said that they wanted to be involved. On September 10, 2004, they announced the Kuali project. Although there were not yet enough resources to go forward with the development, they started planning the project and having conversations with other potential partners. The University of Arizona soon joined up, and in the next six months San Joaquin Delta Community College, Michigan State University, and Cornell came in. In March 2005 the Andrew W. Mellon Foundation announced a grant of $2.5 million to the Kuali project. Together with the $5 million in development resources pledged by the partner institutions, this grant brought the available resources for the project close to its projected $8 million cost, so Kuali was underway! The University of California Office of the President, along with University of California campuses at Davis, Irvine, and Santa Barbara, became a partner in 2006 and contributed an additional $1 million.

Considerable effort went into the choice of the name Kuali. According to Wheeler:

> The name Kuali came from an intensive search. The word *Kuali* means *wok* in Malaysian. We thought that was a very appropriate association because the wok is an essential but very humble dish, and every Asian kitchen has to have one. We thought that Kuali was a wonderful metaphor for administrative systems in a university—humble but essential.

There have been a number of attempts by higher education institutions to band together to jointly develop systems and before Sakai most of them turned out to be failures. But not only has Sakai held together, but it has continued to grow stronger and stronger, and Kuali is following in Sakai's footsteps. Wheeler explains why these projects have been successful:

> We are held together by enlightened self-interest. Through Kuali, Indiana is getting a system that costs $8 million for an investment of a little more than $2.5 million, and all of the other partners can make that same claim or better. And this cost advantage will hold for the entire life of the system—we will be sharing the cost of maintaining the system, which is the dominant part of the total life cycle cost.
>
> Also, we feel strongly that we are a community of institutions that are not just interested in ourselves, but care about each other and are making a significant contribution to the welfare of the entire higher education community. That has been a very energizing motivation.

Furthermore, we are starting from a proven system, upgrading it to modern technology, and modifying it where necessary to make it suitable for everyone, not just IU. If we had tried to start with a clean slate we would still be debating the functional specifications.

Finally, we have taken a date-driven approach to the software development. In system development there is an immutable relationship between completion date, resources employed, and functionality. Problems inevitably arise and you must delay completion, add more resources, or reduce the functionality of the system. We have chosen to keep the completion date and the resources employed relatively fixed and when necessary reduce the functionality of the current release of the system. There will be later releases, and the missing functionality can be added to the next release. In the meantime the users have a system that they can use.

The release of the basic modules of the Kuali Financial System occurred on October 16, 2006. The second release is scheduled for October 2007, and the release of the complete system is scheduled for June 2008.

Legal Issues

Legal issues have become a serious problem for Sakai. The dominant firm in the classroom management systems arena is Blackboard, Inc. The U.S. Patent Office has granted Blackboard a comprehensive patent for classroom management software and Blackboard is suing a small competitor, Desire2Learn, for breach of this patent. Blackboard has asserted that it has no plans to sue Sakai, but it could in the future. Most of the features included in Blackboard's patent were developed and demonstrated over the past 15 years by various researchers, so Sakai leaders believe that the Blackboard patent will be overturned. However, in the meantime Blackboard is using the patent issue to sow FUD (fear, uncertainty, and doubt) to discourage institutions from adopting its competitors' classroom management systems.

Consequently, Kuali is taking great pains to make sure that the developers of Kuali Financials do not inadvertently violate any software patents. According to Walsh:

> Financial people tend to be conservative, so we are doing a lot more due diligence than we might have done otherwise. We had done the due diligence of getting contributor license agreements with everybody that had contributed software from the school saying "I'm not plagiarizing. What I am contributing is my stuff. I am using all the open source constructs that you have asked me to use," etc., etc.
>
> That might have been sufficient, but because we are conservative financial people we are going the extra mile here. We are doing it in two ways. We are having a company do an intellectual property survey for us that is going to look at the code and analyze it very carefully for potential patent violations. We are also paying a software company to run the software

through their system that is similar to plagiarism detection systems and is designed to identify blocks of code that are similar to existing blocks in their extensive database of existing software and thus might be patent violations. We could do one or the other of these, but we are choosing to do both.

The other vexing legal problem that threatened to delay the release of Phase 1 of Kuali Financials was getting the legal departments of the partner institutions to agree on the precise language of the document they would sign to cede their rights to the code their employees wrote to Kuali. Although the institutions had agreed at the start that the Kuali Financial System would be open source, the devil was in the details. Wheeler explains:

> Creating the legal framework for colleges and universities to share all of this stuff has been like moving heaven and earth. I have talked to more university lawyers and technology transfer officers than you can count. I kept having the same conversation over and over and over. First I had to disabuse them of the notion that they were going to sell their software and make money. Nobody makes any money in this market. Then the question was: Under what terms would they share it? Do they maintain control or do they actually give up control to Kuali so it can distribute the system with the Educational Community License? We had to work through all of this to produce a document that everyone could sign. Also, this is international, not just U.S. We had to deal with the peculiarities of the European Union and South Africa, etc. But we finally got it done.

Why Open Source?

Open source software has emerged as a new force in the marketplace in recent years with the appearance of such well-known products as UNIX, Linux, MySQL, Ingres, Apache, Sendmail, etc., which were developed as collaborative efforts by geographically dispersed programmers working on their own time to create and/or improve the product, which was made freely available to all within the technological community. Many people assume that the meaning of the term *open source* refers to how the software was created, but the term is generally understood today to relate to the conditions under which the software can be used (i.e., that it can be used freely by all without compensation as in the Educational Community License mentioned previously). Thus, the Kuali Financial System is open source software.

From the perspective of the organization acquiring it, open source software would present impressive advantages even if it were not free. Wheeler explains some of the advantages of open source:

> If you install software from a typical vendor you do not get the source code and you do not have the right to change the program. You can usually make some add-ons, but no fundamental changes in the system. With open source, if there are things that you don't like you can change them to tailor the system to your needs.

If you install an ERP from PeopleSoft or SAP you are at the mercy of the vendor. For example, the vendor decides when to issue a new release and what that release contains. You have to march lockstep in order to upgrade, and these are all multimillion dollar upgrades. You just don't have control of your destiny. With open source you are free. If you don't like what is going on you can take the software and walk away. You will have to take care of maintaining the software, but you are free to go your own way. So this model fits us very well. We maintain control of destiny. Everybody has walkaway rights to the software.

The open source model allows institutions to decouple producing the software from maintaining the software. In the traditional model you have to buy your maintenance from the intellectual property owner which is a monopoly situation and thus prices are high. But in the new model we can separate producing the software from maintenance and integration services, help desk services, etc. If you hire an implementation partner to install and support Kuali Financials and you work with them for two years, and then for some reason you get upset with them or their prices become too high, you can throw them off campus and go hire somebody else to come in and provide your support services.

Finally, even if you don't choose to install an open source software package you still benefit because the existence of the open source alternative provides competition to the traditional software providers and that competition holds down the price you pay for the system you choose to use.

It is easy to see why the Kuali partner institutions would want to share open source rights to the software among themselves, but it is not immediately obvious why they would insist that it be freely available to all. One advantage to the partners of making the software freely available is that this increases the number of institutions using the software and therefore increases the potential resources available for maintaining the system. Since maintenance costs are such an important component of a system's total life cycle cost, reducing that cost is a significant benefit. And if you give up the idea of making money selling the system, there is no cost to making it open source. But the major reason that Kuali and Sakai are open source is that the founders of these projects, including the Mellon Foundation, believe that every dollar that higher education institutions are spending for administrative systems is a dollar that cannot be spent to support their teaching and research missions. They are passionately committed to the welfare of the entire higher educational community and therefore to open source systems that can reduce the huge expenditures for administrative systems for everyone who would like to use them.

Organization of the Kuali Financials Project

As mentioned previously, the history of interinstitutional cooperation to jointly produce software systems has been littered with failures, so starting out to work together is no guarantee of

EXHIBIT 1
Kuali Financials Project Organization

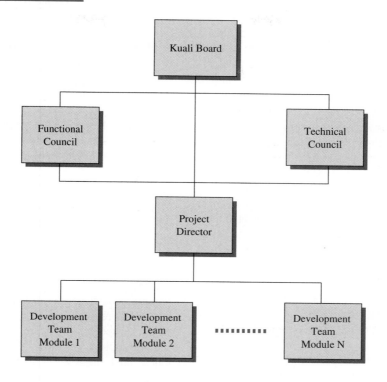

success. It is not easy to successfully develop large, complex financial systems when all the developers and users are in the same organization, and the difficulties are multiplied when both the users and the developers come from different institutions with different cultures that are spread out "from sea to shining sea." Kuali is overcoming these difficulties with innovative organizational and management strategies. Exhibit 1 depicts the Kuali Financial System project's organization.

Kuali Commercial Affiliates

Not shown on the organization chart, but a very important component of the Kuali effort, is the Kuali Commercial Affiliates program. Commercial Affiliates provide for-fee guidance, support, implementation, and integration services related to the Kuali software. Affiliates may offer packaged versions of Kuali that provide value for installation or integration beyond the basic Kuali software. Affiliates may also offer other types of training, documentation, or hosting services.

Although the Kuali Financial System is open source software that is available without cost, the partner institutions have no intention of providing support services to adopters of the Kuali system. The KFS is a large and complex system, and it is not easy to install it to replace your existing financial system. The

partner institutions have worked developing the system and have the resources to install and support it, but most other institutions will need help to make it successful. Thus, if the Kuali Financial System is to be widely adopted and make the broad impact within the higher education community that is hoped for, there will have to be other organizations to provide the necessary support services.

Sakai has a dozen commercial affiliates scattered around the world. At this writing Kuali has enrolled three commercial affiliates—The rSmart Group, IBM, and Huron Consulting. IBM and rSmart have announced that they will be collaborating to support Kuali Financials installations. An rSmart customer, Strathmore University of Nairobi, Kenya, was the first known adopter of the Phase I version of Kuali Financials.

The Kuali Financials Board

The Kuali Financials Board is responsible for directing the development of the Kuali Financial System. It is composed of two representatives from each partner institution, one of whom is a senior IT manager and the other is a senior finance manager. Although both representatives from each institution attend the board meetings and participate in the discussions, only one of them has a vote. Wheeler is the Chairperson and

Walsh is the Executive Director and voting member for Indiana University. NACUBO and rSmart each have one nonvoting member on the board.

The board meets weekly via a telephone conference call and has a face-to-face meeting every three months. The meetings are chaired by Wheeler. An agenda is distributed before the meeting and they follow the agenda. Usually the first thing on the agenda is a 5 to 10 minute discussion of the status report of where the development stands. Then they go on to larger issues that need resolving. While the telephone conferences work well, they try to deal with the more contentious issues at the quarterly face-to-face meetings.

Initially the board was primarily concerned with starting up the project and setting policies and procedures and organizational arrangements that would make for success. The board set up the organizational structure and populated it with employees from the partner institutions. It also formulated the following vision, mission, and scope statements:

Project Vision   Kuali is dedicated to providing and maintaining a richly featured financial system for use by its member institutions. The consortium will work to ensure that:

The baseline of the new system is FIS.

Its financial system modules meet GASB and FASB standards.

The system enables a strong control environment.

Thoughtful and timely changes are made to keep pace with advances in both technology and business.

No one member bears the bulk of the cost for, or reaps the overwhelming majority of the benefit/profit from system development.

An efficient governance and administrative structure is created and maintained to support the member institutions with new or improved functionality, fixes, and service releases.

Project Mission   Create a comprehensive suite of functionality to serve the financial system needs of all Carnegie Class institutions. The design will be an enhancement of the proven functionality of Indiana University's Financial Information System (FIS).

Project Scope   Kuali Financial Systems release 1 and 2 will be based on the existing FIS design. Conformance with FIS provides the fundamental basis for Kuali scope control. The basic presumption of Kuali Financial Systems is conformity with FIS, including preservation of where the FIS software is configurable beyond the IU implementation and configuration decisions.

The following outlines the modules, their expected delivery/release date, and high-level specifics about what is contained in each.

Phase I Deliverables—released October 2006
    Chart of Accounts
    Financial Transactions/General Ledger
    Kuali Nervous System (KNS)
    Kuali Enterprise Workflow (KEW)
Phase IIA Deliverables—scheduled release October 2007
    Accounts Payable/Purchasing
    Budget Construction
    Labor Ledger
    Contracts & Grants
Phase IIB Deliverables—scheduled release July 2008
    Accounts Receivable
    Capital Assets Management System

Detailed information about module specifics was included in the complete Kuali Scope Statement.

The Kuali Nervous System in Phase I is unlike the rest of the modules in that it is a toolbox that has been so useful in developing the system that it is being made available to those who may want to modify or extend the system. It was named the "Nervous System" because, like the human nervous system, it ties together and coordinates everything.

As the project got under way, the board served as the court of last resort when disputes arose. Any partner can escalate a dispute to the board, but fortunately that has been done infrequently because the technical and functional councils have been very effective in working things out at their level. Increasingly as the development process settled down, the board has turned its attention to developing a broader long-term mission for Kuali and modifying the organizational arrangements to accommodate that expanded mission.

The board has provided outstanding leadership to the project. The members of the board are dedicated to the vision of providing open source administrative systems to the educational community. They have consistently put the best interests of the overall project ahead of the interests of their own institutions, so the Kuali Financials project has prospered.

The Technical Council

The Kuali Technical Council (KTC), chaired by Brian McGough of IU, is composed of one representative from each of the partner institutions. The role of the technical council is to provide and enforce technical standards for the Kuali Financial Systems project. Because the systems development is spread out over the IT organizations of seven geographically dispersed institutions, each with its own development culture and practices, without uniform standards the resulting system would be difficult to support and maintain. Without standards two team members from different institutions would find it very difficult to work together on a module.

Eighty percent of the total lifetime cost of software goes to maintenance. The original author of the code often does not perform the maintenance. This is particularly true with open source projects. Applying standard development practices across the Kuali project will result in substantial maintenance savings for everyone. Good standards promote better quality applications, code reuse, and enhanced portability.

If a developer feels it necessary to deviate from a standard, the first step is to communicate with the Kuali Technical Council. The Technical Council then applies its collective knowledge and experience to arrive at a recommended approach. Often the Technical Council can find a way to solve the problem and still adhere to the standards. Otherwise it may decide that an exemption to a particular standard is justified.

The members of the Technical Council are experienced architects, designers, and developers who bring a wealth of experience and wisdom to the table. They have worked together effectively to produce a document titled "The Kuali Architecture and Development Standards" that includes high-level standards on methodology and system architecture and detailed standards concerning the tools and technologies that may be employed.

The following excerpt describes the standard methodology:

In general, the Kuali development methodology is a lightweight, iterative approach to development that focuses on individual components that can be quickly developed and integrated into a larger application taking into account in all cases the knowledge and investment that is being carried forward from the original IU FIS system. Frequent communication and interaction with users is *required* in order for this methodology to succeed. By simplifying the development process and emphasizing frequent feedback, the software product has a much greater likelihood of meeting the user's needs.

Another fundamental rule of the Kuali methodology is to KEEP IT SIMPLE. Developers should resist the temptation to add unnecessary complexity.

The following describes the standard architecture:

The contemporary architecture of applications is a set of distributed, loosely-coupled components and services that provide distinct business services. A Service-Oriented Architecture (SOA) approach to Kuali development is recommended. This architecture assumes service delivery via an enterprise portal framework and the presence of key infrastructure services like a single sign-on solution, an enterprise directory, and an enterprise workflow engine. In addition, a standard Application Program Interface (API) for common services like authentication and authorization should be agreed on.

Components should be designed to build the application into three layers: Presentation, Business, and Persistence layers. Components should be container-agnostic and use standard J2EE proven APIs such as Servlet and JSP. All system-to-system interoperability that cannot be done within the container should be done using Web services technology that uses Apache Axis.

The Presentation layer focuses on the presentation of the data to the user in the context of the user interface, e.g., the Web browser or a rich client. The Presentation layer that we are building for the out-of-the-box version of Kuali is intended to be used through a Web browser as a standard HTML-based Web application.

The Business layer provides the enterprise logic. It includes the components that capture the business rules of the enterprise. It may support multiple Presentation tiers.

The Persistence layer is the data repository for the application. It provides the data storage, retrieval, and maintenance. Data Access Objects (DAOs) should be employed to encapsulate the data sources using the Spring/OJB (Object Relational Bridge) framework to isolate access to the database. No business logic should be present in the data tier. No business object or presentation related object should access the database directly; any need for this should be met through service calls.

The Architecture document suggests some two dozen development tools that should be used for ease of code sharing and consistency in the code base. The coding will be in Java and the eXtensible Markup Language (XML). All secure Internet communications involving Kuali applications should use the Java Secure Socket Extension (JSSE), Sun's Java implementation of the Secure Sockets Layer (SSL). JavaScript should be avoided if at all possible. It should only be used for "value-added" features as approved by the KTC. Kuali should still function properly with JavaScript turned off.

This is only a sampling of the total body of standards promulgated by the Technology Council but it should give the flavor of the approach the council has taken.

The Functional Council

The Functional Council is composed of two or more user representatives from each of the partner institutions, but each institution has only one vote. There are also nonvoting representatives from rSmart and NACUBO. It is chaired by Kathleen T. McNeely, Assistant Vice President for Finance and Executive Director, Financial Management Services at IU and a national leader in higher education on accounting and financial management issues.

According to Wheeler:

The Functional Council, composed of financial people, is God. They speak it and it will be or it will not be. It is the most finely tuned performing group that I have seen in my life, and Kuali could not have been successful without this superb performance by the Functional Council.

The Functional Council meets via an audio telephone link for one hour every Thursday at 1 P.M. Every three months they have a face-to-face meeting for about two and a half days. In these meetings they deal with issues of prioritizing functionality, doing a review of the resources, identifying where they are short on resources, and what functionality gets cut. The Functional Council makes all of those decisions.

The agreement with the Mellon Foundation specified that this would be a rewrite of the IU FIS. But each of the seven institutions has its own ideas about what changes need to be made. There is a subcommittee for each module that is composed of user representatives from the partner institutions. Those subcommittees review the functionality and discuss changes that they want, either changes in current functionality or new functionality for that module. If they suggest a change to the functionality, they write up an enhancement document, which must include an estimate of the hours it will require from the technical side. Then the Functional Council votes on whether or not to allow that change to occur given that they have to manage the overall development resource budget. That is the core of what the Functional Council does. It controls what gets done, what doesn't get done, and when it gets done.

One of the first tasks for the Functional Council was to determine the enhancements to the IU FIS that would be included in the Phase 2 version of the Kuali Financials System. There were far more desirable enhancements than could be accomplished within the resources that were available for development of the first complete version of the system, so the Functional Council had to struggle with very difficult priority decisions.

Each module subcommittee prepared a description of and a resource requirements estimate for each of the enhancements that its members wanted. The Functional Council then considered each of these proposals and assigned each of them one of the following priority levels: essential, high, medium, and low. The essential priority was defined as an enhancement that must be included in Phase 2 or the system would not be acceptable. It was intended that most of the high priority enhancements would be included in Phase 2. After much consideration and several difficult votes, the council agreed upon 16 essential priority and 19 high priority enhancements and included them in the Kuali Financials Scope Statement.

Dynamics of the Council

The weekly council meetings usually include about 20 people in 10 or 12 locations spread out from Ithaca, New York, to Honolulu, Hawaii. They are talking with and listening to each other over a telephone link. You would think that this would never work, but it does. McNeely describes how she manages the meetings:

> Early in the week based on the issues occurring I call the Project Manager, Jim Thomas, and others as appropriate to solicit agenda items. Sometimes Council members will call me and suggest issues the Council needs to deal with. The agenda is created and sent out approximately one day in advance of the

meeting. At the beginning of the meeting I do a roll call to make sure that each school is represented. At the end of each agenda is a miscellaneous item that allows any issues to be brought up if missed.

> The Council follows the agenda items. I usually summarize what the issue is and request that people speak up with their concerns. I usually pause and give them an opportunity to think. The agenda is always completed on time, and all participants are provided an opportunity to speak. If an agenda item has to be deferred or schools indicate they are not ready to vote, the issue goes back on the agenda the next week. We are busy people, so one hour is it.

> At the very end of the meeting I call the roll call again to include those who joined the meeting late. All minutes are taken and posted to the Kuali Web site. If a Functional Council member misses a meeting they can read the minutes. If a lead subject matter expert (SME) wants to know how a vote came about he or she can read the minutes. Roll call includes the names of all in attendance at the meeting, so it is recorded who was in attendance and part of the discussion. If there is disagreement later and somebody indicates they don't remember the decision then the minutes can be reviewed for final resolution. The Functional Council's documentation of the meetings is very good.

> Occasionally a sensitive issue exists that schools are hesitant to speak about in front of everybody. All Functional Council members know that my phone is open for calls. Every few weeks one of the schools will call me and I will spend 20 minutes talking to them. Sometimes I add it to the agenda and the Council discusses it and sometimes the issue is resolved without going to the Functional Council. Overall the communication process for the Council has been very effective.

There have been some very difficult priority issues. For example, at the face-to-face council meeting in November 2005, the project plan for Release 2 showed that they were short 5,000 hours. The Functional Council was charged with identifying items that could be deferred. They agreed that all the planned modules must be delivered and that they should keep the essential priority enhancements. Eliminating all the high-priority enhancements would result in a surplus of 2,000 hours. The difficult part was agreeing on which high-priority enhancements should be moved back in. When the dust settled they were left with six enhancements that would be deferred to future releases.

McNeely recalls another difficult situation:

> Last January we were over budget on our resources and had to make some priority decisions that couldn't wait until the next face to face Functional Council meeting in February. So I called a three-hour Functional Council meeting via teleconferencing. Although effective, it was a very painful conference call since we were cutting scope and some schools were losing functionality they felt they needed. It is hard to do those types of things without face to face, but it worked and we got it done.

Making those kinds of decisions is not easy when you have to get agreement of seven institutions, each of which has its own priorities and culture. McNeely describes the difficulty:

> Higher education institutions have cultures that are very old and very ingrained. There are huge cultural differences between our institutions, not only in the way decisions are made but also in the way we communicate with each other. There have been several instances where people have been offended. In addition, some institutions have a culture of cooperation and compromise, while others have a culture of competition and always being right. Most institutions lie somewhere in between these extremes. Fortunately, most of the Kuali partner institutions lean toward the cooperative end.

> When the Council has had disagreements on functionality we have tried to maintain the focus that the system is not just for the core partners, but for all of higher education. So when roadblocks occur, I try to guide the discussion toward what is best for all of higher education, not just what is best for Indiana or Cornell or Hawaii. With a few exceptions, that has worked.

> Although the Council doesn't vote on everything there are times when a vote finalizes an issue and allows forward movement in the decision-making process. If a school disagrees with a Functional Council decision and feels that it is core to their ability to implement successfully it has the right to escalate the issue to the Kuali Board. That has only happened twice. In general, the Functional Council has been extraordinarily successful in resolving some very difficult issues.

Another key to the success of Kuali has been the close relationship between the Functional Council chair and the project manager. Without trust and close cooperation between the users and the developers it would have been very difficult to succeed with this project. McNeely and Thomas have an excellent personal relationship. Their offices are just a few doors from each other and they communicate face-to-face frequently. This relationship is so important that McNeely questions whether a project like this could succeed if the chair of the Functional Council and the project manager were from different institutions.

The Development Process

The Kuali Financial System has some special characteristics that impact its development. James (Jim) Thomas, Project Manager, explains:

> We are completely re-architecting the technology. The IU FIS is currently a client/server based application which was built using a tool called UNIFACE. At the time the FIS was developed, UNIFACE was a very advanced development tool. Now, we are writing our enterprise applications in Java Web technology. So from a technical standpoint it is completely new. We are leveraging the intellectual property within the system so we know how the system should work. We just need to create it in the new

toolset. We take this document, maybe a Disbursement Voucher, and all the rules and everything behind it, and we create that same document in a Web-based system. The user interface will change because it is Web-based, but there are some things that are consistent. The way the screen is organized will be very similar. However, because of differences between the Web technology and client/server technology it will look a little bit different.

> Going from client/server to the Web presents some challenges. Client/server is a very responsive and rich interface. There are things that you can do which are very difficult with Web-based applications. The Web is more limited in what you can do in the user interface because of technological limitations and browser differences. Something that is really nice and slick that works on Internet Explorer may not work in Firefox or Safari. So there are some challenges with the Web, but we are working through the major user interface problems.

> We are trying to be agnostic in terms of any sort of vended solutions. For example, we are currently running on Oracle database in our development and test environments. However, we are building the system so that someone can use another database system if they wish. In fact, in order to provide a pure open source stack, we are starting to test the code on MySQL, an open source DBMS. This will allow schools who cannot afford Oracle licenses to run on MySQL and avoid the Oracle licensing costs. We are trying to stay open in terms of the technologies that we use to avoid major dependencies on vended software and tools.

> We are "modular" in that our components are not tightly integrated. We do not want to require schools to use the whole ball of wax or nothing. We are really trying to make it more modular and "pluggable." For example, if you have your own purchasing system but want to use our chart of accounts and general ledger, it will be loosely coupled. There is a defined API that is used to interface the modules. There will be work involved with doing so but it will be limited to the interfaces between the two modules as opposed to having to rewrite major components. That said, we also have some pretty aggressive deadlines. True modularity and plugability takes a lot of time to design and develop. Therefore, there are places in terms of modularity where we can do better in the future. To make it the ultimately flexible system takes a lot of time. We don't have a lot of time right now but will improve this aspect as we go. Better yet, other interested developers may want to contribute code and help us do that even sooner.

Managing the Project

Project Manager Jim Thomas is located at Indiana University–Bloomington, but his Kuali staff of 32 developers is spread out over at least a dozen locations. The Mellon grant to Kuali funds a few employees located at IU and other places, but most of the developers are employees of and are paid by their own institutions. Some of them are so valuable that their institutions could not spare them full-time, so they are only part-time with Kuali. Thomas is managing an organization that is virtual in every aspect.

To complete a project of this size and complexity on time and on budget has always been a challenge. Doing it successfully with a virtual organization where the developers are employed by seven different higher education institutions spread over five time zones is exceptionally challenging.

Thomas explains how the development process is organized:

We have broken the project into modules and have a development team for each module. In the first phase, we worked on the core set of modules with teams for Chart of Accounts, General Ledger, and Financial eDocs. Each team has a Development Manager who manages a team of three to seven developers. I work with the Development Managers with the project plans. The Functional Council decides the scope of the things that need to get done based on the development team's time estimates and available resources. The Development Managers assign tasks to their team members and then monitor progress. Some of the Development Managers are located at IU, but others are located at other institutions. The developers on each team are scattered at many different locations.

That presents a challenge. Initially, we wanted each school to have expertise about the whole system. Rather than having all the developers at a particular location work on the same module, we assigned them to different teams. This helped give each institution a set of developers with a broader understanding of the whole system. The scope of this project and different ways in which people manage projects made this difficult. So, while it was a good idea from the perspective of broadening knowledge across institutions, it was not a good idea from the perspective of productivity. Lately I have found that it is good to leverage the fact that people are located together, in some cases sitting right next to each other. I am now more inclined to say that if developers are located at the same institutions, we should try to assign them to the same team when possible. That helps in terms of productivity and communication. The tradeoff is that their institution's technical expertise on the application may be somewhat narrow. With consistent development methodology and standards, this should not be a major problem.

In a virtual organization good communication is critical. We use mail lists, teleconferencing, and do a lot of videoconferencing. We also use Atlassian's Confluence for collaboration and JIRA for task tracking. Confluence is a place where we put documents that people can share and jointly edit. You put documents there and you can share them with a group of people who can make comments and contributions. This is all done online and avoids having to track long e-mail threads around a particular document or discussion. JIRA is a task tracking system. If I have a task that needs to get done, I can create an issue and assign it to a developer. The developer goes into JIRA to see what tasks are assigned to them. The Development Manager can put due dates and priorities on tasks and categorize them by module. These have been useful productivity tools in managing the day to day operations of the project.

With people spread out so widely, face-to-face interaction together in one place is very important. Getting the development teams together in a room for a week or two at a time is really critical. I don't think this project could be successful without doing that. Face time establishes relationships and builds trust. Trust is critical. If teams go too long without that sort of personal contact, trust and communication start to break down a little bit. That can be really problematic. Getting together and establishing and maintaining those relationships, that trust, simply getting to know each other on a personal level, are really important things to do. This is what makes it truly "community source." We always realize the benefits of these gatherings. We will continue to meet face to face on a regular basis.

We are deadline-driven. Deadlines give you targets to shoot for to get things done. The initial product won't be perfect. However, it will be good quality and it will perform the required functionality reliably. We will always have time to refine things and make them better in the future. You can pretty much guarantee that users are going to want some changes anyway after they begin using the system. Our strategy is to get something out in front of the users as soon as possible. They will tell you if it is not what they expected. Getting that feedback sooner rather than later makes the software better. The users are a part of the design and development process throughout the life of the software. In that sense, it becomes THEIR software. They will like it much better. We will continuously improve the system over its lifetime.

Meeting deadlines builds credibility with the users, and the developers get a feeling of accomplishment. Deadlines also encourage progress. You do not have the luxury of spending endless amounts of time debating this or that feature. You make a decision that will work and move on. If it turns out to be a bad decision, you can change it later. Deadlines help you avoid "analysis paralysis" and get the software in front of the users. This type of iterative process has been a successful model for us here at IU.

There are lots of challenges for the manager of a project like this one. Thomas describes some of the difficulties he faces as project manager:

It is hard enough to manage people right here in the same building. Despite the challenges of managing a large group of developers, with those located here at least I can go down the hall and talk to them and see how things are going. When managing a team of developers located in different time zones throughout the country, you can probably multiply the difficulty by about 50. There are logistical issues with scheduling meetings. They are probably used to doing things a bit differently than we are in their shops back home. We do not know each other very well. This presents some challenges when trying to keep them motivated and productive on the project.

We have our own style and culture here at Indiana that may be different from the way they work at Cornell or Hawaii or Arizona or the other schools involved. The way we approach systems development may vary from institution to institution.

The way we manage our project plans may be different. The way we communicate assigned tasks may be different. The way we motivate may be different. It is a challenge to work through these differences when managing developer resources from many different schools. Our managers must find ways to connect with each of their developers and identify the most effective approach for communicating task assignments, monitoring progress, and providing feedback. What works for one developer may not work for another. This is true with developers at the same institution but becomes even more noticeable with developers at different institutions.

In Kuali we have adopted a deadline-driven approach. We are going to deliver the required functionality with good quality code. However, with deadlines, we must also learn what is good enough and move on. KEEP IT SIMPLE is also a basic principle. It is not uncommon for some technical staff to have perfectionist tendencies. They may want to redesign and reanalyze things seeking that "perfect" design or solution. This may involve taking more time than we have to spend. In order to meet our productivity goals, we use deadlines. This can be frustrating to a developer if they aren't happy with the solution they ultimately deliver. We encourage them to log potential improvements in JIRA for future consideration. We can make the software better in the future but do not have unlimited amounts of time for the initial releases.

Another challenge is that I probably manage a project differently than what some of the Kuali developers are accustomed to. These differences in terms of management style, communication, and organizational culture can create problems. The developers have to learn what I expect of them. I have to learn what they expect from me. This is also true for the Development Managers in working both with me and with their development teams. We have to get to know each other better, understand preferred communication and coordination mechanisms, and adjust accordingly. This was particularly difficult in the beginning but has gotten much better over time.

Managing developers from different backgrounds has also been a challenge for the Development Managers. Each of the developers has had his or her own experience with different types of managers and how she or he is used to getting task assignments. There are managers who are very hands-on, very specific with their direction, and have very detailed project plans and assignments. There are managers who are more hands-off giving their staff a general sense of what they want done and give them the freedom to figure out the details on their own. And there is every sort of manager in between. Developers have their own preferences as to how much detailed direction they need. Some developers want autonomy and the ability to design, create, and work mostly on their own with general direction. Other developers want very specific detailed instructions with clearly defined expectations. We can't find an exact match for every developer such that their manager is an exact fit to their preferences. Therefore, building a successful team involves each Development Manager getting to know his or her team members individually. The manager likely will have to manage some differently than others. Developers must also learn to work with managers who may lead with a different style. This takes time to establish working relationships that work effectively. It is particularly challenging when manager and developer are not located in the same place.

We also have the logistical challenges of time zones—I can't schedule a nine o'clock meeting because that is 4 A.M. in Hawaii. It helps that we have e-mail and videoconferencing to bridge that gap a little. We've also had people willing to flex their hours by staying later or getting up earlier to accommodate certain meetings. However, it is still challenging to make things as fair as possible to everyone on the project. We also try to share the travel burden so that no one group ever has to do all of the traveling for our face-to-face meetings.

The Kuali Nervous System

The Kuali Nervous System (KNS) is a module that was included as a part of Release 1 of the KFS, but it is unlike the other modules. Rather, it is a core technical module composed of reusable code components that provide common pieces of functionality. The KNS is a technical framework that enforces consistency in the applications that use it. It promotes adherence to the architectural principles and development standards defined by the Kuali architects. The KNS also provides a stable core of development tools providing a more efficient development paradigm.

The KNS is a toolbox of components that are commonly used across all the modules, such as looking up a value in a table, authorization and authentication, adding notes and attachments to a document, and other things that are done over and over. The Kuali developers spent a great deal of time and effort in the early stages of development designing and developing these core components included in the nervous system. Now they can take those and quickly put together what they call the skeleton, a very fundamental outline of a given document or a given screen of an application. They can put one of those together very rapidly—a matter of half a day or a day. If you need to do a look-up, you just call the look-up component and plug in the right parameters. They have been able to leverage that and develop things fairly quickly later in the project because of it. And they continue to add components to the nervous system.

Another way to think of it is that it also provides some standard approaches. In programming there are always many ways to solve a problem, and if you leave that role open for developers they will come up with every different way. So the KNS is providing some standard ways of doing things, and that will make the system a lot easier to maintain. And, since the components of the nervous system have been debugged, a substantial proportion of new components will be bug-free before system testing is begun.

The KNS has been such a success that they have generalized it to make it independent of the rest of the KFS and Kuali is making it available and promoting it as a valuable asset to any development that is using a Kuali-like architecture. In particular, it will be used in developing other administrative systems that Kuali will develop in the future.

The Future

The installation of the complete Kuali Financial System will require a large, complex, time-consuming, and costly effort. Since the KFS is a technical upgrade of its existing FIS, Indiana University should find installing the KFS to be relatively easy as compared to the effort that other adopters will face. However, IU does not plan to begin installing the new system until the spring of 2008, and it will take most of the rest of that year. The other partners will follow along at their own pace. But it may be several years before a significant number of institutions will be using the KFS.

On the other hand, decisions to adopt the system may come relatively quickly. The partners will feel that it is a success when one or more large prestigious institutions and several smaller ones have announced their intention to install the system. Kuali is already successful in changing the attitude of higher education administrators toward community source application software.

Establishment of the Kuali Foundation

For the Kuali Financial System to continue to evolve and adapt to future circumstances, there must be some mechanism for coordinating ongoing activities over the long run. Also, the success of Kuali in developing the KFS has led the Kuali leadership to conclude that the community source approach should be applied to develop a complete suite of administrative systems for higher education institutions. So the Kuali Board has established the Kuali Foundation to perpetuate the KFS and to expand the Kuali mission to include other administrative systems. Excerpts from the announcement of the establishment of the Kuali Foundation, a 501c3 corporation, follow:

> The Kuali Foundation is a non-profit organization responsible for sustaining and evolving a comprehensive suite of administrative software that meets the needs of all Carnegie Class institutions. Its members are colleges, universities, and interested organizations that share a common vision of open, modular, and distributed systems for their software requirements. The goal of Kuali is to bring the proven functionality of legacy applications to the ease and universality of online services.
>
> The Foundation employs staff to coordinate the efforts of partners, and to manage and protect the Foundation's intellectual property. The Kuali Foundation manages a growing portfolio of enterprise software applications for colleges and universities

such as the Kuali Financial System (KFS), Kuali Enterprise Workflow (KEW), and Kuali Research Administration (KRA). A lightweight Foundation staff coordinates the activities of Foundation members for critical software development and coordination activities such as source code control, release engineering, packaging, documentation, project management, software testing and quality assurance, conference planning, and educating and assisting members of the Kuali Partners Program.

The Kuali Foundation is funded by a combination of grants and support from higher education institutions in the form of memberships in the Kuali Partners Program. The yearly membership dues are based on the institution's annual budget and range from $4,500 to $24,500. Since Kuali systems are open source, an institution does not have to become a member to get the software, but it is anticipated that enough institutions will join up to fund the necessary activities of the Foundation.

Initially the Kuali Financials Board became the Kuali Foundation Board, but additional members have been added to represent new partner institutions and NACUBO. Other members will be added to represent future Kuali partners. The initial staff will include an executive director and someone to control the reference version of the software.

The Research Administration Project

Soon after the release of the Phase I version of the KFS, the Kuali Foundation announced the formation of the Kuali Research Administration (KRA) project. This project will continue the approach and architecture of the KFS. It will be an update of the Massachusetts Institute of Technology's proven COEUS system, one of the first cradle-to-grave award management systems in the nation. The KRA project is funded in part by a $1.5 million grant from the Andrew W. Mellon Foundation. The partner institutions that will be contributing resources to the project include Indiana University, Cornell University and the Weill College of Medicine, MIT, Michigan State University, and the University of Arizona.

The KRA project will be organized like the Kuali Financials project with its own board composed of representatives of the partner institutions and the Functional Council with representatives of the Research Administration people from the partners. However, the Kuali Financials Technical Council will become the overall Kuali Foundation Technical Council so that all the Foundation's projects will have the same technical architecture. As before, the developers will be employees of the partner institutions.

For current information on Kuali Foundation activities, visit *www.kuali.org*.

CASE STUDY III-6

NAVAL SURFACE WARFARE CENTER, CRANE DIVISION: IMPLEMENTING BUSINESS PROCESS REENGINEERING RECOMMENDATIONS

With less than 5 hours of sleep and after a long, hectic day, Bob Matthews was tired. He had not been getting much sleep the last 2 weeks. He wondered, while waiting outside his boss's office, how the business and process reengineering (BPR) project that he was managing would make it through this current rough spot.

He also wondered whether he would be able to see any of his son's baseball game tonight. It was already the last week of May 1999, and there was only one home game left. This was Joey's senior year at Loogootee High School, and Bob hated to miss the last game of the season. It was past 5 P.M. now and he was hoping to make the first pitch at 6 P.M.

However, he and his boss, Deputy Executive Director Bill Kaiser, were continuing a discussion they had started earlier before Kaiser had been called away to a meeting with the commander of the base. All eight of Matthews' BPR teams were running into resistance in planning for implementation. In particular, the implementation plan recommended by the financial management BPR team looked like it was stalled indefinitely.

The team was headed by Cheryl Miller and had the most support of any of the teams throughout its As-Is phase (see Chapter 9 for a discussion of As-Is and To-Be models). They, along with the other seven BPR teams, had even won the union's support for how employee transitions would be handled. But now that the financial management BPR team was ready to implement its recommendations, the leaders of Crane's directorates (the equivalent of business units in the private sector), who served on the BPR steering committee, were withholding their approval.

The financial management BPR team's process change recommendations would potentially save Crane nearly 50 percent compared to the current way of conducting certain processes. The team had recommended the development of some new information systems to automate some currently manual processes, as well as some minor organizational changes. In

talking with the information systems project leader, Matthews had learned of his concern over both gaining cooperation in the systems design phase and achieving actual use of the new systems, given all the resistance.

The team also knew that there were bigger gains to be had. The average cost of financial management in the private sector was 1 to 1.5 percent of sales. Because Crane spent almost 3 percent of revenue on its financial management processes, the financial management BPR team felt there were even more significant savings to be found. To reap these more significant savings, the team had recommended establishing some common business rules across the directorates. Yet the leaders of the directorates had rejected these ideas as well.

"Hope you weren't waiting long," Bill Kaiser said, as he put his briefcase under his desk and flung his suitcoat over his chair.

"No. I was running late myself," Matthews replied. "Cheryl had stopped by my office to ask about what to do next."

"What did you tell her?" Kaiser asked.

"I told her to continue preparing for implementation," Matthews said.

"Good," Kaiser responded. "The directors may be resisting, but we have to move forward. We have a very high profile with the Navy on this project and everyone's watching, so stopping is not an option."

"No. But without the directors' support, it will be impossible for the BPR effort in financial management to succeed," Matthews said.

"We'll need to map out a strategy to make sure that doesn't happen," Kaiser said. "I went ahead and ordered dinner. It should be here in a half hour."

Matthews looked at his watch. He hoped he would catch at least the last inning or two.

Background

In May 1999, Crane was a major acquisition and support division of the Naval Surface Warfare Center, and employed about 3,200 people in 152 populated buildings over almost 100 square miles in southwestern Indiana. Beginning as a munitions production and storage facility, Crane had evolved into primarily an engineering and technical support facility that included ordnance testing and evaluation, design, development, and procurement.

Crane handled diverse and highly technical product lines, including:

- **Electronic warfare** Crane's units provided comprehensive engineering, logistics, and maintenance/repair support for countermeasures systems for the Navy, Marine Corps, and Air Force.
- **Chemical/biological detection** The people at Crane built equipment and provided training and program management, technical support, alteration, installation support, and in-service engineering agent support.
- **Microwave** Crane's departments provided application engineering and product support to help sustain the microwave industry.
- **Microelectronics** The Crane facility had some of the most comprehensive failure analysis and material analysis facilities in the world.
- **Small arms** Crane personnel provided design, development, acquisition, testing, and evaluation of small arms, weapons, night vision devices, laser range finders, laser markers, and individual combat equipment in support of special operations forces.
- **Commercial technologies** Crane executives worked with business and industry leaders to apply commercial products to weapons systems.

Crane's expense budget for FY 1999 was $750 million, including payments to subcontractors. The employee payroll was about $300 million of the total.

Most of Crane's 3,200 employees worked in one of three functions: (1) munitions production and surveillance, (2) procurement of weapons, or (3) adapting commercial products for use in a military environment. There were about 450 employees involved in the munitions function. The procurement function (e.g., development of specifications, testing, evaluation, and qualification of vendors) was done for field weapons systems and employed about 800 people. The third major function, working with private business and industry to adapt commercial products for military use, employed about 700 Crane people. The remaining 1,150 employees were support (about 300) or administrative personnel (about 850).

Command Structure (Organization)

In May 1999, Crane's leadership reported to the Naval Surface Warfare Center (NSWC) which in turn reported to the Naval Sea Systems Command (NAVSEA) and then to the Chief of Naval Operations (CNO). The Chief of Naval Operations served on the Joint Chiefs of Staff for the United States Department of Defense.

NAVSEA was the largest of the Navy's five systems commands. NAVSEA engineered, built, and supported America's fleet of ships and combat systems. The NAVSEA commander, Vice Admiral George P. Nanos, reported to the CNO. As part of the NSWC, Crane's leadership reported to the NSWC commander, Rear Admiral Kathleen K. Paige, and Ira Blatstein, NSWC executive director.

At the Crane facility, there were three mission critical (line) directorates and five support directorates. (See Exhibit 1.) Each directorate was divided into departments and then branches.

The leadership of the BPR project was assigned to four people. A summary of their backgrounds follows:

Captain William E. Shotts, USN Captain Shotts was appointed commander of Crane in June 1997. (Senior Navy personnel typically rotated through this position every 3 years.) He graduated from the Naval Academy and was commissioned in 1969. Shotts served on submarines for about 10 years and then held various line management positions leading to staff leadership positions prior to coming to Crane.

Stephen P. Gootee Gootee was selected as executive director in December 1995. He previously served his entire career at the Naval Air Warfare Center, Indianapolis, working his way up the chain of command (as program manager and then branch, division, department, and directorate head). Gootee received B.A. and B.S. degrees in aerospace engineering from the University of Notre Dame. He was scheduled to retire in June 1999.

William A. Kaiser He was appointed by Gootee to the deputy executive director position at Crane in 1996. Kaiser had been employed at Crane his entire career, performing in a variety of different line and staff positions. Most recently, Kaiser served as head of the microwave systems directorate.

Robert J. Matthews Matthews was appointed as manager of the business and process reengineering project in March 1998. He had more than 25 years experience as a project manager at Crane. Previously, he led the base realignment and closure and competitive analysis activities.

The Road to Business Process Reengineering

When Steve Gootee first arrived at Crane in 1995, he and the top management at Crane attended a management seminar at Indiana University in Bloomington. Bill Kaiser, deputy executive director, said, "We realized during the program that we didn't

EXHIBIT 1
Organization Chart
Naval Surface Warfare Center, Crane Division

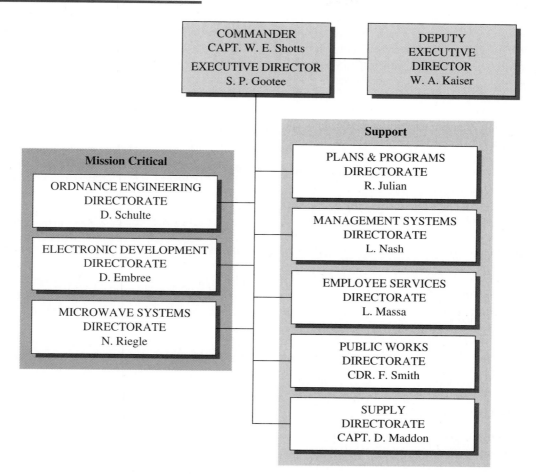

fully understand how our organization actually operated. We found that Crane lacked an overall identity. It was more like an industrial park, a conglomeration of businesses all located at the same place, but with little relationship to each other."

He added, "We realized we needed to do something to become more cohesive, to eliminate redundant operations, and to establish a strong identity. There were signs that Crane might be selected if there was another round of base closings. Our future survival depended on how efficiently we operated and how well we communicated our value to senior leadership in the Navy."

That seminar generated interest among Crane's senior management in identifying ways that the organization could become more efficient. The Navy used a process of competing for who would perform certain jobs like information systems and catering. This process was called A-76. It involved putting certain functions out for bid and allowing the private sector as

well as the government to bid for operating that function. In the summer of 1997, Gootee talked with a senior staff member in the Secretary of the Navy's office. The executive informed Gootee that if Crane developed an alternative method to A-76, he would help secure support for it. The staff member cautioned, however, that any alternative would need to at least meet the 30 percent cost savings currently achieved by employing the A-76 process.

In the fall of 1997, Gootee circulated an article about process reengineering among those he thought would best be able to assess the idea for application at Crane: Bill Kaiser, the deputy executive director, and Bob Matthews, former project manager for both A-76 implementation and base realignment and closure projects. After several meetings, all three felt reengineering both the processes at Crane and the general way Crane "did business" was Crane's best hope for improving operations without cutting into the core strength of the base.

They called the effort business and process reengineering (BPR). On December 20, 1997, Gootee hosted a teleconference to brief NAVSEA and NSWC staff members about BPR.

Gootee next briefed Captain Shotts on the idea and gained his approval of the BPR concept. Shotts then contacted Rear Admiral Paige, NSWC commander. After her conversation with Shotts, Paige presented the idea to the NAVSEA commander at the time, Vice Admiral Sterner, in an e-mail. His initial response was positive, "If they have a better mousetrap, I am ready to test it!" But he added a further constraint—that the implementation timeline would need to beat the time allotted for implementation of A-76.

By March 19, 1998, after Gootee and Shotts presented the idea to top leaders at NAVSEA, the commander of NAVSEA officially designated Crane as NAVSEA's pilot for BPR.

Simultaneously with gaining pilot site approval for BPR, Gootee initiated discussions with William L. Mason, the president of Local 1415 of the American Federation of Government Employees. Mason discussed the idea with his shop stewards and traveled to Washington, D.C., to present the idea at the national headquarters. Gootee and Mason signed a memorandum of agreement in October 1998.

In February of 1998, Gootee and Kaiser set a 2-year budget of $7.5 million for the BPR project. In March 1998, Kaiser recommended to Gootee that Bob Matthews be selected as the manager for the BPR project. Shortly after joining the group, Matthews selected core team members who committed to a full-time position on the team for at least 1 year. The core team reported to Bill Kaiser.

The Financial Management Team

With about 30 years of experience at Crane, Cheryl Miller had been the leader of a financial management team created earlier to look for ways to streamline the processes used to manage the financial function at Crane. Miller recalled:

> Everyone knew something was wrong with the financial management process. But no one had any data to back it up. We had just formed our team and come up with rudimentary definitions for the processes in two directorates when we joined the BPR effort in April 1998 and expanded our scope to include all of Crane. I have been through all kinds of efficiency improvement processes, but BPR is the best. It has structure and methodology and provides data for the guesses we've always had about what was broken. Implementation is tough, though.

Miller was appointed chair of the new financial management BPR team. Like all BPR teams, the financial management BPR team reported to Bob Matthews. In turn, Matthews reported to Bill Kaiser. For the BPR project, Kaiser reported to an executive steering board, made up of the eight Crane directors and the executive team. The executive team was composed of Shotts

(commanding officer), Gootee (executive director), and Mason (union president). (See Exhibit 2 for the BPR organization chart.) BPR teams reported their findings to the executive steering board. The board provided oversight and guidance, reviewed and critiqued progress, acted as advocate for the BPR pilot project, and acted on recommendations.

The responsibility of the financial management BPR team was to identify and model the current financial processes, prioritize opportunities for improvement, gather and analyze data, and develop recommendations. To keep the team size manageable, Miller did not select a representative from each of the directorates.

> I wanted a group that was diverse, but not necessarily all-inclusive. I chose people who had hands-on responsibility—people who worked with the systems every day. Throughout the development of the As-Is baseline model, when we needed additional information about a specific process, we brought in detailed process experts, employees who were familiar with how that specific process actually worked. They described it and walked us through it.

The team was also supported by personnel from an outside consulting firm. Although Miller worked full-time as BPR team leader, team members committed to working about a third of the time on BPR issues. "A lot of team members were already overloaded with their current jobs so getting their supervisors to release them took a lot of effort," Miller said. "It usually took us about 2 weeks and a lot of negotiations by Matthews or Kaiser to get a person released to be on the team."

Building the As-Is Description

The development of the As-Is profile was achieved through five high-level steps and then it was presented to the executive steering board:

1. **Define the financial processes.** The financial management BPR team modeled the financial management processes using Integrated Definition Language (IDEF), the Department of Defense's standard process modeling tool. The IDEF process model is a graphic display of business processes allowing different subprocesses to be modeled independently of each other and then integrated into the overall model. (See Exhibit 3 for an overview of the IDEF process.)

   IDEF models for the current processes in financial management were constructed by the financial management BPR team through a series of facilitated sessions with groups of employees involved in each process. "This is when we brought in the detailed process experts," Miller said. "By getting different user perspectives, we developed one common, detailed description of the business process."

EXHIBIT 2

Business and Process Reengineering Project Organization Chart
Naval Surface Warfare Center, Crane Division

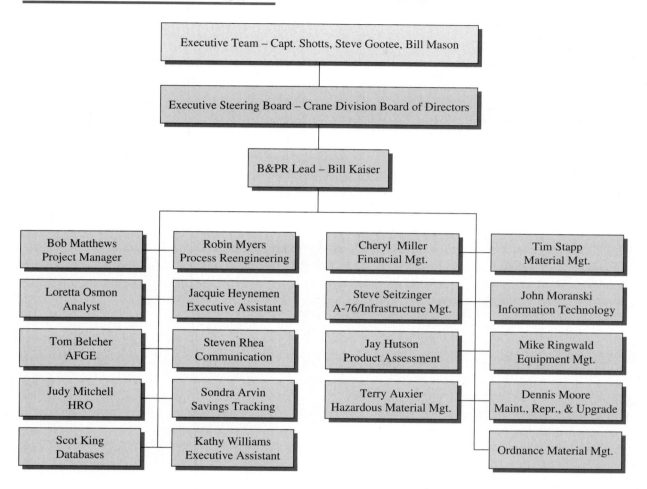

The As-Is modeling process for the financial management BPR team resulted in identifying six high-level work areas that constituted the financial management processes at Crane: workload planning, budgeting, funds administration, fiscal management, financial reporting, and financial analysis. Each high-level process contained three to four subprocesses. The list of all subprocesses is shown in Exhibit 4. The team next developed an overall model that linked together all the high-level work areas, showing how all financial management was carried out at Crane. In addition to the overall model, more detailed diagrams were developed for each subactivity.

Once the model for a process was complete, the team developed an organization-to-process matrix to map the processes into the organizational unit(s) responsible for executing each activity or subactivity. A process-to-information systems matrix was also developed to map the processes to the various information technology systems currently used in financial management at Crane.

2. **Select target processes**   based on customer concerns, recognized opportunities for cost savings, and risk factors.

The financial management BPR team used input from customer assessments and their own analysis to locate the best opportunities for gains in efficiency in order to identify which activities would be best for early reengineering. Based on the team's analysis of all the processes, four sub-subprocesses—validating/signing document, processing funding document, gathering data to monitor costs, and creating/generating reports to monitor costs—were identified as target areas for reengineering in the total financial management process.

EXHIBIT 3
Description of the IDEF Process
Naval Surface Warfare Center, Crane Division

Introduction to Process Modeling with IDEF0

The paradigm for IDEF Modeling is centered around the concept of Activity, which is an active component of a process—i.e., work. An IDEF process is represented by a collection of interrelated activities using graphic and natural language. Relationships between activities, the model, and the external environment are represented by arrows.

In an IDEF0 Model, Activities process Inputs into Outputs using Mechanisms according to the processing rules described in the Controls. This is often described with the acronym ICOM (Input, Control, Output, Mechanism).

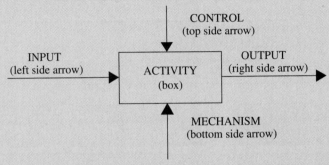

Purpose: This section explains the business reasons for why the model is constructed to help you stay focused.
Viewpoint: This section explains from whose perspective this model has been drawn.

	INPUT (I)	CONTROL (C)	ACTIVITY	MECHANISM (M)	OUTPUT (O)
Language	Describes the Input using a noun or noun phrase	Descibes the Control using a noun or noun phrase	Describes the Activity using an active verb or verb phrase	Describes the Mechanism using a noun or noun phrase	Describes the Output using a noun or noun phrase
Description	An Input is consumed as a result of the Activity process	Controls tell how the Activity should be performed	Transforms Inputs into Outputs through the Activity process	Resources used to accomplish the Activity (people, equipment, computer systems, or facilities)	Result of the Activity
Notes	Every Activity has at least one Input with some minor exceptions	Show Controls ONLY if they add value to the model you are building and support its purpose		Every Activity should show at least one Mechanism	Every Activity has at least one Output

Sample Process Model (Top Level)

Purpose: Document structure of sales order processing department to identify areas of inefficiency.
Viewpoint: Department manager

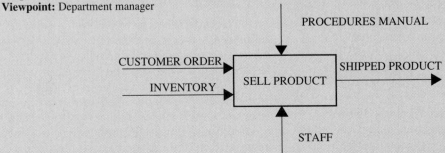

EXHIBIT 3 (*Continued*)

Activity Decomposition

IDEF0 is an hierarchical modeling method using a top-down approach to represent a process. It begins with a summary of the whole process, and progresses to the details. The top-level diagram page (A0) defines the interface of the model with external processes or real world events. The process of refining the top-level description of an Activity is called Decomposition (or drilling down). The first level decomposed pages are numbered A1, A2 A3, etc., and their progeny are A11, A12, A13, etc. (for A1); A21, A22, A23, etc. (for A2); etc., as diagrammed below. From there, the pattern continues indefinitely, adding a digit for each level. As a general rule, a decomposed activity should have 3 to 6 child activities. Node trees aid the understanding of the structure of large IDEF models. Node trees are essentially an indented outline of all the activities in the model as diagrammed below.

Decomposition Page Hierarchy: Decomposition creates a hierarchy of pages. The box numbers are used to provide context for traversing the model.

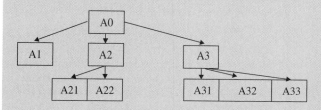

Node Tree: Node trees aid the understanding of the structure of large IDEF models by verbalizing the page hierarchy.

  (A0) Sell Product
    (A2) Process Order
      (A21) Validate Customer Credit
      (A22) Process Rejected Order
    (A3) Ship Product
      (A31) Fill Out Shipping Forms
      (A32) Assemble Shipment
      (A33) Carrier Takes Shipment

Note: The boundary for the decomposition is defined at its preceding level. ICOMs that are carried down between one activity and its decomposition page are called Ports. The port number (C1, O1, M1, I2, etc.) indicates the position of that ICOM on the parent activity ONLY.

3. **Validate the process model** in all directorates and construct a comprehensive profile of the finance function at Crane.

Before collecting data in the directorates, members of the financial management BPR team validated the targeted process model with finance staff in each directorate by asking them to review the targeted process models and note any deviations. In addition, the financial management BPR team conducted focus groups to solicit ideas of which areas to drill down further for data.

4. **Collect data on cost, demographics, systems, and opinions** by conducting a detailed survey of all directorates.

"What I think we did really well," Miller said, "was to go face-to-face with administrative staff in each of the directorates. We showed them our As-Is model and asked them if they had any input. Then we asked them for the names of employees in their directorates who were involved in the financial management process because we found in our initial research that there was no set job title."

In order to calculate cost in the comptroller's office, representatives of the office allocated the cost, work-years, and people among the financial management processes. For the line directorates, the financial management BPR team collected data through a much more comprehensive survey at each line directorate.

The survey was completed by 86 percent of the Crane employees identified as involved in some financial management process. "We conducted the survey in small groups. First we made a presentation about what we were doing. Then we gave them the survey on how they spent their time. There were four of us from the financial management BPR team present to work the room and answer questions," Miller said.

Miller explained that the survey asked each respondent to allocate his/her hours spent in each of the six high-level processes. The survey then asked respondents for additional information in the areas of funds administration and fiscal management. These areas were selected because they contained the subprocesses deemed most fruitful for reengineering. "Overall, we had excellent participation. We had all the data collected by the end of June of 1998," Miller said. The percentage of the total population who completed the work allocation survey is shown in Exhibit 5.

Because the percentage of coverage differed somewhat among the directorates and there was a large sample size, a proportional extrapolation of the data was performed to bring all directorates up to 100 percent,

EXHIBIT 4
Subprocesses and Sub-subprocesses
in Financial Management
Naval Surface Warfare Center, Crane Division

Subprocesses	Sub-subprocesses
[A1] Workload Planning	[A11] Negotiate Workload with Sponsor
	[A12] Issue Data Call
	[A13] Update WIS
	[A14] Perform WIS Reporting
[A2] Budget	[A21] Develop Budget Strategy
	[A22] Develop All Budgets
	[A23] Develop Operating Plan
[A3] Funds Administration	[A31] Process Funding Document
	[A32] Monitor Funding
	[A33] Bill Customer
	[A34] Close Funding Authorization
[A4] Fiscal Management	[A41] Manage Costs
	[A42] Manage Cash
	[A43] Perform Fixed Asset Accounting
	[A44] Maintain Ledger/Subsidiaries
[A5] Financial Reporting	[A51] Publish Corporate Measures
	[A52] Publish Financial Statements
	[A53] Publish Business Systems Reports
	[A54] Publish External Reports
[A6] Financial Analysis	[A61] Analyze Budget to Actual
	[A62] Analyze WIS to Actual
	[A63] Analyze Operating Plan to Actual
	[A64] Perform Ad Hoc Financial Analysis

to provide a common baseline for a more accurate comparison of data between directorates and a more accurate profile of the total cost to perform the financial management function at Crane.

Additional parts of the survey were used to collect contractor costs and noncorporate financial systems information (e.g., personal computers and file servers maintained by the directorate to perform financial management functions).

The hours collected via the survey were converted into cost by using annual labor rates. Personnel information was obtained from human resources information systems containing employee salaries or hourly rates. All salaries were converted into hourly rates and the hourly rate was multiplied by Crane's average fully-burdened labor rate for FY 1997 and FY 1998 to calculate total cost.

Based on the data collected, the total cost of financial management ($22 million) was calculated to be about 3 percent of revenue compared with the private sector range of 1 percent to 1.5 percent for financial management. Due to government regulations and requirements, achieving a cost comparable to the private sector was not considered possible by the team. However, the financial management BPR team found several areas for dramatic improvement. The division of the total cost of financial management across the six high-level processes identified by the team is shown in Exhibit 6.

Matthews said:

A little less than one-third of Crane's workforce was identified as devoting at least part of their time to financial management. Out of the 800 employees identified, about 600 spent less than 20 percent of their time performing financial management functions. Combined with the variety of titles we found, the financial management BPR team thought there may be employees performing financial management who did not have an overall understanding of financial management. We thought that might indicate a higher cost of financial management due to these lost economies of scale.

The two major areas targeted for reengineering, funds administration and fiscal management, made up more than two-thirds of the total cost of financial management. In addition, these two areas accounted for 70 percent of the total personnel hours expended and a little less than half the number of employees identified as performing some financial management function.

Based upon the validation, the financial management processes performed were similar among the directorates. However, there were some differences in the organizational structure of financial management among the directorates—some organized financial management at the directorate/department level whereas others organized it at the branch level.

5. **Reassess target selections for redesign.**   Once all the data were collected and analyzed, the team reassessed its initial target selections to identify Crane-wide reengineering opportunities. As a result of these discussions, five subprocesses in financial management were targeted for redesign: (1) monitor funding, (2) process funding documents (both in funds administration), (3) perform fixed asset accounting, (4) manage costs, and (5) manage cash (all three in fiscal management). Comments by the team about these processes are shown in Exhibit 7.

EXHIBIT 5

Response Rate of the Work Allocation Survey
Naval Surface Warfare Center, Crane Division

Directorate	Number of Employees Identified	Number of Employees Surveyed	Coverage Percent
Command	25	20	80%
Management Systems	37	33	89%
Employee Services	55	46	84%
Public Works	95	82	86%
Purchasing & Supply	75	59	79%
Ordnance Engineering	136	116	85%
Electronic Development	99	87	88%
Electronic Maintenance	126	118	94%
Microwave Systems	163	133	82%
Total	811	694	86%

EXHIBIT 6

Financial Management Processes Total Cost
Naval Surface Warfare Center, Crane Division

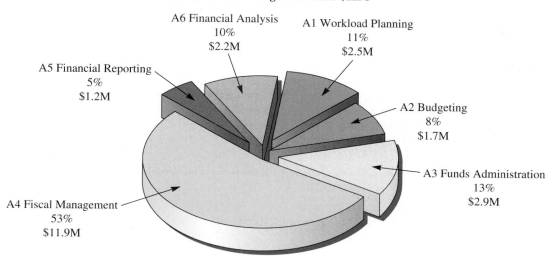

Total Financial Management Cost: $22M

A6 Financial Analysis
10%
$2.2M

A1 Workload Planning
11%
$2.5M

A5 Financial Reporting
5%
$1.2M

A2 Budgeting
8%
$1.7M

A3 Funds Administration
13%
$2.9M

A4 Fiscal Management
53%
$11.9M

6. **Present the results.** The team presented its findings to the executive steering board in late August 1998. Exhibit 8 shows the conclusions from the financial management BPR team's As-Is report.

The board appeared to be extremely pleased with all the work the team had done. One director commented, "I knew we needed to fix some things, but the data the team collected clearly show where we need to focus our attention."

EXHIBIT 7
Financial Management Sub-subprocesses Targeted for Redesign
Naval Surface Warfare Center, Crane Division

Funds Administration
_____

Monitor Funding. The BPR team focused on a subset of monitor funding—time and labor. This sub-subprocesses consists of processing labor and materials/equipment/service expenditures. Processing labor consists of timekeepers' duties, management certification of time, and comptroller's payroll technicians' duties. The financial management BPR team found that a majority of cost/time lies in the timekeepers' duties and that the majority of time is spent resolving errors (e.g., employees failing to clock in/out, malfunction of the time clock, and unanticipated overtime).

Process Funding Documents. Validate/sign funding documents is performed by the comptroller and process funding documents is also performed by the directorates. Funding documents are either received in the comptroller's office or the directorates (typically at the project level). Both processes are manual and circular with duplicate steps (e.g., copy and file) performed at the comptroller, directorate, department, and project levels.

Fiscal Management
_____

Perform Fixed Asset Accounting. There are 112 people performing fixed asset accounting, which is defined as directorate and comptroller equipment custodian duties. Fixed asset accounting also includes comptroller's monitoring and maintenance of items in a property management system. Inventories take a significant amount of time to perform and often result in missing or lost items. The last physical inventory began in FY 1996, was not completed until FY 1997, and resulted in many assets reported missing or lost which have since been identified.

Manage Costs. The process of monitoring costs and funding is functionally distinct, but procedurally connected. Monitoring funding includes tracking and controlling funding from the time it is accepted through completion of the assignment. Monitoring costs is performed at the charge number level. More than 60 percent of the cost spent monitoring costs relates to gathering data and creating/generating reports. Based on information collected through the survey, reports are prepared in part due to employee dissatisfaction with the format of corporate system data and the need to integrate data from multiple sources.

Manage Cash. The team looked at a subset of manage cash—vendor pay/receipt control. This function includes the vendor pay function and consists of matching invoices with receipts and contracts, entering invoice information into a computer system, and mailing copies of all invoices to a facility in Charleston SC that manually inputs the invoice information and pays the bill. Although the vendor pay function is relatively small, it appears it is duplicated in other areas.

The executive team then approved extra funding to immediately begin designing a new vision for financial management at Crane and to construct the To-Be model for the five targeted financial management processes.

Creating the To-Be Models

"Our redesign team started right after we received approval of our report on the As-Is model in August 1998," Miller said. "We thought we could complete the To-Be models in a month or two, but we didn't complete any on schedule."

The financial management BPR team was first increased in size from 9 members to 25 members as there were now five processes to design. For each of the five processes, the team

- reviewed the As-Is model developed earlier
- conducted research on the root causes that might have created such a process
- identified best practices for the same type of process conducted either inside Crane or at another government or commercial agency

EXHIBIT 8
Conclusions of the Financial Management As-Is Report
Naval Surface Warfare Center, Crane Division

Crane has a lack of integrated systems. Finance staff spend a significant amount of time gathering data from numerous systems to create reports for managers and sponsors. The data indicate that this report generation is done to present data in an integrated format versus to perform financial and performance analysis. Crane previously recognized this problem and at the time of data collection was in the process of implementing a data warehouse. As part of the redesign effort, the financial management BPR team will assess the data warehouse design and implementation and identify optimal staffing and organizational structure to complement a data warehouse.

The finance function is decentralized and fragmented. Finance consists of 333 work-years (full-time equivalent) spread over 854 employees. Seventy-five percent of finance costs are expended in the directorates. The financial management BPR team will determine the appropriate mix of centralization/decentralization in the redesign phase.

The finance function is not clearly understood. Finance should serve as a partner to operations, providing meaningful and timely financial information to management. Large numbers of employees at Crane are involved in tabulating and reformatting data. There is little value added since data are not used for analysis or for input to decision making. In the redesign phase, the financial management BPR team will design and deliver performance measurement information to support corporate strategic goals.

Employees performing the finance function do not have the appropriate financial background. Finance activities are performed by staff who are not dedicated to finance and who may not fully understand the role their activities play in Crane's overall financial management. For example, in Crane property management (and other organizations), financial activities are performed by technical staff who, although they understand the technical capabilities of the equipment they are tracking, may not understand the key role that tracking plays in financial control and reporting.

Finance is costly. Depending upon the industry, the finance function in the private sector accounts for 1 to 1.5 percent of total dollars managed. At 3 percent of total dollars managed, there is room for meaningful and substantial reductions in the cost of finance at Crane.

- developed the "ideal" way the process should be handled at Crane (the To-Be model)
- identified actions that could achieve the ideal process
- conducted a business case analysis or cost/benefit analysis for making the suggested change(s)
- selected the best course of action for stakeholder and management review

The new design for the perform fixed asset accounting process was completed in December 1998 and presented to the executive steering board in January 1999. This process tracked all significant fixed assets at Crane throughout their useful life and included updating of the fixed asset database. The team recommended that a centralized team (called the property team) be created to take over this function from smaller groups working in all the directorates. The team also recommended several changes to the information system supporting the fixed asset database. The financial management BPR team estimated that Crane could save at least $550,000 annually by

implementing their recommendations. The investment in information systems development was estimated to be about $25,000.

The To-Be model for process funding documents was completed and reported to the executive steering board in January 1999. The team identified several changes that could be made to automate the processing of funding documents, including electronic processing of paper documents, electronic funds transfer processing, and Web-based funds transfer. The estimated savings exceeded $400,000 per year and would require a one-time investment of $68,000 in systems development and scanning equipment.

The redesign for monitoring funding (called the time and labor effort) was completed and presented to the board in March 1999. This team conducted an extensive best practices analysis, visiting 14 outside agencies/companies as well as several organizations inside Crane. They concluded that none of these organizations did as good a job as Crane in keeping track of personnel time associated with individual jobs.

However, they did find a concept inside Crane that was worthy of organization-wide implementation. Their proposal called for consolidating the job of tracking time and labor effort for each major organization at Crane into the duties of a single person called a scheduler. The estimated savings exceeded $550,000 annually.

The fourth redesign team focused on the receipt control/vendor payment part of the manage cash process. In March 1999, they recommended a series of changes in how this process was handled at Crane and estimated a savings of over $1,000,000 per year. An initial investment of about $70,000 for information systems development would be required.

The redesign for manage costs was put on hold until some common business rules for all Crane operations could be established. Miller said:

> One of the difficulties we ran into was that the finance function is carried out so inconsistently across, and even within, directorates. While we were able to complete most of the redesigns, we found that we really needed some overall rules that would outline how our finance business should be conducted at Crane in order to finish the last process design.
>
> As I told Bob (Matthews), thinking out of the box has also been difficult. We found that some members of the financial management BPR team were too involved in the current process of financial management in their jobs. It was difficult for them to view things objectively. We added more objective members, but the task was still very difficult for many of the members of the team.
>
> We also encountered resistance from people in the directorates. Part of the process of building the To-Be model involves validating our As-Is model, and we encountered a lot of resistance. People questioned how we derived the information. I had one department manager tell me we didn't survey all the people in her department involved in financial management. I then sent her the original list of names she gave me. She was satisfied, but the thing is that it took a great deal of time to answer her concerns. And she's not the only one. I found myself pulling actual surveys and going through them with some people to justify how we collected our data.

By May 1999, only the process funding documents and perform fixed asset accounting redesigns had received approval to start implementation planning. In addition to manage costs, the time and labor effort and vendor pay/receipt control redesigns were stalled until common business rules could be established.

Dealing with the Root Problems

After reading the As-Is report from the financial management BPR team, Bob Matthews and Bill Kaiser concluded that creating the To-Be models was needed, but new processes by themselves could not solve some of the underlying issues in financial management at Crane. Kaiser said:

> The processes observed by our team were rooted in some assumptions and practices that had developed over time at Crane. We could change the individual process but we would never achieve the full benefits of process reengineering until we changed the way we conduct our financial management business here. We had to reengineer our business, too.

Kaiser decided to ask Arthur Andersen, the outside consulting firm working on the project, for some help in surveying how the finance function was conducted at other organizations, to report back by December 1998.

The consultant's report was shared with the financial management BPR team and the resulting conclusions presented to the executive steering board in December 1998. The basic conclusion was that the years of performing financial functions both in the directorates and the central comptroller's office had created a substantial amount of redundant and excess work. As partial proof, they cited some statistics. In FY 1999 Crane had 88 projects underway. These projects in turn had created 4,701 customer order numbers and 16,692 charge numbers. Each of these items required staff processing time and put an excessive load on the organization's information systems. "At the time, there were no rules or constraints, so a project leader could do whatever he/she felt needed to be done," Matthews said.

The consultants recommended that Crane adopt a standard set of rules for conducting the financial function. For example, a single business rule establishing when and how to create customer order numbers and charge numbers would reduce the numbers and redundancy. As a result of that meeting, Kaiser and two senior executives in the corporate financial area decided that they would develop a recommended set of business rules in the finance function for consideration by the executive steering board. They presented their recommendations to senior financial managers in February 1999. About that same time, Cheryl Miller and the financial management BPR team presented their recommendations for process change to the business unit managers. All rejected the recommendations for a variety of reasons.

After several more reviews and revisions, the report on business rules for financial management was presented to the executive steering board at an off-site meeting in May 1999. Exhibit 9 contains part of the report that shows a suggested set of business rules and a set of suggested roles/responsibilities for each of the levels of management involved in the financial management process at Crane. The directors at the meeting listened carefully to the report. Afterwards, one director suggested, "These changes are too radical—do we have to change this much?" Another added, "I haven't gotten a single complaint from my customers." Kaiser asked, "But do your customers know how much it's costing them for these reports?"

EXHIBIT 9

Suggested Business Rules and Roles/Responsibilities for Financial Management
Naval Surface Warfare Center, Crane Division

Business Rules Applied to Financial Management

- The departments at Crane are the primary business units, and financial management (analysis, reports, fund administration, and fiscal management) is focused at that level.

- The controller is the owner of the financial management process, but funds administration reports directly to the department managers.

- Some projects are designed with a specific focus (customer, product, group of customers, etc.) in mind, but all projects have a beginning and end.

- An estimating mechanism (for labor rates) will be established at the corporate level as a tool for the business units.

- While charge numbers are primarily accounting transaction vehicles, there is one charge number per task, instead of a separate charge number for each expense element and organizational unit.

- There is to be one customer order number (CON) per line of accounting. There will be no CON cost overruns.

- The Workload Information System will be developed at the department unit level.

Directorate Directors—Expectations/Responsibilities

- Mentoring of department managers
- Facilitating corporate business development in conjunction with each department
- Advocating and leading corporate (strategic/operational) initiatives
- Overseeing workload initiatives
- Mentoring/developing people to be future leaders
- Improving performance of individuals and the directorate
- Guiding the departments and developing policy
- Providing general oversight of the activities in the directorate

Department Managers—Expectations/Responsibilities

- Ensuring adequate project planning and execution
- Being financially accountable for budgeting, funds administration, and execution
- Planning and executing the workload
- Planning and managing the resources of the department

Funds Administrators—Expectations/Responsibilities

- Overseeing the core financial staff
- Controlling and issuing charge numbers
- Ensuring funds are not over-obligated and are expended as authorized per the CON
- Complying with the financial management business rules
- Ensuring work is planned in accordance with the appropriation requirements
- Providing support to project managers and branch managers

EXHIBIT 9 (*Continued*)

Project Managers—Expectations/Responsibilities

- Interfacing with customer with regards to tasking and meeting customer needs
- Ensuring that cost, schedule, and quality of project meet customer expectations
- Sustaining current business/customers
- Developing new business and customers
- Accepting, validating, and planning the appropriate use of funding (along with department managers)
- Using Microsoft Project (or an agreed-upon off-the-shelf software package) for project planning

Branch Managers—Expectations/Responsibilities

- Acting as the technical process owners, which requires overseeing the quality of the process output and the certification of people, facilities, and equipment, as well as an understanding of process costs, quality, and timeliness
- Delivering an output to the customer
- Managing and leading people
- Developing and maintaining technical capabilities
- Overseeing the financial support provided by the departments
- Ensuring work is accomplished within the planned appropriation

Customer Area Leaders—Expectations/Responsibilities

- Acting as the person visible to and advocate for the customer
- Analyzing existing customers' budgets, technologies, trends, and opportunities
- Focusing on total customer requirements
- Keeping command apprised of political and programmatic issues

---

Another director answered, "No. And they don't seem to mind or else we would have heard about it."

Another director said the changes would seriously interfere with his directorate's management of projects. Others agreed, stating that they had developed their own way of managing the financial part of projects—which was working very well. A director noted, "We created these reports because we needed them." Another director fired a parting shot: "Rather than make us implement all these new rules, just give us some time to reduce personnel since that is what this is all about anyway."

Dealing With Reductions in Personnel

Bob Matthews and Bill Kaiser realized in August 1998 that a likely result of implementing the To-Be models would be the elimination of some jobs at Crane. Yet one of the original objectives of business and process reengineering at Crane had been to make "reductions in force" (RIF) a last resort. So something had to be done to achieve the objective while being able to deliver the savings promised by BPR.

In fall 1998, the Center Resolution Committee (CRC), a group of management and union representatives, provided a framework and recommendations for movement of employees as the result of BPR. The CRC had been formed earlier to address employee grievances before they were escalated off the base. The committee had been very successful, reducing the number of escalated grievances from about 30 per year to almost nothing. But the CRC's recommendations for BPR impacts were rules- and seniority-based with little flexibility for directors to create staffing plans. When the CRC presented their recommendations to the directors in November 1998, the directors rejected the plan.

Matthews, with the help of a consultant, offered to come up with a compromise and presented his plan in early spring 1999. Administrative officers liked the new plan, but not the directors. Absent a solid agreement on employee movement, the BPR teams were stalled in implementing the recommendations in their To-Be models. In April 1999, the executive team (Shotts, Gootee, and Mason) took on the task and came to an agreement. They explained the agreement to the executive steering board during a May 1999 off-site meeting.

The agreement laid out a process for handling personnel whose positions would be eliminated due to BPR. First, each directorate would create a staffing plan when an implementation plan of some process was approved. That plan would show all remaining old positions and any new positions that were to be created. Next, individuals would be slotted into the old positions based on seniority. Any individual could apply for the new positions. All "surplus" personnel would be temporarily transferred to another job in the directorate and registered in Crane's Personnel Transfer Office (PTO) in an inventory of personnel who were to be given priority on job vacancies if they were minimally qualified for the job. In addition, voluntary separation incentives were offered to individuals to encourage retirements. Finally, the PTO manager was instructed to report monthly on the number of people registered. If too many people registered (no number was named in the agreement), discussions about a reduction in force would occur.

Moving Forward

As they sat in Kaiser's office in late May 1999, Matthews reflected, "I find my role has changed and is becoming more important in implementation. And a lot more difficult. We know fixed asset accounting and process funding can move forward. But we need business rules for time and labor effort, manage costs, and vendor pay/receipt control."

Kaiser agreed. "Securing buy-in from the directors is a real brick wall. We charged the chief financial people and the administration with talking to their business managers and directors to decide on business rules and that didn't work. Maybe we could get the executive team to finish the business rules we came up with and make their implementation a mandate—like they did with the Personnel Transfer Office."

Matthews said, "That's a possibility. We know we can't hire a consultant—an outsider can't implement changes to an internal process. The business process owner has to be the one to implement the change if it's to be effective."

Kaiser added, "Another option might be to get the employees to push for the change in business rules and processes. We seem to have the union's support for BPR."

Matthews said, "Our problem is that there are no negative consequences if the directors resist implementation. No one will lose their job for not complying. And we don't know of any upcoming rounds of base closings that would pose a threat. The directors can stall until the BPR project is effectively dead."

Matthews added, "Maybe we took on too much. We could go forward with fixed asset accounting and process funding only. Once they're successful, maybe we'd gain more support for the others."

"That will yield only a small fraction of the savings. Remember that we have to achieve a 30 percent cost savings. I don't think we have any choice other than to continue with full implementation. The project has too high a profile," Kaiser answered.

"Maybe we should back off a little. Not create mandated business rules, but create a team that would come up with less specific rules, more like guidelines, sharing of best practices," Matthews suggested.

"That's a possibility. Of course, we lose control of implementation and possibly forfeit optimal savings," Kaiser said. "It's already 7:00 P.M. We've come up with a couple of options. Let's sleep on them and meet first thing tomorrow morning."

As he drove to the ball field, Matthews thought about his options. Top management at Crane supported BPR. Navy leadership was expecting substantial results. How could middle management hold the project hostage? And if the middle managers got some control over following best practices, would they sabotage the project or would that secure their buy-in? Wasn't the size and scope of BPR bigger than the directors? Could they be successful in getting a mandate from the executive team and proceed without the directors' support? Should they even try to win the directors' support? As he pulled into a parking space, he saw his son out in right field catch a fly ball and throw to first base for a second out. If only he could think how to make a similar play and get the financial management BPR team back on track.

NIBCO's "Big Bang": An SAP Implementation

December 30, 1997, was the "Go-Live" date at NIBCO, Inc., a privately held midsized manufacturer of valves and pipe fittings headquartered in Elkhart, Indiana. In 1996 NIBCO had more than 3,000 employees (called "associates") and annual revenues of $461 million. Although many of the consultants NIBCO had interviewed would not endorse a "big bang" approach, the plan was to convert to SAP R/3 at all ten plants and the four new North American distribution centers at the same time. The price tag for the 15-month project was estimated to be $17 million. One-quarter of the company's senior managers were dedicated to the project, including a leadership triad that included a former VP of operations (Beutler), the information services director (Wilson), and a former quality management director (Davis).

One of the major drivers of the whole thing was that Rex Martin said "I want it done now." That really was the defining moment—because it forced us to stare down these implementation partners and tell them "…. we're going to do this big bang and we're going to do it fast."

Scott Beutler, Project Co-Lead, Business Process

We took ownership: It was our project, not theirs. We used the consultants for what we needed them for and that was technology skills, knowledge transfer, and extra hands.

Gary Wilson, Project Co-Lead, Technology

It was brutal. It was hard on families, but nobody quit, nobody left…Professionally I would say it was unequivocally the highlight of my career.

Jim Davis, Project Co-Lead, Change Management

This case study was published in the *Communications of AIS* 5 (January 2001). Copyright © 2000 by Carol V. Brown and Iris Vessey. The case was prepared for class discussion, rather than to illustrate either effective or ineffective handling of an administrative situation. The authors are indebted to Gary Wilson and the other NIBCO managers who shared their insights with the authors.

Company Background

NIBCO's journey to the Go-Live date began about 3 years earlier, when a significant strategic planning effort took place. At the same time a cross-functional team was charged with reengineering the company's supply chain processes to better meet its customers' needs (see "NIBCO's Big Bang Timeline" in Exhibit 1). One of the key conclusions from these endeavors was that the organization could not prosper with its current information systems. The firm's most recent major investments in information technology had been made over 5 years earlier. Those systems had evolved into a patchwork of legacy systems and reporting tools that could not talk to each other.

After initial talks with several consulting firms, top management brought in the Boston Consulting Group (BCG) in August 1995 to help the company develop a strategic information systems plan to meet its new business objectives.

BCG brought in a team and what they instantly did was to start going through each of the functional areas of the company to determine the need for changes….And so they went into each little nook and cranny of the company and sorted out whether we really needed to change every system we had.

Jim Davis, Project Co-Lead, Change Management

The consensus among NIBCO's management team was that the company was "information poor" and needed to be "cut loose" from its existing systems. There were also major concerns about being able to grow the company and become more global without an integrated information capability. BCG's recommendation on December 1st was that NIBCO replace its legacy systems with common, integrated systems that could be implemented in small chunks over a 3- to 5-year time frame.

They told us, "You really need to look at integration as a major factor in your thought processes—the ability to have common systems with common communication for the manufacturing area, the distribution area, across the enterprise."

Scott Beutler, Project Co-Lead, Business Process

EXHIBIT 1
NIBCO's Big Bang Timeline

Time Frame	Milestone
Early 1995	Cross-functional teams charged with developing NIBCO's strategic plan and reengineering supply chain processes determined that company could not prosper with its current information systems.
May, 1995	Gary Wilson hired as new head of IS department.
August–December, 1995	Boston Consulting Group conducted strategic IT planning study. Recommended that NIBCO replace its legacy systems with integrated enterprise system on client/server platform over 3 to 5 years.
January 1, 1996	Corporation restructured into cross-functional matrix organization. Scott Beutler, former VP of operations, residential division, given responsibility for business system strategic planning, including selection of an ERP package.
July, 1996	Committee recommended purchase of SAP R/3 and "big bang" implementation. Approved by Executive Leadership Team (ELT) and Board of Directors.
August, 1996	Contracts signed with SAP for R/3 modules and IBM as implementation partner. Wilson, Beutler, and Davis form triad leadership team.
September, 1996	Completion of project-team selection and September 30th project kickoff. Begin preparation phase.
December, 1996	Final project scope and resource estimates presented to ELT and Board with Go-Live date of Monday, November 29, 1997 (30-day grace period allowed). Final scope included North America only and consolidation of warehouses to a number yet to be determined. Final project budget was $17 million.
March, 1997	Decision to consolidate warehouses from 17 to 4 by September, 1997. Incentive pay bonus in place a few months after project initiated.
April, 1997	Installation of PCs for customer service associates completed. Weekly newsletter via e-mail initiated.
May, 1997	Business review lead for materials management leaves company; role filled by business review lead for production planning.
Summer, 1997	Maintenance of legacy systems discontinued except for emergency repairs.
September, 1997	User training begins at NIBCO World Headquarters and at remote sites. Sandbox practice system becomes available.
November, 1997	Go-Live date moved from Monday following Thanksgiving to December 30 due to delays in completion of warehouse consolidation and master data load testing.
December 30, 1997	Go Live without consultants.

The company began to reorganize into a cross-functional, matrix structure in January 1996. It also initiated a new cross-functional strategic planning process. Scott Beutler was relieved of his line management responsibilities to focus on the development of a new IT strategy. Beutler had joined NIBCO in early 1990 as general manager of the retail business unit. When this business unit was restructured, he became the VP of operations, residential division. Beutler was charged with learning whether a new type of integrated systems package called enterprise resource planning systems (ERP) would be the best IT investment to move the company forward.

Information Systems at NIBCO

Gary Wilson was hired as the new head of the IS department in May 1995 and became a member of the BCG study team soon after. Wilson had more than 20 years of IS experience, including managing an IS group in a multidivisional company and leading four major project implementations. He reported to Dennis Parker, the chief financial officer.

Wilson inherited an IS department of about 30 NIBCO IS specialists, including those who ran mainframe applications on HP3000 and IBM/MVS platforms. About one-half were COBOL programmers. The IS payroll also included a number of contractors who had been at NIBCO for up to 5 years.

Four major legacy systems supported the order entry, manufacturing, distribution, and accounting functions (see Exhibit 2). The business units had purchased their own packages for some applications and plants were running their own versions of the same manufacturing software package with separate databases.

> We had a neat manufacturing package that ran on a Hewlett Packard, an accounting system that ran on an IBM, and a distribution package that was repackaged to run on the IBM. Nothing talked to each other. Distribution couldn't see what manufacturing was doing and manufacturing couldn't see what distribution and sales were doing.
>
> *Jan Bleile, Power User*

At the time of the BCG study, there was widespread dissatisfaction with the functionality of the legacy environment and data were suspect, at best, because of multiple points of access and multiple databases. The systems development staff spent most of their time building custom interfaces between the systems and trying to resolve the "disconnects."

> The systems blew up on a regular basis because we made lots of ad hoc changes. As a result, the IS people weren't a particularly happy lot…no one really had a great deal of respect for them.
>
> *Dennis Parker, Chief Financial Officer*

The ERP Selection Team

Beutler set up a cross-functional team to select an ERP package early in 1996. CFO Parker was the executive sponsor and it included eight other, primarily director-level, managers. Wilson played an internal technology consultant role for Beutler while still managing the IS group, which was heavily immersed in a new data warehousing project.

EXHIBIT 2
Legacy Systems at NIBCO

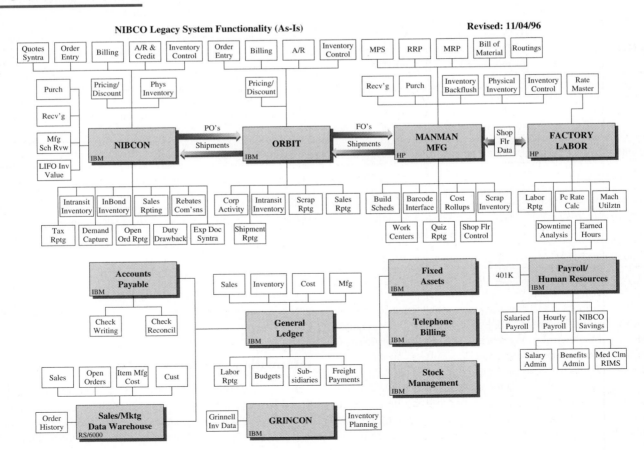

Seven ERP packages were evaluated in depth. Representatives from the various functional areas participated in walk-throughs of specific modules, and the selection team also visited several different vendors' customers. The strengths and weaknesses of each package were mapped into an evaluation matrix. One of the key decisions was whether to wrap a series of best-in-class finance and supply chain solutions around a common database, or whether to select a single ERP system that integrated all the modules.

The selection team also did some benchmarking on implementation approaches and success rates. Some of the team members sensed that the BCG recommendation for a 3- to 5-year phased ERP implementation was not the best approach for NIBCO. The fear was that the company would just get to the point where it would say "enough is enough" without executing the whole plan. Team members had also observed that some of the companies that had used a phased, "go-slow" approach were not among the most successful. At the same time business initiatives were demanding a quicker implementation.

Jim Davis, who had led a reengineering team for the strategic planning process, was asked to facilitate the selection team's formulation of a recommendation to the executive leadership team (ELT).

> Because of my facilitation experience, I was asked to facilitate that meeting so that there would be an objective person who had no particular interest or bias to help lead the discussion… It actually was a bit of a breakthrough because in the context of that meeting we changed our approach from the point solution over 3 to 5 years to an ERP big bang.
>
> *Jim Davis, Project Co-Lead, Change Management*

In July 1996, the ERP selection team recommended to the ELT that NIBCO purchase a single ERP system: SAP R/3. Among the benefits would be multimillion dollar operational improvements and reductions in inventory costs; the ROI was based on a 6 percent forecast growth rate in NIBCO's revenues. The cost estimates included the move from a mainframe to a client/server platform and an estimated number of R/3 licenses. Although consulting costs under the big bang approach were still expected to be high—about one-third of the project budget—they would be lower than the 1,000 days estimated for the 3- to 5-year phased approach. Either approach would involve a big increase in IS spending. The ELT supported the recommendation to implement R/3 as quickly as possible—pull the people out of the business to work on it, focus, and get it done.

The R/3 purchase and big bang implementation plan were then presented to NIBCO's Board of Directors. The Board viewed the big bang approach as a high-risk, high-reward scenario. In order to quickly put in place the systems to execute the new supply chain and customer-facing strategies, which had come out of the strategic planning process, the company would have to commit a significant portion of its resources. This meant dedicating its best people to the project to ensure that the implementation risks were well managed.

A contract was signed with SAP for the FI/CO, MM, PP, SD, and HR modules and for about 620 user licenses soon afterward. The HR (human resources) module would be implemented later. Rex Martin, chairman, president, and CEO of NIBCO, assumed the senior oversight role.

The TIGER Triad

Once the team's big bang recommendation was endorsed, Beutler began to focus on the R/3 implementation project. The initial idea was to have Wilson co-lead the R/3 project with Beutler. In an earlier position, Wilson had worked on equal footing with a business manager as co-leads of a project involving a major platform change, and it had been a huge success. He therefore quickly endorsed the idea of co-leading the project with Beutler. Between the two of them there was both deep NIBCO business knowledge and large-scale IT project management knowledge. Although Beutler was already dedicated full-time to the ERP project, Wilson would continue to manage the IS department as well as co-lead the project for the next 18 months.

Shortly after the Board decision in late July, Rex Martin asked Jim Davis to join Beutler and Wilson as a third co-lead out of concern for the high strategic risk of the project. Martin had been the executive sponsor of a team led by Davis that reengineered strategic planning at NIBCO. The morning after Davis agreed, Martin introduced Davis as the third co-lead of the project, and then let the three directors work out what roles they were going to play.

As the three co-leads looked at what needed to be accomplished, it became clear that Davis' experience with total quality management initiatives could bring focus to the change management aspects of the project. Davis split his time between his quality management job and the R/3 project for about a month, and then began to work full-time on the ERP implementation.

> One of the things we did was a lot of benchmarking…and one of the things we kept hearing over and over was that the change management was a killer. Having been in the IT business for a long time, I realized it was a very, very key element. With the opportunity to give it equal footing, it sounded like we could really focus on the change management piece.
>
> *Gary Wilson, Project Co-Lead, Technology*

I was pretty sensitive to change management because of my TQM role and so in the conversation I could say, "Look guys, if we don't get people to play the new instrument here, it could be a great cornet—but it's never gonna blow a note."

Jim Davis, Project Co-Lead, Change Management

The R/3 project team came to be called the TIGER team: Total Information Generating Exceptional Results. The project was depicted as a growling tiger with a "break away" motto, symbolizing the need to dramatically break away from the old processes and infrastructure (see Exhibit 3). A triangle symbolized the triad leadership with responsibilities for technology (Wilson), business coordination (Beutler), and change management (Davis).

The three co-leads spent significant amounts of time together on a daily basis, including Saturday mornings. Each brought completely different perspectives to the project. They talked through all the issues together and most major decisions, even more technical decisions, were made as a triad.

Rex Martin was the executive sponsor for the team, and also came to be viewed as the project champion. It was Martin's responsibility to ensure that the VPs supported the project and were willing to empower the project leaders to make decisions. The project co-leads informed him of the key issues and Martin eliminated any roadblocks. Together they decided what decisions to refer to the ELT level and provided the ELT with regular project updates. In turn, the ELT was expected to respond quickly. Of the three key project variables—time, scope, and resources—the time schedule was not negotiable: The project was to be completed by year-end 1997.

EXHIBIT 3
TIGER Leadership

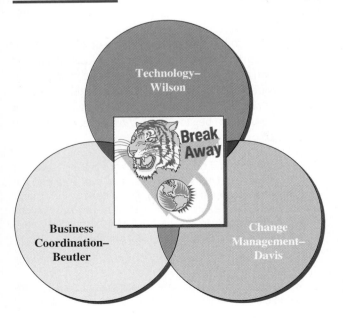

Technology–
Wilson

Break
Away

Business
Coordination–
Beutler

Change
Management–
Davis

Selecting an Implementation Partner

The same NIBCO team that selected the ERP software vendor was responsible for selecting an implementation partner. It was critical that this third-party consulting firm support NIBCO's decision to take a big bang approach, which was viewed as high risk.

I remember serious counsel where people came back and said: "What you've described cannot be done. And here are all the failures that describe why it can't be done." We just kept looking at them and said: "Then we'll get somebody else to tell us how it can be done."

Scott Beutler, Project Co-Lead, Business Process

After considering several consulting firms, IBM and Cap Gemini were chosen as finalists due to different strengths: NIBCO was already an IBM shop from a hardware standpoint, but Cap Gemini had a superior change management program. The team elected to employ IBM. By contracting for a large number of services (implementation consulting, change management consulting, technical consulting, and infrastructure), NIBCO's management hoped it would have enough leverage to get a quick response when problems arose.

Not all of the potential IBM project leaders that the team interviewed believed in the viability of the big bang approach.

When we hired IBM, we hired them with the agreement that they were going to help us to do a big bang in the time frame we wanted. As far as I know, IBM had not done a successful big bang up to that point. In fact, [Michael] Hammer[1] got on the bandwagon about halfway through our project and preached that big bangs are death.

Jim Davis, Project Co-Lead, Change Management

NIBCO's triad leadership design was also not viewed as optimal for decision making, and the consultants recommended that a single project leader be designated. The three co-leads considered their suggestion, but turned it down: The triad ran the project, but designated Beutler as the primary spokesperson.

Another risk was that IBM's change management approach in mid-1996 was an off-the-shelf, generic approach that was not ERP-specific. However, it had been used successfully for business process reengineering projects, and it included communications activities and job redesign initiatives. The intent was to tailor it to the TIGER project.

When the change management consultants came to NIBCO, none of them had ever heard of ERP or SAP, so it was difficult to directly apply their principles to NIBCO's situation. They

---

[1]Michael Hammer has been a reengineering guru since the early 1990s. (See M. Hammer and J. Champy, *Reengineering the Corporation: A Manifesto for Business Revolution*. New York: HarperCollins, 1993.)

stayed with us for 4 or 5 months into the project so that we could get enough learning from them, couple that with our own internal understanding, and then tailor these ideas to the specific ERP change issues.

Jim Davis, Project Co-Lead, Change Management

The IBM contract was signed in late August 1996. Six functional consultants would work with the project team throughout the project. Consultants with ABAP development and training development expertise would be added as needed. Knowledge transfer from the consultants to NIBCO's associates was part of the contract: NIBCO's employees were to be up to speed in R/3 by the Go-Live date.

Selecting the Rest of the TIGER Team

The TIGER project team had a core team that included three business process teams, a technical team, and a change management team. Each business process team had seven or eight people with primary responsibility for a subset of the R/3 modules (see Exhibit 4): (1) sales/distribution, (2) financial control, or (3) materials management/production planning. NIBCO associates on the three business process teams played the following roles:

- *Business review* roles were filled by business leaders who could make the high-level business process

redesign decisions based on their own knowledge and experience, without having to ask for permission.
- *Power user* roles were filled by business people who knew how transactions were processed on a daily basis using the existing legacy systems and were able to capture operational details from people in the organization who understood the problem areas.
- *Business systems analyst* roles were filled by persons with strong technical credentials who were also able to understand the business.

Wilson led the technical team of IS specialists, which was responsible for designing and building the new client/server infrastructure as well as providing ABAP programming support, PC training, and help desk support. The new infrastructure would link more than 60 servers and 1,200 desktop PCs (with standardized e-mail and personal productivity tools) to a WAN. Almost every existing PC was to be either upgraded or replaced, and the WAN would be upgraded to a frame relay network that would link headquarters with all North American plants and distribution centers. New technical capabilities would also be required for the product bar-code scanning and labeling functions that were to be implemented as part of the warehouse management changes.

Jim Davis led the three-person change management team. A public relations manager, Don Hoffman, served as the project

EXHIBIT 4
Project Team Composition

Sales Distribution Team	Finance Controlling Team	Materials Management Production Planning Team	Technical Team
Business Review Role	Business Review Role	Business Review Role	
Power User Role	Power User Role	Power User Role	
Business Systems Analyst	Business Systems Analyst	Business Systems Analyst	
Consultant	Consultant	Consultant	
Change Management Team			Consultants

team's communications/PR person. Steve Hall, an environmental engineer, was responsible for ensuring that all team members and users received the training they needed. Davis had witnessed some training that Hall had done and selected him to lead the training effort for the project.

The R/3 package was to be implemented in a "vanilla" form with essentially no customization. The intent was not to try to reconfigure R/3 to look like the old legacy systems. Rather, the company would adapt to the R/3 "best-practice" processes.

> We felt like SAP had enough functionality within it that we could make, by and large, the choices that we needed to configure the system to accomplish those high-level goals…We would identify what core processes we would need, we would look at the choices within SAP, we would pick the one that most closely mirrored our need, and we would adjust to the difference.
>
> We had to have some senior-level business people who could make the call on those business decisions: how would we configure and why, and what would we let go of and why… We did not have a situation where we had to go ask permission; we had a situation of continuous communication and contact [with top management].
>
> *Jim Davis, Project Co-Lead, Change Management*

To find the best business people for the TIGER team, the three co-leads brainstormed with executives and managers to identify a list of 50 or 60 NIBCO associates who had the skills and competencies needed; the project would require almost half of them. A human resources representative interviewed the candidates with Jim Davis and helped to develop personality profiles, including personal ability to lead and adapt to change, and emotional fit. At some point, the core team would need to put in long hours, 7 days a week.

Four director-level leaders were chosen for business review roles, including the two leaders for sales and distribution. This meant that seven of NIBCO's twenty-eight directors (counting the three project co-leads) would be committed full-time to the project. Because the other directors were needed to keep the business running during the project, the remaining business review roles were filled with managers who had deep enough business knowledge to identify issues as well as strong enough organizational credibility to settle conflicts as they arose.

Two business systems analysts were on each business process team. As liaisons with the technical team, the analysts were to make sure that the technical implementation matched the business requirements. Because few of the IS personnel inherited by Wilson had the appropriate IT-business skill mix for this type of analyst role, Wilson started early in his tenure to use job vacancies to hire people who could fill these anticipated analyst roles. One of these new hires was

Rod Masney, who had worked under Wilson a year earlier in another company.

> One of the exciting things about coming to this company was being a part of an ERP implementation. It was very exciting from a personal and career standpoint. I had been a part of a number of implementations for manufacturing businesses and those types of things, but never anything quite this large.
>
> *Rod Masney, Business Systems Analyst*

Early in the project it was decided that the project team members would be dedicated full-time to the project, but there would be no backfilling of their old jobs. Team members were expected to remain on the team throughout the project plus 4 additional months following the Go-Live date. They would then be redeployed back to business units.

IBM consultants were also assigned to each of the five project teams. The IBM project team members brought their technical knowledge to the project not only so that the business could make smart decisions among the R/3 options, but also for knowledge transfer to the NIBCO core team. Many of these consultants also brought experiences from R/3 implementations at other companies that could be used to help NIBCO avoid similar pitfalls. Consultants from the software vendor (SAP) were also occasionally brought in throughout the project— including BASIS and security consultants.

> We said all along, from day one, that we expected to become competent with the tools. We didn't take the approach of "do it to us" like it's done in many places. We took the approach of "show us how" to be an oil painter, and we'll be the artist. We wanted them to show us how the tools work and what the possibilities were. Then we'd decide how we were going to operate. We started with that from day one.
>
> *Scott Beutler, Project Co-Lead, Business Process*

> Their job was to bring to the table a deep knowledge of SAP and how it functions and enough business savvy to be able to understand the business case to help us best configure it in SAP. But we were responsible for all the decisions. We considered them critical members of the team, not somebody separate and apart. But our goal all along was that as soon as we went live, the consultants would go away and we'd manage the business on our own. We didn't want to have to live with them forever.
>
> *Jim Davis, Project Co-Lead, Change Management*

> We used the consultants for what we needed them for—and that was knowledge transfer, extra hands, and technical skills.
>
> *Gary Wilson, Project Co-Lead, Technology*

In addition to these formal team roles, extended team members would be called on to help with documenting the gaps between old and new business processes and helping with master data loads and testing. Because the business employees designated to these roles would continue to work in their business areas during the project, several of them would also be the primary user trainers in preparation for Go Live. After the cutover, many would also serve in local-expert roles.

> We probably consumed anywhere between 150 to 200 resources throughout the project in one way or another—either scrubbing master data, or training, or who knows what else. If we needed hands to key, we went and got them. That's how many people really got involved—and there were a lot.
>
> *Rod Masney, Business Systems Analyst*

The project kickoff was September 30th. It took the company 14 months of planning to get to the kickoff, and the team had 15 months to deliver the ERP system. During the first week, formal team-building exercises were conducted offsite. During the second week, IBM facilitators led the entire team through discussions about the kinds of changes the project would necessitate. For example, team members were asked to think through what it would mean to change to standardized processes from 10 different ways of doing things in 10 different plants with 10 different databases. The intent was to sensitize the entire team to potential sources of resistance and the need for early communication efforts.

Introductory-level training and training on R/3 modules were held on site; team members were sent to various SAP training sites in North America for more in-depth, 2- to 5-day courses. Altogether, the team received almost 800 days of training.

Working in the TIGER Den

Rex Martin was committed to housing the entire project team in a single physical location. The original plan was to move the team to a building across town, but Martin wanted the group to be located closer to NIBCO's senior managers.

A major remodeling project was in progress at the headquarters building, and the team was allocated 5,000 square feet on the first floor. Beutler and Davis read books on team management and came up with a plan to configure the space, which came to be called the TIGER den. The company's furniture manufacturer designed a movable desk (Nomad), which would enable flexible workspace configurations.

> In the end, we were less mobile than we thought we might be, but it created an environment of total teamwork and lack of individual space that forced us to work together and get done what we needed to get done.
>
> *Jim Davis, Project Co-Lead, Change Management*

The TIGER den had no closed doors and no private offices. A large open space called the "war room" had whiteboards on every wall. It was used for meetings of the whole project team,

open meetings with other NIBCO associates, system prototyping, and for core-team training during the project. Beutler and his administrative assistant, the change management team, and the IBM project manager used an area with a 6-foot partition, that had a U-shaped conference table and workstations. Wilson kept his office within the IS area in another section of the same building, but spent about 40 percent of his time in the den.

Each business process team had its own small "concentration" room for team meetings. They configured their Nomads in different ways, and each team's space took on its own personality. There was also another open space where extended team members could work and that could be reconfigured as needed.

At one end of the TIGER den was a room with soft couches and chairs designed to facilitate informal meetings. It was also used for formal meetings as well as celebrations around significant project milestones or team members' birthdays.

Because up to 70 people could be working in the den at the same time, phones would have been very distracting. The administrative area had a few phones for outbound calls only, and all team members were given private voice mailboxes and pagers; their pager alerted them when a message went into their voice mailbox. A bank of phones was installed in a small hallway leading out of the den, and emergency numbers were given to family members.

The directors on the project team were used to having private offices, so working without privacy in an open arena alongside the rest of the team took some adjustment. They were told: "Here's a chance to 'live' change management."

Final Project Plan

During the initial months of the project, the co-leads worked with the IBM project leaders to hone in on the scope, cost, and magnitude of the project in order to develop a final project plan with a realistic budget. In early December 1996, the final project scope and resource estimates were presented to the ELT and the Board, based on a Go-Live date 12 months later.

The final project budget was estimated to be $17 million, which was 30 percent higher than the midsummer estimate. One of the major reasons for the significant increase was the inclusion of change management costs (including training) that had been missing from the summer budget. About one-third of the final budget was for technology infrastructure costs, including the R/3 software. Another third was for team costs and the education of NIBCO associates. The final third was for third-party consulting.

The December plan also addressed two major changes in project scope. One was a recommendation to include North America only. For example, sales offices outside of the United States (such as operations in Poland) would not be included in the big bang implementation.

A second scope change was driven by technology issues. At the end of 1996, NIBCO had 17 distribution centers, but its long-term strategy was to consolidate to at least half that number. An R/3 project involving 17 distribution centers would have high technology installation and operations costs as well as high project complexity due to the sheer number of locations. A distribution center consolidation prior to the ERP Go-Live date would therefore reduce both technology costs and implementation complexity.

Although the detailed planning for the distribution center (DC) consolidation was not complete when the final project plan was presented to the Board, by March 1997 the company had committed to consolidate from seventeen small DCs to four large ones: one existing facility would be enlarged, and new managers and associates would be hired to run the three new DC facilities. The goal was to complete the consolidation by September 1997 to allow time to prepare for the cutover to the ERP system.

> SAP provides opportunities for consolidation, so it's not uncommon for companies to decide on a certain amount of consolidation for something . . . The original timing had the warehouse consolidation getting done ahead of SAP by a couple of months.
>
> *Gary Wilson, Project Co-Lead, Technology*

There were several major business risks associated with the project that also would have to be managed. First, the integration really had to work, because otherwise any one part of the organization could claim that they were no better off, or even less well off, than before the project. This meant the team would have to make decisions focused on the integration goals, which would result in killing some "sacred cows" along the way.

Second, the company could be significantly harmed during the project because most other company initiatives would basically be put on hold. The exception was the distribution center consolidation, and this would involve large-scale personnel changes and increased demands for training. At the same time, it would be important to maintain as much customer satisfaction as possible.

Management also knew that if the project ran late, it could really hurt the company. So the project had to be completed on time with a quality result.

> You can't pull 27 full-time people out of a business that runs fairly lean, and then not backfill and expect business to go merrily on its way. We actually watched one competitor of ours go live with SAP during the course of our implementation, and the first 2 weeks they were live they could not take a customer order. And so we were seeing some real-life horror stories in front of us. So, the risk management from our perspective was: We're gonna deep six this company if we do this poorly or if we don't do it on time.
>
> *Jim Davis, Project Co-Lead, Change Management*

Because there was no backfilling of the jobs held by the project team members, NIBCO associates not on the project team had to take on extra work to sustain normal operations. This meant that the whole organization needed to be committed to the ERP project. An up-front goal of participation by one-third of NIBCO's salaried associates was established to be sure they understood where the project was going, to promote buy-in, and to get the work done.

> There was a team of people who were living and breathing it everyday, but it truly was a whole company effort. I had two individuals that left my organization and were full-time members of the team. We did their work; we absorbed it. That was universal throughout the company.
>
> *Diane Krill, Director, Customer and Marketing Services*

A few months after the project began, a special incentive pay bonus was established for every salaried NIBCO associate. The bonus was tied to a half-dozen criteria (see Exhibit 5). The Go-Live schedule had to be met, or no incentive pay would be distributed: A 30-day grace period, only, would be allowed from the original date set, which was the Monday after Thanksgiving (November 29th). The incentive pay pool would be reduced by 50 cents for every dollar over budget. Four overall project "success" criteria were also established, along with specific measures. The results of these measures would be available for review by the ELT within 2 months after implementation, and the Board would make the final decision as to whether or not these results collectively met the success criteria.

> In the end, being that solid or fierce in holding firm on the timeline was probably one of the main things that made us successful. . . . There was never an option. Slippage was not an option. We had to make the milestones as we went.
>
> *Scott Beutler, Project Co-Lead, Business Process*

Stock options were also granted to all core team members in April 1997 as a retention incentive.

Achieving the Milestones

The project was conducted in four large phases: preparation, analysis, design, and implementation (see Exhibit 6).

Because few tools were available for purchase, the IS team built a number of tools to help with process scripting as well as project management. For example, Project Office was a NIBCO-developed tool for project management and project tracking that used an Access database (MS Office 95). Project Office became the repository for all project planning documents, As-Is and To-Be process scripts, tables to support the documentation for the project, testing plans and results, site visit and training schedules, issue logging, and much more. The

EXHIBIT 5
Criteria for Incentive Pay

Criterion	Measures	Impact on Incentive Pay
On Time	SAP must be live on or before 12/31/97	Required for any incentive pay
Successful	1) Client/server environment measures: - available 90% of agreed-upon time - 95% of real-time response times less than 2 seconds	Executive leadership team will review the results of these four measures and make a recommendation to the board of directors as to whether or not project was a success
	2) Business processes supported by SAP: - 1 day after Go Live, no transaction data entered into legacy systems - 45 days after implementation, less than 15 open data integrity problem reports	
	3) Core management and administrative processes supported by SAP: - close books through SAP within 15 days at first month end	
	4) Training of NIBCO associates in use of SAP and processes: - a minimum of 95% attendance at training classes across the organization	
Within Budget	Control spending to at or below project plan approved by Board 1/28/97	Every $1 over budget reduces the incentive pool by 50 cents

sales order processing script, for example, consisted of more than 100 pages of detailed documentation, and was used as the basis for classroom training documentation. This tool allowed team members to access the latest project documents and to gauge where they were in relation to the project's key milestones.

Due to the time demands of the project, all team members were provided with laptops so that they could work 24 hours a day, 7 days a week, from anywhere they wanted. Because there was no support for mobile (remote access) computing prior to the TIGER project, providing anytime/anywhere support was also symbolic of NIBCO's new commitment to helping its employees leverage their time better using information technology.

> There wasn't much of an e-mail culture before this...but before this project was over, we basically had pulled the whole company into this way of life.
>
> *Gary Wilson, Project Co-Lead, Technology*

Business Responsibilities

Finance and Controlling Team   The business review lead for the controlling function was Steve Swartzenberg, who had spent more than 5 years in different plant positions, starting as an industrial engineer and working his way up through plant administration; he had recently been promoted to product manager. During the project Swartzenberg worked not only with his current boss, the VP of marketing, but also with the CFO—because the tactical managers of the new controlling module would be controllers within the accounting/finance group.

> My business review role responsibility was to make sure that the functional organizations who would be taking ownership for the controlling module, once we turned it on, were pulling for it. I kept them up to speed on how we were doing on the issues, on the things they needed to help with along the way, so that they knew that their role was to hit each of these critical milestones. None of us wanted to *not* make it, so we knew

EXHIBIT 6
Implementation Phases

Phase	Major Activities
Preparation	Final project plan—scope and cost. As-Is business analysis. Technical infrastructure specifications. Project management and tracking tools developed.
Analysis	Document As-Is processes as To-Be processes. Analyze gap between To-Be processes and R/3 processes. Identify process improvements and changes to fit R/3. Documentation of inputs, outputs, triggers, business activities, (process) roles, change categories, training requirements.

Design	Configure R/3.
	Develop training materials.
	Develop and document specifications (master data, external systems interfaces, reports).
	Develop prototypes:
	  1. Operational: module-oriented; prototyping and testing of business processes; reviewed by business review team.
	  2. Management: module-oriented; demonstrated functionality needed to run business.
	  3. Business: integrated; all key deliverables configured.

Implementation	Some overlap with design phase.
	New tactical teams formed with directors heading up risky areas:
	  1. Master data teams: data cleanup.
	  2. Customization team: determine customization needed across plants.
	  3. Implementation infrastructure team: address outstanding hardware issues; plan transition to new system.
	  4. Help desk team: develop post-live support processes.

how it had to knit together—we knew our job was to hit the milestone.

Steve Swartzenberg, Business Review Lead

There were two IBM consultants on the controlling team. One helped with the controlling (CO) module functions of product costing, cost center accounting, and internal orders; team members relied on this consultant to answer detailed questions about what the package could and could not do. The second consultant supported the team on the profitability analysis (PA) and profit center accounting (PCA) sub-modules. When the second consultant left the project, Swartzenberg helped select a replacement who not only understood R/3 details, but also had a strong financial background.

> Not coming from accounting, I kind of used him as my accounting consultant—as a kind of sanity check.... The controlling module in SAP really is the spot where it all comes together. What you find out is no part of the organization is disconnected

from another. It's all connected; the processes are all integrated. If one part falls out, it doesn't link up.

Steve Swartzenberg, Business Review Lead

A major business process change would be to centralize all accounts payable entries that had been decentralized to the plants in the past. Swartzenberg spent extra time developing documentation that included flow charts and other tools to help with the transition. For example, a check-and-balance process was designed for looking at transactions in specific areas where problems would first be visible. The accounting group did these checks every day for the first month after Go Live so that problems could be fixed as they happened, and to avoid snags at the time of the first financial close.

An extended team member from marketing helped develop profitability reporting (P&Ls) for each of the product lines—copper fittings, cast fittings, plumbing, heating valves, etc.—information that was not available under the old systems.

Materials Management/Production Planning Team

The business review lead for the manufacturing production planning (PP) module was John Hall, a NIBCO veteran of 20 years. Hall had been a member of the BCG study team and was involved in the decision to take the big bang approach. Six months prior to the TIGER project kickoff, Hall had become director of plastics manufacturing.

> The business review teams had 100 percent support from Rex Martin and the ELT. They allowed us to only go to them for major issues. We had the freedom to make decisions.
>
> *John Hall, Business Review Lead*

One of the two power users on the PP team was Jan Bleile, a 25-year NIBCO veteran in production control who had worked on the manufacturing legacy system (Man-Man) and its predecessors. He also had a good rapport with all the old-timers in the plants.

> I was a supply chain master scheduler at that time and the position I was recruited for on the TIGER project was as a power user for the MM/PP team. One of the reasons that I was chosen was that I had been in on all the manufacturing systems implementations that have happened here at NIBCO since we've been computerized.... So it really was a natural for me to accept this, when offered, because of the three other implementations that I was on. This one was different in that it was 100 percent dedicated.
>
> *Jan Bleile, Power User*

From the outset, there were concerns about all the changes that would need to take place to implement both new processes and new systems at the plants. Hall worked with other manufacturing directors, the VP of manufacturing, and Scott Beutler to set up 3- to 4-day meetings with TIGER team members at every plant during December 1996. At these meetings the core project team emphasized that R/3 was the system that would be used at all plants, and that all data would reside in it. In turn, the team learned how things were done in each of the plants, including what each plant thought it did that was unique.

Although it was not initially clear whether common processes could be implemented across all NIBCO plants, the project team was able to reframe each plant's tasks into high-level generic processes. The idea was to keep things relatively simple at first. Then, as people became comfortable in using the system, the number of complex features and functionality could be increased. The project team then gained consensus for this common way of doing things, plant by plant—whether the manufacturing process was for plastics, copper, foundry materials, etc.

> We kept pounding the message home that you don't have to believe us, but just give it a try, and do it with an open mind. Every time someone would call and say, "We can't do this, we're different, we need this, we need that" we would say "you're not going to get it, so you've got to give this a try."...Just

having the CEO as the major champion helps overcome any and all obstacles you can think of.

> *Jan Bleile, Power User*

Extended team members for the PP module were formally designated early on. Although they resided at the plants, they also spent time in the TIGER den at headquarters learning about the master data plans and the impacts of real-time online processing. Through these in-person interactions, the project team members learned what process changes would need to be emphasized the most when the plant workers were trained. During the final months of the project, many of these extended team members dedicated 100 percent of their time to conducting training classes at different facilities. Every NIBCO associate who would need an R/3 license was signed up for a certain number of classroom training hours.

The business review lead for the materials management module left the company in May 1997. Although this event was viewed as positive overall (due to internal team conflicts), it also left a major gap. Because this happened so late in the project, John Hall took on this role as well, with help from Beutler.

Sales/Distribution Team

Several major process changes were also to be implemented for these functions. First, national accounts (which accounted for a large percentage of sales) would have dedicated NIBCO associates. Second, a much more controlled processing environment would be set up for making changes to customer master data. In the past, changes to customer data, including pricing data, could be made by all customer services (CS) personnel. Under SAP, a new, centralized marketing services group would be formed and customer master data changes would be limited to this group. This more centralized, focused approach would yield revenue gains from better response to national accounts. It would also yield dollar savings because fewer price deductions would have to be given to customers due to internal processing errors.

One of the major challenges facing the project team was the structuring of the customer master data. For example, terms of sale at NIBCO had not been defined in terms of the sales channel of the customer in the past, but in R/3, pricing distinctions are made between wholesalers and retailers. This meant that all NIBCO customers had to be classified by their sales channel. Training was also a major hurdle because about half of the CS staff had used green screen terminals in the past and had to be trained in using a PC with a mouse and graphical user interface (Windows). PCs for the CS group were installed about 8 months before the Go-Live date, and each member of this group had over 45 hours of mandatory R/3 training.

NIBCO's warehouse operations had not been highly disciplined in the past, so large-scale process changes would also be implemented for the distribution function. The risk of the warehouse management implementation was increased by the distribution center consolidation that was going on during the same time period.

> We used to run distribution centers with notebooks. John, who put stock away, put it over in bin 12 in the corner, and would write it down. He knew where the overstock was and you could get away with that in a 50,000-square-foot facility. But when running 250,000-square-foot facilities, you can't do that; you've got to have a system run your facility for you.
>
> *Larry Conn, Extended Team Member*

Technical Responsibilities

During the preparation phase, while the business process teams worked on As-Is analysis, about six IS specialists under Wilson developed a 250-page technical document that became the blueprint for building the new technology infrastructure—the PCs, servers, and networks for every NIBCO location. Over the next 9 months, the technical team worked through the installations for all the plants and distribution centers, and a trainer would travel right behind the technical team and do PC and Windows training as needed.

The TIGER project and the new client/server architecture also required new work processes for the IS organization. New processes for network management, backup and recovery procedures, system change controls, and business-client relationship management needed to be developed. Many of these changes were made under the TIGER project umbrella, and the IBM consultants helped with the IT process design and IT worker reskilling.

> The project leaders worked very hard to manage our consultants. We expanded when we needed to and we contracted very quickly. When a consultant no longer held value for us, we cut him loose. At one time, we counted 50 consultants here.
>
> *Rod Masney, Business Systems Analyst*

During the preparation phase, a new director-level position for systems development was filled with an outside hire, Greg Tipton, who began to take over the day-to-day program management responsibilities from Wilson. Tipton became the primary liaison between the TIGER team and the IS development resources during the design phase as ABAP programming needs increased. All maintenance support for legacy systems was essentially shut down by the summer of 1997 as the entire IS group focused on the R/3 implementation.

In the last months of the project, the IS area was running multiple R/3 environments: the development system, a production system, two training systems, and a test system. IS specialists were also dedicated to cleaning up and converting master data, loading master data, and stress testing the system with real data. Data from 85 different legacy system files and lots of Access databases

had to be converted. Although discussions on how to accomplish these critical activities began as early as March 1997, the master data loading processes proved to be more complex than expected, and four complete heavy-duty-testing trials were run.

Change Management Responsibilities

> We were convinced we could configure a system. We were convinced we could build a technical infrastructure that would support it. We were NOT convinced that we could change people's attitudes and behaviors in a way that we could successfully use what we came up with.
>
> *Jim Davis, Project Co-Lead, Change Management*

Because IBM's change management approach was not ERP-specific, the NIBCO team had to learn how to apply it to an R/3 big bang implementation. Some of the IBM change management people had been trained in methods developed by Daryl Conner, CEO of Organizational Development Resources, Inc. Conner's book[2] heightened the leadership team's understanding of the importance of dealing with change management issues at the level of the individual. The overall change management thrust became how to ensure that the R/3 implementation would not drive NIBCO users beyond their abilities to adapt to change.

Although only Davis and two other team members were working full-time on change management issues, all team members were expected to be change leaders. During the selection process they were told that the rest of the organization would be looking to them to understand where the TIGER project was heading and why it made sense to be going in that direction. The team members also had to understand the change implications of their decisions: They were asked to identify what the major impacts would be for people performing a particular function—how they would work together differently, or need different information. The change management team used this knowledge to develop communication and training plans that would help NIBCO associates make those changes.

Identifying the Key Changes   Information to help the change management team was captured as part of the business process documentation. For example, as a business process team was preparing To-Be business process documentation, the team members were asked to identify the changes a given process introduced and to categorize them (see Exhibit 7). No process documentation (and later no training script) would be approved until the change management elements were complete.

For example, an associate in accounts payable who worked with NIBCO's legacy systems in the past really had no need to

---

[2] Daryl R. Conner, *Managing at the Speed of Change*. New York: Villard Books, 1992.

EXHIBIT 7
Change Management Categories

New work (New) The purpose of this category is to highlight where a new job is required. Please reference which role (responsible, accountable, consulted or informed) you are referring to and any details about the job you think would be useful in defining or designing the new job. (Example: Master data is going to be managed and controlled in a centralized location. This would require the creation of a new job which is focused solely on this set of activities.)

Automation of old work (Automate) This should be used when an activity which was previously performed manually will now be automated either in whole or in part. Please note whether this activity should still remain in the same functional area or whether the automation would support its movement to another functional area. (Example: The system will automatically perform the three-way match of a PO, receiver and invoice which we currently reconcile manually.)

Elimination of related activities (Eliminate) This should be used when activities previously performed associated with this activity are no longer required because of a changed process. Please note which function previously performed this eliminated work. (Example: People spend significant time creating special reporting to summarize data in a meaningful way for analysis. The system will provide that data online in a way which allows the analysis to occur without the offline work.)

Work moved from one group to another (Transfer) This should be used when work moves from one function/department to another or when work is moved up or down from one level of management to another. The goal for this element is to track how you expect work to shift as a result of the new activity or process. (Example: Accounts receivable activities occur as a part of the customer service function because of the need for communication with CSRs. The system will now provide information in a way that allows the A/R activities to be performed in the treasury area.)

Risk of process not being done well (Risk) It is important that all new processes be performed efficiently and effectively. This change element should be used when the activity is particularly critical to activities performed downstream and you want to highlight that to the organization. (Example: The new demand pull methodology has a particular "triggering event" which drives all of the downstream events. It is imperative that this activity is performed effectively, or in a particular time frame, or with a particular frequency.)

Increased level of difficulty (Difficulty) This should be used when a new activity or process is substantially more complex or involved than previously. This will give us a heads-up for training and organizational readiness to prepare for a more difficult application. (Example: The current process calls for data to be input without any quality review or analysis. The new process requires a specific analysis to be performed or data to be reviewed and approved prior to entry into the system.)

New business partnerships (Relationships) This should be used to identify where the new activity or process requires people to work together or collaborate in new ways. This could include where information must be shared between groups that don't ordinarily work together. (Example: I currently work with the logistics function to get input for an activity I perform. In the new process, that information will come from manufacturing.)

Miscellaneous (Other) This should be used when you want to highlight an issue or concern that is not covered by one of the other change categories.

talk to the procurement department. In R/3, however, the procurement process has a significant bearing on the transaction documentation that finds its way to accounts payable. So the communication and information sharing between those two groups becomes very important. The change category here would be *relationships*.

Team members were also asked to help determine the training needs for these specific change examples. In all, 450 different business activities in 15 locations had to be addressed.

Internal Communication Plan A critical part of the change management efforts was to provide information and to keep open the communication lines between the project team

and the other NIBCO associates. This involved several types of activities—some at headquarters and some onsite at the plants and distribution centers across North America.

> We basically followed the rule…somebody has to hear something five different times from three different sources for it to hold. So we looked for every different way that we could get ahold of somebody to get their input and to share information with them, too.
>
> *Jim Davis, Project Co-Lead, Change Management*

A communication analysis of three or four hundred people at NIBCO yielded a type of "spider web" map of internal communication linkages from which the "best connected" associates could be determined. The supervisors of associates with a score above a certain level were then asked for their permission to have these associates invited to participate in a TIGER focus group. About fifteen people at corporate, and three to six people at each plant and distribution center, were then personally invited to join the focus group. Their job was to be a "hub" within the business, to provide bidirectional feedback to the team and to those with whom they were connected in the workplace.

> We didn't say: "You have to be a cheerleader for the project." As a matter of fact we said: "We prefer that you fight back because it is only at the point of resistance that we can identify how to react".…. Their job was to get in our face and say: "You know what? You've got a deep problem—people are just not buying into this." Or: "Here's where you're gonna fall off the edge."
>
> *Jim Davis, Project Co-Lead, Change Management*

Another key communications activity was holding monthly "TIGER talks" in the auditorium at corporate headquarters. Jim Davis and selected TIGER team members made presentations and answered questions, and Don Hoffman facilitated the meetings. Each TIGER talk had a different main message, such as project phases, process-focused organizations, training and education plans, technology infrastructure, plans for prototype sessions, organization/role/job design, implementation phase issues, "homestretch" issues, SAP start-up plans, and post-live status.

These face-to-face sessions were open to all NIBCO associates; each session was run four times, so that people could pick a time slot to fit their schedules. Attendance was voluntary, but there was an expectation that members of the focus group would be among the attendees. A summary and internal news release highlighting the main message were published to the entire organization within 48 hours. On a monthly basis, information would be sent out to focus group members and other key players who were not at the meeting, and videotapes of the sessions were also made available.

Team members also conducted two or three rounds of onsite visits to each NIBCO plant and distribution center. That meant that all associates had an opportunity for a physical face-to-face meeting with team members once every 3 to 4 months. Again, questions and answers from these meetings were summarized and distributed within 48 hours to the entire organization.

At each meeting, the team attempted to measure the level of individual commitment to change. A change adoption curve was posted on a flip chart and the meeting leaders pointed out that their goal was to get every NIBCO associate to the buy-in point on the curve. Each participant was given a red sticker and asked to place the sticker on the curve to record "where they were" at the end of each meeting, out of sight of the TIGER

team members. Over the course of the project, these scatter-grams became a way to measure progress toward an effective implementation. The team could also identify which plants or distribution centers were lagging behind, and then focus on the ability of those associates to assimilate the anticipated changes.

About halfway through the project, a weekly newsletter for those associates who would be using R/3 began to be distributed via e-mail. After training had begun, the newsletter included questions asked in the training classes and the answers provided by the classroom trainers.

User Training   Over 1,200 hours of training were delivered at three NIBCO training sites over the 4-month period before Go Live. Depending on their job, users received between 8 and 68 hours of training that focused on the new processes, not just individual tasks. In addition, a user ID was issued during the training classes that entitled associates to access a training "sandbox" where they could try things out and practice transactions or scenarios. User attendance at the training sessions was tracked as part of the organizational incentive scheme, but sandbox practice was not.

Delaying the "Go Live"

The original plan was to go live the Monday after Thanksgiving. This date proved not to be feasible for two primary reasons.

First, the distribution center consolidation was significantly delayed. This resulted in a somewhat chaotic state, as most of the DC managers were still focused on the consolidation, rather than on preparations for the R/3 system. The new staff hardly had a chance to get to know NIBCO's business partners, let alone be prepared for a new system by the Go-Live date.

> These new people who were in all the new facilities never had time to get involved in the SAP project. They never went through appropriate training because they were focused on the consolidation. You cannot do two astronomical projects at the same time. Distribution was not prepared for the SAP start-up and we paid for it.
>
> *Larry Conn, Extended Team Member*

Second, a complete master data load was taking about 17 to 18 days round the clock. The first loading of the master data for manufacturing was sufficiently bad that the consultants had warned them that they were in trouble. The manufacturing data alone was loaded six times. A "stress test" at the beginning of November also reinforced the need for another "full load" test, and time was running out.

> We were probably right out there at the maximum extreme as far as time to get something like this done. There were other small companies out there that had done it in like six or seven months where they just slammed it in. We didn't buy into that.

We had a ton of master data to move around, which was a big deal for us. It was a major, major effort that slowed us down

Scott Beutler, Project Co-Lead, Business Process

The Go-Live date was moved back to the latest possible date—the end of the 30-day grace period. The change management team used the project delay to emphasize scenario training that focused more on business process changes. Although the attendance at training had been very high, there was no formal user-certification process and user readiness continued to be a concern.

The Big Bang: December 30, 1997

On the Go-Live date, there were no consultants on site. Instead of paying the consultants to come in for 2 days in the middle of a holiday week, they were cut loose for the last week in December. Management knew that even if they struggled for those 2 days, they would be bringing the system back down and would have time to work on it over the New Year's holiday weekend to make any fixes. Core team members were on site at plants out in the field, and a help desk was manned by project team members. Besides saving some consultant costs, it was a symbolic move: The company was ready to operate R/3 on its own.

The co-leads had warned the business that "it was going to be ugly" in the beginning. Everything they had read and heard suggested that there would be an initial drop in productivity. The key was not to deny it, but to plan for it and manage through it. On Day 1 they were prepared to be able to operate at only the 50 percent level.

The project team members were kept on the team for only 2 months after the Go-Live date, rather than 4 months. The business units were clamoring for people to come back, and just did not want to wait any longer.

Ideally, we should have had them for another 60 days because we went through a lot of growing pains, and we could have done much better if we had the team together longer. But…it was unraveling on us and we just had to let people go.

Jim Davis, Project Co-Lead, Change Management

By the time they went live, most team members knew where they would be redeployed. Some went back to their old jobs, but several received promotions or new opportunities and many went into newly created jobs. Some of the extended team members found that their business groups continued to rely on them for their in-depth R/3 knowledge. A few of the power users went into SAP support positions within the IS organization.

BAT TAIWAN: IMPLEMENTING SAP FOR A STRATEGIC TRANSITION

We needed a new system to support the new business model. A/P and A/R had never been done in Taiwan before, and the timeline was very short. We told them SAP is not new to Asia, and if it works in operating companies similar to ours (like Singapore) there is no reason why it should not work for us. Furthermore, the integrated information derived from the SAP system is going to help make our jobs more efficient and meaningful. There was a huge buy-in.

Mr. Ma, BAT Taiwan Country Manager

Very few of our people had any experience in actually using an ERP system; they didn't have an integrated system view of things. So we depended a lot on the proven template. As a team we said there should be minimal, minimal changes to the template. We don't want to change the system and get away from those embedded best practices.

Mr. Lee, Project Co-Lead, BAT Taiwan

The Asia Pacific Regional IT Manager, Mr. Ponce, was reflecting on the recent SAP implementation in Taiwan. The project marked an important business transition for the Taiwan market, and it also represented a big victory for insourcing an SAP implementation at BAT. What were the important lessons from the implementation approach and management of this project? How could they be amplified as best practices to other parts of the Asia Pacific region and BAT as a whole?

Company Background

British American Tobacco (BAT) is a 99-year-old company in the tobacco industry that has grown to be one of the top three global players through organic growth and acquisitions. Formerly B.A.T. Industries, it spun off its financial services business in 1998

and merged with the global cigarette company Rothmans International in 1999. BAT's local and international brands are sold in six world regions: Africa, America Pacific, Asia Pacific, Europe, Latin America, and Mesca (Middle East and Central Asia). A seventh division, STC (Smoking Tobacco and Cigars), is a global division operating in more than 100 countries. Corporate headquarters for BAT is based at Globe House in London.

The profit centers are end markets, typically at the country level. Small- to medium-sized end-markets typically report into an area cluster, a self-sufficient management unit led by an area director. An end market is headed by a country manager who reports to an area director, and each area director reports to a regional director.

For example, the Asia Pacific region has five management units: Asia Pacific North (APN), Asia Pacific South (APS), Malaysia, Australasia, and Indonesia. BAT Taiwan is part of the APN management unit, which also includes Hong Kong, The People's Republic of China, and Macau. The country manager for Taiwan has a report line to the managing director for APN, who is also the country manager for China. The APN offices are based in Hong Kong.

BAT Taiwan

BAT Taiwan is a branch office of BAT Services, Ltd., UK (BATUKE), with responsibilities for trade and brand marketing. After the tobacco market in Taiwan was liberalized in 1987, imported cigarettes were allowed to be sold via local agents. Initially, BAT brands were sold in Taiwan by Brown & Williamson and BATUKE through different distributors. Beginning in 1992, all Brown & Williamson's brands were sold through the BATUKE network worldwide. As a result of this global initiative, the importation and distribution of all BAT brands in Taiwan was consolidated, with China Merchants, Ltd., being appointed as the sole importer/distributor for Taiwan. In 1999, the BAT-Rothmans merger resulted in another realignment. Rothmans used a local agent, Taiwan International Tobacco Company, as its sole distributor. In April 2000, both distributors were merged

EXHIBIT 1
Tax Law Change in Taiwan

Old Tax Law	New Tax Law
Monopoly tax at NT$830 per 1,000 sticks of cigarettes (mille)	1) Import duty levied 27% of CIF (import) price
	2) Excise tax @ NT$590 per 1,000 sticks
	3) Health tax @ NT$250 per 1,000 sticks
	4) Value added tax (VAT) @ 5% of consumer price

and now operate under a new corporate entity known as Concord Tobacco Company.

The Rothmans merger also resulted in a more progressive portfolio of brands being available to the BAT Taiwan market. Prior to the merger, BAT's major brand was SE555, but its 2.5-percent market share was declining due to its older consumer profile. After the merger, the BAT market share was slightly boosted from 4.9 percent to 5.3 percent, and the spend focus was shifted to Dunhill, an ex-Rothmans brand, which was more appealing to younger adults.[1] The Taiwan management team also rationalized its brands' stock keeping units (SKUs) to improve its marketing focus and use of resources.

Taiwan has more than 70,000 retail outlets, of which about 4,000 outlets are under five large convenience store chains: 7-11 (about 2,600 outlets), Family Mart (about 1,000), Circle K, Hi Life, and Niko Mart. These five large chain stores are still growing at a rapid pace, at the expense of the independent "mom and pop" stores and "beetle hawkers," and currently account for 43 percent of BAT's volume.

Taiwan's business environment has also been undergoing some major changes due to major bilateral negotiations in preparation for entry into the World Trade Organization (WTO). To provide a more level playing field for international tobacco companies, the Taiwan Tobacco and Wine Monopoly will have to be dissolved. Two new laws relating to the new administration and taxation of tobacco products were passed in April 2000, but have yet to be enforced, pending Taiwan's accession—which has been delayed by the deferment of China's entry. The legislated

change in Tobacco Tax legislation from a specific tax per mille to a mixed tax regime will have significant impacts on pricing, market size and profitability. (See Exhibit 1.)

In the face of these changing market dynamics, and the BAT-Rothmans merger, BAT Taiwan commissioned Bain Consulting to do a full market potential study, to assess the size of the market opportunities and to identify the investment opportunities. This study identified Taiwan as one of the key profitable growth markets in the Asia Pacific region. It also highlighted various strategic options to pursue in order to realize BAT potential in this market: Besides a higher level of investment behind its "drive brand" (Dunhill), a change in business model would be necessary to grow the business and to reap supply-chain savings.

Under the new business model, Taiwan would be directly importing its own products and selling directly to key accounts (e.g., big 5 convenience chains) and its distributor, who would also focus on direct store delivery, as opposed to selling only to the wholesale trade as it had in the past. The plan was to begin direct importing by January 1, 2001. The direct-sales operation would be piloted first in Taipei and then rolled out to the rest of Taiwan sometime before mid-year 2001.

The IT Function at BAT

The information technology (IT) function within BAT mirrors the overall company structure. The global CIO is located at Globe House and has direct reports with responsibilities for IT infrastructure, IT service delivery, e-business and business system initiatives, and IT people and processes. Under the global CIO, there has been an increased emphasis on global strategies to help reduce the costs of implementing integrated IT solutions

---

[1]The launch of Dunhill 1mg in July 2000 contributed to the growth of the Dunhill brand family by 170 percent in 2000.

and ongoing IT service delivery. For example, the newly appointed head of business integration at Globe House has global responsibilities for IT standardization and consolidation initiatives.

BAT currently delivers IT services via three data centers geographically located in Europe (Hamburg, Germany), North America (Macon, Georgia), and Asia Pacific (Kuala Lumpur, Malaysia), and are governed by regional management. All three data centers now operate under a shared services model: by consolidating IT operational support functions at the regional level, economies can be achieved, and these cost savings contribute to the profitability of the BAT end markets that purchase their IT services via a chargeback arrangement.

Europe was the first region to extend the shared services concept beyond data center operations to include application services: In 1997 an Enterprise Center of Excellence (ECoE) began to offer hard-to-find SAP expertise to northern European countries for their R/3 implementation projects. Today the ECoE is also providing SAP services for Latin America.

In the Asia Pacific region, a data center (APDC) was established in Technology Park, Malaysia, in early 1999. Since that time, the APDC has evolved into a shared services organization (APSS) that combines two business streams: a data center and a competency center (center of excellence) for SAP. Personnel with SAP and other IT skill sets are readily available in Malaysia at a cost quite low compared to the other markets, due in part to early SAP installations in the oil and gas industries and recent government incentives for economic growth in high-technology industries.

While the data centers/shared services units are providing support for shared business system solutions, IT organizations that exist at each management unit are responsible for managing the use of IT for their respective end markets. These responsibilities include identifying business requirements, identifying IT solutions, building business cases for IT projects, and managing support services (including local, shared and outsourced services). For example, APN has an IT organization based in Hong Kong with responsibilities covering all the end markets in APN, including China, Hong Kong, and Taiwan. The smaller end markets typically operate with very few IT resources of their own but share resources from the management unit center. For example, BAT Taiwan only has one IT technical support resource onsite for desktop and LAN support, who has a dotted-line report to the IT organization for APN.

New Computer Systems for Taiwan: The ERP Choice

The new business model for BAT Taiwan created a need for a new computer system for functions and processes not previously performed. The Taiwan end market needed to have its own accounts payable and accounts receivable systems because these functions had previously been handled by BAT U.K. It also needed a system to support direct selling and inventory management for multiple sales channels, not just for a single distributor.

Two ERP platform standards had been prescribed for all BAT solutions by 1998: SAP R/3 and Sage Tetra CS/3. The Sage system was selected for less complex, smaller operations that did not need the functionality of SAP and that required a low-cost ERP solution. SAP R/3 was initially viewed as the standard solution for larger, more complex BAT markets only, because it had proven to be a very expensive system to implement and maintain. However, because the Sage system did not scale well, it was no longer viewed as the best solution for BAT organizations in rapidly growing markets. In mid-1999, for example, the former head of IT for APN (now the Asia Pacific Regional IT manager) had put an ERP implementation for the Hong Kong end market on hold because of the weaknesses of both standard options: CS/3 was not viewed as a sufficiently robust system for the Hong Kong market, but the costs of an SAP solution at that time appeared astronomical.

Although Globe House sets strategy and dictates the standard IT platforms, each end market chooses which ERP platform standard to implement, as well as when to implement it. During 1999 and the first 6 months of 2000, however, several BAT regions had gained much more expertise in implementing both ERP platforms. Some of these implementations were brought forward to achieve Y2K compliance. Other projects were undertaken as part of data integration initiatives for the Rothmans merger: Rothmans brands were transferred to BAT (according to local government restrictions) and BAT's processes and standard systems were adopted for all operations.[2]

Within the Asia Pacific region, SAP R/3 projects had been carried out in Australia, Malaysia, and Singapore. Malaysia and Singapore were originally implemented based on the Symphony template; following the merger with Rothmans, however, the Malaysian implementation was changed significantly and it is now regarded as using a different template. Australia is currently using a BAT SAP system for manufacturing, and a Rothmans SAP system for sales. Hence, the Asia Pacific region is currently using three different SAP R/3 templates to satisfy area needs. Many of these projects had been done with Andersen Consulting (now Accenture) as the implementation partner, some using SAP's rapid implementation methodology (Accelerated SAP or ASAP). Because of the success of these projects and growing pressures for common data standards, it was expected that SAP would become the

---

[2]Some of Rothmans' business units had implemented SAP, and other business units were using BPCS on an AS/400 platform.

solution for all end markets over time, if it could be implemented at a reasonable cost.

> When reviewing the APSS model for implementing SAP, we found that the difference in total cost of ownership between CS3 and SAP became insignificant if we use the common configuration approach. Rather than taking an interim solution for cost reason, it's more effective for us to commit a marginally higher investment and advance directly to the endgame solution—which is SAP.
>
> *Head of IT, APN*

In July 2000, a 2-day study of the SAP project for Taiwan was conducted by the APSS Applications Manager for SAP with a team that had representatives from APN, BAT Australia, BAT Singapore, and APSS. The outcome was a high-level system specification document for implementing SAP R/3. The recommendation was that R/3 modules for sales and distribution (SD), materials management (MM—purchasing and inventory management), financials (FI including fixed assets), and controlling (CO including profitability analysis) be implemented in two phases. Phase 1 would support direct importing and distribution to one customer (a former distributor) and would be operational by January 1, 2001. Phase 2 would support direct sales and distribution to key accounts and be operational within 6 months later.

Selecting an IT Partner

Although APN IT could provide project management expertise as well as PC desktop and LAN support, it had no SAP R/3 expertise. An implementation partner with functional and technical SAP experience was therefore needed. Further, Taiwan needed a contract for IT services with a BAT global data center to host the SAP application as well as a contract for ongoing application maintenance: IT resources would need to be contracted for periodic system requests such as new reports, as well as for the periodic software upgrades provided by SAP.

Following the high-level study, both the European and the Asia Pacific shared services organizations were invited to submit proposals for Taiwan's R/3 implementation as well as ongoing operations and support. Taiwan would then select the best proposal based on the R/3 template and other considerations.

The European shared services groups already provided computer support for BAT Taiwan as a user of SAP financials for the BAT U.K. operations. Because Taiwan had experienced the European data center's high-quality operational support first-hand, continuing to work with this data center was a clear option. In addition, the SAP Center of Excellence in Europe was a viable partner for the R/3 implementation project.

The SAP application services group that was part of APSS was a newer group, but had played a part in the other SAP implementations in the AP region. APSS had also been running SAP applications for Australia, Malaysia, and Singapore for more than 16 months at the time of the Taiwan proposal, so APSS also had a proven track record as a regional data center for SAP.

Although Andersen Consulting (now Accenture) had been the implementation partner on a number of BAT R/3 implementations for the AP region, such as those in Australia and Singapore, R/3 project costs using an external implementation partner had been quite expensive. For a new, still small, Taiwan end market, project costs were a very important consideration, so the decision was made to not request a bid from an external consulting firm. In addition, a regional BAT partner would be more knowledgeable about BAT business processes and existing BAT templates for SAP implementations

Proposals were received from the shared services organizations in Europe (EDC and EcoE) and the Asia Pacific (APSS). The decision was made to go with APSS for the R/3 implementation, as well as for SAP hosting and ongoing support, for a number of reasons.

First, the proposals from both Europe (EcoE) and APSS were quite similar with respect to implementing R/3. Although the European shared services group had more extensive SAP implementation experience, APSS had recently used a template (code-named "Symphony") for an SAP implementation with a similar business model in BAT Singapore. Thus, there was high confidence in the SAP functional and technical expertise in the AP region.

Second, for the ongoing operations and maintenance roles, APSS had two major advantages over the EDC: lower personnel costs in the AP region compared to Europe and the same time zone. By mid-2000, the annual operational costs at APSS for hosting an SAP R/3 user were U.S.$3,500, and were expected to drop further in 2001. BAT Taiwan would not have to purchase the SAP software licenses, which would be held by APSS.

> BAT Taiwan saves a lot of time and effort by letting APSS purchase and own the licenses and we only pay a monthly fee. We don't have to track the licenses as assets, manage maintenance contracts and payments, process procurement and track global pricing policies and terms. We also do not have to worry about selling excess licenses when the number of users comes down.
>
> *Head of IT, APN*

> It does not matter where the support group sits. What is crucial is the skill competencies, at the right price, in a politically stable region. Since we're using standard BAT operations, the quality aspect is assured. So cost and support capability become the most critical.
>
> *Mr. Ma, BAT Taiwan Country Manager*

Because Taiwan was in the same time zone as the APSS organization, its people would be able to communicate more easily about their support needs with the shared services group in APSS than with the shared services group located 7 hours away in Europe.

There were also some "natural synergies" with APSS that would help with communications: Taiwan, unlike the rest of the Mandarin-speaking world, uses only the Chinese language for business transactions.[3] The APSS staff in Kuala Lumpur, like other Malaysian businesses, includes many people of Chinese heritage, including some who speak Mandarin.

> The significant time difference between Taiwan and Europe was problematic, as was the lack of knowledge of the Chinese language. Taiwanese are not all fluent in English, and the local system requirements would include preparing invoices and printing reports in Chinese.
>
> *Major Project Management Manager, APN IT*

Taiwan's R/3 Project

The APSS project plan for Taiwan outlined a fixed-cost implementation budget of U.S.$100,000 for Phase 1 and an estimated budget of U.S.$50,000 for Phase 2. Phase 1 would involve 250 APSS man-days and consulting fees of U.S.$77,700. The other costs would include technology upgrades and direct expenses for travel and living expenses for the APSS consultants. The Phase 2 costs would include an estimated U.S.$30,000 for software development costs for unique local requirements.

The Taiwan office named this project Confucius because the project kickoff took place during the week of Confucius' birthday and it was hoped that the intellectual capability pooled from a number of areas within BAT would be as good as that of the renowned Chinese philosopher, if not better.

The project cost was based on several assumptions. (See Exhibit 2.) One key assumption of the plan related to the use of the Symphony template developed by APSS and used in Singapore (BATS). By using this template, Taiwan could leverage BAT's best practices for the new business processes, as well as take advantage of a template that was recently reported to be 95 percent compliant with the corporate data standards set by Globe House.[4]

The Symphony template initially included configuration for the financial and controlling modules, with other modules added later.

---

[3]Taiwan uses the traditional Chinese language, rather than simplified Chinese, as its official language. Chinese is the written form of the language; Mandarin is the spoken form of the language.

[4]A recent review of BAT templates across the regions sponsored by Globe House concluded that the Symphony template had the highest compliance with the corporate data template among all the current templates.

The four primary business processes would be order-to-cash (accounts receivable), requisition-to-payment (accounts payable), inventory management, and plan-and-manage-enterprise, which includes profitability analysis. However, because many of the business processes would be new to the Taiwan office and few staff members had prior in-depth experience with integrated systems in general, few changes to the template itself were anticipated. Customization would only be done for legal or statutory reporting purposes. Further, BAT Taiwan was very mindful of the dangers of customizing standard systems.

> One of the things I learned from my previous company and in BAT was that when we modified the system to suit our local operational needs, normally in the name of enhancement, we changed the system to a point beyond recognition. That's where the problems start. Later, we found that it was difficult to fit in vendors' enhancements, modules, and whatever. To me, it's the resistance to take on processes that have been established and tested as a more efficient way of doing things; we tend to hold onto old habits. It's a mind-set challenge.
>
> *Mr. Ma, BAT Taiwan Country Manager*

For Phase 1, a three-stage implementation approach, developed by APSS with reference to the ASAP methodology, was to be used. (See Exhibit 3.) The business users would participate in the detailed requirements study, in cleaning up data to be converted, verifying the data conversion, and participating in system testing and system rollout. The system would be configured by APSS personnel to reflect Taiwan's business environment, with such details as the number of warehouses and the accounts to be debited or credited in specific circumstances. The development environment would consist of a three-instance development landscape with DEV (development), QAS (quality assurance), and PRD (production) servers, all housed in Kuala Lumpur. R/3 version 3.1H would be implemented for Phase 1.

The plan for Phase 2 included potential solutions to two system requirements unique to doing business in the Taiwan end market. First, an invoicing system required by the Taiwan government (Government Universal Invoice, referred to as GUI) would need to be purchased and integrated with the SAP system. Because this capability would be required for doing business in Taiwan, it was anticipated that the module would be developed by SAP Taiwan. Second, a Chinese language module would be required because Taiwan conducts business communications almost exclusively in its official language. All reports, including those produced by the GUI, and certain parts of the system needed to be in the official Chinese language. APSS planned to request help from SAP Malaysia in producing such a module.

For Phase 1, APSS would provide an application team leader and three other full-time application consultants onsite (which could include contract employees hired by APSS from

EXHIBIT 2
APSS Assumptions for Cost Estimating Phases 1 and 2

- BATS template is extended to include BAT Taiwan in this implementation, and business requirements not supported by BATS template are considered out of scope, with the exception of Fixed Assets, which is not part of the template but will be set up for BAT Taiwan.

- BATS template remains at v3.1H and will be upgraded to v4.6x in Q2 2001. There will be no SAP upgrade during the course of this project. The cost of v4.6x upgrade shall be shared with BATS and BAT Mkt. The cost of upgrade to BAT Taiwan is estimated to be at U.S.$57,000 but the amount will be reviewed again before the upgrade commences.

- BAT Taiwan project is to commence not earlier than mid-September 2000 and a lead time of 4–6 weeks is required to mobilize the resources once the project is awarded to APSS.

- Estimate is based on the high-level understanding gathered during the 2-day SAP study in July 2000. The system specification, documented after the study, forms the basis of this proposal.

- The estimate takes into consideration efforts for 18 customized reports (please refer to Appendix B) in Phase 1.

- A total of 24 business processes will be covered in this project. Refer to Appendix A for details.

- Documents printed in Chinese are not a requirement in Phase 1.

- BAT Taiwan will use the data center services from APSS and will use the existing hardware in APSS. Please refer to Appendix C for the service-level agreement.

- Existing WAN bandwidth is sufficient but will need to reconfirm during the project.

- BAT Taiwan will assume project management, communication plan and execution, development of user procedures, and local infrastructure management.

- Project site and resources are based in Taiwan and there is no necessity to travel outside of Taiwan head office.

- Full-time resources are identified and assigned to the project as per project plan to ensure on-time delivery and quality output of project deliverables.

- The business resources assigned to the project are subject-matter experts in their respective functional areas, and are either decision makers or are in a position to influence the process owners.

- BAT Taiwan resources assigned to the project will be equipped with the knowledge to be the first-level support after Go Live.

- A single set of chart of accounts is used by BATS, BAT Mkt and BAT Taiwan. BATS finance manager has been appointed as custodian for COA. Any request for COA maintenance shall be forwarded by the respective end markets to the custodian for action.

their local market). These four APSS team members would work at the BAT Taiwan offices, beginning with the project kick-off at the end of September 2000 until 2 weeks after the implementation date. A part-time APSS programmer would also be assigned to the project, but would primarily work out of the APSS offices in Kuala Lumpur.

Initial Schedule

The original schedule was to implement the R/3 modules in two phases. Phase 1, to be initiated September 25 and completed by January 2, involved the modules to support direct importation: parts of the SD, MM (purchasing and inventory

EXHIBIT 3
Eight-Week, Three-Stage Project Approach

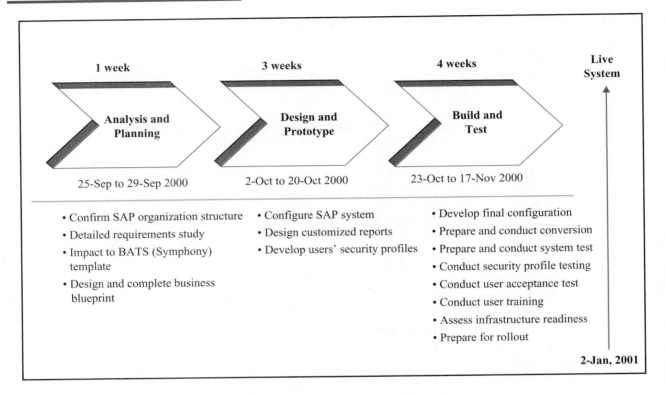

1 week	3 weeks	4 weeks	Live System
Analysis and Planning	**Design and Prototype**	**Build and Test**	
25-Sep to 29-Sep 2000	2-Oct to 20-Oct 2000	23-Oct to 17-Nov 2000	

- Confirm SAP organization structure
- Detailed requirements study
- Impact to BATS (Symphony) template
- Design and complete business blueprint

- Configure SAP system
- Design customized reports
- Develop users' security profiles

- Develop final configuration
- Prepare and conduct conversion
- Prepare and conduct system test
- Conduct security profile testing
- Conduct user acceptance test
- Conduct user training
- Assess infrastructure readiness
- Prepare for rollout

2-Jan, 2001

management), and FI/CO modules. Phase 2, to be completed by June 2001, would involve implementing the additional modules needed for direct sales and distribution to key accounts, as well as the specific invoicing system required by the Taiwan government and software to support the reports in Chinese for the area offices. The Phase 1 system would therefore support importing to just one customer: Taiwan's current distributor. The distributor's system would continue to be used for the GUI reporting until Phase 2 provided these customized capabilities.

Initially, the plan was to complete the Phase 1 development and testing within 8 weeks (by the end of November) to provide a buffer for training the business users in not only the new system, but also in the process changes associated with the new business model. The business users would begin with 18 customized reports.

Although the APSS staff would be full-time, the team members from Taiwan needed to continue to perform some of their current functions during the project. Further, the team members would also need to help train temporary or new personnel that would be brought in near the end of the project.

The Project Team

The leaders for the project team brought together three sources of expertise from the three organizations involved: IT project management from APN; BAT template, SAP package, and technical knowledge from APSS; and local business needs from BAT Taiwan. The country manager for Taiwan, Mr. Ma, served as the business sponsor for the project. The project leaders from APN, Taiwan, and APSS were empowered to make project decisions and formally reported to Mr. Ma and the head of IT for APN, via a project steering committee. (See Exhibit 4.)

The Major Project Manager in the IT APN organization, who had previously been a consultant for one of the Big Five consulting firms but did not have any SAP training, was the IT co-lead responsible for overall management of the project. He developed the schedule and task breakdown, the timing of each task, and the resources needed. His work plan became the final project plan, and he was responsible for monitoring the achievement of the milestones and verifying the quality and scope of the resulting system.

Initially, the lead business role for the project was played by the manager of finance for BAT Taiwan. However, at the time of

EXHIBIT 4
Project Team Composition at Time of Kickoff

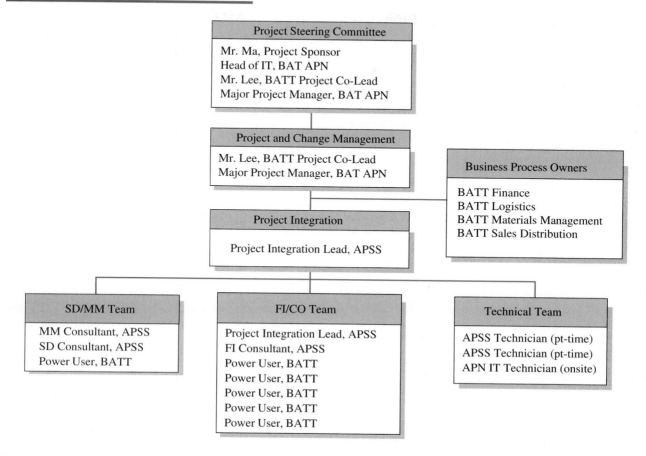

the project kickoff, she announced her resignation from BAT. The lead business manager role for the project was then assumed by Mr. Lee, who was at the time the trade marketing manager for BAT Taiwan and was the logistics process owner on the project. Lee had been Country Manager in Thailand and had experience with the core processes (such as accounts receivable and inventory management) during earlier employment at Johnson & Johnson in the U.S.

For the remainder of the project, Lee took responsibility for the business process owner role for finance as well as logistics. As project co-lead, he was also responsible for co-leading the change management efforts for the project. Two other Taiwan managers also played business process owner roles.

An APSS manager, who was a certified accountant with an MBA, was selected to play the Project Integration Lead role and to lead the APSS development team for the Taiwan project.

This APSS manager was selected to lead the project integration because he had strong knowledge of financials, the business, and the [SAP] FI module. Plus he had managed other ERP

project implementations. He also was able to speak Mandarin, to foster communications.

SAP Applications Manager, APSS

The APSS Project Integration lead was responsible for process integration as well as the day-to-day progress of the project and the work by the APSS team members. He and one other APSS consultant were assigned to the FI/CO modules; one APSS consultant each was assigned to the SD and MM modules. There were two part-time technical team members at APSS (see Exhibit 4).

The initial plan was for the four full-time members of the APSS development team to go to Taiwan for 3 weeks at a time and then return to Kuala Lumpur (KL) for the following weekend for personal reasons. However, government regulations permitted nonresidents to work in Taiwan for only 2 weeks at a time. Therefore the return weekend visits to KL became biweekly. Further, because they could obtain a visa for only 2 months, they remained in Kuala Lumpur for 1 week every

2 months to renew their visas. The week-long visa stays in KL were staggered so that two APSS team members always remained onsite in Taiwan. Pressing issues were discussed with absent team members by phone as needed, and the Project Integration Lead provided a weekly progress report by phone to the APSS Applications manager, who was serving as the APSS lead on an R/3 project in Thailand during several weeks of the Taiwan project.

> Everything was coordinated with timelines. You could do the project at a distance, but being co-located made it a lot easier: when you hit an issue, you could say, "Let's have a meeting to discuss this."
>
> *SAP Application Consultant, APSS*

The manager of finance for BAT Taiwan was initially responsible for choosing the "power users" for the project team based on information provided by APSS about the user expertise that would be needed. Five Taiwan employees were selected to work on the FI/CO modules (see Exhibit 4). Only one user was assigned to work on the SD and MM modules because no one in the Taiwan office had previously been performing these functions; the person had gained experience with sales and logistics functions when employed at Rothmans.

None of the Taiwan users had prior experience on SAP projects, but some users had entered data into the SAP R/3 financials system (of BATUKE) and one user had some experience with Oracle systems. All team members were considered fast learners who would be able to pick up the new system quickly.

> The good thing about Taiwan is that most of the managers here are pretty new in the organization. They are young, well-educated (many have MBAs), and have a high level of computer literacy. They are open-minded and are more prepared to take on changes. They knew that whatever we were doing in the past, things were going to be different, and they knew that what we had was cumbersome, that we could not go forward with a bunch of non-integrated systems. They welcomed the [SAP] system; this was going to help them do their job. Their commitment level was extremely high. So the credit is due to the people themselves.
>
> *Mr. Ma, BAT Taiwan Country Manager*

All of the Taiwan team members continued to also do their regular jobs during the project. One manager, who had just rejoined the Taiwan office in a supervisory role, was able to devote 70 percent of his efforts to the project. The BAT Taiwan Project Co-Lead was able to juggle the workloads of the part-time project team members that reported to him. The trade marketing position was left open, but the country manager helped with that role.

The Taiwan operations were small at that time. This made it more difficult for the project team, because they had to deal with day-to-day activities as well as the project. But they also had full senior management support.

> *Major Project Manager, APN IT*

There were three technical team members (see Exhibit 4). The APN IT resource already based in Taiwan was responsible for the telecommunications infrastructure to support system access by five business partners in Taiwan. The R/3 Basis expert from APSS worked offsite until a week before the Go-Live date, when he spent 2 weeks in Taiwan. The third person on the technical team was responsible for creating ABAP reports. Later in the project, she was replaced by a programmer from SAP Malaysia. Just prior to Go Live, this programmer spent 3 weeks in Taiwan to ensure that all the reports were functioning correctly.

Kickoff Meeting

A 1-day project kickoff meeting was held in Taiwan at the end of September and was run by the manager of finance for BAT Taiwan. Most of the project team members and all of the business process owners were present, as were the brand and trade marketing managers. The project co-leads from APSS and APN talked to the whole office staff—both expert and casual users—about the need to be supportive of the project team members over the coming months.

> They made a presentation to the whole office—whether they would be actual users or a final user at the end of the day. They said, "These people are taking on a lot in a short period of time...and you should not make too many unreasonable demands during this time period." They were told that the project was a critical part of the full potential initiative, so let's pull together on this one.
>
> *Mr. Lee, Project Co-Lead, BAT Taiwan*

The APSS team members worked in a conference room just down the hall from the other managers. All the team members got along well together, both in the work environment and socially—including some weekend get-togethers.

Exhibit 5 documents the High-Level Work Plan with the 8-week project milestones. During the Business Blueprint Phase (high-level requirements), the APSS team members met with the key users to explain the processes in the template and to learn about local needs. The fact that the APSS personnel knew BAT's business really helped, because Taiwan had not had to deal with accounts payable, accounts receivable, or inventory in the past.

> They added a lot of value. When we needed to decide how we wanted to configure something, they would say, "The BAT way is this."
>
> *Mr. Lee, Project Co-Lead, BAT Taiwan*

EXHIBIT 5
Work Plan and Milestones for Phase 1

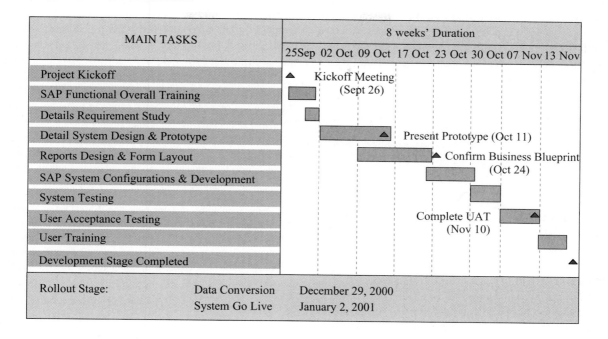

MAIN TASKS	8 weeks' Duration
	25Sep 02 Oct 09 Oct 17 Oct 23 Oct 30 Oct 07 Nov 13 Nov
Project Kickoff	▲ Kickoff Meeting (Sept 26)
SAP Functional Overall Training	
Details Requirement Study	
Detail System Design & Prototype	▲ Present Prototype (Oct 11)
Reports Design & Form Layout	▲ Confirm Business Blueprint (Oct 24)
SAP System Configurations & Development	
System Testing	
User Acceptance Testing	Complete UAT (Nov 10) ▲
User Training	
Development Stage Completed	▲

Rollout Stage:	Data Conversion	December 29, 2000
	System Go Live	January 2, 2001

They knew the alternatives and the impact on the user and the actual process. For example, online approval of a purchase order sounds good, but they asked, "Who will approve it when the person is out of the office?" because someone must go into the system to do it. [Singapore implemented online approval, but it was not effective—so in the end it was not used.] APSS could advise us on these issues.

Major Project Manager, APN IT

The APSS people knew BAT's processes. They asked us to review the blueprint. I had worked with Oracle systems and knew how to link modules—Materials Management and Finance.

FI/CO Team Member, BAT Taiwan

The initial configuration was really good. We worked really hard. The APSS team understands our operations and our industry. Also, they spoke my primary language [Mandarin].

MM/SD Team Member, BAT Taiwan

Because BAT Taiwan had no experience with direct distribution, help was sought from some workers at the distributor. Some configuration was also done to take into account the expected future changes in government regulations regarding the payment of taxes that would affect product pricing, as well as the key accounts that would be introduced in a future phase. These changes could be activated when needed. A prototype was ready by the third week.

Scope Change: Moving Forward Phase 2

In October, the project leaders recognized that some of the Phase 2 changes would already be done in the initial configuration, so it might be possible to move Phase 2 forward. They believed that Phase 1 could be completed easily within the 8-week period and that the team had the resources to also complete Phase 2 by January, 2001. They consulted with the APSS Applications Manager, the Head of IT at APN, and the other project team members, and it was agreed to move Phase 2 forward. A revised proposal was prepared by APSS, and the phase was renamed 1A to signal that the Phase 1 resources would continue on the project team, rather than have a totally different implementation.

Changing the schedule for the two-phase implementation greatly increased the risks of the project from both an IT and a business perspective. Phase 1A included the two requirements that were specific to the Taiwan implementation: the government-designed invoicing system (GUI) and the Chinese language module. These additional requirements increased the technical complexity of the initial implementation, as well as the need for training on additional business processes. APN management therefore initiated a formal review before the end of October to reassess the risks and to determine whether the project was under-resourced.

The APN review team consisted of the IT head at APN and two finance managers from Hong Kong. The team leads walked through the project and discussions were held in

Taiwan with the business sponsor. As a result of this review, BAT Taiwan made plans to hire additional temporary staff prior to the user acceptance testing phase to help relieve the business team members who would be involved. In addition, Hong Kong-based APN staff (mostly from finance, but also logistics and IT) would receive training prior to implementation in case they were needed for emergency backup support. Further, APSS staff would stay longer than originally anticipated following the rollout.

> There were a lot of concerns. It was a short timeframe and for the first time it was managed by APSS—not jointly managed with Andersen Consulting. A lot of 'teething problems' had been experienced in other project rollouts, so APSS consultants were requested to stay longer to provide onsite support.
>
> *APSS Project Integration Lead*

The functionality required for the GUI system[5] was originally expected to be part of the version 4.6 upgrade of SAP R/3 proposed for the Phase 2 project. At the end of November it was learned that SAP could not deliver a version of the GUI for the 3.1H system prior to January 1. Another vendor's GUI system would therefore need to be purchased and interfaced to the R/3 system (as a bolt-on). With advice from BAT's auditors (PricewaterhouseCoopers), a system from a local supplier that had been implemented by a number of other companies in Taiwan was identified and a contract was signed in mid-December.

The Chinese language module was needed to print reports. SAP Malaysia offered to help, but would not have the resources to do it before mid-March. Some other companies that were developing the software as a bolt-on were asked to make presentations, and a system was purchased from E-Com. The APSS Basis team member was scheduled to come to Taiwan a week before Go Live to ensure that the system would print correctly.

User Acceptance Testing and Change Management

Because of the change in Taiwan's business model, the change management activities associated with the SAP implementation involved defining new staff roles and communicating with all personnel, as well as providing training for those involved in the new system. The Project Co-lead at BAT Taiwan, Mr. Lee, was largely responsible for change management as the business lead on the project team, although all the training was done by APSS.

Temporary personnel were brought in before user acceptance testing (UAT) to perform functions usually done by project team members. Three temporary accountants were trained for 2 weeks on the general ledger, issuing checks, and paying employees. Similarly, two extra people were brought on to help in the MM/SD areas. One of these people had previously worked for the distributor and knew the existing system very well; she later became a permanent BAT employee. The other person, who used to work for a consumer products company, had considerable experience in order processing.

The UAT phase involved all of the users on the project team. Most of the other finance personnel had received exposure to the new processes during earlier phases of the project. Other Taiwan personnel were trained in early November as part of the UAT phase of the project. Few changes were required as a result of the testing. However, the integrated nature of the system did cause some problems.

> There were some hiccups here and there. During the user test phase, there were some apprehensions, partly due to the lack of understanding of the system, and the process adjustments that need to be made. With motivation and support from each other within the team, they managed to pull it through with great success.
>
> *Mr. Ma, BAT Taiwan Country Manager*

Following the UAT, an additional 20 people—mostly in marketing functions—received overview training from the APSS consultants. A key challenge here was how to convey the integrated nature of the system when most people were used to focusing on a single function.

Quality Reviews

Globe House provided funding for two quality reviews. The first one was to be a quality review after the user acceptance test, prior to implementation. The second one would be part of a post-implementation review process a few months after implementation.

The country manager decided that having a third-party independent of BAT to do the review would be a good idea, and SAP Taiwan was selected. The first review took place in early December and took the form of the quality check for the Final Preparation Phase in the ASAP methodology. The results were positive and the project team prepared for the final steps: Data Conversion on December 29 and Go Live on January 2, 2001.

> We were unconcerned about whether someone from SAP or an internal auditor did the review. The issue was: Is the system quality up to the mark? Is there anything substandard that could cause a system failure?
>
> *Mr. Ma, BAT Taiwan Country Manager*

Globe House has sponsored some of the quality reviews. It depends on whether the project management would like to have

---

[5]The GUI is an official invoice that must be prepared using invoice numbers issued by the government. When a business uses up its assigned range of numbers, it must reapply for a further set of numbers, and so on. Six to eight such reports must be submitted to the government for tax purposes every 4 to 8 weeks.

it done or not. In Brazil, the reviews are being done by an external consulting partner, but it's a much bigger project: Once a week a person comes in and reviews the implementation progress.

SAP Program Manager,
Business Integration, Globe House

Go Live

Phases 1 and 1A went live according to the revised project plan on January 2, 2001, with one major exception: The functionality for processing the key accounts and for printing the reports with the Chinese language module were included in this release, but the GUI interface was not integrated with SAP until mid-January. Instead, the team's contingency plan was used for the first 2 weeks in January: the sales orders were entered into BAT Taiwan's R/3 system and then submitted to the system used by the country's long-time distributor to produce the required government reports. This process made the January close very difficult, although it was still completed within a week.

There was also a delay in the installation of a new telecommunications line leased from the government-owned telecommunications company in Taiwan. This meant that a more expensive international dial-up line had to be used to connect to Kuala Lumpur via Hong Kong until early in February, when the leased line could be phased in.

Initially, there were also some order processing problems. The Go Live date was close to the Chinese New Year (January 24), which meant heavy numbers of orders had to be processed at the same time as the new business processes were being implemented. Some orders were delivered late and sometimes an order contained the wrong pricing, but within 6 weeks, these problems were worked out. The second close in February went smoothly.

The original Phase 1 plan was for all APSS consultants to remain onsite in Taiwan for 2 weeks after Go Live. Because of the new Phase 1A schedule, the business sponsor asked for 4 weeks of support. A compromise solution was to provide two APSS team members onsite for 6 weeks following Go Live. In addition to the Project Integration lead, the MM consultant from APSS remained onsite for the first 2 weeks and helped coach the users through the new processes, and then the second financial consultant and SD consultant from APSS were onsite for the succeeding 2 weeks.

As of January 2001, APSS is running three separate SAP systems for (1) Singapore, Taiwan, and Thailand, (2) Malaysia, and (3) Australia. BAT Taiwan's R/3 system is run on the same client system as those of Singapore and Thailand.[6] Because all three systems use the same template, each country shares the same organizational hierarchy, chart of accounts, and data definitions. For example, finance is subdivided into the three areas of operating, marketing, and corporate finance, while marketing is subdivided into trade and brand marketing. Each country is defined by a company code, which represents a legal entity for reporting purposes. Although the basic processes within the client are the same, some configuration is specific to the company code. For example, a country can have its own configuration to reflect how it wants to manage costs, how it structures its departments, and with codes for its own area offices and key accounts. Further, controlling area and operating concern are defined at the company code level. There is no consolidation of financials or profitability analysis at the regional level. Exhibit 6 shows the cost center hierarchy for BAT Taiwan.

Ongoing Operational Support by APSS

In the first 3 months of service, the production server running the Taiwan system had been down only once for a period of approximately 2 hours. However, in the weeks immediately following Go Live, procedural errors led to a few processing errors. For example, incorrect data was recorded on some occasions when the users specified an incorrect company code (equivalent to a country code).

A multi-tier support plan is in place. Tier 1 support is provided locally and APSS provides support services via their help line based on six priority levels. (See Exhibit 7.) Contacts with an APSS consultant on the original Taiwan project team are sometimes feasible, but not guaranteed. However, learnings from the Taiwan project and the modifications to the Symphony template for the local system requirements have been captured in a Lotus Notes database accessible to other members of the APSS support team.

User ID and authorization changes are authorized by designated business managers, and these requests are submitted to APSS via an Excel spreadsheet format. As noted earlier, APSS owns the SAP licenses and leases them to the end market as needed.

Requests for system changes (new functionality, new configuration, or new reports) for Taiwan are reviewed and authorized by the Project Co-Lead at BAT Taiwan, who is now head of finance for the Taiwan office. Some problems have surfaced over time and certain changes have been requested as users have learned more about how the system works. For instance, a differential pricing policy was not initially specified, but has been added to the configuration.

Post-Implementation in Taiwan

A project celebration was held as part of a Chinese New Year celebration for the BAT Taiwan office. It involved dinner for the heads of the Taiwan departments and all of the business users on the team. At the dinner, each Taiwan project member who

---

[6]The Thailand R/3 implementation was also completed in Fall 2000.

EXHIBIT 6
Cost Center Hierarchy for Taiwan's R/3 System

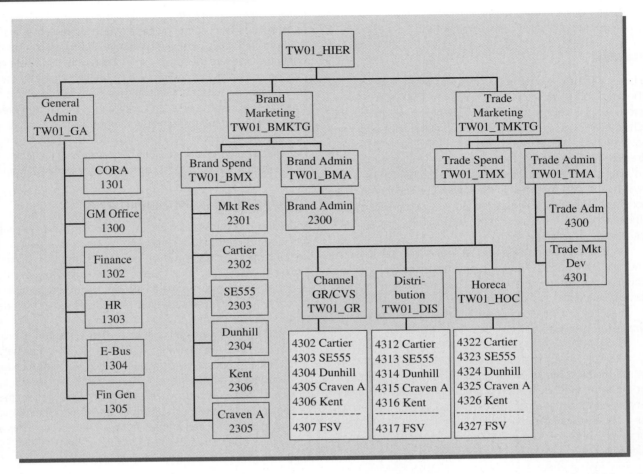

was not a department head received a surprise bonus of a month's salary in recognition of their effort and extra-long hours.

People say that it usually takes a year to do an SAP implementation, or maybe only 6 months when you have the experience. Here it was 4 months for the implementation; it was so fast you're maybe a little afraid that things may still go wrong. But now we're starting to feel proud.

FI/CO Team Member, BAT Taiwan

Over the past few years, BAT Taiwan has grown from 20 to 100 personnel as it first absorbed Rothmans and then evolved into a full trading company. All data entry is now done in the Taipei office, and invoices are printed at the five area offices. Within the Taipei office a few work imbalances still continued to exist because of the lack of widespread SAP expertise and the loss of some expert business users. For example, the MM/SD lead still regularly worked a few hours of overtime each evening even after the new GUI system was in place.

A system upgrade to R/3 version 4.6C is planned for July 2001, and some improvements to the process configurations could be made at the same time.

SAP is a very powerful application for a small market. Initially you go through a stage where you learn the basics but you don't yet know all the functionality. When you become proficient with the system, you begin to look at other needs. APSS needs to be ready to show the business how to use the system better—what the more complex processes are that they couldn't absorb before.

Mr. Ponce, Asia Pacific Regional IT Manager

A formal post-implementation review, sponsored by Globe House, was to be conducted toward the end of March 2001. Other BAT managers are expected to be interested in learning how the implementation was accomplished so quickly, at such a low cost, and whether the business users were happy with the quality of the system. Within APN, Hong Kong would probably be the next end market to implement SAP.

EXHIBIT 7

Help Desk Support by APSS

Priority	Definition	Users Affected	Examples	Minimum Service Level *
P1	The entire business is stopped, a business process has failed and/or an entire site is affected.	All	System is unavailable, billing and delivery cannot be processed, month-end processing cannot be completed.	95% resolved in 1 hour = Application & APSS (HD, Sec, Ops) – Resolution External Engineer (third party, i.e., Equant/IBM) – Active assistance
P2	Issue impacts a module, prevents a large number of users from doing their work, and/or a workaround is not available.	Group	Sales and Distribution module fails, orders cannot be taken, volume is too large for a manual workaround.	90% resolved in 2 business hours
P3	Issue impacts a module and prevents a large number of users from doing their work and a workaround is available.	Group	Financial journals cannot be posted but it does not affect third parties, volume is small for a manual workaround.	90% resolved in 3 business hours
P4	User is prevented from doing work due to critical task failure, no workaround exists.	Single	User cannot print documentation, user profile is not complete.	90% resolved in 4 business hours
P5	A user is prevented from completing a function, but a workaround can be provided, and/or problem is minor.	Single	Automatic check printing fails but critical payments can still be processed with manual checks.	90% resolved in 2 business days
P6	Query or request.	N/A	How to extract data for reporting	90% resolved in 3 business days

* Minimum service level: a resolution (including workarounds) is handed to the user to confirm acceptance before it is implemented in the production environment.

A TROUBLED PROJECT AT MODERN MATERIALS, INC.

Modern Materials, Inc. (MMI) manufactures products that are used as raw materials by large manufacturers and the construction industry. With yearly sales exceeding $3 billion, over 10,000 employees, and four large manufacturing facilities in the United States, MMI is one of the giants in the manufacturing materials industry. Two of the facilities produce basic products and the other two process these materials further to produce products with special properties and shapes.

MMI was established under another name in 1927 and grew over time through a series of small mergers and acquisitions until 1991, when it took over a major competitor and the resulting company took the name MMI. Two of its manufacturing facilities came with this merger, which broadened MMI's product line.

The last several years have been difficult ones for the manufacturing materials industry, with overcapacity, foreign competition, and a depressed manufacturing economy putting intense pressure on profits. MMI has fared better than most of its competitors, but as can be noted in Exhibit 1, MMI has lost money in 2 of the past 5 years. Furthermore, at this time it looks like the year 2003 will be worse than 2002. MMI went through a wrenching downsizing in 1998 that has left the remaining workers stretched thin and working at a hectic pace.

Information Services at MMI

Up until 1994 MMI had a conventional internal IS structure, with a small corporate IS group and decentralized organizations serving the two major divisions created with the merger in 1991. Each premerger company became a division in MMI, and each division inherited the IS organization of the company from which it was formed. Each division had its legacy people and legacy systems modified to provide the necessary enterprise data to corporate IS.

In 1994 MMI outsourced its IS organization to STC, a major player in the IT outsourcing business. As a part of the contract, STC offered employment to all of MMI's IS people, and most of them accepted jobs with STC. Thus MMI's IS staff was pretty much the same as before, but under new management. And the hardware and software were also taken over by STC. MMI retained a small group of analysts concerned with problem definition and process analysis.

Initiation of the Supply-Chain Management System (SCMS) Project

In 1995 Harvey Woodson was hired from a smaller competitor to become executive vice president for quality at MMI. Woodson brought with him a passionate vision of how to improve MMI's competitive position and profitability through exemplary customer service—being able to take orders, produce the product, and get it to the customer with the desired quality and package type when it was needed. Everyone in the industry had similar products and similar quality, and Woodson believed that outstanding customer service could make MMI stand apart from its competition.

Providing outstanding customer service depends upon excellent supply-chain management, which involves entering an order, creating a manufacturing order to guide it through the required manufacturing processes, scheduling it into production, producing it, warehousing it, shipping and routing it so that it arrives at the proper time, invoicing and billing it, and handling any testing issues or claims that might arise. This chain of events starts with the initial order and carries all the way through the customer receiving and using the product in his manufacturing process.

Woodson understood that excellent supply-chain management depends upon efficient processes supported by appropriate information processing systems. MMI's production processes were highly automated, with exceptional computer controls, but the business processes and the supporting information systems were clearly inadequate to provide outstanding customer service. As previously noted, the information systems were mainly legacy systems from the premerger companies

EXHIBIT 1
Selected MMI Financial Data (in Millions)

Statement of Operations	1998	1999	2000	2001	2002
Net sales	$ 3,544	$ 3,142	$ 3,230	$ 3,349	$ 3,277
Cost of goods sold	3,032	2,825	2,837	2,938	3,071
Depreciation	149	147	142	154	168
Gross margin	363	170	251	257	38
Selling, general & admin.	155	160	169	163	166
Financing costs	16	15	14	32	60
Downsizing costs	30				
Net income	162	(5)	68	62	(188)

that had been jury-rigged to provide the necessary enterprise information, and each location had its own way of doing things and its own systems.

In 1996 Woodson proposed that MMI undertake a massive effort to make a quantum leap in its supply-chain management performance by reengineering its business processes corporatewide and providing adequate information systems support for the new supply-chain management (SCM) process. A task force, composed of four senior executives and chaired by Woodson, was established to develop a proposal to present to the MMI board.

MMI's senior management enthusiastically bought into the vision of gaining competitive advantage through outstanding customer service. There was unanimous agreement that making this vision a reality depended upon radical improvements in the SCM process by reengineering MMI's business processes and supporting these new processes with adequate information technology. The question was how to do this, how long it would take, and what it would cost.

The company from which Woodson had come had completed reengineering and systems development for its SCM process, and Woodson had been involved in that effort. The development of that system had been outsourced to United Consultants Associates (UCA). That system was developed for only a single-plant operation, and Woodson envisioned a much more comprehensive system, but UCA could be employed to begin with that system and expand and enhance it to suit the needs of MMI. The task force estimated that the existing UCA-developed system contained about 50 to 60 percent of the functionality that MMI would require.

Hiring UCA to develop a new SCMS for MMI was the major alternative developed by the task force. The task force also considered the alternatives of enhancing MMI's existing systems to support the reengineered processes or acquiring enterprise software, but both alternatives were rejected as impractical.

The proposal cited the following business objectives of a new SCMS:

- Reduce inventories
- Increase market share
- Enhance profits
- Reduce operating costs
- Increase customer satisfaction

The new system would be based upon reengineered processes and replace the following existing MMI systems:

- Sales-order entry
- Sales forecasting
- Order status
- Pricing
- Scheduling and planning
- Manufacturing data collection
- Inventory control
- Quality tracking
- Traffic
- Shipping
- Invoicing
- Billing
- EDI

UCA, the contractor who would provide the code for the system developed for MMI's competitor, would lead the requirements definition effort and develop the system design and program specifications for the new SCMS. UCA would also assist MMI people in reengineering the business processes. Coding, testing, and installation of the system would be done by MMI's IS outsourcer, STC. The initial system provided by UCA did not include a production scheduling module, so an existing scheduling and planning module would be purchased from another qualified vendor and integrated into the system by STC.

The SCMS project was planned to take 3 years at a cost of $60 million. This proposal was approved by the board of MMI in late 1997 and work on the project began in early 1998, with completion scheduled for early 2001.

Building the System

The project was driven by Woodson, who headed a small steering committee of MMI managers. He was the project's champion, providing the enthusiasm and push within MMI. Woodson had been through this process before, and he knew that radical reengineering was necessary to achieve the dramatic improvements in customer service that MMI was seeking. He also understood that radical reengineering was terribly hard to accomplish because it would require enthusiastic participation by workers who would have to make radical changes in how they did their jobs, and that degree of change is hard for most people. Furthermore, one of the first things business process reengineering involves is looking for work that does not contribute to what is being accomplished. Eliminating that work may eliminate people, perhaps some of the same people being asked to participate in the reengineering process. So Woodson devoted a lot of time and energy to cheerleading—generating enthusiasm and support for the project throughout the company. He spent a lot of time out at the plants explaining how important the project was to the future success of the company, encouraging people to give their best efforts, and using his clout as an executive vice president to coerce people when necessary.

Early in 1998, just as the project was getting started, the industry was hit by a serious downturn, and MMI was forced to reduce its workforce by more than 8 percent. Morale plummeted, and as the remaining workers had to assume the duties of those who were downsized, it was difficult for them to find the time to get involved in reengineering and defining requirements of the system. In order to not fall too far behind the schedule, UCA people began to design the system and develop program specifications on the basis of what they thought the processes and requirements should be. This resulted in huge problems later, when the code had been written and the systems were to be tested and installed, requiring

much expensive and time-consuming rework, so the project fell further and further behind schedule.

In 1999 management realized that MMI had a serious problem with Y2K compatibility and decided that it was necessary to devote most of the STC resources at MMI to dealing with that problem, so the time spent on the SCMS project was substantially reduced during that year.

In 2000 Woodson, the driving force behind the project, suddenly left for greener pastures, and the project lost its original champion. The task force that had been driving the project was reorganized, with senior managers replaced with middle-level managers, and Woodson replaced as its leader and de facto project manager by George Leach, director of planning in the construction division.

Leach had no experience in an IS organization, but was very knowledgeable about how to run the business, and had a great reputation as a sophisticated user of information technology, having developed several impressive personal systems to assist management in running the division. These systems used PC software such as Microsoft Excel and Access to manipulate and analyze data extracted from MMI's existing IS systems, but had no documentation and were outside the regular production environment of the IS department.

Leach was an enthusiastic and forceful leader of the SCMS development effort and had a good understanding of the SCM process. When the requirements definition process for a system component fell behind schedule, Leach would step into the breach and assist in defining the requirements and specifying appropriate processes.

The first component of the system, order entry, was completed and ready for final testing in early 2001, about the time the entire project was originally scheduled for completion. Final testing did not go smoothly. The various locations insisted that the new uniform processes the system was based upon were not feasible and much rework was required to make the system acceptable. It was early 2002 before the order entry system was fully installed and in use.

New Chief Information Officer Hired

By early 2002 it was obvious that the SCMS project was seriously behind schedule and over budget, and MMI's senior management became more and more concerned with perceived problems with the project. In March 2002, Charles Hastings was brought in as chief information officer (CIO) and given the mission of straightening out the problem. Hastings was a long-time MMI manager who had been director of IS at one of the plants before becoming plant manager.

Matthew West, MMI financial vice president, had served in that position for many years. Before MMI established the CIO position, IS had reported to West, so West had some familiarity with IS projects. Shortly after Hastings became CIO, West expressed concern about the project:

> We need to admit that the supply-chain management project is a failure, minimize our losses by killing it, and move on. I realize that it is hard to abandon a project that we have invested so much time and effort in, but times are so tough for MMI that we cannot continue to pour money down a rat hole.

It took only 2 months for Hastings to agree that the project was in serious trouble. Although MMI senior management continued to believe in the vision of improved competitiveness through better customer service and the need for a new SCMS to support reengineered processes, the project had lost much of its drive when Woodson left MMI. Due to other serious business concerns, there had been no consistent personal involvement on the part of any senior manager. Consequently, there had been no top management clout to enforce the project's intent to make radical changes in how MMI did business. Furthermore, although people from MMI and at least three different outside contractors were working on the project, there was no overall project management responsibility. Hastings found a lot of finger-pointing with, for example, people from UCA saying "I'm waiting for MMI people to complete this," and MMI people saying "I'm waiting for STC." They were all correct because there was little overall coordination of what they were doing.

Hastings expressed concern about the project to George Leach, and Leach maintained that, although the project was well behind schedule and over budget, the underlying problems had been overcome and the project was now under control:

> We have had some serious problems to overcome—the downsizing that slowed down our requirements definition effort, the Y2K problem that diverted resources from the project, and Woodson's leadership was lost. We have also had some coordination problems between the four organizations that have been working on the project. We are now well past the planned completion date of the project and $4 million over the initial budget of $60 million, which is not surprising given the problems we have had.
>
> On the other hand, we have successfully installed the order-entry system and many of the rest of the components are almost completed. We are dealing with the coordination problems, have recently redone the project plan, and I am confident that we can complete the system in 18 months at a total cost of $84 million. Given the importance of a supply-chain management process to MMI's future, there is no question in my mind that we should complete the project as planned.

Wishing to get a more comprehensive picture of the health of the project, Hastings prevailed upon STC to bring in an experienced consultant, Carol Young, to study the situation and make recommendations about how to deal with any remaining problems.

Young's Findings

Carol Young was an experienced project manager who was brought in from a different STC location to conduct the study at MMI. Young had just completed an STC assignment as the project manager of a large system development project that was completed on time and on budget.

The first thing Young did was to run a quick "health check" of the project using a questionnaire that STC has used in many places. On a scale of 1 to 10, it evaluates how the project is doing in seven critical areas such as risk management, financial management, and schedule management. A score of 1 or 2 is in intensive care, 3 or 4 is critical condition, etc. When she analyzed the results, the average score was 3.1, so the project was in deep, deep trouble (see Exhibit 2).

Then Young examined the newest version of the schedule that Leach asserted would get the project completed in 18 months at a cost of an additional $20 million. She reported:

> I took two additional people and interviewed every functional person and every end user person that had anything to do with the next phase of the schedule, which was planned to take three months. All of those people said that the project was in the toilet. The major problems were that the requirements had not been correctly identified, so they were going to have to do a lot of rework to get the requirements right, and the users were terrified because there was almost no testing in the schedule—only a little time for user acceptance testing. There was no unit testing and no integration testing. The users knew that installing the system would be a disaster.
>
> I also carefully reviewed the project plan and found that it does not take into account staffing needs. Often more work is scheduled over a time period than there are people available to do the necessary work. Thus the schedule is not feasible. Furthermore, the new systems do not have the documentation and controls necessary in a production environment. It is a mess.
>
> When we included the time to define the requirements, make the necessary changes, upgrade the controls and documentation, and adequately test and install the system, the time to complete that phase went from 3 months to 6 months. All of the succeeding phases had the same problems, so the time to complete the project went from 18 months to at least 3 years, assuming that it is done right. If MMI doesn't define the requirements and do the needed testing, the project will be a complete disaster. But Leach is still planning to complete and convert to the use of each new system in about half the time it will actually take. Because MMI is burning money on this project at over $1.2 million a month, the cost goes from $20 million to $40 million.
>
> In summary, the current schedule that envisions the completion of the project in 18 months at a total cost of $84 million is totally unrealistic. The minimum time and cost that will be required for Leach to complete the system is 3 more years at a total cost of $104 million.

EXHIBIT 2
Project Health Check by Carol Young

PM Functional Area	Intensive Care		Critical		Fair		Good		Excellent	
	1	2	3	4	5	6	7	8	9	10
Communication Management		X								
Risk Management				X						
Scope Management			X							
Schedule Management						X				
Quality Management	X									
Financial/Contractual Management				X						
Resource Management		X								

Note: The average score is 3.1, which means the project is in critical condition.

When Hastings asked why the project was in such deep trouble, Young replied:

In the first place, there has been no overall project management in the professional IS sense. No one has been given overall project management responsibility and authority. What little project management the project has had has been by Leach as head of the project steering committee. There has been little coordination between the various contractors who are working on the project so one contractor has often wasted time waiting on another to complete something. During this waiting time the workers continue to work and draw their pay even though they are not accomplishing anything, wasting MMI's money as well as time.

Although Leach is an enthusiastic, hard-working, dedicated manager who knows MMI and its supply-chain management problems, unfortunately he has no concept of how to develop an IS system of this complexity. His experience is in user development, where he has done an outstanding job. But in user development, where data are extracted from an existing system and manipulated with PC tools, one can get away with just building a system without too much concern for the requirements because you can easily modify it until you get it right. One does not need thorough documentation because the user is also the developer and understands the details of the system. You don't have to worry about security, risk management controls, configuration management controls, data capture issues, etc. And you do not have to coordinate the activities of various groups that are all working on the project. So Leach has tried his best to lead this project without understanding any of these crucial aspects of project management.

Furthermore, the MMI legacy systems had little usable documentation, so the development team did not know the details of what these systems did or how they did it. When the

downsizing came about and the users did not have time to participate in the reengineering and defining the requirements, UCA and Leach assumed that they understood the requirements and began defining the system and writing program specs without really understanding the requirements or obtaining buy-in from the users. They did not realize they had serious problems until they tried to install the systems and the users rebelled.

Hastings asked Young what she would suggest that MMI do, and this was her reply:

I have devoted a good deal of time to determining what needs to be done, how it could best be accomplished, and how it should be managed. The bad news is that the best plan I could come up with would take 2 years for completion of the system. The good news is that the total cost would be only $84 million.

My suggestion would be for MMI to designate me as the overall project manager and make sure that the entire project, including all the contractors and MMI personnel, would be directly responsible to me. Leach would continue to head the steering committee and provide vision and knowledge of MMI's supply-chain management process, but I would have direct responsibility for managing the project. The $84 million cost includes STC's fee for managing the project.

I have reworked Leach's schedule to eliminate the inefficiencies, do things in the proper sequence, provide the time needed to perform the necessary activities with the people available, involve the users in requirements definition and system testing, and so on. It will take 2 years to complete the work.

The project bottleneck was the rate at which the users and functional people could define the requirements. Everyone on the project had been spending a lot of useless time waiting for the users and for each other or writing code on the basis of incomplete requirements. They were busy working, but they were not doing anything productive. When I lengthened the schedule to what was feasible and assigned the work properly, I was able to drastically reduce the staffing on the project, so we would only be spending $800,000 a month rather than $1.2 million.

Leach had been using a "big bang" approach where they worked simultaneously on all five of the remaining phases. I plan to use a "rolling wave" approach where we will concentrate on defining the requirements of the first phase. When that is completed, we will move on to programming on that phase. The people who were defining requirements for the first phase can then move on to the same task for the second phase, and so on. This way we will work at the pace at which they can define requirements and everyone working on the project will be doing useful work all the time.

Leach's Reaction

In response to Young's critique of the project and its management, George Leach made the following points:

Carol went out and talked to a number of malcontents who do not know what is currently going on in the development process and do not understand the quality that we are now building into the system. Carol hasn't worked on this project, knows little about conditions in MMI, and just represents the viewpoint that nobody who is not an IS professional can manage a systems development project. Carol heard what Carol wanted to hear. I suspect that Carol is influenced by the desire to develop more business for STC and criticizing me is the way for STC to take over the project.

I would argue that given the obstacles we have faced, the project has been remarkably successful. Remember that we lost a year to downsizing and a year to Y2K. The downsizing has made it much more difficult to reengineer the processes and to define requirements because the users are so busy trying to keep production going. Also, we lost Woodson's leadership at a crucial time.

Secondly, it looks like we are farther behind than we really are. Although we have only installed the order entry system, quite a number of additional systems are almost complete and ready to go into final testing. So we are set to make a lot of progress in the next few months.

Finally, experience has taught us a lot about managing development. I have thoroughly reworked our development approach, project plan, and schedule to make it more effective. I am now conducting weekly meetings with the managers of all the contractors to discuss and deal with our coordination problems. I am confident that we can complete the system in 18 months for only an additional $20 million.

Young was quick to respond to Leach's accusation that she was criticizing his leadership in order to get more business for STC:

If my proposal to manage the project is accepted it will result in less, not more, revenue for STC than if I had recommended that the project continue under its present management. Our people are working steadily on the project now and would continue to do so for at least 3 years. Under my proposal, the number of our people working on the project would be reduced and our people would only be on the project for 2 years, so our total revenue would be substantially less. If I were trying to maximize STC's revenue I would have let things go on as they are.

West's Concerns

Vice President of Finance West believed that MMI was in such dire financial condition that the SCMS project should be shut down immediately. He asserted:

We are losing substantial amounts of money, and if this continues for too long we will be in big trouble. We hope things turn around before long and are taking every possible measure to make sure that it does.

Our stock has tanked. Our stockholders' equity, cash, and working capital have declined significantly over the last 5 years, and they will continue to decline this year. [See Exhibit 3.] We are borrowing money to cover deficits in our cash flow. We project that this year will be very tough, but we expect the economy to turn around and our position to begin to improve during 2003. [See Exhibit 4.] Although we are not in immediate danger of bankruptcy, we will be in desperate straits if our projections turn out to have been too optimistic. Borrowing more money to cover cash-flow deficits will be exceedingly difficult.

It is not responsible management to spend $20 million on any project in our present situation even if that amount would not bankrupt us. There are too many better ways to use those resources. For example, that would be $20 million we would not have to borrow and $20 million less in losses. Also, we may have to downsize again in the near future, and $20 million would save the jobs of some people we desperately need.

Furthermore, I doubt that this project can be completed as proposed under either Leach's or Young's proposals. Since the downsizing we do not have the user manpower to define the requirements well enough, and we also have serious political problems that are holding us back. Young will find that the lack of project management is not the only serious problem that we face in completing this project.

But more importantly, even if it were to be completed it would not achieve the purpose that motivated the project in the first place, namely providing competitive advantage by a quantum jump in customer service. We might get marginally improved data processing systems, but we have not done the reengineering to obtain the radical changes in how we do business that would set us apart from our competitors. This project was never justified on the basis of quantitative returns, only on strategic grounds, and it has been doomed ever since our downsizing and the departure of Woodson. We should have killed it years ago.

However, in the final analysis it doesn't matter whether or not the project is a complete failure. Even if it would be a moderate success, in these difficult times we cannot afford the huge drain on our resources that it involves. Perhaps we could

EXHIBIT 3
Selected MMI End-of-Year Financial Data (Dollars in Millions)

	1998	1999	2000	2001	2002
Cash & cash equivalents	$307	$241	$193	$215	$160
Working capital	410	305	300	350	107
Stockholders' equity	845	691	740	752	620
Stock price/share	27.25	14.00	17.75	11.50	6.25

mothball it so that if conditions improve it could be resumed, but we need to get rid of it for now.

Leach contested West's assertion that the new system would not provide the competitive advantage originally envisioned:

We have only installed one subsystem, and you cannot expect overall performance to be improved much until the entire system is installed and working. The results of this effort will be apparent when the full system is completed and installed.

Our legacy systems that run production at the plants are stand-alone systems that are not integrated with other production systems or with the support systems—administrative, financial, personnel, etc. The new system will integrate everything from the time the customer calls in an order through ordering the raw materials, scheduling and following through the production process, entering it into inventory, shipping it, billing it, and handling any problems with the use of the product.

As a result, the customer will be able to get exactly what he wants in the shortest possible time. When the customer calls with an order, it can be entered, scheduled, and the delivery date determined while the customer is on the phone. Changes to an order can be made quickly and easily. The lead time to deliver an order will be reduced from today's 120 days to 45 days, which is just a little more than a third of what it is today! That will be a huge improvement in customer service. No one else in our industry will be able to match this.

Also, this reduction in the time to deliver an order will result in tremendous savings for MMI because in-process inventory will be reduced so dramatically. And time is money for us as well as for our customers. We will be saving huge amounts of money.

Furthermore, with this integrated system, management information will be available in real time rather than months after the fact. We will be able to determine the profitability of each product and focus our marketing efforts on the most profitable products, and we will be able to plan our production and load it on our facilities so as to minimize the cost of production. Not only will we be able to radically improve customer service, but we will also be able to improve the profitability of what we produce.

I admit that the project has had its problems, but I am sure that we can complete it in 18 months for an additional $20 million. Although our financial condition is not good, this is a strategic project that will greatly improve our competitiveness. It represents a crucial top management vision, and I can't believe that we would abandon it because of temporary difficulties. MMI's future depends upon it!

Mary J. Ellis, the construction division's representative on the project steering committee, believed that the project should be continued and that Leach should continue to lead it. She asserted:

Admittedly our financial condition is not the best, but $20 million is not going to make or break us. We must not let short-range problems cause us to lose the vision that can make such an important contribution to MMI's long-term success.

George has the vision, the enthusiasm, and the experience needed to complete the project. George has provided outstanding leadership, fighting through difficulty after difficulty. Without George's drive and enthusiasm the project would have failed long ago. It would be disastrous to change leadership now when the project is so close to completion.

EXHIBIT 4
Selected MMI Projections, End of Year (in millions)

	Projections			
	2003	2004	2005	2006
Sales	$3,217	$3,250	$3,372	$3,516
Net Income	(287)	(50)	70	180
Stockholders' equity	342	286	350	522

PURCHASING A STUDENT MANAGEMENT SYSTEM AT JEFFERSON COUNTY SCHOOL SYSTEM (REVISED)

The Jefferson County School System (JCSS) educates about 10,000 students in fourteen elementary schools, two middle schools, and two high schools. It serves a diverse community consisting of a county seat of 80,000 with a substantial industrial base and a major state university, and the surrounding rural area.

Central High School and Roosevelt High School, located on the eastern edge of town, are spirited athletic rivals whose attendance districts split the county into approximately equal areas, with each district including about 1,450 city and rural patrons. The two middle schools each have about 750 pupils in the seventh and eighth grades and also serve diversified areas. The elementary schools are located throughout the county and range in size from rural schools with about 250 students up to almost 700 students for the largest city school.

History of Administrative Computing in JCSS

Administrative computing at JCSS began in the early 1970s when computing resources at the university were leased to do scheduling and grade reporting and to keep student enrollment data. In 1976 the school corporation purchased a DEC PDP 11/34 computer, and the student management applications were converted from the university computer. During the next few years, financial applications were added and more student management applications were developed. Over the years there have been many changes to the JCSS technical architecture. They now have four Dell servers operating under UNIX, and PCs in all JCSS locations are connected to the system via a high-speed TCP/IP network.

All JCSS applications, both financial and student management, were custom developed by the longtime director of data processing, David Meyer, and the two programmers on his staff. The users of these systems were satisfied with them, and when they wanted changes and improvements, Meyer and

his programmers would make them. There was no end-user capability—if anyone needed a special report, a program to produce it was written by one of the programmers.

Three years ago the long-time JCSS superintendent of schools retired and Dr. Harvey Greene was hired as his replacement. Dr. Greene had been the superintendent of a smaller school system and had attended a conference where a speaker convinced him that software had become a commodity and that it no longer made sense for a school system to develop and maintain its own software.

After a few months to get his feet on the ground, Dr. Greene established a small task force of administrators to evaluate the JCSS data processing systems and to recommend directions for the future. Not surprisingly, this task force recommended that:

- The JCSS systems should be replaced with purchased software packages with maintenance agreements.

- The new systems should utilize an integrated database and report-generation software so that people could share data from various applications.

- Because JCSS would no longer be doing custom development, the programming staff of the data processing department could be eliminated.

David Meyer was not included on the task force, and Director of Data Processing Meyer was quite upset with the decision to gut his staff without even consulting him. When these recommendations were accepted by Dr. Greene and the school board, he chose to resign from his position as DP Director. He was replaced by Carol Andrews, who had 13 years of experience as an applications programmer, systems programmer, and systems analyst with a nearby federal government installation.

Purchasing the New System

After spending several months getting acclimated to the JCSS and her new job, Andrews set about the task of selecting a vendor to provide the hardware and software to replace the current administrative computing applications at JCSS. In late

November a computer selection committee was appointed to evaluate available systems and recommend a vendor to the JCSS School Board. This 14-member committee included representatives of most of the major users of the system—assistant principals who did scheduling and were responsible for student records, deans who were responsible for attendance and student discipline, counselors, teachers, the personnel director, and the chief accountant. It also included representatives of the different levels of schools in the system and from each of the larger school locations.

By late March Andrews and the committee had prepared a 71-page request for proposal (RFP) that was sent to 23 possible vendors, asking that proposals be submitted by May 4. The RFP stated that "The proposals will be evaluated on functional requirements, support services, and a 5-year life cycle cost." The table of contents of the RFP is included as Exhibit 1. Appendices A through E listed in the contents were in the form of fill-in-the-blank questionnaires that defined the information that JCSS desired from the vendors.

The RFP was sent to vendors that would contract to accept responsibility for all the software and support and training services required to install and maintain the new system. Appendix C of the RFP described the JCSS hardware and communications architecture and specified that any required changes to the existing environment must be described and the associated costs presented. The desired requirements for the application software were described in Appendix D in the form of characteristics that could be checked off as included or not.

Although members of the selection committee made suggestions, Andrews determined most of the requirements for the application systems by examining what the existing systems did and talking with people throughout the JCSS. The application specifications for the attendance accounting and student scheduling systems from Appendix D are included as Exhibit 2.

EXHIBIT 1
Jefferson County School System Request for Proposal

Table of Contents

I. Introduction 1

II. General Conditions 2

- Non-collusions Affidavit and Bid Security
- Acceptance or Rejection of Bids
- Explanation to Vendors
- Quality of the Proposal
- Prime Point of Contact
- Basis of Selection
- Test Demonstrations
- Method of Payment
- Award of Contract

III. Vendor Response Format 4

A. Management Summary
B. Vendor Profile
C. Vendor Services Summary
D. Hardware and Communications Requirements
E. Application Software Specifications
F. Cost Summary
G. Project Plan and Management
H. Application Software Support
I. Contract Exhibits

IV. Appendices

A. Vendor Profile 11
B. Vendor Services Summary 12
C. Hardware and Communications Configuration 14
D. Application Specifications 21
E. Cost Summary 61
F. JCSS Enrollment Table 70

EXHIBIT 2
Application Specifications, Appendix D

Student Administration System
Attendance Accounting

Included	
Yes	No

_____ _____ 1. Provide for interactive entry and correction of daily attendance information.

_____ _____ 2. Provide for interactive entry and correction of YTD attendance information.

_____ _____ 3. Provide for interactive entry of period by period, and half or whole day attendance.

_____ _____ 4. Capable of input of attendance by online entry or optional scanning devices(s).

_____ _____ 5. Provide online access to student attendance records by date or course, showing period by period attendance and reason for absence for any date.

_____ _____ 6. Provide "user defined" definition of ADA and ADM calculation requirements.

_____ _____ 7. Provide for entry of absence reason codes by exception.

_____ _____ 8. Provide for multiple attendance periods with "user defined" number of days in each.

_____ _____ 9. Provide for entry of entire year school calendar.

_____ _____ 10. Provide for student registers.

_____ _____ 11. Provide for entry and withdrawal. Provide for student withdrawal, which retains all student information and tracks the withdrawn student's attendance as "not enrolled"; in the event the student returns to the district and reenrolls all attendance calculations will automatically be current and up to date.

Included	
Yes	No

_____ _____ 12. Daily absence worksheet phone list.

_____ _____ 13. Daily absence report.

_____ _____ 14. Absence report by reason.

_____ _____ 15. Student Attendance Register Report. List by class and section.

_____ _____ 16. Student Absence by Reason listing.

_____ _____ 17. School Absence by Reason listing.

_____ _____ 18. Provide attendance reports with ADA and ADM calculations from any beginning date through any ending date.

19. Provide attendance reports by:
_____ _____ Student
_____ _____ Absence and Absence reason(s)
_____ _____ Sex
_____ _____ Grade level
_____ _____ Course and section
_____ _____ Multiple combinations of the preceding requirements

20. Provide ADA and ADM calculation reports, with any "from" and "through" dates for the following:
_____ _____ Any and all schools
_____ _____ The entire district
_____ _____ Each attendance register

_____ _____ 21. Provide M-F absence reports by any "from" and "through" dates, also by student, grade, sex, course and section, and/or absence reason code.

_____ _____ 22. Provide daily entry and withdrawal reports.

Selection of the Vendor

Seven proposals were submitted in response to the RFP. Andrews was able to winnow them down easily to three serious contenders that were evaluated in detail. Each of the three finalists was invited to demonstrate its system to the selection committee. The vendors were not told in detail what to show,

but they were asked to demonstrate the operation of several of the major systems. The three vendors brought in their own computers for the demonstration, and all of the demonstrations were quite satisfactory to the committee.

The committee originally intended to visit a school that used each vendor's system, but because of time and money constraints they were only able to visit two sites—one Data Systems, Inc.,

EXHIBIT 2 (*Continued*)

Student Administration System
Student Scheduling

Included
Yes   No

1. Provide for interactive entry and correction of student course requests and master schedule data.

2. Automatically process student course requests against the master schedule to produce class schedules for each student.

3. Provide for Arena Scheduling.

4. Provide for interactive drop/add of students from classes after initial schedules are established, at any time.

5. Scheduling data must interface with student records.

6. Provide for course restrictions by grade level and/or sex.

7. Allow for addition of new courses and sections at any time.

8. Provide current enrollment summary of each course and section both online and via printed report.

9. Provide for mass adds, deletes or changes based on grade, sex, etc.

10. Online editing of valid course number requests during entry is required.

11. Provide for scheduling retries without erasing previous scheduling runs.

12. Provide for override of maximum enrollment.

Included
Yes   No

13. Provide for each student a year-long schedule, with up to 20 different courses (excluding lunch and study hall).

14. Provide for "prioritizing" scheduling runs by grade level and/or student number.

15. Provide master schedule by teacher listing.

16. Preregistration "by student" course request report.

17. Preregistration "by course" request listing.

18. Provide course request tally report.

19. Provide potential conflict matrix.

20. Provide student conflict report.

21. Provide student schedules.

22. Provide course and section status summary.

23. Provide course rosters by teacher.

24. Provide room utilization report with conflict alert.

25. Provide teacher utilization report with conflict alert.

26. Provide schedule exception listing showing student and open periods (by either closed or conflict status), also show all filled periods.

27. Provide scheduling by quarter, semester, year-long, or trimester options.

installation and one Scholastic Systems Corporation installation. Andrews and Dr. Paul Faris, Assistant Principal at Roosevelt High, spent one day at each of these locations observing their systems in action and talking with users. In addition, members of the committee made telephone calls to their counterparts at other schools that used each vendor's systems without unearthing any major problems or concerns. Everyone seemed quite positive about all three vendors and their products.

The committee had a difficult time deciding between the three finalists. Each of the vendors proposed software packages in all the areas that JCSS had asked for, but none of these systems did exactly what they wanted in exactly the way the current systems did things. The committee finally chose Data Systems, Inc. (DSI) because the members felt they could work

well with the DSI people and they felt that the DSI proposal was best on balance, as indicated in Exhibit 3, which they presented to the JCSS School Board. This table rates six factors on a scale from 1 to 5, with a total rating for each of the finalist vendors at the bottom. DSI was rated highest in "Application Software" because its system was a Web-based system, and the committee felt that this was the technology of the future. DSI had recently converted the functionality of its legacy systems to the Web-based architecture and had only installed it at three school systems, so the committee was aware that it might have more bugs than if the system had been in use for several years. The "cost of ownership" includes the purchase price of the software, installation, training, and five years of maintenance and support. The "bid exceptions" rating refers to

EXHIBIT 3
Evaluation of Bids

Selection Criteria	Data Systems	Scholastic Systems	Orian Computer Systems
1. Vendor Profile	5	5	3
2. Vendor Services	5	4	3
3. Application Software	5	4	3
4. 5 yr. Cost of Ownership (Rating)	$502,000 4	$655,000 3	$430,000 5
5. Software support	5	4	3
6. Bid Exceptions	5	4	3
TOTAL RATING	29	24	20

how well the proposed software fits the JCSS specifications and thus a high rating indicates that little modification of the software would be needed.

The JCSS School Board awarded the contract to DSI in June. It included the following systems: financial, payroll/personnel, fixed assets, warehouse inventory, registration, scheduling, grades/transcripts, attendance, book bills, office assistant, electronic mail, and special education. These systems utilize a standard relational database management system that includes a query language that generates ad hoc reports.

DSI agreed to make specific changes in the software packages where the committee had indicated that the packages did not meet the JCSS specifications. The contract also provided that DSI would devote up to 100 hours of programming time to making other modifications (not yet specified) in its software. Any additional changes requested by JCSS would be billed at $100 per programmer hour. JCSS also purchased DSI's standard software maintenance contract.

Implementation of the Systems

With the help of DSI people, the software for the new systems was loaded on the JCSS servers in December. Although they had some problems with the financial systems, they successfully

converted most of them from the old systems to the new DSI systems. However, they had major problems in installing and using the student management systems.

Andrews planned to follow the cycle of the academic year when implementing the student systems. First, they would transfer all the student demographic information from the present system to the new system's database. Then they would complete the students' fall class schedules by the end of the spring semester, as they had been doing with the old system, so that the students' schedules would be on the new system and ready to go in the fall. During the summer they would pick up the attendance accounting on the new system so it would be ready for the fall. Then they would implement grade reporting so it would be ready for use at the end of the first six-week grading period in the fall. Finally, they would convert the student transcript information from the old system so that fall semester grades could be transferred to the transcripts at the end of the semester.

They successfully transferred the student demographic information from the old system to the new in February. Then they started to work on student scheduling. Things did not go well. The training provided by DSI for the scheduling officers was a disaster. Then, after entering the student class requests and the available faculty data, they started the first scheduling run. After it had run all day without completing the schedules, they decided that there was something definitely wrong. Andrews never completely resolved this problem with DSI's experts. DSI claimed that it was caused by the way the scheduling officer set up the scheduling system—the various parameters that the system uses. Andrews was still convinced that there was some sort of bug in the scheduling program.

DSI did make some minor modifications to the program, and they sent some people out to consult with Andrews and her staff on how to set up the schedule, but they were unable to get the schedules done by the end of the spring semester as planned. This caused severe problems because the assistant principals in charge of scheduling were not on the payroll during the summer. Fortunately, Paul Faris, the scheduling officer at Roosevelt, was working summer school, and with his assistance they were just able to get all the schedules done two weeks before school started.

Preparation for the fall was also hindered by the fact that neither the school secretaries, who entered much of the data for the attendance module, nor the counselors, who had to work with the scheduling of new students in the system and changes to schedules of continuing students, were on the payroll during the summer. The administration would not spend the money to pay these people to come in during the summer for training on the system, so all training was delayed until the week before school started, when everyone reported back to work. The training was rushed, and again DSI did a poor job with it.

When school started in the fall, the system was a total disaster. The people who were working with the system did not understand it or know what they were doing with it. When the counselors tried to schedule a new student into his classes, the system might take 20 minutes to produce his new schedule. Needless to say, there were long lines of students waiting in the halls, and the students, their parents, the counselors, teachers, and administrators were upset and terribly frustrated.

Also, the attendance officers did not know what they were doing and could not make the system work for the first few weeks of the semester. Things were so bad that at the end of the first grading period Andrews decided that, although the grade reporting system was working correctly, it was not feasible to have the teachers enter their grades directly into the system as had been planned. Instead, she hired several outside clerical people to enter the grades from forms the teachers filled out. After some well-executed training, the teachers successfully entered their grades at the end of the semester.

By the end of the fall semester most of those working with the student systems had learned enough to make them work adequately, and a few of them were beginning to recognize that the new systems had some significant advantages over the old ones. They did get the second semester underway without major problems, and in early February of the next year they were getting ready to bring up the transcript system and start the scheduling process for the fall.

Perspectives of the Participants

Given everything that had transpired in acquiring and implementing the new system to this stage, it is not surprising that there were many different opinions on the problems that were encountered, whether or not the new system was satisfactory, and what the future would hold. The following presents the perspectives of a number of those who had been involved with the new system.

Dr. Harold Whitney, Assistant Principal, Central High School

Dr. Whitney asserts that the previous system was an excellent system that really did the job for them.

> It was fast, efficient, and effective. And when we needed something, rather than having to call DSI in Virginia to get it done, our own people would do it for us in a matter of 2 or 3 days. However, the study committee (which probably didn't have enough good school people on it) decided on the new system, and we were told that we would start with the new scheduling software package early in the year.

The first acquaintance that Whitney had with the new system was in early February when DSI sent someone in to train four or five of the scheduling people on how to use the new system to construct a master schedule. Whitney recalls:

> Over a 3-day period we took 50 students and tried to construct a master schedule. And at the end of the 3 days, we still hadn't been able to do it. It was apparent that the lady they sent out to train us, while she may have known the software, had no idea of what we wanted in a master schedule, and had never experienced the master schedule-building process in a large high school.
>
> The master schedule is the class schedule of all of the courses that we offer—when and where they will be taught, and by whom. In the past, I would take the course requests from our students and summarize them to determine the demand for each course, and then I would develop a master schedule that assigned our available teachers to the courses that they could best teach while meeting the student demand as well as possible. I had to take into account the fact that, among all the teachers who are certified to teach mathematics, some are more effective teaching algebra and geometry than they are in calculus, and similarly for other subject areas. Also, we have 15 or so teachers who are part-time in our school and therefore can only teach here during the morning (or the afternoon). Furthermore, we need to lock our 2-semester courses so that a student will have the same teacher for both semesters.

With the new system we were supposed to input our teachers and their certifications and the student requests for courses, and the DSI software would generate the ideal master schedule to satisfy that demand. But we had to place quite a number of restrictions on what and when the teachers could teach and into what sections a student could be scheduled. When we tried to run the software, it just ran and ran, but it never produced a satisfactory schedule.

DSI sent one of its top executives out to talk with Whitney about these problems. The executive told Whitney that "the reason that you're unhappy is that you're placing too many restrictions on the schedule." Whitney replied, "All well and good. But are you telling me that your software package should dictate our curriculum? That it should dictate who teaches calculus, who teaches general math, who teaches advanced and who teaches beginning grammar? That's hardly sound educationally!"

Whitney ended up doing the schedule by hand, as he had done before, and the students were scheduled by the end of the spring semester. Some of the other schools continued to try to use the full system, and they had a hard time getting the schedules out by the start of school.

Whitney had a very bad impression of the system until the end of the year when he began to believe things were improving somewhat. The DSI people were beginning to listen to him, and he was more receptive: "I've always been able to see that somewhere down the road the new system will have capabilities that improve on our old system."

Dr. Paul Faris, Assistant Principal, Roosevelt High School

Dr. Faris, an active member of the computer study committee that chose the new system, is responsible for class scheduling at Roosevelt High. Unlike Harold Whitney at Central High, he used the system as it was intended to be used both to develop the master schedule and to schedule the students into their classes. He had a struggle with the system at first and had not completed the master schedule by the end of spring. However, he was on the payroll during the summer and was able to complete the master schedule a few weeks before the beginning of school in the fall. In doing so he learned a great deal about how the scheduling system worked.

The way your master schedule is set up and the search patterns you establish determine how the system performs. The individual principals have control over many aspects of the process, and there is a lot of leeway—whether you set up for one semester or two, whether you strictly enforce class sizes, whether or not you have alternatives to search for with specific courses, and so on. We set it up for double semester, which is the hard one, but I had generous limits on my class size and we had limited search for alternatives, which

kicked the difficult ones out of the system to handle on a manual basis. And I limited certain courses to seniors, or sophomores, et cetera, and that restricted the search pattern somewhat.

Dr. Faris knew that the beginning of the fall semester would be crunch time, when lots of work would have to be done with the new system in a limited amount of time. So he prepared his people for the transition ahead of time. His secretary was skilled on the old system. Early in the spring Faris told her: "We are going to change over our entire system in 4 months. And week by week I want you to tell me what files have to be changed over, and you and I are going to do it." Again, it was a matter of making sure things were done in a nonpressure situation where they could learn what they had to know.

Dr. Faris and his counselors still had many problems during the first few weeks of school in the fall, but nothing that they could not cope with. Things are going well in his area now. When they recently started the second semester it was a crunch time again, but the counselors got along fine with schedule changes and they completed the new schedules faster than they had with the old system. Dr. Faris believes that the new system is a substantial improvement over the old one.

I can follow through and find the kids' attendance, current program, grades, past history and transcripts, and probably have everything I need in 2 or 3 minutes. Before the new system I could barely walk to the filing cabinet and find his folder in that time. And then I'd still have to go to the counseling office and get the current schedule, and then to the attendance office and get the attendance record.

I'm really pleased with the new file structures. And Carol's programmer is starting to add back some of the custom things that we had in the old system. I'm looking forward to being trained on the report generator so that I can produce my own special reports without getting a programmer involved.

Dr. Ruth Gosser, Assistant Principal, Central High School

Dr. Gosser is the attendance and disciplinary officer at Central High and was a member of the computer selection committee. Ruth recalls:

We looked at about four different companies. Several had very good packages, although I will admit that by the time you sit through four or five different presentations, they all tend to run into one another.

My participation in specifying the requirements and evaluating the proposed systems was minimal. It was a big committee, and I was busy with other things, so I didn't even read the materials very carefully. I disliked spending the time that I did, and I was really turned off by the details, especially the technical details. I remember thinking: Ugh! I'm sick of this. Just go ahead and buy something!

She and her people had only two days of training on the system before the start of school, and Gosser thought the training provided was pretty useless. "They weren't very well-organized, and they spent too much time on the technical aspects of the system. I just wanted to know how to use the system, but they tried to give me a lot more and it really confused me and made me angry."

When school started in the fall, it was a disaster. Ruth remembers it vividly:

It was awful! Awful! I didn't get home till after 6:30 for weeks. Just getting the information in and out was a nightmare. We had a terrible time trying to change the unexcused to excused, and doing all the little things that go with that. It was so bad that we seriously considered abandoning the system and trying to do it by hand. It was horrible!

But we've just gone through second-semester class changes, and I haven't heard anyone weeping and wailing about what a crummy system this is. We're beginning to recognize that we've got the new system, and we're going to have it for a long time. They're not going to junk a system that we have paid all that money for, so we'd better work to make the very best out of it that we can. And I can see that there are some really good things about the new system that the old system didn't have, and never could have.

Looking back, I don't think that the computer selection committee did a very good job. If I had known then what I know now I'd have put a lot more effort into it than I did. Since most of us didn't put in the effort to get down to the details of exactly what we needed, Carol pretty much had to do it herself. Unfortunately, we only gave her enough information to get her off our backs. Like "I need something that will chart attendance for me." That wasn't much help. Every system we considered would chart attendance, so we had no basis for deciding which system would have been best for us.

Dr. Helen Davis, Assistant Principal, Roosevelt High

Dr. Davis is the attendance and disciplinary officer at Roosevelt High School. She was not a member of the computer selection committee, and she does not think it did a very good job.

The committee looked at a lot of different kinds of things, but they didn't communicate. Even though we all were supposed to have representatives on the committee, we didn't know what they were doing, nor did we have the opportunity to discuss any of the systems that they were looking at and whether those systems would help us or satisfy our needs.

When the new system was put in last fall a lot of us had no training, no information, and didn't know what was going on. My secretary had a day and a half training in August, but I had

no training at all. Some training was offered to me in August, but I had already made arrangements to be out of town, and no flexibility was provided as to when the training would be available. Furthermore, there are no user-friendly manuals for the system—the manual they gave me is written in computerese. So I've had to learn the system by bitter experience, and I still don't know what it offers me. I could go through a hundred menus and not find what I want because I don't know what they are for.

Last fall when school opened my blood pressure probably went to about 300 every day! We couldn't do attendance—it wouldn't work. We couldn't print an absence list for the teachers. We couldn't put out an unexcused list. We couldn't get an excessive absence report, so it was mid-semester before I could start sending letters to parents whose kids weren't attending regularly. That really impedes the work of trying to keep kids in school.

The thing that frustrated Helen the most was that she resented being controlled by the software system.

The system is dictating what we can do with kids and their records. It needs to be the opposite way. We ought to be driving that machine to service what we need to do as easily as possible. But the machine is driving us, and I'm really displeased with that.

We're stuck with DSI and their software because we've got so much money invested in it. In time Carol will be able to make this system as compatible with our needs as it can be, but it will never be as suitable as it should be. And it will take a long, long time before we get all the things that we need.

Catherine Smith, Counselor, Central High School

Catherine Smith has been a counselor at Central High School for 20 years, but she had no experience with the computer before the training session that was held the Thursday and Friday before school started. According to Catherine:

The first day of school was just unbelievable! It took 2 hours to schedule one new student. Everyone was running up and down the halls asking each other questions. No one knew what was going on.

The first 2 days I had absolutely no control over that computer! It would bleep, and you didn't know why. But by Wednesday morning I began to get control. I knew that if I pushed this button, this would happen. And I knew how to make it do some of the things I wanted it to do.

Now that I've worked with it for a semester, I'm happy with it. The system contains a tremendous amount of information that I need to help the students. The thing I like most about the system is that when I want to put a kid in a class and it's full, I can find out instantly how many kids are in each section, and I can usually find a place for the kid. I can even override it if the section is closed. Despite the fact that we almost died during that first week, now that I have control over it I think it's tremendous!

Murphey Ford, English Teacher, Roosevelt High School

Murphey has taught English at Roosevelt for 12 years, and he has had no experience with a computer beyond entering his grades into the old system.

This new computer has been a disaster from the word go. Last fall they didn't produce a class schedule until 2 weeks before classes were to start, so I had no time to prepare to teach a class I hadn't taught for 5 years! And I wasn't even asked if I would be willing to teach it—the computer just assigned me to it.

Then they relaxed the limits on class size. We ended up having some classes with 30 students and others with 40. That's not fair to either the students or the teachers. And it was a zoo around here at the beginning of the fall. It was 3 weeks before they got all the new students into their classes and things settled down a little.

In this community we have very high expectations for the education system, but we never have enough money to provide the special programs we want, or get adequate supplies, or pay decent salaries. It really burns me up that we spent so much on this new system that doesn't work anything like as well as the old one.

Carol Andrews, Director of Data Processing

The 15 months since the new software arrived have been very difficult and stressful for Carol:

I often wonder what it was that caused things to have gotten so difficult and to have raised so much negative reaction to the new system. One explanation is that we have a history of custom-developed systems, so anything that users wanted got done exactly the way they wanted it. Now we have a set of generic software that is meant to serve many school systems and it doesn't do exactly what they want in exactly the way they want it.

It was hard to get effective participation from the members of the computer selection committee. Coming from the government our RFP wasn't very big to me, but when I passed it around to the committee they couldn't believe it. I couldn't even get the people to really read the RFP, let alone the responses. Actually, it should have been even more detailed. It was the lack of detail that really caused us most of our problems, because it has been the details that have determined whether or not the systems were suitable to our people.

We should have paid a lot more attention to training. DSI hasn't had much experience with training, and they just didn't do a good job with it. They left me, a new user, with too much responsibility for setting up the training and making sure that everything in the system was ready for it. And they didn't provide me with the training that I needed.

Money is a big constraint to the JCSS. I needed a lot more programming help in-house, and someone from DSI—a week here and a week there—to fill in for our lack of knowledge in being able to support our users.

Looking back at it, 15 months seems like an extremely long time to implement a new system. But it might have been better to take even more time to do it. Maybe we should have piloted the system at one school for a year and worked the bugs out of it before installing it systemwide.

Where do we go from here? How do we handle the negative reaction that has been generated from all the stumbles and falls? How do we get things turned around to take advantage of some of the things that are really positive for the school system now that we have access to all this information? I'm beginning to see little pockets here and there where people are starting to use the capabilities of the new system and are developing positive attitudes. I hope that we're getting over the hump!

If we had it to do over again, would we make the decision to go with DSI? That's a question I ask myself every day! Could we have done better? Would we have had fewer problems? I don't know.

PART IV
THE INFORMATION MANAGEMENT SYSTEM

A COMMON THEME OF THIS TEXTBOOK IS THAT MANAGING IT INVESTMENTS IS A responsibility shared by business managers and IS leaders. The importance of the role of senior business managers is therefore especially evident in the Part IV chapters that address planning and managing an organization's IT assets.

Chapter 14 describes an overall process for setting a direction for investing in and planning an organization's information resources. The first step in establishing an effective "management system" is for the business and IS leadership to first agree on a shared vision for the IS role within their organization. From this vision, an overall IT architecture and the plans to enable it are developed. Annual IS planning typically begins with an assessment of the current IS organization performance, revisiting the vision for the IS role in the business and IT architecture, and then developing or revising strategic and operational plans. Short descriptions of some planning tools (such as critical success factors, value-chain analyses, scenario planning) and examples of documents from these planning steps are provided. The chapter also emphasizes the linkage between business and IS planning, and the steps in which business manager participation is essential for ensuring business-IT alignment.

Chapter 15 presents current practices and trends for managing all three IT assets introduced in Chapter 1: technology, IT human resources, and the IT–business relationship. Alternative designs for IT governance (such as what role should be played by a central IS group versus groups in business divisions) are described to set the context for IS leadership in an organization. Then current practices for managing IT service delivery and an organization's portfolio of IT applications are discussed in some detail. The section on managing IT human resources includes research on what IT skills are critical for keeping in-house and the section on the IT-business relationship asset includes mechanisms found to be important for building and fostering effective relationships. The chapter ends with a discussion of unique issues associated with managing a global IS organization and managing offshore IT outsourcing arrangements.

Chapter 16, a chapter totally devoted to the topic of information security, presents some recent statistics for external and internal e-crimes and some technical approaches to prevent and deter them. However, the primary focus of the chapter is on managerial approaches. Information risk management is discussed early in the chapter, and recent laws that impact IT security practices are summarized. Current thinking about the development and distribution of security policies, business continuity planning, electronic records management approaches, and the new organizational role of chief information security officer are also covered in this chapter.

Chapter 17, entitled "Legal, Ethical, and Social Issues," begins with short frameworks for understanding ethical issues related to IT and examples of codes of ethics for IT professionals. The focus then changes from organizational issues to broader IT-related issues of importance to individuals and the societies we live in—including privacy issues, identity theft, and intellectual property rights.

Part IV (and this textbook) closes with nine original case studies written by the textbook authors. The Clarion School for Boys case study addresses the assessment of IT investment opportunities and developing a plan to implement them within a small organization. The Teletron case study describes a business proposal to convert a company from a services firm to a software firm, which would involve major IT investments. The Sallie Mae case study describes a successful example of a "fast track" project to integrate the technology assets of two merging companies using an internally led IT project team and a proven project management office (PMO) capability.

The next pair of cases describes how a (disguised) $2 billion company with multiple business units and aggressive growth goals manages its first major IT outsourcing decision and vendor contract for computer and telecommunications operations for all of its business units. The Schaeffer A case study presents the decision process and opposing views of various stakeholders. The Schaeffer B case study describes the management challenges the company faces during the multiyear outsourcing relationship with a Tier 1 service provider that the company selected, including responding to ongoing business restructurings at Schaeffer.

The next two cases have even more of an international focus. The Baxter case study in Part IV describes a small company facing decisions about how to provide IT support for a new manufacturing plant being built in Mexico. The BAT case study in Part IV is an example of a shared services arrangement for providing IT service delivery and applications development support to country-level offices within the company's Asia Pacific region.

Finally, two short case studies, "Mary Morrison's Ethical Dilemma" and "A Security Breach on the Indiana University Computer Network," extend the discussions on information security and ethical issues found in the two final chapters of this textbook.

CHAPTER 14
PLANNING INFORMATION SYSTEMS RESOURCES

IN PREVIOUS CHAPTERS THE TECHNICAL AND OPERATIONAL GROUNDWORK crucial to an understanding of the management of the information resources in an organization was established. You should now be familiar with many of the issues of computing hardware and software, telecommunications and networking, the variety of information technology (IT) applications, and the development and maintenance of application software systems. The successful management of an organization's information resources in today's competitive business environment must combine this knowledge with a thorough understanding of business strategy to guide the development of information resources for the firm.

This chapter deals with a critical component for effectively managing IT in an organization—setting a direction for its information resources. To set a direction that is aligned with the organization's business strategy requires an information resource planning system that includes: (1) an assessment of current information resources (the status quo), (2) the establishment of an information vision and an IT architecture for that vision, (3) the formulation of an IS strategic plan to move an organization's information resources from their current status toward the desired vision and architecture, and (4) the formulation of IS operational plans (including systems project plans) to achieve short-term IS objectives.

It would not be appropriate here to outline detailed instructions for a specific planning system because planning needs and styles differ greatly from organization to organization and many approaches seem to work. Instead, the basic issues and concepts for an effective information resources planning effort are addressed in this chapter.

Likewise, as will be discussed in Chapter 15, IT governance designs vary widely across firms, and many large organizations in particular have multiple IS units that report to different business managers. However, in this chapter we will discuss the information resources planning process from the perspective of a single IS department. Finally, although some parts of the detailed planning process are typically internal to the IS organization, business managers should also be involved. Examples from a variety of organizations are used to explain the concepts.

This chapter begins with a discussion of some of the reasons companies should set a direction for information resources and definitions of some key terms. Then the overall planning process and each of the steps in it are explained. The chapter ends with some guidelines for developing an information resources plan and outlines the benefits to business managers and IS professionals of having a clear direction for the development of the entire organization's information resources.

THE NEED FOR A DIRECTION FOR INFORMATION RESOURCES

Organizations need a plan for the development of their information resources for several reasons. In some firms, the management of all the diverse applications of IT is not organized under a single person. Yet most firms want to share information among diverse parts of the firm (and sometimes outside the firm) and use that information for strategic or operational advantage. Discussion and agreement on a common IT architecture (as defined later in this chapter) for the varied applications of IT in an organization can provide a shared understanding among IS professionals and business managers of how the company can make best use of its information resources.

Developing a plan for a company's information resources helps communicate the future to others and provides a consistent rationale for making individual decisions. Sometimes an information resources plan is created because business managers have expressed concern about whether there is some grand scheme within which to make individual decisions. The plan for information resources development provides this grand scheme. In organizations where some IS decisions and information resources are decentralized to business units, the establishment of a well-understood overall information resources direction is critical for making consistent, timely decisions by both business managers and IS professionals that ensure business and IT alignment (see the box entitled "Business and IT Alignment").

Planning discussions often help business managers and IS professionals in making basic decisions about how the "business" of IS will be conducted—defining the organization's basic style and values. Such discussions might be part of comprehensive programs that attempt to define or refine the culture of the overall company. For example, a growing medical device manufacturing company believed it was necessary to instill a greater awareness about the concept of quality in the entire business to compete more effectively in the global marketplace. The effort led that company's IS director to consider more precisely the quality-related values to be embraced by the IS organization. For the first time, the IS organization began to consider the role of quality in the shared beliefs of people within the IS organization. Discussion focused on various IS quality issues such as excessive rework in the design of major systems.

Traumatic incidents sometimes create the need for an information resources direction-setting process. For example, telecommunications network redundancy was recently a significant architecture discussion topic among some IS directors within the financial services industry. A tornado had destroyed much of a telecommunications carrier's critical switching center, and the extensive damage reduced data and voice circuit availability for several days. As a result, banks and other organizations that depended on the constant availability of the public telephone network for certain operations, such as automatic teller machines (ATMs), were forced to reexamine contingency plans associated with the unavailability of telecommunications service. Some organizations realized that IS management had not thought seriously about what to do when faced with such a loss. The result in many firms was an extended set of discussions on network architecture and network plans.

BUSINESS AND IT ALIGNMENT

Alignment of IT strategy with the organization's business strategy is a fundamental principle. IS managers must be knowledgeable about how new technologies can be integrated into the business (in addition to the integration among the different technologies and architectures) and must be privy to senior management's tactical and strategic plans. Both IS and business executives must be present when corporate strategies are discussed. IS executives must be able to delineate the strengths and weaknesses of the technologies in question.

[Adapted from Luftman and Brier, 1996]

THE OUTPUTS OF THE DIRECTION-SETTING PROCESS

IS managers have developed project plans and budgets for many years. However, the task of formally developing and communicating an overall information resources plan, with an explicit information vision and architecture, is relatively new to some organizations, whereas other organizations may have had several years of experience in such a process. Creating an information vision, for example, might be a very new activity. As a result, the deliverables at each step in the process take on somewhat different meanings from organization to organization. We therefore first define each output or deliverable in the information resources planning process.

Information Resources Assessment

As outlined in earlier chapters, any organization has a set of information resources—both technological and human—through which business managers conduct the business of the organization.

> An **information resources assessment** includes inventorying and critically evaluating an organization's technical and human resources in terms of how well they are meeting the organization's business needs and IS mission.

An information resources assessment includes reviewing the quality and quantity of the organization's technological resources—the hardware, software, networks, and data components of the information resources system. The human asset portion of an information resources assessment includes a review of the quantity and training/experience level of both users and IS professionals, as well as the management systems and values that drive IS decisions in the organization.

Information Vision and Architecture

Information vision and *architecture* are new terms to many business managers and IS professionals. At a recent meeting of IS directors, the following ideas emerged about the meaning of the information vision and architecture concept. Some executives described the term as a "shared understanding of how computing and telecommunications technology will be used and managed in the business at some point in the future." Others reported that they generate a "comprehensive statement about our future information resources that is part philosophy and part blueprint." The group held that a vision and architecture statement must be "specific enough to guide planning and decision making but flexible enough to avoid restatement each time a new information system is developed." Finally, several in the group asserted that a "vision and architecture statement should provide the long-term goal for the IS planning effort"—the vision and architecture statement represents the overall design target.

Several ideas common to these descriptions suggest a definition. First, the information vision and architecture statement is an ideal view of the future state of the organization's information resources and not the plan on how to get there (the information resources plan is discussed later). Second, the vision and architecture statement must be specific enough to provide policy guidelines for individual decisions. Third, deliberations about vision and architecture must focus on the long term, but exact dates are usually not specified. Finally, there is some difference

between a vision and an architecture although some firms combine the two concepts into a single statement.

With these ideas in mind, the terms can be defined as follows:

> An **information vision** is a written expression of the desired future about how information will be used and managed in the organization.
>
> The information technology **architecture** depicts the way an organization's information resources will be deployed to deliver that vision.

Much like the design of a future complex aircraft or a skyscraper, an information vision and an IT architecture together translate a mental image for the desired future state of information use and management into a comprehensive set of written guidelines, policies, pictures, or mandates within which an organization should operate and make decisions. Other organizations create architectural diagrams or blueprints much like a building architect uses a diagram to represent a mental image of the future. As is true for a business vision, the information vision and architecture might also be a written statement. For example, one organization found it sufficient to define its information vision by stating, "We must provide quality data and computing products and services that meet our clients' needs in a timely and cost-effective manner." Regardless of the form, statements about vision and architecture should provide the business, managerial, and technical platform for planning and executing IS operations in the firm.

Information Resources Plans

The information resources planning process should generate two major plan outputs—the strategic IS plan and the operational IS plan.

> The **strategic IS plan** contains a set of longer-term objectives (often three to five years) that represent measurable movement toward the information vision and IT architecture and a set of associated major initiatives that must be undertaken to achieve these objectives.

At the strategic level, these initiatives are not typically defined precisely enough to be IS projects. Instead, the IS strategic plan lists the major changes that must be made in the deployment of an organization's information resources over some time period, usually multiple years.

> The **operational IS plan** is a precise set of shorter-term goals (one or two years) and an associated project portfolio that will be executed by the IS department and by business managers in support of the strategic IS plan.

The operational IS plan incorporates the precise results that will be accomplished and outlines the set of projects that will be undertaken. Often the budgets for each project are identified in the plan. In essence, the operational plan crystallizes the strategic plan into a series of defined projects that will be accomplished in the short term.

The process of generating each of these outputs and how they are linked together is discussed in more detail in the next section.

THE PROCESS OF SETTING THE DIRECTION

IS and Business Planning

Previous chapters have argued that IS decisions must be tightly aligned with the direction of the business. Such a maxim exists whether for the design of a particular application system or for the overall direction of the organization's information resources. Figure 14.1 depicts the relationship between setting the direction for the business as a whole and setting the overall direction for information use and management in that business. In other words, the strategy for information resources must be tied directly to the strategy for the business. (This linkage process might be applied for the entire company, a division, or an individual business manager's department.)

On the left side of the chart are the general steps required to set a direction for the business. On the right are the required planning steps for the organization's information resources. Note that the many arrows depicting how the output of one IS step (on the right side) impacts the next business step (on the left side) is an ideal view and may not actually occur in practice (as discussed later). However, recent research has shown that senior management involvement in strategic IS planning yields the most successful planning outcomes (Basu et al., 2002). Our focus in this chapter will be on the right side of Figure 14.1, but our overall assumption is that an organization's IS planning and business planning processes are linked and that business managers also play key roles in the IS planning process.

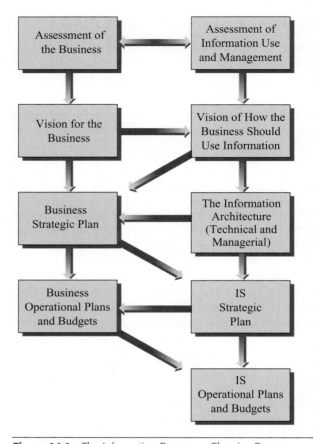

Figure 14.1 The Information Resources Planning Process

Assessment

Any organizational planning process should start with an assessment step, both for the business and for its information resources. Current performance is compared to a previous plan, to competitors, or to a set of past objectives. Operating data are collected. IS surveys are also often conducted to measure internal (business customer) satisfaction with IS performance. Competing organizations are "benchmarked" to determine both what is possible and what is being achieved at other organizations. Both a business assessment and an information resources assessment should be conducted. More on the information assessment step is presented later in this chapter.

Vision

The second basic step in any planning process should be to envision an ideal or intended state at some point in the future. In other words, the entity (the business or its information resources) is described in a way that denotes what the organization wants the entity to become. It does *not* define how to achieve this vision. For the information resources area, an architecture is also generated, and should be a direct input to business and IS strategic plans for the organization.

Strategic Planning

Strategic planning is the third step and should be conducted for both the business and its information resources. **Strategic planning** is the process of constructing a viable fit between the organization's objectives and resources and its changing market and technological opportunities. The aim of any strategic planning effort is to shape the company's resources and products so that they combine to produce the needed results and make progress toward the organization's vision. Strategic *business* planning sets the basic course for the use of all resources, usually over an extended time period. It is designed to be general in nature and typically does not specify precise budgets, schedules, or operating details. Instead, it translates the organization's vision into a set of interim goals and major initiatives that describe how to accomplish the organization's vision of its future. Review of the strategic plan is exercised by regularly examining the status of the major initiatives contained in it.

In parallel with the business plan, a strategic IS plan should be designed to define the path to be taken to lead the organization from its current use and management of its information resources to a future state that is consistent with the information and business vision of the organization. The strategic IS plan also defines the desired results for a specified multiyear time period and the necessary major initiatives to be undertaken.

Operational Planning

Operational planning lays out the major actions the organization needs to carry out in the shorter term (usually a year) to activate its strategic initiatives. It typically includes a portfolio of projects that will be implemented during some time frame in order of priority or urgency. Specific, measurable goals are established, and general estimates of costs and benefits are prepared. New capital expenditures are identified and justified. Responsibility for achievement of the objectives, actions, and projects is also specified in this plan. Review of the operational plan is more precise, often on a time-and-cost basis at the project level. Specific details, responsibilities, and dates of projects that move to the implementation stage are identified in the budget, including staffing requirements, facility scheduling, specific demand and usage forecasts, and detailed expense estimates. Once set in motion, the operational plan is naturally less

flexible than the strategic plan. The operational plan relies heavily on the operating budget for control purposes. In the past, companies developed both long-term (three to five years), as well as short-term (one year) operational business plans. Today, however, an operational planning horizon beyond two or three years is considered unrealistic by many organizations (Heckman, 2003; Philip, 2007).

The operational IS plan is likely even more project-specific than its business plan counterpart, and relies heavily on a balanced (in terms of risk, cost, and expected benefit) portfolio of projects. This difference is a natural result of the operational plan's purpose—to translate the general information resources direction, as defined in the strategic IS plan, into specific systems development projects or other efforts for the IS department (such as a capacity upgrade) that also meet specific initiatives for the business. The operational IS plan also typically includes internal projects designed to enable the IS department to better meet the IS delivery needs of the business.

The operational IS plan also identifies specific accomplishments to be achieved on multiyear applications systems development projects. Suggestions are made for improvements in IS department operating procedures and for increasing infrastructure capacity. Specific goals, actions, due dates, and budgets are proposed for software purchases. The time of professional IS staff is allocated to major systems development projects and other activities.

Traditional Planning in the IS Organization

Until recently, most IS organizations did not have a "seat at the table" when the business planned for its future. Instead, IS leaders might receive a copy of a completed business plan, with little explanation or opportunity for input. In these IS organizations, the process of overall information resources planning is clearly not integrated well with the business planning process, and does not match the input and output arrows in Figure 14.1. As a result, these IS organizations tended to adopt a bottom-up approach to information resources planning, referred to as **needs-based (or project-oriented) IS planning**. That is, when a specific business need called for a new information system, an IS project team was formed to address the situation. Because of this project focus, in many cases not enough consideration was given to the impact that the new proposed IT solution might have on another proposed or existing system, which often resulted in incompatible systems and databases, unacceptable implementation time frames, and a host of other problems.

This reactive orientation toward IS planning, although practical from the perspective of the IS department and perhaps the individual business managers, also typically failed to give adequate consideration to the organization's total information requirements across operating units, including possible economies of scale and avoidance of duplication of efforts, as well as other lost strategic opportunities. As demand for information to be shared across functional organizational lines increased and the distinction between classes of IT blurred, these types of shortcomings led many companies to seek better ways to set a direction for their information resources. Thus, the concept of developing a strategic IS plan, driven by the business strategic plan and seeking to conform to an agreed-upon information vision and architecture for the organization, began to be used more extensively.

Although both the business planning and information resources planning processes are important for overall organizational effectiveness, the rest of this chapter deals in detail only with the right-hand side (IS) steps of Figure 14.1.

ASSESSING CURRENT INFORMATION RESOURCES

The information resources planning process should begin with an assessment of the use of information and IT in the entire organization and an assessment of the IS organization itself. This assessment of the status quo is usually conducted by a committee of business managers and IS professionals, perhaps with the aid of outside experts. Outside facilitators can bring needed objectivity and experience to the process, but their value must be weighed against the added cost. Alternatively, the assessment might be conducted totally by an outside organization and presented to top business and IS department management or the IS oversight committee. As with all such outside studies, there is the possibility that this approach might develop a "not invented here" response by the IS organization and some business managers. If carefully orchestrated, however, an outside information resources assessment can be very successful.

Measuring IS Use and Attitudes

The information resources assessment, however it is conducted, should measure current levels of information resources use within the organization and compare it to a set of standards. These standards may be derived from past performance in the organization, technical benchmarks, industry norms, and "best of class" estimates obtained from other companies. In addition to use measures, the attitudes of users and staff of the IS organization are important. Opinions about the performance of the IS organization in relating its activities to the needs and direction of the business must be measured. Likewise, a technical assessment of the IT infrastructure should be conducted.

Figure 14.2 contains a portion of an information resources assessment conducted for a food products company in response to dissatisfaction with the performance of its IS organization on the part of the company's business managers. As should be clear from the example, the assessment led to substantial changes in the overall information resources direction at this organization.

- **A standard IT platform to integrate our information systems does not exist in our company.** A variety of disconnected information systems exists throughout our organization. Some systems are run on isolated mainframes, others on PCs, at multiple locations. These types of IT "silos" hinder integration and cause needless efforts on the part of IT staff to build interfaces between disparate systems to support decision-making by senior managers.
- **Significant gaps exist in automating "value-added" processes in our company.** Many of the steps involved in value-added processes are conducted manually, or using systems that do not talk to each other. There are work steps that are not supported by the software, and the staff either overrides the software or manually supports these tasks. This results in "lost" opportunities for strategic advantage from our IT investments.
- **There is a consistent perception among business users that the IS department is not responsive to their support needs.** There seems to be a general lack of trust between the user community and the IS organization. Requests for new application systems are not approved and the recent turnover in desktop support personnel has resulted in IT staff not understanding the support needs of their internal business customers.
- **The level of user training is substantially below needs and expectations.** Training on new software is inconsistent. There is a strong feeling among business users that only "tunnel training" exists—they are taught enough to perform a current specific task rather than use software applications in more innovative ways.

Figure 14.2 Sample Items from Information Resources Assessment

Reviewing the IS Organizational Mission

Another important part of the assessment step is a review of the IS department's mission. The **IS mission** (or IS role) statement should set forth the fundamental rationale (or reason to exist) for the activities of the IS department. As introduced in Chapter 1, the IS organization's mission can vary substantially from one organization to another. Some IS departments may be in a more "defensive" mode, focusing primarily on IS operations, while others take a more "offensive" role, focusing on how to use new technologies to achieve strategic advantage in the marketplace, or are truly in a strategic role, focusing on excellent IS operations as well as delivering strategic advantage from newer technologies (Nolan and McFarlan, 2005).

Involving business managers in the assessment exercise is one way to ensure that the IS mission statement defines the most appropriate role for the IS department. This involvement also allows business managers throughout the organization to understand better why the IS department needs a mission statement and a strategic plan. Some examples of questions that require key business management involvement are provided in the box entitled "Assessing the IS Mission."

Figure 14.3 provides an example of a major mismatch between what IS leaders and business managers in the same manufacturing organization understood the IS department's mission to be. The top of the figure is the mission statement developed by the organization's IS staff, which emphasized technical capabilities and a more "defensive" posture—including an emphasis on secure data storage, maintaining processing capacity, managing the data network, providing access to external information resources, and integrated systems development services.

In contrast, the mission statement developed by nine senior managers in this organization makes it clear that these business managers see the IS role as supporting business strategy *and* operations, including being the provider of "new management tools" to improve decision making in

Mission Statement Prepared by IS Managers

Information Services is responsible for designing, acquiring (including custom developing), and maintaining a wide variety of computing systems and services for the people of our corporation.

In this role, the department:

- Provides a secure location for housing and accessing the official electronic data records of the company.
- Maintains computer processing capacity and support for file maintenance and information reporting.
- Provides access to approved external data sources on the Internet.
- Manages a corporate data network that delivers services to departmental and individual workstations linked to its data center.
- Provides integrated IS development for departments in order to advance organizational strategies (systems development services are available for central systems, local area network, workstations, and supply chain applications).

Mission Statement Prepared by Business Managers

In order to meet the challenges outlined within the company's Vision Statement and support the strategic objectives and values of our company, the mission of Information Services is to provide reliable information, data, and computing services to all clients, both within and, where appropriate, outside of the company.

To accomplish this role, the IS department will exercise leadership in identifying new management tools based on evolving information technology that enables management to increase their effectiveness in operating and managing the business. The department's ultimate objective is the development of an integrated information infrastructure and associated services required to facilitate the decision-making process.

Figure 14.3   Conflicting Mission Statements

the business. Leading an IS department with this more "offensive" mission statement would clearly require a major transformation of the IS organization role. In this situation, a mismatch in business and IS manager perceptions of the IS mission was found to be a root cause of internal customer dissatisfaction with the IS department's past performance.

Assessing Performance versus Goals

An annual IS assessment should also include actual performance data. Figure 14.4 provides an example from a regional bank in the Midwest where some of an IS department's

---

ASSESSING THE IS MISSION

- What is the impact of IT on the company's competitive position?
- Have the opportunities for current and forthcoming technologies been fully considered?
- Will changing IT capabilities and economies of scale change the way the business is operated and managed in the future?
- Has the right balance between IT innovation and managing IT costs been achieved?

Achievement Area	Prior Year Objectives	Prior Year Performance[*]
Internal customer satisfaction with applications development services	80%	(71%)
Departmental computing equipment purchases that comply with the supported standards	85%	88%
Scheduled network availability to internal customers	99%	99%
Percent of total organization computing resource capacity connected to data network	80%	85%
Cost per transaction on common systems (lower means higher performance)	$0.025	($0.0285)
IS department personnel turnover (lower means higher performance)	12%	(14%)

[*]Parentheses indicate performance did not meet the IS objective

Figure 14.4 Assessing the Achievements of Prior Year IS Objectives

operational objectives for the prior year are compared against actual performance metrics. The reasons for the shortfalls can be assessed, and this information can be used as input to later steps in the information resources planning process (as shown in Figure 14.1) and to set specific operational objectives for the following year.

CREATING AN INFORMATION VISION

After assessing the current use and management of an organization's information resources, the shared business and IS leadership expectations of how information will be used in the future should be specified. Developing these expectations requires both an understanding of the future direction of the business and an understanding of the role information can play in winning the competitive race.

Vision creation starts with speculation on how the business's competitive environment will change and how the company should take advantage of it. Once this business vision is specified (and written), the implications for how information should be used in the firm in the future should be outlined. The information vision for the organization can then be written.

An example might be useful to explain the process. A small printing company in Atlanta was taken over by new management as the result of an acquisition. During three off-site,

full-day discussion sessions that were held to create a new vision and direction for the overall company, a task force developed a set of basic specifications and fundamental propositions about the company in the future, which led to new business strategy decisions. Senior managers and professional experts in the IS department then reviewed these business priorities along with the new business vision. After several sessions, they jointly arrived at a shared vision for information use and management in the company, as stated below:

- Business managers will know how to use information to make decisions and how to use the capabilities of our information resources effectively.

- Each business unit and functional department will manage its information resources within an overall IT architecture.

- All existing business support processes (e.g., purchase order processing) will be automated (with business rules) to free up time of critical human resources.

- All internal customers (employees) will have desktop tools with easy access to internal and external networks (the Internet) for research and communications.

- Our corporate network will be able to service a large number of remote nodes (to be able to send and receive large files from external customers) at high speed.

■ User demand on our information system each year will experience:

1. Medium growth in transaction volume on existing common systems.
2. High growth in ad hoc requests for information on all shared and personal systems.
3. High growth in transaction volume from new applications on shared and personal systems.

■ The order fulfillment cycle (for external customers) will be supported by an integrated, comprehensive, and accurate database.

Taken together, these statements specify how senior management wants information to be used and managed in the future. These statements are not a plan—how the IS department working with business managers will create this environment must still be determined. Instead, these statements represent a vision of what is desired. The architectural decisions on how to deploy the company's data, software, people, and other IS assets are also not all specified. That is the next step.

DESIGNING THE IT ARCHITECTURE

Now that a vision for future information use in the organization has been formulated, the IS organization, often in cooperation with business managers, must design an IT architecture. This architecture specifies how the technological and human assets and the IS organization should be deployed in the future to meet the information vision. In particular, it reflects the IT integration and standardization requirements required by the firm's operating model for the business (Ross et al., 2006). The actual plan for migrating the organization's current information resources to the specified IT architecture is developed later.

Several models have been developed that define the elements that make up an architecture for IT. Traditionally, these models take on a very technical definition of an IT architecture. In keeping with the classification of IS assets, Figure 14.5 presents a high-level list of the elements for both a technological component and a human component.

The **technological component** of the IT architecture contains desired specifications about future hardware and operating systems, network, data and data management systems, and applications software. One approach is to consider these elements as IT services to be provided to the business

> **TECHNOLOGICAL COMPONENT**
> • Hardware (and Operating Systems)
> • Application Software
> • Network
> • Data
>
> **HUMAN COMPONENT**
> • Personnel
> • Values/Culture
> • Management System

Figure 14.5 Elements of an IT Architecture

(Weill and Vitale, 2001). For example, Figure 14.6 presents a list of five categories of IT services that a typical IS organization today needs to plan for, beginning with channels for customers to communicate with the business. Some of the tradeoffs and issues in developing the specifications about these elements are dealt with in more detail in other chapters; business continuity planning and other risk management considerations are discussed in Chapter 16.

The **human assets** component of an IT architecture outlines the ideal state of the personnel, values, and management systems aspects of an IT system. Together, these elements specify the "business" parts of managing the IS department,

> **External Customer Channel Management:** Provide electronic channels to end consumers or business customers to support one or more applications (e.g., Web sites, call centers, IVR, mobile phones, etc.).
>
> **Communications Management:** Wide area and local area communications network services, including Internet, extranet, and EDI linkages with business partners; intranet access to support employees and groups.
>
> **Data Management:** Management of data independent of applications, including database administration, transaction processing, data storage, data warehouses for business intelligence.
>
> **Application Infrastructure Management:** Centralized management of enterprise and workgroup application services, wireless applications, and applications for workflow support.
>
> **Data Center Facilities Management:** Management of large-scale data processing facilities, including mainframes and other servers.

Figure 14.6 Examples of IT Services to Be Considered in Designing an IT Architecture

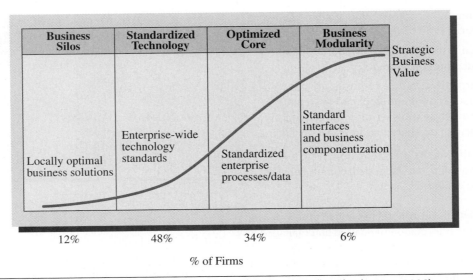

Business Silos	Standardized Technology	Optimized Core	Business Modularity
Locally optimal business solutions	Enterprise-wide technology standards	Standardized enterprise processes/data	Standard interfaces and business componentization

Strategic Business Value

| 12% | 48% | 34% | 6% |

% of Firms

Figure 14.7   Business Value at Different Stages of IT Architecture Maturity (Ross, Weill, and Robertson, 2006)

how business managers will be involved, and how IS decisions will be made. Chapter 15 will specifically address managing the human resources for the IT organization.

Recent researchers have also proposed that there are four IT architecture "maturity" stages that differ in their ability to provide support for business operating models, and therefore the value IT provides to the business (Ross et al., 2006):

1. **Business Silos:**   companies seek to maximize individual business unit or functional needs
2. **Standardized Technology:**   companies seek to enable IT efficiencies through shared services and application rationalization, resulting in enterprise-wide IT standardization
3. **Optimized Core:**   companies implement enterprise-wide business processes and data with tightly linked systems and processes (such as with ERP systems)
4. **Business Modularity:**   companies seek global flexibility with loosely coupled IT-enabled business process components, which enable local differences but also preserve enterprise-wide standards

As shown in Figure 14.7, almost half of the companies studied were found to be in only the second stage. However, even these firms have achieved greater business benefits by moving from multiple, local IT platforms (stage 1) to enterprise-wide IT standards (stage 2). Significantly greater business benefits were also found to have accrued to those firms that have "optimized" their IT architectures to support standardized business processes and integrated data (stage 3). Although very few firms had achieved stage 4, the authors argue that firms must achieve

stage 3 before moving on to stage 4, since the business value of the final stage is based on preserving enterprise-wide standards while also increasing the flexibility at the local business unit (or functional) level.

THE STRATEGIC IS PLAN

According to Figure 14.1, after assessing the current information resources situation and establishing an information vision and IT architecture, a strategic IS plan is developed. This plan is a statement of the major objectives and initiatives (not yet defined precisely enough to be projects) that the IS organization and business managers must accomplish over some time period to enable the information vision and the IT architecture, and to be aligned with the strategic plan for the overall business. The strategic IS plan should also contain a set of measurable results to be achieved during this time period for assessing progress toward the vision. The plan might also contain the results of an internal *and external* strategic analysis.

The Strategic IS Planning Process

The development of the IS strategic plan is accomplished in four basic steps: setting objectives or goals, conducting an external analysis, conducting an internal analysis, and establishing strategic initiatives. Although they are treated here in sequence, most planning processes involve iterations through these four steps.

Setting Objectives The setting of IS objectives is done in much the same way as strategic objectives are specified for any business or functional organization. Measures are identified for each of the key result areas for the organization. IS objectives are often established in such areas as IS department service image, IS personnel productivity, and the appropriateness of technology applications. Goals relating to increased effectiveness, access to external resources, and breadth of business manager involvement in IS applications are also possible.

A sample of strategic IS objectives for a regional bank in the Midwest was shown in Figure 14.4. This organization assigned IS department goals in several areas, including internal customer satisfaction, compliance with standards, network availability, and IS department personnel turnover. Although the choice of which goals to set will vary with the organization's circumstances, each objective should provide some clear benchmark toward achieving the vision and architecture for IT.

Conducting Internal and External Analyses The second step in the development of a strategic IS plan is a review of the external environment within which the organization's information resources must be developed over the planning period, say three to five years. This step should include reviews of the company's strategic business plan as well as an IT industry forecast. Quite often the result of this process is a series of statements called opportunities (areas in which new systems could be created or where the IS organization could take some action to the company's long-term advantage) and threats (external factors that might affect IS performance that could be corrected or for which some countermeasure could be developed).

Along with the external analysis, a review of the internal strengths and weaknesses of the IS department and how well business managers play their role in the entire IT process is also conducted. The list of strengths indicates areas where the IS department is particularly strong. Likewise, the list of weaknesses displays areas where the IS department or the role of the business manager should improve. The internal analysis parts of this step are often conducted during the assessment phase of the planning process described earlier in this chapter. These four statements together make up a **SWOT** (strengths, weaknesses, opportunities, and threats) strategic situation analysis.

A sample SWOT analysis that was input into a company's strategic IS plan is shown in Figure 14.8. Note that the company (via a working group of business managers and IS managers) identified seven strengths related to the organization's information resources. Most relate to

technical skills of IS professionals and the quality of their transaction processing systems. Six weaknesses in the use or management of information are listed, ranging from personnel issues within the IS organization to limited departmental applications beyond routine transaction processing.

These strengths and weaknesses act as either leverage points (strengths) or as limiting factors (weaknesses) for new strategic initiatives. The threats and opportunities lists contain both factual and attitudinal issues that must be dealt with in the plan. Both user and technology issues should be mentioned in the opportunities and threats sections.

Establishing Strategic Initiatives Figure 14.9 contains a set of strategic initiatives resulting from a strategic information resources planning effort for a medium-sized energy company. Each statement represents an important initiative needed to enhance the role of IT at this corporation. Some of these initiatives will require substantial investment and create new operating costs for implementation. Yet none of the initiatives is spelled out in enough detail to be immediately translated into action. The operational planning step is required to translate these initiatives into actual projects.

Tools for Identifying IT Strategic Opportunities

While building the strategic IS plan, organizations often seek help in identifying ways in which IT can provide strategic advantage for the firm. Several tools for finding new strategic insights have proven useful. None of the tools discussed here explicitly considers how an opportunity, once identified, can be translated into a comprehensive IS plan for the organization. The tools, however, have proven valuable in finding specific opportunities for IT applications and showing the role that IT might play in achieving certain business objectives.

Critical Success Factors One well-known method for identifying strategic IT opportunities is to define information needs and processes critical to the success of a business function like sales or to the entire organization, called **critical success factors (CSFs)**. Any recent text on strategic management should contain a fuller discussion of CSFs. Generally, however, CSFs define a limited number of areas (usually four to six) that, if executed satisfactorily, will contribute most to the success of the overall performance of the firm or function. Many CSFs have either short-term or long-term impact on the use of IT. Once

Strengths	Weaknesses
Opportunities	Threats

Strengths

- Major transaction control systems are relatively new, functionally adequate, well-documented, maintainable, and operationally efficient.
- The IS department has demonstrated effectiveness in adding new technologies (e.g., Web-enabling certain systems).
- There is a stable, competent professional IS staff with expertise in designing and programming transaction processing systems.
- Our IS outsourcing partner seems to manage a reliable, cost-effective data center.
- There is substantial use of our in-house electronic mail operation, frequented by most business managers in the company.
- There is substantial information technology expertise among business managers in both line and staff organizations.

Weaknesses

- A single point of IS contact for internal customer operational problem diagnosis and resolution has not been established.
- There are limited data center performance measurement systems.
- There is a lack of emphasis on transaction-based systems development productivity.
- There is a high degree of technology specialization (narrowness) among IS professional staff and a limited degree of business orientation.
- There is limited departmental use of information technology beyond simple decision support and participation in common transaction processing systems.
- Few business managers make effective use of the Internet.

Opportunities

- The IS department enjoys a high degree of credibility among the large and growing internal customer community.
- The role of the business manager in collaborating with the IS department has been institutionalized, facilitating ease of future system implementation.
- There is a growing base of internal customers who understand a wide range of information technologies and want to use IT for their business.
- The Internet provides data and interaction capability that would be of substantial strategic use to the firm.

Threats

- The IS department's effectiveness is threatened by pockets of internal customer negativism, especially among top management.
- Some business managers are developing a high degree of technical competence, which they employ in a nonintegrated fashion by developing separate workstation-based systems.
- The accelerating pace of technological change and proliferation of information technologies pose risks of control, obsolescence, and difficulty in maintaining IS professional staff competence.
- Extensive internal communication networks and internal customer access to external databases pose security risks to our data.
- The IS department is still not an integral part of company's business planning process.

Figure 14.8   Swot Analysis Example

identified, the factors can be stated as opportunities for the application of IT. An analysis might then be conducted to determine more precisely how IT can be used to accomplish the needed task.

Analysis of Competitive Forces   It is generally accepted that competitive advantage can come about by changing the balance of power between a business and the other actors in the industry. As seen from the strategic systems

Management wants the Information Services and Systems (ISS) department to develop its own long-range plan utilizing the vision, mission, values, and principles of operation outlined previously. The following is a listing of initiatives we feel should be undertaken in the ultimate formulation of this plan:

1. Manage development and operations of network architecture and security in accordance with business and internal customer requirements.

2. Help departments build individual information plans, utilizing ISS departmental expertise and knowledge of overall company system requirements.

3. Create and maintain a short list of approved hardware and software that can be efficiently utilized within the designed network to meet end-user requirements.

4. Coordinate with other departments in the evaluation and design of telecommunication and data communication systems that meet the company's strategic and operational needs.

5. Provide and annually update a prioritized list of uses of external data that would strategically help the company.

6. Encourage active client participation in network utilization through training programs and help sessions that increase the efficiency and effectiveness of the overall company decision-making process.

7. Restructure the information services and systems departmental organization to better accomplish the mission of the department.

8. Develop a structured timetable and system of application backlog reductions.

9. Formulate a written standardization process for application development.

Figure 14.9   Sample Strategy Agenda

examples in earlier chapters, a company interested in finding a strategic initiative can:

- Inhibit the entry of new competitors by raising the stakes for competing in the market or by redefining the basis for competition in at least one dimension (e.g., price, image, customer service, product features).

- Slow the application of substitute products/services by providing difficult-to-duplicate features.

- Make products/services more desirable than those of current competitors by providing unique product features or customer services or by shifting some customer product selection criterion (e.g., by being a low-cost provider).

- More strongly link with customers by making it easy for them to do business with the company and difficult to switch to a competitor.

- More strongly link with suppliers to obtain lower-cost, higher-quality materials.

An analysis of these competitive sources can identify ways in which competitive advantage can be achieved through the creative use of IT. But where exactly might opportunities exist? Figure 14.10 lists questions that IS strategic planners can ask about suppliers, customers, and competitors to identify opportunities for the strategic use of IT. An individual manager can study these questions as well and use them to stimulate discussion in a brainstorming session aimed at suggesting possible applications of IT.

Value Chain Analysis   Another technique frequently used to suggest strategic IS initiatives is the classic **value chain analysis** method described by Porter and Millar

(1985). As depicted in Figure 14.11, the value chain includes five primary and four support activities within an organization that can each add value for the customer in the process of producing, delivering, and servicing a product or service.

IT can be used in each activity to capture, manipulate, and distribute the data necessary to support that activity and its linkages to other activities. To be of strategic or competitive importance, automating an activity in this chain must, for instance, make the process run more efficiently or lead to differentiation of the product or service.

For example, an organization's goal of market differentiation by a high level of on-time delivery of products

---

Suppliers

- Can we use IT to gain leverage over our suppliers?
  - Improve our bargaining power?
  - Reduce their bargaining power?
- Can we use IT to reduce purchasing costs?
  - Reduce our order processing costs?
  - Reduce supplier's billing costs?
- Can we use IT to identify alternative supply sources?
  - Locate substitute products?
  - Identify lower-price suppliers?
- Can we use IT to improve the quality of products and services we receive from suppliers?
  - Reduce order lead time?
  - Monitor quality?
  - Leverage supplier service data for better service to our customers?
- Can we use IT to give us access to vital information about our suppliers that will help us reduce our costs?
  - Select the most appropriate products?
  - Negotiate price breaks?
  - Monitor work progress and readjust our schedules?
  - Assess quality control?
- Can we use IT to give our suppliers information important to them that will in turn yield a cost, quality, or service reliability advantage to us?
  - Conduct electronic exchange of data to reduce their costs?
  - Provide master production schedule changes?

Customers

- Can we use IT to reduce our customers' cost of doing business with us?
  - Reduce paperwork for ordering or paying?
  - Provide status information more rapidly?
  - By reducing our costs and prices?
- Can we provide some unique information to our customers that will make them buy our products/services?
  - Billing or account status data?
  - Options to switch to higher-value substitutes?
  - By being first with an easy-to-duplicate feature that will simply provide value by being first?
- Can we use IT to increase our customers' costs of switching to a new supplier?
  - By providing proprietary hardware or software?
  - By making them dependent upon us for their data?
  - By making our customer service more personalized?
- Can we use external database sources to learn more about our customers and discover possible market niches?
  - By relating buyer behavior from us to buying other products?
  - By analyzing customer interactions and questions to us to develop customized products/services or methods of responding to customer needs?

continued on next page

Figure 14.10 Questions to Identify Strategic IT Application Opportunities

- Can we use IT to help our customers increase their revenues?
  — By providing proprietary market data to them?
  — By supporting their access to their markets through our channels?

Competitors

- Can we use IT to raise the entry barriers of new competitors into our markets?
  — By redefining product features around IT components?
  — By providing customer services through IT?
- Can we use IT to differentiate our products/services?
  — By highlighting existing differentiators?
  — By creating new differentiators?
- Can we use IT to make a preemptive move over our competition?
  — By offering something new because we have proprietary data?
- Can we use IT to provide substitutes?
  — By simulating other products?
  — By enhancing our existing products?
- Can we use IT to match an existing competitor's offerings?
  — Are competitor products/services based on unique IT capabilities or technologies and capabilities generally available?

Figure 14.10   *Continued*

SUPPORT ACTIVITIES	Firm infrastructure	Planning models				
	Human resource management	Automated personnel scheduling				
	Technology development	Computer-aided design			Electronic market research	
	Procurement	Online procurement of parts				
PRIMARY ACTIVITIES		Inbound logistics	Operations	Outbound logistics	Marketing and sales	Service
	Examples of IT application	Automated warehouse	Flexible manufacturing	Automated order processing	Telemarketing Laptops for sales representatives	Remote servicing of equipment Computer scheduling and routing of repair trucks

Figure 14.11   Strategic IT Application Opportunities in the Value Chain

requires that operations, outbound logistics, and service activities (such as installation) be highly coordinated, and the whole process might need to be reengineered to be Web-enabled. Thus, an automated IS in support of such coordination could have significant strategic value. In automotive manufacturing, for example, Internet-based systems that facilitate sharing of design specifications among design, engineering, and manufacturing (which might be widely separated geographically) can greatly reduce new vehicle development time and cost. Significant advantage can also be gained at the interfaces between the activities, where incompatibility in departmental objectives and technologies can slow the transition process or provide misinformation between major activities.

From a broader perspective, an organization's value chain is actually part of a larger system of value creation, called a supply chain, that flows from suppliers, through the firm, to other firms providing distribution, and ultimately to the end customer. Opportunities for improvement in the supply chain could thus be intercompany, such as using the Internet to automate the automobile ordering process from customers to dealers to manufacturers. As a result, exchanging information over the Internet has been of strategic importance in several industries. It is also important to remember that activities in a value chain are not necessarily sequential because many activities can occur in parallel. In fact, significant competitive advantage can occur by using IT to allow these activities to be done in parallel, thereby developing or delivering products sooner. Thus, competitive advantage can result from improvements in either the internal value chain or the interorganizational supply chain.

A series of idea-generation and action-planning sessions is often used to generate possible strategic applications of IT for the organization. The idea-generation sessions typically include example strategic applications from other organizations (to stimulate ideas by analogy). Small groups then brainstorm on possible strategic opportunities that address the competitive assessment. Questions such as those in Figure 14.10 can be used to stimulate ideas for IT application. A critical element of this brainstorming process is that criticism and negative comments about new ideas are prohibited.

Subsequent evaluation of these ideas involves the degree of competitive advantage expected, cost to implement, technical and resource feasibility, and risk. Based upon these criteria, ideas are then grouped into ranked categories. Top priority ideas are identified and used in the strategic IS planning process.

The constructs and opportunity identification techniques discussed here are nothing more than tools for creating a strategic IS plan. Like any tool, they can be misused or misinterpreted to the detriment of the information resources planning process and ultimately the organization. Although tools and concepts help, the key to the development of a viable strategic IS plan is clearly the ability of the IS department and business managers to work together in designing and executing an IS strategic plan.

Scenario Planning   Another technique that has frequently been used by business leaders to address an uncertain future has been to develop alternative scenarios for what the future might look like. Typically, a few major drivers are focused on to create the "scenario space" and then characteristics of the scenarios are used to help the company plan for the future.

For example, four scenarios for the future of the IS organization were recently proposed by Gray and Hovav (2007) based on high or low levels of two IT-related drivers:

1. telecommunications reliability (which is assumed to impact IT reliability in general), and
2. IT alignment with business and socioeconomic conditions.

Based on these two drivers, four very different alternatives for the IS organization are proposed, ranging from a "return to the dark ages"—in which, for example, the strategic use of IT is low and cyberterrorism reigns—and "nirvana" in which strategic use of IT is high, and there is essentially no cyberterrorism. Although these are admittedly extreme alternatives, the intent is to describe differences for important variables for each scenario to help planners do more "out-of-the-box" thinking.

THE OPERATIONAL IS PLAN

After the strategic IS plan has been developed, the initiatives identified in it must be translated into an action plan incorporating a set of defined IS projects with precise expected results, due dates, priorities, and responsibilities.

Operational planning differs from strategic planning in its focus, its linkage to the business, and in the specificity with which IS projects are defined and addressed (see Figure 14.1). A multiyear operational IS plan, which may be developed for up to a three-year time period, focuses on project definition, selection, and prioritization. Resource allocation among projects and tools for providing continuity among ongoing projects are also components of the long-term plan.

The first step is to define multiyear IS operating objectives. Key changes in the business direction should be identified and their possible impact on IS activities should be assessed. The inventory of available information resources is then reviewed to determine which needs can be met over the planning period. Alternatives to new systems are developed in light of the constraints identified by the information resource inventory process conducted earlier.

IS development or acquisition projects must next be defined and selected. The criteria for evaluating projects include availability of resources, degree of risk, and potential of the project to contribute value to the organization's objectives. Clearly, organizational politics often play more than a minor role in the final project selection process, as different business leaders argue for projects that they sponsor (see the sponsor role discussion in Chapter 12).

Many IS planners have taken a cue from financial analysts by adopting a *portfolio view* of the IS operational plan. They select new systems to be developed or purchased based on their association with and impact on other projects in the current systems development portfolio. Factors to consider include, but are not limited to, the level of risk of the various projects in the portfolio, the expected time until completion, their interrelation with other projects, their nature (for example, transaction processing versus business intelligence), and the amount of resources required. IS and business mangers then seek to balance the projects in the portfolio.

Firms that ignore portfolio balance and concentrate solely on implementing low risk transaction processing systems for a single function, for example, might lose the opportunity to develop higher risk systems offering higher potential business returns. Conversely, a project portfolio of nothing but risky applications with unknown chances for success and uncertain economic benefits might place the firm itself in financial jeopardy. Figure 14.12 shows a portion of the systems project portfolio (both new systems and enhancements of existing systems) developed for a company with its own sales organization.

Each IS project in the portfolio must then be subjected to a more detailed project planning process, in the form of a budget review. Once the operational IS plan has been approved, it should be shared to help instill a sense of commitment on the part of the organization. As with all business functions, a multiyear IS plan should be reviewed and updated as necessary, at least annually.

Finally, the operational IS plan for a one-year time period focuses on specific tasks to be completed on projects that are currently underway or ready to be started. It is linked to the firm's business priorities by the annual budget. Hardware, software, and staffing needs, scheduled maintenance, and other operational factors are highlighted in detail.

System/Project	This Year	Next Year	In Two Years	New (N) or Replacement (R)	Make (M) or Buy (B)	Risk Assessment	Project Size	Comments
Executive and retiree personal income tax assistance		X		N	B	Low	Small	Manual assistance currently provided
Fixed assets accounting		X	X	R	B	Medium	Large	Improved asset management and ability to respond to tax law changes
Corporate competitive database	X	X		N	M	High	Medium	Improved analytical capabilities, access
Common tactical sales information system		X	X	N	M/B	High	Large	An ongoing series of installations of capabilities to enhance the effectiveness of the sales organization
Order entry by field organization	X			N	M	Medium	Small	Provide more timely processing of customer orders

Figure 14.12 IS Operational Plan: Project Portfolio

Sometimes the long-term and short-term operational plans are combined into a single document. As business and technology changes have become more constant, the planning horizons have shortened and the need for more frequent reviews and updating have increased. Quarterly reviews are now increasingly being used in today's organizations.

GUIDELINES FOR EFFECTIVE IS PLANNING

Planning for the development of an organization's information resources can be a very complex, time-consuming process. Planning efforts attempt to make provisions for the rapid rate of change in IT and capture the often hazy definition of exactly what a strategic system is supposed to do. The first step in developing an organizational planning focus, as opposed to only a project focus, is to change the way in which the IS organization's professionals view their jobs. These changes include adoption of a service orientation by the IS staff in order to view users as partners. Change must also be viewed by IS professionals as a constant process to be exploited, not just an intermittent disturbance to be controlled.

By taking the following actions, managers can also increase the likelihood of a successful IS planning effort:

1. *Early clarification of the purpose of the planning process is essential.*   IS and business managers will not adopt the shared vision necessary for success of the direction-setting process if they do not understand the purpose of the effort, its scope, and its relevance to their individual efforts.
2. *The information resources planning effort should be viewed as an iterative effort.*   An extended planning process that generates reams of paper that are left untouched will not be as effective as a short process that generates a plan that is reviewed and then *modified on a regular basis* to reflect the new realities facing the organization. Many IS plans have lengthy implementation periods, and needs and situations change.
3. *The plan should reflect realistic expectations.*   Input into the planning process by business managers can result in much more feasible plans, greater probability of acceptance of new application solutions, and systems that more closely resemble those needed by the business.
4. *A unified approach to delivering IT services should be used.*   The boundaries between technical computing, business computing, collaboration technologies,

Web applications, and other IT application areas are increasingly blurred. An integrated view of all of these application areas will result in the adoption of one cohesive, overall IT service delivery approach. For example, a very confusing message is sent when telecommunications is centrally planned and is a free service while scientific computing is treated as a scarce resource and charged for by the use-unit.

5. *An effective IS plan will also take into consideration potential barriers and constraints.*   The best-planned, most technically well-designed systems often meet with resistance if adequate consideration is not given to how people will react to them on both an individual and group basis.

BENEFITS OF INFORMATION RESOURCES PLANNING

The cost of developing an IS plan can be substantial, especially in terms of IS leaders' and business managers' time, but significant benefits can be achieved from such endeavors (Brown, 2004). Both the resulting documents and the processes used to create the assessment, the vision and architecture, and the strategic and operational plans contribute to these benefits.

Better IS Resource Allocation

A good plan provides the basis for more specific IS resource allocation. In most organizations, IS management is charged with creating budgets that reflect business priorities for the IS organization over the next several years. A planning process that contains a vision and an architecture demonstrates *what* the group should be trying to create. Likewise, a good plan explains *how* the organization will get there. Budget requests then make a lot more sense to those outside the IS department.

Communicating Budget Needs with Top Management

Top management correctly insists on a rationale for major capital or staffing investments in the IT arena. Many IS directors often request significant operating or capital budget increases—well above that available to other departments. A solid IS plan, clearly linked to the business's direction, can help explain the need for such expenditures by showing a nontechnical context for priorities.

Creating a Context for IT Decisions

Another important function of an information resources plan is to create a clear context within which business managers and IS professionals can make individual decisions. In many organizations it is possible to come to work every day, move from one meeting to another and from one project to another, and not really understand the organization's overall direction. It is critical to communicate the overall direction of information use and management widely throughout the firm so everyone can understand that the organization is focused on the same defined target.

Achieving Both Integration and Innovation

Most IS organizations are focused on balancing the needs for tighter integration of their common (shared) systems and networks while simultaneously responding to business unit needs to innovate with new technologies (Segars and Grover, 1999). Developing an overall information resources plan forces discussion on how exactly to go about achieving these seemingly opposite objectives. Such intense discussions might promote a greater understanding of the trade-off between autonomy and integration and result in a commitment to a particular course of action.

Evaluating Vendor Options

The range of architecture options for IT applications is broad and growing. Moreover, the number of IT vendors is growing rapidly. A clear IS plan can provide guidance in selecting one vendor over another. It allows an organization to take advantage of a range of options and see how they best fit into some overall architecture for the future. Otherwise, the organization runs the risk of being "vendor-driven," as well as responding only to current needs rather than designing long-term solutions to major future business problems. Having an explicit IT architecture and plan is also an effective way for IS leaders to communicate with vendors on the need for certain capabilities in future IT products.

Meeting Management Expectations

Today, senior management in most organizations has higher expectations than ever before on what IT can do strategically for the company. Company executives are looking for new sources of competitive advantage. In a global competitive arena, where many organizations have excellent scientists, design engineers, and new product development specialists, company leaders want to use IT

as another source of distinction in the market. The development of an explicit vision and architecture for IT generates discussion on the role of this critical resource in meeting the firm's objectives.

SUMMARY

To ensure that IT is effectively utilized in today's competitive, rapidly changing world, the organization must engage in a proactive, future-based information resources planning process. The process must begin with a thorough assessment of the current situation, including the IS mission, goal accomplishment, and customer satisfaction.

The development of an information vision and architecture is a difficult conceptual task. Organizations often create visions or architectures that explicitly deal with only some of the issues mentioned in this chapter. Therefore, it is important to revisit a vision/mission statement regularly to resolve issues not dealt with earlier. Ongoing attention to IT architecture decisions is also a critical IS leadership role.

Strategic planners must have an understanding of the competitive marketplace in which the company operates, as well as the strengths and weaknesses of its own IS department. The strategic IS plan should mirror and be clearly linked to the business plan, and provide a well-documented road map from which the firm can make IT investment and budgeting decisions. Documentation from the entire IS planning process ranges from the broad objectives stated in the strategic IS plan to the detailed staffing requirements and expense forecasts made in the short-term operational IS plan.

A number of tools exist for identifying strategic opportunities to be assimilated into the strategic IS plan. Whether or not these tools are used, both business managers and IS professionals have crucial roles to play if the IS plan is to be linked to the strategic direction of the overall business.

REVIEW QUESTIONS

1. This chapter emphasizes that an IS plan should be linked to the strategic plan for the overall organization. Why is this important?

2. How does an information vision differ from an IT architecture?

3. Describe the basic steps in the development of the IS strategic plan in Figure 14.1

4. What are some ways that business managers might participate in the Assessment step?

5. Why is it important to assess user attitudes, not just information use?

6. Comment on the differences between the IS mission statements by the IS and business managers in Figure 14.3. What are some conclusions that could be drawn from these differences?

7. How would you respond to the criticism that a proposed IT architecture is not feasible based on today's technology?

8. How could the performance results in Figure 14.4 be used in the remaining IS planning steps?

9. Figure 14.7 suggests that companies evolve their IT architectures through different maturity stages. Why might this be true?

10. Contrast the critical success factors (CSFs) and SWOT (strengths, weaknesses, opportunities, and threats) approaches for assessing opportunities for a strategic IS planning process. Under what circumstances might one of these approaches be more useful than the other?

11. Why might companies today develop IS operational plans that only cover one or two years?

12. Why is it important to include business managers in a process to develop a strategic IS plan? An operational IS plan?

6. Making assumptions when necessary, construct an IT architecture that is consistent with the printing company's new shared vision, as described in the section of this chapter entitled "Creating an Information Vision."

7. Given the rapid rate of change in both information technologies and business environments, do you believe that strategic IS planning efforts continue to be worthwhile for most organizations? Why or why not? Under what circumstances might they not be?

8. Some have argued that a company's existing IT architecture and strategic IS plan should drive the business strategic plan, instead of being driven by it. Can you think of an example where this might be the case?

9. Do you believe that strategic advantages obtained by the effective use of IT are sustainable? Why?

10. In what phases of the IS planning process is the business manager most likely to be involved? What are his or her responsibilities likely to be during each of the steps in Figure 14.1?

11. How might a business manager's role change if the benefits of proposed IT investments are exceedingly difficult to quantify?

DISCUSSION QUESTIONS

1. In addition to the reasons listed in the chapter, what other issues or events might cause an organization that does not have a formal IS plan to recognize the need for developing one?

2. What are the major implications for the business manager if an assessment of current practices indicates substantial inconsistency in the information vision and architecture for the company? What are the major implications for the IS leaders?

3. How might the human components of a company's IT architecture have an impact on the technological components (as described in Figure 14.5) of its architecture, and vice versa?

4. What are some important IT management challenges that would likely be encountered in working toward the Optimized Core architecture in Figure 14.7?

5. Through which media (text, pictures, etc.) can an information vision and architecture be represented? What are the advantages of each approach?

REFERENCES

Applegate, Lynda M., Robert D. Austin, and F. Warren McFarlan. 2007. *Corporate Information Strategy and Management: Text and Cases*, 7th ed. New York: McGraw-Hill/Irwin.

Basu, V. Hartono, Al Lederer and Vijay Sethi. 2002. "The impact of organizational commitment, senior management involvement and team involvement on strategic information systems planning." *Information and Management*, 39: 513–524.

Brown, Irwin T. J. 2004. "Testing and extending theory in strategic information systems planning through literature analysis." *Information Resources Management Journal*, 17:4: 20–48.

Crane, Darlene B., and Margery Mayer. 2003. "A three step assessment." *Darwin Magazine* 4 (September): 4–7.

Daniel, Diann. 2007. "The rising importance of the enterprise architect." *CIO, www. cio.com/article/101401.The_ Rising_Importance_of_the_Enterprise_Architect/1* (March 31).

Evans, Philip, and Thomas S. Wheeler. 2000. *How the New Economics of Information Transforms Strategy*. Boston, MA: Harvard Business School.

Feld, Charlie S., and Donna B. Stoddard. 2004. "Getting IT right." *Harvard Business Review* 54 (February): 1–8.

Gray, Paul and Anat Zeelim Hovav. 2007. "The IS organization of the future: Four scenarios for 2020." *Information Systems Management*, 24:2 (Spring): 113–120.

Heckman, Robert L. 2003. "Strategic Information Technology Planning and the Line Manager's Role." in C.V. Brown and H. Topi (eds.), *IS Management Handbook*, 8th ed. New York: Auerbach, Chapter 4.

Hildebrand, Carol. 2000. "The art of the new deal." *Darwin Magazine* 1 (June/July): 9–15.

Hoenig, Christopher. 2000. "The master planner." *CIO* 13 (May 1): 76, 78.

Luftman, Jerry, and Tom Brier. 1996. "Achieving and sustaining business-IT alignment." *California Management Review* 42 (1): 109–122.

Malan, Ruth, and Dana Bredemeyer. 2003. "Architecture strategy." Bredemeyer Consulting Web site, *www.bredemeyer.com/ArchitectingProcess/ArchitectureStrategy.htm* (April).

McKeen, James D., and Heather A. Smith. 2003. *Making IT Happen: Critical Issues in IT Management*. New York: John Wiley & Sons.

McNurlin, Barbara C., and Ralph H. Sprague. 2006. *Information Systems Management in Practice*, 7th ed. Upper Saddle River, NJ: Pearson Prentice Hall.

Nolan, Richard and F. Warren McFarlan. 2005. "Information technology and the board of directors." *Harvard Business Review* (October). HBR Reprint R0510F.

Oliver, Dan. 2002. "Build your skills: Four steps in building an enterprise data architecture." TechRepublic Web site, *www.techrepublic.com* (March 18).

Pearlson, Keri E., and Carol S. Saunders. 2005. *Managing and Using Information Systems: A Strategic Approach*, 3rd ed. New York: John Wiley & Sons.

Perks, Col, and Tony Beveridge. 2003. *Guide to Enterprise IT Architecture*. New York: Springer.

Philip, George. 2007. "IS strategic planning for operational efficiency." *Information Systems Management*, 24 (3): 247–264.

Porter, Michael E., and Victor E. Millar. 1985. "How information gives you competitive advantage." *Harvard Business Review* 63 (July–August): 149–160.

Rechtin, Eberhardt, and Mark Maier. 1997. *The Art of Systems Architecting*. Boca Raton, FL: CRC Press.

Ross, Jeanne, Peter Weill, and David Robertson. 2006. *Enterprise Architecture as Strategy: Creating a Foundation for Business Execution*. Boston: Harvard Business School Press.

Schekkerman, Jaap. 2006. "Enterprise architecture assessment guide." Version 2.2. Institute for Enterprise Architecture Developments Web site, *www.enterprise-architecture.info/Images/Architecture%20Score%20Card/Enterprise%20Architecture%20Assessment%20Guide%20v2.2.pdf* (January).

Segars, Al, and Varun Grover. 1999. "Profiles of strategic information systems planning." *Information Systems Research*, 10(3): 199–232.

Seger, Katherine, and Donna B. Stoddard. 1993. "Managing information: the IT architecture." Harvard Business School 9-193-059.

U.S. Government Accounting Office. 2003. "Information technology: A framework for assessing and improving enterprise architecture management." Version 1.1. U.S. GAO Report GAO-03-584G. U.S. GAO Web site, *www.geo.gov/docdblite/summary.php?rptno=GAO-03-584G&accno=A06709* (April 1).

Weill, Peter and Michael Vitale. 2002. "Information technology infrastructure for e-business." *MIS Quarterly Executive* 1:1 (March): 17–34.

Wunder, John, and Will Tracz. 2003. "An information architecture strategy." *Journal of Defense Software Engineering* (October): 17–34.

CHAPTER 15
LEADING THE INFORMATION SYSTEMS FUNCTION

As introduced in Chapter 1, an IS department is responsible for managing three IT assets: the technology and human resources that comprise an organization's information resources, as well as what has been called the IT-business relationship asset (Ross et al., 1996). This third asset reflects the reality that whether IS leaders are CIOs of large corporations or are IS directors in much smaller businesses, their effectiveness will be highly dependent on their abilities to work closely with key business managers in their organizations. As described in Chapter 14, this collaboration begins with developing a vision for the IS role in the organization, which sets the boundaries for IT architecture planning and strategic IT investments. IT today is so pervasive that it requires the attention of every major organizational unit and key business manager.

Here in Chapter 15 we focus on the major IS activities that IS leaders need to effectively manage to achieve their organizations' IS vision and current objectives. First we briefly address some of the external and internal influences on the evolving IS role in today's client organizations and the business reasons for different IS governance designs. These choices determine which IT resource decisions will be made centrally (as in a corporate IS unit headed by a CIO) or decentrally (in business units). Then we focus on current practices and performance metrics for managing the three IT assets.

Our discussions about managing the technology asset will be in two major parts:

1. Managing IT service delivery, and
2. Managing IT applications

The chapter ends with a discussion of two special IS leadership challenges that reflect today's increasingly "flat" world: managing a global IS organization, and managing offshore IT outsourcing contracts.

THE EVOLVING IS ROLE

Rapid changes in information technologies and manager expectations for how IT can be utilized in a business have led to significant changes in the IS mission and the way the IS role has been carried out. Some of these external changes are driven by the IT industry itself, while others are anticipated and unanticipated external events (such as the Sarbanes-Oxley legislation in response to a major business debacle in the United States).

Some observers have noted that IS leaders have been pulled in two different directions: commoditization and strategic use (Smith and McKeen, 2006). For example, technical innovations and globalization have increased the drivers for connectivity and collaboration, which promote IT standardization and commoditization. However, the opposite pull is for IT to contribute to innovations that lead toward business strategy transformations that leverage new advances in IT.

Other changes in the IS role have been due to an increased understanding of old and new technologies by business managers, the growth in opportunities to leverage a global Internet, and domestic changes in legal and regulatory environments—including changes to respond to terrorist events, other criminal activities, and increased opportunities to leverage external labor markets.

Despite these common influences, not all organizations desire to invest in information resources at the same level at the same point in time. As introduced in Chapter 1, the extent to which an organization takes an *offensive* or *defensive* approach to their IT investments (see Figure 1.1) depends on the extent to which they are dependent on reliable and "proven" IT for critical business operations and the extent to which the organization's managers seek out new technologies to implement new business strategies.

For example, sometimes an organization moves to a more aggressive posture after a change in business leadership. There is now a greater understanding among business leaders of how to leverage old and new technologies and the business

THE CIO JOB ISN'T WHAT IT USED TO BE

Today's CIO job isn't what it used to be. The computing systems they manage have long been seen as an essential corporate resource with significant costs that need to be controlled. Growth by acquisition brings new consolidation challenges, including whittling down dozens of data centers to a small number of regional centers. Today's CIO is also being asked to help hone corporate strategies to better leverage IT—including how to reach new customers, how to better design products, and how to increase revenue growth rates. Today's Web sites are also now huge direct-sales channels that must be skillfully designed and tightly managed, and IS leaders may work with a company's business unit to design new customer-centric products that can be digitally delivered. Although the average compensation for a firm's top IS leader is now about $200,000, CIOs at some major corporations are reporting salaries more than three times the average.

[Adapted from Tam 2007]

opportunities (and threats) that exist with a global Internet. A new senior executive may want to aggressively invest in enterprise systems to improve an organization's internal or external supply chain processes or integrate data captured by systems

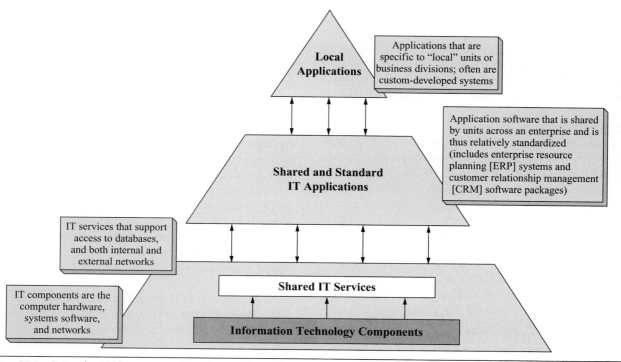

Figure 15.1   Enterprise IT Management (Based on Weill and Broadbent, 1998)

in previously autonomous business units. Other senior managers may want to more aggressively invest in better business intelligence for product development, customer segmentation, or pricing decisions: They want access to enterprise-wide data—and lots of it—as quickly as possible.

Ensuring payback from appropriate IT investments, being able to respond quickly to changing external events, and leveraging technology for increased business value are now basic expectations that an organization's IS leaders must meet (see the sidebar entitled "The CIO Job Isn't What It Used to Be").

To succeed in these objectives, an IS organization may not only have to develop new capabilities, but also the way its IS resources are governed. Different IS governance designs, and the reasons they are chosen, are therefore described in the next section.

DESIGNING THE IS ORGANIZATION STRUCTURE AND GOVERNANCE

The "classic" IS organization of the 1970s had two primary responsibilities: computer operations and software applications. At the outset, these two primary IS activities were typically managed within the same unit: a *centralized* **IS governance** design. However, in large organizations, each business division may have had its own IS staff running its own applications on its own computers—with little or no coordination across the other divisions. This design in large organizations resulted in what came to be called a *decentralized* IS governance design. Decentralized IS designs can still be found in organizations with highly autonomous business units that perceive no major benefits from sharing IS operations or applications with other business units. Stated differently, the business units are given essentially total control over their IS resources.

Another way to view these two primary IS responsibilities is shown in Figure 15.1. Here, a distinction is made between two types of applications:

- "shared" applications, that are used across an organization (such as ERP systems), and
- "local" applications, such as a scheduling system for a particular manufacturing plant or a claims processing system for a particular service unit

By definition, shared applications are likely to be governed under a centralized IS group, whereas "local" applications may or may not be. These more specialized "local"

applications are typically supported by a separate group of IS personnel, and this group might be part of a centralized IS unit or part of a decentralized IS unit that reports to the business manager of the division that the "local" application supports.

Today, highly *centralized* designs are especially common for computer operations activities. This is because greater cost efficiencies can be achieved when expensive computer equipment and networks can be purchased and operated by a central (corporate) IS group for all business units. Some large businesses also have centralized IS designs for most of their applications in an attempt to achieve greater integration across their business processes and the systems to support them.

Two hybrid IS governance designs—which combine elements of centralized and decentralized designs—are also common today. As shown in Figure 15.2, some organizations choose a *federal* design in an attempt to achieve the benefits associated with *both* the centralized and decentralized designs. Specifically, these companies seek to achieve cost efficiencies from centralizing their computer and network operations under a single (corporate) IS unit, but give business units control over their applications by decentralizing these resources. The fourth design, called here a *customized* design, is found in some large, multidivisional firms in which some business divisions choose to have a centralized IS unit handle all of their IT needs, while other divisions choose to have a federal or decentralized design in order to locally address their own IT needs with their own IS staff running their own computers.

It is important to note that decisions on how to distribute IS decision-making authority and oversight are separate from decisions on how to distribute computer-processing power, storage equipment, and network hubs. The discussion here focuses on centralized versus decentralized decision-making authority for a set of IS activities, not the economies of locating data processing operations close to a supplier or a specific business user.

Today, some organizations with centralized designs for their computer operations are also operating as a "business within a business" where the IS unit is treated much like an external vendor, with separate cost and revenue accounting. The most common approach here is to combine the IS organization with other functional support organizations in a **shared services** model. These groups often include human resources, legal, physical facilities maintenance, and transportation, and may or may not be created as a separate legal entity. Multiple shared services organizations may also be set up in large, international firms in different regions, and sometimes these units compete for service contracts with other shared service units that primarily serve a different

	Centralized	Decentralized	Federal	Customized
Operations -Infrastructure Planning -Computer Operations -Telecom/Network Operations -Help Desk -Desktop Support	C	D	C	C or D
Applications -Application Planning -New System Development -Legacy System Maintenance -End-User Development Support	C	D	D	C or D

C = Centralized decision making and accountability for IT resources
D = Decentralized decision making and accountability for IT resources

Figure 15.2   Four Common IS Governance Designs (Adapted from Brown, 2003)

region. (For a detailed example, see the case study IV-7: "BAT APSS: Shared Services at a Multinational Firm.")

How does a firm choose among these IS governance designs? A firm's IS governance design needs to be aligned with characteristics of the overall business. If a company is relatively small, a centralized IS design is most likely. If a company is large and has multiple business units, and the heads of these business units can operate with a high degree of autonomy, then a federal or decentralized design is more likely to be chosen than a centralized IS governance design. If one of the business leaders in this large, multibusiness company is reluctant to take on IS responsibilities, then a custom design may be adopted to accommodate this business leader's preference.

MANAGING IT SERVICE DELIVERY

The physical technology assets of an organization (its computer hardware, telecommunications and data networks, and software) have always represented a very large capital investment. Although hardware costs have decreased, user demands for PCs, laptops, and other portable devices have increased, and the actual purchase costs for these systems is only a fraction of what it costs to support a user

connected to internal and external networks and applications. However, from a *business* perspective, these technology assets are used to deliver a *service*—such as access to e-mail, an application screen for entering order information, or a printer connected to a local area network.

The IT infrastructure decisions that an organization's IS leader is responsible for directly affect IT service delivery. Many technology decisions about the physical location of IT equipment, the choice of a new PC operating system, or a new security application, also involve different kinds of trade-offs that can affect IT service delivery. (Examples of some specific technology trade-off issues are summarized in Figure 15.3.) Although these types of decisions require IT expertise, business manager input is frequently required to adequately assess the trade-offs so that the best decision is made from a service delivery perspective, not just a technology perspective.

Today, employees at all levels in the organization, at multiple locations, typically interact with the computer network for essential aspects of their work. Thus, network or computer failure now has a high degree of visibility—it may disrupt plant managers, division heads, and decision making by senior leaders. Further, with the advent of applications for not only internal operations, but also interorganizational operations, an IT service delivery failure may also have a direct impact on the company's customers or suppliers.

1. **Equipment Location.** Clearly, most organizations today operate in a distributed computing environment. However, the physical location of the hardware on a network can be a critical issue from cost, control, and security standpoints. Physically distributing equipment that supports enterprise systems may create additional costs for managing the hardware and safeguarding data (e.g., many computers and telecommunications switches benefit significantly from being housed in a secure, environmentally controlled location), as well as extra costs for specialized personnel. Nevertheless, there may also be good reasons for locating servers near plant or division managers, rather than in a corporate or regional data center many miles away. Likewise, some countries may be better hosts than others for the location of complex data centers.

2. **Client/Server Allocations.** Policies on the design and role of IT servers and workstations are also driven by not only cost concerns, but also convenience and security trade-offs. Questions that need to be addressed include: What is the most appropriate location of each type of computing work—at the workstation or at a central server or at a remote hardware resource? Which workstations should have independent intelligence and which should be a network device slaved to some central server? Should telecommunications, such as with voice over the Internet protocol (VoIP), and computer components of the workstation be physically integrated? Should video conferencing capability be integrated into the manager workstation, on a local area network, or at some departmental server? What level of access should a given client have to outside resources on the Internet?

3. **Operating System Standards.** Some vendors of technology hardware still offer a proprietary operating system, although more commonality exists now than in the past. How many and which operating systems will the organization support? In particular, will the organization support an "open source" operating system such as Linux, for servers and/or cleints? Each different operating system creates more difficulty in sustaining a seamless network, and support costs increase rapidly as new operating systems are added. Confining the company to one operating system, however, reduces bargaining power, limits access to the best software, and makes the organization more dependent on the fortunes (and security practices) of a particular vendor.

4. **Network Redundancy.** Because organizations are so dependent today on their networks, many business managers want full redundancy of the key nodes and paths in the IT network. Yet full redundancy can be *very* expensive. How much redundancy should there be in the design of the network? Should there be full redundancy only for major nodes and high-volume pathways? The cost for full path redundancy can be very expensive because there must be at least two different paths to every node in the network from every other node. Likewise, "hot" backup sites that allow failed critical nodes to return to operation quickly are also expensive. The lack of redundancy, however, can be very expensive in terms of lost user time if the network or a critical node is not available for some period. The needs of business managers for specific types of applications are key inputs to trade-off decisions between the cost of downtime and the cost to provide continuous access.

5. **Standard Communications Protocols.** As with operating systems, many hardware vendors support their own proprietary communications protocols as well as some mix of standard communications protocols. For example, most vendors support the ASCII file transfer protocol, the Ethernet protocol for local area networks, and the TCP/IP protocol for use of the Internet. However, there are many other protocols to be considered. (See Chapter 4 for a discussion of protocols.) Although the selection process is complex, some set of communications protocols should be established as standards in the firm.

6. **Bandwidth Capacity.** What bandwidth, or transmission capacity, should be provided between hardware nodes in the network? The decision is, of course, dependent on the applications to be used. Image and graphical applications require much greater transmission rates for effective use than do text-only applications. Content-rich applications are growing rapidly on the Internet. Should every client on the network have broadband connectivity? Specifications about the desired technical infrastructure to meet the vision for information use are critical to help drive bandwidth investments.

7. **Network Response Time.** In many organizations, hundreds of users are simultaneously interacting with the network, and each of them is directly affected by the response time of the system—the delay between when the return key is pressed and when the response from the system appears on the screen. If this delay is reasonably short, and consistent, users are generally satisfied. If the delay is perceived by the user as excessively long—three or four seconds when one is used to subsecond responses—it can be very frustrating and significantly hamper productivity. Yet the costs needed to reduce response delays tend to increase exponentially at some level, so input from business managers is again critical in making such decisions.

8. **Security, Privacy, and Network Access.** If steps are taken to make the network and its nodes more secure, quite often the result is to reduce ease of access for users of the network. Organizations should make an explicit decision to operate somewhere along the spectrum between maximum ease of access and maximum security, based on an up-to-date understanding of the legal and regulatory environments for their business. In addition, how ubiquitous should access be to specific networks and data? Should all managers in the organization have essentially the same access rights, or is there a need to provide different levels of access support—including remote access—to specific employees? To what extent should employees have unrestricted Internet access? At many firms, viewing the results of athletic events (or even the events themselves) is permitted from the desktop, but others prohibit such access.

Figure 15.3 Technology Trade-off Decisions

Today's information "utility" is like electrical power—if it goes out, everything comes to a halt until service is restored. For example, problems with a bank's network can affect those customers who enter transactions into the bank's ATM system, and problems with an airline traffic control system at a major hub can create havoc for travelers and business partners worldwide.

Chargeback systems and service level agreements are two management mechanisms typically used by IS leaders to help ensure that the costs of providing a specific service are recognized by the business units that use the service, and that business unit expectations for delivering the service (for example, the response time for displaying an online application screen) are met by the IS unit providing the service. These mechanisms therefore also establish some of the metrics for assessing an IS department's overall performance in delivering IT services.

Chargeback Systems

Some senior business managers believe that the best way to hold both IS and the business units accountable for IT costs is to have the IS unit operate like a profit center, with a flexible budget and an agreed-upon transfer pricing scheme. This approach places control of IT spending directly in the hands of those business managers who use the services. Instead of a vague annual negotiation process of capital expenditure approvals and cost allocations, the IS leader and senior business managers agree on prices for IT services that allow the IS department to effectively manage IS department costs.

If implemented well, a **chargeback system** can be a way to better understand true costs: business managers adapt their behavior to take advantage of the agreed upon price of a service. For example, discounts for overnight processing might cause a business manager to rely less on online reporting in real time. Other potential benefits associated with chargeback systems are summarized in Figure 15.4.

Transfer prices can be developed for a broad and comprehensive range of IS activities, including charges for:

- ■ IS personnel (time spent and rate for specific skills)
- ■ Computer usage (or computer cycles used)
- ■ Disk file space (data storage costs based on type of storage unit)
- ■ Number of transactions processed
- ■ Amount of computer main memory used (per unit of time)
- ■ Number of users of an application

Charges might be cost-based (to recover all costs) or market-based (to be comparable to market alternatives). A combination of clearly identifiable direct costs, plus an allocation of other overhead costs (space, administrative staff, and so on), might also be used.

However, a major problem with implementing any chargeback system is that many IT costs are joint costs, not easily attributed to one single unit—such as the cost to store and maintain a shared database or to place an order fulfillment process on the Internet. Further, some costs are essentially fixed, such as systems software costs, and all of the components of a data center are complex. Thus, calculating data processing costs, and having the capability to reduce expenditures as processing demands vary, can be difficult to accomplish.

Another potential problem is that chargeback systems can become a source of tension between the IS organization and business managers unless the structure for determining the IS service charges is jointly developed and clearly understood. As summarized in Figure 15.5, successful chargeback systems have charges that are understandable, promptly reported, controllable by the business manager, and consistent with the organization's IS role and goals. Once implemented, it's important to periodically evaluate the chargeback formulas to ensure that the desired results are being achieved.

Service Level Agreements (SLAs)

Another mechanism for managing the delivery of IT services is to develop formal **service level agreements** for individual business units. Similar to an agreement that

- Assigning costs to those who consume and benefit from IT.
- Controlling wasteful use of IT resources by encouraging users to compare the benefits with the costs and eliminate unprofitable use.
- Overcoming erroneous perceptions that IT costs may be unnecessarily high.
- Providing incentives by subsidizing the price of certain services or innovative uses of technologies.
- Changing the IS department's budgeting process to be more business driven, thus rewarding the IS organization for improved service and greater efficiency rather than technological change for its own sake.
- Encouraging line managers to be knowledgeable consumers of IS because they must directly pay for such support.

Figure 15.4 Potential Benefits from Chargeback Systems

- **Understandable:** An understandable chargeback system reports use in business terms that user-managers can relate to their own activities, not just computer operations. For example, charges per customer order, invoice, or report relate more to business activity than does the number of computer input/output operations performed or machine cycles used.
- **Prompt and regular feedback:** Charges should be reported soon after the activity to which they are related so that use and cost can be closely linked and total costs can be accurately monitored by those who can control the costs.
- **Controllable:** The activity for which business managers are charged must be something they can control. For example, charges for rerun computer jobs because of operator errors would not be controllable. Further, business managers must have a choice to use alternative services or to substitute one kind of usage with another (for example, switching between two alternative database management systems or trading computer time for data storage).
- **Accountable:** Managers responsible for generating IS activity must be identifiable and must be held accountable for their charges. Otherwise, the charges are meaningless and useless.
- **Relate to benefits:** Managers must see a link between costs and benefits so they can balance the value of the IS services against what is being spent.
- **Consistent with IS and organizational goals:** Charges should be designed to achieve the goals set for the business and the goals of the IS organization. Thus, charges should encourage use of important information technology services, efficient use of scarce technology and services, the desired balance of internal and external sourcing of IS services, and development of systems that comply with accepted architectural standards.

Figure 15.5 Characteristics of Good Chargeback Systems

would be written with an external supplier, an SLA explicitly defines client expectations (here, the business unit) for a specific type of IT service, and procedures to be followed when there is an IT service delivery failure.

At a minimum, an SLA should include the following elements:

- A simple definition of the service to be provided (e.g., help desk support)
- The name(s) and contact information of IS personnel to contact for this service

- A table listing the services to be provided and their costs (e.g., how quickly different types of problems will be responded to, and the costs associated with providing this type of service level)
- Escalation procedures (e.g., who to contact if the agreed upon service response is not being provided)
- A sign-off page for the appropriate business client and the IS liaison preparing the SLA document

Service Delivery Process Improvements with ITIL

In recent years, IS leaders have also adopted new process-oriented approaches to help their IS departments improve their internal delivery of IT services. In particular, several organizations have begun to implement processes that are part of the **Information Technology Infrastructure Library (ITIL)**.

First developed in the late 1980s by a branch of the British government, ITIL documents a set of 12 processes to deploy and operate computer systems, such as processes to ensure:

- adequate *computer capacity* exists for new IT applications or other IT infrastructure changes
- tracking of a *computer incident* (such as a service interruption or security breach) from the time it first appears until a system change is made to permanently fix the problem
- all changes to any component of an IT system follow a formal *change management* process

In addition to providing a common language for operational processes for communicating with other internal IT staff as well as contractors and suppliers, the ITIL framework can be used to train IT staff to think of IT services more from a business-oriented perspective than a technology-component perspective. The overall objective is for IT operations staff to better anticipate service delivery impacts before an IT infrastructure change is made, and to more quickly and effectively resolve delivery problems after they are detected (see the box entitled "ITIL at Work").

Outsourcing IT Service Delivery

Because of the high degree of specialized IT skills and training required to effectively manage data centers and networks, and especially the complexities involved with transborder computer and network operations, many organizations of all sizes have chosen to outsource some, or most, of their IT service delivery activities. One of the

ITIL AT WORK

When a business user at the brokerage firm Pershing has an IT system or hardware problem, their call to a service desk is transferred to one of four specialty areas: desktop, network, mainframe, or distributed systems. The staff member who answers the phone has a list of previous incidents and how they were resolved. If the user's problem cannot be resolved within 10 minutes, a subject matter expert is automatically notified. If the problem is not resolved by the SME after one hour, a senior IT manager is conferred with. And if the IT department can't solve a problem after two hours, the CIO is required to call a top business executive. Since the use of ITIL guidelines to restructure their handling of service desk calls 12 months ago, Pershing's incident response time has been reduced by 50 percent. Since all incidents are tracked using a common language, it's also easier to spot trends across the specialty areas, and to perform a "root-cause" analysis on chronic problems to identify underlying flaws in the IT systems that are causing them.

[Adapted from Worthen, 2005]

primary benefits with **outsourcing** these types of IT activities is cost savings: large, experienced IT service providers may be able to do it cheaper than a client organization for which IT service delivery is not considered a "core competence."

However, outsourcing contracts for managing computer processing and communications networks for larger organizations are typically multiyear contracts—spanning five, seven, or ten years. Because of the complexity of the outsourced activities, security concerns about the organizational data and processing being managed, and the time length of these outsourcing arrangements, entering into such a contract typically requires many months of preparation and contract negotiations under the purview of an organization's legal department and procurement specialists. Once IT service delivery is outsourced, it's also hard to bring it back in-house.

It's therefore important for organizations to carefully assess the potential costs and benefits of *not* having internal IS personnel perform these critical activities. (See the section "Insourcing and Outsourcing IT Skills.")

MANAGING IT APPLICATIONS

Most organizations have a substantial investment in software applications used throughout the business. Some have thousands of programs and millions of lines of code

that are the result of investing millions of dollars in thousands of staff-years for custom systems development by in-house personnel and/or with the help of outside contractors. Software applications become critical assets without which the company could not operate. One of the key application management dilemmas is when to abandon a legacy system and invest in a new IT solution, versus continue to incur the costs of maintaining an aging **legacy system**. In the early 1990s, it was not uncommon for large organizations to be spending 80 percent of their application software budget on legacy system maintenance, rather than on new software—both new custom-developed applications and purchased packages.

An Applications Portfolio Approach

Thinking about a firm's software assets as an **IT applications portfolio** to be continuously managed helps an organization make these types of difficult decisions. The company should know what software it owns, where it is located, what it does, how effective it is, and what risks are associated with its continued use and maintenance. Any company should treat maintenance of software just as they treat plant maintenance: an activity that is necessary to preserve the value of the asset, based on a regular assessment of the return that this asset provides to the company.

Decisions about the development of new applications and the maintenance of legacy applications should be subject to a set of guidelines derived from the organization's current vision, IT architecture, and strategic IS plans for the future. These guidelines should also provide a corporate-level policy as to what degree application investments at the "local" (functional, divisional) level are appropriate, as opposed to the implementation of "shared" IT applications (as described earlier in Figure 15.1), as well as the extent to which corporate IS resources are involved in the development and maintenance of such "local" applications.

Other issues that applications portfolio policies should deal with include the organization's preferences for purchased packages versus custom-developed applications. As discussed in Chapter 11, software packages frequently require major changes in business processes that would not be required if a custom application were built. However, for many organizations the benefits of more quickly implementing a software package that may already have been proven (in other organizations that purchased it) to be a reliable, well-designed application may outweigh the business costs of having to undertake custom application development.

All but very small organizations typically have a formal process for making any IT investment decision. Most of these organizations also require that some kind of return on investment (ROI) and risk assessment be performed for new IT application projects of a certain size. The payback period for a given investment then becomes one of the criteria used by a committee (with representatives from relevant business and IS units) charged with approving and prioritizing project requests on an annual or more frequent basis.

As described in the chapters in Part III, sometimes it is difficult to quantify the potential benefits from a new application, especially when the proposed application will be custom-built with new technologies. In these situations, prototyping and pilot techniques are typically used (see Chapter 10).

Organizational guidelines should also exist for assessing IT investments for smaller projects that may not go through a formal approval process—including policies and guidelines for application development by employees who are not IS professionals. (For a discussion of guidelines for user-developed applications, see Chapter 13.)

Metrics for IT Applications Management

The performance metrics for a new application project are well established: both custom and packaged system implementation projects should result in (1) a high-quality application, (2) delivered on time and (3) within budget. However, large system projects—such as multimodule ERP systems that will be implemented at multiple sites—should also be tracked to ensure that the potential benefits calculated at the time of the investment decision are actually realized. For this type of investment, a one-year lag in capturing the benefits is not unusual—and the responsibility for ensuring that the benefits are achieved clearly resides with not only IS managers, but also business managers.

Recently, there have also been significant efforts to improve the quality of IS processes to manage and deliver IT applications. In particular, for example, many IS leaders have adopted the process guidelines embedded in the **Capability Maturity Model** developed over a decade ago by the Software Engineering Institute (SEI) at Carnegie Mellon University. Since that time, adoptions of the process model have significantly increased, although by 2003 the majority of organizations had not yet reached Level 3. Descriptions of the five levels and the levels achieved by reporting organizations are provided in Figure 15.6. (As noted in the exhibit, a revised version of the model, named **CMMI**, was released in 2002.)

However, recent researchers have shown that many organizations seek to achieve certification only up to CMMI Level 3, and that in many situations this is a wise decision. That is, moving to Levels 4 and 5 requires a significant amount of additional IS development discipline and IS specialist time to document and test systems. Level 5 processes are certainly appropriate for certain types of systems (such as government defense systems) but may not be appropriate for many other types of business applications (Adler et al., 2005).

Many of today's organizations have also invested in process improvements under a **project management office (PMO)** or similar program management structure. In addition to improved performance metrics due to training in project management techniques, benefits have also accrued to those firms that have developed repeatable processes, change management capabilities, and post-project reviews. (See also the PMO discussion in Chapter 12.)

MANAGING IT HUMAN RESOURCES

The most important asset in the IS organization is clearly its people—and personnel costs are typically the largest item in an IS organization's annual budget. The specific skills needed for effective IT service delivery and IT application solutions vary based on the IT infrastructure standards and nature of the business. However, IS personnel skills needed for today's organizations can be classified into five categories (Zwieg et al., 2006): technical, project management, business domain, sourcing, and IT administration. A listing of specific skills and capabilities for each of these categories can be found in Figure 15.7.

The overall performance metrics for managing IS personnel are similar to those for other business functions, and have remained relatively constant. In the second half of the 1990s, however, IT staffing issues escalated in importance in many organizations due to a shortfall in IT skills and lots of job-hopping by IT professionals. More recently, attracting, developing, and retaining IT professionals has again become one of the top five concerns of IS leaders (Agarwal et al., 2006).

In recent years, one common approach to expanding IS managers' involvement in managing IT human resources has been to establish a direct reporting relationship with the HR staff members responsible for recruiting IT workers so that they better understand the skill needs of the IS organization. Another common initiative has been to develop formal "coaching" programs for mentoring IT personnel to reduce job-hopping.

CMM*	Focus and Description	Key Process Areas	Distribution of Levels Achieved	
			1987–1991 (132 organizations)	1999–2003 (1.343 organizations)
Level 1: Initial	*Competent people and heroics:* The software process is ad hoc, occasionally even chaotic. Few processes are defined, and success depends on individual effort and heroics.		80.0%	13.3%
Level 2: Repeatable	*Program management processes:* Basic program management processes are established to track cost, schedule, and functionality. The necessary process discipline is in place to repeat earlier successes on programs with similar applications.	• software configuration management • software quality assurance • software subcontract management • software project tracking and oversight • software project planning • requirements management	12.3%	43.5%
Level 3: Defined	*Engineering processes and organizational support:* The software process for both management and engineering activities is documented, standardized, and integrated into a standard software process for the organization. All programs use an approved, tailored version of the organization's standard software process for developing and maintaining software.	• peer reviews • intergroup coordination • software product engineering • integrated software management • training program • organization process definition • organization process focus	6.9%	25.6%
Level 4: Managed	*Product and process quality:* Detailed measures of the software process and product quality are collected. Both the software process and products are quantitatively understood and controlled.	• software quality management • quantitative process management	0.0%	8.5%
Level 5: Optimizing	*Continuous process improvement:* Improvement is enabled by quantitative feedback from the process and from piloting innovative ideas and technologies.	• process change management • technology change management • defect prevention	0.8%	9.2%

*In the revised Capability Maturity Model Integrated (CMMI) model, Level 4 is "Quantitatively Managed."

Figure 15.6 Five Levels of Capability Maturity for Software Development (Based on Adler et al., 2005)

Technical
>   Systems analysis
>   Systems design
>   Programming
>   Systems testing
>
>   Database design/administration
>   IT architecture/standards
>
>   Operations (Service delivery/ITIL)
>   Mainframe
>   Distributed systems
>   Operating systems
>   Voice/data telecommunications
>
>   Help desk/desktop support
>   Continuity/disaster recovery

Project Management
>   Project team leadership
>   Project planning, budgeting & scheduling
>   Project risk management
>   User relationship management
>   CMM utilization
>   Working globally/virtual teaming

Business Domain
>   Account management & communications
>   Industry application knowledge
>   Company-specific knowledge
>   Function-specific knowledge
>   Business process design & reengineering
>   Change management/readiness

Sourcing
>   Sourcing strategy
>   Third-party provider selection
>   Contracting & legal
>   Vendor relationship management

IT Administration
>   IT governance
>   Financial management
>   Internal HR management

Figure 15.7   IT Skills and Capabilities by Categories (Adapted from Zwieg et al., 2006)

Most IS leaders also regularly monitor their IT staff retention rates, and typically compare these to their annual goals, usually stated as "turnover" rates. However, the ideal turnover rate for one organization may not be similar to that for another organization. This can be due to several reasons,

including the need for an organization to focus on newer emerging technologies, for which a higher turnover rate for older skills not needed is ideal. Or an organization may need to retain industry-specific or company-specific knowledge of its employees, and thus a lower turnover rate is ideal.

A list of common practices that organizations have used to retain IT workers is provided in Figure 15.8. Note that many of these practices are devoted to the continuing professional development of IS staff—including career planning, skill and competency training, and mentor-based development. The IS field is diverse and includes some highly specialized skill needs. Although senior IS executives are more and more becoming general business managers, most IS professionals have specific technical

Work Environment	Interesting work
	Empowerment/Participation
	Teams
	Communication by senior
	management
	Market-anchored
	compensation
Career Development	Promotion from within
	Career paths
	Career planning activities
	Management training &
	development
	Building business/leadership
	skills
	Dev. plan & competency/skill
	training
	Individual or mentor-based
	development
	In-house/other mentor-based
	formal training program
	More frequent appraisals
Community-Building Initiatives	Newsletters
	Intranets
	Social activities
	Socially responsible activities
Monetary Incentives	Monetary rewards/bonuses
	Variable compensation
Employment Incentives	Employment security
	Financial stability of company

Figure 15.8   Common Practices for Retaining IT Workers (Agarwal et al., *MIS Quarterly Executive*, Sept. 2006 p. 139)

Enterprise Resource Planning (ERP business domain, SAP, PeopleSoft)

Sarbanes-Oxley (SOX business domain)

Customer Relationship Management (CRM business domain, Siebel)

Database (Sybase, Oracle DB, DB2, RDMS general)

Simple Object Access Protocol (SOAP)

Unix (AIX, other)

PL/SQL

COBOL, C, C++, C#

XML, Perl

Java/J2EE

Visual C++, Visual Basic

Websphere, ASP.net, .net

Microsoft Project

SAS

Figure 15.9   Top-Paying IT Professional Skills in 2006 (Based on Dice, 2006)

duties and require specialized training. With product life cycles for software shortening, it is not uncommon for large organizations to have some of its IT workforce in training most of the time.

The salaries and retention rates of IS professionals are highly dependent on current labor markets. In mid-2007, there were reports of greater turnover rates in many organizations as the number of new college graduates with computer science and business technology backgrounds remained low and the demand for IT services from large and specialized consulting firms grew. The most in-demand IT professional skills and experiences actually cover a broad range of technical and IT application knowledge. Figure 15.9 provides a listing of those highest rated in 2006, based on survey responses from about 20,000 IT professionals in client companies as well as IT industry firms and consultancies.

Insourcing and Outsourcing IT Skills

Decisions about the mix of internal and external IS staffing have become more complex in recent years as the sourcing alternatives have grown. However, a recent survey of IS leaders in client organizations based in the United States suggests that some technical, project management, and especially business domain skills of IT professionals are highly valued—and most critical for keeping in-house. Stated differently, client organizations are most reluctant to outsource the skills shown in Figure 15.10. As expected, the top skills that firms are most likely to outsource to third-party providers were all technical skills (see the full list in Figure 15.7).

For those readers aspiring to be entry-level IT professionals, it should be kept in mind that the outsourced technical skills still are needed by client organizations, and

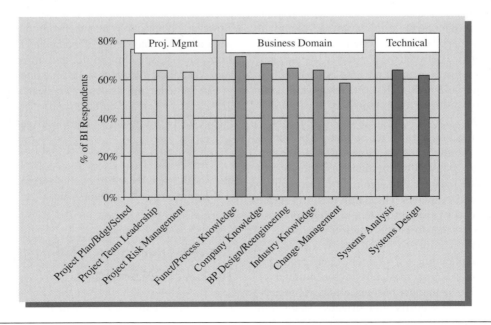

Figure 15.10   IT Skills Most Critical to Keep In-House (Zwieg et al., "The Information Technology Workforce: Trends and Implications 2005–2008," *MIS Quarterly Executive*, Sept. 2006, p. 103.)

in many cases the vendors providing them are domestic firms that specialize in specific IT services or application solutions for a specific industry—such as health care or financial services. Further, several U.S.-based service providers are also multinational firms, with IT service centers around the world (such as IBM and EDS).

What types of IT work should be outsourced? IT service delivery and IT applications development and maintenance are often being outsourced for different reasons. With the cost-cutting emphasis in business in recent years, there has been a renewed interest in outsourcing data center operations (sometimes called IS facilities management) to external service organizations. When data centers are outsourced, it is also common to outsource the management of data networks and telecommunications, as well as the IT help desk. The most common benefit associated with this type of IT infrastructure outsourcing is cost savings, and some companies have reported 10 to 20 percent cost savings due to the economies of scale available to the vendor that could not be achieved by the client organization alone.

However, there are also other potential benefits to outsourcing IT service delivery activities, including leveraging the expertise and presence of a major multinational service provider. In other words, an outsourcer who already operates in geographies that the client company is, or intends to, expand to may provide not only the needed equipment and skills at a lower cost, but also provide valued knowledge about operating in a specific world region.

Beginning with the Y2K compliance work in the late 1990s, many firms also began to increase their usage of external service providers for application development work. Here the primary benefit may be cost, if there is a labor market difference between the contracted workers and the in-house staff. However, there are also other benefits, including access to specific IT skill sets (such as skills with newer technologies) or improved productivity tools, as well as the ability to hire specialists for a short time period during the life of a project rather than for permanent positions.

More recently, some vendors have offered another sourcing alternative: not only hiring their firms to configure a given software package, but also to host the applications on the vendor's computers. These **application service providers (ASPs)** range from providers of single purpose applications (like a sales-force automation capability as offered by Salesforce.com) to broad applications (like enterprise resource planning systems). The client organization often pays an ASP on the basis of the number of "seats" (users) or on the number of transactions per month.

On the other hand, security and privacy issues and the strategic value of some data may mean that certain applications should not be developed by or operated on computers owned by another organization. For example, applications to support new product research and development may be considered too sensitive to outsource. Sometimes an outsourcer will specialize in particular industries (for example, retail or health care) to gain a depth of relevant application knowledge; in such instances, steps should be taken to ensure that the outsourcer is not put in a situation where its personnel could leak competitive information.

Other outsourcing advantages include the ability for the client firm to downsize or to respond to other significant business restructurings (e.g., mergers, smaller acquisitions, and divestitures). With these types of business restructurings often come sudden shifts in demands for computing power or systems integration work, and an outsourcing vendor may be in a better position to increase or decrease support. The client firm may only need to pay for what it uses, rather than building a data center for peak load, and letting it sit underutilized during other periods. However, the outsourcing contract needs to be written so that it accommodates this type of growth or downsizing in the business. [For example, see case IV-5: "IT Infrastructure Outsourcing at Schaeffer (B)."]

Some firms have chosen to outsource because it is difficult to keep pace with technological change. Keeping up with the latest technologies and IT service delivery techniques requires hiring and retaining highly skilled IS staff, which may be difficult, especially in non-urban areas. In other situations, outsourcing at least a portion of IT activities is motivated by a lack of satisfaction with IT service delivery or application development by an in-house IS department. However, organizations that engage in outsourcing contracts without a good knowledge of their own IT costs and resource strengths risk spending more, and incurring more delays, than when those functions were done internally.

Similar to buying a software application (see Chapter 11), the selection of an outsourcing vendor should include several factors about the vendor, not just its products, including:

- Vendor reputation as a vendor partner, and health as a company
- Established record of quality service, including responsiveness to client issues

MANAGING THE IT-BUSINESS RELATIONSHIP

If the CIO is truly an officer of the business, then he or she will not be the only person at that level concerned with IT issues in the business: by appointing a CIO, the organization is signaling that IT leadership needs to be a concern of all senior managers. Cross-functional management, in which problems are addressed in partnership among business peers, is also becoming more common.

However, when the IS leader is not a CIO, or a strong consensus or collaborative culture is not present, the senior IS leader should still not address all IT concerns without business manager input. As discussed earlier, this is because an IS department's *relationship* with the business is one of the three IT assets that needs to be managed well. The building and fostering of this relationship asset needs to begin at "the top" of the IS organization, with the CIO or other top IS leader.

A strong IT-business relationship asset is characterized by a true business-IS partnership, a cooperative relationship. Business managers need to be encouraged to work with senior IS managers, with the intent of sustaining a long-term relationship, not just a relationship based on collaboration for a single IT project. Partners share key common goals and develop a relationship based on mutual trust, as well as share a project's benefits and risks. The common goal is to achieve a greater contribution from investing in information resources than could be achieved by IS managers alone. Each partner respects the distinctive resources and competencies of other partners.

In organizations where there has not been a strong IT-business relationship, it may be useful to start by clearly defining the authority of the partners (as a sort of "prenuptial agreement"). Figure 15.11 contains an example of an agreement developed by a midsized organization to try and *rebuild* a failing IT-business relationship.

Partnering with Horizontal Mechanisms

Four types of **horizontal mechanisms** can be used to help build and foster IT-business partnerships (see Figure 15.12). The most frequently used mechanism is to implement a formal group (a council or committee) with key business stakeholders and senior IS leaders as members. For example, a high-level committee is typically charged with the responsibility of approving and prioritizing IT investments for an annual budget cycle. This type of committee is also increasingly being given the responsibility of serving as an oversight committee for current IT projects of a certain size. This means that the committee meets on a

---

Expectations/Responsibilities Statement

1. All user departments will be fully accountable for their use of information resources, including the skill level of people using information technology resources.
2. User departments will pay an annual fee to the IS department for workstations to include capital, software, and maintenance costs.
3. The IS department will set and enforce standards for user workstation hardware, software, and network connections.
4. User departments will pay for use of shareable information technology resources through a fair division of overhead.
5. Senior management will be kept engaged in information technology issues via regular communications by IS staff.
6. The IS department will actively initiate communication with all user departments.
7. The IS department will build its plan and budget with full knowledge of company business plans.
8. Members of the IS department will serve as internal business process improvement consultants and consultants on the use of the Internet in making the supply chain more efficient.
9. The IS department will be represented on issue-oriented or business planning teams where information definition and/or collection is crucial.
10. Policy affecting users will be determined by the IS Policy Committee, which will be chaired by a senior business executive.

Figure 15.11   Rebuilding an IT-Business Relationship

Mechanisms for IT-Business Partnering	
Mechanism	**Description**
Formal Groups	Formally established councils or teams with specific linking or oversight responsibilities for IT activities (such as IS steering committees)
Formal Roles	Individual positions with formal responsibility for linking activities between a central IT unit and one or more business units (such as IS managers serving as account managers for specific business units)
Informal Networking Practices	Intentional activities or practices to link managers in two or more organizational units who may engage in or impact cross-unit problem-solving (such as physical co-location)
Human Resource Practices	Human resource management initiatives to facilitate voluntary cross-unit problem-solving (such as temporary job rotations, cross-unit input to performance reviews)

Figure 15.12   Four Mechanisms for IT-Business Partnering (Based on Brown, 2003)

quarterly basis, or more frequently, to manage the company's IT application portfolio.

A summary of such a committee's expanded responsibilities might therefore include:

- Approve requests for new technology investments
- Set priorities for application development and implementation
- Monitor progress of IT projects against established timelines and budgets
- Share responsibility and ownership for achieving business value from IT investments

However, the use of such committees is not a substitute for an effective CIO and good IS management. Instead, this mechanism works best when proactive and responsive IS management is also in place.

Recent research has also found that formal integrator role positions are also viewed by some organizations as critical for achieving a strong IT-business relationship. For example, in firms with a centralized IS organization design, an **account manager** may be assigned to "manage the account" of a specific business unit. Often the person in this integrator role will have an office physically adjacent to other business managers in the company.

Two other types of mechanisms in Figure 15.12 (informal networking practices and human resource practices) are used to link IS and business managers, or IS managers that report to different business units, in a less formal way. These mechanisms help build interpersonal networks among organizational members that can be used for information and knowledge sharing across different units.

MEASURING OVERALL IS PERFORMANCE

Several performance metrics were mentioned in the previous discussion of the technology and human resource assets. However, an organization's IT-business relationship asset can be more difficult to evaluate. Certainly business unit leaders can be asked to measure the effectiveness of an IS account manager assigned to their business unit, and many organizations collect evaluations of the performance of an IS project team after a project for a given business unit has been completed. Some organizations also conduct an annual survey to assess business manager satisfaction with IS activities in general. However, these measures may not capture well the higher-level contributions of an IS organization in terms of its ability to provide "business value."

One increasingly popular approach to assessing these higher level outcomes has been to mirror metrics used by the overall organization. For example, in the early 1990s, a now popular tool called the **balanced scorecard** was introduced by Kaplan and Norton (1992) with the objective of providing an approach for organizations to provide a more "balanced" view of organizational performance than financial performance measures alone. The original model included four metrics, namely (1) customer satisfaction, (2) internal processes, (3) innovation and learning, in addition to (4) financial performance.

Applying these metrics to an *IS organization* assessment, some CIOs have adopted a balanced scorecard approach that captures not only the IS role as service provider, but also its ability to serve as a key resource for enabling business process improvements. Some organizations have reported that the process of aligning a balanced scorecard for the IS department with a corporate (or business unit) scorecard has also helped the organization to develop a common "language" for business and IS leaders to more openly discuss IS performance objectives and how well they are being achieved (Huang and Hu, 2007).

HOW GLOBAL IT STANDARDIZATION ENABLES "ONE COMPANY, ONE TEAM"

Part of the mission of a global company such as Johnson Controls, Inc., is to transfer people, products, and processes seamlessly across the world. According to CIO Sam Valanju, IT standardization helps to make this vision of "one company, one team" a reality. For example:

- The company has one e-mail system and one e-meeting system (for collaboration) around the world.
- An employee can take their company laptop to any Johnson Controls site around the world, and its wireless connection will work in any facility—whether the employee came from China, the United States, or Europe, it will work.
- The same vendor's telephone products are used at company sites around the world, so when you are at a different site, pushing buttons to retrieve voice mail, it just gives you the feeling that you are in your own office.
- Workers in eight automotive design centers around the world are seamlessly connected, working with the same standardized systems, in the same standardized way.

[Adapted from Brown, 2006]

SPECIAL ISSUE: MANAGING A GLOBAL IS ORGANIZATION

Today, virtually all organizations, regardless of size, must deal with the impacts of competing in a global economy. At an organization level, this can require not only an in-depth knowledge of technological and business issues, but also of world history, culture, geography, religion, politics, and international law. With ever-improving global communication networks and connectivity, global IS management has also become much more pervasive, and brings with it some new leadership challenges.

For example, systems integration has long been acknowledged as a critical process for most organizations, and the additional problems associated with integrating a multitude of diverse systems across multiple geographies is especially challenging. To avoid some of the pitfalls of integration, many IT leaders are increasingly relying on worldwide IT standards (see the box entitled "How Global IT Standardization Enables 'One Company, One Team'").

Nevertheless, several unique factors at the region and country level also need to be taken into account, such as:

Country Telecommunications Infrastructures   To fully realize the benefits of integrated global information systems, countries must be able to provide transnational companies the necessary telecommunications infrastructure and its associated worldwide connectivity. Landlines in many developing countries are still limited and are often supplanted by easy-to-set-up wireless infrastructures. Unfortunately, not all cellular networks provide the bandwidth necessary for enterprise-wide applications, and satellite connections can be expensive.

Many global companies base their Asian headquarters in the tiny island nation of Singapore to take advantage of the fact that it is one of the most wired countries in the world (Collett, 2003). Other emerging economies in Asia—such as Malaysia—created special zones for foreign subsidiaries where the telecommunications was world-class, even when the infrastructure in the rest of the country was limited. Global IT managers must be aware of what different countries will be able to provide before making decisions on global systems rollouts and multinational development efforts.

Legal and Security Considerations   In addition to being technically knowledgeable and culturally sensitive, the global IT manager must also keep constantly abreast of current legal and ethical issues in the countries of operation. Governmental regulations on technology transfers, intellectual property and copyrights, privacy laws, and transborder data flows are but a few of the areas that must be constantly monitored. For example, the European Union's Data Protection Directive requires that companies exporting data about EU citizens across borders meet Europe's very stringent privacy standards, and failure to comply can lead to hefty fines.

In addition, global electronic commerce has led to considerable legal arguments over issues of jurisdiction regarding intellectual property and Web content. For example, which country's laws should apply when objectionable Web content may be viewed in any country in the world? Network security has also become a global concern for IT managers. With the promise of global connectivity comes the danger of network attacks from locations around the world.

Language and Culture   Among the most common problems facing global IT managers dealing with a culturally diverse group of international workers is the issue of differences in language. Fluency in English is often mistaken for an understanding of Western idioms. A baseball expression ("hit a home run") may make as little sense in a country whose national sport is cricket as would "bowling a googly" in the United States. Further, body language and gestures have different connotations in different countries.

Cultural differences also play an important role in determining the effectiveness of global technology implementations. Figure 15.13 summarizes nine dimensions identified by House et al. (2002) that managers need to be aware of. For example, when dealing with individuals from a society characterized by high power distance, the manager should be aware that those employees may be less comfortable with contradicting their superiors than are their Western counterparts. This may require, for example, different communication mechanisms for project team members to avoid potential problems.

Time Zone Differences   With employees around the world separated by up to as much as 10 to 15 hours, finding times for synchronous meetings and discussions can be frustrating. For example, setting a 10:00 A.M. meeting in a Seattle corporate headquarters translates to 10:30 P.M. in the New Delhi office and 4:00 A.M. in Sydney, Australia. To deal with the problem fairly and avoid resentment in foreign offices, meeting times are sometimes rotated through time zones, alternating between the local workday times of the foreign and domestic offices.

On the other hand, there can also be advantages to operating across multiple time zones. By handing off work from one location to another, projects can "follow-the-sun." For example, when an employee leaves for the day at

- **Uncertainty avoidance**   Extent to which members of a society avoid uncertainty (through social norms or bureaucratic processes) to improve predictability of future events
- **Power distance**   Degree to which members of a society expect and accept that power is distributed unequally within a firm.
- **Collectivism-I**   Extent to which organizations and society reward collective distribution of resources and collective action
- **Collectivism-II**   Degree to which individuals see themselves as part of a group, whether it is an organization or family
- **Gender egalitarianism**   Extent to which a society or organization minimizes gender role differences and gender discrimination
- **Assertiveness**   Degree to which individuals are assertive, confrontational, and aggressive in societal relationships
- **Future orientation**   Extent to which society engages in future-oriented activities such as planning, investing in the future, and delaying gratification
- **Performance orientation**   Extent to which group members are encouraged and rewarded for performance improvement and excellence
- **Human orientation**   Extent to which a collective encourages and rewards individuals for being fair, generous, altruistic, caring and kind to others

Figure 15.13   Nine Dimensions of Cultural Differences (Adapted from House et al., 2002)

the U.S. office, he or she can hand-off the project work to an employee in the Bangalore, India, office who is just coming in for the day. Under this model, project work continues around the world, around the clock.

SPECIAL ISSUE: MANAGING OFFSHORE OUTSOURCING ARRANGEMENTS

Since the intensive Y2K reprogramming efforts of the mid- and late-1990s, companies have looked increasingly beyond their own national borders for partners to help design, develop, and maintain their information systems. While India remains the leader in *offshore outsourcing*, many other countries vie for a share of this market. The Philippines, Vietnam, Malaysia, Brazil, Russia, Bulgaria, and South Africa are some locations that offer highly trained IS personnel at costs that seem to be a fraction of what is available domestically.

However, not all offshore arrangements are the same. For example, some U.S. companies have established offshore development centers in which foreign technology workers are actually employees of the U.S.-based company and use the same software tools and development processes as their domestic counterparts. The main difference is the salaries paid for these workers: Recent estimates are that it will take about a quarter of a century before average salaries in India will converge with average salaries in the United States (Luftman and Kempaiah, 2007).

The term *near-shore* has also been introduced to distinguish offshore locations that are geographically closer to a company's home office, often with overlapping time zones.

For example, several companies in the United States are looking more closely at sites in South America. Many multinational firms have the option of choosing what is referred to as *best-shore* sites—meaning there are multiple options available to them, and time zones and skill sets can be taken into account. Sometimes a "follow-the-sun" approach is deliberately chosen in order to leverage the ability to hand off development work from workers in one geographic area to another, to decrease the time to complete a given project.

A recent study of successful application development projects that involved an offshore outsourcing vendor resulted in the identification of 10 IS capabilities considered to be critical to the effectiveness of these projects (see the left-hand column of Figure 15.14). These capabilities included not only the ability to select an offshore vendor,

10 Capabilities	Questions for Capability Assessment
Capability to Strategize	1. Is offshore outsourcing an integral part of our IT strategy?
	2. Is our top management routinely involved in the offshore decision making?
	3. Do we have clear specific guiding principles for how to conduct offshore outsourcing?
	4. Do we have realistic expectations about cost savings from offshore outsourcing?
	5. Do we have clear procedures for evaluating which functions to keep in-house and which to offshore?
	6. Do we routinely consider multiple vendors and/or multiple locations for risky projects?
Offshore Readiness	1. Do we have a clear idea about in-house costs of existing IT activities and services?
	2. Do we have clear goals for offshore outsourcing?
	3. Can we quickly alter our offshoring arrangement characteristics (e.g., size, duration) if outcomes are not as expected?
	4. Do all the key organizational stakeholders support offshore outsourcing?
Vendor Selection	1. Do we continuously update our knowledge of offshore vendors (e.g., through trade publications and conferences)?
	2. Do we constantly learn about best practices in vendor selection and governance?
	3. Do we have clear procedures for selecting offshore vendors (e.g., RFPs, country visits)?
	4. Do we have standard processes to evaluate if vendor matches our needs (e.g., location, expertise)?
	5. Do we ensure that vendor matches our values, goals, and objectives?
Contract Facilitation	1. Can we effectively negotiate pricing for the global context?
	2. Do we have clear procedures for negotiating SLAs?
	3. Can we establish safeguards to protect our proprietary information from possible leaks?
	4. Can we ensure that unanticipated legal issues will be handled in our country?
	5. Can we clearly assign roles and responsibilities for domestic and offshore personnel?
	6. Do we establish specific offices, liaisons for offshore outsourcing?
Relationship Governance	1. Can we adapt to the business practices, norms in the vendor country?
	2. Can we adapt to the offshore vendor's "way of doing things"?
	3. Do we invest resources to understand the culture in the vendor country?
	4. Do we organize events and training programs to alleviate cultural differences?
	5. Do we ensure the offsite team members are actively involved in the arrangement?
	6. Do we foster friendly relationships with the onsite personnel through informal meetings and social events?

Figure 15.14

HR Management	1.	Do we have standard processes to determine percentage of vendor personnel needed onsite (e.g., 30:70 rule)?
	2.	Can we effectively 'interview' new vendor personnel to recruit for our on-site needs?
	3.	Can we effectively collocate with vendor personnel based on the stage of the project?
	4.	Can we create joint teams of our personnel and vendor personnel to manage global team members?
	5.	Do we assign joint leadership for certain aspects of the offshore outsourcing project?
Knowledge Management	1.	Do we have standard processes for transferring knowledge across global locations?
	2.	Do we retain and encourage our "Knowledge Experts" (key IT personnel) for knowledge transfer?
	3.	Do we have the necessary IT infrastructure (e.g., online conferences) that supports global knowledge transfer?
	4.	Do we facilitate knowledge integration between client and vendor team members (e.g., through online communication tools)?
	5.	Do we have standard processes and IT infrastructure (e.g., KMS) to manage knowledge (i.e., capture, store, share, and exploit knowledge from other projects)?
Distributed Work Management	1.	Do we use 24/7 development to our advantage?
	2.	Do we meet regularly with global team members to coordinate efforts?
	3.	Do we ensure that electronic meetings are balanced with periodic face-to-face contacts?
	4.	Do we use advanced communication and coordination tools (e.g., videoconferencing and Web-based collaboration tools)?
	5.	Do we post offshore updates regularly on the company intranet or on the web?
IS Organization Change	1.	Can we quickly incorporate changing work patterns to match offshore outsourcing demands?
	2.	Can we quickly 'ramp-up' our existing processes to match offshore outsourcing demands?
	3.	Do we provide good incentives to our IS personnel to move to other firms, as part of restructuring?
	4.	Do we effectively re-skill our IS personnel, to accommodate offshoring demands?
	5.	Do we regularly communicate with our existing IS personnel, to remove any negative reactions to offshoring?
User Change	1.	Are we prepared for changes in our organization due to offshore outsourcing?
	2.	Do we clearly communicate the pros and cons of offshore outsourcing to our employees?
	3.	Do we address employee concerns about offshoring (e.g., directly interacting with vendor personnel located elsewhere)?
	4.	Do we quickly address anxiety or anger towards offshoring and/or offshore vendor personnel?

Figure 15.14 A Checklist for Assessing Offshore Outsourcing Capabilities (Ranganathan and Balaji, 2007) (continued)

develop comprehensive SLAs for the offshore contract, and establish a trust-based relationship between the client and the vendor, but also capabilities to recognize and overcome cultural and geographical difficulties, such as described earlier.

SUMMARY

The IS role in organizations has continued to evolve as new technologies and external events have increased the dependence on IT for business operations and achieving strategic business goals. The importance of IT is reflected in many organizations by the establishment of a chief information officer (CIO) position. There has also been an increasing focus on business manager participation in IT investment and prioritization decisions to help ensure IT-business alignment.

Although IS resources can be centralized, decentralized, or both centralized *and* decentralized, IS leaders are responsible for managing the same three IT assets: technology, human resources, and the IT-business relationship. In recent years, improved processes for both IT service delivery and IT application development have been adopted. It is also common in large organizations today to find a mixture of sourcing arrangements, including an internal IT workforce with skills critical to keep "in-house" as well as contracts with external service providers, both domestic and offshore.

The increased globalization of companies has led to an increased reliance on IT standards to integrate IT operations and applications. IS managers are also becoming more effective at managing workers and projects that are being conducted in different countries.

REVIEW QUESTIONS

1. Why has the IS role in organizations undergone so much change?
2. What benefits are associated with centralized IT governance, and how do these differ from the benefits associated with decentralized governance?
3. What are some of the major IT services provided to business users?
4. What are some of the ways that IS leaders can ensure that the costs of providing a service such as help desk support are aligned with the service levels wanted by business leaders?
5. What is meant by the term *IT applications portfolio*?
6. Why is it important for business managers to participate in IT investment decisions?
7. Why might a financial measure like return on investment (ROI) be important for assessing a proposal to develop or purchase a new software application?
8. What are some of the key issues associated with managing an IS organization's personnel?
9. Why are many organizations contracting with outside organizations (i.e., outsourcing) to provide some of their IT services or develop some of their applications?
10. What structural and nonstructural mechanisms can be used to help increase the likelihood that business and IS leaders are working together as "business partners"?
11. What is a balanced scorecard approach, and why might it be used by a CIO to help measure overall IS performance?
12. What are some of the global IS management challenges facing many IS leaders today?
13. What are some special issues associated with managing offshore staff (or contractors) versus staff in the client organization's home country?

DISCUSSION QUESTIONS

1. What types of skills and experiences should be considered when choosing a person to fill a chief information officer (CIO) position? Why might these skills and experiences be weighted differently by different organizations or by the same organization at different times?
2. This chapter emphasizes the need for partnering relationships between IS and business managers for managing IT. Define your concept of a management partnership and describe why you think it may, or may not, be more important for managing IT than managing other business functions.
3. What business or IT initiative might lead an entire organization (or business unit) with a federal IT governance design to change to a centralized IT governance design?
4. Research some examples of "shared services" organizations that include IT. What are the primary advantages associated with this "business within a business" structure? Why might an organization implement this structure, instead of a structure in which these IT responsibilities are centralized under a CIO?
5. Many chargeback systems result in "tensions" between IS and business leaders. Why do you think this often happens, and what might an IS leader do to resolve these?
6. Why have many organizations decided to purchase applications when they can, rather than custom-develop them? How does this type of policy impact the IT skill sets needed for the IS organization?
7. If you were a vice president of consumer marketing for a major appliance manufacturer, what metrics might you personally use to evaluate the performance of the IS organization in your company?
8. Review the list of IT professional skill sets that were among the highest paying jobs for IT professionals working in client organizations. Which types of jobs would you find the most interesting, and why?
9. How might the role of IS leaders and other IS employees change as more B2B e-business applications are conducted over the Internet?
10. Develop a list of pros and cons for an IS leader to consider when deciding whether or not to outsource (a) its IT operations (data center, networks, helpdesk) and (b) an application development project. What are the differences (if any) between your two lists, and why?
11. Select one of the special challenges discussed for managing a global IS organization. What types of education and training programs would you like to participate in to help you better prepare for this type of challenge?

REFERENCES

Adler, Paul S., Frank E. McGarry, Wendy B. Irion-Talbot, and Derek J. Binney. 2005. "Enabling process discipline: Lessons from the journey to CMM Level 5." *MIS Quarterly Executive* 4:1 (March): 215–227.

Agarwal, Ritu, Carol V. Brown, Thomas W. Ferratt, and Jo Ellen Moore. 2006. "Five mindsets for retaining IT staff." *MIS Quarterly Executive* 5:3 (September): 137–150.

Allen, Julia H. 2006. "Integrating Security and IT." *Build Security In: Setting a Higher Standard for Software Assurance*, sponsored by U.S. Department of Homeland Security. http://buildsecurityin.us-cert.gov/daisy/bsi/articles/best-practices/deployment/576.html.

Bennis, Warren. 1999. "Lessons in leadership." *CIO* 12 (June 15): 14–16.

Birge, Eileen M. 1999. "How to measure IT performance." *Beyond Computing* 8 (January/February): 67–71.

Brown, C. V. 1999. "Horizontal mechanisms under differing IS contexts." *MIS Quarterly* 23 (September): 421–454.

Brown, C. V. 2003. "The IT organization of the future." in Jerry Luftman (ed.), *Competing in the Information Age*. Oxford University Press, Chapter 8.

Brown, C. V. 2006. "Interview with Sam Valanju." *MIS Quarterly Executive* 5:4 (December): 193–197.

Clawson, James G. 2000. "The new infocracies: Implications for leadership." *Ivey Business Journal* 14 (May/June): 76–80.

[Dice]. 2006. *Dice Tech Salary Survey Results*. Internal publication, Urbandale, IA.

Duffy, D. 2002. "Continental divide." *CIO* 15 (April 15): 14–15.

Edberg, D., F. H. Grupe, and W. Kuechler. 2001. "Practical issues in global IT management." *Information Systems Management* 39 (Winter): 34–46.

Golden, William. 2007. "The practical value of the IT Infrastructure Library (ITIL)." *CIO* (May 18).

Gupta, Anil K., and Vivay Govindaranjan. 2000. "The rising cost of waiting." *CIO* 13 (July 15): 27–29.

House, R., M., Javidan, P. Hanges, and P. Dorfman. 2002. "Understanding cultures and implicit leadership theories across the globe: An introduction to Project GLOBE", *Journal of World Business* 37 (July): 3–10.

Huang, C. Derrick, and Qing Hu. 2007. "Achieving IT-business strategic alignment via enterprise-wide implementation of balanced scorecards." *Information Systems Management* 24:2 (Spring): 173–184.

Hubbard, Douglas. 1999. "The IT measurement inversion." *CIO* 12 (April 15): 67–69.

Judge, Paul C. 1998. "What've you done for us lately?" *BusinessWeek* 64 (September 7): 68–70.

Kaplan, Robert S., and David P. Norton. 1992. "The balanced scorecard—measures that drive performance." *Harvard Business Review* 70 (January–February): 71–79.

Karlgaard, Rich. 2003. "What makes a great CIO?" *Forbes* 163 (November 24): 43.

King, J. 2003. "IT's global itinerary." *Computerworld* 37 (September 15): 43–47.

King, J. 2003. "The best of both shores." *Computerworld* 37 (April 21): 12–14.

Koch, Christopher. 2000. "ASP and ye shall receive." *CIO* 13 (May 1): 47–50.

Luftman, Jerry, and Rajkumar Kempaiah. 2007. "The IS organization of the future: The IT talent challenge." *Information Systems Management* 24:2 (Spring): 129–138.

Machiavelli, Niccolo. (ca. 1513, trans 1988). *The Prince*. Hill Thompson (trans.). Palm Springs, CA: ETC Publications.

Mearian, L. 2002. "MasterCard nears finish of payment system rollout." *Computerworld* 36 (December 13): 2.

Nolan, Richard, and F. Warren McFarlan. 2005. "Information technology and the board of directors." *Harvard Business Review* (October).

Odo, A. 2003. "Improved telecom has increased investments." *Daily Trust* (Abuja), (October 31): 4.

Pearlson, Keri E. 2001. *Managing and Using Information Systems: A Strategic Approach*. Hoboken, NJ: John Wiley & Sons.

Ranganathan, C., and S. Balaji. 2007. "Critical capabilities for offshore outsourcing of information systems." *MIS Quarterly Executive*, 6:3 (September): 147–164

Riemenschneider, Cynthia. 2000. "What small business executives have learned about managing information technology." *Information & Management* 15 (August): 257–263.

Ross, Jeanne W., and Peter Weill. 2002. "Six IT decisions your IT people shouldn't make." *Harvard Business Review*. 80 (November 2002): 3–9.

Tam, Pui-Wing. 2007. "CIO posts morph from tech support into strategy." *Wall Street Journal* (February 20): B5.

Weill, Peter, and Marianne Broadbent. 1998. *Leveraging the New Infrastructure: How Market Leaders Capitalize on Information Technology*. Boston: Harvard Business School.

Wheatley, M. 2001. "Nestlé's worldwide squeeze." *CIO* 14 (June 1): 22–24.

Worthen, Ben. 2005. "IT governance—ITIL power." *CIO* (September 1).

Zwieg, Phil, et al. 2006. "The information technology workforce: trends and implications 2005–2008." *MIS Quarterly Executive* 5:2 (September): 101–108.

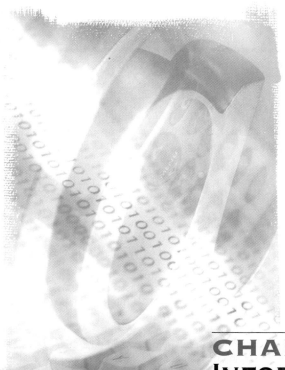

CHAPTER 16
INFORMATION SECURITY

EMPLOYMENT OPPORTUNITIES FOR INFORMATION SECURITY SPECIALISTS have increased significantly in the last several years. There is good reason for this: As industrial economies move toward information-based economies, their information and its confidentiality and security become more important. We need only look at the ascendancy of the information industries such as banking, insurance, investment, and increased investments in data warehouses and business intelligence applications to see this increasing importance of information in business.

Early in the field of information security, the standard mantra was that better passwords, firewall rules, encryption, and other security technologies would solve most security breaches. However, although these types of technologies certainly help to reduce the risk for external attacks, they are much less effective in thwarting attacks by an insider (or former employee). For example, the primary sources of thefts of intellectual property rights, trade secrets, and research and development knowledge are employees who are authorized to have access to the information that they are stealing. No amount of technology investments will stop this kind of loss.

In addition, the protection of the confidentiality and integrity of an organization's information is also now *required by law* in the United States. For example, as we will discuss in more detail later in this chapter:

- the Sarbanes-Oxley law requires proper controls on information for all publicly traded companies,

- the Gramm-Leach-Bliley law mandates strict standards in confidentiality for all financial and credit-reporting organizations, whether they are public or private, and

- the Health Insurance Portability and Accountability Act (HIPAA) requires a high standard of privacy for medical records.

The penalties for noncompliance or violation of these laws can range from civil charges and severe fines to criminal charges for repeated and flagrant violations.

This chapter will therefore focus in particular on the *managerial* aspects of information security—including risk management, security policies, business continuity planning, and enterprise records management approaches to system controls, auditing, and compliance. This is not meant to negate the importance of security technologies in any way. IT managers are responsible for identifying and implementing appropriate technologies for information security, based on the organization's assessment of its risks.

We begin this chapter with a brief discussion of e-crime threats, which sets the stage for a discussion of some basic information risk management approaches for determining what actions should be taken for information protection from a cost/benefit perspective. Then we provide summaries of today's most important U.S. laws on information security and confidentiality and some of the consequences of noncompliance. Then we discuss information security policies (what they include, who should develop them, how to disseminate them), business continuity planning, and electronic records management. The chapter ends with an introduction to a new managerial role that frequently, but not always, has a reporting relationship with the CIO: the chief information security officer.

E-CRIME

Electronic crime (e-crime) is defined today as any criminal violation in which a computer or e-media is used in the commission of the crime (*CSO Magazine*, 2005) A recent survey of security executives and law enforcement personnel found that the average number of e-crimes in the year was 86 and the average loss was over $500,000 per organization, although several of the respondents were unable to determine the actual dollar loss.

The types of losses from e-crimes can take many forms. In the same survey (*CSO Magazine*, 2005), only 12 percent of the respondents said their organizations experienced some type of critical financial or operational loss, but another 12 percent reported harm to the organization's reputation (due to publicity of the crime). Within just the past few years, major security breaches have led to the exposure of credit and debit card data stored by retailers (see Figure 16.1). The largest of these breaches to date took place over an 18-month period, and involved the records of over 45 million cardholders (see the box entitled "Customer Data Theft at TJX").

CUSTOMER DATA THEFT AT TJX

For a period of 18 months beginning in the summer of 2005, TJX, a $17 billion retailer, had the credit card information of at least 45 million customers stolen. Some investigators believe that the information thieves may have stolen the records of as many as 200 million credit card holders.

How did the information thieves do this? The evidence suggests that it was not that difficult: they tapped into highly insecure wireless connections, gained administrative control of large databases, and freely downloaded immense amounts of unencrypted information from the company's data warehouse. By any reasonable auditing standards, TJX was guilty of gross negligence.

What was the cost of this theft? TJX will also be spending well over $100 million for badly needed security upgrades, but this dollar amount does not come close to the dollar amount associated with the loss of reputation, goodwill, and opportunity costs for TJX. In addition, financial institutions are projected to spend over $300 million to replace the credit cards of these TJX customers, and retailers and credit card issuers have absorbed many tens of millions in false card billings. Industry experts estimate that the total business losses will be close to $1 billion.

Is it fair that the credit card companies have to pay for these losses when the security problems lie with a retailer such as TJX, and not the issuers of the cards themselves? The United States will likely pass new laws in the near future that will put the liability for such information heists directly upon the parties who were responsible for the thefts—due to negligence or lack of due diligence.

[Adapted from Pereira, 2007]

Company with Security Breach	Number of Credit or Debit Cards Compromised	Date of Breach
BJ's Wholesale Club	40,000 cards	March 2004
DSW Retail Ventures	1.4 million cards	March 2005
CardSystems Inc	40 million cards	June 2005
TJX Cos	45+ million cards	July 2005–Dec. 2006

Figure 16.1 Major Data Card Breaches from 2004 to 2006 (Adapted from Pereira 2007)

Type of E-Crime Experienced in Past Year	% of Respondents
Virus or other malicious code	82
Spyware	61
Phishing	57
Illegal generation of spam e-mail	48
Unauthorized access to information, systems, or networks	43
Denial of service attacks	32
Rogue wireless access point	21
Exposure of private or sensitive information	19
Fraud	19
Identity theft (of employee)	17
Password sniffing	16
Theft of intellectual property	14
Zombie machines on organization's network	13
Theft of other proprietary information	12
Sabotage	11
Web site defacement	9

Figure 16.2   Types of E-Crimes Experienced: Based on 554 Survey Responses in 2005 (*CSO Magazine*, 2005)

The most prevalent type of crime in recent years, however, has been a **virus** or other malicious code, or **spyware** and **phishing** attacks, generated from outside the organization. In a recent survey, over half of the organizational respondents had experienced this type of crime (see Figure 16.2). Although outsiders therefore pose the greatest cyber-security threat to organizations, insiders (both current employees and former employees—including temporary employees and contractors) still continue to be the source of e-crime in about 20 percent of incidents (in which the source is identified). Typical insider crimes are gaining unauthorized access to information, systems, or networks, or causing an exposure of an organization's private or sensitive information.

Committing a crime against a current or former employer can also sometimes be a way that individuals "get back" at a company for real or perceived transgressions. For example, an insurance company employee who was fired from his IT job planted a "logic bomb" that went off after he left the firm and destroyed more than 160,000 records used to pay monthly payroll commissions (Baase, 1997). Many companies attempt to minimize this type of risk by immediately canceling the computer passwords of an employee who quits, or is fired; the employee may even be watched as they clean out their belongings and are escorted off the premises.

Cyberattacks on computers and Web sites have of course greatly increased over the past decade as organizations have increased their Internet connectivity. Some attacks involve single computers, and some are intended to involve thousands. The perpetrator can be a **hacker** or a **cracker**. Hackers usually intend no harm to humans, and justify their actions as helpful in pointing out vulnerabilities in computer security practices or particular software products (most notably Microsoft operating systems). In contrast, crackers use hacking techniques to intentionally steal information, wipe out hard drives, or to do other harm. Descriptions of some of the most common techniques used to attack computers from the outside are described in Figure 16.3.

Other e-crimes are directed at stealing information or money from individuals—including employees. For example, unwary users can be defrauded by **spoofing**—a technique in which a Web site that mimics a legitimate site is set up for the purpose of misleading or defrauding an Internet user. A message board or e-mail might be used to direct the victim to the spurious site, or the spoofer might simply use a close variant of another site's URL to con people who make an innocent typing mistake.

Most of today's organizations typically have invested in a variety of technologies, including firewalls, automated virus scanning technologies, physical security systems, spyware/adware detection software, automated or manual "patch" management, and other sophisticated network traffic monitoring and tracking tools—or have contracted with service providers to provide such security. (According to Gartner, the worldwide **antivirus software** market alone will total about $5 billion in 2007.)

Identifying and justifying these types of technologies is an IT manager's responsibility, but all managers responsible for information security compliance should be kept apprised of the basics of such technologies (see Figure 16.4) so that they can participate in decisions about capital investments as part of an organization's approach to risk management.

Good security management also depends on alert and dedicated IT employees. For examples of thwarted (or minimized) e-crimes due to actions taken by employees responsible for maintaining information security, see the box entitled "The E-Crime I'm Most Proud of Preventing or Solving."

Techniques Used to Attack Computers

1. A **virus** is a small unit of code that invades a computer program or file. When the invaded program is executed or the file is opened, the virus makes copies of itself that are released to invade other programs or files in that computer. It may also do nasty things like erase files or corrupt programs. Viruses are transmitted from one computer to another when an invaded computer program or file is transmitted to another computer.

2. A **worm** is a virus that has the ability to copy itself from machine to machine, normally over a network.

3. A **Trojan horse** is a security-breaking program that is introduced into a computer and serves as a way for an intruder to reenter the computer in the future. It may be disguised as something innocent such as a screen saver or a game.

4. A **logic bomb** is a program that is introduced into a computer and set to take action at a certain time or when a specified event occurs.

5. A **denial of service attack** is implemented by invading a large number of computers on the Internet and instructing them to simultaneously send repeated messages to a target computer, thus either overloading that computer's input buffer or jamming the communications lines into the computer so badly that legitimate users cannot obtain access.

Figure 16.3   Descriptions of Some Common Techniques Used to Attack Computers

- *Firewalls and Proxy Servers*   Managers should understand the basics of packet filtering; stateful, stateless, kernel, and application level firewalls; and the strategies of positioning layered defenses of multiple firewalls at the enterprise, departmental, and client levels.
- *Encryption and VPNs*   Managers should have a general understanding of how encryption works, and what a public key infrastructure (PKI) is. Encrypted information can be the last level of defense against information thieves. In fact, being able to prove that stolen information was highly encrypted can protect an organization from legal liabilities.
- *Identity and Access Management Systems (IAM)*   Managing the authentication and authorization rights of all of an organization's employees, contractors, auditors, and other authorized business partners is too complex for many organizations to effectively control without a commercially available IAM software system. IAM systems are also especially helpful for adding, limiting access for, or removing large numbers of users when an organization is buying another company, downsizing large numbers of staff, spinning off a business, or going through some other major restructuring.
- *Content-Filtering Tools*   Managers must know how to keep their employees from accessing inappropriate sites from their organizational networks. Current laws like Sarbanes-Oxley virtually mandate the use of content-filtering for information protection.
- *Penetration-Testing Tools*   Managers need to be able to set up regular probes on their internal networks to determine potential vulnerabilities.

Figure 16.4   Information Security Technology Basics

THE E-CRIME I'M MOST PROUD OF PREVENTING OR SOLVING

- Defacement of our Web site: We tracked down the defacer, arrested him, prosecuted him and convicted him. He is currently serving three years in federal prison.

- Attempts to plant logic bombs and password sniffers by foreign hackers (originating in Asia and Eastern Europe) were detected and prevented.

- An infected PC of a contractor that was spreading a virus was caught in the first hour of being online.

[Extracted from *CSO Magazine*, 2005]

INFORMATION RISK MANAGEMENT

All information security should begin with **risk management**. One of the important issues is to determine the best balance between the costs versus benefits of risk management practices. For example, you personally wouldn't want to pay $10,000 to protect yourself from an estimated potential loss of $5,000, and organizations don't either. But how do you determine these amounts? The challenge here is in estimating potential losses, as determining how much the organization is paying for security is relatively easy.

First, management must determine what their real information assets are and assign values and priorities for them. It is easy to overlook valuable information assets, and organizations often do not know what they are dependent upon until they lose access to it. So it is imperative that managers take a systematic approach to identifying all of their critical information assets and what business processes are dependent upon what specific information systems.

Second, management must determine how long the organization can function without a specific information asset—which is typically one hour, half a day, one day, two days, one week, or about one month.

Third, departmental managers and the owners of the information assets then need to develop and implement the security procedures to protect these assets. The security budget should include both the dollar outlays and the personnel dedicated to the task.

After a major system intrusion, top management may order security managers to do 'whatever it takes' to secure the system. But these of course are temporary orders. Those responsible for security management need to be able to answer the following:

What human resources and financial assets are to be deployed, in what proportions, to protect what assets?

This is the essence of information security management, and both quantitative and qualitative means are used to provide the answers to these questions.

Quantitative risk analysis approaches are used to provide real dollar figures as to what an organization's risks can be. As shown in Figure 16.5, for each information asset and the business goals they enable, the known vulnerabilities are explicitly stated, and an estimate is provided for what a single loss expectancy (SLE) would cost. An SLE can be difficult to determine because the variance can be large. For example, one intrusion can be somewhat harmless, but another can cost many thousands of dollars.

The best sources to use here are based on the (1) historical experiences of the organization and (2) industry averages. For example, the organization in Figure 16.5 had experienced laptop theft in the past two years, which it concluded had led to the loss of several contracts. If an organization

Information Asset	Goal	Vulnerability	Single Loss Expectancy (SLE)	Annual Occurrence Rate (AOR)	Annualized Expected Losses (AEL)
Private corporate information on laptops	Complete privacy of all important corporate information on laptops	Laptop theft and copying of information from them	$50,000	1.5 times*	$75,000
Company email	Complete e-mail privacy of all important communications	Intercepting e-mail	$10,000	6 times	$60,000

*Based on the theft of 3 laptops in the past two years.

Figure 16.5 Risk Management Assessment by Information Asset

SILENCE IS NO LONGER AN OPTION

When someone steals your camera, you know it is stolen, and the thieves do not leave a copy of it. But information theft is different: It can be stolen, but you still can have your copy of it. In fact, if the thieves are skillful, you actually may never know that it happened: The true information criminal will never tell you that he or she has stolen your information because they will want to come back and do it again, and again. Another reason for poor statistics on information theft is the reality that the victims historically have been unwilling to admit that it has happened. Companies have been silent about information theft in the past because of the bad publicity and legal liabilities that accompany it.

But new laws for the reporting of information theft have led to new behaviors in the last few years. For example, California's State Law 1386 went into effect on July 1, 2003. This law requires all organizations that store information on California residents to report to their citizens any information theft within 96 hours. Failure to do so can have both civil and criminal remedies. So, company silence is no longer an option.

However, many information crime statistics are actually somewhat "grey areas" due to the difficulties of knowing that an information theft has occurred and a reluctance on the part of companies that were victims in the past to make an information theft public (see the box entitled "Silence Is No Longer an Option").

After performing a quantitative risk analysis for all information assets, the annual expected losses (AEL) figures are used in a **security cost-benefit analysis** (see Figure 16.6). For example, using strong third-party encryption technology to ensure the confidentiality of laptop information was estimated to cost $100 per laptop, and the organization had about 200 laptops that were exposed to such loss. Security prevention solutions are listed in an Actions column, and both one-time and continuing costs are determined for each action. The total costs of the actions are then subtracted from the annualized expected losses (AEL) to determine the benefits to the organization from taking these actions.

Finally, importance data can be collected from management to help justify and prioritize investments in information security technologies (such as those discussed earlier in this chapter). Qualitative scales on the relative importance of each information asset—such as using a scale of 1 through 5, where 1 is the most important, 5 the least important—can be used to help determine what assets are the most important for the organization as a whole, and to use this information to determine what percentage of a security budget should be allocated to the different information risks identified.

More recently, managers performing information risk assessments have also been required to take into account the risks of financial penalties due to an organization's noncompliance with U.S. laws, as described in the next section.

has experienced this type of loss before, the impacts will be easier to estimate. If not, industry statistics may be available to help determine potential losses from specific vulnerabilities.

The annual occurrence rate (AOR) is simply your estimation of how often this loss happens each year. You multiply this times SLE to get the annualized expected losses (AEL).

$$\text{SLE} \times \text{AOR} = \text{AEL}$$

Similar to Figure 16.5, precise numbers can be calculated to justify security budgets and resource deployments.

Information Asset	Goal	Annualized Expected Losses (AEL)	Actions	Annualized Cost of Actions	Return Benefit
Private corporate information on laptops	Complete privacy of all important corporate information on laptops	$75,000	implement strong third-party encryption on all laptops	$20,000*	$55,000
Company e-mail	Complete e-mail privacy of all important communications	$60,000	implement a client-to-client e-mail encryption system	$20,000	$40,000

*Based on $100 per laptop for 200 laptops.

Figure 16.6 Security Cost-Benefit Analysis by Information Asset

COMPLIANCE WITH CURRENT INFORMATION SECURITY LAWS

In this section we summarize the relevant characteristics of five recent U.S. laws that have important impacts on information security practices in organizations. Brief descriptions of the overall purpose of the laws and penalties for noncompliance, in order of the dates they were enacted, are provided in Figure 16.7. Next we discuss them in more detail, beginning with the laws that have had the greatest corporate impacts.

Sarbanes-Oxley (SOX)

The **Sarbanes-Oxley Act of 2002 (SOX)** was passed in response to the corporate scandals at companies such as Enron, in which many employees lost not only their jobs but also their savings for retirement. SOX has had a major impact on the accounting, record-keeping, and controls landscape for all publicly traded corporations doing business and/or being traded in the United States.

To avoid serious legal liabilities, managers need to know the following:

Records Retention: SOX specifically states that corporations must retain all relevant e-mail in an indexed, accessible form for a minimum number of years, to guarantee that the auditors can easily obtain the necessary documents. This rule has spurred the growth of **electronic records management (ERM)** software. As described in more detail later in this chapter, these systems can categorize the type and retention time for specific electronic documents, and these systems will insure their retention.

IT Audit Controls: Section 404 of SOX states that publicly traded companies in the United States must establish, document, and maintain internal controls for financial reporting. Company officers are required to have evaluated the effectiveness of the internal controls within 90 days prior to the report. Section 404 also requires management to produce an internal control report as part of each annual SEC report.

Law	Date Enacted	Purpose	Penalties
Health Insurance Portability and Accountability Act (HIPAA)	08/21/1996	Standardization and confidentiality of health data.	Both civil and criminal, with maximums of $250,000 in fines and 10 years in prison.
Gramm-Leach-Bliley Act (GLBA)	11/11/1999	Privacy of personal financial and credit information.	
The PATRIOT Act	10/26/2001	(relating to information security) Keep records of all financial transactions over $10,000. To allow the government to see all telephone, e-mail, and financial information without a search warrant.	Varies, depending upon intent. Deliberate violation and/or noncooperation with governmental inquiry is a felony.
Sarbanes-Oxley Act (SOX)	7/30/2002	Integrity in financial statements and disclosures, internal controls, and auditor independence.	Organizations can be fined up to $100,000. Individuals up to $10,000 and 5 years in prison.
California Information Practice Act (Senate Bill 1386)	07/01/2003	Mandates full and quick disclosure to anyone who has had their information lost or stolen from any company doing business in California.	Allows civil lawsuits for loss of information. The most serious penalty is negative publicity from public exposure.

Figure 16.7 Recent U.S. Laws with Information Security Impacts

The Committee of Sponsoring Organizations (COSO) has created a framework for auditors to assess controls. The COSO guidelines now require the chief information officer (CIO) to be directly responsible for the security, accuracy, and reliability of the information systems that manage and report the financial data. Because the CEO and CFO of companies are typically dependent upon the CIO's controls, the CIO is now critically involved in the sign-offs of a company's financial statements.

The COSO framework specifically impacts information technology in the following five areas:

Risk Assessment: Management must first conduct a risk assessment of the information systems affecting the validity of the financial statements.

Control Environment: Management's philosophy regarding whether employees are involved in the decisions affecting the quality assurance, security, and confidentiality of their information systems.

Control Activities: The design, implementation, and quality assurance teams should be independent. The organization must document usage rules and demonstrate the reliability of audit trails. Management must be able to demonstrate segregation of duties (SOD) within their critical processes where there can be conflicts of interest and increased opportunities for fraud.

Monitoring: Management must create systems that allow for quick and accurate internal audits, and should perform these audits on a schedule appropriate to their level of risk. Management must clearly understand that they are responsible for the results of these audits.

Information and Communication: IT management must be able to demonstrate to management that they are in compliance with SOX. They must be able to demonstrate that they can quickly respond to any changes in information that would affect financial reporting and SOX requirements.

Gramm-Leach-Bliley Act of 1999 (GLBA)

The GLBA mandates all organizations to maintain a high level of confidentiality of all financial information of their clients or customers. The GLB Act gives authority to eight federal agencies and states to enforce the Financial Privacy Rule and the Safeguards Rule. These two regulations apply to all banks and lending companies, securities firms, insurance companies, credit reporting, and consumer loan agencies. It applies to anyone involved in transferring or safeguarding money, preparing of individual tax returns, providing financial advice, credit counseling, residential real estate settlement services, or collecting consumer debts. With such a broad scope, it seems fair to say that some aspect of most businesses comes under the jurisdiction of the GLB Act.

The Financial Privacy Rule The Financial Privacy Rule requires financial institutions to give their customers privacy notices that explain the financial institution's information collection and sharing practices. GLBA requires that the organization must clearly state their privacy policy at the time of establishing the relationship. In turn, customers have the right to limit some sharing of their information.

Financial institutions and other companies that receive personal financial information from a financial institution are now limited in their ability to use that information. Financial institutions may not disclose to a third party any nonpublic personal information. This includes account and credit card numbers, social security numbers, or any otherwise private information that could allow someone to obtain more information from it. Failure to do so can lead to serious civil penalties.

Health Insurance Portability and Accountability Act (HIPAA)

Organizations that deal with electronic transactions of medical records, medical payments or remittance advice, insurance claims, eligibility requirements, or medical referral information must be in compliance with **HIPAA**. Organizations that have insurance policies for their employees must also comply. Noncompliance with HIPAA's confidentiality standards can lead to serious civil penalties and fines.

If HIPAA applies to an organization, its management must do the following:

1. Assign a person/persons to be responsible for HIPAA compliance
2. Familiarize staff with the key HIPAA compliance issues
3. Know how the law specifically affects the organization
4. Insure in writing and with audits that all of the relevant business organizations it works with also are HIPAA compliant.

The PATRIOT Act

The PATRIOT Act greatly reduces the requirements for the government to access information. U.S. law enforcement agencies are now permitted to request business and financial records and use electronic surveillance from organizations without court search warrants. These provisions apply especially to banks for searching money trails and in the use of roving wiretaps for communication companies.

The PATRIOT Act allows victims of computer hacking to request law enforcement assistance in monitoring the "trespassers" on their computers. This change made the law technology-neutral. It placed electronic trespassers on the same footing as physical trespassers. Now, hacking victims can seek law enforcement assistance to combat hackers, just as burglary victims have been able to invite officers into their homes to catch burglars.

The PATRIOT Act extends the money-laundering act of 1986 so that it is mandatory for financial institutions to file a Currency Transaction Report (CTR) for all cash transactions greater than $10,000. It also amends the Bank Secrecy Act of 1970 to lower the legal standards for disclosure.

DEVELOPING AN INFORMATION SECURITY POLICY

Every organization today needs to have a clear information security policy that takes into account the information risks to be managed and the compliance needs with laws such as those discussed previously. There are no "implied" security policies: If your policy is not written down, then you have **no** security policy, and publicly traded organizations with no written security policy are automatically out of compliance with Sarbanes-Oxley.

If your security policy is not written down, your organization has no security policy.

Insurance companies today will not insure an organization that does not have a clearly written security policy. This is the current business environment, and it is likely to continue to be this way well into the twenty-first century.

Security policies should be written at a high level, and should state what is, and what *is not*, permissible. There should be no ambiguity in the policy. One should also not substitute existing civil or criminal laws for an organization's security policy. Instead, the policy should explicitly state that such acts are prohibited.

Policies should also clearly state what the punishments are for violation of the policy.

This gives management the justification they need to quickly remove any employees who behave improperly: The organization may not yet know whether they have violated the law or not, but if you can prove that they have clearly violated the security policy, then you have clear grounds for employee dismissal.

Although another company's security policy will never be a perfect fit, "boilerplate" information security policies can often be found on the Internet or in other sources. The actual implementation details of the policy, however, should be in a procedures manual, not in the security policy itself.

Who Should Develop the Security Policy?   Unless an organization is quite small, it should establish a security policy committee with representatives for as many affected user groups and other stakeholders as possible. This helps ensure not only good policy content but also employee support for the written policy. If a security policy does not have the support of the managers who must administer and abide by it, it will fail.

Then, all relevant employees should be asked to read any new policy developed by the committee (on company time) and be given an easy way to ask any questions about it; if the policy isn't clear, it should be rewritten to be more understandable for the internal worker. Whenever significant changes are made to a policy, this process should be repeated with all affected employees.

Because the technological and legal environments constantly change, the security policy committee should have regular, scheduled meetings to develop and vote on any changes or additions to the policy. Developing a security policy is an ongoing task, rather than an end goal.

What Should Be in the Security Policy?   A security policy needs to be written for everything that affects the information integrity and confidentiality of the organization. It should state what the organization does to be in compliance with current laws, and what exactly an employee can, and cannot, do with organizational information.

An organization may actually have many security policies (Barman, 2002), or it may have a single, comprehensive security policy that is a compendium. Common policy areas are:

- *Access Control Policies:*   password log-in and access controls, encryption, public key infrastructures
- *External Access Policies:*   Internet security, VPN access, Web and Internet, e-mail
- *User and Physical Policies:*   Acceptable use, network architecture and address, physical security

Password management policies and formal policies on acceptable use are most commonly used to prevent or reduce e-crime. An example of an **acceptable use policy** is shown in Figure 16.8.

This document sets forth the policy of _____ (the Company) with regard to the use of, access to, review, and disclosure of various electronic communications, including those sent or received by Company employees. This information systems policy applies to all individuals using the Company's computer and network systems, including employees, subcontractors, and consultants.

For the purposes of this document, "electronic communications" includes, but is not limited to, the sending, receipt, and use of information through the corporate electronic information network, the Internet, voice mail, facsimiles, teleconferencing, and all other online information services.

Information Systems Are for Business Purposes

Information systems offered by the Company are provided to its users for the primary purpose of Company-related use.

Personal use is permissible on a limited bases. This limited personal use should not be during charged time and should not interfere with job performance. Personal messages may not be broadcast to groups of people or other employees except to appropriate forums (such as designated Usenet news groups). Permission for Company-wide broadcasting of personal messages must be obtained from your manager.

Monitoring and Privacy

Electronic communications through the Company's information systems are the property of the Company to assist it in carrying out business. The Company treats all electronic communications sent, received, or stored as business messages, including those for personal use. All users shall have no expectations of privacy with respect to any electronic message. While the Company will not do this routinely, it reserves the right to monitor, access, review, copy, store, or delete any electronic communications, including personal messages, from the system for any purpose and to disclose them to others, as deemed appropriate.

Data Retention Policy

The Company will retain e-mail messages and any backup of such e-mail for six months. Other computer system backups will be stored for only one year or longer if required by contract.

Prohibited Activity and Use of Good Judgment

Use of electronic communications to engage in any communication or action that is threatening, discriminatory (based on language that can be viewed as harassing others based on race, creed, color, age, sex, physical handicap, sexual orientation, or otherwise, defamatory, slanderous, obscene, or harassing) is prohibited. Electronic communications shall not disclose personnel information without authorization. The destruction or alteration of electronic communications with the intent to cause harm or injury to the Company or an employee of the Company is strictly prohibited.

Electronic communications shall not be used for any illegal purposes or violate the intellectual property rights of others. Employees shall not break into the computers or intercept the communications of other individuals.

Employees will use the same good judgment to prepare electronic communications as they would use in preparing a hard copy of a memorandum. The content of electronic communications may have significant business and financial consequences for individuals of the Company and may be inappropriately taken out of context. Because of the ease of sending these documents, extra care must be taken to ensure that they are not sent hastily. Please keep in mind that your messages may be read by someone other than the addressee. Accordingly, please ensure that your messages are courteous, professional, and business-like.

Intellectual Property and Licensing

The ease of copying through various electronic communications systems poses a serious risk of intellectual property infringement. Each user must be aware and respect the rights of others.

Software that may be marked as "free," "public domain," and "public use" may be free for personal use but not corporate use. In downloading software from the Internet, use of this software can violate copyright or licensing requirements. Always obtain approval from your manager or the Legal Department before using any publicly available software package.

Do not copy software licensed to the Company unless you are authorized under the Company's license to do so.

Users may not install software that originally came from your home computer or elsewhere unless you can demonstrate from a written license that such use is permitted.

Do not copy software owned by the company without appropriate permissions.

Do not remove intellectual property notices of others.

Virus Protection

Users may not knowingly create, execute, forward, or introduce any computer code designed to self-replicate, damage, or otherwise impede the performance of any computer's memory, storage, operating system, or software.

Software and other files may not be loaded on the Company's computers unless a virus check is performed using an approved virus-scanning program. It is a violation of this policy to disable any virus-checking facilities installed on any system or network.

Figure 16.8 Acceptable Use Policy Example (Example published in Barman, 2002)

Disciplinary Action

Management reserves the right to revoke any user's access privileges at any time for violations of this policy and conduct that disrupts the normal operation of the company's information systems. Any conduct that adversely affects the ability of others to use the company's systems and networks or which can harm others, will not be permitted. Violations to this policy can result in termination.

Authority may be exercised without notice, and management disclaims responsibility for loss or damage to data and software as a result.

Acknowledgement

I acknowledge that I have read and will abide by the Company's Information Security Policy.

Name _____   Date _____

Figure 16.8   (continued)

How Strict Should a Security Policy Be?   The rigidity of the policy should be appropriate for the estimated risks to the organization. A mantra used by some is: Tighten it up until it hurts, and then loosen it up until it works.

When and How Should an Organization Develop a Security Policy to Address a New Situation?   A new policy should be developed as soon as possible: The longer an organization operates without a complete policy, the greater are the information and legal risks.

How Should Policies Be Disseminated?   The organization should make it easy for all employees (including contractors) to know where they can find the most current version of a security policy. Hard-copy distribution of policies is still common: Manuals are typically made available to all employees, and policies are included in training materials. More recently, organizations have been distributing policies by e-mail or posting them online (on the organization's intranet or other secured internal network).

Organizations should save and archive all approval transactions for proof of agreement, should they be needed in the future. New employees should be asked to thoroughly read existing security policies and then sign them as a condition of employment. Some organizations require all of their employees to review and accept their appropriate usage policy on an annual basis. In some situations, the employee may be asked to acknowledge acceptance of the policy each time data is accessed.

PLANNING FOR BUSINESS CONTINUITY

In the past, IT organizations focused on "disaster recovery planning"—which were contingency plans for how to recover from an unexpected natural disaster such as a flood, tornado, hurricane, or fire. For example, many organizations have contacts with external service providers to provide backup data center processing and telecommunications support. Research has shown that an organization's inability to resume in a reasonable time span to normal business activities after a major disruption is a key predictor of business failure.

However, **business continuity planning (BCP)** involves much more than recovering from a natural disaster. It involves putting plans in place to ensure that employees and business processes can continue when faced with any major unanticipated disruption. As many organizations learned after the 9/11 terrorist attacks (McNurlin and Sprague, 2004), business continuity also requires having:

- Alternate workspaces for people with working computers and phone lines
- Backup IT sites that are not too close but not too far away (to be within driving distance but not affected by a regional telecommunication disaster)
- Up-to-date evacuation plans that everyone knows and has practiced
- Backed-up laptops and departmental servers, because a lot of corporate information is housed on these machines rather than in the data center
- Helping people cope with a disaster by having easily accessible phone lists, e-mail lists, and even instant-messenger lists so that people can communicate with loved ones and colleagues

The process for creating a BCP begins with a business impact analysis, which can include the following:

1. Define the critical business processes and departments
2. Identify interdependencies between them
3. Examine all possible disruptions to these systems

4. Gather quantitative and qualitative information on these threats
5. Provide remedies for restoring systems

For item 3, some dependencies that affect access to organizational information are obvious—such as electricity, communications, and Internet connections. Others may be less obvious, such as the maximum tolerable downtime for each application system. Traditionally, these have been measured in categories like the following:

- Lower-priority = 30 days
- Normal = 7 days
- Important = 72 hours
- Urgent = 24 hours
- Critical = < 1/2 day

This should result in quantitative rankings, along with qualitative judgments, about the severity of the disruption, which are then used to determine an appropriate remedy for system restoration.

The BCP should also state who is responsible for doing what under which conditions. Logs and other documentation should be available to implement the plan. Finally, BCP plans should be tested. Depending on the organization's industry, auditors may require periodic testing within a certain time frame.

Testing a BCP may in fact be the most costly part of the process, as it demands pulling staff away from their normal work to simulate a parallel situation to which a disruption occurs. Testing a BCP therefore costs the organization money, time, and resources in the short term, and it can also temporarily lower productivity.

ELECTRONIC RECORDS MANAGEMENT (ERM)

The importance of electronic records management has grown as recent U.S. laws have required that an organization must retain certain records for a minimum period of time. For example, Section 802 of Sarbanes-Oxley requires that public companies and their public accounting firms maintain all audit and review work papers for five years. The Internal Revenue Service can require a period of seven years, and willful destruction of corporate audit records can result in sentences of imprisonment for up to ten years. The Health Information Portability and Accountability Act (HIPAA) requires a minimum retention period of six years for medical records, and penalties include both large civil fines and even criminal imprisonment. There are currently over a dozen major laws within the United States alone that require information retention and protection, and in December 2006 more explicit rules were developed for how organizations must handle a response to a litigation request for electronic documents.

In general, most businesses have greatly underestimated their **digital liability** for actions their employees have taken. For example, Microsoft executives clearly did not think out the consequences when sending e-mails about Netscape (see the box entitled "Is E-Mail Forever?").

Digital liability management requires ensuring that managers are knowledgeable about the risks involved in information mismanagement, the need for precise policies, and the legal and regulatory environment that its organization faces. All digital liability management must be based upon risk analysis. This may seem obvious, but business history is littered with cases of companies that did not assess the risks of their actions.

The sheer complexity of large organizations, in combination with changing national and international laws and the increased use of electronic documents, requires a

---

IS E-MAIL FOREVER?

The basis of a U.S. government antitrust case against Microsoft was that Microsoft conspired to use its monopoly on the desktop computer market to drive Netscape (which introduced the first commercial browser) out of business. Microsoft denied it—but were there copies of incriminating e-mails somewhere to prove otherwise? Yes—there were hundreds of e-mails, all on servers outside of Microsoft.

How can this happen? If an organization is using Open Shortest Path First (OSPF) routing, then it is allowing the network to choose the quickest route to send its information, including its e-mail. This means that an e-mail could pass through a number of public servers anyplace on the continent. The sending organization has no control over these servers, and these machines are constantly backing up the information passing through them. Thus, it is very reasonable to assume that there will be discoverable electronic copies archived somewhere.

Recent history has also shown that companies cannot even control their e-mail on their own private subnets. Individuals can make copies, save them, forward them, and most definitely do not "wash" them forever off their storage devices.

So: **Is e-mail forever?** As users and managers, you should assume that yes—it is. In other words, it is much more probable that a computer forensics specialist will be able to recreate the e-mail than the user will be able to erase it forever from everyplace.

centralized approach to electronic records management (ERM). In many organizations, an investment in not only ERM specialists but also commercial, off-the-shelf ERM software may be justified.

In general, an ERM manager (or an ERM committee) should be responsible for the following:

1. *Defining*   what constitutes an electronic record. Electronic records include not just e-mail, but financial records, research and development, IM messages, customer and transaction databases, and many others.
2. *Analyzing*   the current business environment and developing appropriate ERM policies. For example, what should be kept, and for how long? When and how should records be destroyed? Who can make copies, and on what types of media? Where are these media copies kept, and who has access to them?
3. *Classifying*   specific records based upon their importance, regulatory requirements, and duration.
4. *Authenticating records*   by maintaining accurate logs and procedures to prove that these are the actual records, and that they have not been altered.
5. *Managing policy compliance*   The ERM policies must have precise controls, explaining what is to be done, when it is to be done, who is to do it, with logs and controls to prove that the policy has been complied with.

Amendments to the U.S. Federal Rules of Civil Procedure that took effect in December 2006 place a new burden on records managers for the purposes of records retention and timely information gathering in response to potential litigation. Since failure to comply with these **eDiscovery amendments** can lead to severe financial penalties, good ERM practices are becoming an important part of information risk management (Volonino et al., 2007).

THE CHIEF INFORMATION SECURITY ROLE

Many organizations have also recently implemented the role of **chief information security officer (CISO)**. The CISO is responsible for continually assessing an organization's information security risks and for developing and implementing effective countermeasures. A CISO does not need to have a computer engineer's level of understanding of security technologies. However, a CISO does need to be able to talk knowledgeably with technical staff about mature and emerging technologies for information security.

The goal of the CISO is not to eliminate all information risk. Rather, the goal is to identify and prioritize all relevant risks, totally eliminate those risks that can be eliminated with a reasonable investment, and to mitigate other risks until the point of diminished returns for security investments. Of course determining that point of diminished returns can be quite difficult.

The globalization of business also brings increased information security risks. For example, many organizations enter into joint ventures or other strategic alliances for research and development, new product manufacturing, or product testing. Offshore outsourcing has also become increasingly common, with third-party firms processing an organization's payroll or claims data. Some firms also use application service providers (ASPs) that host applications and store customer data for multiple client organizations. All of these organizational arrangements increase information security risks, and contribute to the need to create high-level management positions to manage them.

For understanding the potential value of having a highly competent CISO, one need look no further than the most recent front page headline about a data breach or credit card theft.

SUMMARY

Organizations are increasing their investments in not only information security technologies but also electronic records management and information security specialists. The goal is to minimize an organization's risks at an acceptable cost level. This does not mean that organizations strive to be completely secure. Rather, it means that, to the best of current technical and information management knowledge, an organization must mitigate risks to the highest level of security that it can, based upon risk management assessments, its resources, and its current legal and regulatory environment. The goal is to find the appropriate balance between accessibility, integrity, and confidentiality, based upon a thorough risk analysis.

An organization must be in compliance with current laws. Noncompliance is not an option, and a company's employees need to be educated on all of the relevant laws for their position and their organization.

Information security management needs to be viewed as a process, and never as an achievable end state. IT managers are responsible for assessing and implementing security technologies, as well as assessing new risks associated with new technologies. A CISO, other high-level manager, or organizational committee needs to be responsible for assessing the impacts of changing regulations or other work environment changes, and developing and implementing new information security policies to address them. Information security requires continuous adjustments, based on imperfect information, about a potentially hostile external environment.

Review Questions

1. What kind of criminal act would be considered an e-crime?
2. What is the difference between a hacker and a cracker?
3. What are the overall goals of information risk management?
4. What resources can organizations use to calculate an expected annual financial loss for a given information asset?
5. Why does the Sarbanes-Oxley Act impact the work of IT personnel?
6. What is HIPAA, and what are some of its potential impacts on IT workers in hospitals and other health care provider organizations?
7. Why is it important for an organization to have an information security policy?
8. What is the specific purpose of an acceptable use policy?
9. What were some of the lessons learned about business continuity planning that can be derived from organizational experiences following the 9/11 attack on the World Trade Center in New York? Do you think these also apply to BCP in the event of a natural disaster, such as a major flood?
10. What information security issues does electronic records management address?
11. What is the role of a chief information security officer, and why is this organizational role a relatively new one?

3. The importance of having vigilant IT professionals who are capable of detecting and minimizing the damage from a security breach has become increasingly important. Is this a type of job position that you would like to hold, and why—or why not?
4. To achieve SOX compliance has required many organizations to significantly change their business processes and invest in new software products. Use the Internet to research some examples of these types of impacts that SOX has had on U.S.-based organizations in particular.
5. HIPAA compliance even affects the physician's office. Comment on how procedures at one of your own physicians' offices appear to have changed (or not changed) because of this relatively recent law.
6. Concerns about the misuse of the PATRIOT Act continue to be discussed in the media. What are some examples of recent concerns that have been reported?
7. Reflect on when you last received authority to have a computer account with an organization (such as your university), and comment on your own experience when you were asked to sign (or otherwise signify acceptance) of an organizational policy similar to the acceptable use policy in Figure 16.8. Would you recommend any changes to the organization for how to present this policy to a new account holder?
8. How easy is it to find an information security policy (such as an acceptable use policy) at your university? At an organization where you are an employee?
9. Use the Internet to research some of the IT-related issues that had to be addressed by organizations (or individuals) in a recent natural disaster in your own country.
10. What are some of the potential impacts of the eDiscovery amendments on organizations?
11. If you were offered the position of a CISO for a large organization, would you accept this role, and why or why not? Under what circumstances might you request a reporting relationship to the CIO of that organization, if it did not already exist?

Discussion Questions

1. Do you think the acts of hackers should be punished the same as those by crackers? Why or why not?
2. Use the Internet to identify a recent report of a spoofing or phishing crime, and summarize what it involved, and what the punishment (if any) was.

References

Baase, Sara. 1997. *A Gift of Fire—Social, Legal, and Ethical Issues in Computing.* Upper Saddle River, NJ: Pearson Prentice Hall.

Barman, Scott. 2002. *Writing Information Security Policies.* Indianapolis, IN: New Riders Publishing.

Cerullo, Virginia, and M. J. Cerullo. 2004. "Business continuity planning: A comprehensive approach." *Information Systems Management*, 21:3 (Summer): 65–69.

CSO Magazine. 2005. "E-Crime Watch™ Survey: Summary of Findings." In cooperation with the U.S. Secret Service and CERT Coordination Center (Carnegie Mellon University).

Knapp, K. J., and W. R. Boulton. 2006. "Cyber-warfare threatens corporations: Expansion into commercial environments." *Information Systems Management*, 23:2 (Spring): 76–87.

McNurlin, Barbara C., and Ralph H. Sprague, Jr. 2004. *Information Systems Management in Practice*, 6th ed. Upper Saddle River, NJ: Pearson Prentice Hall.

Pereira, Joseph. 2007. "How credit-card data went out wireless door." *Wall Street Journal* (May 4): A1, A12.

Sager, Ira, Steve Hamm, Neil Gross, John Carey, and Robert D. Hoff. 2000. "Cyber crime." *Business Week* (February 21).

Volonino, Linda, Janice C. Sipior, and Burke T. Ward. 2007. "Managing the lifecycle of electronically stored information." *Information Systems Management*, 24:3 (Summer): 231–238.

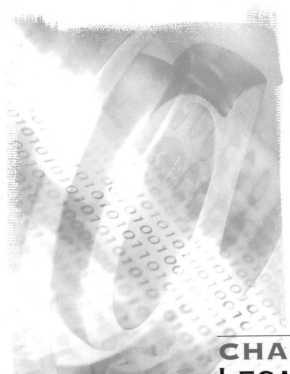

CHAPTER 17
LEGAL, ETHICAL, AND SOCIAL ISSUES

As we have seen, information technology (IT) is becoming a core resource for organizations in today's global economy and is affecting, if not determining, what organizations produce and how they are managed. Anyone with casual familiarity with today's news knows that IT is influencing the whole of society, not just the business arena. Today's generation can hardly conceive of living without the cell phone, the PC, communication satellites, fax machines, and the Internet. IT is rapidly changing our lives, and this process of change is ongoing. The information revolution is often compared with the industrial revolution in terms of the overall impact that the industrial revolution had on civilization.

In spite of all the benefits that IT has brought, it has also given rise to a number of troubling social problems, such as loss of privacy, intellectual property issues, identity theft, spam, **computer viruses** and **worms**, sexual exploitation of children, obsolescence of workers' skills, global outsourcing of jobs, and deterioration of working conditions. It would require an entire book to do justice to the legal, ethical, and social issues in IT, but we will explore a select number of these social issues and consider their ethical and legal implications.

In the next section we discuss some of the challenges associated with establishing laws related to IT. Then we explore some ways that managers can identify and analyze problems from an ethical perspective. Next we discuss three selected

issues in more depth: privacy, identity theft, and intellectual property rights. Finally, we briefly introduce the topics of computer crime, access to the technology, freedom of speech, the hazards of inaccuracy, and the impact on workers.

THE LEGAL ENVIRONMENT

In dealing with the use of IT, individuals and organizations must work within a complex legal environment. This legal environment is incomplete and sometimes less than satisfactory, yet it is a manager's duty to know and obey the existing laws. Ignorance of the law is no excuse.

The purpose of law is to constrain behavior within a society so that its needs are satisfied and harm within it is prevented. Thus, law is related to, but not necessarily identical to, ethics. Laws are rules that must be obeyed, but it is difficult to write a rule that applies to every possible situation, especially in the case of IT, which is changing so rapidly. Also, laws must be enforceable—there must be meaningful sanctions that are invoked if the law is broken. A law that cannot be enforced or that people will not obey simply engenders a lack of respect for all law.

The information revolution has put great strain on the legal system. IT has made new forms of crime, such as identity theft, feasible. And it has changed the mechanisms for reproducing printed material, photos, art, and music to the point where what was once laborious and expensive has become a simple matter of downloading from the Web. Technology has evolved quite rapidly, and the legal system has inevitably lagged behind.

The first reaction has been to try to reinterpret existing laws to apply to new conditions, which they often do not quite fit. Then writing and adopting new laws takes time, and it is hard to write a law that exactly suits the problem, especially when the problems are always changing. It might take a number of iterations before a satisfactory law emerges.

Ideally, the law should reflect the best interests of society as a whole, but there is always controversy on what best serves the public interest. Laws, then, are typically compromises between the views of various interest groups. Also, the issues in regulating technology can be very complex, and members of Congress might have little expertise in dealing with these issues. Therefore, representatives may depend on the expertise and advice of lobbyists who can devote resources to developing logical positions that reflect the interests of those who are paying them.

Organizations are increasingly global, and the Internet covers most of the world. Different countries have different values and different legal systems. Whose laws apply when a possible crime has been committed? There are serious problems in determining who has jurisdiction when the person who is injured is in one jurisdiction and the perpetrator of the crime is in another. It might be virtually impossible to enforce any law in a situation where essentially anonymous people in multiple countries are involved.

The impact of IT law on organizations has been discussed in Chapter 16. In this chapter we will discuss the impact of IT law on individuals and society.

ETHICS FRAMEWORKS

Why are we discussing ethics in a book on management of IT? First, IT has a growing impact on our lives, and anything that has such powerful effects on people's lives gives rise to ethical issues. Second, managers determine how IT is used, and therefore managers are responsible for the effects of the use of IT and the ethical implications of these effects.

To act ethically requires that we take *responsibility* for our actions. We need to clearly understand that the technology

itself is not to blame for any harm that results from its use. Too often we hear: "We can't do that because our computer won't allow it." That might be true for the person who is making the statement, but it does not absolve the organization from responsibility—someone designed the system and programmed the computer to act in that way. And saying "the computer won't let me do that" is equivalent to saying "our organizational policy won't let me do that." Likewise, blaming the computer for a mistake is just an excuse—those who decided to use the computer and designed and implemented a system without adequate controls are responsible for any harm, not the computer! People and organizations are responsible for the results, good or bad, of the use of IT.

Most of us consider ourselves ethical persons. Most of us have an internal set of ethical standards, and we are uncomfortable when we violate these standards. Furthermore, in our careers as managers or professionals, there are very practical reasons to act ethically according to the society's standards. As individuals, if we are perceived as unethical we are in deep, deep trouble. If we get a reputation for being unethical, our jobs, or even our careers, might come to an inglorious end. Likewise, if an organization is perceived as unethical it might quickly be out of business. Whether it belongs to an individual or an organization, a reputation for integrity is crucial to success. Consider, for example, what happened to Enron and its managers when its books were found to be dishonest. Thus, managers must be concerned both with their individual ethics and the ethics of their organization. Managers are involved in determining the organization's ethical standards as well as in making sure that these standards are followed.

Identifying Ethical Problems

The first step in acting ethically is to recognize that a decision or action has ethical implications. In our use of IT we might do harm because we simply did not realize that our actions might be harmful—we might not consider all the implications of our actions. Therefore, we need to think about the ethical issues associated with our decisions before we take action. One purpose of this chapter is to sensitize you to the ethical issues that might arise in your use of IT so that you will not neglect the ethical implications.

How do we identify decisions where ethical problems might arise? Because our ethical makeup lies deep within us, the most common way we recognize ethical problems is by feel—when we don't feel right about a situation there might be an ethical problem. When we suspect that there might be ethical problems, a number of questions can be of help: Is this fair to everyone who will be affected? Would I want my mother to know about this? Would I care if everyone knew about this? What would be the result if everyone did this?

Identifying ethical problems associated with the use of IT might be complicated by the fact that its effects can be so pervasive. The effects of the use of IT might extend to many stakeholders—managers, workers, stockholders, customers, suppliers, communities, and the general public—and might affect them in ways that are not immediately obvious. For example, collecting information on customers for use in serving their needs might be beneficial to both the customer and the organization, but if this information is not protected against intrusion, someone might break into the system, steal personal information, and use it to harm the individual. Furthermore, if this information is sold to outside parties it might be used to harm the individual. Therefore, when trying to determine if there are ethical problems in the use of IT, a good place to start is to carefully consider all the potential stakeholders who might be affected by the system and determine how each one could be affected. If one or more of the stakeholders might be harmed, there is likely to be an ethical problem.

Analyzing Ethical Problems

There is no universally accepted way to determine whether an action is ethically justified or unethical. There are examples where almost everyone would agree that an action, such as murder, is unethical, but still there are those who believe that they are acting ethically when they kill women and children in an act of terrorism or in war. Even though there are no universally accepted rules, many concepts are helpful in analyzing ethical problems.

A number of professional organizations have recognized that IT presents many ethical issues. The Institute of Electrical and Electronic Engineers (IEEE) and the Association for Computing Machinery (ACM) have jointly developed a comprehensive code of ethics for the software engineering profession. The preamble to this Code of Ethics and Professional Practice, developed by the IEEE-CS/ACM Joint Task Force on Software Engineering Ethics and Professional Practices, contains the following paragraph:

Ethical tensions can best be addressed by thoughtful consideration of fundamental principles, rather than blind reliance on detailed regulations. These Principles should influence software engineers to consider broadly who is affected by their work; to examine if they and their colleagues are treating other human beings with due respect; to consider how the public, if reasonably well informed, would

view their decisions; to analyze how the least empowered will be affected by their decisions; and to consider whether their acts would be judged worthy of the ideal professional working as a software engineer. In all these Judgments concern for the health, safety and welfare of the public is primary; that is, the "Public Interest" is central to this Code.

The Association for Computing Machinery (ACM) code of ethics for its members explicitly recognizes that managers and organizations have special responsibilities as expressed in Section 3 of this code (see Figure 17.1).

Quite a number of basic principles to guide ethical behavior have been suggested over the years. Some of these principles come from religious traditions, while others come from philosophers and others concerned with ethics. The ancient Hippocratic oath advises physicians to "do no harm." The Ten Commandments of the Hebrew scripture forbid killing, adultery, stealing, bearing false witness, and coveting. Most world religions advocate the same ethic as Christianity's Golden Rule: Treat others as you would like them to treat you.

Some ethical issues are viewed differently depending upon the culture in which they arise. For example, in some Islamic cultures charging interest and drinking alcohol are unethical while polygamy is permissible. In some cultures bribery is not considered unethical; it is just the way you get things done. In cultures where there is respect for the law, breaking the law is considered unethical. However, the reverse—if it is not illegal it is ethical—is usually not an accepted interpretation.

In some cases the situation is so complex that it is not immediately obvious what action is ethical. When there are several interests that are affected in different ways by the decision one needs to carefully consider the impact on all those affected. Here *all* the parties who will be affected by the action must be identified and the consequences for each party delineated. Then it is tempting to argue that the action is ethically justified if the good outweighs the bad. However, when you harm some parties in order to benefit others it is usually questionable. Most people would be offended if, for example, all the benefits go to the decision maker at the expense of others who are harmed.

In these complex situations we should remember that there usually are a number of possible alternative actions—not just "do it" or "not do it." Especially in the case of developing and using IT, we can often devise alternatives that obtain adequate benefits while minimizing the harmful effects. And we need to be sure that we identify and include *all* those who will be affected by the system, not just those who will benefit from it. We might be inclined to include ourselves, those we know, members of

---

Section 3 of the ACM Code of Ethics

3. **Organizational Leadership Imperatives.** As an ACM member and an organizational leader, I will …

3.1   Articulate social responsibilities of members of an organizational unit and encourage full acceptance of those responsibilities.

3.2   Manage personnel and resources to design and build information systems that enhance the quality of working life.

3.3   Acknowledge and support proper and authorized uses of an organization's computing and communication resources.

3.4   Ensure that users and those who will be affected by a system have their needs clearly articulated during the assessment and design of requirements; later the system must be validated to meet requirements.

3.5   Articulate and support policies that protect the dignity of users and others affected by a computing system.

3.6   Create opportunities for members of the organization to learn the principles and limitations of computer systems.

Figure 17.1   Section 3 of the ACM Code of Ethics (Copyright © 2003, Association for Computing Machinery, Inc., Reprinted by permission.)

---

our organization, members of our community, or members of our segment of society, while excluding "outsiders" from consideration. Ignoring affected parties is a common flaw in ethical reasoning.

Despite occasional problems, ethical reasoning is seldom difficult. If we recognize that there is an ethical issue involved and take some time to think it through we usually have little difficulty knowing what is ethical and what is unethical. Problems arise, however, when we face decisions where being ethical has a cost. How we deal with these situations is what distinguishes the ethical person or organization from the unethical ones.

Some social issues that are important, but are not discussed in depth in this chapter, are e-mail, cyberstalking, sexual abuse via the Internet, and pornography. An employee might harass others via hate e-mail. Cyberstalking is the use of the Internet, e-mail, or other electronic communications devices to stalk another person. Employees can be sexual predators who are contacting minors through chat rooms using company facilities. And employees might use their office computers to access pornography while at work. These activities might subject the organization to significant penalties as well as public embarrassment, so it behooves prudent managers to make sure that policies and other relevant controls are in place so that they do not occur in their area of responsibility (see the discussion of security policies in Chapter 16).

PRIVACY

Privacy is important to people, but it is a difficult concept to define. Violating your privacy can relate to unwanted access to your person, or to intruding into your home or office, or to observing you, or to obtaining information about you. We would like to think that we have a "right" to privacy, but legally that right is much weaker than property rights or the right to free speech.

As a legal right *privacy* was defined by Samuel D. Warren and Louis D. Brandeis in 1890 as "the right to be let alone." However, this broad right has not been enacted into law in the United States.

In our discussion we will define privacy as *the ability to control access to information about ourselves.* Control is a key word in this definition because there is information about us that we willingly share with family, or friends, or those we trust, but that we would not want to share with the general public. Note that there is information about us— public information—to which we cannot control access. And there is critical information about us, such as our social security number, that by law we must provide to financial institutions so that income can be reported to the Internal Revenue Service (IRS). This is another instance of why the concept of control is so important, for we want to be able to keep our social security number away from potential identity thieves.

A person might give up his or her claim to privacy by giving permission to collect and use certain personal information. Therefore, if, after fully informing a person of how the information is to be used, you receive the person's permission to obtain and use personal information, you are not invading that person's privacy. People routinely give up personal information to someone they trust in exchange for some benefit or in order to transact business. However, privacy has been invaded when that information is used in ways that the person never intended or agreed to.

Privacy Problems

It is clear that IT has radically affected our ability to control access to information about ourselves and thus presents serious privacy problems. Before the computer, when transactions and records were on paper, there was quite limited access even to public information about ourselves. To find information someone had to go to where it was located, find it in the file, and copy it down. Today, when the same information is in an online database, it can often be obtained from anywhere in the world in a few seconds and at no cost. That ability has provided an enormous boost to productivity in our economy, but without substantial safeguards it can devastate our personal privacy.

The Web has enormously magnified the privacy problem. Once information is available on the Web it is instantly available worldwide. Moreover, this information can no longer be controlled because it may be copied and made available in numerous other places.

Explosive growth of the use of IT has produced a situation where huge amounts of personal information are easily available without any need for criminal activities. For reasons of convenience and efficiency, government agencies are putting official records into online databases—birth and death records, marriages, divorces, property sales, business licenses, legal proceedings, driving records, and so on. Furthermore, personal information is valuable for marketing purposes, and there are data brokers whose business is to collect and sell such information to whomever wishes to purchase it.

In the normal activities of transacting business, we often must provide sensitive personal information such as name, address, and credit card number. To take out a loan from a financial institution we must provide much more personal information and allow a credit check so that the lending institution can decide whether we are likely to repay the loan. This is quite legitimate and, because we agree to provide the information in order to transact the business, there is no invasion of privacy. However, when the business uses the information for purposes that we did not authorize or sells the information, serious privacy problems arise.

People differ widely in their attitude toward this kind of invasion of their privacy. Surveys over the years have shown that about 25 percent of the public is not at all concerned with these privacy issues, 25 percent is quite sensitive to loss of privacy, and the remaining 50 percent is willing to consider trading some privacy for other benefits if given the right to make that decision.

Personal information is so valuable to marketers that they go to great lengths to obtain it. Purchasers are encouraged to fill out and return warranty cards that sometimes include a questionnaire with questions about age, income, hobbies, favorite magazines, and so forth. If you enter a sweepstakes you might have to fill out an entry form with similar questions. If you have a special shopper card that provides discounts at your supermarket, you probably filled out an application that included personal information. Credit card records can provide comprehensive information about your shopping habits (see the box entitled "Credit Cards"). All this personal information is likely to end up in databases that are used to target marketing efforts.

When individuals do not know what data are being collected or by whom or how it is used, they have no control over their personal information and therefore by definition their privacy has been invaded. Furthermore, if all these marketing databases were to be combined with official

---

CREDIT CARDS

In 1992, General Motors Corp. joined with MasterCard International, Inc., to offer the GM Card. As a result, GM now has a database of 12 million GM cardholders, and it surveys them to learn what they're driving, when they next plan to buy a car or truck, and what kind of vehicle they would like. GM went into the credit-card business not just to build loyalty and offer cardholders rebates on cars but also because it saw the billing process as a way to harvest reams of data about consumers.

American Express Co., using massively parallel processors from Thinking Machines, Inc., stores every credit card transaction. Then 70 workstations at the American Express Decision Sciences Center in Phoenix race through mountains of data on millions of American Express cardholders—the stores they shop in, the places they travel to, the restaurants they've eaten in, and even the economic conditions and weather in the areas where they live—in order to target special promotions to customers through its billing process.

[Adapted from Berry, Verity, Kerwin and DeGeorge, 1994]

information databases and financial information databases into one database, the result would be a very comprehensive dossier on each person. So far this has not been done in the democracies of the world, but it would be possible. Repressive governments have developed and used these comprehensive dossiers as a means to control their citizens.

E-Commerce Privacy Concerns

We know that unencrypted communications on the Web can be intercepted and that there are sites that mimic trusted companies for the purpose of enticing the unwary to give their personal identifying information and credit card number to potential identity thieves. But we might not be aware that legitimate, trusted businesses are collecting personal information about us and our shopping activities and selling them to others. As described in Chapter 8, some companies participate in independent certification programs, such as TRUSTe, and declare this association on their Web site (such as displaying the TRUSTe seal).

When you visit a Web site, that site might deposit a **cookie** on your computer in a cookie file provided by your Web browser. The cookie is a small record that identifies you to the Web site you visited and allows it to set up a file on its computer that can record information about the actions you take with that site. When you visit that site again, the cookie is retrieved and that data are used to access your file on the site. This can be very helpful to you. For example, if you have made a purchase from that store, it might have saved your name, address, and credit card number so you do not have to enter that information again (but only verify it) when you wish to make another purchase. The Web store might also maintain a record of the particular items you looked at and the purchases you made and analyze that information to determine your interests and target its advertising and promotions to those interests. (As described in Chapter 8, this type of personalization capability was pioneered by Amazon.com, and considered today a characteristic of a good retailing site.)

From the standpoint of your privacy, this use of cookies is relatively benign. Furthermore, it provides the basis for "target marketing" that is very beneficial to the marketer and also helps provide you with promotional material that might be of interest to you instead of just junk mail. However, you might not know about the cookie or the information that the Web site maintains about you. Further, if the Web site sells that information to others without your permission that is a definite violation of your privacy because you have lost control of your personal information. This information, along with similar information from other Web sites that you visit, might end up in the database of a data broker whose business is building comprehensive dossiers on people and selling them. You might or might not care about whether a comprehensive picture of your buying habits and interests is freely available, but some people consider this to be a gross invasion of their privacy.

Cookies can also be used to develop more comprehensive information on your interests and preferences as you surf across a number of Web sites. For example, DoubleClick Inc., a leading Internet advertising service, places ads for thousands of advertisers on thousands of Web sites that employ their services. When you visit one of these client Web sites, a cookie is deposited on your computer that identifies you as described previously. However, that cookie also identifies you when you visit any other DoubleClick client Web site, so your record in DoubleClick's computer includes information about your viewing and purchasing behavior across all of DoubleClick's client sites. This information is extremely valuable to advertisers, for they can then display ads to you that fit your interests and you have a higher than normal probability of responding to their ads. Any improvement in the response rate is of great value to an advertiser, and you might also benefit by not being subjected to as many ads in which you have no interest.

The data collected by the use of a cookie is anonymous—the cookie only identifies your browser to DoubleClick's computers. However, in 2001 DoubleClick made a strategic investment in Abacus Direct, a direct marketing service that served direct mail and catalog marketers. Abacus had buying information on 88 million households, including name, address, telephone number, credit card numbers, income, and purchases. DoubleClick soon announced a product that provided advertising services based upon merging its Internet database with the Abacus database to serve cross-channel marketers. When this linking of databases was publicized by the news media it elicited a storm of protest and DoubleClick announced that it was withdrawing that product until suitable privacy standards had been developed. The product has since been returned to DoubleClick's product line under the following privacy guidelines (selected from the DoubleClick Web site, *www.doubleclick.com*):

- DoubleClick will not use any personal information to target Internet ads.

- DoubleClick will allow you to opt out of its depositing a cookie on your computer.

- DoubleClick encourages its clients to also allow you to opt out of the client depositing cookies and to provide notice to its customers of the DoubleClick technologies that they use.

■ DoubleClick does not develop marketing scores that indicate a user's individual health condition, detailed financial information, sexual orientation or behavior, information that appears to relate to children under 13, racial and ethnic origin, political opinions, religious or philosophical opinions, and trade union membership.

As of this writing Google is in the process of obtaining approval to purchase DoubleClick. The prospect of combining the search information that Google has access to with DoubleClick's information is very disturbing to some privacy advocates who are opposing approval of this merger. (See also the discussion of Google in Chapter 8.)

One of the most rapidly growing types of software that covertly gathers a user's personal information without the user's knowledge is called **spyware** (or adware), which may or may not use cookies (Sipior et al., 2005). Spyware usually is a hidden component within a downloaded screen saver, music-swapping software, or other freeware or shareware, or may be automatically downloaded when a user visits a specific Web site or clicks on an ad. Some spyware programs scan computer hard drives for user files or track every mouse click and every keystroke, usually for targeted advertising purposes.

Except for the financial industry, in the United States there are no laws regulating the collection and sharing of such data. Although many proposals have been introduced in the U.S. Congress, legislation is difficult to craft, as broad wording could prohibit legitimate and useful practices and stifle innovation (Sipior et al., 2005). Most companies today do post a privacy policy, but many of these do not fully explain what data they collect or how they use or share the data. In addition, companies can change their privacy policies at any time without notifying those whose data they have collected, and when companies merge or enter into other alliances, what used to be illegal external sharing can become legal internal sharing.

A list of organizational actions that can lead to negative responses by an organization's online customers is provided in Figure 17.2. Other authors have also emphasized the need for organizations to strengthen their "human firewalls," such as by requiring customer service representatives for telecommunications companies to call back a person at their registered phone number to verify their identify, and other identity-verifying tactics (Armstrong, 2006).

Workplace Privacy

There is no expectation of privacy in the workplace. The U.S. courts have held that a company can monitor anything done using company computers. (See the box entitled "Legal Liability for Employee Conduct.") Employees need to be aware that e-mail is archived on company computers, so deleting an e-mail message from a personal folder does not remove it from company records. Furthermore, if the company is investigated by a government agency, the e-mail archives might be turned over to the investigating agency. Enron employees were dismayed in March 2003 when 1.6 million personal e-mails and documents were posted on a government Web site (Berman, 2003). (Embarrassing personal messages, as well as sensitive information such as social security numbers, were among the data posted.) This and other well-publicized litigation have resulted in managers reassessing their document retention policies for e-mail in particular. An organization's policy impacts its procedures if the company is faced with litigation (as dictated by the recent eDiscovery amendments to the Federal Rules of Civil Procedure).

Companies do not want their employees to waste company time and resources on inappropriate activities such as personal online shopping, chatting with friends, gambling online, or visiting pornographic Web sites. Managers can be held accountable for certain illegal activities of employees even if they were unaware that these activities were taking place, so companies often monitor employees in self defense. The only federal law that limits employer surveillance is the 1986 Electronic Communications Privacy Act, which bans employers from eavesdropping on spoken personal conversations. For practical as well as ethical reasons, it is important that the company policies for monitoring employee activities and communications be carefully considered and that they be clearly communicated to company employees.

LEGAL LIABILITY FOR EMPLOYEE CONDUCT

Corporate executives are becoming increasingly aggressive about spying on their employees, and with good reason: Now, in addition to job shirkers and office-supply thieves, they have to worry about being held accountable for the misconduct of their subordinates.

Even one offensive e-mail message circulated around the office by a single employee can pose a liability risk for a company. Not only that, but a wave of laws—including the federal Health Insurance Portability and Accountability Act (HIPAA) of 1996 and the anticorruption and corporate-governance Sarbanes-Oxley Act of 2002—have imposed new record-keeping and investigative burdens on companies. Not complying with some laws can result in the personal liability of officers and directors.

[Nusbaum, 2003]

Action Area	Possible Negative Consequence(s) of Mismanagement	Frequently Observed Types of Mismanagement
COLLECTION AND STORAGE	• Data subjects reluctant to provide accurate personal data to, or engage in transactions with, the organization in future	• Organization collecting more data than needed • Organization unclear or obfuscating about future uses of data
SECONDARY USE	• Possible legal liability for organization • Data subjects reluctant to provide personal data to, or engage in transactions with, the organization in future	• Organizational policies/practices ignore privacy implications of internal data re-use • Organizational inattentiveness to privacy implications of external data sharing • Excessive liberalism regarding "affiliate sharing"
DATA ACCURACY	• Incorrect inferences and decisions regarding data subjects • Possible legal liability for some organizations • Data subjects reluctant to provide personal data to, or engage in transactions with, the organization in future	• Organizational security controls lacking (enable deliberate errors) • Organizational quality control lapses in data collection or manipulation (accidental errors)
AUTHORIZED ACCESS	• Possible legal liability for some organizations (e.g., health care providers) • If discovered, data subjects reluctant to provide personal data to, or engage in transactions with, the organization in future (assuming they have a reasonable option).	• Weak security controls (technical) • Organizational inattentiveness to "need to know" implementation (managerial)
AUTOMATED JUDGMENT	• Inappropriate approval/denial of products and services with respect to some data subjects • Data subjects reluctant to provide personal data to, or engage in transactions with, the organization in future	• Excessive reliance on implementation of standard operating procedures (without rational referrals for human judgments)
PROFILING	• Data subjects form resentment towards organizations that contributed to the combined profiles • General backlash	• Lack of clarity regarding provisions on external sharing of data (or violations of clear provisions)

Figure 17.2 Privacy Mismanagement (Smith, 2004)

Ethics of Invasion of Privacy

Most of us would argue that invasion of privacy is unethical, for if you invade someone's privacy you are not treating that person as you would want to be treated. However, some argue that in some cases the resulting good can exceed the harm that has been caused. This, of course, can be tricky as it might be very difficult to accurately value the harm caused by a loss of privacy, and it is common to ignore or to undervalue the potential harm to others.

Laws on Privacy

In the United States there is no comprehensive legal right to privacy, but there is a great deal of legislation that purports to offer some privacy protection. For example, privacy laws in existence by the new millennium were as follows (Baron, 2000):

- The Fair Credit Reporting Act regulates the disclosure of credit application data and credit histories.

- The Privacy Act restricts a government agency from gathering information for one purpose and using it for another purpose or sharing it with another government agency. For example, the IRS has been prohibited from sharing income tax information with other agencies.

- The Family Education Rights and Privacy Act protects the privacy of students by restricting access to their student grade and disciplinary information.

- The Electronic Communications Privacy Act prohibits unauthorized access to e-mail.

- The Video Protection Privacy Act prohibits videotape service providers from disclosing information about video rentals.

- The Driver's Privacy Protection Act prohibits states from selling driver's license information.

- The Health Insurance Portability and Accountability Act protects your electronic medical records from unauthorized disclosure.

- The Children's Online Privacy Protection Act prohibits collecting information from children under the age of 13 unless their parents authorize it.

In total, U.S. laws provide a great deal of protection in certain areas. Student information, electronic medical information, and electronic communications are reasonably well protected. However, although several federal laws relate to protection of financial data, the total result is not very impressive. First, there is no federal protection of the privacy of information collected by other businesses such as merchants. Second, financial institutions— businesses that engage in banking, credit card issuing, insuring, stocks and bonds, financial advice, and investing—often buy and sell the information that they collect on you.

However, the Gramm-Leach-Bliley Act (GLBA) does provide some limited privacy protections against the sale of private financial information. According to the Web sites of the American Civil Liberties Union and the Federal Trade Commission:

- Financial institutions must develop precautions to ensure the security and confidentiality of customer records and information and to protect against unauthorized access to such records.

- Financial institutions must provide the customer with written notice of their information sharing policies when he [or she] first becomes a customer and annually thereafter.

- The customer has the right to opt out of sharing his [or her] information with certain third parties, and the above privacy policy notice must explain how, and offer a reasonable way, for the customer to opt out. However, the customer cannot prevent sharing this information with affiliated companies or companies that the financial institution has employed to provide certain services, or with credit reporting agencies, or as part of the sale of a business.

The requirement that the customer "opt out" to obtain this limited privacy protection is a significant concern. Because the ability to sell this information has substantial value, the financial institution has the motivation to reduce the likelihood that the opt-out option will be exercised. So the required privacy notice might be long, written so only a lawyer can understand it, printed in small type, and included in the envelope with the customer's bill along with several advertising inserts. It takes a dedicated person to take the time and effort to read through and understand the notice, to figure out how to opt out, and to follow the required procedure. From the standpoint of the consumer, an "opt-in" policy would be much preferred, for it would force the companies to explain clearly what would be shared, with whom, and how the information would be used in order to persuade the customer to agree to the sharing.

Judging by their laws, many European countries in particular seem to value privacy more highly than the United States does. According to Grupe, Kuechler, and Sweeney (2003), the U.S. position on privacy can be characterized as:

- unprotective of data about individuals collected by businesses and government

- an unrestricted flow of data among companies

- a market-driven view of people as consumers under which data are seen as a saleable, usable commodity that belongs to the corporations

- reliant on self-regulation by companies to respect an individual's privacy

- regulated by specific pieces of legislation (i.e., by sector) that relate to particular aspects of privacy, but not to privacy generally

In contrast, the European position can be characterized as:

- protective of personal rights with respect to data about individuals

- restrictive regarding the flow of personal data out of the country of origin, except to other countries honoring certain privacy principles

- having a view of the people as citizens who are in control of their personal data

- regulated by general laws, principles, procedures, and standards adopted to oversee the collection of data by governmental agencies established for this purpose

These differences in approach have led to conflicts that managers should be aware of. For example, in 1998 the European Union issued a directive that requires that countries allow transborder personal data transfers only to countries that adhere to standards substantially equivalent to those of the European Union. That does not include the United States, which threatened to interrupt European operations of U.S. companies. After some intense negotiations, an accommodation has been worked out that allows U.S. companies to continue to transfer data back to the United States if they certify that they adhere to agreed-to "safe harbor" standards that are roughly equivalent to those that the GLBA requires for financial institutions.

The PATRIOT Act, passed by Congress soon after the terrorist attacks of September 11, 2001, with the purpose of protecting Americans against terrorism, significantly weakened Americans' constitutional protection against unreasonable search and seizure by allowing the FBI to force anyone—including doctors, libraries, bookstores, universities, and Internet service providers (ISPs)—to turn over records on their clients or customers by simply telling a judge that the request is related to an ongoing terrorism or foreign intelligence investigation. Some sections of the PATRIOT Act had sunset provisions that were due to expire, but in 2005 Congress reauthorized the act. At this time a number of changes were made, some of which strengthened the powers of the government and others that provided more judicial oversight of the most controversial provisions including the section forcing doctors and libraries to turn over records as mentioned previously. Future assessment of the PATRIOT Act by U.S. lawmakers is anticipated, due to growing public concerns.

IDENTITY THEFT

Identity theft is a particularly detestable invasion of privacy. According to the Federal Trade Commission (FTC), **identity theft** is "someone appropriating your personal information without your knowledge to commit fraud or theft." An identity thief uses information about you, such as your name, address, social security number, credit card number, and/or other identifying information to impersonate you and obtain loans or purchase items using your credit. When the thief does not make the required payments, it is reported to credit bureaus and your personal credit rating could be ruined. Furthermore, the thief's creditors might hound you to repay the debts that have been run up in your name. Although more than half of the incidents involving credit card theft are typically resolved within just a few days, about 12 percent of incidents can take one to two months, and about 8 percent of thefts that involve personal information can take three or more months (Baum, 2006). However, besides taking a lot of personal time and effort, some cases also exact a heavy emotional toll (see the box entitled "Identity Theft Nightmare").

IDENTITY THEFT NIGHTMARE

John Harrison's nightmare began on July 27, 2001, when an identity thief used Harrison's social security number to acquire a military photo ID and began a four-month spending rampage that left more than 60 bogus accounts and close to $260,000 worth of purchases in his victim's name. Using Harrison's good credit rating, the thief had been able to open new credit card, checking, and utility accounts, and then purchase two new pickups, mobile phones, clothing, and more than $7,000 in home improvements. He rented an apartment as Harrison and even bought a vacation time-share.

Police arrested and prosecuted the thief, Jerry Phillips, and he even went to prison for three years. With an apologetic thief behind bars, Harrison thought he was lucky—but he was wrong. Despite letters from the Justice Department confirming that he was a victim, Harrison is still being harassed by creditors. In fact, he remains nearly $140,000 in debt.

Harrison has struggled for over four years and spent over 2,000 hours to clear his name. "I'll spend 10 minutes explaining that I'm a victim of identity theft," says Harrison of his daily battles with unremitting debt collectors. "Then they'll say, 'OK, can you start paying some of this debt?' It keeps coming and you don't have a choice but to deal with it."

Harrison's personal credit also dried up as banks revoked his spending limits. And when his 15-year-old daughter needed his help to open up her first savings account, they were turned away. "I can't put a price tag on the humiliation I felt," Harrison reported.

[Abstracted from Moritz, 2003, and CBS News, 2005]

Technically, identity theft might not be solely a computer crime, for the identity information about you might be obtained by stealing your wallet or bills out of your mailbox, by obtaining your credit card number from a credit card receipt, by "dumpster diving" to find discarded paper records, or by disclosure by someone who has legitimate access to your personal information. However, the information can also be obtained by breaking into a computer and examining files that contain this information, by **phishing** (sending an e-mail to a user falsely claiming to be a legitimate enterprise in an attempt to scam the user into providing private information), or even by intercepting information flowing through the Internet or dedicated communication lines. The fraud that makes identity theft lucrative would not be possible without the heavy dependence on IT by national credit card companies and credit bureaus. (Information security actions, from an organizational perspective, are discussed in Chapter 16.)

Impact of Identity Theft

Identity theft crime has become a serious problem, both for businesses and individuals. In 2004, 3.6 million households in the United States (roughly 3 percent) had at least one member who had been an identity theft victim within the previous six months. According to a government study, the households most likely to experience such a crime had household income of $75,000 or higher; were headed by persons ages 18 to 24; and were in urban or suburban areas.

However, financial institutions and merchants bear most of the dollar costs of identity theft, which are estimated to be about $50 billion annually. If your credit card is misused, either the merchant or the credit card company absorbs the loss. If someone borrows money in your name, the lender is stuck with the loss. In addition, today's laws require that companies notify individuals about known incidents that involve identity theft, which also can be costly.

However, the dollar figures do not tell the full story of the impact of identity theft on the victim. In the first place, the victim must prove his or her innocence to every business that has been victimized, and the business might not be happy about its loss and be reluctant to admit that it erred, so it might make it difficult to erase what it assumes to be the victim's debt. Furthermore, by the time the victim finds out about the crime, the thief could have run up a lot of bad debts that end up on the victim's credit record, thus destroying the victim's reputation and creditworthiness. Getting these records corrected can be a long, laborious process and might have to be repeated over and over as the thief continues more thievery using the victim's identity. Although the typical victim may spend only 30 or 40 hours clearing up his or her record, there are certainly cases where the victim's life has been severely impacted (as described previously in the box entitled "Identity Theft Nightmare").

Punishment of Identity Theft

Sometimes it is only the person whose identity has been stolen who has any direct motivation to stop the thief from further activity. The banks and merchants from whom the identity thief has stolen money do not always pursue the identity and prosecution of the thief, unless the loss was quite large. In addition, members of the police force are also sometimes reluctant to pursue identity thieves. Police agencies are underfunded, overworked, and might be untrained in how to handle identity theft investigations, and if the identity thief has not taken any money from the person whose identity has been stolen, many police officers feel that no crime has been committed and a report of the crime may not be made. According to a 2003 ITRC study, 26 percent of the victims were unable to get the local police to take a report of the crime, even after multiple attempts, and only 29 percent of the victims were able to get a written report from the police. This can be particularly frustrating for individuals affected, because many businesses and banks require a copy of a police report to clear the record of the identity theft victim.

There is no question that an identity thief is acting unethically. But how about the banks and merchants who simply ignore the crime rather than pursuing the thief? It is clear that the identity theft victim is often injured by that lack of action as it allows the identity thief to continue to take advantage of the victim. The banks and merchants justify their inaction on the grounds that the cost of taking action exceeds the amount that might be recovered from the thief, so taking action is not economically justified for them. This raises very tough ethical issues, because these institutions are victims also. How much cost should they be expected to bear in order to reduce the potential harm to the person whose identity has been stolen?

Laws on Identity Theft

The Identity Theft and Assumption Deterrence Act of 1998 amended Title 18 of the United States Code Section 1028 to make it a federal crime when anyone "knowingly transfers or uses, without lawful authority, a means of identification of another person with the intent to commit, or to aid or abet, any unlawful activity that constitutes a violation of

Federal law, or that constitutes a felony under any applicable State or local law."

Violations of the act are investigated by federal investigative agencies such as the U.S. Secret Service, the FBI, and the U.S. Postal Inspection Service and prosecuted by the Department of Justice. The act also requires the FTC to log and acknowledge such complaints, provide victims with relevant information, and refer their complaints to appropriate entities (e.g., the major national consumer reporting agencies and other law enforcement agencies).

Preventing Identity Theft

There are a number of precautions one should take to reduce the danger of identity theft:

- Protect your social security number. Do not reveal it to anyone unless you know that it is necessary and will be used legitimately. Do not carry your social security card or your social security number in your wallet.
- Protect your credit cards. Carry as few cards as possible in your wallet. Keep them in sight when you use them in restaurants to make sure that they are not copied.
- Protect your computer by using a firewall and installing antivirus and antispyware software.
- Pay bills online rather than by receiving paper bills.
- Do not throw bills, credit card offers, etc., into the trash. Shred them instead.
- Check your credit card bills and bank statements carefully to detect any unauthorized activity.
- Check your credit reports frequently, at least once a year.

The Fair Credit Reporting Act as amended sets the rules for how credit bureaus maintain information and what victims of identity theft must do to clear their credit records. The act is a large, complex law, and it does not adequately address the needs of identity theft victims. For example, at a time when speed is very important to the victim, the law allows 30 days for the credit bureaus to make corrections, and the credit bureau is the judge of whether any correction should be made. Always the burden of proof is on the victim.

However, creditors victimized by identity theft have a legitimate interest in making sure that the bad debts they cover are truly identity theft rather than the doings of a deadbeat who is swindling them, so it is not easy to write and pass laws that protect the creditors and also provide adequate relief for identity theft victims. Nevertheless, it is clear that the law on identity theft is inadequate and enforcement of the law is poor.

Identity theft has, however, also led to some new business opportunities: Several financial services companies now offer insurance products to protect individuals from identity theft losses.

INTELLECTUAL PROPERTY RIGHTS

There are a number of definitions of **intellectual property**, but we will use the following:

> *Intellectual property is any product of the human mind, such as an idea, an invention, a literary creation, a work of art, a business method, an industrial process, a chemical formula, a computer program, or a presentation.*

Intellectual property is quite different from physical property. If one sells or gives away something physical, you no longer have it, but an idea can be shared without losing it. With the invention of the printing press, the widespread sharing of intellectual property became feasible, and succeeding waves of technological development have made sharing easier. With digital representation increasingly becoming the norm, sharing intellectual property has become easy, rapid, and inexpensive.

What property can be owned differs from one society to another. For example, in a communist society individuals cannot own land and the means of production. Many Native Americans had no concept of land ownership. And in many societies today private ownership of intellectual property is uncommon. Even in the United States you cannot own an idea, but only the particular expression of that idea, and others can take that idea and use it in other ways.

Most Western societies have long recognized that intellectual property is so valuable to society that its creation should be rewarded, so they have copyright and patent laws that grant its creator exclusive ownership rights that allow that person to profit from the creation of the intellectual property. But societies also recognize that eventually intellectual property should be in the public domain, so the ownership rights to intellectual property are granted for only a limited time. Societies differ widely in exactly what is to be protected, how it is to be protected, and for how long. Protection for intellectual property is built into the U.S. Constitution in Section 8 on the powers of Congress, which includes these words: "To promote the Progress of Science and useful Arts, by securing for limited Times to

Authors and Inventors the exclusive Right to their respective Writings and Discoveries."

The patent and copyright laws were first devised when printing was the primary medium of expression that needed protection. However, IT separates the information from the media that contains it—one can no longer protect information by controlling the piece of paper on which it is written. The development of photography, motion pictures, sound recorders, copiers, computers, CDs, and the Internet have continuously changed the environment, and it has been quite a challenge to adapt these laws to each new reality. This is further complicated by the fact that each country has its own history of laws, which differ from one another.

Although we cannot begin to cover all aspects of intellectual property rights in this chapter, we discuss next two areas that are currently of great interest—software piracy and digital entertainment piracy—including some of the problems generated by globalization and the international reach of the Internet.

Software Piracy

Software piracy is a serious problem for the software industry. According to the Business Software Alliance (2007), 35 percent of the business and consumer PC software installed worldwide in 2006 was pirated, which cost the software industry nearly $40 billion. This does not include software installed on servers and mainframes.

Software piracy rates vary significantly by region (Business Software Alliance, 2007), with North America the lowest at 22 percent, Western Europe at 34 percent, Asia/Pacific at 55 percent, Middle East/Africa at 60 percent, Latin America at 66 percent, and Central/Eastern Europe leading the pack at 68 percent. In dollar terms Asia/Pacific leads with $11.6 billion in losses, followed by Western Europe with $10.6 billion and North America with $8.1 billion. Several countries have over an 80 percent piracy rate, including Armenia, Vietnam, Venezuela, Pakistan, and Indonesia. Until the last few years China had the highest piracy rate, but more aggressive government action has brought the rate down to 82 percent.

Many of the highest software piracy rates are in formerly communist areas where there is no tradition of intellectual property rights. Also, in emerging and developing economies there are strong incentives for the government to ignore (or even encourage) software piracy. Software is essential to becoming a modern economy, it is expensive to purchase legally, and foreign exchange resources are scarce, so low-cost domestic copies can be a significant advantage to less developed countries.

Copyright Protection

The ownership rights of developers of computer software are protected by both copyrights and patents. One cannot copyright an idea, but one can copyright a specific written expression of that idea, whether it is on paper, magnetic disk, CD, or in some other electronic form. Except for certain "fair use" exceptions, the copyrighted material cannot be copied without the copyright holder's permission. Computer programs can be copyrighted, and that means that they cannot be used without the developer's permission because they must be copied into your computer memory in order to be used. For most software, the copyright owner does not sell the software itself, but only the right to use it under certain specified conditions. If the user violates those conditions he or she is deemed to have violated the copyright.

U.S. copyright laws make it illegal to copy software and use it without the software vendor's permission, and there are severe penalties for violating these laws. Although this is difficult to enforce against individuals, software vendors have become vigilant in prosecuting large companies that have (knowingly or unknowingly) allowed software to be copied. Most well-managed companies have strict policies against copying software, and they check periodically to make sure that an individual's office PC hard drive contains only authorized software. That is why the business software piracy rate is so low in the United States. However, individuals can copy software for personal use without much fear of prosecution, so whether or not one copies software depends primarily upon one's ethical position on that issue.

Patent Protection

A copyright provides effective protection against software piracy, but it does not prevent someone else from creating another computer program that does the same thing as the copyrighted program. This is where patents come in. A patent on an invention or process gives its creator the exclusive right to the manufacture and use of the new design or method for a limited period of time. One cannot patent laws of nature, natural phenomena, mathematics, or other universal truths. We used to think of patents as protecting the inventors of machines, but in recent years some very strange things have been granted patents: plants, animals, and even genes.

Patenting computer programs has had a controversial history. At first, courts viewed computer programs as algorithms similar to mathematical algorithms that cannot be patented. However, in recent years the U.S. Patent Office has begun to issue patents on computer-implemented processes. For example, Amazon.com was issued a patent on "one-click ordering" on the Web: If you are a previous customer, Amazon.com retrieves a cookie to locate its record containing your name, address, and credit card number, and thus can process your order without you having to reenter that information. That process seems obvious today, as cookies are being widely used for many similar purposes, but the patent was issued in the mid-1990s. Amazon.com sued Barnes and Noble over infringement of this patent, but in March 2002 the suit was settled out of court so that patent has not yet been tested in court.

Over the past several years software patents have been a contentious issue in the European Parliament, and the outcome is still in doubt. However, in the United States each year thousands of computer programs and basic business processes are patented by such software giants as Microsoft and IBM. IBM alone was issued nearly 3,000 patents in 2005, a substantial number of which were computer program patents. This has created a great deal of controversy because it can inhibit the growth of small software firms who do not have the resources to find their way through the maze of what is allowable and what is not or to defend against infringement lawsuits. With so many software patents granted, how can any software developer be confident that he or she has not infringed on one or more of them without employing an army of lawyers?

In May 2007, Microsoft executives asserted that 235 Microsoft patents were being infringed by the Linux operating system, OpenOffice desktop applications, and other open source programs. The executives declined to specify what patents had been violated by whom and said that they had no present intentions to sue to enforce these patents. However, this announcement provoked a firestorm of reactions, some asserting that if Microsoft decided to litigate it would open the floodgates of countersuits and that Microsoft's vast trove of patents would be at risk. Nevertheless, this announcement probably produced the intended result: It reportedly cast a pall over the open source software community, scared smaller software developers, and disturbed large Microsoft customers that are using some popular open source software. Clearly the software patent situation needs the attention of Congress and the courts.

Digital Entertainment Piracy

Growing volumes of digital music, digital videos, and digital movies are being pirated worldwide. In developing countries much of this piracy is carried out by copying or counterfeiting CD and DVD disks. The mission of the International Federation of the Phonographic Industry (IFPI), which represents the international recording industry, includes participating in the identification and prosecution of piracy operations. Some of these foreign operations are even purported to help finance organized crime and international terrorism activities. CD piracy rates vary widely from country to country, from over 90 percent in Indonesia and Paraguay down to less than 10 percent in the United States, Japan, and most of Western Europe.

Internet File Sharing

In the United States, file downloading and file sharing via the Internet have been a major problem for the entertainment industry. Sharing entertainment files on the Internet has become an emotional and contentious issue, with some claiming that it is leading to the demise of the entertainment industry as we know it and others claiming that the industry can continue to prosper and even profit from downloading.

The Recording Industry Association of America (RIAA) has launched a crusade against sharing music on the Internet, undertaking a publicity and educational campaign, lobbying lawmakers for help, and instituting legal action against those trafficking in copyrighted files. According to Berman (2004), speaking for the recording industry:

> *Internet piracy means lost livelihoods and lost jobs, not just in record companies but also across the entire music community. For those who think the 10.9 percent first half sales fall in 2003 does not speak for itself, look at the other evidence. Artist rosters have been cut, thousands of jobs have been lost, from retailers to sound engineers, from truck drivers to music journalists. Surveys in five major markets— USA, Canada, Germany, Japan and the UK—show that Internet copying and file-sharing is reducing CD sales significantly more than it is promoting them.*

Swapping music on the Internet gained widespread popularity with the advent of Napster. Napster developed software that enabled people to make **MP3** files stored on their computers available to others through a peer-to-peer (P2P) network so that others could download music at no cost. Downloading free music became so popular on college campuses that many colleges started banning access to Napster on their networks because it used up so much bandwidth. The major record labels sued Napster in federal court on the grounds that it was violating their copyrights, and after a good deal of legal maneuvering, the judge ordered Napster to shut down. Napster then converted its business model to be a service provider through which music could be legally downloaded by paying a fee.

Similar fates were met by other firms that used P2P software. For example, Sharman Networks developed different P2P software that provided the same service as the Napster software and started the Kazaa service to distribute the file-sharing software. By 2003 some 143 million copies of the Kazaa software had been downloaded and the volume of free music files being downloaded on the Web continued to grow. After another protracted legal battle with the major record labels, Kazaa was also shut down as a free downloading site.

In 2003 the RIAA began another approach—filing lawsuits against those individuals making large quantities of copyrighted music available through a P2P network. These individuals were identified through a complex process that involved lookups of the Internet addresses of users. The Digital Millennium Copyright Act relieves the ISP of legal responsibility for what the user transmits over the Internet, but it has a provision that allows organizations such as the RIAA to easily subpoena the names and addresses of suspected users so that they can be contacted and lawsuits can be filed.

Such a lawsuit is not a trivial matter, for U.S. copyright law provides penalties of up to $150,000 for each violation. Because so many individuals are involved in this type of activity, the RIAA's strategy for a time was to file a number of highly publicized lawsuits as a scare tactic and thereby substantially reduce the amount of music being downloaded (see the box entitled "Early Downloading Lawsuits"). Most of those sued have settled out of court for a few thousand dollars, but the message has been sent that those who share copyrighted music on the Web are not anonymous and might be subjected to expensive penalties.

The entertainment industry is hoping that these lawsuits will motivate increasing numbers of people to sign up and use *legal* for-pay Internet sites. The widespread usage of iPods and other MP3 players has also helped to reduce the demand for illegal downloads: By 2005, 29 percent of current music and video downloaders reported owning an iPod or other MP3 player and used online music services like iTunes. However, e-mail and instant messaging are other sources: 20 percent of current downloaders said they also received music or video files in this way. Although the majority of the general public believes that U.S. government enforcement could reduce illegal file sharing, more than half of broadband users, and most young adults surveyed, strongly believed that illegal file sharing was "beyond government control" (Madden and Rainie, 2005).

Ethical Questions

It seems clear that large numbers of people are comfortable illegally downloading copyrighted entertainment on the Internet. A survey by Public Affairs (2003) of 1,000 U.S. college and university students found the following about student attitudes and behavior:

1. 69 percent of the students surveyed have downloaded music from the Internet, and three-fourths of the downloaders admitted to never paying for the music they download. Thus, over half of the students surveyed had been downloading music and never paid for any of it.
2. Only 24 percent of the students said that it is always wrong to pirate music and movies, 55 percent said it depends on the circumstances, and 21 percent said it is always right.

Most ethical rules conclude that taking something of value from others without their consent is unethical. For example, the music companies assert that downloading someone's music that they are trying to sell is stealing. However, many people do not believe that intellectual property has the same ownership rights as real property. They do not think that downloading a song is the equivalent of stealing so it does not violate the ethical rules against stealing.

Some persons assert that when downloading music that you would not purchase, the artist has not forgone any income and you have had the pleasure of hearing the music. They argue that no one is harmed by this downloading so it is not unethical. However, that is a slippery slope because it is so easy to assume that you would not have purchased the music, although you might have if you could not download it for free.

There are many who assert that downloading does not hurt companies in the entertainment industry, and might even be helpful. These arguments are based on the assumption that the industries have been too slow to satisfy consumer

EARLY DOWNLOADING LAWSUITS

Twelve-year-old Brianna LaHara was frightened to learn that she was among the hundreds of people sued yesterday by giant music companies in federal courts. "I got really scared. My stomach is all turning," Brianna said. "I thought it was OK to download music because my mom paid a service fee for it. Out of all people, why did they pick on me?"

Those sued included a working mom, a college football player, and a 71-year-old grandpa who blamed his grandkids for the legal mess.

[Adapted from the Fox News Channel and Wired News on the Internet, September 9 and 10, 2003]

FREE DIGITAL ENTERTAINMENT!

James Phung saw *Phone Booth* before you did. What's more, he saw it for free, in the comfort of his private home-screening room. Phung isn't a movie star or a Hollywood insider; he's a junior at the University of Texas who makes $8 an hour at the campus computer lab. But many big-budget Hollywood movies have their North American premieres in his humble off-campus apartment. Like millions of other people, Phung downloads movies for free from the Internet, often before they hit theaters. *Phone Booth* will fit nicely on his 120-GB hard drive alongside *Anger Management*, *Tears of the Sun*, and about 125 other films, not to mention more than 2,000 songs. Phung is the entertainment industry's worst nightmare, but he's very real, and there are a lot more like him.

In late July 2007, some of the most sought-after downloads were for copies of TV shows planned for the fall season: NBC's *Bionic Woman*, ABC's *Pushing Daisies*, the CW's *Reaper*, and several other TV shows were available for illegal download on sites such as Torrent Spy, The Pirate Bay, and Mininova. Other leaked shows included Fox's midseason *The Sarah Connor Chronicles* (a spin-off from *The Terminator*), ABC's *Cavemen*, NBC's *Chuck*, and NBC's *Lipstick Jungle*.

Television Week confirmed that the video downloads were of reasonably high quality, akin to the streaming programs on broadcast network Web sites. Viewer comments were already being posted. One viewer wrote: "A lot better than I'd expected...."

Although some network representatives said they anticipated that copies sent to critics and other industry screeners would eventually leak out, most of those interviewed expressed surprise that their full-length pilots were already available on the Web. However, since most of the leaked shows are among the more anticipated, buzz-heavy titles of the fall season, some downloaders wondered if the networks and studios had actually leaked the programs themselves.

The network and studio representatives, however, denied uploading the shows. "We're doing everything we can to fight piracy," said one. "Our piracy department is playing whack-a-mole with these things."

Newly released movies turn up online before they hit the theaters. Record albums debut on the Internet before they have a chance to hit the charts. TV pilots are available for viewing months ahead of the next season. Somewhere along the line, millions of computer users everywhere have made a collective decision that since no one can make them pay for entertainment, they're not going to. And it doesn't appear that "whack-a-mole" tactics are enough to stop them.

[Adapted from Grossman, 2003; and Hibberd, 2007]

---

demands for digitized delivery. That might be true, but it appears to be a rather tenuous basis for an ethical analysis.

Today's headlines continue to suggest that pirating is still prominent in the United States, including the online "leaking" of the pilots of the new season's TV shows (see the box entitled "Free Digital Entertainment!").

OTHER SOCIAL ISSUES

In this section we introduce other important social issues that we cannot cover more thoroughly because of space limitations.

Computer Crime

Computer crime takes many forms, including financial crimes, businesses stealing competitors' secrets, espionage agents stealing military intelligence, attacks on computers by terrorists, grudge attacks by disgruntled employees or ex-employees, attacks by "hackers" who do it for fun, and the use of IT by criminals to run their criminal businesses and facilitate their criminal activities. Chapter 16 described several examples of computer crime.

Access to the Technology

IT has become such an essential ingredient of a modern economy that people who do not have access to IT are precluded from full participation in the benefits of the economy. Similarly, societies are doomed to third-world status if they do not have a computer-literate population provided with access to modern IT.

The United States is in reasonably good shape in regard to computer access and computer literacy. As reported by the National Center for Education Statistics, 91 percent of children in nursery school and students in grades kindergarten through 12 use computers and 59 percent use the Internet (DeBell and Chapman, 2006). Furthermore, this participation rate is growing year after year. On the other hand, there is a "digital divide"—computer and Internet use are divided along demographic and socioeconomic lines with whites having more usage than blacks, who have more usage than Hispanics. Also, those living in households with higher family incomes are more likely to use computers and the Internet than those living in lower-income households, and the lower-income children tend to have access to these technologies only at school while the higher-income children have access at both home and school. The good news is that the digital divide is getting smaller and smaller over the years as the total participation rate is growing. Rather than access to technology, our problem is likely to be functional illiteracy in both reading and mathematics.

Europe and Japan lag behind the United States in access to the computer, but are in relatively good shape. The developing countries lag far behind the developed world, but are making progress. However, in the undeveloped world the situation is virtually hopeless, for the problem is not computer literacy but any kind of literacy, and huge numbers of people have no access to any technology—80 percent of the world's population has never made a phone call, let alone used the Internet.

Freedom of Speech

The Internet is such a powerful and pervasive technology for presenting information that the question arises: Is there information that is so harmful or dangerous that for the good of society it should be prohibited from being posted on the Internet? How about detailed plans for an atomic bomb? Or instructions for making a bomb from readily available materials such as the one used in the Oklahoma City bombing? Or several different suggestions for how to poison a city's water supply? Or the names and addresses of physicians who perform abortions along with assertions that they are murderers who must be punished? Or child pornography? Or the spam that jams your e-mail inbox and consumes vast amounts of bandwidth? Or blogs that spread vicious rumors? Or cyberbullying?

The increasingly pervasive use of the Internet and the World Wide Web has led to renewed controversy over the conflicts between our right to freedom of speech and the right of society to protect itself against terrorists or criminals or those who would tear down the moral basis on which our society depends. It is clear that there are limits to free speech—you cannot libel someone or threaten to harm someone without risking legal action. However, when it comes to prohibiting other types of speech, the U.S. courts have generally upheld the free speech rights granted by the First Amendment. Furthermore, the legal status might be moot because of the practical difficulties of policing the Internet, as the offender's identity might be concealed or he or she might be anywhere in the world and therefore out of the jurisdiction of U.S. law.

Hazards of Inaccuracy

As mentioned earlier, comprehensive data about individuals are contained in numerous large databases that are used to make important decisions that affect the individual.

Unfortunately, much of this data is highly inaccurate or incomplete, or both. When these erroneous data items are used to make decisions about individuals, the results can have serious consequences for those unfortunate persons.

For example, the FBI's National Crime Information Center maintains an integrated, real-time transaction processing and online fingerprint-matching database that includes data about suspected terrorists, fugitives, outstanding arrest warrants, missing people, gang members, and stolen vehicles, guns, or boats. This system handles millions of transactions a day while serving law enforcement officials at all levels by providing information on people who have been arrested or who have arrest warrants outstanding, stolen cars, and other items. It is used at airports to screen people who are boarding airplanes. Many police agencies have terminals in police cars so that when a police officer stops a car for a traffic violation, the officer can check whether the driver is potentially dangerous or the car is stolen before approaching the car. You can imagine the problems that result when these data are not accurate.

The three large credit reporting services in the United States—Experian (formerly TRW), Equifax, and TransUnion LLC—maintain huge databases on 90 percent of American adults. These services purchase computer records from banks and other creditors and from public records of lawsuits, tax liens, and legal judgments. These records are compiled and then sold to credit grantors, rental property owners, employers, insurance companies, and many others interested in a consumer's credit record. If a person's records are not accurate, he or she might be unable to get a credit card or a loan to buy a home or an automobile or might even be denied employment. Today, the reasons for credit ratings are sometimes being shared with individuals as part of reports to other institutions (such as mortgage lenders).

Businesses also maintain data whose accuracy might affect many people and whose accuracy and security might be very important to those affected. Thus, there are many legal and ethical issues associated with accuracy. These are particularly difficult issues because accuracy is quite costly for those maintaining the data while others are the ones being harmed by the inaccuracies. How much accuracy is reasonable and who should pay the associated costs are difficult legal, ethical, and social issues.

Impact on Workers

Information technology has tremendous impacts on workers. A major advantage of IT is that it increases productivity by providing tools for individual employees. However, the introduction of a new IT solution also can lead to a reduction in the workforce, and the jobs of those workers that are not replaced may be significantly altered. Sometimes the new jobs are more challenging and rewarding; at other times, the jobs can be deskilled—and workers can feel like they are mere cogs in an assembly line of routine tasks. Ethical issues arise here because managers are responsible for the design of work systems, and they can choose to consider or to ignore quality of working life issues in deciding among possible alternative designs.

Furthermore, IT has facilitated global outsourcing of work. Were it not for IT, help desks and IS programming activities for companies in developed countries like the United States could not be located in Asian countries or at other offshore locations. From the perspective of a corporation's bottom line, outsourcing these IT tasks—and, more recently, other business tasks such as accounting, claim processing, and payroll processing—has been very beneficial.

The ethical question then becomes: Are workers merely one factor of production or are they worthy of further consideration because they are human beings and citizens of a specific country? This question is applicable far beyond the impact of IT and is of continuing importance not just in the United States but throughout the world. What, if any, legal protection should be provided for workers is a continuing ethical and legal question.

THE FUTURE

As we have seen, the pervasive growth of IT has presented a number of vexing legal, ethical, and social problems. For the foreseeable future it is clear that computers will continue to get faster, more powerful, and less costly, just as they have over the past 50 years. The question is: What will individuals and organizations do with all the increased IT power that will be available for less and less money?

The computer was first used as a big, fast calculator, but soon it began to support decision making in well-structured but complex areas, such as deciding how to segment a customer base or how to minimize the cost of materials while still meeting government regulations. In the military, command and control systems based on IT have allowed humans and computers to share complex analysis and decision-making tasks, with both computers and humans doing what each does best. However, just as the industrial revolution replaced human and animal muscle power with machines, and in the process caused painful dislocations to displaced workers, IT has also enabled the downsizing of organizations—in this case, by streamlining processes, automating tasks, and providing visibility to data, when and where it is needed.

Today the computer can also take the place of humans in areas where we always thought that human brainpower was required. Expert systems are commonly used in troubleshooting applications from automobile maintenance to medical diagnosis, and neural networks are routinely used to sift through mountains of data and discover relationships that humans probably would not be able to find. In May 1997 Deep Blue, an IBM supercomputer with very sophisticated software developed by a long-term IBM-sponsored research project, finally beat the reigning world chess champion, Garry Kasparov, in a challenge match. Although the field of artificial intelligence (AI) has advanced far more slowly than some predicted in its early days, it is now clear that the computer is capable of competing with any human chess player. IT is also intertwined with other exciting technological developments: Robotics, nanotechnology, and genetic engineering all have exciting possibilities for improving human life, but they could also lead to some unintended consequences.

So what new social and ethical issues will the future bring? We have no clear answers to this question, but we are confident that business and IT managers will need to continue to address the types of issues discussed in this chapter.

REVIEW QUESTIONS

1. What is meant by the term *identity theft*? What can happen to a person who is the victim of identity theft?
2. Why is a person's social security number so valuable that someone might steal it?
3. Describe the services provided by a credit reporting service such as Experian, Equifax, and TransUnion. How are these services provided?
4. What do U.S. laws require a financial company to do in regard to sharing information that it has collected on its customers?
5. What is the difference between a copyright and a patent on a computer program?
6. In reference to a company sharing information that it has collected about a customer, what is meant by "opt in"? By "opt out"? In your opinion, which of these is preferable?
7. Has IT created an ethical problem for you or someone you know? Explain.

DISCUSSION QUESTIONS

1. Suppose you are the victim of an identity thief who continues to use your identity and to ruin your credit rating after you have discovered the problem. What problems do you have in clearing your name? How could the laws be changed to help you in this process?

2. Some people believe that "access to computers should be unlimited and total" and that "all information should be free." Do you agree with these statements? Why or why not?

3. Spam on the Internet is a growing problem. Why is spam so attractive to some marketers? Can spam be controlled by laws? Are there other ways that spam might be controlled if laws fail? How?

4. What do we mean by "intellectual property?" What are the differences between intellectual property and real property? Should someone be able to own intellectual property? Why or why not?

5. The U.S. Patent Office is granting patents on computer processes such as Amazon.com's "one-click ordering." Should patents be granted on such computer-supported business processes? Why or why not?

6. In your opinion, what is the most important social issue raised by the explosion of IT? Why? How can society best deal with this issue?

7. The RIAA asserts that downloading copyrighted music on the Internet without paying for it is stealing, but lots of people are doing it. Is this ethical? Why or why not? If this is not ethical, why are so many people doing it?

8. In the United States, information that a company collects about the customer is legally the company's property. In the European Union this information is the individual's property. Explain why there is this difference in the legal treatment of this information.

9. In order to protect against terrorists, the U.S. government is collecting more and more data on individuals into comprehensive databases. Have you any concerns about this? Why or why not?

10. Although this practice might invade individual privacy, many companies use IT to measure the quality and quantity of an employee's work. Discuss the ethical implications of this practice.

REFERENCES

Armstrong, Ross. 2006. "Ease of access to AT&T records by HP investigators shows need for better privacy protection." Info-Tech Research Group News Release, *www.infotech.com*.

Associated Press. 1997. "Survey: Bosses watching workers." *Bloomington Herald-Times* 120 (May 5): A3.

Baase, Sara. 1997. *A Gift of Fire—Social, Legal, and Ethical Issues in Computing*. Upper Saddle River, NJ: Pearson Prentice Hall.

Baron, David P. 2000. "DoubleClick and Internet privacy." Case Number P-32, Graduate School of Business, Stanford University.

Baum, Katrina. 2006. "First Estimates from the National Crime Victimization Survey: Identity Theft, 2004." *Bureau of Justice Statistics Bulletin* NCJ 212213, *www.ojp.gov/bjs/pub/pdf/it04.pdf* (April).

Berman, Dennis K. 2003. "Online laundry: Government posts Enron's e-mail." *Wall Street Journal* (October 6).

Berman, Jay. 2004. "IFPI's Jay Berman sets out industry's global Internet strategy for 2004." *IFPI Quarterly Newsletter*, *www.ifpi.org/site-content/press/20031216.html* (January 7).

Berry, Jonathan, John Verity, Kathleen Kerwin, and Gail DeGeorge. 1994. "Database marketing." *BusinessWeek* (September 5): 56–62.

Business Software Alliance. 2007. "Fourth annual BSA and IDC global software piracy study." Business Software Alliance Web site, *w3.bsa.org/globalstudy* (May).

CBS News. 2005. "An identity theft nightmare: Victim still battling his creditors four years later." CBS News Web site, *www.cbsnews.com/stories/2005/02/25/eveningnews/consumer/main676597.shtml*. Hartford, CT (February 25).

Cortese, Amy. 1995. "Warding off the cyberspace invaders." *BusinessWeek* (March 13): 92–93.

DeBell, Matthew, and Chris Chapman. 2006. "Computer and Internet use by students in 2003." National Center for Education Statistics Web site, *nces.ed.gov/pubsearch/pubsinfo.asp?pubid=2006065* (September).

DeGeorge, Richard T. 1999. *Business Ethics*, 5th ed. Upper Saddle River, NJ: Pearson Prentice Hall.

FTC. 2003. "Federal Trade Commission—Identity Theft Survey Report." Prepared by Synovate, *www.ftc.gov/os/2003/09/synovaterepor.pdf* (September).

Gaudin, Sharon. 2003. "May breaks record for digital attacks." IT Management Web site, *itmanagement.earthweb.com/secu/article.php/2210321* (May 21).

Grossman, Lev. 2003. "It's all FREE!" *Time* (May 5): 61.

Grupe, Fritz H., William Kuechler, and Scot Sweeney. 2003. "Dealing with data privacy protection: An issue for the 21st century." *IS Management Handbook*. Carol V. Brown and Heikki Topi (eds.). Boca Raton, FL: Auerbach, 697–713.

Hamm, Steve, Jay Greene, Cliff Edwards, and Jim Kerstetter. 2003. "Epidemic." *BusinessWeek* (September 8): 28.

Hibberd, James. 2007. "Top fall pilots leaked online." TV Week Web site, *www.tvweek.com/news/2007/07/top_fall_pilots_leaked_online.php* (July 29).

Horowitz, Janice M. 1992. "Crippled by computers." *Time* 140 (October 12): 70–72.

IFPI. 2003. "The recording industry commercial piracy report 2003." International Federation of the Phonographic Industry Web site, *www.ifpi.org/content/library/ piracy2003.pdf.*

IFPI. 2006. "The recording industry 2006 piracy report." International Federation of the Phonographic Industry Web site, *www.ifpi.org/content/library/piracy-report2006.pdf.*

ITRC. 2003. "Identity theft: The aftermath—2003." Identity Theft Resource Center Web site, *www.idtheftcenter.org.*

Koepp, Stephen, Charles Pelton, and Seth Shulman. 1986. "The boss that never blinks." *Time* 135 (July 28): 46–47.

Madden, Mary, and Lee Rainie. 2005. "Music and video downloading moves beyond P2P." Pew Internet Project Data Memo, *www.pewinternet.org/pdfs/ PIP_Filesharing_March05.pdf* (March).

McCollum, Scott. 2002. "Mi2g: Digital attacks decline worldwide while attacks on USA rise." *WorldTech Tribune,* *www.worldtechtribune.com/worldtechtribune/asparticles/ buzz/bz12022002.asp* (December 2).

Moritz, Robert. 2003. "When someone steals your identity." *Parade Magazine* (July 6): 3–4.

Newman, Matthew. 2003. "EU improves software patent, but outlaws Amazon One Click." Dow Jones, *news.morningstar. com/news/DJ/Mo6/D17/1055868063730.html* (June 17).

Nusbaum, Marci Alboher. 2003. "New kind of snooping arrives at the office." *New York Times* (July 11).

Pew Internet Project. "Spam: How it is hurting e-mail and degrading life on the Internet." A report funded by the Pew Charitable Trusts.

PIRG. 1998. "Mistakes do happen." The sixth study on credit report accuracy by the Public Interest Research Group (March).

Public Affairs. 2003. "Internet piracy on campus, a survey of 1000 U.S. college and university students and 300 U.S. college and university educators." Washington, D.C. (September 16).

Reno, Janet. 2000. "The electronic frontier: The challenge of unlawful conduct involving the use of the Internet." *Report of the President's Working Group on Unlawful Conduct on the Internet* (March).

Sager, Ira, Steve Hamm, Neil Gross, John Carey, and Robert D. Hoff. 2000. "Cyber crime," *BusinessWeek* (February 21).

Sipior, Janice C., Burke T. Ward, and Georgina R. Roselli. 2005. "The ethical and legal concerns of spyware." *Information Systems Management* 22 (Spring): 39–49.

Smith, H. Jeff. 2004. "Information privacy and its management." *MIS Quarterly Executive* 3 (December): 201–213.

Sorkin, David E. 2003. Spam Laws Web page, *www.spamlaws.com* (November 26).

Stoll, Cliff. 1989. *The Cuckoo's Egg: Tracking a Spy Through the Maze of Computer Espionage.* New York: Pocket Books.

Swartz, Jon, and Paul Davidson. 2003. "Spam thrives despite effort to screen it out." *USA Today* (May 8).

THE CLARION SCHOOL FOR BOYS, INC.—MILWAUKEE DIVISION: MAKING INFORMATION SYSTEMS INVESTMENTS

John Young, Controller of the Clarion School for Boys, Inc.—Milwaukee Division, hung up the telephone as the school bell signaled the end of another day's classes. Young's conversation with Sean McHardy, the Superintendent and Chief Operating Officer of Clarion—Milwaukee Division, was short and to the point. McHardy had called to confirm that Young would be prepared to present his assessment of the current information systems (IS) at Clarion and propose a direction for information systems at the organization for the next fiscal year at the quarterly Board of Directors meeting scheduled for next week (June 13, 2006) in Chicago.

As an MBA student, Young had learned about the importance of an overall information systems strategy. McHardy's request, however, required Young to formalize a full plan, complete with an assessment of the current situation as well as future projects and budgets. As Controller, Young knew that the members of the Board of Directors were anxious to hear how Clarion—Milwaukee's current investment in information technology was paying off. Since 1998, when the Board had approved a sizable investment in hardware and software, there had been little formal monitoring of the system's benefit.

Young had joined the Milwaukee Division of Clarion in November 2005. His previous job had been as assistant controller in one of the divisions of American Chemical Company (ACC) in Chicago; he had worked at ACC for 10 years after receiving his MBA in finance from a well-known Midwestern business school.

After 10 years, Young had tired of big companies and narrow jobs and decided to move into a position with broader responsibility. However, most of his days at Clarion—Milwaukee had been spent "fighting fires" rather than planning business strategy. Although his position was quite different than he had expected, he felt the intangible rewards clearly surpassed those at American Chemical. Young had developed several good friends at Clarion—Milwaukee and enjoyed his daily routine.

The Clarion School for Boys, Inc.

The Clarion School for Boys, Inc., was founded in 1989 as "a refuge for wayward boys" by a group of investors from Chicago, all of whom had grown up in foster homes but accumulated considerable wealth during their lives. Their vision was to create an environment for boys who had got into trouble that would provide them with a diagnosis and treatment plan as well as the discipline and support needed to become productive members of society. They felt that they could operate these schools efficiently and make a small profit in the process. During the next 10 years, Clarion established a diverse program of care that relied on the dedication and devotion of this group of investors. The first school was opened near Chicago, Illinois, in 1991. Later, Clarion opened additional schools near Detroit, Michigan (1995); Indianapolis, Indiana (1998); and St. Louis, Missouri (2000).

The Milwaukee division was the second oldest school in the Clarion system, opened in 1993. It was housed on the grounds of a former monastery and contained several buildings and 80 acres of land on the edge of the city. As in other states, Clarion—Milwaukee Division depended somewhat on the parents for financial tuition. However, over 80 percent of the revenue came from per diem charges paid by government agencies for the housing and treatment of problem boys.

The Clarion School for Boys—Milwaukee Division was classified as a private, for-profit residential treatment facility for delinquent boys between the ages of 10 and 18. In 2006, there were 128 full- and part-time employees who provided care and treatment to 120 students. Of the 9 residential child-care facilities operating in Wisconsin, Clarion—Milwaukee was the second largest in terms of enrollment and the third most expensive in per diem charges. Unlike Clarion—Milwaukee, most other child-care facilities were not designed to help children who were exhibiting severe behavioral problems. As a result, Clarion—Milwaukee often functioned as a "last resort" before a child was placed in a mental hospital or state correctional institution.

Clarion—Milwaukee's ability to manage difficult cases was largely the result of its comprehensive treatment program. The treatment effort was supported by a faculty-managed school program along with modern crisis-management facilities and tracking devices. Since 1999, Clarion—Milwaukee's strategy to differentiate itself from its competitors emphasized the importance of using modern information technology in combination with a caring staff attitude. Because the school typically dealt with potentially dangerous students, the ability to contact support staff and access student records quickly was considered essential to effective performance.

As operational expenses and capital requirements continued to rise, the Milwaukee school became more dependent on increased per diem charges and higher enrollments to balance the budget. During the 2005–2006 fiscal year (ending June 30, 2006), Clarion charged placement agencies or families $150.50 per day for each student enrolled in the regular treatment program. For students enrolled in the ISIS program, a premium care/rehabilitation facility opened in 2001 for students whose next option was a juvenile delinquency institution, the charge was $197.00 per day. Total per diem revenue for the 2005–2006 fiscal year was budgeted at $4,891,000, but enrollment had been running well ahead of projections. As a result, there was considerable interest in expanding the school's capacity in fiscal 2006–2007.

All capital expenditures were allocated from the Capital Assets Fund of Clarion, Inc. Each division competed with the other operations for access to this fund. Clarion—Milwaukee was proposing three major projects for fiscal year 2006–2007:

1. a major upgrade to the IBM AS/400 computing system and associated software, personal computers, and network,
2. the remodeling of a living unit to expand the ISIS program, and
3. the construction of a cottage that would accommodate 10 additional students for the regular program.

Young would have responsibility for managing each of these major capital projects. All capital projects exceeding $25,000 had to be approved by the Board of Directors of Clarion, Inc. The Board was known for reviewing each capital request carefully.

Information Systems (IS) Planning

With labor costs representing 68 percent of the school's operating budget, Young's predecessor (Jacob Miller) considered computerization as one way to increase staff effectiveness and productivity in accessing information and to improve communications among the staff. Miller did not emphasize using automation to reduce cost directly (e.g., by reducing staff). On the recommendation of Miller in January 1998, the Clarion, Inc., board of directors approved the purchase of an IBM AS/400 computer and associated applications software.

Because Clarion, Inc., had many demands for its capital, Miller knew that capital expenditures for computers were considered difficult to justify, especially if the purchases were not connected directly to a new revenue stream. Nevertheless, members of the Board of Directors exhibited interest in the new information systems project even before the approval in 1998. As Miller began to describe the capabilities of the system in detail, the Board's interest rose even further. Likewise, staff from all treatment programs and support areas expressed enthusiasm for the proposed benefits. Based mostly on the treatment staff's support, the Board approved the project.

The stated objective of the hardware and software investment was to save staff time by using electronic communications, to accelerate routine tasks, and to provide easier, faster access to computerized student data. Critical functions at the time were considered to be electronic mail, student database access, analysis of the data held in the student database, and appointment/room scheduling. Applications software was purchased for each of these functions as well as support packages for accounting and human resources. The AS/400 system acquisition was supplemented by the purchase of 60 personal computers, replacing those that had been purchased from 1993 through 1997.

In order to synchronize implementation of the 1998 computer acquisition project with the needs of all departments, the Clarion Board of Directors had also approved a long-range organization plan for the Milwaukee Division. A joint effort between Board members and staff from all levels had led to the adoption of the division's first five-year plan. This comprehensive plan focused on both administrative and treatment issues and was also approved in January 1998.

Clarion—Milwaukee's Computer System

While no longer considered by some as state of the art, Clarion—Milwaukee's computer network was custom-designed for its application needs in 1998. The distributed system was networked campuswide and linked the 60 IBM personal computers and attached laser printers. Each personal computer was provided with the latest version of Microsoft Windows as well as the Microsoft Office applications software suite. According to the IBM sales representative, the network architecture allowed for 40 to 50 more personal computers to be added over time. Additional AS/400 computers could also be networked to provide peer-to-peer communications if more central computing power was needed at the school. No access to the Internet was allowed at the time due to concerns over providing students access to potentially harmful material.

Because of severe budget constraints at Clarion from 2000 through 2004, no major upgrades to the AS/400 system were made. While all 60 personal computers were replaced in 2004 with the latest IBM desktops, the main system and its

EXHIBIT 1
Campus Computing Network:
The Clarion School for Boys, Inc.—Milwaukee Division

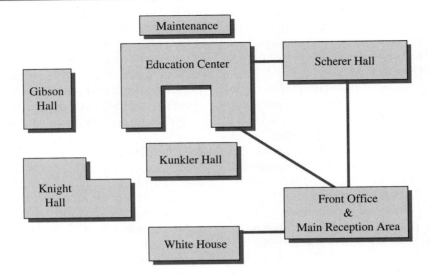

associated software remained the same as in 1998. Five IBM laptops were purchased for checkout by staff, and staff access to the Internet was allowed at that time.

The school's AS/400 computer was located in the front office building, where 14 personal computers were also located (see Exhibit 1). The primary system console—used for initial program loads and file backups by Jean Baker (the senior bookkeeper who worked for Young)—and the school's PBX unit (for the telephone system) were also located in the front office. The "white house," where the offices of the Assistant to the Superintendent and the Controller were located, housed 10 of the 60 personal computers as well.

The education center contained all of Clarion—Milwaukee's classrooms and was by far the largest building on campus. Of the 60 total, 24 personal computers were available in a pool in the staff lounge of the center for teachers and the education supervisor, who also shared these systems with personnel who worked under the supervisor of services and other staff who worked in the east wing of the center.

The ISIS treatment program was located in Sherer Hall. Twelve personal computers were available in a community cubicle office environment for shared use by treatment and support staff. The Knight, Gibson, and Kunkler Hall dormitories (that could each house up to 45 students) were not equipped with computers, nor were the maintenance facilities. The proposed addition would place personal computers in each of the dormitories for student use, but still would not permit Internet

access for fear that residents might access inappropriate materials.

Evaluating the Current System

After having the same system (except for new PCs) for over eight years, Young thought that the computing system should be formally evaluated. During his first staff meeting in November 2005, Young asked whether the administrative and treatment staff thought the current campuswide IS architecture was sufficient for Clarion. He also asked the group if they viewed the network as an advantage Clarion—Milwaukee had over other schools providing similar services.

In order to focus the discussion, Young asked, "What are your opinions of the system?" A sampling of the answers follows (the organizations these people belong to are described in Exhibit 2):

"We use e-mail to distribute weekly teaching plans to our aides." (Teacher)

"We put the whole report card process on the system. Each teacher can input grades from a PC—it saves a lot of time since the cards don't have to go to each instructor individually." (Education Supervisor)

"I recently talked with an old classmate of mine who is using a computerized database to store addresses for frequent mailings. He addresses envelopes through the

EXHIBIT 2
Unit Duties and Organizational Chart:
The Clarion School for Boys, Inc.—Milwaukee Division

Social Services Department

The social services department is responsible for ensuring that those under care receive the appropriate clinical treatment. Because of the involvement of this department with the boys and their placing agencies as well as the wide variety of treatment options, access to the treatment files as well as e-mail, mail routing, and dictation is extremely important. The supervisor of social services functions as department head and is a member of the administrative council. She is also a member of the institutional treatment team.

Social services counselors handle direct counseling and casework functions, enter various progress data, and serve as members of the institutional treatment team and unit treatment teams. Most of the documents and reports that are the responsibility of the unit treatment teams require user data entry and report generation on the part of counselors.

Program Department

The program department is responsible for the group living environment as well as activities such as crisis intervention, recreation, and special events of the treatment program. Staff members in this department supervise part-time employees within their treatment area (child-care workers, recreation workers, and program aides). One lead program supervisor functions as the primary department head and needs access to computer treatment data and all other information resources. Seven associate program supervisors share direct supervisory responsibility for the child-care and recreation data.

Education Department

The education department is responsible for the operation of Clarion—Milwaukee's comprehensive year-round education program. Because the education department coordinates its activities with the program department, effective communication between these departments is critical. The education supervisor functions as the principal for the school. She is a member of the administrative council and the institutional treatment team. Within this department, 20 teachers provide instruction to the boys in a regular classroom environment. Some teachers have telephones while others do not. Most communication is through direct contact and written memos.

Transition Department

The transition department is responsible for the treatment and care of 20 boys enrolled in Clarion—Milwaukee's "transitional living" program. In most respects, the transition program is a separate treatment entity with its own supervisory, counseling, and care staff, but most supplementary functions are still performed by main campus personnel. The transition supervisor serves as the department head and is on the institutional treatment team and the administrative council.

ISIS Department

The ISIS department was created in response to the development of the ISIS rehabilitation program. The ISIS department reports to the supervisor of social services but has its own program supervisor. ISIS social service counselors perform some of the same functions as their counterparts in the regular program. Certain treatment needs require computer access to specialized treatment data.

Development Department

The development department is responsible for all human resource issues and a variety of other tasks, including the fund-raising efforts and public relations of Clarion—Milwaukee. The development director also serves as assistant to the superintendent. This department has access to the AS/400-based human resources data, telecommunications, dictation, and mail routing. The director is a member of the administrative council.

Controller's Department

The controller's department performs purchasing, information systems, and financial control functions as well as all accounting and treasury functions. The controller, who also assumes overall responsibility for finance, leads the department. The head bookkeeper reports to the controller and spends about one-quarter of her time performing system operator

EXHIBIT 2 (*Continued*)

responsibilities. Typical daily tasks included answering users' questions and performing file backups for the AS/400. The controller is also responsible for the housekeeping and maintenance departments. Neither of these departments is tied into the computer network.

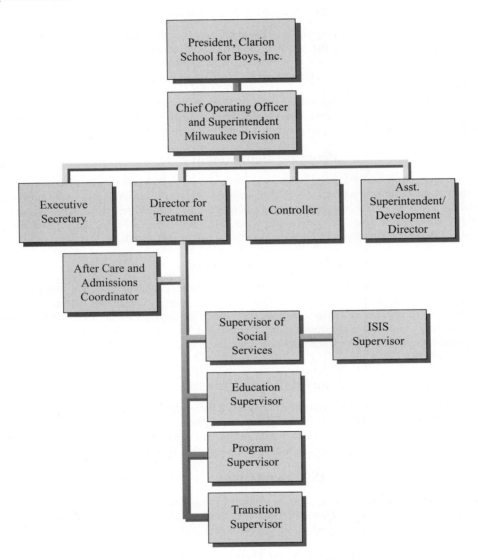

printer in a fraction of the time it used to take. I send a lot of mail to local businesses every month. Can we do that on the system?" (Executive Secretary)

"We had two programmers working for us at my last school. They would ask us about our needs in admissions and would customize software that we licensed. I enjoyed using the system since I helped design the applications. Why don't we have that kind of help?" (After Care and Admissions Coordinator)

"Since I just joined the Clarion staff about a month and a half ago, I'm not sure what is available on the system. We used

computers extensively at my university. Are there training sessions offered so I can learn more about the system?" (Associate Program Supervisor for Activities and Honor Jobs)

Following the staff meeting, Young spent time trying to determine if the current system was really cost-effective for Clarion—Milwaukee Division. Although it was clear that the system had potential, his inquiry showed it was not getting the level of use his predecessor had envisioned.

Young realized he faced a challenge in convincing his boss of the need for any improvement in the current system.

Superintendent McHardy had always been hesitant to incorporate any new technology into the school's operations. Young once overheard McHardy mention to a Board member that he felt that "computer technology and the treatment of troubled boys just don't mesh."

A New Long-Range IS Plan

In December 2005, McHardy called Young into his office. "John," he began, "I'm hearing that you're asking questions about the computer system. Your inquiry matches my concerns about the way we are managing our information system—or should I say *not* managing it? From what I can tell, few people on Clarion–Milwaukee's staff fully understand how our current systems are functioning and what capabilities are available. Furthermore, we have only sketchy ideas of what our IS objectives should be over the next few years—and most of those are probably only in your head."

Young nodded in agreement, as if he truly had a vision of Clarion–Milwaukee's IS strategy. McHardy continued, "We've also got to get a handle on the cost situation. Are you aware that we have spent more than $80,000 on hardware and software maintenance agreements alone in the last 12 months? I want you to really dig into the information systems area so you can include an assessment of where we are now and a long-term direction for information systems for the Clarion Board of Directors next June along with your regular business plan and budget presentation. Can you do it?"

In mid-January 2006, Young formed the Information Systems (IS) Task Force to help develop the IS assessment and plan. Besides Young, the six-member task force included Christopher Larson, Director for Treatment; Brian Thomas, Assistant to the Superintendent; Ann Lyman, Supervisor of Social Services; Lara Kirk, Education Supervisor; and Michael Todd, Program Supervisor. As indicated on the organization chart in Exhibit 2, the task force was composed primarily of department-level management.

At its first meeting, Young defined the objectives of the IS Task Force—to explore the IS needs of Clarion–Milwaukee employees and determine what enhancements (if any) should be made to the hardware, network, database, and software so that the information system would better fulfill the staff's mission-critical requirements. At the meeting, Young suggested that task force responsibilities would require only minimal time commitment by the staff. He told the group simply "to keep your ear to the ground and listen for needs that are not being met."

The IS Assessment Process

By their mid-February 2006 meeting, the IS Task Force members had not developed a list of new needs. Instead, they reported that they had received substantial informal input from staff indicating that the current system was not living up to expectations. In an effort to identify the root causes of these

disappointments, the task force decided to conduct a staff survey with the goal of understanding the most common complaint—the lack of communications throughout the organization and the failure of the school's information system to remedy the situation. The survey was distributed by Young's office during March 2006. Some responses were not received until a full month later. Results of the survey are shown in Exhibit 3.

An initial review of the results of the IS Task Force's survey indicated that personal contact was seen by the respondents as the most important form of communication among staff at Clarion–Milwaukee. Second was the telephone system. Third on the staff's list was the AS/400's electronic mail system. Most staff members were aware of the communications software products available on the AS/400, but many were not using them. Further down on the list of ways to communicate was reports. Although hundreds of different paper reports were processed regularly, the importance of these types of written communication was perceived as low.

The task force considered the possibility that the current information system had not proved as effective as hoped simply because it was not being used extensively by staff. By checking the system logs (an automatic record of system usage generated by the operating system), it was determined that while an employee might have been logged on the system for most of the day, he or she was actively using it less than 15 minutes each day. The task force members were not sure why the system was not being used as expected.

In addition to conducting the survey, task force members allotted time at their own departmental meetings in March 2006 and during one-on-one conversations to solicit responses from other members of the units for which they had primary responsibility. Discussion of these issues was awkward for some of the task force members because they were not well educated in the area of information systems.

Task Force Interviews

Highlights from the IS Task Force's personal interviews helped better define the attitudes of Clarion–Milwaukee's staff. One task force member, Lara Kirk, reported to the committee at its late-March 2006 meeting that she had conducted a group interview with instructors who had used the system for electronic mail. She recalled one teacher saying, "It was great during the first month or two when we could actually find a PC available, but after that, they got so crowded. I don't have time to wait in line. I thought these were supposed to be *personal* computers." Another added, "I have found PCs available early in the morning, say between eight o'clock and nine, but whenever I try to log on, I get a message telling me the system is not available. I think it says something about backups—whatever that means."

When Kirk pursued these problems, she learned from Jean Baker that the system backup schedule took place

EXHIBIT 3
Information Systems Survey:
The Clarion School for Boys, Inc.—Milwaukee Division

Background

A questionnaire was distributed to all full-time employees except for janitorial and temporary services personnel. A one-week turnaround time was requested. Although the employees were not required to identify themselves on the form, department names were noted on each questionnaire before it was distributed. The overall survey response rate was 71 percent. Lower return rates were apparent in the education and social services departments. No surveys were returned from the maintenance department. Some returned surveys contained questions that were not answered.

Findings

The following summary of the information resources survey has three main sections: Mechanisms for Verbal Communication, Mechanisms for Written Communication, and a Summary of Detailed Data Analysis.

Mechanisms for Verbal Communication

Type	Frequency
Large formal staff gatherings	
• General staff meetings	1 per year, or when there was a major crisis
• Convocations	3 per year
• Institutional treatment team meetings	1–2 hours, once per week
• In-service training sessions	1 per month
Large informal staff gatherings	
• Weekday lunches	Most staff were required to eat with the students
• Holiday parties and banquets	5 per year
Small formal staff gatherings	
• Unit treatment team meetings	1 or 2 per week
• Administrative Council meetings	1 per week
• Departmental meetings	1 per week
• Teachers' meetings	Every weekday morning
• Supervisory sessions	Approximately 1 per month
• Performance reviews	Annual, with supervisor
• Scheduled one-on-one meetings	Various
• Long-range planning committee meetings	4 per year
Other informal staff gatherings	
• Teachers' lounge discussions	
• Work space area conversations by coffee machine and mailboxes	
• Service staff's break room conversations	
• Unscheduled one-on-one meetings	
• "Parking lot" conversations	

Mechanisms for Written Communication

- Scrap notes: notes of all shapes and sizes, no format
- Memos: a standard 4-copy form, many per day
- Weekly treatment services calendar: 4 to 6 pages

EXHIBIT 3 (*Continued*)

- Special request forms: various requests
- Minutes of formal meetings and supervisory sessions: 1 to 6 pages
- *The Clarion Record:* 5 to 10 page quarterly internal report of the corporation
- Semester calendar: 20 to 26 pages three times per year
- Financial statements: 6 pages issued monthly
- Departmental one-year goals: 2 to 6 pages annually
- Annual audit: 10 to 12 pages annually
- Five-year plan: 40 to 60 pages, updated annually

Summary of Detailed Data Analysis

For each of the following questions, the survey question (as it appeared on the questionnaire) precedes the summary analyses.

Question: What information sources do you rely on most to accomplish your daily job tasks?

	Direct	*Telephone*	*Written*	*Computer*	*Other*	*Total*
Responses	32	11	6	8	0	57
Percent (rounded)	56%	19%	11%	14%	0%	100%

Data from the above question displayed by job classification (percent rounded):

	Direct	*Telephone*	*Written*	*Computer*	*Total*
Treatment	65%	15%	10%	10%	100%
Management/Administration	67%	11%	11%	11%	100%
Instructional	30%	20%	10%	40%	100%
Clerical	0%	70%	0%	30%	100%
Social Services	80%	0%	20%	0%	100%

Question: Which of the following information resources would you most like to use more?

	Direct	*Telephone*	*Written*	*Computer*	*Other*	*Total*
Responses	8	5	5	19	0	37
Percent (rounded)	22%	14%	14%	51%	0%	100%

Data from the above question displayed by job classification (percent rounded):

	Direct	*Telephone*	*Written*	*Computer*	*Total*
Treatment	24%	24%	24%	28%	100%
Management/Administration	10%	0%	10%	80%	100%
Instructional	50%	0%	0%	50%	100%
Clerical	0%	25%	0%	75%	100%
Social Services	0%	0%	50%	50%	100%

EXHIBIT 3 (*Continued*)

Question: Which of the following computing functions have you used? (Select more than one if necessary.)

"Percent of respondents" designates percent of respondents who indicated the specific answer for this question if they indicated at least one answer for this question. "Percent of all" indicates the percent of responses as a portion of all Clarion employees.

	E-mail	Database Entry	Database Query	Calendaring	Spreadsheet	Accounting
Responses	36	32	23	7	3	10
Percent of respondents (rounded)	80%	71%	51%	16%	7%	22%
Percent of all (rounded)	28%	25%	18%	5%	2%	8%

Question: How much formal training have you had on the computer system?

"Percent of respondents" designates percent of respondents who indicated the specific answer for this question if they indicated an answer for this question. "Percent of all" indicates the percent of responses as a portion of all Clarion employees.

	None	Demo	1–3 hr	4–7 hr	8–16 hr	17–32 hr	32+ hr
Responses	2	5	11	7	7	6	7
Percent of respondents (rounded)	4%	11%	24%	16%	16%	13%	16%
Percent of all (rounded)	2%	4%	9%	5%	5%	5%	5%

Question: Circle either I am satisfied or dissatisfied with the amount of training I have received.

"Percent of respondents" designates percent of respondents who indicated the specific answer for this question if they indicated an answer for this question. "Percent of all" indicates the percent of responses as a portion of all Clarion employees.

	Satisfied	Dissatisfied
Responses	18	25
Percent of Respondents (rounded)	42%	58%
Percent of All (rounded)	14%	20%

Question: How much time do you spend working on a PC or the central system on the average each day?

(For this question, answers were compiled only by job classification.)

	None	< 1 hr	1–2 hr	3–4 hr	> 4 hr
Treatment	0%	50%	31%	14%	5%
Management/Administrative	0%	31%	38%	15%	15%
Instructional	0%	60%	10%	20%	10%
Clerical	0%	0%	67%	33%	0%
Social Services	0%	90%	10%	0%	0%

each morning between 8:00 and 9:30. When Baker was backing up the system, she specified that no other users could log on.

Christopher Larson also relayed comments from one of his group interview sessions. "We have found that it is easier to use our old file card system to look up student records rather than walk all the way down the hall to the nearest PC to use the system. But I heard the same information is actually available online. I just don't have time to go stand in line and wait to use the system."

Michael Todd reported that although he had thought the clerical staff was using the calendaring software product on the AS/400 to help his associate program supervisors with room scheduling and personal calendar services, they were actually using the functions very infrequently. When he questioned the secretaries during the group interview, they told him that "the associate program supervisors like to keep their own calendars and they never give us enough time to schedule activities ahead of time. We usually end up rushing around trying to find an open classroom or conference room for their needs at the last minute."

Brian Thomas discovered that his assistant and the director of planned giving were using the system less than he had thought as well. "To make a long story short," he said, "no one ever told me what value I would get from the new computer system. I could use a better phone system so I could hold conference calls among potential donors rather than a better computer system. I'm sure I could raise more money if I could put donors in contact with each other one on one. I have heard that we spent a lot of money on the AS/400. Who is using it?"

Young also heard reports that staff members at Clarion—Milwaukee felt defensive when faced by what they perceived as an "interrogation" by their supervisors on the IS Task Force. It was obvious that some employees were sugarcoating their answers while others simply avoided giving their opinions.

Obtaining Outside Help

One important result of the task force assessment survey and the individual interviews was the conclusion that the task force needed additional planning assistance from an objective source. At the special request of the task force, Clarion's Board of Directors approved funding in late April 2006 for Young to hire a consulting firm to assist with his assessment and plan.

In a hurried search for a consulting firm to assist at Clarion—Milwaukee, the IS task force selected LTM Consultants, Inc., from among three companies that submitted proposals, largely because LTM had a local office in Milwaukee and had done some work for other divisions of Clarion.

LTM was a growing firm of 47 professionals and 18 support staff members based in Chicago. The firm had offices in three states, and its expertise included accounting, information technology, and general management consulting. Young believed that LTM would provide the best value to Clarion—Milwaukee. The final engagement letter from LTM is included as Exhibit 4. Young expected LTM to deliver an IS assessment and plan for the school by the first week of June 2006. Although Young would assume ultimate responsibility for the recommendations he would deliver to the Clarion Board of Directors, he considered an outside set of recommendations as well as the task force work critical to his success with the Directors in June.

Young spent a full day briefing the three LTM consultants on the history of Clarion—Milwaukee's IS situation, including the results of the recent IS Task Force survey. In his position as Controller, Young explained that he was responsible for making sure that major capital investments were paying off. He wanted to know if the system was filling the information needs at Clarion—Milwaukee and which long-term improvements should be made. He also pointed out organizational change issues to LTM that he thought might have affected system usage. For example, Clarion—Milwaukee had grown in three years from 90 to 120 students. A number of new positions had been created to take on the extra load. Full- and part-time staff had increased by almost 30 percent, and turnover and absenteeism were very low.

"I'm not sure," Young told the LTM team, "but my biggest challenge may be in selling McHardy that the system was a good investment for Clarion—Milwaukee and that further investment is warranted." He went on to describe a brief discussion he had with McHardy when they bumped into each other on the way to the parking lot one evening. "When I asked Sean's opinion of the school's information system, he said that he hadn't found any practical use for computers so far besides the word-processing software on his PC (he uses it for his daily to-do lists)." Young recalled McHardy's words, "I don't use e-mail, I just make a phone call or walk over to someone's office." McHardy continued, as he headed for his car, "Sometimes I wonder if our investment was worthwhile, John. I know the Clarion Board of Directors is counting on you to make sure that Clarion—Milwaukee is getting full value from the system."

Regarding his own concern about the use of the current information system, Young remembered that his own department had a difficult time with specialized billing needs. Most of the billing was done directly through the system's accounting software, but about 10 percent was first done by hand and then manually entered into the invoicing system as adjustments at the end of a period. Young admitted to the consultants, "If I can't get invoicing to work consistently for my own staff, how can I expect others to be excited about other applications?"

During the visit by the LTM team to Clarion—Milwaukee in May, the lead consultant mentioned that she had done some investigation of basic hardware and software options for the school. First, she had contacted several other users of the AS/400 in Milwaukee and Chicago to see how they were handling ongoing issues of maintenance. She discovered that while Clarion's current AS/400 is no longer supported by IBM, there are several reputable third-party maintenance organizations in Milwaukee that could service the hardware. She also learned that continuing software maintenance and upgrades would be somewhat more difficult, but she found several independent software specialists who could provide support for the current operating system and applications software. While she

EXHIBIT 4
Engagement Letter from LTM Consultants, Inc.,
to the Clarion School for Boys, Inc.—Milwaukee Division

April 20, 2006

LTM Consultants
765 Corporate Circle
Milwaukee, WI 51744

John F. Young
Controller
The Clarion School for Boys, Inc.—Milwaukee Division
Post Office Box 2217
Milwaukee, WI 51740-2217

Dear John:

LTM appreciates the opportunity to work with the Clarion School for Boys, Inc.—
Milwaukee Division in identifying critical issues related to its future information
systems environment and determining its future systems strategy. The primary
objectives of our engagement are to:

- Evaluate the current strengths and weaknesses of Clarion—Milwaukee's
  information systems.
- Determine the information systems strategy required to achieve Clarion—
  Milwaukee's short-term and long-term business goals.

In consideration of the importance of this engagement, we have combined the
unique talents of LTM consultants from three of our offices. A three-person team of
consultants from LTM's Information Technology Group in Milwaukee, the Human
Factors Group in Indianapolis, and the Strategy Group in Chicago will ensure that
this engagement is approached from both a business and technical solution perspective.

One critical success factor of this project is to quickly gain an in-depth
understanding of the needs, issues, and constraints related to Clarion—Milwaukee's
information systems environment. Only then can we convert the present functional
needs into a broad set of systems requirements and a subsequent strategy.

We estimate this analysis will require approximately four weeks to complete at an
estimated cost for professional services of $42,500. Costs for travel and lodging
expenses will be billed as incurred. An initial invoice of $20,000 will be issued
fifteen days after start-up, and a reconciling invoice will be submitted upon
completion of the engagement.

John, we look forward to working with you and the Clarion—Milwaukee School on
this important assignment. I can assure you that we will bring the value that will
make a difference to your school in the future.

Sincerely,

C. J. VanZant

Carl John VanZant
Vice President

Approved: ___John F. Young_____   ___4/23/06___
                 Clarion School for Boys, Inc.   Date

would not recommend this alternative, Clarion—Milwaukee could continue its operation as is at least for the next few years.

The consultant had also contacted the local IBM sales office. She found that the AS/400 had gone through several iterations since the machine was purchased by the school. The AS/400 series had been replaced by the IBM eServer iSeries line, which in turn was replaced by the IBM System i family of hardware. Most recently, IBM had announced a version of the System i for smaller organizations that needed to upgrade from an AS/400. The sales representative mentioned that the new operating system is called the i5/OS and still supports the AS/400 DB/2 database applications. The IBM sales representative also

mentioned that a new System i Model 525 would be four to five times faster than Clarion's AS/400 and could handle a full complement of eight disk drives (560 gigabytes) for all the online data storage the school could ever need. The consultant found that pricing for software is now user-based so the operating system and user software licenses would need to be relicensed for the conversion to a System i. The sales representative's estimate for a conversion to a System i at Clarion—Milwaukee would be between $100,000 and $130,000, including project management and professional services to support the conversion. The consultant mentioned that the IBM salesperson would be happy to visit with Young as

EXHIBIT 5
LTM's Consulting Report:
The Clarion School for Boys, Inc.—Milwaukee Division

LTM Consultants
765 Corporate Circle
Milwaukee, WI 51744

June 3, 2006

John F. Young
The Clarion School for Boys, Inc.—Milwaukee Division
Post Office Box 2217
Milwaukee, WI 51740-2217

Dear John:

LTM has completed our study at Clarion and we submit the enclosed written report per our agreement. As I mentioned to you during our telephone conversation, we would be happy to present our findings to Clarion, Inc.'s Board of Directors meeting in Chicago if you wish.

Please note the four main sections of the report. First, a sampling of comments from Clarion—Milwaukee's staff characterize the general attitude toward information systems (IS). Strengths and weaknesses of the current information system are highlighted. Finally, specific recommendations are presented for improving Clarion—Milwaukee's information system.

As I am sure you will agree, there are many opportunities to improve Clarion—Milwaukee's daily IS operations. We would like to meet with you soon to discuss how LTM can assist you in making our recommendations operational.

Sincerely,

C. J. VanZant

Carl John VanZant
Vice President

Enclosure

EXHIBIT 5 (*Continued*)

Long-Range IS Plan Final Report

Findings in this report are a result of analysis during the last week of April and the first three weeks of May 2006. Eighteen person-days were spent on site at the Clarion—Milwaukee school. LTM consultants began with a kickoff meeting that included six department supervisors, three directors, and the superintendent. In this meeting, the scope and purpose of LTM's engagement was defined: to identify critical issues related to Clarion—Milwaukee's future information system (IS) environment with the goal of defining Clarion—Milwaukee's future IS strategy.

Included in this report is a selection of comments made by Clarion—Milwaukee staff during both formal and informal interactions with LTM consultants. The following six questions were used as a starting point for each interview. A majority of the interview time was devoted to exploring responses to initial questions using follow-up questions.

1. Are there any recommendations you would like to make regarding how the Clarion—Milwaukee Division school handles information—written, computer, telephone, or direct (face-to-face)?
2. What is the most useful form of information you receive?
3. In what ways do you feel this form of information is vital to your work objectives?
4. What could be done to make Clarion—Milwaukee's information system even more beneficial to your work?
5. Summarize the strengths of the current information system.
6. Are there any additional comments you would like to make regarding future enhancements to Clarion—Milwaukee's information system?

The following interviews were conducted during the first three weeks of the study:

- Six 2-hour two-on-one interviews with department supervisors (two LTM consultants and one supervisor)
- Six 1-hour interviews with the unit directors
- Twenty-three 1-hour two-on-one interviews with nonsupervisory staff

LTM consultants attended the following meetings during the last three weeks of the study:

- Two weekly administrative council meetings (comprised of the nine supervisors and the superintendent)
- One weekly institutional treatment team meeting (comprised of the superintendent, director of treatment services, deputy director of treatment services, supervisor of the program department, associate program supervisors, supervisor of social services, social service counselors, education department supervisor, and transition department supervisor)
- Two scheduled department meetings and four impromptu department meetings
- Five daily teachers' meetings
- One weekly unit treatment team meeting (comprised of one teacher, two members of the child-care workers staff, and a member of the social service staff)

LTM consultants randomly queried 17 of Clarion—Milwaukee's employees in the halls of the school and in the parking lot by asking questions about their uses of current IS resources at the school. Staff comments were recorded during both formal and informal conversations.

The remainder of this report is divided into four main sections: Sampling of Staff's Comments, Strengths of Clarion—Milwaukee's Information System, Weaknesses of Clarion—Milwaukee's Information System, and Information System Strategy.

Sampling of Staff's Comments

"I have been trying to finish this month's books for the last two days, but I am having the same problems as last month. The accounts receivable software program is still giving me difficulties. I think I'll just do them by hand again this month."

(Bookkeeper)

EXHIBIT 5 (*Continued*)

"I use the scheduling module all the time for my event scheduling since most of the work I do runs in biweekly cycles. The automatic messages remind me when I have something due."

(Clerical Worker)

"There was a lot of initial excitement about e-mail, but I haven't heard much about it since then. I know I've been too busy to learn it myself, and I missed the training sessions because of other meetings. The only thing I've heard is that a few of the teachers sent out e-mail to others, but never got a reply. Maybe the interest died down because everyone didn't get training right away."

(Education Supervisor)

"I'll be honest with you. Although I have been using the system for almost a year now, it is not easy to use. I think my daughter's Mac is much easier."

(Development Staff Member)

"I remember someone mentioning that there is an inventory management software package we might use for our kitchen supplies, but I haven't checked into it yet."

(Kitchen Manager)

"In my last job, we used a program on our computer to monitor the progress of our students. It was a custom package written for us by a consulting group. Although it took about 10 months to complete the software, it worked very well for our special needs."

(Transition Counselor)

"It would help us if we had a reliable system for keeping the student's medical records. Sometimes the note cards get misplaced, and you don't know about it until you really need one."

(Nurse)

"I just bypass the menu system since it slows me down ...especially since I have set up generic templates for all the common reports."

(Secretary)

"I am responsible for producing the weekly treatment services calendar. Because I am continually making updates, my biggest complaint is that I have to walk down the hall whenever I want to get a printed copy."

(Associate Program Supervisor)

Strengths of Clarion—Milwaukee's Information System

Hardware and Software

1. Dictation equipment is used extensively by treatment personnel. This use increases efficiency for both treatment staff and the secretarial staff who transcribe the dictations.
2. Personal computers are used by the controller and the director of development to generate overhead slides for presentations.
3. Software application programs are flexible enough to be useful for both beginners and advanced users.
4. Adequate software documentation manuals are available for users.
5. The AS/400 file transfer product allows data transfer between PC and mainframe units. It allows flexibility for those who use PCs a lot.
6. The AS/400 is expandable in case additional workstations or processors are needed.

Policy and Procedures

1. System backups are done on a daily basis and are well organized.
2. Quarterly preventive maintenance schedules coordinated through IBM representatives have been effective in the past.

EXHIBIT 5 (*Continued*)

Staff Perceptions

In general, interviews revealed that most of the staff, although not totally satisfied with Clarion—Milwaukee's information system, felt that the system was likely better than what existed in comparable facilities. Most frequently noted comparisons were with a local mental health facility that is experiencing severe system difficulties.

Weaknesses of Clarion—Milwaukee's Information System

Hardware and Software

1. Resultant quality of dictated memos is largely dependent on the level of experience of the secretary.
2. Some needed software is not available on the AS/400, necessitating use of personal computers for some reporting functions.
3. Self-paced tutorial software is not available for users.
4. A number of users stated that PCs were not available when they needed them late in the day. PCs are used heavily from 3:00 P. M. to 5:00 P. M.

Policy and Procedures

1. At least 90 minutes each day of the senior bookkeeper's time is spent running system back-ups and initial program loads (IPLs). Consequently, others cannot use the system during that time, and Ms. Baker is not available to perform her regular supervisory functions.
2. Requests for report changes are routed through department supervisors to either John Young or Jean Baker. Once each month they are reviewed and reprioritized by Baker and Young. Baker then works on requests according to priority, as time permits. Day-to-day operations require Young or Baker to answer user questions as they come up, which reduces the time they have for their primary responsibilities.
3. Only two individuals have attended college-level computer courses. A formal training schedule does not exist.

Staff Perceptions

1. Administrative council members were given very limited opportunities to provide input for the original computerization project in 1998. Thus, they perceive the current system as incapable of providing for their needs.
2. Direct personal communication has become more difficult as staff size has increased and departmental specialization has evolved.
3. Many of Clarion—Milwaukee's would-be IS users have decided not to use the system because they find it difficult to find an open PC.
4. Secretarial staff use the AS/400 application software more than any other personnel. The AS/400 is regarded by many as only a tool for performing reporting tasks.
5. Staff who use accounting applications have a sense that they are "the shoemaker's children" whose applications receive lowest priority.

Information System Strategy

The following recommendations are arranged in general categories, with more specific suggestions offered in the conclusion:

1. **Establish a permanent staff position for IS management.** It is difficult for a staff member to handle an information system project as a part-time assignment when she has a multitude of other responsibilities and projects to oversee at the same time. For this reason, a new manager-level position should be created with primary responsibility to manage Clarion—Milwaukee's information system (including computing networks, personal computers, and telephone systems). Additional responsibility should include evaluation

EXHIBIT 5 (*Continued*)

and implementation of IS training needs. The new IS manager should report to the controller and have permanent membership on the long-range planning committee. The individual selected for the IS manager position should have extensive computer science background and information systems experience.

2. **Establish a team approach to planning.** Planning should initially be conducted by a small team with strong leadership, making sure that feedback is obtained from the various user groups in each of the departments. A feedback process should be used to motivate staff toward cooperation and support of IS projects. This feedback can be accomplished by soliciting their input and explaining system benefits so they will develop a sense of ownership. Potential "stakeholders" should also be identified as this process reduces the barriers to change.

3. **Involve and evaluate the entire system when considering all IS projects.** Telecommunications, central computer, and PC decisions should not be made in a vacuum. When IS-related decisions need to be made, Clarion—Milwaukee's entire IS must be considered. The new IS manager's responsibilities should include researching "high-impact" issues. This procedure should be regarded as an integral part of Clarion—Milwaukee's information system evolution. Overall evaluation should include input from experts within each department.

   A formal impact assessment methodology should be established to ensure a comprehensive and consistent evaluation. The methodology should include consideration of the following:

   • What are the attitudes of employees regarding the introduction and use of the new system?
   • How should Clarion—Milwaukee's business practices change as a result of the new system?
   • Should organizational restructuring occur, including changes, additions, or eliminations of staff positions?
   • How much experience does Clarion—Milwaukee have in this particular area?
   • What other current projects or strategic issues could compete with this project?

   Use of a formal impact assessment methodology will allow identification of opportunities with low, medium, and high risk that can be considered when appraising the response to future change. Furthermore, in concert with an evaluation of the entire information system, this technique facilitates development of a rolling, long-range IS plan.

4. **Install a formal approach to IS planning.** A variety of techniques can be used for IS planning. "Critical success factors" and "investment strategy analysis" are common frameworks. Elements of several of these techniques should be combined in structuring planning activities. It is also vital for the Milwaukee superintendent and the Clarion, Inc., board of directors to have proposals that can be judged according to the same criteria in the process of decision making. Although the formal process will undoubtedly be time-consuming, our experience with IS projects suggests that this practice will benefit the school in the long term by reducing the likelihood of inappropriate projects being implemented. A specific planning framework should include the following features:

   A. **Master IS Plan.** A master IS plan involves identification of the school's strategic issues and the development of the planning infrastructure for the future. The master plan is based on an examination of Clarion—Milwaukee's formal mission statement with respect to current strategic emphases. Workshops should be held for staff with the goals of educating them as to the strategic process of IS planning and providing an understanding of broad IS management objectives. All employees at Clarion—Milwaukee should be aware of the necessity to manage all information—including text documents, voice messages, diagrams, and statistics—as valuable corporate assets. Staff should understand that computers, software, written documents, and telephones are not "theirs." Decisions and procedures regarding these assets will be based on the treatment of these elements as "Clarion—Milwaukee Division" resources addressed within the master plan. Staff should also be instructed to identify "critical success

EXHIBIT 5 (*Continued*)

factors" vital for accomplishing Clarion—Milwaukee's objectives. This process will link specific task activities to the master IS plan.

    B. Top Management Involvement. Primary attention should be given to techniques that facilitate top management involvement and support. The superintendent, along with the new IS manager, should play a critical role in long-range IS planning. All future IS planning decisions should also include substantial input from members of the administrative council.

    C. Systems Life Cycle Methodology. A "systems life cycle" methodology is recommended for use on each specific application system. It is also useful for establishing requirements and project timetables. When evaluating new application systems, consideration should be given to the life-cycle stage of each component. Avoid decisions that lead to purchase of an application just prior to the release of a new option. A formal system should be developed that facilitates identification of a software product's evolutionary position with respect to Clarion—Milwaukee's current technology. Only after application systems are characterized within the spectrum of "cutting edge" to "nearing obsolescence" and compared to the Clarion—Milwaukee Division's ability to manage new technology, should tactical decisions be made.

    D. Rolling Timetable. The master IS plan should include a rolling timetable in order to coordinate various project efforts and make effective IS investment decisions.

5. Incorporate IS requirements in proposed long-range planning objectives.
Long-range planning (LRP) objectives must include information regarding a standard set of topics relevant to information systems. Each LRP objective should address its potential impact on Clarion—Milwaukee's information system and specifically identify any additional requirements. It is because of the highly integrated nature of IS planning and other long-range planning that the new IS manager will have to work closely with Clarion—Milwaukee's controller.

6. Establish IS objectives within Clarion—Milwaukee Division's five-year plan. As Clarion—Milwaukee's IS planning requirements become more complex, it will be imperative to continually seek out new ways to make strategic decisions. For this reason, Clarion—Milwaukee should include ongoing evaluation of computer-based methodologies, which would increase planning efficiency and integrity, as part of the long-range planning process. The role of IS management must be evaluated and redefined in light of technological changes.

---

soon as he was ready to make his recommendations to the board. Young expressed his appreciation to the lead LTM consultant for this information.

Decision Time

It was 4:35 P.M. on June 6, 2006—one week before his presentation. Knowing he would have to work with his IS Task Force to finalize the report, Young poured himself a cup of coffee and flipped open the consultants' findings, which he had received earlier that day (the report's text is included as Exhibit 5). He read LTM's report with the vigor of a graduate student, hoping the findings would be a panacea for Clarion—Milwaukee's information systems problems.

Young had intended to make LTM's report the basis of his own report to the Board of Directors. Now that he had read it,

he thought it included some good ideas and suggestions, but it seemed lacking as a full IS plan.

As Young was reviewing the plan, Jean Baker brought an envelope into his office. She said "a nice young man dropped this off just now. I told him that you were too busy to see someone without an appointment. He asked that I deliver it to you as soon as possible. He mentioned that he had heard from one of the members of the Board of Directors that you were considering an upgrade to the AS/400 system. He thought you would be interested in what he brought." Young opened the envelope and found a proposal to replace the AS/400 system with a Microsoft-based system (see Exhibit 6).

Young was now really unsure exactly what he needed to do, but he knew he would be burning a lot of midnight oil during the next few days.

EXHIBIT 6
Proposal: Hooper Technology Services, Inc.,
for the Clarion School for Boys, Inc.—Milwaukee Division

Hooper Technology Services, Inc.
5517 Technology Place
Milwaukee, WI 51740

June 6, 2006

John F. Young
Controller
The Clarion School for Boys, Inc.—Milwaukee Division
Post Office Box 2217
Milwaukee, WI 51740-2217

Dear Mr. Young,

Hooper Technology Services is an authorized Microsoft value-added reseller, specializing in providing state-of-the-art solutions for midsize organizations based on the Microsoft suite of products.

We have learned that you are considering an upgrade to your existing IBM AS/400. As I am sure you have heard, IBM no longer provides full support to that system and has changed its focus to the follow-on System i.

We believe that your school would be well-served by converting your information technology system to one based on industry-leading Microsoft products. Your existing AS/400 applications would continue to run as a server on this network but additional applications would be deployed on a Microsoft platform.

You would not have to complete this migration all at once. We would propose two phases:

1. Install MS Exchange, MS Office, and MS Outlook and implement e-mail and shared calendaring on the MS network, plus provide DS-1 level connectivity to the Internet.
2. Install MS Dynamics CRM and implement an application for the Development Department and an application for care coordination for the Social Services, Program, Education, Transition, and ISIS departments.

The budget for Phase 1 includes servers ($28,000), operating system licenses ($6,000), client licenses ($10,000), and professional services ($10,000) for a total of $54,000. For Phase 2, the cost is estimated at $10,000 for more servers, $2,000 for additional operating system licenses, $10,000 for client licenses, and between $40,000 and $100,000 for professional services, for a grand total of between $62,000 and $122,000. While we cannot specify the cost of professional services in Phase 2 at this time, we would work with Clarion personnel to create a detailed statement of work and budget for Phase 2. However, we think you should seriously consider spending at least $50,000 in staff training on the new system.

We would also strongly recommend that you add the personal computers (notebooks) needed for each staff member's use at home. This change would require another 120 notebooks, software, and printers at a cost of $220,000 installed. The current set of desktop personal computers would be used for students as well as administrative staff use while at school.

We strongly believe that a migration to a modern architecture for the school will be of significant benefit to staff and students.

I would be please to discuss this proposal with you in more detail at your convenience.

Sincerely,

J. Caleb Hooper
Vice President

TELETRON, INC.: USING INFORMATION TECHNOLOGY TO TRANSFORM A COMPANY

"Come on in, guys," said Timothy C. Lybrook, founder and chief executive officer of Teletron, Inc., a Bloomington, Indiana, provider of telecommunications expense management services for corporate telecommunications users. It was April 25, 1999, and Teletron was considering the implementation of a new strategy to grow the company from about $10 million in sales to about $100 million, in part through the use of information technology.

"Thanks," replied Robert N. Jonas, director of information technology at Teletron, and Dennis M. Kirin, vice president of client services at the company, simultaneously, as they entered Tim's office.

"We want to show you the plans for the development of Virtual Analyzer and get your approval," said Bob.

"The investment will not be small, but the benefits are huge," said Dennis.

"OK," said Tim. "I am anxious to see your analysis and plan. As you know, this is one of the three legs in the transformation of our company. We gotta get it right."

Expense Management in the Telecommunications Industry

In 1999, there were approximately 6,000 telecommunications providers in the United States. However, only about 45 companies accounted for approximately 95 percent of the dollar value of the telecommunications services provided. The providers signed their customers to various plans or contracts that carried costs for specific services. The providers then invoiced the users each month.

Traditionally, telecommunications invoices from providers were sent to customers on paper—thick stacks of paper for large corporations. Often, these invoices contained internal provider codes that offered little explanation of their exact meaning. Customers were forced to determine what each charge on the invoice was for and to compare the charge to their particular plan or contract. Needless to say, this situation made the process of verifying invoices very time-consuming for the customer. As a result, many corporations merely accepted the invoice as accurate. Even checking invoices sent electronically was very difficult.

Surveys of corporate telecommunications managers often showed major dissatisfaction with the providers' billing practices, especially about errors that seemed "always in the favor of the provider." Most customers believed that these billing overcharges occurred because of poor record-keeping by the provider, complexity of the contracts, inadequate operational support systems at the provider, lack of time by the customer to verify the invoices, and internal miscommunication within either organization. These mistakes were considered by most telecommunications managers to be significant—telecommunications expenses were often rated as the fifth or sixth largest expense item in corporations, and were growing rapidly.

The size and complexity of the telecommunications expense problem increased significantly during the 1990s, and was forecast to grow significantly during the first decade of the new century. Additional services, such as broadband technology, were enabling enterprises to transfer vast amounts of digital information rapidly. In addition, cell phone use by corporate customers grew rapidly during the 1990s and was forecast to grow substantially in the new century as well. Finally, the old voice-centric telecommunications infrastructure was being replaced with new service offerings that combined voice, data, and video using the Internet Protocol (IP).

According to Gartner-Dataquest, an industry tracking firm, total telecommunications spending by the business market was estimated to grow to $175 billion in 2000 and continue to expand rapidly to over $350 billion by 2005. One reason given for this rapid growth was that many corporations recognized that their telecommunications infrastructure was critical for their company's revenue growth. Yet the cost of errors in operating this infrastructure could well be greater than the revenue benefits.

The expense management environment, characterized by numerous service offerings, frequent errors in billing, and multiple telecommunications providers, created a significant opportunity for service firms to assist enterprises in realizing cost savings and operating efficiencies. Most corporate customers did not consider telecommunications expense management to be a core competency. They typically did not possess the time, expertise, and access to the necessary information that would enable them to analyze their telecommunications bills in-house for accuracy or to investigate money-saving opportunities. According to a recent research report, procuring telecommunications services was "a pain for everyone." The researchers concluded that companies of all sizes were unhappy at every stage of the telecommunications procurement process, from ordering to installation to billing.

In the late 1990s, several experts recognized an opportunity for service firms with expertise in telecommunications billing to review complicated invoices from several providers (each with different codes) for accuracy as well as searching for and negotiating the lowest prices and the highest quality service for a corporation. Furthermore, these experts forecast a large incremental market opportunity for such firms that would go beyond traditional outsourcing to provide software tools that would empower enterprises to analyze easily and proactively their telecommunications services.

Company History

In the 1980s, Tim Lybrook was working as a consultant to the resort industry. His business took him to a variety of resort operations across the United States. As part of his work, he reviewed how his clients were spending their money. While reviewing the cost structure of his clients, Tim often noticed inaccuracies in their telephone bills. Resort operators were consistently being overcharged for their telecommunications services, often by as much as 30 percent.

After seeing this situation existing for several customers, Tim wondered if there was a business opportunity there. During 1990–1991, Lybrook investigated several other industries and found that the same problem existed. Companies were routinely overpaying their local, long distance, data, and wireless providers. These overpayments were due to the complexity of the bills, the size of the organizations, the diversity of services, and errors of the service providers. So in 1990 Lybrook incorporated Teletron to assist "companies throughout the United States to reduce their telecommunication expenditures by identifying inefficiencies and errors in their phone bills." He finished a business plan in late 1991, and Teletron started hiring employees in February 1992.

Teletron targeted customers in the United States that spent between $10,000 and $500,000 per month on telecommunications services. An inside Teletron salesperson would call the telecommunications manager, and propose that Teletron audit the company's last 12 months of telecommunications invoices. If Teletron found errors and had them corrected, Teletron would receive 50 percent of the savings. If no savings were found, the company owed Teletron nothing. A typical proposal call went something like:

> Mr. Jones, I am Mary Johnson with the Teletron Corporation. We are a telecommunications expense management firm located in Bloomington, Indiana. In our work with clients, we have discovered that over 95 percent of the telecommunications bills received from carriers or providers contain errors, often in the provider's favor. Have you ever seen that problem? . . . I thought you might have. We provide a no-risk service for our corporate clients—you send us your telecommunications bills for last month. If we find errors in the bills, we will contact the carriers and get them to send the rest of the past year bills. When we correct the errors, you pay us 50 percent of the documented savings. If we don't find anything, you owe us nothing. Therefore, our service is risk-free to you. Would you be interested in talking further?

Teletron then assigned the client to an account manager who in turn often used former telephone company personnel to conduct manual audits of the provider bills. The company maintained a library of relevant telecommunications contracts and tariffs against which the auditors would compare the bills. When errors were found, the Teletron auditor contacted the billing personnel at the telecommunication provider and worked with the provider to adjust the bill. When all the bills were audited, Teletron compiled the savings and invoiced the client for its fee. Teletron personnel also attempted to identify better plans or contracts for their clients. If future savings could be achieved by the client by implementing one of their suggestions, Teletron invoiced the client for a share of the next 12 months of savings.

After the initial engagement with the client, Teletron personnel attempted to build a longer-term relationship with the client, auditing their bills on an ongoing basis. But clients accepted this additional service very rarely. Most client engagements lasted from 6 months to a year. New clients had to be solicited on a continuing basis.

Lybrook considered the core competencies of Teletron to be its ability to interpret telecommunications bills, find errors, compare contracts and tariffs with current invoices, and effectively deal with telecommunications providers. He considered this expertise to apply equally well to the local, long distance, wireless, Internet, and data markets.

Teletron faced strong competition from a few larger firms and hundreds of "mom-and-pop" operations. However, there was no company that held more than 1 percent of the market. Most firms that audited telecommunications invoices were small operations, usually owned by a retired telephone company employee who knew contracts. Others were captives of certain service providers. Likewise, some telecommunications departments of user companies offered to audit the telecommunications invoices of other companies as a way to earn revenue.

Most competitors were privately held. Several of these privately held companies had grown to significant size. They were:

- **Cost Management Consultants:** This company assisted clients in making decisions regarding both energy and telecommunications costs. The company performed both energy and telecommunications invoice audits.
- **Optimizers:** Optimizers helped midsize businesses manage telecommunications expenses via invoice auditing, selecting and integrating telecommunications equipment, providing telecommunications management advice, and negotiating rates for telecommunications needs.
- **Teledata Control, Inc.:** TCI specialized in providing cost control solutions for voice, data, and information services. The company offered invoice auditing among a range of other services. In 1999, TCI had approximately $7 million in revenue and employed 93 people.

Teletron was very successful in its strategy from 1992–1998, amassing over 5,000 clients that ranged from small businesses to Fortune 500 companies. Exhibit 1 contains a map of where Teletron's past and current customers were located in 1999. Exhibit 2 shows a selected list of past and current clients as of December 1998.

In addition to serving many well-known clients, Teletron was generally successful from a financial standpoint, achieving a compounded revenue growth of more than 200 percent from 1992 through1998. In addition, Teletron maintained EBITDA margins on revenue in the 10 to 30 percent range during this period. See Exhibit 3 for the financial results of Teletron during 1992–1998.

Despite the financial success, in 1998 Lybrook began to question whether the company could continue to grow under its current business model. The company experienced over 90 percent yearly customer "churn," requiring a costly ongoing customer acquisition process. As carriers corrected their billing mistakes, many of Teletron's customers felt that they no longer needed Teletron's services. Other customers hired a person for finding billing errors so as to keep 100 percent of the savings rather than splitting the savings with Teletron. In addition to churn, Lybrook recognized that the auditing process was a labor-intensive operation. While the process of searching the contracts for the correct charge for a particular customer could be

EXHIBIT 1
Location of Clients in 1999
Teletron, Inc.

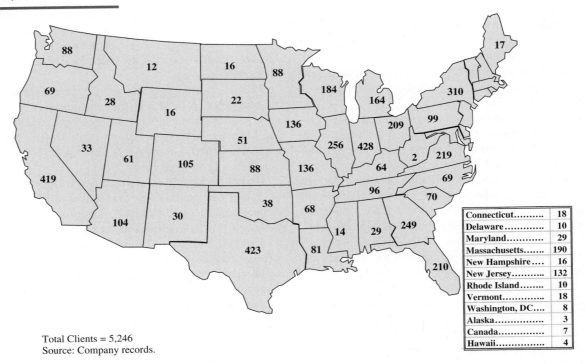

Connecticut	18
Delaware	10
Maryland	29
Massachusetts	190
New Hampshire	16
New Jersey	132
Rhode Island	10
Vermont	18
Washington, DC	8
Alaska	3
Canada	7
Hawaii	4

Total Clients = 5,246
Source: Company records.

EXHIBIT 2

Examples of Past and Current Clients
Teletron, Inc.

Marconi Medical	Shell Oil	Masterbrand/Schrock
BMW North America	Epsilon	Harland Financial
North American Mortgage	AGI Klearfold	Kohl's Department Store
Saint Mary's SMDC	Humana	La-Z-Boy Chairs
Relizon	Disney Stores	Talbots
LaQuinta Inns	Dollar General Corp.	Red Roof Inns
Earthlink	Bungee	

Source: Company records.

EXHIBIT 3

1992 to 1998 Financial Results
Teletron, Inc.

Year	Revenue (in $000)	EBITDA (in $000)	EBT (in $000)	Headcount
1992	$14	$(115)	($115)	4
1993	76	(143)	(143)	4
1994	253	26	26	4
1995	557	106	106	12
1996	1,636	345	345	35
1997	4,107	1,122	1,134	62
1998	7,268	904	854	157

Source: Company records.

taught, automating the process would require significant effort. In mid-1998, Lybrook began to wonder how to keep customers longer and how to automate some of his internal processes.

A New Business Model

By the end of 1998, Lybrook decided that he wanted to grow the company to become a $100 million business by 2006. He was no longer interested in owning just a "lifestyle" business. He also felt that the existing business model, while profitable, was not scalable to that level. Finally, he believed that merely automating some of Teletron's processes would not result in a profitable $100 million operation—labor costs grew too rapidly as sales increased.

At the January 5, 1999, board of directors meeting, Lybrook presented his new vision for the company. He saw Teletron acting as an intermediary between the providers of telecommunications services and the users of those services. Teletron would help its clients (the users) solve problems, whatever they were. His conversations with many corporate telecommunications managers convinced him that while minimizing invoicing errors and seeking better contracts for customers were important, they were not the only problems these customers had. Teletron would continue to offer consulting and auditing services to clients but would now provide a software product to its clients on a subscription basis.

In order to achieve his vision, Lybrook proposed to the board that three major transformations take place at Teletron. First, the senior management in the company who reported to Tim should be replaced. Teletron needed senior management who had been successful in $100 million companies. Tim immediately hired a new vice president of client services.

Exhibit 4 contains brief biographies of the key management team at Teletron as of April 1999.

Second, Tim proposed the creation of a new, complex piece of software (called Virtual Analyzer) that could be delivered from Teletron's server in an application service provider (ASP) mode. He believed that the ASP delivery vehicle would be more acceptable to the client than licensing the software. He reasoned that most telecommunications users did not want

EXHIBIT 4
Biographies of Key Management Staff
Teletron, Inc.

Timothy C. Lybrook is Teletron's chairman and chief executive officer. Prior to founding Teletron, he spent 14 years as a consultant in the resort industry, where he implemented call centers, established sales teams, marketed trade shows, developed direct mail programs, and created strategic alliances/partnerships. He founded Teletron in 1990 to take advantage of the inefficiencies in the telecommunications industry which he witnessed in the resort industry. Mr. Lybrook serves on the board of directors for the Bloomington Economic Development Corporation and the Greater Bloomington Chamber of Commerce.

William L. Bennett is vice president of finance. He brings more than 7 years of diversified corporate financial experience to Teletron. His background includes work in several positions, ranging from financial analyst to controller to director of financial planning. Mr. Bennett has been instrumental in supporting Teletron's financial initiatives through its past rapid growth, with sound financial planning and responsible cost management. Mr. Bennett is a CPA.

Mary Ellen Pastor is director of human resources. Mary Ellen provides Teletron with human resource strategies acquired during her 10 years of experience in the telecommunications industry. Ms. Pastor manages recruitment, employee relations, compensation and benefits, and organizational development for Teletron.

Robert N. Jonas is director of information technology. Bob brings technology, business, and leadership skills to Teletron's information technology division. In Mr. Jonas's 16 years of experience, he has held positions as systems analyst, manager of telecommunications, and director of systems development for a series of privately-held companies in the Midwest.

Charles A. Bentley is director of sales. Chuck has more than 13 years of sales execution and leadership in the telecommunications and high technology industries. Most recently, he was the vice president of sales and business development for a Silicon Valley startup. Prior to that, Chuck was a regional sales director, where he increased sales by an average of 16 percent over 5 years.

Dennis M. Kirin joined Teletron in February of 1999. He brings to Teletron more than 10 years of customer service, information technology, and operations management experience. He has designed, built, and managed multi-vendor customer service, training, and maintenance operations for both large and small businesses and is experienced in new products and services, pricing, business models, and operational infrastructure. Mr. Kirin leads Teletron's client services department where his focus is on creating clients for life.

Source: Company records.

the upkeep responsibilities of a complex piece of licensed software. This software product had to have a great deal of knowledge imbedded in it, reflecting what highly experienced Teletron employees had formerly done.

Third, Tim knew that he had to change the entire culture at Teletron, especially the way the company went to market. While past growth was impressive on a percentage basis, Teletron needed large increases in dollar revenue to reach the target of $100 million by 2006 from an existing $7.3 million level. In particular, the sales process had to change drastically. From 1992 to 1998, Teletron used a cadre of inside salespeople to sell a service directly to many clients, most of whom did not continue as clients after the initial engagement. This effort had to be replaced with a process that developed long-term relationships in which clients would subscribe to a software solution developed by Teletron that resided on Teletron's server. The size of the call center would be reduced. Different kinds of salespeople would have to be hired—those who could sell complex software to clients not used to buying it. New channels to reach the customer would have to be developed.

Making the New Business Model a Reality

Creating a new software package became a major part of implementing the new business model for Teletron. On February 10, 1999, Lybrook assigned the director of information technology, Robert N. Jonas, and the newly hired vice president of client services, Dennis M. Kirin, to co-chair a task force that would design a new system. Their day-to-day duties were to be delegated to someone in their unit. In his memo, Tim laid out the following goals for the new system:

- Expand the range of services that Teletron provided.
- Allow the client (purchaser of the software) to manage his telecommunications environment efficiently and effectively.
- Meet the broad range of needs of the telecommunications manager in corporations.

Tim asked for a proposal by the end of April 1999. When Bob and Dennis returned with their proposal, Tim opened the meeting by saying:

Thanks for putting all your effort into this project. I realize that you have had to perform double duty for the last 2 months. Even though I asked you to delegate your day-to-day responsibilities to someone else, I know that you still had to run your shop as well as lead this task force. And, Dennis, you were new! But you and I both know that this system is very much the future of the firm. Rather than listen to a formal presentation, let me ask you some questions. Let's start with the size of the market we can go after. Dennis?

Dennis replied,

There is some good news here. The market is huge. Gartner-Dataquest estimates that the addressable telecommunications cost management market will grow from a little under $2 billion now to over $5 billion by 2005, a 26 percent compound annual growth rate. With no dominant player in the market, this market is largely underserved. If we capture just 5 percent of that market, we are talking about a huge sales opportunity. We can easily grow to your $100 million revenue goal in 7 years. And cost management is only one part of the functions that Virtual Analyzer will provide our clients.

"Outstanding! I knew the potential was large, but I had no idea that it was that large," said Tim. "But, let me ask you . . . what does your market research show has to be included in a software offering to meet customer needs?"

Bringing up his PowerPoint presentation, Dennis responded,

Let me first describe our research process. We first pulled 1,200 company names of current and past clients from our database. We then designed a four-page questionnaire that asked some questions about their satisfaction with our current services and asked about their needs. The questionnaires were sent to telecommunications managers in medium- to large-size corporations. We got 157 usable responses out of the 1,200 questionnaires sent.

Basically, there are six needs. The first is inventory management. They all have a massive problem determining the equipment and features installed in every part of their telecommunications environment. They want a way to keep track of all of the telecommunications services used at each site. These services include the features, the service provider providing the service, the accounts that the service provider bills for the service, and the equipment used to provide the service.

Second, they want better access to the provider plans and contracts the company is using. Currently, most customers do not have a central database for this kind of information. In short, they don't know exactly what they are buying. They use lots of providers, each with many different plans or contracts. And they want to receive this information electronically. They argued that in order to realize any significant cost savings, a customer must first understand exactly what plans and services they are subscribing to and the extent of their usage of that telecommunications service. For example, many large companies do not take the time to review their paper bills to determine what their long distance charges are to a particular state or country. This is primarily due to the sheer size of their paper bills and the complexity of those bills.

Third was expense management. This is our traditional area of expertise. Even if the customer can organize all their telecommunications data, there is still a level of expertise that is needed to analyze the data fully, and thereby realize significant cost savings. While some companies seem to have this solved by hiring people to do the auditing or by using our service or the services of one of our competitors, most still believe that they are missing lots of opportunities here. In addition to finding problems in current bills, the customers want help in recommending changes to existing plans and services.

Fourth, our customers need help in vendor invoice processing and payment. They need to collect all the bills for analysis first. Once they have analyzed the bills, the company wants to be able to send the corrected bills to accounts payable to issue payment. Obviously, they need to do this for each vendor. Many need an interface to the company's accounts payable system.

Fifth, they still have the old standby needs—moves, adds, and changes. Given all the organizational change in our customers these days, services at a particular site change very frequently. They may install a T1 line today only to have it removed in 2 months because the demand at that site has changed significantly. The customer needs a central point of contact for making these changes and providing oversight of the day-to-day duties to make sure the move, add, or change occurs on the most economical basis. It would be great if the change were then updated in the overall inventory list of telecommunications services.

Finally, they expressed a need for some analytical capability. Some of the reports they want include usage studies, service assessments and recommendations, market comparisons with other companies to determine if they are getting a good rate, vendor analyses to see if they have the best set of vendors, and risk assessment.

"OK, that is a good list. I am not surprised by any of those needs," replied Tim. "But will they buy a commercial software product to help them manage these issues? Or will they have their internal systems development department design a home-grown system? Or maybe they will just continue to do it manually? Or use an outside service?"

"Let me handle that question," replied Jonas.

We specifically asked that question in the survey. The first thing that we found is that there is no way that they can get enough staff to perform these functions manually. Most have had staff cuts. And while the telecommunications managers would generally like to have an internal system tailored to their specific needs and processes, they are ready to buy a piece of commercial software. They recognize that with all the Y2K issues capturing the attention of their information technology departments now, they are not going to be successful in getting such a system designed internally. And even when the Y2K issues go away, there is going to be such a backlog of other demands that they don't think they will be successful in getting a system written any time soon.

"I sure hope you are right," replied Tim. "The people I am talking to tell me that acquisition of anything that is not Y2K related is being delayed. Of course, this product won't be out for 2 to 3 years so maybe that is not a big worry. Tell me, are we the first company to think of this idea or are there competitors out there with software packages they offer to telecommunications managers?"

"Well," replied Bob. "We're not the first, but I think that we can be the best. We found five companies that seemed to represent real competition. If we look at this chart, they are:

- **QuantumShift:** QuantumShift operates a B2B e-commerce business model focusing on outsourcing and cost management. It has an Internet platform called "InterAct" that uses the Internet to automate and accelerate the telecommunications supply chain. QuantumShift also has a professional services team to assist clients with telecommunications equipment selection. The company has recently secured approximately $110 million through three rounds of venture financing, and its revenues are in the $15 to 20 million range. Unlike Teletron, most customers do not see QuantumShift as vendor-neutral as it markets telecommunications services to its customers.

- **Tenet International:** Tenet is a small, independent, cost management service provider. It helps clients control and manage telecommunications expenses through financial analysis and customer service support. Tenet can transmit information with a customized feed to the client based on client specifications. Tenet also offers Web-based management and control reports in addition to a vendor payment service. The company's revenues are estimated to be in the $1 to 5 million range.

- **Simplexity:** Simplexity is an Internet-based trading hub where buyers and sellers of telecommunications services can connect and transact with each other. It targets a broad spectrum of customers ranging from home-based, small, and medium-sized businesses, to telecommunications carriers. Simplexity seeks to help its customers compare and select the best products, plans, and service providers. Simplexity recently raised $53.5 million through three rounds of venture financing. The company has approximately $7 million in revenue and employs about 90 people.

- **Intera Communications:** Intera's Smart Partner platform provides solutions for managing its clients' telecommunications services. It offers an online inventory of a client's telecommunications services, vendors, and equipment. In addition, the client can compare, select, and order voice, data, Internet, and wireless services through Smart Partner. The company has approximately $49 million in annual revenues and 150 employees.

- **ProfitLine:** ProfitLine provides business process outsourcing solutions that manage the life cycle of voice and data services and reduce communications costs for enterprise-level companies. These services include service ordering and optimization, inventory management, bill management and auditing, accounts payable processing, telecommunications contract negotiations, and project management. Delivery of these services is done via a proprietary Web application, providing real-time visibility into their outsourcing services."

"Hmm... very interesting," said Tim. "Two out of these five companies recently received venture capital funding... and in large amounts. If we can develop something better, maybe we can go to the VC market as well. But that is for later... after we decide if we want to develop this package or not. Tell me, given all the competition out there, is what we are planning any better than the others? Or are we just being a 'me too'?"

"We figured that you might ask that question," replied Dennis. "We were able to inspect each of the competing products. From that process, we prepared a comparison table (Exhibit 5) that shows what each of these offerings can do compared to what we are planning to put in as features and capabilities of Virtual Analyzer. As you can see from the table, Virtual Analyzer will be the best offering in this market. It looks to us that Tenet is our most robust competitor, but it is targeting a different size market and the company is pretty small."

"I'm impressed so far," said Tim. "But let's discuss what you are proposing that Virtual Analyzer actually be able to do. What is the functionality you see in the product?"

"OK," said Bob. "Let's answer that question three ways:"

First, Virtual Analyzer will have six major modules corresponding to the needs we found in the market. They are Client Information Management; Move, Add, and Change Processing; Vendor Invoice Processing and Vendor Invoice Payment; Invoice Analyzer; Rate Optimizer; and Industry Information Management.

Second, Virtual Analyzer provides six primary reporting and analysis capabilities. Let me define each one:

1. Inventory management reports show the exact telecommunications services used at each site, including the exact features, the service provider, and any other tracking information desired by the client.

2. Detail tracking reports provide data on costs by site, service provider, and user-defined categories.

3. Cost allocation reports show cost by site, service, service provider, and user-defined categories. Our clients will use this report to charge back costs to groups within their organizations.

4. Usage allocation reports provide the client with a flexible way to allocate usage to projects or entities in

EXHIBIT 5

Comparison of Virtual Analyzer to its Competition
Teletron, Inc.

Company	Teletron	Quantum-Shift	Tenet International	Simplexity	Intera	Profit-Line
Service Offerings:						
Cost Management	Yes	Yes	Yes	Yes	Yes	Yes
Bill Optimization	Yes	Yes	Yes	Yes	Yes	Yes
Bill Management	Yes	No	Yes	Likely	Yes	Yes
Full Service	Yes	Some	Yes	Yes	Some	Some
Inventory/Infrastructure Management	Yes	Yes	Yes	No	Yes	Yes
Target Market	Medium to Large	Medium to Large	Small to Medium	Residential, SOHO, Medium, Carriers	Small to Medium	Small to Medium
Internet Capability	Full	Nearly Full	Nearly Full	Some	Nearly Full	Some
Name of Platform	Virtual Analyzer	InterAct	Copyrighted ASP Software	N/A	Smart Partner	Bill Management

Source: Company records.

case they want to study the actual cost of a project or organization.

5. Trend analysis reports track usage and cost trends by a variety of dimensions, allowing the user to detect abuses and areas for improved services.

6. Variance analysis reports identify any significant changes in cost or usage measures.

Through these capabilities, our clients will be able to generate many unique and customizable reports. They can create reports based on certain factors they define and produce a report that is specific to their individual needs. The software will

reside on our server here in Bloomington. We will be linked electronically to the carriers or providers as well as our clients. As clients update their database, the system will automatically contact the carriers for adjustments. Likewise, when there is a new contract or an invoice for one of our customers, the carrier will send it electronically to us, and Virtual Analyzer will update the customer's database.

Third, there is a more detailed and technical description of the features and capabilities of each major routine in the software being designed. If you are interested, I have a handout on the capabilities of each of the major routines. (See Exhibit 6.)

EXHIBIT 6
Virtual Analyzer's Features and Capabilities
Teletron, Inc.

Client Information Management—Reports and Analysis	
Client Information Management	The Client Information Management System collects, processes, and presents all of a client's telecom information. This includes all of the services they use, who provides the service, locations where the services are used, what equipment is used to provide the service, how much it costs, and how it is used.
Data Acquisition	Cost and usage data are acquired from service providers in three ways: EDI, CD, and from paper bills. EDI is the preferred mechanism and will be used whenever possible. CD data will be used when EmDI is not available. Paper bills will be used when they are the only available source.
Data Processing	When the data has been collected, it is processed. Processing includes aggregation and allocation of cost and usage data into user-defined categories based on user-defined time periods.
Inventory Management	An inventory of the services used, the providers of the service, the locations where the services are used, and the components (equipment) used to provide the services are maintained in the inventory. The inventory provides the basic structure by which all cost and usage information is aggregated and allocated.
Monthly Detail Tracking	All of the cost and usage information provided monthly by the service providers is captured and tracked. This includes translating each service provider's charge codes into standard (Teletron) charge codes. The data can be presented in the form of a "Teletron" invoice that breaks down the data (cost and usage) into easy to read and understandable formats.
Cost Allocation	Costs are aggregated and allocated by location, service provider, type of service, type of component, any user defined code, or any combination of these. For example, Virtual Analyzer can aggregate and allocate by service type by location. If locations are assigned a user-defined code for "Office Type," Virtual Analyzer can aggregate and allocate by service type by office type by type of component, etc.
Usage Allocation	Usage is aggregated and allocated by up to 13 categories that include the basic inventory items (location, service type, service provider, etc.) as well as categories that can be defined by the client. These include time of day, time of month, length of call, type of call, etc. Each client determines the categories into which usage data are aggregated.
Trend Analysis	Trend Analysis is performed and reported on both cost and usage data. The reports will provide the information in both words and graphical representations. Trends analyzed will include month to previous month, other time periods (such as quarter to previous quarter and year-to-date to previous year-to-date), current month to same month of previous year, etc. These reports can be run by location, service provider, service type, user-defined codes, etc.
Variance Reporting	Variance Reporting refers to reports that show changes to the client's information. This includes new accounts/components, missing accounts/components, changes in charges from one month to the next, changes to the inventory, etc.

EXHIBIT 6 (*Continued*)

User-Defined Codes	Users have the ability to assign codes to locations, services, and/or components. The user defines a category for each code, identifies the valid codes for each category, and then assigns the code(s) to the appropriate inventory item. For example, the client may have their locations assigned to "Regions." They can also assign codes that identify the type of location (sales office, distribution center, manufacturing facility, warehouse, etc.).
Chargebacks	Virtual Analyzer will create a standard ASCII delimited file that will contain user-specified data for input into the client's accounting system.

Move, Add, Change (MAC) Processing

MAC Processing	MAC Processing tracks the processing required for implementing a change. It is an external system in that it tracks the work done by the service provider and not work done by Teletron.
Online Request	Users will input their requests for changes to service through a Web-based request system. This will be linked to Virtual Analyzer's inventory so that the user can select the service provider, service, and/or component.
Service Order Creation	Service Orders will be created from the MAC Request. Templates will be developed and used for each type of Service Order. Multiple Service Orders can be generated from a single MAC Request. For example, a client may change its long distance provider from MCI to AT&T. Service Orders are created for AT&T, MCI, and every local service provider. The Service Orders created are sent electronically via e-mail or fax to the service provider.
Service Order Tracking	The progress of every Service Order issued is tracked. Each Service Order type has milestones associated with it that detail what needs to be done and when it should be done. If a milestone date passes, the person assigned to manage the Service Order is notified. As each milestone is completed, the system updates the status of the Service Order. The client can view the status of its requests at any time.
Issue Tracking	Each issue that arises during the completion of a Service Order is logged. The Teletron employee assigned to manage a Service Order, the service provider, and the client can communicate through the Issue Log.
Update Inventory	Virtual Analyzer Inventory will automatically be updated by the MAC system. New services requested will be added to the Inventory. Cancelled services will be marked and tracked until the service provider has sent the final bill.
Reporting	The MAC system will provide multiple reports that will detail information by service provider, by location, by type of MAC, by type of service, etc.

Vendor Invoice Processing (VIP) and Vendor Invoice Payment Program (VIPP)

VIP/VIPP Processing	The VIP/VIPP Processing system presents each invoice to the client. The client determines which invoice to pay, how much to pay, and when to make the payments. A payment is made for each invoice from the service providers.
Account Setup	A payment account is set up with the bank that is used to pay the bills for the client. If a service provider accepts electronic payments, the billing accounts are set up for electronic payment.
Payment Authorization	The client views each invoice and enters the amount they authorize to pay and when payment should be released. Multiple payments can be authorized for a single invoice.
Money Transfer	The money to pay the authorized amounts is transferred from an account in the client's bank to the payment account.
Payment Creation	There are two ways payments can be made: electronic and check. Electronic payments are transfers from the payment account directly into an account specified by the service provider. This is the preferred method of payment. Checks are created and mailed to those service providers that cannot accept electronic payments. One payment is created for each invoice received.

EXHIBIT 6 (*Continued*)

Payment Tracking	The date each payment (electronic or check) is processed is tracked, including the dates the payments are created, sent, and cleared in the payment account.
Reporting	The VIP/VIPP system has reports that identify the payment accounts, monthly payment log by client by account, outstanding balances, etc.

Invoice Analyzer

Invoice Analyzer	The Invoice Analyzer reviews each invoice against a set of rules that are maintained in a database, then logs every violation for evaluation by an analyst. The client determines what to do with each finding.
Specify Rules	The rules used to analyze an invoice are maintained in a database. The rules are developed by the analysts and can be applied for a specific service provider, type of service, specific billing plan, etc. For example, a rule may be to identify all short calls (i.e., calls that are less than 30 seconds). Another rule may be to identify all long calls (i.e., calls longer than 2 hours).
Review Invoices	The main logic of the system is to apply each rule to an invoice. When invoice data are found to violate a rule, this is logged in the Findings table. It is possible for a single invoice data item (such as a specific call) to violate more than one rule.
Analyze Findings	The violations identified and logged are summarized for the analyst. An analyst reviews the findings and determines whether a specific finding is legitimate or not. If legitimate, it is marked as an "opportunity" for a savings or for a credit. Analysts can review aggregate findings or each specific finding. For example, the review may have found 300 short calls and 25 long calls. All of the short calls can be classified as an opportunity at one time. Alternatively, each long call can be reviewed and only those that are questioned are marked as opportunities.
Authorize Findings	The opportunities are reviewed with the client. The client authorizes which opportunities to pursue and which ones to ignore.
Savings & Credits	Savings and Credits tables are updated with authorized opportunities. The Savings and Credits table is used to track implementation of the findings.
Generate MACs	MACs are generated for the authorized opportunities. Each MAC is for a specific service provider and can contain one or more opportunities. A Teletron analyst determines whether to combine opportunities or to submit them separately. The MAC system is used to track the progress of implementing an authorized opportunity.
Reporting	The Invoice Analyzer has reports that identify the findings, opportunities, authorized opportunities, etc.

Rate Optimizer

Rate Optimizer	The Rate Optimizer system maintains a database of Billing Plans with rates. It is used by the Invoice Analyzer to verify that proper rates were used for an invoice item. It is also used to identify rate plans that can save money. There are two primary types of Billing Plans that are kept, commercial and private. Commercial Plans are plans that are available to the general public. Private Plans are contracts negotiated between a service provider and a company. All Billing Plans must be published.
Database Maintenance	The Billing Plans database can be maintained manually. This includes adding new plans, modifying existing plans, etc. Notes about specific plans, features, rates, etc. can be made by analysts.
Database Population	Most of the data in the Billing Plans database will come from a third party. The system will use this data to populate and maintain the data. It is able to distinguish data between the third party information and the data entered manually.
Build Billing Plan Profile	Rate Optimizer analyzes the Billing Plans and develops a profile that identifies the services covered, the qualifications to obtain the lowest rates, the probability that the vendor will give discounts, etc.

EXHIBIT 6 (*Continued*)

Build Client Profile	Rate Optimizer analyzes a client's telecom requirements and builds a profile that identifies the services required, the number of sites, components, and the mix of each.
Find Potential Plans	Rate Optimizer will match a client profile against the Billing Plan profiles and identify all Billing Plans that are candidates for supplying the services needed at lower cost.
Calculate Potential Savings	For each candidate Billing Plan, the potential savings are calculated. This is done by applying the client's profile against the qualifications of the potential plans and usage and calculating the cost of the candidate plan.
Reporting	Rate Optimizer generates reports on the Billing Plans, including updates, special offers, etc. The primary report identifies potential plans for saving money with the calculated potential savings.

Industry Information Management

Industry Information Management	The Industry Information Management system aggregates client telecommunication information into a database that views the information by industry rather than by client.
Maintain Aggregation Criteria	The primary criterion for aggregation is the industry. There are additional criteria that can be specified to further refine the data such as annual revenue, number of employees, geographic region, etc.
Data Aggregation	Each client's data is aggregated into the industry database as specified by the criteria established. Once in the industry database, the identity of the client is lost.
Cost Analysis	Costs are analyzed by industry, service type, service provider, component type, time of year, etc., and any combination. It includes calculating average costs by cost category, service type, etc. For example, the average cost of a long distance call by service provider can be calculated.
Usage Analysis	Usage is analyzed by industry, service type, service provider, component type, time of day, time of month, time of year, etc., and any combination.
Service Provider Analysis	Service provider analysis includes analyzing what the actual average cost of a call is for a service provider for different volumes of calls (100 per month vs. 5,000 month vs. 10,000 per month, etc.) for calls from different geographic regions. It also includes an evaluation of performance for completing service orders, annual volume of billing errors, etc.
Trend Analysis	The system also analyzes trends in the industry, such as percent of telecom expense by service type, total expenditures, total costs by service type, etc.
Industry Reports	Virtual Analyzer will provide both standard industry reports and custom reports requested by service providers, industry analysts, and corporations who want to evaluate their performance against industry standards.

Source: Company records.

"Maybe later," replied Tim. "Right now, I'm more interested in exactly how you are planning to bring Virtual Analyzer to market."

"OK," replied Dennis. "That is my area, at least for now. While we want the client to use all of the Virtual Analyzer modules as a single package, we will allow some customers to pick and choose among the various services. However, we believe that a customer must at least subscribe to the Client Information Management and Vendor Invoice Processing and Vendor Invoice Payment modules in order to realize any significant advantages from the Virtual Analyzer system."

"Next," Dennis continued. "We think that parts of the software are 'protectable'. . . we intend to file a patent application when we finish the beta test in two years."

"Great, great . . . tell me how we are planning to price the product," asked Tim. "You mentioned the customers will be able to pick and choose between the various services . . . how is that going to be figured into the pricing?" Dennis explained,

Tim, pricing will be based on the size of the company and the number of modules they choose to use. Larger companies using only two modules would be charged about two percent of their monthly telecommunications cost while smaller companies using all the modules would be billed around six percent of their monthly telecommunications expense. So we expect our average customer revenue to be about $25,000 per month which is roughly four percent of their average monthly telecommunications bill.

"Good," replied Tim. "Tell me, how do we get to market? We have no experience in selling software. What are the channels?"

"We have three choices," replied Dennis.

We can create a sales force and go after the clients one at a time. Clearly, we will have to do some of that, but it is very expensive. Alternatively, we can use our Web site to sell the software. That method is cheap and will work for some clients, but we think that most customers won't buy our solution by seeing a demonstration package on the Internet. They will want someone to visit them. Finally, we can create a series of channel partners. These are companies who sell complementary services, like help desk companies or information technology consulting companies. Some examples might be IBM, EDS, and some of the large accounting firms. We give them a piece of the revenue in exchange for their selling the product for us. Our guess is that we will have to use all three approaches.

"OK. Well done, you guys. Give my thanks to the rest of your team," replied Tim. "You have clearly thought about the issues from our customers' standpoint. I like what I am hearing. But I can't invest money without a return, despite how good an idea we have here. Have you estimated how much this part of our transformation will cost us?"

"Now comes the bad news," offered Bob.

This is one complex piece of software. I have worked on some big projects before and this one will be among the most complex ones I have seen. We have to imbed the thought processes our auditing analysts have been using for ten plus years into computer code. So the analysis time will be significant. We looked at going outside for the systems development work, but the cost right now is out of sight. And most of the consultants don't have any capacity anyway since they are all working on Y2K problems. So we are going to have to hire our own staff.

In addition to designing and testing the software itself, there are lots of other costs that have to be considered as part of the investment. We need to buy lots of big servers. And we will need to translate all the data tables used by the providers in their contracts and invoices into a standard table that our system can use. This task by itself will be huge. We found out that AT&T alone has something like 800 different billing systems—each with a different data structure. Plus what we worked on already—the market research—costs money. And the time we are going to spend contacting customers and providers must be considered as part of the investment as well.

Our best estimate is that the project will take the rest of this year, all of next year, and be ready for alpha and beta testing by early 2001. We should not count on any revenue from Virtual Analyzer before 2002. Any revenue we get until then will come from operating our old business model.

"Yeah," added Dennis.

As this chart (Exhibit 7) shows, we expect the total investment needed to achieve this transformation will cost

EXHIBIT 7
Investment and Financial Projections for 1999 to 2006 Teletron, Inc.

Year	Revenue (in $000)	EBITDA (in $000)	Investment (in $000)
1999	$11,061	$971	$3,173
2000	12,585	1,801	2,838
2001	10,271	1,124	3,382
2002	5,393	(891)	1,000
2003	16,575	5,540	1,000
2004	33,601	15,612	1,500
2005	60,343	27,947	2,000
2006	108,368	49,598	3,000

Source: Company records.

us over $9 million spread out over 1999 through 2001. Plus, we have to count on added costs for enhancements of between $1 million and $3 million each year from then on. That is definitely the bad news. But . . . we think that we can definitely hit your revenue targets coming from this new business model. Getting to $100 million in revenue with nearly $50 million in EBITDA is really doable. After all, look at the size of the market. We only need a tiny percent of the $5 billion market to hit our 2006 target revenue.

"That sucking sound you hear is my gasping for air!!" replied Tim. "I had no idea that our transformation would cost this much. So . . . you are telling me that to make this part of our transformation work, we have to spend over $9 million. That is quite a load for a $7 million company. We will have to raise that money . . . clearly Teletron won't generate that kind of cash internally."

Decision Time

"Guys," said Tim. "Again, let me thank you for your effort on this project. I need to consider whether I want to bet this company's future on this idea. And . . . I have to prepare a presentation for the board of directors that includes the return on investment from this endeavor for them to consider at its May 4 meeting in Bloomington."

As the two task force leaders left his office, Tim Lybrook began to construct his presentation to the board. (See Exhibit 8.) He started by listing some of the benefits of the idea. Tim wondered what other benefits he was missing. He then started to make a list of risks. Tim stopped for now. He knew that there were additional risks he had not yet considered. He had to go to a meeting with the builder of his new building. But he knew that he had to finish the presentation. Of course, he first had to decide whether he really wanted to go ahead with the project.

EXHIBIT 8
Preliminary List of Benefits and Risks of Making the Investment
Teletron, Inc.

Benefits

- A huge market with generally weak competitors.

- A steady revenue stream as an application service provider (ASP)—remember the value of an annuity.

- Simple support process as an ASP with all software directly under Teletron's control.

- Ease of initial installation with no on-site activity since an ASP.

- Ease of software upgrades with no requirement to change client software.

- Simpler and less expensive EDI/XML connectivity to carriers from one site.

- Simple pricing model ($ per month per user for each module subscribed to).

- An ROI of ? percent.

- High barriers to entry—requires expertise and lots of capital.

Risks

- Required reliance on the Internet, but we have no experience using this communications medium.

- Relatively untried concept.

- Market acceptance is subject to a high level of uncertainty and risk.

- Difficulty in predicting future growth rates.

- Sales cycle may be long.

- Excessive length of time until revenue starts flowing from the offering.

- Difficulty in reaching the market—have to use channel partners not under our control.

FastTrack IT Integration for the Sallie Mae Merger

This transaction combines our capital strength and sales capabilities with USA Group's premier service quality. . . . It would be difficult to overstate the significance of this deal to our three principal constituencies: students, schools, and shareholders.[1]

—Albert L. Lord, Vice Chairman and Chief Executive Officer,
Sallie Mae

In June 2000, the two largest players in the education finance industry announced their intent to merge: Sallie Mae of Reston, Virginia, would acquire USA Group of Indianapolis, Indiana. The merger announcement in *The Wall Street Journal* highlighted the strategic role that USA Group's software applications would play in the new combined company: USA Group's loan-guarantee-processing business and its campus-loan origination and loan-processing products were expected to make the combined company more competitive.[2]

Although Sallie Mae held a teleconference for all employees on the day of the merger announcement, new tensions about the future set in quickly. People were stunned. USA Group was our largest competitor, and there was a lot of uncertainty about how this could impact employment for all of us. There was so much anxiety on both sides. People had built their careers at these companies.

—Cindy Gunn, Vice President of Computer Operations
for Sallie Mae

Sallie Mae planned to cut its work force by 1,700 employees, or 25 percent, by the end of 2001, as it integrated its operations with USA Group. Most of these reductions (1,400) would be in its information-technology and customer-service areas; the remainder (300) would be administration and headquarters jobs.[3]

The busy season for the education-financing industry is in the summer: about 60 percent of loan processing occurs during the summer months in preparation for the fall semester, with June as the peak month. When the government's Direct Lending program had undergone a major software change about 1 year earlier, there had been a number of publicized bottlenecks and processing errors with student loans during the busy season. Sallie Mae's management team didn't want to make the same mistakes; to ensure that its own customers would not go to a competitor, customer-facing operations would need to be completed before the coming summer season, with no perceived loss of service.

Some were afraid the merger might meet shareholder objectives but would hurt the customer. The customer concerns were that service would suffer, agility would be low, and we would create a large bureaucracy. We were combining the volume of two company's loans on one system with a new management team and brand-new architecture. And we were doing it just before peak season.

—Hamed Omar, Senior Vice President, Technology Group

Company Histories

Sallie Mae was founded in 1972 as a government-sponsored enterprise (GSE) in Reston, Virginia, to provide a secondary market for banks and other lenders to sell their student loans. Prior to the merger, Sallie Mae had a $50 billion portfolio of student loans and was the largest funding source and servicer for student loans in the United States. The company's primary role was to purchase student loans from banks and other lenders, creating a secondary market and freeing up funds for the institutions to lend out money to other borrowers.

Albert L. Lord, Sallie Mae's CEO, had been a major catalyst in transforming the company from a GSE to a publicly held

[1]PR Newswire (SLM Holding Corporation), June 15, 2000, "Sallie Mae and USA Group Reach Agreement to Combine."

[2]The Wall Street Journal, June 16, 2000, "Sallie Mae Is Set to Buy Assets of USA Group In Cash-Stock Deal."

[3]The Wall Street Journal, Sept. 1, 2000, "Sallie Mae Will Cut Jobs After Acquiring USA Group."

business. In the early 1990s he helped streamline the company's operations, but then left the company in 1993 when the board opposed his plans for restructuring the company. Two years later, he led a dissident slate of eight directors that was elected to the 21-member board and was able successfully to launch a plan to reposition the company from a buyer of loans to a competitive lender to students.[4]

As CEO since 1997, Lord began phasing out the company's government-sponsored status, despite some internal opposition.[5] Lord also switched its marketing focus to get closer to the customer. Rather than working solely with banks and financial institutions, the company began marketing to students through the schools. At the time of the merger announcement in June 2000, Sallie Mae was a $14 billion public firm.

USA Group was originally founded in 1960 as USA Funds, a not-for-profit company based in the Indianapolis, Indiana, area. At the time of the merger, USA Group had a $16 billion portfolio of student loans, was the largest guarantor of student loans in the U.S., and had been aggressively growing its fee-based businesses of loan origination and default collection. In 1999, the company had an excess of $150 million in revenues over expenses, and employed 3,000 people, across 20 states, the District of Columbia, and Canada.

Laying the Groundwork for the Merger

As Sallie Mae entered the new millennium, its executive team was concerned that the company could not maintain its double-digit growth in 2004 and beyond if it did not expand its servicing role. At the same time, USA Group's executive team was seeking a buyer to gain access to the capital it needed to take advantage of market opportunities to grow the company's private loans and for-profit collections businesses. USA Group became an acquisition target for Sallie Mae for three primary reasons:

1. Its complementary student loan services would result in Sallie Mae having a role in the entire life cycle of the student loan, from origination to default collection.
2. Economies of scale from combining operations would allow Sallie Mae to continue being profitable in the face of narrowing margins.
3. Sallie Mae leaders could leverage the information technology and marketing prowess of USA Group to grow revenues.

Prior to nailing down the final offer, Sallie Mae sent a team of four IT leaders to Indianapolis in May 2000 to conduct due diligence for the merger. The goals of the visit were to validate the information about the company that had been received and to report back to the CEO about any previously unforeseen issues that could materially impact the purchase offer.

> My colleagues and I were pretty impressed with what USA Group was doing from a technical standpoint. Their approach was thoughtful, strategic, and focused. We were impressed with their ability to make progress on strategic activities . . . and they had executed very effectively . . . . They were a good step ahead of us in the rollout and deployment of automated call-center technologies as well as tools to manage their hardware and software assets. We had languished behind and couldn't get focused on newer technologies. I believe this was due in part to a period of several changes in IT management in the previous years, making it difficult to focus on long-term projects. In contrast, the USA Group management team was very stable and had worked together for a long time.
>
> —Cindy Gunn, Vice President of Computer Operations
> for Sallie Mae

The New Merged Company

USA Group was acquired by Sallie Mae for $770 million on July 31, 2000. The new Sallie Mae became a single source of service for customers—from the point of loan application to successful repayment (see Exhibit 1).

The immediate financial goals for the merger were to reduce headcount by 1,700 (25 percent) and to reduce costs by 40 percent. Due to significant redundancies across the two companies, nine customer service centers would be reduced to six, and four data centers would be consolidated into one. In addition to successfully achieving its cost reduction goals for the merger, the combined company sought to attain double-digit growth in its business as a result of the merger.

Stock options were issued to all USA Group employees when the merger was finalized. Since USA Group was founded as a not-for-profit company, this was a new financial opportunity for many of its managers.

> We were really excited about getting stock options. We could exercise half of them in June 2001 and half of them in June 2002. A lot of people took advantage of the options since the stock price more than doubled.
>
> —Paula Lohss, Manager, Application Development
> Support Services

Another major change for USA Group employees was adjusting to a results-driven, for-profit culture in which risk-taking was viewed as positive as long as the risks were well managed.

> One of the biggest differences between USA Group and Sallie Mae is the increased adherence to plan and budget. We now have shareholders. Many of our employees have always

---

[4]Investor's Business Daily (Los Angeles, CA), July 11, 2001, "Sallie Mae's Albert Lord: Hard Work Helped Him Repair Lender."

[5]The privatization process is scheduled to be completed in 2006.

EXHIBIT 1
Three Basic Steps of the Student Loan Business

1) The student application originates either with a lending institution, a school financial aid office, or online through a student loan originator such as Sallie Mae.

2) After the application is submitted, a loan guarantor processes the loan; a loan approval comes with a federal government guarantee that the lender will be paid back. Guarantors are either state agencies or not-for-profit entities that provide loan insurance to lenders or holders of Federal Family Education Loan Program (FFELP) loans.

3) The loan is serviced throughout its life, which at Sallie Mae is an average of 10 years. Most students begin repayment after graduation. Default prevention and collection services work together to ensure that the highest possible percentage of loans are repaid.

worked in a not-for-profit environment and the change was somewhat of a shock.

> —*Larry Morgan, Senior Vice President, Application System Development*

Within one calendar year from the June announcement of the merger, the IT group of the new company would integrate its most critical system applications and IT operations. To realize the publicized cost savings, a single IT headquarters location would be selected, the data centers would be consolidated, and 500 technologies within the two companies would need to be rationalized, transitioned, or retired. One of the most contentious decisions would be which of the two homegrown loan-servicing systems to eliminate.

> Many mergers and acquisitions fail; more fail than succeed. So it's very important to do the right things when you're trying to bring two corporations together. You also have to do this with very good execution—do it right—or you will go out of business, or will definitely flounder.
>
> —*Hamed Omar, Senior Vice President, Technology Group*

The IT Organizations

The Sallie Mae IT organization had undergone a great deal of change in the years prior to the merger. CIO turnover had been high, making it difficult for the company to maintain a coherent IT architecture. Plans for integrating the IT operations for two recent acquisitions (Nellie Mae of Braintree, Massachusetts, and Student Loan Funding Resources of Cincinnati) had not yet been completed. Several strategic applications had been totally outsourced, and the IT work force had been cut back to less than 500 just prior to the merger announcement.

In contrast, the IT organization at USA Group had a fairly stable history and had grown to 600 personnel: approximately 400 developers and 200 operations staff. CIO Greg Clancy had

a 20-year tenure with the company, and his IT management team of the past 6 to 7 years was well-oiled, with a proven track record for developing complex systems and keeping operational costs low.

Within the 5 years prior to the merger, more than $100 million had been invested by USA Group in two internally developed service applications: (1) the Eagle II guarantee agency system, which tracked all federal loan origination and guarantee activities administered on behalf of guarantors, and (2) the Unity loan-servicing system.

A new call-center routing application, which routes incoming customer calls based on loan-record characteristics and the skill base of available call-center representatives, had won a Smithsonian innovation award in 1999 and led to a recognition for outstanding customer service in *CIO Magazine* Top 100 in 2000.[6]

PeopleSoft modules for financials and human resources had also been implemented under project teams led by IT groups within the business units.

> The former USA Group teams had worked together for a long time. One of the major secrets of our success is that we know how to work with each other. The group in Reston didn't have the same cohesion. CIO turnover had been very high, projects took longer to complete, and there seemed to be more infighting.
>
> —*Greg Clancy, Chief Information Officer*

On June 15, Clancy was privately informed that he would be CIO of the new Sallie Mae. Although the public announcement of his appointment was not made until August 1, both internal and external communications made it apparent to the Reston IT group that IT leadership at the new Sallie Mae would

---

[6]CIO Magazine, Aug. 15, 2000, "IDG's CIO Magazine Honors Top 100 Companies," "CIO-100 Winners Recognized for Outstanding Customer Service."

be primarily in the hands of the former USA Group team. For example, according to a report in *The Washington Post*, a Sallie Mae executive vice president stated in a June 16 announcement that, "Indianapolis has a . . . very high-quality work force, and in terms of the technology environment, probably a more stable one."[7]

> Those of us in [Sallie Mae] IT leadership quickly made the decision to make this work. I was 98 percent certain that I would not have a job after the merger was completed, but as a shareholder and longtime member of Sallie Mae's management team, I believed it was absolutely the best thing for Sallie Mae to do this.
>
> —*Cindy Gunn, Vice President of Computer Operations for Sallie Mae*

> Cindy Gunn really helped on the Reston side: she kept a great attitude . . . and her group was still motivated, despite the fact that many of them would lose their jobs after the merger was completed. She was the linchpin.
>
> —*Greg Clancy, Chief Information Officer*

Soon after the merger was announced, all critical systems were assigned to teams of two technology "champions"—one from Sallie Mae and one from USA Group. Together, the two champions were responsible for conducting a full disclosure and comparative analysis of the relevant systems. Knowing that Sallie Mae executives would need to have a high degree of confidence in the capabilities of the acquired USA Group team as each system alternative was examined, the USA Group IT managers encouraged their people to take advantage of every opportunity to demonstrate their abilities to develop innovative applications and to handle operations that would be triple the size of the systems they had managed in the past. They also changed their decision processes so that they could make decisions faster:

> We had to focus on making decisions quickly, so our decision-making process had to change. We went from presenting highly detailed written justifications to presenting key bullet points on PowerPoint slides. You also had only one meeting to present your case. Over time we have moved from a 5-year to a 3-year NPV [net present value]. We still use this macro-level decision-making process today.
>
> —*Sharon Vincent, Director of Network Services*

> We were told to have confidence in our ability as we exchanged and gathered information. For each application decision, we spent a lot of time and effort trying to prove that our systems were the best choice. We took charge, and we were very assertive. I think all of these interactions really helped us gain their confidence.
>
> —*Becky Robinson, Director of Systems Management*

---

[7]*The Washington Post*, Sept. 1, 2000, "Sallie Mae to Cut Staff 25 Percent."

> We were to be assertive, yet not burn bridges. We kept it professional . . . .And when an announcement was made, there wasn't a lot of animosity.
>
> —*Jon Jones, Director of Client Server Computing*

The IT Headquarters Decision

The decision about the physical location of the consolidated data center was not formally made until October 2000. Sallie Mae had established measurable cost-cutting goals with their merger consultants (McKinsey & Company), and each side (Reston and Indianapolis) was charged with developing a formal cost/benefit analysis for having the IT headquarters located in their city. The cost advantages became pretty clear: operating a consolidated data center out of Reston, Virginia, would be much more expensive than out of the acquired Indianapolis area facility.

- IT personnel costs in Indianapolis were estimated to be about 30 percent less than in the Reston area, which had become a mid-Atlantic Silicon Valley phenomenon.
- Running the data center out of an expanded Indianapolis facility would save an estimated annual $2 million or more in occupancy costs due to the significantly lower costs in this Midwest city.
- The new Sallie Mae data-center facility in Reston could be leased out at an attractive price.

Shortly after the relocation decision, a lease agreement with a new tenant, beginning July 1, 2001, was signed for the Reston data center.

The First Data Center Consolidation

In the months prior to the USA Group merger, Sallie Mae had been working to integrate the operations of Nellie Mae, a company Sallie Mae had purchased in 1999. Nellie Mae was a major originator of student loans based in Braintree, Massachusetts, with 150 employees. However, the integration project had been slow going. The 16 IT professionals at Nellie Mae already had severance packages in hand, but their severance pay was dependent on a successful operational move and knowledge transfer to Sallie Mae.

When Jo Lee Hayes of USA Group took on this small data center consolidation project, severance of IT professionals was only 3 months away. Working side-by-side with Nellie Mae's IT operations head and a team of six to eight people, Hayes defined the current Nellie Mae systems, established a move strategy, and worked through the systems integration and knowledge transfer issues. Successful on-time completion of this data center project was a visible early win for the Indianapolis-based IT team.

> Everybody knew where he or she stood, and there was no question about what needed to be done. We had a hard-and-fast

date, and people were motivated to combine operations successfully because severance was tied to successful knowledge transfer. . . . It was thrilling, impossible, and such a rush when we actually pulled it off.

—*Jo Lee Hayes, Vice President, Business Solutions Group*

Critical Application Decisions

The types of factors used to determine the fate of current applications included system functionality, scalability, performance, the number and types of interactions with other systems, whether the system was custom or purchased, and if purchased, whether the latest version of the application was currently installed.

Now you're talking about jobs. Now you're talking about changing people's lives in a big way with whatever system is selected.

—*Allan Horn, Vice President, Technology Operations*

The analyses under the two assigned champions (one for Sallie Mae, one for USA Group) led to one of three outcomes:

- A consensus recommendation was reached amicably.
- A consensus recommendation was reached, but after much conflict and strife.
- A consensus recommendation could not be reached, which meant escalating the decision to the executive level.

Champions were technology owners who had a chance to show top management that they could make decisions and execute them. It didn't reflect well if the decision had to be turned over to senior officers.

—*Jo Lee Hayes, Vice President, Business Solutions Group*

The choice between the two custom-developed loan-servicing applications was the most contentious decision and had major IT work-force effects. Larry Morgan, head of application development for USA Group at the time of the merger, had been responsible for managing the development of both loan-servicing systems. Morgan first joined Sallie Mae in the mid-1980s: he was hired away from Pennsylvania Higher Education, where he had helped to develop a loan-servicing system being used by both Sallie Mae and USA Group. Due to Sallie Mae's fast growth, a new loan-servicing system (Class) had to be developed and installed within a 2-year time frame. In 1991, USA Group lured him to Indianapolis to build a system with even more functionality (Unity), installed in 1994.

At the time of the merger, Sallie Mae's Class system was a 15-year-old application written in COBOL and CICS, maintained by more than 75 IT people in Reston. The only major change to the system had been converting it from an IMS (networked) database to IBM's DB2 (relational) database. USA Group's Unity system used a network IDMS database supported by Computer Associates.

The gap analysis that was performed for the two loan-servicing applications (see criteria in Exhibit 2) did not result in a clear choice. Although there were some concerns about the scalability of the IDMS database application, the functionality of the Unity system was more advanced. Since no consensus recommendation could be reached, the loan-servicing system decision was put into the hands of the senior officers of the company, who depended heavily on the advice of their merger consultants.

Integration risk issues began to weigh heavily on the final decision by top management. One major risk factor was the need for extensive manual review during the conversion process due to transaction complexities that had been coded into the systems to accommodate special situations. For example, updates involving retroactive changes (such as student status changes) required access to record histories, and unique decision rules (for student payment amounts) had been coded into the Unity loan processing system for lenders who had implemented incentive programs for timely student payments. Another major risk factor stemmed from the fact that these systems were servicing a population with little financial management experience (i.e., undergraduate students): System changes visible to customers therefore typically resulted in significantly higher service call volumes.

McKinsey weighed in heavily in this decision. They generally agreed with us that the Unity system was better, but there wasn't enough difference in functionality for them to break their standard decision rule: adopt the system of the dominant company in order to reduce the merger risks.

—*Greg Clancy, Chief Information Officer*

EXHIBIT 2
Gap Analysis Criteria for Loan Servicing Applications

Scalability
Cost
Performance (response time, concurrent users)
Reliability
Partnership (including customization for external partners)
Marketplace Differentiation
Quality (robustness, customer satisfaction)
Technology/Architecture
Customer Service Security
Flexibility
Compliance
Functionality Differences
Vendor Relationships
Resource Skill Set (including market availability)
Recoverability
Interdependencies

The final point came down to risk and timing. If the conversion was to be done by April, it simply wasn't possible to convert $50 billion in loans from Class to Unity, within the time constraints required, without presenting serious problems to our operational areas.

—Larry Morgan, Senior Vice President, Application System Development

Although the employees of both companies fought hard to keep the custom systems they had developed, and the battles were fierce, once the application decisions were made, they began working together to implement them. In the end, about 78 IT employees were retained in Reston to maintain the Class system. The plan was to add new Web functionality and to complete the implementation of an advanced call-center capability for the Class system within the second year of the new merged company.

When you build a system, it becomes a part of you . . . both sides wanted to keep their system alive, and the battles were fierce. I was fortunate enough to have worked with both the Class and Unity teams in the construction of those systems. I was an insider to both teams. I also had established relationships with the new senior management team. . . . I had perhaps the easiest job during the integration period.

—Larry Morgan, Senior Vice President, Application System Development

In contrast, implementation time was not the same critical concern when the back-office system for the finance function was selected. USA Group had implemented PeopleSoft modules for both finance and human resources during the second half of the 1990s. Sallie Mae was using an older and clearly less functional package for finance (Walker Interactive). Here the key trade-off was between capturing cost savings as quickly as possible by converting to the Sallie Mae package, or postponing these cost savings in order to have a more robust packaged solution that would be newly configured for the combined company.

Since this was a back-office application, rather than a customer-facing application, the Sallie Mae executive team accepted the technical team recommendation to adopt the PeopleSoft suite for both finance and human resources for the new Sallie Mae. By delaying the implementation until the fall of 2001, the company would also be one of the first large corporations to implement a Web-based version of the PeopleSoft package (version 8.0).

Retaining IT Staff

At the time when the company announced that the bulk of IT operations would move to Indianapolis, the HR department was ready with a detailed severance package program for the people in Reston who chose not to move to Indianapolis. IT jobs in the Mid-Atlantic area were plentiful at the time, and Sallie Mae's Reston data center was just across the street from Oracle's East Coast headquarters.

One third of the Reston IT staff (the most critical IT employees) were offered generous retention bonuses on top of severance pay to encourage them to stay until the merger was complete. Performance measures, including successful knowledge transfer, were built into the retention bonus contracts for the Reston staff.

You can't pull off a project like this just through a project plan. Good people make the difference. Even if people were losing their jobs, they needed to know they had value.

—John Bennett, Project Manager for Data Center Relocation

The company decided to err on giving too much, and that left a good feeling in the company—that you can't be a loser in this merger. . . . When you do the right thing with employees, they pitch in and make sure that the merger is successful.

—Hamed Omar, Senior Vice President, Technology Group

The team had pride in what it had built and wanted to turn it over with their heads held high. The severance packages and retention bonuses were certainly better than industry standard . . . . Members of my team also knew early on when their jobs were scheduled to end. . . . All of these factors contributed to the success of the transition. . . . We leveraged what could have been negative into something positive. . . . Several took their severance money and used it to start a business and pursue a dream. Others took a year off to do something that was important to them personally.

—Cindy Gunn, Vice President of Computer Operations for Sallie Mae

Only a small number of Indianapolis staff (e.g., critical Unity team members) were offered retention packages, because other IT jobs in the company were likely to be available to them. USA Group was viewed as a great place to work by people in central Indiana. Since there was a high differential in skill costs between Indianapolis and the DC area (e.g., $65 in Indianapolis compared to $75 or more in DC for application developers), the IT leaders could expect to retain the Indianapolis-based IT employees that they wanted to keep.

Placing the Bet on Internal Project Management

The McKinsey consultants strongly recommended that IT consultants be brought in to help with the data-center consolidation project and put forth several conditions for selecting the consulting firm. This narrowed the field to five very large players. Reston VP Cindy Gunn strongly encouraged hiring a specific IT firm because of an already established vendor relationship with Sallie Mae and the firm's recognized expertise in risk management.

The IT consultants were brought in at the end of November 2000 to work on a plan for moving the Reston data center. The consulting team hosted an IT integration kickoff meeting in Reston, during which they provided instruction on how to move equipment and applications effectively across the country. But the meeting did not go well.

Their approach was not received well by those of us who had to carry out this move. The approach seemed generic, and they weren't showing us how their tactics could be applied in our situation.

—*John Bennett, Project Manager for Data Center Relocation*

From the beginning, we felt as if we were stretching them. They had one methodology, and if we wanted to succeed, we needed to adhere to it pretty closely. From day 1, they said it would take 12 to 18 months. We asked if we could accelerate the methodology, and they were uncomfortable with approaching it that way.

—*Becky Robinson, Director of Systems Management*

Following the kickoff meeting, the IT consulting team lead advised Sallie Mae's executive team that the aggressiveness of the Indianapolis group's (FastTrack) approach was high risk. Instead of attempting to complete the data center move in 7 months, as proposed by the internal team, the consultants recommended that it be scheduled across 12 to 18 months, under their leadership.

This event proved to be a catalyst for the Indianapolis and Reston IT leaders to join together and take over the leadership for the data-center relocation project from the consultants. CIO Clancy presented to his Chief Operating Officer a counterproposal prepared by the internal IT team that would complete the data-center relocation project, including the conversion of the $15 billion loans from Unity to Class, by May 2001 (see timeline in Exhibit 3).

The CIO's plan called for managing the project internally using a project management office (PMO) structure that had been used for the $80 million USA Group Eagle II guarantee

EXHIBIT 3
IT Integration Timeline and Market Responses

Activity	Date Accomplished	Stock Price
Merger announced	June 15, 2000	$36.63 (June15)
Merger finalized; CIO announced	Aug. 1, 2000	$43.88 (Aug.1)
Data center location and Unity/Class decisions announced	October 2000	$48.69 (Oct.2)
IT consultants hired for data center relocation (DCR) project	November 2000	$57.56 (Nov.1)
Decision to lead DCR project internally	December 2000	$57.87 (Dec.1)
Move elements identified and major milestones established	January 2001	$62.81 (Jan.2)
Reston data center moves began	February 2001	$66.00 (Feb.1)
Initial enhancements to customer-facing applications completed	April 2001	$74.80 (April2)
Reston mainframe move completed	May 13, 2001	$66.20 (May 14)
Peak loan processing season begins	June 1, 2001	$69.60 (June1)
	Date Scheduled	
PeopleSoft Financials implementation	November 2001	
Full enhancements to call center routing application	April 2002	

system a few years earlier. Because of the minimal consulting role, the savings in consulting fees were projected to be $3.5 million.

Sallie Mae's executives knew that in this day and age where everything has to be done at Internet speed, the merger had to be incredibly fast and incredibly successful. Otherwise the marketplace would really punish you. . . . The longer a merger goes, the more uncertainty there is of how well you're going to pull it off, the more your products or services have a mixed reception by your customer, and the more your leadership is uncertain. In two or three quarters, if you're not saying, "we're getting it done," you will see your stock price being affected. . . . We decided that if the consultants weren't helping us reach our goals, we didn't need them.

—*Hamed Omar, Senior Vice President, Technology Group*

Sallie Mae's management decided to back the internal IT leaders. For the Indianapolis team members, an extra motivation to succeed was a rumor that a consulting partner on the loan-servicing system gap analysis had bet a Sallie Mae executive that the Indianapolis team could not pull off the FastTrack integration plan. This had made everyone mad, and created a reason for breaking the boundaries of 60-hour weeks.

The Data Center Relocation Team

The team structure for moving the IT headquarters to Indianapolis is shown in Exhibit 4. The data center relocation (DCR) team had its own steering committee of six direct reports to the CIO, chosen because of the criticality of their areas of responsibility within the two IT organizations. The primary objectives of the steering

EXHIBIT 4
Data Center Relocation Team Structure

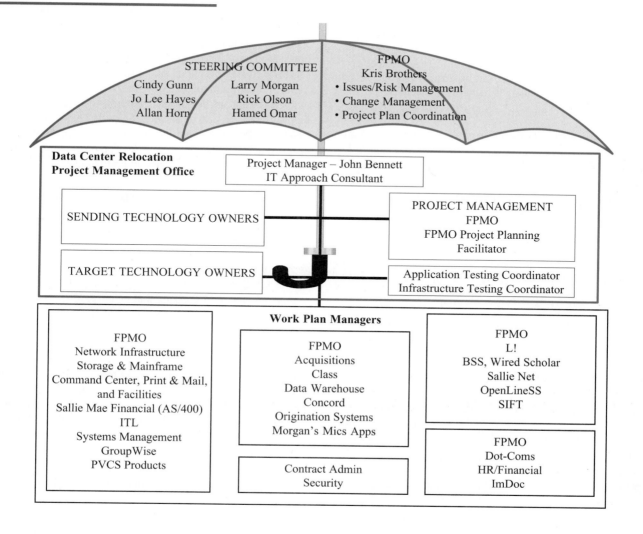

committee were to make top-level decisions and to keep obstacles out of the way so that the project team members could get the job done. They were responsible for setting strategic direction and mitigating the risks of the project, while still actively managing their own IT functions.

> Along the way, I questioned things quite a bit from a financial and risk standpoint. I didn't want to put the company at risk by moving the integration along too quickly. We had a number of checkpoint meetings to ensure we'd be successful at a reasonable cost.
>
> —*Greg Clancy, Chief Information Officer*

> You have to trust your people. Give them autonomy. Listen, and don't hold them back. A jockey who pulls too hard on the reins will never have a winning horse. We told them, "Guys, run like your hair's on fire." . . . We only got involved with approvals if the group couldn't agree on what needed to be done, or if the decision involved a high-risk issue. For example, the steering committee got involved when we were deciding whether to have two or three T1 lines.
>
> —*Allan Horn, Vice President, Technology Operations*

> In merger mode, you have to behave a certain way. People are watching your confidence. You're not only managing the project, but you're managing perceptions. You need to keep confidence high that the merger can be done within budget, with acceptable risks, and that the management team can pull it off.
>
> —*Hamed Omar, Senior Vice President, Technology Group*

The project office for the DCR employed some of the same team members who had managed the Eagle II system a few years earlier. The detailed processes and review mechanisms developed for Eagle II had been extensively reviewed by the McKinsey consultants before the decision was made to manage the IT integration internally.

> After our processes were reviewed at an executive level, [the consultants] spent about two weeks with us hand in hand to evaluate whether our project office was ready to manage this integration. They were very impressed with the size of Eagle II and how we handled risk management, change management, and progress stewardship.
>
> —*Cheri E. Dayton, Senior Manager, Guarantee Systems Development*

Oversight for the integration activities for the merger as a whole was provided by Rob Autor, who was Sallie Mae's VP for integration. Autor and his group of three global project managers, based in Reston, monitored the data-center move from a business perspective, keeping the key players (the board, CEO, McKinsey, institutional clients, and auditors) informed of the DCR team's progress.

Under the authority of the larger project office, the focused project-management office (FPMO) for the DCR initiative was responsible for monitoring and reporting global issues related

EXHIBIT 5
Success Criteria for Data Center Relocation

1) No unplanned interruptions
2) Meet scheduled dates
3) Meet budget
4) Continuity of staffing
5) Knowledge transfer
6) Maintain data integrity
7) Resulting service levels will be consistent, with contractual agreements met
8) Successful integration of application and infrastructure teams

to the data-center integration, including status of project plans, timing, codependencies, risks, and financial issues. The criteria for success for the DCR project are presented in Exhibit 5.

The project leader for the DCR team was John Bennett, who had started as a Unity programmer at USA Group 15 years earlier. Bennett had overall accountability for planning, management, and communications. One member of the IT consulting team was kept on the project full time to help infuse best industry practices and to serve as a coach. During the kickoff meeting in Reston, Bennett had seen this particular consultant in action and liked his strong collaboration and communication skills, strong work ethic, and willingness to listen.

Defining and Implementing by Move Element

Based on guidelines from both the steering committee and the project manager, the other managers on the DCR team were responsible for specific deliverables from each phase. Sending-technology owners (primarily based in Reston) were responsible for assuring the viability and functionality of the pre-move technology area and ensuring that all necessary activities had taken place for the target (receiving) technology owner (primarily based in Indianapolis) effectively to take over the assigned technology.

Each work-plan manager had overall accountability for a specific area, and managed the tasks that needed to be done prior to the move, shutting down the application, and executing the move. This required a detailed understanding of the infrastructure and business requirements of each move element.

Move-element leaders helped create the detailed plans with their work-plan managers and were held technically accountable for relocating assigned move elements within the scheduled time frame, with no unplanned application outage and minimal customer impact.

As shown in Exhibit 6, move elements were defined in an early planning phase. Greater detail was then added to each move plan: Equipment and software were specified, dependencies defined, and testing plans prescribed. Templates were provided to improve communication across work plans, projects, and aggregate planning activities. Each move was considered complete after the relocated application had been successfully put into operation. The post-move execution ended when all unused infrastructure was disposed of, and the support of the application had become a responsibility of the regular operational support team. (See Exhibit 7 for the move-element project plan.)

One major difference between the approach adopted by Sallie Mae and the approach introduced by their IT consultants was that move elements were first identified, and managed, from a business-application perspective, rather than a technology-infrastructure perspective. As described in Exhibit 8, the software application view provided a vertical business perspective, and the technology infrastructure view provided a horizontal cross-application perspective. Move elements were therefore managed as a set of interdependent hardware and software components. Large business applications were divided into smaller logical move elements to better facilitate project planning and move flexibility.

[The IT consultants] had us looking at this move from a technology viewpoint. The way we looked at it, the superstructure was the application. We defined move elements as a set of hardware and/or software components that can and should move together because of interdependencies.

—John Bennett, Project Manager for Data Center Relocation

The systems development people became the team leads. They understood the dependencies, the integration points. . . . It was a hard decision to make, and it was difficult to let someone else be in charge of the data-center move. But it was critical that we didn't lose sight of the applications because they were our primary concern. It then became our job to focus on a higher level of coordination, resolving the dependencies. It took time to get to an organized state . . . the whole structure shook out over about two months.

—Becky Robinson, Director of Systems Management

The plans were incredibly detailed, and they were written from an application-owner point of view. The trick was to see the dependencies. The IT applications people knew those dependencies and were able to align them with what they had to do.

—Allan Horn, Vice President, Technology Operations

Move-element freeze policies (see Exhibit 9) required that no application changes be implemented for a 2-week period

EXHIBIT 6
Data Center Relocation Approach

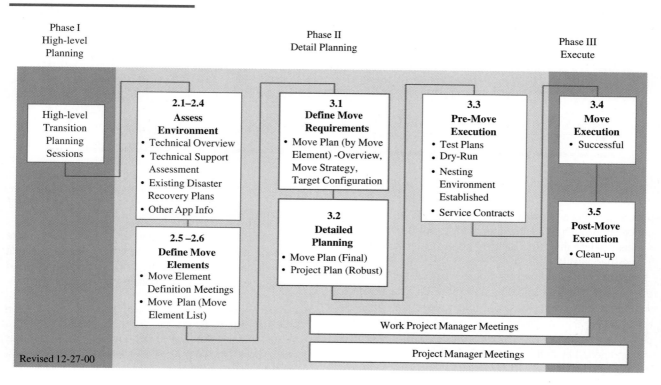

EXHIBIT 7
Move Element Project Plan

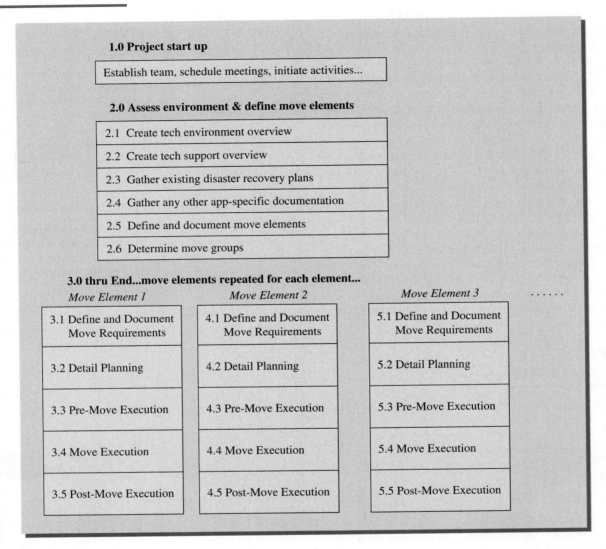

1.0 Project start up

Establish team, schedule meetings, initiate activities...

2.0 Assess environment & define move elements

2.1 Create tech environment overview
2.2 Create tech support overview
2.3 Gather existing disaster recovery plans
2.4 Gather any other app-specific documentation
2.5 Define and document move elements
2.6 Determine move groups

3.0 thru End...move elements repeated for each element...

Move Element 1	*Move Element 2*	*Move Element 3*	. . . . . .
3.1 Define and Document Move Requirements	4.1 Define and Document Move Requirements	5.1 Define and Document Move Requirements	
3.2 Detail Planning	4.2 Detail Planning	5.2 Detail Planning	
3.3 Pre-Move Execution	4.3 Pre-Move Execution	5.3 Pre-Move Execution	
3.4 Move Execution	4.4 Move Execution	5.4 Move Execution	
3.5 Post-Move Execution	4.5 Post-Move Execution	5.5 Post-Move Execution	

prior to the move-element implementation and for a 1-week period afterwards. Infrastructure changes were not allowed 4 weeks before the move element implementation and for a 1-week period afterwards.

All plans, policies, timelines, progress reports, and other relevant documents were coordinated by the FPMO staff for each area of the integration. These documents were then e-mailed to key managers and posted on Sallie Mae Central, the company's intranet. This provided companywide access to the information needed by both IT and business managers to manage the project effectively as well as to manage ongoing operations.

Equipment Move Strategies

One of the first steps in moving the data center was to make decisions on how all of the equipment from Reston would fit into the Indianapolis facility. A number of approaches were used to redesign the space to accommodate the new equipment.

Our first impression, and theirs, was "this will never fit." The Sallie Mae data center was the length of a football field. Once we started doing floor plans, we found that Sallie Mae was underutilizing their space. We used a number of strategies here. We eliminated local monitors and keyboards on storage racks,

EXHIBIT 8
Move Element Definition Approach

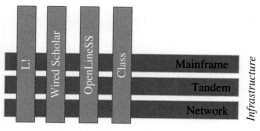

> 1) Define move element from the applications point of view (vertical).
>
> 2) Then define from the infrastructure point of view, to catch any gaps (horizontal).

for example. This saved a lot of space. Replacing old equipment with smaller new equipment helped too.

—Jon Jones, Director of Client Server Computing

Excellent vendor relationships were key to rationalizing equipment, making infrastructure improvements, and carrying out the project on time and within budget.

> When we were negotiating with vendors for USA Group, we weren't really a big player in the market and had less latitude. . . . As part of Sallie Mae, we were nearly able to write our own terms and conditions. In some cases, we were working with vendor reps in D.C., and they were able to make better and faster deals and were more flexible. We told them what we wanted, and they delivered.

—Becky Robinson, Director of Systems Management

Three different strategies were used for installing computer equipment in the Indianapolis facility that had been used in Reston. (Improvements to infrastructure components—such as backup equipment and more secure firewalls—were also built into the migration plans.)

1. The *Asset Swap* method was used for equipment in Reston ready to be retired. New equipment was purchased from the hardware vendor for the Indianapolis facility. Once the applications on the old equipment had been moved to (installed on) the new equipment in Indianapolis, the old equipment in Reston was traded in to the vendor.

2. The *Push/Pull* strategy was used for select equipment in Reston that was not ready to be retired and difficult to replace: the old equipment was taken out, moved, and reinstalled in Indianapolis.

3. The *Swing* method was used for equipment that existed in multiples. New equipment was purchased for Indianapolis for the earliest moves. After the initial applications were successfully installed on the new equipment, the relevant piece of equipment was removed from Reston and shipped to Indianapolis for the next move, and so on.

The strategy choice for each move element was based on allowable downtime for the application(s) involved, vendor prices for replacement equipment and trade-ins, and physical move costs. The overall objective was to decrease integration risks by minimizing the hardware assets that would be physically moved from Reston to Indianapolis. For example, a Reston data warehouse was stored on a Sun E10K server. Since this was a very expensive piece of equipment, an asset swap strategy would have been very costly. However, it was learned that the business could tolerate up to a week of downtime outside of the peak processing season, so a push/pull strategy was used instead. The vendor tore down the machine in Reston, trucked it to Indiana, and rebuilt it at the Indianapolis facility.

> Lack of backup was the biggest risk. We determined the maximum downtime that the operation could handle without losing customers, and we established backup and system redundancies as needed.

—John Bennett, Project Manager for Data Center Relocation

In contrast, the company couldn't afford much downtime for the mainframe on which the Class loan-servicing system was run: the service centers needed to be able to communicate with customers. The push/pull method required too much downtime, so the asset swap method was used. For DASD storage, a new vendor was selected in order to provide newer technology that would better handle the company's increased storage needs, as well as reduce the maintenance risks associated with older technologies.

Redundancies were built in wherever possible to minimize the business impact of the "go live" dates of critical applications. For example, beginning in March 2001, three T1 lines were leased from AT&T in order to have a fast electronic backup for the major moves.

> We spent a lot of money, almost a million dollars in two months, to create a pretty significant pipe between the two centers, in order to have a very fast link, so that you could essentially run the business out of either center if your migration had a problem. Fortunately, most of our migrations went well, and they did not have any problems, but that was a great big insurance.

—Hamed Omar, Senior Vice President, Technology Group

Prior to any move, the sending technology owners worked with the target (receiving) technology owners to transfer the knowledge needed by the Indianapolis operations staff to

EXHIBIT 9
Move Element Freeze Policies

Production Environment

The production environment move element freeze standard requires that:

- No application changes affecting the move element to be moved are implemented for a two-week period prior and one-week period after the move element implementation date.
- No infrastructure changes affecting the move element to be moved are implemented for a four-week period prior and one-week period after the move element implementation date.

In addition it is desirable that any application changes be implemented in time to have been executed successfully in production.

This generally would mean the following:

1) For changes that impact monthly processing, no changes should be made after the month-end execution proceeding the move element transition date.

2) For changes that impact weekly processing, no changes should be made after the weekly processing immediately proceeding the move element transition date.

3) For changes that impact daily processing, no changes should be made for two weeks prior to the move element transition date.

Example: If a move element is scheduled to move on 3/17, any application changes affecting month-end processing should be implemented in time to process for February month end. If the application change cannot make the February month-end implementation, it should be held and implemented after 2/24.

Quality Assurance and Development Environment

The QA and Development Environment move element freeze standard requires that:

- No application changes affecting the move element to be moved are implemented for a three-day period prior and three-day period after the move element implementation date. Any changes made during the two-week period prior to the move must be documented and given to the WPM for inclusion in the Move Control Book prior to the move occurring. This way issues caused by normal development will not be mistaken for move issues.
- No infrastructure changes affecting the move element to be moved are implemented for a four-week period prior and one-week period after the move element implementation date.

Appeal Process

In cases where the move freeze policy presents unusual hardships for the business, an appeal process is available. Any change requests falling within the standard move-freeze period require prior approval bythe Data Center Relocation Steering Committee. Information to be presented to the Steering Committee for them to consider a change within the freeze period includes:

- Explanation of the move element, the move approach, and the level of complexity
- Explanation of the requested change and primary business contact
- Increased risk associated with implementing the change during the freeze period
- Effect on the business of holding the change
- Benefits associated with completing the change during the freeze period

Questions concerning the freeze should be directed to the individual Work Plan Managers and then to their vice presidents for initial resolution. Issues that cannot be resolved through the Work Plan Manager should be documented and raised to the Data Center Relocation project manager (John Bennett). If not resolvable, the project manager will raise the issue to the Data Center Relocation steering committee and if necessary to Greg Clancy.

Move Element Freeze Communication Responsibility

Work Plan Managers are responsible for communicating to affected technology and business area management the freeze periods associated with each move element. The freeze dates will also be posted on the Data Center Relocation Web site. Any freeze period issues must be communicated to the Work Plan Manager and, if necessary, to the Data Center Relocation project manager (John Bennett).

handle the changes in applications, hardware, and large increases in transaction volume.

Early in the process, we asked teams to start planning and scheduling tasks related to training. The approach was tell them, show them, watch them.

—Allan Horn, Vice President, Technology Operations

The Major Data Center Moves

The DCR team began moving applications in February 2001, as they were ready (see Exhibit 10). From the director level down, the IT staffs at Reston and Indianapolis were paired by function to work on knowledge-transfer issues—including computer operators, help-desk people, database administrators, and other technical support people.

Trial runs were conducted as needed to determine the length of time that various transitions would take. Individual

move element teams met every day, and a project room was dedicated for this purpose. Anyone on the DCR team was authorized to call a meeting.

The Data Center Relocation team had an action orientation. They weren't waiting for someone to tell them what to do . . . they were off doing it. We had a number of moves from March to mid-June, and none were failures. Very little didn't work. It was truly amazing.

—Greg Clancy, Chief Information Officer

We clicked. We had a mission. No confusion, illusions, or secrets. . . . It was critical that we maintained people's confidence.

—Allan Horn, Vice President, Technology Operations

Starting February 1, DCR team members were responsible for written status reports and updated project plans on a weekly basis. Plans were submitted to the FMPO staff on Mondays, and 2-hour meetings were held via videoconference every Tuesday to discuss project status. About 20 people in

EXHIBIT 10
Calendar for Data Center Moves

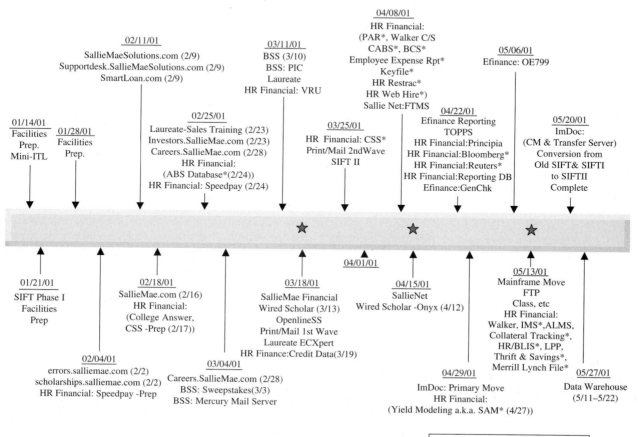

Indianapolis participated in the meetings, with about 15 people participating from Reston. Meetings were held with the steering committee two times a week.

> Videoconferencing was a key medium for us. This merger was an emotional event. In Reston, people were losing their jobs, and in Indianapolis, people were struggling to keep their jobs. Body language was everything. If you couldn't see people, you didn't know what was going on. Videoconferencing also helped us create the impression of a big group working together toward a common goal.
>
> —*John Bennett, Project Managerfor Data Center Relocation*

During this time, the typical workday was 12 hours long. Since weekends afforded some downtime for executing a move element, there were many weekends when IT people couldn't go home. A command center was set up in the Indianapolis office every weekend to help monitor move activities; full command centers were set up for the three most critical weekend moves in mid-March, mid-April, and mid-May.

> On the weekends with very large numbers of move elements, complicated moves, or very integrated move elements, we created move control books that listed everything that would be moving, implementation plans, vendor information, contingency plans, risks, disaster-recovery plans, and the possible impact to the business if a move failed. We manned the PMO communications center with team members, PMO members, vendors, and specific key contacts related to the implementation.
>
> —*Cheri E. Dayton, Senior Manager, Guarantee Systems Development*

> We took every opportunity for community building. On those long weekends we set up games for them to play. About once a week, we held informal luncheons to recognize successes along the way. We had an open budget on food: it was delivered around the clock every day. You can't take too good care of your people, and you can't communicate too much.
>
> —*Allan Horn, Vice President, Technology Operations*

The movement of the Reston mainframe operations for the loan-servicing application was studied the most. Timings were made for truck hauls between Reston and Indianapolis, including loading and unloading times. The T-1 lines would allow the company to revert back to operations in Reston if a glitch in Indianapolis precluded running the loan-servicing system from its new location.

The mainframe move was scheduled to take place over a weekend in mid-May. A full command center was in place, and about a dozen representatives from hardware and software vendors were required to be on site for the weekend. In addition, all vendors were required to have plans in place to provide immediate access to other people and resources should

there be a problem with their equipment or software. The team members were on location round the clock.

> The technical part of that weekend was challenging, but it wasn't the hardest part. The political and business ramifications of that move were huge. The mainframe is the lifeblood of the company. The call centers use it every minute of every day. It was the most critical part of the entire move.
>
> —*John Bennett, Project Manager for Data Center Relocation*

You have to tell yourself that you can be the first ones to do it, that you're not an average company and can find a way to succeed. That can-do attitude is critical to success.

> —*Hamed Omar, Senior Vice President, Technology Group*

Before the mainframe switch was flipped, John Bennett pulled the team together for a go/no-go decision at 2 a.m. Sunday morning.

> I got a lot of flack for having a meeting at that time of morning: people wanted to know why it couldn't wait until 7 a.m. We couldn't wait that long to know if there was a problem. We had duplicated enough tapes so that we could start installing manually in Reston, and a corporate Learjet was waiting to fly the other tapes back to Reston. We never used this backup, but it was good to know it was there. We had spent a lot of time working to make sure the mainframe move went smoothly, and it went grand.
>
> —*John Bennett, Project Manager for Data Center Relocation*

A month before the Reston data center move was even completed [the IT consultant firm that lost the contract] knew we would be successful. They told us that they planned to come up with a "FastTrack" method for mergers based on what they had learned through the engagement.

> —*Greg Clancy, Chief Information Officer*

The Challenges Ahead

The new IT group at Sallie Mae would soon be tested during peak lending season: not only would the transaction processing load be larger, but the systems would also be running on newly upgraded hardware and communications lines. Would they be able to avoid the bottlenecks and processing errors the government's direct lending program changeover had caused in a previous year? So far, the stock market reaction had been positive, but if there were a servicing failure, how would the market react? Would Sallie Mae be able to retain its customer base?

Still ahead were more IT application challenges—including implementing the advanced call-center routing capability for the new combined company, getting both companies on the same intranet and e-mail systems, and moving the corporate staff based in Reston onto PeopleSoft financial and human resource systems. With IT headquarters in Indianapolis and corporate headquarters in Reston, would the IT project team be able to successfully navigate the political challenges of these integrations as well?

IT INFRASTRUCTURE OUTSOURCING AT SCHAEFFER (A): THE OUTSOURCING DECISION

Schaeffer Corporation, headquartered in the small Midwestern town of Vilonia, is a diversified manufacturer. In 2002 Schaeffer Corporation's consolidated sales were around $2 billion and its profit after taxes was about $200 million. Schaeffer's stock is publicly held and its value has been consistently recognized by the marketplace over the past few years.

Founded by Frederick W. Schaeffer in 1877, Schaeffer Corporation originally manufactured small farm machines, such as churns, cream separators, corn shellers, apple peelers, and the like. Frederick had one son and three daughters, and the daughters married men who joined the business: Hiram C. Colbert, George Kinzer, and Heinrich Reitzel. Each of them led the transformation of the companies into new product lines, and today Schaeffer Corporation sells very different products within three very different divisions, named the Colbert division, the Kinzer division, and the Reitzel (pronounced "rightsell") division.

Each division is relatively autonomous, with the responsibility for product development and marketing of its own product lines. Two of the divisions have their own manufacturing plants and distribution facilities; the third division is now in financial services, providing agribusiness loans, estate and equipment loans, etc. The products are all branded with their division's name rather than with the Schaeffer name. Although the financials of the divisions are closely monitored by Schaeffer corporate headquarters, each division is held responsible by corporate management for its bottom-line performance, and the bonuses of the managers of each division depend upon the bottom-line performance of that division.

The Colbert and Kinzer divisions have profitable, but relatively stable, product lines. However, the Reitzel division is in a more dynamic industrial market with substantial opportunity for growth in both sales and profitability. The other divisions only operate in North America, but Reitzel has operations in 10 European countries as well as South America. In recent years,

Reitzel has contributed about two-thirds of Schaeffer's total dollar sales and about 80 percent of its total profits.

Historically, Schaeffer's board of directors has been satisfied to have a profitable and well run, but slow growth, company. However, new board members have recently targeted the Reitzel division as the corporate growth engine, and at year-end 2001 set ambitious goals for Reitzel to generate 10 percent annual growth in Schaeffer's corporate revenues and 15 percent growth in Schaeffer's corporate profits over each of the next five years. Reitzel management expected to achieve these goals by expanding into new geographical areas outside the United States and by expansion of its product lines, including acquiring other companies.

Information Technology at Schaeffer Corporation

In the past, each of the business divisions had its own information technology resources—including data centers, network operations and systems development people, help desk and desktop support staff. However, four years ago the corporation implemented a "shared services" approach that included IT, and most of the IT resources in the three divisions were centralized into this shared services unit for the entire corporation. They consolidated three data centers into one, eliminated a large number of servers, brought their support and system development people together, and established a corporate help desk, etc. However, the vice presidents of IT that previously reported to each division head were retained, and now had a dual report to both their business division head and the corporate vice president of IT that now headed the shared services unit.

Prior to this consolidation each division also had its own unique applications systems for all of its systems. However, soon after the consolidation, the corporate IT group purchased an ERP system that would replace the finance, human resources, production, and distribution systems in all three divisions. The system was installed so that each division had its own "instance" of the ERP package, since their products and customers were so different. It had been a difficult migration, but moving to a common "shared" enterprise system would bring cost savings to all the divisions in the future.

In 2002, the corporate data center had about 300 servers, and a staff of 100, including desktop support and help desk people for all divisions. Computer operations were reliable and secure, with good response time and excellent availability. However, there had been complaints about the help desk, and the performance of the wide area network (WAN) had not been as good as anticipated, but the central IT staff was working to improve performance in these areas. The system development group was separate and consisted of about 70 additional staff.

The Colbert and Kinzer divisions have a relatively small portfolio of company-specific applications that are now well integrated with their ERP system and easily maintained. The Reitzel division, on the other hand, has a much more complex application infrastructure, primarily due to their recent acquisitions. As compared with any other division, Reitzel also had triple the network capacity, triple the number of servers, and more help desk problems than the other two divisions combined. Reitzel also had a long history of making decisions about applications that created integration headaches.

The Outsourcing Study

In early 2002, shortly after the Schaeffer board announced its ambitious growth goals for the Reitzel division, Pedro A. Moreno, Reitzel's Vice President of Human Resources, proposed that Schaeffer consider outsourcing some of its IT resources. Moreno argued:

Information technology is not one of Schaeffer's core competencies, and I am confident that we can save some money by outsourcing. The other reason that we must do it is that for us to achieve our ambitious growth goals, we must have improved information technology services. Expanding into additional countries and acquiring new companies will require extraordinary information technology support efforts. We are doing reasonably well now, but our information technology people are stretched to the limit just supporting our day-to-day activities. There is no way that we are capable of crash efforts of the magnitude that we will need. But an outsourcer has a large supply of well-trained, capable people, as well as redundant hardware and software resources, so they can adjust to our dynamic, unforeseeable needs with little difficulty.

Schaeffer Corporation is a relatively conservative company and Moreno's proposal to outsource information technology was met with skepticism from many directions. However, Alan Harding, the corporate vice president of IT, thought that Moreno's proposal had sufficient merit and that it should be carefully considered. A corporate task force, that included Moreno, was established to thoroughly investigate whether or not Schaeffer Corporation should outsource any of its IT or not.

Knowing very little about how to approach outsourcing, the task force engaged Gartner Consulting Group to assist in exploring this issue. It quickly became apparent that this would not be a quick or easy study. Moreno recalls:

Gartner was very helpful. They said: "Before you decide to outsource you have to know what IT services you provide in great detail, and right now we don't think you know that. You need to know each piece of equipment in every location. You need to understand your IT processes. You need to know what your employees are doing, both in the scope of what might be outsourced and out of that scope, because they are related. And most of all, you have to know every service that you are providing in each operations area that you are considering outsourcing. There usually are 'assumed' services that are done without much thought, but if they are not specified in a contract they will not be provided by the outsourcer and you will have to continue to provide them or pay extra to the outsourcer."

Gartner gave us dozens and dozens of templates to be filled out and the IT folks spent months collecting data about ourselves. We did not consider outsourcing our development resources. Instead, we studied what the outsourcers call our "towers," which were the data center, distributed computing (all the desktops), voice (telephones), data networks, and our help desk. We spent about a year collecting data about the local and wide area data networks, the data center, our help desk, and our voice communications. We took our time to do it right.

Then we spent several months preparing a 200-page Request for Proposal (RFP) to give to potential outsourcing vendors. The RFP described our IT infrastructure and services, indicated exactly what we wanted to outsource, and asked for bids specifying how these services would be provided and what it would cost. We did not want to take the risk of moving our operations to a big remote data center, so we also specified that the data center facility in Vilonia would continue to be operated by the vendor.

Because of Reitzel's international scope, Gartner advised us that there were only a few U.S.-based companies that could satisfy our needs, and we decided to focus on ABC Corporation and DEF Corporation. We brought each vendor in for an all-day kickoff meeting where we shared with them what we had learned about out IT operations and what we wanted them to do for us. We gave them the 200-page RFP, and they had about two months to analyze the RFP and formulate a response for us.

Outsourcing information technology is different from buying an automobile where you have a car, negotiate its price and options, and that is it. If Schaeffer outsources its IT operations, it is contracting for services for a number of years in the future, and neither Schaeffer nor an outsourcer knows what will happen to the volume of transactions to be processed or even the locations to be served during that time. Therefore, the bids from the outsourcers could not be in the form of a total dollar cost over the seven-year length of the contract. Rather the bids would need to include a detailed set of costs for each of the services at the service levels that Schaeffer had requested, together with the penalties that would be incurred by the vendor if they did not provide the specified level of service. The quoted costs were unit costs, and Moreno describes how they evaluated the two proposals:

> Everything that they will do has a price. If they go touch a desktop, there is a price for that. If they answer a phone, there is a price for that. If they replace a phone, there is a price for that. If we increase the number of servers or databases, we will have to pay a specified amount more. And it works both ways—if things decrease we will pay less. We started with a base-line level of activity to get the projected cost to compare with our current costs, but it took us some time to go through the process of calculating things out so that we could arrive at a projected cost for each bidder.

When the bids had been evaluated, ABC Corporation was the lowest bidder. The good news was that the people on the task force felt very comfortable with the idea of having ABC as their business partner. The bad news was that the bid was projected to cost $220 million over the seven years, which was about $20 million more than it was projected to cost Schaeffer to continue to provide these IT services in-house. There was no way that Schaeffer Corporation management was going to go for that. Corporate Vice President of IT Harding explains:

> We were quite disappointed when the bids came in. Instead of saving some money as we had originally hoped, we were going to have to spend substantially more to outsource. Although I had become persuaded that there were still good reasons to outsource, even if it cost more, I knew that our management would never agree to a deal costing that much.
>
> Gartner had warned us during the data gathering part of the study that we were not likely to save any money by outsourcing because we were already pretty efficient. The work we had done ourselves in creating a consolidated shared services infrastructure had already picked all the low-hanging fruit. We had already consolidated three data centers into one. We had already eliminated about 50 headcount out of 150 and were down to 100. We had already done server consolidation and reduced our server count from 300 to 200. So the things that an outsourcer comes in and does for you we had already done. We had very lean, efficient operations to outsource.
>
> The reason that the bids were so much higher was that when we developed the specifications in the RFP we had asked for a number of improvements over what we were currently doing. We had asked for a Cadillac when we could only afford our current Buick. The representatives of ABC understood this and agreed to work with us to get the total cost down to something that we could afford.

Moreno added:

> The negotiation process was arduous and detailed. This was a big agreement, and we had 10 countries in Europe that we had to include under separate agreements as well. It ended up taking weeks, but it was a good process. In the end we changed

some of our ideas about what we needed. We took away some of the whiz-bang options that we had told ABC we absolutely had to have, which allowed them to come down in price somewhat, and they also took out some of their margin. We got the projected cost down to $200 million over the seven years, about the same as the projected cost of doing it ourselves. Given that we had been able to make it cost neutral, I strongly believed that we should outsource because of the quality and flexibility we could obtain with having a Tier 1 service provider.

Reactions to the Outsourcing Proposal

The task force recommended to Schaeffer's top management that Schaeffer outsource all of its IT operations, but keep systems development in-house. The task force's report included a description of the process that had been followed to obtain the bids and negotiate the proposed contract with ABC Corporation, and included the following argument in support of the recommendation:

> Schaeffer's board has set the strategic growth goals based on growth through acquisition and geographic expansion overseas. However, we cannot achieve these goals without high quality and very flexible IT resources. We have solid staffing for serving a static situation, but our staff and data center cannot handle the global and dynamic requirements that these new strategic directions will place upon us.
>
> When we have an acquisition, our demand for IT resources initially is going to spike, but then it will flatten out after a few months. Not only will ABC bring access to larger numbers of people, but they will also be capable of expanding and contracting staff. It is difficult for us to temporarily hire 20 experts in the field to help us for a relatively short time and then not have permanent opportunities for them.
>
> We are global and intend to expand into other countries. We are in 10 countries in Europe, and Europe is much more complex than domestically. We have only seven people working in infrastructure for all of Europe, so we are going to have to double or triple our staff over there. So it makes sense to give the responsibility to ABC who already has resources in all these countries, both where we are now and where we will be going in the future.
>
> ABC has a very deep bench—hundreds of thousands of employees for them to pick from to serve our needs as opposed to our one hundred. If someone leaves, it generally takes us three to six months to find a suitable replacement because it is hard to get people to move to Vilonia. ABC provides an attractive career path for its employees and can attract and keep people with outstanding talent that would never come to Vilonia to work for Schaeffer. ABC can afford to invest in extensive training and can offer a variety of challenging technical opportunities to its people, so we will have access to substantially higher-quality technical knowledge.
>
> In short, Schaeffer is anticipating exciting opportunities that will be impossible to achieve with our existing IT staff. With

ABC as our business partner, we will be much better positioned to exploit the dynamic opportunities for growth that we are seeking.

When the task force report was circulated, there was quite a reaction throughout Schaeffer Corporation, with some managers voicing enthusiastic support and others equally strongly opposed. Vivian D. Johnson, vice president of IT for the Kinzer division, expressed the following concerns:

Perhaps IT is not one of Schaeffer's core competencies, but it is a critical factor in our long-term success. Do we want to turn over such critical resources to an outside organization?

It will be like "getting married" to ABC Corporation. Although it has a good reputation and we feel comfortable with its people, what happens three years down the road when these people have gone on to greener pastures within ABC? Today Schaeffer may be a high priority with ABC, but before long other opportunities will appear and the good people that we will start out with will be replaced with others who do not know us as well. What will happen when a new situation arises that is not covered in our contract and we have to renegotiate, and we have lost our bargaining position?

Quite a number of outsourcing relationships have not worked out well. If we become unhappy with ABC's performance, we will have eliminated these internal IT capabilities and the cost of bringing it back will be tremendous—there is no way our management would go for that. What will that mean for our dreams of growth that depend so heavily on good information technology support? There is a lot of unrecognized risk inherent in this proposal.

What will happen to our current information technology people, many of whom have served Schaeffer faithfully for years? I don't know the exact numbers, but I am sure that many of them will no longer be employed by Schaeffer. Is that fair? This is a small-town company and our greatest asset has always been our loyal, dedicated, and hard-working labor force. We are mostly nonunion, and we have never had a strike. We have never done anything like this, and I am concerned about the effect this may have on the morale of all of our workers and on their future commitment to the company.

I understand that our company is changing and that we face new and different challenges that require expanding our IT resources. But have we considered the available alternatives? Traditionally when we needed special skills or additional people we have employed contractors, and that approach has worked out well in the past. Under the proposed contract we will be paying ABC for every bit of help we get just as we would any contractor, but we would be married to them—if the relationship sours you can't just employ another vendor.

Also, it is clear that we have underfunded our information technology area, so it should be no surprise that we do not have all the resources that we will need in the future. Under the contract with ABC, we will be paying extra for any additional resources that it provides. Would we not be better off investing some of that money in acquiring and developing our own

people? Then we would have our own resources for the long run instead of having to depend on an outside organization over which we have little control when push-comes-to-shove.

Carol J. Hanna, vice president for finance of the Colbert division, expressed the following concerns:

The proposal to outsource is very expensive and risky. Although it appears to be no more expensive than our in-house Information Technology organization, there is no question in my mind that we will be paying substantially more. With such complex services I am sure that we have not been able to define them all to include in the contract and there will be things that are not included that will still have to be done at additional cost. Furthermore, it is common knowledge that outsourcers "low-ball" the first-year costs of a contract because they know that they can make it up in the later years, and because their clients will have no bargaining position when inevitable changes have to be negotiated. We will be writing a blank check since there is no way of knowing what our costs in the future will be as conditions change. Also, there will be substantial unanticipated costs involved in administering the contract and managing the relationships with ABC people.

As the financial officer of Colbert, I am particularly concerned because I am convinced that whatever benefits this proposal will bring will go to our Reitzel division, while the other divisions will bear additional costs without additional benefits. Both ABC and Gartner have said that our present IT organization is very efficient. We are getting along fine with our current IT services, and can continue to do so in the future. This is not a fair deal for Colbert.

If it is so important that IT support for Reitzel be outsourced, why not outsource Reitzel's part of the data center, the network, and the phone system, and leave the rest of our support as it is? That would have the added benefit of maintaining a nucleus of IT professionals within Schaeffer so that if the outsourcing deal does not work out there would be something to build on if we wanted to bring it back in house for Reitzel. While the data center will remain in Vilonia, we have heard that most of ABC's people, including the help desk staff, will be located far away. Only a handful (less than 20) of information technology people will be located here. What happens if we have a problem? How are we going to get someone to help us? Today we know where our IT support people sit. We can go to their office, beg them for help, and stay there until things get fixed. We know and trust these people. Not only are they long-time colleagues, but they are our neighbors as well. With a big outsourcing company, how are we going to work with them? All of the processes are going to change, because the people can be all over the world. We are afraid of that and we do not like it at all!

Charles T. Gibbs, vice president of IT for the Reitzel division, enthusiastically supported the recommendation to outsource:

Schaeffer's world changed when our top management set such aggressive growth goals for the corporation. To get a corporate-wide sales growth of 10 percent a year, Reitzel's sales are going to have to grow over 14 percent, and for corporate profits to grow 15 percent a year, Reitzel's profits will have to increase about 18 percent each year. Those are daunting goals, and they can't be achieved by business as usual. We can't continue to be the conservative, risk-averse company that we have always been. We are going to have to be nimble and daring in expanding into new markets and in acquiring outside companies. And it is amply clear that our in-house information technology organization does not have the skills or the flexibility to support the rate of change that we must undertake. With its vast reservoir of talented and skilled people, and experience managing change, ABC Corporation is the ideal business partner to enable our new strategy.

There is no question that ABC can manage technology well. The data center will perform at least as well as it does today, and our telephone services will continue to be excellent. ABC can manage our data networks far better than we have been able to do, so we will be able to substantially reduce the outages that have been disrupting critical business activities.

There has been a great deal of FUD [fear, uncertainty, and doubt] about the performance of the help desk and desktop support services that are more people-intensive. But there have been lots of complaints about the performance of our present help desk, so people's concern in this area may be a case of preferring our familiar mediocre service to the unknown. However, the task force understood people's fears and put a lot of effort into defining performance criteria, both for response to help desk calls and time to resolve problems. We have involved large numbers of our users in defining these service criteria, and ABC has agreed that they are attainable, and they will pay significant penalties if they are not met.

In Europe, each country has its local help desk support. With all the divided responsibility, this is hard to manage with a hodgepodge of processes and no global view of our support issues. ABC will provide a global help desk with a single process and an integrated database that all countries will work off of. Furthermore, ABC's help desk will be globally redundant as it can be supported from any site where ABC provides help desk services. We believe that help desk support will be a shining example of the value outsourcing brings to the table.

In the final analysis we have to recognize that Schaeffer's world has changed. We have to move our mind-set into the twenty-first century where information technology organizations will also become managers of IT service providers rather than providing all the services themselves. The challenge of our IT people will be to manage a long-term relationship with ABC, and at the same time to establish closer relationships with users in the divisions so that information technology can more effectively support the essential needs and strategic directions of the business.

Harding responded to some of the concerns that had been expressed:

We have been very concerned about what may happen to our IT people who may be displaced. Many people who worked in this organization were worried about what outsourcing would mean for them. We tried to engage them with ABC so that they could learn about what it would mean to work for ABC. We brought in ABC people who joined them from a client firm who talked with our people about how wonderful it had been for their career. We tried to convince our people that if you are a technical person, working for ABC is a good thing because you have so many more opportunities for technical career development and advancement. Instead of working in Vilonia in an IT organization with only 100 positions, you are going to work with a company that is global and has 100,000 employees. Unfortunately, that argument worked with a few people, but the bulk of the people had the attitude—"Look, I care about my career advancement, but I want to stay in Vilonia."

We had about 100 headcount when we started studying outsourcing. However, during the outsourcing decision process, 10 people decided to leave for other jobs; and we did not fill these vacancies with Schaeffer employees—we filled these positions with temps—so now we have 90 Schaeffer IT employees who will be affected. ABC will likely offer jobs to about 40 of our current employees, but some of them may not take them because in the long run they might have to leave Vilonia. So at least 50 people will be terminated if they can't find other jobs somewhere within Schaeffer. They will be given six months' pay and help in finding other employment. Fifty is a very small number when compared to the thousands of Schaeffer's people in Vilonia.

It has been suggested that we could use the resources that we will devote to outsourcing to build up our internal IT resources and employ more contractors and thereby satisfy our future needs. This suggestion simply reflects a lack of understanding of how different our future must be. Although we have good information technology resources today, "good" will not be good enough. We are going to have to change our corporate aspiration level from being satisfied with our insular way of doing things, to a situation where in critical areas we aspire to be the very best. To accomplish our goals, our IT support must be the very best, and ABC is clearly outstanding in providing that support. ABC brings IT resources that we simply cannot match given our size and location.

It has been suggested that we outsource IT for Reitzel only, and leave all IT in-house for the other divisions. That would be very expensive because we would lose economies of scale. We would have to restart negotiations with our current vendors as well as ABC, and would not be able to get the same deals because of the smaller scale. Furthermore, today our IT operations for all three divisions are consolidated into a shared infrastructure. To break this infrastructure apart to take out Reitzel would be very expensive and take many months. That would be a logistical nightmare for Reitzel, especially when they are attempting to concentrate management attention on leveraging their core competencies. Our management is going to have all it can handle just striving to meet its ambitious growth goals.

It was now up to Schaeffer's corporate management to make a decision on the task force recommendation.

IT INFRASTRUCTURE OUTSOURCING AT SCHAEFFER (B): MANAGING THE CONTRACT

In March 2007, Alan Harding, the Vice President of IT at Schaeffer Corporation, was busy preparing to meet with top management at their corporate offices in Vilonia. In light of the recent business developments at Schaeffer, important IT decisions had to be made—and they had to be made soon.

Four years ago, Schaeffer had signed a seven-year, $200 million outsourcing contract with ABC Corporation to outsource its centralized IT infrastructure. The deal meant that Schaeffer would retain its systems development activities in-house, and outsource data center operations, voice and data telecommunications, distributed computing support (including desktops), and help desk support for employees throughout the company.

But being a multidivisional firm had posed its own problems when it came to the outsourcing decision. The concerns centered on Schaeffer's aggressive growth targets for Reitzel (one of its three divisions). Senior management in the other divisions believed that Reitzel was the only division that would benefit from outsourcing what was being efficiently run in-house. However, the concerns of the divisions were addressed, and the deal was signed in June 2003. What followed was a period of outsourcing challenges for Schaeffer's management, and although the differences between the divisions resurfaced, Schaeffer's managers had deftly handled every situation.

Now a new business restructuring meant that the outsourcing deal had to be changed. Schaeffer's management had recently decided to split its divisions into two independent business entities and dissolve the corporate parent. With almost three years remaining in the outsourcing contract, Schaeffer's management had several options to consider—and Harding thought it was beginning to look every bit as complicated as the initial decision to outsource.

Company Background

Founded by Fredrick W. Schaeffer in 1877, Schaeffer Corporation is the parent firm for three divisions, with total annual sales of about $2 billion in 2002. Fredrick's three son-in-laws—Hiram C. Colbert, Heinrich Reitzel, and George Kinzer—each managed a division, and ran them as autonomous business units out of the small Midwestern town of Vilonia. Originally, the company manufactured only small farm machines, but today Schaeffer's three divisions sell very different products. The Colbert and Reitzel (pronounced "right-sell") divisions have their own manufacturing plants and distribution facilities; the third division is now in financial services, providing agribusiness loans, estate and equipment loans, etc. The products are all branded with their division's name rather than with the Schaeffer name.

Colbert and Kinzer have operations only in the United States. Their markets are relatively mature, with minimal to modest opportunities for growth. Reitzel, however, has grown rapidly in recent years through new products and acquisitions, and was continuing to expand globally. As the "corporate growth engine" for Schaeffer, it operated in 10 European countries and South America, and still contributed about two-thirds of Schaeffer's dollar sales and about 80 percent of its total profits.

In the past, each of Schaeffer's divisions had managed its own IT infrastructure—separate data centers, its own computer operations and systems development specialists, and separate help desk staff. However, in the late 1990s Schaeffer realized the need for consolidating and centralizing IT infrastructure operations for the entire corporation. The corporate vice president of IT championed this cost efficiency initiative by eliminating a number of servers, reducing the number of IT personnel, establishing a corporate help desk, and so on. During this time, Schaeffer also purchased licenses for and installed enterprise software (an ERP system) to support finance, human resources, manufacturing, and distribution processes. Each division was, however, allowed to implement separate instances of the ERP package to accommodate their own business needs. The result of this consolidation was a single data center for all three divisions, with centralized computer and telecommunications operations staff in a "shared services" unit.

Even though significant cost savings were achieved through this IT consolidation, Schaeffer still felt the need to improve its IT services. In particular, there was a growing need to provide IT support for Schaeffer's aggressive growth strategy for its Reitzel division. As the internal IT capability was deemed insufficient, Schaeffer began the process to choose an outsourcer for its IT infrastructure in early 2002.

The Outsourcing Contract

> We wanted the capability to execute on the business strategy, which was aggressive growth through acquisition. And we didn't think our IT organization could support that strategy by ourselves . . .
>
> *Alan Harding, vice president of IT at Schaeffer*

Unlike most companies choosing to outsource IT infrastructure, cost savings from outsourcing was the least of Schaeffer's priorities. In fact, the outsourcing deal would cost Schaeffer as much as it had cost to manage it internally (about $200 million). Rather, the primary goal was to give Schaeffer greater IT flexibility to achieve the aggressive growth goals set by its board. The "selective outsourcing" strategy adopted by Schaeffer was in line with this overall strategy. While outsourcing the infrastructure components promoted the global growth strategy, retaining systems development in-house would provide the agility to respond to rapid business changes.

With help from Gartner consulting group, and after a thorough process of documenting internal processes and creating metrics for service levels, an RFP was created for the IT infrastructure activities. Proposals from two large vendor firms were considered, and after several months of negotiations, the contract was signed with ABC Corporation in June 2003:

> We basically decided to look at the entire infrastructure—lock, stock, and barrel. We'd keep a few people back to manage the outsourcer [ABC]. But for the most part, everything was going to ABC.
>
> *Alan Harding*

The outsourcing contract with ABC included data center operations for over 300 servers, help desk support for all computer users in the three divisions, local and wide area network support for voice and data communications, and technical support for over 6,000 PCs at domestic locations. Separate agreements were signed for each of the 10 European countries where Reitzel operated:

> There were ten country agreements. ABC proposed, and our legal department agreed, that we set up country agreements with ABC. Each country had different laws and you want to make sure that all those different local requirements are contemplated. So we have a country agreement for every place we do business.
>
> *Alan Harding*

Schaeffer also needed a contract that would be favorable to their aggressive growth goals for Reitzel. This meant that the contract needed to be structured in a flexible enough way to allow Schaeffer to add newly acquired companies and/or spin off divisions under the existing outsourcing contract without penalties or additional charges. Schaeffer had been growing for years through related and unrelated acquisitions, and had also spun off several divisions in the prior decade. It was therefore anticipated that both types of restructuring would need to be accommodated in the contract:

> We structured the deal with a concept called Additional Resource Charges (ARCs—called "Arcs") and Reduced Resource Charges (RRCs—called "Rooks"). We certainly expected to buy a bunch of companies, but we might sell one.
>
> *Alan Harding*

Other stipulations in the contract were that the data center would continue to be run out of Vilonia, the small Midwestern town where all of the divisions were headquartered. In addition, it was agreed that about half of Schaeffer's current IT infrastructure employees would be transferred to ABC. The transferred employees would maintain the same seniority at ABC as they had at Schaeffer at the time of the transition. These employees were also protected from any potential layoffs by ABC for the first year.

A critical aspect of the contract negotiations was the creation of detailed Service Level Agreements (SLAs) to which the vendor would be held accountable. The majority of the SLAs were focused on technology measures. For example, SLAs were used to establish the acceptable server and networking uptimes, help desk response times, and resolution times for other operational problems. Severity levels for different types of problems were established, and different service levels were contracted for each severity level with the vendor, depending on the business impact and vendor costs.

> There are hundreds of different pieces of hardware. We'd say, "this group of servers is absolutely critical so we're going to call those 'gold.' This group of servers is important so we'll call those 'silvers,' and this group of servers is used for application development, so we're going to call those 'bronze.'" We then set levels of service and we defined the SLA based on level of service.
>
> *Alan Harding*

For example, 80 percent of Severity 1 help desk issues had to be resolved in less than four hours, but 80 percent of Severity 3 issues had to be resolved within three business days (see Exhibit 1). Compliance statistics for all the SLAs in the contract were tracked and reported by the vendor during monthly meetings with Schaeffer. Noncompliance with an SLA would result in explicit financial penalties for the vendor. While negotiating the contract, Schaeffer also had to make some compromises with respect to service levels, to keep costs within current budget levels. For example, Schaeffer chose a longer response time for Severity 1 help desk issues because management thought the benefits of a quicker response than four hours would not warrant the vendor's higher costs.

EXHIBIT 1
SLA for Help Desk Problem Resolution by Vendor

Severity Level	Service Level Agreement (SLA)
Severity 1	80% in 4 Hours; 95% in 24 Hours
Severity 2	80% in 8 Hours; 95% in 24 Hours
Severity 3	80% in 3 Business Days; 95% in 5 Business Days
Severity 4	80% in 5 Business Days; 95% in 15 Business Days

The Transition Period

After the outsourcing contract was signed, there was an official six-month transition period as ABC took over Schaeffer's IT operations. A few key subject matter experts (SMEs) were retained by Schaeffer to help manage the outsourcing arrangement, but most of the IT personnel (about 50) in infrastructure support positions at Schaeffer were moved to ABC. By this time, only about a dozen IT personnel had to find other jobs because many had already done so in the months prior to the contract bidding and negotiation processes.

During the transition process, Schaeffer provided ABC with extensive documentation, access to all relevant computer systems, and information about IT processes already in place. During the transition period, none of the SLAs were in effect, which meant that ABC could perfect their processes during this time frame to match the SLAs. The Schaeffer employees that were transferred to ABC provided invaluable technical and business knowledge about Schaeffer's operational environment:

> When we brought ABC on board, we were very open with them. We gave them everything—including our help desk scripts—to get them up to speed.
>
> *Rusty Evans, IT Director, Colbert division*

On the flip side however, the transition affected every remaining IT employee at Schaeffer, because their processes and workflows changed dramatically.

Transitioning to any outsourcing provider in the first six months is about the most painful process you can possibly imagine because every process is changing for every individual. You've got the people kept at Schaeffer: all their processes are changing. You've got the people who were at Schaeffer who went to ABC in the deal: They're probably not that thrilled and they have to deal with their own personal issues after just kind of getting "thrown over the wall." And then you've got ABC employees hitting the ground who know technology, but don't know anything about us. So you've got these three groups all with their own agendas, all with their own issues to deal with, all trying to get to a single integrated process, and it's just hard. It's just really hard.

Alan Harding

Facing the Challenges

The first couple years after the signing of the outsourcing deal, several management challenges surfaced for Schaeffer. Some of the underlying precontract differences between the IT needs for Reitzel and the other two divisions also resurfaced. These differences between the divisions seemed to stem from the primary objective of the outsourcing arrangement. The contract was written to be flexible to accommodate growth: Outsourcing provided the capability to scale up IT operations quickly, so that Reitzel could pursue an aggressive series of acquisitions and global expansion. The vendor's technical capability and expertise were also viewed as better than what the company could provide on its own, because IT infrastructure management was the vendor's (ABC's) core competency.

But what worked for Reitzel did not necessarily work for the other divisions. For example, Colbert was in a mature industry that faced little growth, and its IT management was focused on cost reduction and efficient operations. Colbert had over half of its IT budget tied up in outsourced IT infrastructure costs, which could have been reduced if it hadn't been bound by the corporate outsourcing contract:

> Colbert and Reitzel are two different companies. At Colbert, we are very focused on cost: we know what the costs are, and we're trying to improve those costs. Reitzel is on the uptake: they don't care as much about the cost. They value the ABC services because they're growing. . . . We're trying to figure out how to cut the costs of this table in half. But they need three more tables.
>
> *Rusty Evans*

The approaches to maintaining the ERP systems at these two companies were also different. A year into the outsourcing agreement, Reitzel set up a separate contract with ABC for offshore workers in India to maintain their ERP applications, which had been customized to fit Reitzel's specific business needs.

Colbert's ERP maintenance needs were simpler because they had done a "vanilla" ERP implementation, and they continued to maintain their ERP applications in-house:

> We find we can be a lot more nimble and responsive with our own team when it comes to supporting our ERP applications. Since we don't change code, we just keep it up and running. When we have a problem, the people are right there. Reitzel actually changed the code in their ERP applications, and they have a whole lot more internal and ABC people maintaining it.
>
> *Rusty Evans*

Divestiture of Kinzer

The first actual contractual change with ABC was due to the divestiture of Kinzer about one year into the contract. Operating in the financial services industry, Kinzer was the smallest of the three divisions in both sales and IT expenditures, and barely fit the corporate profile. Even though the divestiture made good business sense, it created an additional layer of complexity for Schaeffer with respect to its IT activities. The issue was: Who would support Kinzer's IT from now on?

Schaeffer's managers had anticipated during the contract negotiation phase that such a spin-off might occur. As per the RRC condition in the contract, Schaeffer could scale down IT operations up to 40 percent without incurring any penalty. This simple provision helped them avoid penalty costs with ABC during the divestiture process for Kinzer:

> What we negotiated with ABC is, when we sign the deal we're going to count everything—PCs, servers, network switches, voice mail boxes—and these go into the contract as a baseline. Then we'll have a unit rate where every PC costs X dollars to support, every server costs Y; everything has a unit cost. So if we go buy a company, and this adds 500 desktops and 50 servers, no contract renegotiation is necessary. We just get an ARC at the unit cost that we agreed to. We also negotiated a 40% floor on the RRCs—so we could take volume down 40% without penalty.
>
> *Alan Harding*

Given Kinzer's geographic proximity to Reitzel, it was decided that Kinzer would buy its IT services from Schaeffer, which in effect meant that there was no impact on the outsourcing revenues earned by ABC:

> The TSA [Transition Services Agreement] acknowledges that Schaeffer will deliver services to Kinzer through the ABC contract, and ABC agrees in an amendment to the contract to support Kinzer in that way.
>
> *Alan Harding*

Setting Up a PMO Structure

By late 2004, Schaeffer decided that they needed a better approach to managing a large IT infrastructure outsourcing arrangement as well as Reitzel's new offshore contract for ERP maintenance. In December 2004, ABC's consulting arm conducted a study to provide Schaeffer with recommendations on how to improve their management of the outsourcing relationship. They made two major recommendations.

The first recommendation was to establish a governance model with an IT lead (a director of outsourcing) directly accountable for managing the relationship, and for overseeing the day-to-day activities of the contract:

> Initially, we struggled with managing the ABC contract, as we were inexperienced. Our governance model put structure around our decision-making process and brought clarity to the relationship.
>
> *Virginia King, Director of Outsourcing, Schaeffer*

The second recommendation was to establish a Project Management Office (PMO) structure, with an IT lead and several enterprise architects. Schaeffer also implemented this recommendation and established a Project Management Office (PMO) for approving IT investments as well as coordinating in-house systems development initiatives with the IT infrastructure teams at ABC. Another important change was to implement a Portfolio Review Board for large projects:

> What we have established is a Portfolio Review Board (PRB). Each senior VP has a designee on this board. Their job is to meet once a month, review all project requests that are submitted, and prioritize them. Any project that requires shared services between the divisions has to come through our PMO organization.
>
> *Penelope Overton, Director of PMO, Schaeffer*

The Colbert executive who served as the liaison with ABC for that division attended the weekly outsourcing meetings chaired by the new director of outsourcing and also was a representative at the monthly PRB meetings.

Insourcing European Operations

Around the same time that the PMO was kicked off, the IT infrastructure costs in Reitzel's European business units were rising alarmingly. Domestically, the IT infrastructure costs were as anticipated, but in Europe the costs seemed to be spiraling out of control. Despite the fact that a key benefit from the original outsourcing contract was the ability to expand globally with very little difficulty, Reitzel was having a difficult time justifying these skyrocketing expenses, especially since its European computer operations were being primarily run out of its Vilonia center on the same ERP system as its domestic operations:

> I learned a very painful lesson. If there's anybody talking about global outsourcing, I'm going to say: "Europe is very difficult—be very careful in this geography." They're all country towers. You've got tons of management fees layered on top because none of the country managers talk to each other. The cultures are very, very different. As any other company trying to deal with multi-cultures, it costs more money . . . and I would be willing to bet that every outsourcer has that same problem.
>
> *Alan Harding, vice president of IT at Schaeffer*

The insourcing of computer operations for its European units would provide Schaeffer with more operational control, as well as more control over its costs. Schaeffer's IT leadership team therefore renegotiated with the vendor to insource the entire European computer operations. (Global support was a centralized service based out of the United States, and the termination of the local country agreements in Europe did not change this part of the agreement.) Since the contract stipulated high contract termination costs, a compromise plan was worked out. ABC would not invoke the termination costs if Schaeffer would agree to allow ABC to move some of its infrastructure support offshore to South America. The ongoing benefit for ABC would be that it could provide the same services for Schaeffer using its own offshore center, but at a cheaper cost—due to labor market differences.

Unlike offshore locations in Asia, moving the support to South America would also provide no new coordination problems due to different time zones. However, there was considerable skepticism among Schaeffer's top management about moving IT infrastructure support offshore. An on-site visit was arranged for the vice president of IT and his leadership team, and they were impressed with what they saw. The contract with ABC was revised, and the new agreements took effect in early 2005.

> The director of outsourcing, the project executive and I—we all took a trip to Argentina so that we could see that infrastructure. Not the infrastructure of ABC, but the infrastructure of the city to make sure we weren't sending it to some backwoods. I was absolutely overwhelmed with how European this city in South America was. Like any transition, it was a little rocky in the beginning . . . but since my team doesn't come to me complaining about it, I know that it's working fine.
>
> *Alan Harding*

Bringing Back Desktop Support

Even after two changes in the contract, some Schaeffer employees still expressed frustrations about the quality of service that ABC was providing. In particular, simmering discontent with ABC's handling of desktop support was surfacing within Schaeffer. As

time went on, it had become apparent that the contract with ABC was not fully meeting the needs of Schaeffer's business users: The technical SLAs were generally being met, but Schaeffer employees expected more—especially when it came to resolving their desktop support problems. Before the contract, Schaeffer's employees could call their own centralized help desk, and their issues would often be addressed over the telephone during the first call. But ABC's processes called for new help desk requests to first be logged into their support system. Problem tickets were then issued, which were then prioritized and assigned to an ABC technician. The personal touch that symbolized Schaeffer was lost after the outsourcing deal with ABC:

> People used to walk down the hallway and say, "Hey, can you come over here and look at this?" And I had to now say, "I am sorry—if you can put in a ticket, I will come back and look at it."
>
> *Larry Brown, Desktop Support Technician*

Although ABC was a Tier 1 outsource service provider, the vendor's ticketing system for help desk calls and the support levels that Schaeffer had purchased led to performance gaps with user expectations. One of the many Schaeffer employee names for the help desk was the "helpless desk."

Citing poor performance by ABC and mounting cost pressures at the Colbert division in particular, Schaeffer renegotiated with ABC to exclude desktop support from the contract. From ABC's perspective, desktop support was the least profitable part of its contract with Schaeffer, and it had subcontracted some of the work to a small regional vendor located close to Schaeffer's divisions. ABC therefore readily accepted the contract change without termination fines.

But Schaeffer's management then faced the dilemma of who would provide desktop support for Schaeffer. At first, they considered using the same regional vendor that ABC had used, but this idea was abandoned due to concerns about the survival of the small outsourcing company. Instead, the decision was made to bring all of the desktop support back in-house. The IT support personnel that were moved to ABC as part of the original outsourcing deal became Schaeffer employees again. Essentially, this meant that the ABC personnel that had been located in the basement of the Colbert facility were moved to the same floor as other Colbert IT employees, and the desktop support activities were now managed by this division for all of Schaeffer.

As part of this change, Colbert's IT managers set up new SLAs for its internal workers. During the ABC contract, 80 percent of the desktop support issues were to be resolved in the time specified, but Colbert changed this to 95 percent. For example, under the ABC contract 80 percent of level 1 issues were to be resolved within four hours, and under Colbert's new SLA 95 percent of level 1 issues were to be resolved within four hours. The quality of the service for Schaeffer's desktop and remote users, which had been one of the primary sources of user dissatisfaction with the

EXHIBIT 2
Compliance Statistics for Severity 3 Desktop Support Under New Target

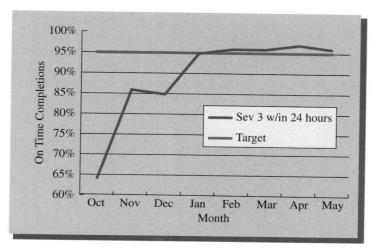

ABC contract, increased dramatically—even exceeding the new 95 percent targets for 24-hour resolution (see Exhibit 2).

> Morale improved after I came back here. ABC is just such a big company—it was "No Ticket—No Work." Schaeffer people hated that, because they were so used to me walking down the hall to fix an issue. Now, we are given the liberty to respond if someone stops us, and they don't have a ticket. We can spend an hour at somebody's desk—turn in an AIP (Action in Progress)—and get credit for the time we spent on what we did. You are still not doing it as "freebie" work, but accounting for your time. So within this last year here, we have had tons of compliments on the way things are working.
>
> *Larry Brown*

> Part of that was morale. There were people in the [desktop] team that were just frustrated with being in that middle position—being in between your customer and your employer. They felt they were caught is this "tug-of-war." Once it came in house, everybody saw the opportunities that were available, and realized that things were going to be better—but at the same time that expectations were going to be higher.
>
> *Evan McGreary, Desktop Support Lead*

Several business users expressed their happiness with the improved customer service in writing (see Exhibit 3).

The New Outsourcing Dilemma for Schaeffer

About four years into the contract with ABC, Schaeffer announced a more radical business restructuring plan: The parent entity would be dissolved, and two separate business entities

EXHIBIT 3
Quotes from Business Users

1. It is so paralyzing not to have a computer in this day and age, and Sam was of great help. I thought you should know that I was very pleased with your staff.

2. Two words come to mind regarding the implementation of my new laptop–"AWESOME SERVICE!" From the time the e-mail was sent to the final installation of the laptop, everyone involved was very professional, and extremely helpful in getting this done so quickly for me. You all did an awesome job and should feel good about what you do for our organization.

3. Thanks for the excellent job in setting up my new laptop. This will make my transition to Germany much smoother.

4. Tina and John have been awesome! I was blown away at how quickly you turned around my computer! You were both available by phone for me. My computer is great! I feel like it's Christmas all over again. . . . I can't tell you how much I appreciate your seamless response!

5. I wanted to let you know that Jack came up this AM, to work on my problematic printer. He arrived early and was very cheerful and took a lot of time to work on it. He even gave me his cell number in case I ran into any more problems. I know this printer has been difficult and with Jack's help, it now seems to be working wonderfully!

would be created for its two remaining divisions. The news of the split was received positively by Schaeffer's shareholders, as Colbert currently had about $700 million in annual revenues and 3,500 employees, but Reitzel was almost twice that size and still growing.

An agreement was reached with ABC to transfer the outsourcing contract from the parent (Schaeffer) to the new Reitzel Corporation, with no financial penalty. This meant that the new Colbert Corporation could decide whether to continue in an outsourcing arrangement with ABC via Reitzel, start a new outsourcing contract of its own, or insource all of its IT infrastructure activities. The current IT leadership team at Colbert included several seasoned IT managers, including one manager with deep experience working for a different large outsourcing vendor. These same managers had been responsible for Colbert's recent success at insourcing the desktop support for all of Schaeffer. A few weeks after the business restructuring announcement, Colbert's IT leaders began assessing what insourcing would mean in terms of not only IT costs but also the hiring of new IT talent in the current regional labor market:

> We think we can do it cheaper, better, and faster internally. There's always a markup with a vendor: the vendor has to make 15–30% markup with their people and leveraging is very difficult. When you need a dedicated onsite facility, a vendor can't do it cheaper than you can—unless you do offshoring.
>
> *Rusty Evans*

Pursuing an agreement with a regional IT outsourcer that is not burdened with global support needs also might be an attractive option. But every one of Colbert's IT managers agreed that the complaints about customer service under any new arrangement would need to go away.

As for the new Reitzel Corporation, its managers must decide whether or not to renew the IT infrastructure contract with ABC when it expires, and whether or not to continue to purchase desktop support from Colbert. Another key outsourcing issue to be addressed is whether to continue to sole-source its IT infrastructure activities, or whether to open up negotiations with other vendors for competitive bids. Sole-sourcing may not lead to the lowest cost or best SLA contract terms. Competitive bidding might lead to lower IT contract costs for Reitzel, but even going through the decision process would be resource-intensive. Changing to a different vendor or adding another vendor for a multisourcing arrangement would also mean another painful transition period:

> As a company, we haven't acquired as many companies as we initially thought. But when we have acquired, it has definitely been beneficial to have ABC. They have a deeper bench and can bring in the necessary resources at a last minute's notice.
>
> *Virginia King*

Before the latest restructuring announcement, the plan had been to start the renegotiation process with ABC in about six months. That would have given Schaeffer a year to decide whether to renew the sole-source agreement with ABC, and if it chose not to, there would still be ample time to explore other alternative arrangements. But with the public announcement about separating the companies, Reitzel's management team decided to start conversations with ABC several months sooner. In preparation for discussions with Reitzel's top management, the vice president of IT began to prepare a document that would capture what the company had learned under the current outsourcing arrangement, and what might be done differently in the future.

It was beginning to look like the outsourcing decisions for the two new companies would be as complicated and time-consuming as the original decision to contract with ABC had been several years earlier.

SYSTEMS SUPPORT FOR A NEW BAXTER MANUFACTURING COMPANY PLANT IN MEXICO

Baxter Manufacturing Company (BMC), located in a small midwestern town, is a leading manufacturer of metal stampings, particularly deep-drawn electric motor housings. The company was founded in 1978 by its chairman, Walter R. Baxter, as a supplier of tools and dies, but it soon expanded into the stamping business. BMC is a closely held corporation, with the Baxter family holding most of the stock.

BMC's major customers include Ford, General Motors, Honda of America, General Electric, Whirlpool, Amana, and Maytag. BMC has two markets. It makes brackets and other components sold directly to appliance and automotive assemblers to go straight into the end product. But BMC also makes motor casings and the like that go to intermediate suppliers that make components (such as motors) that then go to the appliance and automotive assemblers of the finished products. For example, BMC ships a motor housing to a motor manufacturer who makes the motor, and BMC also makes the bracket that holds the motor onto the frame and ships it directly to the manufacturer who assembles the motor and bracket into the finished product.

BMC's 170,000-square-foot manufacturing facility is one of the best in the country, with 43 presses that range from 50- to 800-ton capacity. Every press is equipped with accessory items such as feeds, reels, and electronic detection systems. In addition to the presses, BMC has recently added the capacity to weld, drill, tap, and assemble stampings into more complex parts to suit the needs and desires of its customers.

BMC employs about 420 people and is nonunion. Over its 22-year history, BMC has had steady growth. The most recent 6 years of sales were:

1994	$49,900,000	1997	$85,785,000
1995	$61,976,000	1998	$97,550,000
1996	$74,130,000	1999	$112,337,000

Before joining BMC in 1994, MIS manager Don Collins had 20 years of experience as a lead systems analyst with a large manufacturer and broad experience with manufacturing systems. In 1997 the MIS department had five people, but there was some turnover and Collins was unable to hire replacements because of the high salaries commanded by people with the necessary skills. Therefore, the MIS department was down to three people, including Collins, and in a maintenance mode for the past 3 years. BMC management has recognized that improved systems are a high priority, and Collins has recently been authorized to hire two more people at competitive salaries.

BMC managers have generated so many requests for new systems that an MIS steering committee has been established to approve projects and set systems development priorities. The members of the MIS steering committee are President Kyle Baxter, Vice President for Customer Service Sue Barkley, Controller Lou Wilcox, and Don Collins. Sue Barkley is a sister of Kyle Baxter and has been a champion of information technology within BMC.

Recent Developments

In May 1999, a major appliance manufacturer customer contacted BMC President Kyle Baxter and encouraged BMC to consider building a plant in Mexico to serve the needs of the customer's Mexican operations. This customer had carefully studied its suppliers and selected a small number to invite to become favored parts suppliers in Mexico.

In January 2000, the BMC board approved the decision to build a plant in Mexico. BMC management had been thinking about building a plant in Mexico for some time, for about 20 percent of BMC's production was being shipped to factories located in Mexico. Although Mexican wage rates are much lower than those in the United States, BMC management was not primarily motivated by the prospect of low Mexican wages. Stamping is very capital intensive and semiautomated, so labor costs are not a big part of the total cost of production, and there will be additional costs that will make up for any wage savings. But the cost of shipping, the problems in getting products across the border, and the difficulty in predicting exactly when a shipment will be delivered all make customers prefer to have their parts produced locally for their Mexican factories. BMC management decided that in order to be an important factor in the growing Mexican market, BMC must have a factory in Mexico.

BMC has assured its U.S. workers and the community in which its current plant is located that no present production will be moved to Mexico—everything produced there will be new business. The U.S. plant has been expanded 18 times since the first unit was built, and there is little room for further expansion on the site. If BMC's sales are to continue to grow, new plants will have to be built, and those in the United States will probably be built closer to major customers.

BMC decided to build the new plant in Queretaro, a thriving metropolis located about a 3-hour drive northwest of Mexico City. The city of Queretaro has a population of about 500,000, and its metropolitan area has a population of about a million. It has excellent infrastructure for Mexico, with progressive city leadership and a university. This university is paperless. All course work and homework is completed on computers—no paper at all! There is a lot of technology education available, including tool and die training programs. Also, some major U.S. consulting firms have offices there. This environment is why BMC's customer and other manufacturers are locating in Queretaro.

The new factory will be located reasonably close to the customer plant that it will serve. However, Kyle Baxter intends to expand BMC's business in Mexico, so in the long run this plant will supply parts to other customers. The new plant will start out small, but BMC has plenty of land and the plant has been designed so that it can be easily expanded as the need arises. The plant's initial planned dimensions are about 200 by 200 feet, providing 40,000 square feet of space. It will start with six presses (two 125-ton, two 200-ton, and two 300-ton presses) but with none of the huge 600- to 800-ton presses that BMC has in the main plant. It will have some welders, a toolroom, and a tooling facility where dies can be maintained. There will be offices in the plant for quality control, plant engineering, and a shift supervisor, and office space along the front for the plant manager, accounting manager, human resources manager, clerical workers, and a computer room. In addition it will have a break room, a training room, and shower and locker facilities—most plants provide shower facilities in that part of Mexico. And there will be a small kitchen where the workers can cook meals.

Don Collins designed the computer room for the Mexican plant. It is located in a secure area next to a permanent wall and will have adequate power, air conditioning, emergency lighting, and everything that is needed for a computer room. The plant will be wired with category-5 copper wiring throughout. There are plans for fiber-optic cable as the plant expands, so internal communications will not be a problem. They may or may not install a central computer at the start. An Ethernet LAN will connect the PCs in the plant.

Initially this plant will employ about 35 people in a single shift operation. As of May 1, 2000, the plant manager, Jesus Salazar, and the financial and human resources manager, Maria Alvarez, had been hired. Both were from the locality and speak some English. It is expected that the other managers will speak some English, although they may not be completely fluent. But the rest of the workers will not be English-speaking. Initially two experienced BMC managers, one from the toolroom facility and the other from plant engineering, will be sent to Queretaro to help with the start-up and training. These two expatriate managers have no international experience and neither speaks Spanish. They are scheduled to return to the United States within 2 years, after which the staff in Mexico should be entirely local.

For the foreseeable future BMC will do all engineering, designing, and building of the dies in its U.S. facility and ship them to the Mexican plant. They will have to do some final tuning down there. Die maintenance will be done locally, so BMC will have to develop some skilled people there. That is one reason BMC is sending the two managers from the United States to help them get started.

The Mexican plant was designed, the land was acquired, and ground was broken for construction in January 2000. The Mexican plant was scheduled to begin to deliver parts to its major customer in December 2000.

For tax and legal reasons, BMC has established a wholly owned subsidiary corporation to own and operate the Mexican plant. BMC will treat the Mexican plant just like an outside contractor—customers will place orders with the BMC home office and pay the home office for the parts. Then the home office will pay the Mexican subsidiary for the work it performs and the service it provides. The Mexican plant will ship the parts it produces directly to the customer, and will work directly with the customer on operational issues such as quality.

IS Issues

When BMC management decided to build a plant in Mexico, Don Collins' first concern was how to deal with the systems needs of a plant in Mexico. When this question arose BMC President Kyle Baxter's first reaction was:

> We want to have good systems down there, and we ought to use this opportunity to consider the long-range systems needs of the entire company. It would be nice if we could get something in Mexico that we can use for the entire company.

In January 2000, Kyle Baxter established a small task force to develop a plan for systems support of the Mexican plant and report to the BMC executive committee. The designated task force leaders were Collins and Virginia (Ginnie) Mease, BMC's controller. The task force also included Sue Barkley, Jesus Salazar, and Maria Alvarez.

The stated mission of the task force was:

To implement the desired business processes and to select, implement, and support the appropriate business system that will exceed the needs of BMC Mexico.

The goals of the task force included the following:

1. Business processes will be defined to facilitate optimum effectiveness.
2. Software will match the business processes.
3. Software will enable integrated processes.
4. The business system selected can also be implemented throughout BMC.
5. Language and currency needs will be met.
6. The business system investment will provide the best cost/benefit.
7. Support of the system will be available in Mexico.

For some time BMC managers had been thinking about the possibility of acquiring an enterprise resource planning (ERP) system to replace and expand the operational systems of the company, and an ERP would meet most of the previously stated goals, so the initial focus of the task force was to investigate the possibility of acquiring an ERP.

Collins was a member of an IS management group sponsored by a local university, and through this contact he was able to get access to three nearby companies who had experience with an ERP. Collins and Mease developed an interview guide covering the questions they thought were important, interviewed managers at the three companies, and summarized the results of the interviews. Two things stood out from the interviews: First, there was not enough time to implement an ERP package properly by the end of the year, and, second, BMC management could not simultaneously cope with the disruption of starting a new plant and the disruption of installing an ERP. Therefore, on May 25, 2000, the BMC executive committee decided to eliminate the goal of considering the long-term needs of BMC from the task force charter and to concentrate exclusively on developing systems support for the Mexican plant.

Alternatives Considered

After the decision to abandon consideration of an ERP, Collins and Mease defined the following three approaches to supporting the Mexican plant:

1. Connect the Mexican plant to BMC's existing systems through a high-speed communications line.
2. Contract through an application service provider (ASP) to provide systems support to the Mexican plant.
3. Employ a piecemeal solution where they would acquire a number of software packages that could run on the

networked PCs in Mexico that would serve the basic needs of the Mexican plant.

Initially the Mexican plant would be a relatively small operation, and transaction volumes would be quite small. Collins and Mease felt that at the start they would only need to handle basic things—control inventory, ship, print reports, handle EDI to and from the major customer—the things necessary for the operation to run. On the other hand, they expected the Mexican operation to grow rapidly, so transaction volumes and the complexity of managing production would grow over time.

The first alternative—using the existing BMC systems in Mexico through a high-speed communications line—was quickly eliminated. In the first place, there was the language problem. BMC's existing systems were in English and would have to be translated into Spanish for use in Mexico, and that was deemed impractical. Second, because of the language problem, they could not support these systems in Mexico. The availability of local support was a crucial factor in determining how to serve the systems needs of the Mexican plant. There must be people who can help install the applications software, handle any problems that arise, and train people in using the software. And there must be support for the hardware platform that the applications run on.

An application service provider (ASP) is a company that has one or more large data centers and furnishes a portion of that processing and file storage capacity to each of its clients via communications facilities. For years it has been anticipated that, sometime in the future, information processing power would be available through a wall plug just like electrical power. An ASP is the current embodiment of that dream. Thus, the customer of an ASP does not have to invest in computer hardware and systems software or manage a data center. Rather, the customer pays a monthly fee to the ASP based on the amount of file storage, RAM, and computer processing cycles used. The customer also pays for the use of the communications facilities used.

The ASP may also provide some applications software, but the customer usually buys applications software from software vendors that work with the ASP. The ASP provides help desk support and deals with hardware problems, but applications software problems are handed off to the individual software vendors.

Collins had difficulty exploring the ASP option. He contacted his local IBM representative, but it took a long time to get in touch with a person who represented IBM's ASP business. It was early August before Collins could get definite information on what ASP services IBM could provide to the Mexican plant. IBM would be able to serve the Mexican plant through communications facilities linking the Mexican plant to IBM's Rochester, N.Y., data center. Applications software would be obtained from a number of software vendors with whom IBM has partnership arrangements. Many of these vendors provide Spanish language versions of some of their software. IBM provides a Spanish language help desk that hands off applications software problems to the appropriate vendor's Spanish language help desk.

The cost of IBM's ASP service would be $60,000 per year. There would, of course, be additional charges for the applications software, training, data conversion, and start-up. These costs seemed excessive in comparison to the third alternative and the ASP solution seemed overly complicated for the start-up operation, so BMC abandoned consideration of the ASP option and concluded that the piecemeal solution was the only viable option for supporting the Mexican operation at the start. However, after the Mexican plant is in operation and things have settled down, BMC intends to reconsider both the ERP and the ASP options for the entire company.

Nagging Difficulties

Collins, Mease, and Barkley had encountered major communications difficulties in dealing with the BMC people in Mexico. Salazar and Alvarez had not been active participants in the task force, and there had been little effective communication with either of them. According to Collins, there were four things contributing to these communications problems:

1. **Language.**   When we talk to each other we don't always understand the true meaning of what the other guy is saying. We nod our heads, but we may not be on the same page.
2. **Cultural.**   They give the distinct impression of wanting to be self-sufficient, and therefore any help we give may be considered paternalistic. This may be the result of sensitivities relating to America's dominant position ever since the Mexican War.
3. **Distance.**   It would be different if we could drive there in a couple of hours. But it is a major disruption for them to come up here or us to go down there.
4. **Mind-set.**   Their mind-set has been on getting up and running and producing parts, not on any supporting activities. We just cannot get their attention, and you can't communicate without attention!

Collins, Mease, and Barkley have also begun to reconsider the task force's role in providing systems support to the Mexican plant. Barkley explains their dilemma:

We feel that we are responsible for helping them get started right, but it is clear that they would like to do it on their own. We don't want their local pride to result in them falling on their faces, but if they have the capability they definitely need to have a major role in making the decisions. But we can't tell whether they have the capability.

Right now they are concentrating on getting the plant operational so that they can get parts out the door. We are

ready to help, but they don't seem to have the time or the urgency. We are afraid that once they get past the hurdle of getting into production, then they are going to expect to get the systems installed and running in the next week.

The broader question is: How much should we dictate to them in all areas down there? Do we want to let them reinvent the wheel because of the cultural gap between us and them? Or should we insist on providing some guidance from our functional areas (human resources, quality, materials control, production planning, etc.) to assist them with getting the basics up and going? On the other hand, do we really want to pass on any of our "bad habits" to them?

Status on September 12, 2000

Construction of the Mexican plant is on schedule, and it will be ready to begin production no later than December 1. As of September 12, Collins and Mease felt that they had made little progress in providing systems support for the Mexican operation. They had decided to pursue a piecemeal approach, so they needed to find vendors who could provide and support the basic Spanish language software packages that would be needed to support the small start-up operation.

Maria Alvarez, the human resources/financial manager, had experience with a small financial software package from Contpaq and she would like very much to use that package at the Mexican plant. Contpaq has a Web site, but it is in Spanish, so Collins has not been able to find out much about the software from that source. Grant Thornton, BMC's U.S. consultant for establishing a Mexican operation, has an office in Queretaro. This firm will be the Mexican plant's auditor, and it recommends the Contpaq financial software, so it appears that local support for that package would be available. Unfortunately, Collins has been unable to find out if this package will run on the peer-to-peer PC network planned for the Mexican plant. Collins has contacted Grant Thornton's Mexican office, but has not been able to get this information from its people. Collins is also trying to determine if Grant Thornton can provide local support for the Mexican plant's PCs.

The Mexican plant now has two customers. Collins and Mease have contacted both of them to determine what kind of interaction they will require at the start. Fortunately, neither of them is using EDI in Mexico, so they will fax shipping orders and schedules to the plant. They are both using standard labels, so it should be possible to find a simple barcode package to produce the labels. They also do not have any special requirements for packing slips and bills of lading, so BMC should be able to find a simple package to produce this paperwork. If not, this paperwork could be created manually on a typewriter at the start. Collins and Mease are confident that Spanish language software to do these things is available in Mexico, and that support for it will also be available locally.

Collins believes that the task force has responsibility for three things:

One is to make sure that we have the infrastructure in place—plant wiring that is tested and secure, a secure computer room for a server if it is needed, desktop PCs set up and working on the LAN—and make sure that we have support for those. Next is communications—Internet access and a digital line so that they can route their network into ours so that we can share files and communicate through a dedicated connection. The third area is applications.

We have the first two under control except for local support. We sent Jim Walters from my staff down there and he tested their wiring and it is fine. We also sent Paul Adams from my staff down to set up all the desktop PCs and the peer-to-peer network, and he also gave them Internet access. We still do not have the dedicated digital line, but the phone company will provide that in its own due time.

The weak link right now is support down there. When things don't work on a PC or the network, it is very hard—whether it is English or Spanish—to solve those kinds of problems over the phone. We must have support down there for the desktop, and so far we don't have it.

They also are a long way from obtaining the needed applications software. Collins assesses this problem as follows:

I think that we can get a simple package to produce the bar-code labels for the parts, and a package to produce the shipping documents. But the people down there have not been concerned with some fundamental questions such as: How do you schedule production? How do you order materials? What is needed on the factory floor? How are you going to provide instructions to the operators on how to run the parts?

Ginnie and I are struggling with whether to go down there, pull some people aside, take them to a hotel for a couple of days, and try to settle some of those questions. Time is growing short!

BAT APSS: SHARED SERVICES AT A MULTINATIONAL FIRM

The shared services approach provides significant economies of scale for very small operations. The only way that we could do SAP in these end markets was to use a template so that support would be at a marginal cost. We also revised the implementation process to make it quicker and affordable.

— *Mr. Ponce, Asia Pacific Regional IT Manager*

The conclusion was that we couldn't achieve any additional cost efficiencies by outsourcing. The cost is already low and [an external provider] couldn't do it any cheaper. The challenge is whether we can do it any better.

— *Mr. Tan, Head, APSS*

One of the biggest challenges for shared services is to grow credibility within the BAT world. It all comes back to skills, resource costs, and credibility.

— *Mr. Lam, IT Director, Malaysia*

Background on BAT and the IT Function

British American Tobacco (BAT) is a 99-year-old company in the tobacco industry that has grown to be one of the top three global players through organic growth and acquisitions. Formerly B.A.T. Industries, it spun off its financial services business in 1998 and merged with the global cigarette company Rothmans International in 1999. BAT's local and international brands are sold in six world regions: Africa, America Pacific, Asia Pacific, Europe, Latin America, and Mesca (Middle East and Central Asia). A seventh division, STC (Smoking Tobacco and Cigars), is a global division operating in more than 100 countries.

The profit centers are end markets typically at the country level.[1] Small- to medium-sized end markets typically report into an area cluster, a self-sufficient management unit. The area

directors report to regional directors, who are members of BAT's executive board (TMB, Tobacco Management Board). For example, the Asia Pacific region, which is headquartered in Kuala Lumpur, has five management units: Asia Pacific North (APN), Asia Pacific South (APS), Malaysia, Australasia, and Indonesia. The Asia Pacific regional director has a team of functional managers who provide functional leadership for the region.

The information technology (IT) function within BAT mirrors the overall company structure. The global CIO is located at Globe House in London and has direct reports with responsibilities for IT infrastructure, IT service delivery, e-business and business systems initiatives, and IT people and processes. Each region's IT manager, who has a solid-line report to the regional director, has a dotted-line report to the global CIO. The IT heads in the management units have a solid-line report to the managing director of the cluster.

For example, the IT manager for the Asia Pacific region, Mr. Ponce, is located at the Asia Pacific regional headquarters in Kuala Lumpur, Malaysia. APN has an IT organization based in Hong Kong, with responsibilities for identifying business requirements, identifying IT solutions, building business cases for IT projects, and managing support services (including local, shared, and outsourced services) for all the end markets in APN, including China, Hong Kong, and Taiwan.

The smaller end markets typically operate with very few IT resources of their own but share resources from the management unit center. For example, BAT Taiwan only has one IT technical support resource onsite for desktop and LAN support, who has a dotted-line report to the IT organization for APN.

Achieving IT Convergence

Under the global CIO, there has been an increased emphasis on business integration and IT convergence. A number of common global platforms have been designated as BAT standards. These initiatives include Project Hermes for consolidation of global telecommunications, GENA for deployment of a global standard desktop, either SAP R/3 or Sage Tetra CS/3 for enterprise resource planning, IBM's MQ series for enterprise application integration, and Lotus Notes for knowledge sharing.

[1]In early 2001, there were approximately 120 end markets.

Mr. Pottrick, the head of business integration, has global responsibilities for IT standardization and consolidation initiatives. On Pottrick's team there are two global ERP program managers: one for Sage Tetra CS/3 and one for SAP R/3. When these two ERP platforms were selected as standards in 1998, SAP R/3 was viewed as the standard solution for larger, more complex BAT markets only, because it had proven to be a very expensive system to implement and maintain. The Sage system was for less complex, smaller operations that did not need the functionality of SAP and that required a low-cost ERP solution. However, by early 2001, SAP had become a less expensive solution to implement.

> There is an implied strategy that SAP will become the solution for all end markets over time. However, that will depend on reducing costs so that it can be implemented at reasonable cost. This will mean template-based, out-of-the-box implementations (vanilla) or ASP delivery so that the cost is reasonable for those end markets.
>
> *— Mr. Pottrick, Head of Business Integration, Globe House*

Prior to the Rothmans merger, Globe House formed a committee with representatives from the regions and end markets to work with Ernst & Young consultants to develop a standard BAT template for SAP. The original template focused on global data standards sufficient for integrating high-level business data. However, although Globe House sets strategy and mandates the standard IT platforms, each end market chooses which ERP platform standard to implement, as well as when to implement it. Unique business pressures and the need to deal with Y2K issues at the local level had resulted in considerable deviation from the template standards.

For example, by early 2001 three different templates were being used for SAP R/3 configurations for end markets in the AP region: (1) the Symphony template used by the Singapore, Taiwan, and Thailand end markets; (2) the Malaysia template, which was a modification of the Symphony template to accommodate the merger with Rothmans; and (3) the Australian template, which has undergone a lot of customization. A recent study sponsored by Globe House to determine how close the various BAT templates were to the global template concluded that the AP region's Symphony template had the highest data standard compliance (95%) across BAT. The BAT Malaysia template had 85% compliance, while the Australian template was 50% compliant.

The lack of data standards is a key constraint to several e-business initiatives that BAT, like most international firms, has recently mounted. The lack of common processes also results in consolidations being done manually. These needs for standardization led to the revitalization of the Global ERP program management function. For example, under the SAP program manager, representatives from all regions and markets belong to a design reference group for SAP that is concerned with sharing best practices and lessons learned about end market initiatives. Global IT is also seeking ways to get stronger business unit buy-in for the use of common data and processes.

> The challenge is how to influence the regions and end markets to move on it.
>
> *— Mr. Pottrick, Head of Business Integration, Globe House*

IT Shared Services

BAT currently delivers IT services via three data centers geographically located in Europe (Hamburg, Germany), North America (Macon, Georgia), and the Asia Pacific (Kuala Lumpur, Malaysia) that are governed by regional management. All three data centers now operate under a shared services model: By consolidating IT operational support functions at the regional level, economies can be achieved, and these cost savings contribute to the profitability of the BAT end markets that purchase their IT services. Shared services is therefore a very powerful approach for providing services to small but growing markets: Each country can leverage the best practices of the enterprise at marginal cost.

Europe was the first region to extend the shared services concept to include application services: In 1997 they began to offer hard-to-find SAP expertise to northern European countries for their R/3 implementation projects. Since that time, both the Asia Pacific and Middle East regions have also been exploring how to leverage IT applications expertise within their regions. For example, Sri Lanka in the MESCA region is one of the leaders in implementing CS/3.

Asia Pacific Shared Services (APSS): Evolving from a Data Center

As part of their Y2K compliance projects, several end markets in the Asia Pacific region needed to migrate from an AS/400 application (BPCS) to SAP R/3 about the same time. Representatives from their business and IT organizations came together in late 1997 to develop the template code-named "Symphony" and to share SAP technical expertise.

The following year, IT leaders in the AP region started to consider establishing an independent company to provide data center services for SAP and other applications, and the decision was made to take advantage of a government initiative in the region: the Malaysia Multi-media Super Corridor (MMSC) in Technology Park, Malaysia. The APDC was granted MMSC status in 1998 and started operations within the corridor in Kuala Lumpur in early 1999. Other countries in the region had similar high technology incentives, but Malaysia had a more advantageous cost structure.

MMSC companies receive various economic benefits, including reduced costs for utilities and additional tax incentives.

MMSC companies also are able to hire workers from outside the country more easily. For example, work permits can be made available within 1 to 2 weeks instead of 3 to 4 months. The cost for skilled IT personnel in Malaysia is quite low compared to the other labor markets. Malaysia is also a cultural melting pot where West meets East: the Malaysian population is a mixture of Chinese, Indian, and Malay. In addition to the Malay language, Bahasa, its residents commonly speak various Chinese dialects (e.g., Cantonese, Mandarin) and are proficient in English, which is the most effective language for communicating among all the countries in the region. There is also a cultural history of collaboration rather than conflict.

Since 1999, the APDC has evolved into a shared services organization that includes not only a data center but also a competency center (center of excellence) for SAP. (See Exhibit 1.) The regional IT head, Mr. Ponce, brought in Andersen Consulting (now Accenture) to help identify the best opportunities for shared services in early 2000. Today, the APSS mission is to maximize economies of scale in the delivery of application support, technical support, and operations support for the end markets in the region. Service level agreements are used to ensure responsiveness to the customer.

APSS is currently governed by two BAT organizations. (See Exhibit 2.) The regional IT Council, chaired by the managing director of BAT Malaysia, consists of the regional IT head and the heads of the IT organizations for APN, APS, Australia, Malaysia, and Indonesia, sets the strategic IT direction for the APSS organization. APSS also has a dotted-line report to the ASEAN Synergies Group, which consists of all the top business managers in the ASEAN sub-region. The formation of APSS required buy-in from these business heads, who became convinced of the potential benefits of APSS operations for their end markets.

Mr. Tan currently heads the APSS organization. (See Exhibit 3.) He joined BAT in mid-1999 after a long tenure with companies in the oil-and-gas industry in Malaysia, in which he gained extensive SAP experience. On a day-to-day basis, Mr. Tan reports to the IT head for Malaysia, Mr. Lam, who developed an early vision for the shared services concept within the region.

The earliest component of APSS was the data center, which today includes computer operations, network management, and technical support for common BAT platforms, such as GENA (standard desktop infrastructure), and application software such as Lotus Notes and SAP R/3. APSS also manages regional and local IT infrastructures, which in some instances involves the management of outsourcing contracts. APSS also runs other shared systems for the region, such as a human resources system (Bucks), which is used by eight countries. An SAP applications manager is responsible for the SAP development and

EXHIBIT 1
Asia Pacific Shared Services Framework

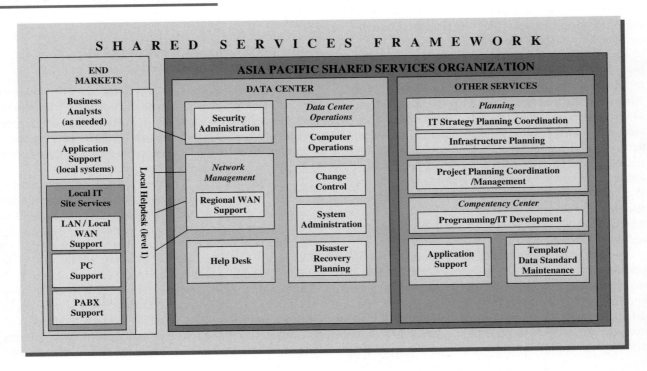

EXHIBIT 2

IT Governance at Asia Pacific Shared Services

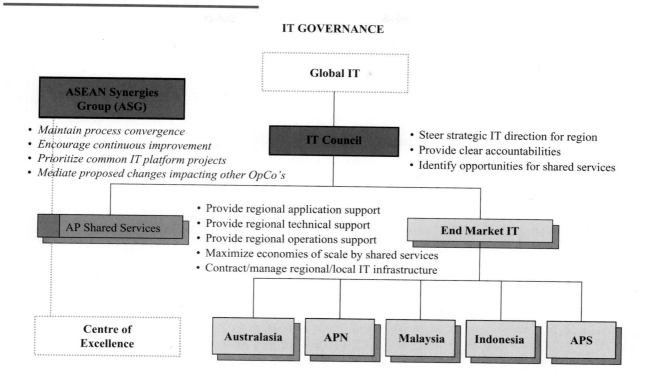

maintenance projects. A second applications manager provides other application development services for Malaysia and other countries in the region. Other centers of excellence for information technology also exist in the AP region outside of Malaysia. For example, Australia and Hong Kong provide Internet access for other end markets in the region.

In a recent 9 to 12 month APSS study, the costs for the data center, the servers, and desktop machines were examined for the whole AP region. The conclusion was that they could not achieve any additional cost efficiencies by outsourcing. In the year 2000, the annual cost via APSS for hosting an SAP R/3 user, which includes hardware, software lease, and support for hardware and applications, was U.S.$3,500. The expectation is that this figure will decrease still further by the end of 2001: three SAP instances will be running systems for ten end markets in the region and a total of 1,500 users, at an average cost of U.S.$3,000 per user. In contrast, if those end markets were to host SAP R/3 by country, their annual costs were estimated to be in excess of U.S.$9,000 per user.

Staffing Issues

External contract personnel are regularly used by APSS in order to expand and contract their resources for application development projects. APSS has formed partnerships with local service providers who can provide experienced personnel. APSS also has contracts with freelance consultants. Contract personnel are generally put first on new projects so that they understand the problems of the end markets and are then rotated into support roles. On average, APSS employs 10 to 15 contractors, with a mix of short- and long-term contracts.

For example, a new APSS contract employee with extensive SAP knowledge who was hired for the BAT Taiwan implementation was given about 3 weeks' training on the Symphony template and APSS methodology prior to going onsite to Taiwan for the kickoff of their R/3 implementation project. During those weeks, she had access to written documentation and an APSS staff member who provided support for another end market walked through the template with her.

Currently, APSS is concentrating on cross-training full-time personnel to gain more flexibility. For example, APSS personnel go to SAP training for multiple modules as well as cross-functional training so that they have exposure to how R/3 is integrated across modules. Expertise is also built via a Lotus Notes database that is used for knowledge transfer. This tool is used as a repository for project documentation and for a help desk system. Knowledge transfer also occurs following each implementation: When project team members complete an implementation, they run through the design and any special

EXHIBIT 3
Organization Chart for Asia Pacific Shared Services

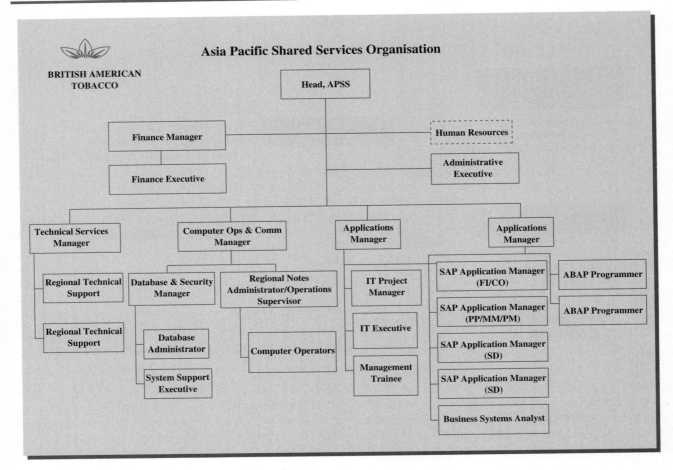

requirements the country has with all members of the SAP application team.

Managing IT resources for a growing shared services operation will continue to be a challenge. APSS needs not only to recruit the best people, but also to train them and retain them.

> A key challenge is how to quickly mobilize resources and put the right people on projects.
>
> — *SAP Applications Manager, APSS*

BAT sells itself as a company that is human-centric: it cares for its people and their development. There are numerous opportunities to grow within BAT: high-potential employees can move into many different functions worldwide throughout their career. Given that there may be limitations to grow within certain end markets, opportunities will be made available to high-potential employees and especially to those who are mobile.

> — *Mr. Lam, IT Director, Malaysia*

Leveraging SAP Templates and Implementation Expertise

During the past 2 years, the APSS staff has gained a lot of expertise in implementing SAP systems. An external consulting partner (Andersen Consulting) had been used for the Australia, Malaysia, and Singapore projects, and also projects that involved data integration initiatives for the Rothmans merger. Much of this experience was used to good advantage in Fall 2000 for the Taiwan and Thailand R/3 implementation projects that were completed by APSS without external consultants. However, the opportunity for the Taiwan implementation almost eluded them.

> We were deploying resources for the merger and were not really thinking about how to bring the figure down for Taiwan because it didn't have the resources. The thinking behind it was not whether they needed ERP or not, because they needed it: we wanted them to have the scalability to grow, and grow fast.

But Taiwan had an offer from ECoE [European Center of Excellence for SAP] and we realized that someone would be eating our own grass. We revised the implementation process and found that we could take time out of it.

— Mr. Ponce, Asia Pacific Regional IT Manager

The fixed-cost contract for the two-phase Taiwan implementation was U.S.$150,000, and the less complex Thailand implementation was U.S.$50,000. The Taiwan implementation required two functions specific to Taiwan: a government-mandated invoicing system and Chinese (Mandarin) language capabilities. These projects were considered a quantum leap from the earlier Singapore implementation, which included manufacturing modules and was done with external consultants (Andersen Consulting) at a cost of U.S.$5 million.

Both the Taiwan and Thailand implementations involved converting the end markets to a new business model by January 2001. These business model changes involved not only direct importation, but also direct distribution, two activities that had been done previously by independent distributors of BAT products. Although neither of the markets was very large, the change in business model meant a big change in operations. In addition to their prior functions, both needed an ERP system for accounts receivable, accounts payable, as well as purchasing and inventory management, and they needed it in less than 6 months.

The two implementations had overlapping schedules. The first phase of the Taiwan implementation (without bolt-ons) was scheduled for 8 weeks, and the kickoff was the end of September 2000. The Thailand implementation was scheduled for 5 weeks, initiated in October, and completed before the Taiwan implementation. BAT's operations in Taiwan were much larger than those in Thailand: The office has evolved from a 20-person to a 100-person office in less than 5 years. In addition, the Taiwan implementation had two unique requirements (a government-required invoicing system and a Chinese-language module), neither of which was supplied by the R/3 version currently used by APSS. The BAT Thailand office had only two finance people prior to the R/3 implementation, and the project had one unique requirement: invoices in the Thai language.

Each project had a project manager from the area IT organization (APS for Thailand, APN for Taiwan), a full-time APSS development team, and a technical team with part-time APSS resources. For both projects, the APSS development team members worked onsite and part-time ABAP and Basis personnel worked primarily from Kuala Lampur. The SAP applications manager at APSS served as the APSS lead for the Thailand project. She also did the high-level project plan for Taiwan and had an oversight role for that project. One of her direct reports was the APSS lead on the Taiwan project. Because the Symphony template was to be implemented for both Taiwan and Thailand

in the same client in a single R/3 instance along with the Singapore system, it was critical that changes made to the template for either site were carefully coordinated. APSS had formal procedures for how to go about changing the template, as well as the time frames for doing it.

The Taiwan project was treated as a one-off implementation and the project team spent a lot of time in a business blueprint stage, in which users typically determine the R/3 best practices that will be used for their company.[2] When the business processes were new to the end market, however, the APSS team members explained how the processes in the template worked, and then asked the users about local requirements. This approach was modified for the Thailand implementation: The APSS team set up the template in a conference room pilot (CRP), which allowed users to interact with a working model of the proposed system. In this way, a few special requirements were identified. Because Thailand would be using shared services out of Singapore for their finance function, the finance module for the Symphony template had to be strictly adhered to. The Thailand project was therefore more of a "straightjacket" implementation in which the APSS team drove the project.

> Thailand could not have transformed itself from Rep Office to Trading Co. with the speed required if the processes had not been determined already; it enabled Thailand to scale up its operations with very few additional resources.
>
> *— Mr. Ponce, Asia Pacific Regional IT Manager*

The Taiwan case is a demonstration of how you can take a complex enterprise application and deploy it in a business situation in reasonable cost and time.

> *— Mr. Pottrick, Head of Business Integration, Globe House*

The approaches used for the Taiwan and Thailand implementations are expected to be applicable to other small locations with changing business models and few unique business requirements. However, some countries will require more complex implementations. For example, some end markets will have additional modules to implement their manufacturing operations. Other end markets that currently operate manually will require a totally new technical infrastructure as well as additional types of training.

> The oil-and-gas industry had 50 to 60 organizations sharing the same template. The same convergence can also be achieved in the tobacco industry because the industry is not that complex. The challenge is to find the right balance between convergence and flexibility.
>
> *— Mr. Tan, Head, APSS*

---

[2]In a one-off implementation, the business problem has distinct characteristics that need to be assessed independently.

IT Shared Services: The Future

APSS is a young organization building credibility based on BAT process knowledge and low-cost solutions. The next challenges will be to expand its services and to learn to market its shared services to a broader arena.

Partnerships with other BAT shared services units may also become increasingly important. Although the AP region has demonstrated that SAP R/3 implementations can be affordable to smaller end markets, IT cost efficiencies alone may not be a strong enough business driver for an end market to adopt a standard template. For example, a business model that includes a price discount for subscribing to financial shared services as well as SAP R/3 was "proven" in Thailand and is likely to be adopted by other country managers. That is, a discount per named SAP user is given to the end market based on cost savings from the sharing of help desk services: The APSS help center funnels finance calls to the financial shared center in Singapore.

> There are some restrictions when using a template, which a business is more willing to accept if it sees that it is possible to have business-focused shared services, such as for financials.
>
> — *SAP Programme Manager, Globe House*

In Thailand there is a very conscious recognition that "I don't need to worry about all this back office work. This is all done for me. I have more time to focus on the business, just look at [the output from SAP] and analyze my profitability and what we need to do."

> — *Mr. Ponce, Asia Pacific Regional IT Manager*

In the future, APSS may also be in a position to offer its services outside the AP region. The European shared-services organizations already support end markets in Latin America and other regions outside of Europe, and the AP end countries are beginning to see that SAP is affordable. The learnings from template-based R/3 implementations could also be leveraged for other package implementations— such as a standard customer relationship-management (CRM) system. Global BAT could also decide to commercialize its shared services organizations, rather than retaining these units as internal service providers.

MARY MORRISON'S ETHICAL ISSUE (REVISED)

Mary Morrison, a second-semester sophomore business major at Big State University, was unpacking the new PC that her family had given her for Christmas when she discovered that, except for the Windows operating system, no software was included with the machine. Although the new PC was an adequate computer, it was an inexpensive machine, and one way that the store kept the price low was to not include software. Mary was concerned because she knew that she would need a good word processor, a spreadsheet program, and some presentation software, and she thought that this software would be included with the computer.

According to her friends, Microsoft Office Professional was the recommended suite of software for business students. Mary quickly checked around the university and found that she could buy Microsoft Office Professional at the special price of $199. However, a friend, Frank Taylor, offered to let her copy his Microsoft Office Professional onto the new machine. Mary was uneasy about accepting Frank's offer because she had learned in her computer literacy class that copying copyrighted software was illegal and was tantamount to stealing it. She told Frank that she needed to think about it. Frank could not understand her hesitation. "Everybody does it," he explained.

Mary's Background

Mary's family was reasonably well-to-do. Her mother and father had met at Big State University and had gotten married when they both graduated. Mary was the oldest child and had two younger brothers. Mary's parents valued education and expected to send all of their children to college. Although they had a comfortable income and had saved money for their children's education for years, the rapidly rising cost of a college education forced them to establish a home equity loan that they could use to help with college expenses. Their oldest son would be in college next year, and the financial crunch would increase when they had two children in college at the same time. That situation would last several years.

Mary grew up to be a good student and graduated from high school in the top third of her class. Because of the high cost, Mary did not consider going to a private school, but she and her parents had always expected her to attend Big State University so she started there in the fall after her high school graduation.

Mary's parents paid her tuition and room and board and provided her an additional amount each semester to cover books and incidentals, and they expected her to live within that amount. She worked a few hours a week in the college bookstore at minimum wage to provide more spending money and had saved several hundred dollars that she had planned to use to pay for a Spring Break trip to Florida with a group of her friends. She could use part of that money to pay for Microsoft Office, but she would have to work extra hours at the bookstore to afford her Spring Break trip.

Mary's Analysis

Mary considered herself to be an ethical person, and she was uneasy about accepting Frank's offer to let her copy his software, so she decided to consider the pros and cons of this decision. Her choices were to accept Frank's offer to install his Microsoft Office or to buy it for $199.

Mary considered the following rationale for accepting Frank's offer:

- Although it was illegal, there was no chance that she would get caught.
- It would not cost Frank anything, and although Microsoft would be losing revenue, it would go to Bill Gates, who already had more millions than he could spend.
- Everybody did it.
- Working extra hours at the bookstore would put pressure on both her studying and recreational time.

Mary considered the following arguments against copying Frank's software:

- She knew that copying Frank's software was stealing the product of someone else's effort. She viewed herself as an honest person. She had never stolen any-thing, and she knew that she would never consider shoplifting something worth $199 from a store, even if she knew she would not get caught. In fact, if she had found a wallet containing $200 in cash, she would go to great lengths to return the wallet and its contents to its owner.

• She had the money to buy the software.

After carefully considering her analysis, Mary picked up the phone to call Frank and tell him her decision.

A SECURITY BREACH ON THE INDIANA UNIVERSITY COMPUTER NETWORK

On Wednesday, March 12, 1997, over 2,000 Indiana University (IU) faculty received the following e-mail message: "Are you aware that Indiana University put your privacy at risk? Have they contacted you about it?"

The sender of this message was Glen Roberts of Oil City, Pennsylvania, who describes himself on his Web home page as a talk show host, privacy advocate, and Internet entrepreneur. Searching the Internet, Roberts had located an IU file containing the names of 2,760 IU faculty, along with their Social Security numbers, addresses, and phone numbers, which Roberts had downloaded and posted on his Web site. The file had been created by the University Graduate School to provide information on the research interests of the faculty members so that they could be notified of funding opportunities that might be of interest to them.

All IU information on the Web is supposed to be protected by a "safeword card." According to Norma Holland, director of university computing services: "We have what is called a 'firewall,' an Internet term that essentially prevents access to data which are not public. The safeword card allows only authorized and authenticated users to get to those data." But this sensitive file apparently was not protected. According to Jeffrey Alberts, associate dean, this was an obsolete file that escaped unnoticed when the system was being upgraded to make it more secure. The university immediately removed the file and disabled the old gateway service.

The situation was called "an eye-opener" by IU vice president for public affairs Christopher Simpson: "It was fortunate that more sensitive data was not compromised. Although we are very sensitive to the release of information like this, this is vastly different from having individual access to the university's most sensitive proprietary information. This is a good wake-up call. That is exactly how we are viewing it."

But Roberts posed a question of other potential security problems. "You must remember that even though my page may have brought this to your attention in an unpleasant man-

ner, the real danger lies in those who may have silently obtained the information from your site with no one the wiser," he wrote in a Web page dialogue with Mark S. Bruhn, IU information security officer.

Roberts claims the Privacy Act of 1974 "forbids such agencies (as IU) from even asking for Social Security numbers in other than specifically enumerated situations. That the SSN is included in any such faculty Internet research database is outrageous," Roberts wrote on his Web conversation with Bruhn. "Even if the files are not meant to be available to the public, the wholesale collection of such information in an 'Internet database' demonstrates a clear failure to understand even the most basic precepts of personal privacy."

Roberts' Justification

Roberts was described by people at two Pennsylvania newspapers as "an interesting fellow and a computer whiz-bang." According to the *Erie Times*, which did a profile on Roberts several months prior to this incident, he came to Oil City from the Chicago area, where he published a paper that dealt with privacy issues. He has done a short-wave radio program and now does a radio program on the Internet. Also, he has been a network television consultant and appeared on local talk shows. Roberts also publishes several Web pages and works as a computer consultant.

Roberts said he came across the IU file during a check of his own domain. By typing "SSN" into the Infoseek search engine, Roberts said, he called up a list of entries that showed a name and Social Security number. By opening that file, he found the IU research database.

Roberts said he has been involved in publicizing privacy issues for about 15 years. His interest began, he said, by using the Freedom of Information Act and obtaining copies of government documents. He said he was surprised at the amount of information available of which people are not usually aware. He has been particularly interested in the seemingly widespread availability of individuals' Social Security numbers, which are pathways to other information and whose disclosure raises the potential of unauthorized use of a person's identity.

Roberts states that the issue is this: "Should the university be collecting this information and putting it in databases, with maybe not the intent to pass it out all over the world but with intent that a fair number of people may be accessing that information?"

Roberts said he published the IU list because the privacy issue does not usually become tangible to people until they experience an invasion themselves. "The bottom line is privacy is an extremely important issue but it is only important when you see it affect yourself firsthand," he said. "That's what I have done with other Web pages. People can experience it firsthand, and with that experience can be more public debate and action on the issues."

He added that he is disturbed that people are unhappy with him for posting names and Social Security numbers where they can be obtained free, but no one seems concerned that the same kind of information is being sold all over the country. "The same outrage should apply to companies for however long they've been selling this kind of information," Roberts said. "Unless it is in your face, it does not seem to matter."

Faculty Reaction

Many of the IU faculty members on the published list disagree with Roberts' tactics. They were primarily concerned, for the obvious reasons, that their Social Security numbers were made easily available, and over a hundred faculty e-mailed protests to Roberts.

"I go to Roberts and say 'I like people who are watchdogs, but do you need to post this information in a convenient location to make your point?'" said Kurt Zorn, of the IU School of Public and Environmental Affairs. "I think he might have done more damage by doing this than the university did in its oversight. There might have been more effective ways of calling attention to the problem."

Law professor Ed Greenebaum added that he believes Roberts made a judgment about the university without any information, which is unfair. "The impact is to expose us to a danger he says he is trying to prevent, and it's much more than it otherwise would have been," Greenebaum said. "My concern is not with the university's intent but why this individual feels the need, inconsistently in my view, to facilitate the distribution of our Social Security numbers."

With IU threatening to take legal action and the heavy volume of protests from IU faculty, Roberts removed the IU file from his Web page and said he has no intention of posting the names and Social Security numbers again.

The Consequences

On March 27, religious studies professor James Ackerman said he had recently been billed for phone lines, Internet access, and credit card accounts that are not his own. Although it has not been verified, he believes someone picked up his name and Social Security number from Roberts' Web page.

Within two weeks of the posting, Ackerman received a bill for a month's Internet time, had a call from AT&T saying it was ready with a conference call he did not order, got an inquiry from Ameritech asking if he made a call from Germany to Portland, Oregon, and discovered there were calling card accounts opened in his name.

William Boone, an education professor, said his wife received an inquiry from MCI's fraud department about calls originating from Germany using the Boones' calling card number. Although there has been no proof that Roberts' Web page was the source of the information used in the fraud, Boone and others believe the incidents are more than a coincidence. "What are the chances two IU professors are getting unauthorized calls from Germany? What are the chances this is not related to the World Wide Web issue?" Boone said.

Boone's wife said the issue is unsettling. "It feels like such a violation," she said. "You feel like someone knows you but you don't know them. That is very uncomfortable."

The situation has been frustrating to Ackerman, who said the credit card companies told him they could not put a block on his Social Security number. He was told he could contact three credit agencies, which many banks use to check a person's credit, and they could put a hold on his records.

Ackerman also contacted the office of IU's legal counsel, which was unable to offer much assistance. "At this point, we don't even know if his experience relates in any way to Roberts' Web page," said Michael Klein, associate university counsel. "There are some timing coincidences, but you just don't know." However, the university is exploring whether there is any legal liability Roberts might incur if faculty members are damaged, financially or otherwise.

Klein added that the university is reviewing the issue of using Social Security numbers in the course of running the school. "As an institution, we are taking a look inward to determine if there are some alternatives," he said.

GLOSSARY

1 GbE, 10 GbE, 40 GbE   Variations of Gigabit Ethernet, operating at 1 billion bits per second (1 gbps), 10 billion bits per second (10 gbps), and 40 billion bits per second (40 gbps), respectively. 1 GbE and 10 GbE are often used in backbone networks, and 40 GbE is currently under development. *See also* Backbone network, Gigabit Ethernet.

Acceptable use policy   A company-specific policy for employee usage of computers and networks owned by the organization.

Account manager   A manager given the responsibility and accountability for managing a relationship with a specific business unit, either on a full-time basis or as part of his/her IS position responsibilities. Typically, an IS account manager will have an office physically close to business managers in the business unit for which he/she serves as the key point-of-contact and IS relationship manager.

Aggregator   Another name for an RSS reader. *See* RSS reader.

AI   *See* Artificial intelligence, Expert systems shell.

Alpha site   An organization that is involved as one of the first sites to use a software package before it is generally released to the market. An alpha site can influence all aspects of the package.

American National Standards Institute (ANSI)   The United States standard-setting body for many IT standards.

Analog network   The electronic linking of devices, where messages are sent over the links by having some analogous physical quantity (e.g., voltage) continuously vary as a function of time. Historically, the telephone network has been an analog network.

ANSI   *See* American National Standards Institute.

Antivirus software   Software designed to identify, block, and eliminate harmful computer files and program code. To be effective, antivirus software installed on a personal computer needs to be regularly updated with data about new known viruses.

Applet   An application program, written in the Java object-oriented programming language, which is usually stored on a Web server and downloaded to a microcomputer with a mouse click and then executed by a Java-compatible Web browser. A major advantage of a Java applet is that it can be run on virtually any IT platform. *See also* Web browser, IT platform.

Application independence   The separation, or decoupling, of data from application systems. Application independence means that applications are built separately from the databases from which applications draw their data; application independence results in lower long-term costs for systems development.

Application portfolio approach   *See* IT application portfolio.

Application service provider (ASP)   An information technology vendor that hosts applications for which it holds the licenses, typically using Web-based front-ends and Internet access. The vendor provides one or more complete applications to client organizations on a pay-per-use or flat-fee basis. The vendor may be the vendor of the software (e.g., Salesforce.com) or a third-party service provider. ASP aggregators host multiple applications with a common interface. Also called Software as a Service. *See also* Outsourcing, Software as a Service.

Application suite   *See* Office suite.

Applications software   All programs written to accomplish particular tasks for computer users. Examples include programs for payroll computation, inventory record-keeping, word processing, and producing a summarized report for top management.

Arithmetic/logical unit   The portion of a computer system in which arithmetic operations (such as addition and multiplication) and logical operations (such as comparing two numbers for equality) are carried out.

ARPANET   The forerunner of the Internet; a network created by the U.S. Department of Defense to link leading U.S. research universities and research centers.

Artificial intelligence (AI)   The study of how to make computers do things that are presently done better by people. AI research includes six separate but related areas: natural languages, robotics, perceptive systems (vision and hearing), genetic programming (also called evolutionary design), expert systems, and neural networks.

Artificial intelligence (AI) shell   *See* Expert system shell.

ASP   *See* Application service provider.

Assembler   A program (software) that translates an assembly language program—a program containing mnemonic operation codes and symbolic addresses—into an equivalent machine language program.

Assembly language   Second generation computer language in which the programmer uses easily remembered mnemonic operation codes instead of machine language operation codes and symbolic addresses instead of memory cell addresses. Such a language is considerably easier to use than machine language, but it still requires the programmer to employ the same small steps that the computer has been built to understand.

Asynchronous Transfer Mode (ATM)   An approach to implementing a network, especially a WAN or a backbone network, based on high-speed switching technology to accomplish fast packet switching with short, fixed-length packets. With ATM, connectivity between devices is provided through a switch rather through a shared bus or ring, with line speeds of up to 1.24 billion bits per second (1.24 gbps) possible. *See also* Packet switching.

ATM   *See* Asynchronous Transfer Mode.

Attribute   Characteristics of data entities about which we wish to maintain data, such as name and address for customers.

Audit trail   An EDP auditing technique that allows a business transaction to be traced from the time of input through all the processes and reports in which the transaction data are used. An audit trail is used to identify where errors are introduced or security breaches may have occurred.

B2B   Business-to-business e-commerce utilizing electronic applications for transactions and communications between two or more businesses. B2B e-commerce includes direct-to-customer sales with business customers.

B2C   Business-to-consumer e-commerce utilizing electronic applications for transactions and communications between a business seller (or a business intermediary or distributor) and individual end-consumers.

Backbone   In a telecommunications network, the underlying foundation to which the other elements attach. For example, NSFNET served as the backbone for the Internet until 1995 by providing the underlying high-volume links of the Internet to which other elements attached. *See also* Backbone network.

Backbone network   A middle-distance network that interconnects local area networks in a single organization with each other and with the organization's wide area network and the Internet. The technology employed is at the high end of that used for LANs, such as Fast Ethernet, Gigabit Ethernet, or ATM running over fiber-optic or twisted-pair cabling. *See also* Asynchronous Transfer Mode, Fast Ethernet, Gigabit Ethernet.

Balanced scorecard   A management model (by Kaplan and Norton) that translates an organization's goals and strategy into a "scorecard" of "balanced" measures that include not only financial metrics, but also customer satisfaction, internal processes, and innovation and learning. Some firms have adopted the same approach for assessing the performance of an IS organization.

Bandwidth   The difference between the highest and the lowest frequencies (cycles per second) that can be transmitted on a single medium. Bandwidth is important because it is a measure of the capacity of the transmission medium.

Bar code label   A label consisting of a series of bars used to identify an item; when the bar code is scanned, the data are entered into a computer. There are a variety of bar code languages, the most widely known of which is the Universal Product Code, or UPC, used by the grocery industry. The use of bar codes is very popular for high-volume supermarket checkout, department store sales, inventory tracking, time and attendance records, and health care records.

Baseband coax   A simple-to-use and inexpensive-to-install type of coaxial cable that offers a single digital transmission channel with maximum transmission speeds ranging from 10 million bits per second (bps) up to 1 billion bps. Baseband coax was widely used for LANs and for long-distance transmission within the telephone network, although much of this coax has now been replaced by fiber-optic cabling.

Batch processing   A mode of transaction processing in which a group or "batch" of transactions of a particular type is accumulated and then processed as a single batch at one time. For example, all sales for a firm would be accumulated during the day and then processed as a single batch at night.

Baud   Number of signals sent per second; one measure of data transmission speed. Baud is often equivalent to hertz (another measure of transmission speed) and to bits per second.

Benchmarking A procedure to compare the capabilities of various computers in a particular organizational setting by running a representative set of real jobs (jobs regularly run on the organization's existing computer) on each of the machines and comparing the resulting elapsed times.

Beta site An organization that is involved in user acceptance testing of a software package before it is released to the market. A beta site has influence on fine tuning the package, as well as possible enhancements for later releases of the software.

Bit Widely used abbreviation for a *bi*nary digi*t*, i.e., a 0 or a 1. Coding schemes used in computer systems employ particular sequences of bits to represent the decimal numbers, alphabetic characters, and special characters.

Blade Shorthand for blade server; *see* Blade server.

Blade server A server so thin (like a "blade") that several of them can be housed in a single chassis, thus saving space in the computer center. As an example, one particular chassis, which is less than 16 inches tall, offers up to 14 bays, each of which can hold a two-processor blade. The blade servers are about 1.2 inches wide and are mounted vertically in the chassis—much like sliding a book into a bookshelf. The blade server slides into a bay and plugs into the chassis, sharing power, fans, floppy drives, switches, and ports with the other blade servers in the chassis.

Blog A user-generated Web site where entries are made in journal style; blogs often provide commentary on a particular subject or serve as a personal online diary.

Bluetooth Short-range radio technology that has been built into a microchip, enabling data to be transmitted wirelessly at speeds of 1 million bits per second (bps) up to 3 million bps. Bluetooth technology eliminates the need for many cables and permits the control of Bluetooth-equipped appliances from a cellular phone–all from a remote location, if desired.

Boundary Identifies the scope of a system. A boundary segregates the system from its environment.

BPR *See* Business process reengineering.

Bricks-and-clicks A term used for traditional companies that have integrated their *offline* and *online* business channels as part of a multichannel e-business strategy. *See also* Click-and-mortar.

Bridge A hardware device employed in a telecommunications network to connect two local area networks (LANs) or LAN segments when the LANs use the same protocols, or set of rules. A bridge is smart enough to forward only messages that need to go to the other LAN.

Broadband A general designation applied to the higher-speed alternatives for accessing the Internet from a home or small office, namely Digital Subscriber Line (DSL), cable modem, and satellite connections.

Broadband coax A type of coaxial cable—more expensive and harder to use than baseband coax—that originally used analog transmission, but increasingly employs digital transmission. A single broadband coax can be divided into multiple channels so that a single cable can support simultaneous transmission of data, voice, and television. Broadband data transmission rates are similar to those for baseband coax, and high transmission speeds are possible over much longer distances than are feasible for baseband coax. Broadband coax is still widely used for cable television and LANs that span a significant area, often called metropolitan area networks.

Browser *See* Web browser.

Bus topology A network topology in which a single length of cable (coax, fiber-optic, or twisted pair)—not connected at the ends—is shared by all network devices; also called a linear topology.

Business continuity plan Contingency plans for an organization to follow in the event of a natural or man-made disaster to ensure that the company can continue to do business within an agreed upon time period. For IS managers, this includes having appropriate data center and network backup plans in place to resume transaction processing and electronic communication within a specified time period.

Business intelligence The focus of newer fourth generation languages; these software tools are designed to answer queries relating to the business by analyzing data (often massive quantities of data), thereby providing "intelligence" to the business that will help it become more competitive.

Business intelligence system *See* Competitive intelligence system.

Business process The chain of activities required to achieve an outcome such as order fulfillment or materials acquisition.

Business process reengineering (BPR) The redesign of business processes to achieve dramatic improvements in efficiency and responsiveness by taking advantage of information technology. Also referred to as business process redesign.

Byte A memory cell that can store only one character of data. *See also* Memory.

Cable modem A high-speed, or broadband, connection to the Internet using the coaxial cables already used by television. Cable television companies had to reengineer the cable television system to permit the two-way data flow required for Internet connections. Cable modem speeds may be degraded as the number of users goes up because users are sharing the bandwidth of the coaxial cable.

Cache memory A very high-speed storage unit used as an intermediary between elements of a computer system that have a significant mismatch in speeds (e.g., fetching data from main memory and the much faster execution of an instruction by the arithmetic/logical unit). An entire block of data is moved from the slower element (main memory) to cache memory, so that most requests for data from the faster element (arithmetic/logical unit) can be satisfied directly from the very high-speed cache memory.

CAD *See* Computer-aided design.

CAE *See* Computer-aided engineering.

CAM *See* Computer-aided manufacturing.

Capability Maturity Model (CMM) A five-stage model of software development and IT project management processes that are designed to increase software quality and decrease development costs due to standard, repeatable approaches across multiple projects within the same organization. The model was developed by the Software Engineering Institute at Carnegie Mellon University. A level-5 CMM certification is required for some contractors to bid on software development projects for high-risk, government-sponsored projects, such as for custom development projects for the U.S. Department of Defense.

CAPP *See* Computer-aided process planning.

CASE *See* Computer-aided software engineering.

CD An abbreviation for compact disk, a commonly used optical storage device with a standard capacity of 700 megabytes of data or 80 minutes of audio recording. *See also* CD-ROM, CD-R, CD-RW, DVD, DVD-ROM, DVD-R, DVD-RW, Optical disk.

CD-R An abbreviation for compact disk-recordable, formerly called a WORM (write once-read many) disk, a type of optical disk that can be written on by the user once and can then be read many times. CD-R technology is appropriate for archiving documents, engineering drawings, and records of all types.

CD-ROM An abbreviation for compact disk-read only memory; the first common type of optical disk storage for personal computers. CD-ROM can only be read and cannot be erased and is particularly useful for distributing large amounts of relatively stable data to many locations.

CD-RW An abbreviation for compact disk-rewritable, a type of optical disk that can be written on and read many times, then rewritten and read many times, and so on. Rewritable optical disks are the most versatile form of optical storage, and falling prices make them an attractive alternative to the standard floppy disk.

Cellular telephone A telephone instrument that can be installed in a car or carried in a pocket or briefcase; this instrument can be used anywhere as long as it is within the 8 to 10 mile range of a cellular switching station.

Center of excellence An organizational structure in which employees, who are experts in a technology, process, or both, provide internal consulting and transfer their knowledge to others in the same organization. For example, a multinational firm might establish an SAP center of excellence in order to leverage what has been learned about how best to configure and implement various SAP software modules.

Central processing unit (CPU) The name given to the combination of the control unit, which controls all other components of a computer, and the arithmetic/logical unit, in which computations and logical comparisons are carried out; also referred to as the processor.

Change management A term that refers to activities directed at successfully managing changes in the business that involve major changes in the ways that employees do their work (e.g., changes that involve new business processes and data transactions that impact employees in different work groups).

Chargeback system The process that is used to internally charge client units for IS services provided. These internal charges might be established to recover costs or might represent market prices for the IS service.

Check digit One or more digits appended to a critical value for validation purposes; the check digit has some mathematical relationship to the other digits in the number.

Chief information officer (CIO) The executive leader responsible for information technology strategy, policy, and service delivery. The corporate CIO typically reports to a CEO or President, COO, or CFO of the company. In addition to a corporate-level CIO, some organizations might have decentralized major IS responsibilities to leaders in the organization's business divisions. *See also* Chief technology officer.

Chief information security officer (CISO)   A corporate officer responsible for continually assessing an organization's information security risks and for developing and implementing effective countermeasures. The CISO might or might not have a reporting relationship to the organization's CIO.

Chief technology officer (CTO)   Senior manager responsible for identifying and recommending ways in which information technology (IT) can be applied in an organization. The title is most often used in dot-com businesses or companies with a substantial presence on the Internet. *See also* Chief information officer.

CIM   *See* Computer-integrated manufacturing.

CIO   *See* Chief information officer.

CISO   *See* Chief information security officer.

Click-and-mortar   A term that emerged in the late 1990s to refer to traditional (brick-and-mortar) companies that had also implemented e-business strategies; the term is synonymous with "bricks-and-clicks."

Client/server system   A particular type of distributed system in which the processing power is distributed between a central server computer, such as a midrange system, and a number of client computers, which are usually desktop microcomputers. The split in responsibilities between the server and the client varies considerably between applications, but the client often handles data entry and the immediate output, while the server maintains the larger database against which the new data are processed. *See also* Distributed systems.

CMM   *See* Capability Maturity Model.

CMMI   A revised version of the CMM model, released in 2002. *See* Capability Maturity Model.

Coax   *See* Coaxial cable.

Coaxial cable (coax)   A common transmission medium that consists of a heavy copper wire at the center, surrounded by insulating material, then a cylindrical conductor such as a woven braided mesh, and finally an outer protective plastic covering. The two kinds of coaxial cable in widespread use are baseband coax for digital transmission and broadband coax for both analog and digital transmission. *See also* Baseband coax, Broadband coax.

Collaboration   A term used as a synonym for groupware. *See also* Groupware.

Collaborative environment   *See* Collaboration.

COM   *See* Computer output microfilm.

Compact disk   *See* CD.

Competitive forces model   A model of five competitive forces faced by companies within the same industry, developed by Michael E. Porter for strategic assessment and planning.

Competitive intelligence system   An executive information system (EIS) that emphasizes competitive information. *See also* Executive information system.

Compiler   A program (software) that translates a third generation or fourth generation language program into an equivalent machine language program, translating the entire program into machine language before any of the program is executed.

Computer-aided design (CAD)   The use of computer graphics (both two-dimensional and three-dimensional) and a database to create and modify engineering designs.

Computer-aided engineering (CAE)   The analysis of the functional characteristics of an engineering design by simulating the product performance under various conditions.

Computer-aided manufacturing (CAM)   The use of computers to plan and control manufacturing processes. CAM incorporates computer programs to control automated equipment on the shop floor, automated guided vehicles to move material, and a communications network to link all the pieces.

Computer-aided process planning (CAPP)   A computer-based system that plans the sequence of processes that produce or assemble a part. During the design process, the engineer retrieves the closest standard plan from a database and modifies that plan rather than starting from scratch.

Computer-aided software engineering (CASE)   A set of integrated software tools used by IS specialists to automate some or all phases of an SDLC process. Upper-CASE tools support project management, the Definition phase, and the initial steps of the Construction phase, including the creation of a DD/D. Lower-CASE tools are back-end code generators and maintenance support tools. *See also* Integrated-CASE.

Computer-integrated manufacturing (CIM)   A broad term that encompasses many uses of the computer to help manufacturers operate more effectively and efficiently. CIM systems fall into three major categories: engineering systems, which are aimed at increasing the productivity of engineers; manufacturing administration, which includes systems that develop production schedules and monitor production; and factory operations, which include those systems that actually control the operation of machines on the factory floor.

Computer output microfilm (COM)   A computer output method using microfilm or microfiche (a sheet of film) as the output medium. A computer output device called a COM recorder accepts the data from memory and prepares the microfilm output at very high speeds.

Computer telecommunications network   The type of network emanating from a single medium-sized, large, or very large computer or a group of closely linked computers; usually arranged in a tree topology.

Computer virus   A small unit of code that invades a computer program or file. When the invaded program is executed or the file is opened, the virus makes copies of itself that invade other programs or files in that computer. It might also erase files or corrupt programs. Viruses are transmitted from one computer to another when an invaded computer program or file is transmitted to another computer.

Computer worm   A computer virus that has the ability to copy itself from machine to machine over a network.

Contention bus   A design standard for a local area network based on a bus topology and contention for the use of the bus by all devices on the network. Any device may transmit a message if the bus is idle, but if two devices start to transmit at the same time, a collision will occur and both messages will be lost. *See also* CSMA/CD protocol.

Context diagram   A logical model that identifies the entities outside the boundaries of a system with which the system must interface. *See also* Data flow diagram.

Control unit   The component of a computer system that controls all the remaining components. The control unit brings instructions (operations to be performed) from memory one at a time, interprets each instruction, and carries it out—all at electronic speed. *See also* Central processing unit, Stored-program concept.

Controller   A hardware unit to link input/output or file devices to the CPU and memory of large computer systems. The controller is a highly specialized microprocessor that manages the operation of its attached devices to free the CPU from these tasks.

Cookie   As used with the Web, a cookie is a message given to a Web browser by a Web server. The browser stores the message on the user's hard drive, and then sends it back to the server each time the browser requests a page from the server. The main purpose of cookies is to identify users and possibly prepare customized Web pages for them.

Cordless telephone   A portable telephone instrument that can be used up to about 1,000 feet from its wired telephone base unit; this permits the user to carry the instrument to various rooms in a house or take it outdoors.

Corporate data model   A chart that describes all the data requirements of a given organization. This chart shows what data entities and relationships between the entities are important for the organization.

Corporate information policy   The foundation for managing the ownership of data; a policy describing the use and handling of data and information within the corporation.

Cost-benefit analysis   A process to identify the potential costs and benefits of a new initiative as part of an organization's decision making about whether or not to proceed with the initiative. For example, a rough cost-benefit analysis is typically conducted prior to the approval of a new application software project, and a more detailed analysis is conducted after the project requirements are better defined to ensure that the organizational benefits outweigh the project costs.

Coverage model   A common data model used in geographic information systems in which different layers or themes represent similar types of geographic features in the same area (e.g., counties, highways, customers) and are stacked on top of one another.

CPU   *See* Central processing unit.

Cracker   A person who breaks into a computer system to steal information, wipe out hard drives, or do other harm. *See also* Hacker.

Critical success factors (CSFs)   A limited number of organizational activities that, if done well, will contribute the most to the successful performance of an organization or function.

CRM   *See* Customer relationship management system.

CSFs   *See* Critical success factors.

CSMA/CA Protocol   An abbreviation for Carrier Sense Multiple Access with Collision Avoidance, the protocol used in a wireless design for a local area network. CSMA/CA is quite similar to CSMA/CD used in traditional Ethernet, but it makes greater efforts to avoid collisions. *See also* CSMA/CD Protocol.

CSMA/CD Protocol   An abbreviation for Carrier Sense Multiple Access with Collision Detection, the protocol used in the contention bus design for a local area network. With this protocol, any device may transmit a message if the bus is idle. However, if two devices start to transmit at the same time, a collision will occur and the messages will become garbled. Both devices must recognize that this collision has occurred, stop transmitting, wait some random period of time, and then try again.

CTO   *See* Chief technology officer.

Customer relationship management (CRM) system   A computer application that attempts to provide an integrated approach to all aspects of interaction a company has with its customers, including marketing, sales, and support. A CRM system often pulls much of its data from the organization's data warehouse; most CRM packages depend upon capturing, updating, and utilizing extensive profiles of individual customers.

DASD   *See* Direct access storage device.

Data administration   The name typically given to an organizational unit created to lead the efforts in data management; the group often reports as a staff unit to the IS director, although other structures are possible.

Data analysis and presentation application   An application that manipulates data and then distributes information to authorized users. These applications concentrate on creating useful information from established data sources and, because they are separate from data capture and transfer systems, can be individually changed without the expense of changing the data capture and transfer systems.

Data architecture   *See* Data model.

Data capture application   An application that gathers data and populates databases. These applications allow the simplification of all other applications that then transfer or report data and information.

Data center   A computer installation that stores, maintains, and provides access to vast quantities of data; includes computer hardware (servers, midrange systems, mainframes, and/or supercomputers), communications facilities, system software, and technical support and operations staff.

Data dictionary/directory (DD/D)   Support software that provides a repository of metadata for each data element in a system—including the meaning, alternative names, storage format, integrity rules, security clearances, and physical location of data—that is used by the DBMS and system users.

Data flow diagram (DFD)   A common diagrammatic technique for logical As-Is and To-Be models. Symbols are used to represent the movement, processing, and

storage of data in a system and both inputs from and outputs to the environment. Each process in a top-level DFD is decomposed to a lower level, and so on.

Data governance   An organizational process for establishing strategy, objectives, and policies for organizational data.

Data independence   A highly desirable characteristic of data stored in a database in which the data are independent of the database structure or the physical organization of the data. Thus data can be selected from a disk file by referring to the content of records, and systems professionals responsible for database design can reorganize the physical organization of data without affecting the logic of programs.

Data mart   A smaller, more focused version of a data warehouse created for "drop-in shopping," much like a neighborhood convenience mart. *See also* Data warehouse, Data warehousing.

Data mining   Searching or "mining" for "nuggets" of information from the vast quantities of data stored in an organization's data warehouse, employing a variety of technologies such as decision trees and neural networks. *See also* Data warehousing.

Data model   A map or blueprint for organizational data. A data model shows the data entities and relationships that are important to an organization. *See also* Entity-relationship diagram.

Data standards   A clear and useful way to uniquely identify every instance of data and to give unambiguous business meaning to all data. Types of standards include identifiers, naming, definition, integrity rules, and usage rights.

Data steward   A business manager responsible for the quality of data in a particular subject or process area, such as customer, product, or billing.

Data transfer and integration application   An application that moves data from one database to another or otherwise brings together data from various databases. These applications permit one source of data to serve many localized systems within an organization.

Data warehouse   A very large database or collection of databases, created to make data accessible to many people in an organization. *See also* Data warehousing.

Data warehousing   The establishment and maintenance of a large data storage facility containing data on all or at least many aspects of the enterprise; less formally, a popular method for making data accessible to many people in an organization. To create a data warehouse, a firm pulls data from its operational transaction processing systems and puts the data in a separate "data warehouse" so that users may access and analyze the data without endangering the operational systems. *See also* Data mining.

Database A shared collection of logically related data that is organized to meet the needs of an organization.

Database administrator (DBA) The person in the data administration unit who is responsible for computerized databases. A DBA is concerned with efficiency, integrity, and security of database processing.

Database architecture A description of the way in which the data are structured and stored in a database.

Database management system (DBMS) Support software that is used to create, manage, and protect organizational data. A DBMS is the software that manages a database; it works with the operating system to store and modify data and to make data accessible in a variety of meaningful and authorized ways.

DBA *See* Database administrator.

DBMS *See* Database management system.

DDD *See* Direct Distance Dialing.

DD/D *See* Data dictionary/directory.

Decision support system (DSS) A computer-based system, almost always interactive, designed to assist managers in making decisions. A DSS incorporates both data and models and is usually intended to assist in the solution of semistructured or unstructured problems. An actual application that assists in the decision-making process is properly called a specific DSS; examples of specific DSSs include a police-beat allocation system, a capacity planning and production scheduling system, and a capital investment decision system.

DSS generator Computer software that provides a set of capabilities to build a specific DSS quickly and easily. For example, Microsoft Excel, a spreadsheet package, can be used as a DSS generator to construct specific financial models that can be used in decision making.

Denial of service attack A method of crippling a computer by invading a large number of computers on the Internet and instructing them to simultaneously send repeated messages to a target computer, thus either overloading that computer's input buffer or jamming the communication lines into the target computer so badly that legitimate users cannot obtain access.

Desktop computer The most common type of personal computer, which is large enough that it can not be moved around easily. The monitor and the keyboard, and sometimes the computer case itself, sit on a table or "desktop." If the computer case sits on the floor under the table or desk, it is called a "tower" unit.

DFD *See* Data flow diagram.

Digital liability An organization's liability related to the mismanagement of electronic records.

Digital network The electronic linking of devices, where messages are sent over the links by directly transmitting the zeros and ones used by computers and other digital devices. Computer telecommunications networks are digital networks, and the telephone network is gradually being shifted from an analog to a digital network.

Digital Subscriber Line A high-speed, or broadband, connection to the Internet using already installed telephone lines. DSL service, which is available from telephone companies in many parts of the United States, uses a sophisticated modulation scheme to move data over the wires without interfering with voice traffic.

Digital video disk *See* DVD.

Direct access file A basic type of computer file from which it is possible for the computer to obtain a record immediately, without regard to where the record is located on the file; usually stored on magnetic disk. Computer files, also called secondary memory or secondary storage, are added to a computer system to keep vast quantities of data accessible within the computer system at more reasonable costs than main memory.

Direct access storage device (DASD) The device on which direct access files are stored. *See also* Direct access file.

Direct Distance Dialing (DDD) The normal way of using the long-distance telephone network in the United States in which the user directly dials the number with which he or she wishes to communicate and pays for the service based on the duration of the call and the geographical distance; may be used for voice and data communications between any two spots served by the telephone network.

Direct file organization *See* Direct access file.

Disposable application An application that can be discarded when it becomes obsolete without affecting the operation of any other application; this is made possible by application independence. Also referred to as a disposable system. *See also* Application independence.

Distributed data processing *See* Distributed systems.

Distributed systems Application systems in which the processing power is distributed to multiple sites, which are then tied together via telecommunications lines. Distributed systems have computers of possibly varying sizes located at various physical sites at which the organization does business, and these computers are linked by telecommunications lines in order to support some business process.

Documentation Written descriptions produced during the systems development process for those who use the system (user documentation) and for IS specialists who operate and maintain the system (system documentation).

Dot-com A term used to describe a cyber business that receives revenues entirely based on customer transactions or other usage of its Web site. Also referred to as a "pure-play" dot-com business, as distinguished from a "bricks-and-clicks" business.

DSL *See* Digital Subscriber Line.

DSS *See* Decision support system.

Dual-core system A multiprocessor computer system that has two complete processors manufactured as part of a single chip. There are now quad-core chips available, and there will eventually be 8-core and 16-core chips. *See also* Dual-processor system, Multiprocessor.

Dual-processor system A multiprocessor computer system that contains two physically separate processors (two integrated circuits, or chips) located in the same box (called a chassis). *See also* Dual-core system, Multiprocessor.

DVD An abbreviation for digital video disk, an optical storage device that holds much more data than a conventional CD and therefore can be used for very large files such as video; standard capacity varies from 4.7 gigabytes up to 17 gigabytes. Also called a digital versatile disk. *See also* CD, CD-ROM, CD-R, CD-RW, DVD-ROM, DVD-R, DVD-RW, Optical disk.

DVD-R An abbreviation for digital video disk-recordable, a type of optical disk that can be written on by the user once and can then be read many times. DVD-R technology is appropriate for archiving documents, engineering drawings, and records of all types.

DVD-ROM An abbreviation for digital video disk-read only memory, a type of optical disk that can only be read and cannot be erased. DVD-ROM is particularly useful for distributing large amounts of relatively stable data to many locations.

DVD-RW An abbreviation for digital video disk-rewritable, a type of optical disk that can be written on and read many times, then rewritten and read many times, and so on. Rewritable optical disks are the most versatile form of optical storage, and falling prices make them an attractive alternative to the standard floppy disk.

E-business systems Applications that enable the electronic transmission of business transactions or other related information between a buyer and seller or other business partners. *See also* B2B, B2C.

E-commerce *See* Electronic commerce.

E-crime *See* Electronic crime.

E-mail *See* Electronic mail.

EDI *See* Electronic data interchange.

eDiscovery amendments Amendments to the U.S. Federal Rules of Civil Procedure effective December 2006 that establish procedures for records retention and electronic information gathering that U.S. organizations must follow in response to potential litigation as well as penalties for non-compliance.

EDP auditing A variety of methods used by trained auditors to ensure the correct processing of data. EDP auditing combines data processing controls with classical accounting auditing methods.

EIS *See* Executive information system.

Electronic commerce The electronic transmission of buyer/seller transactions and other related communications between individuals and businesses or between two or more businesses that are trading partners. By the late 1990s the Internet became the major platform for conducting electronic commerce or e-commerce. *See also* B2B, B2C, Dot-com.

Electronic crime (E-crime) Criminal acts that involve the usage of electronic communication and/or computers.

Electronic data interchange (EDI) A set of standards and hardware and software technology that enable computers in independent organizations to exchange business documents electronically. Although typical transactions include purchase orders, order acknowledgments, invoices, price quotes, shipping notices, and insurance claims, any document can potentially be exchanged using EDI. The transaction standards are typically established by an industry consortium or a national or international standards body (such as ANSI).

Electronic mail   A system whereby users send and receive messages electronically at their workstations. Electronic mail, or e-mail, can help eliminate telephone tag and usually incorporates such features as sending a message to a distribution list, resending a message to someone else with an appended note, and filing messages in electronic file folders for later recall.

Electronic records management (ERM)   A disciplined approach to managing electronic records (including e-mail documents) for efficient storage and retrieval over their useful lifecycle, including the establishment and enforcement of time periods for records retention and destruction.

Encapsulation   A principle of object-oriented modeling and programming in which both data and operations (methods) to be performed using the data are stored together as an object.

Encryption   An encoding system used for transmission of computer data to ensure confidentiality and security of the data.

End-user computing   *See* User computing.

Enterprise modeling   A top-down approach to detailing the data requirements of an organization. Enterprise modeling employs a high-level, three-tier approach, first dividing the work of the organization into its major functions (such as selling and manufacturing), and then dividing each of these functions into processes and each process into activities.

Enterprise resource planning (ERP) system   A set of integrated business applications, or modules, to carry out most common business functions, including inventory control, general ledger accounting, accounts payable, accounts receivable, material requirements planning, order management, and human resources. ERP modules are integrated, primarily through a common set of definitions and a common database, and the modules have been designed to reflect a particular way of doing business, i.e., a particular set of business processes. The leading ERP vendors are Oracle and SAP.

Enterprise system   A large application designed to integrate a set of business functions or processes. Enterprise resource planning (ERP) systems were the first wave of such systems, which today include customer relationship management (CRM) systems and supply chain management (SCM) systems.

Entity   In data modeling, the things about which data are collected, for example, a customer or a product.

Entity-relationship diagram (ERD)   A common notation for modeling organizational data requirements. ER diagramming uses specific symbols to represent data entities, relationships, and attributes.

ERD   *See* Entity-relationship diagram.

ERM   *See* Electronic records management.

ERP   *See* Enterprise resource planning system.

Ethernet   The name of the original Xerox version of a contention bus local area network design, which has come to be used as a synonym for a contention bus design. *See also* Local area network, Contention bus.

Evolutionary design   *See* Genetic programming.

Evolutionary development   Any development approach that does not depend upon defining complete requirements early in the development process, but, like prototyping, evolves the system by building successive versions until the system is acceptable. *See also* Prototyping, Rapid application development.

Executive information system (EIS)   A computer application designed to be used directly by managers, without the assistance of intermediaries, to provide the executive easy on-line access to current information about the status of the organization and its environment. Such information includes filtered and summarized internal transactions data and also "soft" data such as assessments, rumors, opinions, and ideas.

Expert systems   The branch of artificial intelligence concerned with building systems that incorporate the decision-making logic of a human expert. Expert systems can diagnose and prescribe treatment for diseases, analyze proposed bank loans, and determine the optimal sequence of stops on a truck route.

Expert systems shell   Computer software that provides the basic framework of an expert system and a limited but user-friendly special language to develop the expert system. With the purchase of such a shell, the organization's system builder can concentrate on the details of the business decision being modeled and the development of the knowledge base.

eXtensible Markup Language (XML)   A markup language standard to facilitate data interchange across applications on the Web. An XML specification consists of tags that convey the meaning of data, not the presentation format.

Extranet   A private network that is a portion of a company's intranet, which is made accessible (normally over the Internet) to business partners outside the company (such as customers or suppliers). *See also* Intranet.

eXtreme Programming (XP)   A so-called "agile" software development approach in which programmers develop computer code in a very short time period using programming pairs, common coding approaches, and frequent testing of each other's work.

Factory automation   The use of information technology to automate various aspects of factory operations. Factory automation includes numerically controlled machines, material requirements planning (MRP) systems, computer-integrated manufacturing (CIM), and computer-controlled robots.

Fast Ethernet   An approach to implementing a high-speed local area network, operating at 100 million bits per second (mbps). Fast Ethernet uses the same CSMA/CD architecture as traditional Ethernet and is usually implemented using either a cable of four twisted pairs (this is called 100 Base-T) or a multimode fiber-optic cable (this is 100 Base-F). *See also* Contention bus, CSMA/CD protocol, Ethernet.

FDDI   *See* Fiber Distributed Data Interface.

Feasibility analysis   An analysis step in the systems development life cycle in which the economic, operational, and technical feasibility of a proposed system is assessed.

Federal design   An IS organization design in which responsibilities are both centralized and decentralized to maximize the organization's IT resources. Typically, IS operational activities are centralized to a corporate IS unit, and systems development activities are decentralized to business units to increase their control over local application needs.

Fiber Distributed Data Interface (FDDI)   An American National Standards Institute (ANSI) standard for building a local area network that offers a transmission speed of 100 million bits per second (mbps) and fault tolerance because of its double-ring architecture; FDDI utilizes either fiber-optic cabling or a cable containing four twisted pairs.

Fiber optics   A transmission medium in which data are transmitted by sending pulses of light through a thin fiber of glass or fused silica. Although expensive to install and difficult to work with, the high transmission speeds possible with fiber-optic cabling—100 million bits per second (mbps) to 640 billion bps (gbps)—are leading to its use in most new long-distance telephone lines, in backbone networks to connect multiple LANs,

and in LANs where very high speeds or high security needs exist.

File Transfer Protocol (FTP)   An Internet application, or tool, that allows users to send and receive files, including programs, from one computer system to another over the Internet. The user logs into the two computer systems at the same time and then copies files from one system to the other.

Firewall   Usually implemented through software operating on a router, server, or personal computer, a firewall inhibits access to an organization's internal network or to an individual's personal computer.

Flash memory   A type of memory used in digital cameras and music players, as well as in keychain drives for PCs. *See also* Keychain drive.

Formal system   The way an organization or business process was designed to work. *See also* Informal system.

Fourth generation language   A computer language in which the user gives a precise statement of what is to be accomplished, not how to do it. No procedure is necessary; the order of statements is usually inconsequential. Examples include SAS, FOCUS, and CA-Ramis.

Free agent   A type of telecommuter who independently contracts out his or her services without becoming an employee of any organization.

FTP   *See* File Transfer Protocol.

Full-duplex transmission   A type of data transmission in which data can travel in both directions at once over the communication line.

Functional information system   An information system, usually composed of multiple interrelated subsystems, that provides the information necessary to accomplish various tasks within a specific functional area of the business, such as production, marketing, accounting, personnel, or engineering.

Gateway   A hardware device employed in a telecommunications network to connect two or more local area networks (LANs) or to connect two different types of networks, such as a backbone network and the Internet, where the networks may use different protocols. The gateway, which is really a sophisticated router, forwards only those messages that need to be forwarded from one network to another. *See also* Router.

Genetic programming   The branch of artificial intelligence that divides a problem into multiple segments, and then links solutions to these segments together in different ways to breed new "child" solutions; after many generations of breeding, genetic programming might produce results superior to anything devised by a human. Genetic programming has been most useful in the design of innovative products, such as a satellite support arm and an energy-efficient light bulb.

Geographic information system (GIS)   A computer-based system designed to capture, store, manipulate, display, and analyze data spatially referenced to the earth; a GIS links data to maps so that the data's spatial characteristics can be easily understood.

Gigabit Ethernet   An approach to implementing a very high-speed local area network or a backbone network, operating at 1 billion bits per second (gbps) and higher; comes in several versions which run over either Category 5e cable (four twisted pairs of wires), multimode fiber-optic cabling, or single-mode fiber-optic cabling. *See also* 1 GbE, 10 GbE, 40 GbE, Backbone network, Fast Ethernet.

GIS   *See* Geographic information system.

Graphical user interface (GUI)   An interface between a computer and a human user based on graphical screen images such as icons. With a GUI (pronounced gooey), the user selects an application or makes other choices by using a mouse to click on an appropriate icon or label appearing on the screen. Apple's Mac OS and Microsoft's Windows XP and Vista employ a GUI.

Grid computing   The cooperative utilization of many (even several thousand) computers in a network to solve a problem that requires a lot of parallel computer processing power.

Group support system (GSS)   A variant of a decision support system (DSS) in which the system is designed to support a group rather than an individual. The purpose of a GSS is to make group sessions more productive by supporting such group activities as brainstorming, issue structuring, voting, and conflict resolution.

Group technology (GT)   A computer-based system that logically groups parts according to physical characteristics, machine routings through the factory, and similar machine operations. Based on these logical groupings, GT is able to identify existing parts that engineers can use or modify rather than design new parts.

Groupware   Application software designed to support groups; the functionality varies but may include electronic mail, electronic bulletin boards, computer conferencing, electronic calendaring, group scheduling, sharing documents, meeting support systems, electronic forms, and desktop videoconferencing.

GSS   *See* Group support system.

GT   *See* Group technology.

GUI   *See* Graphical user interface.

Hacker   A person who breaks into a computer for the challenge of it without intending to do any harm.

Half-duplex transmission   A type of data transmission in which data can travel in both directions over the communication line, but not simultaneously.

Handheld computer   The smallest type of computing device, which can easily be held in one hand while using the other hand to enter instructions or data via a keyboard or stylus; also called palmtop computer or personal digital assistant.

Hardware   The physical pieces of a computer or telecommunications system, such as a central processing unit, a printer, and a terminal.

Help desk   A support service for IT users that can be accessed via phone or e-mail. The service might be provided by IS specialists who are employees in the same organization or by IS specialists who are under contract to provide this service (i.e., an outsourcing vendor).

Hertz   Cycles per second; one measure of data transmission speed. Hertz is usually equivalent to baud (another measure of transmission speed) and to bits per second.

Hierarchical decomposition   The process of breaking down a system into successive levels of subsystems. This recursive decomposition allows a system to be described at various levels of detail, each appropriate for a different kind of analysis or for a different audience.

HIPAA   The Health Information Portability and Accountability Act (HIPAA), passed by the U.S. government in 1996, sets standards for U.S. organizations to maintain the privacy of medical record information and related payment data; it also establishes both civil and criminal penalties for non-compliance.

Horizontal mechanisms   Intentional management actions to link employees that work in business units that don't have a direct reporting relationship. Horizontal linking mechanisms include structural designs (such as formal groups and integrator roles) as well as other linking devices (such as job rotations) that are intended to help build and foster relationships across different workgroups. Common structural mechanisms to link IS and business groups are IS advisory councils (with senior business leaders) and IS account managers (individuals that serve as a key point-of-contact for a specific business unit).

Hosted solution   A method of using a software package (such as an ERP or CRM system) in which the software runs on the vendor's hardware, and the customer pays a subscription fee on a per user, per month basis to use the application; also called an on-demand solution or Software as a Service (SaaS).

HTML   *See* Hypertext Markup Language.

HTTP   *See* Hypertext Transfer Protocol.

Hub   A simple hardware device employed in a telecommunications network to connect one section of a local area network (LAN) to another. A hub forwards every message it receives to the other section of the LAN, whether or not the messages need to go there. Another use of a hub is to create a shared Ethernet LAN; in this case, the hub is a junction box containing up to 24 ports into which cables can be plugged. Embedded inside the hub is a linear bus connecting all the ports.

Human assets   A component of the IT architecture that includes IS department employees in terms of their values, skill sets, and IS management expertise; also, one of three IT assets that must be effectively managed by IT leaders (the other two are the technology and relationship assets).

Hypertext   As used on the World Wide Web, this is the linking of objects, such as text, pictures, sound clips, and video clips, to each other so that by clicking on highlighted text or a small icon, the user is taken to the related object.

Hypertext Markup Language (HTML)   A specialized language to "mark up" pages to be viewed on the World Wide Web. The "markups" consist of special codes inserted in the text to indicate headings, bold-faced text, italics, where images or photographs are to be placed, and links to other Web pages, among other things.

Hypertext Transfer Protocol (HTTP)   The underlying protocol used by the World Wide Web. HTTP defines how messages are formatted and transmitted and what actions Web browsers and Web servers should take in response to various commands.

I-CASE   *See* Integrated-CASE.

Identity theft   The act of appropriating an individual's personal information without that person's knowledge to commit fraud or theft. An identity thief uses information such as name, address, social security number, credit card number, and/or other identifying information to impersonate someone else and obtain loans or purchase items using his or her credit.

IM   *See* Instant messaging.

Imaging   A computer input/output method by which any type of paper document—including business forms, reports, charts, graphs, and photographs—can be read by a scanner and translated into digital form so that it can be stored in the computer system; this process can also be reversed so that the digitized image stored in the computer system can be displayed on a video display unit, printed on paper, or transmitted to another computer or workstation.

In-line system   A computer system in which data entry is accomplished online (i.e., a transaction is entered directly into the computer via some input device) but the processing is deferred until a suitable batch of transactions has been accumulated.

Incremental commitment   A strategy in systems analysis and design in which the project is reviewed after each phase and continuation of the project is rejustified.

Indexed file organization   A method of organizing a computer file or database in which the control keys only are arranged in sequence in a separate table, along with a pointer to the complete records associated with each key. The records themselves can then be arranged in any order.

Informal system   The way the organization or business process actually works. *See also* Formal system.

Information   Data (usually processed data) that are useful to a decision maker.

Information resources assessment   The act of taking inventory and critically evaluating technological and human resources in terms of how well they meet the organization's business and IS needs.

Information system (IS)   A computer-based system that uses information technology, procedures (processes), and people to capture, move, store, and distribute data and information.

Information systems (IS) department   An organizational unit that has the primary responsibility for managing information technology within a business or other type of organization.

Information technology (IT) Computer hardware and software for processing and storing data, as well as communications technology (networks) for transmitting data.

Information technology architecture An IT architecture is an organization-specific set of requirements for current and future hardware, software, network, and data assets, as well as the human assets needed to acquire, deploy, and maintain them, to meet the organization's information vision.

Information vision A written expression of the desired future for information use and management in an organization.

Inheritance A principle of object-oriented approaches in which subclasses inherit all of the properties and methods of the class to which they belong.

Instant messaging (IM) A synchronous communication system (a variant of electronic mail) that enables the user to establish a private "chat room" with another individual to carry out text-based communication in real time over the Internet. Typically, the IM system signals the user when someone on his or her private list is online, and then the user can initiate a chat session with that individual.

Instruction An individual step or operation in a program, particularly in a machine language program. *See also* Machine language, Program.

Integrated-CASE (I-CASE) A set of full-cycle, integrated CASE tools, in which system specifications supported by the front-end tools can be converted into computer code by the back-end tools included in the system. *See also* Computer-aided software engineering.

Integrated Services Digital Network (ISDN) A set of international standards by which the public telephone network offers additional telecommunications capabilities—including simultaneous transmission of both voice and data over the same line—to telephone users worldwide.

Intellectual property Any product of the human mind, such as an idea, an invention, a literary creation, a work of art, a business method, an industrial process, a chemical formula, a computer program, or a presentation.

Interactive system A computer system in which the user directly interacts with the computer. In such a system, the user would enter data into the computer via some type of input device and the computer would provide a response almost immediately, as in an airline reservation system. An interactive system is an online system in which the computer provides an immediate response to the user.

Interface The point of contact where the environment meets a system or where two subsystems meet. Special functions such as filtering, coding/decoding, error detection and correction, buffering, security, and summarizing occur at an interface, which allows compatibility between the environment and system or two subsystems. *See also* Graphical user interface.

Internet A network of networks that use the TCP/IP protocol, with gateways (connections) to even more networks that do not use the TCP/IP protocol. The two primary applications on the Internet are electronic mail and the World Wide Web. *See also* B2B, B2C, Electronic commerce, Electronic mail, Extranet, Intranet, Transmission Control Protocol/Internet Protocol, World Wide Web.

Internet2 A not-for-profit consortium of more than 200 universities, working in partnership with 70 leading technology companies and the U.S. government, to develop and deploy advanced network applications and technologies. Internet2 operates a very high-performance network as the backbone network for the Internet2 universities; the initial version of this network was named Abilene, and the present even higher-speed network has the confusing name Internet2.

Internet telephony Also called Voice over Internet Protocol (VoIP) or IP telephony, this approach to telephony allows the user to make voice calls using a broadband Internet connection instead of a regular (analog) telephone line. Internet telephony requires an analog telephone adapter for a standard telephone, an IP (digital) phone, or an appropriately equipped computer, as well as a broadband Internet connection.

Interpreter A software program that translates a third generation or fourth generation language program into an equivalent machine language program, executing each source program statement as soon as that single statement is translated.

Intranet A private network operating within an organization that employs the TCP/IP protocol; an intranet is used by employees for information sharing, collaboration, and other applications. A firewall typically is used to separate the intranet from the public Internet.

IP telephony *See* Internet telephony.

IS *See* Information system.

IS advisory committee A committee of senior business managers for the purpose of advising the IS leadership on IT strategy and policy, which might include decision making related to new systems approvals and prioritization; also sometimes called an IS steering committee. *See also* Horizontal mechanisms.

IS governance An organization's formal design for IS-related responsibilities and accountabilities. Common designs today include highly centralized, highly decentralized, and federal IS organizations. Under a typical federal IS governance design, computer and network operations are highly centralized, but software application development and maintenance are highly decentralized.

IS mission The reason(s) for the existence of the IS organization. *See also* IS vision.

IS outsourcing Contracting with an outside organization to perform one or more IS functions or activities. For example, outsourcing might involve a multiyear contract with a vendor to operate an organization's computers and networks, or shorter contracts for application development and maintenance. *See also* Offshore IS outsourcing.

ISDN *See* Integrated Services Digital Network.

IT *See* Information technology.

IT application portfolio The set of software applications in an organization that are installed and being utilized, currently under development, and/or on a list of approved IS projects not yet underway. *See also* IT portfolio management.

IT platform The set of hardware, software, communications, and standards an organization uses to build and operate its information systems.

IT portfolio management A disciplined approach to managing IT investments to best align with the current and anticipated needs of a business for not only the short term, but also the long term. The typical IT investment portfolio includes investments in hardware, custom software, packaged software, and communications networks.

ITIL An acronym for Information Technology Infrastructure Library, a process-based IS management approach—first developed by a branch of the British government—that documents a set of 12 processes for deploying and operating information systems and services.

J2EE *See* Java 2 Enterprise Edition.

JAD *See* Joint application design.

Java 2 Enterprise Edition A platform for application development on the Web, using the OOP paradigm, created by an alliance of companies led by Sun Microsystems. J2EE programming is done in Java, and the programs will run on any platform. J2EE is a collection of Java-based technologies for Web application development; popular J2EE products are WebSphere from IBM and WebLogic from BEA.

Java virtual machine A self-contained operating environment, existing for all major operating systems, in which Java programs are run. The Java virtual machine behaves as if it is a separate computer and thus implements the "write once, run anywhere" portability that is Java's goal.

JCL *See* Job control language.

Job control language (JCL) The specialized computer language by which computer users communicate with the operating system. The term JCL is used primarily in the context of IBM mainframe computers.

Joint application design (JAD) A technique in which system requirements are defined by a team of users and IS specialists during an intensive effort led by a trained facilitator. JAD sessions are often held at special facilities with CASE tool support.

Keychain drive The newest and smallest portable direct access storage device for PCs, making use of flash memory rather than a magnetizable disk. This device, which plugs into the USB port of a PC, goes by various names, of which keychain drive is perhaps the most descriptive, because the device is not much larger than the average car key.

KM *See* Knowledge management.

KMS *See* Knowledge management system.

Knowledge management (KM) The sharing and transferring of knowledge in an organization in order to enhance learning and improve performance; in other words, the strategies and processes of identifying, creating, capturing, organizing, transferring, and leveraging knowledge to help individuals and firms compete.

Knowledge management system (KMS) A system for managing organizational knowledge that enables individuals and organizations to enhance learning, improve performance, and, hopefully, produce long-term sustainable competitive advantage.

LAN *See* Local area network.

Laptop computer The type of personal computer that can easily be carried by a user and used on the user's "lap." A laptop PC is the size of a small briefcase and weighs less than 10 pounds. The terms "laptop" and "notebook" PC are now used almost interchangeably, although the notebook PC originally was a smaller machine than a laptop.

Legacy system A term used to refer to a system that has already been deployed in an organization, especially one that was initially deployed several years ago.

Lewin/Schein change model A 3-stage model for planning and managing change in an organization: unfreezing, moving, and refreezing.

Life-cycle process *See* Systems development life cycle.

Listserv An Internet application, or tool, that is essentially a mailing list such that members of a group can send a single electronic mail message and have it delivered to everyone in the group.

Local area network (LAN) A local data-only network, usually within a single organization and generally operating within an area no more than two or three miles in diameter, that contains a number of intelligent devices (usually microcomputers) capable of data processing. LANs usually follow one of five designs: contention bus, token bus, token ring, Wi-Fi wireless, and WiMAX wireless. *See also* Contention bus, Token bus, Token ring, Wi-Fi LAN, WiMAX LAN, Wireless LAN.

Location intelligence The application of spatial technologies to identifying where someone or something is in real time; the technology most responsible for achieving location intelligence is the Global Positioning System (GPS).

Logic bomb A program that is introduced into a computer and set to take action at a certain time or when a specified event occurs.

Logical system or model A depiction of the function and purpose (the what) of a system without reference to, or implications for, how the system is implemented; includes both As-Is and To-Be models. *See also* Physical system or model.

Lower-CASE *See* Computer-aided software engineering.

M-commerce Shorthand for mobile e-commerce; the utilization of electronic applications and communications via handheld devices and wireless technologies for e-commerce.

Machine language The form of a computer program that the control unit of the computer has been built to understand. In general, each machine language instruction consists of an operation code that tells the control unit what basic machine function is to be performed and one or more addresses that identify the specific memory cells whose contents will be involved in the operation.

Magnetic ink character recognition (MICR) A computer input method used for check processing in the United States. Identifying information and the amount are recorded in magnetizable ink at the bottom of the check; a computer input device called a magnetic ink character reader magnetizes the ink, recognizes the numbers, and transmits the data to the memory of the bank's computer to permit the check to be processed.

Magnetic tape unit A computer file device that stores (writes) data on magnetic tape and retrieves (reads) data from tape back into memory; the usual device on which sequential access files are stored. *See also* Sequential access file.

Mainframe The type of computer system that is used as the main, central computing system of most major corporations and government agencies, ranging in cost from $500,000 to $20,000,000 or more and in power from 400 to 10,000 MFLOPS; used for large business general processing, as the server in client/server applications, as a large Web server, and for a wide range of other applications.

Maintenance The process of making changes to a system after it has been placed in operation, including changes required to correct errors, to adapt the system to changes in the environment, and to enhance the system's functionality. Vendors of a purchased system may be contracted to carry out maintenance as part of the purchase contract.

Make-or-buy decision Within the context of systems development, the choice between customized application development and purchasing a software package.

Manufacturing Automation Protocol (MAP) A communications protocol (a set of rules) for communicating between automated equipment on a factory floor. MAP, which was pioneered by General Motors and has now been accepted by most major manufacturers and IT vendors, ensures an open manufacturing system in which communication between equipment from various vendors is possible.

Manufacturing resources planning (MRP II) A computer-based manufacturing administration system that usually incorporates three major components—the master production schedule, which sets the overall production goals; material requirements planning, which develops the detailed production schedule; and shop floor control, which releases orders to the shop floor based on the detailed schedule and actual production to date.

MAP   *See* Manufacturing Automation Protocol.

Massively parallel processor (MPP)   A parallel processor computer with some large number of parallel CPUs; in general, 32 or more parallel CPUs is considered an MPP if the different CPUs are capable of performing different instructions at the same time, or 1,000 or more parallel CPUs is considered an MPP if the different CPUs must all carry out the same instruction at the same time. *See also* Parallel processor.

Master data management   The disciplines, technologies, and methods to ensure the currency, meaning, and quality of reference data within and across various subject areas.

Material requirements planning (MRP)   A computer-based system that accepts the master production schedule for a factory as input and then develops a detailed production schedule, using parts explosion, production capacity, inventory, and lead time data; usually a component of a manufacturing resources planning (MRP II) system.

MegaFLOPS (MFLOPS)   Shorthand for millions of floating point operations per second, a commonly used speed rating for computers. MegaFLOPS ratings are derived by running a particular set of programs in a particular language on the machines being investigated.

Memory   The primary area for storage of data in a computer system; also referred to as main memory or primary memory. In a computer system all data flows to and from memory. Memory is divided into cells, and a fixed amount of data can be stored in each cell.

Mesh topology   A network topology in which most devices are connected to two, three, or more other devices in a seemingly irregular pattern that resembles a woven net, or a mesh. Examples of a mesh topology include the public telephone network and the network of networks that makes up the Internet.

Metadata   Data about data, or documentation about the business and technical characteristics of data, such as the description and maximum length of customer name.

Metadata repository   *See* Data dictionary/directory (DD/D).

Metcalfe's Law   A theory in which the value of a network to each of its members is a nonlinear increasing function of the number of users; more formally, the value is proportional to $(n^2 - n)/2$, where "n" is the number of nodes on the network.

MFLOPS   *See* MegaFLOPS.

MICR   *See* Magnetic ink character recognition.

Microcomputer   The category of computers with the least cost ($200 to $4,000) and the least power (50 to 1,000 MFLOPS), generally used for personal computing and small business processing and as a Web client and a client in client/server applications; also called micros or personal computers (PCs).

Microwave   Considered as a transmission medium, although strictly speaking it is line-of-sight broadcast technology in which radio signals are sent out into the air. With transmission speeds of 500 thousand bits per second (bps) to 100 million bps, microwave transmission is widely used for long-distance telephone communication and for corporate voice and data networks.

Middleware   A term that covers all of the software needed to support interactions between clients and servers in client/server systems. Middleware usually includes three categories of software: server operating systems to create a "single-system image" for all services on the network; transport software to allow communications employing a standard protocol to be sent across the network; and service-specific software to carry out specific services such as electronic mail.

Midrange system   This broadest category of computer systems, which stretches all the way from microcomputers to the much larger mainframes and supercomputers, has evolved from two earlier categories of computers—workstations and minicomputers. Prices vary from $4,000 to $1,000,000, with power ranging from 100 to 10,000 MFLOPS; applications include departmental computing, midsized business general processing, server in client/server applications, Web server, file server, local area network server, and specific tasks such as office automation, computer-aided design, and graphics. *See also* Workstation, Minicomputer.

Minicomputer   A category of computer systems that has now been subsumed into the midrange systems category, these "small mainframes" were just like the larger mainframe machines, except that they were less powerful and less expensive; applications included departmental computing, specific tasks such as office automation, server in client/server applications, and midsized business general processing. *See also* Midrange system, Superminicomputer.

MIPS An acronym for millions of instructions per second executed by the control unit of a computer; a commonly used maximum speed rating for computers.

Modem An abbreviation for modulator/demodulator, a device that converts data from digital form to analog form so that it can be sent over the analog telephone network and reconverts data from analog to digital form after it has been transmitted.

Module A self-contained unit of software that performs one or more functions. Ideally it has well-defined interfaces with the other modules in the program so that changes in a module affect the rest of the program only through the outputs from that module. *See also* Subsystem.

MP3 A standard coding scheme for compressing audio signals into a very small file (about one-twelfth the size of the original file) while preserving the original level of sound quality when it is played. MP3 is the most popular Internet audio format that allows users to download music from the Internet.

MPP *See* Massively parallel processor.

MRP *See* Material requirements planning.

MRP II *See* Manufacturing resources planning.

Multiprocessing The method of processing when two or more CPUs are installed as part of the same computer system; all CPUs are under control of a single operating system.

Multiprocessor A computer configuration in which multiple processors (CPUs) are installed as part of the same computer system, with all CPUs under control of a single operating system. *See* Massively parallel processor, Parallel processor, Symmetric multiprocessor.

Multiprogramming A procedure by which the operating system switches back and forth among a number of programs, all located in memory at the same time, to keep the CPU busy while input/output operations are taking place; more specifically, this is called event-driven multiprogramming.

Multitasking The terminology used for microcomputers to describe essentially the same function as multiprogramming on larger machines. In preemptive multitasking, the operating system allocates slices of CPU time to each program (the same as time-driven multiprogramming); in cooperative multitasking, each program can control the CPU for as long as it needs it (the same as event-driven multiprogramming). *See also* Multiprogramming, Time-sharing.

Multithreading Almost the same as multitasking except that the multiple threads (*thread* is short for *thread of execution*) are different parts of the same program that are being executed near simultaneously, with the operating system controlling the switching back and forth among threads of the single program. *See also* Multitasking.

Natural language A computer language in which the user writes a program in ordinary English (or something very close to it); little or no training will be required to use a natural language. At present, there are no true natural languages, but some restricted natural language products have been developed that can be used with a variety of DBMSs and fourth generation languages.

.NET A platform for application development on the Web, using the OOP paradigm, created by Microsoft. .NET programming can be done in a variety of languages, including VB.NET, C#, and J#, but can only be run on a Windows platform.

Network interface card (NIC) In general, a specialized card that must be installed in a computer to permit it to access a particular type of network, usually a local area network. For wireless LANs, the NIC is a short-range radio transceiver that can send and receive radio signals.

Network operating system (NOS) *See* Server operating system.

Network protocol An agreed-upon set of rules or conventions governing communication among elements of a network, or, more specifically, among layers or levels of a network.

Networking The electronic linking of geographically dispersed devices.

Neural networks The branch of artificial intelligence concerned with recognizing patterns from vast amounts of data by a process of adaptive learning; named after the study of how the human nervous system works, but in fact uses extensive statistical analysis to identify meaningful patterns from the data.

NIC *See* Network interface card.

Nonprocedural language *See* Fourth generation language.

Normalization The process of creating simple data structures from more complex ones; this process consists of a set of rules that yields a data structure that is very stable and useful across many different requirements.

NOS *See* Network operating system.

Notebook computer The type of personal computer that can easily be carried by the user; this type of PC is similar in size to a student's notebook and it typically weighs no more than 5 or 6 pounds. The terms "laptop" and "notebook" PC are now used almost interchangeably, although the notebook PC originally was a smaller machine than a laptop.

Object A person, place, or thing including data and methods, as used in physical To-Be modeling; a chunk of program code encompassing both data and methods, as used in object-oriented programming. *See also* Object-oriented programming.

Object-oriented programming (OOP) A type of computer programming based on the creation and use of a set of objects and the development of relationships among the objects. The most popular OOP languages are C++ and Java. *See also* Object, Object-oriented techniques.

Object-oriented techniques A broad term that includes object-oriented analysis and design techniques as well as object-oriented programming.

Object program The machine language program that is the result of translating a second, third, or fourth generation source program.

OCR *See* Optical character recognition.

Office automation The use of information technology to automate various aspects of office operations. Office automation involves a set of office-related functions that might or might not be integrated in a single system, including electronic mail, word processing, photocopying, document preparation, voice mail, desktop publishing, personal databases, and electronic calendaring.

Office suite A collection of personal productivity software packages for use in the office (e.g., word processing, spreadsheet, presentation graphics, database management system) that are integrated to some extent and marketed as a set. Microsoft Office is the leading office suite; other suites include Corel WordPerfect Office, Lotus SmartSuite, and Sun StarOffice.

Offshore IS outsourcing Outsourcing IS functions or activities to IS employees of a vendor that is located in a different nation than the client organization. In contrast, the term "offshoring" alone has recently come to mean allocating work to IS employees of the same organization, but who are located in a different nation.

OLAP *See* Online analytical processing.

On-demand solution *See* Hosted solution.

Online analytical processing (OLAP) Querying against a database, employing OLAP software that makes it easy to pose complex queries along multiple dimensions, such as time, organizational unit, and geography. The chief component of OLAP is the OLAP server, which sits between a client machine and a database server; the OLAP server understands how data are organized in the database and has special functions for analyzing the data. *See also* Data mining.

Online processing A mode of transaction processing in which each transaction is entered directly into the computer when it occurs and the associated processing is carried out immediately. For example, sales would be entered into the computer (probably via a microcomputer) as soon as they occurred, and sales records would be updated immediately.

Online system *See* Online processing.

OOP *See* Object-oriented programming.

Open source software Software that is distributed at no cost to the acquirer, with the acquirer having the right to modify the source code. Software derived from open source software, if distributed, must also be distributed as open source.

Open systems Systems (usually operating systems and other support software) that are not tied to a particular computer system or software vendor. Examples include the UNIX operating system, with versions available for a wide variety of hardware platforms, and the Linux operating system, which runs on all of the major IT platforms.

Open Systems Interconnection (OSI) Reference Model An evolving set of network protocols developed by the International Standards Organization (ISO), which deals with connecting all systems that are open for communication with other systems (i.e., systems that conform to certain minimal standards) by defining seven layers, each of which will have one or more protocols.

Operating system Very complex software that controls the operation of the computer hardware and coordinates all the other software. The purposes of an operating system are to get as much work done as possible with the available resources and to be convenient to use.

Operational IS plan Short-term goals (typically 1 to 2 years) and associated projects to be executed by the IS department and business managers, in support of the strategic IS plan.

Optical character recognition (OCR) A computer input method that directly scans typed, printed, or hand-printed material. A computer input device called an optical character reader scans and recognizes the characters and then transmits the data to the memory or records them on a magnetic media.

Optical disk A medium upon which computer files can be stored. Data are recorded on an optical disk by using a laser to burn microscopic pits on its surface. Optical disks have a much greater capacity than magnetic disks.

OSI *See* Open Systems Interconnection Reference Model.

Outsourcing *See* IS outsourcing.

Packet assembly/disassembly device (PAD) A telecommunication device used to connect an organization's internal networks (at each of its locations) to the common carrier network in order to set up a packet-switched network.

Packet-switched network A network employing packet switching; examples include Abilene, the Internet, and many WANs. *See also* Packet switching.

Packet switching A method of operating a digital telecommunications network (especially a WAN) in which information is divided into packets of some fixed length that are then sent over the network separately. Rather than tying up an entire end-to-end circuit for the duration of the session, the packets from various users can be interspersed with one another to permit more efficient use of the network.

PAD *See* Packet assembly/disassembly device.

Palmtop computer *See* Handheld computer.

Parallel processor (PP) A multiprocessor configuration (multiple CPUs installed as part of the same computer system) designed to give a separate piece of the same program to each of the processors so that work on the program can proceed in parallel on the separate pieces.

PC *See* Microcomputer, Laptop computer, Notebook computer.

PDA *See* Personal digital assistant.

Perceptive systems The branch of artificial intelligence that involves creating machines possessing a visual or aural perceptual ability, or both, that affects their physical behavior; in other words, creating robots that can "see" or "hear" and react to what they see or hear.

Performance management (PM) A software package—an expanded version of an executive information system—that is intended to give all levels of management the information they need to ensure that the organization performs successfully. *See also* Competitive intelligence system, Executive information system.

Personal computer *See* Microcomputer.

Personal digital assistant (PDA) The smallest microcomputers, also called palmtop or handheld computers, which weigh under a pound and cost from $200 to $600.

Personal productivity software Software products, usually microcomputer-based, designed to increase the productivity of a manager or other knowledge worker; examples are word processing, spreadsheets, database management systems, presentation graphics, and Web browsers.

Phishing A technique used to fool computer users into giving away sensitive personal information (e.g., usernames, passwords, credit card details) via their responses to a fraudulent e-mail or instant messaging communication.

Physical system or model A depiction of the physical form (the how) of an information system. *See also* Logical system or model.

PM *See* Performance management.

PMO *See* Project Management Office.

Portal A standardized entry point to key information on the corporate network. Many organizations have created carefully designed portals to enable employees (and perhaps customers and suppliers) to gain easy access to information they need. *See also* Intranet.

Portlet A specialized content area, or window, within an intranet opening page, or within a portal. *See also* Portal.

PP *See* Parallel processor.

Privacy policy An organizational policy that describes the organization's rules for the protection (nondisclosure) of information collected as part of its business transactions and other interactions with consumers of its products and services, including online transactions using its Web site.

Procedural language *See* Third generation language.

Procedural-oriented techniques *See* Structured techniques.

Processor *See* Central processing unit.

Productivity language Another name for a fourth generation language. This type of language tends to make the programmer or user more productive, which explains the name.

Program 1)A complete listing of what the computer is to do for a particular application, expressed in a form that the control unit of the computer has been built to understand or that can be translated into such a form. A program is made up of a sequence of individual steps or operations called instructions. *See also* Control unit, Instruction. 2) A group of projects managed in a coordinated way—as a program—rather than separately.

Program management The management of multiple, related projects in a coordinated way, with the objective of achieving greater benefits to the organization than would be achieved from managing the projects individually.

Program structure chart A common diagrammatic technique for showing the flow of control for a computer program.

Project A temporary initiative to create a unique product or service in a specific time period, including activities that require coordination and control.

Project champion A project role played by a business manager who has high credibility among those workers who will be most affected by the implementation of the new product or service being created by the project team. The role might not be a formally designated one, but the project champion is relied upon to use his or her influence to remove obstacles and motivate users to accept changes that will enable the project to meet its formal milestones and overall activities. *See also* Project sponsor.

Project management The application of people knowledge, skills, tools, and techniques to multiple activities designed to meet the objectives of a particular project.

Project Management Office (PMO) An organizational unit (sometimes called a "project office") staffed with experienced project managers to ensure projects are run well and coordinated as necessary. The PMO might be a temporary unit set up for a complex project or a permanent unit measured on project performance. The unit might be responsible for only IS projects or for both IS and non-IS projects.

Project manager The manager accountable for delivering a project of high quality, on time and within budget; might be an IS manager, a business manager, or both.

Project milestone A significant deliverable for a project and its assigned deadline date for completion.

Project sponsor A project role typically played by the manager who financially "owns" the project, which includes not just funding the project but also participating in its oversight. For IS projects that are not just IT infrastructure investments, a business manager typically is in this role.

Proprietary systems Systems (usually referring to operating systems) that are the property of a particular software vendor and, in most cases, were written expressly for a particular computer system. Examples are Windows XP and Vista, which are Microsoft's current operating systems for personal computers, and z/OS and z/VM, which are two alternative large machine operating systems offered by IBM.

Prototyping A systems methodology in which an initial version of a system is built very quickly using fourth generation tools and then is tried out by users, who recommend changes that are the basis for building an improved version. This iterative process is continued until the result is accepted. *See also* Rapid application development.

Pull technology Refers to the mode of operation on the Internet where the client must request data before the data are sent to the client. For example, a Web browser represents pull technology in that the browser must request a Web page before it is sent to the user's screen. *See also* Push technology.

Push technology Refers to the mode of operation on the Internet where data are sent to the client without the client requesting the data. Examples of push technology include electronic mail and the distribution of software updates to the client. *See also* Pull technology.

Query language A 4 GL, nonprocedural special-purpose language for posing queries to the database, often built into the DBMS, that allows users to produce reports by specifying their content and format.

RAD *See* Rapid application development.

Radio frequency identification (RFID) A growing approach to item identification employing RFID tags—often the size of a postage stamp or smaller—that combine tiny chips with an antenna. When a tag is placed on an item, it automatically radios its location to RFID readers on store shelves, checkout counters, loading bay doors, and possibly shopping carts. With RFID tags, inventory is taken automatically and continuously. RFID tags can cut costs by requiring fewer workers for scanning items; they can also provide more current and more accurate information to the entire supply chain.

RAID *See* Redundant array of independent disks.

Rapid application development (RAD) A hybrid systems development methodology based upon a combination of SDLC, prototyping, JAD techniques, and CASE tools, in which the end-prototype becomes the actual system. *See also* Prototyping, Joint application design, CASE.

Raster-based GIS One of two basic approaches for representation and analysis of spatial data in which space is divided into small, equal-sized cells arranged in a grid; these cells (or rasters) can take on a range of values and are "aware" of their location relative to other cells. Weather forecasting employs a raster-based approach.

Reduced instruction set computing chip *See* RISC chip.

Redundant array of independent disks (RAID) A type of storage system for large computers in which a large number of inexpensive, small disk drives (such as those used in microcomputers) are linked together to substitute for the giant disk drives that were previously used.

Relational DBMS A particular type of database management system (DBMS) that views each data entity as a simple table, with the columns as data elements and the rows as different instances of the entity. The records are then related by storing common data, e.g., customer number, in each of the associated tables. Relational DBMSs are the most popular type of DBMS today.

Relationship A relevant association between organizational entities, such as a customer (entity) submits (relationship) an order (entity).

Release management A documented process for migrating a new system, or a new version of an older system, from a development environment to a production (operations) environment within a given organization.

Remote login An Internet application that permits a user to log into and perform work on a computer that is remote to the user's current location.

Request for proposal (RFP) A document that is sent to potential vendors inviting them to submit a proposal for a system purchase. It provides the objectives and requirements of the desired system, including the technical environment in which it must operate; specifies what the vendor must provide as input to the selection process; and explains the conditions for submitting proposals and the general criteria that will be used to evaluate them.

RFID *See* Radio frequency identification.

RFP *See* Request for proposal.

Ring topology A network topology in which all network devices share a single length of cable—with the ends of the cable connected to form a ring.

Ripple effect The result that occurs when a change in one part of a program or system causes unanticipated problems in a different part of the program or system. Then changes necessary to correct that problem may cause problems somewhere else, and so on.

RISC chip Very fast processor chip based on the idea of reduced instruction set computing, or RISC; originally developed for use in high-powered workstations, but now used in other machines, especially midrange systems.

Risk management A term used to refer to activities directed at successfully managing risks to an organization. For example, organizations need to assess the potential business-related losses associated with computer, software, and network failures of various types to determine the amount to spend on solutions that decrease the likelihood of these business losses.

Router A hardware device employed in a telecommunications network to connect two or more local area networks (LANs), where the networks might use different protocols. The router forwards only those messages that need to be forwarded from one network to another. *See also* Gateway.

RSS reader Software built into today's browsers and some e-mail programs that—after a user has subscribed to an RSS feed from a particular site—checks for new content at user-determined intervals and retrieves syndicated Web content such as Weblogs, podcasts, and mainstream mass media reports.

SA&D *See* Systems analysis and design.

SAA *See* Systems Application Architecture.

SaaS *See* Software as a Service.

Sarbanes-Oxley Act (SOX) Legislation passed by the U.S. government in 2002 that requires stricter accounting procedures and financial record certifications for publicly-traded corporations in response to recent corporate scandals in large U.S. companies (such as Enron). The passing of this act led to significant investments in information technologies by many companies to implement better controls to ensure the reliability and integrity of enterprise data.

Satellite communication   A variation of microwave transmission in which a communications satellite is used to relay microwave signals over long distances.

Satellite connection   A high-speed, or broadband, connection to the Internet using a satellite dish at the home or office to communicate with a satellite.

SCM   *See* Supply chain management system.

Scrum   One of the so-called "agile" methodologies in which small work teams, utilizing frequent and varied meetings, coordinate a series of very small projects that together develop an information system.

SDLC   *See* System development life cycle.

Search engine   An information retrieval program that permits the user to search for content that meets a specific criterion (typically containing a given word or phrase) and retrieves a list of items that match the criterion.

Sequential access file   A basic type of computer file in which all of the records that make up the file are stored in sequence according to the file's control key (e.g., a payroll file will contain individual employee records stored in sequence according to the employee identification number); usually stored on magnetic tape. Computer files, also called secondary memory or secondary storage, are added to a computer system to keep vast quantities of data accessible within the computer system at more reasonable costs than main memory.

Sequential file organization   *See* Sequential access file.

Server operating system   Support software installed on the network server that manages network resources and controls the network's operation. The primary server operating systems are Microsoft's Windows Server 2003 and Windows Server 2008, several variations of UNIX, and Linux.

Service-oriented architecture   An application architecture based on a collection of functions, or services, where these services can communicate (or be connected) with one another. Once services are created, they can be used over and over again in different applications—only the connections will vary.

Service level agreement (SLA)   An agreement between IS and a client that specifies a set of services to be provided, the amount of those services to be provided, the quality of these services and how it is to be

measured, and the price to be charged for these services.

Servlet   An application program, written in the Java object-oriented programming language, which resides on a Web server and is executed on the Web server (not downloaded to the client like an applet). *See also* Applet.

SFC   *See* Shop floor control.

Shared Ethernet   The original Ethernet design, which employs a contention bus as its logical topology but is usually implemented as a physical star arrangement. The usual way of creating a shared Ethernet LAN is to plug the cables from all the devices on the LAN into a hub, which is a junction box containing up to 24 ports into which cables can be plugged. Embedded inside the hub is a linear bus connecting all the ports. *See also* Ethernet, Switched Ethernet.

Shared services   A type of centralized governance design in which IS decision making and accountability is "shared" across multiple business units. Shared services units often are responsible for not only IS activities (typically computer and network operations), but also other functional support activities—such as entities responsible for recruiting and retaining human resources.

Shop floor control (SFC) system   A computer-based system that provides online, real-time control and monitoring of machines on the shop floor; for example, the SFC system might recognize that a tool on a particular milling machine is getting dull (by measuring the metal that the machine is cutting per second) and signal this fact to the human operator on duty.

Simplex transmission   A type of data transmission in which data can travel only in one direction over the communication line. Simplex transmission might be used from a monitoring device at a remote site back to a central computer.

SLA   *See* Service level agreement.

SMP   *See* Symmetric multiprocessor.

SNA   *See* Systems Network Architecture.

Social networking application   An Internet application that permits users to post information about themselves and to view information posted by others; examples include MySpace and Facebook.

Software   The set of programs (made up of instructions) that control the operations of the computer system.

Software as a Service (SaaS) A label sometimes given to a hosted solution or an on-demand solution. *See also* Hosted solution.

Software package Computer software that is sold as a self-contained "package" so that it may be distributed widely. In addition to the computer programs, a package might include comprehensive documentation of the system, assistance in installing the system, training, a hot-line consulting service for dealing with problems, and even maintenance of the system.

SOA *See* Service-oriented architecture.

SONET *See* Synchronous Optical Network.

Source program A program written in a second, third, or fourth generation language.

SOW *See* Statement of work.

SOX *See* Sarbanes-Oxley Act.

Spam Unsolicited electronic mail that is broadcast to a large list of e-mail users in an attempt to reach potential customers. Spam is the Internet equivalent to the "junk mail" that is physically sent as bulk mail and delivered by a postal service to recipients who often discard it without even opening it.

Specific DSS *See* Decision support system.

Speech recognition software Software package used to convert the human voice into digitized computer input, so that users can "dictate" a document or message to the computer and, eventually, control the computer by oral commands.

Sponsor *See* Project sponsor.

Spoofing A way of misleading or defrauding a Web surfer by setting up a Web site that mimics a legitimate site. The spoofer might use some means, such as a message board, to direct the victim to the spurious site, or he or she might simply use a close variant of the legitimate site's Uniform Resource Locator (URL) to con people who make a typing mistake.

Spyware Any software that covertly gathers user information through the user's Internet connection without his or her knowledge, usually for advertising purposes. Spyware typically is a hidden component within a downloaded screen saver, music-swapping software, or other freeware or shareware, or may be automatically downloaded when a user visits a specific Web site or clicks on an ad. Also called adware.

SQL A standard query and data definition language for relational DBMSs. This standard, endorsed by the American National Standards Institute (ANSI), is used in many personal computer, midrange system, and mainframe computer DBMSs.

Star topology A network topology that has some primary device at its center with cables radiating from the primary device to all the other network devices.

Statement of work A high-level document that describes the deliverables of the project and the key project milestones, which can be used as a contract between the project manager and the project sponsor to guide and manage the delivery of the project. *See also* Project milestone.

Stored-program concept The concept of preparing a precise list of exactly what the computer is to do (this list is called a program), loading or storing this program in the computer's memory, and then letting the control unit carry out the program at electronic speed. The listing or program must be in a form that the control unit of the computer has been built to understand.

Strategic business planning The process of constructing plans to enable the organization's vision for its future, taking into account marketplace changes and technological opportunities.

Strategic IS plan A set of long-term IS objectives (typically 3 to 5 years) and the major IS initiatives to be undertaken to support an organization's information vision and the information technology architecture to achieve these objectives.

Structure chart *See* Program structure chart.

Structured programming A technique of writing programs so that each program is divided into modules or blocks, where each block has only one entry point and one exit point. In this form, the program logic is easy to follow and understand, and thus the maintenance and correction of such a program should be easier than for a nonstructured program.

Structured techniques A body of structured approaches and tools to document system needs and requirements, functional features and dependencies, and design decisions. Also referred to as procedurally oriented techniques. *See also* Structured programming.

Subsystem A component of a system that is itself viewed as a set of interrelated components. A subsystem has a well-defined purpose that must contribute to the purpose of the system as a whole. *See also* Module, Hierarchical decomposition.

Supercomputer The most expensive and most powerful category of computers, ranging in cost from $1,000,000 to $100,000,000 or more and power from

10,000 to 1,000,000,000,000 MFLOPS; used for numerically-intensive computing and as a very large Web server.

Superminicomputer Large minicomputers; the upper end of the minicomputer category. Both minicomputers and superminicomputers have now disappeared, subsumed by the broader midrange systems category. *See also* Midrange systems, Minicomputers.

Supply chain management (SCM) system A computer-based system for the distribution and transportation of raw materials and finished products throughout the supply chain and for incorporating constraints caused by the supply chain into the production scheduling process.

Support software Programs that do not directly produce output needed by users, but instead support applications software in producing the needed output. Support software provides a computing environment in which it is relatively easy and efficient for humans to work, enables applications programs written in a variety of languages to be carried out, and ensures that computer hardware and software resources are used efficiently. Support software includes operating systems, language compilers, and virus protection programs.

Switch A hardware device employed in a telecommunications network to connect more than two local area networks (LANs) or LAN segments that use the same protocols. For example, a switch might connect several low-speed LANs (12 Ethernet LANs running at 10 mbps) into a single 100-mbps backbone network running Fast Ethernet.

Switched Ethernet A newer variant of Ethernet that provides better performance than shared Ethernet at a higher price. A switch is substituted for the shared Ethernet's hub, and the LAN operates as a logical star as well as a physical star. The switch is smarter than a hub—rather than passing all communications through to all devices on the LAN, which is what a hub does, the switch establishes separate point-to-point circuits to each device and then forwards communications only to the appropriate device. *See also* Ethernet, Shared Ethernet.

SWOT analysis A situation analysis conducted as part of strategic planning or when comparing opportunities for IT investment. SWOT refers to strengths, weaknesses, opportunities, and threats.

Symmetric multiprocessor (SMP) A multiprocessor computer configuration in which all the processors

(CPUs) are identical, with each processor acting independently of the others. The multiple CPUs equally share functional and timing access to and control over all other system components, including memory and the various peripheral devices, with each CPU working in its own allotted portion of memory.

Synchronous Optical Network (SONET) American National Standards Institute (ANSI) approved standard for connecting fiber-optic transmission systems; this standard is employed in a range of high-capacity lines varying from the OC-1 level of nearly 52 mbps to the OC-768 level of 39.812 gbps.

System A set of interrelated components that must work together to achieve some common purpose.

System decoupling Reducing the need to coordinate two system components. Decoupling is accomplished by creating slack and flexible resources, buffers, sharing resources, and standards.

System development methodology A framework of guidelines, tools, and techniques for developing computer systems. *See also* Systems development life cycle, Prototyping.

System requirements A set of logical and physical capabilities and characteristics that a new (or modified) system is required to have upon its implementation (or installation).

Systems analysis and design (SA&D) Major activities performed by IS specialists that are part of systems development and implementation methodologies. *See also* Systems development life cycle, Prototyping, Rapid application development.

Systems analyst IS specialist who works with users to develop systems requirements and help plan implementations and who works with systems designers, programmers, and other information technology (IT) specialists to construct systems based on the user requirements.

Systems Application Architecture (SAA) A statement of architectural philosophy developed by IBM, beginning in the late 1980s; SAA supports SNA as well as TCP/IP and elements of OSI. *See also* Systems Network Architecture, TCP/IP, and OSI.

Systems development life cycle (SDLC) The traditional methodology used by IS professionals to develop a new computer application that includes three general phases: Definition, Construction, and Implementation. Also referred to as a "waterfall" process because of its sequential steps. The SDLC methodology defines the activities necessary for these three phases, as well as a framework for planning and managing a development project. Operations and maintenance are included in the Implementation phase. A modified SDLC approach is used to purchase packaged systems.

Systems Network Architecture (SNA)   A set of network protocols created by IBM to allow its customers to construct their own private networks using the wide variety of IBM communication products, teleprocessing access methods, and data link protocols. SNA was first created in 1974 and is still in widespread use.

Systems software   *See* Support software.

T-1 lines   The most common leased communication lines, operating at a data transmission rate of 1.544 million bits per second. These lines, which may be leased from AT&T or another long-distance carrier, often provide the basis for a wide area network (WAN).

Tablet computer   A variation of a notebook computer (PC) where the user writes on an electronic tablet (usually the video screen folded flat on top of the PC) with a digital pen. Please note that a tablet PC can also be used as a standard notebook computer.

TCO   *See* Total cost of ownership.

TCP/IP   *See* Transmission Control Protocol/Internet Protocol.

Telecommunications   Communications at a distance, including voice (telephone) and data (text/image) communications. Other similar terms used almost interchangeably with telecommunications include data communications, datacom, teleprocessing, telecom, and networking.

Telecommuter   A person who works at home or at another location that is not part of a regular office environment and who uses computers and communications to connect to organizational resources to accomplish his or her work; includes mobile workers, other "road warriors," and free agents. *See also* Free agent.

Telnet   An Internet application, or tool, that allows a user to log into a remote computer from whatever computer he or she is using at the time, as long as both computers are attached to the Internet.

Terminal   A computer-related device that has input (keyboard, mouse) and output (video display) capabilities, but does essentially no processing, and thus operates as a "slave" to a "master" computer, usually a midrange system or a mainframe. For some

applications, a microcomputer may emulate a terminal so that it can operate with a large computer system.

Third generation language   A programming language in which the programmer expresses a step-by-step procedure devised to accomplish the desired task. Examples include FORTRAN, COBOL, BASIC, and C.

Third-party implementation partner   Outside consultants who are contracted to manage a packaged software implementation project at a client's site as employees of an independent consulting firm, not employees of the vendor of the software package. For example, the large enterprise system vendors typically certify large consulting firms (such as the "Big 4"), IT industry consultants (such as IBM), and smaller consulting firms on different versions of their software packages, and these third-party businesses provide employees who work on project teams at the client site, while the vendors' employees only provide on-site technical support as needed.

Three-tier client/server system   A variation of a client/server system in which the processing is split across three tiers, the client and two servers. In the most popular three-tier system, the user interface is housed on the client, usually a PC (tier 1); the processing is performed on a midrange system operating as the applications server (tier 2); and the data are stored on a large machine (often a mainframe or midrange system) that operates as the database server (tier 3).

Timeboxing   Establishing a maximum time limit for the delivery of a project or project module; typically 6 months or less.

Time-sharing   A procedure by which the operating system switches among a number of programs, all stored in memory at the same time, giving each program a small slice of CPU time before moving on to the next program; this is also called time-driven multiprogramming.

Token bus   A design standard for a local area network based on a bus topology and the passing of a token around the bus to all devices in a specified order. In this design, a given device can only transmit when it has the token and thus collisions can never occur. The token bus design is central to the Manufacturing Automation Protocol (MAP).

Token ring   A design standard for a local area network based on a ring topology and the passing of a token around the ring to all devices in a specified order. In this design, a given device can only transmit when it has the token and thus collisions can never occur.

Total cost of ownership (TCO)   Total cost of ownership for a computer system or device, including initial purchase or development costs, initial implementation costs, as well as ongoing support costs. For example, the TCO for a desktop PC includes not only the purchase and installation of the PC hardware and the software and network installation costs, but also the cost of supporting the use of the PC (e.g., user training, help desk, software upgrades, file storage backup, IT-related investments, etc.)

Transaction processing system   A very common type of computer application in which transactions (of a particular type) are processed in order to provide desired output. Examples include the processing of employee work records (transactions) to produce payroll checks and accompanying reports and the processing of orders (transactions) to produce invoices and associated reports. Transaction processing systems might be batch, online, or in-line.

Transborder data flow   Electronic movement of data across a country's national boundary. Such data flows may be restricted by laws that protect a country's economic, political, or personal privacy interests.

Transmission Control Protocol/Internet Protocol (TCP/IP)   A popular network protocol used in the Internet, as well as in intranets operating within organizations and many packet-switched networks. Although not part of the OSI model, TCP/IP corresponds roughly to the network and transport layers of the seven-layer model.

Tree topology   A network topology that has some primary device at the top of the tree, with cables radiating from this primary device to devices further down the tree that, in turn, may have cables radiating from them to other devices still further down the tree, and so on; also called hierarchical topology.

Twisted pair   The most common transmission medium, with two insulated copper wires (about 1 millimeter thick) twisted together in a long helix. Data transmission speeds up to 56,000 bits per second (bps) are possible with twisted pairs on the analog telephone network, with higher speeds of 256,000 bps up to 7 million bps attainable over a digital telephone line or up to 1 billion bps on local area networks.

Two-tier client/server system   The original implementation of a client/server system in which the processing is split between the client (usually a PC) and the server (midrange system or mainframe). If most of the processing is done on the client, this is called a fat client or thin server model; if most of the processing is done on the server, this is called a thin client or fat server model.

UML   *See* Unified Modeling Language.

Unified Modeling Language (UML)   A general-purpose notational system for specifying and visualizing complex software, especially large, object-oriented projects. Examples of such UML-based CASE tools are IBM's Rational Rose and Borland's Together.

Universal Resource Locator (URL)   An address for an Internet file; the address includes the name of the protocol to access the resource (usually http), a domain name for the computer on which the file is located, and perhaps specific locator information. For example, the Web URL for the publisher of this textbook is *http://www.prenhall.com*. Also known as Uniform Resource Locator.

Upper-CASE   *See* Computer-aided software engineering.

URL   *See* Universal Resource Locator.

Usenet newsgroups   An Internet application, or tool, setting up discussion groups, which are essentially huge electronic bulletin boards on which group members can read and post messages.

User application development   Development of business applications by employees who are not IS professionals, but rather are primarily in traditional business roles such as accountants, financial analysts, production schedulers, engineers, and brand managers. In most but not all instances, the people who develop the applications also directly use them in their work.

User computing   Hands-on use of computer resources by workers who are not IS specialists to enter data, make data queries, prepare reports, communicate, perform statistical analyses, analyze problems, navigate online applications, develop Web pages, and so forth.

User interface   That part of a system through which the user interacts with the system. As examples, it may use a mouse, a touch-screen, menus, commands, voice recognition, a telephone keypad, output screens, voice response, and printed reports. *See also* Graphical user interface.

Value added network (VAN)   Formerly, the name given to the practice of contracting with an outside vendor to operate a packet-switched wide area network (WAN) for an organization. Today such a packet-switched WAN is usually called a managed network.

Value chain analysis   A method developed by Michael E. Porter to identify possible strategic initiatives by examining the primary and support activities of an organization that can add value to a firm's products or services from a customer perspective.

VAN   *See* Value added network.

Vector-based GIS   One of two basic approaches for representation and analysis of spatial data in which features in the landscape are associated with either a point (e.g., customer address, power pole), a line (road, river), or a polygon (lake, county, zip code area). The vector-based approach is in widespread use in public administration, public utilities, and business.

Vertically integrated information system   An information system that serves more than one vertical level in an organization or an industry, such as a system designed to be used by an automobile manufacturer and the associated independent dealers.

View integration   A bottom-up approach to detailing an organization's data requirements. View integration analyzes each report, screen, form, and document in the organization and combines each of these views into one consolidated and consistent picture of all organizational data.

Virtual memory   A procedure by which the operating system switches portions of programs (called pages) between main memory and DASD so that portions of enough programs are stored in main memory to enable efficient multiprogramming. To the user, it appears as though an unlimited amount of main memory available, whereas in fact most of each program is stored in DASD.

Virtual private network (VPN)   The equivalent of a private packet-switched network that has been created using the public Internet. A VPN provides a moderate data rate at a very reasonable cost, but the network's reliability is low; a VPN employs encryption and other security mechanisms to ensure that only authorized users can access the network and that the data cannot be intercepted.

Virtual reality (VR)   The use of computer-based systems to create an environment that seems real to one or more senses (usually including sight) of the human user or users. Practical uses of VR include tank crew training for the U.S. Army, the design of an automobile dashboard and controls, and retail store layout.

Virtual teams   Work teams where members of the team are not co-located and might not even be in the same time zone or country. Groupware and other communication tools facilitate electronic meetings and same time or asynchronous document sharing.

Virtualization   The increasingly popular practice of running multiple applications under control of multiple operating systems on a single physical server in order to reduce the number of servers needed, thus saving costs and space.

Virus   *See* Computer virus.

Voice over Internet Protocol (VoIP)   *See* Internet telephony.

Voice response unit   A computer output method using the spoken voice to provide a response to the user. This output method is gaining increasing acceptance as a provider of limited, tightly programmed computer output, often in conjunction with touch-tone telephone input.

VoIP   *See* Internet telephony.

VPN   *See* Virtual private network.

VR   *See* Virtual reality.

W3C   World Wide Web Consortium, an international consortium of companies involved with the management of the Internet and the World Wide Web. W3C is the chief standards body for the Web; among its open standards are Hypertext Transfer Protocol (HTTP) and Hypertext Markup Language (HTML).

WAN   *See* Wide area network.

WAP   *See* Wireless access point.

WATS   *See* Wide Area Telephone Service.

Web   Shorthand for World Wide Web. *See* World Wide Web.

Web 2.0   A phrase that refers to a perceived second generation of Web-based services that emphasize online collaboration and sharing among users; such second generation Web-based services include blogs, wikis, and a variety of social networking applications such as the very popular MySpace, Facebook, and Classmates. *See also* Blog, Social networking application, Wiki.

Web browser   A software application that enables users to access and navigate Web sites; the most common Web browsers are Internet Explorer (Microsoft) and Firefox.

Web services   A particular collection of technologies built around the XML standard of communicating. Web services might be the means by which SOA services communicate with one another, but that does not have to be the case. *See also* Service-oriented architecture.

Wi-Fi LAN The most common type of wireless LAN, based on the IEEE 802.11 family of specifications; Wi-Fi is short for wireless fidelity. Wi-Fi LANs are rapidly proliferating, with obvious advantages for people on the move who need access to the Internet in airports, restaurants, and hotels and on university campuses. Wi-Fi is also gaining acceptance as a home or neighborhood network. Wi-Fi LANs use the shared Ethernet design (logical bus, physical star) and the CSMA/CA Protocol.

Wide area network (WAN) A type of network over which both voice and data for a single organization are communicated among the multiple locations (often far apart) where the organization operates, usually employing point-to-point transmission over facilities owned by several organizations, including the public telephone network; also called a long-haul network.

Wide Area Telephone Service (WATS) A service available from the telephone company in which an organization pays a monthly fee for unlimited long distance telephone service using ordinary voice circuits. WATS is an easy way to set up a wide area network (WAN) and costs less per hour than standard Direct Distance Dialing (DDD).

Wiki A Web site that permits users to add, remove, or modify the content of the site, often without the need for registration, thus making a wiki an effective tool for mass collaborative authoring.

WiMAX LAN The newest type of wireless LAN, based on the IEEE 802.16 family of specifications; WiMAX is short for worldwide interoperability for microwave access. WiMAX is projected to grow rapidly because of its significant advantages—it will operate very much like Wi-Fi, but at higher speeds, over greater distances, and for a greater number of users.

Wireless Considered as a transmission medium, although strictly speaking it is broadcast technology in which radio signals are sent out into the air. Examples are cordless telephone, cellular telephone, wireless LAN, and microwave.

Wireless access point (WAP) A radio transceiver that serves as the central device in a wireless LAN and that connects the LAN to other networks. The WAP receives the signals of all computers within its range and repeats them to ensure that all other computers within the range can hear them; it also forwards all messages for recipients not on this wireless LAN via the wired network.

Wireless LAN A local area network employing wireless communication between the various devices in the network. Compared to a wired LAN, a wireless LAN is easier to plan and install, less secure, and more susceptible to interference. Most wireless LANs operate in the range of 6 to 54 million bits per second (bps), with a few newer wireless LANs operating at speeds of 100 million bps or more. *See also* Wi-Fi LAN, WiMAX LAN.

Word A memory cell that can store two or more characters of data; alternatively, the amount of data handled by the CPU as a single unit. *See also* Memory.

Work breakdown analysis Identification of the project phases and detailed activities for each phase, including the task sequencing and time estimates, usually based on a particular systems methodology.

Workstation Generally, any computer-related device at which an individual may work, such as a personal computer or a terminal. Specifically, a subcategory of the midrange computer category (now difficult to distinguish from other midrange systems) consisting of computers based on powerful microprocessor chips and RISC chips—really grown-up, more powerful microcomputers, but not usually used by a single individual. *See also* Midrange system, RISC chip.

World Wide Web An Internet application, or tool, that uses a hypertext-based approach to traverse, or "surf," the Internet by clicking on a link contained in one document to move to another document, and so on; these links might also connect to video clips, recordings, photographs, and images.

Worm *See* Computer worm.

WORM disk *See* CD-R.

WWW *See* World Wide Web.

XML *See* eXtensible Markup Language.

XP *See* eXtreme Programming.

Y2K *See* Year 2000 problem.

Year 2000 (Y2K) problem Computer calculation errors that would have occurred (without programming changes) beginning with the year 2000 due to the earlier coding of a four-digit year as a two-digit data element; sometimes called the "millennium bug." Billions of dollars were spent worldwide to achieve Y2K compliance for computer software and hardware.

INDEX